MW00632912

OLD TESTAMENT PARSING GUIDE

GENESIS-ESTHER

TODD S. BEALL, Ph.D.
WILLIAM A. BANKS, Th.M.

MOODY PRESS
Chicago

Library of Congress Cataloging in Publication Data

Beall, Todd S., 1952-
Old Testament parsing guide.

Contents: [1] Genesis–Esther.
1. Hebrew language–Verb. 2. Bible. O.T.–
Language, style. I. Banks, William A., 1943-
II. Title.
PJ4645.B43 1986 492.4'5 86-16304
ISBN 0-8024-6315-0 (v. 1)

2 3 4 5 6 Printing/AK/Year 93 92 91 90 89

Printed in the United States of America

Contents

ACKNOWLEDGEMENTS

A work of this nature could not have become a reality without the assistance of numerous people along the way. First, we would like to thank Dr. Homer Heater, former Dean of Capital Bible Seminary, who instilled in both of us a love for the Hebrew language, which has resulted in this project. His suggestions and input during the course of the project have been invaluable. Special thanks also go to Dr. Richard A. Taylor, Professor of Old Testament Literature and Exegesis at Capital, for his careful proofing of the Aramaic portions of the work.

In addition, we would like to thank several past and present Capital Bible Seminary students who gave unstintingly of their time to check the work, and make it a better publication: Carol Hedegard, Paul Liebert, Doug Lyon, Ron Satta, Jeff Silvieus, Joe Sperty, and Tom Strubert. In particular, we would like to thank Rev. Colin Smith, who, although a busy pastor and a student at Capital, found the time to check large sections of the work with Mandelkern's Concordance, thus eliminating further errors. To each of these individuals we owe an enormous debt of gratitude.

We would also like to acknowledge the assistance of Michael Bushell, whose word processing program (with Hebrew font capabilities) we utilized extensively in our work. His gracious assistance on numerous occasions enabled us to expedite the production of this volume.

Finally, we would both like to thank our wives and families for their patience with us during the past five years as we labored for countless hours on this work. Without their willingness to sacrifice in many ways, this project would not have been possible.

Todd S. Beall
William A. Banks

INTRODUCTION

Purpose of the Work

Over the past fifteen years, numerous aids for students of the New Testament have appeared, making the task of translating and understanding the original Greek text much easier. Interlinear Greek-English New Testaments, verse-by-verse vocabulary lists, grammatical aids, and New Testament parsing guides all have enabled the serious student of the Scripture (whether pastor or layperson) to delve into the original Greek text with greater ease than ever before.

Comparable works for the Old Testament, however, have been lacking until recently. The now completed *Interlinear Hebrew-English Old Testament* by J. Kohlenberger III (Zondervan) and *A Reader's Hebrew-English Lexicon of the Old Testament* by T. Armstrong, D. Busby, and C. Carr (Zondervan) have helped to make the study of the Old Testament in Hebrew easier, as has B. Einspahr's *Index to Brown, Driver and Briggs Hebrew Lexicon* (Moody). But one of the chief difficulties in studying Hebrew is in mastering its verbal system, and until now a verse-by-verse parsing aid (similar to N. Han's *A Parsing Guide to the Greek New Testament* [Herald]) for the Old Testament did not exist.

The purpose of this work, then, is to supply a verse-by-verse parsing aid for *every* verb in the Old Testament, so that the busy pastor or serious Bible student will be aided in translating more rapidly any portion of the Old Testament text. Rather than spending his time searching for a verb's root in the lexicon, or looking up the form in Davidson's *Analytical Hebrew and Chaldee Lexicon of the Old Testament* (Zondervan; where words are listed alphabetically by their form, not verse by verse), the student may spend his time more profitably in the interpretation of the text at hand. To this end, the page number of Brown, Driver and Briggs' *Hebrew and English Lexicon of the Old Testament* (BDB; Oxford) is listed beside each verb entry, so that the student may look up the word rapidly in this standard lexicon should he need further help on a word's use or meaning.

Scope of the Work

This work, issued in two volumes, lists every verb form in order of occurrence in the Old Testament according to verse. If the same form occurs twice within a verse, it is parsed twice. Consideration was given to eliminating the most common verb forms (for example, לאמר and ויהי), but it was thought that it would be most helpful for those whose Hebrew is weak to include all verb forms. The more advanced Hebrew student may simply skip over the more obvious forms.

The Hebrew text used is the *Biblia Hebraica Stuttgartensia* (BHS), which reproduces the Leningrad Codex. In addition, the textual variants represented by the *Kethib-Qere* of the Masoretes are represented in the parsing guide whenever either the *Kethib* (what is written in the text) or the *Qere* (what is to be read instead of the *Kethib*) is a verb form. (In the parsing guide the *Kethib* is noted by a "k" after the verb form, while the *Qere* is marked by a "q".) Help in parsing some of the *Kethib-Qere* forms has been provided by R. Gordis, *The Biblical Text in the Making: A Study of the Kethib-Qere* (Ktav), although Gordis has not been followed in all instances.

Sample Parsing Guide Entry

To explain the features of the parsing guide, it will be helpful to consider a sample parsing guide entry:

Ch	Vs	Form	Stem	Tnse	Pgn	Root	BDB	Sfx	Meaning
1:	28	כבשה	qal	impv	mp	כבש	461	3fs	subdue

Each entry begins with the chapter and verse location of the form in question ("1: 28"). Next, the unpointed verb form is given ("כבשה"), *without* any prefixes (even ו ["and"] and the ל ["to"] used for construct infinitives are omitted from the form written in the parsing guide). Suffixes are, however, included. Next, the stem, tense, and person, gender, and number of the form are given ("qal impv mp"). The root of the form is then indicated ("כבשׁ"), followed by the page number in BDB where discussion of the verb root begins ("461"). Note that the BDB page numbers do not reference the page a particular citation is discussed, as in Einspahr, but rather the page where discussion of the verb root begins. (The former method could not have been chosen, since BDB does not necessarily cite *all* occurrences of a particular verb, whereas the parsing guide does). Next, where applicable, the person, gender, and number of the suffix attached to the verb are indicated ("3fs"). Finally, a definition of the verb is provided ("subdue"). This definition is *not* intended to replace a more thorough lexical study, but rather reflects the most common meaning of the word in the stem indicated. Because of space limitations, sometimes the definition is abbreviated (note especially the abbreviation "c" for "cause" used in hiphil stems).

Parsing of Waw Consecutive and Volitive Forms

While other Old Testament parsing aids (such as Davidson's) do not specifically indicate *waw* consecutive perfect (wcp), *waw* consecutive imperfect (wci), cohortative, or jussive forms, the present work has attempted to delineate such forms. Little problem is encountered in parsing *waw* consecutive imperfect forms, since these forms have a particular orthography that distinguishes the *waw* consecutive imperfect from the simple *waw*. In the case of *waw* consecutive perfects, however, the situation is more complicated because there is no difference in form between a *waw* consecutive perfect and a simple *waw* (sometimes there is a change of tone, but many times there is not). Thus, the recognition of *waw* consecutive perfects is not determined simply by form, but rather by meaning. Hence, the recognition of *waw* consecutive perfects is sometimes a subjective process.

A similar problem is met with the determination of cohortatives and jussives. In the case of cohortatives, sometimes the orthography is unclear, since final א and final ה verbs rarely take the ה of the cohortative, and suffixed forms never do. Furthermore, occasionally the cohortative *form* is used, but the meaning is not cohortative (see Gesenius' *Hebrew Grammar* [Oxford], §108g,h). The same is true for the jussives. The jussives look the same as the normal imperfects in all the third person plural forms and in most of the singular forms as well (the jussive differs in form only in the hiphil and in the middle weak and final ה verbs). Because of this similarity in form, as Gesenius notes, "it is frequently doubtful which of the two the writer intended" (*Hebrew Grammar*, §109k). Sometimes the jussive form is used, but the meaning seems to be imperfect; at other times the meaning appears to be jussive, but the jussive form (where it would be distinctive) is not used (see further, S. R. Driver, *A Treatise on the Use of the Tenses in Hebrew* [Oxford], §170-75). Hence, as P. Joüon observes, it is often necessary to distinguish between the syntactical jussive "mode" and the jussive "form" (*Grammaire de l'hébreu biblique* [Pontifical Biblical Institute], §114g n. 2).

To help distinguish between those cases where the *form* is clearly jussive or cohortative and those where the form does not show it, but the *meaning* seems to be jussive or cohortative, the following abbreviations are used in the parsing guide:

1) *jus* indicates jussive in form and meaning;

2) *jusf* indicates jussive in form only, not meaning (rare);

and 3) *jusm* indicates jussive in meaning, but no unique form to indicate jussive is used. Similar sigla are used for cohortatives (*coh*, *cohf*, and *cohm*).

It is recognized that there is a great deal of subjectivity involved in the determination of some of the *waw* consecutive perfect forms, and many of the jussive and cohortative forms (especially those designated with jusf, jusm, cohf, and cohm), since in many cases the *context*, not form alone, is the determining factor. Hence, the parsing guide should not be regarded as the "last word" in these cases. However, it was thought that the benefits of designating the *waw* consecutive perfects, cohortatives, and jussives in the parsing guide outweighed the increased subjectivity involved.

Other Difficult Forms

Aside from the problems with *waw* consecutive perfects, cohortatives, and jussives mentioned above, there are other forms which present particular difficulties in parsing.

Often it is difficult to decide whether a form is a verb or an adjective (for example, טוב). Similarly, for some weak verbs the forms for perfect 3ms and for participle are the same, and it is often difficult to decide between the two (especially troublesome are בא and מת). In such cases we have normally followed BDB, if it made reference to the specific form. We have also made abundant use of S. Mandelkern's *Veteris Testamenti Concordantiae Hebraicae atque Chaldaicae* (Tel Aviv: Schocken) and A. Even-Shoshan's *A New Concordance of the Old Testament* (Baker) for help in disputed forms. Throughout the work, we have striven for consistency as much as possible in such matters.

Because the Masoretes did not recognize qal passive forms, they pointed such forms as Pual perfects or Hophal imperfects, and the forms are so listed in BDB. In the parsing guide, however, we have noted numerous qal passive forms, in accordance with Gesenius (*Hebrew Grammar*, §52e,53u) and Joüon (*Grammaire de l'hébreu biblique*, §58).

In the case of one particular verb, חוה, the root indicated in the parsing guide does not match the BDB page number given. BDB regarded such forms as השתחות (Gen 37:10) as a hithpalel from the root שחה, but in reality the form should be parsed as a hishtaphel from the root חוה. The BDB page number for all references to this root is given as page 1005, where the forms are discussed under the (incorrect) root שחה.

Finally, some forms seem nearly impossible to parse as pointed (for example, ילדת in Gen 16:11: its pointing is a hybrid of qal participle and qal perfect). Such forms have been marked with a "?" after the BDB page number to indicate that the parsing of this form is uncertain. We have tried to keep the number of forms marked with a "?" to a strict minimum.

Accuracy of the Work

Every effort has been made to ensure a high degree of accuracy in this work. Each form has been parsed and checked in context by both co-authors as well as at least one other person. In addition, the entire work was then sorted and compared by hand with Mandelkern's Concordance. Thus, in addition to the original work, each entry has been checked at least four different times.

Yet, by no means are we claiming inerrancy for this work! With over 42,000 verbs in Genesis through Esther, and eight pieces of information about each form, this volume contains about 340,000 items, or over 2,000,000 characters of information. Undoubtedly some typos (Hebrew and English) and parsing errors have slipped through our careful checking procedures. The authors would be most grateful for information as to any errors encountered, so that they may be corrected in future editions.

May the Lord be glorified, and the study of His Word be enhanced by those who use this work.

PREFACE TO THE SECOND PRINTING

We are gratified at the excellent reception of the first printing of this work. We have received enthusiastic letters of appreciation from places as diverse as New Zealand and Burma! Very few suggested corrections have been received, which means either that 1) the work is reasonably accurate or 2) users of the volume are not looking carefully enough! Some corrections have been made in this second printing, most of a quite minor nature. In this regard we would like to express special appreciation to Dr. Alan Groves, Associate Professor of Old Testament at Westminister Seminary, and his staff, who found a number of discrepancies while checking *every verb* in this work during their preparation of a morphologically tagged text of the Hebrew Bible.

Our continued hope is that this volume will be instrumental in making the process of translating the Hebrew text less tedious, to the end that more and more students and pastors will uncover the richness of the Hebrew language in their preaching and teaching of the Word of God.

ABBREVIATIONS

The following abbreviations are used in the *Old Testament Parsing Guide*:

Stem Abbreviations

Hebrew

niph=niphal
hiph=hiphil
hoph=hophal
hith=hithpael

(less common)
hish=hishtaphel
hoth=hothpaal
htpo=hithpolel
htpp=hithpalpel
nith=nithpael
pal=palel
pall=pealal
pil=pilel
pilp=pilpel
pol=polel
pola=polal
polp=polpal
pul=pulal
qalp=qal passive

Aramaic

aph=aphel
haph=haphel
hish=hishtaphel
htap=hithaphel
htpa=hithpaal
htpe=hithpeel
htpo=hithpolel
htpp=hithpalpel
ish=ishtaphel
ith=ithpeel
itho=ithpoel
pol=polel
shap=shaphel

Tense Abbreviations

coh=cohortative in form and meaning
cohf=cohortative in form, not meaning
cohm=cohortative in meaning, but no unique form to indicate cohortative
impf=imperfect
impv=imperative
infa=infinitive absolute
infc=infinitive construct
jus=jussive in form and meaning
jusf=jussive in form, not meaning
jusm=jussive in meaning, but no unique form to indicate jussive
pft=perfect
pptc=passive participle (only in qal)
ptc=participle
wci=*waw* consecutive imperfect
wcp=*waw* consecutive perfect

Special Symbols (see Introduction for further explanation)

k=*Kethib* form
q=*Qere* form
?=Parsing of this form is unclear
c. (in Meaning section)=cause

ChVs	Form	Stem	Tnse	PGN	Root	BDB	Sfx	Meaning
GENESIS								
1:1	ברא	qal	pft	3ms	ברא	135		create
1:2	היתה	qal	pft	3fs	היה	224		be,become
	מרחפת	piel	ptc	fs	רחף	934		hover
1:3	יאמר	qal	wci	3ms	אמר	55		say
	יהי	qal	jus	3ms	היה	224		be,become
	יהי	qal	wci	3ms	היה	224		be,become
1:4	ירא	qal	wci	3ms	ראה	906		see
	יבדל	hiph	wci	3ms	בדל	95		divide
1:5	יקרא	qal	wci	3ms	קרא	894		call,proclaim
	קרא	qal	pft	3ms	קרא	894		call,proclaim
	יהי	qal	wci	3ms	היה	224		be,become
	יהי	qal	wci	3ms	היה	224		be,become
1:6	יאמר	qal	wci	3ms	אמר	55		say
	יהי	qal	jus	3ms	היה	224		be,become
	יהי	qal	jus	3ms	היה	224		be,become
	מבדיל	hiph	ptc	ms	בדל	95		divide
1:7	יעשׂ	qal	wci	3ms	עשׂה	793		do,make
	יבדל	hiph	wci	3ms	בדל	95		divide
	יהי	qal	wci	3ms	היה	224		be,become
1:8	יקרא	qal	wci	3ms	קרא	894		call,proclaim
	יהי	qal	wci	3ms	היה	224		be,become
	יהי	qal	wci	3ms	היה	224		be,become
1:9	יאמר	qal	wci	3ms	אמר	55		say
	יקוו	niph	jusm	3mp	קוה	876		be collected
	תראה	niph	jusm	3fs	ראה	906		appear,be seen
	יהי	qal	wci	3ms	היה	224		be,become
1:10	יקרא	qal	wci	3ms	קרא	894		call,proclaim
	קרא	qal	pft	3ms	קרא	894		call,proclaim
	ירא	qal	wci	3ms	ראה	906		see
1:11	יאמר	qal	wci	3ms	אמר	55		say
	תדשא	hiph	jus	3fs	דשא	205		cause to sprout
	מזריע	hiph	ptc	ms	זרע	281		produce seed
	עשׂה	qal	ptc	ms	עשׂה	793		do,make
	יהי	qal	wci	3ms	היה	224		be,become
1:12	תוצא	hiph	wci	3fs	יצא	422		bring out
	מזריע	hiph	ptc	ms	זרע	281		produce seed
	עשׂה	qal	ptc	ms	עשׂה	793		do,make
	ירא	qal	wci	3ms	ראה	906		see
1:13	יהי	qal	wci	3ms	היה	224		be,become
	יהי	qal	wci	3ms	היה	224		be,become
1:14	יאמר	qal	wci	3ms	אמר	55		say
	יהי	qal	jus	3ms	היה	224		be,become
	הבדיל	hiph	infc		בדל	95		divide
	היו	qal	wcp	3cp	היה	224		be,become
1:15	היו	qal	wcp	3cp	היה	224		be,become
	האיר	hiph	infc		אור	21		cause to shine
	יהי	qal	wci	3ms	היה	224		be,become
1:16	יעשׂ	qal	wci	3ms	עשׂה	793		do,make
1:17	יתן	qal	wci	3ms	נתן	678		give,set
	האיר	hiph	infc		אור	21		cause to shine
1:18	משׁל	qal	infc		משׁל	605		rule
	הבדיל	hiph	infc		בדל	95		divide
	ירא	qal	wci	3ms	ראה	906		see

ChVs	Form	Stem	Tnse	PGN	Root	BDB	Sfx	Meaning
1:19	יהי	qal	wci	3ms	היה	224		be,become
	יהי	qal	wci	3ms	היה	224		be,become
1:20	יאמר	qal	wci	3ms	אמר	55		say
	ישׁרצו	qal	jusm	3mp	שׁרץ	1056		swarm,teem
	יעופף	pol	jusm	3ms	עוף	733		fly about
1:21	יברא	qal	wci	3ms	ברא	135		create
	רמשׂת	qal	ptc	fs	רמשׂ	942		creep
	שׁרצו	qal	pft	3cp	שׁרץ	1056		swarm,teem
	ירא	qal	wci	3ms	ראה	906		see
1:22	יברך	piel	wci	3ms	ברך	138		bless
	אמר	qal	infc		אמר	55		say
	פרו	qal	impv	mp	פרה	826		bear fruit
	רבו	qal	impv	mp	רבה	915		be many,great
	מלאו	qal	impv	mp	מלא	569		be full,fill
	ירב	qal	jus	3ms	רבה	915		be many,great
1:23	יהי	qal	wci	3ms	היה	224		be,become
	יהי	qal	wci	3ms	היה	224		be,become
1:24	יאמר	qal	wci	3ms	אמר	55		say
	תוצא	hiph	jus	3fs	יצא	422		bring out
	יהי	qal	wci	3ms	היה	224		be,become
1:25	יעשׂ	qal	wci	3ms	עשׂה	793		do,make
	ירא	qal	wci	3ms	ראה	906		see
1:26	יאמר	qal	wci	3ms	אמר	55		say
	נעשׂה	qal	cohm	1cp	עשׂה	793		do,make
	ירדו	qal	jusm	3mp	רדה	921		rule
	רמשׂ	qal	ptc	ms	רמשׂ	942		creep
1:27	יברא	qal	wci	3ms	ברא	135		create
	ברא	qal	pft	3ms	ברא	135		create
	ברא	qal	pft	3ms	ברא	135		create
1:28	יברך	piel	wci	3ms	ברך	138		bless
	יאמר	qal	wci	3ms	אמר	55		say
	פרו	qal	impv	mp	פרה	826		bear fruit
	רבו	qal	impv	mp	רבה	915		be many,great
	מלאו	qal	impv	mp	מלא	569		be full,fill
	כבשׁה	qal	impv	mp	כבשׁ	461	3fs	subdue
	רדו	qal	impv	mp	רדה	921		rule
	רמשׂת	qal	ptc	fs	רמשׂ	942		creep
1:29	יאמר	qal	wci	3ms	אמר	55		say
	נתתי	qal	pft	1cs	נתן	678		give,set
	זרע	qal	ptc	ms	זרע	281		sow
	זרע	qal	ptc	ms	זרע	281		sow
	יהיה	qal	impf	3ms	היה	224		be,become
1:30	רומשׂ	qal	ptc	ms	רמשׂ	942		creep
	יהי	qal	wci	3ms	היה	224		be,become
1:31	ירא	qal	wci	3ms	ראה	906		see
	עשׂה	qal	pft	3ms	עשׂה	793		do,make
	יהי	qal	wci	3ms	היה	224		be,become
	יהי	qal	wci	3ms	היה	224		be,become
2:1	יכלו	pual	wci	3mp	כלה	477		be finished
2:2	יכל	piel	wci	3ms	כלה	477		complete,finish
	עשׂה	qal	pft	3ms	עשׂה	793		do,make
	ישׁבת	qal	wci	3ms	שׁבת	991		cease,desist
	עשׂה	qal	pft	3ms	עשׂה	793		do,make
2:3	יברך	piel	wci	3ms	ברך	138		bless

ChVs	Form	Stem	Tnse	PGN	Root	BDB	Sfx	Meaning
2: 3	יקדש	piel	wci	3ms	קדש	872		consecrate
	שבת	qal	pft	3ms	שבת	991		cease,desist
	ברא	qal	pft	3ms	ברא	135		create
	עשׂות	qal	infc		עשׂה	793		do,make
2: 4	הבראם	niph	infc		ברא	135	3mp	be created
	עשׂות	qal	infc		עשׂה	793		do,make
2: 5	יהיה	qal	impf	3ms	היה	224		be,become
	יצמח	qal	impf	3ms	צמח	855		sprout up
	המטיר	hiph	pft	3ms	מטר	565		rain
	עבד	qal	infc		עבד	712		work,serve
2: 6	יעלה	qal	impf	3ms	עלה	748		go up
	השקה	hiph	wcp	3ms	שקה	1052		give to drink
2: 7	ייצר	qal	wci	3ms	יצר	427		form,create
	יפח	qal	wci	3ms	נפח	655		breathe,blow
	יהי	qal	wci	3ms	היה	224		be,become
2: 8	יטע	qal	wci	3ms	נטע	642		plant
	ישׂם	qal	wci	3ms	שׂים	962		put,set
	יצר	qal	pft	3ms	יצר	427		form,create
2: 9	יצמח	hiph	wci	3ms	צמח	855		cause to grow
	נחמד	niph	ptc	ms	חמד	326		desirable
2: 10	יצא	qal	ptc	ms	יצא	422		go out
	השקות	hiph	infc		שקה	1052		give to drink
	יפרד	niph	impf	3ms	פרד	825		divide
	היה	qal	wcp	3ms	היה	224		be,become
2: 11	סבב	qal	ptc	ms	סבב	685		surround
2: 13	סובב	qal	ptc	ms	סבב	685		surround
2: 14	הלך	qal	ptc	ms	הלך	229		walk,go
2: 15	יקח	qal	wci	3ms	לקח	542		take
	ינחהו	hiph	wci	3ms	נוח	628	3ms	give rest,put
	עבדה	qal	infc		עבד	712	3fs	work,serve
	שמרה	qal	infc		שמר	1036	3fs	keep,watch
2: 16	יצו	piel	wci	3ms	צוה	845		command
	אמר	qal	infc		אמר	55		say
	אכל	qal	infa		אכל	37		eat,devour
	תאכל	qal	impf	2ms	אכל	37		eat,devour
2: 17	תאכל	qal	impf	2ms	אכל	37		eat,devour
	אכלך	qal	infc		אכל	37	2ms	eat,devour
	מות	qal	infa		מות	559		die
	תמות	qal	impf	2ms	מות	559		die
2: 18	יאמר	qal	wci	3ms	אמר	55		say
	היות	qal	infc		היה	224		be,become
	אעשׂה	qal	impf	1cs	עשׂה	793		do,make
2: 19	יצר	qal	wci	3ms	יצר	427		form,create
	יבא	hiph	wci	3ms	בוא	97		bring in
	ראות	qal	infc		ראה	906		see
	יקרא	qal	impf	3ms	קרא	894		call,proclaim
	יקרא	qal	impf	3ms	קרא	894		call,proclaim
2: 20	יקרא	qal	wci	3ms	קרא	894		call,proclaim
	מצא	qal	pft	3ms	מצא	592		find
2: 21	יפל	hiph	wci	3ms	נפל	656		cause to fall
	יישן	qal	wci	3ms	ישן	445		sleep
	יקח	qal	wci	3ms	לקח	542		take
	יסגר	qal	wci	3ms	סגר	688		shut
2: 22	יבן	qal	wci	3ms	בנה	124		build
2: 22	לקח	qal	pft	3ms	לקח	542		take
	יבאה	hiph	wci	3ms	בוא	97	3fs	bring in
2: 23	יאמר	qal	wci	3ms	אמר	55		say
	יקרא	niph	impf	3ms	קרא	894		be called
	לקחה	qalp	pft	3fs	לקח	542		be taken
2: 24	יעזב	qal	impf	3ms	עזב	736		leave,loose
	דבק	qal	wcp	3ms	דבק	179		cling,cleave
	היו	qal	wcp	3cp	היה	224		be,become
2: 25	יהיו	qal	wci	3mp	היה	224		be,become
	יתבששו	htpo	impf	3mp	בוש	101		ashamed
3: 1	היה	qal	pft	3ms	היה	224		be,become
	עשׂה	qal	pft	3ms	עשׂה	793		do,make
	יאמר	qal	wci	3ms	אמר	55		say
	אמר	qal	pft	3ms	אמר	55		say
	תאכלו	qal	impf	2mp	אכל	37		eat,devour
3: 2	תאמר	qal	wci	3fs	אמר	55		say
	נאכל	qal	impf	1cp	אכל	37		eat,devour
3: 3	אמר	qal	pft	3ms	אמר	55		say
	תאכלו	qal	impf	2mp	אכל	37		eat,devour
	תגעו	qal	impf	2mp	נגע	619		touch,strike
	תמתון	qal	impf	2mp	מות	559		die
3: 4	יאמר	qal	wci	3ms	אמר	55		say
	מות	qal	infa		מות	559		die
	תמתון	qal	impf	2mp	מות	559		die
3: 5	ידע	qal	ptc	ms	ידע	393		know
	אכלכם	qal	infc		אכל	37	2mp	eat,devour
	נפקחו	niph	wcp	3cp	פקח	824		be opened
	הייתם	qal	wcp	2mp	היה	224		be,become
	ידעי	qal	ptc	mp	ידע	393		know
3: 6	תרא	qal	wci	3fs	ראה	906		see
	נחמד	niph	ptc	ms	חמד	326		desirable
	השׂכיל	hiph	infc		שׂכל	968		look at,prosper
	תקח	qal	wci	3fs	לקח	542		take
	תאכל	qal	wci	3fs	אכל	37		eat,devour
	תתן	qal	wci	3fs	נתן	678		give,set
	יאכל	qal	wci	3ms	אכל	37		eat,devour
3: 7	תפקחנה	niph	wci	3fp	פקח	824		be opened
	ידעו	qal	wci	3mp	ידע	393		know
	יתפרו	qal	wci	3mp	תפר	1074		sew together
	יעשׂו	qal	wci	3mp	עשׂה	793		do,make
3: 8	ישמעו	qal	wci	3mp	שמע	1033		hear
	מתהלך	hith	ptc	ms	הלך	229		walk to and fro
	יתחבא	hith	wci	3ms	חבא	285		hide oneself
3: 9	יקרא	qal	wci	3ms	קרא	894		call,proclaim
	יאמר	qal	wci	3ms	אמר	55		say
3: 10	יאמר	qal	wci	3ms	אמר	55		say
	שמעתי	qal	pft	1cs	שמע	1033		hear
	אירא	qal	wci	1cs	ירא	431		fear
	אחבא	niph	wci	1cs	חבא	285		hide oneself
3: 11	יאמר	qal	wci	3ms	אמר	55		say
	הגיד	hiph	pft	3ms	נגד	616		declare,tell
	צויתיך	piel	pft	1cs	צוה	845	2ms	command
	אכל	qal	infc		אכל	37		eat,devour
	אכלת	qal	pft	2ms	אכל	37		eat,devour

ChVs	Form	Stem	Tnse	PGN	Root	BDB	Sfx	Meaning
3:12	יאמר	qal	wci	3ms	אמר	55		say
	נתתה	qal	pft	2ms	נתן	678		give,set
	נתנה	qal	pft	3fs	נתן	678		give,set
	אכל	qal	wci	1cs	אכל	37		eat,devour
3:13	יאמר	qal	wci	3ms	אמר	55		say
	עשׂית	qal	pft	2fs	עשׂה	793		do,make
	תאמר	qal	wci	3fs	אמר	55		say
	השׁיאני	hiph	pft	3ms	נשׁא	674	1cs	beguile
	אכל	qal	wci	1cs	אכל	37		eat,devour
3:14	יאמר	qal	wci	3ms	אמר	55		say
	עשׂית	qal	pft	2ms	עשׂה	793		do,make
	ארור	qal	pptc	ms	ארר	76		curse
	תלך	qal	impf	2ms	הלך	229		walk,go
	תאכל	qal	impf	2ms	אכל	37		eat,devour
3:15	אשׁית	qal	impf	1cs	שׁית	1011		put,set
	ישׁופך	qal	impf	3ms	שׁוף	1003	2ms	bruise,cover
	תשׁופנו	qal	impf	2ms	שׁוף	1003	3ms	bruise,cover
3:16	אמר	qal	pft	3ms	אמר	55		say
	הרבה	hiph	infa		רבה	915		make many
	ארבה	hiph	impf	1cs	רבה	915		make many
	תלדי	qal	impf	2fs	ילד	408		bear,beget
	ימשׁל	qal	impf	3ms	משׁל	605		rule
3:17	אמר	qal	pft	3ms	אמר	55		say
	שׁמעת	qal	pft	2ms	שׁמע	1033		hear
	תאכל	qal	wci	2ms	אכל	37		eat,devour
	צויתיך	piel	pft	1cs	צוה	845	2ms	command
	אמר	qal	infc		אמר	55		say
	תאכל	qal	impf	2ms	אכל	37		eat,devour
	ארורה	qal	pptc	fs	ארר	76		curse
	תאכלנה	qal	impf	2ms	אכל	37	3fs	eat,devour
3:18	תצמיח	hiph	impf	3fs	צמח	855		cause to grow
	אכלת	qal	wcp	2ms	אכל	37		eat,devour
3:19	תאכל	qal	impf	2ms	אכל	37		eat,devour
	שׁובך	qal	infc		שׁוב	996	2ms	turn,return
	לקחת	qalp	pft	2ms	לקח	542		be taken
	תשׁוב	qal	impf	2ms	שׁוב	996		turn,return
3:20	יקרא	qal	wci	3ms	קרא	894		call,proclaim
	היתה	qal	pft	3fs	היה	224		be,become
3:21	יעשׂ	qal	wci	3ms	עשׂה	793		do,make
	ילבשׁם	hiph	wci	3ms	לבשׁ	527	3mp	clothe
3:22	יאמר	qal	wci	3ms	אמר	55		say
	היה	qal	pft	3ms	היה	224		be,become
	דעת	qal	infc		ידע	393		know
	ישׁלח	qal	impf	3ms	שׁלח	1018		send
	לקח	qal	wcp	3ms	לקח	542		take
	אכל	qal	wcp	3ms	אכל	37		eat,devour
	חי	qal	wcp	3ms	חיה	310		live
3:23	ישׁלחהו	piel	wci	3ms	שׁלח	1018	3ms	send away,shoot
	עבד	qal	infc		עבד	712		work,serve
	לקח	qalp	pft	3ms	לקח	542		be taken
3:24	יגרשׁ	piel	wci	3ms	גרשׁ	176		drive out
	ישׁכן	hiph	wci	3ms	שׁכן	1014		cause to dwell
	מתהפכת	hith	ptc	fs	הפך	245		turn every way
	שׁמר	qal	infc		שׁמר	1036		keep,watch
4:1	ידע	qal	pft	3ms	ידע	393		know
	תהר	qal	wci	3fs	הרה	247		conceive
	תלד	qal	wci	3fs	ילד	408		bear,beget
	תאמר	qal	wci	3fs	אמר	55		say
	קניתי	qal	pft	1cs	קנה	888		get,buy
4:2	תסף	hiph	wci	3fs	יסף	414		add,do again
	לדת	qal	infc		ילד	408		bear,beget
	יהי	qal	wci	3ms	היה	224		be,become
	רעה	qal	ptc	ms	רעה	944		pasture,tend
	היה	qal	pft	3ms	היה	224		be,become
	עבד	qal	ptc	ms	עבד	712		work,serve
4:3	יהי	qal	wci	3ms	היה	224		be,become
	יבא	hiph	wci	3ms	בוא	97		bring in
4:4	הביא	hiph	pft	3ms	בוא	97		bring in
	ישׁע	qal	wci	3ms	שׁעה	1043		gaze,regard
4:5	שׁעה	qal	pft	3ms	שׁעה	1043		gaze,regard
	יחר	qal	wci	3ms	חרה	354		be kindled,burn
	יפלו	qal	wci	3mp	נפל	656		fall
4:6	יאמר	qal	wci	3ms	אמר	55		say
	חרה	qal	pft	3ms	חרה	354		be kindled,burn
	נפלו	qal	pft	3cp	נפל	656		fall
4:7	תיטיב	hiph	impf	2ms	יטב	405		do good
	שׂאת	qal	infc		נשׂא	669		lift,carry
	תיטיב	hiph	impf	2ms	יטב	405		do good
	רבץ	qal	ptc	ms	רבץ	918		lie down
	תמשׁל	qal	impf	2ms	משׁל	605		rule
4:8	יאמר	qal	wci	3ms	אמר	55		say
	יהי	qal	wci	3ms	היה	224		be,become
	היותם	qal	infc		היה	224	3mp	be,become
	יקם	qal	wci	3ms	קום	877		arise,stand
	יהרגהו	qal	wci	3ms	הרג	246	3ms	kill
4:9	יאמר	qal	wci	3ms	אמר	55		say
	יאמר	qal	wci	3ms	אמר	55		say
	ידעתי	qal	pft	1cs	ידע	393		know
	שׁמר	qal	ptc	ms	שׁמר	1036		keep,watch
4:10	יאמר	qal	wci	3ms	אמר	55		say
	עשׂית	qal	pft	2ms	עשׂה	793		do,make
	צעקים	qal	ptc	mp	צעק	858		cry out
4:11	ארור	qal	pptc	ms	ארר	76		curse
	פצתה	qal	pft	3fs	פצה	822		open,set free
	קחת	qal	infc		לקח	542		take
4:12	תעבד	qal	impf	2ms	עבד	712		work,serve
	תסף	hiph	jusf	3fs	יסף	414		add,do again
	תת	qal	infc		נתן	678		give,set
	נע	qal	ptc	ms	נוע	631		totter,wave
	נד	qal	ptc	ms	נוד	626		wander,lament
	תהיה	qal	impf	2ms	היה	224		be,become
4:13	יאמר	qal	wci	3ms	אמר	55		say
	נשׂא	qal	infc		נשׂא	669		lift,carry
4:14	גרשׁת	piel	pft	2ms	גרשׁ	176		drive out
	אסתר	niph	impf	1cs	סתר	711		hide,be hid
	הייתי	qal	wcp	1cs	היה	224		be,become
	נע	qal	ptc	ms	נוע	631		totter,wave
	נד	qal	ptc	ms	נוד	626		wander,lament

ChVs	Form	Stem	Tnse	PGN	Root	BDB	Sfx	Meaning
4: 14	היה	qal	wcp	3ms	היה	224		be, become
	מצאי	qal	ptc	ms	מצא	592	1cs	find
	יהרגני	qal	impf	3ms	הרג	246	1cs	kill
4: 15	יאמר	qal	wci	3ms	אמר	55		say
	הרג	qal	ptc	ms	הרג	246		kill
	יקם	hoph	impf	3ms	נקם	667		be avenged
	ישׂם	qal	wci	3ms	שׂים	962		put, set
	הכות	hiph	infc		נכה	645		smite
	מצאו	qal	ptc	ms	מצא	592	3ms	find
4: 16	יצא	qal	wci	3ms	יצא	422		go out
	ישׁב	qal	wci	3ms	ישׁב	442		sit, dwell
4: 17	ידע	qal	wci	3ms	ידע	393		know
	תהר	qal	wci	3fs	הרה	247		conceive
	תלד	qal	wci	3fs	ילד	408		bear, beget
	יהי	qal	wci	3ms	היה	224		be, become
	בנה	qal	ptc	ms	בנה	124		build
	יקרא	qal	wci	3ms	קרא	894		call, proclaim
4: 18	יולד	niph	wci	3ms	ילד	408		be born
	ילד	qal	pft	3ms	ילד	408		bear, beget
	ילד	qal	pft	3ms	ילד	408		bear, beget
	ילד	qal	pft	3ms	ילד	408		bear, beget
4: 19	יקח	qal	wci	3ms	לקח	542		take
4: 20	תלד	qal	wci	3fs	ילד	408		bear, beget
	היה	qal	pft	3ms	היה	224		be, become
	ישׁב	qal	ptc	ms	ישׁב	442		sit, dwell
4: 21	היה	qal	pft	3ms	היה	224		be, become
	תפשׂ	qal	ptc	ms	תפשׂ	1074		seize, grasp
4: 22	ילדה	qal	pft	3fs	ילד	408		bear, beget
	לטשׁ	qal	ptc	ms	לטשׁ	538		hammer, sharpen
	חרשׁ	qal	ptc	ms	חרשׁ	360		engrave, plough
4: 23	יאמר	qal	wci	3ms	אמר	55		say
	שׁמען	qal	impv	fp	שׁמע	1033		hear
	האזנה	hiph	impv	fp	אזן	24		hear
	הרגתי	qal	pft	1cs	הרג	246		kill
4: 24	יקם	hoph	impf	3ms	נקם	667		be avenged
4: 25	ידע	qal	wci	3ms	ידע	393		know
	תלד	qal	wci	3fs	ילד	408		bear, beget
	תקרא	qal	wci	3fs	קרא	894		call, proclaim
	שׁת	qal	pft	3ms	שׁית	1011		put, set
	הרגו	qal	pft	3ms	הרג	246	3ms	kill
4: 26	ילד	qalp	pft	3ms	ילד	408		be born
	יקרא	qal	wci	3ms	קרא	894		call, proclaim
	הוחל	hoph	pft	3ms	חלל	320		be begun
	קרא	qal	infc		קרא	894		call, proclaim
5: 1	ברא	qal	infc		ברא	135		create
	עשׂה	qal	pft	3ms	עשׂה	793		do, make
5: 2	בראם	qal	pft	3ms	ברא	135	3mp	create
	יברך	piel	wci	3ms	ברך	138		bless
	יקרא	qal	wci	3ms	קרא	894		call, proclaim
	הבראם	niph	infc		ברא	135	3mp	be created
5: 3	יחי	qal	wci	3ms	חיה	310		live
	יולד	hiph	wci	3ms	ילד	408		beget
	יקרא	qal	wci	3ms	קרא	894		call, proclaim
5: 4	יהיו	qal	wci	3mp	היה	224		be, become
5: 4	הולידו	hiph	infc		ילד	408	3ms	beget
	יולד	hiph	wci	3ms	ילד	408		beget
5: 5	יהיו	qal	wci	3mp	היה	224		be, become
	חי	qal	pft	3ms	חיה	310		live
	ימת	qal	wci	3ms	מות	559		die
5: 6	יחי	qal	wci	3ms	חיה	310		live
	יולד	hiph	wci	3ms	ילד	408		beget
5: 7	יחי	qal	wci	3ms	חיה	310		live
	הולידו	hiph	infc		ילד	408	3ms	beget
	יולד	hiph	wci	3ms	ילד	408		beget
5: 8	יהיו	qal	wci	3mp	היה	224		be, become
	ימת	qal	wci	3ms	מות	559		die
5: 9	יחי	qal	wci	3ms	חיה	310		live
	יולד	hiph	wci	3ms	ילד	408		beget
5: 10	יחי	qal	wci	3ms	חיה	310		live
	הולידו	hiph	infc		ילד	408	3ms	beget
	יולד	hiph	wci	3ms	ילד	408		beget
5: 11	יהיו	qal	wci	3mp	היה	224		be, become
	ימת	qal	wci	3ms	מות	559		die
5: 12	יחי	qal	wci	3ms	חיה	310		live
	יולד	hiph	wci	3ms	ילד	408		beget
5: 13	יחי	qal	wci	3ms	חיה	310		live
	הולידו	hiph	infc		ילד	408	3ms	beget
	יולד	hiph	wci	3ms	ילד	408		beget
5: 14	יהיו	qal	wci	3mp	היה	224		be, become
	ימת	qal	wci	3ms	מות	559		die
5: 15	יחי	qal	wci	3ms	חיה	310		live
	יולד	hiph	wci	3ms	ילד	408		beget
5: 16	יחי	qal	wci	3ms	חיה	310		live
	הולידו	hiph	infc		ילד	408	3ms	beget
	יולד	hiph	wci	3ms	ילד	408		beget
5: 17	יהיו	qal	wci	3mp	היה	224		be, become
	ימת	qal	wci	3ms	מות	559		die
5: 18	יחי	qal	wci	3ms	חיה	310		live
	יולד	hiph	wci	3ms	ילד	408		beget
5: 19	יחי	qal	wci	3ms	חיה	310		live
	הולידו	hiph	infc		ילד	408	3ms	beget
	יולד	hiph	wci	3ms	ילד	408		beget
5: 20	יהיו	qal	wci	3mp	היה	224		be, become
	ימת	qal	wci	3ms	מות	559		die
5: 21	יחי	qal	wci	3ms	חיה	310		live
	יולד	hiph	wci	3ms	ילד	408		beget
5: 22	יתהלך	hith	wci	3ms	הלך	229		walk to and fro
	הולידו	hiph	infc		ילד	408	3ms	beget
	יולד	hiph	wci	3ms	ילד	408		beget
5: 23	יהי	qal	wci	3ms	היה	224		be, become
5: 24	יתהלך	hith	wci	3ms	הלך	229		walk to and fro
	לקח	qal	pft	3ms	לקח	542		take
5: 25	יחי	qal	wci	3ms	חיה	310		live
	יולד	hiph	wci	3ms	ילד	408		beget
5: 26	יחי	qal	wci	3ms	חיה	310		live
	הולידו	hiph	infc		ילד	408	3ms	beget
	יולד	hiph	wci	3ms	ילד	408		beget
5: 27	יהיו	qal	wci	3mp	היה	224		be, become

ChVs	Form	Stem	Tnse	PGN	Root	BDB	Sfx	Meaning
5:27	ימת	qal	wci	3ms	מות	559		die
5:28	יחי	qal	wci	3ms	חיה	310		live
	יולד	hiph	wci	3ms	ילד	408		beget
5:29	יקרא	qal	wci	3ms	קרא	894		call,proclaim
	אמר	qal	infc		אמר	55		say
	ינחמנו	piel	impf	3ms	נחם	636	1cp	comfort
	אררה	piel	pft	3ms	ארר	76	3fs	curse
5:30	יחי	qal	wci	3ms	חיה	310		live
	הולידו	hiph	infc		ילד	408	3ms	beget
	יולד	hiph	wci	3ms	ילד	408		beget
5:31	יהי	qal	wci	3ms	היה	224		be,become
	ימת	qal	wci	3ms	מות	559		die
5:32	יהי	qal	wci	3ms	היה	224		be,become
	יולד	hiph	wci	3ms	ילד	408		beget
6:1	יהי	qal	wci	3ms	היה	224		be,become
	החל	hiph	pft	3ms	חלל	320		begin,profane
	רב	qal	infc		רבב	912		be many
	ילדו	qalp	pft	3cp	ילד	408		be born
6:2	יראו	qal	wci	3mp	ראה	906		see
	יקחו	qal	wci	3mp	לקח	542		take
	בחרו	qal	pft	3cp	בחר	103		choose
6:3	יאמר	qal	wci	3ms	אמר	55		say
	ידון	qal	impf	3ms	דין	192		judge
	שׁגם	qal	infc		שׁגג	992	3mp	err,sin
	היו	qal	wcp	3cp	היה	224		be,become
6:4	היו	qal	pft	3cp	היה	224		be,become
	יבאו	qal	impf	3mp	בוא	97		come in
	ילדו	qal	wcp	3cp	ילד	408		bear,beget
6:5	ירא	qal	wci	3ms	ראה	906		see
6:6	ינחם	niph	wci	3ms	נחם	636		be sorry
	עשׂה	qal	pft	3ms	עשׂה	793		do,make
	יתעצב	hith	wci	3ms	עצב	780		be vexed
6:7	יאמר	qal	wci	3ms	אמר	55		say
	אמחה	qal	impf	1cs	מחה	562		wipe,blot out
	בראתי	qal	pft	1cs	ברא	135		create
	נחמתי	niph	pft	1cs	נחם	636		be sorry
	עשׂיתם	qal	pft	1cs	עשׂה	793	3mp	do,make
6:8	מצא	qal	pft	3ms	מצא	592		find
6:9	היה	qal	pft	3ms	היה	224		be,become
	התהלך	hith	pft	3ms	הלך	229		walk to and fro
6:10	יולד	hiph	wci	3ms	ילד	408		beget
6:11	תשחת	niph	wci	3fs	שׁחת	1007		be marred
	תמלא	niph	wci	3fs	מלא	569		be filled
6:12	ירא	qal	wci	3ms	ראה	906		see
	נשחתה	niph	pft	3fs	שׁחת	1007		be marred
	השחית	hiph	pft	3ms	שׁחת	1007		spoil,ruin
6:13	יאמר	qal	wci	3ms	אמר	55		say
	בא	qal	ptc	ms	בוא	97		come in
	מלאה	qal	pft	3fs	מלא	569		be full,fill
	משחיתם	hiph	ptc	ms	שׁחת	1007	3mp	spoil,ruin
6:14	עשׂה	qal	impv	ms	עשׂה	793		do,make
	תעשׂה	qal	impf	2ms	עשׂה	793		do,make
	כפרת	qal	wcp	2ms	כפר	498		cover w/pitch
6:15	תעשׂה	qal	impf	2ms	עשׂה	793		do,make

ChVs	Form	Stem	Tnse	PGN	Root	BDB	Sfx	Meaning
6:16	תעשׂה	qal	impf	2ms	עשׂה	793		do,make
	תכלנה	piel	impf	2ms	כלה	477	3fs	complete,finish
	תשׂים	qal	impf	2ms	שׂים	962		put,set
	תעשׂה	qal	impf	2ms	עשׂה	793	3fs	do,make
6:17	מביא	hiph	ptc	ms	בוא	97		bring in
	שׁחת	piel	infc		שׁחת	1007		spoil,ruin
	יגוע	qal	impf	3ms	גוע	157		expire,die
6:18	הקמתי	hiph	wcp	1cs	קום	877		raise,build,set
	באת	qal	wcp	2ms	בוא	97		come in
6:19	תביא	hiph	impf	2ms	בוא	97		bring in
	החית	hiph	infc		חיה	310		preserve
	יהיו	qal	impf	3mp	היה	224		be,become
6:20	יבאו	qal	impf	3mp	בוא	97		come in
	החיות	hiph	infc		חיה	310		preserve
6:21	קח	qal	impv	ms	לקח	542		take
	יאכל	niph	impf	3ms	אכל	37		be eaten
	אספת	qal	wcp	2ms	אסף	62		gather
	היה	qal	wcp	3ms	היה	224		be,become
6:22	יעשׂ	qal	wci	3ms	עשׂה	793		do,make
	צוה	piel	pft	3ms	צוה	845		command
	עשׂה	qal	pft	3ms	עשׂה	793		do,make
7:1	יאמר	qal	wci	3ms	אמר	55		say
	בא	qal	impv	ms	בוא	97		come in
	ראיתי	qal	pft	1cs	ראה	906		see
7:2	תקח	qal	impf	2ms	לקח	542		take
7:3	חיות	piel	infc		חיה	310		preserve,revive
7:4	ממטיר	hiph	ptc	ms	מטר	565		rain
	מחיתי	qal	wcp	1cs	מחה	562		wipe,blot out
	עשׂיתי	qal	pft	1cs	עשׂה	793		do,make
7:5	יעשׂ	qal	wci	3ms	עשׂה	793		do,make
	צוהו	piel	pft	3ms	צוה	845	3ms	command
7:6	היה	qal	pft	3ms	היה	224		be,become
7:7	יבא	qal	wci	3ms	בוא	97		come in
7:8	רמשׂ	qal	ptc	ms	רמשׂ	942		creep
7:9	באו	qal	pft	3cp	בוא	97		come in
	צוה	piel	pft	3ms	צוה	845		command
7:10	יהי	qal	wci	3ms	היה	224		be,become
	היו	qal	pft	3cp	היה	224		be,become
7:11	נבקעו	niph	pft	3cp	בקע	131		be cleft
	נפתחו	niph	pft	3cp	פתח	834		be opened
7:12	יהי	qal	wci	3ms	היה	224		be,become
7:13	בא	qal	pft	3ms	בוא	97		come in
7:14	רמשׂ	qal	ptc	ms	רמשׂ	942		creep
7:15	יבאו	qal	wci	3mp	בוא	97		come in
7:16	באים	qal	ptc	mp	בוא	97		come in
	באו	qal	pft	3cp	בוא	97		come in
	צוה	piel	pft	3ms	צוה	845		command
	יסגר	qal	wci	3ms	סגר	688		shut
7:17	יהי	qal	wci	3ms	היה	224		be,become
	ירבו	qal	wci	3mp	רבה	915		be many,great
	ישׂאו	qal	wci	3mp	נשׂא	669		lift,carry
	תרם	qal	wci	3fs	רום	926		be high
7:18	יגברו	qal	wci	3mp	גבר	149		be strong
	ירבו	qal	wci	3mp	רבה	915		be many,great

ChVs	Form	Stem	Tnse	PGN	Root	BDB	Sfx	Meaning
7: 18	תלך	qal	wci	3fs	הלך	229		walk,go
7: 19	גברו	qal	pft	3cp	גבר	149		be strong
	יכסו	pual	wci	3mp	כסה	491		be covered
7: 20	גברו	qal	pft	3cp	גבר	149		be strong
	יכסו	pual	wci	3mp	כסה	491		be covered
7: 21	יגוע	qal	wci	3ms	גוע	157		expire,die
	רמשׂ	qal	ptc	ms	רמשׂ	942		creep
	שׁרץ	qal	ptc	ms	שׁרץ	1056		swarm,teem
7: 22	מתו	qal	pft	3cp	מות	559		die
7: 23	ימח	qal	wci	3ms	מחה	562		wipe,blot out
	ימחו	niph	wci	3mp	מחה	562		be wiped out
	ישׁאר	niph	wci	3ms	שׁאר	983		be left
7: 24	יגברו	qal	wci	3mp	גבר	149		be strong
8: 1	יזכר	qal	wci	3ms	זכר	269		remember
	יעבר	hiph	wci	3ms	עבר	716		cause to pass
	ישׁכו	qal	wci	3mp	שׁכך	1013		abate,crouch
8: 2	יסכרו	niph	wci	3mp	סכר	698		be stopped
	יכלא	niph	wci	3ms	כלא	476		be restrained
8: 3	ישׁבו	qal	wci	3mp	שׁוב	996		turn,return
	הלוך	qal	infa		הלך	229		walk,go
	שׁוב	qal	infa		שׁוב	996		turn,return
	יחסרו	qal	wci	3mp	חסר	341		lack
8: 4	תנח	qal	wci	3fs	נוח	628		rest
8: 5	היו	qal	pft	3cp	היה	224		be,become
	הלוך	qal	infa		הלך	229		walk,go
	חסור	qal	infa		חסר	341		lack
	נראו	niph	pft	3cp	ראה	906		appear,be seen
8: 6	יהי	qal	wci	3ms	היה	224		be,become
	יפתח	qal	wci	3ms	פתח	834		open
	עשׂה	qal	pft	3ms	עשׂה	793		do,make
8: 7	ישׁלח	piel	wci	3ms	שׁלח	1018		send away,shoot
	יצא	qal	wci	3ms	יצא	422		go out
	יצוא	qal	infa		יצא	422		go out
	שׁוב	qal	infa		שׁוב	996		turn,return
	יבשׁת	qal	infc		יבשׁ	386		be dry
8: 8	ישׁלח	piel	wci	3ms	שׁלח	1018		send away,shoot
	ראות	qal	infc		ראה	906		see
	קלו	qal	pft	3cp	קלל	886		be slight,swift
8: 9	מצאה	qal	pft	3fs	מצא	592		find
	תשׁב	qal	wci	3fs	שׁוב	996		turn,return
	ישׁלח	qal	wci	3ms	שׁלח	1018		send
	יקחה	qal	wci	3ms	לקח	542	3fs	take
	יבא	hiph	wci	3ms	בוא	97		bring in
8: 10	יחל	qal	wci	3ms	חול	296		dance,writhe
	יסף	hiph	wci	3ms	יסף	414		add,do again
	שׁלח	piel	infc		שׁלח	1018		send away,shoot
8: 11	תבא	qal	wci	3fs	בוא	97		come in
	ידע	qal	wci	3ms	ידע	393		know
	קלו	qal	pft	3cp	קלל	886		be slight,swift
8: 12	ייחל	niph	wci	3ms	יחל	403		wait
	ישׁלח	piel	wci	3ms	שׁלח	1018		send away,shoot
	יספה	qal	pft	3fs	יסף	414		add,increase
	שׁוב	qal	infc		שׁוב	996		turn,return
8: 13	יהי	qal	wci	3ms	היה	224		be,become

ChVs	Form	Stem	Tnse	PGN	Root	BDB	Sfx	Meaning
8: 13	חרבו	qal	pft	3cp	חרב	351		be dried up
	יסר	hiph	wci	3ms	סור	693		take away
	ירא	qal	wci	3ms	ראה	906		see
	חרבו	qal	pft	3cp	חרב	351		be dried up
8: 14	יבשׁה	qal	pft	3fs	יבשׁ	386		be dry
8: 15	ידבר	piel	wci	3ms	דבר	180		speak
	אמר	qal	infc		אמר	55		say
8: 16	צא	qal	impv	ms	יצא	422		go out
8: 17	רמשׂ	qal	ptc	ms	רמשׂ	942		creep
	הוצאk	hiph	impv	ms	יצא	422		bring out
	היצאq	hiph	impv	ms	יצא	422		bring out
	שׁרצו	qal	wcp	3cp	שׁרץ	1056		swarm,teem
	פרו	qal	wcp	3cp	פרה	826		bear fruit
	רבו	qal	wcp	3cp	רבה	915		be many,great
8: 18	יצא	qal	wci	3ms	יצא	422		go out
8: 19	רומשׂ	qal	ptc	ms	רמשׂ	942		creep
	יצאו	qal	pft	3cp	יצא	422		go out
8: 20	יבן	qal	wci	3ms	בנה	124		build
	יקח	qal	wci	3ms	לקח	542		take
	יעל	hiph	wci	3ms	עלה	748		bring up,offer
8: 21	ירח	hiph	wci	3ms	ריח	926		smell
	יאמר	qal	wci	3ms	אמר	55		say
	אסף	hiph	impf	1cs	יסף	414		add,do again
	קלל	piel	infc		קלל	886		curse
	אסף	hiph	impf	1cs	יסף	414		add,do again
	הכות	hiph	infc		נכה	645		smite
	עשׂיתי	qal	pft	1cs	עשׂה	793		do,make
8: 22	ישׁבתו	qal	impf	3mp	שׁבת	991		cease,desist
9: 1	יברך	piel	wci	3ms	ברך	138		bless
	יאמר	qal	wci	3ms	אמר	55		say
	פרו	qal	impv	mp	פרה	826		bear fruit
	רבו	qal	impv	mp	רבה	915		be many,great
	מלאו	qal	impv	mp	מלא	569		be full,fill
9: 2	יהיה	qal	impf	3ms	היה	224		be,become
	תרמשׂ	qal	impf	3fs	רמשׂ	942		creep
	נתנו	niph	pft	3cp	נתן	678		be given
9: 3	יהיה	qal	impf	3ms	היה	224		be,become
	נתתי	qal	pft	1cs	נתן	678		give,set
9: 4	תאכלו	qal	impf	2mp	אכל	37		eat,devour
9: 5	אדרשׁ	qal	impf	1cs	דרשׁ	205		resort to,seek
	אדרשׁנו	qal	impf	1cs	דרשׁ	205	3ms	resort to,seek
	אדרשׁ	qal	impf	1cs	דרשׁ	205		resort to,seek
9: 6	שׁפך	qal	ptc	ms	שׁפך	1049		pour out
	ישׁפך	niph	impf	3ms	שׁפך	1049		be poured out
	עשׂה	qal	pft	3ms	עשׂה	793		do,make
9: 7	פרו	qal	impv	mp	פרה	826		bear fruit
	רבו	qal	impv	mp	רבה	915		be many,great
	שׁרצו	qal	impv	mp	שׁרץ	1056		swarm,teem
	רבו	qal	impv	mp	רבה	915		be many,great
9: 8	יאמר	qal	wci	3ms	אמר	55		say
	אמר	qal	infc		אמר	55		say
9: 9	מקים	hiph	ptc	ms	קום	877		raise,build,set
9: 10	יצאי	qal	ptc	mp	יצא	422		go out
9: 11	הקמתי	hiph	wcp	1cs	קום	877		raise,build,set

ChVs	Form	Stem	Tnse	PGN	Root	BDB	Sfx	Meaning
9:11	יכרת	niph	impf	3ms	כרת	503		be cut off
	יהיה	qal	impf	3ms	היה	224		be,become
	שׁחת	piel	infc		שׁחת	1007		spoil,ruin
9:12	יאמר	qal	wci	3ms	אמר	55		say
	נתן	qal	ptc	ms	נתן	678		give,set
9:13	נתתי	qal	pft	1cs	נתן	678		give,set
	היתה	qal	wcp	3fs	היה	224		be,become
9:14	היה	qal	wcp	3ms	היה	224		be,become
	ענני	piel	infc		ענן	778	1cs	bring clouds
	נראתה	niph	wcp	3fs	ראה	906		appear,be seen
9:15	זכרתי	qal	wcp	1cs	זכר	269		remember
	יהיה	qal	impf	3ms	היה	224		be,become
	שׁחת	piel	infc		שׁחת	1007		spoil,ruin
9:16	היתה	qal	wcp	3fs	היה	224		be,become
	ראיתיה	qal	wcp	1cs	ראה	906	3fs	see
	זכר	qal	infc		זכר	269		remember
9:17	יאמר	qal	wci	3ms	אמר	55		say
	הקמתי	hiph	pft	1cs	קום	877		raise,build,set
9:18	יהיו	qal	wci	3mp	היה	224		be,become
	יצאים	qal	ptc	mp	יצא	422		go out
9:19	נפצה	qal	pft	3fs	נפץ	659		disperse
9:20	יחל	hiph	wci	3ms	חלל	320		begin,profane
	יטע	qal	wci	3ms	נטע	642		plant
9:21	ישׁת	qal	wci	3ms	שׁתה	1059		drink
	ישׁכר	qal	wci	3ms	שׁכר	1016		be drunk
	יתגל	hith	wci	3ms	גלה	162		be uncovered
9:22	ירא	qal	wci	3ms	ראה	906		see
	יגד	hiph	wci	3ms	נגד	616		declare,tell
9:23	יקח	qal	wci	3ms	לקח	542		take
	ישׂימו	qal	wci	3mp	שׂים	962		put,set
	ילכו	qal	wci	3mp	הלך	229		walk,go
	יכסו	piel	wci	3mp	כסה	491		cover
	ראו	qal	pft	3cp	ראה	906		see
9:24	ייקץ	qal	wci	3ms	יקץ	429		awake
	ידע	qal	wci	3ms	ידע	393		know
	עשׂה	qal	pft	3ms	עשׂה	793		do,make
9:25	יאמר	qal	wci	3ms	אמר	55		say
	ארור	qal	pptc	ms	ארר	76		curse
	יהיה	qal	impf	3ms	היה	224		be,become
9:26	יאמר	qal	wci	3ms	אמר	55		say
	ברוך	qal	pptc	ms	ברך	138		kneel,bless
	יהי	qal	jus	3ms	היה	224		be,become
9:27	יפת	hiph	jus	3ms	פתה	834		make wide
	ישׁכן	qal	jusm	3ms	שׁכן	1014		settle,dwell
	יהי	qal	jus	3ms	היה	224		be,become
9:28	יחי	qal	wci	3ms	חיה	310		live
9:29	יהיו	qal	wci	3mp	היה	224		be,become
	ימת	qal	wci	3ms	מות	559		die
10:1	יולדו	niph	wci	3mp	ילד	408		be born
10:5	נפרדו	niph	pft	3cp	פרד	825		divide
10:8	ילד	qal	pft	3ms	ילד	408		bear,beget
	החל	hiph	pft	3ms	חלל	320		begin,profane
	היות	qal	infc		היה	224		be,become
10:9	היה	qal	pft	3ms	היה	224		be,become
10:9	יאמר	niph	impf	3ms	אמר	55		be said,called
10:10	תהי	qal	wci	3fs	היה	224		be,become
10:11	יצא	qal	pft	3ms	יצא	422		go out
	יבן	qal	wci	3ms	בנה	124		build
10:13	ילד	qal	pft	3ms	ילד	408		bear,beget
10:14	יצאו	qal	pft	3cp	יצא	422		go out
10:15	ילד	qal	pft	3ms	ילד	408		bear,beget
10:18	נפצו	niph	pft	3cp	פוץ	806		be scattered
10:19	יהי	qal	wci	3ms	היה	224		be,become
	באכה	qal	infc		בוא	97	2ms	come in
	באכה	qal	infc		בוא	97	2ms	come in
10:21	ילד	qalp	pft	3ms	ילד	408		be born
10:24	ילד	qal	pft	3ms	ילד	408		bear,beget
	ילד	qal	pft	3ms	ילד	408		bear,beget
10:25	ילד	qalp	pft	3ms	ילד	408		be born
	נפלגה	niph	pft	3fs	פלג	811		be divided
10:26	ילד	qal	pft	3ms	ילד	408		bear,beget
10:30	יהי	qal	wci	3ms	היה	224		be,become
	באכה	qal	infc		בוא	97	2ms	come in
10:32	נפרדו	niph	pft	3cp	פרד	825		divide
11:1	יהי	qal	wci	3ms	היה	224		be,become
11:2	יהי	qal	wci	3ms	היה	224		be,become
	נסעם	qal	infc		נסע	652	3mp	pull up,set out
	ימצאו	qal	wci	3mp	מצא	592		find
	ישׁבו	qal	wci	3mp	ישׁב	442		sit,dwell
11:3	יאמרו	qal	wci	3mp	אמר	55		say
	הבה	qal	impv	ms	יהב	396		give
	נלבנה	qal	coh	1cp	לבן	527		make brick
	נשׂרפה	qal	coh	1cp	שׂרף	976		burn
	תהי	qal	wci	3fs	היה	224		be,become
	היה	qal	pft	3ms	היה	224		be,become
11:4	יאמרו	qal	wci	3mp	אמר	55		say
	הבה	qal	impv	ms	יהב	396		give
	נבנה	qal	cohm	1cp	בנה	124		build
	נעשׂה	qal	cohm	1cp	עשׂה	793		do,make
	נפוץ	qal	impf	1cp	פוץ	806		be scattered
11:5	ירד	qal	wci	3ms	ירד	432		come down
	ראת	qal	infc		ראה	906		see
	בנו	qal	pft	3cp	בנה	124		build
11:6	יאמר	qal	wci	3ms	אמר	55		say
	החלם	hiph	infc		חלל	320	3mp	begin,profane
	עשׂות	qal	infc		עשׂה	793		do,make
	יבצר	niph	impf	3ms	בצר	130		be withheld
	יזמו	qal	impf	3mp	זמם	273		consider,devise
	עשׂות	qal	infc		עשׂה	793		do,make
11:7	הבה	qal	impv	ms	יהב	396		give
	נרדה	qal	coh	1cp	ירד	432		come down
	נבלה	qal	coh	1cp	בלל	117		mingle,mix
	ישׁמעו	qal	impf	3mp	שׁמע	1033		hear
11:8	יפץ	hiph	wci	3ms	פוץ	806		scatter
	יחדלו	qal	wci	3mp	חדל	292		cease
	בנת	qal	infc		בנה	124		build
11:9	קרא	qal	pft	3ms	קרא	894		call,proclaim
	בלל	qal	pft	3ms	בלל	117		mingle,mix

ChVs	Form	Stem	Tnse	PGN	Root	BDB	Sfx	Meaning
11:9	הפיצם	hiph	pft	3ms	פוץ	806	3mp	scatter
11:10	יולד	hiph	wci	3ms	ילד	408		beget
11:11	יחי	qal	wci	3ms	חיה	310		live
	הולידו	hiph	infc		ילד	408	3ms	beget
	יולד	hiph	wci	3ms	ילד	408		beget
11:12	חי	qal	pft	3ms	חיה	310		live
	יולד	hiph	wci	3ms	ילד	408		beget
11:13	יחי	qal	wci	3ms	חיה	310		live
	הולידו	hiph	infc		ילד	408	3ms	beget
	יולד	hiph	wci	3ms	ילד	408		beget
11:14	חי	qal	pft	3ms	חיה	310		live
	יולד	hiph	wci	3ms	ילד	408		beget
11:15	יחי	qal	wci	3ms	חיה	310		live
	הולידו	hiph	infc		ילד	408	3ms	beget
	יולד	hiph	wci	3ms	ילד	408		beget
11:16	יחי	qal	wci	3ms	חיה	310		live
	יולד	hiph	wci	3ms	ילד	408		beget
11:17	יחי	qal	wci	3ms	חיה	310		live
	הולידו	hiph	infc		ילד	408	3ms	beget
	יולד	hiph	wci	3ms	ילד	408		beget
11:18	יחי	qal	wci	3ms	חיה	310		live
	יולד	hiph	wci	3ms	ילד	408		beget
11:19	יחי	qal	wci	3ms	חיה	310		live
	הולידו	hiph	infc		ילד	408	3ms	beget
	יולד	hiph	wci	3ms	ילד	408		beget
11:20	יחי	qal	wci	3ms	חיה	310		live
	יולד	hiph	wci	3ms	ילד	408		beget
11:21	יחי	qal	wci	3ms	חיה	310		live
	הולידו	hiph	infc		ילד	408	3ms	beget
	יולד	hiph	wci	3ms	ילד	408		beget
11:22	יחי	qal	wci	3ms	חיה	310		live
	יולד	hiph	wci	3ms	ילד	408		beget
11:23	יחי	qal	wci	3ms	חיה	310		live
	הולידו	hiph	infc		ילד	408	3ms	beget
	יולד	hiph	wci	3ms	ילד	408		beget
11:24	יחי	qal	wci	3ms	חיה	310		live
	יולד	hiph	wci	3ms	ילד	408		beget
11:25	יחי	qal	wci	3ms	חיה	310		live
	הולידו	hiph	infc		ילד	408	3ms	beget
	יולד	hiph	wci	3ms	ילד	408		beget
11:26	יחי	qal	wci	3ms	חיה	310		live
	יולד	hiph	wci	3ms	ילד	408		beget
11:27	הוליד	hiph	pft	3ms	ילד	408		beget
	הוליד	hiph	pft	3ms	ילד	408		beget
11:28	ימת	qal	wci	3ms	מות	559		die
11:29	יקח	qal	wci	3ms	לקח	542		take
11:30	תהי	qal	wci	3fs	היה	224		be,become
11:31	יקח	qal	wci	3ms	לקח	542		take
	יצאו	qal	wci	3mp	יצא	422		go out
	לכת	qal	infc		הלך	229		walk,go
	יבאו	qal	wci	3mp	בוא	97		come in
	ישבו	qal	wci	3mp	ישב	442		sit,dwell
11:32	יהיו	qal	wci	3mp	היה	224		be,become
	ימת	qal	wci	3ms	מות	559		die

ChVs	Form	Stem	Tnse	PGN	Root	BDB	Sfx	Meaning
12:1	יאמר	qal	wci	3ms	אמר	55		say
	לך	qal	impv	ms	הלך	229		walk,go
	אראך	hiph	impf	1cs	ראה	906	2ms	show,exhibit
12:2	אעשׂך	qal	cohm	1cs	עשׂה	793	2ms	do,make
	אברכך	piel	cohm	1cs	ברך	138	2ms	bless
	אגדלה	piel	coh	1cs	גדל	152		cause to grow
	היה	qal	impv	ms	היה	224		be,become
12:3	אברכה	piel	coh	1cs	ברך	138		bless
	מברכיך	piel	ptc	mp	ברך	138	2ms	bless
	מקללך	piel	ptc	ms	קלל	886	2ms	curse
	אאר	qal	impf	1cs	ארר	76		curse
	נברכו	niph	wcp	3cp	ברך	138		bless oneself
12:4	ילך	qal	wci	3ms	הלך	229		walk,go
	דבר	piel	pft	3ms	דבר	180		speak
	ילך	qal	wci	3ms	הלך	229		walk,go
	צאתו	qal	infc		יצא	422	3ms	go out
12:5	יקח	qal	wci	3ms	לקח	542		take
	רכשׁו	qal	pft	3cp	רכשׁ	940		collect
	עשׂו	qal	pft	3cp	עשׂה	793		do,make
	יצאו	qal	wci	3mp	יצא	422		go out
	לכת	qal	infc		הלך	229		walk,go
	יבאו	qal	wci	3mp	בוא	97		come in
12:6	יעבר	qal	wci	3ms	עבר	716		pass over
12:7	ירא	niph	wci	3ms	ראה	906		appear,be seen
	יאמר	qal	wci	3ms	אמר	55		say
	אתן	qal	impf	1cs	נתן	678		give,set
	יבן	qal	wci	3ms	בנה	124		build
	נראה	niph	ptc	ms	ראה	906		appear,be seen
12:8	יעתק	hiph	wci	3ms	עתק	801		move,remove
	יט	qal	wci	3ms	נטה	639		stretch,incline
	יבן	qal	wci	3ms	בנה	124		build
	יקרא	qal	wci	3ms	קרא	894		call,proclaim
12:9	יסע	qal	wci	3ms	נסע	652		pull up,set out
	הלוך	qal	infa		הלך	229		walk,go
	נסוע	qal	infa		נסע	652		pull up,set out
12:10	יהי	qal	wci	3ms	היה	224		be,become
	ירד	qal	wci	3ms	ירד	432		come down
	גור	qal	infc		גור	157		sojourn
12:11	יהי	qal	wci	3ms	היה	224		be,become
	הקריב	hiph	pft	3ms	קרב	897		bring near
	בוא	qal	infc		בוא	97		come in
	יאמר	qal	wci	3ms	אמר	55		say
	ידעתי	qal	pft	1cs	ידע	393		know
12:12	היה	qal	wcp	3ms	היה	224		be,become
	יראו	qal	impf	3mp	ראה	906		see
	אמרו	qal	wcp	3cp	אמר	55		say
	הרגו	qal	wcp	3cp	הרג	246		kill
	יחיו	piel	impf	3mp	חיה	310		preserve,revive
12:13	אמרי	qal	impv	fs	אמר	55		say
	ייטב	qal	impf	3ms	יטב	405		be good
	חיתה	qal	wcp	3fs	חיה	310		live
12:14	יהי	qal	wci	3ms	היה	224		be,become
	בוא	qal	infc		בוא	97		come in
	יראו	qal	wci	3mp	ראה	906		see

ChVs	Form	Stem	Tnse	PGN	Root	BDB	Sfx	Meaning
12:15	יראו	qal	wci	3mp	ראה	906		see
	יהללו	piel	wci	3mp	הלל	237		praise
	תקח	qalp	wci	3fs	לקח	542		be taken
12:16	היטיב	hiph	pft	3ms	יטב	405		do good
	יהי	qal	wci	3ms	היה	224		be,become
12:17	ינגע	piel	wci	3ms	נגע	619		strike
12:18	יקרא	qal	wci	3ms	קרא	894		call,proclaim
	יאמר	qal	wci	3ms	אמר	55		say
	עשׂית	qal	pft	2ms	עשׂה	793		do,make
	הגדת	hiph	pft	2ms	נגד	616		declare,tell
12:19	אמרת	qal	pft	2ms	אמר	55		say
	אקח	qal	wci	1cs	לקח	542		take
	קח	qal	impv	ms	לקח	542		take
	לך	qal	impv	ms	הלך	229		walk,go
12:20	יצו	piel	wci	3ms	צוה	845		command
	ישׁלחו	piel	wci	3mp	שׁלח	1018		send away,shoot
13:1	יעל	qal	wci	3ms	עלה	748		go up
13:3	ילך	qal	wci	3ms	הלך	229		walk,go
	היה	qal	pft	3ms	היה	224		be,become
13:4	עשׂה	qal	pft	3ms	עשׂה	793		do,make
	יקרא	qal	wci	3ms	קרא	894		call,proclaim
13:5	הלך	qal	ptc	ms	הלך	229		walk,go
	היה	qal	pft	3ms	היה	224		be,become
13:6	נשׂא	qal	pft	3ms	נשׂא	669		lift,carry
	שׁבת	qal	infc		ישׁב	442		sit,dwell
	היה	qal	pft	3ms	היה	224		be,become
	יכלו	qal	pft	3cp	יכל	407		be able
	שׁבת	qal	infc		ישׁב	442		sit,dwell
13:7	יהי	qal	wci	3ms	היה	224		be,become
	רעי	qal	ptc	mp	רעה	944		pasture,tend
	רעי	qal	ptc	mp	רעה	944		pasture,tend
	ישׁב	qal	ptc	ms	ישׁב	442		sit,dwell
13:8	יאמר	qal	wci	3ms	אמר	55		say
	תהי	qal	jus	3fs	היה	224		be,become
	רעי	qal	ptc	mp	רעה	944	1cs	pasture,tend
	רעיך	qal	ptc	mp	רעה	944	2ms	pasture,tend
13:9	הפרד	niph	impv	ms	פרד	825		divide
	אימנה	hiph	coh	1cs	ימן	412		go to right
	אשׂמאילה	hiph	coh	1cs	שׂמאל	970		go to left
13:10	ישׂא	qal	wci	3ms	נשׂא	669		lift,carry
	ירא	qal	wci	3ms	ראה	906		see
	שׁחת	piel	infc		שׁחת	1007		spoil,ruin
	באכה	qal	infc		בוא	97	2ms	come in
13:11	יבחר	qal	wci	3ms	בחר	103		choose
	יסע	qal	wci	3ms	נסע	652		pull up,set out
	יפרדו	niph	wci	3mp	פרד	825		divide
13:12	ישׁב	qal	pft	3ms	ישׁב	442		sit,dwell
	ישׁב	qal	pft	3ms	ישׁב	442		sit,dwell
	יאהל	qal	wci	3ms	אהל	14		pitch tent
13:14	אמר	qal	pft	3ms	אמר	55		say
	הפרד	niph	infc		פרד	825		divide
	שׂא	qal	impv	ms	נשׂא	669		lift,carry
	ראה	qal	impv	ms	ראה	906		see
13:15	ראה	qal	ptc	ms	ראה	906		see

ChVs	Form	Stem	Tnse	PGN	Root	BDB	Sfx	Meaning
13:15	אתננה	qal	impf	1cs	נתן	678	3fs	give,set
13:16	שׂמתי	qal	wcp	1cs	שׂים	962		put,set
	יוכל	qal	impf	3ms	יכל	407		be able
	מנות	qal	infc		מנה	584		count,allot
	ימנה	niph	impf	3ms	מנה	584		be counted
13:17	קום	qal	impv	ms	קום	877		arise,stand
	התהלך	hith	impv	ms	הלך	229		walk to and fro
	אתננה	qal	impf	1cs	נתן	678	3fs	give,set
13:18	יאהל	qal	wci	3ms	אהל	14		pitch tent
	יבא	qal	wci	3ms	בוא	97		come in
	ישׁב	qal	wci	3ms	ישׁב	442		sit,dwell
	יבן	qal	wci	3ms	בנה	124		build
14:1	יהי	qal	wci	3ms	היה	224		be,become
14:2	עשׂו	qal	pft	3cp	עשׂה	793		do,make
14:3	חברו	qal	pft	3cp	חבר	287		unite
14:4	עבדו	qal	pft	3cp	עבד	712		work,serve
	מרדו	qal	pft	3cp	מרד	597		rebel
14:5	בא	qal	pft	3ms	בוא	97		come in
	יכו	hiph	wci	3mp	נכה	645		smite
14:7	ישׁבו	qal	wci	3mp	שׁוב	996		turn,return
	יבאו	qal	wci	3mp	בוא	97		come in
	יכו	hiph	wci	3mp	נכה	645		smite
	ישׁב	qal	ptc	ms	ישׁב	442		sit,dwell
14:8	יצא	qal	wci	3ms	יצא	422		go out
	יערכו	qal	wci	3mp	ערך	789		set in order
14:10	ינסו	qal	wci	3mp	נוס	630		flee,escape
	יפלו	qal	wci	3mp	נפל	656		fall
	נשׁארים	niph	ptc	mp	שׁאר	983		be left
	נסו	qal	pft	3cp	נוס	630		flee,escape
14:11	יקחו	qal	wci	3mp	לקח	542		take
	ילכו	qal	wci	3mp	הלך	229		walk,go
14:12	יקחו	qal	wci	3mp	לקח	542		take
	ילכו	qal	wci	3mp	הלך	229		walk,go
	ישׁב	qal	ptc	ms	ישׁב	442		sit,dwell
14:13	יבא	qal	wci	3ms	בוא	97		come in
	יגד	hiph	wci	3ms	נגד	616		declare,tell
	שׁכן	qal	ptc	ms	שׁכן	1014		settle,dwell
14:14	ישׁמע	qal	wci	3ms	שׁמע	1033		hear
	נשׁבה	niph	pft	3ms	שׁבה	985		be held captive
	ירק	hiph	wci	3ms	ריק	937		make empty
	ירדף	qal	wci	3ms	רדף	922		pursue
14:15	יחלק	niph	wci	3ms	חלק	323		be divided
	יכם	hiph	wci	3ms	נכה	645	3mp	smite
	ירדפם	qal	wci	3ms	רדף	922	3mp	pursue
14:16	ישׁב	hiph	wci	3ms	שׁוב	996		bring back
	השׁיב	hiph	pft	3ms	שׁוב	996		bring back
14:17	יצא	qal	wci	3ms	יצא	422		go out
	קראתו	qal	infc		קרא	896	3ms	meet,encounter
	שׁובו	qal	infc		שׁוב	996	3ms	turn,return
	הכות	hiph	infc		נכה	645		smite
14:18	הוציא	hiph	pft	3ms	יצא	422		bring out
14:19	יברכהו	piel	wci	3ms	ברך	138	3ms	bless
	יאמר	qal	wci	3ms	אמר	55		say
	ברוך	qal	pptc	ms	ברך	138		kneel,bless

ChVs	Form	Stem	Tnse	PGN	Root	BDB	Sfx	Meaning
14:19	קנה	qal	ptc	ms	קנה	888		get,buy
14:20	ברוך	qal	pptc	ms	ברך	138		kneel,bless
	מגן	piel	pft	3ms	מגן	171		deliver up
	יתן	qal	wci	3ms	נתן	678		give,set
14:21	יאמר	qal	wci	3ms	אמר	55		say
	תן	qal	impv	ms	נתן	678		give,set
	קח	qal	impv	ms	לקח	542		take
14:22	יאמר	qal	wci	3ms	אמר	55		say
	הרימתי	hiph	pft	1cs	רום	926		raise,lift
	קנה	qal	ptc	ms	קנה	888		get,buy
14:23	אקח	qal	impf	1cs	לקח	542		take
	תאמר	qal	impf	2ms	אמר	55		say
	העשרתי	hiph	pft	1cs	עשר	799		make rich
14:24	אכלו	qal	pft	3cp	אכל	37		eat,devour
	הלכו	qal	pft	3cp	הלך	229		walk,go
	יקחו	qal	jusm	3mp	לקח	542		take
15:1	היה	qal	pft	3ms	היה	224		be,become
	אמר	qal	infc		אמר	55		say
	תירא	qal	jusm	2ms	ירא	431		fear
	הרבה	hiph	infa		רבה	915		make many
15:2	יאמר	qal	wci	3ms	אמר	55		say
	תתן	qal	impf	2ms	נתן	678		give,set
	הולך	qal	ptc	ms	הלך	229		walk,go
15:3	יאמר	qal	wci	3ms	אמר	55		say
	נתתה	qal	pft	2ms	נתן	678		give,set
	יורש	qal	ptc	ms	ירש	439		possess,inherit
15:4	אמר	qal	infc		אמר	55		say
	יירשך	qal	impf	3ms	ירש	439	2ms	possess,inherit
	יצא	qal	impf	3ms	יצא	422		go out
	יירשך	qal	impf	3ms	ירש	439	2ms	possess,inherit
15:5	יוצא	hiph	wci	3ms	יצא	422		bring out
	יאמר	qal	wci	3ms	אמר	55		say
	הבט	hiph	impv	ms	נבט	613		look,regard
	ספר	qal	impv	ms	ספר	707		count
	תוכל	qal	impf	2ms	יכל	407		be able
	ספר	qal	infc		ספר	707		count
	יאמר	qal	wci	3ms	אמר	55		say
	יהיה	qal	impf	3ms	היה	224		be,become
15:6	האמן	hiph	pft	3ms	אמן	52		believe
	יחשבה	qal	wci	3ms	חשב	362	3fs	think,devise
15:7	יאמר	qal	wci	3ms	אמר	55		say
	הוצאתיך	hiph	pft	1cs	יצא	422	2ms	bring out
	תת	qal	infc		נתן	678		give,set
	רשתה	qal	infc		ירש	439	3fs	possess,inherit
15:8	יאמר	qal	wci	3ms	אמר	55		say
	אדע	qal	impf	1cs	ידע	393		know
	אירשנה	qal	impf	1cs	ירש	439	3fs	possess,inherit
15:9	יאמר	qal	wci	3ms	אמר	55		say
	קחה	qal	impv	ms	לקח	542		take
	משלשת	pual	ptc	fs	שלש	1026		be threefold
	משלשת	pual	ptc	fs	שלש	1026		be threefold
	משלש	pual	ptc	ms	שלש	1026		be threefold
15:10	יקח	qal	wci	3ms	לקח	542		take
	יבתר	piel	wci	3ms	בתר	144		cut in two
15:10	יתן	qal	wci	3ms	נתן	678		give,set
	קראת	qal	infc		קרא	896		meet,encounter
	בתר	qal	pft	3ms	בתר	144		cut in two
15:11	ירד	qal	wci	3ms	ירד	432		come down
	ישב	hiph	wci	3ms	נשב	674		cause to blow
15:12	יהי	qal	wci	3ms	היה	224		be,become
	בוא	qal	infc		בוא	97		come in
	נפלה	qal	pft	3fs	נפל	656		fall
	נפלת	qal	ptc	fs	נפל	656		fall
15:13	יאמר	qal	wci	3ms	אמר	55		say
	ידע	qal	infa		ידע	393		know
	תדע	qal	impf	2ms	ידע	393		know
	יהיה	qal	impf	3ms	היה	224		be,become
	עבדום	qal	wcp	3cp	עבד	712	3mp	work,serve
	ענו	piel	wcp	3cp	ענה	776		humble
15:14	יעבדו	qal	impf	3mp	עבד	712		work,serve
	דן	qal	ptc	ms	דין	192		judge
	יצאו	qal	impf	3mp	יצא	422		go out
15:15	תבוא	qal	impf	2ms	בוא	97		come in
	תקבר	niph	impf	2ms	קבר	868		be buried
15:16	ישובו	qal	impf	3mp	שוב	996		turn,return
15:17	יהי	qal	wci	3ms	היה	224		be,become
	באה	qal	pft	3fs	בוא	97		come in
	היה	qal	pft	3ms	היה	224		be,become
	עבר	qal	pft	3ms	עבר	716		pass over
15:18	כרת	qal	pft	3ms	כרת	503		cut,destroy
	אמר	qal	infc		אמר	55		say
	נתתי	qal	pft	1cs	נתן	678		give,set
16:1	ילדה	qal	pft	3fs	ילד	408		bear,beget
16:2	תאמר	qal	wci	3fs	אמר	55		say
	עצרני	qal	pft	3ms	עצר	783	1cs	restrain
	לדת	qal	infc		ילד	408		bear,beget
	בא	qal	impv	ms	בוא	97		come in
	אבנה	niph	impf	1cs	בנה	124		be built
	ישמע	qal	wci	3ms	שמע	1033		hear
16:3	תקח	qal	wci	3fs	לקח	542		take
	שבת	qal	infc		ישב	442		sit,dwell
	תתן	qal	wci	3fs	נתן	678		give,set
16:4	יבא	qal	wci	3ms	בוא	97		come in
	תהר	qal	wci	3fs	הרה	247		conceive
	תרא	qal	wci	3fs	ראה	906		see
	הרתה	qal	pft	3fs	הרה	247		conceive
	תקל	qal	wci	3fs	קלל	886		be slight,swift
16:5	תאמר	qal	wci	3fs	אמר	55		say
	נתתי	qal	pft	1cs	נתן	678		give,set
	תרא	qal	wci	3fs	ראה	906		see
	הרתה	qal	pft	3fs	הרה	247		conceive
	אקל	qal	wci	1cs	קלל	886		be slight,swift
	ישפט	qal	jusm	3ms	שפט	1047		judge
16:6	יאמר	qal	wci	3ms	אמר	55		say
	עשׂי	qal	impv	fs	עשׂה	793		do,make
	תענה	piel	wci	3fs	ענה	776	3fs	humble
	תברח	qal	wci	3fs	ברח	137		go thru,flee
16:7	ימצאה	qal	wci	3ms	מצא	592	3fs	find

ChVs	Form	Stem	Tnse	PGN	Root	BDB	Sfx	Meaning
16: 8	יאמר	qal	wci	3ms	אמר	55		say
	באת	qal	pft	2fs	בוא	97		come in
	תלכי	qal	impf	2fs	הלך	229		walk, go
	תאמר	qal	wci	3fs	אמר	55		say
	ברחת	qal	ptc	fs	ברח	137		go thru, flee
16: 9	יאמר	qal	wci	3ms	אמר	55		say
	שובי	qal	impv	fs	שוב	996		turn, return
	התעני	hith	impv	fs	ענה	776		humble oneself
16: 10	יאמר	qal	wci	3ms	אמר	55		say
	הרבה	hiph	infa		רבה	915		make many
	ארבה	hiph	impf	1cs	רבה	915		make many
	יספר	niph	impf	3ms	ספר	707		be counted
16: 11	יאמר	qal	wci	3ms	אמר	55		say
	ילדת	qal	wcp	2fs	ילד	408?		bear, beget
	קראת	qal	wcp	2fs	קרא	894		call, proclaim
	שמע	qal	pft	3ms	שמע	1033		hear
16: 12	יהיה	qal	impf	3ms	היה	224		be, become
	ישכן	qal	impf	3ms	שכן	1014		settle, dwell
16: 13	תקרא	qal	wci	3fs	קרא	894		call, proclaim
	דבר	qal	ptc	ms	דבר	180		speak
	אמרה	qal	pft	3fs	אמר	55		say
	ראיתי	qal	pft	1cs	ראה	906		see
	ראי	qal	ptc	ms	ראה	906	1cs	see
16: 14	קרא	qal	pft	3ms	קרא	894		call, proclaim
16: 15	תלד	qal	wci	3fs	ילד	408		bear, beget
	יקרא	qal	wci	3ms	קרא	894		call, proclaim
	ילדה	qal	pft	3fs	ילד	408		bear, beget
16: 16	לדת	qal	infc		ילד	408		bear, beget
17: 1	יהי	qal	wci	3ms	היה	224		be, become
	ירא	niph	wci	3ms	ראה	906		appear, be seen
	יאמר	qal	wci	3ms	אמר	55		say
	התהלך	hith	impv	ms	הלך	229		walk to and fro
	היה	qal	impv	ms	היה	224		be, become
17: 2	אתנה	qal	coh	1cs	נתן	678		give, set
	ארבה	hiph	cohm	1cs	רבה	915		make many
17: 3	יפל	qal	wci	3ms	נפל	656		fall
	ידבר	piel	wci	3ms	דבר	180		speak
	אמר	qal	infc		אמר	55		say
17: 4	היית	qal	wcp	2ms	היה	224		be, become
17: 5	יקרא	niph	impf	3ms	קרא	894		be called
	היה	qal	wcp	3ms	היה	224		be, become
	נתתיך	qal	pft	1cs	נתן	678	2ms	give, set
17: 6	הפרתי	hiph	wcp	1cs	פרה	826		make fruitful
	נתתיך	qal	wcp	1cs	נתן	678	2ms	give, set
	יצאו	qal	impf	3mp	יצא	422		go out
17: 7	הקמתי	hiph	wcp	1cs	קום	877		raise, build, set
	היות	qal	infc		היה	224		be, become
17: 8	נתתי	qal	wcp	1cs	נתן	678		give, set
	הייתי	qal	wcp	1cs	היה	224		be, become
17: 9	יאמר	qal	wci	3ms	אמר	55		say
	תשמר	qal	impf	2ms	שמר	1036		keep, watch
17: 10	תשמרו	qal	impf	2mp	שמר	1036		keep, watch
	המול	niph	infa		מול	557		be circumcised
17: 11	נמלתם	niph	wcp	2mp	מול	557		be circumcised
17: 11	היה	qal	wcp	3ms	היה	224		be, become
17: 12	ימול	niph	impf	3ms	מול	557		be circumcised
17: 13	המול	niph	infa		מול	557		be circumcised
	ימול	niph	impf	3ms	מול	557		be circumcised
	היתה	qal	wcp	3fs	היה	224		be, become
17: 14	ימול	niph	impf	3ms	מול	557		be circumcised
	נכרתה	niph	wcp	3fs	כרת	503		be cut off
	הפר	hiph	pft	3ms	פרר	830		break, frustrate
17: 15	יאמר	qal	wci	3ms	אמר	55		say
	תקרא	qal	impf	2ms	קרא	894		call, proclaim
17: 16	ברכתי	piel	wcp	1cs	ברך	138		bless
	נתתי	qal	pft	1cs	נתן	678		give, set
	ברכתיה	piel	wcp	1cs	ברך	138	3fs	bless
	היתה	qal	wcp	3fs	היה	224		be, become
	יהיו	qal	impf	3mp	היה	224		be, become
17: 17	יפל	qal	wci	3ms	נפל	656		fall
	יצחק	qal	wci	3ms	צחק	850		laugh
	יאמר	qal	wci	3ms	אמר	55		say
	יולד	niph	impf	3ms	ילד	408		be born
	תלד	qal	impf	3fs	ילד	408		bear, beget
17: 18	יאמר	qal	wci	3ms	אמר	55		say
	יחיה	qal	impf	3ms	חיה	310		live
17: 19	יאמר	qal	wci	3ms	אמר	55		say
	ילדת	qal	ptc	fs	ילד	408		bear, beget
	קראת	qal	wcp	2ms	קרא	894		call, proclaim
	הקמתי	hiph	wcp	1cs	קום	877		raise, build, set
17: 20	שמעתיך	qal	pft	1cs	שמע	1033	2ms	hear
	ברכתי	piel	pft	1cs	ברך	138		bless
	הפריתי	hiph	wcp	1cs	פרה	826		make fruitful
	הרביתי	hiph	wcp	1cs	רבה	915		make many
	יוליד	hiph	impf	3ms	ילד	408		beget
	נתתיו	qal	wcp	1cs	נתן	678	3ms	give, set
17: 21	אקים	hiph	impf	1cs	קום	877		raise, build, set
	תלד	qal	impf	3fs	ילד	408		bear, beget
17: 22	יכל	piel	wci	3ms	כלה	477		complete, finish
	דבר	piel	infc		דבר	180		speak
	יעל	qal	wci	3ms	עלה	748		go up
17: 23	יקח	qal	wci	3ms	לקח	542		take
	ימל	qal	wci	3ms	מול	557		circumcise
	דבר	piel	pft	3ms	דבר	180		speak
17: 24	המלו	niph	infc		מול	557	3ms	be circumcised
17: 25	המלו	niph	infc		מול	557	3ms	be circumcised
17: 26	נמול	niph	pft	3ms	מול	557		be circumcised
17: 27	נמלו	niph	pft	3cp	מול	557		be circumcised
18: 1	ירא	niph	wci	3ms	ראה	906		appear, be seen
	ישב	qal	ptc	ms	ישב	442		sit, dwell
18: 2	ישא	qal	wci	3ms	נשא	669		lift, carry
	ירא	qal	wci	3ms	ראה	906		see
	נצבים	niph	ptc	mp	נצב	662		stand
	ירא	qal	wci	3ms	ראה	906		see
	ירץ	qal	wci	3ms	רוץ	930		run
	קראתם	qal	infc		קרא	896	3mp	meet, encounter
	ישתחו	hish	wci	3ms	חוה	1005		bow down
18: 3	יאמר	qal	wci	3ms	אמר	55		say

ChVs	Form	Stem	Tnse	PGN	Root	BDB	Sfx	Meaning
18: 3	מצאתי	qal	pft	1cs	מצא	592		find
	תעבר	qal	jusm	2ms	עבר	716		pass over
18: 4	יקח	qalp	jusm	3ms	לקח	542		be taken
	רחצו	qal	impv	mp	רחץ	934		wash,bathe
	השענו	niph	impv	mp	שען	1043		lean,support
18: 5	אקחה	qal	coh	1cs	לקח	542		take
	סעדו	qal	impv	mp	סעד	703		support
	תעברו	qal	impf	2mp	עבר	716		pass over
	עברתם	qal	pft	2mp	עבר	716		pass over
	יאמרו	qal	wci	3mp	אמר	55		say
	תעשה	qal	impf	2ms	עשה	793		do,make
	דברת	piel	pft	2ms	דבר	180		speak
18: 6	ימהר	piel	wci	3ms	מהר	554		hasten
	יאמר	qal	wci	3ms	אמר	55		say
	מהרי	piel	impv	fs	מהר	554		hasten
	לושי	qal	impv	fs	לוש	534		knead
	עשי	qal	impv	fs	עשה	793		do,make
18: 7	רץ	qal	pft	3ms	רוץ	930		run
	יקח	qal	wci	3ms	לקח	542		take
	יתן	qal	wci	3ms	נתן	678		give,set
	ימהר	piel	wci	3ms	מהר	554		hasten
	עשות	qal	infc		עשה	793		do,make
18: 8	יקח	qal	wci	3ms	לקח	542		take
	עשה	qal	pft	3ms	עשה	793		do,make
	יתן	qal	wci	3ms	נתן	678		give,set
	עמד	qal	ptc	ms	עמד	763		stand,stop
	יאכלו	qal	wci	3mp	אכל	37		eat,devour
18: 9	יאמרו	qal	wci	3mp	אמר	55		say
	יאמר	qal	wci	3ms	אמר	55		say
18: 10	יאמר	qal	wci	3ms	אמר	55		say
	שוב	qal	infa		שוב	996		turn,return
	אשוב	qal	impf	1cs	שוב	996		turn,return
	שמעת	qal	ptc	fs	שמע	1033		hear
18: 11	באים	qal	ptc	mp	בוא	97		come in
	חדל	qal	pft	3ms	חדל	292		cease
	היות	qal	infc		היה	224		be,become
18: 12	תצחק	qal	wci	3fs	צחק	850		laugh
	אמר	qal	infc		אמר	55		say
	בלתי	qal	infc		בלה	115	1cs	wear out
	היתה	qal	pft	3fs	היה	224		be,become
	זקן	qal	pft	3ms	זקן	278		be old
18: 13	יאמר	qal	wci	3ms	אמר	55		say
	צחקה	qal	pft	3fs	צחק	850		laugh
	אמר	qal	infc		אמר	55		say
	אלד	qal	impf	1cs	ילד	408		bear,beget
	זקנתי	qal	pft	1cs	זקן	278		be old
18: 14	יפלא	niph	impf	3ms	פלא	810		be wonderful
	אשוב	qal	impf	1cs	שוב	996		turn,return
18: 15	תכחש	piel	wci	3fs	כחש	471		deceive
	אמר	qal	infc		אמר	55		say
	צחקתי	qal	pft	1cs	צחק	850		laugh
	יראה	qal	pft	3fs	ירא	431		fear
	יאמר	qal	wci	3ms	אמר	55		say
	צחקת	qal	pft	2fs	צחק	850		laugh
18: 16	יקמו	qal	wci	3mp	קום	877		arise,stand
	ישקפו	hiph	wci	3mp	שקף	1054		look down
	הלך	qal	ptc	ms	הלך	229		walk,go
	שלחם	piel	infc		שלח	1018	3mp	send away,shoot
18: 17	אמר	qal	pft	3ms	אמר	55		say
	מכסה	piel	ptc	ms	כסה	491		cover
	עשה	qal	ptc	ms	עשה	793		do,make
18: 18	היו	qal	infa		היה	224		be,become
	יהיה	qal	impf	3ms	היה	224		be,become
	נברכו	niph	wcp	3cp	ברך	138		bless oneself
18: 19	ידעתיו	qal	pft	1cs	ידע	393	3ms	know
	יצוה	piel	impf	3ms	צוה	845		command
	שמרו	qal	wcp	3cp	שמר	1036		keep,watch
	עשות	qal	infc		עשה	793		do,make
	הביא	hiph	infc		בוא	97		bring in
	דבר	piel	pft	3ms	דבר	180		speak
18: 20	יאמר	qal	wci	3ms	אמר	55		say
	רבה	qal	pft	3fs	רבב	912		be many
	כבדה	qal	pft	3fs	כבד	457		be heavy
18: 21	ארדה	qal	coh	1cs	ירד	432		come down
	אראה	qal	cohm	1cs	ראה	906		see
	באה	qal	pft	3fs	בוא	97		come in
	עשו	qal	pft	3cp	עשה	793		do,make
	אדעה	qal	coh	1cs	ידע	393		know
18: 22	יפנו	qal	wci	3mp	פנה	815		turn
	ילכו	qal	wci	3mp	הלך	229		walk,go
	עמד	qal	ptc	ms	עמד	763		stand,stop
18: 23	יגש	qal	wci	3ms	נגש	620		draw near
	יאמר	qal	wci	3ms	אמר	55		say
	תספה	qal	impf	2ms	ספה	705		sweep away
18: 24	תספה	qal	impf	2ms	ספה	705		sweep away
	תשא	qal	impf	2ms	נשא	669		lift,carry
18: 25	עשת	qal	infc		עשה	793		do,make
	המית	hiph	infc		מות	559		kill
	היה	qal	wcp	3ms	היה	224		be,become
	שפט	qal	ptc	ms	שפט	1047		judge
	יעשה	qal	impf	3ms	עשה	793		do,make
18: 26	יאמר	qal	wci	3ms	אמר	55		say
	אמצא	qal	impf	1cs	מצא	592		find
	נשאתי	qal	wcp	1cs	נשא	669		lift,carry
18: 27	יען	qal	wci	3ms	ענה	772		answer
	יאמר	qal	wci	3ms	אמר	55		say
	הואלתי	hiph	pft	1cs	יאל	383		be willing
	דבר	piel	infc		דבר	180		speak
18: 28	יחסרון	qal	impf	3mp	חסר	341		lack
	תשחית	hiph	impf	2ms	שחת	1007		spoil,ruin
	יאמר	qal	wci	3ms	אמר	55		say
	אשחית	hiph	impf	1cs	שחת	1007		spoil,ruin
	אמצא	qal	impf	1cs	מצא	592		find
18: 29	יסף	hiph	wci	3ms	יסף	414		add,do again
	דבר	piel	infc		דבר	180		speak
	יאמר	qal	wci	3ms	אמר	55		say
	ימצאון	niph	impf	3mp	מצא	592		be found
	יאמר	qal	wci	3ms	אמר	55		say

ChVs	Form	Stem	Tnse	PGN	Root	BDB	Sfx	Meaning
18:29	אעשה	qal	impf	1cs	עשה	793		do,make
18:30	יאמר	qal	wci	3ms	אמר	55		say
	יחר	qal	jus	3ms	חרה	354		be kindled,burn
	אדברה	piel	coh	1cs	דבר	180		speak
	ימצאון	niph	impf	3mp	מצא	592		be found
	יאמר	qal	wci	3ms	אמר	55		say
	אעשה	qal	impf	1cs	עשה	793		do,make
	אמצא	qal	impf	1cs	מצא	592		find
18:31	יאמר	qal	wci	3ms	אמר	55		say
	הואלתי	hiph	pft	1cs	יאל	383		be willing
	דבר	piel	infc		דבר	180		speak
	ימצאון	niph	impf	3mp	מצא	592		be found
	יאמר	qal	wci	3ms	אמר	55		say
	אשחית	hiph	impf	1cs	שחת	1007		spoil,ruin
18:32	יאמר	qal	wci	3ms	אמר	55		say
	יחר	qal	jus	3ms	חרה	354		be kindled,burn
	אדברה	piel	coh	1cs	דבר	180		speak
	ימצאון	niph	impf	3mp	מצא	592		be found
	יאמר	qal	wci	3ms	אמר	55		say
	אשחית	hiph	impf	1cs	שחת	1007		spoil,ruin
18:33	ילך	qal	wci	3ms	הלך	229		walk,go
	כלה	piel	pft	3ms	כלה	477		complete,finish
	דבר	piel	infc		דבר	180		speak
	שב	qal	pft	3ms	שוב	996		turn,return
19:1	יבאו	qal	wci	3mp	בוא	97		come in
	ישב	qal	ptc	ms	ישב	442		sit,dwell
	ירא	qal	wci	3ms	ראה	906		see
	יקם	qal	wci	3ms	קום	877		arise,stand
	קראתם	qal	infc		קרא	896	3mp	meet,encounter
	ישתחו	hish	wci	3ms	חוה	1005		bow down
19:2	יאמר	qal	wci	3ms	אמר	55		say
	סורו	qal	impv	mp	סור	693		turn aside
	לינו	qal	impv	mp	לון	533		lodge,remain
	רחצו	qal	impv	mp	רחץ	934		wash,bathe
	השכמתם	hiph	wcp	2mp	שכם	1014		rise early
	הלכתם	qal	wcp	2mp	הלך	229		walk,go
	יאמרו	qal	wci	3mp	אמר	55		say
	נלין	qal	impf	1cp	לון	533		lodge,remain
19:3	יפצר	qal	wci	3ms	פצר	823		push
	יסרו	qal	wci	3mp	סור	693		turn aside
	יבאו	qal	wci	3mp	בוא	97		come in
	יעש	qal	wci	3ms	עשה	793		do,make
	אפה	qal	pft	3ms	אפה	66		bake
	יאכלו	qal	wci	3mp	אכל	37		eat,devour
19:4	ישכבו	qal	impf	3mp	שכב	1011		lie,lie down
	נסבו	niph	pft	3cp	סבב	685		turn round
19:5	יקראו	qal	wci	3mp	קרא	894		call,proclaim
	יאמרו	qal	wci	3mp	אמר	55		say
	באו	qal	pft	3cp	בוא	97		come in
	הוציאם	hiph	impv	ms	יצא	422	3mp	bring out
	נדעה	qal	coh	1cp	ידע	393		know
19:6	יצא	qal	wci	3ms	יצא	422		go out
	סגר	qal	pft	3ms	סגר	688		shut
19:7	יאמר	qal	wci	3ms	אמר	55		say
19:7	תרעו	hiph	impf	2mp	רעע	949		hurt,do evil
19:8	ידעו	qal	pft	3cp	ידע	393		know
	אוציאה	hiph	coh	1cs	יצא	422		bring out
	עשו	qal	impv	mp	עשה	793		do,make
	תעשו	qal	jusm	2mp	עשה	793		do,make
	באו	qal	pft	3cp	בוא	97		come in
19:9	יאמרו	qal	wci	3mp	אמר	55		say
	גש	qal	impv	ms	נגש	620		draw near
	יאמרו	qal	wci	3mp	אמר	55		say
	בא	qal	pft	3ms	בוא	97		come in
	גור	qal	infc		גור	157		sojourn
	ישפט	qal	wci	3ms	שפט	1047		judge
	שפוט	qal	infa		שפט	1047		judge
	נרע	hiph	impf	1cp	רעע	949		hurt,do evil
	יפצרו	qal	wci	3mp	פצר	823		push
	יגשו	qal	wci	3mp	נגש	620		draw near
	שבר	qal	infc		שבר	990		break
19:10	ישלחו	qal	wci	3mp	שלח	1018		send
	יביאו	hiph	wci	3mp	בוא	97		bring in
	סגרו	qal	pft	3cp	סגר	688		shut
19:11	הכו	hiph	pft	3cp	נכה	645		smite
	ילאו	qal	wci	3mp	לאה	521		be weary
	מצא	qal	infc		מצא	592		find
19:12	יאמרו	qal	wci	3mp	אמר	55		say
	הוצא	hiph	impv	ms	יצא	422		bring out
19:13	משחתים	hiph	ptc	mp	שחת	1007		spoil,ruin
	גדלה	qal	pft	3fs	גדל	152		be great,grow
	ישלחנו	piel	wci	3ms	שלח	1018	1cp	send away,shoot
	שחתה	piel	infc		שחת	1007	3fs	spoil,ruin
19:14	יצא	qal	wci	3ms	יצא	422		go out
	ידבר	piel	wci	3ms	דבר	180		speak
	לקחי	qal	ptc	mp	לקח	542		take
	יאמר	qal	wci	3ms	אמר	55		say
	קומו	qal	impv	mp	קום	877		arise,stand
	צאו	qal	impv	mp	יצא	422		go out
	משחית	hiph	ptc	ms	שחת	1007		spoil,ruin
	יהי	qal	wci	3ms	היה	224		be,become
	מצחק	piel	ptc	ms	צחק	850		jest,make sport
19:15	עלה	qal	pft	3ms	עלה	748		go up
	יאיצו	hiph	wci	3mp	אוץ	21		hasten
	אמר	qal	infc		אמר	55		say
	קום	qal	impv	ms	קום	877		arise,stand
	קח	qal	impv	ms	לקח	542		take
	נמצאת	niph	ptc	fp	מצא	592		be found
	תספה	niph	impf	2ms	ספה	705		be swept away
19:16	יתמהמה	htpp	wci	3ms	מהה	554		tarry
	יחזקו	hiph	wci	3mp	חזק	304		make firm,seize
	יצאהו	hiph	wci	3mp	יצא	422	3ms	bring out
	ינחהו	hiph	wci	3mp	נוח	628	3ms	give rest,put
19:17	יהי	qal	wci	3ms	היה	224		be,become
	הוציאם	hiph	infc		יצא	422	3mp	bring out
	יאמר	qal	wci	3ms	אמר	55		say
	המלט	niph	impv	ms	מלט	572		escape
	תביט	hiph	jusm	2ms	נבט	613		look,regard

ChVs	Form	Stem	Tnse	PGN	Root	BDB	Sfx	Meaning
19: 17	תעמד	qal	jusm	2ms	עמד	763		stand,stop
	המלט	niph	impv	ms	מלט	572		escape
	תספה	niph	impf	2ms	ספה	705		be swept away
19: 18	יאמר	qal	wci	3ms	אמר	55		say
19: 19	מצא	qal	pft	3ms	מצא	592		find
	תגדל	hiph	wci	2ms	גדל	152		make great
	עשׂית	qal	pft	2ms	עשׂה	793		do,make
	החיות	hiph	infc		חיה	310		preserve
	אוכל	qal	impf	1cs	יכל	407		be able
	המלט	niph	infc		מלט	572		escape
	תדבקני	qal	impf	3fs	דבק	179	1cs	cling,cleave
	מתי	qal	wcp	1cs	מות	559		die
19: 20	נוס	qal	infc		נוס	630		flee,escape
	אמלטה	niph	coh	1cs	מלט	572		escape
	תחי	qal	jus	3fs	חיה	310		live
19: 21	יאמר	qal	wci	3ms	אמר	55		say
	נשׂאתי	qal	pft	1cs	נשׂא	669		lift,carry
	הפכי	qal	infc		הפך	245	1cs	turn,overturn
	דברת	piel	pft	2ms	דבר	180		speak
19: 22	מהר	piel	impv	ms	מהר	554		hasten
	המלט	niph	impv	ms	מלט	572		escape
	אוכל	qal	impf	1cs	יכל	407		be able
	עשׂות	qal	infc		עשׂה	793		do,make
	באך	qal	infc		בוא	97	2ms	come in
	קרא	qal	pft	3ms	קרא	894		call,proclaim
19: 23	יצא	qal	pft	3ms	יצא	422		go out
	בא	qal	pft	3ms	בוא	97		come in
19: 24	המטיר	hiph	pft	3ms	מטר	565		rain
19: 25	יהפך	qal	wci	3ms	הפך	245		turn,overturn
	ישׁבי	qal	ptc	mp	ישׁב	442		sit,dwell
19: 26	תבט	hiph	wci	3fs	נבט	613		look,regard
	תהי	qal	wci	3fs	היה	224		be,become
19: 27	ישׁכם	hiph	wci	3ms	שׁכם	1014		rise early
	עמד	qal	pft	3ms	עמד	763		stand,stop
19: 28	ישׁקף	hiph	wci	3ms	שׁקף	1054		look down
	ירא	qal	wci	3ms	ראה	906		see
	עלה	qal	pft	3ms	עלה	748		go up
19: 29	יהי	qal	wci	3ms	היה	224		be,become
	שׁחת	piel	infc		שׁחת	1007		spoil,ruin
	יזכר	qal	wci	3ms	זכר	269		remember
	ישׁלח	piel	wci	3ms	שׁלח	1018		send away,shoot
	הפך	qal	infc		הפך	245		turn,overturn
	ישׁב	qal	pft	3ms	ישׁב	442		sit,dwell
19: 30	יעל	qal	wci	3ms	עלה	748		go up
	ישׁב	qal	wci	3ms	ישׁב	442		sit,dwell
	ירא	qal	pft	3ms	ירא	431		fear
	שׁבת	qal	infc		ישׁב	442		sit,dwell
	ישׁב	qal	wci	3ms	ישׁב	442		sit,dwell
19: 31	תאמר	qal	wci	3fs	אמר	55		say
	זקן	qal	pft	3ms	זקן	278		be old
	בוא	qal	infc		בוא	97		come in
19: 32	לכה	qal	impv	ms	הלך	229		walk,go
	נשׁקה	hiph	cohm	1cp	שׁקה	1052		give to drink
	נשׁכבה	qal	coh	1cp	שׁכב	1011		lie,lie down
19: 32	נחיה	piel	cohm	1cp	חיה	310		preserve,revive
19: 33	תשׁקין	hiph	wci	3fp	שׁקה	1052		give to drink
	תבא	qal	wci	3fs	בוא	97		come in
	תשׁכב	qal	wci	3fs	שׁכב	1011		lie,lie down
	ידע	qal	pft	3ms	ידע	393		know
	שׁכבה	qal	infc		שׁכב	1011	3fs	lie,lie down
	קומה	qal	infc		קום	877	3fs	arise,stand
19: 34	יהי	qal	wci	3ms	היה	224		be,become
	תאמר	qal	wci	3fs	אמר	55		say
	שׁכבתי	qal	pft	1cs	שׁכב	1011		lie,lie down
	נשׁקנו	hiph	cohm	1cp	שׁקה	1052	3ms	give to drink
	באי	qal	impv	fs	בוא	97		come in
	שׁכבי	qal	impv	ms	שׁכב	1011		lie,lie down
	נחיה	piel	cohm	1cp	חיה	310		preserve,revive
19: 35	תשׁקין	hiph	wci	3fp	שׁקה	1052		give to drink
	תקם	qal	wci	3fs	קום	877		arise,stand
	תשׁכב	qal	wci	3fs	שׁכב	1011		lie,lie down
	ידע	qal	pft	3ms	ידע	393		know
	שׁכבה	qal	infc		שׁכב	1011	3fs	lie,lie down
	קמה	qal	infc		קום	877	3fs	arise,stand
19: 36	תהרין	qal	wci	3fp	הרה	247		conceive
19: 37	תלד	qal	wci	3fs	ילד	408		bear,beget
	תקרא	qal	wci	3fs	קרא	894		call,proclaim
19: 38	ילדה	qal	pft	3fs	ילד	408		bear,beget
	תקרא	qal	wci	3fs	קרא	894		call,proclaim
20: 1	יסע	qal	wci	3ms	נסע	652		pull up,set out
	ישׁב	qal	wci	3ms	ישׁב	442		sit,dwell
	יגר	qal	wci	3ms	גור	157		sojourn
20: 2	יאמר	qal	wci	3ms	אמר	55		say
	ישׁלח	qal	wci	3ms	שׁלח	1018		send
	יקח	qal	wci	3ms	לקח	542		take
20: 3	יבא	qal	wci	3ms	בוא	97		come in
	יאמר	qal	wci	3ms	אמר	55		say
	מת	qal	ptc	ms	מות	559		die
	לקחת	qal	pft	2ms	לקח	542		take
	בעלת	qal	pptc	fs	בעל	127		marry,rule over
20: 4	קרב	qal	pft	3ms	קרב	897		approach
	יאמר	qal	wci	3ms	אמר	55		say
	תהרג	qal	impf	2ms	הרג	246		kill
20: 5	אמר	qal	pft	3ms	אמר	55		say
	אמרה	qal	pft	3fs	אמר	55		say
	עשׂיתי	qal	pft	1cs	עשׂה	793		do,make
20: 6	יאמר	qal	wci	3ms	אמר	55		say
	ידעתי	qal	pft	1cs	ידע	393		know
	עשׂית	qal	pft	2ms	עשׂה	793		do,make
	אחשׂך	qal	wci	1cs	חשׂך	362		withhold
	חטו	qal	infc		חטא	306		sin
	נתתיך	qal	pft	1cs	נתן	678	2ms	give,set
	נגע	qal	infc		נגע	619		touch,strike
20: 7	השׁב	hiph	impv	ms	שׁוב	996		bring back
	יתפלל	hith	impf	3ms	פלל	813		pray
	חיה	qal	impv	ms	חיה	310		live
	משׁיב	hiph	ptc	ms	שׁוב	996		bring back
	דע	qal	impv	ms	ידע	393		know

ChVs	Form	Stem	Tnse	PGN	Root	BDB	Sfx	Meaning
20:7	מות	qal	infa		מות	559		die
	תמות	qal	impf	2ms	מות	559		die
20:8	ישׁכם	hiph	wci	3ms	שׁכם	1014		rise early
	יקרא	qal	wci	3ms	קרא	894		call,proclaim
	ידבר	piel	wci	3ms	דבר	180		speak
	ייראו	qal	wci	3mp	ירא	431		fear
20:9	יקרא	qal	wci	3ms	קרא	894		call,proclaim
	יאמר	qal	wci	3ms	אמר	55		say
	עשׂית	qal	pft	2ms	עשׂה	793		do,make
	חטאתי	qal	pft	1cs	חטא	306		sin
	הבאת	hiph	pft	2ms	בוא	97		bring in
	יעשׂו	niph	impf	3mp	עשׂה	793		be done
	עשׂית	qal	pft	2ms	עשׂה	793		do,make
20:10	יאמר	qal	wci	3ms	אמר	55		say
	ראית	qal	pft	2ms	ראה	906		see
	עשׂית	qal	pft	2ms	עשׂה	793		do,make
20:11	יאמר	qal	wci	3ms	אמר	55		say
	אמרתי	qal	pft	1cs	אמר	55		say
	הרגוני	qal	wcp	3cp	הרג	246	1cs	kill
20:12	תהי	qal	wci	3fs	היה	224		be,become
20:13	יהי	qal	wci	3ms	היה	224		be,become
	התעו	hiph	pft	3cp	תעה	1073		cause to err
	אמר	qal	wci	1cs	אמר	55		say
	תעשׂי	qal	impf	2fs	עשׂה	793		do,make
	נבוא	qal	impf	1cp	בוא	97		come in
	אמרי	qal	impv	fs	אמר	55		say
20:14	יקח	qal	wci	3ms	לקח	542		take
	יתן	qal	wci	3ms	נתן	678		give,set
	ישׁב	hiph	wci	3ms	שׁוב	996		bring back
20:15	יאמר	qal	wci	3ms	אמר	55		say
	שׁב	qal	impv	ms	ישׁב	442		sit,dwell
20:16	אמר	qal	pft	3ms	אמר	55		say
	נתתי	qal	pft	1cs	נתן	678		give,set
	נכחת	niph	ptc	fs	יכח	406		argue
20:17	יתפלל	hith	wci	3ms	פלל	813		pray
	ירפא	qal	wci	3ms	רפא	950		heal
	ילדו	qal	wci	3mp	ילד	408		bear,beget
20:18	עצר	qal	infa		עצר	783		restrain
	עצר	qal	pft	3ms	עצר	783		restrain
21:1	פקד	qal	pft	3ms	פקד	823		attend to,visit
	אמר	qal	pft	3ms	אמר	55		say
	יעשׂ	qal	wci	3ms	עשׂה	793		do,make
	דבר	piel	pft	3ms	דבר	180		speak
21:2	תהר	qal	wci	3fs	הרה	247		conceive
	תלד	qal	wci	3fs	ילד	408		bear,beget
	דבר	piel	pft	3ms	דבר	180		speak
21:3	יקרא	qal	wci	3ms	קרא	894		call,proclaim
	נולד	niph	pft	3ms	ילד	408		be born
	ילדה	qal	pft	3fs	ילד	408		bear,beget
21:4	ימל	qal	wci	3ms	מול	557		circumcise
	צוה	piel	pft	3ms	צוה	845		command
21:5	הולד	niph	infc		ילד	408		be born
21:6	תאמר	qal	wci	3fs	אמר	55		say
	עשׂה	qal	pft	3ms	עשׂה	793		do,make
21:6	שׁמע	qal	ptc	ms	שׁמע	1033		hear
	יצחק	qal	impf	3ms	צחק	850		laugh
21:7	תאמר	qal	wci	3fs	אמר	55		say
	מלל	piel	pft	3ms	מלל	576		speak
	היניקה	hiph	pft	3fs	ינק	413		nurse
	ילדתי	qal	pft	1cs	ילד	408		bear,beget
21:8	יגדל	qal	wci	3ms	גדל	152		be great,grow
	יגמל	niph	wci	3ms	גמל	168		be weaned
	יעשׂ	qal	wci	3ms	עשׂה	793		do,make
	הגמל	niph	infc		גמל	168		be weaned
21:9	תרא	qal	wci	3fs	ראה	906		see
	ילדה	qal	pft	3fs	ילד	408		bear,beget
	מצחק	piel	ptc	ms	צחק	850		jest,make sport
21:10	תאמר	qal	wci	3fs	אמר	55		say
	גרשׁ	piel	impv	ms	גרשׁ	176		drive out
	יירשׁ	qal	impf	3ms	ירשׁ	439		possess,inherit
21:11	ירע	qal	wci	3ms	רעע	949		be evil
21:12	יאמר	qal	wci	3ms	אמר	55		say
	ירע	qal	jusm	3ms	רעע	949		be evil
	תאמר	qal	impf	3fs	אמר	55		say
	שׁמע	qal	impv	ms	שׁמע	1033		hear
	יקרא	niph	impf	3ms	קרא	894		be called
21:13	אשׂימנו	qal	impf	1cs	שׂים	962	3ms	put,set
21:14	ישׁכם	hiph	wci	3ms	שׁכם	1014		rise early
	יקח	qal	wci	3ms	לקח	542		take
	יתן	qal	wci	3ms	נתן	678		give,set
	שׂם	qal	ptc	ms	שׂים	962		put,set
	ישׁלחה	piel	wci	3ms	שׁלח	1018	3fs	send away,shoot
	תלך	qal	wci	3fs	הלך	229		walk,go
	תתע	qal	wci	3fs	תעה	1073		wander,err
21:15	יכלו	qal	wci	3mp	כלה	477		finished,spent
	תשׁלך	hiph	wci	3fs	שׁלך	1020		throw,cast
21:16	תלך	qal	wci	3fs	הלך	229		walk,go
	תשׁב	qal	wci	3fs	ישׁב	442		sit,dwell
	הרחק	hiph	infa		רחק	934		put far away
	מטחוי	pal	ptc	mp	טחה	377		shoot
	אמרה	qal	pft	3fs	אמר	55		say
	אראה	qal	cohm	1cs	ראה	906		see
	תשׁב	qal	wci	3fs	ישׁב	442		sit,dwell
	תשׂא	qal	wci	3fs	נשׂא	669		lift,carry
	תבך	qal	wci	3fs	בכה	113		weep
21:17	ישׁמע	qal	wci	3ms	שׁמע	1033		hear
	יקרא	qal	wci	3ms	קרא	894		call,proclaim
	יאמר	qal	wci	3ms	אמר	55		say
	תיראי	qal	jusm	2fs	ירא	431		fear
	שׁמע	qal	pft	3ms	שׁמע	1033		hear
21:18	קומי	qal	impv	fs	קום	877		arise,stand
	שׂאי	qal	impv	fs	נשׂא	669		lift,carry
	החזיקי	hiph	impv	fs	חזק	304		make firm,seize
	אשׂימנו	qal	impf	1cs	שׂים	962	3ms	put,set
21:19	יפקח	qal	wci	3ms	פקח	824		open
	תרא	qal	wci	3fs	ראה	906		see
	תלך	qal	wci	3fs	הלך	229		walk,go
	תמלא	piel	wci	3fs	מלא	569		fill

ChVs	Form	Stem	Tnse	PGN	Root	BDB	Sfx	Meaning
21: 19	תשק	hiph	wci	3fs	שקה	1052		give to drink
21: 20	יהי	qal	wci	3ms	היה	224		be, become
	יגדל	qal	wci	3ms	גדל	152		be great, grow
	ישב	qal	wci	3ms	ישב	442		sit, dwell
	יהי	qal	wci	3ms	היה	224		be, become
	רבה	qal	ptc	ms	רבה	916		shoot
21: 21	ישב	qal	wci	3ms	ישב	442		sit, dwell
	תקח	qal	wci	3fs	לקח	542		take
21: 22	יהי	qal	wci	3ms	היה	224		be, become
	יאמר	qal	wci	3ms	אמר	55		say
	אמר	qal	infc		אמר	55		say
	עשה	qal	ptc	ms	עשה	793		do, make
21: 23	השבעה	niph	impv	ms	שבע	989		swear
	תשקר	qal	impf	2ms	שקר	1055		deal falsely
	עשיתי	qal	pft	1cs	עשה	793		do, make
	תעשה	qal	impf	2ms	עשה	793		do, make
	גרתה	qal	pft	2ms	גור	157		sojourn
21: 24	יאמר	qal	wci	3ms	אמר	55		say
	אשבע	niph	impf	1cs	שבע	989		swear
21: 25	הוכח	hiph	pft	3ms	יכח	406		decide, reprove
	גזלו	qal	pft	3cp	גזל	159		tear away, rob
21: 26	יאמר	qal	wci	3ms	אמר	55		say
	ידעתי	qal	pft	1cs	ידע	393		know
	עשה	qal	pft	3ms	עשה	793		do, make
	הגדת	hiph	pft	2ms	נגד	616		declare, tell
	שמעתי	qal	pft	1cs	שמע	1033		hear
21: 27	יקח	qal	wci	3ms	לקח	542		take
	יתן	qal	wci	3ms	נתן	678		give, set
	יכרתו	qal	wci	3mp	כרת	503		cut, destroy
21: 28	יצב	hiph	wci	3ms	נצב	662		cause to stand
21: 29	יאמר	qal	wci	3ms	אמר	55		say
	הצבת	hiph	pft	2ms	נצב	662		cause to stand
21: 30	יאמר	qal	wci	3ms	אמר	55		say
	תקח	qal	impf	2ms	לקח	542		take
	תהיה	qal	impf	3fs	היה	224		be, become
	חפרתי	qal	pft	1cs	חפר	343		dig, search
21: 31	קרא	qal	pft	3ms	קרא	894		call, proclaim
	נשבעו	niph	pft	3cp	שבע	989		swear
21: 32	יכרתו	qal	wci	3mp	כרת	503		cut, destroy
	יקם	qal	wci	3ms	קום	877		arise, stand
	ישבו	qal	wci	3mp	שוב	996		turn, return
21: 33	יטע	qal	wci	3ms	נטע	642		plant
	יקרא	qal	wci	3ms	קרא	894		call, proclaim
21: 34	יגר	qal	wci	3ms	גור	157		sojourn
22: 1	יהי	qal	wci	3ms	היה	224		be, become
	נסה	piel	pft	3ms	נסה	650		test, try
	יאמר	qal	wci	3ms	אמר	55		say
	יאמר	qal	wci	3ms	אמר	55		say
22: 2	יאמר	qal	wci	3ms	אמר	55		say
	קח	qal	impv	ms	לקח	542		take
	אהבת	qal	pft	2ms	אהב	12		love
	לך	qal	impv	ms	הלך	229		walk, go
	העלהו	hiph	impv	ms	עלה	748	3ms	bring up, offer
	אמר	qal	impf	1cs	אמר	55		say
22: 3	ישכם	hiph	wci	3ms	שכם	1014		rise early
	יחבש	qal	wci	3ms	חבש	289		bind
	יקח	qal	wci	3ms	לקח	542		take
	יבקע	piel	wci	3ms	בקע	131		cut to pieces
	יקם	qal	wci	3ms	קום	877		arise, stand
	ילך	qal	wci	3ms	הלך	229		walk, go
	אמר	qal	pft	3ms	אמר	55		say
22: 4	ישא	qal	wci	3ms	נשא	669		lift, carry
	ירא	qal	wci	3ms	ראה	906		see
22: 5	יאמר	qal	wci	3ms	אמר	55		say
	שבו	qal	impv	mp	ישב	442		sit, dwell
	נלכה	qal	coh	1cp	הלך	229		walk, go
	נשתחוה	hish	cohf	1cp	חוה	1005		bow down
	נשובה	qal	coh	1cp	שוב	996		turn, return
22: 6	יקח	qal	wci	3ms	לקח	542		take
	ישם	qal	wci	3ms	שים	962		put, set
	יקח	qal	wci	3ms	לקח	542		take
	ילכו	qal	wci	3mp	הלך	229		walk, go
22: 7	יאמר	qal	wci	3ms	אמר	55		say
	יאמר	qal	wci	3ms	אמר	55		say
	יאמר	qal	wci	3ms	אמר	55		say
	יאמר	qal	wci	3ms	אמר	55		say
22: 8	יאמר	qal	wci	3ms	אמר	55		say
	יראה	qal	impf	3ms	ראה	906		see
	ילכו	qal	wci	3mp	הלך	229		walk, go
22: 9	יבאו	qal	wci	3mp	בוא	97		come in
	אמר	qal	pft	3ms	אמר	55		say
	יבן	qal	wci	3ms	בנה	124		build
	יערך	qal	wci	3ms	ערך	789		set in order
	יעקד	qal	wci	3ms	עקד	785		bind
	ישם	qal	wci	3ms	שים	962		put, set
22: 10	ישלח	qal	wci	3ms	שלח	1018		send
	יקח	qal	wci	3ms	לקח	542		take
	שחט	qal	infc		שחט	1006		slaughter
22: 11	יקרא	qal	wci	3ms	קרא	894		call, proclaim
	יאמר	qal	wci	3ms	אמר	55		say
	יאמר	qal	wci	3ms	אמר	55		say
22: 12	יאמר	qal	wci	3ms	אמר	55		say
	תשלח	qal	jusm	2ms	שלח	1018		send
	תעש	qal	jus	2ms	עשה	793		do, make
	ידעתי	qal	pft	1cs	ידע	393		know
	ירא	qal	ptc	ms	ירא	431		fear
	חשכת	qal	pft	2ms	חשך	362		withhold
22: 13	ישא	qal	wci	3ms	נשא	669		lift, carry
	ירא	qal	wci	3ms	ראה	906		see
	נאחז	niph	pft	3ms	אחז	28		possess, caught
	ילך	qal	wci	3ms	הלך	229		walk, go
	יקח	qal	wci	3ms	לקח	542		take
	יעלהו	hiph	wci	3ms	עלה	748	3ms	bring up, offer
22: 14	יקרא	qal	wci	3ms	קרא	894		call, proclaim
	יראה	qal	impf	3ms	ראה	906		see
	יאמר	niph	impf	3ms	אמר	55		be said, called
	יראה	niph	impf	3ms	ראה	906		appear, be seen
22: 15	יקרא	qal	wci	3ms	קרא	894		call, proclaim

ChVs	Form	Stem	Tnse	PGN	Root	BDB	Sfx	Meaning
22:16	יאמר	qal	wci	3ms	אמר	55		say
	נשבעתי	niph	pft	1cs	שבע	989		swear
	עשית	qal	pft	2ms	עשה	793		do,make
	חשכת	qal	pft	2ms	חשך	362		withhold
22:17	ברך	piel	infa		ברך	138		bless
	אברכך	piel	impf	1cs	ברך	138	2ms	bless
	הרבה	hiph	infa		רבה	915		make many
	ארבה	hiph	impf	1cs	רבה	915		make many
	ירש	qal	impf	3ms	ירש	439		possess,inherit
	איביו	qal	ptc	mp	איב	33	3ms	be hostile to
22:18	התברכו	hith	wcp	3cp	ברך	138		bless oneself
	שמעת	qal	pft	2ms	שמע	1033		hear
22:19	ישב	qal	wci	3ms	שוב	996		turn,return
	יקמו	qal	wci	3mp	קום	877		arise,stand
	ילכו	qal	wci	3mp	הלך	229		walk,go
	ישב	qal	wci	3ms	ישב	442		sit,dwell
22:20	יהי	qal	wci	3ms	היה	224		be,become
	יגד	hoph	wci	3ms	נגד	616		be told
	אמר	qal	infc		אמר	55		say
	ילדה	qal	pft	3fs	ילד	408		bear,beget
22:23	ילד	qal	pft	3ms	ילד	408		bear,beget
	ילדה	qal	pft	3fs	ילד	408		bear,beget
22:24	תלד	qal	wci	3fs	ילד	408		bear,beget
23:1	יהיו	qal	wci	3mp	היה	224		be,become
23:2	תמת	qal	wci	3fs	מות	559		die
	יבא	qal	wci	3ms	בוא	97		come in
	ספד	qal	infc		ספד	704		wail,lament
	בכתה	qal	infc		בכה	113	3fs	weep
23:3	יקם	qal	wci	3ms	קום	877		arise,stand
	מתו	qal	ptc	ms	מות	559	3ms	die
	ידבר	piel	wci	3ms	דבר	180		speak
	אמר	qal	infc		אמר	55		say
23:4	תנו	qal	impv	mp	נתן	678		give,set
	אקברה	qal	coh	1cs	קבר	868		bury
	מתי	qal	ptc	ms	מות	559	1cs	die
23:5	יענו	qal	wci	3mp	ענה	772		answer
	אמר	qal	infc		אמר	55		say
23:6	שמענו	qal	impv	ms	שמע	1033	1cp	hear
	קבר	qal	impv	ms	קבר	868		bury
	מתך	qal	ptc	ms	מות	559	2ms	die
	יכלה	qal	impf	3ms	כלא	476		shut up
	קבר	qal	infc		קבר	868		bury
	מתך	qal	ptc	ms	מות	559	2ms	die
23:7	יקם	qal	wci	3ms	קום	877		arise,stand
	ישתחו	hish	wci	3ms	חוה	1005		bow down
23:8	ידבר	piel	wci	3ms	דבר	180		speak
	אמר	qal	infc		אמר	55		say
	קבר	qal	infc		קבר	868		bury
	מתי	qal	ptc	ms	מות	559	1cs	die
	שמעוני	qal	impv	mp	שמע	1033	1cs	hear
	פגעו	qal	impv	mp	פגע	803		meet,encounter
23:9	יתן	qal	jus	3ms	נתן	678		give,set
	יתננה	qal	jusm	3ms	נתן	678	3fs	give,set
23:10	ישב	qal	ptc	ms	ישב	442		sit,dwell

ChVs	Form	Stem	Tnse	PGN	Root	BDB	Sfx	Meaning
23:10	יען	qal	wci	3ms	ענה	772		answer
	באי	qal	ptc	mp	בוא	97		come in
	אמר	qal	infc		אמר	55		say
23:11	שמעני	qal	impv	ms	שמע	1033	1cs	hear
	נתתי	qal	pft	1cs	נתן	678		give,set
	נתתיה	qal	pft	1cs	נתן	678	3fs	give,set
	נתתיה	qal	pft	1cs	נתן	678	3fs	give,set
	קבר	qal	impv	ms	קבר	868		bury
	מתך	qal	ptc	ms	מות	559	2ms	die
23:12	ישתחו	hish	wci	3ms	חוה	1005		bow down
23:13	ידבר	piel	wci	3ms	דבר	180		speak
	אמר	qal	infc		אמר	55		say
	שמעני	qal	impv	ms	שמע	1033	1cs	hear
	נתתי	qal	pft	1cs	נתן	678		give,set
	קח	qal	impv	ms	לקח	542		take
	אקברה	qal	coh	1cs	קבר	868		bury
	מתי	qal	ptc	ms	מות	559	1cs	die
23:14	יען	qal	wci	3ms	ענה	772		answer
	אמר	qal	infc		אמר	55		say
23:15	שמעני	qal	impv	ms	שמע	1033	1cs	hear
	מתך	qal	ptc	ms	מות	559	2ms	die
	קבר	qal	impv	ms	קבר	868		bury
23:16	ישמע	qal	wci	3ms	שמע	1033		hear
	ישקל	qal	wci	3ms	שקל	1053		weigh
	דבר	piel	pft	3ms	דבר	180		speak
	עבר	qal	ptc	ms	עבר	716		pass over
	סחר	qal	ptc	ms	סחר	695		go around
23:17	יקם	qal	wci	3ms	קום	877		arise,stand
23:18	באי	qal	ptc	mp	בוא	97		come in
23:19	קבר	qal	pft	3ms	קבר	868		bury
23:20	יקם	qal	wci	3ms	קום	877		arise,stand
24:1	זקן	qal	pft	3ms	זקן	278		be old
	בא	qal	pft	3ms	בוא	97		come in
	ברך	piel	pft	3ms	ברך	138		bless
24:2	יאמר	qal	wci	3ms	אמר	55		say
	משל	qal	ptc	ms	משל	605		rule
	שים	qal	impv	ms	שים	962		put,set
24:3	אשביעך	hiph	cohm	1cs	שבע	989	2ms	cause to swear
	תקח	qal	impf	2ms	לקח	542		take
	יושב	qal	ptc	ms	ישב	442		sit,dwell
24:4	תלך	qal	impf	2ms	הלך	229		walk,go
	לקחת	qal	wcp	2ms	לקח	542		take
24:5	יאמר	qal	wci	3ms	אמר	55		say
	תאבה	qal	impf	3fs	אבה	2		be willing
	לכת	qal	infc		הלך	229		walk,go
	השב	hiph	infa		שוב	996		bring back
	אשיב	hiph	impf	1cs	שוב	996		bring back
	יצאת	qal	pft	2ms	יצא	422		go out
24:6	יאמר	qal	wci	3ms	אמר	55		say
	השמר	niph	impv	ms	שמר	1036		be kept,guarded
	תשיב	hiph	impf	2ms	שוב	996		bring back
24:7	לקחני	qal	pft	3ms	לקח	542	1cs	take
	דבר	piel	pft	3ms	דבר	180		speak
	נשבע	niph	pft	3ms	שבע	989		swear

ChVs	Form	Stem	Tnse	PGN	Root	BDB	Sfx	Meaning
24:7	אמר	qal	infc		אמר	55		say
	אתן	qal	impf	1cs	נתן	678		give,set
	ישלח	qal	impf	3ms	שלח	1018		send
	לקחת	qal	wcp	2ms	לקח	542		take
24:8	תאבה	qal	impf	3fs	אבה	2		be willing
	לכת	qal	infc		הלך	229		walk,go
	נקית	niph	wcp	2ms	נקה	667		be clean,free
	תשב	hiph	jusf	2ms	שוב	996		bring back
24:9	ישם	qal	wci	3ms	שים	962		put,set
	ישבע	niph	wci	3ms	שבע	989		swear
24:10	יקח	qal	wci	3ms	לקח	542		take
	ילך	qal	wci	3ms	הלך	229		walk,go
	יקם	qal	wci	3ms	קום	877		arise,stand
	ילך	qal	wci	3ms	הלך	229		walk,go
24:11	יברך	hiph	wci	3ms	ברך	138		cause to kneel
	צאת	qal	infc		יצא	422		go out
	שאבת	qal	ptc	fp	שאב	980		draw (water)
24:12	יאמר	qal	wci	3ms	אמר	55		say
	הקרה	hiph	impv	ms	קרה	899		cause to occur
	עשה	qal	impv	ms	עשה	793		do,make
24:13	נצב	niph	ptc	ms	נצב	662		stand
	יצאת	qal	ptc	fp	יצא	422		go out
	שאב	qal	infc		שאב	980		draw (water)
24:14	היה	qal	wcp	3ms	היה	224		be,become
	אמר	qal	impf	1cs	אמר	55		say
	הטי	hiph	impv	fs	נטה	639		turn,incline
	אשתה	qal	cohm	1cs	שתה	1059		drink
	אמרה	qal	wcp	3fs	אמר	55		say
	שתה	qal	impv	ms	שתה	1059		drink
	אשקה	hiph	impf	1cs	שקה	1052		give to drink
	הכחת	hiph	pft	2ms	יכח	406		decide,reprove
	אדע	qal	impf	1cs	ידע	393		know
	עשית	qal	pft	2ms	עשה	793		do,make
24:15	יהי	qal	wci	3ms	היה	224		be,become
	כלה	piel	pft	3ms	כלה	477		complete,finish
	דבר	piel	infc		דבר	180		speak
	יצאת	qal	ptc	fs	יצא	422		go out
	ילדה	qalp	pft	3fs	ילד	408		be born
24:16	ידעה	qal	pft	3ms	ידע	393	3fs	know
	תרד	qal	wci	3fs	ירד	432		come down
	תמלא	piel	wci	3fs	מלא	569		fill
	תעל	qal	wci	3fs	עלה	748		go up
24:17	ירץ	qal	wci	3ms	רוץ	930		run
	קראתה	qal	infc		קרא	896	3fs	meet,encounter
	יאמר	qal	wci	3ms	אמר	55		say
	הגמיאיני	hiph	impv	fs	גמא	167	1cs	give to drink
24:18	תאמר	qal	wci	3fs	אמר	55		say
	שתה	qal	impv	ms	שתה	1059		drink
	תמהר	piel	wci	3fs	מהר	554		hasten
	תרד	hiph	wci	3fs	ירד	432		bring down
	תשקהו	hiph	wci	3fs	שקה	1052	3ms	give to drink
24:19	תכל	piel	wci	3fs	כלה	477		complete,finish
	השקתו	hiph	infc		שקה	1052	3ms	give to drink
	תאמר	qal	wci	3fs	אמר	55		say
24:19	אשאב	qal	impf	1cs	שאב	980		draw (water)
	כלו	piel	pft	3cp	כלה	477		complete,finish
	שתת	qal	infc		שתה	1059		drink
24:20	תמהר	piel	wci	3fs	מהר	554		hasten
	תער	piel	wci	3fs	ערה	788		lay bare
	תרץ	qal	wci	3fs	רוץ	930		run
	שאב	qal	infc		שאב	980		draw (water)
	תשאב	qal	wci	3fs	שאב	980		draw (water)
24:21	משתאה	hith	ptc	ms	שאה	981		gaze
	מחריש	hiph	ptc	ms	חרש	361		be silent
	דעת	qal	infc		ידע	393		know
	הצליח	hiph	pft	3ms	צלח	852		cause to thrive
24:22	יהי	qal	wci	3ms	היה	224		be,become
	כלו	piel	pft	3cp	כלה	477		complete,finish
	שתות	qal	infc		שתה	1059		drink
	יקח	qal	wci	3ms	לקח	542		take
24:23	יאמר	qal	wci	3ms	אמר	55		say
	הגידי	hiph	impv	fs	נגד	616		declare,tell
	לין	qal	infc		לון	533		lodge,remain
24:24	תאמר	qal	wci	3fs	אמר	55		say
	ילדה	qal	pft	3fs	ילד	408		bear,beget
24:25	תאמר	qal	wci	3fs	אמר	55		say
	לון	qal	infc		לון	533		lodge,remain
24:26	יקד	qal	wci	3ms	קדד	869		bow down
	ישתחו	hish	wci	3ms	חוה	1005		bow down
24:27	יאמר	qal	wci	3ms	אמר	55		say
	ברוך	qal	pptc	ms	ברך	138		kneel,bless
	עזב	qal	pft	3ms	עזב	736		leave,loose
	נחני	qal	pft	3ms	נחה	634	1cs	lead
24:28	תרץ	qal	wci	3fs	רוץ	930		run
	תגד	hiph	wci	3fs	נגד	616		declare,tell
24:29	ירץ	qal	wci	3ms	רוץ	930		run
24:30	יהי	qal	wci	3ms	היה	224		be,become
	ראת	qal	infc		ראה	906		see
	שמעו	qal	infc		שמע	1033	3ms	hear
	אמר	qal	infc		אמר	55		say
	דבר	piel	pft	3ms	דבר	180		speak
	יבא	qal	wci	3ms	בוא	97		come in
	עמד	qal	ptc	ms	עמד	763		stand,stop
24:31	יאמר	qal	wci	3ms	אמר	55		say
	בוא	qal	impv	ms	בוא	97		come in
	ברוך	qal	pptc	ms	ברך	138		kneel,bless
	תעמד	qal	impf	2ms	עמד	763		stand,stop
	פניתי	piel	pft	1cs	פנה	815		make clear
24:32	יבא	qal	wci	3ms	בוא	97		come in
	יפתח	piel	wci	3ms	פתח	834		loose,free
	יתן	qal	wci	3ms	נתן	678		give,set
	רחץ	qal	infc		רחץ	934		wash,bathe
24:33	יישםk	qalp	wci	3ms	ישם	441		be placed
	יושםq	hoph	wci	3ms	שים	962		be set
	אכל	qal	infc		אכל	37		eat,devour
	יאמר	qal	wci	3ms	אמר	55		say
	אכל	qal	impf	1cs	אכל	37		eat,devour
	דברתי	piel	pft	1cs	דבר	180		speak

ChVs	Form	Stem	Tnse	PGN	Root	BDB	Sfx	Meaning
24:33	יאמר	qal	wci	3ms	אמר	55		say
	דבר	piel	impv	ms	דבר	180		speak
24:34	יאמר	qal	wci	3ms	אמר	55		say
24:35	ברך	piel	pft	3ms	ברך	138		bless
	יגדל	qal	wci	3ms	גדל	152		be great,grow
	יתן	qal	wci	3ms	נתן	678		give,set
24:36	תלד	qal	wci	3fs	ילד	408		bear,beget
	יתן	qal	wci	3ms	נתן	678		give,set
24:37	ישׁבעני	hiph	wci	3ms	שׁבע	989	1cs	cause to swear
	אמר	qal	infc		אמר	55		say
	תקח	qal	impf	2ms	לקח	542		take
	ישׁב	qal	ptc	ms	ישׁב	442		sit,dwell
24:38	תלך	qal	impf	2ms	הלך	229		walk,go
	לקחת	qal	wcp	2ms	לקח	542		take
24:39	אמר	qal	wci	1cs	אמר	55		say
	תלך	qal	impf	3fs	הלך	229		walk,go
24:40	יאמר	qal	wci	3ms	אמר	55		say
	התהלכתי	hith	pft	1cs	הלך	229		walk to and fro
	ישׁלח	qal	impf	3ms	שׁלח	1018		send
	הצליח	hiph	wcp	3ms	צלח	852		cause to thrive
	לקחת	qal	wcp	2ms	לקח	542		take
24:41	תנקה	niph	impf	2ms	נקה	667		be clean,free
	תבוא	qal	impf	2ms	בוא	97		come in
	יתנו	qal	impf	3mp	נתן	678		give,set
	היית	qal	wcp	2ms	היה	224		be,become
24:42	אבא	qal	wci	1cs	בוא	97		come in
	אמר	qal	wci	1cs	אמר	55		say
	מצליח	hiph	ptc	ms	צלח	852		cause to thrive
	הלך	qal	ptc	ms	הלך	229		walk,go
24:43	נצב	niph	ptc	ms	נצב	662		stand
	היה	qal	wcp	3ms	היה	224		be,become
	יצאת	qal	ptc	fs	יצא	422		go out
	שׁאב	qal	infc		שׁאב	980		draw (water)
	אמרתי	qal	wcp	1cs	אמר	55		say
	השׁקיני	hiph	impv	fs	שׁקה	1052	1cs	give to drink
24:44	אמרה	qal	wcp	3fs	אמר	55		say
	שׁתה	qal	impv	ms	שׁתה	1059		drink
	אשׁאב	qal	impf	1cs	שׁאב	980		draw (water)
	הכיח	hiph	pft	3ms	יכח	406		decide,reprove
24:45	אכלה	piel	impf	1cs	כלה	477		complete,finish
	דבר	piel	infc		דבר	180		speak
	יצאת	qal	ptc	fs	יצא	422		go out
	תרד	qal	wci	3fs	ירד	432		come down
	תשׁאב	qal	wci	3fs	שׁאב	980		draw (water)
	אמר	qal	wci	1cs	אמר	55		say
	השׁקיני	hiph	impv	fs	שׁקה	1052	1cs	give to drink
24:46	תמהר	piel	wci	3fs	מהר	554		hasten
	תורד	hiph	wci	3fs	ירד	432		bring down
	תאמר	qal	wci	3fs	אמר	55		say
	שׁתה	qal	impv	ms	שׁתה	1059		drink
	אשׁקה	hiph	impf	1cs	שׁקה	1052		give to drink
	אשׁת	qal	wci	1cs	שׁתה	1059		drink
	השׁקתה	hiph	pft	3fs	שׁקה	1052		give to drink
24:47	אשׁאל	qal	wci	1cs	שׁאל	981		ask,borrow
24:47	אמר	qal	wci	1cs	אמר	55		say
	תאמר	qal	wci	3fs	אמר	55		say
	ילדה	qal	pft	3fs	ילד	408		bear,beget
	אשׂם	qal	wci	1cs	שׂים	962		put,set
24:48	אקד	qal	wci	1cs	קדד	869		bow down
	אשׁתחוה	hish	wci	1cs	חוה	1005		bow down
	אברך	piel	wci	1cs	ברך	138		bless
	הנחני	hiph	pft	3ms	נחה	634	1cs	lead,guide
	קחת	qal	infc		לקח	542		take
24:49	עשׂים	qal	ptc	mp	עשׂה	793		do,make
	הגידו	hiph	impv	mp	נגד	616		declare,tell
	הגידו	hiph	impv	mp	נגד	616		declare,tell
	אפנה	qal	cohm	1cs	פנה	815		turn
24:50	יען	qal	wci	3ms	ענה	772		answer
	יאמרו	qal	wci	3mp	אמר	55		say
	יצא	qal	pft	3ms	יצא	422		go out
	נוכל	qal	impf	1cp	יכל	407		be able
	דבר	piel	infc		דבר	180		speak
24:51	קח	qal	impv	ms	לקח	542		take
	לך	qal	impv	ms	הלך	229		walk,go
	תהי	qal	jus	3fs	היה	224		be,become
	דבר	piel	pft	3ms	דבר	180		speak
24:52	יהי	qal	wci	3ms	היה	224		be,become
	שׁמע	qal	pft	3ms	שׁמע	1033		hear
	ישׁתחו	hish	wci	3ms	חוה	1005		bow down
24:53	יוצא	hiph	wci	3ms	יצא	422		bring out
	יתן	qal	wci	3ms	נתן	678		give,set
	נתן	qal	pft	3ms	נתן	678		give,set
24:54	יאכלו	qal	wci	3mp	אכל	37		eat,devour
	ישׁתו	qal	wci	3mp	שׁתה	1059		drink
	ילינו	qal	wci	3mp	לון	533		lodge,remain
	יקומו	qal	wci	3mp	קום	877		arise,stand
	יאמר	qal	wci	3ms	אמר	55		say
	שׁלחני	piel	impv	mp	שׁלח	1018	1cs	send away,shoot
24:55	יאמר	qal	wci	3ms	אמר	55		say
	תשׁב	qal	jusm	3fs	ישׁב	442		sit,dwell
	תלך	qal	impf	3fs	הלך	229		walk,go
24:56	יאמר	qal	wci	3ms	אמר	55		say
	תאחרו	piel	jusm	2mp	אחר	29		tarry,hinder
	הצליח	hiph	pft	3ms	צלח	852		cause to thrive
	שׁלחוני	piel	impv	mp	שׁלח	1018	1cs	send away,shoot
	אלכה	qal	coh	1cs	הלך	229		walk,go
24:57	יאמרו	qal	wci	3mp	אמר	55		say
	נקרא	qal	cohm	1cp	קרא	894		call,proclaim
	נשׁאלה	qal	coh	1cp	שׁאל	981		ask,borrow
24:58	יקראו	qal	wci	3mp	קרא	894		call,proclaim
	יאמרו	qal	wci	3mp	אמר	55		say
	תלכי	qal	impf	2fs	הלך	229		walk,go
	תאמר	qal	wci	3fs	אמר	55		say
	אלך	qal	impf	1cs	הלך	229		walk,go
24:59	ישׁלחו	piel	wci	3mp	שׁלח	1018		send away,shoot
	מנקתה	hiph	ptc	fs	ינק	413	3fs	nurse
24:60	יברכו	piel	wci	3mp	ברך	138		bless
	יאמרו	qal	wci	3mp	אמר	55		say

ChVs	Form	Stem	Tnse	PGN	Root	BDB	Sfx	Meaning
24:60	היי	qal	impv	fs	היה	224		be,become
	יירשׁ	qal	jusm	3ms	ירשׁ	439		possess,inherit
	שׂנאיו	qal	ptc	mp	שׂנא	971	3ms	hate
24:61	תקם	qal	wci	3fs	קום	877		arise,stand
	תרכבנה	qal	wci	3fp	רכב	938		mount,ride
	תלכנה	qal	wci	3fp	הלך	229		walk,go
	יקח	qal	wci	3ms	לקח	542		take
	ילך	qal	wci	3ms	הלך	229		walk,go
24:62	בא	qal	pft	3ms	בוא	97		come in
	בוא	qal	infc		בוא	97		come in
	יושׁב	qal	ptc	ms	ישׁב	442		sit,dwell
24:63	יצא	qal	wci	3ms	יצא	422		go out
	שׂוח	qal	infc		שׂוח	962		meditate
	פנות	qal	infc		פנה	815		turn
	ישׂא	qal	wci	3ms	נשׂא	669		lift,carry
	ירא	qal	wci	3ms	ראה	906		see
	באים	qal	ptc	mp	בוא	97		come in
24:64	תשׂא	qal	wci	3fs	נשׂא	669		lift,carry
	תרא	qal	wci	3fs	ראה	906		see
	תפל	qal	wci	3fs	נפל	656		fall
24:65	תאמר	qal	wci	3fs	אמר	55		say
	הלך	qal	ptc	ms	הלך	229		walk,go
	קראתנו	qal	infc		קרא	896	1cp	meet,encounter
	יאמר	qal	wci	3ms	אמר	55		say
	תקח	qal	wci	3fs	לקח	542		take
	תתכס	hith	wci	3fs	כסה	491		cover oneself
24:66	יספר	piel	wci	3ms	ספר	707		recount
	עשׂה	qal	pft	3ms	עשׂה	793		do,make
24:67	יבאה	hiph	wci	3ms	בוא	97	3fs	bring in
	יקח	qal	wci	3ms	לקח	542		take
	תהי	qal	wci	3fs	היה	224		be,become
	יאהבה	qal	wci	3ms	אהב	12	3fs	love
	ינחם	niph	wci	3ms	נחם	636		be sorry
25:1	יסף	hiph	wci	3ms	יסף	414		add,do again
	יקח	qal	wci	3ms	לקח	542		take
25:2	תלד	qal	wci	3fs	ילד	408		bear,beget
25:3	ילד	qal	pft	3ms	ילד	408		bear,beget
	היו	qal	pft	3cp	היה	224		be,become
25:5	יתן	qal	wci	3ms	נתן	678		give,set
25:6	נתן	qal	pft	3ms	נתן	678		give,set
	ישׁלחם	piel	wci	3ms	שׁלח	1018	3mp	send away,shoot
25:8	יגוע	qal	wci	3ms	גוע	157		expire,die
	ימת	qal	wci	3ms	מות	559		die
	יאסף	niph	wci	3ms	אסף	62		assemble
25:9	יקברו	qal	wci	3mp	קבר	868		bury
25:10	קנה	qal	pft	3ms	קנה	888		get,buy
	קבר	pual	pft	3ms	קבר	868		be buried
25:11	יהי	qal	wci	3ms	היה	224		be,become
	יברך	piel	wci	3ms	ברך	138		bless
	ישׁב	qal	wci	3ms	ישׁב	442		sit,dwell
25:12	ילדה	qal	pft	3fs	ילד	408		bear,beget
25:17	יגוע	qal	wci	3ms	גוע	157		expire,die
	ימת	qal	wci	3ms	מות	559		die
	יאסף	niph	wci	3ms	אסף	62		assemble
25:18	ישׁכנו	qal	wci	3mp	שׁכן	1014		settle,dwell
	באכה	qal	infc		בוא	97	2ms	come in
	נפל	qal	pft	3ms	נפל	656		fall
25:19	הוליד	hiph	pft	3ms	ילד	408		beget
25:20	יהי	qal	wci	3ms	היה	224		be,become
	קחתו	qal	infc		לקח	542	3ms	take
25:21	יעתר	qal	wci	3ms	עתר	801		pray
	יעתר	niph	wci	3ms	עתר	801		be supplicated
	תהר	qal	wci	3fs	הרה	247		conceive
25:22	יתרצצו	htpo	wci	3mp	רצץ	954		struggle
	תאמר	qal	wci	3fs	אמר	55		say
	תלך	qal	wci	3fs	הלך	229		walk,go
	דרשׁ	qal	infc		דרשׁ	205		resort to,seek
25:23	יאמר	qal	wci	3ms	אמר	55		say
	יפרדו	niph	impf	3mp	פרד	825		divide
	יאמץ	qal	impf	3ms	אמץ	54		be strong
	יעבד	qal	impf	3ms	עבד	712		work,serve
25:24	ימלאו	qal	wci	3mp	מלא	569		be full,fill
	לדת	qal	infc		ילד	408		bear,beget
25:25	יצא	qal	wci	3ms	יצא	422		go out
	יקראו	qal	wci	3mp	קרא	894		call,proclaim
25:26	יצא	qal	pft	3ms	יצא	422		go out
	אחזת	qal	ptc	fs	אחז	28		grasp
	יקרא	qal	wci	3ms	קרא	894		call,proclaim
	לדת	qal	infc		ילד	408		bear,beget
25:27	יגדלו	qal	wci	3mp	גדל	152		be great,grow
	יהי	qal	wci	3ms	היה	224		be,become
	ידע	qal	ptc	ms	ידע	393		know
	ישׁב	qal	ptc	ms	ישׁב	442		sit,dwell
25:28	יאהב	qal	wci	3ms	אהב	12		love
	אהבת	qal	ptc	fs	אהב	12		love
25:29	יזד	hiph	wci	3ms	זיד	267		boil,presume
	יבא	qal	wci	3ms	בוא	97		come in
25:30	יאמר	qal	wci	3ms	אמר	55		say
	הלעיטני	hiph	impv	ms	לעט	542	1cs	eat greedily
	קרא	qal	pft	3ms	קרא	894		call,proclaim
25:31	יאמר	qal	wci	3ms	אמר	55		say
	מכרה	qal	impv	ms	מכר	569		sell
25:32	יאמר	qal	wci	3ms	אמר	55		say
	הולך	qal	ptc	ms	הלך	229		walk,go
	מות	qal	infc		מות	559		die
25:33	יאמר	qal	wci	3ms	אמר	55		say
	השׁבעה	niph	impv	ms	שׁבע	989		swear
	ישׁבע	niph	wci	3ms	שׁבע	989		swear
	ימכר	qal	wci	3ms	מכר	569		sell
25:34	נתן	qal	pft	3ms	נתן	678		give,set
	יאכל	qal	wci	3ms	אכל	37		eat,devour
	ישׁת	qal	wci	3ms	שׁתה	1059		drink
	יקם	qal	wci	3ms	קום	877		arise,stand
	ילך	qal	wci	3ms	הלך	229		walk,go
	יבז	qal	wci	3ms	בזה	102		despise
26:1	יהי	qal	wci	3ms	היה	224		be,become
	היה	qal	pft	3ms	היה	224		be,become
	ילך	qal	wci	3ms	הלך	229		walk,go

ChVs	Form	Stem	Tnse	PGN	Root	BDB	Sfx	Meaning
26: 2	ירא	niph	wci	3ms	ראה	906		appear,be seen
	יאמר	qal	wci	3ms	אמר	55		say
	תרד	qal	jusm	2ms	ירד	432		come down
	שׁכן	qal	impv	ms	שׁכן	1014		settle,dwell
	אמר	qal	impf	1cs	אמר	55		say
26: 3	גור	qal	impv	ms	גור	157		sojourn
	אהיה	qal	cohm	1cs	היה	224		be,become
	אברכך	piel	cohm	1cs	ברך	138	2ms	bless
	אתן	qal	impf	1cs	נתן	678		give,set
	הקמתי	hiph	wcp	1cs	קום	877		raise,build,set
	נשׁבעתי	niph	pft	1cs	שׁבע	989		swear
26: 4	הרביתי	hiph	wcp	1cs	רבה	915		make many
	נתתי	qal	wcp	1cs	נתן	678		give,set
	התברכו	hith	wcp	3cp	ברך	138		bless oneself
26: 5	שׁמע	qal	pft	3ms	שׁמע	1033		hear
	ישׁמר	qal	wci	3ms	שׁמר	1036		keep,watch
26: 6	ישׁב	qal	wci	3ms	ישׁב	442		sit,dwell
26: 7	ישׁאלו	qal	wci	3mp	שׁאל	981		ask, borrow
	יאמר	qal	wci	3ms	אמר	55		say
	ירא	qal	pft	3ms	ירא	431		fear
	אמר	qal	infc		אמר	55		say
	יהרגני	qal	impf	3mp	הרג	246	1cs	kill
26: 8	יהי	qal	wci	3ms	היה	224		be,become
	ארכו	qal	pft	3cp	ארך	73		be long
	ישׁקף	hiph	wci	3ms	שׁקף	1054		look down
	ירא	qal	wci	3ms	ראה	906		see
	מצחק	piel	ptc	ms	צחק	850		jest,make sport
26: 9	יקרא	qal	wci	3ms	קרא	894		call,proclaim
	יאמר	qal	wci	3ms	אמר	55		say
	אמרת	qal	pft	2ms	אמר	55		say
	יאמר	qal	wci	3ms	אמר	55		say
	אמרתי	qal	pft	1cs	אמר	55		say
	אמות	qal	impf	1cs	מות	559		die
26: 10	יאמר	qal	wci	3ms	אמר	55		say
	עשׂית	qal	pft	2ms	עשׂה	793		do,make
	שׁכב	qal	pft	3ms	שׁכב	1011		lie,lie down
	הבאת	hiph	wcp	2ms	בוא	97		bring in
26: 11	יצו	piel	wci	3ms	צוה	845		command
	אמר	qal	infc		אמר	55		say
	נגע	qal	ptc	ms	נגע	619		touch,strike
	מות	qal	infa		מות	559		die
	יומת	hoph	impf	3ms	מות	559		be killed
26: 12	יזרע	qal	wci	3ms	זרע	281		sow
	ימצא	qal	wci	3ms	מצא	592		find
	יברכהו	piel	wci	3ms	ברך	138	3ms	bless
26: 13	יגדל	qal	wci	3ms	גדל	152		be great,grow
	ילך	qal	wci	3ms	הלך	229		walk,go
	הלוך	qal	infa		הלך	229		walk,go
	גדל	qal	pft	3ms	גדל	152		be great,grow
26: 14	יהי	qal	wci	3ms	היה	224		be,become
	יקנאו	piel	wci	3mp	קנא	888		be jealous
26: 15	חפרו	qal	pft	3cp	חפר	343		dig,search
	סתמום	piel	pft	3cp	סתם	711	3mp	stop up
	ימלאום	piel	wci	3mp	מלא	569	3mp	fill
26: 16	יאמר	qal	wci	3ms	אמר	55		say
	לך	qal	impv	ms	הלך	229		walk,go
	עצמת	qal	pft	2ms	עצם	782		be mighty,many
26: 17	ילך	qal	wci	3ms	הלך	229		walk,go
	יחן	qal	wci	3ms	חנה	333		decline,encamp
	ישׁב	qal	wci	3ms	ישׁב	442		sit,dwell
26: 18	ישׁב	qal	wci	3ms	שׁוב	996		turn,return
	יחפר	qal	wci	3ms	חפר	343		dig,search
	חפרו	qal	pft	3cp	חפר	343		dig,search
	יסתמום	piel	wci	3mp	סתם	711	3mp	stop up
	יקרא	qal	wci	3ms	קרא	894		call,proclaim
	קרא	qal	pft	3ms	קרא	894		call,proclaim
26: 19	יחפרו	qal	wci	3mp	חפר	343		dig,search
	ימצאו	qal	wci	3mp	מצא	592		find
26: 20	יריבו	qal	wci	3mp	ריב	936		strive,contend
	רעי	qal	ptc	mp	רעה	944		pasture,tend
	רעי	qal	ptc	mp	רעה	944		pasture,tend
	אמר	qal	infc		אמר	55		say
	יקרא	qal	wci	3ms	קרא	894		call,proclaim
	התעשׂקו	hith	pft	3cp	עשׂק	796		contend
26: 21	יחפרו	qal	wci	3mp	חפר	343		dig,search
	יריבו	qal	wci	3mp	ריב	936		strive,contend
	יקרא	qal	wci	3ms	קרא	894		call,proclaim
26: 22	יעתק	hiph	wci	3ms	עתק	801		move,remove
	יחפר	qal	wci	3ms	חפר	343		dig,search
	רבו	qal	pft	3cp	ריב	936		strive,contend
	יקרא	qal	wci	3ms	קרא	894		call,proclaim
	יאמר	qal	wci	3ms	אמר	55		say
	הרחיב	hiph	pft	3ms	רחב	931		enlarge
	פרינו	qal	wcp	1cp	פרה	826		bear fruit
26: 23	יעל	qal	wci	3ms	עלה	748		go up
26: 24	ירא	niph	wci	3ms	ראה	906		appear,be seen
	יאמר	qal	wci	3ms	אמר	55		say
	תירא	qal	jusm	2ms	ירא	431		fear
	ברכתיך	piel	wcp	1cs	ברך	138	2ms	bless
	הרביתי	hiph	wcp	1cs	רבה	915		make many
26: 25	יבן	qal	wci	3ms	בנה	124		build
	יקרא	qal	wci	3ms	קרא	894		call,proclaim
	יט	qal	wci	3ms	נטה	639		stretch,incline
	יכרו	qal	wci	3mp	כרה	500		dig
26: 26	הלך	qal	pft	3ms	הלך	229		walk,go
26: 27	יאמר	qal	wci	3ms	אמר	55		say
	באתם	qal	pft	2mp	בוא	97		come in
	שׂנאתם	qal	pft	2mp	שׂנא	971		hate
	תשׁלחוני	piel	wci	2mp	שׁלח	1018	1cs	send away,shoot
26: 28	יאמרו	qal	wci	3mp	אמר	55		say
	ראו	qal	infa		ראה	906		see
	ראינו	qal	pft	1cp	ראה	906		see
	היה	qal	pft	3ms	היה	224		be,become
	נאמר	qal	wci	1cp	אמר	55		say
	תהי	qal	jus	3fs	היה	224		be,become
	נכרתה	qal	coh	1cp	כרת	503		cut,destroy
26: 29	תעשׂה	qal	impf	2ms	עשׂה	793		do,make
	נגענוך	qal	pft	1cp	נגע	619	2ms	touch,strike

ChVs	Form	Stem	Tnse	PGN	Root	BDB	Sfx	Meaning
26: 29	עשׂינו	qal	pft	1cp	עשׂה	793		do,make
	נשׁלחך	piel	wci	1cp	שׁלח	1018	2ms	send away,shoot
	ברוך	qal	pptc	ms	ברך	138		kneel,bless
26: 30	יעשׂ	qal	wci	3ms	עשׂה	793		do,make
	יאכלו	qal	wci	3mp	אכל	37		eat,devour
	ישׁתו	qal	wci	3mp	שׁתה	1059		drink
26: 31	ישׁכימו	hiph	wci	3mp	שׁכם	1014		rise early
	ישׁבעו	niph	wci	3mp	שׁבע	989		swear
	ישׁלחם	piel	wci	3ms	שׁלח	1018	3mp	send away,shoot
	ילכו	qal	wci	3mp	הלך	229		walk,go
26: 32	יהי	qal	wci	3ms	היה	224		be,become
	יבאו	qal	wci	3mp	בוא	97		come in
	יגדו	hiph	wci	3mp	נגד	616		declare,tell
	חפרו	qal	pft	3cp	חפר	343		dig,search
	יאמרו	qal	wci	3mp	אמר	55		say
	מצאנו	qal	pft	1cp	מצא	592		find
26: 33	יקרא	qal	wci	3ms	קרא	894		call,proclaim
26: 34	יהי	qal	wci	3ms	היה	224		be,become
	יקח	qal	wci	3ms	לקח	542		take
26: 35	תהיין	qal	wci	3fp	היה	224		be,become
27: 1	יהי	qal	wci	3ms	היה	224		be,become
	זקן	qal	pft	3ms	זקן	278		be old
	תכהין	qal	wci	3fp	כהה	462		grow dim
	ראת	qal	infc		ראה	906		see
	יקרא	qal	wci	3ms	קרא	894		call,proclaim
	יאמר	qal	wci	3ms	אמר	55		say
	יאמר	qal	wci	3ms	אמר	55		say
27: 2	יאמר	qal	wci	3ms	אמר	55		say
	זקנתי	qal	pft	1cs	זקן	278		be old
	ידעתי	qal	pft	1cs	ידע	393		know
27: 3	שׂא	qal	impv	ms	נשׂא	669		lift,carry
	צא	qal	impv	ms	יצא	422		go out
	צודה	qal	impv	ms	צוד	844		hunt
27: 4	עשׂה	qal	impv	ms	עשׂה	793		do,make
	אהבתי	qal	pft	1cs	אהב	12		love
	הביאה	hiph	impv	ms	בוא	97		bring in
	אכלה	qal	coh	1cs	אכל	37		eat,devour
	תברכך	piel	impf	3fs	ברך	138	2ms	bless
	אמות	qal	impf	1cs	מות	559		die
27: 5	שׁמעת	qal	ptc	fs	שׁמע	1033		hear
	דבר	piel	infc		דבר	180		speak
	ילך	qal	wci	3ms	הלך	229		walk,go
	צוד	qal	infc		צוד	844		hunt
	הביא	hiph	infc		בוא	97		bring in
27: 6	אמרה	qal	pft	3fs	אמר	55		say
	אמר	qal	infc		אמר	55		say
	שׁמעתי	qal	pft	1cs	שׁמע	1033		hear
	מדבר	piel	ptc	ms	דבר	180		speak
	אמר	qal	infc		אמר	55		say
27: 7	הביאה	hiph	impv	ms	בוא	97		bring in
	עשׂה	qal	impv	ms	עשׂה	793		do,make
	אכלה	qal	coh	1cs	אכל	37		eat,devour
	אברככה	piel	coh	1cs	ברך	138	2ms	bless
27: 8	שׁמע	qal	impv	ms	שׁמע	1033		hear
27: 8	מצוה	piel	ptc	fs	צוה	845		command
27: 9	לך	qal	impv	ms	הלך	229		walk,go
	קח	qal	impv	ms	לקח	542		take
	אעשׂה	qal	coh	1cs	עשׂה	793		do,make
	אהב	qal	pft	3ms	אהב	12		love
27: 10	הבאת	hiph	wcp	2ms	בוא	97		bring in
	אכל	qal	wcp	3ms	אכל	37		eat,devour
	יברכך	piel	impf	3ms	ברך	138	2ms	bless
27: 11	יאמר	qal	wci	3ms	אמר	55		say
27: 12	ימשׁני	qal	impf	3ms	משׁשׁ	606	1cs	feel
	הייתי	qal	wcp	1cs	היה	224		be,become
	מתעתע	pilp	ptc	ms	תעע	1073		mock
	הבאתי	hiph	wcp	1cs	בוא	97		bring in
27: 13	תאמר	qal	wci	3fs	אמר	55		say
	שׁמע	qal	impv	ms	שׁמע	1033		hear
	לך	qal	impv	ms	הלך	229		walk,go
	קח	qal	impv	ms	לקח	542		take
27: 14	ילך	qal	wci	3ms	הלך	229		walk,go
	יקח	qal	wci	3ms	לקח	542		take
	יבא	hiph	wci	3ms	בוא	97		bring in
	תעשׂ	qal	wci	3fs	עשׂה	793		do,make
	אהב	qal	pft	3ms	אהב	12		love
27: 15	תקח	qal	wci	3fs	לקח	542		take
	תלבשׁ	hiph	wci	3fs	לבשׁ	527		clothe
27: 16	הלבישׁה	hiph	pft	3fs	לבשׁ	527		clothe
27: 17	תתן	qal	wci	3fs	נתן	678		give,set
	עשׂתה	qal	pft	3fs	עשׂה	793		do,make
27: 18	יבא	qal	wci	3ms	בוא	97		come in
	יאמר	qal	wci	3ms	אמר	55		say
	יאמר	qal	wci	3ms	אמר	55		say
27: 19	יאמר	qal	wci	3ms	אמר	55		say
	עשׂיתי	qal	pft	1cs	עשׂה	793		do,make
	דברת	piel	pft	2ms	דבר	180		speak
	קום	qal	impv	ms	קום	877		arise,stand
	שׁבה	qal	impv	ms	ישׁב	442		sit,dwell
	אכלה	qal	impv	ms	אכל	37		eat,devour
	תברכני	piel	impf	3fs	ברך	138	1cs	bless
27: 20	יאמר	qal	wci	3ms	אמר	55		say
	מהרת	piel	pft	2ms	מהר	554		hasten
	מצא	qal	infc		מצא	592		find
	יאמר	qal	wci	3ms	אמר	55		say
	הקרה	hiph	pft	3ms	קרה	899		cause to occur
27: 21	יאמר	qal	wci	3ms	אמר	55		say
	גשׁה	qal	impv	ms	נגשׁ	620		draw near
	אמשׁך	qal	coh	1cs	מושׁ	559	2ms	feel
27: 22	יגשׁ	qal	wci	3ms	נגשׁ	620		draw near
	ימשׁהו	qal	wci	3ms	משׁשׁ	606	3ms	feel
	יאמר	qal	wci	3ms	אמר	55		say
27: 23	הכירו	hiph	pft	3ms	נכר	647	3ms	regard,notice
	היו	qal	pft	3cp	היה	224		be,become
	יברכהו	piel	wci	3ms	ברך	138	3ms	bless
27: 24	יאמר	qal	wci	3ms	אמר	55		say
	יאמר	qal	wci	3ms	אמר	55		say
27: 25	יאמר	qal	wci	3ms	אמר	55		say

ChVs	Form	Stem	Tnse	PGN	Root	BDB	Sfx	Meaning
27: 25	הגשה	hiph	impv	ms	נגש	620		bring near
	אכלה	qal	coh	1cs	אכל	37		eat,devour
	תברכך	piel	impf	3fs	ברך	138	2ms	bless
	יגש	hiph	wci	3ms	נגש	620		bring near
	יאכל	qal	wci	3ms	אכל	37		eat,devour
	יבא	hiph	wci	3ms	בוא	97		bring in
	ישת	qal	wci	3ms	שתה	1059		drink
27: 26	יאמר	qal	wci	3ms	אמר	55		say
	גשה	qal	impv	ms	נגש	620		draw near
	שקה	qal	impv	ms	נשק	676		kiss
27: 27	יגש	qal	wci	3ms	נגש	620		draw near
	ישק	qal	wci	3ms	נשק	676		kiss
	ירח	hiph	wci	3ms	ריח	926		smell
	יברכהו	piel	wci	3ms	ברך	138	3ms	bless
	יאמר	qal	wci	3ms	אמר	55		say
	ראה	qal	impv	ms	ראה	906		see
	ברכו	piel	pft	3ms	ברך	138	3ms	bless
27: 28	יתן	qal	jusm	3ms	נתן	678		give,set
27: 29	יעבדוך	qal	jusm	3mp	עבד	712	2ms	work,serve
	ישתחו k	hish	jusm	3ms	חוה	1005		bow down
	ישתחוו q	hish	jusm	3mp	חוה	1005		bow down
	הוה	qal	impv	ms	הוה	217		become
	ישתחוו	hish	jusm	3mp	חוה	1005		bow down
	ארריך	qal	ptc	mp	ארר	76	2ms	curse
	ארור	qal	pptc	ms	ארר	76		curse
	מברכיך	piel	ptc	mp	ברך	138	2ms	bless
	ברוך	qal	pptc	ms	ברך	138		kneel,bless
27: 30	יהי	qal	wci	3ms	היה	224		be,become
	כלה	piel	pft	3ms	כלה	477		complete,finish
	ברך	piel	infc		ברך	138		bless
	יהי	qal	wci	3ms	היה	224		be,become
	יצא	qal	infa		יצא	422		go out
	יצא	qal	pft	3ms	יצא	422		go out
	בא	qal	pft	3ms	בוא	97		come in
27: 31	יעש	qal	wci	3ms	עשה	793		do,make
	יבא	hiph	wci	3ms	בוא	97		bring in
	יאמר	qal	wci	3ms	אמר	55		say
	יקם	qal	jus	3ms	קום	877		arise,stand
	יאכל	qal	jusm	3ms	אכל	37		eat,devour
	תברכני	piel	impf	3fs	ברך	138	1cs	bless
27: 32	יאמר	qal	wci	3ms	אמר	55		say
	יאמר	qal	wci	3ms	אמר	55		say
27: 33	יחרד	qal	wci	3ms	חרד	353		tremble
	יאמר	qal	wci	3ms	אמר	55		say
	צד	qal	ptc	ms	צוד	844		hunt
	יבא	hiph	wci	3ms	בוא	97		bring in
	אכל	qal	wci	1cs	אכל	37		eat,devour
	תבוא	qal	impf	2ms	בוא	97		come in
	אברכהו	piel	wci	1cs	ברך	138	3ms	bless
	ברוך	qal	pptc	ms	ברך	138		kneel,bless
	יהיה	qal	impf	3ms	היה	224		be,become
27: 34	שמע	qal	infc		שמע	1033		hear
	יצעק	qal	wci	3ms	צעק	858		cry out
	יאמר	qal	wci	3ms	אמר	55		say
27: 34	ברכני	piel	impv	ms	ברך	138	1cs	bless
27: 35	יאמר	qal	wci	3ms	אמר	55		say
	בא	qal	pft	3ms	בוא	97		come in
	יקח	qal	wci	3ms	לקח	542		take
27: 36	יאמר	qal	wci	3ms	אמר	55		say
	קרא	qal	pft	3ms	קרא	894		call,proclaim
	יעקבני	qal	wci	3ms	עקב	784	1cs	attack at heel
	לקח	qal	pft	3ms	לקח	542		take
	לקח	qal	pft	3ms	לקח	542		take
	יאמר	qal	wci	3ms	אמר	55		say
	אצלת	qal	pft	2ms	אצל	69		reserve
27: 37	יען	qal	wci	3ms	ענה	772		answer
	יאמר	qal	wci	3ms	אמר	55		say
	שמתיו	qal	pft	1cs	שים	962	3ms	put,set
	נתתי	qal	pft	1cs	נתן	678		give,set
	סמכתיו	qal	pft	1cs	סמך	701	3ms	lean,support
	אעשה	qal	impf	1cs	עשה	793		do,make
27: 38	יאמר	qal	wci	3ms	אמר	55		say
	ברכני	piel	impv	ms	ברך	138	1cs	bless
	ישא	qal	wci	3ms	נשא	669		lift,carry
	יבך	qal	wci	3ms	בכה	113		weep
27: 39	יען	qal	wci	3ms	ענה	772		answer
	יאמר	qal	wci	3ms	אמר	55		say
	יהיה	qal	impf	3ms	היה	224		be,become
27: 40	תחיה	qal	impf	2ms	חיה	310		live
	תעבד	qal	impf	2ms	עבד	712		work,serve
	היה	qal	wcp	3ms	היה	224		be,become
	תריד	hiph	impf	2ms	רוד	923		rove,ramble
	פרקת	qal	wcp	2ms	פרק	830		tear away
27: 41	ישטם	qal	wci	3ms	שטם	966		bear a grudge
	ברכו	piel	pft	3ms	ברך	138	3ms	bless
	יאמר	qal	wci	3ms	אמר	55		say
	יקרבו	qal	impf	3mp	קרב	897		approach
	אהרגה	qal	coh	1cs	הרג	246		kill
27: 42	יגד	hoph	wci	3ms	נגד	616		be told
	תשלח	qal	wci	3fs	שלח	1018		send
	תקרא	qal	wci	3fs	קרא	894		call,proclaim
	תאמר	qal	wci	3fs	אמר	55		say
	מתנחם	hith	ptc	ms	נחם	636		have compassion
	הרגך	qal	infc		הרג	246	2ms	kill
27: 43	שמע	qal	impv	ms	שמע	1033		hear
	קום	qal	impv	ms	קום	877		arise,stand
	ברח	qal	impv	ms	ברח	137		go thru,flee
27: 44	ישבת	qal	wcp	2ms	ישב	442		sit,dwell
	תשוב	qal	impf	3fs	שוב	996		turn,return
27: 45	שוב	qal	infc		שוב	996		turn,return
	שכח	qal	wcp	3ms	שכח	1013		forget
	עשית	qal	pft	2ms	עשה	793		do,make
	שלחתי	qal	wcp	1cs	שלח	1018		send
	לקחתיך	qal	wcp	1cs	לקח	542	2ms	take
	אשכל	qal	impf	1cs	שכל	1013		be bereaved
27: 46	תאמר	qal	wci	3fs	אמר	55		say
	קצתי	qal	pft	1cs	קוץ	880		loathe,abhor
	לקח	qal	ptc	ms	לקח	542		take

ChVs	Form	Stem	Tnse	PGN	Root	BDB	Sfx	Meaning
28: 1	יקרא	qal	wci	3ms	קרא	894		call,proclaim
	יברך	piel	wci	3ms	ברך	138		bless
	יצוהו	piel	wci	3ms	צוה	845	3ms	command
	יאמר	qal	wci	3ms	אמר	55		say
	תקח	qal	impf	2ms	לקח	542		take
28: 2	קום	qal	impv	ms	קום	877		arise,stand
	לך	qal	impv	ms	הלך	229		walk,go
	קח	qal	impv	ms	לקח	542		take
28: 3	יברך	piel	jusm	3ms	ברך	138		bless
	יפרך	hiph	jusm	3ms	פרה	826	2ms	make fruitful
	ירבך	hiph	jusm	3ms	רבה	915	2ms	make many
	היית	qal	wcp	2ms	היה	224		be,become
28: 4	יתן	qal	jusm	3ms	נתן	678		give,set
	רשתך	qal	infc		ירשׁ	439	2ms	possess,inherit
	נתן	qal	pft	3ms	נתן	678		give,set
28: 5	ישׁלח	qal	wci	3ms	שׁלח	1018		send
	ילך	qal	wci	3ms	הלך	229		walk,go
28: 6	ירא	qal	wci	3ms	ראה	906		see
	ברך	piel	pft	3ms	ברך	138		bless
	שׁלח	piel	pft	3ms	שׁלח	1018		send away,shoot
	קחת	qal	infc		לקח	542		take
	ברכו	piel	infc		ברך	138	3ms	bless
	יצו	piel	wci	3ms	צוה	845		command
	אמר	qal	infc		אמר	55		say
	תקח	qal	impf	2ms	לקח	542		take
28: 7	ישׁמע	qal	wci	3ms	שׁמע	1033		hear
	ילך	qal	wci	3ms	הלך	229		walk,go
28: 8	ירא	qal	wci	3ms	ראה	906		see
28: 9	ילך	qal	wci	3ms	הלך	229		walk,go
	יקח	qal	wci	3ms	לקח	542		take
28: 10	יצא	qal	wci	3ms	יצא	422		go out
	ילך	qal	wci	3ms	הלך	229		walk,go
28: 11	יפגע	qal	wci	3ms	פגע	803		meet,encounter
	ילן	qal	wci	3ms	לון	533		lodge,remain
	בא	qal	pft	3ms	בוא	97		come in
	יקח	qal	wci	3ms	לקח	542		take
	ישׂם	qal	wci	3ms	שׂים	962		put,set
	ישׁכב	qal	wci	3ms	שׁכב	1011		lie,lie down
28: 12	יחלם	qal	wci	3ms	חלם	321		dream
	מצב	hoph	ptc	ms	נצב	662		be fixed
	מגיע	hiph	ptc	ms	נגע	619		reach,arrive
	עלים	qal	ptc	mp	עלה	748		go up
	ירדים	qal	ptc	mp	ירד	432		come down
28: 13	נצב	niph	ptc	ms	נצב	662		stand
	יאמר	qal	wci	3ms	אמר	55		say
	שׁכב	qal	ptc	ms	שׁכב	1011		lie,lie down
	אתננה	qal	impf	1cs	נתן	678	3fs	give,set
28: 14	היה	qal	wcp	3ms	היה	224		be,become
	פרצת	qal	wcp	2ms	פרץ	829		break through
	נברכו	niph	wcp	3cp	ברך	138		bless oneself
28: 15	שׁמרתיך	qal	wcp	1cs	שׁמר	1036	2ms	keep,watch
	תלך	qal	impf	2ms	הלך	229		walk,go
	השׁבתיך	hiph	wcp	1cs	שׁוב	996	2ms	bring back
	אעזבך	qal	impf	1cs	עזב	736	2ms	leave,loose
28: 15	עשׂיתי	qal	pft	1cs	עשׂה	793		do,make
	דברתי	piel	pft	1cs	דבר	180		speak
28: 16	ייקץ	qal	wci	3ms	יקץ	429		awake
	יאמר	qal	wci	3ms	אמר	55		say
	ידעתי	qal	pft	1cs	ידע	393		know
28: 17	יירא	qal	wci	3ms	ירא	431		fear
	יאמר	qal	wci	3ms	אמר	55		say
	נורא	niph	ptc	ms	ירא	431		be feared
28: 18	ישׁכם	hiph	wci	3ms	שׁכם	1014		rise early
	יקח	qal	wci	3ms	לקח	542		take
	שׂם	qal	pft	3ms	שׂים	962		put,set
	ישׂם	qal	wci	3ms	שׂים	962		put,set
	יצק	qal	wci	3ms	יצק	427		pour out,cast
28: 19	יקרא	qal	wci	3ms	קרא	894		call,proclaim
28: 20	ידר	qal	wci	3ms	נדר	623		vow
	אמר	qal	infc		אמר	55		say
	יהיה	qal	impf	3ms	היה	224		be,become
	שׁמרני	qal	wcp	3ms	שׁמר	1036	1cs	keep,watch
	הולך	qal	ptc	ms	הלך	229		walk,go
	נתן	qal	wcp	3ms	נתן	678		give,set
	אכל	qal	infc		אכל	37		eat,devour
	לבשׁ	qal	infc		לבשׁ	527		put on,clothe
28: 21	שׁבתי	qal	wcp	1cs	שׁוב	996		turn,return
	היה	qal	wcp	3ms	היה	224		be,become
28: 22	שׂמתי	qal	pft	1cs	שׂים	962		put,set
	יהיה	qal	impf	3ms	היה	224		be,become
	תתן	qal	impf	2ms	נתן	678		give,set
	עשׂר	piel	infa		עשׂר	797		give tenth
	אעשׂרנו	piel	impf	1cs	עשׂר	797	3ms	give tenth
29: 1	ישׂא	qal	wci	3ms	נשׂא	669		lift,carry
	ילך	qal	wci	3ms	הלך	229		walk,go
29: 2	ירא	qal	wci	3ms	ראה	906		see
	רבצים	qal	ptc	mp	רבץ	918		lie down
	ישׁקו	hiph	impf	3mp	שׁקה	1052		give to drink
29: 3	נאספו	niph	wcp	3cp	אסף	62		assemble
	גללו	qal	wcp	3cp	גלל	164		roll away
	השׁקו	hiph	wcp	3cp	שׁקה	1052		give to drink
	השׁיבו	hiph	wcp	3cp	שׁוב	996		bring back
29: 4	יאמר	qal	wci	3ms	אמר	55		say
	יאמרו	qal	wci	3mp	אמר	55		say
29: 5	יאמר	qal	wci	3ms	אמר	55		say
	ידעתם	qal	pft	2mp	ידע	393		know
	יאמרו	qal	wci	3mp	אמר	55		say
	ידענו	qal	pft	1cp	ידע	393		know
29: 6	יאמר	qal	wci	3ms	אמר	55		say
	יאמרו	qal	wci	3mp	אמר	55		say
	באה	qal	ptc	fs	בוא	97		come in
29: 7	יאמר	qal	wci	3ms	אמר	55		say
	האסף	niph	infc		אסף	62		assemble
	השׁקו	hiph	impv	mp	שׁקה	1052		give to drink
	לכו	qal	impv	mp	הלך	229		walk,go
	רעו	qal	impv	mp	רעה	944		pasture,tend
29: 8	יאמרו	qal	wci	3mp	אמר	55		say
	נוכל	qal	impf	1cp	יכל	407		be able

ChVs	Form	Stem	Tnse	PGN	Root	BDB	Sfx	Meaning
29: 8	יאספו	niph	impf	3mp	אסף	62		assemble
	גללו	qal	wcp	3cp	גלל	164		roll away
	השקינו	hiph	wcp	1cp	שׁקה	1052		give to drink
29: 9	מדבר	piel	ptc	ms	דבר	180		speak
	באה	qal	pft	3fs	בוא	97		come in
	רעה	qal	ptc	fs	רעה	944		pasture, tend
29: 10	יהי	qal	wci	3ms	היה	224		be, become
	ראה	qal	pft	3ms	ראה	906		see
	יגשׁ	qal	wci	3ms	נגשׁ	620		draw near
	יגל	hiph	wci	3ms	גלל	164		roll away
	ישׁק	hiph	wci	3ms	שׁקה	1052		give to drink
29: 11	ישׁק	qal	wci	3ms	נשׁק	676		kiss
	ישׂא	qal	wci	3ms	נשׂא	669		lift, carry
	יבך	qal	wci	3ms	בכה	113		weep
29: 12	יגד	hiph	wci	3ms	נגד	616		declare, tell
	תרץ	qal	wci	3fs	רוץ	930		run
	תגד	hiph	wci	3fs	נגד	616		declare, tell
29: 13	יהי	qal	wci	3ms	היה	224		be, become
	שׁמע	qal	infc		שׁמע	1033		hear
	ירץ	qal	wci	3ms	רוץ	930		run
	קראתו	qal	infc		קרא	896	3ms	meet, encounter
	יחבק	piel	wci	3ms	חבק	287		embrace
	ינשׁק	piel	wci	3ms	נשׁק	676		kiss
	יביאהו	hiph	wci	3ms	בוא	97	3ms	bring in
	יספר	piel	wci	3ms	ספר	707		recount
29: 14	יאמר	qal	wci	3ms	אמר	55		say
	ישׁב	qal	wci	3ms	ישׁב	442		sit, dwell
29: 15	יאמר	qal	wci	3ms	אמר	55		say
	עבדתני	qal	wcp	2ms	עבד	712	1cs	work, serve
	הגידה	hiph	impv	ms	נגד	616		declare, tell
29: 17	היתה	qal	pft	3fs	היה	224		be, become
29: 18	יאהב	qal	wci	3ms	אהב	12		love
	יאמר	qal	wci	3ms	אמר	55		say
	אעבדך	qal	impf	1cs	עבד	712	2ms	work, serve
29: 19	יאמר	qal	wci	3ms	אמר	55		say
	תתי	qal	infc		נתן	678	1cs	give, set
	תתי	qal	infc		נתן	678	1cs	give, set
	שׁבה	qal	impv	ms	ישׁב	442		sit, dwell
29: 20	יעבד	qal	wci	3ms	עבד	712		work, serve
	יהיו	qal	wci	3mp	היה	224		be, become
	אהבתו	qal	infc		אהב	12	3ms	love
29: 21	יאמר	qal	wci	3ms	אמר	55		say
	הבה	qal	impv	ms	יהב	396		give
	מלאו	qal	pft	3cp	מלא	569		be full, fill
	אבואה	qal	coh	1cs	בוא	97		come in
29: 22	יאסף	qal	wci	3ms	אסף	62		gather
	יעשׂ	qal	wci	3ms	עשׂה	793		do, make
29: 23	יהי	qal	wci	3ms	היה	224		be, become
	יקח	qal	wci	3ms	לקח	542		take
	יבא	hiph	wci	3ms	בוא	97		bring in
	יבא	qal	wci	3ms	בוא	97		come in
29: 24	יתן	qal	wci	3ms	נתן	678		give, set
29: 25	יהי	qal	wci	3ms	היה	224		be, become
	יאמר	qal	wci	3ms	אמר	55		say
29: 25	עשׂית	qal	pft	2ms	עשׂה	793		do, make
	עבדתי	qal	pft	1cs	עבד	712		work, serve
	רמיתני	piel	pft	2ms	רמה	941	1cs	beguile
29: 26	יאמר	qal	wci	3ms	אמר	55		say
	יעשׂה	niph	impf	3ms	עשׂה	793		be done
	תת	qal	infc		נתן	678		give, set
29: 27	מלא	piel	impv	ms	מלא	569		fill
	נתנה	qal	coh	1cp	נתן	678		give, set
	תעבד	qal	impf	2ms	עבד	712		work, serve
29: 28	יעשׂ	qal	wci	3ms	עשׂה	793		do, make
	ימלא	piel	wci	3ms	מלא	569		fill
	יתן	qal	wci	3ms	נתן	678		give, set
29: 29	יתן	qal	wci	3ms	נתן	678		give, set
29: 30	יבא	qal	wci	3ms	בוא	97		come in
	יאהב	qal	wci	3ms	אהב	12		love
	יעבד	qal	wci	3ms	עבד	712		work, serve
29: 31	ירא	qal	wci	3ms	ראה	906		see
	שׂנואה	qal	pptc	fs	שׂנא	971		hate
	יפתח	qal	wci	3ms	פתח	834		open
29: 32	תהר	qal	wci	3fs	הרה	247		conceive
	תלד	qal	wci	3fs	ילד	408		bear, beget
	תקרא	qal	wci	3fs	קרא	894		call, proclaim
	אמרה	qal	pft	3fs	אמר	55		say
	ראה	qal	pft	3ms	ראה	906		see
	יאהבני	qal	impf	3ms	אהב	12	1cs	love
29: 33	תהר	qal	wci	3fs	הרה	247		conceive
	תלד	qal	wci	3fs	ילד	408		bear, beget
	תאמר	qal	wci	3fs	אמר	55		say
	שׁמע	qal	pft	3ms	שׁמע	1033		hear
	שׂנואה	qal	pptc	fs	שׂנא	971		hate
	יתן	qal	wci	3ms	נתן	678		give, set
	תקרא	qal	wci	3fs	קרא	894		call, proclaim
29: 34	תהר	qal	wci	3fs	הרה	247		conceive
	תלד	qal	wci	3fs	ילד	408		bear, beget
	תאמר	qal	wci	3fs	אמר	55		say
	ילוה	niph	impf	3ms	לוה	530		join oneself
	ילדתי	qal	pft	1cs	ילד	408		bear, beget
	קרא	qal	pft	3ms	קרא	894		call, proclaim
29: 35	תהר	qal	wci	3fs	הרה	247		conceive
	תלד	qal	wci	3fs	ילד	408		bear, beget
	תאמר	qal	wci	3fs	אמר	55		say
	אודה	hiph	impf	1cs	ידה	392		praise
	קראה	qal	pft	3fs	קרא	894		call, proclaim
	תעמד	qal	wci	3fs	עמד	763		stand, stop
	לדת	qal	infc		ילד	408		bear, beget
30: 1	תרא	qal	wci	3fs	ראה	906		see
	ילדה	qal	pft	3fs	ילד	408		bear, beget
	תקנא	piel	wci	3fs	קנא	888		be jealous
	תאמר	qal	wci	3fs	אמר	55		say
	הבה	qal	impv	ms	יהב	396		give
	מתה	qal	ptc	fs	מות	559		die
30: 2	יחר	qal	wci	3ms	חרה	354		be kindled, burn
	יאמר	qal	wci	3ms	אמר	55		say
	מנע	qal	pft	3ms	מנע	586		withhold

ChVs	Form	Stem	Tnse	PGN	Root	BDB	Sfx	Meaning
30: 3	תאמר	qal	wci	3fs	אמר	55		say
	בא	qal	impv	ms	בוא	97		come in
	תלד	qal	jusm	3fs	ילד	408		bear, beget
	אבנה	niph	cohm	1cs	בנה	124		be built
30: 4	תתן	qal	wci	3fs	נתן	678		give, set
	יבא	qal	wci	3ms	בוא	97		come in
30: 5	תהר	qal	wci	3fs	הרה	247		conceive
	תלד	qal	wci	3fs	ילד	408		bear, beget
30: 6	תאמר	qal	wci	3fs	אמר	55		say
	דנני	qal	pft	3ms	דין	192	1cs	judge
	שמע	qal	pft	3ms	שמע	1033		hear
	יתן	qal	wci	3ms	נתן	678		give, set
	קראה	qal	pft	3fs	קרא	894		call, proclaim
30: 7	תהר	qal	wci	3fs	הרה	247		conceive
	תלד	qal	wci	3fs	ילד	408		bear, beget
30: 8	תאמר	qal	wci	3fs	אמר	55		say
	נפתלתי	niph	pft	1cs	פתל	836		wrestle, twist
	יכלתי	qal	pft	1cs	יכל	407		be able
	תקרא	qal	wci	3fs	קרא	894		call, proclaim
30: 9	תרא	qal	wci	3fs	ראה	906		see
	עמדה	qal	pft	3fs	עמד	763		stand, stop
	לדת	qal	infc		ילד	408		bear, beget
	תקח	qal	wci	3fs	לקח	542		take
	תתן	qal	wci	3fs	נתן	678		give, set
30: 10	תלד	qal	wci	3fs	ילד	408		bear, beget
30: 11	תאמר	qal	wci	3fs	אמר	55		say
	באq	qal	pft	3ms	בוא	97		come in
	תקרא	qal	wci	3fs	קרא	894		call, proclaim
30: 12	תלד	qal	wci	3fs	ילד	408		bear, beget
30: 13	תאמר	qal	wci	3fs	אמר	55		say
	אשרוני	piel	pft	3cp	אשר	80	1cs	call blessed
	תקרא	qal	wci	3fs	קרא	894		call, proclaim
30: 14	ילך	qal	wci	3ms	הלך	229		walk, go
	ימצא	qal	wci	3ms	מצא	592		find
	יבא	hiph	wci	3ms	בוא	97		bring in
	תאמר	qal	wci	3fs	אמר	55		say
	תני	qal	impv	fs	נתן	678		give, set
30: 15	תאמר	qal	wci	3fs	אמר	55		say
	קחתך	qal	infc		לקח	542	2ms	take
	קחת	qal	infc		לקח	542		take
	תאמר	qal	wci	3fs	אמר	55		say
	ישכב	qal	impf	3ms	שכב	1011		lie, lie down
30: 16	יבא	qal	wci	3ms	בוא	97		come in
	תצא	qal	wci	3fs	יצא	422		go out
	קראתו	qal	infc		קרא	896	3ms	meet, encounter
	תאמר	qal	wci	3fs	אמר	55		say
	תבוא	qal	impf	2ms	בוא	97		come in
	שכר	qal	infa		שכר	968		hire
	שכרתיך	qal	pft	1cs	שכר	968	2ms	hire
	ישכב	qal	wci	3ms	שכב	1011		lie, lie down
30: 17	ישמע	qal	wci	3ms	שמע	1033		hear
	תהר	qal	wci	3fs	הרה	247		conceive
	תלד	qal	wci	3fs	ילד	408		bear, beget
30: 18	תאמר	qal	wci	3fs	אמר	55		say
30: 18	נתן	qal	pft	3ms	נתן	678		give, set
	נתתי	qal	pft	1cs	נתן	678		give, set
	תקרא	qal	wci	3fs	קרא	894		call, proclaim
30: 19	תהר	qal	wci	3fs	הרה	247		conceive
	תלד	qal	wci	3fs	ילד	408		bear, beget
30: 20	תאמר	qal	wci	3fs	אמר	55		say
	זבדני	qal	pft	3ms	זבד	256	1cs	bestow upon
	יזבלני	qal	impf	3ms	זבל	259	1cs	honor
	ילדתי	qal	pft	1cs	ילד	408		bear, beget
	תקרא	qal	wci	3fs	קרא	894		call, proclaim
30: 21	ילדה	qal	pft	3fs	ילד	408		bear, beget
	תקרא	qal	wci	3fs	קרא	894		call, proclaim
30: 22	יזכר	qal	wci	3ms	זכר	269		remember
	ישמע	qal	wci	3ms	שמע	1033		hear
	יפתח	qal	wci	3ms	פתח	834		open
30: 23	תהר	qal	wci	3fs	הרה	247		conceive
	תלד	qal	wci	3fs	ילד	408		bear, beget
	תאמר	qal	wci	3fs	אמר	55		say
	אסף	qal	pft	3ms	אסף	62		gather
30: 24	תקרא	qal	wci	3fs	קרא	894		call, proclaim
	אמר	qal	infc		אמר	55		say
	יסף	hiph	jus	3ms	יסף	414		add, do again
30: 25	יהי	qal	wci	3ms	היה	224		be, become
	ילדה	qal	pft	3fs	ילד	408		bear, beget
	יאמר	qal	wci	3ms	אמר	55		say
	שלחני	piel	impv	ms	שלח	1018	1cs	send away, shoot
	אלכה	qal	coh	1cs	הלך	229		walk, go
30: 26	תנה	qal	impv	ms	נתן	678		give, set
	עבדתי	qal	pft	1cs	עבד	712		work, serve
	אלכה	qal	coh	1cs	הלך	229		walk, go
	ידעת	qal	pft	2ms	ידע	393		know
	עבדתיך	qal	pft	1cs	עבד	712	2ms	work, serve
30: 27	יאמר	qal	wci	3ms	אמר	55		say
	מצאתי	qal	pft	1cs	מצא	592		find
	נחשתי	piel	pft	1cs	נחש	638		divine
	יברכני	piel	wci	3ms	ברך	138	1cs	bless
30: 28	יאמר	qal	wci	3ms	אמר	55		say
	נקבה	qal	impv	ms	נקב	666		pierce
	אתנה	qal	coh	1cs	נתן	678		give, set
30: 29	יאמר	qal	wci	3ms	אמר	55		say
	ידעת	qal	pft	2ms	ידע	393		know
	עבדתיך	qal	pft	1cs	עבד	712	2ms	work, serve
	היה	qal	pft	3ms	היה	224		be, become
30: 30	היה	qal	pft	3ms	היה	224		be, become
	יפרץ	qal	wci	3ms	פרץ	829		break through
	יברך	piel	wci	3ms	ברך	138		bless
	אעשה	qal	impf	1cs	עשה	793		do, make
30: 31	יאמר	qal	wci	3ms	אמר	55		say
	אתן	qal	impf	1cs	נתן	678		give, set
	יאמר	qal	wci	3ms	אמר	55		say
	תתן	qal	impf	2ms	נתן	678		give, set
	תעשה	qal	impf	2ms	עשה	793		do, make
	אשובה	qal	coh	1cs	שוב	996		turn, return
	ארעה	qal	cohm	1cs	רעה	944		pasture, tend

ChVs	Form	Stem	Tnse	PGN	Root	BDB	Sfx	Meaning
30:31	אשׁמר	qal	cohm	1cs	שׁמר	1036		keep,watch
30:32	אעבר	qal	cohm	1cs	עבר	716		pass over
	הסר	hiph	infa		סור	693		take away
	טלוא	qal	pptc	ms	טלא	378		patch,spot
	טלוא	qal	pptc	ms	טלא	378		patch,spot
	היה	qal	wcp	3ms	היה	224		be,become
30:33	ענתה	qal	wcp	3fs	ענה	772		answer
	תבוא	qal	impf	2ms	בוא	97		come in
	טלוא	qal	pptc	ms	טלא	378		patch,spot
	גנוב	qal	pptc	ms	גנב	170		steal
30:34	יאמר	qal	wci	3ms	אמר	55		say
	יהי	qal	jus	3ms	היה	224		be,become
30:35	יסר	hiph	wci	3ms	סור	693		take away
	טלאים	qal	pptc	mp	טלא	378		patch,spot
	טלאת	qal	pptc	fp	טלא	378		patch,spot
	יתן	qal	wci	3ms	נתן	678		give,set
30:36	ישׂם	qal	wci	3ms	שׂים	962		put,set
	רעה	qal	ptc	ms	רעה	944		pasture,tend
	נותרת	niph	ptc	fp	יתר	451		be left,remain
30:37	יקח	qal	wci	3ms	לקח	542		take
	יפצל	piel	wci	3ms	פצל	822		peel
30:38	יצג	hiph	wci	3ms	יצג	426		place,establish
	פצל	piel	pft	3ms	פצל	822		peel
	תבאן	qal	impf	3fp	בוא	97		come in
	שׁתות	qal	infc		שׁתה	1059		drink
	יחמנה	qal	wci	3fp	חמם	328		be warm
	באן	qal	infc		בוא	97	3fp	come in
	שׁתות	qal	infc		שׁתה	1059		drink
30:39	יחמו	qal	wci	3mp	חמם	328		be warm
	תלדן	qal	wci	3fp	ילד	408		bear,beget
	טלאים	qal	pptc	mp	טלא	378		patch,spot
30:40	הפריד	hiph	pft	3ms	פרד	825		divide
	יתן	qal	wci	3ms	נתן	678		give,set
	ישׁת	qal	wci	3ms	שׁית	1011		put,set
	שׁתם	qal	pft	3ms	שׁית	1011	3mp	put,set
30:41	היה	qal	wcp	3ms	היה	224		be,become
	יחם	piel	infc		יחם	404		conceive
	מקשׁרות	pual	ptc	fp	קשׁר	905		be strong
	שׂם	qal	pft	3ms	שׂים	962		put,set
	יחמנה	piel	infc		יחם	404	3fp	conceive
30:42	העטיף	hiph	infc		עטף	742		be weak
	ישׂים	qal	impf	3ms	שׂים	962		put,set
	היה	qal	wcp	3ms	היה	224		be,become
	עטפים	qal	pptc	mp	עטף	742		be feeble
	קשׁרים	qal	pptc	mp	קשׁר	905		bind
30:43	יפרץ	qal	wci	3ms	פרץ	829		break through
	יהי	qal	wci	3ms	היה	224		be,become
31:1	ישׁמע	qal	wci	3ms	שׁמע	1033		hear
	אמר	qal	infc		אמר	55		say
	לקח	qal	pft	3ms	לקח	542		take
	עשׂה	qal	pft	3ms	עשׂה	793		do,make
31:2	ירא	qal	wci	3ms	ראה	906		see
31:3	יאמר	qal	wci	3ms	אמר	55		say
	שׁוב	qal	impv	ms	שׁוב	996		turn,return
31:3	אהיה	qal	impf	1cs	היה	224		be,become
31:4	ישׁלח	qal	wci	3ms	שׁלח	1018		send
	יקרא	qal	wci	3ms	קרא	894		call,proclaim
31:5	יאמר	qal	wci	3ms	אמר	55		say
	ראה	qal	ptc	ms	ראה	906		see
	היה	qal	pft	3ms	היה	224		be,become
31:6	ידעתן	qal	pft	2fp	ידע	393		know
	עבדתי	qal	pft	1cs	עבד	712		work,serve
31:7	התל	hiph	pft	3ms	תלל	1068		mock,deceive
	החלף	hiph	pft	3ms	חלף	322		change
	נתנו	qal	pft	3ms	נתן	678	3ms	give,set
	הרע	hiph	infc		רעע	949		hurt,do evil
31:8	יאמר	qal	impf	3ms	אמר	55		say
	יהיה	qal	impf	3ms	היה	224		be,become
	ילדו	qal	wcp	3cp	ילד	408		bear,beget
	יאמר	qal	impf	3ms	אמר	55		say
	יהיה	qal	impf	3ms	היה	224		be,become
	ילדו	qal	wcp	3cp	ילד	408		bear,beget
31:9	יצל	hiph	wci	3ms	נצל	664		snatch,deliver
	יתן	qal	wci	3ms	נתן	678		give,set
31:10	יהי	qal	wci	3ms	היה	224		be,become
	יחם	piel	infc		יחם	404		conceive
	אשׂא	qal	wci	1cs	נשׂא	669		lift,carry
	ארא	qal	wci	1cs	ראה	906		see
	עלים	qal	ptc	mp	עלה	748		go up
31:11	יאמר	qal	wci	3ms	אמר	55		say
	אמר	qal	wci	1cs	אמר	55		say
31:12	יאמר	qal	wci	3ms	אמר	55		say
	שׂא	qal	impv	ms	נשׂא	669		lift,carry
	ראה	qal	impv	ms	ראה	906		see
	עלים	qal	ptc	mp	עלה	748		go up
	ראיתי	qal	pft	1cs	ראה	906		see
	עשׂה	qal	ptc	ms	עשׂה	793		do,make
31:13	משׁחת	qal	pft	2ms	משׁח	602		smear,anoint
	נדרת	qal	pft	2ms	נדר	623		vow
	קום	qal	impv	ms	קום	877		arise,stand
	צא	qal	impv	ms	יצא	422		go out
	שׁוב	qal	impv	ms	שׁוב	996		turn,return
31:14	תען	qal	wci	3fs	ענה	772		answer
	תאמרנה	qal	wci	3fp	אמר	55		say
31:15	נחשׁבנו	niph	pft	1cp	חשׁב	362		be thought
	מכרנו	qal	pft	3ms	מכר	569	1cp	sell
	יאכל	qal	wci	3ms	אכל	37		eat,devour
	אכול	qal	infa		אכל	37		eat,devour
31:16	הציל	hiph	pft	3ms	נצל	664		snatch,deliver
	אמר	qal	pft	3ms	אמר	55		say
	עשׂה	qal	impv	ms	עשׂה	793		do,make
31:17	יקם	qal	wci	3ms	קום	877		arise,stand
	ישׂא	qal	wci	3ms	נשׂא	669		lift,carry
31:18	ינהג	qal	wci	3ms	נהג	624		drive
	רכשׁ	qal	pft	3ms	רכשׁ	940		collect
	רכשׁ	qal	pft	3ms	רכשׁ	940		collect
	בוא	qal	infc		בוא	97		come in
31:19	הלך	qal	pft	3ms	הלך	229		walk,go

ChVs	Form	Stem	Tnse	PGN	Root	BDB	Sfx	Meaning
31:19	גזז	qal	infc		גזז	159		shear
	תגנב	qal	wci	3fs	גנב	170		steal
31:20	יגנב	qal	wci	3ms	גנב	170		steal
	הגיד	hiph	pft	3ms	נגד	616		declare,tell
	ברח	qal	ptc	ms	ברח	137		go thru,flee
31:21	יברח	qal	wci	3ms	ברח	137		go thru,flee
	יקם	qal	wci	3ms	קום	877		arise,stand
	יעבר	qal	wci	3ms	עבר	716		pass over
	ישׂם	qal	wci	3ms	שׂים	962		put,set
31:22	יגד	hoph	wci	3ms	נגד	616		be told
	ברח	qal	pft	3ms	ברח	137		go thru,flee
31:23	יקח	qal	wci	3ms	לקח	542		take
	ירדף	qal	wci	3ms	רדף	922		pursue
	ידבק	hiph	wci	3ms	דבק	179		cause to cling
31:24	יבא	qal	wci	3ms	בוא	97		come in
	יאמר	qal	wci	3ms	אמר	55		say
	השׁמר	niph	impv	ms	שׁמר	1036		be kept,guarded
	תדבר	piel	impf	2ms	דבר	180		speak
31:25	ישׂג	hiph	wci	3ms	נשׂג	673		reach,overtake
	תקע	qal	pft	3ms	תקע	1075		thrust,clap
	תקע	qal	pft	3ms	תקע	1075		thrust,clap
31:26	יאמר	qal	wci	3ms	אמר	55		say
	עשׂית	qal	pft	2ms	עשׂה	793		do,make
	תגנב	qal	wci	2ms	גנב	170		steal
	תנהג	piel	wci	2ms	נהג	624		drive away,lead
	שׁביות	qal	pptc	fp	שׁבה	985		take captive
31:27	נחבאת	niph	pft	2ms	חבא	285		hide oneself
	ברח	qal	infc		ברח	137		go thru,flee
	תגנב	qal	wci	2ms	גנב	170		steal
	הגדת	hiph	pft	2ms	נגד	616		declare,tell
	אשׁלחך	piel	wci	1cs	שׁלח	1018	2ms	send away,shoot
31:28	נטשׁתני	qal	pft	2ms	נטשׁ	643	1cs	leave,forsake
	נשׁק	piel	infc		נשׁק	676		kiss
	הסכלת	hiph	pft	2ms	סכל	698		do foolishly
	עשׂו	qal	infc		עשׂה	793		do,make
31:29	עשׂות	qal	infc		עשׂה	793		do,make
	אמר	qal	pft	3ms	אמר	55		say
	אמר	qal	infc		אמר	55		say
	השׁמר	niph	impv	ms	שׁמר	1036		be kept,guarded
	מדבר	piel	infc		דבר	180		speak
31:30	הלך	qal	infa		הלך	229		walk,go
	הלכת	qal	pft	2ms	הלך	229		walk,go
	נכסף	niph	infa		כסף	493		long for
	נכספתה	niph	pft	2ms	כסף	493		long for
	גנבת	qal	pft	2ms	גנב	170		steal
31:31	יען	qal	wci	3ms	ענה	772		answer
	יאמר	qal	wci	3ms	אמר	55		say
	יראתי	qal	pft	1cs	ירא	431		fear
	אמרתי	qal	pft	1cs	אמר	55		say
	תגזל	qal	impf	2ms	גזל	159		tear away,rob
31:32	תמצא	qal	impf	2ms	מצא	592		find
	יחיה	qal	impf	3ms	חיה	310		live
	הכר	hiph	impv	ms	נכר	647		regard,notice
	קח	qal	impv	ms	לקח	542		take
31:32	ידע	qal	pft	3ms	ידע	393		know
	גנבתם	qal	pft	3fs	גנב	170	3ms	steal
31:33	יבא	qal	wci	3ms	בוא	97		come in
	מצא	qal	pft	3ms	מצא	592		find
	יצא	qal	wci	3ms	יצא	422		go out
	יבא	qal	wci	3ms	בוא	97		come in
31:34	לקחה	qal	pft	3fs	לקח	542		take
	תשׂמם	qal	wci	3fs	שׂים	962	3mp	put,set
	תשׁב	qal	wci	3fs	ישׁב	442		sit,dwell
	ימשׁשׁ	piel	wci	3ms	משׁשׁ	606		grope
	מצא	qal	pft	3ms	מצא	592		find
31:35	תאמר	qal	wci	3fs	אמר	55		say
	יחר	qal	jus	3ms	חרה	354		be kindled,burn
	אוכל	qal	impf	1cs	יכל	407		be able
	קום	qal	infc		קום	877		arise,stand
	יחפשׂ	piel	wci	3ms	חפשׂ	344		search for
	מצא	qal	pft	3ms	מצא	592		find
31:36	יחר	qal	wci	3ms	חרה	354		be kindled,burn
	ירב	qal	wci	3ms	ריב	936		strive,contend
	יען	qal	wci	3ms	ענה	772		answer
	יאמר	qal	wci	3ms	אמר	55		say
	דלקת	qal	pft	2ms	דלק	196		burn,pursue
31:37	משׁשׁת	piel	pft	2ms	משׁשׁ	606		grope
	מצאת	qal	pft	2ms	מצא	592		find
	שׂים	qal	impv	ms	שׂים	962		put,set
	יוכיחו	hiph	jusm	3mp	יכח	406		decide,reprove
31:38	שׁכלו	piel	pft	3cp	שׁכל	1013		make childless
	אכלתי	qal	pft	1cs	אכל	37		eat,devour
31:39	הבאתי	hiph	pft	1cs	בוא	97		bring in
	אחטנה	piel	impf	1cs	חטא	306	3fs	purify
	תבקשׁנה	piel	impf	2ms	בקשׁ	134	3fs	seek
	גנבתי	qal	pptc	fs	גנב	170		steal
	גנבתי	qal	pptc	fs	גנב	170		steal
31:40	הייתי	qal	pft	1cs	היה	224		be,become
	אכלני	qal	pft	3ms	אכל	37	1cs	eat,devour
	תדד	qal	wci	3fs	נדד	622		retreat,flee
31:41	עבדתיך	qal	pft	1cs	עבד	712	2ms	work,serve
	תחלף	hiph	wci	2ms	חלף	322		change
31:42	היה	qal	pft	3ms	היה	224		be,become
	שׁלחתני	piel	pft	2ms	שׁלח	1018	1cs	send away,shoot
	ראה	qal	pft	3ms	ראה	906		see
	יוכח	hiph	wci	3ms	יכח	406		decide,reprove
31:43	יען	qal	wci	3ms	ענה	772		answer
	יאמר	qal	wci	3ms	אמר	55		say
	ראה	qal	ptc	ms	ראה	906		see
	אעשׂה	qal	impf	1cs	עשׂה	793		do,make
	ילדו	qal	pft	3cp	ילד	408		bear,beget
31:44	לכה	qal	impv	ms	הלך	229		walk,go
	נכרתה	qal	coh	1cp	כרת	503		cut,destroy
	היה	qal	wcp	3ms	היה	224		be,become
31:45	יקח	qal	wci	3ms	לקח	542		take
	ירימה	hiph	wci	3ms	רום	926		raise,lift
31:46	יאמר	qal	wci	3ms	אמר	55		say
	לקטו	qal	impv	mp	לקט	544		pick,gather

ChVs	Form	Stem	Tnse	PGN	Root	BDB	Sfx	Meaning
31:46	יקחו	qal	wci	3mp	לקח	542		take
	יעשׂו	qal	wci	3mp	עשׂה	793		do,make
	יאכלו	qal	wci	3mp	אכל	37		eat,devour
31:47	יקרא	qal	wci	3ms	קרא	894		call,proclaim
	קרא	qal	pft	3ms	קרא	894		call,proclaim
31:48	יאמר	qal	wci	3ms	אמר	55		say
	קרא	qal	pft	3ms	קרא	894		call,proclaim
31:49	אמר	qal	pft	3ms	אמר	55		say
	יצף	qal	jus	3ms	צפה	859		keep watch
	נסתר	niph	impf	1cp	סתר	711		hide,be hid
31:50	תענה	piel	impf	2ms	ענה	776		humble
	תקח	qal	impf	2ms	לקח	542		take
	ראה	qal	impv	ms	ראה	906		see
31:51	יאמר	qal	wci	3ms	אמר	55		say
	יריתי	qal	pft	1cs	ירה	434		throw,shoot
31:52	אעבר	qal	impf	1cs	עבר	716		pass over
	תעבר	qal	impf	2ms	עבר	716		pass over
31:53	ישׁפטו	qal	jusm	3mp	שׁפט	1047		judge
	ישׁבע	niph	wci	3ms	שׁבע	989		swear
31:54	יזבח	qal	wci	3ms	זבח	256		slaughter
	יקרא	qal	wci	3ms	קרא	894		call,proclaim
	אכל	qal	infc		אכל	37		eat,devour
	יאכלו	qal	wci	3mp	אכל	37		eat,devour
	ילינו	qal	wci	3mp	לון	533		lodge,remain
32:1	ישׁכם	hiph	wci	3ms	שׁכם	1014		rise early
	ינשׁק	piel	wci	3ms	נשׁק	676		kiss
	יברך	piel	wci	3ms	ברך	138		bless
	ילך	qal	wci	3ms	הלך	229		walk,go
	ישׁב	qal	wci	3ms	שׁוב	996		turn,return
32:2	הלך	qal	pft	3ms	הלך	229		walk,go
	יפגעו	qal	wci	3mp	פגע	803		meet,encounter
32:3	יאמר	qal	wci	3ms	אמר	55		say
	ראם	qal	pft	3ms	ראה	906	3mp	see
	יקרא	qal	wci	3ms	קרא	894		call,proclaim
32:4	ישׁלח	qal	wci	3ms	שׁלח	1018		send
32:5	יצו	piel	wci	3ms	צוה	845		command
	אמר	qal	infc		אמר	55		say
	תאמרון	qal	impf	2mp	אמר	55		say
	אמר	qal	pft	3ms	אמר	55		say
	גרתי	qal	pft	1cs	גור	157		sojourn
	אחר	qal	wci	1cs	אחר	29		tarry
32:6	יהי	qal	wci	3ms	היה	224		be,become
	אשׁלחה	qal	wci	1cs	שׁלח	1018		send
	הגיד	hiph	infc		נגד	616		declare,tell
	מצא	qal	infc		מצא	592		find
32:7	ישׁבו	qal	wci	3mp	שׁוב	996		turn,return
	אמר	qal	infc		אמר	55		say
	באנו	qal	pft	1cp	בוא	97		come in
	הלך	qal	ptc	ms	הלך	229		walk,go
	קראתך	qal	infc		קרא	896	2ms	meet,encounter
32:8	יירא	qal	wci	3ms	ירא	431		fear
	יצר	qal	wci	3ms	צרר	864		bind,be cramped
	יחץ	qal	wci	3ms	חצה	345		divide
32:9	יאמר	qal	wci	3ms	אמר	55		say
32:9	יבוא	qal	impf	3ms	בוא	97		come in
	הכהו	hiph	wcp	3ms	נכה	645	3ms	smite
	היה	qal	wcp	3ms	היה	224		be,become
	נשׁאר	niph	ptc	ms	שׁאר	983		be left
32:10	יאמר	qal	wci	3ms	אמר	55		say
	אמר	qal	ptc	ms	אמר	55		say
	שׁוב	qal	impv	ms	שׁוב	996		turn,return
	איטיבה	hiph	coh	1cs	יטב	405		do good
32:11	קטנתי	qal	pft	1cs	קטן	881		be little
	עשׂית	qal	pft	2ms	עשׂה	793		do,make
	עברתי	qal	pft	1cs	עבר	716		pass over
	הייתי	qal	pft	1cs	היה	224		be,become
32:12	הצילני	hiph	impv	ms	נצל	664	1cs	snatch,deliver
	ירא	qal	ptc	ms	ירא	431		fear
	יבוא	qal	impf	3ms	בוא	97		come in
	הכני	hiph	wcp	3ms	נכה	645	1cs	smite
32:13	אמרת	qal	pft	2ms	אמר	55		say
	היטב	hiph	infa		יטב	405		do good
	איטיב	hiph	impf	1cs	יטב	405		do good
	שׂמתי	qal	wcp	1cs	שׂים	962		put,set
	יספר	niph	impf	3ms	ספר	707		be counted
32:14	ילן	qal	wci	3ms	לון	533		lodge,remain
	יקח	qal	wci	3ms	לקח	542		take
	בא	qal	ptc	ms	בוא	97		come in
32:16	מיניקות	hiph	ptc	fp	ינק	413		nurse
32:17	יתן	qal	wci	3ms	נתן	678		give,set
	יאמר	qal	wci	3ms	אמר	55		say
	עברו	qal	impv	mp	עבר	716		pass over
	תשׂימו	qal	impf	2mp	שׂים	962		put,set
32:18	יצו	piel	wci	3ms	צוה	845		command
	אמר	qal	infc		אמר	55		say
	יפגשׁך	qal	impf	3ms	פגשׁ	803	2ms	meet
	שׁאלך	qal	wcp	3ms	שׁאל	981	2ms	ask,borrow
	אמר	qal	infc		אמר	55		say
	תלך	qal	impf	2ms	הלך	229		walk,go
32:19	אמרת	qal	wcp	2ms	אמר	55		say
	שׁלוחה	qal	pptc	fs	שׁלח	1018		send
32:20	יצו	piel	wci	3ms	צוה	845		command
	הלכים	qal	ptc	mp	הלך	229		walk,go
	אמר	qal	infc		אמר	55		say
	תדברון	piel	impf	2mp	דבר	180		speak
	מצאכם	qal	infc		מצא	592	2mp	find
32:21	אמרתם	qal	wcp	2mp	אמר	55		say
	אמר	qal	pft	3ms	אמר	55		say
	אכפרה	piel	coh	1cs	כפר	497		cover,atone
	הלכת	qal	ptc	fs	הלך	229		walk,go
	אראה	qal	impf	1cs	ראה	906		see
	ישׂא	qal	impf	3ms	נשׂא	669		lift,carry
32:22	תעבר	qal	wci	3fs	עבר	716		pass over
	לן	qal	pft	3ms	לון	533		lodge,remain
32:23	יקם	qal	wci	3ms	קום	877		arise,stand
	יקח	qal	wci	3ms	לקח	542		take
	יעבר	qal	wci	3ms	עבר	716		pass over
32:24	יקחם	qal	wci	3ms	לקח	542	3mp	take

ChVs	Form	Stem	Tnse	PGN	Root	BDB	Sfx	Meaning
32: 24	יעברם	hiph	wci	3ms	עבר	716	3mp	cause to pass
	יעבר	hiph	wci	3ms	עבר	716		cause to pass
32: 25	יותר	niph	wci	3ms	יתר	451		be left, remain
	יאבק	niph	wci	3ms	אבק	7		wrestle
	עלות	qal	infc		עלה	748		go up
32: 26	ירא	qal	wci	3ms	ראה	906		see
	יכל	qal	pft	3ms	יכל	407		be able
	יגע	qal	wci	3ms	נגע	619		touch, strike
	תקע	qal	wci	3fs	יקע	429		be dislocated
	האבקו	niph	infc		אבק	7	3ms	wrestle
32: 27	יאמר	qal	wci	3ms	אמר	55		say
	שלחני	piel	impv	ms	שלח	1018	1cs	send away, shoot
	עלה	qal	pft	3ms	עלה	748		go up
	יאמר	qal	wci	3ms	אמר	55		say
	אשלחך	piel	impf	1cs	שלח	1018	2ms	send away, shoot
	ברכתני	piel	pft	2ms	ברך	138	1cs	bless
32: 28	יאמר	qal	wci	3ms	אמר	55		say
	יאמר	qal	wci	3ms	אמר	55		say
32: 29	יאמר	qal	wci	3ms	אמר	55		say
	יאמר	niph	impf	3ms	אמר	55		be said, called
	שרית	qal	pft	2ms	שרה	975		persist
	תוכל	qal	wci	2ms	יכל	407		be able
32: 30	ישאל	qal	wci	3ms	שאל	981		ask, borrow
	יאמר	qal	wci	3ms	אמר	55		say
	הגידה	hiph	impv	ms	נגד	616		declare, tell
	יאמר	qal	wci	3ms	אמר	55		say
	תשאל	qal	impf	2ms	שאל	981		ask, borrow
	יברך	piel	wci	3ms	ברך	138		bless
32: 31	יקרא	qal	wci	3ms	קרא	894		call, proclaim
	ראיתי	qal	pft	1cs	ראה	906		see
	תנצל	niph	wci	3fs	נצל	664		be delivered
32: 32	יזרח	qal	wci	3ms	זרח	280		rise, appear
	עבר	qal	pft	3ms	עבר	716		pass over
	צלע	qal	ptc	ms	צלע	854		limp
32: 33	יאכלו	qal	impf	3mp	אכל	37		eat, devour
	נגע	qal	pft	3ms	נגע	619		touch, strike
33: 1	ישא	qal	wci	3ms	נשא	669		lift, carry
	ירא	qal	wci	3ms	ראה	906		see
	בא	qal	ptc	ms	בוא	97		come in
	יחץ	qal	wci	3ms	חצה	345		divide
33: 2	ישם	qal	wci	3ms	שים	962		put, set
33: 3	עבר	qal	pft	3ms	עבר	716		pass over
	ישתחו	hish	wci	3ms	חוה	1005		bow down
	גשתו	qal	infc		נגש	620	3ms	draw near
33: 4	ירץ	qal	wci	3ms	רוץ	930		run
	קראתו	qal	infc		קרא	896	3ms	meet, encounter
	יחבקהו	piel	wci	3ms	חבק	287	3ms	embrace
	יפל	qal	wci	3ms	נפל	656		fall
	ישקהו	qal	wci	3ms	נשק	676	3ms	kiss
	יבכו	qal	wci	3mp	בכה	113		weep
33: 5	ישא	qal	wci	3ms	נשא	669		lift, carry
	ירא	qal	wci	3ms	ראה	906		see
	יאמר	qal	wci	3ms	אמר	55		say
	יאמר	qal	wci	3ms	אמר	55		say
33: 5	חנן	qal	pft	3ms	חנן	335		show favor
33: 6	תגשן	qal	wci	3fp	נגש	620		draw near
	תשתחוין	hish	wci	3fp	חוה	1005		bow down
33: 7	תגש	qal	wci	3fs	נגש	620		draw near
	ישתחוו	hish	wci	3mp	חוה	1005		bow down
	נגש	niph	pft	3ms	נגש	620		draw near
	ישתחוו	hish	wci	3mp	חוה	1005		bow down
33: 8	יאמר	qal	wci	3ms	אמר	55		say
	פגשתי	qal	pft	1cs	פגש	803		meet
	יאמר	qal	wci	3ms	אמר	55		say
	מצא	qal	infc		מצא	592		find
33: 9	יאמר	qal	wci	3ms	אמר	55		say
	יהי	qal	jus	3ms	היה	224		be, become
33: 10	יאמר	qal	wci	3ms	אמר	55		say
	מצאתי	qal	pft	1cs	מצא	592		find
	לקחת	qal	wcp	2ms	לקח	542		take
	ראיתי	qal	pft	1cs	ראה	906		see
	ראת	qal	infc		ראה	906		see
	תרצני	qal	wci	2ms	רצה	953	1cs	be pleased
33: 11	קח	qal	impv	ms	לקח	542		take
	הבאת	hoph	pft	3fs	בוא	97		be brought
	חנני	qal	pft	3ms	חנן	335	1cs	show favor
	יפצר	qal	wci	3ms	פצר	823		push
	יקח	qal	wci	3ms	לקח	542		take
33: 12	יאמר	qal	wci	3ms	אמר	55		say
	נסעה	qal	coh	1cp	נסע	652		pull up, set out
	נלכה	qal	coh	1cp	הלך	229		walk, go
	אלכה	qal	coh	1cs	הלך	229		walk, go
33: 13	יאמר	qal	wci	3ms	אמר	55		say
	ידע	qal	ptc	ms	ידע	393		know
	עלות	qal	ptc	fp	עול	732		give suck
	דפקום	qal	wcp	3cp	דפק	200	3mp	beat, knock
	מתו	qal	wcp	3cp	מות	559		die
33: 14	יעבר	qal	jusm	3ms	עבר	716		pass over
	אתנהלה	hith	coh	1cs	נהל	624		journey
	אבא	qal	impf	1cs	בוא	97		come in
33: 15	יאמר	qal	wci	3ms	אמר	55		say
	אציגה	hiph	coh	1cs	יצג	426		place, establish
	יאמר	qal	wci	3ms	אמר	55		say
	אמצא	qal	cohm	1cs	מצא	592		find
33: 16	ישב	qal	wci	3ms	שוב	996		turn, return
33: 17	נסע	qal	pft	3ms	נסע	652		pull up, set out
	יבן	qal	wci	3ms	בנה	124		build
	עשה	qal	pft	3ms	עשה	793		do, make
	קרא	qal	pft	3ms	קרא	894		call, proclaim
33: 18	יבא	qal	wci	3ms	בוא	97		come in
	באו	qal	infc		בוא	97	3ms	come in
	יחן	qal	wci	3ms	חנה	333		decline, encamp
33: 19	יקן	qal	wci	3ms	קנה	888		get, buy
	נטה	qal	pft	3ms	נטה	639		stretch, incline
33: 20	יצב	hiph	wci	3ms	נצב	662		cause to stand
	יקרא	qal	wci	3ms	קרא	894		call, proclaim
34: 1	תצא	qal	wci	3fs	יצא	422		go out
	ילדה	qal	pft	3fs	ילד	408		bear, beget

ChVs	Form	Stem	Tnse	PGN	Root	BDB	Sfx	Meaning
34:1	ראות	qal	infc		ראה	906		see
34:2	ירא	qal	wci	3ms	ראה	906		see
	יקח	qal	wci	3ms	לקח	542		take
	ישכב	qal	wci	3ms	שכב	1011		lie,lie down
	יענה	piel	wci	3ms	ענה	776	3fs	humble
34:3	תדבק	qal	wci	3fs	דבק	179		cling,cleave
	יאהב	qal	wci	3ms	אהב	12		love
	ידבר	piel	wci	3ms	דבר	180		speak
34:4	יאמר	qal	wci	3ms	אמר	55		say
	אמר	qal	infc		אמר	55		say
	קח	qal	impv	ms	לקח	542		take
34:5	שמע	qal	pft	3ms	שמע	1033		hear
	טמא	piel	pft	3ms	טמא	379		defile
	היו	qal	pft	3cp	היה	224		be,become
	החרש	hiph	wcp	3ms	חרש	361		be silent
	באם	qal	infc		בוא	97	3mp	come in
34:6	יצא	qal	wci	3ms	יצא	422		go out
	דבר	piel	infc		דבר	180		speak
34:7	באו	qal	pft	3cp	בוא	97		come in
	שמעם	qal	infc		שמע	1033	3mp	hear
	יתעצבו	hith	wci	3mp	עצב	780		be vexed
	יחר	qal	wci	3ms	חרה	354		be kindled, burn
	עשה	qal	pft	3ms	עשה	793		do,make
	שכב	qal	infc		שכב	1011		lie,lie down
	יעשה	niph	impf	3ms	עשה	793		be done
34:8	ידבר	piel	wci	3ms	דבר	180		speak
	אמר	qal	infc		אמר	55		say
	חשקה	qal	pft	3fs	חשק	365		love
	תנו	qal	impv	mp	נתן	678		give,set
34:9	התחתנו	hith	impv	mp	חתן	368		be son-in-law
	תתנו	qal	impf	2mp	נתן	678		give,set
	תקחו	qal	impf	2mp	לקח	542		take
34:10	תשבו	qal	impf	2mp	ישב	442		sit,dwell
	תהיה	qal	impf	3fs	היה	224		be,become
	שבו	qal	impv	mp	ישב	442		sit,dwell
	סחרוה	qal	impv	mp	סחר	695	3fs	go around
	האחזו	niph	impv	mp	אחז	28		possess,caught
34:11	יאמר	qal	wci	3ms	אמר	55		say
	אמצא	qal	cohm	1cs	מצא	592		find
	תאמרו	qal	impf	2mp	אמר	55		say
	אתן	qal	impf	1cs	נתן	678		give,set
34:12	הרבו	hiph	impv	mp	רבה	915		make many
	אתנה	qal	coh	1cs	נתן	678		give,set
	תאמרו	qal	impf	2mp	אמר	55		say
	תנו	qal	impv	mp	נתן	678		give,set
34:13	יענו	qal	wci	3mp	ענה	772		answer
	ידברו	piel	wci	3mp	דבר	180		speak
	טמא	piel	pft	3ms	טמא	379		defile
34:14	יאמרו	qal	wci	3mp	אמר	55		say
	נוכל	qal	impf	1cp	יכל	407		be able
	עשות	qal	infc		עשה	793		do,make
	תת	qal	infc		נתן	678		give,set
34:15	נאות	niph	impf	1cp	אות	22		consent
	תהיו	qal	impf	2mp	היה	224		be,become
34:15	המל	niph	infc		מול	557		be circumcised
34:16	נתנו	qal	wcp	1cp	נתן	678		give,set
	נקח	qal	impf	1cp	לקח	542		take
	ישבנו	qal	wcp	1cp	ישב	442		sit,dwell
	היינו	qal	wcp	1cp	היה	224		be,become
34:17	תשמעו	qal	impf	2mp	שמע	1033		hear
	המול	niph	infc		מול	557		be circumcised
	לקחנו	qal	wcp	1cp	לקח	542		take
	הלכנו	qal	wcp	1cp	הלך	229		walk,go
34:18	ייטבו	qal	wci	3mp	יטב	405		be good
34:19	אחר	piel	pft	3ms	אחר	29		tarry,hinder
	עשות	qal	infc		עשה	793		do,make
	חפץ	qal	pft	3ms	חפץ	342		delight in
	נכבד	niph	ptc	ms	כבד	457		be honored
34:20	יבא	qal	wci	3ms	בוא	97		come in
	ידברו	piel	wci	3mp	דבר	180		speak
	אמר	qal	infc		אמר	55		say
34:21	ישבו	qal	jusm	3mp	ישב	442		sit,dwell
	יסחרו	qal	jusm	3mp	סחר	695		go around
	נקח	qal	impf	1cp	לקח	542		take
	נתן	qal	impf	1cp	נתן	678		give,set
34:22	יאתו	niph	impf	3mp	אות	22		consent
	שבת	qal	infc		ישב	442		sit,dwell
	היות	qal	infc		היה	224		be,become
	המול	niph	infc		מול	557		be circumcised
	נמלים	niph	ptc	mp	מול	557		be circumcised
34:23	נאותה	niph	coh	1cp	אות	22		consent
	ישבו	qal	jusm	3mp	ישב	442		sit,dwell
34:24	ישמעו	qal	wci	3mp	שמע	1033		hear
	יצאי	qal	ptc	mp	יצא	422		go out
	ימלו	niph	wci	3mp	מול	557		be circumcised
	יצאי	qal	ptc	mp	יצא	422		go out
34:25	יהי	qal	wci	3ms	היה	224		be,become
	היותם	qal	infc		היה	224	3mp	be,become
	כאבים	qal	ptc	mp	כאב	456		be in pain
	יקחו	qal	wci	3mp	לקח	542		take
	יבאו	qal	wci	3mp	בוא	97		come in
	יהרגו	qal	wci	3mp	הרג	246		kill
34:26	הרגו	qal	pft	3cp	הרג	246		kill
	יקחו	qal	wci	3mp	לקח	542		take
	יצאו	qal	wci	3mp	יצא	422		go out
34:27	באו	qal	pft	3cp	בוא	97		come in
	יבזו	qal	wci	3mp	בזז	102		plunder
	טמאו	piel	pft	3cp	טמא	379		defile
34:28	לקחו	qal	pft	3cp	לקח	542		take
34:29	שבו	qal	pft	3cp	שבה	985		take captive
	יבזו	qal	wci	3mp	בזז	102		plunder
34:30	יאמר	qal	wci	3ms	אמר	55		say
	עכרתם	qal	pft	2mp	עכר	747		trouble
	הבאישני	hiph	infc		באש	92	1cs	cause to stink
	ישב	qal	ptc	ms	ישב	442		sit,dwell
	נאספו	niph	wcp	3cp	אסף	62		assemble
	הכוני	hiph	wcp	3cp	נכה	645	1cs	smite
	נשמדתי	niph	wcp	1cs	שמד	1029		be exterminated

ChVs	Form	Stem	Tnse	PGN	Root	BDB	Sfx	Meaning
34:31	יאמרו	qal	wci	3mp	אמר	55		say
	זונה	qal	ptc	fs	זנה	275		act a harlot
	יעשׂה	qal	impf	3ms	עשׂה	793		do,make
35:1	יאמר	qal	wci	3ms	אמר	55		say
	קום	qal	impv	ms	קום	877		arise,stand
	עלה	qal	impv	ms	עלה	748		go up
	שׁב	qal	impv	ms	ישׁב	442		sit,dwell
	עשׂה	qal	impv	ms	עשׂה	793		do,make
	נראה	niph	ptc	ms	ראה	906		appear,be seen
	ברחך	qal	infc		ברח	137	2ms	go thru,flee
35:2	יאמר	qal	wci	3ms	אמר	55		say
	הסרו	hiph	impv	mp	סור	693		take away
	הטהרו	hith	impv	mp	טהר	372		purify oneself
	החליפו	hiph	impv	mp	חלף	322		change
35:3	נקומה	qal	coh	1cp	קום	877		arise,stand
	נעלה	qal	coh	1cp	עלה	748		go up
	אעשׂה	qal	impf	1cs	עשׂה	793		do,make
	ענה	qal	ptc	ms	ענה	772		answer
	יהי	qal	wci	3ms	היה	224		be,become
	הלכתי	qal	pft	1cs	הלך	229		walk,go
35:4	יתנו	qal	wci	3mp	נתן	678		give,set
	יטמן	qal	wci	3ms	טמן	380		hide
35:5	יסעו	qal	wci	3mp	נסע	652		pull up,set out
	יהי	qal	wci	3ms	היה	224		be,become
	רדפו	qal	pft	3cp	רדף	922		pursue
35:6	יבא	qal	wci	3ms	בוא	97		come in
35:7	יבן	qal	wci	3ms	בנה	124		build
	יקרא	qal	wci	3ms	קרא	894		call,proclaim
	נגלו	niph	pft	3cp	גלה	162		uncover self
	ברחו	qal	infc		ברח	137	3ms	go thru,flee
35:8	תמת	qal	wci	3fs	מות	559		die
	מינקת	hiph	ptc	fs	ינק	413		nurse
	תקבר	niph	wci	3fs	קבר	868		be buried
	יקרא	qal	wci	3ms	קרא	894		call,proclaim
35:9	ירא	niph	wci	3ms	ראה	906		appear,be seen
	באו	qal	infc		בוא	97	3ms	come in
	יברך	piel	wci	3ms	ברך	138		bless
35:10	יאמר	qal	wci	3ms	אמר	55		say
	יקרא	niph	impf	3ms	קרא	894		be called
	יהיה	qal	impf	3ms	היה	224		be,become
	יקרא	qal	wci	3ms	קרא	894		call,proclaim
35:11	יאמר	qal	wci	3ms	אמר	55		say
	פרה	qal	impv	ms	פרה	826		bear fruit
	רבה	qal	impv	ms	רבה	915		be many,great
	יהיה	qal	impf	3ms	היה	224		be,become
	יצאו	qal	impf	3mp	יצא	422		go out
35:12	נתתי	qal	pft	1cs	נתן	678		give,set
	אתננה	qal	impf	1cs	נתן	678	3fs	give,set
	אתן	qal	impf	1cs	נתן	678		give,set
35:13	יעל	qal	wci	3ms	עלה	748		go up
	דבר	piel	pft	3ms	דבר	180		speak
35:14	יצב	hiph	wci	3ms	נצב	662		cause to stand
	דבר	piel	pft	3ms	דבר	180		speak
	יסך	hiph	wci	3ms	נסך	650		pour out
35:14	יצק	qal	wci	3ms	יצק	427		pour out,cast
35:15	יקרא	qal	wci	3ms	קרא	894		call,proclaim
	דבר	piel	pft	3ms	דבר	180		speak
35:16	יסעו	qal	wci	3mp	נסע	652		pull up,set out
	יהי	qal	wci	3ms	היה	224		be,become
	בוא	qal	infc		בוא	97		come in
	תלד	qal	wci	3fs	ילד	408		bear,beget
	תקשׁ	piel	wci	3fs	קשׁה	904		make hard
	לדתה	qal	infc		ילד	408	3fs	bear,beget
35:17	יהי	qal	wci	3ms	היה	224		be,become
	הקשׁתה	hiph	infc		קשׁה	904	3fs	harden
	לדתה	qal	infc		ילד	408	3fs	bear,beget
	תאמר	qal	wci	3fs	אמר	55		say
	מילדת	piel	ptc	fs	ילד	408		bear,deliver
	תיראי	qal	jusm	2fs	ירא	431		fear
35:18	יהי	qal	wci	3ms	היה	224		be,become
	צאת	qal	infc		יצא	422		go out
	מתה	qal	pft	3fs	מות	559		die
	תקרא	qal	wci	3fs	קרא	894		call,proclaim
	קרא	qal	pft	3ms	קרא	894		call,proclaim
35:19	תמת	qal	wci	3fs	מות	559		die
	תקבר	niph	wci	3fs	קבר	868		be buried
35:20	יצב	hiph	wci	3ms	נצב	662		cause to stand
35:21	יסע	qal	wci	3ms	נסע	652		pull up,set out
	יט	qal	wci	3ms	נטה	639		stretch,incline
35:22	יהי	qal	wci	3ms	היה	224		be,become
	שׁכן	qal	infc		שׁכן	1014		settle,dwell
	ילך	qal	wci	3ms	הלך	229		walk,go
	ישׁכב	qal	wci	3ms	שׁכב	1011		lie,lie down
	ישׁמע	qal	wci	3ms	שׁמע	1033		hear
	יהיו	qal	wci	3mp	היה	224		be,become
35:26	ילד	qalp	pft	3ms	ילד	408		be born
35:27	יבא	qal	wci	3ms	בוא	97		come in
	גר	qal	pft	3ms	גור	157		sojourn
35:28	יהיו	qal	wci	3mp	היה	224		be,become
35:29	יגוע	qal	wci	3ms	גוע	157		expire,die
	ימת	qal	wci	3ms	מות	559		die
	יאסף	niph	wci	3ms	אסף	62		assemble
	יקברו	qal	wci	3mp	קבר	868		bury
36:2	לקח	qal	pft	3ms	לקח	542		take
36:4	תלד	qal	wci	3fs	ילד	408		bear,beget
	ילדה	qal	pft	3fs	ילד	408		bear,beget
36:5	ילדה	qal	pft	3fs	ילד	408		bear,beget
	ילדו	qalp	pft	3cp	ילד	408		be born
36:6	יקח	qal	wci	3ms	לקח	542		take
	רכשׁ	qal	pft	3ms	רכשׁ	940		collect
	ילך	qal	wci	3ms	הלך	229		walk,go
36:7	היה	qal	pft	3ms	היה	224		be,become
	שׁבת	qal	infc		ישׁב	442		sit,dwell
	יכלה	qal	pft	3fs	יכל	407		be able
	שׂאת	qal	infc		נשׂא	669		lift,carry
36:8	ישׁב	qal	wci	3ms	ישׁב	442		sit,dwell
36:11	יהיו	qal	wci	3mp	היה	224		be,become
36:12	היתה	qal	pft	3fs	היה	224		be,become

ChVs	Form	Stem	Tnse	PGN	Root	BDB	Sfx	Meaning
36:12	תלד	qal	wci	3fs	ילד	408		bear,beget
36:13	היו	qal	pft	3cp	היה	224		be,become
36:14	היו	qal	pft	3cp	היה	224		be,become
	תלד	qal	wci	3fs	ילד	408		bear,beget
36:20	ישׁבי	qal	ptc	mp	ישׁב	442		sit,dwell
36:22	יהיו	qal	wci	3mp	היה	224		be,become
36:24	מצא	qal	pft	3ms	מצא	592		find
	רעתו	qal	infc		רעה	944	3ms	pasture,tend
36:31	מלכו	qal	pft	3cp	מלך	573		be king,reign
	מלך	qal	infc		מלך	573		be king,reign
36:32	ימלך	qal	wci	3ms	מלך	573		be king,reign
36:33	ימת	qal	wci	3ms	מות	559		die
	ימלך	qal	wci	3ms	מלך	573		be king,reign
36:34	ימת	qal	wci	3ms	מות	559		die
	ימלך	qal	wci	3ms	מלך	573		be king,reign
36:35	ימת	qal	wci	3ms	מות	559		die
	ימלך	qal	wci	3ms	מלך	573		be king,reign
	מכה	hiph	ptc	ms	נכה	645		smite
36:36	ימת	qal	wci	3ms	מות	559		die
	ימלך	qal	wci	3ms	מלך	573		be king,reign
36:37	ימת	qal	wci	3ms	מות	559		die
	ימלך	qal	wci	3ms	מלך	573		be king,reign
36:38	ימת	qal	wci	3ms	מות	559		die
	ימלך	qal	wci	3ms	מלך	573		be king,reign
36:39	ימת	qal	wci	3ms	מות	559		die
	ימלך	qal	wci	3ms	מלך	573		be king,reign
37:1	ישׁב	qal	wci	3ms	ישׁב	442		sit,dwell
37:2	היה	qal	pft	3ms	היה	224		be,become
	רעה	qal	ptc	ms	רעה	944		pasture,tend
	יבא	hiph	wci	3ms	בוא	97		bring in
37:3	אהב	qal	pft	3ms	אהב	12		love
	עשׂה	qal	pft	3ms	עשׂה	793		do,make
37:4	יראו	qal	wci	3mp	ראה	906		see
	אהב	qal	pft	3ms	אהב	12		love
	ישׂנאו	qal	wci	3mp	שׂנא	971		hate
	יכלו	qal	pft	3cp	יכל	407		be able
	דברו	piel	infc		דבר	180	3ms	speak
37:5	יחלם	qal	wci	3ms	חלם	321		dream
	יגד	hiph	wci	3ms	נגד	616		declare,tell
	יוספו	hiph	wci	3mp	יסף	414		add,do again
	שׂנא	qal	infc		שׂנא	971		hate
37:6	יאמר	qal	wci	3ms	אמר	55		say
	שׁמעו	qal	impv	mp	שׁמע	1033		hear
	חלמתי	qal	pft	1cs	חלם	321		dream
37:7	מאלמים	piel	ptc	mp	אלם	47		bind
	קמה	qal	pft	3fs	קום	877		arise,stand
	נצבה	niph	pft	3fs	נצב	662		stand
	תסבינה	qal	impf	3fp	סבב	685		surround
	תשׁתחוין	hish	wci	3fp	חוה	1005		bow down
37:8	יאמרו	qal	wci	3mp	אמר	55		say
	מלך	qal	infa		מלך	573		be king,reign
	תמלך	qal	impf	2ms	מלך	573		be king,reign
	משׁול	qal	infa		משׁל	605		rule
	תמשׁל	qal	impf	2ms	משׁל	605		rule
37:8	יוספו	hiph	wci	3mp	יסף	414		add,do again
	שׂנא	qal	infc		שׂנא	971		hate
37:9	יחלם	qal	wci	3ms	חלם	321		dream
	יספר	piel	wci	3ms	ספר	707		recount
	יאמר	qal	wci	3ms	אמר	55		say
	חלמתי	qal	pft	1cs	חלם	321		dream
	משׁתחוים	hish	ptc	mp	חוה	1005		bow down
37:10	יספר	piel	wci	3ms	ספר	707		recount
	יגער	qal	wci	3ms	גער	172		rebuke
	יאמר	qal	wci	3ms	אמר	55		say
	חלמת	qal	pft	2ms	חלם	321		dream
	בוא	qal	infa		בוא	97		come in
	נבוא	qal	impf	1cp	בוא	97		come in
	השׁתחות	hish	infc		חוה	1005		bow down
37:11	יקנאו	piel	wci	3mp	קנא	888		be jealous
	שׁמר	qal	pft	3ms	שׁמר	1036		keep,watch
37:12	ילכו	qal	wci	3mp	הלך	229		walk,go
	רעות	qal	infc		רעה	944		pasture,tend
37:13	יאמר	qal	wci	3ms	אמר	55		say
	רעים	qal	ptc	mp	רעה	944		pasture,tend
	לכה	qal	impv	ms	הלך	229		walk,go
	אשׁלחך	qal	cohm	1cs	שׁלח	1018	2ms	send
	יאמר	qal	wci	3ms	אמר	55		say
37:14	יאמר	qal	wci	3ms	אמר	55		say
	לך	qal	impv	ms	הלך	229		walk,go
	ראה	qal	impv	ms	ראה	906		see
	השׁבני	hiph	impv	ms	שׁוב	996	1cs	bring back
	ישׁלחהו	qal	wci	3ms	שׁלח	1018	3ms	send
	יבא	qal	wci	3ms	בוא	97		come in
37:15	ימצאהו	qal	wci	3ms	מצא	592	3ms	find
	תעה	qal	ptc	ms	תעה	1073		wander,err
	ישׁאלהו	qal	wci	3ms	שׁאל	981	3ms	ask,borrow
	אמר	qal	infc		אמר	55		say
	תבקשׁ	piel	impf	2ms	בקשׁ	134		seek
37:16	יאמר	qal	wci	3ms	אמר	55		say
	מבקשׁ	piel	ptc	ms	בקשׁ	134		seek
	הגידה	hiph	impv	ms	נגד	616		declare,tell
	רעים	qal	ptc	mp	רעה	944		pasture,tend
37:17	יאמר	qal	wci	3ms	אמר	55		say
	נסעו	qal	pft	3cp	נסע	652		pull up,set out
	שׁמעתי	qal	pft	1cs	שׁמע	1033		hear
	אמרים	qal	ptc	mp	אמר	55		say
	נלכה	qal	coh	1cp	הלך	229		walk,go
	ילך	qal	wci	3ms	הלך	229		walk,go
	ימצאם	qal	wci	3ms	מצא	592	3mp	find
37:18	יראו	qal	wci	3mp	ראה	906		see
	יקרב	qal	impf	3ms	קרב	897		approach
	יתנכלו	hith	wci	3mp	נכל	647		deal craftily
	המיתו	hiph	infc		מות	559	3ms	kill
37:19	יאמרו	qal	wci	3mp	אמר	55		say
	בא	qal	ptc	ms	בוא	97		come in
37:20	לכו	qal	impv	mp	הלך	229		walk,go
	נהרגהו	qal	cohm	1cp	הרג	246	3ms	kill
	נשׁלכהו	hiph	cohm	1cp	שׁלך	1020	3ms	throw,cast

ChVs	Form	Stem	Tnse	PGN	Root	BDB	Sfx	Meaning
37: 20	אמרנו	qal	wcp	1cp	אמר	55		say
	אכלתהו	qal	pft	3fs	אכל	37	3ms	eat,devour
	נראה	qal	impf	1cp	ראה	906		see
	יהיו	qal	impf	3mp	היה	224		be,become
37: 21	ישמע	qal	wci	3ms	שמע	1033		hear
	יצלהו	hiph	wci	3ms	נצל	664	3ms	snatch,deliver
	יאמר	qal	wci	3ms	אמר	55		say
	נכנו	hiph	cohm	1cp	נכה	645	3ms	smite
37: 22	יאמר	qal	wci	3ms	אמר	55		say
	תשפכו	qal	jusm	2mp	שפך	1049		pour out
	השליכו	hiph	impv	mp	שלך	1020		throw,cast
	תשלחו	qal	jusm	2mp	שלח	1018		send
	הציל	hiph	infc		נצל	664		snatch,deliver
	השיבו	hiph	infc		שוב	996	3ms	bring back
37: 23	יהי	qal	wci	3ms	היה	224		be,become
	בא	qal	pft	3ms	בוא	97		come in
	יפשיטו	hiph	wci	3mp	פשט	832		strip off
37: 24	יקחהו	qal	wci	3mp	לקח	542	3ms	take
	ישלכו	hiph	wci	3mp	שלך	1020		throw,cast
37: 25	ישבו	qal	wci	3mp	ישב	442		sit,dwell
	אכל	qal	infc		אכל	37		eat,devour
	ישאו	qal	wci	3mp	נשא	669		lift,carry
	יראו	qal	wci	3mp	ראה	906		see
	באה	qal	ptc	fs	בוא	97		come in
	נשאים	qal	ptc	mp	נשא	669		lift,carry
	הולכים	qal	ptc	mp	הלך	229		walk,go
	הוריד	hiph	infc		ירד	432		bring down
37: 26	יאמר	qal	wci	3ms	אמר	55		say
	נהרג	qal	impf	1cp	הרג	246		kill
	כסינו	piel	wcp	1cp	כסה	491		cover
37: 27	לכו	qal	impv	mp	הלך	229		walk,go
	נמכרנו	qal	cohm	1cp	מכר	569	3ms	sell
	תהי	qal	jus	3fs	היה	224		be,become
	ישמעו	qal	wci	3mp	שמע	1033		hear
37: 28	יעברו	qal	wci	3mp	עבר	716		pass over
	סחרים	qal	ptc	mp	סחר	695		go around
	ימשכו	qal	wci	3mp	משך	604		draw,pull
	יעלו	hiph	wci	3mp	עלה	748		bring up,offer
	ימכרו	qal	wci	3mp	מכר	569		sell
	יביאו	hiph	wci	3mp	בוא	97		bring in
37: 29	ישב	qal	wci	3ms	שוב	996		turn,return
	יקרע	qal	wci	3ms	קרע	902		tear,rend
37: 30	ישב	qal	wci	3ms	שוב	996		turn,return
	יאמר	qal	wci	3ms	אמר	55		say
	בא	qal	ptc	ms	בוא	97		come in
37: 31	יקחו	qal	wci	3mp	לקח	542		take
	ישחטו	qal	wci	3mp	שחט	1006		slaughter
	יטבלו	qal	wci	3mp	טבל	371		dip
37: 32	ישלחו	piel	wci	3mp	שלח	1018		send away,shoot
	יביאו	hiph	wci	3mp	בוא	97		bring in
	יאמרו	qal	wci	3mp	אמר	55		say
	מצאנו	qal	pft	1cp	מצא	592		find
	הכר	hiph	impv	ms	נכר	647		regard,notice
37: 33	יכירה	hiph	wci	3ms	נכר	647	3fs	regard,notice
37: 33	יאמר	qal	wci	3ms	אמר	55		say
	אכלתהו	qal	pft	3fs	אכל	37	3ms	eat,devour
	טרף	qal	infa		טרף	382		tear,rend
	טרף	qalp	pft	3ms	טרף	382		be torn
37: 34	יקרע	qal	wci	3ms	קרע	902		tear,rend
	ישם	qal	wci	3ms	שים	962		put,set
	יתאבל	hith	wci	3ms	אבל	5		mourn
37: 35	יקמו	qal	wci	3mp	קום	877		arise,stand
	נחמו	piel	infc		נחם	636	3ms	comfort
	ימאן	piel	wci	3ms	מאן	549		refuse
	התנחם	hith	infc		נחם	636		have compassion
	יאמר	qal	wci	3ms	אמר	55		say
	ארד	qal	impf	1cs	ירד	432		come down
	יבך	qal	wci	3ms	בכה	113		weep
37: 36	מכרו	qal	pft	3cp	מכר	569		sell
38: 1	יהי	qal	wci	3ms	היה	224		be,become
	ירד	qal	wci	3ms	ירד	432		come down
	יט	qal	wci	3ms	נטה	639		stretch,incline
38: 2	ירא	qal	wci	3ms	ראה	906		see
	יקחה	qal	wci	3ms	לקח	542	3fs	take
	יבא	qal	wci	3ms	בוא	97		come in
38: 3	תהר	qal	wci	3fs	הרה	247		conceive
	תלד	qal	wci	3fs	ילד	408		bear,beget
	יקרא	qal	wci	3ms	קרא	894		call,proclaim
38: 4	תהר	qal	wci	3fs	הרה	247		conceive
	תלד	qal	wci	3fs	ילד	408		bear,beget
	תקרא	qal	wci	3fs	קרא	894		call,proclaim
38: 5	תסף	hiph	wci	3fs	יסף	414		add,do again
	תלד	qal	wci	3fs	ילד	408		bear,beget
	תקרא	qal	wci	3fs	קרא	894		call,proclaim
	היה	qal	pft	3ms	היה	224		be,become
	לדתה	qal	infc		ילד	408	3fs	bear,beget
38: 6	יקח	qal	wci	3ms	לקח	542		take
38: 7	יהי	qal	wci	3ms	היה	224		be,become
	ימתהו	hiph	wci	3ms	מות	559	3ms	kill
38: 8	יאמר	qal	wci	3ms	אמר	55		say
	בא	qal	impv	ms	בוא	97		come in
	יבם	piel	impv	ms	יבם	386		be levirate
	הקם	hiph	impv	ms	קום	877		raise,build,set
38: 9	ידע	qal	wci	3ms	ידע	393		know
	יהיה	qal	impf	3ms	היה	224		be,become
	היה	qal	wcp	3ms	היה	224		be,become
	בא	qal	pft	3ms	בוא	97		come in
	שחת	piel	wcp	3ms	שחת	1007		spoil,ruin
	נתן	qal	infc		נתן	678		give,set
38: 10	ירע	qal	wci	3ms	רעע	949		be evil
	עשה	qal	pft	3ms	עשה	793		do,make
	ימת	hiph	wci	3ms	מות	559		kill
38: 11	יאמר	qal	wci	3ms	אמר	55		say
	שבי	qal	impv	fs	ישב	442		sit,dwell
	יגדל	qal	impf	3ms	גדל	152		be great,grow
	אמר	qal	pft	3ms	אמר	55		say
	ימות	qal	impf	3ms	מות	559		die
	תלך	qal	wci	3fs	הלך	229		walk,go

ChVs	Form	Stem	Tnse	PGN	Root	BDB	Sfx	Meaning
38:11	תשב	qal	wci	3fs	ישב	442		sit,dwell
38:12	ירבו	qal	wci	3mp	רבה	915		be many,great
	תמת	qal	wci	3fs	מות	559		die
	ינחם	niph	wci	3ms	נחם	636		be sorry
	יעל	qal	wci	3ms	עלה	748		go up
	גזזי	qal	ptc	mp	גזז	159		shear
38:13	יגד	hoph	wci	3ms	נגד	616		be told
	אמר	qal	infc		אמר	55		say
	עלה	qal	ptc	ms	עלה	748		go up
	גז	qal	infc		גזז	159		shear
38:14	תסר	hiph	wci	3fs	סור	693		take away
	תכס	piel	wci	3fs	כסה	491		cover
	תתעלף	hith	wci	3fs	עלף	763		enwrap oneself
	תשב	qal	wci	3fs	ישב	442		sit,dwell
	ראתה	qal	pft	3fs	ראה	906		see
	גדל	qal	pft	3ms	גדל	152		be great,grow
	נתנה	niph	pft	3fs	נתן	678		be given
38:15	יראה	qal	wci	3ms	ראה	906	3fs	see
	יחשבה	qal	wci	3ms	חשב	362	3fs	think,devise
	זונה	qal	ptc	fs	זנה	275		act a harlot
	כסתה	piel	pft	3fs	כסה	491		cover
38:16	יט	qal	wci	3ms	נטה	639		stretch,incline
	יאמר	qal	wci	3ms	אמר	55		say
	הבה	qal	impv	ms	יהב	396		give
	אבוא	qal	cohm	1cs	בוא	97		come in
	ידע	qal	pft	3ms	ידע	393		know
	תאמר	qal	wci	3fs	אמר	55		say
	תתן	qal	impf	2ms	נתן	678		give,set
	תבוא	qal	impf	2ms	בוא	97		come in
38:17	יאמר	qal	wci	3ms	אמר	55		say
	אשלח	piel	impf	1cs	שלח	1018		send away,shoot
	תאמר	qal	wci	3fs	אמר	55		say
	תתן	qal	impf	2ms	נתן	678		give,set
	שלחך	qal	infc		שלח	1018	2ms	send
38:18	יאמר	qal	wci	3ms	אמר	55		say
	אתן	qal	impf	1cs	נתן	678		give,set
	תאמר	qal	wci	3fs	אמר	55		say
	יתן	qal	wci	3ms	נתן	678		give,set
	יבא	qal	wci	3ms	בוא	97		come in
	תהר	qal	wci	3fs	הרה	247		conceive
38:19	תקם	qal	wci	3fs	קום	877		arise,stand
	תלך	qal	wci	3fs	הלך	229		walk,go
	תסר	hiph	wci	3fs	סור	693		take away
	תלבש	qal	wci	3fs	לבש	527		put on,clothe
38:20	ישלח	qal	wci	3ms	שלח	1018		send
	קחת	qal	infc		לקח	542		take
	מצאה	qal	pft	3ms	מצא	592	3fs	find
38:21	ישאל	qal	wci	3ms	שאל	981		ask,borrow
	אמר	qal	infc		אמר	55		say
	יאמרו	qal	wci	3mp	אמר	55		say
	היתה	qal	pft	3fs	היה	224		be,become
38:22	ישב	qal	wci	3ms	שוב	996		turn,return
	יאמר	qal	wci	3ms	אמר	55		say
	מצאתיה	qal	pft	1cs	מצא	592	3fs	find
38:22	אמרו	qal	pft	3cp	אמר	55		say
	היתה	qal	pft	3fs	היה	224		be,become
38:23	יאמר	qal	wci	3ms	אמר	55		say
	תקח	qal	jusm	3fs	לקח	542		take
	נהיה	qal	impf	1cp	היה	224		be,become
	שלחתי	qal	pft	1cs	שלח	1018		send
	מצאתה	qal	pft	2ms	מצא	592	3fs	find
38:24	יהי	qal	wci	3ms	היה	224		be,become
	יגד	hoph	wci	3ms	נגד	616		be told
	אמר	qal	infc		אמר	55		say
	זנתה	qal	pft	3fs	זנה	275		act a harlot
	יאמר	qal	wci	3ms	אמר	55		say
	הוציאוה	hiph	impv	mp	יצא	422	3fs	bring out
	תשרף	niph	jusm	3fs	שרף	976		be burned
38:25	מוצאת	hoph	ptc	fs	יצא	422		be brought out
	שלחה	qal	pft	3fs	שלח	1018		send
	אמר	qal	infc		אמר	55		say
	תאמר	qal	wci	3fs	אמר	55		say
	הכר	hiph	impv	ms	נכר	647		regard,notice
38:26	יכר	hiph	wci	3ms	נכר	647		regard,notice
	יאמר	qal	wci	3ms	אמר	55		say
	צדקה	qal	pft	3fs	צדק	842		be righteous
	נתתיה	qal	pft	1cs	נתן	678	3fs	give,set
	יסף	qal	pft	3ms	יסף	414		add,increase
	דעתה	qal	infc		ידע	393	3fs	know
38:27	יהי	qal	wci	3ms	היה	224		be,become
	לדתה	qal	infc		ילד	408	3fs	bear,beget
38:28	יהי	qal	wci	3ms	היה	224		be,become
	לדתה	qal	infc		ילד	408	3fs	bear,beget
	יתן	qal	wci	3ms	נתן	678		give,set
	תקח	qal	wci	3fs	לקח	542		take
	מילדת	piel	ptc	fs	ילד	408		bear,deliver
	תקשר	qal	wci	3fs	קשר	905		bind
	אמר	qal	infc		אמר	55		say
	יצא	qal	pft	3ms	יצא	422		go out
38:29	יהי	qal	wci	3ms	היה	224		be,become
	משיב	hiph	ptc	ms	שוב	996		bring back
	יצא	qal	pft	3ms	יצא	422		go out
	תאמר	qal	wci	3fs	אמר	55		say
	פרצת	qal	pft	2ms	פרץ	829		break through
	יקרא	qal	wci	3ms	קרא	894		call,proclaim
38:30	יצא	qal	pft	3ms	יצא	422		go out
	יקרא	qal	wci	3ms	קרא	894		call,proclaim
39:1	הורד	hoph	pft	3ms	ירד	432		be led down
	יקנהו	qal	wci	3ms	קנה	888	3ms	get,buy
	הורדהו	hiph	pft	3cp	ירד	432	3ms	bring down
39:2	יהי	qal	wci	3ms	היה	224		be,become
	יהי	qal	wci	3ms	היה	224		be,become
	מצליח	hiph	ptc	ms	צלח	852		cause to thrive
	יהי	qal	wci	3ms	היה	224		be,become
39:3	ירא	qal	wci	3ms	ראה	906		see
	עשה	qal	ptc	ms	עשה	793		do,make
	מצליח	hiph	ptc	ms	צלח	852		cause to thrive
39:4	ימצא	qal	wci	3ms	מצא	592		find

ChVs	Form	Stem	Tnse	PGN	Root	BDB	Sfx	Meaning
39: 4	ישרת	piel	wci	3ms	שרת	1058		minister,serve
	יפקדהו	hiph	wci	3ms	פקד	823	3ms	set,entrust
	נתן	qal	pft	3ms	נתן	678		give,set
39: 5	יהי	qal	wci	3ms	היה	224		be,become
	הפקיד	hiph	pft	3ms	פקד	823		set,entrust
	יברך	piel	wci	3ms	ברך	138		bless
	יהי	qal	wci	3ms	היה	224		be,become
39: 6	יעזב	qal	wci	3ms	עזב	736		leave,loose
	ידע	qal	pft	3ms	ידע	393		know
	אוכל	qal	ptc	ms	אכל	37		eat,devour
	יהי	qal	wci	3ms	היה	224		be,become
39: 7	יהי	qal	wci	3ms	היה	224		be,become
	תשׂא	qal	wci	3fs	נשׂא	669		lift,carry
	תאמר	qal	wci	3fs	אמר	55		say
	שׁכבה	qal	impv	ms	שׁכב	1011		lie,lie down
39: 8	ימאן	piel	wci	3ms	מאן	549		refuse
	יאמר	qal	wci	3ms	אמר	55		say
	ידע	qal	pft	3ms	ידע	393		know
	נתן	qal	pft	3ms	נתן	678		give,set
39: 9	חשׂך	qal	pft	3ms	חשׂך	362		withhold
	אעשׂה	qal	impf	1cs	עשׂה	793		do,make
	חטאתי	qal	wcp	1cs	חטא	306		sin
39: 10	יהי	qal	wci	3ms	היה	224		be,become
	דברה	piel	infc		דבר	180	3fs	speak
	שׁמע	qal	pft	3ms	שׁמע	1033		hear
	שׁכב	qal	infc		שׁכב	1011		lie,lie down
	היות	qal	infc		היה	224		be,become
39: 11	יהי	qal	wci	3ms	היה	224		be,become
	יבא	qal	wci	3ms	בוא	97		come in
	עשׂות	qal	infc		עשׂה	793		do,make
39: 12	תתפשׂהו	qal	wci	3fs	תפשׂ	1074	3ms	seize,grasp
	אמר	qal	infc		אמר	55		say
	שׁכבה	qal	impv	ms	שׁכב	1011		lie,lie down
	יעזב	qal	wci	3ms	עזב	736		leave,loose
	ינס	qal	wci	3ms	נוס	630		flee,escape
	יצא	qal	wci	3ms	יצא	422		go out
39: 13	יהי	qal	wci	3ms	היה	224		be,become
	ראותה	qal	infc		ראה	906	3fs	see
	עזב	qal	pft	3ms	עזב	736		leave,loose
	ינס	qal	wci	3ms	נוס	630		flee,escape
39: 14	תקרא	qal	wci	3fs	קרא	894		call,proclaim
	תאמר	qal	wci	3fs	אמר	55		say
	אמר	qal	infc		אמר	55		say
	ראו	qal	impv	mp	ראה	906		see
	הביא	hiph	pft	3ms	בוא	97		bring in
	צחק	piel	infc		צחק	850		jest,make sport
	בא	qal	pft	3ms	בוא	97		come in
	שׁכב	qal	infc		שׁכב	1011		lie,lie down
	אקרא	qal	wci	1cs	קרא	894		call,proclaim
39: 15	יהי	qal	wci	3ms	היה	224		be,become
	שׁמעו	qal	infc		שׁמע	1033	3ms	hear
	הרימתי	hiph	pft	1cs	רום	926		raise,lift
	אקרא	qal	wci	1cs	קרא	894		call,proclaim
	יעזב	qal	wci	3ms	עזב	736		leave,loose
39: 15	ינס	qal	wci	3ms	נוס	630		flee,escape
	יצא	qal	wci	3ms	יצא	422		go out
39: 16	תנח	hiph	wci	3fs	נוח	628		give rest,put
	בוא	qal	infc		בוא	97		come in
39: 17	תדבר	piel	wci	3fs	דבר	180		speak
	אמר	qal	infc		אמר	55		say
	בא	qal	pft	3ms	בוא	97		come in
	הבאת	hiph	pft	2ms	בוא	97		bring in
	צחק	piel	infc		צחק	850		jest,make sport
39: 18	יהי	qal	wci	3ms	היה	224		be,become
	הרימי	hiph	infc		רום	926	1cs	raise,lift
	אקרא	qal	wci	1cs	קרא	894		call,proclaim
	יעזב	qal	wci	3ms	עזב	736		leave,loose
	ינס	qal	wci	3ms	נוס	630		flee,escape
39: 19	יהי	qal	wci	3ms	היה	224		be,become
	שׁמע	qal	infc		שׁמע	1033		hear
	דברה	piel	pft	3fs	דבר	180		speak
	אמר	qal	infc		אמר	55		say
	עשׂה	qal	pft	3ms	עשׂה	793		do,make
	יחר	qal	wci	3ms	חרה	354		be kindled, burn
39: 20	יקח	qal	wci	3ms	לקח	542		take
	יתנהו	qal	wci	3ms	נתן	678	3ms	give,set
	אסורים	qal	pptc	mp	אסר	63		tie,bind
	יהי	qal	wci	3ms	היה	224		be,become
39: 21	יהי	qal	wci	3ms	היה	224		be,become
	יט	qal	wci	3ms	נטה	639		stretch,incline
	יתן	qal	wci	3ms	נתן	678		give,set
39: 22	יתן	qal	wci	3ms	נתן	678		give,set
	עשׂים	qal	ptc	mp	עשׂה	793		do,make
	היה	qal	pft	3ms	היה	224		be,become
	עשׂה	qal	ptc	ms	עשׂה	793		do,make
39: 23	ראה	qal	ptc	ms	ראה	906		see
	עשׂה	qal	ptc	ms	עשׂה	793		do,make
	מצליח	hiph	ptc	ms	צלח	852		cause to thrive
40: 1	יהי	qal	wci	3ms	היה	224		be,become
	חטאו	qal	pft	3cp	חטא	306		sin
	אפה	qal	ptc	ms	אפה	66		bake
40: 2	יקצף	qal	wci	3ms	קצף	893		be angry
	אופים	qal	ptc	mp	אפה	66		bake
40: 3	יתן	qal	wci	3ms	נתן	678		give,set
	אסור	qal	pptc	ms	אסר	63		tie,bind
40: 4	יפקד	qal	wci	3ms	פקד	823		attend to,visit
	ישרת	piel	wci	3ms	שרת	1058		minister,serve
	יהיו	qal	wci	3mp	היה	224		be,become
40: 5	יחלמו	qal	wci	3mp	חלם	321		dream
	אפה	qal	ptc	ms	אפה	66		bake
	אסורים	qal	pptc	mp	אסר	63		tie,bind
40: 6	יבא	qal	wci	3ms	בוא	97		come in
	ירא	qal	wci	3ms	ראה	906		see
	זעפים	qal	ptc	mp	זעף	277		be vexed
40: 7	ישאל	qal	wci	3ms	שאל	981		ask,borrow
	אמר	qal	infc		אמר	55		say
40: 8	יאמרו	qal	wci	3mp	אמר	55		say
	חלמנו	qal	pft	1cp	חלם	321		dream

ChVs	Form	Stem	Tnse	PGN	Root	BDB	Sfx	Meaning
40:8	פתר	qal	ptc	ms	פתר	837		interpret
	יאמר	qal	wci	3ms	אמר	55		say
	ספרו	piel	impv	mp	ספר	707		recount
40:9	יספר	piel	wci	3ms	ספר	707		recount
	יאמר	qal	wci	3ms	אמר	55		say
40:10	פרחת	qal	ptc	fs	פרח	827		bud
	עלתה	qal	pft	3fs	עלה	748		go up
	הבשׁילו	hiph	pft	3cp	בשׁל	143		ripen
40:11	אקח	qal	wci	1cs	לקח	542		take
	אשׂחט	qal	wci	1cs	שׂחט	965		squeeze out
	אתן	qal	wci	1cs	נתן	678		give,set
40:12	יאמר	qal	wci	3ms	אמר	55		say
40:13	ישׂא	qal	impf	3ms	נשׂא	669		lift,carry
	השׁיבך	hiph	wcp	3ms	שׁוב	996	2ms	bring back
	נתת	qal	wcp	2ms	נתן	678		give,set
	היית	qal	pft	2ms	היה	224		be,become
40:14	זכרתני	qal	pft	2ms	זכר	269	1cs	remember
	ייטב	qal	impf	3ms	יטב	405		be good
	עשׂית	qal	wcp	2ms	עשׂה	793		do,make
	הזכרתני	hiph	wcp	2ms	זכר	269	1cs	c. to remember
	הוצאתני	hiph	wcp	2ms	יצא	422	1cs	bring out
40:15	גנב	pual	infa		גנב	170		be stolen away
	גנבתי	pual	pft	1cs	גנב	170		be stolen away
	עשׂיתי	qal	pft	1cs	עשׂה	793		do,make
	שׂמו	qal	pft	3cp	שׂים	962		put,set
40:16	ירא	qal	wci	3ms	ראה	906		see
	אפים	qal	ptc	mp	אפה	66		bake
	פתר	qal	pft	3ms	פתר	837		interpret
	יאמר	qal	wci	3ms	אמר	55		say
40:17	אפה	qal	ptc	ms	אפה	66		bake
	אכל	qal	ptc	ms	אכל	37		eat,devour
40:18	יען	qal	wci	3ms	ענה	772		answer
	יאמר	qal	wci	3ms	אמר	55		say
40:19	ישׂא	qal	impf	3ms	נשׂא	669		lift,carry
	תלה	qal	wcp	3ms	תלה	1067		hang
	אכל	qal	wcp	3ms	אכל	37		eat,devour
40:20	יהי	qal	wci	3ms	היה	224		be,become
	הלדת	qalp	infc		ילד	408		be born
	יעשׂ	qal	wci	3ms	עשׂה	793		do,make
	ישׂא	qal	wci	3ms	נשׂא	669		lift,carry
	אפים	qal	ptc	mp	אפה	66		bake
40:21	ישׁב	hiph	wci	3ms	שׁוב	996		bring back
	יתן	qal	wci	3ms	נתן	678		give,set
40:22	אפים	qal	ptc	mp	אפה	66		bake
	תלה	qal	pft	3ms	תלה	1067		hang
	פתר	qal	pft	3ms	פתר	837		interpret
40:23	זכר	qal	pft	3ms	זכר	269		remember
	ישׁכחהו	qal	wci	3ms	שׁכח	1013	3ms	forget
41:1	יהי	qal	wci	3ms	היה	224		be,become
	חלם	qal	ptc	ms	חלם	321		dream
	עמד	qal	ptc	ms	עמד	763		stand,stop
41:2	עלת	qal	ptc	fp	עלה	748		go up
	תרעינה	qal	wci	3fp	רעה	944		pasture,tend
41:3	עלות	qal	ptc	fp	עלה	748		go up
41:3	תעמדנה	qal	wci	3fp	עמד	763		stand,stop
41:4	תאכלנה	qal	wci	3fp	אכל	37		eat,devour
	ייקץ	qal	wci	3ms	יקץ	429		awake
41:5	יישׁן	qal	wci	3ms	ישׁן	445		sleep
	יחלם	qal	wci	3ms	חלם	321		dream
	עלות	qal	ptc	fp	עלה	748		go up
41:6	שׁדופת	qal	pptc	fp	שׁדף	995		scorch,blight
	צמחות	qal	ptc	fp	צמח	855		sprout up
41:7	תבלענה	qal	wci	3fp	בלע	118		swallow
	ייקץ	qal	wci	3ms	יקץ	429		awake
41:8	יהי	qal	wci	3ms	היה	224		be,become
	תפעם	niph	wci	3fs	פעם	821		be disturbed
	ישׁלח	qal	wci	3ms	שׁלח	1018		send
	יקרא	qal	wci	3ms	קרא	894		call,proclaim
	יספר	piel	wci	3ms	ספר	707		recount
	פותר	qal	ptc	ms	פתר	837		interpret
41:9	ידבר	piel	wci	3ms	דבר	180		speak
	אמר	qal	infc		אמר	55		say
	מזכיר	hiph	ptc	ms	זכר	269		c. to remember
41:10	קצף	qal	pft	3ms	קצף	893		be angry
	יתן	qal	wci	3ms	נתן	678		give,set
	אפים	qal	ptc	mp	אפה	66		bake
41:11	נחלמה	qal	wci	1cp	חלם	321		dream
	חלמנו	qal	pft	1cp	חלם	321		dream
41:12	נספר	piel	wci	1cp	ספר	707		recount
	יפתר	qal	wci	3ms	פתר	837		interpret
	פתר	qal	pft	3ms	פתר	837		interpret
41:13	יהי	qal	wci	3ms	היה	224		be,become
	פתר	qal	pft	3ms	פתר	837		interpret
	היה	qal	pft	3ms	היה	224		be,become
	השׁיב	hiph	pft	3ms	שׁוב	996		bring back
	תלה	qal	pft	3ms	תלה	1067		hang
41:14	ישׁלח	qal	wci	3ms	שׁלח	1018		send
	יקרא	qal	wci	3ms	קרא	894		call,proclaim
	יריצהו	hiph	wci	3mp	רוץ	930	3ms	bring quickly
	יגלח	piel	wci	3ms	גלח	164		shave
	יחלף	piel	wci	3ms	חלף	322		change
	יבא	qal	wci	3ms	בוא	97		come in
41:15	יאמר	qal	wci	3ms	אמר	55		say
	חלמתי	qal	pft	1cs	חלם	321		dream
	פתר	qal	ptc	ms	פתר	837		interpret
	שׁמעתי	qal	pft	1cs	שׁמע	1033		hear
	אמר	qal	infc		אמר	55		say
	תשׁמע	qal	impf	2ms	שׁמע	1033		hear
	פתר	qal	infc		פתר	837		interpret
41:16	יען	qal	wci	3ms	ענה	772		answer
	אמר	qal	infc		אמר	55		say
	יענה	qal	impf	3ms	ענה	772		answer
41:17	ידבר	piel	wci	3ms	דבר	180		speak
	עמד	qal	ptc	ms	עמד	763		stand,stop
41:18	עלת	qal	ptc	fp	עלה	748		go up
	תרעינה	qal	wci	3fp	רעה	944		pasture,tend
41:19	עלות	qal	ptc	fp	עלה	748		go up
	ראיתי	qal	pft	1cs	ראה	906		see

ChVs	Form	Stem	Tnse	PGN	Root	BDB	Sfx	Meaning
41: 20	תאכלנה	qal	wci	3fp	אכל	37		eat,devour
41: 21	תבאנה	qal	wci	3fp	בוא	97		come in
	נודע	niph	pft	3ms	ידע	393		be made known
	באו	qal	pft	3cp	בוא	97		come in
	איקץ	qal	wci	1cs	יקץ	429		awake
41: 22	ארא	qal	wci	1cs	ראה	906		see
	עלת	qal	ptc	fp	עלה	748		go up
41: 23	צנמות	qal	pptc	fp	צנם	856		dry up,harden
	שׁדפות	qal	pptc	fp	שׁדף	995		scorch,blight
	צמחות	qal	ptc	fp	צמח	855		sprout up
41: 24	תבלען	qal	wci	3fp	בלע	118		swallow
	אמר	qal	wci	1cs	אמר	55		say
	מגיד	hiph	ptc	ms	נגד	616		declare,tell
41: 25	יאמר	qal	wci	3ms	אמר	55		say
	עשׂה	qal	ptc	ms	עשׂה	793		do,make
	הגיד	hiph	pft	3ms	נגד	616		declare,tell
41: 27	עלת	qal	ptc	fp	עלה	748		go up
	שׁדפות	qal	pptc	fp	שׁדף	995		scorch,blight
	יהיו	qal	impf	3mp	היה	224		be, become
41: 28	דברתי	piel	pft	1cs	דבר	180		speak
	עשׂה	qal	ptc	ms	עשׂה	793		do,make
	הראה	hiph	pft	3ms	ראה	906		show,exhibit
41: 29	באות	qal	ptc	fp	בוא	97		come in
41: 30	קמו	qal	wcp	3cp	קום	877		arise,stand
	נשׁכח	niph	wcp	3ms	שׁכח	1013		be forgotten
	כלה	piel	wcp	3ms	כלה	477		complete,finish
41: 31	יודע	niph	impf	3ms	ידע	393		be made known
41: 32	השׁנות	niph	infc		שׁנה	1040		be repeated
	נכון	niph	ptc	ms	כון	465		be established
	ממהר	piel	ptc	ms	מהר	554		hasten
	עשׂתו	qal	infc		עשׂה	793	3ms	do,make
41: 33	ירא	qal	jus	3ms	ראה	906		see
	נבון	niph	ptc	ms	בין	106		be discerning
	ישׁיתהו	qal	jusm	3ms	שׁית	1011	3ms	put,set
41: 34	יעשׂה	qal	jusm	3ms	עשׂה	793		do,make
	יפקד	hiph	jus	3ms	פקד	823		set,entrust
	חמשׁ	piel	wcp	3ms	חמשׁ	332		take fifth part
41: 35	יקבצו	qal	jusm	3mp	קבץ	867		gather,collect
	באת	qal	ptc	fp	בוא	97		come in
	יצברו	qal	jusm	3mp	צבר	840		heap up
	שׁמרו	qal	wcp	3cp	שׁמר	1036		keep,watch
41: 36	היה	qal	wcp	3ms	היה	224		be,become
	תהיין	qal	impf	3fp	היה	224		be,become
	תכרת	niph	impf	3fs	כרת	503		be cut off
41: 37	ייטב	qal	wci	3ms	יטב	405		be good
41: 38	יאמר	qal	wci	3ms	אמר	55		say
	נמצא	qal	impf	1cp	מצא	592		find
41: 39	יאמר	qal	wci	3ms	אמר	55		say
	הודיע	hiph	infc		ידע	393		declare
	נבון	niph	ptc	ms	בין	106		be discerning
41: 40	תהיה	qal	impf	2ms	היה	224		be, become
	ישׁק	qal	impf	3ms	נשׁק	676		kiss
	אגדל	qal	impf	1cs	גדל	152		be great,grow
41: 41	יאמר	qal	wci	3ms	אמר	55		say
41: 41	ראה	qal	impv	ms	ראה	906		see
	נתתי	qal	pft	1cs	נתן	678		give,set
41: 42	יסר	hiph	wci	3ms	סור	693		take away
	יתן	qal	wci	3ms	נתן	678		give,set
	ילבשׁ	hiph	wci	3ms	לבשׁ	527		clothe
	ישׂם	qal	wci	3ms	שׂים	962		put,set
41: 43	ירכב	hiph	wci	3ms	רכב	938		cause to ride
	יקראו	qal	wci	3mp	קרא	894		call,proclaim
	נתון	qal	infa		נתן	678		give,set
41: 44	יאמר	qal	wci	3ms	אמר	55		say
	ירים	hiph	impf	3ms	רום	926		raise,lift
41: 45	יקרא	qal	wci	3ms	קרא	894		call,proclaim
	יתן	qal	wci	3ms	נתן	678		give,set
	יצא	qal	wci	3ms	יצא	422		go out
41: 46	עמדו	qal	infc		עמד	763	3ms	stand,stop
	יצא	qal	wci	3ms	יצא	422		go out
	יעבר	qal	wci	3ms	עבר	716		pass over
41: 47	תעשׂ	qal	wci	3fs	עשׂה	793		do,make
41: 48	יקבץ	qal	wci	3ms	קבץ	867		gather,collect
	היו	qal	pft	3cp	היה	224		be, become
	יתן	qal	wci	3ms	נתן	678		give,set
	נתן	qal	pft	3ms	נתן	678		give,set
41: 49	יצבר	qal	wci	3ms	צבר	840		heap up
	הרבה	hiph	infa		רבה	915		make many
	חדל	qal	pft	3ms	חדל	292		cease
	ספר	qal	infc		ספר	707		count
41: 50	ילד	qalp	pft	3ms	ילד	408		be born
	תבוא	qal	impf	3fs	בוא	97		come in
	ילדה	qal	pft	3fs	ילד	408		bear, beget
41: 51	יקרא	qal	wci	3ms	קרא	894		call,proclaim
	נשׁני	piel	pft	3ms	נשׁה	674	1cs	cause to forget
41: 52	קרא	qal	pft	3ms	קרא	894		call,proclaim
	הפרני	hiph	pft	3ms	פרה	826	1cs	make fruitful
41: 53	תכלינה	qal	wci	3fp	כלה	477		finished,spent
	היה	qal	pft	3ms	היה	224		be, become
41: 54	תחלינה	hiph	wci	3fp	חלל	320		begin,profane
	בוא	qal	infc		בוא	97		come in
	אמר	qal	pft	3ms	אמר	55		say
	יהי	qal	wci	3ms	היה	224		be, become
	היה	qal	pft	3ms	היה	224		be, become
41: 55	תרעב	qal	wci	3fs	רעב	944		be hungry
	יצעק	qal	wci	3ms	צעק	858		cry out
	יאמר	qal	wci	3ms	אמר	55		say
	לכו	qal	impv	mp	הלך	229		walk,go
	יאמר	qal	impf	3ms	אמר	55		say
	תעשׂו	qal	impf	2mp	עשׂה	793		do,make
41: 56	היה	qal	pft	3ms	היה	224		be, become
	יפתח	qal	wci	3ms	פתח	834		open
	ישׁבר	qal	wci	3ms	שׁבר	991		buy grain
	יחזק	qal	wci	3ms	חזק	304		be strong
41: 57	באו	qal	pft	3cp	בוא	97		come in
	שׁבר	qal	infc		שׁבר	991		buy grain
	חזק	qal	pft	3ms	חזק	304		be strong
42: 1	ירא	qal	wci	3ms	ראה	906		see

ChVs	Form	Stem	Tnse	PGN	Root	BDB	Sfx	Meaning
42: 1	יאמר	qal	wci	3ms	אמר	55		say
	תתראו	hith	impf	2mp	ראה	906		look at each
42: 2	יאמר	qal	wci	3ms	אמר	55		say
	שׁמעתי	qal	pft	1cs	שׁמע	1033		hear
	רדו	qal	impv	mp	ירד	432		come down
	שׁברו	qal	impv	mp	שׁבר	991		buy grain
	נחיה	qal	cohm	1cp	חיה	310		live
	נמות	qal	impf	1cp	מות	559		die
42: 3	ירדו	qal	wci	3mp	ירד	432		come down
	שׁבר	qal	infc		שׁבר	991		buy grain
42: 4	שׁלח	qal	pft	3ms	שׁלח	1018		send
	אמר	qal	pft	3ms	אמר	55		say
	יקראנו	qal	impf	3ms	קרא	896	3ms	meet, encounter
42: 5	יבאו	qal	wci	3mp	בוא	97		come in
	שׁבר	qal	infc		שׁבר	991		buy grain
	באים	qal	ptc	mp	בוא	97		come in
	היה	qal	pft	3ms	היה	224		be, become
42: 6	משׁביר	hiph	ptc	ms	שׁבר	991		sell grain
	יבאו	qal	wci	3mp	בוא	97		come in
	ישׁתחוו	hish	wci	3mp	חוה	1005		bow down
42: 7	ירא	qal	wci	3ms	ראה	906		see
	יכרם	hiph	wci	3ms	נכר	647	3mp	regard, notice
	יתנכר	hith	wci	3ms	נכר	647		be recognized
	ידבר	piel	wci	3ms	דבר	180		speak
	יאמר	qal	wci	3ms	אמר	55		say
	באתם	qal	pft	2mp	בוא	97		come in
	יאמרו	qal	wci	3mp	אמר	55		say
	שׁבר	qal	infc		שׁבר	991		buy grain
42: 8	יכר	hiph	wci	3ms	נכר	647		regard, notice
	הכרהו	hiph	pft	3cp	נכר	647	3ms	regard, notice
42: 9	יזכר	qal	wci	3ms	זכר	269		remember
	חלם	qal	pft	3ms	חלם	321		dream
	יאמר	qal	wci	3ms	אמר	55		say
	מרגלים	piel	ptc	mp	רגל	920		slander, spy
	ראות	qal	infc		ראה	906		see
	באתם	qal	pft	2mp	בוא	97		come in
42: 10	יאמרו	qal	wci	3mp	אמר	55		say
	באו	qal	pft	3cp	בוא	97		come in
	שׁבר	qal	infc		שׁבר	991		buy grain
42: 11	היו	qal	pft	3cp	היה	224		be, become
	מרגלים	piel	ptc	mp	רגל	920		slander, spy
42: 12	יאמר	qal	wci	3ms	אמר	55		say
	באתם	qal	pft	2mp	בוא	97		come in
	ראות	qal	infc		ראה	906		see
42: 13	יאמרו	qal	wci	3mp	אמר	55		say
42: 14	יאמר	qal	wci	3ms	אמר	55		say
	דברתי	piel	pft	1cs	דבר	180		speak
	אמר	qal	infc		אמר	55		say
	מרגלים	piel	ptc	mp	רגל	920		slander, spy
42: 15	תבחנו	niph	impf	2mp	בחן	103		be tried
	תצאו	qal	impf	2mp	יצא	422		go out
	בוא	qal	infc		בוא	97		come in
42: 16	שׁלחו	qal	impv	mp	שׁלח	1018		send
	יקח	qal	jusm	3ms	לקח	542		take
42: 16	האסרו	niph	impv	mp	אסר	63		be bound
	יבחנו	niph	jusm	3mp	בחן	103		be tried
	מרגלים	piel	ptc	mp	רגל	920		slander, spy
42: 17	יאסף	qal	wci	3ms	אסף	62		gather
42: 18	יאמר	qal	wci	3ms	אמר	55		say
	עשׂו	qal	impv	mp	עשׂה	793		do, make
	חיו	qal	impv	mp	חיה	310		live
	ירא	qal	ptc	ms	ירא	431		fear
42: 19	יאסר	niph	jusm	3ms	אסר	63		be bound
	לכו	qal	impv	mp	הלך	229		walk, go
	הביאו	hiph	impv	mp	בוא	97		bring in
42: 20	תביאו	hiph	impf	2mp	בוא	97		bring in
	יאמנו	niph	jusm	3mp	אמן	52		be confirmed
	תמותו	qal	impf	2mp	מות	559		die
	יעשׂו	qal	wci	3mp	עשׂה	793		do, make
42: 21	יאמרו	qal	wci	3mp	אמר	55		say
	ראינו	qal	pft	1cp	ראה	906		see
	התחננו	hith	infc		חנן	335	3ms	seek favor
	שׁמענו	qal	pft	1cp	שׁמע	1033		hear
	באה	qal	pft	3fs	בוא	97		come in
42: 22	יען	qal	wci	3ms	ענה	772		answer
	אמר	qal	infc		אמר	55		say
	אמרתי	qal	pft	1cs	אמר	55		say
	אמר	qal	infc		אמר	55		say
	תחטאו	qal	jusm	2mp	חטא	306		sin
	שׁמעתם	qal	pft	2mp	שׁמע	1033		hear
	נדרשׁ	niph	ptc	ms	דרשׁ	205		be sought out
42: 23	ידעו	qal	pft	3cp	ידע	393		know
	שׁמע	qal	ptc	ms	שׁמע	1033		hear
	מליץ	hiph	ptc	ms	ליץ	539		deride
42: 24	יסב	qal	wci	3ms	סבב	685		surround
	יבך	qal	wci	3ms	בכה	113		weep
	ישׁב	qal	wci	3ms	שׁוב	996		turn, return
	ידבר	piel	wci	3ms	דבר	180		speak
	יקח	qal	wci	3ms	לקח	542		take
	יאסר	qal	wci	3ms	אסר	63		tie, bind
42: 25	יצו	piel	wci	3ms	צוה	845		command
	ימלאו	piel	wci	3mp	מלא	569		fill
	השׁיב	hiph	infc		שׁוב	996		bring back
	תת	qal	infc		נתן	678		give, set
	יעשׂ	qal	wci	3ms	עשׂה	793		do, make
42: 26	ישׂאו	qal	wci	3mp	נשׂא	669		lift, carry
	ילכו	qal	wci	3mp	הלך	229		walk, go
42: 27	יפתח	qal	wci	3ms	פתח	834		open
	תת	qal	infc		נתן	678		give, set
	ירא	qal	wci	3ms	ראה	906		see
42: 28	יאמר	qal	wci	3ms	אמר	55		say
	הושׁב	hoph	pft	3ms	שׁוב	996		be returned
	יצא	qal	wci	3ms	יצא	422		go out
	יחרדו	qal	wci	3mp	חרד	353		tremble
	אמר	qal	infc		אמר	55		say
	עשׂה	qal	pft	3ms	עשׂה	793		do, make
42: 29	יבאו	qal	wci	3mp	בוא	97		come in
	יגידו	hiph	wci	3mp	נגד	616		declare, tell

ChVs	Form	Stem	Tnse	PGN	Root	BDB	Sfx	Meaning
42: 29	קרת	qal	ptc	fp	קרה	899		encounter,meet
	אמר	qal	infc		אמר	55		say
42: 30	דבר	piel	pft	3ms	דבר	180		speak
	יתן	qal	wci	3ms	נתן	678		give,set
	מרגלים	piel	ptc	mp	רגל	920		slander,spy
42: 31	נאמר	qal	wci	1cp	אמר	55		say
	היינו	qal	pft	1cp	היה	224		be,become
	מרגלים	piel	ptc	mp	רגל	920		slander,spy
42: 33	יאמר	qal	wci	3ms	אמר	55		say
	אדע	qal	impf	1cs	ידע	393		know
	הניחו	hiph	impv	mp	נוח	628		give rest,put
	קחו	qal	impv	mp	לקח	542		take
	לכו	qal	impv	mp	הלך	229		walk,go
42: 34	הביאו	hiph	impv	mp	בוא	97		bring in
	אדעה	qal	coh	1cs	ידע	393		know
	מרגלים	piel	ptc	mp	רגל	920		slander,spy
	אתן	qal	impf	1cs	נתן	678		give,set
	תסחרו	qal	impf	2mp	סחר	695		go around
42: 35	יהי	qal	wci	3ms	היה	224		be,become
	מריקים	hiph	ptc	mp	ריק	937		make empty
	יראו	qal	wci	3mp	ראה	906		see
	ייראו	qal	wci	3mp	ירא	431		fear
42: 36	יאמר	qal	wci	3ms	אמר	55		say
	שׁכלתם	piel	pft	2mp	שׁכל	1013		make childless
	תקחו	qal	impf	2mp	לקח	542		take
	היו	qal	pft	3cp	היה	224		be,become
42: 37	יאמר	qal	wci	3ms	אמר	55		say
	אמר	qal	infc		אמר	55		say
	תמית	hiph	impf	2ms	מות	559		kill
	אביאנו	hiph	impf	1cs	בוא	97	3ms	bring in
	תנה	qal	impv	ms	נתן	678		give,set
	אשׁיבנו	hiph	impf	1cs	שׁוב	996	3ms	bring back
42: 38	יאמר	qal	wci	3ms	אמר	55		say
	ירד	qal	impf	3ms	ירד	432		come down
	מת	qal	pft	3ms	מות	559		die
	נשׁאר	niph	ptc	ms	שׁאר	983		be left
	קראהו	qal	wcp	3ms	קרא	896	3ms	meet,encounter
	תלכו	qal	impf	2mp	הלך	229		walk,go
	הורדתם	hiph	wcp	2mp	ירד	432		bring down
43: 2	יהי	qal	wci	3ms	היה	224		be,become
	כלו	piel	pft	3cp	כלה	477		complete,finish
	אכל	qal	infc		אכל	37		eat,devour
	הביאו	hiph	pft	3cp	בוא	97		bring in
	יאמר	qal	wci	3ms	אמר	55		say
	שׁבו	qal	impv	mp	שׁוב	996		turn,return
	שׁברו	qal	impv	mp	שׁבר	991		buy grain
43: 3	יאמר	qal	wci	3ms	אמר	55		say
	אמר	qal	infc		אמר	55		say
	העד	hiph	infa		עוד	729		testify,warn
	העד	hiph	pft	3ms	עוד	729		testify,warn
	אמר	qal	infc		אמר	55		say
	תראו	qal	impf	2mp	ראה	906		see
43: 4	משׁלח	piel	ptc	ms	שׁלח	1018		send away,shoot
	נרדה	qal	coh	1cp	ירד	432		come down
43: 4	נשׁברה	qal	coh	1cp	שׁבר	991		buy grain
43: 5	משׁלח	piel	ptc	ms	שׁלח	1018		send away,shoot
	נרד	qal	impf	1cp	ירד	432		come down
	אמר	qal	pft	3ms	אמר	55		say
	תראו	qal	impf	2mp	ראה	906		see
43: 6	יאמר	qal	wci	3ms	אמר	55		say
	הרעתם	hiph	pft	2mp	רעע	949		hurt,do evil
	הגיד	hiph	infc		נגד	616		declare,tell
43: 7	יאמרו	qal	wci	3mp	אמר	55		say
	שׁאול	qal	infa		שׁאל	981		ask,borrow
	שׁאל	qal	pft	3ms	שׁאל	981		ask,borrow
	אמר	qal	infc		אמר	55		say
	נגד	hiph	wci	1cp	נגד	616		declare,tell
	ידוע	qal	infa		ידע	393		know
	נדע	qal	impf	1cp	ידע	393		know
	יאמר	qal	impf	3ms	אמר	55		say
	הורידו	hiph	impv	mp	ירד	432		bring down
43: 8	יאמר	qal	wci	3ms	אמר	55		say
	שׁלחה	qal	impv	ms	שׁלח	1018		send
	נקומה	qal	coh	1cp	קום	877		arise,stand
	נלכה	qal	coh	1cp	הלך	229		walk,go
	נחיה	qal	cohm	1cp	חיה	310		live
	נמות	qal	impf	1cp	מות	559		die
43: 9	אערבנו	qal	impf	1cs	ערב	786	3ms	take on pledge
	תבקשׁנו	piel	impf	2ms	בקשׁ	134	3ms	seek
	הביאתיו	hiph	pft	1cs	בוא	97	3ms	bring in
	הצגתיו	hiph	wcp	1cs	יצג	426	3ms	place,establish
	חטאתי	qal	wcp	1cs	חטא	306		sin
43: 10	התמהמהנו	htpp	pft	1cp	מהה	554		tarry
	שׁבנו	qal	pft	1cp	שׁוב	996		turn,return
43: 11	יאמר	qal	wci	3ms	אמר	55		say
	עשׂו	qal	impv	mp	עשׂה	793		do,make
	קחו	qal	impv	mp	לקח	542		take
	הורידו	hiph	impv	mp	ירד	432		bring down
43: 12	קחו	qal	impv	mp	לקח	542		take
	מושׁב	hoph	ptc	ms	שׁוב	996		be returned
	תשׁיבו	hiph	impf	2mp	שׁוב	996		bring back
43: 13	קחו	qal	impv	mp	לקח	542		take
	קומו	qal	impv	mp	קום	877		arise,stand
	שׁובו	qal	impv	mp	שׁוב	996		turn,return
43: 14	יתן	qal	jusm	3ms	נתן	678		give,set
	שׁלח	piel	wcp	3ms	שׁלח	1018		send away,shoot
	שׁכלתי	qal	pft	1cs	שׁכל	1013		be bereaved
	שׁכלתי	qal	pft	1cs	שׁכל	1013		be bereaved
43: 15	יקחו	qal	wci	3mp	לקח	542		take
	לקחו	qal	pft	3cp	לקח	542		take
	יקמו	qal	wci	3mp	קום	877		arise,stand
	ירדו	qal	wci	3mp	ירד	432		come down
	יעמדו	qal	wci	3mp	עמד	763		stand,stop
43: 16	ירא	qal	wci	3ms	ראה	906		see
	יאמר	qal	wci	3ms	אמר	55		say
	הבא	hiph	impv	ms	בוא	97		bring in
	טבח	qal	impv	ms	טבח	370		slaughter
	הכן	hiph	impv	ms	כון	465		fix,prepare

ChVs	Form	Stem	Tnse	PGN	Root	BDB	Sfx	Meaning
43:16	יאכלו	qal	impf	3mp	אכל	37		eat,devour
43:17	יעש	qal	wci	3ms	עשה	793		do,make
	אמר	qal	pft	3ms	אמר	55		say
	יבא	hiph	wci	3ms	בוא	97		bring in
43:18	ייראו	qal	wci	3mp	ירא	431		fear
	הובאו	hoph	pft	3cp	בוא	97		be brought
	יאמרו	qal	wci	3mp	אמר	55		say
	שב	qal	ptc	ms	שוב	996		turn,return
	מובאים	hoph	ptc	mp	בוא	97		be brought
	התגלל	htpo	infc		גלל	164		roll oneself
	התנפל	hith	infc		נפל	656		throw oneself
	קחת	qal	infc		לקח	542		take
43:19	יגשו	qal	wci	3mp	נגש	620		draw near
	ידברו	piel	wci	3mp	דבר	180		speak
43:20	יאמרו	qal	wci	3mp	אמר	55		say
	ירד	qal	infa		ירד	432		come down
	ירדנו	qal	pft	1cp	ירד	432		come down
	שבר	qal	infc		שבר	991		buy grain
43:21	יהי	qal	wci	3ms	היה	224		be,become
	באנו	qal	pft	1cp	בוא	97		come in
	נפתחה	qal	wci	1cp	פתח	834		open
	נשב	hiph	wci	1cp	שוב	996		bring back
43:22	הורדנו	hiph	pft	1cp	ירד	432		bring down
	שבר	qal	infc		שבר	991		buy grain
	ידענו	qal	pft	1cp	ידע	393		know
	שם	qal	pft	3ms	שים	962		put,set
43:23	יאמר	qal	wci	3ms	אמר	55		say
	תיראו	qal	jusm	2mp	ירא	431		fear
	נתן	qal	pft	3ms	נתן	678		give,set
	בא	qal	pft	3ms	בוא	97		come in
	יוצא	hiph	wci	3ms	יצא	422		bring out
43:24	יבא	hiph	wci	3ms	בוא	97		bring in
	יתן	qal	wci	3ms	נתן	678		give,set
	ירחצו	qal	wci	3mp	רחץ	934		wash,bathe
	יתן	qal	wci	3ms	נתן	678		give,set
43:25	יכינו	hiph	wci	3mp	כון	465		fix,prepare
	בוא	qal	infc		בוא	97		come in
	שמעו	qal	pft	3cp	שמע	1033		hear
	יאכלו	qal	impf	3mp	אכל	37		eat,devour
43:26	יבא	qal	wci	3ms	בוא	97		come in
	יביאו	hiph	wci	3mp	בוא	97		bring in
	ישתחוו	hish	wci	3mp	חוה	1005		bow down
43:27	ישאל	qal	wci	3ms	שאל	981		ask,borrow
	יאמר	qal	wci	3ms	אמר	55		say
	אמרתם	qal	pft	2mp	אמר	55		say
43:28	יאמרו	qal	wci	3mp	אמר	55		say
	יקדו	qal	wci	3mp	קדד	869		bow down
	ישתחוk	hish	wci	3ms	חוה	1005		bow down
	ישתחווq	hish	wci	3mp	חוה	1005		bow down
43:29	ישא	qal	wci	3ms	נשא	669		lift,carry
	ירא	qal	wci	3ms	ראה	906		see
	יאמר	qal	wci	3ms	אמר	55		say
	אמרתם	qal	pft	2mp	אמר	55		say
	יאמר	qal	wci	3ms	אמר	55		say

ChVs	Form	Stem	Tnse	PGN	Root	BDB	Sfx	Meaning
43:29	יחנך	qal	jusm	3ms	חנן	335	2ms	show favor
43:30	ימהר	piel	wci	3ms	מהר	554		hasten
	נכמרו	niph	pft	3cp	כמר	485		grow warm
	יבקש	piel	wci	3ms	בקש	134		seek
	בכות	qal	infc		בכה	113		weep
	יבא	qal	wci	3ms	בוא	97		come in
	יבך	qal	wci	3ms	בכה	113		weep
43:31	ירחץ	qal	wci	3ms	רחץ	934		wash,bathe
	יצא	qal	wci	3ms	יצא	422		go out
	יתאפק	hith	wci	3ms	אפק	67		restrain self
	יאמר	qal	wci	3ms	אמר	55		say
	שימו	qal	impv	mp	שים	962		put,set
43:32	ישימו	qal	wci	3mp	שים	962		put,set
	אכלים	qal	ptc	mp	אכל	37		eat,devour
	יוכלון	qal	impf	3mp	יכל	407		be able
	אכל	qal	infc		אכל	37		eat,devour
43:33	ישבו	qal	wci	3mp	ישב	442		sit,dwell
	יתמהו	qal	wci	3mp	תמה	1069		be astounded
43:34	ישא	qal	wci	3ms	נשא	669		lift,carry
	תרב	qal	wci	3fs	רבה	915		be many,great
	ישתו	qal	wci	3mp	שתה	1059		drink
	ישכרו	qal	wci	3mp	שכר	1016		be drunk
44:1	יצו	piel	wci	3ms	צוה	845		command
	אמר	qal	infc		אמר	55		say
	מלא	piel	impv	ms	מלא	569		fill
	יוכלון	qal	impf	3mp	יכל	407		be able
	שאת	qal	infc		נשא	669		lift,carry
	שים	qal	impv	ms	שים	962		put,set
44:2	תשים	qal	impf	2ms	שים	962		put,set
	יעש	qal	wci	3ms	עשה	793		do,make
	דבר	piel	pft	3ms	דבר	180		speak
44:3	אור	qal	pft	3ms	אור	21		become light
	שלחו	pual	pft	3cp	שלח	1018		be sent off
44:4	יצאו	qal	pft	3cp	יצא	422		go out
	הרחיקו	hiph	pft	3cp	רחק	934		put far away
	אמר	qal	pft	3ms	אמר	55		say
	קום	qal	impv	ms	קום	877		arise,stand
	רדף	qal	impv	ms	רדף	922		pursue
	השגתם	hiph	wcp	2ms	נשג	673	3mp	reach,overtake
	אמרת	qal	wcp	2ms	אמר	55		say
	שלמתם	piel	pft	2mp	שלם	1022		finish,reward
44:5	ישתה	qal	impf	3ms	שתה	1059		drink
	נחש	piel	infa		נחש	638		divine
	ינחש	piel	impf	3ms	נחש	638		divine
	הרעתם	hiph	pft	2mp	רעע	949		hurt,do evil
	עשיתם	qal	pft	2mp	עשה	793		do,make
44:6	ישגם	hiph	wci	3ms	נשג	673	3mp	reach,overtake
	ידבר	piel	wci	3ms	דבר	180		speak
44:7	יאמרו	qal	wci	3mp	אמר	55		say
	ידבר	piel	impf	3ms	דבר	180		speak
	עשות	qal	infc		עשה	793		do,make
44:8	מצאנו	qal	pft	1cp	מצא	592		find
	השיבנו	hiph	pft	1cp	שוב	996		bring back
	נגנב	qal	impf	1cp	גנב	170		steal

ChVs	Form	Stem	Tnse	PGN	Root	BDB	Sfx	Meaning
44:9	ימצא	niph	impf	3ms	מצא	592		be found
	מת	qal	wcp	3ms	מות	559		die
	נהיה	qal	impf	1cp	היה	224		be, become
44:10	יאמר	qal	wci	3ms	אמר	55		say
	ימצא	niph	impf	3ms	מצא	592		be found
	יהיה	qal	impf	3ms	היה	224		be, become
	תהיו	qal	impf	2mp	היה	224		be, become
44:11	ימהרו	piel	wci	3mp	מהר	554		hasten
	יורדו	hiph	wci	3mp	ירד	432		bring down
	יפתחו	qal	wci	3mp	פתח	834		open
44:12	יחפשׂ	piel	wci	3ms	חפשׂ	344		search for
	החל	hiph	pft	3ms	חלל	320		begin, profane
	כלה	piel	pft	3ms	כלה	477		complete, finish
	ימצא	niph	wci	3ms	מצא	592		be found
44:13	יקרעו	qal	wci	3mp	קרע	902		tear, rend
	יעמס	qal	wci	3ms	עמס	770		load, carry
	ישׁבו	qal	wci	3mp	שׁוב	996		turn, return
44:14	יבא	qal	wci	3ms	בוא	97		come in
	יפלו	qal	wci	3mp	נפל	656		fall
44:15	יאמר	qal	wci	3ms	אמר	55		say
	עשׂיתם	qal	pft	2mp	עשׂה	793		do, make
	ידעתם	qal	pft	2mp	ידע	393		know
	נחשׁ	piel	infa		נחשׁ	638		divine
	ינחשׁ	piel	impf	3ms	נחשׁ	638		divine
44:16	יאמר	qal	wci	3ms	אמר	55		say
	נאמר	qal	impf	1cp	אמר	55		say
	נדבר	piel	impf	1cp	דבר	180		speak
	נצטדק	hith	impf	1cp	צדק	842		justify oneself
	מצא	qal	pft	3ms	מצא	592		find
	נמצא	niph	pft	3ms	מצא	592		be found
44:17	יאמר	qal	wci	3ms	אמר	55		say
	עשׂות	qal	infc		עשׂה	793		do, make
	נמצא	niph	pft	3ms	מצא	592		be found
	יהיה	qal	impf	3ms	היה	224		be, become
	עלו	qal	impv	mp	עלה	748		go up
44:18	יגשׁ	qal	wci	3ms	נגשׁ	620		draw near
	יאמר	qal	wci	3ms	אמר	55		say
	ידבר	piel	jusm	3ms	דבר	180		speak
	יחר	qal	jus	3ms	חרה	354		be kindled, burn
44:19	שׁאל	qal	pft	3ms	שׁאל	981		ask, borrow
	אמר	qal	infc		אמר	55		say
44:20	נאמר	qal	wci	1cp	אמר	55		say
	מת	qal	pft	3ms	מות	559		die
	יותר	niph	wci	3ms	יתר	451		be left, remain
	אהבו	qal	pft	3ms	אהב	12	3ms	love
44:21	תאמר	qal	wci	2ms	אמר	55		say
	הורדהו	hiph	impv	mp	ירד	432	3ms	bring down
	אשׂימה	qal	coh	1cs	שׂים	962		put, set
44:22	נאמר	qal	wci	1cp	אמר	55		say
	יוכל	qal	impf	3ms	יכל	407		be able
	עזב	qal	infc		עזב	736		leave, loose
	עזב	qal	wcp	3ms	עזב	736		leave, loose
	מת	qal	wcp	3ms	מות	559		die
44:23	תאמר	qal	wci	2ms	אמר	55		say
44:23	ירד	qal	impf	3ms	ירד	432		come down
	תספון	hiph	impf	2mp	יסף	414		add, do again
	ראות	qal	infc		ראה	906		see
44:24	יהי	qal	wci	3ms	היה	224		be, become
	עלינו	qal	pft	1cp	עלה	748		go up
	נגד	hiph	wci	1cp	נגד	616		declare, tell
44:25	יאמר	qal	wci	3ms	אמר	55		say
	שׁבו	qal	impv	mp	שׁוב	996		turn, return
	שׁברו	qal	impv	mp	שׁבר	991		buy grain
44:26	נאמר	qal	wci	1cp	אמר	55		say
	נוכל	qal	impf	1cp	יכל	407		be able
	רדת	qal	infc		ירד	432		come down
	ירדנו	qal	wcp	1cp	ירד	432		come down
	נוכל	qal	impf	1cp	יכל	407		be able
	ראות	qal	infc		ראה	906		see
44:27	יאמר	qal	wci	3ms	אמר	55		say
	ידעתם	qal	pft	2mp	ידע	393		know
	ילדה	qal	pft	3fs	ילד	408		bear, beget
44:28	יצא	qal	wci	3ms	יצא	422		go out
	אמר	qal	wci	1cs	אמר	55		say
	טרף	qal	infa		טרף	382		tear, rend
	טרף	qalp	pft	3ms	טרף	382		be torn
	ראיתיו	qal	pft	1cs	ראה	906	3ms	see
44:29	לקחתם	qal	wcp	2mp	לקח	542		take
	קרהו	qal	wcp	3ms	קרה	899	3ms	encounter, meet
	הורדתם	hiph	wcp	2mp	ירד	432		bring down
44:30	באי	qal	infc		בוא	97	1cs	come in
	קשׁורה	qal	pptc	fs	קשׁר	905		bind
44:31	היה	qal	wcp	3ms	היה	224		be, become
	ראותו	qal	infc		ראה	906	3ms	see
	מת	qal	wcp	3ms	מות	559		die
	הורידו	hiph	wcp	3cp	ירד	432		bring down
44:32	ערב	qal	pft	3ms	ערב	786		take on pledge
	אמר	qal	infc		אמר	55		say
	אביאנו	hiph	impf	1cs	בוא	97	3ms	bring in
	חטאתי	qal	wcp	1cs	חטא	306		sin
44:33	ישׁב	qal	jus	3ms	ישׁב	442		sit, dwell
	יעל	qal	jus	3ms	עלה	748		go up
44:34	אעלה	qal	impf	1cs	עלה	748		go up
	אראה	qal	impf	1cs	ראה	906		see
	ימצא	qal	impf	3ms	מצא	592		find
45:1	יכל	qal	pft	3ms	יכל	407		be able
	התאפק	hith	infc		אפק	67		restrain self
	נצבים	niph	ptc	mp	נצב	662		stand
	יקרא	qal	wci	3ms	קרא	894		call, proclaim
	הוציאו	hiph	impv	mp	יצא	422		bring out
	עמד	qal	pft	3ms	עמד	763		stand, stop
	התודע	hith	infc		ידע	393		make self known
45:2	יתן	qal	wci	3ms	נתן	678		give, set
	ישׁמעו	qal	wci	3mp	שׁמע	1033		hear
	ישׁמע	qal	wci	3ms	שׁמע	1033		hear
45:3	יאמר	qal	wci	3ms	אמר	55		say
	יכלו	qal	pft	3cp	יכל	407		be able
	ענות	qal	infc		ענה	772		answer

ChVs	Form	Stem	Tnse	PGN	Root	BDB	Sfx	Meaning
45:3	נבהלו	niph	pft	3cp	בהל	96		be disturbed
45:4	יאמר	qal	wci	3ms	אמר	55		say
	גשו	qal	impv	mp	נגש	620		draw near
	יגשו	qal	wci	3mp	נגש	620		draw near
	יאמר	qal	wci	3ms	אמר	55		say
	מכרתם	qal	pft	2mp	מכר	569		sell
45:5	תעצבו	niph	jusm	2mp	עצב	780		be pained
	יחר	qal	jus	3ms	חרה	354		be kindled, burn
	מכרתם	qal	pft	2mp	מכר	569		sell
	שלחני	qal	pft	3ms	שלח	1018	1cs	send
45:7	ישלחני	qal	wci	3ms	שלח	1018	1cs	send
	שום	qal	infc		שים	962		put,set
	החיות	hiph	infc		חיה	310		preserve
45:8	שלחתם	qal	pft	2mp	שלח	1018		send
	ישימני	qal	wci	3ms	שים	962	1cs	put,set
	משל	qal	ptc	ms	משל	605		rule
45:9	מהרו	piel	impv	mp	מהר	554		hasten
	עלו	qal	impv	mp	עלה	748		go up
	אמרתם	qal	wcp	2mp	אמר	55		say
	אמר	qal	pft	3ms	אמר	55		say
	שמני	qal	pft	3ms	שים	962	1cs	put,set
	רדה	qal	impv	ms	ירד	432		come down
	תעמד	qal	jusm	2ms	עמד	763		stand,stop
45:10	ישבת	qal	wcp	2ms	ישב	442		sit,dwell
	היית	qal	wcp	2ms	היה	224		be,become
45:11	כלכלתי	pilp	wcp	1cs	כול	465		support
	תורש	niph	impf	2ms	ירש	439		be impoverished
45:12	ראות	qal	ptc	fp	ראה	906		see
	מדבר	piel	ptc	ms	דבר	180		speak
45:13	הגדתם	hiph	wcp	2mp	נגד	616		declare,tell
	ראיתם	qal	pft	2mp	ראה	906		see
	מהרתם	piel	wcp	2mp	מהר	554		hasten
	הורדתם	hiph	wcp	2mp	ירד	432		bring down
45:14	יפל	qal	wci	3ms	נפל	656		fall
	יבך	qal	wci	3ms	בכה	113		weep
	בכה	qal	pft	3ms	בכה	113		weep
45:15	ינשק	piel	wci	3ms	נשק	676		kiss
	יבך	qal	wci	3ms	בכה	113		weep
	דברו	piel	pft	3cp	דבר	180		speak
45:16	נשמע	niph	pft	3ms	שמע	1033		be heard
	אמר	qal	infc		אמר	55		say
	באו	qal	pft	3cp	בוא	97		come in
	ייטב	qal	wci	3ms	יטב	405		be good
45:17	יאמר	qal	wci	3ms	אמר	55		say
	אמר	qal	impv	ms	אמר	55		say
	עשו	qal	impv	mp	עשה	793		do,make
	טענו	qal	impv	mp	טען	381		load
	לכו	qal	impv	mp	הלך	229		walk,go
	באו	qal	impv	mp	בוא	97		come in
45:18	קחו	qal	impv	mp	לקח	542		take
	באו	qal	impv	mp	בוא	97		come in
	אתנה	qal	coh	1cs	נתן	678		give,set
	אכלו	qal	impv	mp	אכל	37		eat,devour
45:19	צויתה	pual	pft	2ms	צוה	845		be commanded
45:19	עשו	qal	impv	mp	עשה	793		do,make
	קחו	qal	impv	mp	לקח	542		take
	נשאתם	qal	wcp	2mp	נשא	669		lift,carry
	באתם	qal	wcp	2mp	בוא	97		come in
45:20	תחס	qal	jus	2ms	חוס	299		pity
45:21	יעשו	qal	wci	3mp	עשה	793		do,make
	יתן	qal	wci	3ms	נתן	678		give,set
	יתן	qal	wci	3ms	נתן	678		give,set
45:22	נתן	qal	pft	3ms	נתן	678		give,set
	נתן	qal	pft	3ms	נתן	678		give,set
45:23	שלח	qal	pft	3ms	שלח	1018		send
	נשאים	qal	ptc	mp	נשא	669		lift,carry
	נשאת	qal	ptc	fp	נשא	669		lift,carry
45:24	ישלח	piel	wci	3ms	שלח	1018		send away,shoot
	ילכו	qal	wci	3mp	הלך	229		walk,go
	יאמר	qal	wci	3ms	אמר	55		say
	תרגזו	qal	jusm	2mp	רגז	919		quake
45:25	יעלו	qal	wci	3mp	עלה	748		go up
	יבאו	qal	wci	3mp	בוא	97		come in
45:26	יגדו	hiph	wci	3mp	נגד	616		declare,tell
	אמר	qal	infc		אמר	55		say
	משל	qal	ptc	ms	משל	605		rule
	יפג	qal	wci	3ms	פוג	806		grow numb
	האמין	hiph	pft	3ms	אמן	52		believe
45:27	ידברו	piel	wci	3mp	דבר	180		speak
	דבר	piel	pft	3ms	דבר	180		speak
	ירא	qal	wci	3ms	ראה	906		see
	שלח	qal	pft	3ms	שלח	1018		send
	שאת	qal	infc		נשא	669		lift,carry
	תחי	qal	wci	3fs	חיה	310		live
45:28	יאמר	qal	wci	3ms	אמר	55		say
	אלכה	qal	coh	1cs	הלך	229		walk,go
	אראנו	qal	cohm	1cs	ראה	906	3ms	see
	אמות	qal	impf	1cs	מות	559		die
46:1	יסע	qal	wci	3ms	נסע	652		pull up,set out
	יבא	qal	wci	3ms	בוא	97		come in
	יזבח	qal	wci	3ms	זבח	256		slaughter
46:2	יאמר	qal	wci	3ms	אמר	55		say
	יאמר	qal	wci	3ms	אמר	55		say
	יאמר	qal	wci	3ms	אמר	55		say
46:3	יאמר	qal	wci	3ms	אמר	55		say
	תירא	qal	jusm	2ms	ירא	431		fear
	רדה	qal	infc		ירד	432		come down
	אשימך	qal	impf	1cs	שים	962	2ms	put,set
46:4	ארד	qal	impf	1cs	ירד	432		come down
	אעלך	hiph	impf	1cs	עלה	748	2ms	bring up,offer
	עלה	qal	infa		עלה	748		go up
	ישית	qal	impf	3ms	שית	1011		put,set
46:5	יקם	qal	wci	3ms	קום	877		arise,stand
	ישאו	qal	wci	3mp	נשא	669		lift,carry
	שלח	qal	pft	3ms	שלח	1018		send
	שאת	qal	infc		נשא	669		lift,carry
46:6	יקחו	qal	wci	3mp	לקח	542		take
	רכשו	qal	pft	3cp	רכש	940		collect

ChVs	Form	Stem	Tnse	PGN	Root	BDB	Sfx	Meaning
46: 6	יבאו	qal	wci	3mp	בוא	97		come in
46: 7	הביא	hiph	pft	3ms	בוא	97		bring in
46: 8	באים	qal	ptc	mp	בוא	97		come in
46: 12	ימת	qal	wci	3ms	מות	559		die
	יהיו	qal	wci	3mp	היה	224		be, become
46: 15	ילדה	qal	pft	3fs	ילד	408		bear, beget
46: 18	נתן	qal	pft	3ms	נתן	678		give, set
	תלד	qal	wci	3fs	ילד	408		bear, beget
46: 20	יולד	niph	wci	3ms	ילד	408		be born
	ילדה	qal	pft	3fs	ילד	408		bear, beget
46: 22	ילד	qalp	pft	3ms	ילד	408		be born
46: 25	נתן	qal	pft	3ms	נתן	678		give, set
	תלד	qal	wci	3fs	ילד	408		bear, beget
46: 26	באה	qal	ptc	fs	בוא	97		come in
	יצאי	qal	ptc	mp	יצא	422		go out
46: 27	ילד	qalp	pft	3ms	ילד	408		be born
	באה	qal	pft	3fs	בוא	97		come in
46: 28	שׁלח	qal	pft	3ms	שׁלח	1018		send
	הורת	hiph	infc		ירה	434		shoot, teach
	יבאו	qal	wci	3mp	בוא	97		come in
46: 29	יאסר	qal	wci	3ms	אסר	63		tie, bind
	יעל	qal	wci	3ms	עלה	748		go up
	קראת	qal	infc		קרא	896		meet, encounter
	ירא	niph	wci	3ms	ראה	906		appear, be seen
	יפל	qal	wci	3ms	נפל	656		fall
	יבך	qal	wci	3ms	בכה	113		weep
46: 30	יאמר	qal	wci	3ms	אמר	55		say
	אמותה	qal	coh	1cs	מות	559		die
	ראותי	qal	infc		ראה	906	1cs	see
46: 31	יאמר	qal	wci	3ms	אמר	55		say
	אעלה	qal	cohm	1cs	עלה	748		go up
	אגידה	hiph	coh	1cs	נגד	616		declare, tell
	אמרה	qal	coh	1cs	אמר	55		say
	באו	qal	pft	3cp	בוא	97		come in
46: 32	רעי	qal	ptc	mp	רעה	944		pasture, tend
	היו	qal	pft	3cp	היה	224		be, become
	הביאו	hiph	pft	3cp	בוא	97		bring in
46: 33	היה	qal	wcp	3ms	היה	224		be, become
	יקרא	qal	impf	3ms	קרא	894		call, proclaim
	אמר	qal	wcp	3ms	אמר	55		say
46: 34	אמרתם	qal	wcp	2mp	אמר	55		say
	היו	qal	pft	3cp	היה	224		be, become
	תשבו	qal	impf	2mp	ישב	442		sit, dwell
	רעה	qal	ptc	ms	רעה	944		pasture, tend
47: 1	יבא	qal	wci	3ms	בוא	97		come in
	יגד	hiph	wci	3ms	נגד	616		declare, tell
	יאמר	qal	wci	3ms	אמר	55		say
	באו	qal	pft	3cp	בוא	97		come in
47: 2	לקח	qal	pft	3ms	לקח	542		take
	יצגם	hiph	wci	3ms	יצג	426	3mp	place, establish
47: 3	יאמר	qal	wci	3ms	אמר	55		say
	יאמרו	qal	wci	3mp	אמר	55		say
	רעה	qal	ptc	ms	רעה	944		pasture, tend
47: 4	יאמרו	qal	wci	3mp	אמר	55		say
47: 4	גור	qal	infc		גור	157		sojourn
	באנו	qal	pft	1cp	בוא	97		come in
	ישבו	qal	jusm	3mp	ישב	442		sit, dwell
47: 5	יאמר	qal	wci	3ms	אמר	55		say
	אמר	qal	infc		אמר	55		say
	באו	qal	pft	3cp	בוא	97		come in
47: 6	הושב	hiph	impv	ms	ישב	442		cause to dwell
	ישבו	qal	jusm	3mp	ישב	442		sit, dwell
	ידעת	qal	pft	2ms	ידע	393		know
	שׂמתם	qal	wcp	2ms	שׂים	962	3mp	put, set
47: 7	יבא	hiph	wci	3ms	בוא	97		bring in
	יעמדהו	hiph	wci	3ms	עמד	763	3ms	set up, raise
	יברך	piel	wci	3ms	ברך	138		bless
47: 8	יאמר	qal	wci	3ms	אמר	55		say
47: 9	יאמר	qal	wci	3ms	אמר	55		say
	היו	qal	pft	3cp	היה	224		be, become
	השׂיגו	hiph	pft	3cp	נשׂג	673		reach, overtake
47: 10	יברך	piel	wci	3ms	ברך	138		bless
	יצא	qal	wci	3ms	יצא	422		go out
47: 11	יושב	hiph	wci	3ms	ישב	442		cause to dwell
	יתן	qal	wci	3ms	נתן	678		give, set
	צוה	piel	pft	3ms	צוה	845		command
47: 12	יכלכל	pilp	wci	3ms	כול	465		support
47: 13	תלה	qal	wci	3fs	להה	529		languish
47: 14	ילקט	piel	wci	3ms	לקט	544		gather
	נמצא	niph	ptc	ms	מצא	592		be found
	שׁברים	qal	ptc	mp	שׁבר	991		buy grain
	יבא	hiph	wci	3ms	בוא	97		bring in
47: 15	יתם	qal	wci	3ms	תמם	1070		be finished
	יבאו	qal	wci	3mp	בוא	97		come in
	אמר	qal	infc		אמר	55		say
	הבה	qal	impv	ms	יהב	396		give
	נמות	qal	impf	1cp	מות	559		die
	אפס	qal	pft	3ms	אפס	67		cease
47: 16	יאמר	qal	wci	3ms	אמר	55		say
	הבו	qal	impv	mp	יהב	396		give
	אתנה	qal	coh	1cs	נתן	678		give, set
	אפס	qal	pft	3ms	אפס	67		cease
47: 17	יביאו	hiph	wci	3mp	בוא	97		bring in
	יתן	qal	wci	3ms	נתן	678		give, set
	ינהלם	piel	wci	3ms	נהל	624	3mp	lead, refresh
47: 18	תתם	qal	wci	3fs	תמם	1070		be finished
	יבאו	qal	wci	3mp	בוא	97		come in
	יאמרו	qal	wci	3mp	אמר	55		say
	נכחד	piel	impf	1cp	כחד	470		hide
	תם	qal	pft	3ms	תמם	1070		be finished
	נשׁאר	niph	pft	3ms	שׁאר	983		be left
47: 19	נמות	qal	impf	1cp	מות	559		die
	קנה	qal	impv	ms	קנה	888		get, buy
	נהיה	qal	cohm	1cp	היה	224		be, become
	תן	qal	impv	ms	נתן	678		give, set
	נחיה	qal	cohm	1cp	חיה	310		live
	נמות	qal	impf	1cp	מות	559		die
	תשׁם	qal	impf	3fs	ישׁם	445		be desolate

ChVs	Form	Stem	Tnse	PGN	Root	BDB	Sfx	Meaning
47:20	יקן	qal	wci	3ms	קנה	888		get,buy
	מכרו	qal	pft	3cp	מכר	569		sell
	חזק	qal	pft	3ms	חזק	304		be strong
	תהי	qal	wci	3fs	היה	224		be,become
47:21	העביר	hiph	pft	3ms	עבר	716		cause to pass
47:22	קנה	qal	pft	3ms	קנה	888		get,buy
	אכלו	qal	wcp	3cp	אכל	37		eat,devour
	נתן	qal	pft	3ms	נתן	678		give,set
	מכרו	qal	pft	3cp	מכר	569		sell
47:23	יאמר	qal	wci	3ms	אמר	55		say
	קניתי	qal	pft	1cs	קנה	888		get,buy
	זרעתם	qal	wcp	2mp	זרע	281		sow
47:24	היה	qal	wcp	3ms	היה	224		be,become
	נתתם	qal	wcp	2mp	נתן	678		give,set
	יהיה	qal	impf	3ms	היה	224		be,become
	אכל	qal	infc		אכל	37		eat,devour
47:25	יאמרו	qal	wci	3mp	אמר	55		say
	החיתנו	hiph	pft	2ms	חיה	310	1cp	preserve
	נמצא	qal	cohm	1cp	מצא	592		find
	היינו	qal	wcp	1cp	היה	224		be,become
47:26	ישׂם	qal	wci	3ms	שׂים	962		put,set
	היתה	qal	pft	3fs	היה	224		be,become
47:27	ישׁב	qal	wci	3ms	ישׁב	442		sit,dwell
	יאחזו	niph	wci	3mp	אחז	28		possess,caught
	יפרו	qal	wci	3mp	פרה	826		bear fruit
	ירבו	qal	wci	3mp	רבה	915		be many,great
47:28	יחי	qal	wci	3ms	חיה	310		live
	יהי	qal	wci	3ms	היה	224		be,become
47:29	יקרבו	qal	wci	3mp	קרב	897		approach
	מות	qal	infc		מות	559		die
	יקרא	qal	wci	3ms	קרא	894		call,proclaim
	יאמר	qal	wci	3ms	אמר	55		say
	מצאתי	qal	pft	1cs	מצא	592		find
	שׂים	qal	impv	ms	שׂים	962		put,set
	עשׂית	qal	wcp	2ms	עשׂה	793		do,make
	תקברני	qal	jusm	2ms	קבר	868	1cs	bury
47:30	שׁכבתי	qal	wcp	1cs	שׁכב	1011		lie,lie down
	נשׂאתני	qal	wcp	2ms	נשׂא	669	1cs	lift,carry
	קברתני	qal	wcp	2ms	קבר	868	1cs	bury
	יאמר	qal	wci	3ms	אמר	55		say
	אעשׂה	qal	impf	1cs	עשׂה	793		do,make
47:31	יאמר	qal	wci	3ms	אמר	55		say
	השׁבעה	niph	impv	ms	שׁבע	989		swear
	ישׁבע	niph	wci	3ms	שׁבע	989		swear
	ישׁתחו	hish	wci	3ms	חוה	1005		bow down
48:1	יהי	qal	wci	3ms	היה	224		be,become
	יאמר	qal	wci	3ms	אמר	55		say
	חלה	qal	ptc	ms	חלה	317		be weak,sick
	יקח	qal	wci	3ms	לקח	542		take
48:2	יגד	hiph	wci	3ms	נגד	616		declare,tell
	יאמר	qal	wci	3ms	אמר	55		say
	בא	qal	pft	3ms	בוא	97		come in
	יתחזק	hith	wci	3ms	חזק	304		strengthen self
	ישׁב	qal	wci	3ms	ישׁב	442		sit,dwell
48:3	יאמר	qal	wci	3ms	אמר	55		say
	נראה	niph	pft	3ms	ראה	906		appear,be seen
	יברך	piel	wci	3ms	ברך	138		bless
48:4	יאמר	qal	wci	3ms	אמר	55		say
	מפרך	hiph	ptc	ms	פרה	826	2ms	make fruitful
	הרביתך	hiph	wcp	1cs	רבה	915	2ms	make many
	נתתיך	qal	wcp	1cs	נתן	678	2ms	give,set
	נתתי	qal	wcp	1cs	נתן	678		give,set
48:5	נולדים	niph	ptc	mp	ילד	408		be born
	באי	qal	infc		בוא	97	1cs	come in
	יהיו	qal	impf	3mp	היה	224		be,become
48:6	הולדת	hiph	pft	2ms	ילד	408		beget
	יהיו	qal	impf	3mp	היה	224		be,become
	יקראו	niph	impf	3mp	קרא	894		be called
48:7	באי	qal	infc		בוא	97	1cs	come in
	מתה	qal	pft	3fs	מות	559		die
	בא	qal	infc		בוא	97		come in
	אקברה	qal	wci	1cs	קבר	868	3fs	bury
48:8	ירא	qal	wci	3ms	ראה	906		see
	יאמר	qal	wci	3ms	אמר	55		say
48:9	יאמר	qal	wci	3ms	אמר	55		say
	נתן	qal	pft	3ms	נתן	678		give,set
	יאמר	qal	wci	3ms	אמר	55		say
	קחם	qal	impv	ms	לקח	542	3mp	take
	אברכם	piel	cohm	1cs	ברך	138	3mp	bless
48:10	כבדו	qal	pft	3cp	כבד	457		be heavy
	יוכל	qal	impf	3ms	יכל	407		be able
	ראות	qal	infc		ראה	906		see
	יגשׁ	hiph	wci	3ms	נגשׁ	620		bring near
	ישׁק	qal	wci	3ms	נשׁק	676		kiss
	יחבק	piel	wci	3ms	חבק	287		embrace
48:11	יאמר	qal	wci	3ms	אמר	55		say
	ראה	qal	infc		ראה	906		see
	פללתי	piel	pft	1cs	פלל	813		mediate,judge
	הראה	hiph	pft	3ms	ראה	906		show,exhibit
48:12	יוצא	hiph	wci	3ms	יצא	422		bring out
	ישׁתחו	hish	wci	3ms	חוה	1005		bow down
48:13	יקח	qal	wci	3ms	לקח	542		take
	יגשׁ	hiph	wci	3ms	נגשׁ	620		bring near
48:14	ישׁלח	qal	wci	3ms	שׁלח	1018		send
	ישׁת	qal	wci	3ms	שׁית	1011		put,set
	שׂכל	piel	pft	3ms	שׂכל	968		lay crosswise
48:15	יברך	piel	wci	3ms	ברך	138		bless
	יאמר	qal	wci	3ms	אמר	55		say
	התהלכו	hith	pft	3cp	הלך	229		walk to and fro
	רעה	qal	ptc	ms	רעה	944		pasture,tend
48:16	גאל	qal	ptc	ms	גאל	145		redeem
	יברך	piel	jusm	3ms	ברך	138		bless
	יקרא	niph	jusm	3ms	קרא	894		be called
	ידגו	qal	jusm	3mp	דגה	185		multiply
48:17	ירא	qal	wci	3ms	ראה	906		see
	ישׁית	qal	impf	3ms	שׁית	1011		put,set
	ירע	qal	wci	3ms	רעע	949		be evil
	יתמך	qal	wci	3ms	תמך	1069		grasp,support

ChVs	Form	Stem	Tnse	PGN	Root	BDB	Sfx	Meaning
48:17	הסיר	hiph	infc		סור	693		take away
48:18	יאמר	qal	wci	3ms	אמר	55		say
	שׂים	qal	impv	ms	שׂים	962		put,set
48:19	ימאן	piel	wci	3ms	מאן	549		refuse
	יאמר	qal	wci	3ms	אמר	55		say
	ידעתי	qal	pft	1cs	ידע	393		know
	ידעתי	qal	pft	1cs	ידע	393		know
	יהיה	qal	impf	3ms	היה	224		be,become
	יגדל	qal	impf	3ms	גדל	152		be great,grow
	יגדל	qal	impf	3ms	גדל	152		be great,grow
	יהיה	qal	impf	3ms	היה	224		be,become
48:20	יברכם	piel	wci	3ms	ברך	138	3mp	bless
	אמור	qal	infc		אמר	55		say
	יברך	piel	impf	3ms	ברך	138		bless
	אמר	qal	infc		אמר	55		say
	ישׂמך	qal	jusm	3ms	שׂים	962	2ms	put,set
	ישׂם	qal	wci	3ms	שׂים	962		put,set
48:21	יאמר	qal	wci	3ms	אמר	55		say
	מת	qal	ptc	ms	מות	559		die
	היה	qal	wcp	3ms	היה	224		be,become
	השׁיב	hiph	wcp	3ms	שׁוב	996		bring back
48:22	נתתי	qal	pft	1cs	נתן	678		give,set
	לקחתי	qal	pft	1cs	לקח	542		take
49:1	יקרא	qal	wci	3ms	קרא	894		call,proclaim
	יאמר	qal	wci	3ms	אמר	55		say
	האספו	niph	impv	mp	אסף	62		assemble
	אגידה	hiph	coh	1cs	נגד	616		declare,tell
	יקרא	qal	impf	3ms	קרא	896		meet,encounter
49:2	הקבצו	niph	impv	mp	קבץ	867		assemble,gather
	שׁמעו	qal	impv	mp	שׁמע	1033		hear
	שׁמעו	qal	impv	mp	שׁמע	1033		hear
49:4	תותר	hiph	jus	2ms	יתר	451		leave,spare
	עלית	qal	pft	2ms	עלה	748		go up
	חללת	piel	pft	2ms	חלל	320		pollute
	עלה	qal	pft	3ms	עלה	748		go up
49:6	תבא	qal	jusm	3fs	בוא	97		come in
	תחד	qal	jusm	3fs	יחד	402		be united
	הרגו	qal	pft	3cp	הרג	246		kill
	עקרו	piel	pft	3cp	עקר	785		hamstring
49:7	ארור	qal	pptc	ms	ארר	76		curse
	קשׁתה	qal	pft	3fs	קשׁה	904		be hard,severe
	אחלקם	piel	impf	1cs	חלק	323	3mp	divide
	אפיצם	hiph	impf	1cs	פוץ	806	3mp	scatter
49:8	יודוך	hiph	impf	3mp	ידה	392	2ms	praise
	איביך	qal	ptc	mp	איב	33	2ms	be hostile to
	ישׁתחוו	hish	impf	3mp	חוה	1005		bow down
49:9	עלית	qal	pft	2ms	עלה	748		go up
	כרע	qal	pft	3ms	כרע	502		bow down
	רבץ	qal	pft	3ms	רבץ	918		lie down
	יקימנו	hiph	impf	3ms	קום	877	3ms	raise,build,set
49:10	יסור	qal	impf	3ms	סור	693		turn aside
	מחקק	poel	ptc	ms	חקק	349		prescribe(r)
	יבא	qal	impf	3ms	בוא	97		come in
49:11	אסרי	qal	ptc	ms	אסר	63		tie,bind
49:11	כבס	piel	pft	3ms	כבס	460		wash
49:13	ישׁכן	qal	impf	3ms	שׁכן	1014		settle,dwell
49:14	רבץ	qal	ptc	ms	רבץ	918		lie down
49:15	ירא	qal	wci	3ms	ראה	906		see
	נעמה	qal	pft	3fs	נעם	653		be delightful
	יט	qal	wci	3ms	נטה	639		stretch,incline
	סבל	qal	infc		סבל	687		bear a load
	יהי	qal	wci	3ms	היה	224		be,become
	עבד	qal	ptc	ms	עבד	712		work,serve
49:16	ידין	qal	impf	3ms	דין	192		judge
49:17	יהי	qal	jusf	3ms	היה	224		be,become
	נשׁך	qal	ptc	ms	נשׁך	675		bite
	יפל	qal	wci	3ms	נפל	656		fall
	רכבו	qal	ptc	ms	רכב	938	3ms	mount,ride
49:18	קויתי	piel	pft	1cs	קוה	875		wait for
49:19	יגודנו	qal	impf	3ms	גוד	156	3ms	attack
	יגד	qal	impf	3ms	גוד	156		attack
49:20	יתן	qal	impf	3ms	נתן	678		give,set
49:21	שׁלחה	qal	pptc	fs	שׁלח	1018		send
	נתן	qal	ptc	ms	נתן	678		give,set
49:22	פרת	qal	ptc	fs	פרה	826		bear fruit
	פרת	qal	ptc	fs	פרה	826		bear fruit
	צעדה	qal	pft	3fs	צעד	857		step,march
49:23	ימררהו	piel	wci	3mp	מרר	600	3ms	make bitter
	רבו	qal	pft	3cp	רבב	914		shoot
	ישׂטמהו	qal	wci	3mp	שׂטם	966	3ms	bear a grudge
49:24	תשׁב	qal	wci	3fs	ישׁב	442		sit,dwell
	יפזו	qal	wci	3mp	פזז	808		be supple
	רעה	qal	ptc	ms	רעה	944		pasture,tend
49:25	יעזרך	qal	impf	3ms	עזר	740	2ms	help,aid
	יברכך	piel	impf	3ms	ברך	138	2ms	bless
	רבצת	qal	ptc	fs	רבץ	918		lie down
49:26	גברו	qal	pft	3cp	גבר	149		be strong
	תהיין	qal	jusm	3fp	היה	224		be,become
49:27	יטרף	qal	impf	3ms	טרף	382		tear,rend
	יאכל	qal	impf	3ms	אכל	37		eat,devour
	יחלק	piel	impf	3ms	חלק	323		divide
49:28	דבר	piel	pft	3ms	דבר	180		speak
	יברך	piel	wci	3ms	ברך	138		bless
	ברך	piel	pft	3ms	ברך	138		bless
49:29	יצו	piel	wci	3ms	צוה	845		command
	יאמר	qal	wci	3ms	אמר	55		say
	נאסף	niph	ptc	ms	אסף	62		assemble
	קברו	qal	impv	mp	קבר	868		bury
49:30	קנה	qal	pft	3ms	קנה	888		get,buy
49:31	קברו	qal	pft	3cp	קבר	868		bury
	קברו	qal	pft	3cp	קבר	868		bury
	קברתי	qal	pft	1cs	קבר	868		bury
49:33	יכל	piel	wci	3ms	כלה	477		complete,finish
	צות	piel	infc		צוה	845		command
	יאסף	qal	wci	3ms	אסף	62		gather
	יגוע	qal	wci	3ms	גוע	157		expire,die
	יאסף	niph	wci	3ms	אסף	62		assemble
50:1	יפל	qal	wci	3ms	נפל	656		fall

ChVs	Form	Stem	Tnse	PGN	Root	BDB	Sfx	Meaning
50: 1	יבך	qal	wci	3ms	בכה	113		weep
	ישק	qal	wci	3ms	נשק	676		kiss
50: 2	יצו	piel	wci	3ms	צוה	845		command
	רפאים	qal	ptc	mp	רפא	950		heal
	חנט	qal	infc		חנט	334		make spicy
	יחנטו	qal	wci	3mp	חנט	334		make spicy
	רפאים	qal	ptc	mp	רפא	950		heal
50: 3	ימלאו	qal	wci	3mp	מלא	569		be full, fill
	ימלאו	qal	impf	3mp	מלא	569		be full, fill
	יבכו	qal	wci	3mp	בכה	113		weep
50: 4	יעברו	qal	wci	3mp	עבר	716		pass over
	ידבר	piel	wci	3ms	דבר	180		speak
	אמר	qal	infc		אמר	55		say
	מצאתי	qal	pft	1cs	מצא	592		find
	דברו	piel	impv	mp	דבר	180		speak
	אמר	qal	infc		אמר	55		say
50: 5	השביעני	hiph	pft	3ms	שׁבע	989	1cs	cause to swear
	אמר	qal	infc		אמר	55		say
	מת	qal	ptc	ms	מות	559		die
	כריתי	qal	pft	1cs	כרה	500		dig
	תקברני	qal	impf	2ms	קבר	868	1cs	bury
	אעלה	qal	coh	1cs	עלה	748		go up
	אקברה	qal	coh	1cs	קבר	868		bury
	אשובה	qal	coh	1cs	שׁוב	996		turn, return
50: 6	יאמר	qal	wci	3ms	אמר	55		say
	עלה	qal	impv	ms	עלה	748		go up
	קבר	qal	impv	ms	קבר	868		bury
	השביעך	hiph	pft	3ms	שׁבע	989	2ms	cause to swear
50: 7	יעל	qal	wci	3ms	עלה	748		go up
	קבר	qal	infc		קבר	868		bury
	יעלו	qal	wci	3mp	עלה	748		go up
50: 8	עזבו	qal	pft	3cp	עזב	736		leave, loose
50: 9	יעל	qal	wci	3ms	עלה	748		go up
	יהי	qal	wci	3ms	היה	224		be, become
50: 10	יבאו	qal	wci	3mp	בוא	97		come in
	יספדו	qal	wci	3mp	ספד	704		wail, lament
	יעשׂ	qal	wci	3ms	עשׂה	793		do, make
50: 11	ירא	qal	wci	3ms	ראה	906		see
	יושב	qal	ptc	ms	ישב	442		sit, dwell
	יאמרו	qal	wci	3mp	אמר	55		say
	קרא	qal	pft	3ms	קרא	894		call, proclaim
50: 12	יעשׂו	qal	wci	3mp	עשׂה	793		do, make
	צום	piel	pft	3ms	צוה	845	3mp	command
50: 13	ישׂאו	qal	wci	3mp	נשׂא	669		lift, carry
	יקברו	qal	wci	3mp	קבר	868		bury
	קנה	qal	pft	3ms	קנה	888		get, buy
50: 14	ישב	qal	wci	3ms	שׁוב	996		turn, return
	עלים	qal	ptc	mp	עלה	748		go up
	קבר	qal	infc		קבר	868		bury
	קברו	qal	infc		קבר	868	3ms	bury
50: 15	יראו	qal	wci	3mp	ראה	906		see
	מת	qal	pft	3ms	מות	559		die
	יאמרו	qal	wci	3mp	אמר	55		say
	ישׂטמנו	qal	impf	3ms	שׂטם	966	1cp	bear a grudge
50: 15	השב	hiph	infa		שׁוב	996		bring back
	ישיב	hiph	impf	3ms	שׁוב	996		bring back
	גמלנו	qal	pft	1cp	גמל	168		deal out, ripen
50: 16	יצוו	piel	wci	3mp	צוה	845		command
	אמר	qal	infc		אמר	55		say
	צוה	piel	pft	3ms	צוה	845		command
	אמר	qal	infc		אמר	55		say
50: 17	תאמרו	qal	impf	2mp	אמר	55		say
	שׂא	qal	impv	ms	נשׂא	669		lift, carry
	גמלוך	qal	pft	3cp	גמל	168	2ms	deal out, ripen
	שׂא	qal	impv	ms	נשׂא	669		lift, carry
	יבך	qal	wci	3ms	בכה	113		weep
	דברם	piel	infc		דבר	180	3mp	speak
50: 18	ילכו	qal	wci	3mp	הלך	229		walk, go
	יפלו	qal	wci	3mp	נפל	656		fall
	יאמרו	qal	wci	3mp	אמר	55		say
50: 19	יאמר	qal	wci	3ms	אמר	55		say
	תיראו	qal	jusm	2mp	ירא	431		fear
50: 20	חשבתם	qal	pft	2mp	חשב	362		think, devise
	חשבה	qal	pft	3ms	חשב	362	3fs	think, devise
	עשׂה	qal	infc		עשׂה	793		do, make
	החית	hiph	infc		חיה	310		preserve
50: 21	תיראו	qal	jusm	2mp	ירא	431		fear
	אכלכל	pilp	impf	1cs	כול	465		support
	ינחם	piel	wci	3ms	נחם	636		comfort
	ידבר	piel	wci	3ms	דבר	180		speak
50: 22	ישב	qal	wci	3ms	ישב	442		sit, dwell
	יחי	qal	wci	3ms	חיה	310		live
50: 23	ירא	qal	wci	3ms	ראה	906		see
	ילדו	qalp	pft	3cp	ילד	408		be born
50: 24	יאמר	qal	wci	3ms	אמר	55		say
	מת	qal	ptc	ms	מות	559		die
	פקד	qal	infa		פקד	823		attend to, visit
	יפקד	qal	impf	3ms	פקד	823		attend to, visit
	העלה	hiph	wcp	3ms	עלה	748		bring up, offer
	נשבע	niph	pft	3ms	שׁבע	989		swear
50: 25	ישבע	hiph	wci	3ms	שׁבע	989		cause to swear
	אמר	qal	infc		אמר	55		say
	פקד	qal	infa		פקד	823		attend to, visit
	יפקד	qal	impf	3ms	פקד	823		attend to, visit
	העלתם	hiph	wcp	2mp	עלה	748		bring up, offer
50: 26	ימת	qal	wci	3ms	מות	559		die
	יחנטו	qal	wci	3mp	חנט	334		make spicy
	יישׂם	qalp	wci	3ms	ישׂם	441		be placed

EXODUS

ChVs	Form	Stem	Tnse	PGN	Root	BDB	Sfx	Meaning
1: 1	באים	qal	ptc	mp	בוא	97		come in
	באו	qal	pft	3cp	בוא	97		come in
1: 5	יהי	qal	wci	3ms	היה	224		be, become
	יצאי	qal	ptc	mp	יצא	422		go out
	היה	qal	pft	3ms	היה	224		be, become
1: 6	ימת	qal	wci	3ms	מות	559		die
1: 7	פרו	qal	pft	3cp	פרה	826		bear fruit
	ישרצו	qal	wci	3mp	שׁרץ	1056		swarm, teem

ChVs	Form	Stem	Tnse	PGN	Root	BDB	Sfx	Meaning
1:7	ירבו	qal	wci	3mp	רבה	915		be many,great
	יעצמו	qal	wci	3mp	עצם	782		be mighty,many
	תמלא	niph	wci	3fs	מלא	569		be filled
1:8	יקם	qal	wci	3ms	קום	877		arise,stand
	ידע	qal	pft	3ms	ידע	393		know
1:9	יאמר	qal	wci	3ms	אמר	55		say
1:10	הבה	qal	impv	ms	יהב	396		give
	נתחכמה	hith	coh	1cp	חכם	314		show self wise
	ירבה	qal	impf	3ms	רבה	915		be many,great
	היה	qal	wcp	3ms	היה	224		be,become
	תקראנה	qal	impf	3fp	קרא	896		meet,encounter
	נוסף	niph	wcp	3ms	יסף	414		be joined to
	שׂנאינו	qal	ptc	mp	שׂנא	971	1cp	hate
	נלחם	niph	wcp	3ms	לחם	535		wage war
	עלה	qal	wcp	3ms	עלה	748		go up
1:11	ישׂימו	qal	wci	3mp	שׂים	962		put,set
	ענתו	piel	infc		ענה	776	3ms	humble
	יבן	qal	wci	3ms	בנה	124		build
1:12	יענו	piel	impf	3mp	ענה	776		humble
	ירבה	qal	impf	3ms	רבה	915		be many,great
	יפרץ	qal	impf	3ms	פרץ	829		break through
	יקצו	qal	wci	3mp	קוץ	880		loathe,abhor
1:13	יעבדו	hiph	wci	3mp	עבד	712		cause to serve
1:14	ימררו	piel	wci	3mp	מרר	600		make bitter
	עבדו	qal	pft	3cp	עבד	712		work,serve
1:15	יאמר	qal	wci	3ms	אמר	55		say
	מילדת	piel	ptc	fp	ילד	408		bear,deliver
1:16	יאמר	qal	wci	3ms	אמר	55		say
	ילדכן	piel	infc		ילד	408	2fp	bear,deliver
	ראיתן	qal	wcp	2fp	ראה	906		see
	המתן	hiph	wcp	2fp	מות	559		kill
	חיה	qal	wcp	3fs	חיה	310		live
1:17	תיראן	qal	wci	3fp	ירא	431		fear
	מילדת	piel	ptc	fp	ילד	408		bear,deliver
	עשׂו	qal	pft	3cp	עשׂה	793		do,make
	דבר	piel	pft	3ms	דבר	180		speak
	תחיין	piel	wci	3fp	חיה	310		preserve,revive
1:18	יקרא	qal	wci	3ms	קרא	894		call,proclaim
	מילדת	piel	ptc	fp	ילד	408		bear,deliver
	יאמר	qal	wci	3ms	אמר	55		say
	עשׂיתן	qal	pft	2fp	עשׂה	793		do,make
	תחיין	piel	wci	2fp	חיה	310		preserve,revive
1:19	תאמרן	qal	wci	3fp	אמר	55		say
	מילדת	piel	ptc	fs	ילד	408		bear,deliver
	תבוא	qal	impf	3fs	בוא	97		come in
	מילדת	piel	ptc	fp	ילד	408		bear,deliver
	ילדו	qal	wcp	3cp	ילד	408		bear,beget
1:20	ייטב	hiph	wci	3ms	יטב	405		do good
	מילדת	piel	ptc	fp	ילד	408		bear,deliver
	ירב	qal	wci	3ms	רבה	915		be many,great
	יעצמו	qal	wci	3mp	עצם	782		be mighty,many
1:21	יהי	qal	wci	3ms	היה	224		be,become
	יראו	qal	pft	3cp	ירא	431		fear
	מילדת	piel	ptc	fp	ילד	408		bear,deliver
1:21	יעשׂ	qal	wci	3ms	עשׂה	793		do,make
1:22	יצו	piel	wci	3ms	צוה	845		command
	אמר	qal	infc		אמר	55		say
	תשׁליכהו	hiph	impf	2mp	שׁלך	1020	3ms	throw,cast
	תחיון	piel	impf	2mp	חיה	310		preserve,revive
2:1	ילך	qal	wci	3ms	הלך	229		walk,go
	יקח	qal	wci	3ms	לקח	542		take
2:2	תהר	qal	wci	3fs	הרה	247		conceive
	תלד	qal	wci	3fs	ילד	408		bear,beget
	תרא	qal	wci	3fs	ראה	906		see
	תצפנהו	qal	wci	3fs	צפן	860	3ms	hide
2:3	יכלה	qal	pft	3fs	יכל	407		be able
	הצפינו	hiph	infc		צפן	860	3ms	hide
	תקח	qal	wci	3fs	לקח	542		take
	תחמרה	qal	wci	3fs	חמר	330	3fs	cover w/asphalt
	תשׂם	qal	wci	3fs	שׂים	962		put,set
	תשׂם	qal	wci	3fs	שׂים	962		put,set
2:4	תתצב	hith	wci	3fs	יצב	426		stand oneself
	דעה	qal	infc		ידע	393		know
	יעשׂה	niph	impf	3ms	עשׂה	793		be done
2:5	תרד	qal	wci	3fs	ירד	432		come down
	רחץ	qal	infc		רחץ	934		wash,bathe
	הלכת	qal	ptc	fp	הלך	229		walk,go
	תרא	qal	wci	3fs	ראה	906		see
	תשׁלח	qal	wci	3fs	שׁלח	1018		send
	תקחה	qal	wci	3fs	לקח	542	3fs	take
2:6	תפתח	qal	wci	3fs	פתח	834		open
	תראהו	qal	wci	3fs	ראה	906	3ms	see
	בכה	qal	ptc	ms	בכה	113		weep
	תחמל	qal	wci	3fs	חמל	328		spare
	תאמר	qal	wci	3fs	אמר	55		say
2:7	תאמר	qal	wci	3fs	אמר	55		say
	אלך	qal	impf	1cs	הלך	229		walk,go
	קראתי	qal	wcp	1cs	קרא	894		call,proclaim
	מינקת	hiph	ptc	fs	ינק	413		nurse
	תינק	hiph	impf	3fs	ינק	413		nurse
2:8	תאמר	qal	wci	3fs	אמר	55		say
	לכי	qal	impv	fs	הלך	229		walk,go
	תלך	qal	wci	3fs	הלך	229		walk,go
	תקרא	qal	wci	3fs	קרא	894		call,proclaim
2:9	תאמר	qal	wci	3fs	אמר	55		say
	היליכי	hiph	impv	fs	הלך	229		lead,bring
	הינקהו	hiph	impv	fs	ינק	413	3ms	nurse
	אתן	qal	impf	1cs	נתן	678		give,set
	תקח	qal	wci	3fs	לקח	542		take
	תניקהו	hiph	wci	3fs	ינק	413	3ms	nurse
2:10	יגדל	qal	wci	3ms	גדל	152		be great,grow
	תבאהו	hiph	wci	3fs	בוא	97	3ms	bring in
	יהי	qal	wci	3ms	היה	224		be,become
	תקרא	qal	wci	3fs	קרא	894		call,proclaim
	תאמר	qal	wci	3fs	אמר	55		say
	משׁיתהו	qal	pft	1cs	משׁה	602	3ms	draw out,save
2:11	יהי	qal	wci	3ms	היה	224		be,become
	יגדל	qal	wci	3ms	גדל	152		be great,grow

ChVs	Form	Stem	Tnse	PGN	Root	BDB	Sfx	Meaning
2:11	יצא	qal	wci	3ms	יצא	422		go out
	ירא	qal	wci	3ms	ראה	906		see
	ירא	qal	wci	3ms	ראה	906		see
	מכה	hiph	ptc	ms	נכה	645		smite
2:12	יפן	qal	wci	3ms	פנה	815		turn
	ירא	qal	wci	3ms	ראה	906		see
	יך	hiph	wci	3ms	נכה	645		smite
	יטמנהו	qal	wci	3ms	טמן	380	3ms	hide
2:13	יצא	qal	wci	3ms	יצא	422		go out
	נצים	niph	ptc	mp	נצה	663		struggle
	יאמר	qal	wci	3ms	אמר	55		say
	תכה	hiph	impf	2ms	נכה	645		smite
2:14	יאמר	qal	wci	3ms	אמר	55		say
	שמך	qal	pft	3ms	שים	962	2ms	put,set
	שפט	qal	ptc	ms	שפט	1047		judge
	הרגני	qal	infc		הרג	246	1cs	kill
	אמר	qal	ptc	ms	אמר	55		say
	הרגת	qal	pft	2ms	הרג	246		kill
	יירא	qal	wci	3ms	ירא	431		fear
	יאמר	qal	wci	3ms	אמר	55		say
	נודע	niph	pft	3ms	ידע	393		be made known
2:15	ישמע	qal	wci	3ms	שמע	1033		hear
	יבקש	piel	wci	3ms	בקש	134		seek
	הרג	qal	infc		הרג	246		kill
	יברח	qal	wci	3ms	ברח	137		go thru,flee
	ישב	qal	wci	3ms	ישב	442		sit,dwell
	ישב	qal	wci	3ms	ישב	442		sit,dwell
2:16	תבאנה	qal	wci	3fp	בוא	97		come in
	תדלנה	qal	wci	3fp	דלה	194		draw (water)
	תמלאנה	piel	wci	3fp	מלא	569		fill
	השקות	hiph	infc		שקה	1052		give to drink
2:17	יבאו	qal	wci	3mp	בוא	97		come in
	רעים	qal	ptc	mp	רעה	944		pasture,tend
	יגרשום	piel	wci	3mp	גרש	176	3mp	drive out
	יקם	qal	wci	3ms	קום	877		arise,stand
	יושען	hiph	wci	3ms	ישע	446	3fp	deliver,save
	ישק	hiph	wci	3ms	שקה	1052		give to drink
2:18	תבאנה	qal	wci	3fp	בוא	97		come in
	יאמר	qal	wci	3ms	אמר	55		say
	מהרתן	piel	pft	2fp	מהר	554		hasten
	בא	qal	infc		בוא	97		come in
2:19	תאמרן	qal	wci	3fp	אמר	55		say
	הצילנו	hiph	pft	3ms	נצל	664	1cp	snatch,deliver
	רעים	qal	ptc	mp	רעה	944		pasture,tend
	דלה	qal	infa		דלה	194		draw (water)
	דלה	qal	pft	3ms	דלה	194		draw (water)
	ישק	hiph	wci	3ms	שקה	1052		give to drink
2:20	יאמר	qal	wci	3ms	אמר	55		say
	עזבתן	qal	pft	2fp	עזב	736		leave,loose
	קראן	qal	impv	fp	קרא	894		call,proclaim
	יאכל	qal	jusm	3ms	אכל	37		eat,devour
2:21	יואל	hiph	wci	3ms	יאל	383		be willing
	שבת	qal	infc		ישב	442		sit,dwell
	יתן	qal	wci	3ms	נתן	678		give,set
2:22	תלד	qal	wci	3fs	ילד	408		bear,beget
	יקרא	qal	wci	3ms	קרא	894		call,proclaim
	אמר	qal	pft	3ms	אמר	55		say
	הייתי	qal	pft	1cs	היה	224		be,become
2:23	יהי	qal	wci	3ms	היה	224		be,become
	ימת	qal	wci	3ms	מות	559		die
	יאנחו	niph	wci	3mp	אנח	58		sigh
	יזעקו	qal	wci	3mp	זעק	277		call,cry out
	תעל	qal	wci	3fs	עלה	748		go up
2:24	ישמע	qal	wci	3ms	שמע	1033		hear
	יזכר	qal	wci	3ms	זכר	269		remember
2:25	ירא	qal	wci	3ms	ראה	906		see
	ידע	qal	wci	3ms	ידע	393		know
3:1	היה	qal	pft	3ms	היה	224		be,become
	רעה	qal	ptc	ms	רעה	944		pasture,tend
	ינהג	qal	wci	3ms	נהג	624		drive
	יבא	qal	wci	3ms	בוא	97		come in
3:2	ירא	niph	wci	3ms	ראה	906		appear,be seen
	ירא	qal	wci	3ms	ראה	906		see
	בער	qal	ptc	ms	בער	128		burn
	אכל	qalp	ptc	ms	אכל	37		be consumed
3:3	יאמר	qal	wci	3ms	אמר	55		say
	אסרה	qal	coh	1cs	סור	693		turn aside
	אראה	qal	cohm	1cs	ראה	906		see
	יבער	qal	impf	3ms	בער	128		burn
3:4	ירא	qal	wci	3ms	ראה	906		see
	סר	qal	pft	3ms	סור	693		turn aside
	ראות	qal	infc		ראה	906		see
	יקרא	qal	wci	3ms	קרא	894		call,proclaim
	יאמר	qal	wci	3ms	אמר	55		say
	יאמר	qal	wci	3ms	אמר	55		say
3:5	יאמר	qal	wci	3ms	אמר	55		say
	תקרב	qal	jusm	2ms	קרב	897		approach
	של	qal	impv	ms	נשל	675		draw off
	עומד	qal	ptc	ms	עמד	763		stand,stop
3:6	יאמר	qal	wci	3ms	אמר	55		say
	יסתר	hiph	wci	3ms	סתר	711		hide
	ירא	qal	pft	3ms	ירא	431		fear
	הביט	hiph	infc		נבט	613		look,regard
3:7	יאמר	qal	wci	3ms	אמר	55		say
	ראה	qal	infa		ראה	906		see
	ראיתי	qal	pft	1cs	ראה	906		see
	שמעתי	qal	pft	1cs	שמע	1033		hear
	נגשיו	qal	ptc	mp	נגש	620	3ms	press,exact
	ידעתי	qal	pft	1cs	ידע	393		know
3:8	ארד	qal	wci	1cs	ירד	432		come down
	הצילו	hiph	infc		נצל	664	3ms	snatch,deliver
	העלתו	hiph	infc		עלה	748	3ms	bring up,offer
	זבת	qal	ptc	fs	זוב	264		flow,gush
3:9	באה	qal	pft	3fs	בוא	97		come in
	ראיתי	qal	pft	1cs	ראה	906		see
	לחצים	qal	ptc	mp	לחץ	537		press,oppress
3:10	לכה	qal	impv	ms	הלך	229		walk,go
	אשלחך	qal	cohm	1cs	שלח	1018	2ms	send

ChVs	Form	Stem	Tnse	PGN	Root	BDB	Sfx	Meaning
3:10	הוצא	hiph	impv	ms	יצא	422		bring out
3:11	יאמר	qal	wci	3ms	אמר	55		say
	אלך	qal	impf	1cs	הלך	229		walk,go
	אוציא	hiph	impf	1cs	יצא	422		bring out
3:12	יאמר	qal	wci	3ms	אמר	55		say
	אהיה	qal	impf	1cs	היה	224		be,become
	שׁלחתיך	qal	pft	1cs	שׁלח	1018	2ms	send
	הוציאך	hiph	infc		יצא	422	2ms	bring out
	תעבדון	qal	impf	2mp	עבד	712		work,serve
3:13	יאמר	qal	wci	3ms	אמר	55		say
	בא	qal	ptc	ms	בוא	97		come in
	אמרתי	qal	wcp	1cs	אמר	55		say
	שׁלחני	qal	pft	3ms	שׁלח	1018	1cs	send
	אמרו	qal	wcp	3cp	אמר	55		say
	אמר	qal	impf	1cs	אמר	55		say
3:14	יאמר	qal	wci	3ms	אמר	55		say
	אהיה	qal	impf	1cs	היה	224		be,become
	אהיה	qal	impf	1cs	היה	224		be,become
	יאמר	qal	wci	3ms	אמר	55		say
	תאמר	qal	impf	2ms	אמר	55		say
	אהיה	qal	impf	1cs	היה	224		be,become
	שׁלחני	qal	pft	3ms	שׁלח	1018	1cs	send
3:15	יאמר	qal	wci	3ms	אמר	55		say
	תאמר	qal	impf	2ms	אמר	55		say
	שׁלחני	qal	pft	3ms	שׁלח	1018	1cs	send
3:16	לך	qal	impv	ms	הלך	229		walk,go
	אספת	qal	wcp	2ms	אסף	62		gather
	אמרת	qal	wcp	2ms	אמר	55		say
	נראה	niph	pft	3ms	ראה	906		appear,be seen
	אמר	qal	infc		אמר	55		say
	פקד	qal	infa		פקד	823		attend to,visit
	פקדתי	qal	pft	1cs	פקד	823		attend to,visit
	עשׂוי	qal	pptc	ms	עשׂה	793		do,make
3:17	אמר	qal	wci	1cs	אמר	55		say
	אעלה	hiph	impf	1cs	עלה	748		bring up,offer
	זבת	qal	ptc	ms	זוב	264		flow,gush
3:18	שׁמעו	qal	wcp	3cp	שׁמע	1033		hear
	באת	qal	wcp	2ms	בוא	97		come in
	אמרתם	qal	wcp	2mp	אמר	55		say
	נקרה	niph	pft	3ms	קרה	899		encounter
	נלכה	qal	coh	1cp	הלך	229		walk,go
	נזבחה	qal	coh	1cp	זבח	256		slaughter
3:19	ידעתי	qal	pft	1cs	ידע	393		know
	יתן	qal	impf	3ms	נתן	678		give,set
	הלך	qal	infc		הלך	229		walk,go
3:20	שׁלחתי	qal	wcp	1cs	שׁלח	1018		send
	הכיתי	hiph	wcp	1cs	נכה	645		smite
	נפלאתי	niph	ptc	fp	פלא	810	1cs	be wonderful
	אעשׂה	qal	impf	1cs	עשׂה	793		do,make
	ישׁלח	piel	impf	3ms	שׁלח	1018		send away,shoot
3:21	נתתי	qal	wcp	1cs	נתן	678		give,set
	היה	qal	wcp	3ms	היה	224		be,become
	תלכון	qal	impf	2mp	הלך	229		walk,go
	תלכו	qal	impf	2mp	הלך	229		walk,go
3:22	שׁאלה	qal	wcp	3fs	שׁאל	981		ask,borrow
	גרת	qal	ptc	fs	גור	157		sojourn
	שׂמתם	qal	wcp	2mp	שׂים	962		put,set
	נצלתם	piel	wcp	2mp	נצל	664		strip off
4:1	יען	qal	wci	3ms	ענה	772		answer
	יאמר	qal	wci	3ms	אמר	55		say
	יאמינו	hiph	impf	3mp	אמן	52		believe
	ישׁמעו	qal	impf	3mp	שׁמע	1033		hear
	יאמרו	qal	impf	3mp	אמר	55		say
	נראה	niph	pft	3ms	ראה	906		appear,be seen
4:2	יאמר	qal	wci	3ms	אמר	55		say
	יאמר	qal	wci	3ms	אמר	55		say
4:3	יאמר	qal	wci	3ms	אמר	55		say
	השׁליכהו	hiph	impv	ms	שׁלך	1020	3ms	throw,cast
	ישׁליכהו	hiph	wci	3ms	שׁלך	1020	3ms	throw,cast
	יהי	qal	wci	3ms	היה	224		be,become
	ינס	qal	wci	3ms	נוס	630		flee,escape
4:4	יאמר	qal	wci	3ms	אמר	55		say
	שׁלח	qal	impv	ms	שׁלח	1018		send
	אחז	qal	impv	ms	אחז	28		grasp
	ישׁלח	qal	wci	3ms	שׁלח	1018		send
	יחזק	hiph	wci	3ms	חזק	304		make firm,seize
	יהי	qal	wci	3ms	היה	224		be,become
4:5	יאמינו	hiph	impf	3mp	אמן	52		believe
	נראה	niph	pft	3ms	ראה	906		appear,be seen
4:6	יאמר	qal	wci	3ms	אמר	55		say
	הבא	hiph	impv	ms	בוא	97		bring in
	יבא	hiph	wci	3ms	בוא	97		bring in
	יוצאה	hiph	wci	3ms	יצא	422	3fs	bring out
	מצרעת	pual	ptc	fs	צרע	863		be leprous
4:7	יאמר	qal	wci	3ms	אמר	55		say
	השׁב	hiph	impv	ms	שׁוב	996		bring back
	ישׁב	hiph	wci	3ms	שׁוב	996		bring back
	יוצאה	hiph	wci	3ms	יצא	422	3fs	bring out
	שׁבה	qal	pft	3fs	שׁוב	996		turn,return
4:8	היה	qal	wcp	3ms	היה	224		be,become
	יאמינו	hiph	impf	3mp	אמן	52		believe
	ישׁמעו	qal	impf	3mp	שׁמע	1033		hear
	האמינו	hiph	wcp	3cp	אמן	52		believe
4:9	היה	qal	wcp	3ms	היה	224		be,become
	יאמינו	hiph	impf	3mp	אמן	52		believe
	ישׁמעון	qal	impf	3mp	שׁמע	1033		hear
	לקחת	qal	wcp	2ms	לקח	542		take
	שׁפכת	qal	wcp	2ms	שׁפך	1049		pour out
	היו	qal	wcp	3cp	היה	224		be,become
	תקח	qal	impf	2ms	לקח	542		take
	היו	qal	wcp	3cp	היה	224		be,become
4:10	יאמר	qal	wci	3ms	אמר	55		say
	דברך	piel	infc		דבר	180	2ms	speak
4:11	יאמר	qal	wci	3ms	אמר	55		say
	שׂם	qal	pft	3ms	שׂים	962		put,set
	ישׂום	qal	impf	3ms	שׂים	962		put,set
4:12	לך	qal	impv	ms	הלך	229		walk,go
	אהיה	qal	impf	1cs	היה	224		be,become

ChVs	Form	Stem	Tnse	PGN	Root	BDB	Sfx	Meaning
4:12	הוריתיך	hiph	wcp	1cs	ירה	434	2ms	shoot,teach
	תדבר	piel	impf	2ms	דבר	180		speak
4:13	יאמר	qal	wci	3ms	אמר	55		say
	שׁלח	qal	impv	ms	שׁלח	1018		send
	תשׁלח	qal	impf	2ms	שׁלח	1018		send
4:14	יחר	qal	wci	3ms	חרה	354		be kindled,burn
	יאמר	qal	wci	3ms	אמר	55		say
	ידעתי	qal	pft	1cs	ידע	393		know
	דבר	piel	infa		דבר	180		speak
	ידבר	piel	impf	3ms	דבר	180		speak
	יצא	qal	ptc	ms	יצא	422		go out
	קראתך	qal	infc		קרא	896	2ms	meet,encounter
	ראך	qal	wcp	3ms	ראה	906	2ms	see
	שׂמח	qal	wcp	3ms	שׂמח	970		rejoice
4:15	דברת	piel	wcp	2ms	דבר	180		speak
	שׂמת	qal	wcp	2ms	שׂים	962		put,set
	אהיה	qal	impf	1cs	היה	224		be,become
	הוריתי	hiph	wcp	1cs	ירה	434		shoot,teach
	תעשׂון	qal	impf	2mp	עשׂה	793		do,make
4:16	דבר	piel	wcp	3ms	דבר	180		speak
	היה	qal	wcp	3ms	היה	224		be,become
	יהיה	qal	impf	3ms	היה	224		be,become
	תהיה	qal	impf	2ms	היה	224		be,become
4:17	תקח	qal	impf	2ms	לקח	542		take
	תעשׂה	qal	impf	2ms	עשׂה	793		do,make
4:18	ילך	qal	wci	3ms	הלך	229		walk,go
	ישׁב	qal	wci	3ms	שׁוב	996		turn,return
	יאמר	qal	wci	3ms	אמר	55		say
	אלכה	qal	coh	1cs	הלך	229		walk,go
	אשׁובה	qal	coh	1cs	שׁוב	996		turn,return
	אראה	qal	cohm	1cs	ראה	906		see
	יאמר	qal	wci	3ms	אמר	55		say
	לך	qal	impv	ms	הלך	229		walk,go
4:19	יאמר	qal	wci	3ms	אמר	55		say
	לך	qal	impv	ms	הלך	229		walk,go
	שׁב	qal	impv	ms	שׁוב	996		turn,return
	מתו	qal	pft	3cp	מות	559		die
	מבקשׁים	piel	ptc	mp	בקשׁ	134		seek
4:20	יקח	qal	wci	3ms	לקח	542		take
	ירכבם	hiph	wci	3ms	רכב	938	3mp	cause to ride
	ישׁב	qal	wci	3ms	שׁוב	996		turn,return
	יקח	qal	wci	3ms	לקח	542		take
4:21	יאמר	qal	wci	3ms	אמר	55		say
	לכתך	qal	infc		הלך	229	2ms	walk,go
	שׁוב	qal	infc		שׁוב	996		turn,return
	ראה	qal	impv	ms	ראה	906		see
	שׂמתי	qal	pft	1cs	שׂים	962		put,set
	עשׂיתם	qal	wcp	2ms	עשׂה	793	3mp	do,make
	אחזק	piel	impf	1cs	חזק	304		make strong
	ישׁלח	piel	impf	3ms	שׁלח	1018		send away,shoot
4:22	אמרת	qal	wcp	2ms	אמר	55		say
	אמר	qal	pft	3ms	אמר	55		say
4:23	אמר	qal	wci	1cs	אמר	55		say
	שׁלח	piel	impv	ms	שׁלח	1018		send away,shoot
4:23	יעבדני	qal	jusm	3ms	עבד	712	1cs	work,serve
	תמאן	piel	wci	2ms	מאן	549		refuse
	שׁלחו	piel	infc		שׁלח	1018	3ms	send away,shoot
	הרג	qal	ptc	ms	הרג	246		kill
4:24	יהי	qal	wci	3ms	היה	224		be,become
	יפגשׁהו	qal	wci	3ms	פגשׁ	803	3ms	meet
	יבקשׁ	piel	wci	3ms	בקשׁ	134		seek
	המיתו	hiph	infc		מות	559	3ms	kill
4:25	תקח	qal	wci	3fs	לקח	542		take
	תכרת	qal	wci	3fs	כרת	503		cut,destroy
	תגע	hiph	wci	3fs	נגע	619		reach,arrive
	תאמר	qal	wci	3fs	אמר	55		say
4:26	ירף	qal	wci	3ms	רפה	951		sink,relax
	אמרה	qal	pft	3fs	אמר	55		say
4:27	יאמר	qal	wci	3ms	אמר	55		say
	לך	qal	impv	ms	הלך	229		walk,go
	קראת	qal	infc		קרא	896		meet,encounter
	ילך	qal	wci	3ms	הלך	229		walk,go
	יפגשׁהו	qal	wci	3ms	פגשׁ	803	3ms	meet
	ישׁק	qal	wci	3ms	נשׁק	676		kiss
4:28	יגד	hiph	wci	3ms	נגד	616		declare,tell
	שׁלחו	qal	pft	3ms	שׁלח	1018	3ms	send
	צוהו	piel	pft	3ms	צוה	845	3ms	command
4:29	ילך	qal	wci	3ms	הלך	229		walk,go
	יאספו	qal	wci	3mp	אסף	62		gather
4:30	ידבר	piel	wci	3ms	דבר	180		speak
	דבר	piel	pft	3ms	דבר	180		speak
	יעשׂ	qal	wci	3ms	עשׂה	793		do,make
4:31	יאמן	hiph	wci	3ms	אמן	52		believe
	ישׁמעו	qal	wci	3mp	שׁמע	1033		hear
	פקד	qal	pft	3ms	פקד	823		attend to,visit
	ראה	qal	pft	3ms	ראה	906		see
	יקדו	qal	wci	3mp	קדד	869		bow down
	ישׁתחוו	hish	wci	3mp	חוה	1005		bow down
5:1	באו	qal	pft	3cp	בוא	97		come in
	יאמרו	qal	wci	3mp	אמר	55		say
	אמר	qal	pft	3ms	אמר	55		say
	שׁלח	piel	impv	ms	שׁלח	1018		send away,shoot
	יחגו	qal	jusm	3mp	חגג	290		keep festival
5:2	יאמר	qal	wci	3ms	אמר	55		say
	אשׁמע	qal	impf	1cs	שׁמע	1033		hear
	שׁלח	piel	infc		שׁלח	1018		send away,shoot
	ידעתי	qal	pft	1cs	ידע	393		know
	אשׁלח	piel	impf	1cs	שׁלח	1018		send away,shoot
5:3	יאמרו	qal	wci	3mp	אמר	55		say
	נקרא	niph	pft	3ms	קרא	896		meet
	נלכה	qal	coh	1cp	הלך	229		walk,go
	נזבחה	qal	coh	1cp	זבח	256		slaughter
	יפגענו	qal	impf	3ms	פגע	803	1cp	meet,encounter
5:4	יאמר	qal	wci	3ms	אמר	55		say
	תפריעו	hiph	impf	2mp	פרע	828		make unruly
	לכו	qal	impv	mp	הלך	229		walk,go
5:5	יאמר	qal	wci	3ms	אמר	55		say
	השׁבתם	hiph	pft	2mp	שׁבת	991		destroy,remove

ChVs	Form	Stem	Tnse	PGN	Root	BDB	Sfx	Meaning
5:6	יצו	piel	wci	3ms	צוה	845		command
	נגשׂים	qal	ptc	mp	נגשׂ	620		press,exact
	אמר	qal	infc		אמר	55		say
5:7	תאספון	hiph	impf	2mp	יסף	414		add,do again
	תת	qal	infc		נתן	678		give,set
	לבן	qal	infc		לבן	527		make brick
	ילכו	qal	jusm	3mp	הלך	229		walk,go
	קשׁשׁו	poel	wcp	3cp	קשׁשׁ	905		gather stubble
5:8	עשׂים	qal	ptc	mp	עשׂה	793		do,make
	תשׂימו	qal	impf	2mp	שׂים	962		put,set
	תגרעו	qal	impf	2mp	גרע	175		diminish
	נרפים	niph	ptc	mp	רפה	951		be lazy
	צעקים	qal	ptc	mp	צעק	858		cry out
	אמר	qal	infc		אמר	55		say
	נלכה	qal	coh	1cp	הלך	229		walk,go
	נזבחה	qal	coh	1cp	זבח	256		slaughter
5:9	תכבד	qal	jusm	3fs	כבד	457		be heavy
	יעשׂו	qal	impf	3mp	עשׂה	793		do,make
	ישׁעו	qal	impf	3mp	שׁעה	1043		gaze,regard
5:10	יצאו	qal	wci	3mp	יצא	422		go out
	נגשׂי	qal	ptc	mp	נגשׂ	620		press,exact
	יאמרו	qal	wci	3mp	אמר	55		say
	אמר	qal	infc		אמר	55		say
	אמר	qal	pft	3ms	אמר	55		say
	נתן	qal	ptc	ms	נתן	678		give,set
5:11	לכו	qal	impv	mp	הלך	229		walk,go
	קחו	qal	impv	mp	לקח	542		take
	תמצאו	qal	impf	2mp	מצא	592		find
	נגרע	niph	ptc	ms	גרע	175		be withdrawn
5:12	יפץ	hiph	wci	3ms	פוץ	806		scatter
	קשׁשׁ	poel	infc		קשׁשׁ	905		gather stubble
5:13	נגשׂים	qal	ptc	mp	נגשׂ	620		press,exact
	אצים	qal	ptc	mp	אוץ	21		press,hasten
	אמר	qal	infc		אמר	55		say
	כלו	piel	impv	mp	כלה	477		complete,finish
	היות	qal	infc		היה	224		be,become
5:14	יכו	hoph	wci	3mp	נכה	645		be smitten
	שׂמו	qal	pft	3cp	שׂים	962		put,set
	נגשׂי	qal	ptc	mp	נגשׂ	620		press,exact
	אמר	qal	infc		אמר	55		say
	כליתם	piel	pft	2mp	כלה	477		complete,finish
	לבן	qal	infc		לבן	527		make brick
5:15	יבאו	qal	wci	3mp	בוא	97		come in
	יצעקו	qal	wci	3mp	צעק	858		cry out
	אמר	qal	infc		אמר	55		say
	תעשׂה	qal	impf	2ms	עשׂה	793		do,make
5:16	נתן	niph	ptc	ms	נתן	678		be given
	אמרים	qal	ptc	mp	אמר	55		say
	עשׂו	qal	impv	mp	עשׂה	793		do,make
	מכים	hoph	ptc	mp	נכה	645		be smitten
	חטאת	qal	pft	3fs	חטא	306		sin
5:17	יאמר	qal	wci	3ms	אמר	55		say
	נרפים	niph	ptc	mp	רפה	951		be lazy
	נרפים	niph	ptc	mp	רפה	951		be lazy
5:17	אמרים	qal	ptc	mp	אמר	55		say
	נלכה	qal	coh	1cp	הלך	229		walk,go
	נזבחה	qal	coh	1cp	זבח	256		slaughter
5:18	לכו	qal	impv	mp	הלך	229		walk,go
	עבדו	qal	impv	mp	עבד	712		work,serve
	ינתן	niph	impf	3ms	נתן	678		be given
	תתנו	qal	impf	2mp	נתן	678		give,set
5:19	יראו	qal	wci	3mp	ראה	906		see
	אמר	qal	infc		אמר	55		say
	תגרעו	qal	impf	2mp	גרע	175		diminish
5:20	יפגעו	qal	wci	3mp	פגע	803		meet,encounter
	נצבים	niph	ptc	mp	נצב	662		stand
	קראתם	qal	infc		קרא	896	3mp	meet,encounter
	צאתם	qal	infc		יצא	422	3mp	go out
5:21	יאמרו	qal	wci	3mp	אמר	55		say
	ירא	qal	jus	3ms	ראה	906		see
	ישׁפט	qal	jusm	3ms	שׁפט	1047		judge
	הבאשׁתם	hiph	pft	2mp	באשׁ	92		cause to stink
	תת	qal	infc		נתן	678		give,set
	הרגנו	qal	infc		הרג	246	1cp	kill
5:22	ישׁב	qal	wci	3ms	שׁוב	996		turn,return
	יאמר	qal	wci	3ms	אמר	55		say
	הרעתה	hiph	pft	2ms	רעע	949		hurt,do evil
	שׁלחתני	qal	pft	2ms	שׁלח	1018	1cs	send
5:23	באתי	qal	pft	1cs	בוא	97		come in
	דבר	piel	infc		דבר	180		speak
	הרע	hiph	pft	3ms	רעע	949		hurt,do evil
	הצל	hiph	infa		נצל	664		snatch,deliver
	הצלת	hiph	pft	2ms	נצל	664		snatch,deliver
6:1	יאמר	qal	wci	3ms	אמר	55		say
	תראה	qal	impf	2ms	ראה	906		see
	אעשׂה	qal	impf	1cs	עשׂה	793		do,make
	ישׁלחם	piel	impf	3ms	שׁלח	1018	3mp	send away,shoot
	יגרשׁם	piel	impf	3ms	גרשׁ	176	3mp	drive out
6:2	ידבר	piel	wci	3ms	דבר	180		speak
	יאמר	qal	wci	3ms	אמר	55		say
6:3	ארא	niph	wci	1cs	ראה	906		appear,be seen
	נודעתי	niph	pft	1cs	ידע	393		be made known
6:4	הקמתי	hiph	pft	1cs	קום	877		raise,build,set
	תת	qal	infc		נתן	678		give,set
	גרו	qal	pft	3cp	גור	157		sojourn
6:5	שׁמעתי	qal	pft	1cs	שׁמע	1033		hear
	מעבדים	hiph	ptc	mp	עבד	712		cause to serve
	אזכר	qal	wci	1cs	זכר	269		remember
6:6	אמר	qal	impv	ms	אמר	55		say
	הוצאתי	hiph	wcp	1cs	יצא	422		bring out
	הצלתי	hiph	wcp	1cs	נצל	664		snatch,deliver
	גאלתי	qal	wcp	1cs	גאל	145		redeem
	נטויה	qal	pptc	fs	נטה	639		stretch,incline
6:7	לקחתי	qal	wcp	1cs	לקח	542		take
	הייתי	qal	wcp	1cs	היה	224		be,become
	ידעתם	qal	wcp	2mp	ידע	393		know
	מוציא	hiph	ptc	ms	יצא	422		bring out
6:8	הבאתי	hiph	wcp	1cs	בוא	97		bring in

ChVs	Form	Stem	Tnse	PGN	Root	BDB	Sfx	Meaning
6:8	נשׂאתי	qal	pft	1cs	נשׂא	669		lift,carry
	תת	qal	infc		נתן	678		give,set
	נתתי	qal	wcp	1cs	נתן	678		give,set
6:9	ידבר	piel	wci	3ms	דבר	180		speak
	שׁמעו	qal	pft	3cp	שׁמע	1033		hear
6:10	ידבר	piel	wci	3ms	דבר	180		speak
	אמר	qal	infc		אמר	55		say
6:11	בא	qal	impv	ms	בוא	97		come in
	דבר	piel	impv	ms	דבר	180		speak
	ישׁלח	piel	jusm	3ms	שׁלח	1018		send away,shoot
6:12	ידבר	piel	wci	3ms	דבר	180		speak
	אמר	qal	infc		אמר	55		say
	שׁמעו	qal	pft	3cp	שׁמע	1033		hear
	ישׁמעני	qal	impf	3ms	שׁמע	1033	1cs	hear
6:13	ידבר	piel	wci	3ms	דבר	180		speak
	יצום	piel	wci	3ms	צוה	845	3mp	command
	הוציא	hiph	infc		יצא	422		bring out
6:20	יקח	qal	wci	3ms	לקח	542		take
	תלד	qal	wci	3fs	ילד	408		bear,beget
6:23	יקח	qal	wci	3ms	לקח	542		take
	תלד	qal	wci	3fs	ילד	408		bear,beget
6:25	לקח	qal	pft	3ms	לקח	542		take
	תלד	qal	wci	3fs	ילד	408		bear,beget
6:26	אמר	qal	pft	3ms	אמר	55		say
	הוציאו	hiph	impv	mp	יצא	422		bring out
6:27	מדברים	piel	ptc	mp	דבר	180		speak
	הוציא	hiph	infc		יצא	422		bring out
6:28	יהי	qal	wci	3ms	היה	224		be,become
	דבר	piel	pft	3ms	דבר	180		speak
6:29	ידבר	piel	wci	3ms	דבר	180		speak
	אמר	qal	infc		אמר	55		say
	דבר	piel	impv	ms	דבר	180		speak
	דבר	qal	ptc	ms	דבר	180		speak
6:30	יאמר	qal	wci	3ms	אמר	55		say
	ישׁמע	qal	impf	3ms	שׁמע	1033		hear
7:1	יאמר	qal	wci	3ms	אמר	55		say
	ראה	qal	impv	ms	ראה	906		see
	נתתיך	qal	pft	1cs	נתן	678	2ms	give,set
	יהיה	qal	impf	3ms	היה	224		be,become
7:2	תדבר	piel	impf	2ms	דבר	180		speak
	אצוך	piel	impf	1cs	צוה	845	2ms	command
	ידבר	piel	impf	3ms	דבר	180		speak
	שׁלח	piel	wcp	3ms	שׁלח	1018		send away,shoot
7:3	אקשׁה	hiph	impf	1cs	קשׁה	904		harden
	הרביתי	hiph	wcp	1cs	רבה	915		make many
7:4	ישׁמע	qal	impf	3ms	שׁמע	1033		hear
	נתתי	qal	wcp	1cs	נתן	678		give,set
	הוצאתי	hiph	wcp	1cs	יצא	422		bring out
7:5	ידעו	qal	wcp	3cp	ידע	393		know
	נטתי	qal	infc		נטה	639	1cs	stretch,incline
	הוצאתי	hiph	wcp	1cs	יצא	422		bring out
7:6	יעשׂ	qal	wci	3ms	עשׂה	793		do,make
	צוה	piel	pft	3ms	צוה	845		command
	עשׂו	qal	pft	3cp	עשׂה	793		do,make

ChVs	Form	Stem	Tnse	PGN	Root	BDB	Sfx	Meaning
7:7	דברם	piel	infc		דבר	180	3mp	speak
7:8	יאמר	qal	wci	3ms	אמר	55		say
	אמר	qal	infc		אמר	55		say
7:9	ידבר	piel	impf	3ms	דבר	180		speak
	אמר	qal	infc		אמר	55		say
	תנו	qal	impv	mp	נתן	678		give,set
	אמרת	qal	wcp	2ms	אמר	55		say
	קח	qal	impv	ms	לקח	542		take
	השׁלך	hiph	impv	ms	שׁלך	1020		throw,cast
	יהי	qal	jus	3ms	היה	224		be,become
7:10	יבא	qal	wci	3ms	בוא	97		come in
	יעשׂו	qal	wci	3mp	עשׂה	793		do,make
	צוה	piel	pft	3ms	צוה	845		command
	ישׁלך	hiph	wci	3ms	שׁלך	1020		throw,cast
	יהי	qal	wci	3ms	היה	224		be,become
7:11	יקרא	qal	wci	3ms	קרא	894		call,proclaim
	מכשׁפים	piel	ptc	mp	כשׁף	506		practice magic
	יעשׂו	qal	wci	3mp	עשׂה	793		do,make
7:12	ישׁליכו	hiph	wci	3mp	שׁלך	1020		throw,cast
	יהיו	qal	wci	3mp	היה	224		be,become
	יבלע	qal	wci	3ms	בלע	118		swallow
7:13	יחזק	qal	wci	3ms	חזק	304		be strong
	שׁמע	qal	pft	3ms	שׁמע	1033		hear
	דבר	piel	pft	3ms	דבר	180		speak
7:14	יאמר	qal	wci	3ms	אמר	55		say
	מאן	piel	pft	3ms	מאן	549		refuse
	שׁלח	piel	infc		שׁלח	1018		send away,shoot
7:15	לך	qal	impv	ms	הלך	229		walk,go
	יצא	qal	ptc	ms	יצא	422		go out
	נצבת	niph	wcp	2ms	נצב	662		stand
	קראתו	qal	infc		קרא	896	3ms	meet,encounter
	נהפך	niph	pft	3ms	הפך	245		turn oneself
	תקח	qal	impf	2ms	לקח	542		take
7:16	אמרת	qal	wcp	2ms	אמר	55		say
	שׁלחני	qal	pft	3ms	שׁלח	1018	1cs	send
	אמר	qal	infc		אמר	55		say
	שׁלח	piel	impv	ms	שׁלח	1018		send away,shoot
	יעבדני	qal	jusm	3mp	עבד	712	1cs	work,serve
	שׁמעת	qal	pft	2ms	שׁמע	1033		hear
7:17	אמר	qal	pft	3ms	אמר	55		say
	תדע	qal	impf	2ms	ידע	393		know
	מכה	hiph	ptc	ms	נכה	645		smite
	נהפכו	niph	wcp	3cp	הפך	245		turn oneself
7:18	תמות	qal	impf	3fs	מות	559		die
	באשׁ	qal	wcp	3ms	באשׁ	92		stink
	נלאו	niph	wcp	3cp	לאה	521		tire oneself
	שׁתות	qal	infc		שׁתה	1059		drink
7:19	יאמר	qal	wci	3ms	אמר	55		say
	אמר	qal	impv	ms	אמר	55		say
	קח	qal	impv	ms	לקח	542		take
	נטה	qal	impv	ms	נטה	639		stretch,incline
	יהיו	qal	jusm	3mp	היה	224		be,become
	היה	qal	wcp	3ms	היה	224		be,become
7:20	יעשׂו	qal	wci	3mp	עשׂה	793		do,make

ChVs	Form	Stem	Tnse	PGN	Root	BDB	Sfx	Meaning
7:20	צוה	piel	pft	3ms	צוה	845		command
	ירם	hiph	wci	3ms	רום	926		raise,lift
	יך	hiph	wci	3ms	נכה	645		smite
	יהפכו	niph	wci	3mp	הפך	245		turn oneself
7:21	מתה	qal	pft	3fs	מות	559		die
	יבאש	qal	wci	3ms	באש	92		stink
	יכלו	qal	pft	3cp	יכל	407		be able
	שתות	qal	infc		שתה	1059		drink
	יהי	qal	wci	3ms	היה	224		be, become
7:22	יעשו	qal	wci	3mp	עשה	793		do, make
	יחזק	qal	wci	3ms	חזק	304		be strong
	שמע	qal	pft	3ms	שמע	1033		hear
	דבר	piel	pft	3ms	דבר	180		speak
7:23	יפן	qal	wci	3ms	פנה	815		turn
	יבא	qal	wci	3ms	בוא	97		come in
	שת	qal	pft	3ms	שית	1011		put,set
7:24	יחפרו	qal	wci	3mp	חפר	343		dig,search
	שתות	qal	infc		שתה	1059		drink
	יכלו	qal	pft	3cp	יכל	407		be able
	שתת	qal	infc		שתה	1059		drink
7:25	ימלא	niph	wci	3ms	מלא	569		be filled
	הכות	hiph	infc		נכה	645		smite
7:26	יאמר	qal	wci	3ms	אמר	55		say
	בא	qal	impv	ms	בוא	97		come in
	אמרת	qal	wcp	2ms	אמר	55		say
	אמר	qal	pft	3ms	אמר	55		say
	שלח	piel	impv	ms	שלח	1018		send away,shoot
	יעבדני	qal	jusm	3mp	עבד	712	1cs	work,serve
7:27	שלח	piel	infc		שלח	1018		send away,shoot
	נגף	qal	ptc	ms	נגף	619		smite,strike
7:28	שרץ	qal	wcp	3ms	שרץ	1056		swarm, teem
	עלו	qal	wcp	3cp	עלה	748		go up
	באו	qal	wcp	3cp	בוא	97		come in
7:29	יעלו	qal	impf	3mp	עלה	748		go up
8:1	יאמר	qal	wci	3ms	אמר	55		say
	אמר	qal	impv	ms	אמר	55		say
	נטה	qal	impv	ms	נטה	639		stretch, incline
	העל	hiph	impv	ms	עלה	748		bring up, offer
8:2	יט	qal	wci	3ms	נטה	639		stretch, incline
	תעל	qal	wci	3fs	עלה	748		go up
	תכס	piel	wci	3fs	כסה	491		cover
8:3	יעשו	qal	wci	3mp	עשה	793		do, make
	יעלו	hiph	wci	3mp	עלה	748		bring up, offer
8:4	יקרא	qal	wci	3ms	קרא	894		call, proclaim
	יאמר	qal	wci	3ms	אמר	55		say
	העתירו	hiph	impv	mp	עתר	801		pray
	יסר	hiph	jus	3ms	סור	693		take away
	אשלחה	piel	coh	1cs	שלח	1018		send away, shoot
	יזבחו	qal	jusm	3mp	זבח	256		slaughter
8:5	יאמר	qal	wci	3ms	אמר	55		say
	התפאר	hith	impv	ms	פאר	802		glorify self
	אעתיר	hiph	impf	1cs	עתר	801		pray
	הכרית	hiph	infc		כרת	503		cut off, destroy
	תשארנה	niph	impf	3fp	שאר	983		be left
8:6	יאמר	qal	wci	3ms	אמר	55		say
	יאמר	qal	wci	3ms	אמר	55		say
	תדע	qal	impf	2ms	ידע	393		know
8:7	סרו	qal	wcp	3cp	סור	693		turn aside
	תשארנה	niph	impf	3fp	שאר	983		be left
8:8	יצא	qal	wci	3ms	יצא	422		go out
	יצעק	qal	wci	3ms	צעק	858		cry out
	שם	qal	pft	3ms	שים	962		put,set
8:9	יעש	qal	wci	3ms	עשה	793		do, make
	ימתו	qal	wci	3mp	מות	559		die
8:10	יצברו	qal	wci	3mp	צבר	840		heap up
	תבאש	qal	wci	3fs	באש	92		stink
8:11	ירא	qal	wci	3ms	ראה	906		see
	היתה	qal	pft	3fs	היה	224		be, become
	הכבד	hiph	infa		כבד	457		make heavy
	שמע	qal	pft	3ms	שמע	1033		hear
	דבר	piel	pft	3ms	דבר	180		speak
8:12	יאמר	qal	wci	3ms	אמר	55		say
	אמר	qal	impv	ms	אמר	55		say
	נטה	qal	impv	ms	נטה	639		stretch, incline
	הך	hiph	impv	ms	נכה	645		smite
	היה	qal	wcp	3ms	היה	224		be, become
8:13	יעשו	qal	wci	3mp	עשה	793		do, make
	יט	qal	wci	3ms	נטה	639		stretch, incline
	יך	hiph	wci	3ms	נכה	645		smite
	תהי	qal	wci	3fs	היה	224		be, become
	היה	qal	pft	3ms	היה	224		be, become
8:14	יעשו	qal	wci	3mp	עשה	793		do, make
	הוציא	hiph	infc		יצא	422		bring out
	יכלו	qal	pft	3cp	יכל	407		be able
	תהי	qal	wci	3fs	היה	224		be, become
8:15	יאמרו	qal	wci	3mp	אמר	55		say
	יחזק	qal	wci	3ms	חזק	304		be strong
	שמע	qal	pft	3ms	שמע	1033		hear
	דבר	piel	pft	3ms	דבר	180		speak
8:16	יאמר	qal	wci	3ms	אמר	55		say
	השכם	hiph	impv	ms	שכם	1014		rise early
	התיצב	hith	impv	ms	יצב	426		stand oneself
	יוצא	qal	ptc	ms	יצא	422		go out
	אמרת	qal	wcp	2ms	אמר	55		say
	אמר	qal	pft	3ms	אמר	55		say
	שלח	piel	impv	ms	שלח	1018		send away, shoot
	יעבדני	qal	jusm	3mp	עבד	712	1cs	work, serve
8:17	משלח	piel	ptc	ms	שלח	1018		send away, shoot
	משליח	hiph	ptc	ms	שלח	1018		send
	מלאו	qal	wcp	3cp	מלא	569		be full, fill
8:18	הפליתי	hiph	wcp	1cs	פלה	811		make separate
	עמד	qal	ptc	ms	עמד	763		stand, stop
	היות	qal	infc		היה	224		be, become
	תדע	qal	impf	2ms	ידע	393		know
8:19	שמתי	qal	wcp	1cs	שים	962		put,set
	יהיה	qal	impf	3ms	היה	224		be, become
8:20	יעש	qal	wci	3ms	עשה	793		do, make
	יבא	qal	wci	3ms	בוא	97		come in

ChVs	Form	Stem	Tnse	PGN	Root	BDB	Sfx	Meaning
8: 20	תשחת	niph	impf	3fs	שחת	1007		be marred
8: 21	יקרא	qal	wci	3ms	קרא	894		call,proclaim
	יאמר	qal	wci	3ms	אמר	55		say
	לכו	qal	impv	mp	הלך	229		walk,go
	זבחו	qal	impv	mp	זבח	256		slaughter
8: 22	יאמר	qal	wci	3ms	אמר	55		say
	נכון	niph	ptc	ms	כון	465		be established
	עשות	qal	infc		עשה	793		do,make
	נזבח	qal	impf	1cp	זבח	256		slaughter
	נזבח	qal	impf	1cp	זבח	256		slaughter
	יסקלנו	qal	impf	3mp	סקל	709	1cp	stone to death
8: 23	נלך	qal	impf	1cp	הלך	229		walk,go
	זבחנו	qal	wcp	1cp	זבח	256		slaughter
	יאמר	qal	impf	3ms	אמר	55		say
8: 24	יאמר	qal	wci	3ms	אמר	55		say
	אשלח	piel	impf	1cs	שלח	1018		send away,shoot
	זבחתם	qal	wcp	2mp	זבח	256		slaughter
	הרחק	hiph	infa		רחק	934		put far away
	תרחיקו	hiph	impf	2mp	רחק	934		put far away
	לכת	qal	infc		הלך	229		walk,go
	העתירו	hiph	impv	mp	עתר	801		pray
8: 25	יאמר	qal	wci	3ms	אמר	55		say
	יוצא	qal	ptc	ms	יצא	422		go out
	העתרתי	hiph	wcp	1cs	עתר	801		pray
	סר	qal	wcp	3ms	סור	693		turn aside
	יסף	hiph	jus	3ms	יסף	414		add,do again
	התל	hiph	infc		תלל	1068		mock,deceive
	שלח	piel	infc		שלח	1018		send away,shoot
	זבח	qal	infc		זבח	256		slaughter
8: 26	יצא	qal	wci	3ms	יצא	422		go out
	יעתר	qal	wci	3ms	עתר	801		pray
8: 27	יעש	qal	wci	3ms	עשה	793		do,make
	יסר	qal	wci	3ms	סור	693		turn aside
	נשאר	niph	pft	3ms	שאר	983		be left
8: 28	יכבד	hiph	wci	3ms	כבד	457		make heavy
	שלח	piel	pft	3ms	שלח	1018		send away,shoot
9: 1	יאמר	qal	wci	3ms	אמר	55		say
	בא	qal	impv	ms	בוא	97		come in
	דברת	piel	wcp	2ms	דבר	180		speak
	אמר	qal	pft	3ms	אמר	55		say
	שלח	piel	impv	ms	שלח	1018		send away,shoot
	יעבדני	qal	jusm	3mp	עבד	712	1cs	work,serve
9: 2	שלח	piel	infc		שלח	1018		send away,shoot
	מחזיק	hiph	ptc	ms	חזק	304		make firm,seize
9: 3	הויה	qal	ptc	fs	היה	224		be,become
9: 4	הפלה	hiph	wcp	3ms	פלה	811		make separate
	ימות	qal	impf	3ms	מות	559		die
9: 5	ישם	qal	wci	3ms	שים	962		put,set
	אמר	qal	infc		אמר	55		say
	יעשה	qal	impf	3ms	עשה	793		do,make
9: 6	יעש	qal	wci	3ms	עשה	793		do,make
	ימת	qal	wci	3ms	מות	559		die
	מת	qal	pft	3ms	מות	559		die
9: 7	ישלח	qal	wci	3ms	שלח	1018		send
9: 7	מת	qal	pft	3ms	מות	559		die
	יכבד	qal	wci	3ms	כבד	457		be heavy
	שלח	piel	pft	3ms	שלח	1018		send away,shoot
9: 8	יאמר	qal	wci	3ms	אמר	55		say
	קחו	qal	impv	mp	לקח	542		take
	זרקו	qal	wcp	3ms	זרק	284	3ms	toss,scatter
9: 9	היה	qal	wcp	3ms	היה	224		be,become
	היה	qal	wcp	3ms	היה	224		be,become
	פרח	qal	ptc	ms	פרח	827		break out
9: 10	יקחו	qal	wci	3mp	לקח	542		take
	יעמדו	qal	wci	3mp	עמד	763		stand,stop
	יזרק	qal	wci	3ms	זרק	284		toss,scatter
	יהי	qal	wci	3ms	היה	224		be,become
	פרח	qal	ptc	ms	פרח	827		break out
9: 11	יכלו	qal	pft	3cp	יכל	407		be able
	עמד	qal	infc		עמד	763		stand,stop
	היה	qal	pft	3ms	היה	224		be,become
9: 12	יחזק	piel	wci	3ms	חזק	304		make strong
	שמע	qal	pft	3ms	שמע	1033		hear
	דבר	piel	pft	3ms	דבר	180		speak
9: 13	יאמר	qal	wci	3ms	אמר	55		say
	השכם	hiph	impv	ms	שכם	1014		rise early
	התיצב	hith	impv	ms	יצב	426		stand oneself
	אמרת	qal	wcp	2ms	אמר	55		say
	אמר	qal	pft	3ms	אמר	55		say
	שלח	piel	impv	ms	שלח	1018		send away,shoot
	יעבדני	qal	jusm	3mp	עבד	712	1cs	work,serve
9: 14	שלח	qal	ptc	ms	שלח	1018		send
	תדע	qal	impf	2ms	ידע	393		know
9: 15	שלחתי	qal	pft	1cs	שלח	1018		send
	אך	hiph	wci	1cs	נכה	645		smite
	תכחד	niph	wci	2ms	כחד	470		be hid,effaced
9: 16	העמדתיך	hiph	pft	1cs	עמד	763	2ms	set up,raise
	הראתך	hiph	infc		ראה	906	2ms	show,exhibit
	ספר	piel	infc		ספר	707		recount
9: 17	מסתולל	htpo	ptc	ms	סלל	699		exalt oneself
	שלחם	piel	infc		שלח	1018	3mp	send away,shoot
9: 18	ממטיר	hiph	ptc	ms	מטר	565		rain
	היה	qal	pft	3ms	היה	224		be,become
	הוסדה	niph	infc		יסד	413	3fs	sit together
9: 19	שלח	qal	impv	ms	שלח	1018		send
	העז	hiph	impv	ms	עוז	731		bring to safety
	ימצא	niph	impf	3ms	מצא	592		be found
	יאסף	niph	impf	3ms	אסף	62		assemble
	ירד	qal	wcp	3ms	ירד	432		come down
	מתו	qal	wcp	3cp	מות	559		die
9: 20	ירא	qal	ptc	ms	ירא	431		fear
	הניס	hiph	pft	3ms	נוס	630		put to flight
9: 21	שם	qal	pft	3ms	שים	962		put,set
	יעזב	qal	wci	3ms	עזב	736		leave,loose
9: 22	יאמר	qal	wci	3ms	אמר	55		say
	נטה	qal	impv	ms	נטה	639		stretch,incline
	יהי	qal	jus	3ms	היה	224		be,become
9: 23	יט	qal	wci	3ms	נטה	639		stretch,incline

ChVs	Form	Stem	Tnse	PGN	Root	BDB	Sfx	Meaning
9:23	נתן	qal	pft	3ms	נתן	678		give,set
	תהלך	qal	wci	3fs	הלך	229		walk,go
	ימטר	hiph	wci	3ms	מטר	565		rain
9:24	יהי	qal	wci	3ms	היה	224		be,become
	מתלקחת	hith	ptc	fs	לקח	542		contain oneself
	היה	qal	pft	3ms	היה	224		be,become
	היתה	qal	pft	3fs	היה	224		be,become
9:25	יך	hiph	wci	3ms	נכה	645		smite
	הכה	hiph	pft	3ms	נכה	645		smite
	שׁבר	piel	pft	3ms	שׁבר	990		shatter
9:26	היה	qal	pft	3ms	היה	224		be,become
9:27	ישׁלח	qal	wci	3ms	שׁלח	1018		send
	יקרא	qal	wci	3ms	קרא	894		call,proclaim
	יאמר	qal	wci	3ms	אמר	55		say
	חטאתי	qal	pft	1cs	חטא	306		sin
9:28	העתירו	hiph	impv	mp	עתר	801		pray
	הית	qal	infc		היה	224		be,become
	אשׁלחה	piel	coh	1cs	שׁלח	1018		send away,shoot
	תספון	hiph	impf	2mp	יסף	414		add,do again
	עמד	qal	infc		עמד	763		stand,stop
9:29	יאמר	qal	wci	3ms	אמר	55		say
	צאתי	qal	infc		יצא	422	1cs	go out
	אפרשׂ	qal	impf	1cs	פרשׂ	831		spread out
	יחדלון	qal	impf	3mp	חדל	292		cease
	יהיה	qal	impf	3ms	היה	224		be,become
	תדע	qal	impf	2ms	ידע	393		know
9:30	ידעתי	qal	pft	1cs	ידע	393		know
	תיראון	qal	impf	2mp	ירא	431		fear
9:31	נכתה	pual	pft	3fs	נכה	645		be smitten
9:32	נכו	pual	pft	3cp	נכה	645		be smitten
9:33	יצא	qal	wci	3ms	יצא	422		go out
	יפרשׂ	qal	wci	3ms	פרשׂ	831		spread out
	יחדלו	qal	wci	3mp	חדל	292		cease
	נתך	niph	pft	3ms	נתך	677		be poured
9:34	ירא	qal	wci	3ms	ראה	906		see
	חדל	qal	pft	3ms	חדל	292		cease
	יסף	hiph	wci	3ms	יסף	414		add,do again
	חטא	qal	infc		חטא	306		sin
	יכבד	hiph	wci	3ms	כבד	457		make heavy
9:35	יחזק	qal	wci	3ms	חזק	304		be strong
	שׁלח	piel	pft	3ms	שׁלח	1018		send away,shoot
	דבר	piel	pft	3ms	דבר	180		speak
10:1	יאמר	qal	wci	3ms	אמר	55		say
	בא	qal	impv	ms	בוא	97		come in
	הכבדתי	hiph	pft	1cs	כבד	457		make heavy
	שׁתי	qal	infc		שׁית	1011	1cs	put,set
10:2	תספר	piel	impf	2ms	ספר	707		recount
	התעללתי	hith	pft	1cs	עלל	759		busy,vex
	שׂמתי	qal	pft	1cs	שׂים	962		put,set
	ידעתם	qal	wcp	2mp	ידע	393		know
10:3	יבא	qal	wci	3ms	בוא	97		come in
	יאמרו	qal	wci	3mp	אמר	55		say
	אמר	qal	pft	3ms	אמר	55		say
	מאנת	piel	pft	2ms	מאן	549		refuse
10:3	ענת	niph	infc		ענה	776		be afflicted
	שׁלח	piel	impv	ms	שׁלח	1018		send away,shoot
	יעבדני	qal	jusm	3mp	עבד	712	1cs	work,serve
10:4	שׁלח	piel	infc		שׁלח	1018		send away,shoot
	מביא	hiph	ptc	ms	בוא	97		bring in
10:5	כסה	piel	wcp	3ms	כסה	491		cover
	יוכל	qal	impf	3ms	יכל	407		be able
	ראת	qal	infc		ראה	906		see
	אכל	qal	wcp	3ms	אכל	37		eat,devour
	נשׁארת	niph	ptc	fs	שׁאר	983		be left
	אכל	qal	wcp	3ms	אכל	37		eat,devour
	צמח	qal	ptc	ms	צמח	855		sprout up
10:6	מלאו	qal	wcp	3cp	מלא	569		be full,fill
	ראו	qal	pft	3cp	ראה	906		see
	היותם	qal	infc		היה	224	3mp	be,become
	יפן	qal	wci	3ms	פנה	815		turn
	יצא	qal	wci	3ms	יצא	422		go out
10:7	יאמרו	qal	wci	3mp	אמר	55		say
	יהיה	qal	impf	3ms	היה	224		be,become
	שׁלח	piel	impv	ms	שׁלח	1018		send away,shoot
	יעבדו	qal	jusm	3mp	עבד	712		work,serve
	תדע	qal	impf	2ms	ידע	393		know
	אבדה	qal	pft	3fs	אבד	1		perish
10:8	יושׁב	hoph	wci	3ms	שׁוב	996		be returned
	יאמר	qal	wci	3ms	אמר	55		say
	לכו	qal	impv	mp	הלך	229		walk,go
	עבדו	qal	impv	mp	עבד	712		work,serve
	הלכים	qal	ptc	mp	הלך	229		walk,go
10:9	יאמר	qal	wci	3ms	אמר	55		say
	נלך	qal	impf	1cp	הלך	229		walk,go
	נלך	qal	impf	1cp	הלך	229		walk,go
10:10	יאמר	qal	wci	3ms	אמר	55		say
	יהי	qal	jus	3ms	היה	224		be,become
	אשׁלח	piel	impf	1cs	שׁלח	1018		send away,shoot
	ראו	qal	impv	mp	ראה	906		see
10:11	לכו	qal	impv	mp	הלך	229		walk,go
	עבדו	qal	impv	mp	עבד	712		work,serve
	מבקשׁים	piel	ptc	mp	בקשׁ	134		seek
	יגרשׁ	piel	wci	3ms	גרשׁ	176		drive out
10:12	יאמר	qal	wci	3ms	אמר	55		say
	נטה	qal	impv	ms	נטה	639		stretch,incline
	יעל	qal	jusm	3ms	עלה	748		go up
	יאכל	qal	jusm	3ms	אכל	37		eat,devour
	השׁאיר	hiph	pft	3ms	שׁאר	983		leave,spare
10:13	יט	qal	wci	3ms	נטה	639		stretch,incline
	נהג	piel	pft	3ms	נהג	624		drive away,lead
	היה	qal	pft	3ms	היה	224		be,become
	נשׂא	qal	pft	3ms	נשׂא	669		lift,carry
10:14	יעל	qal	wci	3ms	עלה	748		go up
	ינח	qal	wci	3ms	נוח	628		rest
	היה	qal	pft	3ms	היה	224		be,become
	יהיה	qal	impf	3ms	היה	224		be,become
10:15	יכס	piel	wci	3ms	כסה	491		cover
	תחשׁך	qal	wci	3fs	חשׁך	364		be dark

ChVs	Form	Stem	Tnse	PGN	Root	BDB	Sfx	Meaning
10: 15	יאכל	qal	wci	3ms	אכל	37		eat,devour
	הותיר	hiph	pft	3ms	יתר	451		leave,spare
	נותר	niph	pft	3ms	יתר	451		be left,remain
10: 16	ימהר	piel	wci	3ms	מהר	554		hasten
	קרא	qal	infc		קרא	894		call,proclaim
	יאמר	qal	wci	3ms	אמר	55		say
	חטאתי	qal	pft	1cs	חטא	306		sin
10: 17	שׂא	qal	impv	ms	נשׂא	669		lift,carry
	העתירו	hiph	impv	mp	עתר	801		pray
	יסר	hiph	jus	3ms	סור	693		take away
10: 18	יצא	qal	wci	3ms	יצא	422		go out
	יעתר	qal	wci	3ms	עתר	801		pray
10: 19	יהפך	qal	wci	3ms	הפך	245		turn,overturn
	ישׂא	qal	wci	3ms	נשׂא	669		lift,carry
	יתקעהו	qal	wci	3ms	תקע	1075	3ms	thrust,clap
	נשאר	niph	pft	3ms	שׁאר	983		be left
10: 20	יחזק	piel	wci	3ms	חזק	304		make strong
	שׁלח	piel	pft	3ms	שׁלח	1018		send away,shoot
10: 21	יאמר	qal	wci	3ms	אמר	55		say
	נטה	qal	impv	ms	נטה	639		stretch,incline
	יהי	qal	jus	3ms	היה	224		be,become
	ימשׁ	hiph	jusm	3ms	משׁשׁ	606		feel
10: 22	יט	qal	wci	3ms	נטה	639		stretch,incline
	יהי	qal	wci	3ms	היה	224		be,become
10: 23	ראו	qal	pft	3cp	ראה	906		see
	קמו	qal	pft	3cp	קום	877		arise,stand
	היה	qal	pft	3ms	היה	224		be,become
10: 24	יקרא	qal	wci	3ms	קרא	894		call,proclaim
	יאמר	qal	wci	3ms	אמר	55		say
	לכו	qal	impv	mp	הלך	229		walk,go
	עבדו	qal	impv	mp	עבד	712		work,serve
	יצג	hoph	impf	3ms	יצג	426		be left
	ילך	qal	impf	3ms	הלך	229		walk,go
10: 25	יאמר	qal	wci	3ms	אמר	55		say
	תתן	qal	impf	2ms	נתן	678		give,set
	עשׂינו	qal	wcp	1cp	עשׂה	793		do,make
10: 26	ילך	qal	impf	3ms	הלך	229		walk,go
	תשאר	niph	impf	3fs	שׁאר	983		be left
	נקח	qal	impf	1cp	לקח	542		take
	עבד	qal	infc		עבד	712		work,serve
	נדע	qal	impf	1cp	ידע	393		know
	נעבד	qal	impf	1cp	עבד	712		work,serve
	באנו	qal	infc		בוא	97	1cp	come in
10: 27	יחזק	piel	wci	3ms	חזק	304		make strong
	אבה	qal	pft	3ms	אבה	2		be willing
	שׁלחם	piel	infc		שׁלח	1018	3mp	send away,shoot
10: 28	יאמר	qal	wci	3ms	אמר	55		say
	לך	qal	impv	ms	הלך	229		walk,go
	השמר	niph	impv	ms	שׁמר	1036		be kept,guarded
	תסף	hiph	jus	2ms	יסף	414		add,do again
	ראות	qal	infc		ראה	906		see
	ראתך	qal	infc		ראה	906	2ms	see
	תמות	qal	impf	2ms	מות	559		die
10: 29	יאמר	qal	wci	3ms	אמר	55		say

ChVs	Form	Stem	Tnse	PGN	Root	BDB	Sfx	Meaning
10: 29	דברת	piel	pft	2ms	דבר	180		speak
	אסף	hiph	impf	1cs	יסף	414		add,do again
	ראות	qal	infc		ראה	906		see
11: 1	יאמר	qal	wci	3ms	אמר	55		say
	אביא	hiph	impf	1cs	בוא	97		bring in
	ישׁלח	piel	impf	3ms	שׁלח	1018		send away,shoot
	שׁלחו	piel	infc		שׁלח	1018	3ms	send away,shoot
	גרשׁ	piel	infa		גרשׁ	176		drive out
	יגרשׁ	piel	impf	3ms	גרשׁ	176		drive out
11: 2	דבר	piel	impv	ms	דבר	180		speak
	ישׁאלו	qal	jusm	3mp	שׁאל	981		ask,borrow
11: 3	יתן	qal	wci	3ms	נתן	678		give,set
11: 4	יאמר	qal	wci	3ms	אמר	55		say
	אמר	qal	pft	3ms	אמר	55		say
	יוצא	qal	ptc	ms	יצא	422		go out
11: 5	מת	qal	wcp	3ms	מות	559		die
	ישׁב	qal	ptc	ms	ישׁב	442		sit,dwell
11: 6	היתה	qal	wcp	3fs	היה	224		be,become
	נהיתה	niph	pft	3fs	היה	224		be done
	תסף	hiph	impf	3fs	יסף	414		add,do again
11: 7	יחרץ	qal	impf	3ms	חרץ	358		cut,decide
	תדעון	qal	impf	2mp	ידע	393		know
	יפלה	hiph	impf	3ms	פלה	811		make separate
11: 8	ירדו	qal	wcp	3cp	ירד	432		come down
	השתחוו	hish	wcp	3cp	חוה	1005		bow down
	אמר	qal	infc		אמר	55		say
	צא	qal	impv	ms	יצא	422		go out
	אצא	qal	impf	1cs	יצא	422		go out
	יצא	qal	wci	3ms	יצא	422		go out
11: 9	יאמר	qal	wci	3ms	אמר	55		say
	ישׁמע	qal	impf	3ms	שׁמע	1033		hear
	רבות	qal	infc		רבה	915		be many,great
11: 10	עשׂו	qal	pft	3cp	עשׂה	793		do,make
	יחזק	piel	wci	3ms	חזק	304		make strong
	שׁלח	piel	pft	3ms	שׁלח	1018		send away,shoot
12: 1	יאמר	qal	wci	3ms	אמר	55		say
	אמר	qal	infc		אמר	55		say
12: 3	דברו	piel	impv	mp	דבר	180		speak
	אמר	qal	infc		אמר	55		say
	יקחו	qal	impf	3mp	לקח	542		take
12: 4	ימעט	qal	impf	3ms	מעט	589		be small,few
	הית	qal	infc		היה	224		be,become
	לקח	qal	wcp	3ms	לקח	542		take
	אכלו	qal	infc		אכל	37	3ms	eat,devour
	תכסו	qal	impf	2mp	כסס	493		number,account
12: 5	יהיה	qal	impf	3ms	היה	224		be,become
	תקחו	qal	impf	2mp	לקח	542		take
12: 6	היה	qal	wcp	3ms	היה	224		be,become
	שׁחטו	qal	wcp	3cp	שׁחט	1006		slaughter
12: 7	לקחו	qal	wcp	3cp	לקח	542		take
	נתנו	qal	wcp	3cp	נתן	678		give,set
	יאכלו	qal	impf	3mp	אכל	37		eat,devour
12: 8	אכלו	qal	wcp	3cp	אכל	37		eat,devour
	יאכלהו	qal	impf	3mp	אכל	37	3ms	eat,devour

ChVs	Form	Stem	Tnse	PGN	Root	BDB	Sfx	Meaning
12:9	תאכלו	qal	impf	2mp	אכל	37		eat,devour
	מבשל	pual	ptc	ms	בשל	143		be boiled
12:10	תותירו	hiph	impf	2mp	יתר	451		leave,spare
	נתר	niph	ptc	ms	יתר	451		be left,remain
	תשׂרפו	qal	impf	2mp	שׂרף	976		burn
12:11	תאכלו	qal	impf	2mp	אכל	37		eat,devour
	חגרים	qal	pptc	mp	חגר	291		gird
	אכלתם	qal	wcp	2mp	אכל	37		eat,devour
12:12	עברתי	qal	wcp	1cs	עבר	716		pass over
	הכיתי	hiph	wcp	1cs	נכה	645		smite
	אעשׂה	qal	impf	1cs	עשׂה	793		do,make
12:13	היה	qal	wcp	3ms	היה	224		be,become
	ראיתי	qal	wcp	1cs	ראה	906		see
	פסחתי	qal	wcp	1cs	פסח	820		pass over
	יהיה	qal	impf	3ms	היה	224		be,become
	הכתי	hiph	infc		נכה	645	1cs	smite
12:14	היה	qal	wcp	3ms	היה	224		be,become
	חגתם	qal	wcp	2mp	חגג	290		keep festival
	תחגהו	qal	impf	2mp	חגג	290	3ms	keep festival
12:15	תאכלו	qal	impf	2mp	אכל	37		eat,devour
	תשׁביתו	hiph	impf	2mp	שׁבת	991		destroy,remove
	אכל	qal	ptc	ms	אכל	37		eat,devour
	נכרתה	niph	wcp	3fs	כרת	503		be cut off
12:16	יהיה	qal	impf	3ms	היה	224		be,become
	יעשׂה	niph	impf	3ms	עשׂה	793		be done
	יאכל	niph	impf	3ms	אכל	37		be eaten
	יעשׂה	niph	impf	3ms	עשׂה	793		be done
12:17	שׁמרתם	qal	wcp	2mp	שׁמר	1036		keep,watch
	הוצאתי	hiph	pft	1cs	יצא	422		bring out
	שׁמרתם	qal	wcp	2mp	שׁמר	1036		keep,watch
12:18	תאכלו	qal	impf	2mp	אכל	37		eat,devour
12:19	ימצא	niph	impf	3ms	מצא	592		be found
	אכל	qal	ptc	ms	אכל	37		eat,devour
	נכרתה	niph	wcp	3fs	כרת	503		be cut off
12:20	תאכלו	qal	impf	2mp	אכל	37		eat,devour
	תאכלו	qal	impf	2mp	אכל	37		eat,devour
12:21	יקרא	qal	wci	3ms	קרא	894		call,proclaim
	יאמר	qal	wci	3ms	אמר	55		say
	משׁכו	qal	impv	mp	משׁך	604		draw,pull
	קחו	qal	impv	mp	לקח	542		take
	שׁחטו	qal	impv	mp	שׁחט	1006		slaughter
12:22	לקחתם	qal	wcp	2mp	לקח	542		take
	טבלתם	qal	wcp	2mp	טבל	371		dip
	הגעתם	hiph	wcp	2mp	נגע	619		reach,arrive
	תצאו	qal	impf	2mp	יצא	422		go out
12:23	עבר	qal	wcp	3ms	עבר	716		pass over
	נגף	qal	infc		נגף	619		smite,strike
	ראה	qal	wcp	3ms	ראה	906		see
	פסח	qal	wcp	3ms	פסח	820		pass over
	יתן	qal	impf	3ms	נתן	678		give,set
	משׁחית	hiph	ptc	ms	שׁחת	1007		spoil,ruin
	בא	qal	infc		בוא	97		come in
	נגף	qal	infc		נגף	619		smite,strike
12:24	שׁמרתם	qal	wcp	2mp	שׁמר	1036		keep,watch
12:25	היה	qal	wcp	3ms	היה	224		be,become
	תבאו	qal	impf	2mp	בוא	97		come in
	יתן	qal	impf	3ms	נתן	678		give,set
	דבר	piel	pft	3ms	דבר	180		speak
	שׁמרתם	qal	wcp	2mp	שׁמר	1036		keep,watch
12:26	היה	qal	wcp	3ms	היה	224		be,become
	יאמרו	qal	impf	3mp	אמר	55		say
12:27	אמרתם	qal	wcp	2mp	אמר	55		say
	פסח	qal	pft	3ms	פסח	820		pass over
	נגפו	qal	infc		נגף	619	3ms	smite,strike
	הציל	hiph	pft	3ms	נצל	664		snatch,deliver
	יקד	qal	wci	3ms	קדד	869		bow down
	ישׁתחוו	hish	wci	3mp	חוה	1005		bow down
12:28	ילכו	qal	wci	3mp	הלך	229		walk,go
	יעשׂו	qal	wci	3mp	עשׂה	793		do,make
	צוה	piel	pft	3ms	צוה	845		command
	עשׂו	qal	pft	3cp	עשׂה	793		do,make
12:29	יהי	qal	wci	3ms	היה	224		be,become
	הכה	hiph	pft	3ms	נכה	645		smite
	ישׁב	qal	ptc	ms	ישׁב	442		sit,dwell
12:30	יקם	qal	wci	3ms	קום	877		arise,stand
	תהי	qal	wci	3fs	היה	224		be,become
	מת	qal	ptc	ms	מות	559		die
12:31	יקרא	qal	wci	3ms	קרא	894		call,proclaim
	יאמר	qal	wci	3ms	אמר	55		say
	קומו	qal	impv	mp	קום	877		arise,stand
	צאו	qal	impv	mp	יצא	422		go out
	לכו	qal	impv	mp	הלך	229		walk,go
	עבדו	qal	impv	mp	עבד	712		work,serve
	דברכם	piel	infc		דבר	180	2mp	speak
12:32	קחו	qal	impv	mp	לקח	542		take
	דברתם	piel	pft	2mp	דבר	180		speak
	לכו	qal	impv	mp	הלך	229		walk,go
	ברכתם	piel	wcp	2mp	ברך	138		bless
12:33	תחזק	qal	wci	3fs	חזק	304		be strong
	מהר	piel	infc		מהר	554		hasten
	שׁלחם	piel	infc		שׁלח	1018	3mp	send away,shoot
	אמרו	qal	pft	3cp	אמר	55		say
	מתים	qal	ptc	mp	מות	559		die
12:34	ישׂא	qal	wci	3ms	נשׂא	669		lift,carry
	יחמץ	qal	impf	3ms	חמץ	329		be leavened
	צררת	qal	pptc	fp	צרר	864		bind,be cramped
12:35	עשׂו	qal	pft	3cp	עשׂה	793		do,make
	ישׁאלו	qal	wci	3mp	שׁאל	981		ask,borrow
12:36	נתן	qal	pft	3ms	נתן	678		give,set
	ישׁאלום	hiph	wci	3mp	שׁאל	981	3mp	give,lend
	ינצלו	piel	wci	3mp	נצל	664		strip off
12:37	יסעו	qal	wci	3mp	נסע	652		pull up,set out
12:38	עלה	qal	pft	3ms	עלה	748		go up
12:39	יאפו	qal	wci	3mp	אפה	66		bake
	הוציאו	hiph	pft	3cp	יצא	422		bring out
	חמץ	qal	pft	3ms	חמץ	329		be leavened
	גרשׁו	pual	pft	3cp	גרשׁ	176		be expelled
	יכלו	qal	pft	3cp	יכל	407		be able

ChVs	Form	Stem	Tnse	PGN	Root	BDB	Sfx	Meaning
12: 39	התמהמה	htpp	infc		מהה	554		tarry
	עשׂו	qal	pft	3cp	עשׂה	793		do,make
12: 40	ישׁבו	qal	pft	3cp	ישׁב	442		sit,dwell
12: 41	יהי	qal	wci	3ms	היה	224		be,become
	יהי	qal	wci	3ms	היה	224		be,become
	יצאו	qal	pft	3cp	יצא	422		go out
12: 42	הוציאם	hiph	infc		יצא	422	3mp	bring out
12: 43	יאמר	qal	wci	3ms	אמר	55		say
	יאכל	qal	impf	3ms	אכל	37		eat,devour
12: 44	מלתה	qal	pft	2ms	מול	557		circumcise
	יאכל	qal	impf	3ms	אכל	37		eat,devour
12: 45	יאכל	qal	impf	3ms	אכל	37		eat,devour
12: 46	יאכל	niph	impf	3ms	אכל	37		be eaten
	תוציא	hiph	impf	2ms	יצא	422		bring out
	תשׁברו	qal	impf	2mp	שׁבר	990		break
12: 47	יעשׂו	qal	impf	3mp	עשׂה	793		do,make
12: 48	יגור	qal	impf	3ms	גור	157		sojourn
	עשׂה	qal	wcp	3ms	עשׂה	793		do,make
	המול	niph	infc		מול	557		be circumcised
	יקרב	qal	impf	3ms	קרב	897		approach
	עשׂתו	qal	infc		עשׂה	793	3ms	do,make
	היה	qal	wcp	3ms	היה	224		be,become
	יאכל	qal	impf	3ms	אכל	37		eat,devour
12: 49	יהיה	qal	impf	3ms	היה	224		be,become
	גר	qal	ptc	ms	גור	157		sojourn
12: 50	יעשׂו	qal	wci	3mp	עשׂה	793		do,make
	צוה	piel	pft	3ms	צוה	845		command
	עשׂו	qal	pft	3cp	עשׂה	793		do,make
12: 51	יהי	qal	wci	3ms	היה	224		be,become
	הוציא	hiph	pft	3ms	יצא	422		bring out
13: 1	ידבר	piel	wci	3ms	דבר	180		speak
	אמר	qal	infc		אמר	55		say
13: 2	קדשׁ	piel	impv	ms	קדשׁ	872		consecrate
13: 3	יאמר	qal	wci	3ms	אמר	55		say
	זכור	qal	infa		זכר	269		remember
	יצאתם	qal	pft	2mp	יצא	422		go out
	הוציא	hiph	pft	3ms	יצא	422		bring out
	יאכל	niph	impf	3ms	אכל	37		be eaten
13: 4	יצאים	qal	ptc	mp	יצא	422		go out
13: 5	היה	qal	wcp	3ms	היה	224		be,become
	יביאך	hiph	impf	3ms	בוא	97	2ms	bring in
	נשׁבע	niph	pft	3ms	שׁבע	989		swear
	תת	qal	infc		נתן	678		give,set
	זבת	qal	ptc	fs	זוב	264		flow,gush
	עבדת	qal	wcp	2ms	עבד	712		work,serve
13: 6	תאכל	qal	impf	2ms	אכל	37		eat,devour
13: 7	יאכל	niph	impf	3ms	אכל	37		be eaten
	יראה	niph	impf	3ms	ראה	906		appear,be seen
	יראה	niph	impf	3ms	ראה	906		appear,be seen
13: 8	הגדת	hiph	wcp	2ms	נגד	616		declare,tell
	אמר	qal	infc		אמר	55		say
	עשׂה	qal	pft	3ms	עשׂה	793		do,make
	צאתי	qal	infc		יצא	422	1cs	go out
13: 9	היה	qal	wcp	3ms	היה	224		be,become
13: 9	תהיה	qal	impf	3fs	היה	224		be,become
	הוצאך	hiph	pft	3ms	יצא	422	2ms	bring out
13: 10	שׁמרת	qal	wcp	2ms	שׁמר	1036		keep,watch
13: 11	היה	qal	wcp	3ms	היה	224		be,become
	יבאך	hiph	impf	3ms	בוא	97	2ms	bring in
	נשׁבע	niph	pft	3ms	שׁבע	989		swear
	נתנה	qal	wcp	3ms	נתן	678	3fs	give,set
13: 12	העברת	hiph	wcp	2ms	עבר	716		cause to pass
	יהיה	qal	impf	3ms	היה	224		be,become
13: 13	תפדה	qal	impf	2ms	פדה	804		ransom
	תפדה	qal	impf	2ms	פדה	804		ransom
	ערפתו	qal	wcp	2ms	ערף	791	3ms	break neck
	תפדה	qal	impf	2ms	פדה	804		ransom
13: 14	היה	qal	wcp	3ms	היה	224		be,become
	ישׁאלך	qal	impf	3ms	שׁאל	981	2ms	ask,borrow
	אמר	qal	infc		אמר	55		say
	אמרת	qal	wcp	2ms	אמר	55		say
	הוציאנו	hiph	pft	3ms	יצא	422	1cp	bring out
13: 15	יהי	qal	wci	3ms	היה	224		be,become
	הקשׁה	hiph	pft	3ms	קשׁה	904		harden
	שׁלחנו	piel	infc		שׁלח	1018	1cp	send away,shoot
	יהרג	qal	wci	3ms	הרג	246		kill
	זבח	qal	ptc	ms	זבח	256		slaughter
	אפדה	qal	impf	1cs	פדה	804		ransom
13: 16	היה	qal	wcp	3ms	היה	224		be,become
	הוציאנו	hiph	pft	3ms	יצא	422	1cp	bring out
13: 17	יהי	qal	wci	3ms	היה	224		be,become
	שׁלח	piel	infc		שׁלח	1018		send away,shoot
	נחם	qal	pft	3ms	נחה	634	3mp	lead
	אמר	qal	pft	3ms	אמר	55		say
	ינחם	niph	impf	3ms	נחם	636		be sorry
	ראתם	qal	infc		ראה	906	3mp	see
	שׁבו	qal	wcp	3cp	שׁוב	996		turn,return
13: 18	יסב	hiph	wci	3ms	סבב	685		cause to turn
	עלו	qal	pft	3cp	עלה	748		go up
13: 19	יקח	qal	wci	3ms	לקח	542		take
	השׁבע	hiph	infa		שׁבע	989		cause to swear
	השׁביע	hiph	pft	3ms	שׁבע	989		cause to swear
	אמר	qal	infc		אמר	55		say
	פקד	qal	infa		פקד	823		attend to,visit
	יפקד	qal	impf	3ms	פקד	823		attend to,visit
	העליתם	hiph	wcp	2mp	עלה	748		bring up,offer
13: 20	יסעו	qal	wci	3mp	נסע	652		pull up,set out
	יחנו	qal	wci	3mp	חנה	333		decline,encamp
13: 21	הלך	qal	ptc	ms	הלך	229		walk,go
	נחתם	hiph	infc		נחה	634	3mp	lead,guide
	האיר	hiph	infc		אור	21		cause to shine
	לכת	qal	infc		הלך	229		walk,go
13: 22	ימישׁ	hiph	impf	3ms	מושׁ	559		remove,depart
14: 1	ידבר	piel	wci	3ms	דבר	180		speak
	אמר	qal	infc		אמר	55		say
14: 2	דבר	piel	impv	ms	דבר	180		speak
	ישׁבו	qal	jusm	3mp	שׁוב	996		turn,return
	יחנו	qal	jusm	3mp	חנה	333		decline,encamp

ChVs	Form	Stem	Tnse	PGN	Root	BDB	Sfx	Meaning
14:2	תחנו	qal	impf	2mp	חנה	333		decline,encamp
14:3	אמר	qal	wcp	3ms	אמר	55		say
	נבכים	niph	ptc	mp	בוך	100		be confused
	סגר	qal	pft	3ms	סגר	688		shut
14:4	חזקתי	piel	wcp	1cs	חזק	304		make strong
	רדף	qal	wcp	3ms	רדף	922		pursue
	אכבדה	niph	cohf	1cs	כבד	457		be honored
	ידעו	qal	wcp	3cp	ידע	393		know
	יעשׂו	qal	wci	3mp	עשׂה	793		do,make
14:5	יגד	hoph	wci	3ms	נגד	616		be told
	ברח	qal	pft	3ms	ברח	137		go thru,flee
	יהפך	niph	wci	3ms	הפך	245		turn oneself
	יאמרו	qal	wci	3mp	אמר	55		say
	עשׂינו	qal	pft	1cp	עשׂה	793		do,make
	שׁלחנו	piel	pft	1cp	שׁלח	1018		send away,shoot
	עבדנו	qal	infc		עבד	712	1cp	work,serve
14:6	יאסר	qal	wci	3ms	אסר	63		tie,bind
	לקח	qal	pft	3ms	לקח	542		take
14:7	יקח	qal	wci	3ms	לקח	542		take
	בחור	qal	pptc	ms	בחר	103		choose
14:8	יחזק	piel	wci	3ms	חזק	304		make strong
	ירדף	qal	wci	3ms	רדף	922		pursue
	יצאים	qal	ptc	mp	יצא	422		go out
	רמה	qal	ptc	fs	רום	926		be high
14:9	ירדפו	qal	wci	3mp	רדף	922		pursue
	ישׂיגו	hiph	wci	3mp	נשׂג	673		reach,overtake
	חנים	qal	ptc	mp	חנה	333		decline,encamp
14:10	הקריב	hiph	pft	3ms	קרב	897		bring near
	ישׂאו	qal	wci	3mp	נשׂא	669		lift,carry
	נסע	qal	ptc	ms	נסע	652		pull up,set out
	ייראו	qal	wci	3mp	ירא	431		fear
	יצעקו	qal	wci	3mp	צעק	858		cry out
14:11	יאמרו	qal	wci	3mp	אמר	55		say
	לקחתנו	qal	pft	2ms	לקח	542	1cp	take
	מות	qal	infc		מות	559		die
	עשׂית	qal	pft	2ms	עשׂה	793		do,make
	הוציאנו	hiph	infc		יצא	422	1cp	bring out
14:12	דברנו	piel	pft	1cp	דבר	180		speak
	אמר	qal	infc		אמר	55		say
	חדל	qal	impv	ms	חדל	292		cease
	נעבדה	qal	coh	1cp	עבד	712		work,serve
	עבד	qal	infc		עבד	712		work,serve
	מתנו	qal	infc		מות	559	1cp	die
14:13	יאמר	qal	wci	3ms	אמר	55		say
	תיראו	qal	jusm	2mp	ירא	431		fear
	התיצבו	hith	impv	mp	יצב	426		stand oneself
	ראו	qal	impv	mp	ראה	906		see
	יעשׂה	qal	impf	3ms	עשׂה	793		do,make
	ראיתם	qal	pft	2mp	ראה	906		see
	תסיפו	hiph	impf	2mp	יסף	414		add,do again
	ראתם	qal	infc		ראה	906	3mp	see
14:14	ילחם	niph	impf	3ms	לחם	535		wage war
	תחרישׁון	hiph	impf	2mp	חרשׁ	361		be silent
14:15	יאמר	qal	wci	3ms	אמר	55		say
14:15	תצעק	qal	impf	2ms	צעק	858		cry out
	דבר	piel	impv	ms	דבר	180		speak
	יסעו	qal	jusm	3mp	נסע	652		pull up,set out
14:16	הרם	hiph	impv	ms	רום	926		raise,lift
	נטה	qal	impv	ms	נטה	639		stretch,incline
	בקעהו	qal	impv	ms	בקע	131	3ms	cleave,break
	יבאו	qal	jusm	3mp	בוא	97		come in
14:17	מחזק	piel	ptc	ms	חזק	304		make strong
	יבאו	qal	jusm	3mp	בוא	97		come in
	אכבדה	niph	cohf	1cs	כבד	457		be honored
14:18	ידעו	qal	wcp	3cp	ידע	393		know
	הכבדי	niph	infc		כבד	457	1cs	be honored
14:19	יסע	qal	wci	3ms	נסע	652		pull up,set out
	הלך	qal	ptc	ms	הלך	229		walk,go
	ילך	qal	wci	3ms	הלך	229		walk,go
	יסע	qal	wci	3ms	נסע	652		pull up,set out
	יעמד	qal	wci	3ms	עמד	763		stand,stop
14:20	יבא	qal	wci	3ms	בוא	97		come in
	יהי	qal	wci	3ms	היה	224		be,become
	יאר	hiph	wci	3ms	אור	21		cause to shine
	קרב	qal	pft	3ms	קרב	897		approach
14:21	יט	qal	wci	3ms	נטה	639		stretch,incline
	יולך	hiph	wci	3ms	הלך	229		lead,bring
	ישׂם	qal	wci	3ms	שׂים	962		put,set
	יבקעו	niph	wci	3mp	בקע	131		be cleft
14:22	יבאו	qal	wci	3mp	בוא	97		come in
14:23	ירדפו	qal	wci	3mp	רדף	922		pursue
	יבאו	qal	wci	3mp	בוא	97		come in
14:24	יהי	qal	wci	3ms	היה	224		be,become
	ישׁקף	hiph	wci	3ms	שׁקף	1054		look down
	יהם	qal	wci	3ms	המם	243		confuse,vex
14:25	יסר	hiph	wci	3ms	סור	693		take away
	ינהגהו	piel	wci	3ms	נהג	624	3ms	drive away,lead
	יאמר	qal	wci	3ms	אמר	55		say
	אנוסה	qal	coh	1cs	נוס	630		flee,escape
	נלחם	niph	ptc	ms	לחם	535		wage war
14:26	יאמר	qal	wci	3ms	אמר	55		say
	נטה	qal	impv	ms	נטה	639		stretch,incline
	ישׁבו	qal	jusm	3mp	שׁוב	996		turn,return
14:27	יט	qal	wci	3ms	נטה	639		stretch,incline
	ישׁב	qal	wci	3ms	שׁוב	996		turn,return
	פנות	qal	infc		פנה	815		turn
	נסים	qal	ptc	mp	נוס	630		flee,escape
	קראתו	qal	infc		קרא	896	3ms	meet,encounter
	ינער	piel	wci	3ms	נער	654		shake utterly
14:28	ישׁבו	qal	wci	3mp	שׁוב	996		turn,return
	יכסו	piel	wci	3mp	כסה	491		cover
	באים	qal	ptc	mp	בוא	97		come in
	נשׁאר	niph	pft	3ms	שׁאר	983		be left
14:29	הלכו	qal	pft	3cp	הלך	229		walk,go
14:30	יושׁע	hiph	wci	3ms	ישׁע	446		deliver,save
	ירא	qal	wci	3ms	ראה	906		see
	מת	qal	ptc	ms	מות	559		die
14:31	ירא	qal	wci	3ms	ראה	906		see

ChVs	Form	Stem	Tnse	PGN	Root	BDB	Sfx	Meaning
14:31	עשׂה	qal	pft	3ms	עשׂה	793		do,make
	ייראו	qal	wci	3mp	ירא	431		fear
	יאמינו	hiph	wci	3mp	אמן	52		believe
15:1	ישׁיר	qal	impf	3ms	שׁיר	1010		sing
	יאמרו	qal	wci	3mp	אמר	55		say
	אמר	qal	infc		אמר	55		say
	אשׁירה	qal	coh	1cs	שׁיר	1010		sing
	גאה	qal	infa		גאה	144		rise up
	גאה	qal	pft	3ms	גאה	144		rise up
	רכבו	qal	ptc	ms	רכב	938	3ms	mount,ride
	רמה	qal	pft	3ms	רמה	941		cast,shoot
15:2	יהי	qal	wci	3ms	היה	224		be,become
	אנוהו	hiph	impf	1cs	נוה	627	3ms	beautify,praise
	ארממנהו	pol	impf	1cs	רום	926	3ms	raise,rear
15:4	ירה	qal	pft	3ms	ירה	434		throw,shoot
	טבעו	pual	pft	3cp	טבע	371		be sunk
15:5	יכסימו	piel	impf	3mp	כסה	491	3mp	cover
	ירדו	qal	pft	3cp	ירד	432		come down
15:6	נאדרי	niph	ptc	ms	אדר	12		be great
	תרעץ	qal	impf	3fs	רעץ	950		shatter
	אויב	qal	ptc	ms	איב	33		be hostile to
15:7	תהרס	qal	impf	2ms	הרס	248		throw down
	קמיך	qal	ptc	mp	קום	877	2ms	arise,stand
	תשׁלח	piel	impf	2ms	שׁלח	1018		send away,shoot
	יאכלמו	qal	impf	3ms	אכל	37	3mp	eat,devour
15:8	נערמו	niph	pft	3cp	ערם	790		be heaped up
	נצבו	niph	pft	3cp	נצב	662		stand
	נזלים	qal	ptc	mp	נזל	633		flow
	קפאו	qal	pft	3cp	קפא	891		condense
15:9	אמר	qal	pft	3ms	אמר	55		say
	אויב	qal	ptc	ms	איב	33		be hostile to
	ארדף	qal	impf	1cs	רדף	922		pursue
	אשׂיג	hiph	impf	1cs	נשׂג	673		reach,overtake
	אחלק	piel	impf	1cs	חלק	323		divide
	תמלאמו	qal	impf	3fs	מלא	569	3mp	be full,fill
	אריק	hiph	impf	1cs	ריק	937		make empty
	תורישׁמו	hiph	impf	3fs	ירשׁ	439	3mp	c. to possess
15:10	נשׁפת	qal	pft	2ms	נשׁף	676		blow
	כסמו	piel	pft	3ms	כסה	491	3mp	cover
	צללו	qal	pft	3cp	צלל	853		sink
15:11	נאדר	niph	ptc	ms	אדר	12		be great
	נורא	niph	ptc	ms	ירא	431		be feared
	עשׂה	qal	ptc	ms	עשׂה	793		do,make
15:12	נטית	qal	pft	2ms	נטה	639		stretch,incline
	תבלעמו	qal	impf	3fs	בלע	118	3mp	swallow
15:13	נחית	qal	pft	2ms	נחה	634		lead
	גאלת	qal	pft	2ms	גאל	145		redeem
	נהלת	piel	pft	2ms	נהל	624		lead,refresh
15:14	שׁמעו	qal	pft	3cp	שׁמע	1033		hear
	ירגזון	qal	impf	3mp	רגז	919		quake
	אחז	qal	pft	3ms	אחז	28		grasp
	ישׁבי	qal	ptc	mp	ישׁב	442		sit,dwell
15:15	נבהלו	niph	pft	3cp	בהל	96		be disturbed
	יאחזמו	qal	impf	3ms	אחז	28	3mp	grasp
15:15	נמגו	niph	pft	3cp	מוג	556		melt away
	ישׁבי	qal	ptc	mp	ישׁב	442		sit,dwell
15:16	תפל	qal	impf	3fs	נפל	656		fall
	ידמו	qal	impf	3mp	דמם	198		be silent
	יעבר	qal	impf	3ms	עבר	716		pass over
	יעבר	qal	impf	3ms	עבר	716		pass over
	קנית	qal	pft	2ms	קנה	888		get,buy
15:17	תבאמו	hiph	impf	2ms	בוא	97	3mp	bring in
	תטעמו	qal	impf	2ms	נטע	642	3mp	plant
	שׁבתך	qal	infc		ישׁב	442	2ms	sit,dwell
	פעלת	qal	pft	2ms	פעל	821		do,make
	כוננו	pol	pft	3cp	כון	465		establish
15:18	ימלך	qal	impf	3ms	מלך	573		be king,reign
15:19	בא	qal	pft	3ms	בוא	97		come in
	ישׁב	hiph	wci	3ms	שׁוב	996		bring back
	הלכו	qal	pft	3cp	הלך	229		walk,go
15:20	ותקח	qal	wci	3fs	לקח	542		take
	תצאן	qal	wci	3fp	יצא	422		go out
15:21	תען	qal	wci	3fs	ענה	777		sing
	שׁירו	qal	impv	mp	שׁיר	1010		sing
	גאה	qal	infa		גאה	144		rise up
	גאה	qal	pft	3ms	גאה	144		rise up
	רכבו	qal	ptc	ms	רכב	938	3ms	mount,ride
	רמה	qal	pft	3ms	רמה	941		cast,shoot
15:22	יסע	hiph	wci	3ms	נסע	652		lead out,remove
	יצאו	qal	wci	3mp	יצא	422		go out
	ילכו	qal	wci	3mp	הלך	229		walk,go
	מצאו	qal	pft	3cp	מצא	592		find
15:23	יבאו	qal	wci	3mp	בוא	97		come in
	יכלו	qal	pft	3cp	יכל	407		be able
	שׁתת	qal	infc		שׁתה	1059		drink
	קרא	qal	pft	3ms	קרא	894		call,proclaim
15:24	ילנו	niph	wci	3mp	לון	534		murmur
	אמר	qal	infc		אמר	55		say
	נשׁתה	qal	impf	1cp	שׁתה	1059		drink
15:25	יצעק	qal	wci	3ms	צעק	858		cry out
	יורהו	hiph	wci	3ms	ירה	434	3ms	shoot,teach
	ישׁלך	hiph	wci	3ms	שׁלך	1020		throw,cast
	ימתקו	qal	wci	3mp	מתק	608		be sweet,suck
	שׂם	qal	pft	3ms	שׂים	962		put,set
	נסהו	piel	pft	3ms	נסה	650	3ms	test,try
15:26	יאמר	qal	wci	3ms	אמר	55		say
	שׁמוע	qal	infa		שׁמע	1033		hear
	תשׁמע	qal	impf	2ms	שׁמע	1033		hear
	תעשׂה	qal	impf	2ms	עשׂה	793		do,make
	האזנת	hiph	wcp	2ms	אזן	24		hear
	שׁמרת	qal	wcp	2ms	שׁמר	1036		keep,watch
	שׂמתי	qal	pft	1cs	שׂים	962		put,set
	אשׂים	qal	impf	1cs	שׂים	962		put,set
	רפאך	qal	ptc	ms	רפא	950	2ms	heal
15:27	יבאו	qal	wci	3mp	בוא	97		come in
	יחנו	qal	wci	3mp	חנה	333		decline,encamp
16:1	יסעו	qal	wci	3mp	נסע	652		pull up,set out
	יבאו	qal	wci	3mp	בוא	97		come in

ChVs	Form	Stem	Tnse	PGN	Root	BDB	Sfx	Meaning
16:1	צאתם	qal	infc		יצא	422	3mp	go out
16:2	ילינוk	hiph	wci	3mp	לון	534		murmur
	ילונוq	niph	wci	3mp	לון	534		murmur
16:3	יאמרו	qal	wci	3mp	אמר	55		say
	יתן	qal	impf	3ms	נתן	678		give,set
	מותנו	qal	infc		מות	559	1cp	die
	שׁבתנו	qal	infc		ישׁב	442	1cp	sit,dwell
	אכלנו	qal	infc		אכל	37	1cp	eat,devour
	הוצאתם	hiph	pft	2mp	יצא	422		bring out
	המית	hiph	infc		מות	559		kill
16:4	יאמר	qal	wci	3ms	אמר	55		say
	ממטיר	hiph	ptc	ms	מטר	565		rain
	יצא	qal	wcp	3ms	יצא	422		go out
	לקטו	qal	wcp	3cp	לקט	544		pick,gather
	אנסנו	piel	impf	1cs	נסה	650	3ms	test,try
	ילך	qal	impf	3ms	הלך	229		walk,go
16:5	היה	qal	wcp	3ms	היה	224		be,become
	הכינו	hiph	wcp	3cp	כון	465		fix,prepare
	יביאו	hiph	impf	3mp	בוא	97		bring in
	היה	qal	wcp	3ms	היה	224		be,become
	ילקטו	qal	impf	3mp	לקט	544		pick,gather
16:6	יאמר	qal	wci	3ms	אמר	55		say
	ידעתם	qal	wcp	2mp	ידע	393		know
	הוציא	hiph	pft	3ms	יצא	422		bring out
16:7	ראיתם	qal	wcp	2mp	ראה	906		see
	שׁמעו	qal	infc		שׁמע	1033	3ms	hear
	תלונוk	niph	impf	2mp	לון	534		murmur
	תלינוq	hiph	impf	2mp	לון	534		murmur
16:8	יאמר	qal	wci	3ms	אמר	55		say
	תת	qal	infc		נתן	678		give,set
	אכל	qal	infc		אכל	37		eat,devour
	שׂבע	qal	infc		שׂבע	959		be sated
	שׁמע	qal	infc		שׁמע	1033		hear
	מלינם	hiph	ptc	mp	לון	534		murmur
16:9	יאמר	qal	wci	3ms	אמר	55		say
	אמר	qal	impv	ms	אמר	55		say
	קרבו	qal	impv	mp	קרב	897		approach
	שׁמע	qal	pft	3ms	שׁמע	1033		hear
16:10	יהי	qal	wci	3ms	היה	224		be,become
	דבר	piel	infc		דבר	180		speak
	יפנו	qal	wci	3mp	פנה	815		turn
	נראה	niph	pft	3ms	ראה	906		appear,be seen
16:11	ידבר	piel	wci	3ms	דבר	180		speak
	אמר	qal	infc		אמר	55		say
16:12	שׁמעתי	qal	pft	1cs	שׁמע	1033		hear
	דבר	piel	impv	ms	דבר	180		speak
	אמר	qal	infc		אמר	55		say
	תאכלו	qal	impf	2mp	אכל	37		eat,devour
	תשׂבעו	qal	impf	2mp	שׂבע	959		be sated
	ידעתם	qal	wcp	2mp	ידע	393		know
16:13	יהי	qal	wci	3ms	היה	224		be,become
	תעל	qal	wci	3fs	עלה	748		go up
	תכס	piel	wci	3fs	כסה	491		cover
	היתה	qal	pft	3fs	היה	224		be,become

ChVs	Form	Stem	Tnse	PGN	Root	BDB	Sfx	Meaning
16:14	תעל	qal	wci	3fs	עלה	748		go up
	מחספס	pual	ptc	ms	חספס	341		scale-like
16:15	יראו	qal	wci	3mp	ראה	906		see
	יאמרו	qal	wci	3mp	אמר	55		say
	ידעו	qal	pft	3cp	ידע	393		know
	יאמר	qal	wci	3ms	אמר	55		say
	נתן	qal	pft	3ms	נתן	678		give,set
16:16	צוה	piel	pft	3ms	צוה	845		command
	לקטו	qal	impv	mp	לקט	544		pick,gather
	אכלו	qal	infc		אכל	37	3ms	eat,devour
	תקחו	qal	impf	2mp	לקח	542		take
16:17	יעשׂו	qal	wci	3mp	עשׂה	793		do,make
	ילקטו	qal	wci	3mp	לקט	544		pick,gather
	מרבה	hiph	ptc	ms	רבה	915		make many
	ממעיט	hiph	ptc	ms	מעט	589		make small
16:18	ימדו	qal	wci	3mp	מדד	551		measure
	העדיף	hiph	pft	3ms	עדף	727		have surplus
	מרבה	hiph	ptc	ms	רבה	915		make many
	ממעיט	hiph	ptc	ms	מעט	589		make small
	החסיר	hiph	pft	3ms	חסר	341		cause to lack
	אכלו	qal	infc		אכל	37	3ms	eat,devour
	לקטו	qal	pft	3cp	לקט	544		pick,gather
16:19	יאמר	qal	wci	3ms	אמר	55		say
	יותר	hiph	jus	3ms	יתר	451		leave,spare
16:20	שׁמעו	qal	pft	3cp	שׁמע	1033		hear
	יותרו	hiph	wci	3mp	יתר	451		leave,spare
	ירם	qal	wci	3ms	רמם	942		be wormy
	יבאשׁ	qal	wci	3ms	באשׁ	92		stink
	יקצף	qal	wci	3ms	קצף	893		be angry
16:21	ילקטו	qal	wci	3mp	לקט	544		pick,gather
	אכלו	qal	infc		אכל	37	3ms	eat,devour
	חם	qal	pft	3ms	חמם	328		be warm
	נמס	niph	pft	3ms	מסס	587		melt,despair
16:22	יהי	qal	wci	3ms	היה	224		be,become
	לקטו	qal	pft	3cp	לקט	544		pick,gather
	יבאו	qal	wci	3mp	בוא	97		come in
	יגידו	hiph	wci	3mp	נגד	616		declare,tell
16:23	יאמר	qal	wci	3ms	אמר	55		say
	דבר	piel	pft	3ms	דבר	180		speak
	תאפו	qal	impf	2mp	אפה	66		bake
	אפו	qal	impv	mp	אפה	66		bake
	תבשׁלו	piel	impf	2mp	בשׁל	143		boil,cook
	בשׁלו	piel	impv	mp	בשׁל	143		boil,cook
	עדף	qal	ptc	ms	עדף	727		remain over
	הניחו	hiph	impv	mp	נוח	628		give rest,put
16:24	יניחו	hiph	wci	3mp	נוח	628		give rest,put
	צוה	piel	pft	3ms	צוה	845		command
	הבאישׁ	hiph	pft	3ms	באשׁ	92		cause to stink
	היתה	qal	pft	3fs	היה	224		be,become
16:25	יאמר	qal	wci	3ms	אמר	55		say
	אכלהו	qal	impv	mp	אכל	37	3ms	eat,devour
	תמצאהו	qal	impf	2mp	מצא	592	3ms	find
16:26	תלקטהו	qal	impf	2mp	לקט	544	3ms	pick,gather
	יהיה	qal	impf	3ms	היה	224		be,become

ChVs	Form	Stem	Tnse	PGN	Root	BDB	Sfx	Meaning
16: 27	יהי	qal	wci	3ms	היה	224		be,become
	יצאו	qal	pft	3cp	יצא	422		go out
	לקט	qal	infc		לקט	544		pick,gather
	מצאו	qal	pft	3cp	מצא	592		find
16: 28	יאמר	qal	wci	3ms	אמר	55		say
	מאנתם	piel	pft	2mp	מאן	549		refuse
	שׁמר	qal	infc		שׁמר	1036		keep,watch
16: 29	ראו	qal	impv	mp	ראה	906		see
	נתן	qal	pft	3ms	נתן	678		give,set
	נתן	qal	ptc	ms	נתן	678		give,set
	שׁבו	qal	impv	mp	ישׁב	442		sit,dwell
	יצא	qal	jusm	3ms	יצא	422		go out
16: 30	ישׁבתו	qal	wci	3mp	שׁבת	991		cease,desist
16: 31	יקראו	qal	wci	3mp	קרא	894		call,proclaim
16: 32	יאמר	qal	wci	3ms	אמר	55		say
	צוה	piel	pft	3ms	צוה	845		command
	יראו	qal	impf	3mp	ראה	906		see
	האכלתי	hiph	pft	1cs	אכל	37		cause to eat
	הוציאי	hiph	infc		יצא	422	1cs	bring out
16: 33	יאמר	qal	wci	3ms	אמר	55		say
	קח	qal	impv	ms	לקח	542		take
	תן	qal	impv	ms	נתן	678		give,set
	הנח	hiph	impv	ms	נוח	628		give rest,put
16: 34	צוה	piel	pft	3ms	צוה	845		command
	יניחהו	hiph	wci	3ms	נוח	628	3ms	give rest,put
16: 35	אכלו	qal	pft	3cp	אכל	37		eat,devour
	באם	qal	infc		בוא	97	3mp	come in
	נושׁבת	niph	ptc	fs	ישׁב	442		be inhabited
	אכלו	qal	pft	3cp	אכל	37		eat,devour
	באם	qal	infc		בוא	97	3mp	come in
17: 1	יסעו	qal	wci	3mp	נסע	652		pull up,set out
	יחנו	qal	wci	3mp	חנה	333		decline,encamp
	שׁתת	qal	infc		שׁתה	1059		drink
17: 2	ירב	qal	wci	3ms	ריב	936		strive,contend
	יאמרו	qal	wci	3mp	אמר	55		say
	תנו	qal	impv	mp	נתן	678		give,set
	נשׁתה	qal	jusm	1cp	שׁתה	1059		drink
	יאמר	qal	wci	3ms	אמר	55		say
	תריבון	qal	impf	2mp	ריב	936		strive,contend
	תנסון	piel	impf	2mp	נסה	650		test,try
17: 3	יצמא	qal	wci	3ms	צמא	854		be thirsty
	ילן	hiph	wci	3ms	לון	534		murmur
	יאמר	qal	wci	3ms	אמר	55		say
	העליתנו	hiph	pft	2ms	עלה	748	1cp	bring up,offer
	המית	hiph	infc		מות	559		kill
17: 4	יצעק	qal	wci	3ms	צעק	858		cry out
	אמר	qal	infc		אמר	55		say
	אעשׂה	qal	impf	1cs	עשׂה	793		do,make
	סקלני	qal	wcp	3cp	סקל	709	1cs	stone to death
17: 5	יאמר	qal	wci	3ms	אמר	55		say
	עבר	qal	impv	ms	עבר	716		pass over
	קח	qal	impv	ms	לקח	542		take
	הכית	hiph	pft	2ms	נכה	645		smite
	קח	qal	impv	ms	לקח	542		take
17: 5	הלכת	qal	wcp	2ms	הלך	229		walk,go
17: 6	עמד	qal	ptc	ms	עמד	763		stand,stop
	הכית	hiph	wcp	2ms	נכה	645		smite
	יצאו	qal	wcp	3cp	יצא	422		go out
	שׁתה	qal	wcp	3ms	שׁתה	1059		drink
	יעשׂ	qal	wci	3ms	עשׂה	793		do,make
17: 7	יקרא	qal	wci	3ms	קרא	894		call,proclaim
	נסתם	piel	infc		נסה	650	3mp	test,try
	אמר	qal	infc		אמר	55		say
17: 8	יבא	qal	wci	3ms	בוא	97		come in
	ילחם	niph	wci	3ms	לחם	535		wage war
17: 9	יאמר	qal	wci	3ms	אמר	55		say
	בחר	qal	impv	ms	בחר	103		choose
	צא	qal	impv	ms	יצא	422		go out
	הלחם	niph	impv	ms	לחם	535		wage war
	נצב	niph	ptc	ms	נצב	662		stand
17: 10	יעשׂ	qal	wci	3ms	עשׂה	793		do,make
	אמר	qal	pft	3ms	אמר	55		say
	הלחם	niph	infc		לחם	535		wage war
	עלו	qal	pft	3cp	עלה	748		go up
17: 11	היה	qal	wcp	3ms	היה	224		be,become
	ירים	hiph	impf	3ms	רום	926		raise,lift
	גבר	qal	wcp	3ms	גבר	149		be strong
	יניח	hiph	impf	3ms	נוח	628		give rest,put
	גבר	qal	wcp	3ms	גבר	149		be strong
17: 12	יקחו	qal	wci	3mp	לקח	542		take
	ישׂימו	qal	wci	3mp	שׂים	962		put,set
	ישׁב	qal	wci	3ms	ישׁב	442		sit,dwell
	תמכו	qal	pft	3cp	תמך	1069		grasp,support
	יהי	qal	wci	3ms	היה	224		be,become
	בא	qal	infc		בוא	97		come in
17: 13	יחלשׁ	qal	wci	3ms	חלשׁ	325		prostrate
17: 14	יאמר	qal	wci	3ms	אמר	55		say
	כתב	qal	impv	ms	כתב	507		write
	שׂים	qal	impv	ms	שׂים	962		put,set
	מחה	qal	infa		מחה	562		wipe,blot out
	אמחה	qal	impf	1cs	מחה	562		wipe,blot out
17: 15	יבן	qal	wci	3ms	בנה	124		build
	יקרא	qal	wci	3ms	קרא	894		call,proclaim
17: 16	יאמר	qal	wci	3ms	אמר	55		say
18: 1	ישׁמע	qal	wci	3ms	שׁמע	1033		hear
	עשׂה	qal	pft	3ms	עשׂה	793		do,make
	הוציא	hiph	pft	3ms	יצא	422		bring out
18: 2	יקח	qal	wci	3ms	לקח	542		take
18: 3	אמר	qal	pft	3ms	אמר	55		say
	הייתי	qal	pft	1cs	היה	224		be,become
18: 4	יצלני	hiph	wci	3ms	נצל	664	1cs	snatch,deliver
18: 5	יבא	qal	wci	3ms	בוא	97		come in
	חנה	qal	ptc	ms	חנה	333		decline,encamp
18: 6	יאמר	qal	wci	3ms	אמר	55		say
	בא	qal	ptc	ms	בוא	97		come in
18: 7	יצא	qal	wci	3ms	יצא	422		go out
	קראת	qal	infc		קרא	896		meet,encounter
	ישׁתחו	hish	wci	3ms	חוה	1005		bow down

ChVs	Form	Stem	Tnse	PGN	Root	BDB	Sfx	Meaning
18: 7	ישׁק	qal	wci	3ms	נשׁק	676		kiss
	ישׁאלו	qal	wci	3mp	שׁאל	981		ask, borrow
	יבאו	qal	wci	3mp	בוא	97		come in
18: 8	יספר	piel	wci	3ms	ספר	707		recount
	עשׂה	qal	pft	3ms	עשׂה	793		do, make
	מצאתם	qal	pft	3fs	מצא	592	3mp	find
	יצלם	hiph	wci	3ms	נצל	664	3mp	snatch, deliver
18: 9	יחד	qal	wci	3ms	חדה	292		rejoice
	עשׂה	qal	pft	3ms	עשׂה	793		do, make
	הצילו	hiph	pft	3ms	נצל	664	3ms	snatch, deliver
18: 10	יאמר	qal	wci	3ms	אמר	55		say
	ברוך	qal	pptc	ms	ברך	138		kneel, bless
	הציל	hiph	pft	3ms	נצל	664		snatch, deliver
	הציל	hiph	pft	3ms	נצל	664		snatch, deliver
18: 11	ידעתי	qal	pft	1cs	ידע	393		know
	זדו	qal	pft	3cp	זיד	267		act proudly
18: 12	יקח	qal	wci	3ms	לקח	542		take
	יבא	qal	wci	3ms	בוא	97		come in
	אכל	qal	infc		אכל	37		eat, devour
18: 13	יהי	qal	wci	3ms	היה	224		be, become
	ישׁב	qal	wci	3ms	ישׁב	442		sit, dwell
	שׁפט	qal	infc		שׁפט	1047		judge
	יעמד	qal	wci	3ms	עמד	763		stand, stop
18: 14	ירא	qal	wci	3ms	ראה	906		see
	עשׂה	qal	ptc	ms	עשׂה	793		do, make
	יאמר	qal	wci	3ms	אמר	55		say
	עשׂה	qal	ptc	ms	עשׂה	793		do, make
	יושׁב	qal	ptc	ms	ישׁב	442		sit, dwell
	נצב	niph	ptc	ms	נצב	662		stand
18: 15	יאמר	qal	wci	3ms	אמר	55		say
	יבא	qal	impf	3ms	בוא	97		come in
	דרשׁ	qal	infc		דרשׁ	205		resort to, seek
18: 16	יהיה	qal	impf	3ms	היה	224		be, become
	בא	qal	ptc	ms	בוא	97		come in
	שׁפטתי	qal	wcp	1cs	שׁפט	1047		judge
	הודעתי	hiph	wcp	1cs	ידע	393		declare
18: 17	יאמר	qal	wci	3ms	אמר	55		say
	עשׂה	qal	ptc	ms	עשׂה	793		do, make
18: 18	נבל	qal	infa		נבל	615		sink, droop
	תבל	qal	impf	2ms	נבל	615		sink, droop
	תוכל	qal	impf	2ms	יכל	407		be able
	עשׂהו	qal	infc		עשׂה	793	3ms	do, make
18: 19	שׁמע	qal	impv	ms	שׁמע	1033		hear
	איעצך	qal	cohm	1cs	יעץ	419	2ms	advise, counsel
	יהי	qal	jus	3ms	היה	224		be, become
	היה	qal	impv	ms	היה	224		be, become
	הבאת	hiph	wcp	2ms	בוא	97		bring in
18: 20	הזהרתה	hiph	wcp	2ms	זהר	264		teach
	הודעת	hiph	wcp	2ms	ידע	393		declare
	ילכו	qal	impf	3mp	הלך	229		walk, go
	יעשׂון	qal	impf	3mp	עשׂה	793		do, make
18: 21	תחזה	qal	impf	2ms	חזה	302		see
	יראי	qal	ptc	mp	ירא	431		fear
	שׂנאי	qal	ptc	mp	שׂנא	971		hate
18: 21	שׂמת	qal	wcp	2ms	שׂים	962		put, set
18: 22	שׁפטו	qal	wcp	3cp	שׁפט	1047		judge
	היה	qal	wcp	3ms	היה	224		be, become
	יביאו	hiph	impf	3mp	בוא	97		bring in
	ישׁפטו	qal	impf	3mp	שׁפט	1047		judge
	הקל	hiph	impv	ms	קלל	886		make light
	נשׂאו	qal	wcp	3cp	נשׂא	669		lift, carry
18: 23	תעשׂה	qal	impf	2ms	עשׂה	793		do, make
	צוך	piel	wcp	3ms	צוה	845	2ms	command
	יכלת	qal	wcp	2ms	יכל	407		be able
	עמד	qal	infc		עמד	763		stand, stop
	יבא	qal	impf	3ms	בוא	97		come in
18: 24	ישׁמע	qal	wci	3ms	שׁמע	1033		hear
	יעשׂ	qal	wci	3ms	עשׂה	793		do, make
	אמר	qal	pft	3ms	אמר	55		say
18: 25	יבחר	qal	wci	3ms	בחר	103		choose
	יתן	qal	wci	3ms	נתן	678		give, set
18: 26	שׁפטו	qal	wcp	3cp	שׁפט	1047		judge
	יביאון	hiph	impf	3mp	בוא	97		bring in
	ישׁפוטו	qal	impf	3mp	שׁפט	1047		judge
18: 27	ישׁלח	piel	wci	3ms	שׁלח	1018		send away, shoot
	ילך	qal	wci	3ms	הלך	229		walk, go
19: 1	צאת	qal	infc		יצא	422		go out
	באו	qal	pft	3cp	בוא	97		come in
19: 2	יסעו	qal	wci	3mp	נסע	652		pull up, set out
	יבאו	qal	wci	3mp	בוא	97		come in
	יחנו	qal	wci	3mp	חנה	333		decline, encamp
	יחן	qal	wci	3ms	חנה	333		decline, encamp
19: 3	עלה	qal	pft	3ms	עלה	748		go up
	יקרא	qal	wci	3ms	קרא	894		call, proclaim
	אמר	qal	infc		אמר	55		say
	תאמר	qal	impf	2ms	אמר	55		say
	תגיד	hiph	impf	2ms	נגד	616		declare, tell
19: 4	ראיתם	qal	pft	2mp	ראה	906		see
	עשׂיתי	qal	pft	1cs	עשׂה	793		do, make
	אשׂא	qal	wci	1cs	נשׂא	669		lift, carry
	אבא	hiph	wci	1cs	בוא	97		bring in
19: 5	שׁמוע	qal	infa		שׁמע	1033		hear
	תשׁמעו	qal	impf	2mp	שׁמע	1033		hear
	שׁמרתם	qal	wcp	2mp	שׁמר	1036		keep, watch
	הייתם	qal	wcp	2mp	היה	224		be, become
19: 6	תהיו	qal	impf	2mp	היה	224		be, become
	תדבר	piel	impf	2ms	דבר	180		speak
19: 7	יבא	qal	wci	3ms	בוא	97		come in
	יקרא	qal	wci	3ms	קרא	894		call, proclaim
	ישׂם	qal	wci	3ms	שׂים	962		put, set
	צוהו	piel	pft	3ms	צוה	845	3ms	command
19: 8	יענו	qal	wci	3mp	ענה	772		answer
	יאמרו	qal	wci	3mp	אמר	55		say
	דבר	piel	pft	3ms	דבר	180		speak
	נעשׂה	qal	impf	1cp	עשׂה	793		do, make
	ישׁב	hiph	wci	3ms	שׁוב	996		bring back
19: 9	יאמר	qal	wci	3ms	אמר	55		say
	בא	qal	ptc	ms	בוא	97		come in

ChVs	Form	Stem	Tnse	PGN	Root	BDB	Sfx	Meaning
19:9	ישׁמע	qal	impf	3ms	שׁמע	1033		hear
	דברי	piel	infc		דבר	180	1cs	speak
	יאמינו	hiph	impf	3mp	אמן	52		believe
	יגד	hiph	wci	3ms	נגד	616		declare,tell
19:10	יאמר	qal	wci	3ms	אמר	55		say
	לך	qal	impv	ms	הלך	229		walk,go
	קדשׁתם	piel	wcp	2ms	קדשׁ	872	3mp	consecrate
	כבסו	piel	wcp	3cp	כבס	460		wash
19:11	היו	qal	wcp	3cp	היה	224		be,become
	נכנים	niph	ptc	mp	כון	465		be established
	ירד	qal	impf	3ms	ירד	432		come down
19:12	הגבלת	hiph	wcp	2ms	גבל	148		set bounds for
	אמר	qal	infc		אמר	55		say
	השׁמרו	niph	impv	mp	שׁמר	1036		be kept,guarded
	עלות	qal	infc		עלה	748		go up
	נגע	qal	infc		נגע	619		touch,strike
	נגע	qal	ptc	ms	נגע	619		touch,strike
	מות	qal	infa		מות	559		die
	יומת	hoph	impf	3ms	מות	559		be killed
19:13	תגע	qal	impf	2ms	נגע	619		touch,strike
	סקול	qal	infa		סקל	709		stone to death
	יסקל	niph	impf	3ms	סקל	709		be stoned
	ירה	qal	infa		ירה	434		throw,shoot
	יירה	niph	impf	3ms	ירה	434		be shot
	יחיה	qal	impf	3ms	חיה	310		live
	משׁך	qal	infc		משׁך	604		draw,pull
	יעלו	qal	jusm	3mp	עלה	748		go up
19:14	ירד	qal	wci	3ms	ירד	432		come down
	יקדשׁ	piel	wci	3ms	קדשׁ	872		consecrate
	יכבסו	piel	wci	3mp	כבס	460		wash
19:15	יאמר	qal	wci	3ms	אמר	55		say
	היו	qal	impv	mp	היה	224		be,become
	נכנים	niph	ptc	mp	כון	465		be established
	תגשׁו	qal	jusm	2mp	נגשׁ	620		draw near
19:16	יהי	qal	wci	3ms	היה	224		be,become
	הית	qal	infc		היה	224		be,become
	יהי	qal	wci	3ms	היה	224		be,become
	יחרד	qal	wci	3ms	חרד	353		tremble
19:17	יוצא	hiph	wci	3ms	יצא	422		bring out
	קראת	qal	infc		קרא	896		meet,encounter
	יתיצבו	hith	wci	3mp	יצב	426		stand oneself
19:18	עשׁן	qal	pft	3ms	עשׁן	798		smoke,fume
	ירד	qal	pft	3ms	ירד	432		come down
	יעל	qal	wci	3ms	עלה	748		go up
	יחרד	qal	wci	3ms	חרד	353		tremble
19:19	יהי	qal	wci	3ms	היה	224		be,become
	הולך	qal	ptc	ms	הלך	229		walk,go
	חזק	qal	ptc	ms	חזק	304		be strong
	ידבר	piel	impf	3ms	דבר	180		speak
	יעננו	qal	impf	3ms	ענה	772	3ms	answer
19:20	ירד	qal	wci	3ms	ירד	432		come down
	יקרא	qal	wci	3ms	קרא	894		call,proclaim
	יעל	qal	wci	3ms	עלה	748		go up
19:21	יאמר	qal	wci	3ms	אמר	55		say
19:21	רד	qal	impv	ms	ירד	432		come down
	העד	hiph	impv	ms	עוד	729		testify,warn
	יהרסו	qal	impf	3mp	הרס	248		throw down
	ראות	qal	infc		ראה	906		see
	נפל	qal	wcp	3ms	נפל	656		fall
19:22	נגשׁים	niph	ptc	mp	נגשׁ	620		draw near
	יתקדשׁו	hith	impf	3mp	קדשׁ	872		consecrate self
	יפרץ	qal	impf	3ms	פרץ	829		break through
19:23	יאמר	qal	wci	3ms	אמר	55		say
	יוכל	qal	impf	3ms	יכל	407		be able
	עלת	qal	infc		עלה	748		go up
	העדתה	hiph	pft	2ms	עוד	729		testify,warn
	אמר	qal	infc		אמר	55		say
	הגבל	hiph	impv	ms	גבל	148		set bounds for
	קדשׁתו	piel	wcp	2ms	קדשׁ	872	3ms	consecrate
19:24	יאמר	qal	wci	3ms	אמר	55		say
	לך	qal	impv	ms	הלך	229		walk,go
	רד	qal	impv	ms	ירד	432		come down
	עלית	qal	wcp	2ms	עלה	748		go up
	יהרסו	qal	jusm	3mp	הרס	248		throw down
	עלת	qal	infc		עלה	748		go up
	יפרץ	qal	impf	3ms	פרץ	829		break through
19:25	ירד	qal	wci	3ms	ירד	432		come down
	יאמר	qal	wci	3ms	אמר	55		say
20:1	ידבר	piel	wci	3ms	דבר	180		speak
	אמר	qal	infc		אמר	55		say
20:2	הוצאתיך	hiph	pft	1cs	יצא	422	2ms	bring out
20:3	יהיה	qal	impf	3ms	היה	224		be,become
20:4	תעשׂה	qal	impf	2ms	עשׂה	793		do,make
20:5	תשׁתחוה	hish	impf	2ms	חוה	1005		bow down
	תעבדם	hoph	impf	2ms	עבד	712	3mp	be led to serve
	פקד	qal	ptc	ms	פקד	823		attend to,visit
	שׂנאי	qal	ptc	mp	שׂנא	971	1cs	hate
20:6	עשׂה	qal	ptc	ms	עשׂה	793		do,make
	אהבי	qal	ptc	mp	אהב	12	1cs	love
	שׁמרי	qal	ptc	mp	שׁמר	1036		keep,watch
20:7	תשׂא	qal	impf	2ms	נשׂא	669		lift,carry
	ינקה	piel	impf	3ms	נקה	667		acquit
	ישׂא	qal	impf	3ms	נשׂא	669		lift,carry
20:8	זכור	qal	infa		זכר	269		remember
	קדשׁו	piel	infc		קדשׁ	872	3ms	consecrate
20:9	תעבד	qal	impf	2ms	עבד	712		work,serve
	עשׂית	qal	wcp	2ms	עשׂה	793		do,make
20:10	תעשׂה	qal	impf	2ms	עשׂה	793		do,make
20:11	עשׂה	qal	pft	3ms	עשׂה	793		do,make
	ינח	qal	wci	3ms	נוח	628		rest
	ברך	piel	pft	3ms	ברך	138		bless
	יקדשׁהו	piel	wci	3ms	קדשׁ	872	3ms	consecrate
20:12	כבד	piel	impv	ms	כבד	457		honor,make dull
	יארכון	hiph	impf	3mp	ארך	73		prolong
	נתן	qal	ptc	ms	נתן	678		give,set
20:13	תרצח	qal	impf	2ms	רצח	953		murder,slay
20:14	תנאף	qal	impf	2ms	נאף	610		commit adultery
20:15	תגנב	qal	impf	2ms	גנב	170		steal

ChVs	Form	Stem	Tnse	PGN	Root	BDB	Sfx	Meaning
20:16	תענה	qal	impf	2ms	ענה	772		answer
20:17	תחמד	qal	impf	2ms	חמד	326		desire
	תחמד	qal	impf	2ms	חמד	326		desire
20:18	ראים	qal	ptc	mp	ראה	906		see
	ירא	qal	wci	3ms	ראה	906		see
	ינעו	qal	wci	3mp	נוע	631		totter,wave
	יעמדו	qal	wci	3mp	עמד	763		stand,stop
20:19	יאמרו	qal	wci	3mp	אמר	55		say
	דבר	piel	impv	ms	דבר	180		speak
	נשמעה	qal	coh	1cp	שמע	1033		hear
	ידבר	piel	jusm	3ms	דבר	180		speak
	נמות	qal	impf	1cp	מות	559		die
20:20	יאמר	qal	wci	3ms	אמר	55		say
	תיראו	qal	jusm	2mp	ירא	431		fear
	נסות	piel	infc		נסה	650		test,try
	בא	qal	pft	3ms	בוא	97		come in
	תהיה	qal	impf	3fs	היה	224		be,become
	תחטאו	qal	impf	2mp	חטא	306		sin
20:21	יעמד	qal	wci	3ms	עמד	763		stand,stop
	נגשׁ	niph	pft	3ms	נגשׁ	620		draw near
20:22	יאמר	qal	wci	3ms	אמר	55		say
	תאמר	qal	impf	2ms	אמר	55		say
	ראיתם	qal	pft	2mp	ראה	906		see
	דברתי	piel	pft	1cs	דבר	180		speak
20:23	תעשׂון	qal	impf	2mp	עשׂה	793		do,make
	תעשׂו	qal	impf	2mp	עשׂה	793		do,make
20:24	תעשׂה	qal	impf	2ms	עשׂה	793		do,make
	זבחת	qal	wcp	2ms	זבח	256		slaughter
	אזכיר	hiph	impf	1cs	זכר	269		c. to remember
	אבוא	qal	impf	1cs	בוא	97		come in
	ברכתיך	piel	wcp	1cs	ברך	138	2ms	bless
20:25	תעשׂה	qal	impf	2ms	עשׂה	793		do,make
	תבנה	qal	impf	2ms	בנה	124		build
	הנפת	hiph	pft	2ms	נוף	631		swing,wave
	תחללה	piel	wci	2ms	חלל	320	3fs	pollute
20:26	תעלה	qal	impf	2ms	עלה	748		go up
	תגלה	niph	impf	3fs	גלה	162		uncover self
21:1	תשׂים	qal	impf	2ms	שׂים	962		put,set
21:2	תקנה	qal	impf	2ms	קנה	888		get,buy
	יעבד	qal	impf	3ms	עבד	712		work,serve
	יצא	qal	impf	3ms	יצא	422		go out
21:3	יבא	qal	impf	3ms	בוא	97		come in
	יצא	qal	impf	3ms	יצא	422		go out
	יצאה	qal	wcp	3fs	יצא	422		go out
21:4	יתן	qal	impf	3ms	נתן	678		give,set
	ילדה	qal	wcp	3fs	ילד	408		bear,beget
	תהיה	qal	impf	3fs	היה	224		be,become
	יצא	qal	impf	3ms	יצא	422		go out
21:5	אמר	qal	infa		אמר	55		say
	יאמר	qal	impf	3ms	אמר	55		say
	אהבתי	qal	pft	1cs	אהב	12		love
	אצא	qal	impf	1cs	יצא	422		go out
21:6	הגישׁו	hiph	wcp	3ms	נגשׁ	620	3ms	bring near
	הגישׁו	hiph	wcp	3ms	נגשׁ	620	3ms	bring near
21:6	רצע	qal	wcp	3ms	רצע	954		bore,pierce
	עבדו	qal	wcp	3ms	עבד	712	3ms	work,serve
21:7	ימכר	qal	impf	3ms	מכר	569		sell
	תצא	qal	impf	3fs	יצא	422		go out
	צאת	qal	infc		יצא	422		go out
21:8	יעדה	qal	pft	3ms	יעד	416	3fs	appoint
	הפדה	hiph	wcp	3ms	פדה	804	3fs	c. be ransomed
	ימשׁל	qal	impf	3ms	משׁל	605		rule
	מכרה	qal	infc		מכר	569	3fs	sell
	בגדו	qal	infc		בגד	93	3ms	act faithlessly
21:9	ייעדנה	qal	impf	3ms	יעד	416	3fs	appoint
	יעשׂה	qal	impf	3ms	עשׂה	793		do,make
21:10	יקח	qal	impf	3ms	לקח	542		take
	יגרע	qal	impf	3ms	גרע	175		diminish
21:11	יעשׂה	qal	impf	3ms	עשׂה	793		do,make
	יצאה	qal	wcp	3fs	יצא	422		go out
21:12	מכה	hiph	ptc	ms	נכה	645		smite
	מת	qal	wcp	3ms	מות	559		die
	מות	qal	infa		מות	559		die
	יומת	hoph	impf	3ms	מות	559		be killed
21:13	צדה	qal	pft	3ms	צדה	841		lie in wait
	אנה	piel	pft	3ms	אנה	58		cause to meet
	שׂמתי	qal	wcp	1cs	שׂים	962		put,set
	ינוס	qal	impf	3ms	נוס	630		flee,escape
21:14	יזד	hiph	impf	3ms	זיד	267		boil,presume
	הרגו	qal	infc		הרג	246	3ms	kill
	תקחנו	qal	impf	2ms	לקח	542	3ms	take
	מות	qal	infc		מות	559		die
21:15	מכה	hiph	ptc	ms	נכה	645		smite
	מות	qal	infa		מות	559		die
	יומת	hoph	impf	3ms	מות	559		be killed
21:16	גנב	qal	ptc	ms	גנב	170		steal
	מכרו	qal	wcp	3ms	מכר	569	3ms	sell
	נמצא	niph	wcp	3ms	מצא	592		be found
	מות	qal	infa		מות	559		die
	יומת	hoph	impf	3ms	מות	559		be killed
21:17	מקלל	piel	ptc	ms	קלל	886		curse
	מות	qal	infa		מות	559		die
	יומת	hoph	impf	3ms	מות	559		be killed
21:18	יריבן	qal	impf	3mp	ריב	936		strive,contend
	הכה	hiph	wcp	3ms	נכה	645		smite
	ימות	qal	impf	3ms	מות	559		die
	נפל	qal	wcp	3ms	נפל	656		fall
21:19	יקום	qal	impf	3ms	קום	877		arise,stand
	התהלך	hith	wcp	3ms	הלך	229		walk to and fro
	נקה	niph	wcp	3ms	נקה	667		be clean,free
	מכה	hiph	ptc	ms	נכה	645		smite
	יתן	qal	impf	3ms	נתן	678		give,set
	רפא	piel	infa		רפא	950		heal
	ירפא	piel	impf	3ms	רפא	950		heal
21:20	יכה	hiph	impf	3ms	נכה	645		smite
	מת	qal	wcp	3ms	מות	559		die
	נקם	qal	infa		נקם	667		avenge
	ינקם	niph	impf	3ms	נקם	667		avenge oneself

ChVs	Form	Stem	Tnse	PGN	Root	BDB	Sfx	Meaning
21:21	יעמד	qal	impf	3ms	עמד	763		stand,stop
	יקם	hoph	impf	3ms	נקם	667		be avenged
21:22	ינצו	niph	impf	3mp	נצה	663		struggle
	נגפו	qal	wcp	3cp	נגף	619		smite,strike
	יצאו	qal	wcp	3cp	יצא	422		go out
	יהיה	qal	impf	3ms	היה	224		be,become
	ענוש	qal	infa		ענש	778		punish,fine
	יענש	niph	impf	3ms	ענש	778		be fined
	ישית	qal	impf	3ms	שית	1011		put,set
	נתן	qal	wcp	3ms	נתן	678		give,set
21:23	יהיה	qal	impf	3ms	היה	224		be,become
	נתתה	qal	wcp	2ms	נתן	678		give,set
21:26	יכה	hiph	impf	3ms	נכה	645		smite
	שחתה	piel	wcp	3ms	שחת	1007	3fs	spoil,ruin
	ישלחנו	piel	impf	3ms	שלח	1018	3ms	send away,shoot
21:27	יפיל	hiph	impf	3ms	נפל	656		cause to fall
	ישלחנו	piel	impf	3ms	שלח	1018	3ms	send away,shoot
21:28	יגח	qal	impf	3ms	נגח	618		gore
	מת	qal	wcp	3ms	מות	559		die
	סקול	qal	infa		סקל	709		stone to death
	יסקל	niph	impf	3ms	סקל	709		be stoned
	יאכל	niph	impf	3ms	אכל	37		be eaten
21:29	הועד	hoph	wcp	3ms	עוד	729		be testified
	ישמרנו	qal	impf	3ms	שמר	1036	3ms	keep,watch
	המית	hiph	wcp	3ms	מות	559		kill
	יסקל	niph	impf	3ms	סקל	709		be stoned
	יומת	hoph	impf	3ms	מות	559		be killed
21:30	יושת	qalp	impf	3ms	שית	1011		be imposed
	נתן	qal	wcp	3ms	נתן	678		give,set
	יושת	qalp	impf	3ms	שית	1011		be imposed
21:31	יגח	qal	impf	3ms	נגח	618		gore
	יגח	qal	impf	3ms	נגח	618		gore
	יעשה	niph	impf	3ms	עשה	793		be done
21:32	יגח	qal	impf	3ms	נגח	618		gore
	יתן	qal	impf	3ms	נתן	678		give,set
	יסקל	niph	impf	3ms	סקל	709		be stoned
21:33	יפתח	qal	impf	3ms	פתח	834		open
	יכרה	qal	impf	3ms	כרה	500		dig
	יכסנו	piel	impf	3ms	כסה	491	3ms	cover
	נפל	qal	wcp	3ms	נפל	656		fall
21:34	ישלם	piel	impf	3ms	שלם	1022		finish,reward
	ישיב	hiph	impf	3ms	שוב	996		bring back
	מת	qal	ptc	ms	מות	559		die
	יהיה	qal	impf	3ms	היה	224		be,become
21:35	יגף	qal	impf	3ms	נגף	619		smite,strike
	מת	qal	wcp	3ms	מות	559		die
	מכרו	qal	wcp	3cp	מכר	569		sell
	חצו	qal	wcp	3cp	חצה	345		divide
	מת	qal	ptc	ms	מות	559		die
	יחצון	qal	impf	3mp	חצה	345		divide
21:36	נודע	niph	pft	3ms	ידע	393		be made known
	ישמרנו	qal	impf	3ms	שמר	1036	3ms	keep,watch
	שלם	piel	infa		שלם	1022		finish,reward
	ישלם	piel	impf	3ms	שלם	1022		finish,reward
21:36	מת	qal	ptc	ms	מות	559		die
	יהיה	qal	impf	3ms	היה	224		be,become
21:37	יגנב	qal	impf	3ms	גנב	170		steal
	טבחו	qal	wcp	3ms	טבח	370	3ms	slaughter
	מכרו	qal	pft	3ms	מכר	569	3ms	sell
	ישלם	piel	impf	3ms	שלם	1022		finish,reward
22:1	ימצא	niph	impf	3ms	מצא	592		be found
	הכה	hoph	wcp	3ms	נכה	645		be smitten
	מת	qal	wcp	3ms	מות	559		die
22:2	זרחה	qal	pft	3fs	זרח	280		rise,appear
	שלם	piel	infa		שלם	1022		finish,reward
	ישלם	piel	impf	3ms	שלם	1022		finish,reward
	נמכר	niph	wcp	3ms	מכר	569		be sold
22:3	המצא	niph	infa		מצא	592		be found
	תמצא	niph	impf	3fs	מצא	592		be found
	ישלם	piel	impf	3ms	שלם	1022		finish,reward
22:4	יבער	hiph	jusf	3ms	בער	129		c. to be grazed
	שלח	piel	wcp	3ms	שלח	1018		send away,shoot
	בער	piel	wcp	3ms	בער	129		graze
	ישלם	piel	impf	3ms	שלם	1022		finish,reward
22:5	תצא	qal	impf	3fs	יצא	422		go out
	מצאה	qal	wcp	3fs	מצא	592		find
	נאכל	niph	wcp	3ms	אכל	37		be eaten
	שלם	piel	infa		שלם	1022		finish,reward
	ישלם	piel	impf	3ms	שלם	1022		finish,reward
	מבער	hiph	ptc	ms	בער	128		cause to burn
22:6	יתן	qal	impf	3ms	נתן	678		give,set
	שמר	qal	infc		שמר	1036		keep,watch
	גנב	pual	wcp	3ms	גנב	170		be stolen away
	ימצא	niph	impf	3ms	מצא	592		be found
	ישלם	piel	impf	3ms	שלם	1022		finish,reward
22:7	ימצא	niph	impf	3ms	מצא	592		be found
	נקרב	niph	wcp	3ms	קרב	897		be brought
	שלח	qal	pft	3ms	שלח	1018		send
22:8	יאמר	qal	impf	3ms	אמר	55		say
	יבא	qal	impf	3ms	בוא	97		come in
	ירשיען	hiph	impf	3mp	רשע	957		condemn, be evil
	ישלם	piel	impf	3ms	שלם	1022		finish,reward
22:9	יתן	qal	impf	3ms	נתן	678		give,set
	שמר	qal	infc		שמר	1036		keep,watch
	מת	qal	wcp	3ms	מות	559		die
	נשבר	niph	pft	3ms	שבר	990		be broken
	נשבה	niph	pft	3ms	שבה	985		be held captive
	ראה	qal	ptc	ms	ראה	906		see
22:10	תהיה	qal	impf	3fs	היה	224		be,become
	שלח	qal	pft	3ms	שלח	1018		send
	לקח	qal	wcp	3ms	לקח	542		take
	ישלם	piel	impf	3ms	שלם	1022		finish,reward
22:11	גנב	qal	infa		גנב	170		steal
	יגנב	niph	impf	3ms	גנב	170		be stolen
	ישלם	piel	impf	3ms	שלם	1022		finish,reward
22:12	טרף	qal	infa		טרף	382		tear,rend
	יטרף	niph	impf	3ms	טרף	382		be torn
	יבאהו	hiph	impf	3ms	בוא	97	3ms	bring in

ChVs	Form	Stem	Tnse	PGN	Root	BDB	Sfx	Meaning
22: 12	ישלם	piel	impf	3ms	שלם	1022		finish,reward
22: 13	ישאל	qal	impf	3ms	שאל	981		ask,borrow
	נשבר	niph	wcp	3ms	שבר	990		be broken
	מת	qal	pft	3ms	מות	559		die
	שלם	piel	infa		שלם	1022		finish,reward
	ישלם	piel	impf	3ms	שלם	1022		finish,reward
22: 14	ישלם	piel	impf	3ms	שלם	1022		finish,reward
	בא	qal	pft	3ms	בוא	97		come in
22: 15	יפתה	piel	impf	3ms	פתה	834		entice
	ארשה	pual	pft	3fs	ארש	76		be betrothed
	שכב	qal	wcp	3ms	שכב	1011		lie,lie down
	מהר	qal	infa		מהר	555		exchange,buy
	ימהרנה	qal	impf	3ms	מהר	555	3fs	exchange,buy
22: 16	מאן	piel	infa		מאן	549		refuse
	ימאן	piel	impf	3ms	מאן	549		refuse
	תתה	qal	infc		נתן	678	3fs	give,set
	ישקל	qal	impf	3ms	שקל	1053		weigh
22: 17	מכשפה	piel	ptc	fs	כשף	506		practice magic
	תחיה	piel	impf	2ms	חיה	310		preserve,revive
22: 18	שכב	qal	ptc	ms	שכב	1011		lie,lie down
	מות	qal	infa		מות	559		die
	יומת	hoph	impf	3ms	מות	559		be killed
22: 19	זבח	qal	ptc	ms	זבח	256		slaughter
	יחרם	hoph	impf	3ms	חרם	355		be banned
22: 20	תונה	hiph	impf	2ms	ינה	413		oppress
	תלחצנו	qal	impf	2ms	לחץ	537	3ms	press,oppress
	הייתם	qal	pft	2mp	היה	224		be,become
22: 21	תענון	piel	impf	2mp	ענה	776		humble
22: 22	ענה	piel	infa		ענה	776		humble
	תענה	piel	impf	2ms	ענה	776		humble
	צעק	qal	infa		צעק	858		cry out
	יצעק	qal	impf	3ms	צעק	858		cry out
	שמע	qal	infa		שמע	1033		hear
	אשמע	qal	impf	1cs	שמע	1033		hear
22: 23	חרה	qal	wcp	3ms	חרה	354		be kindled,burn
	הרגתי	qal	wcp	1cs	הרג	246		kill
	היו	qal	wcp	3cp	היה	224		be,become
22: 24	תלוה	hiph	impf	2ms	לוה	531		lend
	תהיה	qal	impf	2ms	היה	224		be,become
	נשה	qal	ptc	ms	נשה	674		lend
	תשימון	qal	impf	2mp	שים	962		put,set
22: 25	חבל	qal	infa		חבל	286		bind
	תחבל	qal	impf	2ms	חבל	286		bind
	בא	qal	infc		בוא	97		come in
	תשיבנו	hiph	impf	2ms	שוב	996	3ms	bring back
22: 26	ישכב	qal	impf	3ms	שכב	1011		lie,lie down
	היה	qal	wcp	3ms	היה	224		be,become
	יצעק	qal	impf	3ms	צעק	858		cry out
	שמעתי	qal	wcp	1cs	שמע	1033		hear
22: 27	תקלל	piel	impf	2ms	קלל	886		curse
	תאר	qal	impf	2ms	ארר	76		curse
22: 28	תאחר	piel	impf	2ms	אחר	29		tarry,hinder
	תתן	qal	impf	2ms	נתן	678		give,set
22: 29	תעשה	qal	impf	2ms	עשה	793		do,make

ChVs	Form	Stem	Tnse	PGN	Root	BDB	Sfx	Meaning
22: 29	יהיה	qal	impf	3ms	היה	224		be,become
	תתנו	qal	impf	2ms	נתן	678	3ms	give,set
22: 30	תהיון	qal	impf	2mp	היה	224		be,become
	תאכלו	qal	impf	2mp	אכל	37		eat,devour
	תשלכון	hiph	impf	2mp	שלך	1020		throw,cast
23: 1	תשא	qal	impf	2ms	נשא	669		lift,carry
	תשת	qal	jus	2ms	שית	1011		put,set
	הית	qal	infc		היה	224		be,become
23: 2	תהיה	qal	impf	2ms	היה	224		be,become
	תענה	qal	impf	2ms	ענה	772		answer
	נטת	qal	infc		נטה	639		stretch,incline
	הטת	hiph	infc		נטה	639		turn,incline
23: 3	תהדר	qal	impf	2ms	הדר	213		swell,honor
23: 4	תפגע	qal	impf	2ms	פגע	803		meet,encounter
	איבך	qal	ptc	ms	איב	33	2ms	be hostile to
	תעה	qal	ptc	ms	תעה	1073		wander,err
	השב	hiph	infa		שוב	996		bring back
	תשיבנו	hiph	impf	2ms	שוב	996	3ms	bring back
23: 5	תראה	qal	impf	2ms	ראה	906		see
	שנאך	qal	ptc	ms	שנא	971	2ms	hate
	רבץ	qal	ptc	ms	רבץ	918		lie down
	חדלת	qal	wcp	2ms	חדל	292		cease
	עזב	qal	infc		עזב	736		leave,loose
	עזב	qal	infa		עזב	736		leave,loose
	תעזב	qal	impf	2ms	עזב	736		leave,loose
23: 6	תטה	hiph	impf	2ms	נטה	639		turn,incline
23: 7	תרחק	qal	impf	2ms	רחק	934		be distant
	תהרג	qal	jusm	2ms	הרג	246		kill
	אצדיק	hiph	impf	1cs	צדק	842		make righteous
23: 8	תקח	qal	impf	2ms	לקח	542		take
	יעור	piel	impf	3ms	עור	734		make blind
	יסלף	piel	impf	3ms	סלף	701		pervert,turn
23: 9	תלחץ	qal	impf	2ms	לחץ	537		press,oppress
	ידעתם	qal	pft	2mp	ידע	393		know
	הייתם	qal	pft	2mp	היה	224		be,become
23: 10	תזרע	qal	impf	2ms	זרע	281		sow
	אספת	qal	wcp	2ms	אסף	62		gather
23: 11	תשמטנה	qal	impf	2ms	שמט	1030	3fs	let drop
	נטשתה	qal	wcp	2ms	נטש	643	3fs	leave,forsake
	אכלו	qal	wcp	3cp	אכל	37		eat,devour
	תאכל	qal	impf	3fs	אכל	37		eat,devour
	תעשה	qal	impf	2ms	עשה	793		do,make
23: 12	תעשה	qal	impf	2ms	עשה	793		do,make
	תשבת	qal	impf	2ms	שבת	991		cease,desist
	ינוח	qal	impf	3ms	נוח	628		rest
	ינפש	niph	impf	3ms	נפש	661		refresh oneself
23: 13	אמרתי	qal	pft	1cs	אמר	55		say
	תשמרו	niph	impf	2mp	שמר	1036		be kept,guarded
	תזכירו	hiph	impf	2mp	זכר	269		c. to remember
	ישמע	niph	impf	3ms	שמע	1033		be heard
23: 14	תחג	qal	impf	2ms	חגג	290		keep festival
23: 15	תשמר	qal	impf	2ms	שמר	1036		keep,watch
	תאכל	qal	impf	2ms	אכל	37		eat,devour
	צויתך	piel	pft	1cs	צוה	845	2ms	command

ChVs	Form	Stem	Tnse	PGN	Root	BDB	Sfx	Meaning
23:15	יצאת	qal	pft	2ms	יצא	422		go out
	יראו	niph	impf	3mp	ראה	906		appear,be seen
23:16	תזרע	qal	impf	2ms	זרע	281		sow
	צאת	qal	infc		יצא	422		go out
	אספך	qal	infc		אסף	62	2ms	gather
23:17	יראה	niph	impf	3ms	ראה	906		appear,be seen
23:18	תזבח	qal	impf	2ms	זבח	256		slaughter
	ילין	qal	impf	3ms	לון	533		lodge,remain
23:19	תביא	hiph	impf	2ms	בוא	97		bring in
	תבשל	piel	impf	2ms	בשל	143		boil,cook
23:20	שלח	qal	ptc	ms	שלח	1018		send
	שמרך	qal	infc		שמר	1036	2ms	keep,watch
	הביאך	hiph	infc		בוא	97	2ms	bring in
	הכנתי	hiph	pft	1cs	כון	465		fix,prepare
23:21	השמר	niph	impv	ms	שמר	1036		be kept,guarded
	שמע	qal	impv	ms	שמע	1033		hear
	תמר	hiph	jusm	2ms	מרר	600		make bitter
	ישא	qal	impf	3ms	נשא	669		lift,carry
23:22	שמע	qal	infa		שמע	1033		hear
	תשמע	qal	impf	2ms	שמע	1033		hear
	עשית	qal	wcp	2ms	עשה	793		do,make
	אדבר	piel	impf	1cs	דבר	180		speak
	איבתי	qal	wcp	1cs	איב	33		be hostile to
	איביך	qal	ptc	mp	איב	33	2ms	be hostile to
	צרתי	qal	wcp	1cs	צור	849		treat as foe
	צרריך	qal	ptc	mp	צרר	865	2ms	show hostility
23:23	ילך	qal	impf	3ms	הלך	229		walk,go
	הביאך	hiph	wcp	3ms	בוא	97	2ms	bring in
	הכחדתיו	hiph	wcp	1cs	כחד	470	3ms	hide,efface
23:24	תשתחוה	hish	impf	2ms	חוה	1005		bow down
	תעבדם	hoph	impf	2ms	עבד	712	3mp	be led to serve
	תעשה	qal	impf	2ms	עשה	793		do,make
	הרס	piel	infa		הרס	248		tear down
	תהרסם	piel	impf	2ms	הרס	248	3mp	tear down
	שבר	piel	infa		שבר	990		shatter
	תשבר	piel	impf	2ms	שבר	990		shatter
23:25	עבדתם	qal	wcp	2mp	עבד	712		work,serve
	ברך	piel	wcp	3ms	ברך	138		bless
	הסרתי	hiph	wcp	1cs	סור	693		take away
23:26	תהיה	qal	impf	3fs	היה	224		be,become
	משכלה	piel	ptc	fs	שכל	1013		make childless
	אמלא	piel	impf	1cs	מלא	569		fill
23:27	אשלח	piel	impf	1cs	שלח	1018		send away,shoot
	המתי	qal	wcp	1cs	המם	243		confuse,vex
	תבא	qal	impf	2ms	בוא	97		come in
	נתתי	qal	wcp	1cs	נתן	678		give,set
	איביך	qal	ptc	mp	איב	33	2ms	be hostile to
23:28	שלחתי	qal	wcp	1cs	שלח	1018		send
	גרשה	piel	wcp	3fs	גרש	176		drive out
23:29	אגרשנו	piel	impf	1cs	גרש	176	3ms	drive out
	תהיה	qal	impf	3fs	היה	224		be,become
	רבה	qal	wcp	3fs	רבב	912		be many
23:30	אגרשנו	piel	impf	1cs	גרש	176	3ms	drive out
	תפרה	qal	impf	2ms	פרה	826		bear fruit

ChVs	Form	Stem	Tnse	PGN	Root	BDB	Sfx	Meaning
23:30	נחלת	qal	wcp	2ms	נחל	635		possess,inherit
23:31	שתי	qal	wcp	1cs	שית	1011		put,set
	אתן	qal	impf	1cs	נתן	678		give,set
	ישבי	qal	ptc	mp	ישב	442		sit,dwell
	גרשתמו	piel	wcp	2ms	גרש	176	3mp	drive out
23:32	תכרת	qal	impf	2ms	כרת	503		cut,destroy
23:33	ישבו	qal	impf	3mp	ישב	442		sit,dwell
	יחטיאו	hiph	impf	3mp	חטא	306		cause to sin
	תעבד	qal	impf	2ms	עבד	712		work,serve
	יהיה	qal	impf	3ms	היה	224		be,become
24:1	אמר	qal	pft	3ms	אמר	55		say
	עלה	qal	impv	ms	עלה	748		go up
	השתחויתם	hish	wcp	2mp	חוה	1005		bow down
24:2	נגש	niph	wcp	3ms	נגש	620		draw near
	יגשו	qal	impf	3mp	נגש	620		draw near
	יעלו	qal	impf	3mp	עלה	748		go up
24:3	יבא	qal	wci	3ms	בוא	97		come in
	יספר	piel	wci	3ms	ספר	707		recount
	יען	qal	wci	3ms	ענה	772		answer
	יאמרו	qal	wci	3mp	אמר	55		say
	דבר	piel	pft	3ms	דבר	180		speak
	נעשה	qal	impf	1cp	עשה	793		do,make
24:4	יכתב	qal	wci	3ms	כתב	507		write
	ישכם	hiph	wci	3ms	שכם	1014		rise early
	יבן	qal	wci	3ms	בנה	124		build
24:5	ישלח	qal	wci	3ms	שלח	1018		send
	יעלו	hiph	wci	3mp	עלה	748		bring up,offer
	יזבחו	qal	wci	3mp	זבח	256		slaughter
24:6	יקח	qal	wci	3ms	לקח	542		take
	ישם	qal	wci	3ms	שים	962		put,set
	זרק	qal	pft	3ms	זרק	284		toss,scatter
24:7	יקח	qal	wci	3ms	לקח	542		take
	יקרא	qal	wci	3ms	קרא	894		call,proclaim
	יאמרו	qal	wci	3mp	אמר	55		say
	דבר	piel	pft	3ms	דבר	180		speak
	נעשה	qal	impf	1cp	עשה	793		do,make
	נשמע	qal	impf	1cp	שמע	1033		hear
24:8	יקח	qal	wci	3ms	לקח	542		take
	יזרק	qal	wci	3ms	זרק	284		toss,scatter
	יאמר	qal	wci	3ms	אמר	55		say
	כרת	qal	pft	3ms	כרת	503		cut,destroy
24:9	יעל	qal	wci	3ms	עלה	748		go up
24:10	יראו	qal	wci	3mp	ראה	906		see
24:11	שלח	qal	pft	3ms	שלח	1018		send
	יחזו	qal	wci	3mp	חזה	302		see
	יאכלו	qal	wci	3mp	אכל	37		eat,devour
	ישתו	qal	wci	3mp	שתה	1059		drink
24:12	יאמר	qal	wci	3ms	אמר	55		say
	עלה	qal	impv	ms	עלה	748		go up
	היה	qal	impv	ms	היה	224		be,become
	אתנה	qal	coh	1cs	נתן	678		give,set
	כתבתי	qal	pft	1cs	כתב	507		write
	הורתם	hiph	infc		ירה	434	3mp	shoot,teach
24:13	יקם	qal	wci	3ms	קום	877		arise,stand

ChVs	Form	Stem	Tnse	PGN	Root	BDB	Sfx	Meaning
24:13	משרתו	piel	ptc	ms	שרת	1058	3ms	minister,serve
	יעל	qal	wci	3ms	עלה	748		go up
24:14	אמר	qal	pft	3ms	אמר	55		say
	שבו	qal	impv	mp	ישב	442		sit,dwell
	נשוב	qal	impf	1cp	שוב	996		turn,return
	יגש	qal	impf	3ms	נגש	620		draw near
24:15	יעל	qal	wci	3ms	עלה	748		go up
	יכס	piel	wci	3ms	כסה	491		cover
24:16	ישכן	qal	wci	3ms	שכן	1014		settle,dwell
	יכסהו	piel	wci	3ms	כסה	491	3ms	cover
	יקרא	qal	wci	3ms	קרא	894		call,proclaim
24:17	אכלת	qal	ptc	fs	אכל	37		eat,devour
24:18	יבא	qal	wci	3ms	בוא	97		come in
	יעל	qal	wci	3ms	עלה	748		go up
	יהי	qal	wci	3ms	היה	224		be,become
25:1	ידבר	piel	wci	3ms	דבר	180		speak
	אמר	qal	infc		אמר	55		say
25:2	דבר	piel	impv	ms	דבר	180		speak
	יקחו	qal	jusm	3mp	לקח	542		take
	ידבנו	qal	impf	3ms	נדב	621	3ms	incite
	תקחו	qal	impf	2mp	לקח	542		take
25:3	תקחו	qal	impf	2mp	לקח	542		take
25:5	מאדמים	pual	ptc	mp	אדם	10		dyed red
25:8	עשו	qal	wcp	3cp	עשה	793		do,make
	שכנתי	qal	wcp	1cs	שכן	1014		settle,dwell
25:9	מראה	hiph	ptc	ms	ראה	906		show,exhibit
	תעשו	qal	impf	2mp	עשה	793		do,make
25:10	עשו	qal	wcp	3cp	עשה	793		do,make
25:11	צפית	piel	wcp	2ms	צפה	860		overlay
	תצפנו	piel	impf	2ms	צפה	860	3ms	overlay
	עשית	qal	wcp	2ms	עשה	793		do,make
25:12	יצקת	qal	wcp	2ms	יצק	427		pour out,cast
	נתתה	qal	wcp	2ms	נתן	678		give,set
25:13	עשית	qal	wcp	2ms	עשה	793		do,make
	צפית	piel	wcp	2ms	צפה	860		overlay
25:14	הבאת	hiph	wcp	2ms	בוא	97		bring in
	שאת	qal	infc		נשא	669		lift,carry
25:15	יהיו	qal	impf	3mp	היה	224		be,become
	יסרו	qal	impf	3mp	סור	693		turn aside
25:16	נתת	qal	wcp	2ms	נתן	678		give,set
	אתן	qal	impf	1cs	נתן	678		give,set
25:17	עשית	qal	wcp	2ms	עשה	793		do,make
25:18	עשית	qal	wcp	2ms	עשה	793		do,make
	תעשה	qal	impf	2ms	עשה	793		do,make
25:19	עשה	qal	impv	ms	עשה	793		do,make
	תעשו	qal	impf	2mp	עשה	793		do,make
25:20	היו	qal	wcp	3cp	היה	224		be,become
	פרשי	qal	ptc	mp	פרש	831		spread out
	סככים	qal	ptc	mp	סכך	696		cover
	יהיו	qal	impf	3mp	היה	224		be,become
25:21	נתת	qal	wcp	2ms	נתן	678		give,set
	תתן	qal	impf	2ms	נתן	678		give,set
	אתן	qal	impf	1cs	נתן	678		give,set
25:22	נועדתי	niph	wcp	1cs	יעד	416		gather
25:22	דברתי	piel	wcp	1cs	דבר	180		speak
	אצוה	piel	impf	1cs	צוה	845		command
25:23	עשית	qal	wcp	2ms	עשה	793		do,make
25:24	צפית	piel	wcp	2ms	צפה	860		overlay
	עשית	qal	wcp	2ms	עשה	793		do,make
25:25	עשית	qal	wcp	2ms	עשה	793		do,make
	עשית	qal	wcp	2ms	עשה	793		do,make
25:26	עשית	qal	wcp	2ms	עשה	793		do,make
	נתת	qal	wcp	2ms	נתן	678		give,set
25:27	תהיין	qal	impf	3fp	היה	224		be,become
	שאת	qal	infc		נשא	669		lift,carry
25:28	עשית	qal	wcp	2ms	עשה	793		do,make
	צפית	piel	wcp	2ms	צפה	860		overlay
	נשא	niph	wcp	3ms	נשא	669		be lifted up
25:29	עשית	qal	wcp	2ms	עשה	793		do,make
	יסך	hoph	impf	3ms	נסך	650		be poured out
	תעשה	qal	impf	2ms	עשה	793		do,make
25:30	נתת	qal	wcp	2ms	נתן	678		give,set
25:31	עשית	qal	wcp	2ms	עשה	793		do,make
	תעשה	niph	impf	3fs	עשה	793		be done
	יהיו	qal	impf	3mp	היה	224		be,become
25:32	יצאים	qal	ptc	mp	יצא	422		go out
25:33	משקדים	pual	ptc	mp	שקד	1052		be almond-shape
	משקדים	pual	ptc	mp	שקד	1052		be almond-shape
	יצאים	qal	ptc	mp	יצא	422		go out
25:34	משקדים	pual	ptc	mp	שקד	1052		be almond-shape
25:35	יצאים	qal	ptc	mp	יצא	422		go out
25:36	יהיו	qal	impf	3mp	היה	224		be,become
25:37	עשית	qal	wcp	2ms	עשה	793		do,make
	העלה	hiph	wcp	3ms	עלה	748		bring up,offer
	האיר	hiph	wcp	3ms	אור	21		cause to shine
25:39	יעשה	qal	impf	3ms	עשה	793		do,make
25:40	ראה	qal	impv	ms	ראה	906		see
	עשה	qal	impv	ms	עשה	793		do,make
	מראה	hoph	ptc	ms	ראה	906		be shown
26:1	תעשה	qal	impf	2ms	עשה	793		do,make
	משזר	hoph	ptc	ms	שזר	1004		be twisted
	חשב	qal	ptc	ms	חשב	362		think,devise
	תעשה	qal	impf	2ms	עשה	793		do,make
26:3	תהיין	qal	impf	3fp	היה	224		be,become
	חברת	qal	ptc	fp	חבר	287		unite
	חברת	qal	ptc	fp	חבר	287		unite
26:4	עשית	qal	wcp	2ms	עשה	793		do,make
	תעשה	qal	impf	2ms	עשה	793		do,make
26:5	תעשה	qal	impf	2ms	עשה	793		do,make
	תעשה	qal	impf	2ms	עשה	793		do,make
	מקבילת	hiph	ptc	fp	קבל	867		stand against
26:6	עשית	qal	wcp	2ms	עשה	793		do,make
	חברת	piel	wcp	2ms	חבר	287		unite
	היה	qal	wcp	3ms	היה	224		be,become
26:7	עשית	qal	wcp	2ms	עשה	793		do,make
	תעשה	qal	impf	2ms	עשה	793		do,make
26:9	חברת	piel	wcp	2ms	חבר	287		unite
	כפלת	qal	wcp	2ms	כפל	495		double over

ChVs	Form	Stem	Tnse	PGN	Root	BDB	Sfx	Meaning
26:10	עשׂית	qal	wcp	2ms	עשׂה	793		do,make
26:11	עשׂית	qal	wcp	2ms	עשׂה	793		do,make
	הבאת	hiph	wcp	2ms	בוא	97		bring in
	חברת	piel	wcp	2ms	חבר	287		unite
	היה	qal	wcp	3ms	היה	224		be,become
26:12	עדף	qal	ptc	ms	עדף	727		remain over
	עדפת	qal	ptc	fs	עדף	727		remain over
	תסרח	qal	impf	3fs	סרח	710		go free,overrun
26:13	עדף	qal	ptc	ms	עדף	727		remain over
	יהיה	qal	impf	3ms	היה	224		be,become
	סרוח	qal	pptc	ms	סרח	710		go free,overrun
	כסתו	piel	infc		כסה	491	3ms	cover
26:14	עשׂית	qal	wcp	2ms	עשׂה	793		do,make
	מאדמים	pual	ptc	mp	אדם	10		dyed red
26:15	עשׂית	qal	wcp	2ms	עשׂה	793		do,make
	עמדים	qal	ptc	mp	עמד	763		stand,stop
26:17	משׁלבת	pual	ptc	fp	שׁלב	1016		be bound
	תעשׂה	qal	impf	2ms	עשׂה	793		do,make
26:18	עשׂית	qal	wcp	2ms	עשׂה	793		do,make
26:19	תעשׂה	qal	impf	2ms	עשׂה	793		do,make
26:22	תעשׂה	qal	impf	2ms	עשׂה	793		do,make
26:23	תעשׂה	qal	impf	2ms	עשׂה	793		do,make
26:24	יהיו	qal	impf	3mp	היה	224		be,become
	תאמים	qal	ptc	mp	תאם	1060		be double
	יהיו	qal	impf	3mp	היה	224		be,become
	יהיה	qal	impf	3ms	היה	224		be,become
	יהיו	qal	impf	3mp	היה	224		be,become
26:25	היו	qal	wcp	3cp	היה	224		be,become
26:26	עשׂית	qal	wcp	2ms	עשׂה	793		do,make
26:28	מברח	hiph	ptc	ms	ברח	137		cause to flee
26:29	תצפה	piel	impf	2ms	צפה	860		overlay
	תעשׂה	qal	impf	2ms	עשׂה	793		do,make
	צפית	piel	wcp	2ms	צפה	860		overlay
26:30	הקמת	hiph	wcp	2ms	קום	877		raise,build,set
	הראית	hoph	pft	2ms	ראה	906		be shown
26:31	עשׂית	qal	wcp	2ms	עשׂה	793		do,make
	משׁזר	hoph	ptc	ms	שׁזר	1004		be twisted
	חשׁב	qal	ptc	ms	חשׁב	362		think,devise
	יעשׂה	qal	impf	3ms	עשׂה	793		do,make
26:32	נתתה	qal	wcp	2ms	נתן	678		give,set
	מצפים	pual	ptc	mp	צפה	860		be overlaid
26:33	נתתה	qal	wcp	2ms	נתן	678		give,set
	הבאת	hiph	wcp	2ms	בוא	97		bring in
	הבדילה	hiph	wcp	3fs	בדל	95		divide
26:34	נתת	qal	wcp	2ms	נתן	678		give,set
26:35	שׂמת	qal	wcp	2ms	שׂים	962		put,set
	תתן	qal	impf	2ms	נתן	678		give,set
26:36	עשׂית	qal	wcp	2ms	עשׂה	793		do,make
	משׁזר	hoph	ptc	ms	שׁזר	1004		be twisted
	רקם	qal	ptc	ms	רקם	955		variegate
26:37	עשׂית	qal	wcp	2ms	עשׂה	793		do,make
	צפית	piel	wcp	2ms	צפה	860		overlay
	יצקת	qal	wcp	2ms	יצק	427		pour out,cast
27:1	עשׂית	qal	wcp	2ms	עשׂה	793		do,make
27:1	רבוע	qal	pptc	ms	רבע	917		be square
	יהיה	qal	impf	3ms	היה	224		be,become
27:2	עשׂית	qal	wcp	2ms	עשׂה	793		do,make
	תהיין	qal	impf	3fp	היה	224		be,become
	צפית	piel	wcp	2ms	צפה	860		overlay
27:3	עשׂית	qal	wcp	2ms	עשׂה	793		do,make
	דשנו	piel	infc		דשן	206	3ms	make fat
	תעשׂה	qal	impf	2ms	עשׂה	793		do,make
27:4	עשׂית	qal	wcp	2ms	עשׂה	793		do,make
	עשׂית	qal	wcp	2ms	עשׂה	793		do,make
27:5	נתתה	qal	wcp	2ms	נתן	678		give,set
	היתה	qal	wcp	3fs	היה	224		be,become
27:6	עשׂית	qal	wcp	2ms	עשׂה	793		do,make
	צפית	piel	wcp	2ms	צפה	860		overlay
27:7	הובא	hoph	wcp	3ms	בוא	97		be brought
	היו	qal	wcp	3cp	היה	224		be,become
	שׂאת	qal	infc		נשׂא	669		lift,carry
27:8	נבוב	qal	pptc	ms	נבב	612		hollow out
	תעשׂה	qal	impf	2ms	עשׂה	793		do,make
	הראה	hiph	pft	3ms	ראה	906		show,exhibit
	יעשׂו	qal	impf	3mp	עשׂה	793		do,make
27:9	עשׂית	qal	wcp	2ms	עשׂה	793		do,make
	משׁזר	hoph	ptc	ms	שׁזר	1004		be twisted
27:16	משׁזר	hoph	ptc	ms	שׁזר	1004		be twisted
	רקם	qal	ptc	ms	רקם	955		variegate
27:17	מחשׁקים	pual	ptc	mp	חשׁק	366		fastened
27:18	משׁזר	hoph	ptc	ms	שׁזר	1004		be twisted
27:20	תצוה	piel	impf	2ms	צוה	845		command
	יקחו	qal	jusm	3mp	לקח	542		take
	העלת	hiph	infc		עלה	748		bring up,offer
27:21	יערך	qal	impf	3ms	ערך	789		set in order
28:1	הקרב	hiph	impv	ms	קרב	897		bring near
	כהנו	piel	infc		כהן	464	3ms	act as priest
28:2	עשׂית	qal	wcp	2ms	עשׂה	793		do,make
28:3	תדבר	piel	impf	2ms	דבר	180		speak
	מלאתיו	piel	pft	1cs	מלא	569	3ms	fill
	עשׂו	qal	wcp	3cp	עשׂה	793		do,make
	קדשׁו	piel	infc		קדשׁ	872	3ms	consecrate
	כהנו	piel	infc		כהן	464	3ms	act as priest
28:4	יעשׂו	qal	impf	3mp	עשׂה	793		do,make
	עשׂו	qal	wcp	3cp	עשׂה	793		do,make
	כהנו	piel	infc		כהן	464	3ms	act as priest
28:5	יקחו	qal	impf	3mp	לקח	542		take
28:6	עשׂו	qal	wcp	3cp	עשׂה	793		do,make
	משׁזר	hoph	ptc	ms	שׁזר	1004		be twisted
	חשׁב	qal	ptc	ms	חשׁב	362		think,devise
28:7	חברת	qal	ptc	fp	חבר	287		unite
	יהיה	qal	impf	3ms	היה	224		be,become
	חבר	pual	wcp	3ms	חבר	287		be joined
28:8	יהיה	qal	impf	3ms	היה	224		be,become
	משׁזר	hoph	ptc	ms	שׁזר	1004		be twisted
28:9	לקחת	qal	wcp	2ms	לקח	542		take
	פתחת	piel	wcp	2ms	פתח	836		engrave
28:10	נותרים	niph	ptc	mp	יתר	451		be left,remain

ChVs	Form	Stem	Tnse	PGN	Root	BDB	Sfx	Meaning
28: 11	תפתח	piel	impf	2ms	פתח	836		engrave
	מסבת	hoph	ptc	fp	סבב	685		be turned
	תעשׂה	qal	impf	2ms	עשׂה	793		do, make
28: 12	שׂמת	qal	wcp	2ms	שׂים	962		put, set
	נשׂא	qal	wcp	3ms	נשׂא	669		lift, carry
28: 13	עשׂית	qal	wcp	2ms	עשׂה	793		do, make
28: 14	תעשׂה	qal	impf	2ms	עשׂה	793		do, make
	נתתה	qal	wcp	2ms	נתן	678		give, set
28: 15	עשׂית	qal	wcp	2ms	עשׂה	793		do, make
	חשׁב	qal	ptc	ms	חשׁב	362		think, devise
	תעשׂנו	qal	impf	2ms	עשׂה	793	3ms	do, make
	משׁזר	hoph	ptc	ms	שׁזר	1004		be twisted
	תעשׂה	qal	impf	2ms	עשׂה	793		do, make
28: 16	רבוע	qal	pptc	ms	רבע	917		be square
	יהיה	qal	impf	3ms	היה	224		be, become
	כפול	qal	pptc	ms	כפל	495		double over
28: 17	מלאת	piel	wcp	2ms	מלא	569		fill
28: 20	משׁבצים	pual	ptc	mp	שׁבץ	990		be inwoven
	יהיו	qal	impf	3mp	היה	224		be, become
28: 21	תהיין	qal	impf	3fp	היה	224		be, become
	תהיין	qal	impf	3fp	היה	224		be, become
28: 22	עשׂית	qal	wcp	2ms	עשׂה	793		do, make
28: 23	עשׂית	qal	wcp	2ms	עשׂה	793		do, make
	נתת	qal	wcp	2ms	נתן	678		give, set
28: 24	נתתה	qal	wcp	2ms	נתן	678		give, set
28: 25	תתן	qal	impf	2ms	נתן	678		give, set
	נתתה	qal	wcp	2ms	נתן	678		give, set
28: 26	עשׂית	qal	wcp	2ms	עשׂה	793		do, make
	שׂמת	qal	wcp	2ms	שׂים	962		put, set
28: 27	עשׂית	qal	wcp	2ms	עשׂה	793		do, make
	נתתה	qal	wcp	2ms	נתן	678		give, set
28: 28	ירכסו	qal	impf	3mp	רכס	940		bind
	היות	qal	infc		היה	224		be, become
	יזח	niph	impf	3ms	זחח	267		be displaced
28: 29	נשׂא	qal	wcp	3ms	נשׂא	669		lift, carry
	באו	qal	infc		בוא	97	3ms	come in
28: 30	נתת	qal	wcp	2ms	נתן	678		give, set
	היו	qal	wcp	3cp	היה	224		be, become
	באו	qal	infc		בוא	97	3ms	come in
	נשׂא	qal	wcp	3ms	נשׂא	669		lift, carry
28: 31	עשׂית	qal	wcp	2ms	עשׂה	793		do, make
28: 32	היה	qal	wcp	3ms	היה	224		be, become
	יהיה	qal	impf	3ms	היה	224		be, become
	ארג	qal	ptc	ms	ארג	70		weave
	יהיה	qal	impf	3ms	היה	224		be, become
	יקרע	niph	impf	3ms	קרע	902		be rent, split
28: 33	עשׂית	qal	wcp	2ms	עשׂה	793		do, make
28: 35	היה	qal	wcp	3ms	היה	224		be, become
	שׁרת	piel	infc		שׁרת	1058		minister, serve
	נשׁמע	niph	wcp	3ms	שׁמע	1033		be heard
	באו	qal	infc		בוא	97	3ms	come in
	צאתו	qal	infc		יצא	422	3ms	go out
	ימות	qal	impf	3ms	מות	559		die
28: 36	עשׂית	qal	wcp	2ms	עשׂה	793		do, make
28: 36	פתחת	piel	wcp	2ms	פתח	836		engrave
28: 37	שׂמת	qal	wcp	2ms	שׂים	962		put, set
	היה	qal	wcp	3ms	היה	224		be, become
	יהיה	qal	impf	3ms	היה	224		be, become
28: 38	היה	qal	wcp	3ms	היה	224		be, become
	נשׂא	qal	wcp	3ms	נשׂא	669		lift, carry
	יקדישׁו	hiph	impf	3mp	קדשׁ	872		consecrate
	היה	qal	wcp	3ms	היה	224		be, become
28: 39	שׁבצת	piel	wcp	2ms	שׁבץ	990		weave
	עשׂית	qal	wcp	2ms	עשׂה	793		do, make
	תעשׂה	qal	impf	2ms	עשׂה	793		do, make
	רקם	qal	ptc	ms	רקם	955		variegate
28: 40	תעשׂה	qal	impf	2ms	עשׂה	793		do, make
	עשׂית	qal	wcp	2ms	עשׂה	793		do, make
	תעשׂה	qal	impf	2ms	עשׂה	793		do, make
28: 41	הלבשׁת	hiph	wcp	2ms	לבשׁ	527		clothe
	משׁחת	qal	wcp	2ms	משׁח	602		smear, anoint
	מלאת	piel	wcp	2ms	מלא	569		fill
	קדשׁת	piel	wcp	2ms	קדשׁ	872		consecrate
	כהנו	piel	wcp	3cp	כהן	464		act as priest
28: 42	עשׂה	qal	impv	ms	עשׂה	793		do, make
	כסות	piel	infc		כסה	491		cover
	יהיו	qal	impf	3mp	היה	224		be, become
28: 43	היו	qal	wcp	3cp	היה	224		be, become
	באם	qal	infc		בוא	97	3mp	come in
	גשׁתם	qal	infc		נגשׁ	620	3mp	draw near
	שׁרת	piel	infc		שׁרת	1058		minister, serve
	ישׂאו	qal	impf	3mp	נשׂא	669		lift, carry
	מתו	qal	wcp	3cp	מות	559		die
29: 1	תעשׂה	qal	impf	2ms	עשׂה	793		do, make
	קדשׁ	piel	infc		קדשׁ	872		consecrate
	כהן	piel	infc		כהן	464		act as priest
	לקח	qal	impv	ms	לקח	542		take
29: 2	בלולת	qal	pptc	fp	בלל	117		mingle, mix
	משׁחים	qal	pptc	mp	משׁח	602		smear, anoint
	תעשׂה	qal	impf	2ms	עשׂה	793		do, make
29: 3	נתת	qal	wcp	2ms	נתן	678		give, set
	הקרבת	hiph	wcp	2ms	קרב	897		bring near
29: 4	תקריב	hiph	impf	2ms	קרב	897		bring near
	רחצת	qal	wcp	2ms	רחץ	934		wash, bathe
29: 5	לקחת	qal	wcp	2ms	לקח	542		take
	הלבשׁת	hiph	wcp	2ms	לבשׁ	527		clothe
	אפדת	qal	wcp	2ms	אפד	65		gird on ephod
29: 6	שׂמת	qal	wcp	2ms	שׂים	962		put, set
	נתת	qal	wcp	2ms	נתן	678		give, set
29: 7	לקחת	qal	wcp	2ms	לקח	542		take
	יצקת	qal	wcp	2ms	יצק	427		pour out, cast
	משׁחת	qal	wcp	2ms	משׁח	602		smear, anoint
29: 8	תקריב	hiph	impf	2ms	קרב	897		bring near
	הלבשׁתם	hiph	wcp	2ms	לבשׁ	527	3mp	clothe
29: 9	חגרת	qal	wcp	2ms	חגר	291		gird
	חבשׁת	qal	wcp	2ms	חבשׁ	289		bind
	היתה	qal	wcp	3fs	היה	224		be, become
	מלאת	piel	wcp	2ms	מלא	569		fill

ChVs	Form	Stem	Tnse	PGN	Root	BDB	Sfx	Meaning
29: 10	הקרבת	hiph	wcp	2ms	קרב	897		bring near
	סמך	qal	wcp	3ms	סמך	701		lean,support
29: 11	שחטת	qal	wcp	2ms	שחט	1006		slaughter
29: 12	לקחת	qal	wcp	2ms	לקח	542		take
	נתתה	qal	wcp	2ms	נתן	678		give,set
	תשפך	qal	impf	2ms	שפך	1049		pour out
29: 13	לקחת	qal	wcp	2ms	לקח	542		take
	מכסה	piel	ptc	ms	כסה	491		cover
	הקטרת	hiph	wcp	2ms	קטר	882		make sacrifices
29: 14	תשרף	qal	impf	2ms	שרף	976		burn
29: 15	תקח	qal	impf	2ms	לקח	542		take
	סמכו	qal	wcp	3cp	סמך	701		lean,support
29: 16	שחטת	qal	wcp	2ms	שחט	1006		slaughter
	לקחת	qal	wcp	2ms	לקח	542		take
	זרקת	qal	wcp	2ms	זרק	284		toss,scatter
29: 17	תנתח	piel	impf	2ms	נתח	677		cut in pieces
	רחצת	qal	wcp	2ms	רחץ	934		wash,bathe
	נתת	qal	wcp	2ms	נתן	678		give,set
29: 18	הקטרת	hiph	wcp	2ms	קטר	882		make sacrifices
29: 19	לקחת	qal	wcp	2ms	לקח	542		take
	סמך	qal	wcp	3ms	סמך	701		lean,support
29: 20	שחטת	qal	wcp	2ms	שחט	1006		slaughter
	לקחת	qal	wcp	2ms	לקח	542		take
	נתתה	qal	wcp	2ms	נתן	678		give,set
	זרקת	qal	wcp	2ms	זרק	284		toss,scatter
29: 21	לקחת	qal	wcp	2ms	לקח	542		take
	הזית	hiph	wcp	2ms	נזה	633		cause to spurt
	קדש	qal	wcp	3ms	קדש	872		be set apart
29: 22	לקחת	qal	wcp	2ms	לקח	542		take
	מכסה	piel	ptc	ms	כסה	491		cover
29: 24	שמת	qal	wcp	2ms	שים	962		put,set
	הנפת	hiph	wcp	2ms	נוף	631		swing,wave
29: 25	לקחת	qal	wcp	2ms	לקח	542		take
	הקטרת	hiph	wcp	2ms	קטר	882		make sacrifices
29: 26	לקחת	qal	wcp	2ms	לקח	542		take
	הנפת	hiph	wcp	2ms	נוף	631		swing,wave
	היה	qal	wcp	3ms	היה	224		be,become
29: 27	קדשת	piel	wcp	2ms	קדש	872		consecrate
	הונף	hoph	pft	3ms	נוף	631		be waved
	הורם	hoph	pft	3ms	רום	926		be taken away
29: 28	היה	qal	wcp	3ms	היה	224		be,become
	יהיה	qal	impf	3ms	היה	224		be,become
29: 29	יהיו	qal	impf	3mp	היה	224		be,become
	משחה	qal	infc		משח	602		smear,anoint
	מלא	piel	infc		מלא	569		fill
29: 30	ילבשם	qal	impf	3ms	לבש	527	3mp	put on,clothe
	יבא	qal	impf	3ms	בוא	97		come in
	שרת	piel	infc		שרת	1058		minister,serve
29: 31	תקח	qal	impf	2ms	לקח	542		take
	בשלת	piel	wcp	2ms	בשל	143		boil,cook
29: 32	אכל	qal	wcp	3ms	אכל	37		eat,devour
29: 33	אכלו	qal	wcp	3cp	אכל	37		eat,devour
	כפר	pual	pft	3ms	כפר	497		be atoned for
	מלא	piel	infc		מלא	569		fill
29: 33	קדש	piel	infc		קדש	872		consecrate
	זר	qal	ptc	ms	זור	266		be stranger
	יאכל	qal	impf	3ms	אכל	37		eat,devour
29: 34	יותר	niph	impf	3ms	יתר	451		be left,remain
	שרפת	qal	wcp	2ms	שרף	976		burn
	נותר	niph	ptc	ms	יתר	451		be left,remain
	יאכל	niph	impf	3ms	אכל	37		be eaten
29: 35	עשית	qal	wcp	2ms	עשה	793		do,make
	צויתי	piel	pft	1cs	צוה	845		command
	תמלא	piel	impf	2ms	מלא	569		fill
29: 36	תעשה	qal	impf	2ms	עשה	793		do,make
	חטאת	piel	wcp	2ms	חטא	306		purify
	כפרך	piel	infc		כפר	497	2ms	cover,atone
	משחת	qal	wcp	2ms	משח	602		smear,anoint
	קדשו	piel	infc		קדש	872	3ms	consecrate
29: 37	תכפר	piel	impf	2ms	כפר	497		cover,atone
	קדשת	piel	wcp	2ms	קדש	872		consecrate
	היה	qal	wcp	3ms	היה	224		be,become
	נגע	qal	ptc	ms	נגע	619		touch,strike
	יקדש	qal	impf	3ms	קדש	872		be set apart
29: 38	תעשה	qal	impf	2ms	עשה	793		do,make
29: 39	תעשה	qal	impf	2ms	עשה	793		do,make
	תעשה	qal	impf	2ms	עשה	793		do,make
29: 40	בלול	qal	pptc	ms	בלל	117		mingle,mix
29: 41	תעשה	qal	impf	2ms	עשה	793		do,make
	תעשה	qal	impf	2ms	עשה	793		do,make
29: 42	אועד	niph	impf	1cs	יעד	416		gather
	דבר	piel	infc		דבר	180		speak
29: 43	נעדתי	niph	wcp	1cs	יעד	416		gather
	נקדש	niph	wcp	3ms	קדש	872		be sacred
29: 44	קדשתי	piel	wcp	1cs	קדש	872		consecrate
	אקדש	piel	impf	1cs	קדש	872		consecrate
	כהן	piel	infc		כהן	464		act as priest
29: 45	שכנתי	qal	wcp	1cs	שכן	1014		settle,dwell
	הייתי	qal	wcp	1cs	היה	224		be,become
29: 46	ידעו	qal	wcp	3cp	ידע	393		know
	הוצאתי	hiph	pft	1cs	יצא	422		bring out
	שכני	qal	infc		שכן	1014	1cs	settle,dwell
30: 1	עשית	qal	wcp	2ms	עשה	793		do,make
	תעשה	qal	impf	2ms	עשה	793		do,make
30: 2	רבוע	qal	pptc	ms	רבע	917		be square
	יהיה	qal	impf	3ms	היה	224		be,become
30: 3	צפית	piel	wcp	2ms	צפה	860		overlay
	עשית	qal	wcp	2ms	עשה	793		do,make
30: 4	תעשה	qal	impf	2ms	עשה	793		do,make
	תעשה	qal	impf	2ms	עשה	793		do,make
	היה	qal	wcp	3ms	היה	224		be,become
	שאת	qal	infc		נשא	669		lift,carry
30: 5	עשית	qal	wcp	2ms	עשה	793		do,make
	צפית	piel	wcp	2ms	צפה	860		overlay
30: 6	נתתה	qal	wcp	2ms	נתן	678		give,set
	אועד	niph	impf	1cs	יעד	416		gather
30: 7	הקטיר	hiph	wcp	3ms	קטר	882		make sacrifices
	היטיבו	hiph	infc		יטב	405	3ms	do good

ChVs	Form	Stem	Tnse	PGN	Root	BDB	Sfx	Meaning
30: 7	יקטירנה	hiph	impf	3ms	קטר	882	3fs	make sacrifices
30: 8	העלת	hiph	infc		עלה	748		bring up,offer
	יקטירנה	hiph	impf	3ms	קטר	882	3fs	make sacrifices
30: 9	תעלו	hiph	impf	2mp	עלה	748		bring up,offer
	זרה	qal	ptc	fs	זור	266		be stranger
	תסכו	qal	impf	2mp	נסך	650		pour out
30: 10	כפר	piel	wcp	3ms	כפר	497		cover,atone
	יכפר	piel	impf	3ms	כפר	497		cover,atone
30: 11	ידבר	piel	wci	3ms	דבר	180		speak
	אמר	qal	infc		אמר	55		say
30: 12	תשׂא	qal	impf	2ms	נשׂא	669		lift,carry
	פקדיהם	qal	pptc	mp	פקד	823	3mp	attend to,visit
	נתנו	qal	wcp	3cp	נתן	678		give,set
	פקד	qal	infc		פקד	823		attend to,visit
	יהיה	qal	impf	3ms	היה	224		be,become
	פקד	qal	infc		פקד	823		attend to,visit
30: 13	יתנו	qal	impf	3mp	נתן	678		give,set
	עבר	qal	ptc	ms	עבר	716		pass over
	פקדים	qal	pptc	mp	פקד	823		attend to,visit
30: 14	עבר	qal	ptc	ms	עבר	716		pass over
	פקדים	qal	pptc	mp	פקד	823		attend to,visit
	יתן	qal	impf	3ms	נתן	678		give,set
30: 15	ירבה	hiph	impf	3ms	רבה	915		make many
	ימעיט	hiph	impf	3ms	מעט	589		make small
	תת	qal	infc		נתן	678		give,set
	כפר	piel	infc		כפר	497		cover,atone
30: 16	לקחת	qal	wcp	2ms	לקח	542		take
	נתת	qal	wcp	2ms	נתן	678		give,set
	היה	qal	wcp	3ms	היה	224		be,become
	כפר	piel	infc		כפר	497		cover,atone
30: 17	ידבר	piel	wci	3ms	דבר	180		speak
	אמר	qal	infc		אמר	55		say
30: 18	עשׂית	qal	wcp	2ms	עשׂה	793		do,make
	רחצה	qal	infc		רחץ	934		wash,bathe
	נתת	qal	wcp	2ms	נתן	678		give,set
	נתת	qal	wcp	2ms	נתן	678		give,set
30: 19	רחצו	qal	wcp	3cp	רחץ	934		wash,bathe
30: 20	באם	qal	infc		בוא	97	3mp	come in
	ירחצו	qal	impf	3mp	רחץ	934		wash,bathe
	ימתו	qal	impf	3mp	מות	559		die
	גשׁתם	qal	infc		נגשׁ	620	3mp	draw near
	שׁרת	piel	infc		שׁרת	1058		minister,serve
	הקטיר	hiph	infc		קטר	882		make sacrifices
30: 21	רחצו	qal	wcp	3cp	רחץ	934		wash,bathe
	ימתו	qal	impf	3mp	מות	559		die
	היתה	qal	wcp	3fs	היה	224		be,become
30: 22	ידבר	piel	wci	3ms	דבר	180		speak
	אמר	qal	infc		אמר	55		say
30: 23	קח	qal	impv	ms	לקח	542		take
30: 25	עשׂית	qal	wcp	2ms	עשׂה	793		do,make
	רקח	qal	ptc	ms	רקח	955		mix,compound
	יהיה	qal	impf	3ms	היה	224		be,become
30: 26	משׁחת	qal	wcp	2ms	משׁח	602		smear,anoint
30: 29	קדשׁת	piel	wcp	2ms	קדשׁ	872		consecrate
30: 29	היו	qal	wcp	3cp	היה	224		be,become
	נגע	qal	ptc	ms	נגע	619		touch,strike
	יקדשׁ	qal	impf	3ms	קדשׁ	872		be set apart
30: 30	תמשׁח	qal	impf	2ms	משׁח	602		smear,anoint
	קדשׁת	piel	wcp	2ms	קדשׁ	872		consecrate
	כהן	piel	infc		כהן	464		act as priest
30: 31	תדבר	piel	impf	2ms	דבר	180		speak
	אמר	qal	infc		אמר	55		say
	יהיה	qal	impf	3ms	היה	224		be,become
30: 32	ייסך	qalp	impf	3ms	סוך	691		anoint oneself
	תעשׂו	qal	impf	2mp	עשׂה	793		do,make
	יהיה	qal	impf	3ms	היה	224		be,become
30: 33	ירקח	qal	impf	3ms	רקח	955		mix,compound
	יתן	qal	impf	3ms	נתן	678		give,set
	זר	qal	ptc	ms	זור	266		be stranger
	נכרת	niph	wcp	3ms	כרת	503		be cut off
30: 34	יאמר	qal	wci	3ms	אמר	55		say
	קח	qal	impv	ms	לקח	542		take
	יהיה	qal	impf	3ms	היה	224		be,become
30: 35	עשׂית	qal	wcp	2ms	עשׂה	793		do,make
	רוקח	qal	ptc	ms	רקח	955		mix,compound
	ממלח	pual	ptc	ms	מלח	572		be salted
30: 36	שׁחקת	qal	wcp	2ms	שׁחק	1006		rub away
	הדק	hiph	infa		דקק	200		pulverize
	נתתה	qal	wcp	2ms	נתן	678		give,set
	אועד	niph	impf	1cs	יעד	416		gather
	תהיה	qal	impf	3fs	היה	224		be,become
30: 37	תעשׂה	qal	impf	2ms	עשׂה	793		do,make
	תעשׂו	qal	impf	2mp	עשׂה	793		do,make
	תהיה	qal	impf	3fs	היה	224		be,become
30: 38	יעשׂה	qal	impf	3ms	עשׂה	793		do,make
	הריח	hiph	infc		ריח	926		smell
	נכרת	niph	wcp	3ms	כרת	503		be cut off
31: 1	ידבר	piel	wci	3ms	דבר	180		speak
	אמר	qal	infc		אמר	55		say
31: 2	ראה	qal	impv	ms	ראה	906		see
	קראתי	qal	pft	1cs	קרא	894		call,proclaim
31: 3	אמלא	piel	wci	1cs	מלא	569		fill
31: 4	חשׁב	qal	infc		חשׁב	362		think,devise
	עשׂות	qal	infc		עשׂה	793		do,make
31: 5	מלאת	piel	infc		מלא	569		fill
	עשׂות	qal	infc		עשׂה	793		do,make
31: 6	נתתי	qal	pft	1cs	נתן	678		give,set
	נתתי	qal	pft	1cs	נתן	678		give,set
	עשׂו	qal	wcp	3cp	עשׂה	793		do,make
	צויתך	piel	pft	1cs	צוה	845	2ms	command
31: 10	כהן	piel	infc		כהן	464		act as priest
31: 11	צויתך	piel	pft	1cs	צוה	845	2ms	command
	יעשׂו	qal	impf	3mp	עשׂה	793		do,make
31: 12	יאמר	qal	wci	3ms	אמר	55		say
	אמר	qal	infc		אמר	55		say
31: 13	דבר	piel	impv	ms	דבר	180		speak
	אמר	qal	infc		אמר	55		say
	תשׁמרו	qal	impf	2mp	שׁמר	1036		keep,watch

ChVs	Form	Stem	Tnse	PGN	Root	BDB	Sfx	Meaning
31:13	דעת	qal	infc		ידע	393		know
	מקדשׁכם	piel	ptc	ms	קדשׁ	872	2mp	consecrate
31:14	שׁמרתם	qal	wcp	2mp	שׁמר	1036		keep,watch
	מחלליה	piel	ptc	mp	חלל	320	3fs	pollute
	מות	qal	infa		מות	559		die
	יומת	hoph	impf	3ms	מות	559		be killed
	עשׂה	qal	ptc	ms	עשׂה	793		do,make
	נכרתה	niph	wcp	3fs	כרת	503		be cut off
31:15	יעשׂה	niph	impf	3ms	עשׂה	793		be done
	עשׂה	qal	ptc	ms	עשׂה	793		do,make
	מות	qal	infa		מות	559		die
	יומת	hoph	impf	3ms	מות	559		be killed
31:16	שׁמרו	qal	wcp	3cp	שׁמר	1036		keep,watch
	עשׂות	qal	infc		עשׂה	793		do,make
31:17	עשׂה	qal	pft	3ms	עשׂה	793		do,make
	שׁבת	qal	pft	3ms	שׁבת	991		cease,desist
	ינפשׁ	niph	wci	3ms	נפשׁ	661		refresh oneself
31:18	יתן	qal	wci	3ms	נתן	678		give,set
	כלתו	piel	infc		כלה	477	3ms	complete,finish
	דבר	piel	infc		דבר	180		speak
	כתבים	qal	pptc	mp	כתב	507		write
32:1	ירא	qal	wci	3ms	ראה	906		see
	בשׁשׁ	pol	pft	3ms	בושׁ	101		delay
	רדת	qal	infc		ירד	432		come down
	יקהל	niph	wci	3ms	קהל	874		assemble
	יאמרו	qal	wci	3mp	אמר	55		say
	קום	qal	impv	ms	קום	877		arise,stand
	עשׂה	qal	impv	ms	עשׂה	793		do,make
	ילכו	qal	impf	3mp	הלך	229		walk,go
	העלנו	hiph	pft	3ms	עלה	748	1cp	bring up,offer
	ידענו	qal	pft	1cp	ידע	393		know
	היה	qal	pft	3ms	היה	224		be,become
32:2	יאמר	qal	wci	3ms	אמר	55		say
	פרקו	piel	impv	mp	פרק	830		tear off
	הביאו	hiph	impv	mp	בוא	97		bring in
32:3	יתפרקו	hith	wci	3mp	פרק	830		tear off
	יביאו	hiph	wci	3mp	בוא	97		bring in
32:4	יקח	qal	wci	3ms	לקח	542		take
	יצר	qal	wci	3ms	צור	849		fashion
	יעשׂהו	qal	wci	3ms	עשׂה	793	3ms	do,make
	יאמרו	qal	wci	3mp	אמר	55		say
	העלוך	hiph	pft	3cp	עלה	748	2ms	bring up,offer
32:5	ירא	qal	wci	3ms	ראה	906		see
	יבן	qal	wci	3ms	בנה	124		build
	יקרא	qal	wci	3ms	קרא	894		call,proclaim
	יאמר	qal	wci	3ms	אמר	55		say
32:6	ישׁכימו	hiph	wci	3mp	שׁכם	1014		rise early
	יעלו	hiph	wci	3mp	עלה	748		bring up,offer
	יגשׁו	hiph	wci	3mp	נגשׁ	620		bring near
	ישׁב	qal	wci	3ms	ישׁב	442		sit,dwell
	אכל	qal	infc		אכל	37		eat,devour
	שׁתו	qal	infa		שׁתה	1059		drink
	יקמו	qal	wci	3mp	קום	877		arise,stand
	צחק	piel	infc		צחק	850		jest,make sport
32:7	ידבר	piel	wci	3ms	דבר	180		speak
	לך	qal	impv	ms	הלך	229		walk,go
	רד	qal	impv	ms	ירד	432		come down
	שׁחת	piel	pft	3ms	שׁחת	1007		spoil,ruin
	העלית	hiph	pft	2ms	עלה	748		bring up,offer
32:8	סרו	qal	pft	3cp	סור	693		turn aside
	צויתם	piel	pft	1cs	צוה	845	3mp	command
	עשׂו	qal	pft	3cp	עשׂה	793		do,make
	ישׁתחוו	hish	wci	3mp	חוה	1005		bow down
	יזבחו	qal	wci	3mp	זבח	256		slaughter
	יאמרו	qal	wci	3mp	אמר	55		say
	העלוך	hiph	pft	3cp	עלה	748	2ms	bring up,offer
32:9	יאמר	qal	wci	3ms	אמר	55		say
	ראיתי	qal	pft	1cs	ראה	906		see
32:10	הניחה	hiph	impv	ms	נוח	628		give rest,put
	יחר	qal	jus	3ms	חרה	354		be kindled,burn
	אכלם	piel	cohm	1cs	כלה	477	3mp	complete,finish
	אעשׂה	qal	impf	1cs	עשׂה	793		do,make
32:11	יחל	piel	wci	3ms	חלה	318		pacify,appease
	יאמר	qal	wci	3ms	אמר	55		say
	יחרה	qal	impf	3ms	חרה	354		be kindled,burn
	הוצאת	hiph	pft	2ms	יצא	422		bring out
32:12	יאמרו	qal	impf	3mp	אמר	55		say
	אמר	qal	infc		אמר	55		say
	הוציאם	hiph	pft	3ms	יצא	422	3mp	bring out
	הרג	qal	infc		הרג	246		kill
	כלתם	piel	infc		כלה	477	3mp	complete,finish
	שׁוב	qal	impv	ms	שׁוב	996		turn,return
	הנחם	niph	impv	ms	נחם	636		be sorry
32:13	זכר	qal	impv	ms	זכר	269		remember
	נשׁבעת	niph	pft	2ms	שׁבע	989		swear
	תדבר	piel	wci	2ms	דבר	180		speak
	ארבה	hiph	impf	1cs	רבה	915		make many
	אמרתי	qal	pft	1cs	אמר	55		say
	אתן	qal	impf	1cs	נתן	678		give,set
	נחלו	qal	wcp	3cp	נחל	635		possess,inherit
32:14	ינחם	niph	wci	3ms	נחם	636		be sorry
	דבר	piel	pft	3ms	דבר	180		speak
	עשׂות	qal	infc		עשׂה	793		do,make
32:15	יפן	qal	wci	3ms	פנה	815		turn
	ירד	qal	wci	3ms	ירד	432		come down
	כתבים	qal	pptc	mp	כתב	507		write
	כתבים	qal	pptc	mp	כתב	507		write
32:16	חרות	qal	pptc	ms	חרת	362		engrave
32:17	ישׁמע	qal	wci	3ms	שׁמע	1033		hear
	יאמר	qal	wci	3ms	אמר	55		say
32:18	יאמר	qal	wci	3ms	אמר	55		say
	ענות	qal	infc		ענה	777		sing
	ענות	qal	infc		ענה	777		sing
	ענות	piel	infc		ענה	777		sing
	שׁמע	qal	ptc	ms	שׁמע	1033		hear
32:19	יהי	qal	wci	3ms	היה	224		be,become
	קרב	qal	pft	3ms	קרב	897		approach
	ירא	qal	wci	3ms	ראה	906		see

ChVs	Form	Stem	Tnse	PGN	Root	BDB	Sfx	Meaning
32: 19	יחר	qal	wci	3ms	חרה	354		be kindled, burn
	ישלך	hiph	wci	3ms	שלך	1020		throw, cast
	ישבר	piel	wci	3ms	שבר	990		shatter
32: 20	יקח	qal	wci	3ms	לקח	542		take
	עשׂו	qal	pft	3cp	עשׂה	793		do, make
	ישׂרף	qal	wci	3ms	שׂרף	976		burn
	יטחן	qal	wci	3ms	טחן	377		grind
	דק	qal	pft	3ms	דקק	200		crush, be fine
	יזר	qal	wci	3ms	זרה	279		scatter
	ישק	hiph	wci	3ms	שקה	1052		give to drink
32: 21	יאמר	qal	wci	3ms	אמר	55		say
	עשׂה	qal	pft	3ms	עשׂה	793		do, make
	הבאת	hiph	pft	2ms	בוא	97		bring in
32: 22	יאמר	qal	wci	3ms	אמר	55		say
	יחר	qal	jus	3ms	חרה	354		be kindled, burn
	ידעת	qal	pft	2ms	ידע	393		know
32: 23	יאמרו	qal	wci	3mp	אמר	55		say
	עשׂה	qal	impv	ms	עשׂה	793		do, make
	ילכו	qal	impf	3mp	הלך	229		walk, go
	העלנו	hiph	pft	3ms	עלה	748	1cp	bring up, offer
	ידענו	qal	pft	1cp	ידע	393		know
	היה	qal	pft	3ms	היה	224		be, become
32: 24	אמר	qal	wci	1cs	אמר	55		say
	התפרקו	hith	impv	mp	פרק	830		tear off
	יתנו	qal	wci	3mp	נתן	678		give, set
	אשלכהו	hiph	wci	1cs	שלך	1020	3ms	throw, cast
	יצא	qal	wci	3ms	יצא	422		go out
32: 25	ירא	qal	wci	3ms	ראה	906		see
	פרע	qal	pptc	ms	פרע	828		let go
	פרעה	qal	pft	3ms	פרע	828	3ms	let go
	קמיהם	qal	ptc	mp	קום	877	3mp	arise, stand
32: 26	יעמד	qal	wci	3ms	עמד	763		stand, stop
	יאמר	qal	wci	3ms	אמר	55		say
	יאספו	niph	wci	3mp	אסף	62		assemble
32: 27	יאמר	qal	wci	3ms	אמר	55		say
	אמר	qal	pft	3ms	אמר	55		say
	שׂימו	qal	impv	mp	שׂים	962		put, set
	עברו	qal	impv	mp	עבר	716		pass over
	שובו	qal	impv	mp	שוב	996		turn, return
	הרגו	qal	impv	mp	הרג	246		kill
32: 28	יעשׂו	qal	wci	3mp	עשׂה	793		do, make
	יפל	qal	wci	3ms	נפל	656		fall
32: 29	יאמר	qal	wci	3ms	אמר	55		say
	מלאו	qal	impv	mp	מלא	569		be full, fill
	תת	qal	infc		נתן	678		give, set
32: 30	יהי	qal	wci	3ms	היה	224		be, become
	יאמר	qal	wci	3ms	אמר	55		say
	חטאתם	qal	pft	2mp	חטא	306		sin
	אעלה	qal	impf	1cs	עלה	748		go up
	אכפרה	piel	coh	1cs	כפר	497		cover, atone
32: 31	ישב	qal	wci	3ms	שוב	996		turn, return
	יאמר	qal	wci	3ms	אמר	55		say
	חטא	qal	pft	3ms	חטא	306		sin
	יעשׂו	qal	wci	3mp	עשׂה	793		do, make

ChVs	Form	Stem	Tnse	PGN	Root	BDB	Sfx	Meaning
32: 32	תשׂא	qal	impf	2ms	נשׂא	669		lift, carry
	מחני	qal	impv	ms	מחה	562	1cs	wipe, blot out
	כתבת	qal	pft	2ms	כתב	507		write
32: 33	יאמר	qal	wci	3ms	אמר	55		say
	חטא	qal	pft	3ms	חטא	306		sin
	אמחנו	qal	impf	1cs	מחה	562	3ms	wipe, blot out
32: 34	לך	qal	impv	ms	הלך	229		walk, go
	נחה	qal	impv	ms	נחה	634		lead
	דברתי	piel	pft	1cs	דבר	180		speak
	ילך	qal	impf	3ms	הלך	229		walk, go
	פקדי	qal	infc		פקד	823	1cs	attend to, visit
	פקדתי	qal	wcp	1cs	פקד	823		attend to, visit
32: 35	יגף	qal	wci	3ms	נגף	619		smite, strike
	עשׂו	qal	pft	3cp	עשׂה	793		do, make
	עשׂה	qal	pft	3ms	עשׂה	793		do, make
33: 1	ידבר	piel	wci	3ms	דבר	180		speak
	לך	qal	impv	ms	הלך	229		walk, go
	עלה	qal	impv	ms	עלה	748		go up
	העלית	hiph	pft	2ms	עלה	748		bring up, offer
	נשבעתי	niph	pft	1cs	שבע	989		swear
	אמר	qal	infc		אמר	55		say
	אתננה	qal	impf	1cs	נתן	678	3fs	give, set
33: 2	שלחתי	qal	wcp	1cs	שלח	1018		send
	גרשתי	piel	wcp	1cs	גרש	176		drive out
33: 3	זבת	qal	ptc	fs	זוב	264		flow, gush
	אעלה	qal	impf	1cs	עלה	748		go up
	אכלך	piel	impf	1cs	כלה	477	2ms	complete, finish
33 4	ישמע	qal	wci	3ms	שמע	1033		hear
33: 4	יתאבלו	hith	wci	3mp	אבל	5		mourn
	שתו	qal	pft	3cp	שית	1011		put, set
33: 5	יאמר	qal	wci	3ms	אמר	55		say
	אמר	qal	impv	ms	אמר	55		say
	אעלה	qal	impf	1cs	עלה	748		go up
	כליתיך	piel	wcp	1cs	כלה	477	2ms	complete, finish
	הורד	hiph	impv	ms	ירד	432		bring down
	אדעה	qal	coh	1cs	ידע	393		know
	אעשׂה	qal	impf	1cs	עשׂה	793		do, make
33: 6	יתנצלו	hith	wci	3mp	נצל	664		strip oneself
33: 7	יקח	qal	impf	3ms	לקח	542		take
	נטה	qal	wcp	3ms	נטה	639		stretch, incline
	הרחק	hiph	infa		רחק	934		put far away
	קרא	qal	wcp	3ms	קרא	894		call, proclaim
	היה	qal	wcp	3ms	היה	224		be, become
	מבקשׁ	piel	ptc	ms	בקשׁ	134		seek
	יצא	qal	impf	3ms	יצא	422		go out
33: 8	היה	qal	wcp	3ms	היה	224		be, become
	צאת	qal	infc		יצא	422		go out
	יקומו	qal	impf	3mp	קום	877		arise, stand
	נצבו	niph	wcp	3cp	נצב	662		stand
	הביטו	hiph	wcp	3cp	נבט	613		look, regard
	באו	qal	infc		בוא	97	3ms	come in
33: 9	היה	qal	wcp	3ms	היה	224		be, become
	בא	qal	infc		בוא	97		come in
	ירד	qal	impf	3ms	ירד	432		come down

ChVs	Form	Stem	Tnse	PGN	Root	BDB	Sfx	Meaning
33:9	עמד	qal	wcp	3ms	עמד	763		stand,stop
	דבר	piel	wcp	3ms	דבר	180		speak
33:10	ראה	qal	wcp	3ms	ראה	906		see
	עמד	qal	ptc	ms	עמד	763		stand,stop
	קם	qal	wcp	3ms	קום	877		arise,stand
	השתחוו	hish	wcp	3cp	חוה	1005		bow down
33:11	דבר	piel	wcp	3ms	דבר	180		speak
	ידבר	piel	impf	3ms	דבר	180		speak
	שׁב	qal	wcp	3ms	שׁוב	996		turn,return
	משרתו	piel	ptc	ms	שרת	1058	3ms	minister,serve
	ימישׁ	hiph	impf	3ms	מושׁ	559		remove,depart
33:12	יאמר	qal	wci	3ms	אמר	55		say
	ראה	qal	impv	ms	ראה	906		see
	אמר	qal	ptc	ms	אמר	55		say
	העל	hiph	impv	ms	עלה	748		bring up,offer
	הודעתני	hiph	pft	2ms	ידע	393	1cs	declare
	תשלח	qal	impf	2ms	שׁלח	1018		send
	אמרת	qal	pft	2ms	אמר	55		say
	ידעתיך	qal	pft	1cs	ידע	393	2ms	know
	מצאת	qal	pft	2ms	מצא	592		find
33:13	מצאתי	qal	pft	1cs	מצא	592		find
	הודעני	hiph	impv	ms	ידע	393	1cs	declare
	אדעך	qal	cohm	1cs	ידע	393	2ms	know
	אמצא	qal	impf	1cs	מצא	592		find
	ראה	qal	impv	ms	ראה	906		see
33:14	יאמר	qal	wci	3ms	אמר	55		say
	ילכו	qal	impf	3mp	הלך	229		walk,go
	הנחתי	hiph	wcp	1cs	נוח	628		give rest,put
33:15	יאמר	qal	wci	3ms	אמר	55		say
	הלכים	qal	ptc	mp	הלך	229		walk,go
	תעלנו	hiph	jusm	2ms	עלה	748	1cp	bring up,offer
33:16	יודע	niph	impf	3ms	ידע	393		be made known
	מצאתי	qal	pft	1cs	מצא	592		find
	לכתך	qal	infc		הלך	229	2ms	walk,go
	נפלינו	niph	wcp	1cp	פלה	811		be distinct
33:17	יאמר	qal	wci	3ms	אמר	55		say
	דברת	piel	pft	2ms	דבר	180		speak
	אעשׂה	qal	impf	1cs	עשׂה	793		do,make
	מצאת	qal	pft	2ms	מצא	592		find
	אדעך	qal	wci	1cs	ידע	393	2ms	know
33:18	יאמר	qal	wci	3ms	אמר	55		say
	הראני	hiph	impv	ms	ראה	906	1cs	show,exhibit
33:19	יאמר	qal	wci	3ms	אמר	55		say
	אעביר	hiph	impf	1cs	עבר	716		cause to pass
	קראתי	qal	wcp	1cs	קרא	894		call,proclaim
	חנתי	qal	wcp	1cs	חנן	335		show favor
	אחן	qal	impf	1cs	חנן	335		show favor
	רחמתי	piel	wcp	1cs	רחם	933		have compassion
	ארחם	piel	impf	1cs	רחם	933		have compassion
33:20	יאמר	qal	wci	3ms	אמר	55		say
	תוכל	qal	impf	2ms	יכל	407		be able
	ראת	qal	infc		ראה	906		see
	יראני	qal	impf	3ms	ראה	906	1cs	see
	חי	qal	wcp	3ms	חיה	310		live
33:21	יאמר	qal	wci	3ms	אמר	55		say
	נצבת	niph	wcp	2ms	נצב	662		stand
33:22	היה	qal	wcp	3ms	היה	224		be,become
	עבר	qal	infc		עבר	716		pass over
	שׂמתיך	qal	wcp	1cs	שׂים	962	2ms	put,set
	שׂכתי	qal	wcp	1cs	שׂכך	967		cover,lay over
	עברי	qal	infc		עבר	716	1cs	pass over
33:23	הסרתי	hiph	wcp	1cs	סור	693		take away
	ראית	qal	wcp	2ms	ראה	906		see
	יראו	niph	impf	3mp	ראה	906		appear,be seen
34:1	יאמר	qal	wci	3ms	אמר	55		say
	פסל	qal	impv	ms	פסל	820		hew out
	כתבתי	qal	wcp	1cs	כתב	507		write
	היו	qal	pft	3cp	היה	224		be,become
	שׁברת	piel	pft	2ms	שׁבר	990		shatter
34:2	היה	qal	impv	ms	היה	224		be,become
	נכון	niph	ptc	ms	כון	465		be established
	עלית	qal	wcp	2ms	עלה	748		go up
	נצבת	niph	wcp	2ms	נצב	662		stand
34:3	יעלה	qal	impf	3ms	עלה	748		go up
	ירא	niph	jus	3ms	ראה	906		appear,be seen
	ירעו	qal	jusm	3mp	רעה	944		pasture,tend
34:4	יפסל	qal	wci	3ms	פסל	820		hew out
	ישׁכם	hiph	wci	3ms	שׁכם	1014		rise early
	יעל	qal	wci	3ms	עלה	748		go up
	צוה	piel	pft	3ms	צוה	845		command
	יקח	qal	wci	3ms	לקח	542		take
34:5	ירד	qal	wci	3ms	ירד	432		come down
	יתיצב	hith	wci	3ms	יצב	426		stand oneself
	יקרא	qal	wci	3ms	קרא	894		call,proclaim
34:6	יעבר	qal	wci	3ms	עבר	716		pass over
	יקרא	qal	wci	3ms	קרא	894		call,proclaim
34:7	נצר	qal	ptc	ms	נצר	665		watch,guard
	נשׂא	qal	ptc	ms	נשׂא	669		lift,carry
	נקה	piel	infa		נקה	667		acquit
	ינקה	piel	impf	3ms	נקה	667		acquit
	פקד	qal	ptc	ms	פקד	823		attend to,visit
34:8	ימהר	piel	wci	3ms	מהר	554		hasten
	יקד	qal	wci	3ms	קדד	869		bow down
	ישׁתחו	hish	wci	3ms	חוה	1005		bow down
34:9	יאמר	qal	wci	3ms	אמר	55		say
	מצאתי	qal	pft	1cs	מצא	592		find
	ילך	qal	jusm	3ms	הלך	229		walk,go
	סלחת	qal	wcp	2ms	סלח	699		forgive,pardon
	נחלתנו	qal	wcp	2ms	נחל	635	1cp	possess,inherit
34:10	יאמר	qal	wci	3ms	אמר	55		say
	כרת	qal	ptc	ms	כרת	503		cut,destroy
	אעשׂה	qal	impf	1cs	עשׂה	793		do,make
	נפלאת	niph	ptc	fp	פלא	810		be wonderful
	נבראו	niph	pft	3cp	ברא	135		be created
	ראה	qal	wcp	3ms	ראה	906		see
	נורא	niph	ptc	ms	ירא	431		be feared
	עשׂה	qal	ptc	ms	עשׂה	793		do,make
34:11	שׁמר	qal	impv	ms	שׁמר	1036		keep,watch

ChVs	Form	Stem	Tnse	PGN	Root	BDB	Sfx	Meaning
34:11	מצוך	piel	ptc	ms	צוה	845	2ms	command
	גרש	qal	ptc	ms	גרש	176		cast out
34:12	השמר	niph	impv	ms	שמר	1036		be kept,guarded
	תכרת	qal	impf	2ms	כרת	503		cut,destroy
	יושב	qal	ptc	ms	ישב	442		sit,dwell
	בא	qal	ptc	ms	בוא	97		come in
	יהיה	qal	impf	3ms	היה	224		be,become
34:13	תתצון	qal	impf	2mp	נתץ	683		pull down
	תשברון	piel	impf	2mp	שבר	990		shatter
	תכרתון	qal	impf	2mp	כרת	503		cut,destroy
34:14	תשתחוה	hish	impf	2mp	חוה	1005		bow down
34:15	תכרת	qal	impf	2ms	כרת	503		cut,destroy
	יושב	qal	ptc	ms	ישב	442		sit,dwell
	זנו	qal	wcp	3cp	זנה	275		act a harlot
	זבחו	qal	wcp	3cp	זבח	256		slaughter
	קרא	qal	wcp	3ms	קרא	894		call,proclaim
	אכלת	qal	wcp	2ms	אכל	37		eat,devour
34:16	לקחת	qal	wcp	2ms	לקח	542		take
	זנו	qal	wcp	3cp	זנה	275		act a harlot
	הזנו	hiph	wcp	3cp	זנה	275		commit harlotry
34:17	תעשה	qal	impf	2ms	עשה	793		do,make
34:18	תשמר	qal	impf	2ms	שמר	1036		keep,watch
	תאכל	qal	impf	2ms	אכל	37		eat,devour
	צויתך	piel	pft	1cs	צוה	845	2ms	command
	יצאת	qal	pft	2ms	יצא	422		go out
34:19	תזכר	niph	impf	3fs	זכר	269?		be remembered
34:20	תפדה	qal	impf	2ms	פדה	804		ransom
	תפדה	qal	impf	2ms	פדה	804		ransom
	ערפתו	qal	wcp	2ms	ערף	791	3ms	break neck
	תפדה	qal	impf	2ms	פדה	804		ransom
	יראו	niph	impf	3mp	ראה	906		appear,be seen
34:21	תעבד	qal	impf	2ms	עבד	712		work,serve
	תשבת	qal	impf	2ms	שבת	991		cease,desist
	תשבת	qal	impf	2ms	שבת	991		cease,desist
34:22	תעשה	qal	impf	2ms	עשה	793		do,make
34:23	יראה	niph	impf	3ms	ראה	906		appear,be seen
34:24	אוריש	hiph	impf	1cs	ירש	439		c. to possess
	הרחבתי	hiph	wcp	1cs	רחב	931		enlarge
	יחמד	qal	impf	3ms	חמד	326		desire
	עלתך	qal	infc		עלה	748	2ms	go up
	ראות	niph	infc		ראה	906		appear,be seen
34:25	תשחט	qal	impf	2ms	שחט	1006		slaughter
	ילין	qal	impf	3ms	לון	533		lodge,remain
34:26	תביא	hiph	impf	2ms	בוא	97		bring in
	תבשל	piel	impf	2ms	בשל	143		boil,cook
34:27	יאמר	qal	wci	3ms	אמר	55		say
	כתב	qal	impv	ms	כתב	507		write
	כרתי	qal	pft	1cs	כרת	503		cut,destroy
34:28	יהי	qal	wci	3ms	היה	224		be,become
	אכל	qal	pft	3ms	אכל	37		eat,devour
	שתה	qal	pft	3ms	שתה	1059		drink
	יכתב	qal	wci	3ms	כתב	507		write
34:29	יהי	qal	wci	3ms	היה	224		be,become
	רדת	qal	infc		ירד	432		come down
34:29	רדתו	qal	infc		ירד	432	3ms	come down
	ידע	qal	pft	3ms	ידע	393		know
	קרן	qal	pft	3ms	קרן	902		send out
	דברו	piel	infc		דבר	180	3ms	speak
34:30	ירא	qal	wci	3ms	ראה	906		see
	קרן	qal	pft	3ms	קרן	902		send out
	ייראו	qal	wci	3mp	ירא	431		fear
	גשת	qal	infc		נגש	620		draw near
34:31	יקרא	qal	wci	3ms	קרא	894		call,proclaim
	ישבו	qal	wci	3mp	שוב	996		turn,return
	ידבר	piel	wci	3ms	דבר	180		speak
34:32	נגשו	niph	pft	3cp	נגש	620		draw near
	יצום	piel	wci	3ms	צוה	845	3mp	command
	דבר	piel	pft	3ms	דבר	180		speak
34:33	יכל	piel	wci	3ms	כלה	477		complete,finish
	דבר	piel	infc		דבר	180		speak
	יתן	qal	wci	3ms	נתן	678		give,set
34:34	בא	qal	infc		בוא	97		come in
	דבר	piel	infc		דבר	180		speak
	יסיר	hiph	impf	3ms	סור	693		take away
	צאתו	qal	infc		יצא	422	3ms	go out
	יצא	qal	wcp	3ms	יצא	422		go out
	דבר	piel	wcp	3ms	דבר	180		speak
	יצוה	pual	impf	3ms	צוה	845		be commanded
34:35	ראו	qal	wcp	3cp	ראה	906		see
	קרן	qal	pft	3ms	קרן	902		send out
	השיב	hiph	wcp	3ms	שוב	996		bring back
	באו	qal	infc		בוא	97	3ms	come in
	דבר	piel	infc		דבר	180		speak
35:1	יקהל	hiph	wci	3ms	קהל	874		call assembly
	יאמר	qal	wci	3ms	אמר	55		say
	צוה	piel	pft	3ms	צוה	845		command
	עשת	qal	infc		עשה	793		do,make
35:2	תעשה	niph	impf	3fs	עשה	793		be done
	יהיה	qal	impf	3ms	היה	224		be,become
	עשה	qal	ptc	ms	עשה	793		do,make
	יומת	hoph	impf	3ms	מות	559		be killed
35:3	תבערו	piel	impf	2mp	בער	128		burn,consume
35:4	יאמר	qal	wci	3ms	אמר	55		say
	אמר	qal	infc		אמר	55		say
	צוה	piel	pft	3ms	צוה	845		command
	אמר	qal	infc		אמר	55		say
35:5	קחו	qal	impv	mp	לקח	542		take
	יביאה	hiph	jusm	3ms	בוא	97	3fs	bring in
35:7	מאדמים	pual	ptc	mp	אדם	10		dyed red
35:10	יבאו	qal	jusm	3mp	בוא	97		come in
	יעשו	qal	jusm	3mp	עשה	793		do,make
	צוה	piel	pft	3ms	צוה	845		command
35:19	שרת	piel	infc		שרת	1058		minister,serve
	כהן	piel	infc		כהן	464		act as priest
35:20	יצאו	qal	wci	3mp	יצא	422		go out
35:21	יבאו	qal	wci	3mp	בוא	97		come in
	נשאו	qal	pft	3ms	נשא	669	3ms	lift,carry
	נדבה	qal	pft	3fs	נדב	621		incite

ChVs	Form	Stem	Tnse	PGN	Root	BDB	Sfx	Meaning
35: 21	הביאו	hiph	pft	3cp	בוא	97		bring in
35: 22	יבאו	qal	wci	3mp	בוא	97		come in
	הביאו	hiph	pft	3cp	בוא	97		bring in
	הניף	hiph	pft	3ms	נוף	631		swing,wave
35: 23	נמצא	niph	pft	3ms	מצא	592		be found
	מאדמים	pual	ptc	mp	אדם	10		dyed red
	הביאו	hiph	pft	3cp	בוא	97		bring in
35: 24	מרים	hiph	ptc	ms	רום	926		raise,lift
	הביאו	hiph	pft	3cp	בוא	97		bring in
	נמצא	niph	pft	3ms	מצא	592		be found
	הביאו	hiph	pft	3cp	בוא	97		bring in
35: 25	טוו	qal	pft	3cp	טוה	376		spin
	יביאו	hiph	wci	3mp	בוא	97		bring in
35: 26	נשא	qal	pft	3ms	נשא	669		lift,carry
	טוו	qal	pft	3cp	טוה	376		spin
35: 27	הביאו	hiph	pft	3cp	בוא	97		bring in
35: 29	נדב	qal	pft	3ms	נדב	621		incite
	הביא	hiph	infc		בוא	97		bring in
	צוה	piel	pft	3ms	צוה	845		command
	עשות	qal	infc		עשה	793		do,make
	הביאו	hiph	pft	3cp	בוא	97		bring in
35: 30	יאמר	qal	wci	3ms	אמר	55		say
	ראו	qal	impv	mp	ראה	906		see
	קרא	qal	pft	3ms	קרא	894		call,proclaim
35: 31	ימלא	piel	wci	3ms	מלא	569		fill
35: 32	חשב	qal	infc		חשב	362		think,devise
	עשת	qal	infc		עשה	793		do,make
35: 33	מלאת	piel	infc		מלא	569		fill
	עשות	qal	infc		עשה	793		do,make
35: 34	הורת	hiph	infc		ירה	434		shoot,teach
	נתן	qal	pft	3ms	נתן	678		give,set
35: 35	מלא	piel	pft	3ms	מלא	569		fill
	עשות	qal	infc		עשה	793		do,make
	חשב	qal	ptc	ms	חשב	362		think,devise
	רקם	qal	ptc	ms	רקם	955		variegate
	ארג	qal	ptc	ms	ארג	70		weave
	עשי	qal	ptc	mp	עשה	793		do,make
	חשבי	qal	ptc	mp	חשב	362		think,devise
36: 1	עשה	qal	wcp	3ms	עשה	793		do,make
	נתן	qal	pft	3ms	נתן	678		give,set
	דעת	qal	infc		ידע	393		know
	עשת	qal	infc		עשה	793		do,make
	צוה	piel	pft	3ms	צוה	845		command
36: 2	יקרא	qal	wci	3ms	קרא	894		call,proclaim
	נתן	qal	pft	3ms	נתן	678		give,set
	נשאו	qal	pft	3ms	נשא	669	3ms	lift,carry
	קרבה	qal	infc		קרב	897		approach
	עשת	qal	infc		עשה	793		do,make
36: 3	יקחו	qal	wci	3mp	לקח	542		take
	הביאו	hiph	pft	3cp	בוא	97		bring in
	עשת	qal	infc		עשה	793		do,make
	הביאו	hiph	pft	3cp	בוא	97		bring in
36: 4	יבאו	qal	wci	3mp	בוא	97		come in
	עשים	qal	ptc	mp	עשה	793		do,make
36: 4	עשים	qal	ptc	mp	עשה	793		do,make
36: 5	יאמרו	qal	wci	3mp	אמר	55		say
	אמר	qal	infc		אמר	55		say
	מרבים	hiph	ptc	mp	רבה	915		make many
	הביא	hiph	infc		בוא	97		bring in
	צוה	piel	pft	3ms	צוה	845		command
	עשת	qal	infc		עשה	793		do,make
36: 6	יצו	piel	wci	3ms	צוה	845		command
	יעבירו	hiph	wci	3mp	עבר	716		cause to pass
	אמר	qal	infc		אמר	55		say
	יעשו	qal	jusm	3mp	עשה	793		do,make
	יכלא	niph	wci	3ms	כלא	476		be restrained
	הביא	hiph	infc		בוא	97		bring in
36: 7	היתה	qal	pft	3fs	היה	224		be,become
	עשות	qal	infc		עשה	793		do,make
	הותר	hiph	infa		יתר	451		leave,spare
36: 8	יעשו	qal	wci	3mp	עשה	793		do,make
	עשי	qal	ptc	mp	עשה	793		do,make
	משזר	hoph	ptc	ms	שזר	1004		be twisted
	חשב	qal	ptc	ms	חשב	362		think,devise
	עשה	qal	pft	3ms	עשה	793		do,make
36: 10	יחבר	piel	wci	3ms	חבר	287		unite
	חבר	piel	pft	3ms	חבר	287		unite
36: 11	יעש	qal	wci	3ms	עשה	793		do,make
	עשה	qal	pft	3ms	עשה	793		do,make
36: 12	עשה	qal	pft	3ms	עשה	793		do,make
	עשה	qal	pft	3ms	עשה	793		do,make
	מקבילת	hiph	ptc	fp	קבל	867		stand against
36: 13	יעש	qal	wci	3ms	עשה	793		do,make
	יחבר	piel	wci	3ms	חבר	287		unite
	יהי	qal	wci	3ms	היה	224		be,become
36: 14	יעש	qal	wci	3ms	עשה	793		do,make
	עשה	qal	pft	3ms	עשה	793		do,make
36: 16	יחבר	piel	wci	3ms	חבר	287		unite
36: 17	יעש	qal	wci	3ms	עשה	793		do,make
	עשה	qal	pft	3ms	עשה	793		do,make
36: 18	יעש	qal	wci	3ms	עשה	793		do,make
	חבר	piel	infc		חבר	287		unite
	הית	qal	infc		היה	224		be,become
36: 19	יעש	qal	wci	3ms	עשה	793		do,make
	מאדמים	pual	ptc	mp	אדם	10		dyed red
36: 20	יעש	qal	wci	3ms	עשה	793		do,make
	עמדים	qal	ptc	mp	עמד	763		stand,stop
36: 22	משלבת	pual	ptc	fp	שלב	1016		be bound
	עשה	qal	pft	3ms	עשה	793		do,make
36: 23	יעש	qal	wci	3ms	עשה	793		do,make
36: 24	עשה	qal	pft	3ms	עשה	793		do,make
36: 25	עשה	qal	pft	3ms	עשה	793		do,make
36: 27	עשה	qal	pft	3ms	עשה	793		do,make
36: 28	עשה	qal	pft	3ms	עשה	793		do,make
36: 29	היו	qal	wcp	3cp	היה	224		be,become
	תואמם	qal	ptc	mp	תאם	1060		be double
	יהיו	qal	impf	3mp	היה	224		be,become
	תמים	qal	ptc	mp	תאם	1060		be double

ChVs	Form	Stem	Tnse	PGN	Root	BDB	Sfx	Meaning
36: 29	עשׂה	qal	pft	3ms	עשׂה	793		do,make
36: 30	היו	qal	wcp	3cp	היה	224		be,become
36: 31	יעשׂ	qal	wci	3ms	עשׂה	793		do,make
36: 33	יעשׂ	qal	wci	3ms	עשׂה	793		do,make
	ברח	qal	infc		ברח	137		go thru,flee
36: 34	צפה	piel	pft	3ms	צפה	860		overlay
	עשׂה	qal	pft	3ms	עשׂה	793		do,make
	יצף	piel	wci	3ms	צפה	860		overlay
36: 35	יעשׂ	qal	wci	3ms	עשׂה	793		do,make
	משזר	hoph	ptc	ms	שׁזר	1004		be twisted
	חשב	qal	ptc	ms	חשב	362		think,devise
	עשׂה	qal	pft	3ms	עשׂה	793		do,make
36: 36	יעשׂ	qal	wci	3ms	עשׂה	793		do,make
	יצפם	piel	wci	3ms	צפה	860	3mp	overlay
	יצק	qal	wci	3ms	יצק	427		pour out,cast
36: 37	יעשׂ	qal	wci	3ms	עשׂה	793		do,make
	משזר	hoph	ptc	ms	שׁזר	1004		be twisted
	רקם	qal	ptc	ms	רקם	955		variegate
36: 38	צפה	piel	pft	3ms	צפה	860		overlay
37: 1	יעשׂ	qal	wci	3ms	עשׂה	793		do,make
37: 2	יצפהו	piel	wci	3ms	צפה	860	3ms	overlay
	יעשׂ	qal	wci	3ms	עשׂה	793		do,make
37: 3	יצק	qal	wci	3ms	יצק	427		pour out,cast
37: 4	יעשׂ	qal	wci	3ms	עשׂה	793		do,make
	יצף	piel	wci	3ms	צפה	860		overlay
37: 5	יבא	hiph	wci	3ms	בוא	97		bring in
	שׂאת	qal	infc		נשׂא	669		lift,carry
37: 6	יעשׂ	qal	wci	3ms	עשׂה	793		do,make
37: 7	יעשׂ	qal	wci	3ms	עשׂה	793		do,make
	עשׂה	qal	pft	3ms	עשׂה	793		do,make
37: 8	עשׂה	qal	pft	3ms	עשׂה	793		do,make
37: 9	יהיו	qal	wci	3mp	היה	224		be,become
	פרשׂי	qal	ptc	mp	פרשׂ	831		spread out
	סככים	qal	ptc	mp	סכך	696		cover
	היו	qal	pft	3cp	היה	224		be,become
37: 10	יעשׂ	qal	wci	3ms	עשׂה	793		do,make
37: 11	יצף	piel	wci	3ms	צפה	860		overlay
	יעשׂ	qal	wci	3ms	עשׂה	793		do,make
37: 12	יעשׂ	qal	wci	3ms	עשׂה	793		do,make
	יעשׂ	qal	wci	3ms	עשׂה	793		do,make
37: 13	יצק	qal	wci	3ms	יצק	427		pour out,cast
	יתן	qal	wci	3ms	נתן	678		give,set
37: 14	היו	qal	pft	3cp	היה	224		be,become
	שׂאת	qal	infc		נשׂא	669		lift,carry
37: 15	יעשׂ	qal	wci	3ms	עשׂה	793		do,make
	יצף	piel	wci	3ms	צפה	860		overlay
	שׂאת	qal	infc		נשׂא	669		lift,carry
37: 16	יעשׂ	qal	wci	3ms	עשׂה	793		do,make
	יסך	hoph	impf	3ms	נסך	650		be poured out
37: 17	יעשׂ	qal	wci	3ms	עשׂה	793		do,make
	עשׂה	qal	pft	3ms	עשׂה	793		do,make
	היו	qal	pft	3cp	היה	224		be,become
37: 18	יצאים	qal	ptc	mp	יצא	422		go out
37: 19	משׂקדים	pual	ptc	mp	שׁקד	1052		be almond-shape
37: 19	משׂקדים	pual	ptc	mp	שׁקד	1052		be almond-shape
	יצאים	qal	ptc	mp	יצא	422		go out
37: 20	משׂקדים	pual	ptc	mp	שׁקד	1052		be almond-shape
37: 21	יצאים	qal	ptc	mp	יצא	422		go out
37: 22	היו	qal	pft	3cp	היה	224		be,become
37: 23	יעשׂ	qal	wci	3ms	עשׂה	793		do,make
37: 24	עשׂה	qal	pft	3ms	עשׂה	793		do,make
37: 25	יעשׂ	qal	wci	3ms	עשׂה	793		do,make
	רבוע	qal	pptc	ms	רבע	917		be square
	היו	qal	pft	3cp	היה	224		be,become
37: 26	יצף	piel	wci	3ms	צפה	860		overlay
	יעשׂ	qal	wci	3ms	עשׂה	793		do,make
37: 27	עשׂה	qal	pft	3ms	עשׂה	793		do,make
	שׂאת	qal	infc		נשׂא	669		lift,carry
37: 28	יעשׂ	qal	wci	3ms	עשׂה	793		do,make
	יצף	piel	wci	3ms	צפה	860		overlay
37: 29	יעשׂ	qal	wci	3ms	עשׂה	793		do,make
	רקח	qal	ptc	ms	רקח	955		mix,compound
38: 1	יעשׂ	qal	wci	3ms	עשׂה	793		do,make
	רבוע	qal	pptc	ms	רבע	917		be square
38: 2	יעשׂ	qal	wci	3ms	עשׂה	793		do,make
	היו	qal	pft	3cp	היה	224		be,become
	יצף	piel	wci	3ms	צפה	860		overlay
38: 3	יעשׂ	qal	wci	3ms	עשׂה	793		do,make
	עשׂה	qal	pft	3ms	עשׂה	793		do,make
38: 4	יעשׂ	qal	wci	3ms	עשׂה	793		do,make
38: 5	יצק	qal	wci	3ms	יצק	427		pour out,cast
38: 6	יעשׂ	qal	wci	3ms	עשׂה	793		do,make
	יצף	piel	wci	3ms	צפה	860		overlay
38: 7	יבא	hiph	wci	3ms	בוא	97		bring in
	שׂאת	qal	infc		נשׂא	669		lift,carry
	נבוב	qal	pptc	ms	נבב	612		hollow out
	עשׂה	qal	pft	3ms	עשׂה	793		do,make
38: 8	יעשׂ	qal	wci	3ms	עשׂה	793		do,make
	צבאת	qal	ptc	fp	צבא	838		wage war
	צבאו	qal	pft	3cp	צבא	838		wage war
38: 9	יעשׂ	qal	wci	3ms	עשׂה	793		do,make
	משזר	hoph	ptc	ms	שׁזר	1004		be twisted
38: 16	משזר	hoph	ptc	ms	שׁזר	1004		be twisted
38: 17	מחשקים	pual	ptc	mp	חשק	366		fastened
38: 18	רקם	qal	ptc	ms	רקם	955		variegate
	משזר	hoph	ptc	ms	שׁזר	1004		be twisted
38: 21	פקודי	qal	pptc	mp	פקד	823		attend to,visit
	פקד	pual	pft	3ms	פקד	823		be mustered
38: 22	עשׂה	qal	pft	3ms	עשׂה	793		do,make
	צוה	piel	pft	3ms	צוה	845		command
38: 23	חשב	qal	ptc	ms	חשב	362		think,devise
	רקם	qal	ptc	ms	רקם	955		variegate
38: 24	עשׂוי	qal	pptc	mp	עשׂה	793		do,make
	יהי	qal	wci	3ms	היה	224		be,become
38: 25	פקודי	qal	pptc	mp	פקד	823		attend to,visit
38: 26	עבר	qal	ptc	ms	עבר	716		pass over
	פקדים	qal	pptc	mp	פקד	823		attend to,visit
38: 27	יהי	qal	wci	3ms	היה	224		be,become

ChVs	Form	Stem	Tnse	PGN	Root	BDB	Sfx	Meaning
38:27	צקת	qal	infc		יצק	427		pour out,cast
38:28	עשׂה	qal	pft	3ms	עשׂה	793		do,make
	צפה	piel	pft	3ms	צפה	860		overlay
	חשׁק	piel	pft	3ms	חשׁק	366		furnish w/rings
38:30	יעשׂ	qal	wci	3ms	עשׂה	793		do,make
39:1	עשׂו	qal	pft	3cp	עשׂה	793		do,make
	שׁרת	piel	infc		שׁרת	1058		minister,serve
	יעשׂו	qal	wci	3mp	עשׂה	793		do,make
	צוה	piel	pft	3ms	צוה	845		command
39:2	יעשׂ	qal	wci	3ms	עשׂה	793		do,make
	משׁזר	hoph	ptc	ms	שׁזר	1004		be twisted
39:3	ירקעו	piel	wci	3mp	רקע	955		overlay
	קצץ	piel	pft	3ms	קצץ	893		cut off
	עשׂות	qal	infc		עשׂה	793		do,make
	חשׁב	qal	ptc	ms	חשׁב	362		think,devise
39:4	עשׂו	qal	pft	3cp	עשׂה	793		do,make
	חברת	qal	ptc	fp	חבר	287		unite
	חבר	pual	pft	3ms	חבר	287		be joined
39:5	משׁזר	hoph	ptc	ms	שׁזר	1004		be twisted
	צוה	piel	pft	3ms	צוה	845		command
39:6	יעשׂו	qal	wci	3mp	עשׂה	793		do,make
	מסבת	hoph	ptc	fp	סבב	685		be turned
	מפתחת	pual	ptc	fp	פתח	836		be engraved
39:7	ישׂם	qal	wci	3ms	שׂים	962		put,set
	צוה	piel	pft	3ms	צוה	845		command
39:8	יעשׂ	qal	wci	3ms	עשׂה	793		do,make
	חשׁב	qal	ptc	ms	חשׁב	362		think,devise
	משׁזר	hoph	ptc	ms	שׁזר	1004		be twisted
39:9	רבוע	qal	pptc	ms	רבע	917		be square
	היה	qal	pft	3ms	היה	224		be,become
	כפול	qal	pptc	ms	כפל	495		double over
	עשׂו	qal	pft	3cp	עשׂה	793		do,make
	כפול	qal	pptc	ms	כפל	495		double over
39:10	ימלאו	piel	wci	3mp	מלא	569		fill
39:13	מוסבת	hoph	ptc	fp	סבב	685		be turned
39:15	יעשׂו	qal	wci	3mp	עשׂה	793		do,make
39:16	יעשׂו	qal	wci	3mp	עשׂה	793		do,make
	יתנו	qal	wci	3mp	נתן	678		give,set
39:17	יתנו	qal	wci	3mp	נתן	678		give,set
39:18	נתנו	qal	pft	3cp	נתן	678		give,set
	יתנם	qal	wci	3mp	נתן	678	3mp	give,set
39:19	יעשׂו	qal	wci	3mp	עשׂה	793		do,make
	ישׂימו	qal	wci	3mp	שׂים	962		put,set
39:20	יעשׂו	qal	wci	3mp	עשׂה	793		do,make
	יתנם	qal	wci	3mp	נתן	678	3mp	give,set
39:21	ירכסו	qal	wci	3mp	רכס	940		bind
	היות	qal	infc		היה	224		be,become
	יזח	niph	impf	3ms	זחח	267		be displaced
	צוה	piel	pft	3ms	צוה	845		command
39:22	יעשׂ	qal	wci	3ms	עשׂה	793		do,make
	ארג	qal	ptc	ms	ארג	70		weave
39:23	יקרע	niph	impf	3ms	קרע	902		be rent,split
39:24	יעשׂו	qal	wci	3mp	עשׂה	793		do,make
	משׁזר	hoph	ptc	ms	שׁזר	1004		be twisted
39:25	יעשׂו	qal	wci	3mp	עשׂה	793		do,make
	יתנו	qal	wci	3mp	נתן	678		give,set
39:26	שׁרת	piel	infc		שׁרת	1058		minister,serve
	צוה	piel	pft	3ms	צוה	845		command
39:27	יעשׂו	qal	wci	3mp	עשׂה	793		do,make
	ארג	qal	ptc	ms	ארג	70		weave
39:28	משׁזר	hoph	ptc	ms	שׁזר	1004		be twisted
39:29	משׁזר	hoph	ptc	ms	שׁזר	1004		be twisted
	רקם	qal	ptc	ms	רקם	955		variegate
	צוה	piel	pft	3ms	צוה	845		command
39:30	יעשׂו	qal	wci	3mp	עשׂה	793		do,make
	יכתבו	qal	wci	3mp	כתב	507		write
39:31	יתנו	qal	wci	3mp	נתן	678		give,set
	תת	qal	infc		נתן	678		give,set
	צוה	piel	pft	3ms	צוה	845		command
39:32	תכל	qal	wci	3fs	כלה	477		finished,spent
	יעשׂו	qal	wci	3mp	עשׂה	793		do,make
	צוה	piel	pft	3ms	צוה	845		command
	עשׂו	qal	pft	3cp	עשׂה	793		do,make
39:33	יביאו	hiph	wci	3mp	בוא	97		bring in
39:34	מאדמים	pual	ptc	mp	אדם	10		dyed red
39:41	שׁרת	piel	infc		שׁרת	1058		minister,serve
	כהן	piel	infc		כהן	464		act as priest
39:42	צוה	piel	pft	3ms	צוה	845		command
	עשׂו	qal	pft	3cp	עשׂה	793		do,make
39:43	ירא	qal	wci	3ms	ראה	906		see
	עשׂו	qal	pft	3cp	עשׂה	793		do,make
	צוה	piel	pft	3ms	צוה	845		command
	עשׂו	qal	pft	3cp	עשׂה	793		do,make
	יברך	piel	wci	3ms	ברך	138		bless
40:1	ידבר	piel	wci	3ms	דבר	180		speak
	אמר	qal	infc		אמר	55		say
40:2	תקים	hiph	impf	2ms	קום	877		raise,build,set
40:3	שׂמת	qal	wcp	2ms	שׂים	962		put,set
	סכת	qal	wcp	2ms	סכך	696		cover
40:4	הבאת	hiph	wcp	2ms	בוא	97		bring in
	ערכת	qal	wcp	2ms	ערך	789		set in order
	הבאת	hiph	wcp	2ms	בוא	97		bring in
	העלית	hiph	wcp	2ms	עלה	748		bring up,offer
40:5	נתתה	qal	wcp	2ms	נתן	678		give,set
	שׂמת	qal	wcp	2ms	שׂים	962		put,set
40:6	נתתה	qal	wcp	2ms	נתן	678		give,set
40:7	נתת	qal	wcp	2ms	נתן	678		give,set
	נתת	qal	wcp	2ms	נתן	678		give,set
40:8	שׂמת	qal	wcp	2ms	שׂים	962		put,set
	נתת	qal	wcp	2ms	נתן	678		give,set
40:9	לקחת	qal	wcp	2ms	לקח	542		take
	משׁחת	qal	wcp	2ms	משׁח	602		smear,anoint
	קדשׁת	piel	wcp	2ms	קדשׁ	872		consecrate
	היה	qal	wcp	3ms	היה	224		be,become
40:10	משׁחת	qal	wcp	2ms	משׁח	602		smear,anoint
	קדשׁת	piel	wcp	2ms	קדשׁ	872		consecrate
	היה	qal	wcp	3ms	היה	224		be,become
40:11	משׁחת	qal	wcp	2ms	משׁח	602		smear,anoint

ChVs	Form	Stem	Tnse	PGN	Root	BDB	Sfx	Meaning
40:11	קדשת	piel	wcp	2ms	קדשׁ	872		consecrate
40:12	הקרבת	hiph	wcp	2ms	קרב	897		bring near
	רחצת	qal	wcp	2ms	רחץ	934		wash,bathe
40:13	הלבשׁת	hiph	wcp	2ms	לבשׁ	527		clothe
	משׁחת	qal	wcp	2ms	משׁח	602		smear,anoint
	קדשׁת	piel	wcp	2ms	קדשׁ	872		consecrate
	כהן	piel	wcp	3ms	כהן	464		act as priest
40:14	תקריב	hiph	impf	2ms	קרב	897		bring near
	הלבשׁת	hiph	wcp	2ms	לבשׁ	527		clothe
40:15	משׁחת	qal	wcp	2ms	משׁח	602		smear,anoint
	משׁחת	qal	pft	2ms	משׁח	602		smear,anoint
	כהנו	piel	wcp	3cp	כהן	464		act as priest
	היתה	qal	wcp	3fs	היה	224		be,become
	הית	qal	infc		היה	224		be,become
	משׁחתם	qal	infc		משׁח	602	3mp	smear,anoint
40:16	יעשׂ	qal	wci	3ms	עשׂה	793		do,make
	צוה	piel	pft	3ms	צוה	845		command
	עשׂה	qal	pft	3ms	עשׂה	793		do,make
40:17	יהי	qal	wci	3ms	היה	224		be,become
	הוקם	hoph	pft	3ms	קום	877		be raised up
40:18	יקם	hiph	wci	3ms	קום	877		raise,build,set
	יתן	qal	wci	3ms	נתן	678		give,set
	ישׂם	qal	wci	3ms	שׂים	962		put,set
	יתן	qal	wci	3ms	נתן	678		give,set
	יקם	hiph	wci	3ms	קום	877		raise,build,set
40:19	יפרשׂ	qal	wci	3ms	פרשׂ	831		spread out
	ישׂם	qal	wci	3ms	שׂים	962		put,set
	צוה	piel	pft	3ms	צוה	845		command
40:20	יקח	qal	wci	3ms	לקח	542		take
	יתן	qal	wci	3ms	נתן	678		give,set
	ישׂם	qal	wci	3ms	שׂים	962		put,set
	יתן	qal	wci	3ms	נתן	678		give,set
40:21	יבא	hiph	wci	3ms	בוא	97		bring in
	ישׂם	qal	wci	3ms	שׂים	962		put,set
	יסך	hiph	wci	3ms	סכך	696		cover
	צוה	piel	pft	3ms	צוה	845		command
40:22	יתן	qal	wci	3ms	נתן	678		give,set
40:23	יערך	qal	wci	3ms	ערך	789		set in order
	צוה	piel	pft	3ms	צוה	845		command
40:24	ישׂם	qal	wci	3ms	שׂים	962		put,set
40:25	יעל	hiph	wci	3ms	עלה	748		bring up,offer
	צוה	piel	pft	3ms	צוה	845		command
40:26	ישׂם	qal	wci	3ms	שׂים	962		put,set
40:27	יקטר	hiph	wci	3ms	קטר	882		make sacrifices
	צוה	piel	pft	3ms	צוה	845		command
40:28	ישׂם	qal	wci	3ms	שׂים	962		put,set
40:29	שׂם	qal	pft	3ms	שׂים	962		put,set
	יעל	hiph	wci	3ms	עלה	748		bring up,offer
	צוה	piel	pft	3ms	צוה	845		command
40:30	ישׂם	qal	wci	3ms	שׂים	962		put,set
	יתן	qal	wci	3ms	נתן	678		give,set
	רחצה	qal	infc		רחץ	934		wash,bathe
40:31	רחצו	qal	wcp	3cp	רחץ	934		wash,bathe
40:32	באם	qal	infc		בוא	97	3mp	come in
40:32	קרבתם	qal	infc		קרב	897	3mp	approach
	ירחצו	qal	impf	3mp	רחץ	934		wash,bathe
	צוה	piel	pft	3ms	צוה	845		command
40:33	יקם	hiph	wci	3ms	קום	877		raise,build,set
	יתן	qal	wci	3ms	נתן	678		give,set
	יכל	piel	wci	3ms	כלה	477		complete,finish
40:34	יכס	piel	wci	3ms	כסה	491		cover
	מלא	qal	pft	3ms	מלא	569		be full,fill
40:35	יכל	qal	pft	3ms	יכל	407		be able
	בוא	qal	infc		בוא	97		come in
	שׁכן	qal	pft	3ms	שׁכן	1014		settle,dwell
	מלא	qal	pft	3ms	מלא	569		be full,fill
40:36	העלות	niph	infc		עלה	748		be brought up
	יסעו	qal	impf	3mp	נסע	652		pull up,set out
40:37	יעלה	niph	impf	3ms	עלה	748		be brought up
	יסעו	qal	impf	3mp	נסע	652		pull up,set out
	העלתו	niph	infc		עלה	748	3ms	be brought up
40:38	תהיה	qal	impf	3fs	היה	224		be,become
LEVITICUS								
1:1	יקרא	qal	wci	3ms	קרא	894		call,proclaim
	ידבר	piel	wci	3ms	דבר	180		speak
	אמר	qal	infc		אמר	55		say
1:2	דבר	piel	impv	ms	דבר	180		speak
	אמרת	qal	wcp	2ms	אמר	55		say
	יקריב	hiph	impf	3ms	קרב	897		bring near
	תקריבו	hiph	impf	2mp	קרב	897		bring near
1:3	יקריבנו	hiph	impf	3ms	קרב	897	3ms	bring near
	יקריב	hiph	impf	3ms	קרב	897		bring near
1:4	סמך	qal	wcp	3ms	סמך	701		lean,support
	נרצה	niph	wcp	3ms	רצה	953		be accepted
	כפר	piel	infc		כפר	497		cover,atone
1:5	שׁחט	qal	wcp	3ms	שׁחט	1006		slaughter
	הקריבו	hiph	wcp	3cp	קרב	897		bring near
	זרקו	qal	wcp	3cp	זרק	284		toss,scatter
1:6	הפשׁיט	hiph	wcp	3ms	פשׁט	832		strip off
	נתח	piel	wcp	3ms	נתח	677		cut in pieces
1:7	נתנו	qal	wcp	3cp	נתן	678		give,set
	ערכו	qal	wcp	3cp	ערך	789		set in order
1:8	ערכו	qal	wcp	3cp	ערך	789		set in order
1:9	ירחץ	qal	impf	3ms	רחץ	934		wash,bathe
	הקטיר	hiph	wcp	3ms	קטר	882		make sacrifices
1:10	יקריבנו	hiph	impf	3ms	קרב	897	3ms	bring near
1:11	שׁחט	qal	wcp	3ms	שׁחט	1006		slaughter
	זרקו	qal	wcp	3cp	זרק	284		toss,scatter
1:12	נתח	piel	wcp	3ms	נתח	677		cut in pieces
	ערך	qal	wcp	3ms	ערך	789		set in order
1:13	ירחץ	qal	impf	3ms	רחץ	934		wash,bathe
	הקריב	hiph	wcp	3ms	קרב	897		bring near
	הקטיר	hiph	wcp	3ms	קטר	882		make sacrifices
1:14	הקריב	hiph	wcp	3ms	קרב	897		bring near
1:15	הקריבו	hiph	wcp	3ms	קרב	897	3ms	bring near
	מלק	qal	wcp	3ms	מלק	577		nip off
	הקטיר	hiph	wcp	3ms	קטר	882		make sacrifices

ChVs	Form	Stem	Tnse	PGN	Root	BDB	Sfx	Meaning
1:15	נמצה	niph	wcp	3ms	מצה	594		be drained out
1:16	הסיר	hiph	wcp	3ms	סור	693		take away
	השׁליך	hiph	wcp	3ms	שׁלך	1020		throw,cast
1:17	שׁסע	piel	wcp	3ms	שׁסע	1042		tear in two
	יבדיל	hiph	impf	3ms	בדל	95		divide
	הקטיר	hiph	wcp	3ms	קטר	882		make sacrifices
2:1	תקריב	hiph	impf	3fs	קרב	897		bring near
	יהיה	qal	impf	3ms	היה	224		be,become
	יצק	qal	wcp	3ms	יצק	427		pour out,cast
	נתן	qal	wcp	3ms	נתן	678		give,set
2:2	הביאה	hiph	wcp	3ms	בוא	97	3fs	bring in
	קמץ	qal	wcp	3ms	קמץ	888		grasp
	הקטיר	hiph	wcp	3ms	קטר	882		make sacrifices
2:3	נותרת	niph	ptc	fs	יתר	451		be left,remain
2:4	תקרב	hiph	impf	2ms	קרב	897		bring near
	בלולת	qal	pptc	fp	בלל	117		mingle,mix
	משׁחים	qal	pptc	mp	משׁח	602		smear,anoint
2:5	בלולה	qal	pptc	fs	בלל	117		mingle,mix
	תהיה	qal	impf	3fs	היה	224		be,become
2:6	פתות	qal	infa		פתת	837		crumble
	יצקת	qal	wcp	2ms	יצק	427		pour out,cast
2:7	תעשׂה	niph	impf	3fs	עשׂה	793		be done
2:8	הבאת	hiph	wcp	2ms	בוא	97		bring in
	יעשׂה	niph	impf	3ms	עשׂה	793		be done
	הקריבה	hiph	wcp	3ms	קרב	897	3fs	bring near
	הגישׁה	hiph	wcp	3ms	נגשׁ	620	3fs	bring near
2:9	הרים	hiph	wcp	3ms	רום	926		raise,lift
	הקטיר	hiph	wcp	3ms	קטר	882		make sacrifices
2:10	נותרת	niph	ptc	fs	יתר	451		be left,remain
2:11	תקריבו	hiph	impf	2mp	קרב	897		bring near
	תעשׂה	niph	impf	3fs	עשׂה	793		be done
	תקטירו	hiph	impf	2mp	קטר	882		make sacrifices
2:12	תקריבו	hiph	impf	2mp	קרב	897		bring near
	יעלו	qal	impf	3mp	עלה	748		go up
2:13	תמלח	qal	impf	2ms	מלח	572		salt
	תשׁבית	hiph	impf	2ms	שׁבת	991		destroy,remove
	תקריב	hiph	impf	2ms	קרב	897		bring near
2:14	תקריב	hiph	impf	2ms	קרב	897		bring near
	קלוי	qal	pptc	ms	קלה	885		roast
	תקריב	hiph	impf	2ms	קרב	897		bring near
2:15	נתת	qal	wcp	2ms	נתן	678		give,set
	שׂמת	qal	wcp	2ms	שׂים	962		put,set
2:16	הקטיר	hiph	wcp	3ms	קטר	882		make sacrifices
3:1	מקריב	hiph	ptc	ms	קרב	897		bring near
	יקריבנו	hiph	impf	3ms	קרב	897	3ms	bring near
3:2	סמך	qal	wcp	3ms	סמך	701		lean,support
	שׁחטו	qal	wcp	3ms	שׁחט	1006	3ms	slaughter
	זרקו	qal	wcp	3cp	זרק	284		toss,scatter
3:3	הקריב	hiph	wcp	3ms	קרב	897		bring near
	מכסה	piel	ptc	ms	כסה	491		cover
3:4	יסירנה	hiph	impf	3ms	סור	693	3fs	take away
3:5	הקטירו	hiph	wcp	3cp	קטר	882		make sacrifices
3:6	יקריבנו	hiph	impf	3ms	קרב	897	3ms	bring near
3:7	מקריב	hiph	ptc	ms	קרב	897		bring near
3:7	הקריב	hiph	wcp	3ms	קרב	897		bring near
3:8	סמך	qal	wcp	3ms	סמך	701		lean,support
	שׁחט	qal	wcp	3ms	שׁחט	1006		slaughter
	זרקו	qal	wcp	3cp	זרק	284		toss,scatter
3:9	הקריב	hiph	wcp	3ms	קרב	897		bring near
	יסירנה	hiph	impf	3ms	סור	693	3fs	take away
	מכסה	piel	ptc	ms	כסה	491		cover
3:10	יסירנה	hiph	impf	3ms	סור	693	3fs	take away
3:11	הקטירו	hiph	wcp	3ms	קטר	882	3ms	make sacrifices
3:12	הקריבו	hiph	wcp	3ms	קרב	897	3ms	bring near
3:13	סמך	qal	wcp	3ms	סמך	701		lean,support
	שׁחט	qal	wcp	3ms	שׁחט	1006		slaughter
	זרקו	qal	wcp	3cp	זרק	284		toss,scatter
3:14	הקריב	hiph	wcp	3ms	קרב	897		bring near
	מכסה	piel	ptc	ms	כסה	491		cover
3:15	יסירנה	hiph	impf	3ms	סור	693	3fs	take away
3:16	הקטירם	hiph	wcp	3ms	קטר	882	3mp	make sacrifices
3:17	תאכלו	qal	impf	2mp	אכל	37		eat,devour
4:1	ידבר	piel	wci	3ms	דבר	180		speak
	אמר	qal	infc		אמר	55		say
4:2	דבר	piel	impv	ms	דבר	180		speak
	אמר	qal	infc		אמר	55		say
	תחטא	qal	impf	3fs	חטא	306		sin
	תעשׂינה	niph	impf	3fp	עשׂה	793		be done
	עשׂה	qal	wcp	3ms	עשׂה	793		do,make
4:3	יחטא	qal	impf	3ms	חטא	306		sin
	הקריב	hiph	wcp	3ms	קרב	897		bring near
	חטא	qal	pft	3ms	חטא	306		sin
4:4	הביא	hiph	wcp	3ms	בוא	97		bring in
	סמך	qal	wcp	3ms	סמך	701		lean,support
	שׁחט	qal	wcp	3ms	שׁחט	1006		slaughter
4:5	לקח	qal	wcp	3ms	לקח	542		take
	הביא	hiph	wcp	3ms	בוא	97		bring in
4:6	טבל	qal	wcp	3ms	טבל	371		dip
	הזה	hiph	wcp	3ms	נזה	633		cause to spurt
4:7	נתן	qal	wcp	3ms	נתן	678		give,set
	ישׁפך	qal	impf	3ms	שׁפך	1049		pour out
4:8	ירים	hiph	impf	3ms	רום	926		raise,lift
	מכסה	piel	ptc	ms	כסה	491		cover
4:9	יסירנה	hiph	impf	3ms	סור	693	3fs	take away
4:10	יורם	hoph	impf	3ms	רום	926		be taken away
	הקטירם	hiph	wcp	3ms	קטר	882	3mp	make sacrifices
4:12	הוציא	hiph	wcp	3ms	יצא	422		bring out
	שׂרף	qal	wcp	3ms	שׂרף	976		burn
	ישׂרף	niph	impf	3ms	שׂרף	976		be burned
4:13	ישׁגו	qal	impf	3mp	שׁגה	993		err,go astray
	נעלם	niph	wcp	3ms	עלם	761		be concealed
	עשׂו	qal	wcp	3cp	עשׂה	793		do,make
	תעשׂינה	niph	impf	3fp	עשׂה	793		be done
	אשׁמו	qal	wcp	3cp	אשׁם	79		offend
4:14	נודעה	niph	wcp	3fs	ידע	393		be made known
	חטאו	qal	pft	3cp	חטא	306		sin
	הקריבו	hiph	wcp	3cp	קרב	897		bring near
	הביאו	hiph	wcp	3cp	בוא	97		bring in

ChVs	Form	Stem	Tnse	PGN	Root	BDB	Sfx	Meaning
4:15	סמכו	qal	wcp	3cp	סמך	701		lean,support
	שׁחט	qal	wcp	3ms	שׁחט	1006		slaughter
4:16	הביא	hiph	wcp	3ms	בוא	97		bring in
4:17	טבל	qal	wcp	3ms	טבל	371		dip
	הזה	hiph	wcp	3ms	נזה	633		cause to spurt
4:18	יתן	qal	impf	3ms	נתן	678		give,set
	ישׁפך	qal	impf	3ms	שׁפך	1049		pour out
4:19	ירים	hiph	impf	3ms	רום	926		raise,lift
	הקטיר	hiph	wcp	3ms	קטר	882		make sacrifices
4:20	עשׂה	qal	wcp	3ms	עשׂה	793		do,make
	עשׂה	qal	pft	3ms	עשׂה	793		do,make
	יעשׂה	qal	impf	3ms	עשׂה	793		do,make
	כפר	piel	wcp	3ms	כפר	497		cover,atone
	נסלח	niph	wcp	3ms	סלח	699		be forgiven
4:21	הוציא	hiph	wcp	3ms	יצא	422		bring out
	שׂרף	qal	wcp	3ms	שׂרף	976		burn
	שׂרף	qal	pft	3ms	שׂרף	976		burn
4:22	יחטא	qal	impf	3ms	חטא	306		sin
	עשׂה	qal	wcp	3ms	עשׂה	793		do,make
	תעשׂינה	niph	impf	3fp	עשׂה	793		be done
	אשׁם	qal	wcp	3ms	אשׁם	79		offend
4:23	הודע	hoph	pft	3ms	ידע	393		be made known
	חטא	qal	pft	3ms	חטא	306		sin
	הביא	hiph	wcp	3ms	בוא	97		bring in
4:24	סמך	qal	wcp	3ms	סמך	701		lean,support
	שׁחט	qal	wcp	3ms	שׁחט	1006		slaughter
	ישׁחט	qal	impf	3ms	שׁחט	1006		slaughter
4:25	לקח	qal	wcp	3ms	לקח	542		take
	נתן	qal	wcp	3ms	נתן	678		give,set
	ישׁפך	qal	impf	3ms	שׁפך	1049		pour out
4:26	יקטיר	hiph	impf	3ms	קטר	882		make sacrifices
	כפר	piel	wcp	3ms	כפר	497		cover,atone
	נסלח	niph	wcp	3ms	סלח	699		be forgiven
4:27	תחטא	qal	impf	3fs	חטא	306		sin
	עשׂתה	qal	infc		עשׂה	793	3fs	do,make
	תעשׂינה	niph	impf	3fp	עשׂה	793		be done
	אשׁם	qal	wcp	3ms	אשׁם	79		offend
4:28	הודע	hoph	pft	3ms	ידע	393		be made known
	חטא	qal	pft	3ms	חטא	306		sin
	הביא	hiph	wcp	3ms	בוא	97		bring in
	חטא	qal	pft	3ms	חטא	306		sin
4:29	סמך	qal	wcp	3ms	סמך	701		lean,support
	שׁחט	qal	wcp	3ms	שׁחט	1006		slaughter
4:30	לקח	qal	wcp	3ms	לקח	542		take
	נתן	qal	wcp	3ms	נתן	678		give,set
	ישׁפך	qal	impf	3ms	שׁפך	1049		pour out
4:31	יסיר	hiph	impf	3ms	סור	693		take away
	הוסר	hoph	pft	3ms	סור	693		be taken away
	הקטיר	hiph	wcp	3ms	קטר	882		make sacrifices
	כפר	piel	wcp	3ms	כפר	497		cover,atone
	נסלח	niph	wcp	3ms	סלח	699		be forgiven
4:32	יביא	hiph	impf	3ms	בוא	97		bring in
	יביאנה	hiph	impf	3ms	בוא	97	3fs	bring in
4:33	סמך	qal	wcp	3ms	סמך	701		lean,support
4:33	שׁחט	qal	wcp	3ms	שׁחט	1006		slaughter
	ישׁחט	qal	impf	3ms	שׁחט	1006		slaughter
4:34	לקח	qal	wcp	3ms	לקח	542		take
	נתן	qal	wcp	3ms	נתן	678		give,set
	ישׁפך	qal	impf	3ms	שׁפך	1049		pour out
4:35	יסיר	hiph	impf	3ms	סור	693		take away
	יוסר	hoph	impf	3ms	סור	693		be taken away
	הקטיר	hiph	wcp	3ms	קטר	882		make sacrifices
	כפר	piel	wcp	3ms	כפר	497		cover,atone
	חטא	qal	pft	3ms	חטא	306		sin
	נסלח	niph	wcp	3ms	סלח	699		be forgiven
5:1	תחטא	qal	impf	3fs	חטא	306		sin
	שׁמעה	qal	wcp	3fs	שׁמע	1033		hear
	ראה	qal	pft	3ms	ראה	906		see
	ידע	qal	pft	3ms	ידע	393		know
	יגיד	hiph	impf	3ms	נגד	616		declare,tell
	נשׂא	qal	wcp	3ms	נשׂא	669		lift,carry
5:2	תגע	qal	impf	3fs	נגע	619		touch,strike
	נעלם	niph	wcp	3ms	עלם	761		be concealed
	אשׁם	qal	wcp	3ms	אשׁם	79		offend
5:3	יגע	qal	impf	3ms	נגע	619		touch,strike
	יטמא	qal	impf	3ms	טמא	379		become unclean
	נעלם	niph	wcp	3ms	עלם	761		be concealed
	ידע	qal	pft	3ms	ידע	393		know
	אשׁם	qal	wcp	3ms	אשׁם	79		offend
5:4	תשׁבע	niph	impf	3fs	שׁבע	989		swear
	בטא	piel	infc		בטה	104		speak rashly
	הרע	hiph	infc		רעע	949		hurt,do evil
	היטיב	hiph	infc		יטב	405		do good
	יבטא	piel	impf	3ms	בטה	104		speak rashly
	נעלם	niph	wcp	3ms	עלם	761		be concealed
	ידע	qal	pft	3ms	ידע	393		know
	אשׁם	qal	wcp	3ms	אשׁם	79		offend
5:5	היה	qal	wcp	3ms	היה	224		be,become
	יאשׁם	qal	impf	3ms	אשׁם	79		offend
	התודה	hith	wcp	3ms	ידה	392		confess
	חטא	qal	pft	3ms	חטא	306		sin
5:6	הביא	hiph	wcp	3ms	בוא	97		bring in
	חטא	qal	pft	3ms	חטא	306		sin
	כפר	piel	wcp	3ms	כפר	497		cover,atone
5:7	תגיע	hiph	impf	3fs	נגע	619		reach,arrive
	הביא	hiph	wcp	3ms	בוא	97		bring in
	חטא	qal	pft	3ms	חטא	306		sin
5:8	הביא	hiph	wcp	3ms	בוא	97		bring in
	הקריב	hiph	wcp	3ms	קרב	897		bring near
	מלק	qal	wcp	3ms	מלק	577		nip off
	יבדיל	hiph	impf	3ms	בדל	95		divide
5:9	הזה	hiph	wcp	3ms	נזה	633		cause to spurt
	נשׁאר	niph	ptc	ms	שׁאר	983		be left
	ימצה	niph	impf	3ms	מצה	594		be drained out
5:10	יעשׂה	qal	impf	3ms	עשׂה	793		do,make
	כפר	piel	wcp	3ms	כפר	497		cover,atone
	חטא	qal	pft	3ms	חטא	306		sin
	נסלח	niph	wcp	3ms	סלח	699		be forgiven

ChVs	Form	Stem	Tnse	PGN	Root	BDB	Sfx	Meaning
5:11	תשׂיג	hiph	impf	3fs	נשׂג	673		reach,overtake
	הביא	hiph	wcp	3ms	בוא	97		bring in
	חטא	qal	pft	3ms	חטא	306		sin
	ישׂים	qal	impf	3ms	שׂים	962		put,set
	יתן	qal	impf	3ms	נתן	678		give,set
5:12	הביאה	hiph	wcp	3ms	בוא	97	3fs	bring in
	קמץ	qal	wcp	3ms	קמץ	888		grasp
	הקטיר	hiph	wcp	3ms	קטר	882		make sacrifices
5:13	כפר	piel	wcp	3ms	כפר	497		cover,atone
	חטא	qal	pft	3ms	חטא	306		sin
	נסלח	niph	wcp	3ms	סלח	699		be forgiven
	היתה	qal	wcp	3fs	היה	224		be,become
5:14	ידבר	piel	wci	3ms	דבר	180		speak
	אמר	qal	infc		אמר	55		say
5:15	תמעל	qal	impf	3fs	מעל	591		act faithlessly
	חטאה	qal	wcp	3fs	חטא	306		sin
	הביא	hiph	wcp	3ms	בוא	97		bring in
5:16	חטא	qal	pft	3ms	חטא	306		sin
	ישׁלם	piel	impf	3ms	שׁלם	1022		finish,reward
	יוסף	hiph	jus	3ms	יסף	414		add,do again
	נתן	qal	wcp	3ms	נתן	678		give,set
	יכפר	piel	impf	3ms	כפר	497		cover,atone
	נסלח	niph	wcp	3ms	סלח	699		be forgiven
5:17	תחטא	qal	impf	3fs	חטא	306		sin
	עשׂתה	qal	wcp	3fs	עשׂה	793		do,make
	תעשׂינה	niph	impf	3fp	עשׂה	793		be done
	ידע	qal	pft	3ms	ידע	393		know
	אשׁם	qal	wcp	3ms	אשׁם	79		offend
	נשׂא	qal	wcp	3ms	נשׂא	669		lift,carry
5:18	הביא	hiph	wcp	3ms	בוא	97		bring in
	כפר	piel	wcp	3ms	כפר	497		cover,atone
	שׁגג	qal	pft	3ms	שׁגג	992		err,sin
	ידע	qal	pft	3ms	ידע	393		know
	נסלח	niph	wcp	3ms	סלח	699		be forgiven
5:19	אשׁם	qal	infa		אשׁם	79		offend
	אשׁם	qal	pft	3ms	אשׁם	79		offend
5:20	ידבר	piel	wci	3ms	דבר	180		speak
	אמר	qal	infc		אמר	55		say
5:21	תחטא	qal	impf	3fs	חטא	306		sin
	מעלה	qal	wcp	3fs	מעל	591		act faithlessly
	כחשׁ	piel	wcp	3ms	כחשׁ	471		deceive
	עשׁק	qal	pft	3ms	עשׁק	798		oppress,extort
5:22	מצא	qal	pft	3ms	מצא	592		find
	כחשׁ	piel	wcp	3ms	כחשׁ	471		deceive
	נשׁבע	niph	wcp	3ms	שׁבע	989		swear
	יעשׂה	qal	impf	3ms	עשׂה	793		do,make
	חטא	qal	infc		חטא	306		sin
5:23	היה	qal	wcp	3ms	היה	224		be,become
	יחטא	qal	impf	3ms	חטא	306		sin
	אשׁם	qal	wcp	3ms	אשׁם	79		offend
	השׁיב	hiph	wcp	3ms	שׁוב	996		bring back
	גזל	qal	pft	3ms	גזל	159		tear away,rob
	עשׁק	qal	pft	3ms	עשׁק	798		oppress,extort
	הפקד	hoph	pft	3ms	פקד	823		be appointed
5:23	מצא	qal	pft	3ms	מצא	592		find
5:24	ישׁבע	niph	impf	3ms	שׁבע	989		swear
	שׁלם	piel	wcp	3ms	שׁלם	1022		finish,reward
	יסף	hiph	jus	3ms	יסף	414		add,do again
	יתננו	qal	impf	3ms	נתן	678	3ms	give,set
5:25	יביא	hiph	impf	3ms	בוא	97		bring in
5:26	כפר	piel	wcp	3ms	כפר	497		cover,atone
	נסלח	niph	wcp	3ms	סלח	699		be forgiven
	יעשׂה	qal	impf	3ms	עשׂה	793		do,make
6:1	ידבר	piel	wci	3ms	דבר	180		speak
	אמר	qal	infc		אמר	55		say
6:2	צו	piel	impv	ms	צוה	845		command
	אמר	qal	infc		אמר	55		say
	תוקד	hoph	impf	3fs	יקד	428		be kindled
6:3	לבשׁ	qal	wcp	3ms	לבשׁ	527		put on,clothe
	ילבשׁ	qal	impf	3ms	לבשׁ	527		put on,clothe
	הרים	hiph	wcp	3ms	רום	926		raise,lift
	תאכל	qal	impf	3fs	אכל	37		eat,devour
	שׂמו	qal	wcp	3ms	שׂים	962	3ms	put,set
6:4	פשׁט	qal	wcp	3ms	פשׁט	832		strip off
	לבשׁ	qal	wcp	3ms	לבשׁ	527		put on,clothe
	הוציא	hiph	wcp	3ms	יצא	422		bring out
6:5	תוקד	hoph	impf	3fs	יקד	428		be kindled
	תכבה	qal	impf	3fs	כבה	459		be quenched
	בער	piel	wcp	3ms	בער	128		burn,consume
	ערך	qal	wcp	3ms	ערך	789		set in order
	הקטיר	hiph	wcp	3ms	קטר	882		make sacrifices
6:6	תוקד	hoph	impf	3fs	יקד	428		be kindled
	תכבה	qal	impf	3fs	כבה	459		be quenched
6:7	הקרב	hiph	infa		קרב	897		bring near
6:8	הרים	hiph	wcp	3ms	רום	926		raise,lift
	הקטיר	hiph	wcp	3ms	קטר	882		make sacrifices
6:9	נותרת	niph	ptc	fs	יתר	451		be left,remain
	יאכלו	qal	impf	3mp	אכל	37		eat,devour
	תאכל	niph	impf	3fs	אכל	37		be eaten
	יאכלוה	qal	impf	3mp	אכל	37	3fs	eat,devour
6:10	תאפה	niph	impf	3fs	אפה	66		be baked
	נתתי	qal	pft	1cs	נתן	678		give,set
6:11	יאכלנה	qal	impf	3ms	אכל	37	3fs	eat,devour
	יגע	qal	impf	3ms	נגע	619		touch,strike
	יקדשׁ	qal	impf	3ms	קדשׁ	872		be set apart
6:12	ידבר	piel	wci	3ms	דבר	180		speak
	אמר	qal	infc		אמר	55		say
6:13	יקריבו	hiph	impf	3mp	קרב	897		bring near
	המשח	niph	infc		משח	602		be anointed
6:14	תעשׂה	niph	impf	3fs	עשׂה	793		be done
	מרבכת	hoph	ptc	fs	רבך	916		be mixed
	תביאנה	hiph	impf	2ms	בוא	97	3fs	bring in
	תקריב	hiph	impf	2ms	קרב	897		bring near
6:15	יעשׂה	qal	impf	3ms	עשׂה	793		do,make
	תקטר	hoph	impf	3fs	קטר	882		be offered
6:16	תהיה	qal	impf	3fs	היה	224		be,become
	תאכל	niph	impf	3fs	אכל	37		be eaten
6:17	ידבר	piel	wci	3ms	דבר	180		speak

ChVs	Form	Stem	Tnse	PGN	Root	BDB	Sfx	Meaning
6:17	אמר	qal	infc		אמר	55		say
6:18	דבר	piel	impv	ms	דבר	180		speak
	אמר	qal	infc		אמר	55		say
	תשחט	niph	impf	3fs	שחט	1006		be slaughtered
	תשחט	niph	impf	3fs	שחט	1006		be slaughtered
6:19	מחטא	piel	ptc	ms	חטא	306		purify
	יאכלנה	qal	impf	3ms	אכל	37	3fs	eat,devour
	תאכל	niph	impf	3fs	אכל	37		be eaten
6:20	יגע	qal	impf	3ms	נגע	619		touch,strike
	יקדש	qal	impf	3ms	קדש	872		be set apart
	יזה	qal	impf	3ms	נזה	633		spatter
	יזה	qal	impf	3ms	נזה	633		spatter
	תכבס	piel	impf	2ms	כבס	460		wash
6:21	תבשל	pual	impf	3fs	בשל	143		be boiled
	ישבר	niph	impf	3ms	שבר	990		be broken
	בשלה	pual	pft	3fs	בשל	143		be boiled
	מרק	pual	wcp	3ms	מרק	599		be scoured
	שטף	pual	wcp	3ms	שטף	1009		be rinsed
6:22	יאכל	qal	impf	3ms	אכל	37		eat,devour
6:23	יובא	hoph	impf	3ms	בוא	97		be brought
	כפר	piel	infc		כפר	497		cover,atone
	תאכל	niph	impf	3fs	אכל	37		be eaten
	תשרף	niph	impf	3fs	שרף	976		be burned
7:2	ישחטו	qal	impf	3mp	שחט	1006		slaughter
	ישחטו	qal	impf	3mp	שחט	1006		slaughter
	יזרק	qal	impf	3ms	זרק	284		toss,scatter
7:3	יקריב	hiph	impf	3ms	קרב	897		bring near
	מכסה	piel	ptc	ms	כסה	491		cover
7:4	יסירנה	hiph	impf	3ms	סור	693	3fs	take away
7:5	הקטיר	hiph	wcp	3ms	קטר	882		make sacrifices
7:6	יאכלנו	qal	impf	3ms	אכל	37	3ms	eat,devour
	יאכל	niph	impf	3ms	אכל	37		be eaten
7:7	יכפר	piel	impf	3ms	כפר	497		cover,atone
	יהיה	qal	impf	3ms	היה	224		be,become
7:8	מקריב	hiph	ptc	ms	קרב	897		bring near
	הקריב	hiph	pft	3ms	קרב	897		bring near
	יהיה	qal	impf	3ms	היה	224		be,become
7:9	תאפה	niph	impf	3fs	אפה	66		be baked
	נעשה	niph	pft	3ms	עשה	793		be done
	מקריב	hiph	ptc	ms	קרב	897		bring near
	תהיה	qal	impf	3fs	היה	224		be,become
7:10	בלולה	qal	pptc	fs	בלל	117		mingle,mix
	תהיה	qal	impf	3fs	היה	224		be,become
7:11	יקריב	hiph	impf	3ms	קרב	897		bring near
7:12	יקריבנו	hiph	impf	3ms	קרב	897	3ms	bring near
	הקריב	hiph	wcp	3ms	קרב	897		bring near
	בלולת	qal	pptc	fp	בלל	117		mingle,mix
	משחים	qal	pptc	mp	משח	602		smear,anoint
	מרבכת	hoph	ptc	fs	רבך	916		be mixed
	בלולת	qal	pptc	fp	בלל	117		mingle,mix
7:13	יקריב	hiph	impf	3ms	קרב	897		bring near
7:14	הקריב	hiph	wcp	3ms	קרב	897		bring near
	זרק	qal	ptc	ms	זרק	284		toss,scatter
	יהיה	qal	impf	3ms	היה	224		be,become

ChVs	Form	Stem	Tnse	PGN	Root	BDB	Sfx	Meaning
7:15	יאכל	niph	impf	3ms	אכל	37		be eaten
	יניח	hiph	impf	3ms	נוח	628		give rest,put
7:16	הקריבו	hiph	infc		קרב	897	3ms	bring near
	יאכל	niph	impf	3ms	אכל	37		be eaten
	נותר	niph	ptc	ms	יתר	451		be left,remain
	יאכל	niph	impf	3ms	אכל	37		be eaten
7:17	נותר	niph	ptc	ms	יתר	451		be left,remain
	ישרף	niph	impf	3ms	שרף	976		be burned
7:18	האכל	niph	infa		אכל	37		be eaten
	יאכל	niph	impf	3ms	אכל	37		be eaten
	ירצה	niph	impf	3ms	רצה	953		be accepted
	מקריב	hiph	ptc	ms	קרב	897		bring near
	יחשב	niph	impf	3ms	חשב	362		be thought
	יהיה	qal	impf	3ms	היה	224		be,become
	אכלת	qal	ptc	fs	אכל	37		eat,devour
	תשא	qal	impf	3fs	נשא	669		lift,carry
7:19	יגע	qal	impf	3ms	נגע	619		touch,strike
	יאכל	niph	impf	3ms	אכל	37		be eaten
	ישרף	niph	impf	3ms	שרף	976		be burned
	יאכל	qal	impf	3ms	אכל	37		eat,devour
7:20	תאכל	qal	impf	3fs	אכל	37		eat,devour
	נכרתה	niph	wcp	3fs	כרת	503		be cut off
7:21	תגע	qal	impf	3fs	נגע	619		touch,strike
	אכל	qal	wcp	3ms	אכל	37		eat,devour
	נכרתה	niph	wcp	3fs	כרת	503		be cut off
7:22	ידבר	piel	wci	3ms	דבר	180		speak
	אמר	qal	infc		אמר	55		say
7:23	דבר	piel	impv	ms	דבר	180		speak
	אמר	qal	infc		אמר	55		say
	תאכלו	qal	impf	2mp	אכל	37		eat,devour
7:24	יעשה	niph	impf	3ms	עשה	793		be done
	אכל	qal	infa		אכל	37		eat,devour
	תאכלהו	qal	impf	2mp	אכל	37	3ms	eat,devour
7:25	אכל	qal	ptc	ms	אכל	37		eat,devour
	יקריב	hiph	impf	3ms	קרב	897		bring near
	נכרתה	niph	wcp	3fs	כרת	503		be cut off
	אכלת	qal	ptc	fs	אכל	37		eat,devour
7:26	תאכלו	qal	impf	2mp	אכל	37		eat,devour
7:27	תאכל	qal	impf	3fs	אכל	37		eat,devour
	נכרתה	niph	wcp	3fs	כרת	503		be cut off
7:28	ידבר	piel	wci	3ms	דבר	180		speak
	אמר	qal	infc		אמר	55		say
7:29	דבר	piel	impv	ms	דבר	180		speak
	אמר	qal	infc		אמר	55		say
	מקריב	hiph	ptc	ms	קרב	897		bring near
	יביא	hiph	impf	3ms	בוא	97		bring in
7:30	תביאינה	hiph	impf	3fp	בוא	97		bring in
	יביאנו	hiph	impf	3ms	בוא	97	3ms	bring in
	הניף	hiph	infc		נוף	631		swing,wave
7:31	הקטיר	hiph	wcp	3ms	קטר	882		make sacrifices
	היה	qal	wcp	3ms	היה	224		be,become
7:32	תתנו	qal	impf	2mp	נתן	678		give,set
7:33	מקריב	hiph	ptc	ms	קרב	897		bring near
	תהיה	qal	impf	3fs	היה	224		be,become

ChVs	Form	Stem	Tnse	PGN	Root	BDB	Sfx	Meaning
7:34	לקחתי	qal	pft	1cs	לקח	542		take
	אתן	qal	wci	1cs	נתן	678		give,set
7:35	הקריב	hiph	pft	3ms	קרב	897		bring near
	כהן	piel	infc		כהן	464		act as priest
7:36	צוה	piel	pft	3ms	צוה	845		command
	תת	qal	infc		נתן	678		give,set
	משחו	qal	infc		משח	602	3ms	smear,anoint
7:38	צוה	piel	pft	3ms	צוה	845		command
	צותו	piel	infc		צוה	845	3ms	command
	הקריב	hiph	infc		קרב	897		bring near
8:1	ידבר	piel	wci	3ms	דבר	180		speak
	אמר	qal	infc		אמר	55		say
8:2	קח	qal	impv	ms	לקח	542		take
8:3	הקהל	hiph	impv	ms	קהל	874		call assembly
8:4	יעשׂ	qal	wci	3ms	עשׂה	793		do,make
	צוה	piel	pft	3ms	צוה	845		command
	תקהל	niph	wci	3fs	קהל	874		assemble
8:5	יאמר	qal	wci	3ms	אמר	55		say
	צוה	piel	pft	3ms	צוה	845		command
	עשׂות	qal	infc		עשׂה	793		do,make
8:6	יקרב	hiph	wci	3ms	קרב	897		bring near
	ירחץ	qal	wci	3ms	רחץ	934		wash,bathe
8:7	יתן	qal	wci	3ms	נתן	678		give,set
	יחגר	qal	wci	3ms	חגר	291		gird
	ילבשׁ	hiph	wci	3ms	לבשׁ	527		clothe
	יתן	qal	wci	3ms	נתן	678		give,set
	יחגר	qal	wci	3ms	חגר	291		gird
	יאפד	qal	wci	3ms	אפד	65		gird on ephod
8:8	ישׂם	qal	wci	3ms	שׂים	962		put,set
	יתן	qal	wci	3ms	נתן	678		give,set
8:9	ישׂם	qal	wci	3ms	שׂים	962		put,set
	ישׂם	qal	wci	3ms	שׂים	962		put,set
	צוה	piel	pft	3ms	צוה	845		command
8:10	יקח	qal	wci	3ms	לקח	542		take
	ימשח	qal	wci	3ms	משח	602		smear,anoint
	יקדשׁ	piel	wci	3ms	קדשׁ	872		consecrate
8:11	יז	hiph	wci	3ms	נזה	633		cause to spurt
	ימשח	qal	wci	3ms	משח	602		smear,anoint
	קדשׁם	piel	infc		קדשׁ	872	3mp	consecrate
8:12	יצק	qal	wci	3ms	יצק	427		pour out,cast
	ימשח	qal	wci	3ms	משח	602		smear,anoint
	קדשׁו	piel	infc		קדשׁ	872	3ms	consecrate
8:13	יקרב	hiph	wci	3ms	קרב	897		bring near
	ילבשׁם	hiph	wci	3ms	לבשׁ	527	3mp	clothe
	יחגר	qal	wci	3ms	חגר	291		gird
	יחבשׁ	qal	wci	3ms	חבשׁ	289		bind
	צוה	piel	pft	3ms	צוה	845		command
8:14	יגשׁ	hiph	wci	3ms	נגשׁ	620		bring near
	יסמך	qal	wci	3ms	סמך	701		lean,support
8:15	ישׁחט	qal	wci	3ms	שׁחט	1006		slaughter
	יקח	qal	wci	3ms	לקח	542		take
	יתן	qal	wci	3ms	נתן	678		give,set
	יחטא	piel	wci	3ms	חטא	306		purify
	יצק	qal	pft	3ms	יצק	427		pour out,cast
8:15	יקדשׁהו	piel	wci	3ms	קדשׁ	872	3ms	consecrate
	כפר	piel	infc		כפר	497		cover,atone
8:16	יקח	qal	wci	3ms	לקח	542		take
	יקטר	hiph	wci	3ms	קטר	882		make sacrifices
8:17	שׂרף	qal	pft	3ms	שׂרף	976		burn
	צוה	piel	pft	3ms	צוה	845		command
8:18	יקרב	hiph	wci	3ms	קרב	897		bring near
	יסמכו	qal	wci	3mp	סמך	701		lean,support
8:19	ישׁחט	qal	wci	3ms	שׁחט	1006		slaughter
	יזרק	qal	wci	3ms	זרק	284		toss,scatter
8:20	נתח	piel	pft	3ms	נתח	677		cut in pieces
	יקטר	hiph	wci	3ms	קטר	882		make sacrifices
8:21	רחץ	qal	pft	3ms	רחץ	934		wash,bathe
	יקטר	hiph	wci	3ms	קטר	882		make sacrifices
	צוה	piel	pft	3ms	צוה	845		command
8:22	יקרב	hiph	wci	3ms	קרב	897		bring near
	יסמכו	qal	wci	3mp	סמך	701		lean,support
8:23	ישׁחט	qal	wci	3ms	שׁחט	1006		slaughter
	יקח	qal	wci	3ms	לקח	542		take
	יתן	qal	wci	3ms	נתן	678		give,set
8:24	יקרב	hiph	wci	3ms	קרב	897		bring near
	יתן	qal	wci	3ms	נתן	678		give,set
	יזרק	qal	wci	3ms	זרק	284		toss,scatter
8:25	יקח	qal	wci	3ms	לקח	542		take
8:26	לקח	qal	pft	3ms	לקח	542		take
	ישׂם	qal	wci	3ms	שׂים	962		put,set
8:27	יתן	qal	wci	3ms	נתן	678		give,set
	ינף	hiph	wci	3ms	נוף	631		swing,wave
8:28	יקח	qal	wci	3ms	לקח	542		take
	יקטר	hiph	wci	3ms	קטר	882		make sacrifices
8:29	יקח	qal	wci	3ms	לקח	542		take
	יניפהו	hiph	wci	3ms	נוף	631	3ms	swing,wave
	היה	qal	pft	3ms	היה	224		be,become
	צוה	piel	pft	3ms	צוה	845		command
8:30	יקח	qal	wci	3ms	לקח	542		take
	יז	hiph	wci	3ms	נזה	633		cause to spurt
	יקדשׁ	piel	wci	3ms	קדשׁ	872		consecrate
8:31	יאמר	qal	wci	3ms	אמר	55		say
	בשׁלו	piel	impv	mp	בשׁל	143		boil,cook
	תאכלו	qal	impf	2mp	אכל	37		eat,devour
	צויתי	piel	pft	1cs	צוה	845		command
	אמר	qal	infc		אמר	55		say
	יאכלהו	qal	impf	3mp	אכל	37	3ms	eat,devour
8:32	נותר	niph	ptc	ms	יתר	451		be left,remain
	תשׂרפו	qal	impf	2mp	שׂרף	976		burn
8:33	תצאו	qal	impf	2mp	יצא	422		go out
	מלאת	qal	infc		מלא	569		be full,fill
	ימלא	piel	impf	3ms	מלא	569		fill
8:34	עשׂה	qal	pft	3ms	עשׂה	793		do,make
	צוה	piel	pft	3ms	צוה	845		command
	עשׂת	qal	infc		עשׂה	793		do,make
	כפר	piel	infc		כפר	497		cover,atone
8:35	תשׁבו	qal	impf	2mp	ישׁב	442		sit,dwell
	שׁמרתם	qal	wcp	2mp	שׁמר	1036		keep,watch

ChVs	Form	Stem	Tnse	PGN	Root	BDB	Sfx	Meaning
8:35	תמותו	qal	impf	2mp	מות	559		die
	צויתי	pual	pft	1cs	צוה	845		be commanded
8:36	יעשׂ	qal	wci	3ms	עשׂה	793		do,make
	צוה	piel	pft	3ms	צוה	845		command
9:1	יהי	qal	wci	3ms	היה	224		be,become
	קרא	qal	pft	3ms	קרא	894		call,proclaim
9:2	יאמר	qal	wci	3ms	אמר	55		say
	קח	qal	impv	ms	לקח	542		take
	הקרב	hiph	impv	ms	קרב	897		bring near
9:3	תדבר	piel	impf	2ms	דבר	180		speak
	אמר	qal	infc		אמר	55		say
	קחו	qal	impv	mp	לקח	542		take
9:4	זבח	qal	infc		זבח	256		slaughter
	בלולה	qal	pptc	fs	בלל	117		mingle,mix
	נראה	niph	pft	3ms	ראה	906		appear,be seen
9:5	יקחו	qal	wci	3mp	לקח	542		take
	צוה	piel	pft	3ms	צוה	845		command
	יקרבו	qal	wci	3mp	קרב	897		approach
	יעמדו	qal	wci	3mp	עמד	763		stand,stop
9:6	יאמר	qal	wci	3ms	אמר	55		say
	צוה	piel	pft	3ms	צוה	845		command
	תעשׂו	qal	impf	2mp	עשׂה	793		do,make
	ירא	niph	jus	3ms	ראה	906		appear,be seen
9:7	יאמר	qal	wci	3ms	אמר	55		say
	קרב	qal	impv	ms	קרב	897		approach
	עשׂה	qal	impv	ms	עשׂה	793		do,make
	כפר	piel	impv	ms	כפר	497		cover,atone
	עשׂה	qal	impv	ms	עשׂה	793		do,make
	כפר	piel	impv	ms	כפר	497		cover,atone
	צוה	piel	pft	3ms	צוה	845		command
9:8	יקרב	qal	wci	3ms	קרב	897		approach
	ישׁחט	qal	wci	3ms	שׁחט	1006		slaughter
9:9	יקרבו	hiph	wci	3mp	קרב	897		bring near
	יטבל	qal	wci	3ms	טבל	371		dip
	יתן	qal	wci	3ms	נתן	678		give,set
	יצק	qal	pft	3ms	יצק	427		pour out,cast
9:10	הקטיר	hiph	pft	3ms	קטר	882		make sacrifices
	צוה	piel	pft	3ms	צוה	845		command
9:11	שׂרף	qal	pft	3ms	שׂרף	976		burn
9:12	ישׁחט	qal	wci	3ms	שׁחט	1006		slaughter
	ימצאו	hiph	wci	3mp	מצא	592		cause to find
	יזרקהו	qal	wci	3ms	זרק	284	3ms	toss,scatter
9:13	המציאו	hiph	pft	3cp	מצא	592		cause to find
	יקטר	hiph	wci	3ms	קטר	882		make sacrifices
9:14	ירחץ	qal	wci	3ms	רחץ	934		wash,bathe
	יקטר	hiph	wci	3ms	קטר	882		make sacrifices
9:15	יקרב	hiph	wci	3ms	קרב	897		bring near
	יקח	qal	wci	3ms	לקח	542		take
	ישׁחטהו	qal	wci	3ms	שׁחט	1006	3ms	slaughter
	יחטאהו	piel	wci	3ms	חטא	306	3ms	purify
9:16	יקרב	hiph	wci	3ms	קרב	897		bring near
	יעשׂה	qal	wci	3ms	עשׂה	793	3fs	do,make
9:17	יקרב	hiph	wci	3ms	קרב	897		bring near
	ימלא	piel	wci	3ms	מלא	569		fill

ChVs	Form	Stem	Tnse	PGN	Root	BDB	Sfx	Meaning
9:17	יקטר	hiph	wci	3ms	קטר	882		make sacrifices
9:18	ישׁחט	qal	wci	3ms	שׁחט	1006		slaughter
	ימצאו	hiph	wci	3mp	מצא	592		cause to find
	יזרקהו	qal	wci	3ms	זרק	284	3ms	toss,scatter
9:20	ישׂימו	qal	wci	3mp	שׂים	962		put,set
	יקטר	hiph	wci	3ms	קטר	882		make sacrifices
9:21	הניף	hiph	pft	3ms	נוף	631		swing,wave
	צוה	piel	pft	3ms	צוה	845		command
9:22	ישׂא	qal	wci	3ms	נשׂא	669		lift,carry
	יברכם	piel	wci	3ms	ברך	138	3mp	bless
	ירד	qal	wci	3ms	ירד	432		come down
	עשׂת	qal	infc		עשׂה	793		do,make
9:23	יבא	qal	wci	3ms	בוא	97		come in
	יצאו	qal	wci	3mp	יצא	422		go out
	יברכו	piel	wci	3mp	ברך	138		bless
	ירא	niph	wci	3ms	ראה	906		appear,be seen
9:24	תצא	qal	wci	3fs	יצא	422		go out
	תאכל	qal	wci	3fs	אכל	37		eat,devour
	ירא	qal	wci	3ms	ראה	906		see
	ירנו	qal	wci	3mp	רנן	943		cry aloud
	יפלו	qal	wci	3mp	נפל	656		fall
10:1	יקחו	qal	wci	3mp	לקח	542		take
	יתנו	qal	wci	3mp	נתן	678		give,set
	ישׂימו	qal	wci	3mp	שׂים	962		put,set
	יקרבו	hiph	wci	3mp	קרב	897		bring near
	צוה	piel	pft	3ms	צוה	845		command
10:2	תצא	qal	wci	3fs	יצא	422		go out
	תאכל	qal	wci	3fs	אכל	37		eat,devour
	ימתו	qal	wci	3mp	מות	559		die
10:3	יאמר	qal	wci	3ms	אמר	55		say
	דבר	piel	pft	3ms	דבר	180		speak
	אמר	qal	infc		אמר	55		say
	אקדשׁ	niph	impf	1cs	קדשׁ	872		be sacred
	אכבד	niph	impf	1cs	כבד	457		be honored
	ידם	qal	wci	3ms	דמם	198		be silent
10:4	יקרא	qal	wci	3ms	קרא	894		call,proclaim
	יאמר	qal	wci	3ms	אמר	55		say
	קרבו	qal	impv	mp	קרב	897		approach
	שׂאו	qal	impv	mp	נשׂא	669		lift,carry
10:5	יקרבו	qal	wci	3mp	קרב	897		approach
	ישׂאם	qal	wci	3mp	נשׂא	669	3mp	lift,carry
	דבר	piel	pft	3ms	דבר	180		speak
10:6	יאמר	qal	wci	3ms	אמר	55		say
	תפרעו	qal	jusm	2mp	פרע	828		let go
	תפרמו	qal	impf	2mp	פרם	827		tear,rend
	תמתו	qal	impf	2mp	מות	559		die
	יקצף	qal	impf	3ms	קצף	893		be angry
	יבכו	qal	impf	3mp	בכה	113		weep
	שׂרף	qal	pft	3ms	שׂרף	976		burn
10:7	תצאו	qal	impf	2mp	יצא	422		go out
	תמתו	qal	impf	2mp	מות	559		die
	יעשׂו	qal	wci	3mp	עשׂה	793		do,make
10:8	ידבר	piel	wci	3ms	דבר	180		speak
	אמר	qal	infc		אמר	55		say

ChVs	Form	Stem	Tnse	PGN	Root	BDB	Sfx	Meaning
10:9	תשת	qal	jus	2ms	שתה	1059		drink
	באכם	qal	infc		בוא	97	2mp	come in
	תמתו	qal	impf	2mp	מות	559		die
10:10	הבדיל	hiph	infc		בדל	95		divide
10:11	הורת	hiph	infc		ירה	434		shoot,teach
	דבר	piel	pft	3ms	דבר	180		speak
10:12	ידבר	piel	wci	3ms	דבר	180		speak
	נותרים	niph	ptc	mp	יתר	451		be left,remain
	קחו	qal	impv	mp	לקח	542		take
	נותרת	niph	ptc	fs	יתר	451		be left,remain
	אכלוה	qal	impv	mp	אכל	37	3fs	eat,devour
10:13	אכלתם	qal	wcp	2mp	אכל	37		eat,devour
	צויתי	pual	pft	1cs	צוה	845		be commanded
10:14	תאכלו	qal	impf	2mp	אכל	37		eat,devour
	נתנו	niph	pft	3cp	נתן	678		be given
10:15	יביאו	hiph	impf	3mp	בוא	97		bring in
	הניף	hiph	infc		נוף	631		swing,wave
	היה	qal	wcp	3ms	היה	224		be,become
	צוה	piel	pft	3ms	צוה	845		command
10:16	דרש	qal	infa		דרש	205		resort to,seek
	דרש	qal	pft	3ms	דרש	205		resort to,seek
	שׂרף	pual	pft	3ms	שׂרף	976		be burnt up
	יקצף	qal	wci	3ms	קצף	893		be angry
	נותרם	niph	ptc	mp	יתר	451		be left,remain
	אמר	qal	infc		אמר	55		say
10:17	אכלתם	qal	pft	2mp	אכל	37		eat,devour
	נתן	qal	pft	3ms	נתן	678		give,set
	שׂאת	qal	infc		נשׂא	669		lift,carry
	כפר	piel	infc		כפר	497		cover,atone
10:18	הובא	hoph	pft	3ms	בוא	97		be brought
	אכול	qal	infa		אכל	37		eat,devour
	תאכלו	qal	impf	2mp	אכל	37		eat,devour
	צויתי	piel	pft	1cs	צוה	845		command
10:19	ידבר	piel	wci	3ms	דבר	180		speak
	הקריבו	hiph	pft	3cp	קרב	897		bring near
	תקראנה	qal	wci	3fp	קרא	896		meet,encounter
	אכלתי	qal	wcp	1cs	אכל	37		eat,devour
	ייטב	qal	impf	3ms	יטב	405		be good
10:20	ישמע	qal	wci	3ms	שמע	1033		hear
	ייטב	qal	wci	3ms	יטב	405		be good
11:1	ידבר	piel	wci	3ms	דבר	180		speak
	אמר	qal	infc		אמר	55		say
11:2	דברו	piel	impv	mp	דבר	180		speak
	אמר	qal	infc		אמר	55		say
	תאכלו	qal	impf	2mp	אכל	37		eat,devour
11:3	מפרסת	hiph	ptc	fs	פרס	828		divide
	שסעת	qal	ptc	fs	שסע	1042		cleave,divide
	מעלת	hiph	ptc	fs	עלה	748		bring up,offer
	תאכלו	qal	impf	2mp	אכל	37		eat,devour
11:4	תאכלו	qal	impf	2mp	אכל	37		eat,devour
	מעלי	hiph	ptc	mp	עלה	748		bring up,offer
	מפריסי	hiph	ptc	mp	פרס	828		divide
	מעלה	hiph	ptc	ms	עלה	748		bring up,offer
	מפריס	hiph	ptc	ms	פרס	828		divide
11:5	מעלה	hiph	ptc	ms	עלה	748		bring up,offer
	יפריס	hiph	impf	3ms	פרס	828		divide
11:6	מעלת	hiph	ptc	fs	עלה	748		bring up,offer
	הפריסה	hiph	pft	3fs	פרס	828		divide
11:7	מפריס	hiph	ptc	ms	פרס	828		divide
	שסע	qal	ptc	ms	שסע	1042		cleave,divide
	יגר	niph	impf	3ms	גרר	176		chew
11:8	תאכלו	qal	impf	2mp	אכל	37		eat,devour
	תגעו	qal	impf	2mp	נגע	619		touch,strike
11:9	תאכלו	qal	impf	2mp	אכל	37		eat,devour
	תאכלו	qal	impf	2mp	אכל	37		eat,devour
11:11	יהיו	qal	impf	3mp	היה	224		be,become
	תאכלו	qal	impf	2mp	אכל	37		eat,devour
	תשקצו	piel	impf	2mp	שקץ	1055		detest
11:13	תשקצו	piel	impf	2mp	שקץ	1055		detest
	יאכלו	niph	impf	3mp	אכל	37		be eaten
11:20	הלך	qal	ptc	ms	הלך	229		walk,go
11:21	תאכלו	qal	impf	2mp	אכל	37		eat,devour
	הלך	qal	ptc	ms	הלך	229		walk,go
	נתר	piel	infc		נתר	684		leap,spring
11:22	תאכלו	qal	impf	2mp	אכל	37		eat,devour
11:24	תטמאו	hith	impf	2mp	טמא	379		defile oneself
	נגע	qal	ptc	ms	נגע	619		touch,strike
	יטמא	qal	impf	3ms	טמא	379		become unclean
11:25	נשׂא	qal	ptc	ms	נשׂא	669		lift,carry
	יכבס	piel	impf	3ms	כבס	460		wash
	טמא	qal	wcp	3ms	טמא	379		become unclean
11:26	מפרסת	hiph	ptc	fs	פרס	828		divide
	שסעת	qal	ptc	fs	שסע	1042		cleave,divide
	מעלה	hiph	ptc	fs	עלה	748		bring up,offer
	נגע	qal	ptc	ms	נגע	619		touch,strike
	יטמא	qal	impf	3ms	טמא	379		become unclean
11:27	הולך	qal	ptc	ms	הלך	229		walk,go
	הלכת	qal	ptc	fs	הלך	229		walk,go
	נגע	qal	ptc	ms	נגע	619		touch,strike
	יטמא	qal	impf	3ms	טמא	379		become unclean
11:28	נשׂא	qal	ptc	ms	נשׂא	669		lift,carry
	יכבס	piel	impf	3ms	כבס	460		wash
	טמא	qal	wcp	3ms	טמא	379		become unclean
11:29	שׁרץ	qal	ptc	ms	שׁרץ	1056		swarm,teem
11:31	נגע	qal	ptc	ms	נגע	619		touch,strike
	יטמא	qal	impf	3ms	טמא	379		become unclean
11:32	יפל	qal	impf	3ms	נפל	656		fall
	יטמא	qal	impf	3ms	טמא	379		become unclean
	יעשׂה	niph	impf	3ms	עשׂה	793		be done
	יובא	hoph	impf	3ms	בוא	97		be brought
	טמא	qal	wcp	3ms	טמא	379		become unclean
	טהר	qal	wcp	3ms	טהר	372		be clean,pure
11:33	יפל	qal	impf	3ms	נפל	656		fall
	יטמא	qal	impf	3ms	טמא	379		become unclean
	תשברו	qal	impf	2mp	שׁבר	990		break
11:34	יאכל	niph	impf	3ms	אכל	37		be eaten
	יבוא	qal	impf	3ms	בוא	97		come in
	יטמא	qal	impf	3ms	טמא	379		become unclean

ChVs	Form	Stem	Tnse	PGN	Root	BDB	Sfx	Meaning
11:34	ישתה	niph	impf	3ms	שתה	1059		be drunk
	יטמא	qal	impf	3ms	טמא	379		become unclean
11:35	יפל	qal	impf	3ms	נפל	656		fall
	יטמא	qal	impf	3ms	טמא	379		become unclean
	יתץ	qalp	impf	3ms	נתץ	683		be broken down
	יהיו	qal	impf	3mp	היה	224		be, become
11:36	יהיה	qal	impf	3ms	היה	224		be, become
	נגע	qal	ptc	ms	נגע	619		touch, strike
	יטמא	qal	impf	3ms	טמא	379		become unclean
11:37	יפל	qal	impf	3ms	נפל	656		fall
	יזרע	niph	impf	3ms	זרע	281		be sown
11:38	יתן	qalp	impf	3ms	נתן	678		be given
	נפל	qal	wcp	3ms	נפל	656		fall
11:39	ימות	qal	impf	3ms	מות	559		die
	נגע	qal	ptc	ms	נגע	619		touch, strike
	יטמא	qal	impf	3ms	טמא	379		become unclean
11:40	אכל	qal	ptc	ms	אכל	37		eat, devour
	יכבס	piel	impf	3ms	כבס	460		wash
	טמא	qal	wcp	3ms	טמא	379		become unclean
	נשׂא	qal	ptc	ms	נשׂא	669		lift, carry
	יכבס	piel	impf	3ms	כבס	460		wash
	טמא	qal	wcp	3ms	טמא	379		become unclean
11:41	שׁרץ	qal	ptc	ms	שׁרץ	1056		swarm, teem
	יאכל	niph	impf	3ms	אכל	37		be eaten
11:42	הולך	qal	ptc	ms	הלך	229		walk, go
	הולך	qal	ptc	ms	הלך	229		walk, go
	מרבה	hiph	ptc	ms	רבה	915		make many
	שׁרץ	qal	ptc	ms	שׁרץ	1056		swarm, teem
	תאכלום	qal	impf	2mp	אכל	37	3mp	eat, devour
11:43	תשׁקצו	piel	jusm	2mp	שׁקץ	1055		detest
	שׁרץ	qal	ptc	ms	שׁרץ	1056		swarm, teem
	תטמאו	hith	impf	2mp	טמא	379		defile oneself
	נטמתם	niph	wcp	2mp	טמא	379		defile oneself
11:44	התקדשׁתם	hith	wcp	2mp	קדשׁ	872		consecrate self
	הייתם	qal	wcp	2mp	היה	224		be, become
	תטמאו	piel	impf	2mp	טמא	379		defile
	רמשׂ	qal	ptc	ms	רמשׂ	942		creep
11:45	מעלה	hiph	ptc	ms	עלה	748		bring up, offer
	הית	qal	infc		היה	224		be, become
	הייתם	qal	wcp	2mp	היה	224		be, become
11:46	רמשׂת	qal	ptc	fs	רמשׂ	942		creep
	שׁרצת	qal	ptc	fs	שׁרץ	1056		swarm, teem
11:47	הבדיל	hiph	infc		בדל	95		divide
	נאכלת	niph	ptc	fs	אכל	37		be eaten
	תאכל	niph	impf	3fs	אכל	37		be eaten
12:1	ידבר	piel	wci	3ms	דבר	180		speak
	אמר	qal	infc		אמר	55		say
12:2	דבר	piel	impv	ms	דבר	180		speak
	אמר	qal	infc		אמר	55		say
	תזריע	hiph	impf	3fs	זרע	281		produce seed
	ילדה	qal	wcp	3fs	ילד	408		bear, beget
	טמאה	qal	wcp	3fs	טמא	379		become unclean
	דותה	qal	infc		דוה	188	3fs	be ill
	תטמא	qal	impf	3fs	טמא	379		become unclean
12:3	ימול	niph	impf	3ms	מול	557		be circumcised
12:4	תשׁב	qal	impf	3fs	ישׁב	442		sit, dwell
	תגע	qal	impf	3fs	נגע	619		touch, strike
	תבא	qal	impf	3fs	בוא	97		come in
	מלאת	qal	infc		מלא	569		be full, fill
12:5	תלד	qal	impf	3fs	ילד	408		bear, beget
	טמאה	qal	wcp	3fs	טמא	379		become unclean
	תשׁב	qal	impf	3fs	ישׁב	442		sit, dwell
12:6	מלאת	qal	infc		מלא	569		be full, fill
	תביא	hiph	impf	3fs	בוא	97		bring in
12:7	הקריבו	hiph	wcp	3ms	קרב	897	3ms	bring near
	כפר	piel	wcp	3ms	כפר	497		cover, atone
	טהרה	qal	wcp	3fs	טהר	372		be clean, pure
	ילדת	qal	ptc	fs	ילד	408		bear, beget
12:8	תמצא	qal	impf	3fs	מצא	592		find
	לקחה	qal	wcp	3fs	לקח	542		take
	כפר	piel	wcp	3ms	כפר	497		cover, atone
	טהרה	qal	wcp	3fs	טהר	372		be clean, pure
13:1	ידבר	piel	wci	3ms	דבר	180		speak
	אמר	qal	infc		אמר	55		say
13:2	יהיה	qal	impf	3ms	היה	224		be, become
	היה	qal	wcp	3ms	היה	224		be, become
	הובא	hoph	wcp	3ms	בוא	97		be brought
13:3	ראה	qal	wcp	3ms	ראה	906		see
	הפך	qal	pft	3ms	הפך	245		turn, overturn
	ראהו	qal	wcp	3ms	ראה	906	3ms	see
	טמא	piel	wcp	3ms	טמא	379		defile
13:4	הפך	qal	pft	3ms	הפך	245		turn, overturn
	הסגיר	hiph	wcp	3ms	סגר	688		shut up, deliver
13:5	ראהו	qal	wcp	3ms	ראה	906	3ms	see
	עמד	qal	pft	3ms	עמד	763		stand, stop
	פשׂה	qal	pft	3ms	פשׂה	832		spread
	הסגירו	hiph	wcp	3ms	סגר	688	3ms	shut up, deliver
13:6	ראה	qal	wcp	3ms	ראה	906		see
	פשׂה	qal	pft	3ms	פשׂה	832		spread
	טהרו	piel	wcp	3ms	טהר	372	3ms	cleanse
	כבס	piel	wcp	3ms	כבס	460		wash
	טהר	qal	wcp	3ms	טהר	372		be clean, pure
13:7	פשׂה	qal	infa		פשׂה	832		spread
	תפשׂה	qal	impf	3fs	פשׂה	832		spread
	הראתו	niph	infc		ראה	906	3ms	appear, be seen
	נראה	niph	wcp	3ms	ראה	906		appear, be seen
13:8	ראה	qal	wcp	3ms	ראה	906		see
	פשׂתה	qal	pft	3fs	פשׂה	832		spread
	טמאו	piel	wcp	3ms	טמא	379	3ms	defile
13:9	תהיה	qal	impf	3fs	היה	224		be, become
	הובא	hoph	wcp	3ms	בוא	97		be brought
13:10	ראה	qal	wcp	3ms	ראה	906		see
	הפכה	qal	pft	3fs	הפך	245		turn, overturn
13:11	נושׁנת	niph	ptc	fs	ישׁן	445		be old
	טמאו	piel	wcp	3ms	טמא	379	3ms	defile
	יסגרנו	hiph	impf	3ms	סגר	688	3ms	shut up, deliver
13:12	פרוח	qal	infa		פרח	827		break out
	תפרח	qal	impf	3fs	פרח	827		break out

ChVs	Form	Stem	Tnse	PGN	Root	BDB	Sfx	Meaning
13:12	כסתה	piel	wcp	3fs	כסה	491		cover
13:13	ראה	qal	wcp	3ms	ראה	906		see
	כסתה	piel	pft	3fs	כסה	491		cover
	טהר	piel	wcp	3ms	טהר	372		cleanse
	הפך	qal	pft	3ms	הפך	245		turn,overturn
13:14	הראות	niph	infc		ראה	906		appear,be seen
	יטמא	qal	impf	3ms	טמא	379		become unclean
13:15	ראה	qal	wcp	3ms	ראה	906		see
	טמאו	piel	wcp	3ms	טמא	379	3ms	defile
13:16	ישוב	qal	impf	3ms	שוב	996		turn,return
	נהפך	niph	wcp	3ms	הפך	245		turn oneself
	בא	qal	wcp	3ms	בוא	97		come in
13:17	ראהו	qal	wcp	3ms	ראה	906	3ms	see
	נהפך	niph	pft	3ms	הפך	245		turn oneself
	טהר	piel	wcp	3ms	טהר	372		cleanse
13:18	יהיה	qal	impf	3ms	היה	224		be,become
	נרפא	niph	wcp	3ms	רפא	950		be healed
13:19	היה	qal	wcp	3ms	היה	224		be,become
	נראה	niph	wcp	3ms	ראה	906		appear,be seen
13:20	ראה	qal	wcp	3ms	ראה	906		see
	הפך	qal	pft	3ms	הפך	245		turn,overturn
	טמאו	piel	wcp	3ms	טמא	379	3ms	defile
	פרחה	qal	pft	3fs	פרח	827		break out
13:21	יראנה	qal	impf	3ms	ראה	906	3fs	see
	הסגירו	hiph	wcp	3ms	סגר	688	3ms	shut up,deliver
13:22	פשׂה	qal	infa		פשׂה	832		spread
	תפשׂה	qal	impf	3fs	פשׂה	832		spread
	טמא	piel	wcp	3ms	טמא	379		defile
13:23	תעמד	qal	impf	3fs	עמד	763		stand,stop
	פשׂתה	qal	pft	3fs	פשׂה	832		spread
	טהרו	piel	wcp	3ms	טהר	372	3ms	cleanse
13:24	יהיה	qal	impf	3ms	היה	224		be,become
	היתה	qal	wcp	3fs	היה	224		be,become
13:25	ראה	qal	wcp	3ms	ראה	906		see
	נהפך	niph	pft	3ms	הפך	245		turn oneself
	פרחה	qal	pft	3fs	פרח	827		break out
	טמא	piel	wcp	3ms	טמא	379		defile
13:26	יראנה	qal	impf	3ms	ראה	906	3fs	see
	הסגירו	hiph	wcp	3ms	סגר	688	3ms	shut up,deliver
13:27	ראהו	qal	wcp	3ms	ראה	906	3ms	see
	פשׂה	qal	infa		פשׂה	832		spread
	תפשׂה	qal	impf	3fs	פשׂה	832		spread
	טמא	piel	wcp	3ms	טמא	379		defile
13:28	תעמד	qal	impf	3fs	עמד	763		stand,stop
	פשׂתה	qal	pft	3fs	פשׂה	832		spread
	טהרו	piel	wcp	3ms	טהר	372	3ms	cleanse
13:29	יהיה	qal	impf	3ms	היה	224		be,become
13:30	ראה	qal	wcp	3ms	ראה	906		see
	טמא	piel	wcp	3ms	טמא	379		defile
13:31	יראה	qal	impf	3ms	ראה	906		see
	הסגיר	hiph	wcp	3ms	סגר	688		shut up,deliver
13:32	ראה	qal	wcp	3ms	ראה	906		see
	פשׂה	qal	pft	3ms	פשׂה	832		spread
	היה	qal	pft	3ms	היה	224		be,become
13:33	התגלח	hith	wcp	3ms	גלח	164		shave oneself
	יגלח	piel	impf	3ms	גלח	164		shave
	הסגיר	hiph	wcp	3ms	סגר	688		shut up,deliver
13:34	ראה	qal	wcp	3ms	ראה	906		see
	פשׂה	qal	pft	3ms	פשׂה	832		spread
	טהר	piel	wcp	3ms	טהר	372		cleanse
	כבס	piel	wcp	3ms	כבס	460		wash
	טהר	qal	wcp	3ms	טהר	372		be clean,pure
13:35	פשׂה	qal	infa		פשׂה	832		spread
	יפשׂה	qal	impf	3ms	פשׂה	832		spread
13:36	ראהו	qal	wcp	3ms	ראה	906	3ms	see
	פשׂה	qal	pft	3ms	פשׂה	832		spread
	יבקר	piel	impf	3ms	בקר	133		seek,inquire
13:37	עמד	qal	pft	3ms	עמד	763		stand,stop
	צמח	qal	pft	3ms	צמח	855		sprout up
	נרפא	niph	pft	3ms	רפא	950		be healed
	טהרו	piel	wcp	3ms	טהר	372	3ms	cleanse
13:38	יהיה	qal	impf	3ms	היה	224		be,become
13:39	ראה	qal	wcp	3ms	ראה	906		see
	פרח	qal	pft	3ms	פרח	827		break out
13:40	ימרט	niph	impf	3ms	מרט	598		be made bald
13:41	ימרט	niph	impf	3ms	מרט	598		be made bald
13:42	יהיה	qal	impf	3ms	היה	224		be,become
	פרחת	qal	ptc	fs	פרח	827		break out
13:43	ראה	qal	wcp	3ms	ראה	906		see
13:44	צרוע	qal	pptc	ms	צרע	863		be leprous
	טמא	piel	infa		טמא	379		defile
	יטמאנו	piel	impf	3ms	טמא	379	3ms	defile
13:45	צרוע	qal	pptc	ms	צרע	863		be leprous
	יהיו	qal	impf	3mp	היה	224		be,become
	פרמים	qal	pptc	mp	פרם	827		tear,rend
	יהיה	qal	impf	3ms	היה	224		be,become
	פרוע	qal	pptc	ms	פרע	828		let go
	יעטה	qal	impf	3ms	עטה	741		wrap oneself
	יקרא	qal	impf	3ms	קרא	894		call,proclaim
13:46	יטמא	qal	impf	3ms	טמא	379		become unclean
	ישב	qal	impf	3ms	ישב	442		sit,dwell
13:47	יהיה	qal	impf	3ms	היה	224		be,become
13:49	היה	qal	wcp	3ms	היה	224		be,become
	הראה	hoph	wcp	3ms	ראה	906		be shown
13:50	ראה	qal	wcp	3ms	ראה	906		see
	הסגיר	hiph	wcp	3ms	סגר	688		shut up,deliver
13:51	ראה	qal	wcp	3ms	ראה	906		see
	פשׂה	qal	pft	3ms	פשׂה	832		spread
	יעשׂה	niph	impf	3ms	עשׂה	793		be done
	ממארת	hiph	ptc	fs	מאר	549		prick,pain
13:52	שׂרף	qal	wcp	3ms	שׂרף	976		burn
	יהיה	qal	impf	3ms	היה	224		be,become
	ממארת	hiph	ptc	fs	מאר	549		prick,pain
	תשׂרף	niph	impf	3fs	שׂרף	976		be burned
13:53	יראה	qal	impf	3ms	ראה	906		see
	פשׂה	qal	pft	3ms	פשׂה	832		spread
13:54	צוה	piel	wcp	3ms	צוה	845		command
	כבסו	piel	wcp	3cp	כבס	460		wash

ChVs	Form	Stem	Tnse	PGN	Root	BDB	Sfx	Meaning
13:54	הסגירו	hiph	wcp	3ms	סגר	688	3ms	shut up,deliver
13:55	ראה	qal	wcp	3ms	ראה	906		see
	הכבס	hoth	infc		כבס	460		be washed out
	הפך	qal	pft	3ms	הפך	245		turn,overturn
	פשׂה	qal	pft	3ms	פשׂה	832		spread
	תשׂרפנו	qal	impf	2ms	שׂרף	976	3ms	burn
13:56	ראה	qal	pft	3ms	ראה	906		see
	הכבס	hoth	infc		כבס	460		be washed out
	קרע	qal	wcp	3ms	קרע	902		tear,rend
13:57	תראה	niph	impf	3fs	ראה	906		appear,be seen
	פרחת	qal	ptc	fs	פרח	827		break out
	תשׂרפנו	qal	impf	2ms	שׂרף	976	3ms	burn
13:58	תכבס	piel	impf	2ms	כבס	460		wash
	סר	qal	wcp	3ms	סור	693		turn aside
	כבס	pual	wcp	3ms	כבס	460		be washed
	טהר	qal	wcp	3ms	טהר	372		be clean,pure
13:59	טהרו	piel	infc		טהר	372	3ms	cleanse
	טמאו	piel	infc		טמא	379	3ms	defile
14:1	ידבר	piel	wci	3ms	דבר	180		speak
	אמר	qal	infc		אמר	55		say
14:2	תהיה	qal	impf	3fs	היה	224		be,become
	מצרע	pual	ptc	ms	צרע	863		be leprous
	הובא	hoph	wcp	3ms	בוא	97		be brought
14:3	יצא	qal	wcp	3ms	יצא	422		go out
	ראה	qal	wcp	3ms	ראה	906		see
	נרפא	niph	pft	3ms	רפא	950		be healed
	צרוע	qal	pptc	ms	צרע	863		be leprous
14:4	צוה	piel	wcp	3ms	צוה	845		command
	לקח	qal	wcp	3ms	לקח	542		take
	מטהר	hith	ptc	ms	טהר	372		purify oneself
14:5	צוה	piel	wcp	3ms	צוה	845		command
	שׁחט	qal	wcp	3ms	שׁחט	1006		slaughter
14:6	יקח	qal	impf	3ms	לקח	542		take
	טבל	qal	wcp	3ms	טבל	371		dip
	שׁחטה	qal	pptc	fs	שׁחט	1006		slaughter
14:7	הזה	hiph	wcp	3ms	נזה	633		cause to spurt
	מטהר	hith	ptc	ms	טהר	372		purify oneself
	טהרו	piel	wcp	3ms	טהר	372	3ms	cleanse
	שׁלח	piel	wcp	3ms	שׁלח	1018		send away,shoot
14:8	כבס	piel	wcp	3ms	כבס	460		wash
	מטהר	hith	ptc	ms	טהר	372		purify oneself
	גלח	piel	wcp	3ms	גלח	164		shave
	רחץ	qal	wcp	3ms	רחץ	934		wash,bathe
	טהר	qal	wcp	3ms	טהר	372		be clean,pure
	יבוא	qal	impf	3ms	בוא	97		come in
	ישׁב	qal	wcp	3ms	ישׁב	442		sit,dwell
14:9	היה	qal	wcp	3ms	היה	224		be,become
	יגלח	piel	impf	3ms	גלח	164		shave
	יגלח	piel	impf	3ms	גלח	164		shave
	כבס	piel	wcp	3ms	כבס	460		wash
	רחץ	qal	wcp	3ms	רחץ	934		wash,bathe
	טהר	qal	wcp	3ms	טהר	372		be clean,pure
14:10	יקח	qal	impf	3ms	לקח	542		take
	בלולה	qal	pptc	fs	בלל	117		mingle,mix
14:11	העמיד	hiph	wcp	3ms	עמד	763		set up,raise
	מטהר	piel	ptc	ms	טהר	372		cleanse
	מטהר	hith	ptc	ms	טהר	372		purify oneself
14:12	לקח	qal	wcp	3ms	לקח	542		take
	הקריב	hiph	wcp	3ms	קרב	897		bring near
	הניף	hiph	wcp	3ms	נוף	631		swing,wave
14:13	שׁחט	qal	wcp	3ms	שׁחט	1006		slaughter
	ישׁחט	qal	impf	3ms	שׁחט	1006		slaughter
14:14	לקח	qal	wcp	3ms	לקח	542		take
	נתן	qal	wcp	3ms	נתן	678		give,set
	מטהר	hith	ptc	ms	טהר	372		purify oneself
14:15	לקח	qal	wcp	3ms	לקח	542		take
	יצק	qal	wcp	3ms	יצק	427		pour out,cast
14:16	טבל	qal	wcp	3ms	טבל	371		dip
	הזה	hiph	wcp	3ms	נזה	633		cause to spurt
14:17	יתן	qal	impf	3ms	נתן	678		give,set
	מטהר	hith	ptc	ms	טהר	372		purify oneself
14:18	נותר	niph	ptc	ms	יתר	451		be left,remain
	יתן	qal	impf	3ms	נתן	678		give,set
	מטהר	hith	ptc	ms	טהר	372		purify oneself
	כפר	piel	wcp	3ms	כפר	497		cover,atone
14:19	עשׂה	qal	wcp	3ms	עשׂה	793		do,make
	כפר	piel	wcp	3ms	כפר	497		cover,atone
	מטהר	hith	ptc	ms	טהר	372		purify oneself
	ישׁחט	qal	impf	3ms	שׁחט	1006		slaughter
14:20	העלה	hiph	wcp	3ms	עלה	748		bring up,offer
	כפר	piel	wcp	3ms	כפר	497		cover,atone
	טהר	qal	wcp	3ms	טהר	372		be clean,pure
14:21	משׂגת	hiph	ptc	fs	נשׂג	673		reach,overtake
	לקח	qal	wcp	3ms	לקח	542		take
	כפר	piel	infc		כפר	497		cover,atone
	בלול	qal	pptc	ms	בלל	117		mingle,mix
14:22	תשׂיג	hiph	impf	3fs	נשׂג	673		reach,overtake
	היה	qal	wcp	3ms	היה	224		be,become
14:23	הביא	hiph	wcp	3ms	בוא	97		bring in
14:24	לקח	qal	wcp	3ms	לקח	542		take
	הניף	hiph	wcp	3ms	נוף	631		swing,wave
14:25	שׁחט	qal	wcp	3ms	שׁחט	1006		slaughter
	לקח	qal	wcp	3ms	לקח	542		take
	נתן	qal	wcp	3ms	נתן	678		give,set
	מטהר	hith	ptc	ms	טהר	372		purify oneself
14:26	יצק	qal	impf	3ms	יצק	427		pour out,cast
14:27	הזה	hiph	wcp	3ms	נזה	633		cause to spurt
14:28	נתן	qal	wcp	3ms	נתן	678		give,set
	מטהר	hith	ptc	ms	טהר	372		purify oneself
14:29	נותר	niph	ptc	ms	יתר	451		be left,remain
	יתן	qal	impf	3ms	נתן	678		give,set
	מטהר	hith	ptc	ms	טהר	372		purify oneself
	כפר	piel	infc		כפר	497		cover,atone
14:30	עשׂה	qal	wcp	3ms	עשׂה	793		do,make
	תשׂיג	hiph	impf	3fs	נשׂג	673		reach,overtake
14:31	תשׂיג	hiph	impf	3fs	נשׂג	673		reach,overtake
	כפר	piel	wcp	3ms	כפר	497		cover,atone
	מטהר	hith	ptc	ms	טהר	372		purify oneself

ChVs	Form	Stem	Tnse	PGN	Root	BDB	Sfx	Meaning
14: 32	תשׂיג	hiph	impf	3fs	נשׂג	673		reach,overtake
14: 33	ידבר	piel	wci	3ms	דבר	180		speak
	אמר	qal	infc		אמר	55		say
14: 34	תבאו	qal	impf	2mp	בוא	97		come in
	נתן	qal	ptc	ms	נתן	678		give,set
	נתתי	qal	wcp	1cs	נתן	678		give,set
14: 35	בא	qal	wcp	3ms	בוא	97		come in
	הגיד	hiph	wcp	3ms	נגד	616		declare,tell
	אמר	qal	infc		אמר	55		say
	נראה	niph	pft	3ms	ראה	906		appear,be seen
14: 36	צוה	piel	wcp	3ms	צוה	845		command
	פנו	piel	wcp	3cp	פנה	815		make clear
	יבא	qal	impf	3ms	בוא	97		come in
	ראות	qal	infc		ראה	906		see
	יטמא	qal	impf	3ms	טמא	379		become unclean
	יבא	qal	impf	3ms	בוא	97		come in
	ראות	qal	infc		ראה	906		see
14: 37	ראה	qal	wcp	3ms	ראה	906		see
14: 38	יצא	qal	wcp	3ms	יצא	422		go out
	הסגיר	hiph	wcp	3ms	סגר	688		shut up,deliver
14: 39	שׁב	qal	wcp	3ms	שׁוב	996		turn,return
	ראה	qal	wcp	3ms	ראה	906		see
	פשׂה	qal	pft	3ms	פשׂה	832		spread
14: 40	צוה	piel	wcp	3ms	צוה	845		command
	חלצו	piel	wcp	3cp	חלץ	322		deliver
	השׁליכו	hiph	wcp	3cp	שׁלך	1020		throw,cast
14: 41	יקצע	hiph	impf	3ms	קצע	892		scrape off
	שׁפכו	qal	wcp	3cp	שׁפך	1049		pour out
	הקצו	hiph	pft	3cp	קצה	891		scrape off
14: 42	לקחו	qal	wcp	3cp	לקח	542		take
	הביאו	hiph	wcp	3cp	בוא	97		bring in
	יקח	qal	impf	3ms	לקח	542		take
	טח	qal	wcp	3ms	טוח	376		overlay
14: 43	ישׁוב	qal	impf	3ms	שׁוב	996		turn,return
	פרח	qal	wcp	3ms	פרח	827		break out
	חלץ	piel	pft	3ms	חלץ	322		deliver
	הקצות	hiph	infc		קצה	891		scrape off
	הטוח	niph	infc		טוח	376		be coated
14: 44	בא	qal	wcp	3ms	בוא	97		come in
	ראה	qal	wcp	3ms	ראה	906		see
	פשׂה	qal	pft	3ms	פשׂה	832		spread
	ממארת	hiph	ptc	fs	מאר	549		prick,pain
14: 45	נתץ	qal	wcp	3ms	נתץ	683		pull down
	הוציא	hiph	wcp	3ms	יצא	422		bring out
14: 46	בא	qal	ptc	ms	בוא	97		come in
	הסגיר	hiph	pft	3ms	סגר	688		shut up,deliver
	יטמא	qal	impf	3ms	טמא	379		become unclean
14: 47	שׁכב	qal	ptc	ms	שׁכב	1011		lie,lie down
	יכבס	piel	impf	3ms	כבס	460		wash
	אכל	qal	ptc	ms	אכל	37		eat,devour
	יכבס	piel	impf	3ms	כבס	460		wash
14: 48	בא	qal	infa		בוא	97		come in
	יבא	qal	impf	3ms	בוא	97		come in
	ראה	qal	wcp	3ms	ראה	906		see
14: 48	פשׂה	qal	pft	3ms	פשׂה	832		spread
	הטח	niph	infc		טוח	376		be coated
	טהר	piel	wcp	3ms	טהר	372		cleanse
	נרפא	niph	pft	3ms	רפא	950		be healed
14: 49	לקח	qal	wcp	3ms	לקח	542		take
	חטא	piel	infc		חטא	306		purify
14: 50	שׁחט	qal	wcp	3ms	שׁחט	1006		slaughter
14: 51	לקח	qal	wcp	3ms	לקח	542		take
	טבל	qal	wcp	3ms	טבל	371		dip
	שׁחוטה	qal	pptc	fs	שׁחט	1006		slaughter
	הזה	hiph	wcp	3ms	נזה	633		cause to spurt
14: 52	חטא	piel	wcp	3ms	חטא	306		purify
14: 53	שׁלח	piel	wcp	3ms	שׁלח	1018		send away,shoot
	כפר	piel	wcp	3ms	כפר	497		cover,atone
	טהר	qal	wcp	3ms	טהר	372		be clean,pure
14: 57	הורת	hiph	infc		ירה	434		shoot,teach
15: 1	ידבר	piel	wci	3ms	דבר	180		speak
	אמר	qal	infc		אמר	55		say
15: 2	דברו	piel	impv	mp	דבר	180		speak
	אמרתם	qal	wcp	2mp	אמר	55		say
	יהיה	qal	impf	3ms	היה	224		be,become
	זב	qal	ptc	ms	זוב	264		flow,gush
15: 3	תהיה	qal	impf	3fs	היה	224		be,become
	רר	qal	pft	3ms	ריר	938		flow
	החתים	hiph	pft	3ms	חתם	367		seal
15: 4	ישׁכב	qal	impf	3ms	שׁכב	1011		lie,lie down
	זב	qal	ptc	ms	זוב	264		flow,gush
	יטמא	qal	impf	3ms	טמא	379		become unclean
	ישׁב	qal	impf	3ms	ישׁב	442		sit,dwell
	יטמא	qal	impf	3ms	טמא	379		become unclean
15: 5	יגע	qal	impf	3ms	נגע	619		touch,strike
	יכבס	piel	impf	3ms	כבס	460		wash
	רחץ	qal	wcp	3ms	רחץ	934		wash,bathe
	טמא	qal	wcp	3ms	טמא	379		become unclean
15: 6	ישׁב	qal	ptc	ms	ישׁב	442		sit,dwell
	ישׁב	qal	impf	3ms	ישׁב	442		sit,dwell
	זב	qal	ptc	ms	זוב	264		flow,gush
	יכבס	piel	impf	3ms	כבס	460		wash
	רחץ	qal	wcp	3ms	רחץ	934		wash,bathe
	טמא	qal	wcp	3ms	טמא	379		become unclean
15: 7	נגע	qal	ptc	ms	נגע	619		touch,strike
	זב	qal	ptc	ms	זוב	264		flow,gush
	יכבס	piel	impf	3ms	כבס	460		wash
	רחץ	qal	wcp	3ms	רחץ	934		wash,bathe
	טמא	qal	wcp	3ms	טמא	379		become unclean
15: 8	ירק	qal	impf	3ms	רקק	956		spit
	זב	qal	ptc	ms	זוב	264		flow,gush
	כבס	piel	wcp	3ms	כבס	460		wash
	רחץ	qal	wcp	3ms	רחץ	934		wash,bathe
	טמא	qal	wcp	3ms	טמא	379		become unclean
15: 9	ירכב	qal	impf	3ms	רכב	938		mount,ride
	זב	qal	ptc	ms	זוב	264		flow,gush
	יטמא	qal	impf	3ms	טמא	379		become unclean
15: 10	נגע	qal	ptc	ms	נגע	619		touch,strike

ChVs	Form	Stem	Tnse	PGN	Root	BDB	Sfx	Meaning
15:10	יהיה	qal	impf	3ms	היה	224		be,become
	יטמא	qal	impf	3ms	טמא	379		become unclean
	נושׂא	qal	ptc	ms	נשׂא	669		lift,carry
	יכבס	piel	impf	3ms	כבס	460		wash
	רחץ	qal	wcp	3ms	רחץ	934		wash,bathe
	טמא	qal	wcp	3ms	טמא	379		become unclean
15:11	יגע	qal	impf	3ms	נגע	619		touch,strike
	זב	qal	ptc	ms	זוב	264		flow,gush
	שׁטף	qal	pft	3ms	שׁטף	1009		overflow
	כבס	piel	wcp	3ms	כבס	460		wash
	רחץ	qal	wcp	3ms	רחץ	934		wash,bathe
	טמא	qal	wcp	3ms	טמא	379		become unclean
15:12	יגע	qal	impf	3ms	נגע	619		touch,strike
	זב	qal	ptc	ms	זוב	264		flow,gush
	ישׁבר	niph	impf	3ms	שׁבר	990		be broken
	ישׁטף	niph	impf	3ms	שׁטף	1009		be overwhelmed
15:13	יטהר	qal	impf	3ms	טהר	372		be clean,pure
	זב	qal	ptc	ms	זוב	264		flow,gush
	ספר	qal	wcp	3ms	ספר	707		count
	כבס	piel	wcp	3ms	כבס	460		wash
	רחץ	qal	wcp	3ms	רחץ	934		wash,bathe
	טהר	qal	wcp	3ms	טהר	372		be clean,pure
15:14	יקח	qal	impf	3ms	לקח	542		take
	בא	qal	wcp	3ms	בוא	97		come in
	נתנם	qal	wcp	3ms	נתן	678	3mp	give,set
15:15	עשׂה	qal	wcp	3ms	עשׂה	793		do,make
	כפר	piel	wcp	3ms	כפר	497		cover,atone
15:16	תצא	qal	impf	3fs	יצא	422		go out
	רחץ	qal	wcp	3ms	רחץ	934		wash,bathe
	טמא	qal	wcp	3ms	טמא	379		become unclean
15:17	יהיה	qal	impf	3ms	היה	224		be,become
	כבס	pual	wcp	3ms	כבס	460		be washed
	טמא	qal	wcp	3ms	טמא	379		become unclean
15:18	ישׁכב	qal	impf	3ms	שׁכב	1011		lie,lie down
	רחצו	qal	wcp	3cp	רחץ	934		wash,bathe
	טמאו	qal	wcp	3cp	טמא	379		become unclean
15:19	תהיה	qal	impf	3fs	היה	224		be,become
	זבה	qal	ptc	fs	זוב	264		flow,gush
	יהיה	qal	impf	3ms	היה	224		be,become
	תהיה	qal	impf	3fs	היה	224		be,become
	נגע	qal	ptc	ms	נגע	619		touch,strike
	יטמא	qal	impf	3ms	טמא	379		become unclean
15:20	תשׁכב	qal	impf	3fs	שׁכב	1011		lie,lie down
	יטמא	qal	impf	3ms	טמא	379		become unclean
	תשׁב	qal	impf	3fs	ישׁב	442		sit,dwell
	יטמא	qal	impf	3ms	טמא	379		become unclean
15:21	נגע	qal	ptc	ms	נגע	619		touch,strike
	יכבס	piel	impf	3ms	כבס	460		wash
	רחץ	qal	wcp	3ms	רחץ	934		wash,bathe
	טמא	qal	wcp	3ms	טמא	379		become unclean
15:22	נגע	qal	ptc	ms	נגע	619		touch,strike
	תשׁב	qal	impf	3fs	ישׁב	442		sit,dwell
	יכבס	piel	impf	3ms	כבס	460		wash
	רחץ	qal	wcp	3ms	רחץ	934		wash,bathe
15:22	טמא	qal	wcp	3ms	טמא	379		become unclean
15:23	ישׁבת	qal	ptc	fs	ישׁב	442		sit,dwell
	נגעו	qal	infc		נגע	619	3ms	touch,strike
	יטמא	qal	impf	3ms	טמא	379		become unclean
15:24	שׁכב	qal	infa		שׁכב	1011		lie,lie down
	ישׁכב	qal	impf	3ms	שׁכב	1011		lie,lie down
	תהי	qal	jus	3fs	היה	224		be,become
	טמא	qal	wcp	3ms	טמא	379		become unclean
	ישׁכב	qal	impf	3ms	שׁכב	1011		lie,lie down
	יטמא	qal	impf	3ms	טמא	379		become unclean
15:25	יזוב	qal	impf	3ms	זוב	264		flow,gush
	תזוב	qal	impf	3fs	זוב	264		flow,gush
	תהיה	qal	impf	3fs	היה	224		be,become
15:26	תשׁכב	qal	impf	3fs	שׁכב	1011		lie,lie down
	יהיה	qal	impf	3ms	היה	224		be,become
	תשׁב	qal	impf	3fs	ישׁב	442		sit,dwell
	יהיה	qal	impf	3ms	היה	224		be,become
15:27	נוגע	qal	ptc	ms	נגע	619		touch,strike
	יטמא	qal	impf	3ms	טמא	379		become unclean
	כבס	piel	wcp	3ms	כבס	460		wash
	רחץ	qal	wcp	3ms	רחץ	934		wash,bathe
	טמא	qal	wcp	3ms	טמא	379		become unclean
15:28	טהרה	qal	pft	3fs	טהר	372		be clean,pure
	ספרה	qal	wcp	3fs	ספר	707		count
	תטהר	qal	impf	3fs	טהר	372		be clean,pure
15:29	תקח	qal	impf	3fs	לקח	542		take
	הביאה	hiph	wcp	3fs	בוא	97		bring in
15:30	עשׂה	qal	wcp	3ms	עשׂה	793		do,make
	כפר	piel	wcp	3ms	כפר	497		cover,atone
15:31	הזרתם	hiph	wcp	2mp	נזר	634		refrain
	ימתו	qal	impf	3mp	מות	559		die
	טמאם	piel	infc		טמא	379	3mp	defile
15:32	זב	qal	ptc	ms	זוב	264		flow,gush
	תצא	qal	impf	3fs	יצא	422		go out
	טמאה	qal	infc		טמא	379		become unclean
15:33	זב	qal	ptc	ms	זוב	264		flow,gush
	ישׁכב	qal	impf	3ms	שׁכב	1011		lie,lie down
16:1	ידבר	piel	wci	3ms	דבר	180		speak
	קרבתם	qal	infc		קרב	897	3mp	approach
	ימתו	qal	wci	3mp	מות	559		die
16:2	יאמר	qal	wci	3ms	אמר	55		say
	דבר	piel	impv	ms	דבר	180		speak
	יבא	qal	jusm	3ms	בוא	97		come in
	ימות	qal	impf	3ms	מות	559		die
	אראה	niph	impf	1cs	ראה	906		appear,be seen
16:3	יבא	qal	impf	3ms	בוא	97		come in
16:4	ילבשׁ	qal	impf	3ms	לבשׁ	527		put on,clothe
	יהיו	qal	impf	3mp	היה	224		be,become
	יחגר	qal	impf	3ms	חגר	291		gird
	יצנף	qal	impf	3ms	צנף	857		wrap together
	רחץ	qal	wcp	3ms	רחץ	934		wash,bathe
	לבשׁם	qal	wcp	3ms	לבשׁ	527	3mp	put on,clothe
16:5	יקח	qal	impf	3ms	לקח	542		take
16:6	הקריב	hiph	wcp	3ms	קרב	897		bring near

ChVs	Form	Stem	Tnse	PGN	Root	BDB	Sfx	Meaning
16:6	כפר	piel	wcp	3ms	כפר	497		cover,atone
16:7	לקח	qal	wcp	3ms	לקח	542		take
	העמיד	hiph	wcp	3ms	עמד	763		set up,raise
16:8	נתן	qal	wcp	3ms	נתן	678		give,set
16:9	הקריב	hiph	wcp	3ms	קרב	897		bring near
	עלה	qal	pft	3ms	עלה	748		go up
	עשׂהו	qal	wcp	3ms	עשׂה	793	3ms	do,make
16:10	עלה	qal	pft	3ms	עלה	748		go up
	יעמד	hoph	impf	3ms	עמד	763		be placed
	כפר	piel	infc		כפר	497		cover,atone
	שׁלח	piel	infc		שׁלח	1018		send away,shoot
16:11	הקריב	hiph	wcp	3ms	קרב	897		bring near
	כפר	piel	wcp	3ms	כפר	497		cover,atone
	שׁחט	qal	wcp	3ms	שׁחט	1006		slaughter
16:12	לקח	qal	wcp	3ms	לקח	542		take
	הביא	hiph	wcp	3ms	בוא	97		bring in
16:13	נתן	qal	wcp	3ms	נתן	678		give,set
	כסה	piel	wcp	3ms	כסה	491		cover
	ימות	qal	impf	3ms	מות	559		die
16:14	לקח	qal	wcp	3ms	לקח	542		take
	הזה	hiph	wcp	3ms	נזה	633		cause to spurt
	יזה	hiph	impf	3ms	נזה	633		cause to spurt
16:15	שׁחט	qal	wcp	3ms	שׁחט	1006		slaughter
	הביא	hiph	wcp	3ms	בוא	97		bring in
	עשׂה	qal	wcp	3ms	עשׂה	793		do,make
	עשׂה	qal	pft	3ms	עשׂה	793		do,make
	הזה	hiph	wcp	3ms	נזה	633		cause to spurt
16:16	כפר	piel	wcp	3ms	כפר	497		cover,atone
	יעשׂה	qal	impf	3ms	עשׂה	793		do,make
	שׁכן	qal	ptc	ms	שׁכן	1014		settle,dwell
16:17	יהיה	qal	impf	3ms	היה	224		be,become
	באו	qal	infc		בוא	97	3ms	come in
	כפר	piel	infc		כפר	497		cover,atone
	צאתו	qal	infc		יצא	422	3ms	go out
	כפר	piel	wcp	3ms	כפר	497		cover,atone
16:18	יצא	qal	wcp	3ms	יצא	422		go out
	כפר	piel	wcp	3ms	כפר	497		cover,atone
	לקח	qal	wcp	3ms	לקח	542		take
	נתן	qal	wcp	3ms	נתן	678		give,set
16:19	הזה	hiph	wcp	3ms	נזה	633		cause to spurt
	טהרו	piel	wcp	3ms	טהר	372	3ms	cleanse
	קדשׁו	piel	wcp	3ms	קדשׁ	872	3ms	consecrate
16:20	כלה	piel	wcp	3ms	כלה	477		complete,finish
	כפר	piel	infc		כפר	497		cover,atone
	הקריב	hiph	wcp	3ms	קרב	897		bring near
16:21	סמך	qal	wcp	3ms	סמך	701		lean,support
	התודה	hith	wcp	3ms	ידה	392		confess
	נתן	qal	wcp	3ms	נתן	678		give,set
	שׁלח	piel	wcp	3ms	שׁלח	1018		send away,shoot
16:22	נשׂא	qal	wcp	3ms	נשׂא	669		lift,carry
	שׁלח	piel	wcp	3ms	שׁלח	1018		send away,shoot
16:23	בא	qal	wcp	3ms	בוא	97		come in
	פשׁט	qal	wcp	3ms	פשׁט	832		strip off
	לבשׁ	qal	pft	3ms	לבשׁ	527		put on,clothe
16:23	באו	qal	infc		בוא	97	3ms	come in
	הניחם	hiph	wcp	3ms	נוח	628	3mp	give rest,put
16:24	רחץ	qal	wcp	3ms	רחץ	934		wash,bathe
	לבשׁ	qal	wcp	3ms	לבשׁ	527		put on,clothe
	יצא	qal	wcp	3ms	יצא	422		go out
	עשׂה	qal	wcp	3ms	עשׂה	793		do,make
	כפר	piel	wcp	3ms	כפר	497		cover,atone
16:25	יקטיר	hiph	impf	3ms	קטר	882		make sacrifices
16:26	משׁלח	piel	ptc	ms	שׁלח	1018		send away,shoot
	יכבס	piel	impf	3ms	כבס	460		wash
	רחץ	qal	wcp	3ms	רחץ	934		wash,bathe
	יבוא	qal	impf	3ms	בוא	97		come in
16:27	הובא	hoph	pft	3ms	בוא	97		be brought
	כפר	piel	infc		כפר	497		cover,atone
	יוציא	hiph	impf	3ms	יצא	422		bring out
	שׂרפו	qal	wcp	3cp	שׂרף	976		burn
16:28	שׂרף	qal	ptc	ms	שׂרף	976		burn
	יכבס	piel	impf	3ms	כבס	460		wash
	רחץ	qal	wcp	3ms	רחץ	934		wash,bathe
	יבוא	qal	impf	3ms	בוא	97		come in
16:29	היתה	qal	wcp	3fs	היה	224		be,become
	תענו	piel	impf	2mp	ענה	776		humble
	תעשׂו	qal	impf	2mp	עשׂה	793		do,make
	גר	qal	ptc	ms	גור	157		sojourn
16:30	יכפר	piel	impf	3ms	כפר	497		cover,atone
	טהר	piel	infc		טהר	372		cleanse
	תטהרו	qal	impf	2mp	טהר	372		be clean,pure
16:31	עניתם	piel	wcp	2mp	ענה	776		humble
16:32	כפר	piel	wcp	3ms	כפר	497		cover,atone
	ימשׁח	qal	impf	3ms	משׁח	602		smear,anoint
	ימלא	piel	impf	3ms	מלא	569		fill
	כהן	piel	infc		כהן	464		act as priest
	לבשׁ	qal	wcp	3ms	לבשׁ	527		put on,clothe
16:33	כפר	piel	wcp	3ms	כפר	497		cover,atone
	יכפר	piel	impf	3ms	כפר	497		cover,atone
	יכפר	piel	impf	3ms	כפר	497		cover,atone
16:34	היתה	qal	wcp	3fs	היה	224		be,become
	כפר	piel	infc		כפר	497		cover,atone
	יעשׂ	qal	wci	3ms	עשׂה	793		do,make
	צוה	piel	pft	3ms	צוה	845		command
17:1	ידבר	piel	wci	3ms	דבר	180		speak
	אמר	qal	infc		אמר	55		say
17:2	דבר	piel	impv	ms	דבר	180		speak
	אמרת	qal	wcp	2ms	אמר	55		say
	צוה	piel	pft	3ms	צוה	845		command
	אמר	qal	infc		אמר	55		say
17:3	ישׁחט	qal	impf	3ms	שׁחט	1006		slaughter
	ישׁחט	qal	impf	3ms	שׁחט	1006		slaughter
17:4	הביאו	hiph	pft	3ms	בוא	97	3ms	bring in
	הקריב	hiph	infc		קרב	897		bring near
	יחשׁב	niph	impf	3ms	חשׁב	362		be thought
	שׁפך	qal	pft	3ms	שׁפך	1049		pour out
	נכרת	niph	wcp	3ms	כרת	503		be cut off
17:5	יביאו	hiph	impf	3mp	בוא	97		bring in

ChVs	Form	Stem	Tnse	PGN	Root	BDB	Sfx	Meaning
17:5	זבחים	qal	ptc	mp	זבח	256		slaughter
	הביאם	hiph	wcp	3cp	בוא	97	3mp	bring in
	זבחו	qal	wcp	3cp	זבח	256		slaughter
17:6	זרק	qal	wcp	3ms	זרק	284		toss,scatter
	הקטיר	hiph	wcp	3ms	קטר	882		make sacrifices
17:7	יזבחו	qal	impf	3mp	זבח	256		slaughter
	זנים	qal	ptc	mp	זנה	275		act a harlot
	תהיה	qal	impf	3fs	היה	224		be,become
17:8	תאמר	qal	impf	2ms	אמר	55		say
	יגור	qal	impf	3ms	גור	157		sojourn
	יעלה	hiph	impf	3ms	עלה	748		bring up,offer
17:9	יביאנו	hiph	impf	3ms	בוא	97	3ms	bring in
	עשות	qal	infc		עשׂה	793		do,make
	נכרת	niph	wcp	3ms	כרת	503		be cut off
17:10	גר	qal	ptc	ms	גור	157		sojourn
	יאכל	qal	impf	3ms	אכל	37		eat,devour
	נתתי	qal	wcp	1cs	נתן	678		give,set
	אכלת	qal	ptc	fs	אכל	37		eat,devour
	הכרתי	hiph	wcp	1cs	כרת	503		cut off,destroy
17:11	נתתיו	qal	pft	1cs	נתן	678	3ms	give,set
	כפר	piel	infc		כפר	497		cover,atone
	יכפר	piel	impf	3ms	כפר	497		cover,atone
17:12	אמרתי	qal	pft	1cs	אמר	55		say
	תאכל	qal	impf	3fs	אכל	37		eat,devour
	גר	qal	ptc	ms	גור	157		sojourn
	יאכל	qal	impf	3ms	אכל	37		eat,devour
17:13	גר	qal	ptc	ms	גור	157		sojourn
	יצוד	qal	impf	3ms	צוד	844		hunt
	יאכל	niph	impf	3ms	אכל	37		be eaten
	שפך	qal	wcp	3ms	שׁפך	1049		pour out
	כסהו	piel	wcp	3ms	כסה	491	3ms	cover
17:14	אמר	qal	wci	1cs	אמר	55		say
	תאכלו	qal	impf	2mp	אכל	37		eat,devour
	אכליו	qal	ptc	mp	אכל	37	3ms	eat,devour
	יכרת	niph	impf	3ms	כרת	503		be cut off
17:15	תאכל	qal	impf	3fs	אכל	37		eat,devour
	כבס	piel	wcp	3ms	כבס	460		wash
	רחץ	qal	wcp	3ms	רחץ	934		wash,bathe
	טמא	qal	wcp	3ms	טמא	379		become unclean
	טהר	qal	wcp	3ms	טהר	372		be clean,pure
17:16	יכבס	piel	impf	3ms	כבס	460		wash
	ירחץ	qal	impf	3ms	רחץ	934		wash,bathe
	נשׂא	qal	wcp	3ms	נשׂא	669		lift,carry
18:1	ידבר	piel	wci	3ms	דבר	180		speak
	אמר	qal	infc		אמר	55		say
18:2	דבר	piel	impv	ms	דבר	180		speak
	אמרת	qal	wcp	2ms	אמר	55		say
18:3	ישבתם	qal	pft	2mp	ישׁב	442		sit,dwell
	תעשׂו	qal	impf	2mp	עשׂה	793		do,make
	מביא	hiph	ptc	ms	בוא	97		bring in
	תעשׂו	qal	impf	2mp	עשׂה	793		do,make
	תלכו	qal	impf	2mp	הלך	229		walk,go
18:4	תעשׂו	qal	impf	2mp	עשׂה	793		do,make
	תשמרו	qal	impf	2mp	שׁמר	1036		keep,watch
18:4	לכת	qal	infc		הלך	229		walk,go
18:5	שמרתם	qal	wcp	2mp	שׁמר	1036		keep,watch
	יעשׂה	qal	impf	3ms	עשׂה	793		do,make
	חי	qal	wcp	3ms	חיה	310		live
18:6	תקרבו	qal	impf	2mp	קרב	897		approach
	גלות	piel	infc		גלה	162		uncover
18:7	תגלה	piel	impf	2ms	גלה	162		uncover
	תגלה	piel	impf	2ms	גלה	162		uncover
18:8	תגלה	piel	impf	2ms	גלה	162		uncover
18:9	תגלה	piel	impf	2ms	גלה	162		uncover
18:10	תגלה	piel	impf	2ms	גלה	162		uncover
18:11	תגלה	piel	impf	2ms	גלה	162		uncover
18:12	תגלה	piel	impf	2ms	גלה	162		uncover
18:13	תגלה	piel	impf	2ms	גלה	162		uncover
18:14	תגלה	piel	impf	2ms	גלה	162		uncover
	תקרב	qal	impf	2ms	קרב	897		approach
18:15	תגלה	piel	impf	2ms	גלה	162		uncover
	תגלה	piel	impf	2ms	גלה	162		uncover
18:16	תגלה	piel	impf	2ms	גלה	162		uncover
18:17	תגלה	piel	impf	2ms	גלה	162		uncover
	תקח	qal	impf	2ms	לקח	542		take
	גלות	piel	infc		גלה	162		uncover
18:18	תקח	qal	impf	2ms	לקח	542		take
	צרר	qal	infc		צרר	865		make rival-wife
	גלות	piel	infc		גלה	162		uncover
18:19	תקרב	qal	impf	2ms	קרב	897		approach
	גלות	piel	infc		גלה	162		uncover
18:20	תתן	qal	impf	2ms	נתן	678		give,set
	טמאה	qal	infc		טמא	379		become unclean
18:21	תתן	qal	impf	2ms	נתן	678		give,set
	העביר	hiph	infc		עבר	716		cause to pass
	תחלל	piel	impf	2ms	חלל	320		pollute
18:22	תשכב	qal	impf	2ms	שׁכב	1011		lie,lie down
18:23	תתן	qal	impf	2ms	נתן	678		give,set
	טמאה	qal	infc		טמא	379		become unclean
	תעמד	qal	impf	3fs	עמד	763		stand,stop
	רבעה	qal	infc		רבע	918	3fs	lie down
18:24	תטמאו	hith	impf	2mp	טמא	379		defile oneself
	נטמאו	niph	pft	3cp	טמא	379		defile oneself
	משלח	piel	ptc	ms	שׁלח	1018		send away,shoot
18:25	תטמא	qal	wci	3fs	טמא	379		become unclean
	אפקד	qal	wci	1cs	פקד	823		attend to,visit
	תקא	hiph	wci	3fs	קיא	883		vomit up
	ישביה	qal	ptc	mp	ישׁב	442	3fs	sit,dwell
18:26	שמרתם	qal	wcp	2mp	שׁמר	1036		keep,watch
	תעשׂו	qal	impf	2mp	עשׂה	793		do,make
	גר	qal	ptc	ms	גור	157		sojourn
18:27	עשׂו	qal	pft	3cp	עשׂה	793		do,make
	תטמא	qal	wci	3fs	טמא	379		become unclean
18:28	תקיא	hiph	impf	3fs	קיא	883		vomit up
	טמאכם	piel	infc		טמא	379	2mp	defile
	קאה	qal	pft	3fs	קיא	883		vomit up
18:29	יעשׂה	qal	impf	3ms	עשׂה	793		do,make
	נכרתו	niph	wcp	3cp	כרת	503		be cut off

ChVs	Form	Stem	Tnse	PGN	Root	BDB	Sfx	Meaning
18:29	עשׂת	qal	ptc	fp	עשׂה	793		do,make
18:30	שׁמרתם	qal	wcp	2mp	שׁמר	1036		keep,watch
	עשׂות	qal	infc		עשׂה	793		do,make
	נעשׂו	niph	pft	3cp	עשׂה	793		be done
	תטמאו	hith	impf	2mp	טמא	379		defile oneself
19:1	ידבר	piel	wci	3ms	דבר	180		speak
	אמר	qal	infc		אמר	55		say
19:2	דבר	piel	impv	ms	דבר	180		speak
	אמרת	qal	wcp	2ms	אמר	55		say
	תהיו	qal	impf	2mp	היה	224		be,become
19:3	תיראו	qal	impf	2mp	ירא	431		fear
	תשׁמרו	qal	impf	2mp	שׁמר	1036		keep,watch
19:4	תפנו	qal	jusm	2mp	פנה	815		turn
	תעשׂו	qal	impf	2mp	עשׂה	793		do,make
19:5	תזבחו	qal	impf	2mp	זבח	256		slaughter
	תזבחהו	qal	impf	2mp	זבח	256	3ms	slaughter
19:6	יאכל	niph	impf	3ms	אכל	37		be eaten
	נותר	niph	ptc	ms	יתר	451		be left,remain
	ישׂרף	niph	impf	3ms	שׂרף	976		be burned
19:7	האכל	niph	infa		אכל	37		be eaten
	יאכל	niph	impf	3ms	אכל	37		be eaten
	ירצה	niph	impf	3ms	רצה	953		be accepted
19:8	אכליו	qal	ptc	mp	אכל	37	3ms	eat,devour
	ישׂא	qal	impf	3ms	נשׂא	669		lift,carry
	חלל	piel	pft	3ms	חלל	320		pollute
	נכרתה	niph	wcp	3fs	כרת	503		be cut off
19:9	קצרכם	qal	infc		קצר	894	2mp	reap,harvest
	תכלה	piel	impf	2ms	כלה	477		complete,finish
	קצר	qal	infc		קצר	894		reap,harvest
	תלקט	piel	impf	2ms	לקט	544		gather
19:10	תעולל	poel	impf	2ms	עלל	760		glean
	תלקט	piel	impf	2ms	לקט	544		gather
	תעזב	qal	impf	2ms	עזב	736		leave,loose
19:11	תגנבו	qal	impf	2mp	גנב	170		steal
	תכחשׁו	piel	impf	2mp	כחשׁ	471		deceive
	תשׁקרו	piel	impf	2mp	שׁקר	1055		deal falsely
19:12	תשׁבעו	niph	impf	2mp	שׁבע	989		swear
	חללת	piel	wcp	2ms	חלל	320		pollute
19:13	תעשׁק	qal	impf	2ms	עשׁק	798		oppress,extort
	תגזל	qal	impf	2ms	גזל	159		tear away,rob
	תלין	qal	impf	3fs	לון	533		lodge,remain
19:14	תקלל	piel	impf	2ms	קלל	886		curse
	תתן	qal	impf	2ms	נתן	678		give,set
	יראת	qal	wcp	2ms	ירא	431		fear
19:15	תעשׂו	qal	impf	2mp	עשׂה	793		do,make
	תשׂא	qal	impf	2ms	נשׂא	669		lift,carry
	תהדר	qal	impf	2ms	הדר	213		swell,honor
	תשׁפט	qal	impf	2ms	שׁפט	1047		judge
19:16	תלך	qal	impf	2ms	הלך	229		walk,go
	תעמד	qal	impf	2ms	עמד	763		stand,stop
19:17	תשׂנא	qal	impf	2ms	שׂנא	971		hate
	הוכח	hiph	infa		יכח	406		decide,reprove
	תוכיח	hiph	impf	2ms	יכח	406		decide,reprove
	תשׂא	qal	impf	2ms	נשׂא	669		lift,carry
19:18	תקם	qal	impf	2ms	נקם	667		avenge
	תטר	qal	impf	2ms	נטר	643		keep
	אהבת	qal	wcp	2ms	אהב	12		love
19:19	תשׁמרו	qal	impf	2mp	שׁמר	1036		keep,watch
	תרביע	hiph	impf	2ms	רבע	918		c. to lie down
	תזרע	qal	impf	2ms	זרע	281		sow
	יעלה	qal	impf	3ms	עלה	748		go up
19:20	ישׁכב	qal	impf	3ms	שׁכב	1011		lie,lie down
	נחרפת	niph	ptc	fs	חרף	358		acquire
	הפדה	hoph	infa		פדה	804		be ransomed
	נפדתה	niph	pft	3fs	פדה	804		be ransomed
	נתן	niph	pft	3ms	נתן	678		be given
	תהיה	qal	impf	3fs	היה	224		be,become
	יומתו	hoph	impf	3mp	מות	559		be killed
19:21	הביא	hiph	wcp	3ms	בוא	97		bring in
19:22	כפר	piel	wcp	3ms	כפר	497		cover,atone
	חטא	qal	pft	3ms	חטא	306		sin
	נסלח	niph	wcp	3ms	סלח	699		be forgiven
	חטא	qal	pft	3ms	חטא	306		sin
19:23	תבאו	qal	impf	2mp	בוא	97		come in
	נטעתם	qal	wcp	2mp	נטע	642		plant
	ערלתם	qal	wcp	2mp	ערל	790		count as uncirc
	יהיה	qal	impf	3ms	היה	224		be,become
	יאכל	niph	impf	3ms	אכל	37		be eaten
19:24	יהיה	qal	impf	3ms	היה	224		be,become
19:25	תאכלו	qal	impf	2mp	אכל	37		eat,devour
	הוסיף	hiph	infc		יסף	414		add,do again
19:26	תאכלו	qal	impf	2mp	אכל	37		eat,devour
	תנחשׁו	piel	impf	2mp	נחשׁ	638		divine
	תעוננו	poel	impf	2mp	ענן	778		soothsay
19:27	תקפו	hiph	impf	2mp	נקף	668		surround
	תשׁחית	hiph	impf	2ms	שׁחת	1007		spoil,ruin
19:28	תתנו	qal	impf	2mp	נתן	678		give,set
	תתנו	qal	impf	2mp	נתן	678		give,set
19:29	תחלל	piel	jusm	2ms	חלל	320		pollute
	הזנותה	hiph	infc		זנה	275	3fs	commit harlotry
	תזנה	qal	impf	3fs	זנה	275		act a harlot
	מלאה	qal	wcp	3fs	מלא	569		be full,fill
19:30	תשׁמרו	qal	impf	2mp	שׁמר	1036		keep,watch
	תיראו	qal	impf	2mp	ירא	431		fear
19:31	תפנו	qal	jusm	2mp	פנה	815		turn
	תבקשׁו	piel	jusm	2mp	בקשׁ	134		seek
	טמאה	qal	infc		טמא	379		become unclean
19:32	תקום	qal	impf	2ms	קום	877		arise,stand
	הדרת	qal	wcp	2ms	הדר	213		swell,honor
	יראת	qal	wcp	2ms	ירא	431		fear
19:33	יגור	qal	impf	3ms	גור	157		sojourn
	תונו	hiph	impf	2mp	ינה	413		oppress
19:34	יהיה	qal	impf	3ms	היה	224		be,become
	גר	qal	ptc	ms	גור	157		sojourn
	אהבת	qal	wcp	2ms	אהב	12		love
	הייתם	qal	pft	2mp	היה	224		be,become
19:35	תעשׂו	qal	impf	2mp	עשׂה	793		do,make
19:36	יהיה	qal	impf	3ms	היה	224		be,become

ChVs	Form	Stem	Tnse	PGN	Root	BDB	Sfx	Meaning
19:36	הוצאתי	hiph	pft	1cs	יצא	422		bring out
19:37	שׁמרתם	qal	wcp	2mp	שׁמר	1036		keep,watch
	עשׂיתם	qal	wcp	2mp	עשׂה	793		do,make
20:1	ידבר	piel	wci	3ms	דבר	180		speak
	אמר	qal	infc		אמר	55		say
20:2	תאמר	qal	impf	2ms	אמר	55		say
	גר	qal	ptc	ms	גור	157		sojourn
	יתן	qal	impf	3ms	נתן	678		give,set
	מות	qal	infa		מות	559		die
	יומת	hoph	impf	3ms	מות	559		be killed
	ירגמהו	qal	impf	3mp	רגם	920	3ms	stone
20:3	אתן	qal	impf	1cs	נתן	678		give,set
	הכרתי	hiph	wcp	1cs	כרת	503		cut off,destroy
	נתן	qal	pft	3ms	נתן	678		give,set
	טמא	piel	infc		טמא	379		defile
	חלל	piel	infc		חלל	320		pollute
20:4	העלם	hiph	infa		עלם	761		conceal,hide
	יעלימו	hiph	impf	3mp	עלם	761		conceal,hide
	תתו	qal	infc		נתן	678	3ms	give,set
	המית	hiph	infc		מות	559		kill
20:5	שׂמתי	qal	wcp	1cs	שׂים	962		put,set
	הכרתי	hiph	wcp	1cs	כרת	503		cut off,destroy
	זנים	qal	ptc	mp	זנה	275		act a harlot
	זנות	qal	infc		זנה	275		act a harlot
20:6	תפנה	qal	impf	3fs	פנה	815		turn
	זנות	qal	infc		זנה	275		act a harlot
	נתתי	qal	wcp	1cs	נתן	678		give,set
	הכרתי	hiph	wcp	1cs	כרת	503		cut off,destroy
20:7	התקדשׁתם	hith	wcp	2mp	קדשׁ	872		consecrate self
	הייתם	qal	wcp	2mp	היה	224		be,become
20:8	שׁמרתם	qal	wcp	2mp	שׁמר	1036		keep,watch
	עשׂיתם	qal	wcp	2mp	עשׂה	793		do,make
	מקדשׁכם	piel	ptc	ms	קדשׁ	872	2mp	consecrate
20:9	יקלל	piel	impf	3ms	קלל	886		curse
	מות	qal	infa		מות	559		die
	יומת	hoph	impf	3ms	מות	559		be killed
	קלל	piel	pft	3ms	קלל	886		curse
20:10	ינאף	qal	impf	3ms	נאף	610		commit adultery
	ינאף	qal	impf	3ms	נאף	610		commit adultery
	מות	qal	infa		מות	559		die
	יומת	hoph	impf	3ms	מות	559		be killed
	נאף	qal	ptc	ms	נאף	610		commit adultery
	נאפת	qal	ptc	fs	נאף	610		commit adultery
20:11	ישׁכב	qal	impf	3ms	שׁכב	1011		lie,lie down
	גלה	piel	pft	3ms	גלה	162		uncover
	מות	qal	infa		מות	559		die
	יומתו	hoph	impf	3mp	מות	559		be killed
20:12	ישׁכב	qal	impf	3ms	שׁכב	1011		lie,lie down
	מות	qal	infa		מות	559		die
	יומתו	hoph	impf	3mp	מות	559		be killed
	עשׂו	qal	pft	3cp	עשׂה	793		do,make
20:13	ישׁכב	qal	impf	3ms	שׁכב	1011		lie,lie down
	עשׂו	qal	pft	3cp	עשׂה	793		do,make
	מות	qal	infa		מות	559		die
20:13	יומתו	hoph	impf	3mp	מות	559		be killed
20:14	יקח	qal	impf	3ms	לקח	542		take
	ישׂרפו	qal	impf	3mp	שׂרף	976		burn
	תהיה	qal	impf	3fs	היה	224		be,become
20:15	יתן	qal	impf	3ms	נתן	678		give,set
	מות	qal	infa		מות	559		die
	יומת	hoph	impf	3ms	מות	559		be killed
	תהרגו	qal	impf	2mp	הרג	246		kill
20:16	תקרב	qal	impf	3fs	קרב	897		approach
	רבעה	qal	infc		רבע	918		lie down
	הרגת	qal	wcp	2ms	הרג	246		kill
	מות	qal	infa		מות	559		die
	יומתו	hoph	impf	3mp	מות	559		be killed
20:17	יקח	qal	impf	3ms	לקח	542		take
	ראה	qal	wcp	3ms	ראה	906		see
	תראה	qal	impf	3fs	ראה	906		see
	נכרתו	niph	wcp	3cp	כרת	503		be cut off
	גלה	piel	pft	3ms	גלה	162		uncover
	ישׂא	qal	impf	3ms	נשׂא	669		lift,carry
20:18	ישׁכב	qal	impf	3ms	שׁכב	1011		lie,lie down
	גלה	piel	wcp	3ms	גלה	162		uncover
	הערה	hiph	pft	3ms	ערה	788		make naked
	גלתה	piel	pft	3fs	גלה	162		uncover
	נכרתו	niph	wcp	3cp	כרת	503		be cut off
20:19	תגלה	piel	impf	2ms	גלה	162		uncover
	הערה	hiph	pft	3ms	ערה	788		make naked
	ישׂאו	qal	impf	3mp	נשׂא	669		lift,carry
20:20	ישׁכב	qal	impf	3ms	שׁכב	1011		lie,lie down
	גלה	piel	pft	3ms	גלה	162		uncover
	ישׂאו	qal	impf	3mp	נשׂא	669		lift,carry
	ימתו	qal	impf	3mp	מות	559		die
20:21	יקח	qal	impf	3ms	לקח	542		take
	גלה	piel	pft	3ms	גלה	162		uncover
	יהיו	qal	impf	3mp	היה	224		be,become
20:22	שׁמרתם	qal	wcp	2mp	שׁמר	1036		keep,watch
	עשׂיתם	qal	wcp	2mp	עשׂה	793		do,make
	תקיא	hiph	impf	3fs	קיא	883		vomit up
	מביא	hiph	ptc	ms	בוא	97		bring in
	שׁבת	qal	infc		ישׁב	442		sit,dwell
20:23	תלכו	qal	impf	2mp	הלך	229		walk,go
	משׁלח	piel	ptc	ms	שׁלח	1018		send away,shoot
	עשׂו	qal	pft	3cp	עשׂה	793		do,make
	אקץ	qal	wci	1cs	קוץ	880		loathe,abhor
20:24	אמר	qal	wci	1cs	אמר	55		say
	תירשׁו	qal	impf	2mp	ירשׁ	439		possess,inherit
	אתננה	qal	impf	1cs	נתן	678	3fs	give,set
	רשׁת	qal	infc		ירשׁ	439		possess,inherit
	זבת	qal	ptc	fs	זוב	264		flow,gush
	הבדלתי	hiph	pft	1cs	בדל	95		divide
20:25	הבדלתם	hiph	wcp	2mp	בדל	95		divide
	תשׁקצו	piel	impf	2mp	שׁקץ	1055		detest
	תרמשׂ	qal	impf	3fs	רמשׂ	942		creep
	הבדלתי	hiph	pft	1cs	בדל	95		divide
	טמא	piel	infc		טמא	379		defile

ChVs	Form	Stem	Tnse	PGN	Root	BDB	Sfx	Meaning
20:26	הייתם	qal	wcp	2mp	היה	224		be,become
	אבדל	hiph	wci	1cs	בדל	95		divide
	היות	qal	infc		היה	224		be,become
20:27	יהיה	qal	impf	3ms	היה	224		be,become
	מות	qal	infa		מות	559		die
	יומתו	hoph	impf	3mp	מות	559		be killed
	ירגמו	qal	impf	3mp	רגם	920		stone
21:1	יאמר	qal	wci	3ms	אמר	55		say
	אמר	qal	impv	ms	אמר	55		say
	אמרת	qal	wcp	2ms	אמר	55		say
	יטמא	hith	impf	3ms	טמא	379		defile oneself
21:3	היתה	qal	pft	3fs	היה	224		be,become
	יטמא	hith	impf	3ms	טמא	379		defile oneself
21:4	יטמא	hith	impf	3ms	טמא	379		defile oneself
	החלו	niph	infc		חלל	320	3ms	pollute oneself
21:5	יקרחהk	qal	impf	3fs	קרח	901		make bald
	יקרחוq	qal	impf	3mp	קרח	901		make bald
	יגלחו	piel	impf	3mp	גלח	164		shave
	ישׂרטו	qal	impf	3mp	שׂרט	976		incise
21:6	יהיו	qal	impf	3mp	היה	224		be,become
	יחללו	piel	impf	3mp	חלל	320		pollute
	מקריבם	hiph	ptc	mp	קרב	897		bring near
	היו	qal	wcp	3cp	היה	224		be,become
21:7	זנה	qal	ptc	fs	זנה	275		act a harlot
	יקחו	qal	impf	3mp	לקח	542		take
	גרושה	qal	pptc	fs	גרשׁ	176		cast out
	יקחו	qal	impf	3mp	לקח	542		take
21:8	קדשׁתו	piel	wcp	2ms	קדשׁ	872	3ms	consecrate
	מקריב	hiph	ptc	ms	קרב	897		bring near
	יהיה	qal	impf	3ms	היה	224		be,become
	מקדשׁכם	piel	ptc	ms	קדשׁ	872	2mp	consecrate
21:9	תחל	niph	impf	3fs	חלל	320		pollute oneself
	זנות	qal	infc		זנה	275		act a harlot
	מחללת	piel	ptc	fs	חלל	320		pollute
	תשׂרף	niph	impf	3fs	שׂרף	976		be burned
21:10	יוצק	hoph	impf	3ms	יצק	427		be poured,firm
	מלא	piel	wcp	3ms	מלא	569		fill
	לבשׁ	qal	infc		לבשׁ	527		put on,clothe
	יפרע	qal	impf	3ms	פרע	828		let go
	יפרם	qal	impf	3ms	פרם	827		tear,rend
21:11	מת	qal	ptc	ms	מות	559		die
	יבא	qal	impf	3ms	בוא	97		come in
	יטמא	hith	impf	3ms	טמא	379		defile oneself
21:12	יצא	qal	impf	3ms	יצא	422		go out
	יחלל	piel	impf	3ms	חלל	320		pollute
21:13	יקח	qal	impf	3ms	לקח	542		take
21:14	גרושה	qal	pptc	fs	גרשׁ	176		cast out
	זנה	qal	ptc	fs	זנה	275		act a harlot
	יקח	qal	impf	3ms	לקח	542		take
	יקח	qal	impf	3ms	לקח	542		take
21:15	יחלל	piel	impf	3ms	חלל	320		pollute
	מקדשׁו	piel	ptc	ms	קדשׁ	872	3ms	consecrate
21:16	ידבר	piel	wci	3ms	דבר	180		speak
	אמר	qal	infc		אמר	55		say
21:17	דבר	piel	impv	ms	דבר	180		speak
	אמר	qal	infc		אמר	55		say
	יהיה	qal	impf	3ms	היה	224		be,become
	יקרב	qal	impf	3ms	קרב	897		approach
	הקריב	hiph	infc		קרב	897		bring near
21:18	יקרב	qal	impf	3ms	קרב	897		approach
	חרם	qal	pptc	ms	חרם	356		slit
	שׂרוע	qal	pptc	ms	שׂרע	976		extend
21:19	יהיה	qal	impf	3ms	היה	224		be,become
21:21	יגשׁ	qal	impf	3ms	נגשׁ	620		draw near
	הקריב	hiph	infc		קרב	897		bring near
	יגשׁ	qal	impf	3ms	נגשׁ	620		draw near
	הקריב	hiph	infc		קרב	897		bring near
21:22	יאכל	qal	impf	3ms	אכל	37		eat,devour
21:23	יבא	qal	impf	3ms	בוא	97		come in
	יגשׁ	qal	impf	3ms	נגשׁ	620		draw near
	יחלל	piel	impf	3ms	חלל	320		pollute
	מקדשׁם	piel	ptc	ms	קדשׁ	872	3mp	consecrate
21:24	ידבר	piel	wci	3ms	דבר	180		speak
22:1	ידבר	piel	wci	3ms	דבר	180		speak
	אמר	qal	infc		אמר	55		say
22:2	דבר	piel	impv	ms	דבר	180		speak
	ינזרו	niph	jusm	3mp	נזר	634		dedicate self
	יחללו	piel	impf	3mp	חלל	320		pollute
	מקדשׁים	hiph	ptc	mp	קדשׁ	872		consecrate
22:3	אמר	qal	impv	ms	אמר	55		say
	יקרב	qal	impf	3ms	קרב	897		approach
	יקדישׁו	hiph	impf	3mp	קדשׁ	872		consecrate
	נכרתה	niph	wcp	3fs	כרת	503		be cut off
22:4	צרוע	qal	pptc	ms	צרע	863		be leprous
	זב	qal	ptc	ms	זוב	264		flow,gush
	יאכל	qal	impf	3ms	אכל	37		eat,devour
	יטהר	qal	impf	3ms	טהר	372		be clean,pure
	נגע	qal	ptc	ms	נגע	619		touch,strike
	תצא	qal	impf	3fs	יצא	422		go out
22:5	יגע	qal	impf	3ms	נגע	619		touch,strike
	יטמא	qal	impf	3ms	טמא	379		become unclean
	יטמא	qal	impf	3ms	טמא	379		become unclean
22:6	תגע	qal	impf	3fs	נגע	619		touch,strike
	טמאה	qal	wcp	3fs	טמא	379		become unclean
	יאכל	qal	impf	3ms	אכל	37		eat,devour
	רחץ	qal	pft	3ms	רחץ	934		wash,bathe
22:7	בא	qal	wcp	3ms	בוא	97		come in
	טהר	qal	wcp	3ms	טהר	372		be clean,pure
	יאכל	qal	impf	3ms	אכל	37		eat,devour
22:8	יאכל	qal	impf	3ms	אכל	37		eat,devour
	טמאה	qal	infc		טמא	379		become unclean
22:9	שׁמרו	qal	wcp	3cp	שׁמר	1036		keep,watch
	ישׂאו	qal	impf	3mp	נשׂא	669		lift,carry
	מתו	qal	wcp	3cp	מות	559		die
	יחללהו	piel	impf	3mp	חלל	320	3ms	pollute
	מקדשׁם	piel	ptc	ms	קדשׁ	872	3mp	consecrate
22:10	יאכל	qal	impf	3ms	אכל	37		eat,devour
	יאכל	qal	impf	3ms	אכל	37		eat,devour

ChVs	Form	Stem	Tnse	PGN	Root	BDB	Sfx	Meaning
22: 11	יקנה	qal	impf	3ms	קנה	888		get, buy
	יאכל	qal	impf	3ms	אכל	37		eat, devour
	יאכלו	qal	impf	3mp	אכל	37		eat, devour
22: 12	תהיה	qal	impf	3fs	היה	224		be, become
	תאכל	qal	impf	3fs	אכל	37		eat, devour
22: 13	תהיה	qal	impf	3fs	היה	224		be, become
	גרושה	qal	pptc	fs	גרשׁ	176		cast out
	שׁבה	qal	wcp	3fs	שׁוב	996		turn, return
	תאכל	qal	impf	3fs	אכל	37		eat, devour
	יאכל	qal	impf	3ms	אכל	37		eat, devour
22: 14	יאכל	qal	impf	3ms	אכל	37		eat, devour
	יסף	qal	wcp	3ms	יסף	414		add, increase
	נתן	qal	wcp	3ms	נתן	678		give, set
22: 15	יחללו	piel	impf	3mp	חלל	320		pollute
	ירימו	hiph	impf	3mp	רום	926		raise, lift
22: 16	השׂיאו	hiph	wcp	3cp	נשׂא	669		cause to bring
	אכלם	qal	infc		אכל	37	3mp	eat, devour
	מקדשׁם	piel	ptc	ms	קדשׁ	872	3mp	consecrate
22: 17	ידבר	piel	wci	3ms	דבר	180		speak
	אמר	qal	infc		אמר	55		say
22: 18	דבר	piel	impv	ms	דבר	180		speak
	אמרת	qal	wcp	2ms	אמר	55		say
	יקריב	hiph	impf	3ms	קרב	897		bring near
	יקריבו	hiph	impf	3mp	קרב	897		bring near
22: 20	תקריבו	hiph	impf	2mp	קרב	897		bring near
	יהיה	qal	impf	3ms	היה	224		be, become
22: 21	יקריב	hiph	impf	3ms	קרב	897		bring near
	פלא	piel	infc		פלא	810		offer
	יהיה	qal	impf	3ms	היה	224		be, become
	יהיה	qal	impf	3ms	היה	224		be, become
22: 22	שׁבור	qal	pptc	ms	שׁבר	990		break
	חרוץ	qal	pptc	ms	חרץ	358		cut, decide
	תקריבו	hiph	impf	2mp	קרב	897		bring near
	תתנו	qal	impf	2mp	נתן	678		give, set
22: 23	שׂרוע	qal	pptc	ms	שׂרע	976		extend
	קלוט	qal	pptc	ms	קלט	886		be stunted
	תעשׂה	qal	impf	2ms	עשׂה	793		do, make
	ירצה	niph	impf	3ms	רצה	953		be accepted
22: 24	מעוך	qal	pptc	ms	מעך	590		press
	כתות	qal	pptc	ms	כתת	510		beat, crush
	נתוק	qal	pptc	ms	נתק	683		draw away, pull
	כרות	qal	pptc	ms	כרת	503		cut, destroy
	תקריבו	hiph	impf	2mp	קרב	897		bring near
	תעשׂו	qal	impf	2mp	עשׂה	793		do, make
22: 25	תקריבו	hiph	impf	2mp	קרב	897		bring near
	ירצו	niph	impf	3mp	רצה	953		be accepted
22: 26	ידבר	piel	wci	3ms	דבר	180		speak
	אמר	qal	infc		אמר	55		say
22: 27	יולד	niph	impf	3ms	ילד	408		be born
	היה	qal	wcp	3ms	היה	224		be, become
	ירצה	niph	impf	3ms	רצה	953		be accepted
22: 28	תשׁחטו	qal	impf	2mp	שׁחט	1006		slaughter
22: 29	תזבחו	qal	impf	2mp	זבח	256		slaughter
	תזבחו	qal	impf	2mp	זבח	256		slaughter
22: 30	יאכל	niph	impf	3ms	אכל	37		be eaten
	תותירו	hiph	impf	2mp	יתר	451		leave, spare
22: 31	שׁמרתם	qal	wcp	2mp	שׁמר	1036		keep, watch
	עשׂיתם	qal	wcp	2mp	עשׂה	793		do, make
22: 32	תחללו	piel	impf	2mp	חלל	320		pollute
	נקדשׁתי	niph	wcp	1cs	קדשׁ	872		be sacred
	מקדשׁכם	piel	ptc	ms	קדשׁ	872	2mp	consecrate
22: 33	מוציא	hiph	ptc	ms	יצא	422		bring out
	היות	qal	infc		היה	224		be, become
23: 1	ידבר	piel	wci	3ms	דבר	180		speak
	אמר	qal	infc		אמר	55		say
23: 2	דבר	piel	impv	ms	דבר	180		speak
	אמרת	qal	wcp	2ms	אמר	55		say
	תקראו	qal	impf	2mp	קרא	894		call, proclaim
23: 3	תעשׂה	niph	impf	3fs	עשׂה	793		be done
	תעשׂו	qal	impf	2mp	עשׂה	793		do, make
23: 4	תקראו	qal	impf	2mp	קרא	894		call, proclaim
23: 6	תאכלו	qal	impf	2mp	אכל	37		eat, devour
23: 7	יהיה	qal	impf	3ms	היה	224		be, become
	תעשׂו	qal	impf	2mp	עשׂה	793		do, make
23: 8	הקרבתם	hiph	wcp	2mp	קרב	897		bring near
	תעשׂו	qal	impf	2mp	עשׂה	793		do, make
23: 9	ידבר	piel	wci	3ms	דבר	180		speak
	אמר	qal	infc		אמר	55		say
23: 10	דבר	piel	impv	ms	דבר	180		speak
	אמרת	qal	wcp	2ms	אמר	55		say
	תבאו	qal	impf	2mp	בוא	97		come in
	נתן	qal	ptc	ms	נתן	678		give, set
	קצרתם	qal	wcp	2mp	קצר	894		reap, harvest
	הבאתם	hiph	wcp	2mp	בוא	97		bring in
23: 11	הניף	hiph	wcp	3ms	נוף	631		swing, wave
	יניפנו	hiph	impf	3ms	נוף	631	3ms	swing, wave
23: 12	עשׂיתם	qal	wcp	2mp	עשׂה	793		do, make
	הניפכם	hiph	infc		נוף	631	2mp	swing, wave
23: 13	בלולה	qal	pptc	fs	בלל	117		mingle, mix
23: 14	תאכלו	qal	impf	2mp	אכל	37		eat, devour
	הביאכם	hiph	infc		בוא	97	2mp	bring in
23: 15	ספרתם	qal	wcp	2mp	ספר	707		count
	הביאכם	hiph	infc		בוא	97	2mp	bring in
	תהיינה	qal	impf	3fp	היה	224		be, become
23: 16	תספרו	qal	impf	2mp	ספר	707		count
	הקרבתם	hiph	wcp	2mp	קרב	897		bring near
23: 17	תביאו	hiph	impf	2mp	בוא	97		bring in
	תהיינה	qal	impf	3fp	היה	224		be, become
	תאפינה	niph	impf	3fp	אפה	66		be baked
23: 18	הקרבתם	hiph	wcp	2mp	קרב	897		bring near
	יהיו	qal	impf	3mp	היה	224		be, become
23: 19	עשׂיתם	qal	wcp	2mp	עשׂה	793		do, make
23: 20	הניף	hiph	wcp	3ms	נוף	631		swing, wave
	יהיו	qal	impf	3mp	היה	224		be, become
23: 21	קראתם	qal	wcp	2mp	קרא	894		call, proclaim
	יהיה	qal	impf	3ms	היה	224		be, become
	תעשׂו	qal	impf	2mp	עשׂה	793		do, make
23: 22	קצרכם	qal	infc		קצר	894	2mp	reap, harvest

ChVs	Form	Stem	Tnse	PGN	Root	BDB	Sfx	Meaning
23:22	תכלה	piel	impf	2ms	כלה	477		complete,finish
	קצרך	qal	infc		קצר	894	2ms	reap,harvest
	תלקט	piel	impf	2ms	לקט	544		gather
	תעזב	qal	impf	2ms	עזב	736		leave,loose
23:23	ידבר	piel	wci	3ms	דבר	180		speak
	אמר	qal	infc		אמר	55		say
23:24	דבר	piel	impv	ms	דבר	180		speak
	אמר	qal	infc		אמר	55		say
	יהיה	qal	impf	3ms	היה	224		be,become
23:25	תעשׂו	qal	impf	2mp	עשׂה	793		do,make
	הקרבתם	hiph	wcp	2mp	קרב	897		bring near
23:26	ידבר	piel	wci	3ms	דבר	180		speak
	אמר	qal	infc		אמר	55		say
23:27	יהיה	qal	impf	3ms	היה	224		be,become
	עניתם	piel	wcp	2mp	ענה	776		humble
	הקרבתם	hiph	wcp	2mp	קרב	897		bring near
23:28	תעשׂו	qal	impf	2mp	עשׂה	793		do,make
	כפר	piel	infc		כפר	497		cover,atone
23:29	תענה	pual	impf	3fs	ענה	776		be afflicted
	נכרתה	niph	wcp	3fs	כרת	503		be cut off
23:30	תעשׂה	qal	impf	3fs	עשׂה	793		do,make
	האבדתי	hiph	wcp	1cs	אבד	1		destroy
23:31	תעשׂו	qal	impf	2mp	עשׂה	793		do,make
23:32	עניתם	piel	wcp	2mp	ענה	776		humble
	תשׁבתו	qal	impf	2mp	שׁבת	991		cease,desist
23:33	ידבר	piel	wci	3ms	דבר	180		speak
	אמר	qal	infc		אמר	55		say
23:34	דבר	piel	impv	ms	דבר	180		speak
	אמר	qal	infc		אמר	55		say
23:35	תעשׂו	qal	impf	2mp	עשׂה	793		do,make
23:36	תקריבו	hiph	impf	2mp	קרב	897		bring near
	יהיה	qal	impf	3ms	היה	224		be,become
	הקרבתם	hiph	wcp	2mp	קרב	897		bring near
	תעשׂו	qal	impf	2mp	עשׂה	793		do,make
23:37	תקראו	qal	impf	2mp	קרא	894		call,proclaim
	הקריב	hiph	infc		קרב	897		bring near
23:38	תתנו	qal	impf	2mp	נתן	678		give,set
23:39	אספכם	qal	infc		אסף	62	2mp	gather
	תחגו	qal	impf	2mp	חגג	290		keep festival
23:40	לקחתם	qal	wcp	2mp	לקח	542		take
	שׂמחתם	qal	wcp	2mp	שׂמח	970		rejoice
23:41	חגתם	qal	wcp	2mp	חגג	290		keep festival
	תחגו	qal	impf	2mp	חגג	290		keep festival
23:42	תשׁבו	qal	impf	2mp	ישׁב	442		sit,dwell
	ישׁבו	qal	impf	3mp	ישׁב	442		sit,dwell
23:43	ידעו	qal	impf	3mp	ידע	393		know
	הושׁבתי	hiph	pft	1cs	ישׁב	442		cause to dwell
	הוציאי	hiph	infc		יצא	422	1cs	bring out
23:44	ידבר	piel	wci	3ms	דבר	180		speak
24:1	ידבר	piel	wci	3ms	דבר	180		speak
	אמר	qal	infc		אמר	55		say
24:2	צו	piel	impv	ms	צוה	845		command
	יקחו	qal	impf	3mp	לקח	542		take
	העלת	hiph	infc		עלה	748		bring up,offer

ChVs	Form	Stem	Tnse	PGN	Root	BDB	Sfx	Meaning
24:3	יערך	qal	impf	3ms	ערך	789		set in order
24:4	יערך	qal	impf	3ms	ערך	789		set in order
24:5	לקחת	qal	wcp	2ms	לקח	542		take
	אפית	qal	wcp	2ms	אפה	66		bake
	יהיה	qal	impf	3ms	היה	224		be,become
24:6	שׂמת	qal	wcp	2ms	שׂים	962		put,set
24:7	נתת	qal	wcp	2ms	נתן	678		give,set
	היתה	qal	wcp	3fs	היה	224		be,become
24:8	יערכנו	qal	impf	3ms	ערך	789	3ms	set in order
24:9	היתה	qal	wcp	3fs	היה	224		be,become
	אכלהו	qal	wcp	3cp	אכל	37	3ms	eat,devour
24:10	יצא	qal	wci	3ms	יצא	422		go out
	ינצו	niph	wci	3mp	נצה	663		struggle
24:11	יקב	qal	wci	3ms	קבב	866		curse
	יקלל	piel	wci	3ms	קלל	886		curse
	יביאו	hiph	wci	3mp	בוא	97		bring in
24:12	יניחהו	hiph	wci	3mp	נוח	628	3ms	give rest,put
	פרשׁ	qal	infc		פרשׁ	831		make distinct
24:13	ידבר	piel	wci	3ms	דבר	180		speak
	אמר	qal	infc		אמר	55		say
24:14	הוצא	hiph	impv	ms	יצא	422		bring out
	מקלל	piel	ptc	ms	קלל	886		curse
	סמכו	qal	wcp	3cp	סמך	701		lean,support
	שׁמעים	qal	ptc	mp	שׁמע	1033		hear
	רגמו	qal	wcp	3cp	רגם	920		stone
24:15	תדבר	piel	impf	2ms	דבר	180		speak
	אמר	qal	infc		אמר	55		say
	יקלל	piel	impf	3ms	קלל	886		curse
	נשׂא	qal	wcp	3ms	נשׂא	669		lift,carry
24:16	נקב	qal	ptc	ms	נקב	666		curse
	מות	qal	infa		מות	559		die
	יומת	hoph	impf	3ms	מות	559		be killed
	רגום	qal	infa		רגם	920		stone
	ירגמו	qal	impf	3mp	רגם	920		stone
	נקבו	qal	infc		נקב	666	3ms	curse
	יומת	hoph	impf	3ms	מות	559		be killed
24:17	יכה	hiph	impf	3ms	נכה	645		smite
	מות	qal	infa		מות	559		die
	יומת	hoph	impf	3ms	מות	559		be killed
24:18	מכה	hiph	ptc	ms	נכה	645		smite
	ישׁלמנה	piel	impf	3ms	שׁלם	1022	3fs	finish,reward
24:19	יתן	qal	impf	3ms	נתן	678		give,set
	עשׂה	qal	pft	3ms	עשׂה	793		do,make
	יעשׂה	niph	impf	3ms	עשׂה	793		be done
24:20	יתן	qal	impf	3ms	נתן	678		give,set
	ינתן	niph	impf	3ms	נתן	678		be given
24:21	מכה	hiph	ptc	ms	נכה	645		smite
	ישׁלמנה	piel	impf	3ms	שׁלם	1022	3fs	finish,reward
	מכה	hiph	ptc	ms	נכה	645		smite
	יומת	hoph	impf	3ms	מות	559		be killed
24:22	יהיה	qal	impf	3ms	היה	224		be,become
	יהיה	qal	impf	3ms	היה	224		be,become
24:23	ידבר	piel	wci	3ms	דבר	180		speak
	יוציאו	hiph	wci	3mp	יצא	422		bring out

ChVs	Form	Stem	Tnse	PGN	Root	BDB	Sfx	Meaning
24:23	מקלל	piel	ptc	ms	קלל	886		curse
	ירגמו	qal	wci	3mp	רגם	920		stone
	עשׂו	qal	pft	3cp	עשׂה	793		do,make
	צוה	piel	pft	3ms	צוה	845		command
25:1	ידבר	piel	wci	3ms	דבר	180		speak
	אמר	qal	infc		אמר	55		say
25:2	דבר	piel	impv	ms	דבר	180		speak
	אמרת	qal	wcp	2ms	אמר	55		say
	תבאו	qal	impf	2mp	בוא	97		come in
	נתן	qal	ptc	ms	נתן	678		give,set
	שׁבתה	qal	wcp	3fs	שׁבת	991		cease,desist
25:3	תזרע	qal	impf	2ms	זרע	281		sow
	תזמר	qal	impf	2ms	זמר	274		prune
	אספת	qal	wcp	2ms	אסף	62		gather
25:4	יהיה	qal	impf	3ms	היה	224		be,become
	תזרע	qal	impf	2ms	זרע	281		sow
	תזמר	qal	impf	2ms	זמר	274		prune
25:5	תקצור	qal	impf	2ms	קצר	894		reap,harvest
	תבצר	qal	impf	2ms	בצר	130		cut off
	יהיה	qal	impf	3ms	היה	224		be,become
25:6	היתה	qal	wcp	3fs	היה	224		be,become
	גרים	qal	ptc	mp	גור	157		sojourn
25:7	תהיה	qal	impf	3fs	היה	224		be,become
	אכל	qal	infc		אכל	37		eat,devour
25:8	ספרת	qal	wcp	2ms	ספר	707		count
	היו	qal	wcp	3cp	היה	224		be,become
25:9	העברת	hiph	wcp	2ms	עבר	716		cause to pass
	תעבירו	hiph	impf	2mp	עבר	716		cause to pass
25:10	קדשׁתם	piel	wcp	2mp	קדשׁ	872		consecrate
	קראתם	qal	wcp	2mp	קרא	894		call,proclaim
	ישׁביה	qal	ptc	mp	ישׁב	442	3fs	sit,dwell
	תהיה	qal	impf	3fs	היה	224		be,become
	שׁבתם	qal	wcp	2mp	שׁוב	996		turn,return
	תשׁבו	qal	impf	2mp	שׁוב	996		turn,return
25:11	תהיה	qal	impf	3fs	היה	224		be,become
	תזרעו	qal	impf	2mp	זרע	281		sow
	תקצרו	qal	impf	2mp	קצר	894		reap,harvest
	תבצרו	qal	impf	2mp	בצר	130		cut off
25:12	תהיה	qal	impf	3fs	היה	224		be,become
	תאכלו	qal	impf	2mp	אכל	37		eat,devour
25:13	תשׁבו	qal	impf	2mp	שׁוב	996		turn,return
25:14	תמכרו	qal	impf	2mp	מכר	569		sell
	קנה	qal	infa		קנה	888		get,buy
	תונו	hiph	jusm	2mp	ינה	413		oppress
25:15	תקנה	qal	impf	2ms	קנה	888		get,buy
	ימכר	qal	impf	3ms	מכר	569		sell
25:16	רב	qal	infc		רבב	912		be many
	תרבה	hiph	impf	2ms	רבה	915		make many
	מעט	qal	infc		מעט	589		be small,few
	תמעיט	hiph	impf	2ms	מעט	589		make small
	מכר	qal	ptc	ms	מכר	569		sell
25:17	תונו	hiph	impf	2mp	ינה	413		oppress
	יראת	qal	wcp	2ms	ירא	431		fear
25:18	עשׂיתם	qal	wcp	2mp	עשׂה	793		do,make
ChVs	Form	Stem	Tnse	PGN	Root	BDB	Sfx	Meaning
25:18	תשׁמרו	qal	impf	2mp	שׁמר	1036		keep,watch
	עשׂיתם	qal	wcp	2mp	עשׂה	793		do,make
	ישׁבתם	qal	wcp	2mp	ישׁב	442		sit,dwell
25:19	נתנה	qal	wcp	3fs	נתן	678		give,set
	אכלתם	qal	wcp	2mp	אכל	37		eat,devour
	ישׁבתם	qal	wcp	2mp	ישׁב	442		sit,dwell
25:20	תאמרו	qal	impf	2mp	אמר	55		say
	נאכל	qal	impf	1cp	אכל	37		eat,devour
	נזרע	qal	impf	1cp	זרע	281		sow
	נאסף	qal	impf	1cp	אסף	62		gather
25:21	צויתי	piel	wcp	1cs	צוה	845		command
	עשׂת	qal	wcp	3fs	עשׂה	793		do,make
25:22	זרעתם	qal	wcp	2mp	זרע	281		sow
	אכלתם	qal	wcp	2mp	אכל	37		eat,devour
	בוא	qal	infc		בוא	97		come in
	תאכלו	qal	impf	2mp	אכל	37		eat,devour
25:23	תמכר	niph	impf	3fs	מכר	569		be sold
25:24	תתנו	qal	impf	2mp	נתן	678		give,set
25:25	ימוך	qal	impf	3ms	מוך	557		be low,poor
	מכר	qal	wcp	3ms	מכר	569		sell
	בא	qal	wcp	3ms	בוא	97		come in
	גאלו	qal	ptc	ms	גאל	145	3ms	redeem
	גאל	qal	wcp	3ms	גאל	145		redeem
25:26	יהיה	qal	impf	3ms	היה	224		be,become
	גאל	qal	ptc	ms	גאל	145		redeem
	השׂיגה	hiph	wcp	3fs	נשׂג	673		reach,overtake
	מצא	qal	wcp	3ms	מצא	592		find
25:27	חשׁב	piel	wcp	3ms	חשׁב	362		devise
	השׁיב	hiph	wcp	3ms	שׁוב	996		bring back
	עדף	qal	ptc	ms	עדף	727		remain over
	מכר	qal	pft	3ms	מכר	569		sell
	שׁב	qal	wcp	3ms	שׁוב	996		turn,return
25:28	מצאה	qal	pft	3fs	מצא	592		find
	השׁיב	hiph	infc		שׁוב	996		bring back
	היה	qal	wcp	3ms	היה	224		be,become
	קנה	qal	ptc	ms	קנה	888		get,buy
	יצא	qal	wcp	3ms	יצא	422		go out
	שׁב	qal	wcp	3ms	שׁוב	996		turn,return
25:29	ימכר	qal	impf	3ms	מכר	569		sell
	היתה	qal	wcp	3fs	היה	224		be,become
	תם	qal	infc		תמם	1070		be finished
	תהיה	qal	impf	3fs	היה	224		be,become
25:30	יגאל	niph	impf	3ms	גאל	145		be redeemed
	מלאת	qal	infc		מלא	569		be full,fill
	קם	qal	wcp	3ms	קום	877		arise,stand
	קנה	qal	ptc	ms	קנה	888		get,buy
	יצא	qal	impf	3ms	יצא	422		go out
25:31	יחשׁב	niph	impf	3ms	חשׁב	362		be thought
	תהיה	qal	impf	3fs	היה	224		be,become
	יצא	qal	impf	3ms	יצא	422		go out
25:32	תהיה	qal	impf	3fs	היה	224		be,become
25:33	יגאל	qal	impf	3ms	גאל	145		redeem
	יצא	qal	wcp	3ms	יצא	422		go out
25:34	ימכר	niph	impf	3ms	מכר	569		be sold

ChVs	Form	Stem	Tnse	PGN	Root	BDB	Sfx	Meaning
25:35	ימוך	qal	impf	3ms	מוך	557		be low,poor
	מטה	qal	wcp	3fs	מוט	556		totter
	החזקת	hiph	wcp	2ms	חזק	304		make firm,seize
	חי	qal	wcp	3ms	חיה	310		live
25:36	תקח	qal	jusm	2ms	לקח	542		take
	יראת	qal	wcp	2ms	ירא	431		fear
	חי	qal	wcp	3ms	חיה	310		live
25:37	תתן	qal	impf	2ms	נתן	678		give,set
	תתן	qal	impf	2ms	נתן	678		give,set
25:38	הוצאתי	hiph	pft	1cs	יצא	422		bring out
	תת	qal	infc		נתן	678		give,set
	היות	qal	infc		היה	224		be,become
25:39	ימוך	qal	impf	3ms	מוך	557		be low,poor
	נמכר	niph	wcp	3ms	מכר	569		be sold
	תעבד	qal	impf	2ms	עבד	712		work,serve
25:40	יהיה	qal	impf	3ms	היה	224		be,become
	יעבד	qal	impf	3ms	עבד	712		work,serve
25:41	יצא	qal	wcp	3ms	יצא	422		go out
	שׁב	qal	wcp	3ms	שׁוב	996		turn,return
	ישׁוב	qal	impf	3ms	שׁוב	996		turn,return
25:42	הוצאתי	hiph	pft	1cs	יצא	422		bring out
	ימכרו	niph	impf	3mp	מכר	569		be sold
25:43	תרדה	qal	impf	2ms	רדה	921		rule
	יראת	qal	wcp	2ms	ירא	431		fear
25:44	יהיו	qal	impf	3mp	היה	224		be,become
	תקנו	qal	impf	2mp	קנה	888		get,buy
25:45	גרים	qal	ptc	mp	גור	157		sojourn
	תקנו	qal	impf	2mp	קנה	888		get,buy
	הולידו	hiph	pft	3cp	ילד	408		beget
	היו	qal	wcp	3cp	היה	224		be,become
25:46	התנחלתם	hith	wcp	2mp	נחל	635		possess oneself
	רשׁת	qal	infc		ירשׁ	439		possess,inherit
	תעבדו	qal	impf	2mp	עבד	712		work,serve
	תרדה	qal	impf	2ms	רדה	921		rule
25:47	תשׂיג	hiph	impf	3fs	נשׂג	673		reach,overtake
	מך	qal	wcp	3ms	מוך	557		be low,poor
	נמכר	niph	wcp	3ms	מכר	569		be sold
25:48	נמכר	niph	pft	3ms	מכר	569		be sold
	תהיה	qal	impf	3fs	היה	224		be,become
	יגאלנו	qal	impf	3ms	גאל	145	3ms	redeem
25:49	יגאלנו	qal	impf	3ms	גאל	145	3ms	redeem
	יגאלנו	qal	impf	3ms	גאל	145	3ms	redeem
	השׂיגה	hiph	pft	3fs	נשׂג	673		reach,overtake
	נגאל	niph	wcp	3ms	גאל	145		be redeemed
25:50	חשׁב	piel	wcp	3ms	חשׁב	362		devise
	קנהו	qal	ptc	ms	קנה	888	3ms	get,buy
	המכרו	niph	infc		מכר	569	3ms	be sold
	היה	qal	wcp	3ms	היה	224		be,become
	יהיה	qal	impf	3ms	היה	224		be,become
25:51	ישׁיב	hiph	impf	3ms	שׁוב	996		bring back
25:52	נשׁאר	niph	pft	3ms	שׁאר	983		be left
	חשׁב	piel	wcp	3ms	חשׁב	362		devise
	ישׁיב	hiph	impf	3ms	שׁוב	996		bring back
25:53	יהיה	qal	impf	3ms	היה	224		be,become
25:53	ירדנו	qal	impf	3ms	רדה	921	3ms	rule
25:54	יגאל	niph	impf	3ms	גאל	145		be redeemed
	יצא	qal	wcp	3ms	יצא	422		go out
25:55	הוצאתי	hiph	pft	1cs	יצא	422		bring out
26:1	תעשׂו	qal	impf	2mp	עשׂה	793		do,make
	תקימו	hiph	impf	2mp	קום	877		raise,build,set
	תתנו	qal	impf	2mp	נתן	678		give,set
	השׁתחות	hish	infc		חוה	1005		bow down
26:2	תשׁמרו	qal	impf	2mp	שׁמר	1036		keep,watch
	תיראו	qal	impf	2mp	ירא	431		fear
26:3	תלכו	qal	impf	2mp	הלך	229		walk,go
	תשׁמרו	qal	impf	2mp	שׁמר	1036		keep,watch
	עשׂיתם	qal	wcp	2mp	עשׂה	793		do,make
26:4	נתתי	qal	wcp	1cs	נתן	678		give,set
	נתנה	qal	wcp	3fs	נתן	678		give,set
	יתן	qal	impf	3ms	נתן	678		give,set
26:5	השׂיג	hiph	wcp	3ms	נשׂג	673		reach,overtake
	ישׂיג	hiph	impf	3ms	נשׂג	673		reach,overtake
	אכלתם	qal	wcp	2mp	אכל	37		eat,devour
	ישׁבתם	qal	wcp	2mp	ישׁב	442		sit,dwell
26:6	נתתי	qal	wcp	1cs	נתן	678		give,set
	שׁכבתם	qal	wcp	2mp	שׁכב	1011		lie,lie down
	מחריד	hiph	ptc	ms	חרד	353		terrify
	השׁבתי	hiph	wcp	1cs	שׁבת	991		destroy,remove
	תעבר	qal	impf	3fs	עבר	716		pass over
26:7	רדפתם	qal	wcp	2mp	רדף	922		pursue
	איביכם	qal	ptc	mp	איב	33	2mp	be hostile to
	נפלו	qal	wcp	3cp	נפל	656		fall
26:8	רדפו	qal	wcp	3cp	רדף	922		pursue
	ירדפו	qal	impf	3mp	רדף	922		pursue
	נפלו	qal	wcp	3cp	נפל	656		fall
	איביכם	qal	ptc	mp	איב	33	2mp	be hostile to
26:9	פניתי	qal	wcp	1cs	פנה	815		turn
	הפריתי	hiph	wcp	1cs	פרה	826		make fruitful
	הרביתי	hiph	wcp	1cs	רבה	915		make many
	הקימתי	hiph	wcp	1cs	קום	877		raise,build,set
26:10	אכלתם	qal	wcp	2mp	אכל	37		eat,devour
	נושן	niph	ptc	ms	ישן	445		be old
	תוציאו	hiph	impf	2mp	יצא	422		bring out
26:11	נתתי	qal	wcp	1cs	נתן	678		give,set
	תגעל	qal	impf	3fs	געל	171		abhor,loathe
26:12	התהלכתי	hith	wcp	1cs	הלך	229		walk to and fro
	הייתי	qal	wcp	1cs	היה	224		be,become
	תהיו	qal	impf	2mp	היה	224		be,become
26:13	הוצאתי	hiph	pft	1cs	יצא	422		bring out
	הית	qal	infc		היה	224		be,become
	אשׁבר	qal	wci	1cs	שׁבר	990		break
	אולך	hiph	wci	1cs	הלך	229		lead,bring
26:14	תשׁמעו	qal	impf	2mp	שׁמע	1033		hear
	תעשׂו	qal	impf	2mp	עשׂה	793		do,make
26:15	תמאסו	qal	impf	2mp	מאס	549		reject,refuse
	תגעל	qal	impf	3fs	געל	171		abhor,loathe
	עשׂות	qal	infc		עשׂה	793		do,make
	הפרכם	hiph	infc		פרר	830	2mp	break,frustrate

ChVs	Form	Stem	Tnse	PGN	Root	BDB	Sfx	Meaning
26:16	אעשה	qal	impf	1cs	עשה	793		do,make
	הפקדתי	hiph	wcp	1cs	פקד	823		set,entrust
	מכלות	piel	ptc	fp	כלה	477		complete,finish
	מדיבת	hiph	ptc	fp	דוב	187		pine away
	זרעתם	qal	wcp	2mp	זרע	281		sow
	אכלהו	qal	wcp	3cp	אכל	37	3ms	eat,devour
	איביכם	qal	ptc	mp	איב	33	2mp	be hostile to
26:17	נתתי	qal	wcp	1cs	נתן	678		give,set
	נגפתם	niph	wcp	2mp	נגף	619		be smitten
	איביכם	qal	ptc	mp	איב	33	2mp	be hostile to
	רדו	qal	wcp	3cp	רדה	921		rule
	שנאיכם	qal	ptc	mp	שנא	971	2mp	hate
	נסתם	qal	wcp	2mp	נוס	630		flee,escape
	רדף	qal	ptc	ms	רדף	922		pursue
26:18	תשמעו	qal	impf	2mp	שמע	1033		hear
	יספתי	qal	wcp	1cs	יסף	414		add,increase
	יסרה	piel	infc		יסר	415		correct,chasten
26:19	שברתי	qal	wcp	1cs	שבר	990		break
	נתתי	qal	wcp	1cs	נתן	678		give,set
26:20	תם	qal	wcp	3ms	תמם	1070		be finished
	תתן	qal	impf	3fs	נתן	678		give,set
	יתן	qal	impf	3ms	נתן	678		give,set
26:21	תלכו	qal	impf	2mp	הלך	229		walk,go
	תאבו	qal	impf	2mp	אבה	2		be willing
	שמע	qal	infc		שמע	1033		hear
	יספתי	qal	wcp	1cs	יסף	414		add,increase
26:22	השלחתי	hiph	wcp	1cs	שלח	1018		send
	שכלה	piel	wcp	3fs	שכל	1013		make childless
	הכריתה	hiph	wcp	3fs	כרת	503		cut off,destroy
	המעיטה	hiph	wcp	3fs	מעט	589		make small
	נשמו	niph	wcp	3cp	שמם	1030		be desolate
26:23	תוסרו	niph	impf	2mp	יסר	415		be corrected
	הלכתם	qal	wcp	2mp	הלך	229		walk,go
26:24	הלכתי	qal	wcp	1cs	הלך	229		walk,go
	הכיתי	hiph	wcp	1cs	נכה	645		smite
26:25	הבאתי	hiph	wcp	1cs	בוא	97		bring in
	נקמת	qal	ptc	fs	נקם	667		avenge
	נאספתם	niph	wcp	2mp	אסף	62		assemble
	שלחתי	piel	wcp	1cs	שלח	1018		send away,shoot
	נתתם	niph	wcp	2mp	נתן	678		be given
	אויב	qal	ptc	ms	איב	33		be hostile to
26:26	שברי	qal	infc		שבר	990	1cs	break
	אפו	qal	wcp	3cp	אפה	66		bake
	השיבו	hiph	wcp	3cp	שוב	996		bring back
	אכלתם	qal	wcp	2mp	אכל	37		eat,devour
	תשבעו	qal	impf	2mp	שבע	959		be sated
26:27	תשמעו	qal	impf	2mp	שמע	1033		hear
	הלכתם	qal	wcp	2mp	הלך	229		walk,go
26:28	הלכתי	qal	wcp	1cs	הלך	229		walk,go
	יסרתי	piel	wcp	1cs	יסר	415		correct,chasten
26:29	אכלתם	qal	wcp	2mp	אכל	37		eat,devour
	תאכלו	qal	impf	2mp	אכל	37		eat,devour
26:30	השמדתי	hiph	wcp	1cs	שמד	1029		exterminate
	הכרתי	hiph	wcp	1cs	כרת	503		cut off,destroy
26:30	נתתי	qal	wcp	1cs	נתן	678		give,set
	געלה	qal	wcp	3fs	געל	171		abhor,loathe
26:31	נתתי	qal	wcp	1cs	נתן	678		give,set
	השמותי	hiph	wcp	1cs	שמם	1030		ravage,appall
	אריח	hiph	impf	1cs	ריח	926		smell
26:32	השמתי	hiph	wcp	1cs	שמם	1030		ravage,appall
	שממו	qal	wcp	3cp	שמם	1030		be desolate
	איביכם	qal	ptc	mp	איב	33	2mp	be hostile to
	ישבים	qal	ptc	mp	ישב	442		sit,dwell
26:33	אזרה	piel	impf	1cs	זרה	279		scatter
	הריקתי	hiph	wcp	1cs	ריק	937		make empty
	היתה	qal	wcp	3fs	היה	224		be,become
	יהיו	qal	impf	3mp	היה	224		be,become
26:34	תרצה	qal	impf	3fs	רצה	953		be pleased
	השמה	hoph	infc		שמם	1030	3fs	be desolate
	איביכם	qal	ptc	mp	איב	33	2mp	be hostile to
	תשבת	qal	impf	3fs	שבת	991		cease,desist
	הרצת	hiph	wcp	3fs	רצה	953		pay off
26:35	השמה	hoph	infc		שמם	1030	3fs	be desolate
	תשבת	qal	impf	3fs	שבת	991		cease,desist
	שבתה	qal	pft	3fs	שבת	991		cease,desist
	שבתכם	qal	infc		ישב	442	2mp	sit,dwell
26:36	נשארים	niph	ptc	mp	שאר	983		be left
	הבאתי	hiph	wcp	1cs	בוא	97		bring in
	איביהם	qal	ptc	mp	איב	33	3mp	be hostile to
	רדף	qal	wcp	3ms	רדף	922		pursue
	נדף	niph	ptc	ms	נדף	623		be driven about
	נסו	qal	wcp	3cp	נוס	630		flee,escape
	נפלו	qal	wcp	3cp	נפל	656		fall
	רדף	qal	ptc	ms	רדף	922		pursue
26:37	כשלו	qal	wcp	3cp	כשל	505		stumble,totter
	רדף	qal	ptc	ms	רדף	922		pursue
	תהיה	qal	impf	3fs	היה	224		be,become
	איביכם	qal	ptc	mp	איב	33	2mp	be hostile to
26:38	אבדתם	qal	wcp	2mp	אבד	1		perish
	אכלה	qal	wcp	3fs	אכל	37		eat,devour
	איביכם	qal	ptc	mp	איב	33	2mp	be hostile to
26:39	נשארים	niph	ptc	mp	שאר	983		be left
	ימקו	niph	impf	3mp	מקק	596		rot,decay
	איביכם	qal	ptc	mp	איב	33	2mp	be hostile to
	ימקו	niph	impf	3mp	מקק	596		rot,decay
26:40	התודו	hith	wcp	3cp	ידה	392		confess
	מעלו	qal	pft	3cp	מעל	591		act faithlessly
	הלכו	qal	pft	3cp	הלך	229		walk,go
26:41	אלך	qal	impf	1cs	הלך	229		walk,go
	הבאתי	hiph	wcp	1cs	בוא	97		bring in
	איביהם	qal	ptc	mp	איב	33	3mp	be hostile to
	יכנע	niph	impf	3ms	כנע	488		humble self
	ירצו	qal	impf	3mp	רצה	953		be pleased
26:42	זכרתי	qal	wcp	1cs	זכר	269		remember
	אזכר	qal	impf	1cs	זכר	269		remember
	אזכר	qal	impf	1cs	זכר	269		remember
26:43	תעזב	niph	impf	3fs	עזב	736		be left
	תרץ	qal	jus	3fs	רצה	953		be pleased

ChVs	Form	Stem	Tnse	PGN	Root	BDB	Sfx	Meaning
26: 43	השמה	hoph	infc		שמם	1030	3fs	be desolate
	ירצו	qal	impf	3mp	רצה	953		be pleased
	מאסו	qal	pft	3cp	מאס	549		reject,refuse
	געלה	qal	pft	3fs	געל	171		abhor,loathe
26: 44	היותם	qal	infc		היה	224	3mp	be,become
	איביהם	qal	ptc	mp	איב	33	3mp	be hostile to
	מאסתים	qal	pft	1cs	מאס	549	3mp	reject,refuse
	געלתים	qal	pft	1cs	געל	171	3mp	abhor,loathe
	כלתם	piel	infc		כלה	477	3mp	complete,finish
	הפר	hiph	infc		פרר	830		break,frustrate
26: 45	זכרתי	qal	wcp	1cs	זכר	269		remember
	הוצאתי	hiph	pft	1cs	יצא	422		bring out
	הית	qal	infc		היה	224		be,become
26: 46	נתן	qal	pft	3ms	נתן	678		give,set
27: 1	ידבר	piel	wci	3ms	דבר	180		speak
	אמר	qal	infc		אמר	55		say
27: 2	דבר	piel	impv	ms	דבר	180		speak
	אמרת	qal	wcp	2ms	אמר	55		say
	יפלא	hiph	impf	3ms	פלא	810		do wondrously
27: 3	היה	qal	wcp	3ms	היה	224		be,become
	היה	qal	wcp	3ms	היה	224		be,become
27: 4	היה	qal	wcp	3ms	היה	224		be,become
27: 5	היה	qal	wcp	3ms	היה	224		be,become
27: 6	היה	qal	wcp	3ms	היה	224		be,become
27: 7	היה	qal	wcp	3ms	היה	224		be,become
27: 8	מך	qal	ptc	ms	מוך	557		be low,poor
	העמידו	hiph	wcp	3ms	עמד	763	3ms	set up,raise
	העריך	hiph	wcp	3ms	ערך	790		value,tax
	תשיג	hiph	impf	3fs	נשג	673		reach,overtake
	נדר	qal	ptc	ms	נדר	623		vow
	יעריכנו	hiph	impf	3ms	ערך	790	3ms	value,tax
27: 9	יקריבו	hiph	impf	3mp	קרב	897		bring near
	יתן	qal	impf	3ms	נתן	678		give,set
	יהיה	qal	impf	3ms	היה	224		be,become
27: 10	יחליפנו	hiph	impf	3ms	חלף	322	3ms	change
	ימיר	hiph	impf	3ms	מור	558		change
	המר	hiph	infa		מור	558		change
	ימיר	hiph	impf	3ms	מור	558		change
	היה	qal	wcp	3ms	היה	224		be,become
	יהיה	qal	impf	3ms	היה	224		be,become
27: 11	יקריבו	hiph	impf	3mp	קרב	897		bring near
	העמיד	hiph	wcp	3ms	עמד	763		set up,raise
27: 12	העריך	hiph	wcp	3ms	ערך	790		value,tax
	יהיה	qal	impf	3ms	היה	224		be,become
27: 13	גאל	qal	infa		גאל	145		redeem
	יגאלנה	qal	impf	3ms	גאל	145	3fs	redeem
	יסף	qal	wcp	3ms	יסף	414		add,increase
27: 14	יקדש	hiph	impf	3ms	קדש	872		consecrate
	העריכו	hiph	wcp	3ms	ערך	790	3ms	value,tax
	יעריך	hiph	impf	3ms	ערך	790		value,tax
	יקום	qal	impf	3ms	קום	877		arise,stand
27: 15	מקדיש	hiph	ptc	ms	קדש	872		consecrate
	יגאל	qal	impf	3ms	גאל	145		redeem
	יסף	qal	wcp	3ms	יסף	414		add,increase
27: 15	היה	qal	wcp	3ms	היה	224		be,become
27: 16	יקדיש	hiph	impf	3ms	קדש	872		consecrate
	היה	qal	wcp	3ms	היה	224		be,become
27: 17	יקדיש	hiph	impf	3ms	קדש	872		consecrate
	יקום	qal	impf	3ms	קום	877		arise,stand
27: 18	יקדיש	hiph	impf	3ms	קדש	872		consecrate
	חשב	piel	wcp	3ms	חשב	362		devise
	נותרת	niph	ptc	fp	יתר	451		be left,remain
	נגרע	niph	wcp	3ms	גרע	175		be withdrawn
27: 19	גאל	qal	infa		גאל	145		redeem
	יגאל	qal	impf	3ms	גאל	145		redeem
	מקדיש	hiph	ptc	ms	קדש	872		consecrate
	יסף	qal	wcp	3ms	יסף	414		add,increase
	קם	qal	wcp	3ms	קום	877		arise,stand
27: 20	יגאל	qal	impf	3ms	גאל	145		redeem
	מכר	qal	pft	3ms	מכר	569		sell
	יגאל	niph	impf	3ms	גאל	145		be redeemed
27: 21	היה	qal	wcp	3ms	היה	224		be,become
	צאתו	qal	infc		יצא	422	3ms	go out
	תהיה	qal	impf	3fs	היה	224		be,become
27: 22	יקדיש	hiph	impf	3ms	קדש	872		consecrate
27: 23	חשב	piel	wcp	3ms	חשב	362		devise
	נתן	qal	wcp	3ms	נתן	678		give,set
27: 24	ישוב	qal	impf	3ms	שוב	996		turn,return
	קנהו	qal	pft	3ms	קנה	888	3ms	get,buy
27: 25	יהיה	qal	impf	3ms	היה	224		be,become
	יהיה	qal	impf	3ms	היה	224		be,become
27: 26	יבכר	pual	impf	3ms	בכר	114		born firstling
	יקדיש	hiph	impf	3ms	קדש	872		consecrate
27: 27	פדה	qal	wcp	3ms	פדה	804		ransom
	יסף	qal	wcp	3ms	יסף	414		add,increase
	יגאל	niph	impf	3ms	גאל	145		be redeemed
	נמכר	niph	wcp	3ms	מכר	569		be sold
27: 28	יחרם	hiph	impf	3ms	חרם	355		ban,destroy
	ימכר	niph	impf	3ms	מכר	569		be sold
	יגאל	niph	impf	3ms	גאל	145		be redeemed
27: 29	יחרם	hoph	impf	3ms	חרם	355		be banned
	יפדה	niph	impf	3ms	פדה	804		be ransomed
	מות	qal	infa		מות	559		die
	יומת	hoph	impf	3ms	מות	559		be killed
27: 31	גאל	qal	infa		גאל	145		redeem
	יגאל	qal	impf	3ms	גאל	145		redeem
	יסף	hiph	jus	3ms	יסף	414		add,do again
27: 32	יעבר	qal	impf	3ms	עבר	716		pass over
	יהיה	qal	impf	3ms	היה	224		be,become
27: 33	יבקר	piel	impf	3ms	בקר	133		seek,inquire
	ימירנו	hiph	impf	3ms	מור	558	3ms	change
	המר	hiph	infa		מור	558		change
	ימירנו	hiph	impf	3ms	מור	558	3ms	change
	היה	qal	wcp	3ms	היה	224		be,become
	יהיה	qal	impf	3ms	היה	224		be,become
	יגאל	niph	impf	3ms	גאל	145		be redeemed
27: 34	צוה	piel	pft	3ms	צוה	845		command

ChVs	Form	Stem	Tnse	PGN	Root	BDB	Sfx	Meaning
NUMBERS								
1:1	ידבר	piel	wci	3ms	דבר	180		speak
	צאתם	qal	infc		יצא	422	3mp	go out
	אמר	qal	infc		אמר	55		say
1:2	שׂאו	qal	impv	mp	נשׂא	669		lift,carry
1:3	יצא	qal	ptc	ms	יצא	422		go out
	תפקדו	qal	impf	2mp	פקד	823		attend to,visit
1:4	יהיו	qal	impf	3mp	היה	224		be,become
1:5	יעמדו	qal	impf	3mp	עמד	763		stand,stop
1:16	קרואיq	qal	pptc	mp	קרא	894		call,proclaim
1:17	יקח	qal	wci	3ms	לקח	542		take
	נקבו	niph	pft	3cp	נקב	666		be marked
1:18	הקהילו	hiph	pft	3cp	קהל	874		call assembly
	יתילדו	hith	wci	3mp	ילד	408		be registered
1:19	צוה	piel	pft	3ms	צוה	845		command
	יפקדם	qal	wci	3ms	פקד	823	3mp	attend to,visit
1:20	יהיו	qal	wci	3mp	היה	224		be,become
	יצא	qal	ptc	ms	יצא	422		go out
1:21	פקדיהם	qal	pptc	mp	פקד	823	3mp	attend to,visit
1:22	פקדיו	qal	pptc	mp	פקד	823	3ms	attend to,visit
	יצא	qal	ptc	ms	יצא	422		go out
1:23	פקדיהם	qal	pptc	mp	פקד	823	3mp	attend to,visit
1:24	יצא	qal	ptc	ms	יצא	422		go out
1:25	פקדיהם	qal	pptc	mp	פקד	823	3mp	attend to,visit
1:26	יצא	qal	ptc	ms	יצא	422		go out
1:27	פקדיהם	qal	pptc	mp	פקד	823	3mp	attend to,visit
1:28	יצא	qal	ptc	ms	יצא	422		go out
1:29	פקדיהם	qal	pptc	mp	פקד	823	3mp	attend to,visit
1:30	יצא	qal	ptc	ms	יצא	422		go out
1:31	פקדיהם	qal	pptc	mp	פקד	823	3mp	attend to,visit
1:32	יצא	qal	ptc	ms	יצא	422		go out
1:33	פקדיהם	qal	pptc	mp	פקד	823	3mp	attend to,visit
1:34	יצא	qal	ptc	ms	יצא	422		go out
1:35	פקדיהם	qal	pptc	mp	פקד	823	3mp	attend to,visit
1:36	יצא	qal	ptc	ms	יצא	422		go out
1:37	פקדיהם	qal	pptc	mp	פקד	823	3mp	attend to,visit
1:38	יצא	qal	ptc	ms	יצא	422		go out
1:39	פקדיהם	qal	pptc	mp	פקד	823	3mp	attend to,visit
1:40	יצא	qal	ptc	ms	יצא	422		go out
1:41	פקדיהם	qal	pptc	mp	פקד	823	3mp	attend to,visit
1:42	יצא	qal	ptc	ms	יצא	422		go out
1:43	פקדיהם	qal	pptc	mp	פקד	823	3mp	attend to,visit
1:44	פקדים	qal	pptc	mp	פקד	823		attend to,visit
	פקד	qal	pft	3ms	פקד	823		attend to,visit
	היו	qal	pft	3cp	היה	224		be,become
1:45	יהיו	qal	wci	3mp	היה	224		be,become
	פקודי	qal	pptc	mp	פקד	823		attend to,visit
	יצא	qal	ptc	ms	יצא	422		go out
1:46	יהיו	qal	wci	3mp	היה	224		be,become
	פקדים	qal	pptc	mp	פקד	823		attend to,visit
1:47	התפקדו	hoth	pft	3cp	פקד	823		be mustered
1:48	ידבר	piel	wci	3ms	דבר	180		speak
	אמר	qal	infc		אמר	55		say
1:49	תפקד	qal	impf	2ms	פקד	823		attend to,visit
1:49	תשׂא	qal	impf	2ms	נשׂא	669		lift,carry
1:50	הפקד	hiph	impv	ms	פקד	823		set,entrust
	ישׂאו	qal	impf	3mp	נשׂא	669		lift,carry
	ישׁרתהו	piel	impf	3mp	שׁרת	1058	3ms	minister,serve
	יחנו	qal	impf	3mp	חנה	333		decline,encamp
1:51	נסע	qal	infc		נסע	652		pull up,set out
	יורידו	hiph	impf	3mp	ירד	432		bring down
	חנת	qal	infc		חנה	333		decline,encamp
	יקימו	hiph	impf	3mp	קום	877		raise,build,set
	זר	qal	ptc	ms	זור	266		be stranger
	יומת	hoph	impf	3ms	מות	559		be killed
1:52	חנו	qal	wcp	3cp	חנה	333		decline,encamp
1:53	יחנו	qal	impf	3mp	חנה	333		decline,encamp
	יהיה	qal	impf	3ms	היה	224		be,become
	שׁמרו	qal	wcp	3cp	שׁמר	1036		keep,watch
1:54	יעשׂו	qal	wci	3mp	עשׂה	793		do,make
	צוה	piel	pft	3ms	צוה	845		command
	עשׂו	qal	pft	3cp	עשׂה	793		do,make
2:1	ידבר	piel	wci	3ms	דבר	180		speak
	אמר	qal	infc		אמר	55		say
2:2	יחנו	qal	impf	3mp	חנה	333		decline,encamp
	יחנו	qal	impf	3mp	חנה	333		decline,encamp
2:3	חנים	qal	ptc	mp	חנה	333		decline,encamp
2:4	פקדיהם	qal	pptc	mp	פקד	823	3mp	attend to,visit
2:5	חנים	qal	ptc	mp	חנה	333		decline,encamp
2:6	פקדיו	qal	pptc	mp	פקד	823	3ms	attend to,visit
2:8	פקדיו	qal	pptc	mp	פקד	823	3ms	attend to,visit
2:9	פקדים	qal	pptc	mp	פקד	823		attend to,visit
	יסעו	qal	impf	3mp	נסע	652		pull up,set out
2:11	פקדיו	qal	pptc	mp	פקד	823	3ms	attend to,visit
2:12	חונם	qal	ptc	mp	חנה	333		decline,encamp
2:13	פקדיהם	qal	pptc	mp	פקד	823	3mp	attend to,visit
2:15	פקדיהם	qal	pptc	mp	פקד	823	3mp	attend to,visit
2:16	פקדים	qal	pptc	mp	פקד	823		attend to,visit
	יסעו	qal	impf	3mp	נסע	652		pull up,set out
2:17	נסע	qal	wcp	3ms	נסע	652		pull up,set out
	יחנו	qal	impf	3mp	חנה	333		decline,encamp
	יסעו	qal	impf	3mp	נסע	652		pull up,set out
2:19	פקדיהם	qal	pptc	mp	פקד	823	3mp	attend to,visit
2:21	פקדיהם	qal	pptc	mp	פקד	823	3mp	attend to,visit
2:23	פקדיהם	qal	pptc	mp	פקד	823	3mp	attend to,visit
2:24	פקדים	qal	pptc	mp	פקד	823		attend to,visit
	יסעו	qal	impf	3mp	נסע	652		pull up,set out
2:26	פקדיהם	qal	pptc	mp	פקד	823	3mp	attend to,visit
2:27	חנים	qal	ptc	mp	חנה	333		decline,encamp
2:28	פקדיהם	qal	pptc	mp	פקד	823	3mp	attend to,visit
2:30	פקדיהם	qal	pptc	mp	פקד	823	3mp	attend to,visit
2:31	פקדים	qal	pptc	mp	פקד	823		attend to,visit
	יסעו	qal	impf	3mp	נסע	652		pull up,set out
2:32	פקודי	qal	pptc	mp	פקד	823		attend to,visit
	פקודי	qal	pptc	mp	פקד	823		attend to,visit
2:33	התפקדו	hoth	pft	3cp	פקד	823		be mustered
	צוה	piel	pft	3ms	צוה	845		command
2:34	יעשׂו	qal	wci	3mp	עשׂה	793		do,make

ChVs	Form	Stem	Tnse	PGN	Root	BDB	Sfx	Meaning
2:34	צוה	piel	pft	3ms	צוה	845		command
	חנו	qal	pft	3cp	חנה	333		decline,encamp
	נסעו	qal	pft	3cp	נסע	652		pull up,set out
3:1	דבר	piel	pft	3ms	דבר	180		speak
3:3	משחים	qal	pptc	mp	משח	602		smear,anoint
	מלא	piel	pft	3ms	מלא	569		fill
	כהן	piel	infc		כהן	464		act as priest
3:4	ימת	qal	wci	3ms	מות	559		die
	הקרבם	hiph	infc		קרב	897	3mp	bring near
	זרה	qal	ptc	fs	זור	266		be stranger
	היו	qal	pft	3cp	היה	224		be,become
	יכהן	piel	wci	3ms	כהן	464		act as priest
3:5	ידבר	piel	wci	3ms	דבר	180		speak
	אמר	qal	infc		אמר	55		say
3:6	הקרב	hiph	impv	ms	קרב	897		bring near
	העמדת	hiph	wcp	2ms	עמד	763		set up,raise
	שׁרתו	piel	wcp	3cp	שׁרת	1058		minister,serve
3:7	שׁמרו	qal	wcp	3cp	שׁמר	1036		keep,watch
	עבד	qal	infc		עבד	712		work,serve
3:8	שׁמרו	qal	wcp	3cp	שׁמר	1036		keep,watch
	עבד	qal	infc		עבד	712		work,serve
3:9	נתתה	qal	wcp	2ms	נתן	678		give,set
	נתונם	qal	pptc	mp	נתן	678		give,set
	נתונם	qal	pptc	mp	נתן	678		give,set
3:10	תפקד	qal	impf	2ms	פקד	823		attend to,visit
	שׁמרו	qal	wcp	3cp	שׁמר	1036		keep,watch
	זר	qal	ptc	ms	זור	266		be stranger
	יומת	hoph	impf	3ms	מות	559		be killed
3:11	ידבר	piel	wci	3ms	דבר	180		speak
	אמר	qal	infc		אמר	55		say
3:12	לקחתי	qal	pft	1cs	לקח	542		take
	היו	qal	wcp	3cp	היה	224		be,become
3:13	הכתי	hiph	infc		נכה	645	1cs	smite
	הקדשׁתי	hiph	pft	1cs	קדשׁ	872		consecrate
	יהיו	qal	impf	3mp	היה	224		be,become
3:14	ידבר	piel	wci	3ms	דבר	180		speak
	אמר	qal	infc		אמר	55		say
3:15	פקד	qal	impv	ms	פקד	823		attend to,visit
	תפקדם	qal	impf	2ms	פקד	823	3mp	attend to,visit
3:16	יפקד	qal	wci	3ms	פקד	823		attend to,visit
	צוה	pual	pft	3ms	צוה	845		be commanded
3:17	יהיו	qal	wci	3mp	היה	224		be,become
3:22	פקדיהם	qal	pptc	mp	פקד	823	3mp	attend to,visit
	פקדיהם	qal	pptc	mp	פקד	823	3mp	attend to,visit
3:23	יחנו	qal	impf	3mp	חנה	333		decline,encamp
3:28	שׁמרי	qal	ptc	mp	שׁמר	1036		keep,watch
3:29	יחנו	qal	impf	3mp	חנה	333		decline,encamp
3:31	ישׁרתו	piel	impf	3mp	שׁרת	1058		minister,serve
3:32	שׁמרי	qal	ptc	mp	שׁמר	1036		keep,watch
3:34	פקדיהם	qal	pptc	mp	פקד	823	3mp	attend to,visit
3:35	יחנו	qal	impf	3mp	חנה	333		decline,encamp
3:38	חנים	qal	ptc	mp	חנה	333		decline,encamp
	שׁמרים	qal	ptc	mp	שׁמר	1036		keep,watch
	זר	qal	ptc	ms	זור	266		be stranger

ChVs	Form	Stem	Tnse	PGN	Root	BDB	Sfx	Meaning
3:38	יומת	hoph	impf	3ms	מות	559		be killed
3:39	פקודי	qal	pptc	mp	פקד	823		attend to,visit
	פקד	qal	pft	3ms	פקד	823		attend to,visit
3:40	יאמר	qal	wci	3ms	אמר	55		say
	פקד	qal	impv	ms	פקד	823		attend to,visit
	שׂא	qal	impv	ms	נשׂא	669		lift,carry
3:41	לקחת	qal	wcp	2ms	לקח	542		take
3:42	יפקד	qal	wci	3ms	פקד	823		attend to,visit
	צוה	piel	pft	3ms	צוה	845		command
3:43	יהי	qal	wci	3ms	היה	224		be,become
	פקדיהם	qal	pptc	mp	פקד	823	3mp	attend to,visit
3:44	ידבר	piel	wci	3ms	דבר	180		speak
	אמר	qal	infc		אמר	55		say
3:45	קח	qal	impv	ms	לקח	542		take
	היו	qal	wcp	3cp	היה	224		be,become
3:46	עדפים	qal	ptc	mp	עדף	727		remain over
3:47	לקחת	qal	wcp	2ms	לקח	542		take
	תקח	qal	impf	2ms	לקח	542		take
3:48	נתתה	qal	wcp	2ms	נתן	678		give,set
	עדפים	qal	ptc	mp	עדף	727		remain over
3:49	יקח	qal	wci	3ms	לקח	542		take
	עדפים	qal	ptc	mp	עדף	727		remain over
3:50	לקח	qal	pft	3ms	לקח	542		take
3:51	יתן	qal	wci	3ms	נתן	678		give,set
	צוה	piel	pft	3ms	צוה	845		command
4:1	ידבר	piel	wci	3ms	דבר	180		speak
	אמר	qal	infc		אמר	55		say
4:2	נשׂא	qal	infa		נשׂא	669		lift,carry
4:3	בא	qal	ptc	ms	בוא	97		come in
	עשׂות	qal	infc		עשׂה	793		do,make
4:5	בא	qal	wcp	3ms	בוא	97		come in
	נסע	qal	infc		נסע	652		pull up,set out
	הורדו	hiph	wcp	3cp	ירד	432		bring down
	כסו	piel	wcp	3cp	כסה	491		cover
4:6	נתנו	qal	wcp	3cp	נתן	678		give,set
	פרשׂו	qal	wcp	3cp	פרשׂ	831		spread out
	שׂמו	qal	wcp	3cp	שׂים	962		put,set
4:7	יפרשׂו	qal	impf	3mp	פרשׂ	831		spread out
	נתנו	qal	wcp	3cp	נתן	678		give,set
	יהיה	qal	impf	3ms	היה	224		be,become
4:8	פרשׂו	qal	wcp	3cp	פרשׂ	831		spread out
	כסו	piel	wcp	3cp	כסה	491		cover
	שׂמו	qal	wcp	3cp	שׂים	962		put,set
4:9	לקחו	qal	wcp	3cp	לקח	542		take
	כסו	piel	wcp	3cp	כסה	491		cover
	ישׁרתו	piel	impf	3mp	שׁרת	1058		minister,serve
4:10	נתנו	qal	wcp	3cp	נתן	678		give,set
	נתנו	qal	wcp	3cp	נתן	678		give,set
4:11	יפרשׂו	qal	impf	3mp	פרשׂ	831		spread out
	כסו	piel	wcp	3cp	כסה	491		cover
	שׂמו	qal	wcp	3cp	שׂים	962		put,set
4:12	לקחו	qal	wcp	3cp	לקח	542		take
	ישׁרתו	piel	impf	3mp	שׁרת	1058		minister,serve
	נתנו	qal	wcp	3cp	נתן	678		give,set

ChVs	Form	Stem	Tnse	PGN	Root	BDB	Sfx	Meaning
4:12	כסו	piel	wcp	3cp	כסה	491		cover
	נתנו	qal	wcp	3cp	נתן	678		give,set
4:13	דשנו	piel	wcp	3cp	דשן	206		make fat
	פרשו	qal	wcp	3cp	פרש	831		spread out
4:14	נתנו	qal	wcp	3cp	נתן	678		give,set
	ישרתו	piel	impf	3mp	שרת	1058		minister,serve
	פרשו	qal	wcp	3cp	פרש	831		spread out
	שמו	qal	wcp	3cp	שים	962		put,set
4:15	כלה	piel	wcp	3ms	כלה	477		complete,finish
	כסת	piel	infc		כסה	491		cover
	נסע	qal	infc		נסע	652		pull up,set out
	יבאו	qal	impf	3mp	בוא	97		come in
	שאת	qal	infc		נשא	669		lift,carry
	יגעו	qal	impf	3mp	נגע	619		touch,strike
	מתו	qal	wcp	3cp	מות	559		die
4:17	ידבר	piel	wci	3ms	דבר	180		speak
	אמר	qal	infc		אמר	55		say
4:18	תכריתו	hiph	jusm	2mp	כרת	503		cut off,destroy
4:19	עשו	qal	impv	mp	עשה	793		do,make
	חיו	qal	wcp	3cp	חיה	310		live
	ימתו	qal	impf	3mp	מות	559		die
	גשתם	qal	infc		נגש	620	3mp	draw near
	יבאו	qal	impf	3mp	בוא	97		come in
	שמו	qal	wcp	3cp	שים	962		put,set
4:20	יבאו	qal	impf	3mp	בוא	97		come in
	ראות	qal	infc		ראה	906		see
	בלע	piel	infc		בלע	118		swallow up
	מתו	qal	wcp	3cp	מות	559		die
4:21	ידבר	piel	wci	3ms	דבר	180		speak
	אמר	qal	infc		אמר	55		say
4:22	נשא	qal	infa		נשא	669		lift,carry
4:23	תפקד	qal	impf	2ms	פקד	823		attend to,visit
	בא	qal	ptc	ms	בוא	97		come in
	צבא	qal	infc		צבא	838		wage war
	עבד	qal	infc		עבד	712		work,serve
4:24	עבד	qal	infc		עבד	712		work,serve
4:25	נשאו	qal	wcp	3cp	נשא	669		lift,carry
4:26	יעשה	niph	impf	3ms	עשה	793		be done
	עבדו	qal	wcp	3cp	עבד	712		work,serve
4:27	תהיה	qal	impf	3fs	היה	224		be,become
	פקדתם	qal	wcp	2mp	פקד	823		attend to,visit
4:29	תפקד	qal	impf	2ms	פקד	823		attend to,visit
4:30	תפקדם	qal	impf	2ms	פקד	823	3mp	attend to,visit
	בא	qal	ptc	ms	בוא	97		come in
	עבד	qal	infc		עבד	712		work,serve
4:32	תפקדו	qal	impf	2mp	פקד	823		attend to,visit
4:34	יפקד	qal	wci	3ms	פקד	823		attend to,visit
4:35	בא	qal	ptc	ms	בוא	97		come in
4:36	יהיו	qal	wci	3mp	היה	224		be,become
	פקדיהם	qal	pptc	mp	פקד	823	3mp	attend to,visit
4:37	פקודי	qal	pptc	mp	פקד	823		attend to,visit
	עבד	qal	ptc	ms	עבד	712		work,serve
	פקד	qal	pft	3ms	פקד	823		attend to,visit
4:38	פקודי	qal	pptc	mp	פקד	823		attend to,visit

ChVs	Form	Stem	Tnse	PGN	Root	BDB	Sfx	Meaning
4:39	בא	qal	ptc	ms	בוא	97		come in
4:40	יהיו	qal	wci	3mp	היה	224		be,become
	פקדיהם	qal	pptc	mp	פקד	823	3mp	attend to,visit
4:41	פקודי	qal	pptc	mp	פקד	823		attend to,visit
	עבד	qal	ptc	ms	עבד	712		work,serve
	פקד	qal	pft	3ms	פקד	823		attend to,visit
4:42	פקודי	qal	pptc	mp	פקד	823		attend to,visit
4:43	בא	qal	ptc	ms	בוא	97		come in
4:44	יהיו	qal	wci	3mp	היה	224		be,become
	פקדיהם	qal	pptc	mp	פקד	823	3mp	attend to,visit
4:45	פקודי	qal	pptc	mp	פקד	823		attend to,visit
	פקד	qal	pft	3ms	פקד	823		attend to,visit
4:46	פקדים	qal	pptc	mp	פקד	823		attend to,visit
	פקד	qal	pft	3ms	פקד	823		attend to,visit
4:47	בא	qal	ptc	ms	בוא	97		come in
	עבד	qal	infc		עבד	712		work,serve
4:48	יהיו	qal	wci	3mp	היה	224		be,become
	פקדיהם	qal	pptc	mp	פקד	823	3mp	attend to,visit
4:49	פקד	qal	pft	3ms	פקד	823		attend to,visit
	פקדיו	qal	pptc	mp	פקד	823	3ms	attend to,visit
	צוה	piel	pft	3ms	צוה	845		command
5:1	ידבר	piel	wci	3ms	דבר	180		speak
	אמר	qal	infc		אמר	55		say
5:2	צו	piel	impv	ms	צוה	845		command
	ישלחו	piel	jusm	3mp	שלח	1018		send away,shoot
	צרוע	qal	pptc	ms	צרע	863		be leprous
	זב	qal	ptc	ms	זוב	264		flow,gush
5:3	תשלחו	piel	impf	2mp	שלח	1018		send away,shoot
	תשלחום	piel	impf	2mp	שלח	1018	3mp	send away,shoot
	יטמאו	piel	impf	3mp	טמא	379		defile
	שכן	qal	ptc	ms	שכן	1014		settle,dwell
5:4	יעשו	qal	wci	3mp	עשה	793		do,make
	ישלחו	piel	wci	3mp	שלח	1018		send away,shoot
	דבר	piel	pft	3ms	דבר	180		speak
	עשו	qal	pft	3cp	עשה	793		do,make
5:5	ידבר	piel	wci	3ms	דבר	180		speak
	אמר	qal	infc		אמר	55		say
5:6	דבר	piel	impv	ms	דבר	180		speak
	יעשו	qal	impf	3mp	עשה	793		do,make
	מעל	qal	infc		מעל	591		act faithlessly
	אשמה	qal	wcp	3fs	אשם	79		offend
5:7	התודו	hith	wcp	3cp	ידה	392		confess
	עשו	qal	pft	3cp	עשה	793		do,make
	השיב	hiph	wcp	3ms	שוב	996		bring back
	יסף	hiph	jus	3ms	יסף	414		add,do again
	נתן	qal	wcp	3ms	נתן	678		give,set
	אשם	qal	pft	3ms	אשם	79		offend
5:8	גאל	qal	ptc	ms	גאל	145		redeem
	השיב	hiph	infc		שוב	996		bring back
	מושב	hoph	ptc	ms	שוב	996		be returned
	יכפר	piel	impf	3ms	כפר	497		cover,atone
5:9	יקריבו	hiph	impf	3mp	קרב	897		bring near
	יהיה	qal	impf	3ms	היה	224		be,become
5:10	יהיו	qal	impf	3mp	היה	224		be,become

ChVs	Form	Stem	Tnse	PGN	Root	BDB	Sfx	Meaning
5: 10	יתן	qal	impf	3ms	נתן	678		give,set
	יהיה	qal	impf	3ms	היה	224		be,become
5: 11	ידבר	piel	wci	3ms	דבר	180		speak
	אמר	qal	infc		אמר	55		say
5: 12	דבר	piel	impv	ms	דבר	180		speak
	אמרת	qal	wcp	2ms	אמר	55		say
	תשטה	qal	impf	3fs	שטה	966		turn aside
	מעלה	qal	wcp	3fs	מעל	591		act faithlessly
5: 13	שכב	qal	wcp	3ms	שכב	1011		lie,lie down
	נעלם	niph	wcp	3ms	עלם	761		be concealed
	נסתרה	niph	wcp	3fs	סתר	711		hide,be hid
	נטמאה	niph	pft	3fs	טמא	379		defile oneself
	נתפשה	niph	pft	3fs	תפש	1074		be seized
5: 14	עבר	qal	wcp	3ms	עבר	716		pass over
	קנא	piel	wcp	3ms	קנא	888		be jealous
	נטמאה	niph	pft	3fs	טמא	379		defile oneself
	עבר	qal	pft	3ms	עבר	716		pass over
	קנא	piel	wcp	3ms	קנא	888		be jealous
	נטמאה	niph	pft	3fs	טמא	379		defile oneself
5: 15	הביא	hiph	wcp	3ms	בוא	97		bring in
	הביא	hiph	wcp	3ms	בוא	97		bring in
	יצק	qal	impf	3ms	יצק	427		pour out,cast
	יתן	qal	impf	3ms	נתן	678		give,set
	מזכרת	hiph	ptc	fs	זכר	269		c. to remember
5: 16	הקריב	hiph	wcp	3ms	קרב	897		bring near
	העמדה	hiph	wcp	3ms	עמד	763	3fs	set up,raise
5: 17	לקח	qal	wcp	3ms	לקח	542		take
	יהיה	qal	impf	3ms	היה	224		be,become
	יקח	qal	impf	3ms	לקח	542		take
	נתן	qal	wcp	3ms	נתן	678		give,set
5: 18	העמיד	hiph	wcp	3ms	עמד	763		set up,raise
	פרע	qal	wcp	3ms	פרע	828		let go
	נתן	qal	wcp	3ms	נתן	678		give,set
	יהיו	qal	impf	3mp	היה	224		be,become
	מאררים	piel	ptc	mp	ארר	76		curse
5: 19	השביע	hiph	wcp	3ms	שבע	989		cause to swear
	אמר	qal	wcp	3ms	אמר	55		say
	שכב	qal	pft	3ms	שכב	1011		lie,lie down
	שטית	qal	pft	2fs	שטה	966		turn aside
	הנקי	niph	impv	fs	נקה	667		be clean,free
	מאררים	piel	ptc	mp	ארר	76		curse
5: 20	שטית	qal	pft	2fs	שטה	966		turn aside
	נטמאת	niph	pft	2fs	טמא	379		defile oneself
	יתן	qal	wci	3ms	נתן	678		give,set
5: 21	השביע	hiph	wcp	3ms	שבע	989		cause to swear
	אמר	qal	wcp	3ms	אמר	55		say
	יתן	qal	jusm	3ms	נתן	678		give,set
	תת	qal	infc		נתן	678		give,set
	נפלת	qal	ptc	fs	נפל	656		fall
5: 22	באו	qal	wcp	3cp	בוא	97		come in
	מאררים	piel	ptc	mp	ארר	76		curse
	צבות	hiph	infc		צבה	839		cause to swell
	נפל	hiph	infc		נפל	656		cause to fall
	אמרה	qal	wcp	3fs	אמר	55		say
5: 23	כתב	qal	wcp	3ms	כתב	507		write
	מחה	qal	wcp	3ms	מחה	562		wipe,blot out
5: 24	השקה	hiph	wcp	3ms	שקה	1052		give to drink
	מאררים	piel	ptc	mp	ארר	76		curse
	באו	qal	wcp	3cp	בוא	97		come in
	מאררים	piel	ptc	mp	ארר	76		curse
5: 25	לקח	qal	wcp	3ms	לקח	542		take
	הניף	hiph	wcp	3ms	נוף	631		swing,wave
	הקריב	hiph	wcp	3ms	קרב	897		bring near
5: 26	קמץ	qal	wcp	3ms	קמץ	888		grasp
	הקטיר	hiph	wcp	3ms	קטר	882		make sacrifices
	ישקה	hiph	impf	3ms	שקה	1052		give to drink
5: 27	השקה	hiph	wcp	3ms	שקה	1052	3fs	give to drink
	היתה	qal	wcp	3fs	היה	224		be,become
	נטמאה	niph	pft	3fs	טמא	379		defile oneself
	תמעל	qal	wci	3fs	מעל	591		act faithlessly
	באו	qal	wcp	3cp	בוא	97		come in
	מאררים	piel	ptc	mp	ארר	76		curse
	צבתה	qal	wcp	3fs	צבה	839		swell up
	נפלה	qal	wcp	3fs	נפל	656		fall
	היתה	qal	wcp	3fs	היה	224		be,become
5: 28	נטמאה	niph	pft	3fs	טמא	379		defile oneself
	נקתה	niph	wcp	3fs	נקה	667		be clean,free
	נזרעה	niph	wcp	3fs	זרע	281		be sown
5: 29	תשטה	qal	impf	3fs	שטה	966		turn aside
	נטמאה	niph	wcp	3fs	טמא	379		defile oneself
5: 30	תעבר	qal	impf	3fs	עבר	716		pass over
	קנא	piel	wcp	3ms	קנא	888		be jealous
	העמיד	hiph	wcp	3ms	עמד	763		set up,raise
	עשה	qal	wcp	3ms	עשה	793		do,make
5: 31	נקה	niph	wcp	3ms	נקה	667		be clean,free
	תשא	qal	impf	3fs	נשא	669		lift,carry
6: 1	ידבר	piel	wci	3ms	דבר	180		speak
	אמר	qal	infc		אמר	55		say
6: 2	דבר	piel	impv	ms	דבר	180		speak
	אמרת	qal	wcp	2ms	אמר	55		say
	יפלא	hiph	impf	3ms	פלא	810		do wondrously
	נדר	qal	infc		נדר	623		vow
	הזיר	hiph	infc		נזר	634		be a Nazirite
6: 3	יזיר	hiph	impf	3ms	נזר	634		be a Nazirite
	ישתה	qal	impf	3ms	שתה	1059		drink
	ישתה	qal	impf	3ms	שתה	1059		drink
	יאכל	qal	impf	3ms	אכל	37		eat,devour
6: 4	יעשה	niph	impf	3ms	עשה	793		be done
	יאכל	qal	impf	3ms	אכל	37		eat,devour
6: 5	יעבר	qal	impf	3ms	עבר	716		pass over
	מלאת	qal	infc		מלא	569		be full,fill
	יזיר	hiph	impf	3ms	נזר	634		be a Nazirite
	יהיה	qal	impf	3ms	היה	224		be,become
	גדל	piel	infc		גדל	152		cause to grow
6: 6	הזירו	hiph	infc		נזר	634	3ms	be a Nazirite
	מת	qal	ptc	ms	מות	559		die
	יבא	qal	impf	3ms	בוא	97		come in
6: 7	יטמא	hith	impf	3ms	טמא	379		defile oneself

ChVs	Form	Stem	Tnse	PGN	Root	BDB	Sfx	Meaning
6:7	מתם	qal	infc		מות	559	3mp	die
6:9	ימות	qal	impf	3ms	מות	559		die
	מת	qal	ptc	ms	מות	559		die
	טמא	piel	wcp	3ms	טמא	379		defile
	גלח	piel	wcp	3ms	גלח	164		shave
	יגלחנו	piel	impf	3ms	גלח	164	3ms	shave
6:10	יבא	hiph	impf	3ms	בוא	97		bring in
6:11	עשׂה	qal	wcp	3ms	עשׂה	793		do,make
	כפר	piel	wcp	3ms	כפר	497		cover,atone
	חטא	qal	pft	3ms	חטא	306		sin
	קדשׁ	piel	wcp	3ms	קדשׁ	872		consecrate
6:12	הזיר	hiph	wcp	3ms	נזר	634		be a Nazirite
	הביא	hiph	wcp	3ms	בוא	97		bring in
	יפלו	qal	impf	3mp	נפל	656		fall
	טמא	qal	pft	3ms	טמא	379		become unclean
6:13	מלאת	qal	infc		מלא	569		be full,fill
	יביא	hiph	impf	3ms	בוא	97		bring in
6:14	הקריב	hiph	wcp	3ms	קרב	897		bring near
6:15	בלולת	qal	pptc	fp	בלל	117		mingle,mix
	משׁחים	qal	pptc	mp	משׁח	602		smear,anoint
6:16	הקריב	hiph	wcp	3ms	קרב	897		bring near
	עשׂה	qal	wcp	3ms	עשׂה	793		do,make
6:17	יעשׂה	qal	impf	3ms	עשׂה	793		do,make
	עשׂה	qal	wcp	3ms	עשׂה	793		do,make
6:18	גלח	piel	wcp	3ms	גלח	164		shave
	לקח	qal	wcp	3ms	לקח	542		take
	נתן	qal	wcp	3ms	נתן	678		give,set
6:19	לקח	qal	wcp	3ms	לקח	542		take
	נתן	qal	wcp	3ms	נתן	678		give,set
	התגלחו	hith	infc		גלח	164	3ms	shave oneself
6:20	הניף	hiph	wcp	3ms	נוף	631		swing,wave
	ישׁתה	qal	impf	3ms	שׁתה	1059		drink
6:21	ידר	qal	impf	3ms	נדר	623		vow
	תשׂיג	hiph	impf	3fs	נשׂג	673		reach,overtake
	ידר	qal	impf	3ms	נדר	623		vow
	יעשׂה	qal	impf	3ms	עשׂה	793		do,make
6:22	ידבר	piel	wci	3ms	דבר	180		speak
	אמר	qal	infc		אמר	55		say
6:23	דבר	piel	impv	ms	דבר	180		speak
	אמר	qal	infc		אמר	55		say
	תברכו	piel	impf	2mp	ברך	138		bless
	אמור	qal	infa		אמר	55		say
6:24	יברכך	piel	jusm	3ms	ברך	138	2ms	bless
	ישׁמרך	qal	jusm	3ms	שׁמר	1036	2ms	keep,watch
6:25	יאר	hiph	jus	3ms	אור	21		cause to shine
	יחנך	qal	jusm	3ms	חנן	335	2ms	show favor
6:26	ישׂא	qal	jusm	3ms	נשׂא	669		lift,carry
	ישׂם	qal	jusm	3ms	שׂים	962		put,set
6:27	שׂמו	qal	wcp	3cp	שׂים	962		put,set
	אברכם	piel	impf	1cs	ברך	138	3mp	bless
7:1	יהי	qal	wci	3ms	היה	224		be,become
	כלות	piel	infc		כלה	477		complete,finish
	הקים	hiph	infc		קום	877		raise,build,set
	ימשׁח	qal	wci	3ms	משׁח	602		smear,anoint
7:1	יקדשׁ	piel	wci	3ms	קדשׁ	872		consecrate
	ימשׁחם	qal	wci	3ms	משׁח	602	3mp	smear,anoint
	יקדשׁ	piel	wci	3ms	קדשׁ	872		consecrate
7:2	יקריבו	hiph	wci	3mp	קרב	897		bring near
	עמדים	qal	ptc	mp	עמד	763		stand,stop
	פקדים	qal	pptc	mp	פקד	823		attend to,visit
7:3	יביאו	hiph	wci	3mp	בוא	97		bring in
	יקריבו	hiph	wci	3mp	קרב	897		bring near
7:4	יאמר	qal	wci	3ms	אמר	55		say
	אמר	qal	infc		אמר	55		say
7:5	קח	qal	impv	ms	לקח	542		take
	היו	qal	wcp	3cp	היה	224		be,become
	עבד	qal	infc		עבד	712		work,serve
	נתתה	qal	wcp	2ms	נתן	678		give,set
7:6	יקח	qal	wci	3ms	לקח	542		take
	יתן	qal	wci	3ms	נתן	678		give,set
7:7	נתן	qal	pft	3ms	נתן	678		give,set
7:8	נתן	qal	pft	3ms	נתן	678		give,set
7:9	נתן	qal	pft	3ms	נתן	678		give,set
	ישׂאו	qal	impf	3mp	נשׂא	669		lift,carry
7:10	יקריבו	hiph	wci	3mp	קרב	897		bring near
	המשׁח	niph	infc		משׁח	602		be anointed
	יקריבו	hiph	wci	3mp	קרב	897		bring near
7:11	יאמר	qal	wci	3ms	אמר	55		say
	יקריבו	hiph	impf	3mp	קרב	897		bring near
7:12	יהי	qal	wci	3ms	היה	224		be,become
	מקריב	hiph	ptc	ms	קרב	897		bring near
7:13	בלולה	qal	pptc	fs	בלל	117		mingle,mix
7:18	הקריב	hiph	pft	3ms	קרב	897		bring near
7:19	הקרב	hiph	pft	3ms	קרב	897		bring near
	בלולה	qal	pptc	fs	בלל	117		mingle,mix
7:25	בלולה	qal	pptc	fs	בלל	117		mingle,mix
7:31	בלולה	qal	pptc	fs	בלל	117		mingle,mix
7:37	בלולה	qal	pptc	fs	בלל	117		mingle,mix
7:43	בלולה	qal	pptc	fs	בלל	117		mingle,mix
7:49	בלולה	qal	pptc	fs	בלל	117		mingle,mix
7:55	בלולה	qal	pptc	fs	בלל	117		mingle,mix
7:61	בלולה	qal	pptc	fs	בלל	117		mingle,mix
7:67	בלולה	qal	pptc	fs	בלל	117		mingle,mix
7:73	בלולה	qal	pptc	fs	בלל	117		mingle,mix
7:79	בלולה	qal	pptc	fs	בלל	117		mingle,mix
7:84	המשׁח	niph	infc		משׁח	602		be anointed
7:88	המשׁח	niph	infc		משׁח	602		be anointed
7:89	בא	qal	infc		בוא	97		come in
	דבר	piel	infc		דבר	180		speak
	ישׁמע	qal	wci	3ms	שׁמע	1033		hear
	מדבר	hith	ptc	ms	דבר	180		speak
	ידבר	piel	wci	3ms	דבר	180		speak
8:1	ידבר	piel	wci	3ms	דבר	180		speak
	אמר	qal	infc		אמר	55		say
8:2	דבר	piel	impv	ms	דבר	180		speak
	אמרת	qal	wcp	2ms	אמר	55		say
	העלתך	hiph	infc		עלה	748	2ms	bring up,offer
	יארו	hiph	impf	3mp	אור	21		cause to shine

ChVs	Form	Stem	Tnse	PGN	Root	BDB	Sfx	Meaning
8: 3	יעשׂ	qal	wci	3ms	עשׂה	793		do,make
	העלה	hiph	pft	3ms	עלה	748		bring up,offer
	צוה	piel	pft	3ms	צוה	845		command
8: 4	הראה	hiph	pft	3ms	ראה	906		show,exhibit
	עשׂה	qal	pft	3ms	עשׂה	793		do,make
8: 5	ידבר	piel	wci	3ms	דבר	180		speak
	אמר	qal	infc		אמר	55		say
8: 6	קח	qal	impv	ms	לקח	542		take
	טהרת	piel	wcp	2ms	טהר	372		cleanse
8: 7	תעשׂה	qal	impf	2ms	עשׂה	793		do,make
	טהרם	piel	infc		טהר	372	3mp	cleanse
	הזה	hiph	impv	ms	נזה	633		cause to spurt
	העבירו	hiph	wcp	3cp	עבר	716		cause to pass
	כבסו	piel	wcp	3cp	כבס	460		wash
	הטהרו	hith	wcp	3cp	טהר	372		purify oneself
8: 8	לקחו	qal	wcp	3cp	לקח	542		take
	בלולה	qal	pptc	fs	בלל	117		mingle,mix
	תקח	qal	impf	2ms	לקח	542		take
8: 9	הקרבת	hiph	wcp	2ms	קרב	897		bring near
	הקהלת	hiph	wcp	2ms	קהל	874		call assembly
8: 10	הקרבת	hiph	wcp	2ms	קרב	897		bring near
	סמכו	qal	wcp	3cp	סמך	701		lean,support
8: 11	הניף	hiph	wcp	3ms	נוף	631		swing,wave
	היו	qal	wcp	3cp	היה	224		be,become
	עבד	qal	infc		עבד	712		work,serve
8: 12	יסמכו	qal	impf	3mp	סמך	701		lean,support
	עשׂה	qal	impv	ms	עשׂה	793		do,make
	כפר	piel	infc		כפר	497		cover,atone
8: 13	העמדת	hiph	wcp	2ms	עמד	763		set up,raise
	הנפת	hiph	wcp	2ms	נוף	631		swing,wave
8: 14	הבדלת	hiph	wcp	2ms	בדל	95		divide
	היו	qal	wcp	3cp	היה	224		be,become
8: 15	יבאו	qal	impf	3mp	בוא	97		come in
	עבד	qal	infc		עבד	712		work,serve
	טהרת	piel	wcp	2ms	טהר	372		cleanse
	הנפת	hiph	wcp	2ms	נוף	631		swing,wave
8: 16	נתנים	qal	pptc	mp	נתן	678		give,set
	נתנים	qal	pptc	mp	נתן	678		give,set
	לקחתי	qal	pft	1cs	לקח	542		take
8: 17	הכתי	hiph	infc		נכה	645	1cs	smite
	הקדשׁתי	hiph	pft	1cs	קדשׁ	872		consecrate
8: 18	אקח	qal	wci	1cs	לקח	542		take
8: 19	אתנה	qal	wci	1cs	נתן	678		give,set
	נתנים	qal	pptc	mp	נתן	678		give,set
	עבד	qal	infc		עבד	712		work,serve
	כפר	piel	infc		כפר	497		cover,atone
	יהיה	qal	impf	3ms	היה	224		be,become
	גשׁת	qal	infc		נגשׁ	620		draw near
8: 20	יעשׂ	qal	wci	3ms	עשׂה	793		do,make
	צוה	piel	pft	3ms	צוה	845		command
	עשׂו	qal	pft	3cp	עשׂה	793		do,make
8: 21	יתחטאו	hith	wci	3mp	חטא	306		purify oneself
	יכבסו	piel	wci	3mp	כבס	460		wash
	ינף	hiph	wci	3ms	נוף	631		swing,wave

ChVs	Form	Stem	Tnse	PGN	Root	BDB	Sfx	Meaning
8: 21	יכפר	piel	wci	3ms	כפר	497		cover,atone
	טהרם	piel	infc		טהר	372	3mp	cleanse
8: 22	באו	qal	pft	3cp	בוא	97		come in
	עבד	qal	infc		עבד	712		work,serve
	צוה	piel	pft	3ms	צוה	845		command
	עשׂו	qal	pft	3cp	עשׂה	793		do,make
8: 23	ידבר	piel	wci	3ms	דבר	180		speak
	אמר	qal	infc		אמר	55		say
8: 24	יבוא	qal	impf	3ms	בוא	97		come in
	צבא	qal	infc		צבא	838		wage war
8: 25	ישׁוב	qal	impf	3ms	שׁוב	996		turn,return
	יעבד	qal	impf	3ms	עבד	712		work,serve
8: 26	שׁרת	piel	wcp	3ms	שׁרת	1058		minister,serve
	שׁמר	qal	infc		שׁמר	1036		keep,watch
	יעבד	qal	impf	3ms	עבד	712		work,serve
	תעשׂה	qal	impf	2ms	עשׂה	793		do,make
9: 1	ידבר	piel	wci	3ms	דבר	180		speak
	צאתם	qal	infc		יצא	422	3mp	go out
	אמר	qal	infc		אמר	55		say
9: 2	יעשׂו	qal	wci	3mp	עשׂה	793		do,make
9: 3	תעשׂו	qal	impf	2mp	עשׂה	793		do,make
	תעשׂו	qal	impf	2mp	עשׂה	793		do,make
9: 4	ידבר	piel	wci	3ms	דבר	180		speak
	עשׂת	qal	infc		עשׂה	793		do,make
9: 5	יעשׂו	qal	wci	3mp	עשׂה	793		do,make
	צוה	piel	pft	3ms	צוה	845		command
	עשׂו	qal	pft	3cp	עשׂה	793		do,make
9: 6	יהי	qal	wci	3ms	היה	224		be,become
	היו	qal	pft	3cp	היה	224		be,become
	יכלו	qal	pft	3cp	יכל	407		be able
	עשׂת	qal	infc		עשׂה	793		do,make
	יקרבו	qal	wci	3mp	קרב	897		approach
9: 7	יאמרו	qal	wci	3mp	אמר	55		say
	נגרע	niph	impf	1cp	גרע	175		be withdrawn
	הקרב	hiph	infc		קרב	897		bring near
9: 8	יאמר	qal	wci	3ms	אמר	55		say
	עמדו	qal	impv	mp	עמד	763		stand,stop
	אשׁמעה	qal	coh	1cs	שׁמע	1033		hear
	יצוה	piel	impf	3ms	צוה	845		command
9: 9	ידבר	piel	wci	3ms	דבר	180		speak
	אמר	qal	infc		אמר	55		say
9: 10	דבר	piel	impv	ms	דבר	180		speak
	אמר	qal	infc		אמר	55		say
	יהיה	qal	impf	3ms	היה	224		be,become
	עשׂה	qal	wcp	3ms	עשׂה	793		do,make
9: 11	יעשׂו	qal	impf	3mp	עשׂה	793		do,make
	יאכלהו	qal	impf	3mp	אכל	37	3ms	eat,devour
9: 12	ישׁאירו	hiph	impf	3mp	שׁאר	983		leave,spare
	ישׁברו	qal	impf	3mp	שׁבר	990		break
	יעשׂו	qal	impf	3mp	עשׂה	793		do,make
9: 13	היה	qal	pft	3ms	היה	224		be,become
	חדל	qal	wcp	3ms	חדל	292		cease
	עשׂות	qal	infc		עשׂה	793		do,make
	נכרתה	niph	wcp	3fs	כרת	503		be cut off

ChVs	Form	Stem	Tnse	PGN	Root	BDB	Sfx	Meaning
9:13	הקריב	hiph	pft	3ms	קרב	897		bring near
	ישׂא	qal	impf	3ms	נשׂא	669		lift,carry
9:14	יגור	qal	impf	3ms	גור	157		sojourn
	עשׂה	qal	wcp	3ms	עשׂה	793		do,make
	יעשׂה	qal	impf	3ms	עשׂה	793		do,make
	יהיה	qal	impf	3ms	היה	224		be,become
9:15	הקים	hiph	infc		קום	877		raise,build,set
	כסה	piel	pft	3ms	כסה	491		cover
	יהיה	qal	impf	3ms	היה	224		be,become
9:16	יהיה	qal	impf	3ms	היה	224		be,become
	יכסנו	piel	impf	3ms	כסה	491	3ms	cover
9:17	העלת	niph	infc		עלה	748		be brought up
	יסעו	qal	impf	3mp	נסע	652		pull up,set out
	ישׁכן	qal	impf	3ms	שׁכן	1014		settle,dwell
	יחנו	qal	impf	3mp	חנה	333		decline,encamp
9:18	יסעו	qal	impf	3mp	נסע	652		pull up,set out
	יחנו	qal	impf	3mp	חנה	333		decline,encamp
	ישׁכן	qal	impf	3ms	שׁכן	1014		settle,dwell
	יחנו	qal	impf	3mp	חנה	333		decline,encamp
9:19	האריך	hiph	infc		ארך	73		prolong
	שׁמרו	qal	wcp	3cp	שׁמר	1036		keep,watch
	יסעו	qal	impf	3mp	נסע	652		pull up,set out
9:20	יהיה	qal	impf	3ms	היה	224		be,become
	יחנו	qal	impf	3mp	חנה	333		decline,encamp
	יסעו	qal	impf	3mp	נסע	652		pull up,set out
9:21	יהיה	qal	impf	3ms	היה	224		be,become
	נעלה	niph	wcp	3ms	עלה	748		be brought up
	נסעו	qal	wcp	3cp	נסע	652		pull up,set out
	נעלה	niph	wcp	3ms	עלה	748		be brought up
	נסעו	qal	wcp	3cp	נסע	652		pull up,set out
9:22	האריך	hiph	infc		ארך	73		prolong
	שׁכן	qal	infc		שׁכן	1014		settle,dwell
	יחנו	qal	impf	3mp	חנה	333		decline,encamp
	יסעו	qal	impf	3mp	נסע	652		pull up,set out
	העלתו	niph	infc		עלה	748	3ms	be brought up
	יסעו	qal	impf	3mp	נסע	652		pull up,set out
9:23	יחנו	qal	impf	3mp	חנה	333		decline,encamp
	יסעו	qal	impf	3mp	נסע	652		pull up,set out
	שׁמרו	qal	pft	3cp	שׁמר	1036		keep,watch
10:1	ידבר	piel	wci	3ms	דבר	180		speak
	אמר	qal	infc		אמר	55		say
10:2	עשׂה	qal	impv	ms	עשׂה	793		do,make
	תעשׂה	qal	impf	2ms	עשׂה	793		do,make
	היו	qal	wcp	3cp	היה	224		be,become
10:3	תקעו	qal	wcp	3cp	תקע	1075		thrust,clap
	נועדו	niph	wcp	3cp	יעד	416		gather
10:4	יתקעו	qal	impf	3mp	תקע	1075		thrust,clap
	נועדו	niph	wcp	3cp	יעד	416		gather
10:5	תקעתם	qal	wcp	2mp	תקע	1075		thrust,clap
	נסעו	qal	wcp	3cp	נסע	652		pull up,set out
	חנים	qal	ptc	mp	חנה	333		decline,encamp
10:6	תקעתם	qal	wcp	2mp	תקע	1075		thrust,clap
	נסעו	qal	wcp	3cp	נסע	652		pull up,set out
	חנים	qal	ptc	mp	חנה	333		decline,encamp

ChVs	Form	Stem	Tnse	PGN	Root	BDB	Sfx	Meaning
10:6	יתקעו	qal	impf	3mp	תקע	1075		thrust,clap
10:7	הקהיל	hiph	infc		קהל	874		call assembly
	תתקעו	qal	impf	2mp	תקע	1075		thrust,clap
	תריעו	hiph	impf	2mp	רוע	929		raise a shout
10:8	יתקעו	qal	impf	3mp	תקע	1075		thrust,clap
	היו	qal	wcp	3cp	היה	224		be,become
10:9	תבאו	qal	impf	2mp	בוא	97		come in
	צרר	qal	ptc	ms	צרר	865		show hostility
	הרעתם	hiph	wcp	2mp	רוע	929		raise a shout
	נזכרתם	niph	wcp	2mp	זכר	269		be remembered
	נושׁעתם	niph	wcp	2mp	ישׁע	446		be saved
	איביכם	qal	ptc	mp	איב	33	2mp	be hostile to
10:10	תקעתם	qal	wcp	2mp	תקע	1075		thrust,clap
	היו	qal	wcp	3cp	היה	224		be,become
10:11	יהי	qal	wci	3ms	היה	224		be,become
	נעלה	niph	pft	3ms	עלה	748		be brought up
10:12	יסעו	qal	wci	3mp	נסע	652		pull up,set out
	ישׁכן	qal	wci	3ms	שׁכן	1014		settle,dwell
10:13	יסעו	qal	wci	3mp	נסע	652		pull up,set out
10:14	יסע	qal	wci	3ms	נסע	652		pull up,set out
10:17	הורד	hoph	wcp	3ms	ירד	432		be led down
	נסעו	qal	wcp	3cp	נסע	652		pull up,set out
	נשׂאי	qal	ptc	mp	נשׂא	669		lift,carry
10:18	נסע	qal	wcp	3ms	נסע	652		pull up,set out
10:21	נסעו	qal	wcp	3cp	נסע	652		pull up,set out
	נשׂאי	qal	ptc	mp	נשׂא	669		lift,carry
	הקימו	hiph	wcp	3cp	קום	877		raise,build,set
	באם	qal	infc		בוא	97	3mp	come in
10:22	נסע	qal	wcp	3ms	נסע	652		pull up,set out
10:25	נסע	qal	wcp	3ms	נסע	652		pull up,set out
	מאסף	piel	ptc	ms	אסף	62		gather
10:28	יסעו	qal	wci	3mp	נסע	652		pull up,set out
10:29	יאמר	qal	wci	3ms	אמר	55		say
	נסעים	qal	ptc	mp	נסע	652		pull up,set out
	אמר	qal	pft	3ms	אמר	55		say
	אתן	qal	impf	1cs	נתן	678		give,set
	לכה	qal	impv	ms	הלך	229		walk,go
	הטבנו	hiph	wcp	1cp	יטב	405		do good
	דבר	piel	pft	3ms	דבר	180		speak
10:30	יאמר	qal	wci	3ms	אמר	55		say
	אלך	qal	impf	1cs	הלך	229		walk,go
	אלך	qal	impf	1cs	הלך	229		walk,go
10:31	יאמר	qal	wci	3ms	אמר	55		say
	תעזב	qal	jusm	2ms	עזב	736		leave,loose
	ידעת	qal	pft	2ms	ידע	393		know
	חנתנו	qal	infc		חנה	333	1cp	decline,encamp
	היית	qal	wcp	2ms	היה	224		be,become
10:32	היה	qal	wcp	3ms	היה	224		be,become
	תלך	qal	impf	2ms	הלך	229		walk,go
	היה	qal	wcp	3ms	היה	224		be,become
	ייטיב	hiph	impf	3ms	יטב	405		do good
	הטבנו	hiph	wcp	1cp	יטב	405		do good
10:33	יסעו	qal	wci	3mp	נסע	652		pull up,set out
	נסע	qal	ptc	ms	נסע	652		pull up,set out

ChVs	Form	Stem	Tnse	PGN	Root	BDB	Sfx	Meaning
10:33	תור	qal	infc		תור	1064		seek out,spy
10:34	נסעם	qal	infc		נסע	652	3mp	pull up,set out
10:35	יהי	qal	wci	3ms	היה	224		be,become
	נסע	qal	infc		נסע	652		pull up,set out
	יאמר	qal	wci	3ms	אמר	55		say
	קומה	qal	impv	ms	קום	877		arise,stand
	יפצו	qal	jusm	3mp	פוץ	806		be scattered
	איביך	qal	ptc	mp	איב	33	2ms	be hostile to
	ינסו	qal	jusm	3mp	נוס	630		flee,escape
	משׂנאיך	piel	ptc	mp	שׂנא	971	2ms	hate
10:36	נחה	qal	infc		נוח	628	3ms	rest
	יאמר	qal	impf	3ms	אמר	55		say
	שׁובה	qal	impv	ms	שׁוב	996		turn,return
11:1	יהי	qal	wci	3ms	היה	224		be,become
	מתאננים	htpo	ptc	mp	אנן	59		complain
	ישׁמע	qal	wci	3ms	שׁמע	1033		hear
	יחר	qal	wci	3ms	חרה	354		be kindled,burn
	תבער	qal	wci	3fs	בער	128		burn
	תאכל	qal	wci	3fs	אכל	37		eat,devour
11:2	יצעק	qal	wci	3ms	צעק	858		cry out
	יתפלל	hith	wci	3ms	פלל	813		pray
	תשׁקע	qal	wci	3fs	שׁקע	1054		sink down
11:3	יקרא	qal	wci	3ms	קרא	894		call,proclaim
	בערה	qal	pft	3fs	בער	128		burn
11:4	התאוו	hith	pft	3cp	אוה	16		desire
	ישׁבו	qal	wci	3mp	שׁוב	996		turn,return
	יבכו	qal	wci	3mp	בכה	113		weep
	יאמרו	qal	wci	3mp	אמר	55		say
	יאכלנו	hiph	impf	3ms	אכל	37	1cp	cause to eat
11:5	זכרנו	qal	pft	1cp	זכר	269		remember
	נאכל	qal	impf	1cp	אכל	37		eat,devour
11:8	שׁטו	qal	pft	3cp	שׁוט	1001		go about
	לקטו	qal	wcp	3cp	לקט	544		pick,gather
	טחנו	qal	wcp	3cp	טחן	377		grind
	דכו	qal	pft	3cp	דוך	188		pound,beat
	בשׁלו	piel	wcp	3cp	בשׁל	143		boil,cook
	עשׂו	qal	wcp	3cp	עשׂה	793		do,make
	היה	qal	wcp	3ms	היה	224		be,become
11:9	רדת	qal	infc		ירד	432		come down
	ירד	qal	impf	3ms	ירד	432		come down
11:10	ישׁמע	qal	wci	3ms	שׁמע	1033		hear
	בכה	qal	ptc	ms	בכה	113		weep
	יחר	qal	wci	3ms	חרה	354		be kindled,burn
	רע	qal	pft	3ms	רעע	949		be evil
11:11	יאמר	qal	wci	3ms	אמר	55		say
	הרעת	hiph	pft	2ms	רעע	949		hurt,do evil
	מצתי	qal	pft	1cs	מצא	592		find
	שׂום	qal	infc		שׂים	962		put,set
11:12	הריתי	qal	pft	1cs	הרה	247		conceive
	ילדתיהו	qal	pft	1cs	ילד	408	3ms	bear,beget
	תאמר	qal	impf	2ms	אמר	55		say
	שׂאהו	qal	impv	ms	נשׂא	669	3ms	lift,carry
	ישׂא	qal	impf	3ms	נשׂא	669		lift,carry
	אמן	qal	ptc	ms	אמן	52		nourish
11:12	ינק	qal	ptc	ms	ינק	413		suck
	נשׁבעת	niph	pft	2ms	שׁבע	989		swear
11:13	תת	qal	infc		נתן	678		give,set
	יבכו	qal	impf	3mp	בכה	113		weep
	אמר	qal	infc		אמר	55		say
	תנה	qal	impv	ms	נתן	678		give,set
	נאכלה	qal	coh	1cp	אכל	37		eat,devour
11:14	אוכל	qal	impf	1cs	יכל	407		be able
	שׂאת	qal	infc		נשׂא	669		lift,carry
11:15	עשׂה	qal	ptc	ms	עשׂה	793		do,make
	הרגני	qal	impv	ms	הרג	246	1cs	kill
	הרג	qal	infa		הרג	246		kill
	מצאתי	qal	pft	1cs	מצא	592		find
	אראה	qal	cohm	1cs	ראה	906		see
11:16	יאמר	qal	wci	3ms	אמר	55		say
	אספה	qal	impv	ms	אסף	62		gather
	ידעת	qal	pft	2ms	ידע	393		know
	לקחת	qal	wcp	2ms	לקח	542		take
	התיצבו	hith	wcp	3cp	יצב	426		stand oneself
11:17	ירדתי	qal	wcp	1cs	ירד	432		come down
	דברתי	piel	wcp	1cs	דבר	180		speak
	אצלתי	qal	wcp	1cs	אצל	69		reserve
	שׂמתי	qal	wcp	1cs	שׂים	962		put,set
	נשׂאו	qal	wcp	3cp	נשׂא	669		lift,carry
	תשׂא	qal	impf	2ms	נשׂא	669		lift,carry
11:18	תאמר	qal	impf	2ms	אמר	55		say
	התקדשׁו	hith	impv	mp	קדשׁ	872		consecrate self
	אכלתם	qal	wcp	2mp	אכל	37		eat,devour
	בכיתם	qal	pft	2mp	בכה	113		weep
	אמר	qal	infc		אמר	55		say
	יאכלנו	hiph	impf	3ms	אכל	37	1cp	cause to eat
	טוב	qal	pft	3ms	טוב	373		be pleasing
	נתן	qal	wcp	3ms	נתן	678		give,set
	אכלתם	qal	wcp	2mp	אכל	37		eat,devour
11:19	תאכלון	qal	impf	2mp	אכל	37		eat,devour
11:20	יצא	qal	impf	3ms	יצא	422		go out
	היה	qal	wcp	3ms	היה	224		be,become
	מאסתם	qal	pft	2mp	מאס	549		reject,refuse
	תבכו	qal	wci	2mp	בכה	113		weep
	אמר	qal	infc		אמר	55		say
	יצאנו	qal	pft	1cp	יצא	422		go out
11:21	יאמר	qal	wci	3ms	אמר	55		say
	אמרת	qal	pft	2ms	אמר	55		say
	אתן	qal	impf	1cs	נתן	678		give,set
	אכלו	qal	wcp	3cp	אכל	37		eat,devour
11:22	ישׁחט	niph	impf	3ms	שׁחט	1006		be slaughtered
	מצא	qal	wcp	3ms	מצא	592		find
	יאסף	niph	impf	3ms	אסף	62		assemble
	מצא	qal	wcp	3ms	מצא	592		find
11:23	יאמר	qal	wci	3ms	אמר	55		say
	תקצר	qal	impf	3fs	קצר	894		be short
	תראה	qal	impf	2ms	ראה	906		see
	יקרך	qal	impf	3ms	קרה	899	2ms	encounter,meet
11:24	יצא	qal	wci	3ms	יצא	422		go out

ChVs	Form	Stem	Tnse	PGN	Root	BDB	Sfx	Meaning
11:24	ידבר	piel	wci	3ms	דבר	180		speak
	יאסף	qal	wci	3ms	אסף	62		gather
	יעמד	hiph	wci	3ms	עמד	763		set up,raise
11:25	ירד	qal	wci	3ms	ירד	432		come down
	ידבר	piel	wci	3ms	דבר	180		speak
	יאצל	hiph	wci	3ms	אצל	69		set apart
	יתן	qal	wci	3ms	נתן	678		give,set
	יהי	qal	wci	3ms	היה	224		be,become
	נוח	qal	infc		נוח	628		rest
	יתנבאו	hith	wci	3mp	נבא	612		prophesy
	יספו	qal	pft	3cp	יסף	414		add,increase
11:26	ישארו	niph	wci	3mp	שאר	983		be left
	תנח	qal	wci	3fs	נוח	628		rest
	כתבים	qal	pptc	mp	כתב	507		write
	יצאו	qal	pft	3cp	יצא	422		go out
	יתנבאו	hith	wci	3mp	נבא	612		prophesy
11:27	ירץ	qal	wci	3ms	רוץ	930		run
	יגד	hiph	wci	3ms	נגד	616		declare,tell
	יאמר	qal	wci	3ms	אמר	55		say
	מתנבאים	hith	ptc	mp	נבא	612		prophesy
11:28	יען	qal	wci	3ms	ענה	772		answer
	משרת	piel	ptc	ms	שרת	1058		minister,serve
	יאמר	qal	wci	3ms	אמר	55		say
	כלאם	qal	impv	ms	כלא	476	3mp	shut up
11:29	יאמר	qal	wci	3ms	אמר	55		say
	מקנא	piel	ptc	ms	קנא	888		be jealous
	יתן	qal	impf	3ms	נתן	678		give,set
	יתן	qal	impf	3ms	נתן	678		give,set
11:30	יאסף	niph	wci	3ms	אסף	62		assemble
11:31	נסע	qal	pft	3ms	נסע	652		pull up,set out
	יגז	qal	wci	3ms	גוז	156		pass away
	יטש	qal	wci	3ms	נטש	643		leave,forsake
11:32	יקם	qal	wci	3ms	קום	877		arise,stand
	יאספו	qal	wci	3mp	אסף	62		gather
	ממעיט	hiph	ptc	ms	מעט	589		make small
	אסף	qal	pft	3ms	אסף	62		gather
	ישטחו	qal	wci	3mp	שטח	1008		spread abroad
	שטוח	qal	infa		שטח	1008		spread abroad
11:33	יכרת	niph	impf	3ms	כרת	503		be cut off
	חרה	qal	pft	3ms	חרה	354		be kindled,burn
	יך	hiph	wci	3ms	נכה	645		smite
11:34	יקרא	qal	wci	3ms	קרא	894		call,proclaim
	קברו	qal	pft	3cp	קבר	868		bury
	מתאוים	hith	ptc	mp	אוה	16		desire
11:35	נסעו	qal	pft	3cp	נסע	652		pull up,set out
	יהיו	qal	wci	3mp	היה	224		be,become
12:1	תדבר	piel	wci	3fs	דבר	180		speak
	לקח	qal	pft	3ms	לקח	542		take
	לקח	qal	pft	3ms	לקח	542		take
12:2	יאמרו	qal	wci	3mp	אמר	55		say
	דבר	piel	pft	3ms	דבר	180		speak
	דבר	piel	pft	3ms	דבר	180		speak
	ישמע	qal	wci	3ms	שמע	1033		hear
12:4	יאמר	qal	wci	3ms	אמר	55		say
12:4	צאו	qal	impv	mp	יצא	422		go out
	יצאו	qal	wci	3mp	יצא	422		go out
12:5	ירד	qal	wci	3ms	ירד	432		come down
	יעמד	qal	wci	3ms	עמד	763		stand,stop
	יקרא	qal	wci	3ms	קרא	894		call,proclaim
	יצאו	qal	wci	3mp	יצא	422		go out
12:6	יאמר	qal	wci	3ms	אמר	55		say
	שמעו	qal	impv	mp	שמע	1033		hear
	יהיה	qal	impf	3ms	היה	224		be,become
	אתודע	hith	impf	1cs	ידע	393		make self known
	אדבר	piel	impf	1cs	דבר	180		speak
12:7	נאמן	niph	ptc	ms	אמן	52		be confirmed
12:8	אדבר	piel	impf	1cs	דבר	180		speak
	יביט	hiph	impf	3ms	נבט	613		look,regard
	יראתם	qal	pft	2mp	ירא	431		fear
	דבר	piel	infc		דבר	180		speak
12:9	יחר	qal	wci	3ms	חרה	354		be kindled,burn
	ילך	qal	wci	3ms	הלך	229		walk,go
12:10	סר	qal	pft	3ms	סור	693		turn aside
	מצרעת	pual	ptc	fs	צרע	863		be leprous
	יפן	qal	wci	3ms	פנה	815		turn
	מצרעת	pual	ptc	fs	צרע	863		be leprous
12:11	יאמר	qal	wci	3ms	אמר	55		say
	תשת	qal	jus	2ms	שית	1011		put,set
	נואלנו	niph	pft	1cp	יאל	383		act foolishly
	חטאנו	qal	pft	1cp	חטא	306		sin
12:12	תהי	qal	jus	3fs	היה	224		be,become
	מת	qal	ptc	ms	מות	559		die
	צאתו	qal	infc		יצא	422	3ms	go out
	יאכל	niph	wci	3ms	אכל	37		be eaten
12:13	יצעק	qal	wci	3ms	צעק	858		cry out
	אמר	qal	infc		אמר	55		say
	רפא	qal	impv	ms	רפא	950		heal
12:14	יאמר	qal	wci	3ms	אמר	55		say
	ירק	qal	infa		ירק	439		spit
	ירק	qal	pft	3ms	ירק	439		spit
	תכלם	niph	impf	3fs	כלם	483		be humiliated
	תסגר	niph	impf	3fs	סגר	688		be shut
	תאסף	niph	impf	3fs	אסף	62		assemble
12:15	תסגר	niph	wci	3fs	סגר	688		be shut
	נסע	qal	pft	3ms	נסע	652		pull up,set out
	האסף	niph	infc		אסף	62		assemble
12:16	נסעו	qal	pft	3cp	נסע	652		pull up,set out
	יחנו	qal	wci	3mp	חנה	333		decline,encamp
13:1	ידבר	piel	wci	3ms	דבר	180		speak
	אמר	qal	infc		אמר	55		say
13:2	שלח	qal	impv	ms	שלח	1018		send
	יתרו	qal	jusm	3mp	תור	1064		seek out,spy
	נתן	qal	ptc	ms	נתן	678		give,set
	תשלחו	qal	impf	2mp	שלח	1018		send
13:3	ישלח	qal	wci	3ms	שלח	1018		send
13:16	שלח	qal	pft	3ms	שלח	1018		send
	תור	qal	infc		תור	1064		seek out,spy
	יקרא	qal	wci	3ms	קרא	894		call,proclaim

ChVs	Form	Stem	Tnse	PGN	Root	BDB	Sfx	Meaning
13:17	ישלח	qal	wci	3ms	שלח	1018		send
	תור	qal	infc		תור	1064		seek out,spy
	יאמר	qal	wci	3ms	אמר	55		say
	עלו	qal	impv	mp	עלה	748		go up
	עליתם	qal	wcp	2mp	עלה	748		go up
13:18	ראיתם	qal	wcp	2mp	ראה	906		see
	ישב	qal	ptc	ms	ישב	442		sit,dwell
13:19	ישב	qal	ptc	ms	ישב	442		sit,dwell
	יושב	qal	ptc	ms	ישב	442		sit,dwell
13:20	התחזקתם	hith	wcp	2mp	חזק	304		strengthen self
	לקחתם	qal	wcp	2mp	לקח	542		take
13:21	יעלו	qal	wci	3mp	עלה	748		go up
	יתרו	qal	wci	3mp	תור	1064		seek out,spy
	בא	qal	infc		בוא	97		come in
13:22	יעלו	qal	wci	3mp	עלה	748		go up
	יבא	qal	wci	3ms	בוא	97		come in
	נבנתה	niph	pft	3fs	בנה	124		be built
13:23	יבאו	qal	wci	3mp	בוא	97		come in
	יכרתו	qal	wci	3mp	כרת	503		cut,destroy
	ישאהו	qal	wci	3mp	נשא	669	3ms	lift,carry
13:24	קרא	qal	pft	3ms	קרא	894		call,proclaim
	כרתו	qal	pft	3cp	כרת	503		cut,destroy
13:25	ישבו	qal	wci	3mp	שוב	996		turn,return
	תור	qal	infc		תור	1064		seek out,spy
13:26	ילכו	qal	wci	3mp	הלך	229		walk,go
	יבאו	qal	wci	3mp	בוא	97		come in
	ישיבו	hiph	wci	3mp	שוב	996		bring back
	יראום	hiph	wci	3mp	ראה	906	3mp	show,exhibit
13:27	יספרו	piel	wci	3mp	ספר	707		recount
	יאמרו	qal	wci	3mp	אמר	55		say
	באנו	qal	pft	1cp	בוא	97		come in
	שלחתנו	qal	pft	2ms	שלח	1018	1cp	send
	זבת	qal	ptc	fs	זוב	264		flow,gush
13:28	ישב	qal	ptc	ms	ישב	442		sit,dwell
	בצרות	qal	pptc	fp	בצר	130		cut off
	ראינו	qal	pft	1cp	ראה	906		see
13:29	יושב	qal	ptc	ms	ישב	442		sit,dwell
	יושב	qal	ptc	ms	ישב	442		sit,dwell
	ישב	qal	ptc	ms	ישב	442		sit,dwell
13:30	יהס	hiph	wci	3ms	הסה	245		silence
	יאמר	qal	wci	3ms	אמר	55		say
	עלה	qal	infa		עלה	748		go up
	נעלה	qal	impf	1cp	עלה	748		go up
	ירשנו	qal	wcp	1cp	ירש	439		possess,inherit
	יכול	qal	infa		יכל	407		be able
	נוכל	qal	impf	1cp	יכל	407		be able
13:31	עלו	qal	pft	3cp	עלה	748		go up
	אמרו	qal	pft	3cp	אמר	55		say
	נוכל	qal	impf	1cp	יכל	407		be able
	עלות	qal	infc		עלה	748		go up
13:32	יוציאו	hiph	wci	3mp	יצא	422		bring out
	תרו	qal	pft	3cp	תור	1064		seek out,spy
	אמר	qal	infc		אמר	55		say
	עברנו	qal	pft	1cp	עבר	716		pass over
13:32	תור	qal	infc		תור	1064		seek out,spy
	אכלת	qal	ptc	fs	אכל	37		eat,devour
	יושביה	qal	ptc	mp	ישב	442	3fs	sit,dwell
	ראינו	qal	pft	1cp	ראה	906		see
13:33	ראינו	qal	pft	1cp	ראה	906		see
	נהי	qal	wci	1cp	היה	224		be,become
	היינו	qal	pft	1cp	היה	224		be,become
14:1	תשא	qal	wci	3fs	נשא	669		lift,carry
	יתנו	qal	wci	3mp	נתן	678		give,set
	יבכו	qal	wci	3mp	בכה	113		weep
14:2	ילנו	niph	wci	3mp	לון	534		murmur
	יאמרו	qal	wci	3mp	אמר	55		say
	מתנו	qal	pft	1cp	מות	559		die
	מתנו	qal	pft	1cp	מות	559		die
14:3	מביא	hiph	ptc	ms	בוא	97		bring in
	נפל	qal	infc		נפל	656		fall
	יהיו	qal	impf	3mp	היה	224		be,become
	שוב	qal	infc		שוב	996		turn,return
14:4	יאמרו	qal	wci	3mp	אמר	55		say
	נתנה	qal	coh	1cp	נתן	678		give,set
	נשובה	qal	coh	1cp	שוב	996		turn,return
14:5	יפל	qal	wci	3ms	נפל	656		fall
14:6	תרים	qal	ptc	mp	תור	1064		seek out,spy
	קרעו	qal	pft	3cp	קרע	902		tear,rend
14:7	יאמרו	qal	wci	3mp	אמר	55		say
	אמר	qal	infc		אמר	55		say
	עברנו	qal	pft	1cp	עבר	716		pass over
	תור	qal	infc		תור	1064		seek out,spy
14:8	חפץ	qal	pft	3ms	חפץ	342		delight in
	הביא	hiph	wcp	3ms	בוא	97		bring in
	נתנה	qal	wcp	3ms	נתן	678	3fs	give,set
	זבת	qal	ptc	fs	זוב	264		flow,gush
14:9	תמרדו	qal	jusm	2mp	מרד	597		rebel
	תיראו	qal	jusm	2mp	ירא	431		fear
	סר	qal	pft	3ms	סור	693		turn aside
	תיראם	qal	jusm	2mp	ירא	431	3mp	fear
14:10	יאמרו	qal	wci	3mp	אמר	55		say
	רגום	qal	infc		רגם	920		stone
	נראה	niph	pft	3ms	ראה	906		appear,be seen
14:11	יאמר	qal	wci	3ms	אמר	55		say
	ינאצני	piel	impf	3mp	נאץ	610	1cs	spurn
	יאמינו	hiph	impf	3mp	אמן	52		believe
	עשיתי	qal	pft	1cs	עשה	793		do,make
14:12	אכנו	hiph	impf	1cs	נכה	645	3ms	smite
	אורשנו	hiph	impf	1cs	ירש	439	3ms	c. to possess
	אעשה	qal	impf	1cs	עשה	793		do,make
14:13	יאמר	qal	wci	3ms	אמר	55		say
	שמעו	qal	wcp	3cp	שמע	1033		hear
	העלית	hiph	pft	2ms	עלה	748		bring up,offer
14:14	אמרו	qal	wcp	3cp	אמר	55		say
	יושב	qal	ptc	ms	ישב	442		sit,dwell
	שמעו	qal	pft	3cp	שמע	1033		hear
	נראה	niph	pft	3ms	ראה	906		appear,be seen
	עמד	qal	ptc	ms	עמד	763		stand,stop

ChVs	Form	Stem	Tnse	PGN	Root	BDB	Sfx	Meaning
14:14	הלך	qal	ptc	ms	הלך	229		walk,go
14:15	המתה	hiph	wcp	2ms	מות	559		kill
	אמרו	qal	wcp	3cp	אמר	55		say
	שמעו	qal	pft	3cp	שמע	1033		hear
	אמר	qal	infc		אמר	55		say
14:16	יכלת	qal	infc		יכל	407		be able
	הביא	hiph	infc		בוא	97		bring in
	נשבע	niph	pft	3ms	שבע	989		swear
	ישחטם	qal	wci	3ms	שחט	1006	3mp	slaughter
14:17	יגדל	qal	jusm	3ms	גדל	152		be great,grow
	דברת	piel	pft	2ms	דבר	180		speak
	אמר	qal	infc		אמר	55		say
14:18	נשא	qal	ptc	ms	נשא	669		lift,carry
	נקה	piel	infa		נקה	667		acquit
	ינקה	piel	impf	3ms	נקה	667		acquit
	פקד	qal	ptc	ms	פקד	823		attend to,visit
14:19	סלח	qal	impv	ms	סלח	699		forgive,pardon
	נשאתה	qal	pft	2ms	נשא	669		lift,carry
14:20	יאמר	qal	wci	3ms	אמר	55		say
	סלחתי	qal	pft	1cs	סלח	699		forgive,pardon
14:21	ימלא	niph	impf	3ms	מלא	569		be filled
14:22	ראים	qal	ptc	mp	ראה	906		see
	עשיתי	qal	pft	1cs	עשה	793		do,make
	ינסו	piel	wci	3mp	נסה	650		test,try
	שמעו	qal	pft	3cp	שמע	1033		hear
14:23	יראו	qal	impf	3mp	ראה	906		see
	נשבעתי	niph	pft	1cs	שבע	989		swear
	מנאצי	piel	ptc	mp	נאץ	610	1cs	spurn
	יראוה	qal	impf	3mp	ראה	906	3fs	see
14:24	היתה	qal	pft	3fs	היה	224		be,become
	ימלא	piel	wci	3ms	מלא	569		fill
	הביאתיו	hiph	wcp	1cs	בוא	97	3ms	bring in
	בא	qal	pft	3ms	בוא	97		come in
	יורשנה	hiph	impf	3ms	ירש	439	3fs	c. to possess
14:25	יושב	qal	ptc	ms	ישב	442		sit,dwell
	פנו	qal	impv	mp	פנה	815		turn
	סעו	qal	impv	mp	נסע	652		pull up,set out
14:26	ידבר	piel	wci	3ms	דבר	180		speak
	אמר	qal	infc		אמר	55		say
14:27	מלינים	hiph	ptc	mp	לון	534		murmur
	מלינים	hiph	ptc	mp	לון	534		murmur
	שמעתי	qal	pft	1cs	שמע	1033		hear
14:28	אמר	qal	impv	ms	אמר	55		say
	דברתם	piel	pft	2mp	דבר	180		speak
	אעשה	qal	impf	1cs	עשה	793		do,make
14:29	יפלו	qal	impf	3mp	נפל	656		fall
	פקדיכם	qal	pptc	mp	פקד	823	2mp	attend to,visit
	הלינתם	hiph	pft	2mp	לון	534		murmur
14:30	תבאו	qal	impf	2mp	בוא	97		come in
	נשאתי	qal	pft	1cs	נשא	669		lift,carry
	שכן	piel	infc		שכן	1014		establish
14:31	אמרתם	qal	pft	2mp	אמר	55		say
	יהיה	qal	impf	3ms	היה	224		be,become
	הביאתי	hiph	wcp	1cs	בוא	97		bring in
14:31	ידעו	qal	wcp	3cp	ידע	393		know
	מאסתם	qal	pft	2mp	מאס	549		reject,refuse
14:32	יפלו	qal	impf	3mp	נפל	656		fall
14:33	יהיו	qal	impf	3mp	היה	224		be,become
	רעים	qal	ptc	mp	רעה	944		pasture,tend
	נשאו	qal	wcp	3cp	נשא	669		lift,carry
	תם	qal	infc		תמם	1070		be finished
14:34	תרתם	qal	pft	2mp	תור	1064		seek out,spy
	תשאו	qal	impf	2mp	נשא	669		lift,carry
	ידעתם	qal	wcp	2mp	ידע	393		know
14:35	דברתי	piel	pft	1cs	דבר	180		speak
	אעשה	qal	impf	1cs	עשה	793		do,make
	נועדים	niph	ptc	mp	יעד	416		gather
	יתמו	qal	impf	3mp	תמם	1070		be finished
	ימתו	qal	impf	3mp	מות	559		die
14:36	שלח	qal	pft	3ms	שלח	1018		send
	תור	qal	infc		תור	1064		seek out,spy
	ישבו	qal	wci	3mp	שוב	996		turn,return
	אילונוk	niph	wci	3mp	לון	534		murmur
	ילינוq	hiph	wci	3mp	לון	534		murmur
	הוציא	hiph	infc		יצא	422		bring out
14:37	ימתו	qal	wci	3mp	מות	559		die
	מוצאי	hiph	ptc	mp	יצא	422		bring out
14:38	חיו	qal	pft	3cp	חיה	310		live
	הלכים	qal	ptc	mp	הלך	229		walk,go
	תור	qal	infc		תור	1064		seek out,spy
14:39	ידבר	piel	wci	3ms	דבר	180		speak
	יתאבלו	hith	wci	3mp	אבל	5		mourn
14:40	ישכמו	hiph	wci	3mp	שכם	1014		rise early
	יעלו	qal	wci	3mp	עלה	748		go up
	אמר	qal	infc		אמר	55		say
	עלינו	qal	wcp	1cp	עלה	748		go up
	אמר	qal	pft	3ms	אמר	55		say
	חטאנו	qal	pft	1cp	חטא	306		sin
14:41	יאמר	qal	wci	3ms	אמר	55		say
	עברים	qal	ptc	mp	עבר	716		pass over
	תצלח	qal	impf	3fs	צלח	852		prosper
14:42	תעלו	qal	jusm	2mp	עלה	748		go up
	תנגפו	niph	impf	2mp	נגף	619		be smitten
	איביכם	qal	ptc	mp	איב	33	2mp	be hostile to
14:43	נפלתם	qal	wcp	2mp	נפל	656		fall
	שבתם	qal	pft	2mp	שוב	996		turn,return
	יהיה	qal	impf	3ms	היה	224		be,become
14:44	יעפלו	hiph	wci	3mp	עפל	779		be heedless
	עלות	qal	infc		עלה	748		go up
	משו	qal	pft	3cp	מוש	559		depart,remove
14:45	ירד	qal	wci	3ms	ירד	432		come down
	ישב	qal	ptc	ms	ישב	442		sit,dwell
	יכום	hiph	wci	3mp	נכה	645	3mp	smite
	יכתום	hiph	wci	3mp	כתת	510	3mp	beat in pieces
15:1	ידבר	piel	wci	3ms	דבר	180		speak
	אמר	qal	infc		אמר	55		say
15:2	דבר	piel	impv	ms	דבר	180		speak
	אמרת	qal	wcp	2ms	אמר	55		say

ChVs	Form	Stem	Tnse	PGN	Root	BDB	Sfx	Meaning
15:2	תבאו	qal	impf	2mp	בוא	97		come in
	נתן	qal	ptc	ms	נתן	678		give,set
15:3	עשיתם	qal	wcp	2mp	עשה	793		do,make
	פלא	piel	infc		פלא	810		offer
	עשות	qal	infc		עשה	793		do,make
15:4	הקריב	hiph	wcp	3ms	קרב	897		bring near
	מקריב	hiph	ptc	ms	קרב	897		bring near
	בלול	qal	pptc	ms	בלל	117		mingle,mix
15:5	תעשה	qal	impf	2ms	עשה	793		do,make
15:6	תעשה	qal	impf	2ms	עשה	793		do,make
	בלולה	qal	pptc	fs	בלל	117		mingle,mix
15:7	תקריב	hiph	impf	2ms	קרב	897		bring near
15:8	תעשה	qal	impf	2ms	עשה	793		do,make
	פלא	piel	infc		פלא	810		offer
15:9	הקריב	hiph	wcp	3ms	קרב	897		bring near
	בלול	qal	pptc	ms	בלל	117		mingle,mix
15:10	תקריב	hiph	impf	2ms	קרב	897		bring near
15:11	יעשה	niph	impf	3ms	עשה	793		be done
15:12	תעשו	qal	impf	2mp	עשה	793		do,make
	תעשו	qal	impf	2mp	עשה	793		do,make
15:13	יעשה	qal	impf	3ms	עשה	793		do,make
	הקריב	hiph	infc		קרב	897		bring near
15:14	יגור	qal	impf	3ms	גור	157		sojourn
	עשה	qal	wcp	3ms	עשה	793		do,make
	תעשו	qal	impf	2mp	עשה	793		do,make
	יעשה	qal	impf	3ms	עשה	793		do,make
15:15	גר	qal	ptc	ms	גור	157		sojourn
	יהיה	qal	impf	3ms	היה	224		be,become
15:16	יהיה	qal	impf	3ms	היה	224		be,become
	גר	qal	ptc	ms	גור	157		sojourn
15:17	ידבר	piel	wci	3ms	דבר	180		speak
	אמר	qal	infc		אמר	55		say
15:18	דבר	piel	impv	ms	דבר	180		speak
	אמרת	qal	wcp	2ms	אמר	55		say
	באכם	qal	infc		בוא	97	2mp	come in
	מביא	hiph	ptc	ms	בוא	97		bring in
15:19	היה	qal	wcp	3ms	היה	224		be,become
	אכלכם	qal	infc		אכל	37	2mp	eat,devour
	תרימו	hiph	impf	2mp	רום	926		raise,lift
15:20	תרימו	hiph	impf	2mp	רום	926		raise,lift
	תרימו	hiph	impf	2mp	רום	926		raise,lift
15:21	תתנו	qal	impf	2mp	נתן	678		give,set
15:22	תשגו	qal	impf	2mp	שגה	993		err,go astray
	תעשו	qal	impf	2mp	עשה	793		do,make
	דבר	piel	pft	3ms	דבר	180		speak
15:23	צוה	piel	pft	3ms	צוה	845		command
	צוה	piel	pft	3ms	צוה	845		command
15:24	היה	qal	wcp	3ms	היה	224		be,become
	נעשתה	niph	pft	3fs	עשה	793		be done
	עשו	qal	wcp	3cp	עשה	793		do,make
15:25	כפר	piel	wcp	3ms	כפר	497		cover,atone
	נסלח	niph	wcp	3ms	סלח	699		be forgiven
	הביאו	hiph	pft	3cp	בוא	97		bring in
15:26	נסלח	niph	wcp	3ms	סלח	699		be forgiven
15:26	גר	qal	ptc	ms	גור	157		sojourn
15:27	תחטא	qal	impf	3fs	חטא	306		sin
	הקריבה	hiph	wcp	3fs	קרב	897		bring near
15:28	כפר	piel	wcp	3ms	כפר	497		cover,atone
	שגגת	qal	ptc	fs	שגג	992		err,sin
	חטאה	qal	infc		חטא	306		sin
	כפר	piel	infc		כפר	497		cover,atone
	נסלח	niph	wcp	3ms	סלח	699		be forgiven
15:29	גר	qal	ptc	ms	גור	157		sojourn
	יהיה	qal	impf	3ms	היה	224		be,become
	עשה	qal	ptc	ms	עשה	793		do,make
15:30	תעשה	qal	impf	3fs	עשה	793		do,make
	רמה	qal	ptc	fs	רום	926		be high
	מגדף	piel	ptc	ms	גדף	154		revile
	נכרתה	niph	wcp	3fs	כרת	503		be cut off
15:31	בזה	qal	pft	3ms	בזה	102		despise
	הפר	hiph	pft	3ms	פרר	830		break,frustrate
	הכרת	niph	infa		כרת	503		be cut off
	תכרת	niph	impf	3fs	כרת	503		be cut off
15:32	יהיו	qal	wci	3mp	היה	224		be,become
	ימצאו	qal	wci	3mp	מצא	592		find
	מקשש	poel	ptc	ms	קשש	905		gather stubble
15:33	יקריבו	hiph	wci	3mp	קרב	897		bring near
	מצאים	qal	ptc	mp	מצא	592		find
	מקשש	poel	ptc	ms	קשש	905		gather stubble
15:34	יניחו	hiph	wci	3mp	נוח	628		give rest,put
	פרש	pual	pft	3ms	פרש	831		made distinct
	יעשה	niph	impf	3ms	עשה	793		be done
15:35	יאמר	qal	wci	3ms	אמר	55		say
	מות	qal	infa		מות	559		die
	יומת	hoph	impf	3ms	מות	559		be killed
	רגום	qal	infa		רגם	920		stone
15:36	יציאו	hiph	wci	3mp	יצא	422		bring out
	ירגמו	qal	wci	3mp	רגם	920		stone
	ימת	qal	wci	3ms	מות	559		die
	צוה	piel	pft	3ms	צוה	845		command
15:37	יאמר	qal	wci	3ms	אמר	55		say
	אמר	qal	infc		אמר	55		say
15:38	דבר	piel	impv	ms	דבר	180		speak
	אמרת	qal	wcp	2ms	אמר	55		say
	עשו	qal	wcp	3cp	עשה	793		do,make
	נתנו	qal	wcp	3cp	נתן	678		give,set
15:39	היה	qal	wcp	3ms	היה	224		be,become
	ראיתם	qal	wcp	2mp	ראה	906		see
	זכרתם	qal	wcp	2mp	זכר	269		remember
	עשיתם	qal	wcp	2mp	עשה	793		do,make
	תתרו	qal	impf	2mp	תור	1064		seek out,spy
	זנים	qal	ptc	mp	זנה	275		act a harlot
15:40	תזכרו	qal	impf	2mp	זכר	269		remember
	עשיתם	qal	wcp	2mp	עשה	793		do,make
	הייתם	qal	wcp	2mp	היה	224		be,become
15:41	הוצאתי	hiph	pft	1cs	יצא	422		bring out
	היות	qal	infc		היה	224		be,become
16:1	יקח	qal	wci	3ms	לקח	542		take

ChVs	Form	Stem	Tnse	PGN	Root	BDB	Sfx	Meaning
16:2	יקמו	qal	wci	3mp	קום	877		arise,stand
16:3	יקהלו	niph	wci	3mp	קהל	874		assemble
	יאמרו	qal	wci	3mp	אמר	55		say
	תתנשׂאו	hith	impf	2mp	נשׂא	669		lift self up
16:4	ישׁמע	qal	wci	3ms	שׁמע	1033		hear
	יפל	qal	wci	3ms	נפל	656		fall
16:5	ידבר	piel	wci	3ms	דבר	180		speak
	אמר	qal	infc		אמר	55		say
	ידע	hiph	jus	3ms	ידע	393		declare
	הקריב	hiph	wcp	3ms	קרב	897		bring near
	יבחר	qal	impf	3ms	בחר	103		choose
	יקריב	hiph	impf	3ms	קרב	897		bring near
16:6	עשׂו	qal	impv	mp	עשׂה	793		do,make
	קחו	qal	impv	mp	לקח	542		take
16:7	תנו	qal	impv	mp	נתן	678		give,set
	שׂימו	qal	impv	mp	שׂים	962		put,set
	היה	qal	wcp	3ms	היה	224		be,become
	יבחר	qal	impf	3ms	בחר	103		choose
16:8	יאמר	qal	wci	3ms	אמר	55		say
	שׁמעו	qal	impv	mp	שׁמע	1033		hear
16:9	הבדיל	hiph	pft	3ms	בדל	95		divide
	הקריב	hiph	infc		קרב	897		bring near
	עבד	qal	infc		עבד	712		work,serve
	עמד	qal	infc		עמד	763		stand,stop
	שׁרתם	piel	infc		שׁרת	1058	3mp	minister,serve
16:10	יקרב	hiph	wci	3ms	קרב	897		bring near
	בקשׁתם	piel	wcp	2mp	בקשׁ	134		seek
16:11	נעדים	niph	ptc	mp	יעד	416		gather
	תלונוk	niph	impf	2mp	לון	534		murmur
	תלינוq	hiph	impf	2mp	לון	534		murmur
16:12	ישׁלח	qal	wci	3ms	שׁלח	1018		send
	קרא	qal	infc		קרא	894		call,proclaim
	יאמרו	qal	wci	3mp	אמר	55		say
	נעלה	qal	impf	1cp	עלה	748		go up
16:13	העליתנו	hiph	pft	2ms	עלה	748	1cp	bring up,offer
	זבת	qal	ptc	fs	זוב	264		flow,gush
	המיתנו	hiph	infc		מות	559	1cp	kill
	תשׂתרר	hith	impf	2ms	שׂרר	979		make self ruler
	השׂתרר	hith	infa		שׂרר	979		make self ruler
16:14	זבת	qal	ptc	fs	זוב	264		flow,gush
	הביאתנו	hiph	pft	2ms	בוא	97	1cp	bring in
	תתן	qal	wci	2ms	נתן	678		give,set
	תנקר	piel	impf	2ms	נקר	669		bore out
	נעלה	qal	impf	1cp	עלה	748		go up
16:15	יחר	qal	wci	3ms	חרה	354		be kindled,burn
	יאמר	qal	wci	3ms	אמר	55		say
	תפן	qal	jus	2ms	פנה	815		turn
	נשׂאתי	qal	pft	1cs	נשׂא	669		lift,carry
	הרעתי	hiph	pft	1cs	רעע	949		hurt,do evil
16:16	יאמר	qal	wci	3ms	אמר	55		say
	היו	qal	impv	mp	היה	224		be,become
16:17	קחו	qal	impv	mp	לקח	542		take
	נתתם	qal	wcp	2mp	נתן	678		give,set
	הקרבתם	hiph	wcp	2mp	קרב	897		bring near
16:18	יקחו	qal	wci	3mp	לקח	542		take
	יתנו	qal	wci	3mp	נתן	678		give,set
	ישׂימו	qal	wci	3mp	שׂים	962		put,set
	יעמדו	qal	wci	3mp	עמד	763		stand,stop
16:19	יקהל	hiph	wci	3ms	קהל	874		call assembly
	ירא	niph	wci	3ms	ראה	906		appear,be seen
16:20	ידבר	piel	wci	3ms	דבר	180		speak
	אמר	qal	infc		אמר	55		say
16:21	הבדלו	niph	impv	mp	בדל	95		separate self
	אכלה	piel	cohm	1cs	כלה	477		complete,finish
16:22	יפלו	qal	wci	3mp	נפל	656		fall
	יאמרו	qal	wci	3mp	אמר	55		say
	יחטא	qal	impf	3ms	חטא	306		sin
	תקצף	qal	impf	2ms	קצף	893		be angry
16:23	ידבר	piel	wci	3ms	דבר	180		speak
	אמר	qal	infc		אמר	55		say
16:24	דבר	piel	impv	ms	דבר	180		speak
	אמר	qal	infc		אמר	55		say
	העלו	niph	impv	mp	עלה	748		be brought up
16:25	יקם	qal	wci	3ms	קום	877		arise,stand
	ילך	qal	wci	3ms	הלך	229		walk,go
	ילכו	qal	wci	3mp	הלך	229		walk,go
16:26	ידבר	piel	wci	3ms	דבר	180		speak
	אמר	qal	infc		אמר	55		say
	סורו	qal	impv	mp	סור	693		turn aside
	תגעו	qal	jusm	2mp	נגע	619		touch,strike
	תספו	niph	impf	2mp	ספה	705		be swept away
16:27	יעלו	niph	wci	3mp	עלה	748		be brought up
	יצאו	qal	pft	3cp	יצא	422		go out
	נצבים	niph	ptc	mp	נצב	662		stand
16:28	יאמר	qal	wci	3ms	אמר	55		say
	תדעון	qal	impf	2mp	ידע	393		know
	שׁלחני	qal	pft	3ms	שׁלח	1018	1cs	send
	עשׂות	qal	infc		עשׂה	793		do,make
16:29	ימתון	qal	impf	3mp	מות	559		die
	יפקד	niph	impf	3ms	פקד	823		be visited
	שׁלחני	qal	pft	3ms	שׁלח	1018	1cs	send
16:30	יברא	qal	impf	3ms	ברא	135		create
	פצתה	qal	wcp	3fs	פצה	822		open,set free
	בלעה	qal	wcp	3fs	בלע	118		swallow
	ירדו	qal	wcp	3cp	ירד	432		come down
	ידעתם	qal	wcp	2mp	ידע	393		know
	נאצו	piel	pft	3cp	נאץ	610		spurn
16:31	יהי	qal	wci	3ms	היה	224		be,become
	כלתו	piel	infc		כלה	477	3ms	complete,finish
	דבר	piel	infc		דבר	180		speak
	תבקע	niph	wci	3fs	בקע	131		be cleft
16:32	תפתח	qal	wci	3fs	פתח	834		open
	תבלע	qal	wci	3fs	בלע	118		swallow
16:33	ירדו	qal	wci	3mp	ירד	432		come down
	תכס	piel	wci	3fs	כסה	491		cover
	יאבדו	qal	wci	3mp	אבד	1		perish
16:34	נסו	qal	pft	3cp	נוס	630		flee,escape
	אמרו	qal	pft	3cp	אמר	55		say

ChVs	Form	Stem	Tnse	PGN	Root	BDB	Sfx	Meaning
16:34	תבלענו	qal	impf	3fs	בלע	118	1cp	swallow
16:35	יצאה	qal	pft	3fs	יצא	422		go out
	תאכל	qal	wci	3fs	אכל	37		eat, devour
	מקריבי	hiph	ptc	mp	קרב	897		bring near
17:1	ידבר	piel	wci	3ms	דבר	180		speak
	אמר	qal	infc		אמר	55		say
17:2	אמר	qal	impv	ms	אמר	55		say
	ירם	hiph	jus	3ms	רום	926		raise, lift
	זרה	qal	impv	ms	זרה	279		scatter
	קדשׁו	qal	pft	3cp	קדשׁ	872		be set apart
17:3	עשׂו	qal	wcp	3cp	עשׂה	793		do, make
	הקריבם	hiph	pft	3cp	קרב	897	3mp	bring near
	יקדשׁו	qal	wci	3mp	קדשׁ	872		be set apart
	יהיו	qal	jusm	3mp	היה	224		be, become
17:4	יקח	qal	wci	3ms	לקח	542		take
	הקריבו	hiph	pft	3cp	קרב	897		bring near
	שׂרפים	qal	pptc	mp	שׂרף	976		burn
	ירקעום	piel	wci	3mp	רקע	955	3mp	overlay
17:5	יקרב	qal	impf	3ms	קרב	897		approach
	הקטיר	hiph	infc		קטר	882		make sacrifices
	יהיה	qal	impf	3ms	היה	224		be, become
	דבר	piel	pft	3ms	דבר	180		speak
17:6	ילנו	niph	wci	3mp	לון	534		murmur
	אמר	qal	infc		אמר	55		say
	המתם	hiph	pft	2mp	מות	559		kill
17:7	יהי	qal	wci	3ms	היה	224		be, become
	הקהל	niph	infc		קהל	874		assemble
	יפנו	qal	wci	3mp	פנה	815		turn
	כסהו	piel	pft	3ms	כסה	491	3ms	cover
	ירא	niph	wci	3ms	ראה	906		appear, be seen
17:8	יבא	qal	wci	3ms	בוא	97		come in
17:9	ידבר	piel	wci	3ms	דבר	180		speak
	אמר	qal	infc		אמר	55		say
17:10	הרמו	niph	impv	mp	רמם	942		lift up oneself
	אכלה	piel	cohm	1cs	כלה	477		complete, finish
	יפלו	qal	wci	3mp	נפל	656		fall
17:11	יאמר	qal	wci	3ms	אמר	55		say
	קח	qal	impv	ms	לקח	542		take
	תן	qal	impv	ms	נתן	678		give, set
	שׂים	qal	impv	ms	שׂים	962		put, set
	הולך	hiph	impv	ms	הלך	229		lead, bring
	כפר	piel	impv	ms	כפר	497		cover, atone
	יצא	qal	pft	3ms	יצא	422		go out
	החל	hiph	pft	3ms	חלל	320		begin, profane
17:12	יקח	qal	wci	3ms	לקח	542		take
	דבר	piel	pft	3ms	דבר	180		speak
	ירץ	qal	wci	3ms	רוץ	930		run
	החל	hiph	pft	3ms	חלל	320		begin, profane
	יתן	qal	wci	3ms	נתן	678		give, set
	יכפר	piel	wci	3ms	כפר	497		cover, atone
17:13	יעמד	qal	wci	3ms	עמד	763		stand, stop
	מתים	qal	ptc	mp	מות	559		die
	תעצר	niph	wci	3fs	עצר	783		be restrained
17:14	יהיו	qal	wci	3mp	היה	224		be, become
17:14	מתים	qal	ptc	mp	מות	559		die
	מתים	qal	ptc	mp	מות	559		die
17:15	ישׁב	qal	wci	3ms	שׁוב	996		turn, return
	נעצרה	niph	pft	3fs	עצר	783		be restrained
17:16	ידבר	piel	wci	3ms	דבר	180		speak
	אמר	qal	infc		אמר	55		say
17:17	דבר	piel	impv	ms	דבר	180		speak
	קח	qal	impv	ms	לקח	542		take
	תכתב	qal	impf	2ms	כתב	507		write
17:18	תכתב	qal	impf	2ms	כתב	507		write
17:19	הנחתם	hiph	wcp	2ms	נוח	628	3mp	give rest, put
	אועד	niph	impf	1cs	יעד	416		gather
17:20	היה	qal	wcp	3ms	היה	224		be, become
	אבחר	qal	impf	1cs	בחר	103		choose
	יפרח	qal	impf	3ms	פרח	827		bud
	השׁכתי	hiph	wcp	1cs	שׁכך	1013		still, calm
	מלינם	hiph	ptc	mp	לון	534		murmur
17:21	ידבר	piel	wci	3ms	דבר	180		speak
	יתנו	qal	wci	3mp	נתן	678		give, set
17:22	ינח	hiph	wci	3ms	נוח	628		give rest, put
17:23	יהי	qal	wci	3ms	היה	224		be, become
	יבא	qal	wci	3ms	בוא	97		come in
	פרח	qal	pft	3ms	פרח	827		bud
	יצא	hiph	wci	3ms	יצא	422		bring out
	יצץ	hiph	wci	3ms	צוץ	847		blossom
	יגמל	qal	wci	3ms	גמל	168		deal out, ripen
17:24	יצא	hiph	wci	3ms	יצא	422		bring out
	יראו	qal	wci	3mp	ראה	906		see
	יקחו	qal	wci	3mp	לקח	542		take
17:25	יאמר	qal	wci	3ms	אמר	55		say
	השׁב	hiph	impv	ms	שׁוב	996		bring back
	תכל	piel	jus	3fs	כלה	477		complete, finish
	ימתו	qal	impf	3mp	מות	559		die
17:26	יעשׂ	qal	wci	3ms	עשׂה	793		do, make
	צוה	piel	pft	3ms	צוה	845		command
	עשׂה	qal	pft	3ms	עשׂה	793		do, make
17:27	יאמרו	qal	wci	3mp	אמר	55		say
	אמר	qal	infc		אמר	55		say
	גוענו	qal	pft	1cp	גוע	157		expire, die
	אבדנו	qal	pft	1cp	אבד	1		perish
	אבדנו	qal	pft	1cp	אבד	1		perish
17:28	ימות	qal	impf	3ms	מות	559		die
	תמנו	qal	pft	1cp	תמם	1070		be finished
	גוע	qal	infc		גוע	157		expire, die
18:1	יאמר	qal	wci	3ms	אמר	55		say
	תשׂאו	qal	impf	2mp	נשׂא	669		lift, carry
	תשׂאו	qal	impf	2mp	נשׂא	669		lift, carry
18:2	הקרב	hiph	impv	ms	קרב	897		bring near
	ילוו	niph	jusm	3mp	לוה	530		join oneself
	ישׁרתוך	piel	jusm	3mp	שׁרת	1058	2ms	minister, serve
18:3	שׁמרו	qal	wcp	3cp	שׁמר	1036		keep, watch
	יקרבו	qal	impf	3mp	קרב	897		approach
	ימתו	qal	impf	3mp	מות	559		die
18:4	נלוו	niph	wcp	3cp	לוה	530		join oneself

ChVs	Form	Stem	Tnse	PGN	Root	BDB	Sfx	Meaning
18: 4	שׁמרו	qal	wcp	3cp	שׁמר	1036		keep,watch
	זר	qal	ptc	ms	זור	266		be stranger
	יקרב	qal	impf	3ms	קרב	897		approach
18: 5	שׁמרתם	qal	wcp	2mp	שׁמר	1036		keep,watch
	יהיה	qal	impf	3ms	היה	224		be,become
18: 6	לקחתי	qal	pft	1cs	לקח	542		take
	נתנים	qal	pptc	mp	נתן	678		give,set
	עבד	qal	infc		עבד	712		work,serve
18: 7	תשׁמרו	qal	impf	2mp	שׁמר	1036		keep,watch
	עבדתם	qal	wcp	2mp	עבד	712		work,serve
	אתן	qal	impf	1cs	נתן	678		give,set
	זר	qal	ptc	ms	זור	266		be stranger
	יומת	hoph	impf	3ms	מות	559		be killed
18: 8	ידבר	piel	wci	3ms	דבר	180		speak
	נתתי	qal	pft	1cs	נתן	678		give,set
	נתתים	qal	pft	1cs	נתן	678	3mp	give,set
18: 9	יהיה	qal	impf	3ms	היה	224		be,become
	ישׁיבו	hiph	impf	3mp	שׁוב	996		bring back
18: 10	תאכלנו	qal	impf	2ms	אכל	37	3ms	eat,devour
	יאכל	qal	impf	3ms	אכל	37		eat,devour
	יהיה	qal	impf	3ms	היה	224		be,become
18: 11	נתתים	qal	pft	1cs	נתן	678	3mp	give,set
	יאכל	qal	impf	3ms	אכל	37		eat,devour
18: 12	יתנו	qal	impf	3mp	נתן	678		give,set
	נתתים	qal	pft	1cs	נתן	678	3mp	give,set
18: 13	יביאו	hiph	impf	3mp	בוא	97		bring in
	יהיה	qal	impf	3ms	היה	224		be,become
	יאכלנו	qal	impf	3ms	אכל	37	3ms	eat,devour
18: 14	יהיה	qal	impf	3ms	היה	224		be,become
18: 15	יקריבו	hiph	impf	3mp	קרב	897		bring near
	יהיה	qal	impf	3ms	היה	224		be,become
	פדה	qal	infa		פדה	804		ransom
	תפדה	qal	impf	2ms	פדה	804		ransom
	תפדה	qal	impf	2ms	פדה	804		ransom
18: 16	תפדה	qal	impf	2ms	פדה	804		ransom
18: 17	תפדה	qal	impf	2ms	פדה	804		ransom
	תזרק	qal	impf	2ms	זרק	284		toss,scatter
	תקטיר	hiph	impf	2ms	קטר	882		make sacrifices
18: 18	יהיה	qal	impf	3ms	היה	224		be,become
	יהיה	qal	impf	3ms	היה	224		be,become
18: 19	ירימו	hiph	impf	3mp	רום	926		raise,lift
	נתתי	qal	pft	1cs	נתן	678		give,set
18: 20	יאמר	qal	wci	3ms	אמר	55		say
	תנחל	qal	impf	2ms	נחל	635		possess,inherit
	יהיה	qal	impf	3ms	היה	224		be,become
18: 21	נתתי	qal	pft	1cs	נתן	678		give,set
	עבדים	qal	ptc	mp	עבד	712		work,serve
18: 22	יקרבו	qal	impf	3mp	קרב	897		approach
	שׂאת	qal	infc		נשׂא	669		lift,carry
	מות	qal	infc		מות	559		die
18: 23	עבד	qal	wcp	3ms	עבד	712		work,serve
	ישׂאו	qal	impf	3mp	נשׂא	669		lift,carry
	ינחלו	qal	impf	3mp	נחל	635		possess,inherit
18: 24	ירימו	hiph	impf	3mp	רום	926		raise,lift
18: 24	נתתי	qal	pft	1cs	נתן	678		give,set
	אמרתי	qal	pft	1cs	אמר	55		say
	ינחלו	qal	impf	3mp	נחל	635		possess,inherit
18: 25	ידבר	piel	wci	3ms	דבר	180		speak
	אמר	qal	infc		אמר	55		say
18: 26	תדבר	piel	impf	2ms	דבר	180		speak
	אמרת	qal	wcp	2ms	אמר	55		say
	תקחו	qal	impf	2mp	לקח	542		take
	נתתי	qal	pft	1cs	נתן	678		give,set
	הרמתם	hiph	wcp	2mp	רום	926		raise,lift
18: 27	נחשב	niph	wcp	3ms	חשב	362		be thought
18: 28	תרימו	hiph	impf	2mp	רום	926		raise,lift
	תקחו	qal	impf	2mp	לקח	542		take
	נתתם	qal	wcp	2mp	נתן	678		give,set
18: 29	תרימו	hiph	impf	2mp	רום	926		raise,lift
18: 30	אמרת	qal	wcp	2ms	אמר	55		say
	הרימכם	hiph	infc		רום	926	2mp	raise,lift
	נחשב	niph	wcp	3ms	חשב	362		be thought
18: 31	אכלתם	qal	wcp	2mp	אכל	37		eat,devour
18: 32	תשׂאו	qal	impf	2mp	נשׂא	669		lift,carry
	הרימכם	hiph	infc		רום	926	2mp	raise,lift
	תחללו	piel	impf	2mp	חלל	320		pollute
	תמותו	qal	impf	2mp	מות	559		die
19: 1	ידבר	piel	wci	3ms	דבר	180		speak
	אמר	qal	infc		אמר	55		say
19: 2	צוה	piel	pft	3ms	צוה	845		command
	אמר	qal	infc		אמר	55		say
	דבר	piel	impv	ms	דבר	180		speak
	יקחו	qal	jusm	3mp	לקח	542		take
	עלה	qal	pft	3ms	עלה	748		go up
19: 3	נתתם	qal	wcp	2mp	נתן	678		give,set
	הוציא	hiph	wcp	3ms	יצא	422		bring out
	שׁחט	qal	wcp	3ms	שׁחט	1006		slaughter
19: 4	לקח	qal	wcp	3ms	לקח	542		take
	הזה	hiph	wcp	3ms	נזה	633		cause to spurt
19: 5	שׂרף	qal	wcp	3ms	שׂרף	976		burn
	ישׂרף	qal	impf	3ms	שׂרף	976		burn
19: 6	לקח	qal	wcp	3ms	לקח	542		take
	השׁליך	hiph	wcp	3ms	שׁלך	1020		throw,cast
19: 7	כבס	piel	wcp	3ms	כבס	460		wash
	רחץ	qal	wcp	3ms	רחץ	934		wash,bathe
	יבוא	qal	impf	3ms	בוא	97		come in
	טמא	qal	wcp	3ms	טמא	379		become unclean
19: 8	שׂרף	qal	ptc	ms	שׂרף	976		burn
	יכבס	piel	impf	3ms	כבס	460		wash
	רחץ	qal	wcp	3ms	רחץ	934		wash,bathe
	טמא	qal	wcp	3ms	טמא	379		become unclean
19: 9	אסף	qal	wcp	3ms	אסף	62		gather
	הניח	hiph	wcp	3ms	נוח	628		give rest,put
	היתה	qal	wcp	3fs	היה	224		be,become
19: 10	כבס	piel	wcp	3ms	כבס	460		wash
	אסף	qal	ptc	ms	אסף	62		gather
	טמא	qal	wcp	3ms	טמא	379		become unclean
	היתה	qal	wcp	3fs	היה	224		be,become

ChVs	Form	Stem	Tnse	PGN	Root	BDB	Sfx	Meaning
19: 10	גר	qal	ptc	ms	גור	157		sojourn
19: 11	נגע	qal	ptc	ms	נגע	619		touch,strike
	מת	qal	ptc	ms	מות	559		die
	טמא	qal	wcp	3ms	טמא	379		become unclean
19: 12	יתחטא	hith	impf	3ms	חטא	306		purify oneself
	יטהר	qal	impf	3ms	טהר	372		be clean,pure
	יתחטא	hith	impf	3ms	חטא	306		purify oneself
	יטהר	qal	impf	3ms	טהר	372		be clean,pure
19: 13	נגע	qal	ptc	ms	נגע	619		touch,strike
	מת	qal	ptc	ms	מות	559		die
	ימות	qal	impf	3ms	מות	559		die
	יתחטא	hith	impf	3ms	חטא	306		purify oneself
	טמא	piel	pft	3ms	טמא	379		defile
	נכרתה	niph	wcp	3fs	כרת	503		be cut off
	זרק	qalp	pft	3ms	זרק	284		be sprinkled
	יהיה	qal	impf	3ms	היה	224		be, become
19: 14	ימות	qal	impf	3ms	מות	559		die
	בא	qal	ptc	ms	בוא	97		come in
	יטמא	qal	impf	3ms	טמא	379		become unclean
19: 15	פתוח	qal	pptc	ms	פתח	834		open
19: 16	יגע	qal	impf	3ms	נגע	619		touch,strike
	מת	qal	ptc	ms	מות	559		die
	יטמא	qal	impf	3ms	טמא	379		become unclean
19: 17	לקחו	qal	wcp	3cp	לקח	542		take
	נתן	qal	wcp	3ms	נתן	678		give,set
19: 18	לקח	qal	wcp	3ms	לקח	542		take
	טבל	qal	wcp	3ms	טבל	371		dip
	הזה	hiph	wcp	3ms	נזה	633		cause to spurt
	היו	qal	pft	3cp	היה	224		be, become
	נגע	qal	ptc	ms	נגע	619		touch,strike
	מת	qal	ptc	ms	מות	559		die
19: 19	הזה	hiph	wcp	3ms	נזה	633		cause to spurt
	חטאו	piel	wcp	3ms	חטא	306	3ms	purify
	כבס	piel	wcp	3ms	כבס	460		wash
	רחץ	qal	wcp	3ms	רחץ	934		wash, bathe
	טהר	qal	wcp	3ms	טהר	372		be clean,pure
19: 20	יטמא	qal	impf	3ms	טמא	379		become unclean
	יתחטא	hith	impf	3ms	חטא	306		purify oneself
	נכרתה	niph	wcp	3fs	כרת	503		be cut off
	טמא	piel	pft	3ms	טמא	379		defile
	זרק	qalp	pft	3ms	זרק	284		be sprinkled
19: 21	היתה	qal	wcp	3fs	היה	224		be, become
	מזה	hiph	ptc	ms	נזה	633		cause to spurt
	יכבס	piel	impf	3ms	כבס	460		wash
	נגע	qal	ptc	ms	נגע	619		touch,strike
	יטמא	qal	impf	3ms	טמא	379		become unclean
19: 22	יגע	qal	impf	3ms	נגע	619		touch,strike
	יטמא	qal	impf	3ms	טמא	379		become unclean
	נגעת	qal	ptc	fs	נגע	619		touch,strike
	תטמא	qal	impf	3fs	טמא	379		become unclean
20: 1	יבאו	qal	wci	3mp	בוא	97		come in
	ישב	qal	wci	3ms	ישב	442		sit,dwell
	תמת	qal	wci	3fs	מות	559		die
	תקבר	niph	wci	3fs	קבר	868		be buried
20: 2	היה	qal	pft	3ms	היה	224		be, become
	יקהלו	niph	wci	3mp	קהל	874		assemble
20: 3	ירב	qal	wci	3ms	ריב	936		strive,contend
	יאמרו	qal	wci	3mp	אמר	55		say
	אמר	qal	infc		אמר	55		say
	גוענו	qal	pft	1cp	גוע	157		expire,die
	גוע	qal	infc		גוע	157		expire,die
20: 4	הבאתם	hiph	pft	2mp	בוא	97		bring in
	מות	qal	infc		מות	559		die
20: 5	העליתנו	hiph	pft	2mp	עלה	748	1cp	bring up,offer
	הביא	hiph	infc		בוא	97		bring in
	שתות	qal	infc		שתה	1059		drink
20: 6	יבא	qal	wci	3ms	בוא	97		come in
	יפלו	qal	wci	3mp	נפל	656		fall
	ירא	niph	wci	3ms	ראה	906		appear, be seen
20: 7	ידבר	piel	wci	3ms	דבר	180		speak
	אמר	qal	infc		אמר	55		say
20: 8	קח	qal	impv	ms	לקח	542		take
	הקהל	hiph	impv	ms	קהל	874		call assembly
	דברתם	piel	wcp	2mp	דבר	180		speak
	נתן	qal	wcp	3ms	נתן	678		give,set
	הוצאת	hiph	wcp	2ms	יצא	422		bring out
	השקית	hiph	wcp	2ms	שקה	1052		give to drink
20: 9	יקח	qal	wci	3ms	לקח	542		take
	צוהו	piel	pft	3ms	צוה	845	3ms	command
20: 10	יקהלו	hiph	wci	3mp	קהל	874		call assembly
	יאמר	qal	wci	3ms	אמר	55		say
	שמעו	qal	impv	mp	שמע	1033		hear
	מרים	qal	ptc	mp	מרה	598		be disobedient
	נוציא	hiph	impf	1cp	יצא	422		bring out
20: 11	ירם	hiph	wci	3ms	רום	926		raise, lift
	יך	hiph	wci	3ms	נכה	645		smite
	יצאו	qal	wci	3mp	יצא	422		go out
	תשת	qal	wci	3fs	שתה	1059		drink
20: 12	יאמר	qal	wci	3ms	אמר	55		say
	האמנתם	hiph	pft	2mp	אמן	52		believe
	הקדישני	hiph	infc		קדש	872	1cs	consecrate
	תביאו	hiph	impf	2mp	בוא	97		bring in
	נתתי	qal	pft	1cs	נתן	678		give,set
20: 13	רבו	qal	pft	3cp	ריב	936		strive,contend
	יקדש	niph	wci	3ms	קדש	872		be sacred
20: 14	ישלח	qal	wci	3ms	שלח	1018		send
	אמר	qal	pft	3ms	אמר	55		say
	ידעת	qal	pft	2ms	ידע	393		know
	מצאתנו	qal	pft	3fs	מצא	592	1cp	find
20: 15	ירדו	qal	wci	3mp	ירד	432		come down
	נשב	qal	wci	1cp	ישב	442		sit,dwell
	ירעו	hiph	wci	3mp	רעע	949		hurt,do evil
20: 16	נצעק	qal	wci	1cp	צעק	858		cry out
	ישמע	qal	wci	3ms	שמע	1033		hear
	ישלח	qal	wci	3ms	שלח	1018		send
	יצאנו	hiph	wci	3ms	יצא	422	1cp	bring out
20: 17	נעברה	qal	coh	1cp	עבר	716		pass over
	נעבר	qal	impf	1cp	עבר	716		pass over

ChVs	Form	Stem	Tnse	PGN	Root	BDB	Sfx	Meaning
20:17	נשתה	qal	impf	1cp	שתה	1059		drink
	נלך	qal	impf	1cp	הלך	229		walk,go
	נטה	qal	impf	1cp	נטה	639		stretch,incline
	נעבר	qal	impf	1cp	עבר	716		pass over
20:18	יאמר	qal	wci	3ms	אמר	55		say
	תעבר	qal	impf	2ms	עבר	716		pass over
	אצא	qal	impf	1cs	יצא	422		go out
	קראתך	qal	infc		קרא	896	2ms	meet,encounter
20:19	יאמרו	qal	wci	3mp	אמר	55		say
	נעלה	qal	cohm	1cp	עלה	748		go up
	נשתה	qal	impf	1cp	שתה	1059		drink
	נתתי	qal	wcp	1cs	נתן	678		give,set
	אעברה	qal	coh	1cs	עבר	716		pass over
20:20	יאמר	qal	wci	3ms	אמר	55		say
	תעבר	qal	impf	2ms	עבר	716		pass over
	יצא	qal	wci	3ms	יצא	422		go out
	קראתו	qal	infc		קרא	896	3ms	meet,encounter
20:21	ימאן	piel	wci	3ms	מאן	549		refuse
	נתן	qal	infc		נתן	678		give,set
	עבר	qal	infc		עבר	716		pass over
	יט	qal	wci	3ms	נטה	639		stretch,incline
20:22	יסעו	qal	wci	3mp	נסע	652		pull up,set out
	יבאו	qal	wci	3mp	בוא	97		come in
20:23	יאמר	qal	wci	3ms	אמר	55		say
	אמר	qal	infc		אמר	55		say
20:24	יאסף	niph	impf	3ms	אסף	62		assemble
	יבא	qal	impf	3ms	בוא	97		come in
	נתתי	qal	pft	1cs	נתן	678		give,set
	מריתם	qal	pft	2mp	מרה	598		be disobedient
20:25	קח	qal	impv	ms	לקח	542		take
	העל	hiph	impv	ms	עלה	748		bring up,offer
20:26	הפשט	hiph	impv	ms	פשט	832		strip off
	הלבשתם	hiph	wcp	2ms	לבש	527	3mp	clothe
	יאסף	niph	impf	3ms	אסף	62		assemble
	מת	qal	wcp	3ms	מות	559		die
20:27	יעש	qal	wci	3ms	עשה	793		do,make
	צוה	piel	pft	3ms	צוה	845		command
	יעלו	qal	wci	3mp	עלה	748		go up
20:28	יפשט	hiph	wci	3ms	פשט	832		strip off
	ילבש	hiph	wci	3ms	לבש	527		clothe
	ימת	qal	wci	3ms	מות	559		die
	ירד	qal	wci	3ms	ירד	432		come down
20:29	יראו	qal	wci	3mp	ראה	906		see
	גוע	qal	pft	3ms	גוע	157		expire,die
	יבכו	qal	wci	3mp	בכה	113		weep
21:1	ישמע	qal	wci	3ms	שמע	1033		hear
	ישב	qal	ptc	ms	ישב	442		sit,dwell
	בא	qal	pft	3ms	בוא	97		come in
	ילחם	niph	wci	3ms	לחם	535		wage war
	ישב	qal	wci	3ms	שבה	985		take captive
21:2	ידר	qal	wci	3ms	נדר	623		vow
	יאמר	qal	wci	3ms	אמר	55		say
	נתן	qal	infa		נתן	678		give,set
	תתן	qal	impf	2ms	נתן	678		give,set
21:2	החרמתי	hiph	wcp	1cs	חרם	355		ban,destroy
21:3	ישמע	qal	wci	3ms	שמע	1033		hear
	יתן	qal	wci	3ms	נתן	678		give,set
	יחרם	hiph	wci	3ms	חרם	355		ban,destroy
	יקרא	qal	wci	3ms	קרא	894		call,proclaim
21:4	יסעו	qal	wci	3mp	נסע	652		pull up,set out
	סבב	qal	infc		סבב	685		surround
	תקצר	qal	wci	3fs	קצר	894		be short
21:5	ידבר	piel	wci	3ms	דבר	180		speak
	העליתנו	hiph	pft	2mp	עלה	748	1cp	bring up,offer
	מות	qal	infc		מות	559		die
	קצה	qal	pft	3fs	קוץ	880		loathe,abhor
21:6	ישלח	piel	wci	3ms	שלח	1018		send away,shoot
	ינשכו	piel	wci	3mp	נשך	675		bite
	ימת	qal	wci	3ms	מות	559		die
21:7	יבא	qal	wci	3ms	בוא	97		come in
	יאמרו	qal	wci	3mp	אמר	55		say
	חטאנו	qal	pft	1cp	חטא	306		sin
	דברנו	piel	pft	1cp	דבר	180		speak
	התפלל	hith	impv	ms	פלל	813		pray
	יסר	hiph	jus	3ms	סור	693		take away
	יתפלל	hith	wci	3ms	פלל	813		pray
21:8	יאמר	qal	wci	3ms	אמר	55		say
	עשה	qal	impv	ms	עשה	793		do,make
	שים	qal	impv	ms	שים	962		put,set
	היה	qal	wcp	3ms	היה	224		be,become
	נשוך	qal	pptc	ms	נשך	675		bite
	ראה	qal	wcp	3ms	ראה	906		see
	חי	qal	wcp	3ms	חיה	310		live
21:9	יעש	qal	wci	3ms	עשה	793		do,make
	ישמהו	qal	wci	3ms	שים	962	3ms	put,set
	היה	qal	wcp	3ms	היה	224		be,become
	נשך	qal	pft	3ms	נשך	675		bite
	הביט	hiph	wcp	3ms	נבט	613		look,regard
	חי	qal	wcp	3ms	חיה	310		live
21:10	יסעו	qal	wci	3mp	נסע	652		pull up,set out
	יחנו	qal	wci	3mp	חנה	333		decline,encamp
21:11	יסעו	qal	wci	3mp	נסע	652		pull up,set out
	יחנו	qal	wci	3mp	חנה	333		decline,encamp
21:12	נסעו	qal	pft	3cp	נסע	652		pull up,set out
	יחנו	qal	wci	3mp	חנה	333		decline,encamp
21:13	נסעו	qal	pft	3cp	נסע	652		pull up,set out
	יחנו	qal	wci	3mp	חנה	333		decline,encamp
	יצא	qal	ptc	ms	יצא	422		go out
21:14	יאמר	niph	impf	3ms	אמר	55		be said,called
21:15	נטה	qal	pft	3ms	נטה	639		stretch,incline
	נשען	niph	wcp	3ms	שען	1043		lean,support
21:16	אמר	qal	pft	3ms	אמר	55		say
	אסף	qal	impv	ms	אסף	62		gather
	אתנה	qal	coh	1cs	נתן	678		give,set
21:17	ישיר	qal	impf	3ms	שיר	1010		sing
	עלי	qal	impv	fs	עלה	748		go up
	ענו	qal	impv	mp	ענה	777		sing
21:18	חפרוה	qal	pft	3cp	חפר	343	3fs	dig,search

ChVs	Form	Stem	Tnse	PGN	Root	BDB	Sfx	Meaning
21:18	כרוה	qal	pft	3cp	כרה	500	3fs	dig
	מחקק	poel	ptc	ms	חקק	349		prescribe(r)
21:20	נשקפה	niph	wcp	3fs	שקף	1054		look down
21:21	ישלח	qal	wci	3ms	שלח	1018		send
	אמר	qal	infc		אמר	55		say
21:22	אעברה	qal	coh	1cs	עבר	716		pass over
	נטה	qal	impf	1cp	נטה	639		stretch,incline
	נשתה	qal	impf	1cp	שתה	1059		drink
	נלך	qal	impf	1cp	הלך	229		walk,go
	נעבר	qal	impf	1cp	עבר	716		pass over
21:23	נתן	qal	pft	3ms	נתן	678		give,set
	עבר	qal	infc		עבר	716		pass over
	יאסף	qal	wci	3ms	אסף	62		gather
	יצא	qal	wci	3ms	יצא	422		go out
	קראת	qal	infc		קרא	896		meet,encounter
	יבא	qal	wci	3ms	בוא	97		come in
	ילחם	niph	wci	3ms	לחם	535		wage war
21:24	יכהו	hiph	wci	3ms	נכה	645	3ms	smite
	יירש	qal	wci	3ms	ירש	439		possess,inherit
21:25	יקח	qal	wci	3ms	לקח	542		take
	ישב	qal	wci	3ms	ישב	442		sit,dwell
21:26	נלחם	niph	pft	3ms	לחם	535		wage war
	יקח	qal	wci	3ms	לקח	542		take
21:27	יאמרו	qal	impf	3mp	אמר	55		say
	משלים	qal	ptc	mp	משל	605		use a proverb
	באו	qal	impv	mp	בוא	97		come in
	תבנה	niph	jusm	3fs	בנה	124		be built
	תכונן	htpo	jusm	3fs	כון	465		be established
21:28	יצאה	qal	pft	3fs	יצא	422		go out
	אכלה	qal	pft	3fs	אכל	37		eat,devour
21:29	אבדת	qal	pft	2ms	אבד	1		perish
	נתן	qal	pft	3ms	נתן	678		give,set
21:30	נירם	qal	wci	1cp	ירה	434	3mp	throw,shoot
	אבד	qal	pft	3ms	אבד	1		perish
	נשים	hiph	wci	1cp	שמם	1030		ravage,appall
21:31	ישב	qal	wci	3ms	ישב	442		sit,dwell
21:32	ישלח	qal	wci	3ms	שלח	1018		send
	רגל	piel	infc		רגל	920		slander,spy
	ילכדו	qal	wci	3mp	לכד	539		capture
	ויירשk	qal	wci	3ms	ירש	439		possess,inherit
	ויורשq	hiph	wci	3ms	ירש	439		c. to possess
21:33	יפנו	qal	wci	3mp	פנה	815		turn
	יעלו	qal	wci	3mp	עלה	748		go up
	יצא	qal	wci	3ms	יצא	422		go out
	קראתם	qal	infc		קרא	896	3mp	meet,encounter
21:34	יאמר	qal	wci	3ms	אמר	55		say
	תירא	qal	jusm	2ms	ירא	431		fear
	נתתי	qal	pft	1cs	נתן	678		give,set
	עשית	qal	wcp	2ms	עשה	793		do,make
	עשית	qal	pft	2ms	עשה	793		do,make
	יושב	qal	ptc	ms	ישב	442		sit,dwell
21:35	יכו	hiph	wci	3mp	נכה	645		smite
	השאיר	hiph	pft	3ms	שאר	983		leave,spare
	יירשו	qal	wci	3mp	ירש	439		possess,inherit

ChVs	Form	Stem	Tnse	PGN	Root	BDB	Sfx	Meaning
22:1	יסעו	qal	wci	3mp	נסע	652		pull up,set out
	יחנו	qal	wci	3mp	חנה	333		decline,encamp
22:2	ירא	qal	wci	3ms	ראה	906		see
	עשה	qal	pft	3ms	עשה	793		do,make
22:3	יגר	qal	wci	3ms	גור	158		dread
	יקץ	qal	wci	3ms	קוץ	880		loathe,abhor
22:4	יאמר	qal	wci	3ms	אמר	55		say
	ילחכו	piel	impf	3mp	לחך	535		lick up
	לחך	qal	infc		לחך	535		lick
22:5	ישלח	qal	wci	3ms	שלח	1018		send
	קרא	qal	infc		קרא	894		call,proclaim
	אמר	qal	infc		אמר	55		say
	יצא	qal	pft	3ms	יצא	422		go out
	כסה	piel	pft	3ms	כסה	491		cover
	ישב	qal	ptc	ms	ישב	442		sit,dwell
22:6	לכה	qal	impv	ms	הלך	229		walk,go
	ארה	qal	impv	ms	ארר	76		curse
	אוכל	qal	impf	1cs	יכל	407		be able
	נכה	hiph	impf	1cp	נכה	645		smite
	אגרשנו	piel	wci	1cs	גרש	176	3ms	drive out
	ידעתי	qal	pft	1cs	ידע	393		know
	תברך	piel	impf	2ms	ברך	138		bless
	מברך	pual	ptc	ms	ברך	138		be blessed
	תאר	qal	impf	2ms	ארר	76		curse
	יואר	hoph	impf	3ms	ארר	76		be cursed
22:7	ילכו	qal	wci	3mp	הלך	229		walk,go
	יבאו	qal	wci	3mp	בוא	97		come in
	ידברו	piel	wci	3mp	דבר	180		speak
22:8	יאמר	qal	wci	3ms	אמר	55		say
	לינו	qal	impv	mp	לון	533		lodge,remain
	השבתי	hiph	wcp	1cs	שוב	996		bring back
	ידבר	piel	impf	3ms	דבר	180		speak
	ישבו	qal	wci	3mp	ישב	442		sit,dwell
22:9	יבא	qal	wci	3ms	בוא	97		come in
	יאמר	qal	wci	3ms	אמר	55		say
22:10	יאמר	qal	wci	3ms	אמר	55		say
	שלח	qal	pft	3ms	שלח	1018		send
22:11	יצא	qal	ptc	ms	יצא	422		go out
	יכס	piel	wci	3ms	כסה	491		cover
	לכה	qal	impv	ms	הלך	229		walk,go
	קבה	qal	impv	ms	קבב	866		curse
	אוכל	qal	impf	1cs	יכל	407		be able
	הלחם	niph	infc		לחם	535		wage war
	גרשתיו	piel	wcp	1cs	גרש	176	3ms	drive out
22:12	יאמר	qal	wci	3ms	אמר	55		say
	תלך	qal	impf	2ms	הלך	229		walk,go
	תאר	qal	impf	2ms	ארר	76		curse
	ברוך	qal	pptc	ms	ברך	138		kneel,bless
22:13	יקם	qal	wci	3ms	קום	877		arise,stand
	יאמר	qal	wci	3ms	אמר	55		say
	לכו	qal	impv	mp	הלך	229		walk,go
	מאן	piel	pft	3ms	מאן	549		refuse
	תתי	qal	infc		נתן	678	1cs	give,set
	הלך	qal	infc		הלך	229		walk,go

ChVs	Form	Stem	Tnse	PGN	Root	BDB	Sfx	Meaning
22: 14	יקומו	qal	wci	3mp	קום	877		arise,stand
	יבאו	qal	wci	3mp	בוא	97		come in
	יאמרו	qal	wci	3mp	אמר	55		say
	מאן	piel	pft	3ms	מאן	549		refuse
	הלך	qal	infc		הלך	229		walk,go
22: 15	יסף	hiph	wci	3ms	יסף	414		add,do again
	שלח	qal	infc		שלח	1018		send
	נכבדים	niph	ptc	mp	כבד	457		be honored
22: 16	יבאו	qal	wci	3mp	בוא	97		come in
	יאמרו	qal	wci	3mp	אמר	55		say
	אמר	qal	pft	3ms	אמר	55		say
	תמנע	niph	jusm	2ms	מנע	586		be withholden
	הלך	qal	infc		הלך	229		walk,go
22: 17	כבד	piel	infa		כבד	457		honor,make dull
	אכבדך	piel	impf	1cs	כבד	457	2ms	honor,make dull
	תאמר	qal	impf	2ms	אמר	55		say
	אעשה	qal	impf	1cs	עשה	793		do,make
	לכה	qal	impv	ms	הלך	229		walk,go
	קבה	qal	impv	ms	קבב	866		curse
22: 18	יען	qal	wci	3ms	ענה	772		answer
	יאמר	qal	wci	3ms	אמר	55		say
	יתן	qal	impf	3ms	נתן	678		give,set
	אוכל	qal	impf	1cs	יכל	407		be able
	עבר	qal	infc		עבר	716		pass over
	עשות	qal	infc		עשה	793		do,make
22: 19	שבו	qal	impv	mp	ישב	442		sit,dwell
	אדעה	qal	coh	1cs	ידע	393		know
	יסף	hiph	jus	3ms	יסף	414		add,do again
	דבר	piel	infc		דבר	180		speak
22: 20	יבא	qal	wci	3ms	בוא	97		come in
	יאמר	qal	wci	3ms	אמר	55		say
	קרא	qal	infc		קרא	894		call,proclaim
	באו	qal	pft	3cp	בוא	97		come in
	קום	qal	impv	ms	קום	877		arise,stand
	לך	qal	impv	ms	הלך	229		walk,go
	אדבר	piel	impf	1cs	דבר	180		speak
	תעשה	qal	impf	2ms	עשה	793		do,make
22: 21	יקם	qal	wci	3ms	קום	877		arise,stand
	יחבש	qal	wci	3ms	חבש	289		bind
	ילך	qal	wci	3ms	הלך	229		walk,go
22: 22	יחר	qal	wci	3ms	חרה	354		be kindled, burn
	הולך	qal	ptc	ms	הלך	229		walk,go
	יתיצב	hith	wci	3ms	יצב	426		stand oneself
	רכב	qal	ptc	ms	רכב	938		mount,ride
22: 23	תרא	qal	wci	3fs	ראה	906		see
	נצב	niph	ptc	ms	נצב	662		stand
	שלופה	qal	pptc	fs	שלף	1025		draw out,off
	תט	qal	wci	3fs	נטה	639		stretch,incline
	תלך	qal	wci	3fs	הלך	229		walk,go
	יך	hiph	wci	3ms	נכה	645		smite
	הטתה	hiph	infc		נטה	639	3fs	turn,incline
22: 24	יעמד	qal	wci	3ms	עמד	763		stand,stop
22: 25	תרא	qal	wci	3fs	ראה	906		see
	תלחץ	niph	wci	3fs	לחץ	537		squeeze oneself
22: 25	תלחץ	qal	wci	3fs	לחץ	537		press,oppress
	יסף	hiph	wci	3ms	יסף	414		add,do again
	הכתה	hiph	infc		נכה	645	3fs	smite
22: 26	יוסף	hiph	wci	3ms	יסף	414		add,do again
	עבור	qal	infc		עבר	716		pass over
	יעמד	qal	wci	3ms	עמד	763		stand,stop
	נטות	qal	infc		נטה	639		stretch,incline
22: 27	תרא	qal	wci	3fs	ראה	906		see
	תרבץ	qal	wci	3fs	רבץ	918		lie down
	יחר	qal	wci	3ms	חרה	354		be kindled,burn
	יך	hiph	wci	3ms	נכה	645		smite
22: 28	יפתח	qal	wci	3ms	פתח	834		open
	תאמר	qal	wci	3fs	אמר	55		say
	עשיתי	qal	pft	1cs	עשה	793		do,make
	הכיתני	hiph	pft	2ms	נכה	645	1cs	smite
22: 29	יאמר	qal	wci	3ms	אמר	55		say
	התעללת	hith	pft	2fs	עלל	759		busy,vex
	הרגתיך	qal	pft	1cs	הרג	246	2fs	kill
22: 30	תאמר	qal	wci	3fs	אמר	55		say
	רכבת	qal	pft	2ms	רכב	938		mount,ride
	הסכן	hiph	infa		סכן	698		show habit
	הסכנתי	hiph	pft	1cs	סכן	698		show habit
	עשות	qal	infc		עשה	793		do,make
	יאמר	qal	wci	3ms	אמר	55		say
22: 31	יגל	piel	wci	3ms	גלה	162		uncover
	ירא	qal	wci	3ms	ראה	906		see
	נצב	niph	ptc	ms	נצב	662		stand
	שלפה	qal	pptc	fs	שלף	1025		draw out,off
	יקד	qal	wci	3ms	קדד	869		bow down
	ישתחו	hish	wci	3ms	חוה	1005		bow down
22: 32	יאמר	qal	wci	3ms	אמר	55		say
	הכית	hiph	pft	2ms	נכה	645		smite
	יצאתי	qal	pft	1cs	יצא	422		go out
	ירט	qal	pft	3ms	ירט	437		precipitate
22: 33	תראני	qal	wci	3fs	ראה	906	1cs	see
	תט	qal	wci	3fs	נטה	639		stretch,incline
	נטתה	qal	pft	3fs	נטה	639		stretch,incline
	הרגתי	qal	pft	1cs	הרג	246		kill
	החייתי	hiph	pft	1cs	חיה	310		preserve
22: 34	יאמר	qal	wci	3ms	אמר	55		say
	חטאתי	qal	pft	1cs	חטא	306		sin
	ידעתי	qal	pft	1cs	ידע	393		know
	נצב	niph	ptc	ms	נצב	662		stand
	קראתי	qal	infc		קרא	896	1cs	meet,encounter
	רע	qal	pft	3ms	רעע	949		be evil
	אשובה	qal	coh	1cs	שוב	996		turn,return
22: 35	יאמר	qal	wci	3ms	אמר	55		say
	לך	qal	impv	ms	הלך	229		walk,go
	אדבר	piel	impf	1cs	דבר	180		speak
	תדבר	piel	impf	2ms	דבר	180		speak
	ילך	qal	wci	3ms	הלך	229		walk,go
22: 36	ישמע	qal	wci	3ms	שמע	1033		hear
	בא	qal	pft	3ms	בוא	97		come in
	יצא	qal	wci	3ms	יצא	422		go out

ChVs	Form	Stem	Tnse	PGN	Root	BDB	Sfx	Meaning
22:36	קראתו	qal	infc		קרא	896	3ms	meet,encounter
22:37	יאמר	qal	wci	3ms	אמר	55		say
	שׁלח	qal	infa		שׁלח	1018		send
	שׁלחתי	qal	pft	1cs	שׁלח	1018		send
	קרא	qal	infc		קרא	894		call,proclaim
	הלכת	qal	pft	2ms	הלך	229		walk,go
	אוכל	qal	impf	1cs	יכל	407		be able
	כבדך	piel	infc		כבד	457	2ms	honor,make dull
22:38	יאמר	qal	wci	3ms	אמר	55		say
	באתי	qal	pft	1cs	בוא	97		come in
	יכול	qal	infa		יכל	407		be able
	אוכל	qal	impf	1cs	יכל	407		be able
	דבר	piel	infc		דבר	180		speak
	ישׂים	qal	impf	3ms	שׂים	962		put,set
	אדבר	piel	impf	1cs	דבר	180		speak
22:39	ילך	qal	wci	3ms	הלך	229		walk,go
	יבאו	qal	wci	3mp	בוא	97		come in
22:40	יזבח	qal	wci	3ms	זבח	256		slaughter
	ישׁלח	piel	wci	3ms	שׁלח	1018		send away,shoot
22:41	יהי	qal	wci	3ms	היה	224		be,become
	יקח	qal	wci	3ms	לקח	542		take
	יעלהו	hiph	wci	3ms	עלה	748	3ms	bring up,offer
	ירא	qal	wci	3ms	ראה	906		see
23:1	יאמר	qal	wci	3ms	אמר	55		say
	בנה	qal	impv	ms	בנה	124		build
	הכן	hiph	impv	ms	כון	465		fix,prepare
23:2	יעשׂ	qal	wci	3ms	עשׂה	793		do,make
	דבר	piel	pft	3ms	דבר	180		speak
	יעל	hiph	wci	3ms	עלה	748		bring up,offer
23:3	יאמר	qal	wci	3ms	אמר	55		say
	התיצב	hith	impv	ms	יצב	426		stand oneself
	אלכה	qal	coh	1cs	הלך	229		walk,go
	יקרה	niph	impf	3ms	קרה	899		encounter
	קראתי	qal	infc		קרא	896	1cs	meet,encounter
	יראני	hiph	impf	3ms	ראה	906	1cs	show,exhibit
	הגדתי	hiph	wcp	1cs	נגד	616		declare,tell
	ילך	qal	wci	3ms	הלך	229		walk,go
23:4	יקר	niph	wci	3ms	קרה	899		encounter
	יאמר	qal	wci	3ms	אמר	55		say
	ערכתי	qal	pft	1cs	ערך	789		set in order
	אעל	hiph	wci	1cs	עלה	748		bring up,offer
23:5	ישׂם	qal	wci	3ms	שׂים	962		put,set
	יאמר	qal	wci	3ms	אמר	55		say
	שׁוב	qal	impv	ms	שׁוב	996		turn,return
	תדבר	piel	impf	2ms	דבר	180		speak
23:6	ישׁב	qal	wci	3ms	שׁוב	996		turn,return
	נצב	niph	ptc	ms	נצב	662		stand
23:7	ישׂא	qal	wci	3ms	נשׂא	669		lift,carry
	יאמר	qal	wci	3ms	אמר	55		say
	ינחני	hiph	impf	3ms	נחה	634	1cs	lead,guide
	לכה	qal	impv	ms	הלך	229		walk,go
	ארה	qal	impv	ms	ארר	76		curse
	לכה	qal	impv	ms	הלך	229		walk,go
	זעמה	qal	impv	ms	זעם	276		be indignant
23:8	אקב	qal	impf	1cs	קבב	866		curse
	קבה	qal	pft	3ms	קבב	866	3ms	curse
	אזעם	qal	impf	1cs	זעם	276		be indignant
	זעם	qal	pft	3ms	זעם	276		be indignant
23:9	אראנו	qal	impf	1cs	ראה	906	3ms	see
	אשׁורנו	qal	impf	1cs	שׁור	1003	3ms	behold,regard
	ישׁכן	qal	impf	3ms	שׁכן	1014		settle,dwell
	יתחשׁב	hith	impf	3ms	חשׁב	362		reckon oneself
23:10	מנה	qal	pft	3ms	מנה	584		count,allot
	תמת	qal	jus	3fs	מות	559		die
	תהי	qal	jus	3fs	היה	224		be,become
23:11	יאמר	qal	wci	3ms	אמר	55		say
	עשׂית	qal	pft	2ms	עשׂה	793		do,make
	קב	qal	infc		קבב	866		curse
	איבי	qal	ptc	mp	איב	33	1cs	be hostile to
	לקחתיך	qal	pft	1cs	לקח	542	2ms	take
	ברכת	piel	pft	2ms	ברך	138		bless
	ברך	piel	infa		ברך	138		bless
23:12	יען	qal	wci	3ms	ענה	772		answer
	יאמר	qal	wci	3ms	אמר	55		say
	ישׂים	qal	impf	3ms	שׂים	962		put,set
	אשׁמר	qal	impf	1cs	שׁמר	1036		keep,watch
	דבר	piel	infc		דבר	180		speak
23:13	יאמר	qal	wci	3ms	אמר	55		say
	לךk	qal	impv	ms	הלך	229		walk,go
	qלכה	qal	impv	ms	הלך	229		walk,go
	תראנו	qal	impf	2ms	ראה	906	3ms	see
	תראה	qal	impf	2ms	ראה	906		see
	תראה	qal	impf	2ms	ראה	906		see
	קבנו	qal	impv	ms	קבב	866	3ms	curse
23:14	יקחהו	qal	wci	3ms	לקח	542	3ms	take
	יבן	qal	wci	3ms	בנה	124		build
	יעל	hiph	wci	3ms	עלה	748		bring up,offer
23:15	יאמר	qal	wci	3ms	אמר	55		say
	התיצב	hith	impv	ms	יצב	426		stand oneself
	אקרה	niph	impf	1cs	קרה	899		encounter
23:16	יקר	niph	wci	3ms	קרה	899		encounter
	ישׂם	qal	wci	3ms	שׂים	962		put,set
	יאמר	qal	wci	3ms	אמר	55		say
	שׁוב	qal	impv	ms	שׁוב	996		turn,return
	תדבר	piel	impf	2ms	דבר	180		speak
23:17	יבא	qal	wci	3ms	בוא	97		come in
	נצב	niph	ptc	ms	נצב	662		stand
	יאמר	qal	wci	3ms	אמר	55		say
	דבר	piel	pft	3ms	דבר	180		speak
23:18	ישׂא	qal	wci	3ms	נשׂא	669		lift,carry
	יאמר	qal	wci	3ms	אמר	55		say
	קום	qal	impv	ms	קום	877		arise,stand
	שׁמע	qal	impv	ms	שׁמע	1033		hear
	האזינה	hiph	impv	ms	אזן	24		hear
23:19	יכזב	piel	jusm	3ms	כזב	469		lie,deceive
	יתנחם	hith	jusm	3ms	נחם	636		have compassion
	אמר	qal	pft	3ms	אמר	55		say
	יעשׂה	qal	impf	3ms	עשׂה	793		do,make

ChVs	Form	Stem	Tnse	PGN	Root	BDB	Sfx	Meaning
23: 19	דבר	piel	pft	3ms	דבר	180		speak
	יקימנה	hiph	impf	3ms	קום	877	3fs	raise, build, set
23: 20	ברך	piel	infa		ברך	138		bless
	לקחתי	qal	pft	1cs	לקח	542		take
	ברך	piel	pft	3ms	ברך	138		bless
	אשיבנה	hiph	impf	1cs	שׁוב	996	3fs	bring back
23: 21	הביט	hiph	pft	3ms	נבט	613		look, regard
	ראה	qal	pft	3ms	ראה	906		see
23: 22	מוציאם	hiph	ptc	ms	יצא	422	3mp	bring out
23: 23	יאמר	niph	impf	3ms	אמר	55		be said, called
	פעל	qal	pft	3ms	פעל	821		do, make
23: 24	יקום	qal	impf	3ms	קום	877		arise, stand
	יתנשׂא	hith	impf	3ms	נשׂא	669		lift self up
	ישׁכב	qal	impf	3ms	שׁכב	1011		lie, lie down
	יאכל	qal	impf	3ms	אכל	37		eat, devour
	ישׁתה	qal	impf	3ms	שׁתה	1059		drink
23: 25	יאמר	qal	wci	3ms	אמר	55		say
	קב	qal	infa		קבב	866		curse
	תקבנו	qal	impf	2ms	קבב	866	3ms	curse
	ברך	piel	infa		ברך	138		bless
	תברכנו	piel	impf	2ms	ברך	138	3ms	bless
23: 26	יען	qal	wci	3ms	ענה	772		answer
	יאמר	qal	wci	3ms	אמר	55		say
	דברתי	piel	pft	1cs	דבר	180		speak
	אמר	qal	infc		אמר	55		say
	ידבר	piel	impf	3ms	דבר	180		speak
	אעשׂה	qal	impf	1cs	עשׂה	793		do, make
23: 27	יאמר	qal	wci	3ms	אמר	55		say
	לכה	qal	impv	ms	הלך	229		walk, go
	אקחך	qal	cohm	1cs	לקח	542	2ms	take
	יישׁר	qal	impf	3ms	ישׁר	448		be straight
	קבתו	qal	wcp	2ms	קבב	866	3ms	curse
23: 28	יקח	qal	wci	3ms	לקח	542		take
	נשׁקף	niph	ptc	ms	שׁקף	1054		look down
23: 29	יאמר	qal	wci	3ms	אמר	55		say
	בנה	qal	impv	ms	בנה	124		build
	הכן	hiph	impv	ms	כון	465		fix, prepare
23: 30	יעשׂ	qal	wci	3ms	עשׂה	793		do, make
	אמר	qal	pft	3ms	אמר	55		say
	יעל	hiph	wci	3ms	עלה	748		bring up, offer
24: 1	ירא	qal	wci	3ms	ראה	906		see
	טוב	qal	pft	3ms	טוב	373		be pleasing
	ברך	piel	infc		ברך	138		bless
	הלך	qal	pft	3ms	הלך	229		walk, go
	קראת	qal	infc		קרא	896		meet, encounter
	ישׁת	qal	wci	3ms	שׁית	1011		put, set
24: 2	ישׂא	qal	wci	3ms	נשׂא	669		lift, carry
	ירא	qal	wci	3ms	ראה	906		see
	שׁכן	qal	ptc	ms	שׁכן	1014		settle, dwell
	תהי	qal	wci	3fs	היה	224		be, become
24: 3	ישׂא	qal	wci	3ms	נשׂא	669		lift, carry
	יאמר	qal	wci	3ms	אמר	55		say
	שׁתם	qal	pptc	ms	שׁתם	1060		open
24: 4	שׁמע	qal	ptc	ms	שׁמע	1033		hear
24: 4	יחזה	qal	impf	3ms	חזה	302		see
	נפל	qal	ptc	ms	נפל	656		fall
	גלוי	qal	pptc	ms	גלה	162		uncover
24: 5	טבו	qal	pft	3cp	טוב	373		be pleasing
24: 6	נטיו	niph	pft	3cp	נטה	639		be stretched
	נטע	qal	pft	3ms	נטע	642		plant
24: 7	יזל	qal	jusm	3ms	נזל	633		flow
	ירם	qal	jus	3ms	רום	926		be high
	תנשׂא	hith	jusm	3fs	נשׂא	669		lift self up
24: 8	מוציאו	hiph	ptc	ms	יצא	422	3ms	bring out
	יאכל	qal	impf	3ms	אכל	37		eat, devour
	יגרם	piel	impf	3ms	גרם	175		break bones
	ימחץ	qal	impf	3ms	מחץ	563		smite through
24: 9	כרע	qal	pft	3ms	כרע	502		bow down
	שׁכב	qal	pft	3ms	שׁכב	1011		lie, lie down
	יקימנו	hiph	impf	3ms	קום	877	3ms	raise, build, set
	מברכיך	piel	ptc	mp	ברך	138	2ms	bless
	ברוך	qal	pptc	ms	ברך	138		kneel, bless
	ארריך	qal	ptc	mp	ארר	76	2ms	curse
	ארור	qal	pptc	ms	ארר	76		curse
24: 10	יחר	qal	wci	3ms	חרה	354		be kindled, burn
	יספק	qal	wci	3ms	ספק	706		slap, clap
	יאמר	qal	wci	3ms	אמר	55		say
	קב	qal	infc		קבב	866		curse
	איבי	qal	ptc	mp	איב	33	1cs	be hostile to
	קראתיך	qal	pft	1cs	קרא	894	2ms	call, proclaim
	ברכת	piel	pft	2ms	ברך	138		bless
	ברך	piel	infa		ברך	138		bless
24: 11	ברח	qal	impv	ms	ברח	137		go thru, flee
	אמרתי	qal	pft	1cs	אמר	55		say
	כבד	piel	infa		כבד	457		honor, make dull
	אכבדך	piel	impf	1cs	כבד	457	2ms	honor, make dull
	מנעך	qal	pft	3ms	מנע	586	2ms	withhold
24: 12	יאמר	qal	wci	3ms	אמר	55		say
	שׁלחת	qal	pft	2ms	שׁלח	1018		send
	דברתי	piel	pft	1cs	דבר	180		speak
	אמר	qal	infc		אמר	55		say
24: 13	יתן	qal	impf	3ms	נתן	678		give, set
	אוכל	qal	impf	1cs	יכל	407		be able
	עבר	qal	infc		עבר	716		pass over
	עשׂות	qal	infc		עשׂה	793		do, make
	ידבר	piel	impf	3ms	דבר	180		speak
	אדבר	piel	impf	1cs	דבר	180		speak
24: 14	הולך	qal	ptc	ms	הלך	229		walk, go
	לכה	qal	impv	ms	הלך	229		walk, go
	איעצך	qal	cohm	1cs	יעץ	419	2ms	advise, counsel
	יעשׂה	qal	impf	3ms	עשׂה	793		do, make
24: 15	ישׂא	qal	wci	3ms	נשׂא	669		lift, carry
	יאמר	qal	wci	3ms	אמר	55		say
	שׁתם	qal	pptc	ms	שׁתם	1060		open
24: 16	שׁמע	qal	ptc	ms	שׁמע	1033		hear
	ידע	qal	ptc	ms	ידע	393		know
	יחזה	qal	impf	3ms	חזה	302		see
	נפל	qal	ptc	ms	נפל	656		fall

ChVs	Form	Stem	Tnse	PGN	Root	BDB	Sfx	Meaning
24:16	גלוי	qal	pptc	ms	גלה	162		uncover
24:17	אראנו	qal	impf	1cs	ראה	906	3ms	see
	אשורנו	qal	impf	1cs	שור	1003	3ms	behold,regard
	דרך	qal	pft	3ms	דרך	201		tread,march
	קם	qal	wcp	3ms	קום	877		arise,stand
	מחץ	qal	wcp	3ms	מחץ	563		smite through
24:18	היה	qal	wcp	3ms	היה	224		be,become
	היה	qal	wcp	3ms	היה	224		be,become
	איביו	qal	ptc	mp	איב	33	3ms	be hostile to
	עשה	qal	ptc	ms	עשה	793		do,make
24:19	ירד	qal	jus	3ms	רדה	921		rule
	האביד	hiph	wcp	3ms	אבד	1		destroy
24:20	ירא	qal	wci	3ms	ראה	906		see
	ישא	qal	wci	3ms	נשא	669		lift,carry
	יאמר	qal	wci	3ms	אמר	55		say
24:21	ירא	qal	wci	3ms	ראה	906		see
	ישא	qal	wci	3ms	נשא	669		lift,carry
	יאמר	qal	wci	3ms	אמר	55		say
	שים	qal	pptc	ms	שים	962		put,set
24:22	יהיה	qal	impf	3ms	היה	224		be,become
	בער	piel	infc		בער	128		burn,consume
	תשבך	qal	impf	3fs	שבה	985	2ms	take captive
24:23	ישא	qal	wci	3ms	נשא	669		lift,carry
	יאמר	qal	wci	3ms	אמר	55		say
	יחיה	qal	impf	3ms	חיה	310		live
	שמו	qal	infc		שים	962	3ms	put,set
24:24	ענו	piel	wcp	3cp	ענה	776		humble
	ענו	piel	wcp	3cp	ענה	776		humble
24:25	יקם	qal	wci	3ms	קום	877		arise,stand
	ילך	qal	wci	3ms	הלך	229		walk,go
	ישב	qal	wci	3ms	שוב	996		turn,return
	הלך	qal	pft	3ms	הלך	229		walk,go
25:1	ישב	qal	wci	3ms	ישב	442		sit,dwell
	יחל	hiph	wci	3ms	חלל	320		begin,profane
	זנות	qal	infc		זנה	275		act a harlot
25:2	תקראן	qal	wci	3fp	קרא	894		call,proclaim
	יאכל	qal	wci	3ms	אכל	37		eat,devour
	ישתחוו	hish	wci	3mp	חוה	1005		bow down
25:3	יצמד	niph	wci	3ms	צמד	855		join oneself to
	יחר	qal	wci	3ms	חרה	354		be kindled,burn
25:4	יאמר	qal	wci	3ms	אמר	55		say
	קח	qal	impv	ms	לקח	542		take
	הוקע	hiph	impv	ms	יקע	429		hang
	ישב	qal	jus	3ms	שוב	996		turn,return
25:5	יאמר	qal	wci	3ms	אמר	55		say
	שפטי	qal	ptc	mp	שפט	1047		judge
	הרגו	qal	impv	mp	הרג	246		kill
	נצמדים	niph	ptc	mp	צמד	855		join oneself to
25:6	בא	qal	ptc	ms	בוא	97		come in
	יקרב	hiph	wci	3ms	קרב	897		bring near
	בכים	qal	ptc	mp	בכה	113		weep
25:7	ירא	qal	wci	3ms	ראה	906		see
	יקם	qal	wci	3ms	קום	877		arise,stand
	יקח	qal	wci	3ms	לקח	542		take
25:8	יבא	qal	wci	3ms	בוא	97		come in
	ידקר	qal	wci	3ms	דקר	201		pierce
	תעצר	niph	wci	3fs	עצר	783		be restrained
25:9	יהיו	qal	wci	3mp	היה	224		be,become
	מתים	qal	ptc	mp	מות	559		die
25:10	ידבר	piel	wci	3ms	דבר	180		speak
	אמר	qal	infc		אמר	55		say
25:11	השיב	hiph	pft	3ms	שוב	996		bring back
	קנאו	piel	infc		קנא	888	3ms	be jealous
	כליתי	piel	pft	1cs	כלה	477		complete,finish
25:12	אמר	qal	impv	ms	אמר	55		say
	נתן	qal	ptc	ms	נתן	678		give,set
25:13	היתה	qal	wcp	3fs	היה	224		be,become
	קנא	piel	pft	3ms	קנא	888		be jealous
	יכפר	piel	wci	3ms	כפר	497		cover,atone
25:14	מכה	hoph	ptc	ms	נכה	645		be smitten
	הכה	hoph	pft	3ms	נכה	645		be smitten
25:15	מכה	hoph	ptc	fs	נכה	645		be smitten
25:16	ידבר	piel	wci	3ms	דבר	180		speak
	אמר	qal	infc		אמר	55		say
25:17	צרור	qal	infa		צרר	865		show hostility
	הכיתם	hiph	wcp	2mp	נכה	645		smite
25:18	צררים	qal	ptc	mp	צרר	865		show hostility
	נכלו	piel	pft	3cp	נכל	647		deceive
	מכה	hoph	ptc	fs	נכה	645		be smitten
25:19	יהי	qal	wci	3ms	היה	224		be,become
26:1	יאמר	qal	wci	3ms	אמר	55		say
	אמר	qal	infc		אמר	55		say
26:2	שאו	qal	impv	mp	נשא	669		lift,carry
	יצא	qal	ptc	ms	יצא	422		go out
26:3	ידבר	piel	wci	3ms	דבר	180		speak
	אמר	qal	infc		אמר	55		say
26:4	צוה	piel	pft	3ms	צוה	845		command
	יצאים	qal	ptc	mp	יצא	422		go out
26:7	יהיו	qal	wci	3mp	היה	224		be,become
	פקדיהם	qal	pptc	mp	פקד	823	3mp	attend to,visit
26:9	קרואיk	qal	pptc	mp	קרא	894		call,proclaim
	הצו	hiph	pft	3cp	נצה	663		struggle
	הצתם	hiph	infc		נצה	663	3mp	struggle
26:10	תפתח	qal	wci	3fs	פתח	834		open
	תבלע	qal	wci	3fs	בלע	118		swallow
	מות	qal	infc		מות	559		die
	אכל	qal	infc		אכל	37		eat,devour
	יהיו	qal	wci	3mp	היה	224		be,become
26:11	מתו	qal	pft	3cp	מות	559		die
26:18	פקדיהם	qal	pptc	mp	פקד	823	3mp	attend to,visit
26:19	ימת	qal	wci	3ms	מות	559		die
26:20	יהיו	qal	wci	3mp	היה	224		be,become
26:21	יהיו	qal	wci	3mp	היה	224		be,become
26:22	פקדיהם	qal	pptc	mp	פקד	823	3mp	attend to,visit
26:25	פקדיהם	qal	pptc	mp	פקד	823	3mp	attend to,visit
26:27	פקדיהם	qal	pptc	mp	פקד	823	3mp	attend to,visit
26:29	הוליד	hiph	pft	3ms	ילד	408		beget
26:33	היו	qal	pft	3cp	היה	224		be,become

ChVs	Form	Stem	Tnse	PGN	Root	BDB	Sfx	Meaning
26:34	פקדיהם	qal	pptc	mp	פקד	823	3mp	attend to,visit
26:37	פקדיהם	qal	pptc	mp	פקד	823	3mp	attend to,visit
26:40	יהיו	qal	wci	3mp	היה	224		be,become
26:41	פקדיהם	qal	pptc	mp	פקד	823	3mp	attend to,visit
26:43	פקדיהם	qal	pptc	mp	פקד	823	3mp	attend to,visit
26:47	פקדיהם	qal	pptc	mp	פקד	823	3mp	attend to,visit
26:50	פקדיהם	qal	pptc	mp	פקד	823	3mp	attend to,visit
26:51	פקודי	qal	pptc	mp	פקד	823		attend to,visit
26:52	ידבר	piel	wci	3ms	דבר	180		speak
	אמר	qal	infc		אמר	55		say
26:53	תחלק	niph	impf	3fs	חלק	323		be divided
26:54	תרבה	hiph	impf	2ms	רבה	915		make many
	תמעיט	hiph	impf	2ms	מעט	589		make small
	פקדיו	qal	pptc	mp	פקד	823	3ms	attend to,visit
	יתן	qalp	impf	3ms	נתן	678		be given
26:55	יחלק	niph	impf	3ms	חלק	323		be divided
	ינחלו	qal	impf	3mp	נחל	635		possess,inherit
26:56	תחלק	niph	impf	3fs	חלק	323		be divided
26:57	פקודי	qal	pptc	mp	פקד	823		attend to,visit
26:58	הולד	hiph	pft	3ms	ילד	408		beget
26:59	ילדה	qal	pft	3fs	ילד	408		bear,beget
	תלד	qal	wci	3fs	ילד	408		bear,beget
26:60	יולד	niph	wci	3ms	ילד	408		be born
26:61	ימת	qal	wci	3ms	מות	559		die
	הקריבם	hiph	infc		קרב	897	3mp	bring near
26:62	יהיו	qal	wci	3mp	היה	224		be,become
	פקדיהם	qal	pptc	mp	פקד	823	3mp	attend to,visit
	התפקדו	hoth	pft	3cp	פקד	823		be mustered
	נתן	niph	pft	3ms	נתן	678		be given
26:63	פקודי	qal	pptc	mp	פקד	823		attend to,visit
	פקדו	qal	pft	3cp	פקד	823		attend to,visit
26:64	היה	qal	pft	3ms	היה	224		be,become
	פקודי	qal	pptc	mp	פקד	823		attend to,visit
	פקדו	qal	pft	3cp	פקד	823		attend to,visit
26:65	אמר	qal	pft	3ms	אמר	55		say
	מות	qal	infa		מות	559		die
	ימתו	qal	impf	3mp	מות	559		die
	נותר	niph	pft	3ms	יתר	451		be left,remain
27:1	תקרבנה	qal	wci	3fp	קרב	897		approach
27:2	תעמדנה	qal	wci	3fp	עמד	763		stand,stop
	אמר	qal	infc		אמר	55		say
27:3	מת	qal	pft	3ms	מות	559		die
	היה	qal	pft	3ms	היה	224		be,become
	נועדים	niph	ptc	mp	יעד	416		gather
	מת	qal	pft	3ms	מות	559		die
	היו	qal	pft	3cp	היה	224		be,become
27:4	יגרע	niph	impf	3ms	גרע	175		be withdrawn
	תנה	qal	impv	ms	נתן	678		give,set
27:5	יקרב	hiph	wci	3ms	קרב	897		bring near
27:6	יאמר	qal	wci	3ms	אמר	55		say
	אמר	qal	infc		אמר	55		say
27:7	דברת	qal	ptc	fp	דבר	180		speak
	נתן	qal	infa		נתן	678		give,set
	תתן	qal	impf	2ms	נתן	678		give,set

ChVs	Form	Stem	Tnse	PGN	Root	BDB	Sfx	Meaning
27:7	העברת	hiph	wcp	2ms	עבר	716		cause to pass
27:8	תדבר	piel	impf	2ms	דבר	180		speak
	אמר	qal	infc		אמר	55		say
	ימות	qal	impf	3ms	מות	559		die
	העברתם	hiph	wcp	2mp	עבר	716		cause to pass
27:9	נתתם	qal	wcp	2mp	נתן	678		give,set
27:10	נתתם	qal	wcp	2mp	נתן	678		give,set
27:11	נתתם	qal	wcp	2mp	נתן	678		give,set
	ירשׁ	qal	wcp	3ms	ירשׁ	439		possess,inherit
	היתה	qal	wcp	3fs	היה	224		be,become
	צוה	piel	pft	3ms	צוה	845		command
27:12	יאמר	qal	wci	3ms	אמר	55		say
	עלה	qal	impv	ms	עלה	748		go up
	ראה	qal	impv	ms	ראה	906		see
	נתתי	qal	pft	1cs	נתן	678		give,set
27:13	ראיתה	qal	wcp	2ms	ראה	906		see
	נאספת	niph	wcp	2ms	אסף	62		assemble
	נאסף	niph	pft	3ms	אסף	62		assemble
27:14	מריתם	qal	pft	2mp	מרה	598		be disobedient
	הקדישׁני	hiph	infc		קדשׁ	872	1cs	consecrate
27:15	ידבר	piel	wci	3ms	דבר	180		speak
	אמר	qal	infc		אמר	55		say
27:16	יפקד	qal	jusm	3ms	פקד	823		attend to,visit
27:17	יצא	qal	impf	3ms	יצא	422		go out
	יבא	qal	impf	3ms	בוא	97		come in
	יוציאם	hiph	impf	3ms	יצא	422	3mp	bring out
	יביאם	hiph	impf	3ms	בוא	97	3mp	bring in
	תהיה	qal	impf	3fs	היה	224		be,become
	רעה	qal	ptc	ms	רעה	944		pasture,tend
27:18	יאמר	qal	wci	3ms	אמר	55		say
	קח	qal	impv	ms	לקח	542		take
	סמכת	qal	wcp	2ms	סמך	701		lean,support
27:19	העמדת	hiph	wcp	2ms	עמד	763		set up,raise
	צויתה	piel	wcp	2ms	צוה	845		command
27:20	נתתה	qal	wcp	2ms	נתן	678		give,set
	ישׁמעו	qal	impf	3mp	שׁמע	1033		hear
27:21	יעמד	qal	impf	3ms	עמד	763		stand,stop
	שׁאל	qal	wcp	3ms	שׁאל	981		ask,borrow
	יצאו	qal	impf	3mp	יצא	422		go out
	יבאו	qal	impf	3mp	בוא	97		come in
27:22	יעשׂ	qal	wci	3ms	עשׂה	793		do,make
	צוה	piel	pft	3ms	צוה	845		command
	יקח	qal	wci	3ms	לקח	542		take
	יעמדהו	hiph	wci	3ms	עמד	763	3ms	set up,raise
27:23	יסמך	qal	wci	3ms	סמך	701		lean,support
	יצוהו	piel	wci	3ms	צוה	845	3ms	command
	דבר	piel	pft	3ms	דבר	180		speak
28:1	ידבר	piel	wci	3ms	דבר	180		speak
	אמר	qal	infc		אמר	55		say
28:2	צו	piel	impv	ms	צוה	845		command
	אמרת	qal	wcp	2ms	אמר	55		say
	תשׁמרו	qal	impf	2mp	שׁמר	1036		keep,watch
	הקריב	hiph	infc		קרב	897		bring near
28:3	אמרת	qal	wcp	2ms	אמר	55		say

ChVs	Form	Stem	Tnse	PGN	Root	BDB	Sfx	Meaning
28: 3	תקריבו	hiph	impf	2mp	קרב	897		bring near
28: 4	תעשׂה	qal	impf	2ms	עשׂה	793		do, make
	תעשׂה	qal	impf	2ms	עשׂה	793		do, make
28: 5	בלולה	qal	pptc	fs	בלל	117		mingle, mix
28: 6	עשׂיה	qal	pptc	fs	עשׂה	793		do, make
28: 7	הסך	hiph	impv	ms	נסך	650		pour out
28: 8	תעשׂה	qal	impf	2ms	עשׂה	793		do, make
	תעשׂה	qal	impf	2ms	עשׂה	793		do, make
28: 9	בלולה	qal	pptc	fs	בלל	117		mingle, mix
28: 11	תקריבו	hiph	impf	2mp	קרב	897		bring near
28: 12	בלולה	qal	pptc	fs	בלל	117		mingle, mix
	בלולה	qal	pptc	fs	בלל	117		mingle, mix
28: 13	בלולה	qal	pptc	fs	בלל	117		mingle, mix
28: 14	יהיה	qal	impf	3ms	היה	224		be, become
28: 15	יעשׂה	niph	impf	3ms	עשׂה	793		be done
28: 17	יאכל	niph	impf	3ms	אכל	37		be eaten
28: 18	תעשׂו	qal	impf	2mp	עשׂה	793		do, make
28: 19	הקרבתם	hiph	wcp	2mp	קרב	897		bring near
	יהיו	qal	impf	3mp	היה	224		be, become
28: 20	בלולה	qal	pptc	fs	בלל	117		mingle, mix
	תעשׂו	qal	impf	2mp	עשׂה	793		do, make
28: 21	תעשׂה	qal	impf	2ms	עשׂה	793		do, make
28: 22	כפר	piel	infc		כפר	497		cover, atone
28: 23	תעשׂו	qal	impf	2mp	עשׂה	793		do, make
28: 24	תעשׂו	qal	impf	2mp	עשׂה	793		do, make
	יעשׂה	niph	impf	3ms	עשׂה	793		be done
28: 25	יהיה	qal	impf	3ms	היה	224		be, become
	תעשׂו	qal	impf	2mp	עשׂה	793		do, make
28: 26	הקריבכם	hiph	infc		קרב	897	2mp	bring near
	יהיה	qal	impf	3ms	היה	224		be, become
	תעשׂו	qal	impf	2mp	עשׂה	793		do, make
28: 27	הקרבתם	hiph	wcp	2mp	קרב	897		bring near
28: 28	בלולה	qal	pptc	fs	בלל	117		mingle, mix
28: 30	כפר	piel	infc		כפר	497		cover, atone
28: 31	תעשׂו	qal	impf	2mp	עשׂה	793		do, make
	יהיו	qal	impf	3mp	היה	224		be, become
29: 1	יהיה	qal	impf	3ms	היה	224		be, become
	תעשׂו	qal	impf	2mp	עשׂה	793		do, make
	יהיה	qal	impf	3ms	היה	224		be, become
29: 2	עשׂיתם	qal	wcp	2mp	עשׂה	793		do, make
29: 3	בלולה	qal	pptc	fs	בלל	117		mingle, mix
29: 5	כפר	piel	infc		כפר	497		cover, atone
29: 7	יהיה	qal	impf	3ms	היה	224		be, become
	עניתם	piel	wcp	2mp	ענה	776		humble
	תעשׂו	qal	impf	2mp	עשׂה	793		do, make
29: 8	הקרבתם	hiph	wcp	2mp	קרב	897		bring near
	יהיו	qal	impf	3mp	היה	224		be, become
29: 9	בלולה	qal	pptc	fs	בלל	117		mingle, mix
29: 12	יהיה	qal	impf	3ms	היה	224		be, become
	תעשׂו	qal	impf	2mp	עשׂה	793		do, make
	חגתם	qal	wcp	2mp	חגג	290		keep festival
29: 13	הקרבתם	hiph	wcp	2mp	קרב	897		bring near
	יהיו	qal	impf	3mp	היה	224		be, become
29: 14	בלולה	qal	pptc	fs	בלל	117		mingle, mix
29: 35	תהיה	qal	impf	3fs	היה	224		be, become
	תעשׂו	qal	impf	2mp	עשׂה	793		do, make
29: 36	הקרבתם	hiph	wcp	2mp	קרב	897		bring near
29: 39	תעשׂו	qal	impf	2mp	עשׂה	793		do, make
30: 1	יאמר	qal	wci	3ms	אמר	55		say
	צוה	piel	pft	3ms	צוה	845		command
30: 2	ידבר	piel	wci	3ms	דבר	180		speak
	אמר	qal	infc		אמר	55		say
	צוה	piel	pft	3ms	צוה	845		command
30: 3	ידר	qal	impf	3ms	נדר	623		vow
	השׁבע	niph	infa		שׁבע	989		swear
	אסר	qal	infc		אסר	63		tie, bind
	יחל	hiph	impf	3ms	חלל	320		begin, profane
	יצא	qal	ptc	ms	יצא	422		go out
	יעשׂה	qal	impf	3ms	עשׂה	793		do, make
30: 4	תדר	qal	impf	3fs	נדר	623		vow
	אסרה	qal	wcp	3fs	אסר	63		tie, bind
30: 5	שׁמע	qal	wcp	3ms	שׁמע	1033		hear
	אסרה	qal	pft	3fs	אסר	63		tie, bind
	החרישׁ	hiph	wcp	3ms	חרשׁ	361		be silent
	קמו	qal	wcp	3cp	קום	877		arise, stand
	אסרה	qal	pft	3fs	אסר	63		tie, bind
	יקום	qal	impf	3ms	קום	877		arise, stand
30: 6	הניא	hiph	pft	3ms	נוא	626		restrain
	שׁמעו	qal	infc		שׁמע	1033	3ms	hear
	אסרה	qal	pft	3fs	אסר	63		tie, bind
	יקום	qal	impf	3ms	קום	877		arise, stand
	יסלח	qal	impf	3ms	סלח	699		forgive, pardon
	הניא	hiph	pft	3ms	נוא	626		restrain
30: 7	היו	qal	infa		היה	224		be, become
	תהיה	qal	impf	3fs	היה	224		be, become
	אסרה	qal	pft	3fs	אסר	63		tie, bind
30: 8	שׁמע	qal	wcp	3ms	שׁמע	1033		hear
	שׁמעו	qal	infc		שׁמע	1033	3ms	hear
	החרישׁ	hiph	wcp	3ms	חרשׁ	361		be silent
	קמו	qal	wcp	3cp	קום	877		arise, stand
	אסרה	qal	pft	3fs	אסר	63		tie, bind
	יקמו	qal	impf	3mp	קום	877		arise, stand
30: 9	שׁמע	qal	infc		שׁמע	1033		hear
	יניא	hiph	impf	3ms	נוא	626		restrain
	הפר	hiph	wcp	3ms	פרר	830		break, frustrate
	אסרה	qal	pft	3fs	אסר	63		tie, bind
	יסלח	qal	impf	3ms	סלח	699		forgive, pardon
30: 10	גרושׁה	qal	pptc	fs	גרשׁ	176		cast out
	אסרה	qal	pft	3fs	אסר	63		tie, bind
	יקום	qal	impf	3ms	קום	877		arise, stand
30: 11	נדרה	qal	pft	3fs	נדר	623		vow
	אסרה	qal	pft	3fs	אסר	63		tie, bind
30: 12	שׁמע	qal	wcp	3ms	שׁמע	1033		hear
	החרשׁ	hiph	wcp	3ms	חרשׁ	361		be silent
	הניא	hiph	pft	3ms	נוא	626		restrain
	קמו	qal	wcp	3cp	קום	877		arise, stand
	אסרה	qal	pft	3fs	אסר	63		tie, bind
	יקום	qal	impf	3ms	קום	877		arise, stand

ChVs	Form	Stem	Tnse	PGN	Root	BDB	Sfx	Meaning
30: 13	הפר	hiph	infa		פרר	830		break,frustrate
	יפר	hiph	impf	3ms	פרר	830		break,frustrate
	שמעו	qal	infc		שמע	1033	3ms	hear
	יקום	qal	impf	3ms	קום	877		arise,stand
	הפרם	hiph	pft	3ms	פרר	830	3mp	break,frustrate
	יסלח	qal	impf	3ms	סלח	699		forgive,pardon
30: 14	ענת	piel	infc		ענה	776		humble
	יקימנו	hiph	impf	3ms	קום	877	3ms	raise,build,set
	יפרנו	hiph	impf	3ms	פרר	830	3ms	break,frustrate
30: 15	החרש	hiph	infa		חרש	361		be silent
	יחריש	hiph	impf	3ms	חרש	361		be silent
	הקים	hiph	wcp	3ms	קום	877		raise,build,set
	הקים	hiph	pft	3ms	קום	877		raise,build,set
	החרש	hiph	pft	3ms	חרש	361		be silent
	שמעו	qal	infc		שמע	1033	3ms	hear
30: 16	הפר	hiph	infa		פרר	830		break,frustrate
	יפר	hiph	impf	3ms	פרר	830		break,frustrate
	שמעו	qal	infc		שמע	1033	3ms	hear
	נשא	qal	wcp	3ms	נשא	669		lift,carry
30: 17	צוה	piel	pft	3ms	צוה	845		command
31: 1	ידבר	piel	wci	3ms	דבר	180		speak
	אמר	qal	infc		אמר	55		say
31: 2	נקם	qal	impv	ms	נקם	667		avenge
	תאסף	niph	impf	2ms	אסף	62		assemble
31: 3	ידבר	piel	wci	3ms	דבר	180		speak
	אמר	qal	infc		אמר	55		say
	החלצו	niph	impv	mp	חלץ	323		be equipped
	יהיו	qal	jusm	3mp	היה	224		be,become
	תת	qal	infc		נתן	678		give,set
31: 4	תשלחו	qal	impf	2mp	שלח	1018		send
31: 5	ימסרו	niph	wci	3mp	מסר	588		be delivered to
	חלוצי	qal	pptc	mp	חלץ	323		equipped
31: 6	ישלח	qal	wci	3ms	שלח	1018		send
31: 7	יצבאו	qal	wci	3mp	צבא	838		wage war
	צוה	piel	pft	3ms	צוה	845		command
	יהרגו	qal	wci	3mp	הרג	246		kill
31: 8	הרגו	qal	pft	3cp	הרג	246		kill
	הרגו	qal	pft	3cp	הרג	246		kill
31: 9	ישבו	qal	wci	3mp	שבה	985		take captive
	בזזו	qal	pft	3cp	בזז	102		plunder
31: 10	שרפו	qal	pft	3cp	שרף	976		burn
31: 11	יקחו	qal	wci	3mp	לקח	542		take
31: 12	יבאו	hiph	wci	3mp	בוא	97		bring in
31: 13	יצאו	qal	wci	3mp	יצא	422		go out
	קראתם	qal	infc		קרא	896	3mp	meet,encounter
31: 14	יקצף	qal	wci	3ms	קצף	893		be angry
	פקודי	qal	pptc	mp	פקד	823		attend to,visit
	באים	qal	ptc	mp	בוא	97		come in
31: 15	יאמר	qal	wci	3ms	אמר	55		say
	חייתם	piel	pft	2mp	חיה	310		preserve,revive
31: 16	היו	qal	pft	3cp	היה	224		be,become
	מסר	qal	infc		מסר	588		commit
	תהי	qal	wci	3fs	היה	224		be,become
31: 17	הרגו	qal	impv	mp	הרג	246		kill
31: 17	ידעת	qal	ptc	fs	ידע	393		know
	הרגו	qal	impv	mp	הרג	246		kill
31: 18	ידעו	qal	pft	3cp	ידע	393		know
	החיו	hiph	impv	mp	חיה	310		preserve
31: 19	חנו	qal	impv	mp	חנה	333		decline,encamp
	הרג	qal	ptc	ms	הרג	246		kill
	נגע	qal	ptc	ms	נגע	619		touch,strike
	תתחטאו	hith	impf	2mp	חטא	306		purify oneself
31: 20	תתחטאו	hith	impf	2mp	חטא	306		purify oneself
31: 21	יאמר	qal	wci	3ms	אמר	55		say
	באים	qal	ptc	mp	בוא	97		come in
	צוה	piel	pft	3ms	צוה	845		command
31: 23	יבא	qal	impf	3ms	בוא	97		come in
	תעבירו	hiph	impf	2mp	עבר	716		cause to pass
	טהר	qal	wcp	3ms	טהר	372		be clean,pure
	יתחטא	hith	impf	3ms	חטא	306		purify oneself
	יבא	qal	impf	3ms	בוא	97		come in
	תעבירו	hiph	impf	2mp	עבר	716		cause to pass
31: 24	כבסתם	piel	wcp	2mp	כבס	460		wash
	טהרתם	qal	wcp	2mp	טהר	372		be clean,pure
	תבאו	qal	impf	2mp	בוא	97		come in
31: 25	יאמר	qal	wci	3ms	אמר	55		say
	אמר	qal	infc		אמר	55		say
31: 26	שא	qal	impv	ms	נשא	669		lift,carry
31: 27	חצית	qal	wcp	2ms	חצה	345		divide
	תפשי	qal	ptc	mp	תפש	1074		seize,grasp
	יצאים	qal	ptc	mp	יצא	422		go out
31: 28	הרמת	hiph	wcp	2ms	רום	926		raise,lift
	יצאים	qal	ptc	mp	יצא	422		go out
31: 29	תקחו	qal	impf	2mp	לקח	542		take
	נתתה	qal	wcp	2ms	נתן	678		give,set
31: 30	תקח	qal	impf	2ms	לקח	542		take
	אחז	qal	pptc	ms	אחז	28		grasp
	נתתה	qal	wcp	2ms	נתן	678		give,set
	שמרי	qal	ptc	mp	שמר	1036		keep,watch
31: 31	יעש	qal	wci	3ms	עשה	793		do,make
	צוה	piel	pft	3ms	צוה	845		command
31: 32	יהי	qal	wci	3ms	היה	224		be,become
	בזזו	qal	pft	3cp	בזז	102		plunder
31: 35	ידעו	qal	pft	3cp	ידע	393		know
31: 36	תהי	qal	wci	3fs	היה	224		be,become
	יצאים	qal	ptc	mp	יצא	422		go out
31: 37	יהי	qal	wci	3ms	היה	224		be,become
31: 41	יתן	qal	wci	3ms	נתן	678		give,set
	צוה	piel	pft	3ms	צוה	845		command
31: 42	חצה	qal	pft	3ms	חצה	345		divide
	צבאים	qal	ptc	mp	צבא	838		wage war
31: 43	תהי	qal	wci	3fs	היה	224		be,become
31: 47	יקח	qal	wci	3ms	לקח	542		take
	אחז	qal	pptc	ms	אחז	28		grasp
	יתן	qal	wci	3ms	נתן	678		give,set
	שמרי	qal	ptc	mp	שמר	1036		keep,watch
	צוה	piel	pft	3ms	צוה	845		command
31: 48	יקרבו	qal	wci	3mp	קרב	897		approach

ChVs	Form	Stem	Tnse	PGN	Root	BDB	Sfx	Meaning
31:48	פקדים	qal	pptc	mp	פקד	823		attend to,visit
31:49	יאמרו	qal	wci	3mp	אמר	55		say
	נשׂאו	qal	pft	3cp	נשׂא	669		lift,carry
	נפקד	niph	pft	3ms	פקד	823		be visited
31:50	נקרב	hiph	wci	1cp	קרב	897		bring near
	מצא	qal	pft	3ms	מצא	592		find
	כפר	piel	infc		כפר	497		cover,atone
31:51	יקח	qal	wci	3ms	לקח	542		take
31:52	יהי	qal	wci	3ms	היה	224		be,become
	הרימו	hiph	pft	3cp	רום	926		raise,lift
31:53	בזזו	qal	pft	3cp	בזז	102		plunder
31:54	יקח	qal	wci	3ms	לקח	542		take
	יבאו	hiph	wci	3mp	בוא	97		bring in
32:1	היה	qal	pft	3ms	היה	224		be,become
	יראו	qal	wci	3mp	ראה	906		see
32:2	יבאו	qal	wci	3mp	בוא	97		come in
	יאמרו	qal	wci	3mp	אמר	55		say
	אמר	qal	infc		אמר	55		say
32:4	הכה	hiph	pft	3ms	נכה	645		smite
32:5	יאמרו	qal	wci	3mp	אמר	55		say
	מצאנו	qal	pft	1cp	מצא	592		find
	יתן	qalp	jusm	3ms	נתן	678		be given
	תעברנו	hiph	jusm	2ms	עבר	716	1cp	cause to pass
32:6	יאמר	qal	wci	3ms	אמר	55		say
	יבאו	qal	impf	3mp	בוא	97		come in
	תשבו	qal	impf	2mp	ישב	442		sit,dwell
32:7	תנואוןk	qal	impf	2mp	נוא	626		hinder
	תניאוןq	hiph	impf	2mp	נוא	626		restrain
	עבר	qal	infc		עבר	716		pass over
	נתן	qal	pft	3ms	נתן	678		give,set
32:8	עשׂו	qal	pft	3cp	עשׂה	793		do,make
	שׁלחי	qal	infc		שׁלח	1018	1cs	send
	ראות	qal	infc		ראה	906		see
32:9	יעלו	qal	wci	3mp	עלה	748		go up
	יראו	qal	wci	3mp	ראה	906		see
	יניאו	hiph	wci	3mp	נוא	626		restrain
	בא	qal	infc		בוא	97		come in
	נתן	qal	pft	3ms	נתן	678		give,set
32:10	יחר	qal	wci	3ms	חרה	354		be kindled,burn
	ישׁבע	niph	wci	3ms	שׁבע	989		swear
	אמר	qal	infc		אמר	55		say
32:11	יראו	qal	impf	3mp	ראה	906		see
	עלים	qal	ptc	mp	עלה	748		go up
	נשׁבעתי	niph	pft	1cs	שׁבע	989		swear
	מלאו	piel	pft	3cp	מלא	569		fill
32:12	מלאו	piel	pft	3cp	מלא	569		fill
32:13	יחר	qal	wci	3ms	חרה	354		be kindled,burn
	ינעם	hiph	wci	3ms	נוע	631	3mp	shake,disturb
	תם	qal	infc		תמם	1070		be finished
	עשׂה	qal	ptc	ms	עשׂה	793		do,make
32:14	קמתם	qal	pft	2mp	קום	877		arise,stand
	ספות	qal	infc		ספה	705		sweep away
32:15	תשׁובן	qal	impf	2mp	שׁוב	996		turn,return
	יסף	qal	wcp	3ms	יסף	414		add,increase
32:15	הניחו	hiph	infc		נוח	628	3ms	give rest,put
	שׁחתם	piel	wcp	2mp	שׁחת	1007		spoil,ruin
32:16	יגשׁו	qal	wci	3mp	נגשׁ	620		draw near
	יאמרו	qal	wci	3mp	אמר	55		say
	נבנה	qal	impf	1cp	בנה	124		build
32:17	נחלץ	niph	impf	1cp	חלץ	323		be equipped
	חשׁים	qal	pptc	mp	חושׁ	301		make haste
	הביאנם	hiph	pft	1cp	בוא	97	3mp	bring in
	ישׁב	qal	wcp	3ms	ישׁב	442		sit,dwell
	ישׁבי	qal	ptc	mp	ישׁב	442		sit,dwell
32:18	נשׁוב	qal	impf	1cp	שׁוב	996		turn,return
	התנחל	hith	infc		נחל	635		possess oneself
32:19	ננחל	qal	impf	1cp	נחל	635		possess,inherit
	באה	qal	pft	3fs	בוא	97		come in
32:20	יאמר	qal	wci	3ms	אמר	55		say
	תעשׂון	qal	impf	2mp	עשׂה	793		do,make
	תחלצו	niph	impf	2mp	חלץ	323		be equipped
32:21	עבר	qal	wcp	3ms	עבר	716		pass over
	חלוץ	qal	pptc	ms	חלץ	323		equipped
	הורישׁו	hiph	infc		ירשׁ	439	3ms	c. to possess
	איביו	qal	ptc	mp	איב	33	3ms	be hostile to
32:22	נכבשׁה	niph	wcp	3fs	כבשׁ	461		be subdued
	תשׁבו	qal	impf	2mp	שׁוב	996		turn,return
	הייתם	qal	wcp	2mp	היה	224		be,become
	היתה	qal	wcp	3fs	היה	224		be,become
32:23	תעשׂון	qal	impf	2mp	עשׂה	793		do,make
	חטאתם	qal	pft	2mp	חטא	306		sin
	דעו	qal	impv	mp	ידע	393		know
	תמצא	qal	impf	3fs	מצא	592		find
32:24	בנו	qal	impv	mp	בנה	124		build
	יצא	qal	ptc	ms	יצא	422		go out
	תעשׂו	qal	impf	2mp	עשׂה	793		do,make
32:25	יאמר	qal	wci	3ms	אמר	55		say
	אמר	qal	infc		אמר	55		say
	יעשׂו	qal	impf	3mp	עשׂה	793		do,make
	מצוה	piel	ptc	ms	צוה	845		command
32:26	יהיו	qal	impf	3mp	היה	224		be,become
32:27	יעברו	qal	impf	3mp	עבר	716		pass over
	חלוץ	qal	pptc	ms	חלץ	323		equipped
	דבר	qal	ptc	ms	דבר	180		speak
32:28	יצו	piel	wci	3ms	צוה	845		command
32:29	יאמר	qal	wci	3ms	אמר	55		say
	יעברו	qal	impf	3mp	עבר	716		pass over
	חלוץ	qal	pptc	ms	חלץ	323		equipped
	נכבשׁה	niph	wcp	3fs	כבשׁ	461		be subdued
	נתתם	qal	wcp	2mp	נתן	678		give,set
32:30	יעברו	qal	impf	3mp	עבר	716		pass over
	חלוצים	qal	pptc	mp	חלץ	323		equipped
	נאחזו	niph	wcp	3cp	אחז	28		possess,caught
32:31	יענו	qal	wci	3mp	ענה	772		answer
	אמר	qal	infc		אמר	55		say
	דבר	piel	pft	3ms	דבר	180		speak
	נעשׂה	qal	impf	1cp	עשׂה	793		do,make
32:32	נעבר	qal	impf	1cp	עבר	716		pass over

ChVs	Form	Stem	Tnse	PGN	Root	BDB	Sfx	Meaning
32: 32	חלוצים	qal	pptc	mp	חלץ	323		equipped
32: 33	יתן	qal	wci	3ms	נתן	678		give,set
32: 34	יבנו	qal	wci	3mp	בנה	124		build
32: 37	בנו	qal	pft	3cp	בנה	124		build
32: 38	מוסבת	hoph	ptc	fp	סבב	685		be turned
	יקראו	qal	wci	3mp	קרא	894		call,proclaim
	בנו	qal	pft	3cp	בנה	124		build
32: 39	ילכו	qal	wci	3mp	הלך	229		walk,go
	ילכדה	qal	wci	3mp	לכד	539	3fs	capture
	יורש	hiph	wci	3ms	ירש	439		c. to possess
32: 40	יתן	qal	wci	3ms	נתן	678		give,set
	ישב	qal	wci	3ms	ישב	442		sit,dwell
32: 41	הלך	qal	pft	3ms	הלך	229		walk,go
	ילכד	qal	wci	3ms	לכד	539		capture
	יקרא	qal	wci	3ms	קרא	894		call,proclaim
32: 42	הלך	qal	pft	3ms	הלך	229		walk,go
	ילכד	qal	wci	3ms	לכד	539		capture
	יקרא	qal	wci	3ms	קרא	894		call,proclaim
33: 1	יצאו	qal	pft	3cp	יצא	422		go out
33: 2	יכתב	qal	wci	3ms	כתב	507		write
33: 3	יסעו	qal	wci	3mp	נסע	652		pull up,set out
	יצאו	qal	pft	3cp	יצא	422		go out
	רמה	qal	ptc	fs	רום	926		be high
33: 4	מקברים	piel	ptc	mp	קבר	868		bury
	הכה	hiph	pft	3ms	נכה	645		smite
	עשה	qal	pft	3ms	עשה	793		do,make
33: 5	יסעו	qal	wci	3mp	נסע	652		pull up,set out
	יחנו	qal	wci	3mp	חנה	333		decline,encamp
33: 6	יסעו	qal	wci	3mp	נסע	652		pull up,set out
	יחנו	qal	wci	3mp	חנה	333		decline,encamp
33: 7	יסעו	qal	wci	3mp	נסע	652		pull up,set out
	ישב	qal	wci	3ms	שוב	996		turn,return
	יחנו	qal	wci	3mp	חנה	333		decline,encamp
33: 8	יסעו	qal	wci	3mp	נסע	652		pull up,set out
	יעברו	qal	wci	3mp	עבר	716		pass over
	ילכו	qal	wci	3mp	הלך	229		walk,go
	יחנו	qal	wci	3mp	חנה	333		decline,encamp
33: 9	יסעו	qal	wci	3mp	נסע	652		pull up,set out
	יבאו	qal	wci	3mp	בוא	97		come in
	יחנו	qal	wci	3mp	חנה	333		decline,encamp
33: 10	יסעו	qal	wci	3mp	נסע	652		pull up,set out
	יחנו	qal	wci	3mp	חנה	333		decline,encamp
33: 11	יסעו	qal	wci	3mp	נסע	652		pull up,set out
	יחנו	qal	wci	3mp	חנה	333		decline,encamp
33: 12	יסעו	qal	wci	3mp	נסע	652		pull up,set out
	יחנו	qal	wci	3mp	חנה	333		decline,encamp
33: 13	יסעו	qal	wci	3mp	נסע	652		pull up,set out
	יחנו	qal	wci	3mp	חנה	333		decline,encamp
33: 14	יסעו	qal	wci	3mp	נסע	652		pull up,set out
	יחנו	qal	wci	3mp	חנה	333		decline,encamp
	היה	qal	pft	3ms	היה	224		be,become
	שתות	qal	infc		שתה	1059		drink
33: 15	יסעו	qal	wci	3mp	נסע	652		pull up,set out
	יחנו	qal	wci	3mp	חנה	333		decline,encamp
33: 16	יסעו	qal	wci	3mp	נסע	652		pull up,set out
	יחנו	qal	wci	3mp	חנה	333		decline,encamp
33: 17	יסעו	qal	wci	3mp	נסע	652		pull up,set out
	יחנו	qal	wci	3mp	חנה	333		decline,encamp
33: 18	יסעו	qal	wci	3mp	נסע	652		pull up,set out
	יחנו	qal	wci	3mp	חנה	333		decline,encamp
33: 19	יסעו	qal	wci	3mp	נסע	652		pull up,set out
	יחנו	qal	wci	3mp	חנה	333		decline,encamp
33: 20	יסעו	qal	wci	3mp	נסע	652		pull up,set out
	יחנו	qal	wci	3mp	חנה	333		decline,encamp
33: 21	יסעו	qal	wci	3mp	נסע	652		pull up,set out
	יחנו	qal	wci	3mp	חנה	333		decline,encamp
33: 22	יסעו	qal	wci	3mp	נסע	652		pull up,set out
	יחנו	qal	wci	3mp	חנה	333		decline,encamp
33: 23	יסעו	qal	wci	3mp	נסע	652		pull up,set out
	יחנו	qal	wci	3mp	חנה	333		decline,encamp
33: 24	יסעו	qal	wci	3mp	נסע	652		pull up,set out
	יחנו	qal	wci	3mp	חנה	333		decline,encamp
33: 25	יסעו	qal	wci	3mp	נסע	652		pull up,set out
	יחנו	qal	wci	3mp	חנה	333		decline,encamp
33: 26	יסעו	qal	wci	3mp	נסע	652		pull up,set out
	יחנו	qal	wci	3mp	חנה	333		decline,encamp
33: 27	יסעו	qal	wci	3mp	נסע	652		pull up,set out
	יחנו	qal	wci	3mp	חנה	333		decline,encamp
33: 28	יסעו	qal	wci	3mp	נסע	652		pull up,set out
	יחנו	qal	wci	3mp	חנה	333		decline,encamp
33: 29	יסעו	qal	wci	3mp	נסע	652		pull up,set out
	יחנו	qal	wci	3mp	חנה	333		decline,encamp
33: 30	יסעו	qal	wci	3mp	נסע	652		pull up,set out
	יחנו	qal	wci	3mp	חנה	333		decline,encamp
33: 31	יסעו	qal	wci	3mp	נסע	652		pull up,set out
	יחנו	qal	wci	3mp	חנה	333		decline,encamp
33: 32	יסעו	qal	wci	3mp	נסע	652		pull up,set out
	יחנו	qal	wci	3mp	חנה	333		decline,encamp
33: 33	יסעו	qal	wci	3mp	נסע	652		pull up,set out
	יחנו	qal	wci	3mp	חנה	333		decline,encamp
33: 34	יסעו	qal	wci	3mp	נסע	652		pull up,set out
	יחנו	qal	wci	3mp	חנה	333		decline,encamp
33: 35	יסעו	qal	wci	3mp	נסע	652		pull up,set out
	יחנו	qal	wci	3mp	חנה	333		decline,encamp
33: 36	יסעו	qal	wci	3mp	נסע	652		pull up,set out
	יחנו	qal	wci	3mp	חנה	333		decline,encamp
33: 37	יסעו	qal	wci	3mp	נסע	652		pull up,set out
	יחנו	qal	wci	3mp	חנה	333		decline,encamp
33: 38	יעל	qal	wci	3ms	עלה	748		go up
	ימת	qal	wci	3ms	מות	559		die
	צאת	qal	infc		יצא	422		go out
33: 40	ישמע	qal	wci	3ms	שמע	1033		hear
	ישב	qal	ptc	ms	ישב	442		sit,dwell
	בא	qal	infc		בוא	97		come in
33: 41	יסעו	qal	wci	3mp	נסע	652		pull up,set out
	יחנו	qal	wci	3mp	חנה	333		decline,encamp
33: 42	יסעו	qal	wci	3mp	נסע	652		pull up,set out
	יחנו	qal	wci	3mp	חנה	333		decline,encamp

ChVs	Form	Stem	Tnse	PGN	Root	BDB	Sfx	Meaning
33: 43	יסעו	qal	wci	3mp	נסע	652		pull up,set out
	יחנו	qal	wci	3mp	חנה	333		decline,encamp
33: 44	יסעו	qal	wci	3mp	נסע	652		pull up,set out
	יחנו	qal	wci	3mp	חנה	333		decline,encamp
33: 45	יסעו	qal	wci	3mp	נסע	652		pull up,set out
	יחנו	qal	wci	3mp	חנה	333		decline,encamp
33: 46	יסעו	qal	wci	3mp	נסע	652		pull up,set out
	יחנו	qal	wci	3mp	חנה	333		decline,encamp
33: 47	יסעו	qal	wci	3mp	נסע	652		pull up,set out
	יחנו	qal	wci	3mp	חנה	333		decline,encamp
33: 48	יסעו	qal	wci	3mp	נסע	652		pull up,set out
	יחנו	qal	wci	3mp	חנה	333		decline,encamp
33: 49	יחנו	qal	wci	3mp	חנה	333		decline,encamp
33: 50	ידבר	piel	wci	3ms	דבר	180		speak
	אמר	qal	infc		אמר	55		say
33: 51	דבר	piel	impv	ms	דבר	180		speak
	אמרת	qal	wcp	2ms	אמר	55		say
	עברים	qal	ptc	mp	עבר	716		pass over
33: 52	הורשתם	hiph	wcp	2mp	ירשׁ	439		c. to possess
	ישׁבי	qal	ptc	mp	ישׁב	442		sit,dwell
	אבדתם	piel	wcp	2mp	אבד	1		destroy
	תאבדו	piel	impf	2mp	אבד	1		destroy
	תשׁמידו	hiph	impf	2mp	שׁמד	1029		exterminate
33: 53	הורשתם	hiph	wcp	2mp	ירשׁ	439		c. to possess
	ישׁבתם	qal	wcp	2mp	ישׁב	442		sit,dwell
	נתתי	qal	pft	1cs	נתן	678		give,set
	רשׁת	qal	infc		ירשׁ	439		possess,inherit
33: 54	התנחלתם	hith	wcp	2mp	נחל	635		possess oneself
	תרבו	hiph	impf	2mp	רבה	915		make many
	תמעיט	hiph	impf	2ms	מעט	589		make small
	יצא	qal	impf	3ms	יצא	422		go out
	יהיה	qal	impf	3ms	היה	224		be,become
	תתנחלו	hith	impf	2mp	נחל	635		possess oneself
33: 55	תורישׁו	hiph	impf	2mp	ירשׁ	439		c. to possess
	ישׁבי	qal	ptc	mp	ישׁב	442		sit,dwell
	היה	qal	wcp	3ms	היה	224		be,become
	תותירו	hiph	impf	2mp	יתר	451		leave,spare
	צררו	qal	wcp	3cp	צרר	865		show hostility
	ישׁבים	qal	ptc	mp	ישׁב	442		sit,dwell
33: 56	היה	qal	wcp	3ms	היה	224		be,become
	דמיתי	piel	pft	1cs	דמה	197		liken,think
	עשׂות	qal	infc		עשׂה	793		do,make
	אעשׂה	qal	impf	1cs	עשׂה	793		do,make
34: 1	ידבר	piel	wci	3ms	דבר	180		speak
	אמר	qal	infc		אמר	55		say
34: 2	צו	piel	impv	ms	צוה	845		command
	אמרת	qal	wcp	2ms	אמר	55		say
	באים	qal	ptc	mp	בוא	97		come in
	תפל	qal	impf	3fs	נפל	656		fall
34: 3	היה	qal	wcp	3ms	היה	224		be,become
	היה	qal	wcp	3ms	היה	224		be,become
34: 4	נסב	niph	wcp	3ms	סבב	685		turn round
	עבר	qal	wcp	3ms	עבר	716		pass over
	היהk	qal	wcp	3ms	היה	224		be,become
34: 4	היוq	qal	wcp	3cp	היה	224		be,become
	יצא	qal	wcp	3ms	יצא	422		go out
	עבר	qal	wcp	3ms	עבר	716		pass over
34: 5	נסב	niph	wcp	3ms	סבב	685		turn round
	היו	qal	wcp	3cp	היה	224		be,become
34: 6	היה	qal	wcp	3ms	היה	224		be,become
	יהיה	qal	impf	3ms	היה	224		be,become
34: 7	יהיה	qal	impf	3ms	היה	224		be,become
	תתאו	piel	impf	2mp	תאה	1060		mark out
34: 8	תתאו	piel	impf	2mp	תאה	1060		mark out
	בא	qal	infc		בוא	97		come in
	היו	qal	wcp	3cp	היה	224		be,become
34: 9	יצא	qal	wcp	3ms	יצא	422		go out
	היו	qal	wcp	3cp	היה	224		be,become
	יהיה	qal	impf	3ms	היה	224		be,become
34: 10	התאויתם	hith	wcp	2mp	אוה	16		mark out
34: 11	ירד	qal	wcp	3ms	ירד	432		come down
	ירד	qal	wcp	3ms	ירד	432		come down
	מחה	qal	wcp	3ms	מחה	562		strike
34: 12	ירד	qal	wcp	3ms	ירד	432		come down
	היו	qal	wcp	3cp	היה	224		be,become
	תהיה	qal	impf	3fs	היה	224		be,become
34: 13	יצו	piel	wci	3ms	צוה	845		command
	אמר	qal	infc		אמר	55		say
	תתנחלו	hith	impf	2mp	נחל	635		possess oneself
	צוה	piel	pft	3ms	צוה	845		command
	תת	qal	infc		נתן	678		give,set
34: 14	לקחו	qal	pft	3cp	לקח	542		take
	לקחו	qal	pft	3cp	לקח	542		take
34: 15	לקחו	qal	pft	3cp	לקח	542		take
34: 16	ידבר	piel	wci	3ms	דבר	180		speak
	אמר	qal	infc		אמר	55		say
34: 17	ינחלו	qal	impf	3mp	נחל	635		possess,inherit
34: 18	תקחו	qal	impf	2mp	לקח	542		take
	נחל	qal	infc		נחל	635		possess,inherit
34: 29	צוה	piel	pft	3ms	צוה	845		command
	נחל	piel	infc		נחל	635		allot
35: 1	ידבר	piel	wci	3ms	דבר	180		speak
	אמר	qal	infc		אמר	55		say
35: 2	צו	piel	impv	ms	צוה	845		command
	נתנו	qal	wcp	3cp	נתן	678		give,set
	שׁבת	qal	infc		ישׁב	442		sit,dwell
	תתנו	qal	impf	2mp	נתן	678		give,set
35: 3	היו	qal	wcp	3cp	היה	224		be,become
	שׁבת	qal	infc		ישׁב	442		sit,dwell
	יהיו	qal	impf	3mp	היה	224		be,become
35: 4	תתנו	qal	impf	2mp	נתן	678		give,set
35: 5	מדתם	qal	wcp	2mp	מדד	551		measure
	יהיה	qal	impf	3ms	היה	224		be,become
35: 6	תתנו	qal	impf	2mp	נתן	678		give,set
	תתנו	qal	impf	2mp	נתן	678		give,set
	נס	qal	infc		נוס	630		flee,escape
	רצח	qal	ptc	ms	רצח	953		murder,slay
	תתנו	qal	impf	2mp	נתן	678		give,set

ChVs	Form	Stem	Tnse	PGN	Root	BDB	Sfx	Meaning
35:7	תתנו	qal	impf	2mp	נתן	678		give,set
35:8	תתנו	qal	impf	2mp	נתן	678		give,set
	תרבו	hiph	impf	2mp	רבה	915		make many
	תמעיטו	hiph	impf	2mp	מעט	589		make small
	ינחלו	qal	impf	3mp	נחל	635		possess,inherit
	יתן	qal	impf	3ms	נתן	678		give,set
35:9	ידבר	piel	wci	3ms	דבר	180		speak
	אמר	qal	infc		אמר	55		say
35:10	דבר	piel	impv	ms	דבר	180		speak
	אמרת	qal	wcp	2ms	אמר	55		say
	עברים	qal	ptc	mp	עבר	716		pass over
35:11	הקריתם	hiph	wcp	2mp	קרה	899		cause to occur
	תהיינה	qal	impf	3fp	היה	224		be,become
	נס	qal	wcp	3ms	נוס	630		flee,escape
	רצח	qal	ptc	ms	רצח	953		murder,slay
	מכה	hiph	ptc	ms	נכה	645		smite
35:12	היו	qal	wcp	3cp	היה	224		be,become
	גאל	qal	ptc	ms	גאל	145		redeem
	ימות	qal	impf	3ms	מות	559		die
	רצח	qal	ptc	ms	רצח	953		murder,slay
	עמדו	qal	infc		עמד	763	3ms	stand,stop
35:13	תתנו	qal	impf	2mp	נתן	678		give,set
	תהיינה	qal	impf	3fp	היה	224		be,become
35:14	תתנו	qal	impf	2mp	נתן	678		give,set
	תתנו	qal	impf	2mp	נתן	678		give,set
	תהיינה	qal	impf	3fp	היה	224		be,become
35:15	תהיינה	qal	impf	3fp	היה	224		be,become
	נוס	qal	infc		נוס	630		flee,escape
	מכה	hiph	ptc	ms	נכה	645		smite
35:16	הכהו	hiph	pft	3ms	נכה	645	3ms	smite
	ימת	qal	wci	3ms	מות	559		die
	רצח	qal	ptc	ms	רצח	953		murder,slay
	מות	qal	infa		מות	559		die
	יומת	hoph	impf	3ms	מות	559		be killed
	רצח	qal	ptc	ms	רצח	953		murder,slay
35:17	ימות	qal	impf	3ms	מות	559		die
	הכהו	hiph	pft	3ms	נכה	645	3ms	smite
	ימת	qal	wci	3ms	מות	559		die
	רצח	qal	ptc	ms	רצח	953		murder,slay
	מות	qal	infa		מות	559		die
	יומת	hoph	impf	3ms	מות	559		be killed
	רצח	qal	ptc	ms	רצח	953		murder,slay
35:18	ימות	qal	impf	3ms	מות	559		die
	הכהו	hiph	pft	3ms	נכה	645	3ms	smite
	ימת	qal	wci	3ms	מות	559		die
	רצח	qal	ptc	ms	רצח	953		murder,slay
	מות	qal	infa		מות	559		die
	יומת	hoph	impf	3ms	מות	559		be killed
	רצח	qal	ptc	ms	רצח	953		murder,slay
35:19	גאל	qal	ptc	ms	גאל	145		redeem
	ימית	hiph	impf	3ms	מות	559		kill
	רצח	qal	ptc	ms	רצח	953		murder,slay
	פגעו	qal	infc		פגע	803	3ms	meet,encounter
	ימיתנו	hiph	impf	3ms	מות	559	3ms	kill
35:20	יהדפנו	qal	impf	3ms	הדף	213	3ms	thrust,drive
	השליך	hiph	pft	3ms	שלך	1020		throw,cast
	ימת	qal	wci	3ms	מות	559		die
35:21	הכהו	hiph	pft	3ms	נכה	645	3ms	smite
	ימת	qal	wci	3ms	מות	559		die
	מות	qal	infa		מות	559		die
	יומת	hoph	impf	3ms	מות	559		be killed
	מכה	hiph	ptc	ms	נכה	645		smite
	רצח	qal	ptc	ms	רצח	953		murder,slay
	גאל	qal	ptc	ms	גאל	145		redeem
	ימית	hiph	impf	3ms	מות	559		kill
	רצח	qal	ptc	ms	רצח	953		murder,slay
	פגעו	qal	infc		פגע	803	3ms	meet,encounter
35:22	הדפו	qal	pft	3ms	הדף	213	3ms	thrust,drive
	השליך	hiph	pft	3ms	שלך	1020		throw,cast
35:23	ימות	qal	impf	3ms	מות	559		die
	ראות	qal	infc		ראה	906		see
	יפל	hiph	wci	3ms	נפל	656		cause to fall
	ימת	qal	wci	3ms	מות	559		die
	אויב	qal	ptc	ms	איב	33		be hostile to
	מבקש	piel	ptc	ms	בקש	134		seek
35:24	שפטו	qal	wcp	3cp	שפט	1047		judge
	מכה	hiph	ptc	ms	נכה	645		smite
	גאל	qal	ptc	ms	גאל	145		redeem
35:25	הצילו	hiph	wcp	3cp	נצל	664		snatch,deliver
	רצח	qal	ptc	ms	רצח	953		murder,slay
	גאל	qal	ptc	ms	גאל	145		redeem
	השיבו	hiph	wcp	3cp	שוב	996		bring back
	נס	qal	pft	3ms	נוס	630		flee,escape
	ישב	qal	wcp	3ms	ישב	442		sit,dwell
	משח	qal	pft	3ms	משח	602		smear,anoint
35:26	יצא	qal	infa		יצא	422		go out
	יצא	qal	impf	3ms	יצא	422		go out
	רצח	qal	ptc	ms	רצח	953		murder,slay
	ינוס	qal	impf	3ms	נוס	630		flee,escape
35:27	מצא	qal	wcp	3ms	מצא	592		find
	גאל	qal	ptc	ms	גאל	145		redeem
	רצח	qal	wcp	3ms	רצח	953		murder,slay
	גאל	qal	ptc	ms	גאל	145		redeem
	רצח	qal	ptc	ms	רצח	953		murder,slay
35:28	ישב	qal	impf	3ms	ישב	442		sit,dwell
	ישוב	qal	impf	3ms	שוב	996		turn,return
	רצח	qal	ptc	ms	רצח	953		murder,slay
35:29	היו	qal	wcp	3cp	היה	224		be,become
35:30	מכה	hiph	ptc	ms	נכה	645		smite
	ירצח	qal	impf	3ms	רצח	953		murder,slay
	רצח	qal	ptc	ms	רצח	953		murder,slay
	יענה	qal	impf	3ms	ענה	772		answer
	מות	qal	infc		מות	559		die
35:31	תקחו	qal	impf	2mp	לקח	542		take
	רצח	qal	ptc	ms	רצח	953		murder,slay
	מות	qal	infc		מות	559		die
	מות	qal	infa		מות	559		die
	יומת	hoph	impf	3ms	מות	559		be killed

ChVs	Form	Stem	Tnse	PGN	Root	BDB	Sfx	Meaning
35:32	תקחו	qal	impf	2mp	לקח	542		take
	נוס	qal	infc		נוס	630		flee,escape
	שׁוב	qal	infc		שׁוב	996		turn,return
	שׁבת	qal	infc		ישׁב	442		sit,dwell
35:33	תחניפו	hiph	impf	2mp	חנף	337		pollute
	יחניף	hiph	impf	3ms	חנף	337		pollute
	יכפר	pual	impf	3ms	כפר	497		be atoned for
	שׁפך	qalp	pft	3ms	שׁפך	1049		be poured out
	שׁפכו	qal	ptc	ms	שׁפך	1049	3ms	pour out
35:34	תטמא	piel	impf	2ms	טמא	379		defile
	ישׁבים	qal	ptc	mp	ישׁב	442		sit,dwell
	שׁכן	qal	ptc	ms	שׁכן	1014		settle,dwell
	שׁכן	qal	ptc	ms	שׁכן	1014		settle,dwell
36:1	יקרבו	qal	wci	3mp	קרב	897		approach
	ידברו	piel	wci	3mp	דבר	180		speak
36:2	יאמרו	qal	wci	3mp	אמר	55		say
	צוה	piel	pft	3ms	צוה	845		command
	תת	qal	infc		נתן	678		give,set
	צוה	pual	pft	3ms	צוה	845		be commanded
	תת	qal	infc		נתן	678		give,set
36:3	היו	qal	wcp	3cp	היה	224		be,become
	נגרעה	niph	wcp	3fs	גרע	175		be withdrawn
	נוסף	niph	wcp	3ms	יסף	414		be joined to
	תהיינה	qal	impf	3fp	היה	224		be,become
	יגרע	niph	impf	3ms	גרע	175		be withdrawn
36:4	יהיה	qal	impf	3ms	היה	224		be,become
	נוספה	niph	wcp	3fs	יסף	414		be joined to
	תהיינה	qal	impf	3fp	היה	224		be,become
	יגרע	niph	impf	3ms	גרע	175		be withdrawn
36:5	יצו	piel	wci	3ms	צוה	845		command
	אמר	qal	infc		אמר	55		say
	דברים	qal	ptc	mp	דבר	180		speak
36:6	צוה	piel	pft	3ms	צוה	845		command
	אמר	qal	infc		אמר	55		say
	תהיינה	qal	impf	3fp	היה	224		be,become
	תהיינה	qal	impf	3fp	היה	224		be,become
36:7	תסב	qal	impf	3fs	סבב	685		surround
	ידבקו	qal	impf	3mp	דבק	179		cling,cleave
36:8	ירשׁת	qal	ptc	fs	ירשׁ	439		possess,inherit
	תהיה	qal	impf	3fs	היה	224		be,become
	יירשׁו	qal	impf	3mp	ירשׁ	439		possess,inherit
36:9	תסב	qal	impf	3fs	סבב	685		surround
	ידבקו	qal	impf	3mp	דבק	179		cling,cleave
36:10	צוה	piel	pft	3ms	צוה	845		command
	עשׂו	qal	pft	3cp	עשׂה	793		do,make
36:11	תהיינה	qal	wci	3fp	היה	224		be,become
36:12	היו	qal	pft	3cp	היה	224		be,become
	תהי	qal	wci	3fs	היה	224		be,become
36:13	צוה	piel	pft	3ms	צוה	845		command

DEUTERONOMY

ChVs	Form	Stem	Tnse	PGN	Root	BDB	Sfx	Meaning
1:1	דבר	piel	pft	3ms	דבר	180		speak
1:3	יהי	qal	wci	3ms	היה	224		be,become
	דבר	piel	pft	3ms	דבר	180		speak
1:3	צוה	piel	pft	3ms	צוה	845		command
1:4	הכתו	hiph	infc		נכה	645	3ms	smite
	יושׁב	qal	ptc	ms	ישׁב	442		sit,dwell
	יושׁב	qal	ptc	ms	ישׁב	442		sit,dwell
1:5	הואיל	hiph	pft	3ms	יאל	383		be willing
	באר	piel	pft	3ms	באר	91		make plain
	אמר	qal	infc		אמר	55		say
1:6	דבר	piel	pft	3ms	דבר	180		speak
	אמר	qal	infc		אמר	55		say
	שׁבת	qal	infc		ישׁב	442		sit,dwell
1:7	פנו	qal	impv	mp	פנה	815		turn
	סעו	qal	impv	mp	נסע	652		pull up,set out
	באו	qal	impv	mp	בוא	97		come in
1:8	ראה	qal	impv	ms	ראה	906		see
	נתתי	qal	pft	1cs	נתן	678		give,set
	באו	qal	impv	mp	בוא	97		come in
	רשׁו	qal	impv	mp	ירשׁ	439		possess,inherit
	נשׁבע	niph	pft	3ms	שׁבע	989		swear
	תת	qal	infc		נתן	678		give,set
1:9	אמר	qal	wci	1cs	אמר	55		say
	אמר	qal	infc		אמר	55		say
	אוכל	qal	impf	1cs	יכל	407		be able
	שׂאת	qal	infc		נשׂא	669		lift,carry
1:10	הרבה	hiph	pft	3ms	רבה	915		make many
1:11	יסף	hiph	jus	3ms	יסף	414		add,do again
	יברך	piel	jusm	3ms	ברך	138		bless
	דבר	piel	pft	3ms	דבר	180		speak
1:12	אשׂא	qal	impf	1cs	נשׂא	669		lift,carry
1:13	הבו	qal	impv	mp	יהב	396		give
	נבנים	niph	ptc	mp	בין	106		be discerning
	ידעים	qal	pptc	mp	ידע	393		know
	אשׂימם	qal	cohm	1cs	שׂים	962	3mp	put,set
1:14	תענו	qal	wci	2mp	ענה	772		answer
	תאמרו	qal	wci	2mp	אמר	55		say
	דברת	piel	pft	2ms	דבר	180		speak
	עשׂות	qal	infc		עשׂה	793		do,make
1:15	אקח	qal	wci	1cs	לקח	542		take
	ידעים	qal	pptc	mp	ידע	393		know
	אתן	qal	wci	1cs	נתן	678		give,set
1:16	אצוה	piel	wci	1cs	צוה	845		command
	שׁפטיכם	qal	ptc	mp	שׁפט	1047	2mp	judge
	אמר	qal	infc		אמר	55		say
	שׁמע	qal	infa		שׁמע	1033		hear
	שׁפטתם	qal	wcp	2mp	שׁפט	1047		judge
1:17	תכירו	hiph	impf	2mp	נכר	647		regard,notice
	תשׁמעון	qal	impf	2mp	שׁמע	1033		hear
	תגורו	qal	impf	2mp	גור	158		dread
	יקשׁה	qal	impf	3ms	קשׁה	904		be hard,severe
	תקרבון	hiph	impf	2mp	קרב	897		bring near
	שׁמעתיו	qal	wcp	1cs	שׁמע	1033	3ms	hear
1:18	אצוה	piel	wci	1cs	צוה	845		command
	תעשׂון	qal	impf	2mp	עשׂה	793		do,make
1:19	נסע	qal	wci	1cp	נסע	652		pull up,set out
	נלך	qal	wci	1cp	הלך	229		walk,go

ChVs	Form	Stem	Tnse	PGN	Root	BDB	Sfx	Meaning
1:19	נורא	niph	ptc	ms	ירא	431		be feared
	ראיתם	qal	pft	2mp	ראה	906		see
	צוה	piel	pft	3ms	צוה	845		command
	נבא	qal	wci	1cp	בוא	97		come in
1:20	אמר	qal	wci	1cs	אמר	55		say
	באתם	qal	pft	2mp	בוא	97		come in
	נתן	qal	ptc	ms	נתן	678		give,set
1:21	ראה	qal	impv	ms	ראה	906		see
	נתן	qal	pft	3ms	נתן	678		give,set
	עלה	qal	impv	ms	עלה	748		go up
	רשׁ	qal	impv	ms	ירשׁ	439		possess,inherit
	דבר	piel	pft	3ms	דבר	180		speak
	תירא	qal	jusm	2ms	ירא	431		fear
	תחת	qal	jusm	2ms	חתת	369		be shattered
1:22	תקרבון	qal	wci	2mp	קרב	897		approach
	תאמרו	qal	wci	2mp	אמר	55		say
	נשׁלחה	qal	coh	1cp	שׁלח	1018		send
	יחפרו	qal	jusm	3mp	חפר	343		dig,search
	ישׁבו	hiph	jusm	3mp	שׁוב	996		bring back
	נעלה	qal	impf	1cp	עלה	748		go up
	נבא	qal	impf	1cp	בוא	97		come in
1:23	ייטב	qal	wci	3ms	יטב	405		be good
	אקח	qal	wci	1cs	לקח	542		take
1:24	יפנו	qal	wci	3mp	פנה	815		turn
	יעלו	qal	wci	3mp	עלה	748		go up
	יבאו	qal	wci	3mp	בוא	97		come in
	ירגלו	piel	wci	3mp	רגל	920		slander,spy
1:25	יקחו	qal	wci	3mp	לקח	542		take
	יורדו	hiph	wci	3mp	ירד	432		bring down
	ישׁבו	hiph	wci	3mp	שׁוב	996		bring back
	יאמרו	qal	wci	3mp	אמר	55		say
	נתן	qal	ptc	ms	נתן	678		give,set
1:26	אביתם	qal	pft	2mp	אבה	2		be willing
	עלת	qal	infc		עלה	748		go up
	תמרו	hiph	wci	2mp	מרה	598		rebel
1:27	תרגנו	niph	wci	2mp	רגן	920		murmur,rebel
	תאמרו	qal	wci	2mp	אמר	55		say
	הוציאנו	hiph	pft	3ms	יצא	422	1cp	bring out
	תת	qal	infc		נתן	678		give,set
	השׁמידנו	hiph	infc		שׁמד	1029	1cp	exterminate
1:28	עלים	qal	ptc	mp	עלה	748		go up
	המסו	hiph	pft	3cp	מסס	587		cause to melt
	אמר	qal	infc		אמר	55		say
	רם	qal	ptc	ms	רום	926		be high
	בצורת	qal	pptc	fp	בצר	130		cut off
	ראינו	qal	pft	1cp	ראה	906		see
1:29	אמר	qal	wci	1cs	אמר	55		say
	תערצון	qal	impf	2mp	ערץ	791		frighten,fear
	תיראון	qal	impf	2mp	ירא	431		fear
1:30	הלך	qal	ptc	ms	הלך	229		walk,go
	ילחם	niph	impf	3ms	לחם	535		wage war
	עשׂה	qal	pft	3ms	עשׂה	793		do,make
1:31	ראית	qal	pft	2ms	ראה	906		see
	נשׂאך	qal	pft	3ms	נשׂא	669	2ms	lift,carry

ChVs	Form	Stem	Tnse	PGN	Root	BDB	Sfx	Meaning
1:31	ישׂא	qal	impf	3ms	נשׂא	669		lift,carry
	הלכתם	qal	pft	2mp	הלך	229		walk,go
	באכם	qal	infc		בוא	97	2mp	come in
1:32	מאמינם	hiph	ptc	mp	אמן	52		believe
1:33	הלך	qal	ptc	ms	הלך	229		walk,go
	תור	qal	infc		תור	1064		seek out,spy
	חנתכם	qal	infc		חנה	333	2mp	decline,encamp
	ראתכם	hiph	infc		ראה	906	2mp	show,exhibit
	תלכו	qal	impf	2mp	הלך	229		walk,go
1:34	ישׁמע	qal	wci	3ms	שׁמע	1033		hear
	יקצף	qal	wci	3ms	קצף	893		be angry
	ישׁבע	niph	wci	3ms	שׁבע	989		swear
	אמר	qal	infc		אמר	55		say
1:35	יראה	qal	impf	3ms	ראה	906		see
	נשׁבעתי	niph	pft	1cs	שׁבע	989		swear
	תת	qal	infc		נתן	678		give,set
1:36	יראנה	qal	impf	3ms	ראה	906	3fs	see
	אתן	qal	impf	1cs	נתן	678		give,set
	דרך	qal	pft	3ms	דרך	201		tread,march
	מלא	piel	pft	3ms	מלא	569		fill
1:37	התאנף	hith	pft	3ms	אנף	60		be angry
	אמר	qal	infc		אמר	55		say
	תבא	qal	impf	2ms	בוא	97		come in
1:38	עמד	qal	ptc	ms	עמד	763		stand,stop
	יבא	qal	impf	3ms	בוא	97		come in
	חזק	piel	impv	ms	חזק	304		make strong
	ינחלנה	hiph	impf	3ms	נחל	635	3fs	c. to inherit
1:39	אמרתם	qal	pft	2mp	אמר	55		say
	יהיה	qal	impf	3ms	היה	224		be,become
	ידעו	qal	pft	3cp	ידע	393		know
	יבאו	qal	impf	3mp	בוא	97		come in
	אתננה	qal	impf	1cs	נתן	678	3fs	give,set
	יירשׁוה	qal	impf	3mp	ירשׁ	439	3fs	possess,inherit
1:40	פנו	qal	impv	mp	פנה	815		turn
	סעו	qal	impv	mp	נסע	652		pull up,set out
1:41	תענו	qal	wci	2mp	ענה	772		answer
	תאמרו	qal	wci	2mp	אמר	55		say
	חטאנו	qal	pft	1cp	חטא	306		sin
	נעלה	qal	impf	1cp	עלה	748		go up
	נלחמנו	niph	wcp	1cp	לחם	535		wage war
	צונו	piel	pft	3ms	צוה	845	1cp	command
	תחגרו	qal	wci	2mp	חגר	291		gird
	תהינו	hiph	wci	2mp	הון	223		make light of
	עלת	qal	infc		עלה	748		go up
1:42	יאמר	qal	wci	3ms	אמר	55		say
	אמר	qal	impv	ms	אמר	55		say
	תעלו	qal	impf	2mp	עלה	748		go up
	תלחמו	niph	impf	2mp	לחם	535		wage war
	תנגפו	niph	impf	2mp	נגף	619		be smitten
	איביכם	qal	ptc	mp	איב	33	2mp	be hostile to
1:43	אדבר	piel	wci	1cs	דבר	180		speak
	שׁמעתם	qal	pft	2mp	שׁמע	1033		hear
	תמרו	hiph	wci	2mp	מרה	598		rebel
	תזדו	hiph	wci	2mp	זיד	267		boil,presume

ChVs	Form	Stem	Tnse	PGN	Root	BDB	Sfx	Meaning
1:43	תעלו	qal	wci	2mp	עלה	748		go up
1:44	יצא	qal	wci	3ms	יצא	422		go out
	ישׁב	qal	ptc	ms	ישׁב	442		sit,dwell
	קראתכם	qal	infc		קרא	896	2mp	meet,encounter
	ירדפו	qal	wci	3mp	רדף	922		pursue
	תעשׂינה	qal	impf	3fp	עשׂה	793		do,make
	יכתו	hiph	wci	3mp	כתת	510		beat in pieces
1:45	תשׁבו	qal	wci	2mp	שׁוב	996		turn,return
	תבכו	qal	wci	2mp	בכה	113		weep
	שׁמע	qal	pft	3ms	שׁמע	1033		hear
	האזין	hiph	pft	3ms	אזן	24		hear
1:46	תשׁבו	qal	wci	2mp	ישׁב	442		sit,dwell
	ישׁבתם	qal	pft	2mp	ישׁב	442		sit,dwell
2:1	נפן	qal	wci	1cp	פנה	815		turn
	נסע	qal	wci	1cp	נסע	652		pull up,set out
	דבר	piel	pft	3ms	דבר	180		speak
	נסב	qal	wci	1cp	סבב	685		surround
2:2	יאמר	qal	wci	3ms	אמר	55		say
	אמר	qal	infc		אמר	55		say
2:3	סב	qal	infc		סבב	685		surround
	פנו	qal	impv	mp	פנה	815		turn
2:4	צו	piel	impv	ms	צוה	845		command
	אמר	qal	infc		אמר	55		say
	עברים	qal	ptc	mp	עבר	716		pass over
	ישׁבים	qal	ptc	mp	ישׁב	442		sit,dwell
	ייראו	qal	impf	3mp	ירא	431		fear
	נשׁמרתם	niph	wcp	2mp	שׁמר	1036		be kept,guarded
2:5	תתגרו	hith	jusm	2mp	גרה	173		excite oneself
	אתן	qal	impf	1cs	נתן	678		give,set
	נתתי	qal	pft	1cs	נתן	678		give,set
2:6	תשׁברו	qal	impf	2mp	שׁבר	991		buy grain
	אכלתם	qal	wcp	2mp	אכל	37		eat,devour
	תכרו	qal	impf	2mp	כרה	500		get by trade
	שׁתיתם	qal	wcp	2mp	שׁתה	1059		drink
2:7	ברכך	piel	pft	3ms	ברך	138	2ms	bless
	ידע	qal	pft	3ms	ידע	393		know
	לכתך	qal	infc		הלך	229	2ms	walk,go
	חסרת	qal	pft	2ms	חסר	341		lack
2:8	נעבר	qal	wci	1cp	עבר	716		pass over
	ישׁבים	qal	ptc	mp	ישׁב	442		sit,dwell
	נפן	qal	wci	1cp	פנה	815		turn
	נעבר	qal	wci	1cp	עבר	716		pass over
2:9	יאמר	qal	wci	3ms	אמר	55		say
	תצר	qal	jus	2ms	צור	849		treat as foe
	תתגר	hith	jus	2ms	גרה	173		excite oneself
	אתן	qal	impf	1cs	נתן	678		give,set
	נתתי	qal	pft	1cs	נתן	678		give,set
2:10	ישׁבו	qal	pft	3cp	ישׁב	442		sit,dwell
	רם	qal	ptc	ms	רום	926		be high
2:11	יחשׁבו	niph	impf	3mp	חשׁב	362		be thought
	יקראו	qal	impf	3mp	קרא	894		call,proclaim
2:12	ישׁבו	qal	pft	3cp	ישׁב	442		sit,dwell
	יירשׁום	qal	impf	3mp	ירשׁ	439	3mp	possess,inherit
	ישׁמידום	hiph	wci	3mp	שׁמד	1029	3mp	exterminate
2:12	ישׁבו	qal	wci	3mp	ישׁב	442		sit,dwell
	עשׂה	qal	pft	3ms	עשׂה	793		do,make
	נתן	qal	pft	3ms	נתן	678		give,set
2:13	קמו	qal	impv	mp	קום	877		arise,stand
	עברו	qal	impv	mp	עבר	716		pass over
	נעבר	qal	wci	1cp	עבר	716		pass over
2:14	הלכנו	qal	pft	1cp	הלך	229		walk,go
	עברנו	qal	pft	1cp	עבר	716		pass over
	תם	qal	infc		תמם	1070		be finished
	נשׁבע	niph	pft	3ms	שׁבע	989		swear
2:15	היתה	qal	pft	3fs	היה	224		be,become
	המם	qal	infc		המם	243	3mp	confuse,vex
	תמם	qal	infc		תמם	1070	3mp	be finished
2:16	יהי	qal	wci	3ms	היה	224		be,become
	תמו	qal	pft	3cp	תמם	1070		be finished
	מות	qal	infc		מות	559		die
2:17	ידבר	piel	wci	3ms	דבר	180		speak
	אמר	qal	infc		אמר	55		say
2:18	עבר	qal	ptc	ms	עבר	716		pass over
2:19	קרבת	qal	wcp	2ms	קרב	897		approach
	תצרם	qal	jusm	2ms	צור	849	3mp	treat as foe
	תתגר	hith	jus	2ms	גרה	173		excite oneself
	אתן	qal	impf	1cs	נתן	678		give,set
	נתתיה	qal	pft	1cs	נתן	678	3fs	give,set
2:20	תחשׁב	niph	impf	3fs	חשׁב	362		be thought
	ישׁבו	qal	pft	3cp	ישׁב	442		sit,dwell
	יקראו	qal	impf	3mp	קרא	894		call,proclaim
2:21	רם	qal	ptc	ms	רום	926		be high
	ישׁמידם	hiph	wci	3ms	שׁמד	1029	3mp	exterminate
	יירשׁם	qal	wci	3mp	ירשׁ	439	3mp	possess,inherit
	ישׁבו	qal	wci	3mp	ישׁב	442		sit,dwell
2:22	עשׂה	qal	pft	3ms	עשׂה	793		do,make
	ישׁבים	qal	ptc	mp	ישׁב	442		sit,dwell
	השׁמיד	hiph	pft	3ms	שׁמד	1029		exterminate
	יירשׁם	qal	wci	3mp	ירשׁ	439	3mp	possess,inherit
	ישׁבו	qal	wci	3mp	ישׁב	442		sit,dwell
2:23	ישׁבים	qal	ptc	mp	ישׁב	442		sit,dwell
	יצאים	qal	ptc	mp	יצא	422		go out
	השׁמידם	hiph	pft	3cp	שׁמד	1029	3mp	exterminate
	ישׁבו	qal	wci	3mp	ישׁב	442		sit,dwell
2:24	קומו	qal	impv	mp	קום	877		arise,stand
	סעו	qal	impv	mp	נסע	652		pull up,set out
	עברו	qal	impv	mp	עבר	716		pass over
	ראה	qal	impv	ms	ראה	906		see
	נתתי	qal	pft	1cs	נתן	678		give,set
	החל	hiph	impv	ms	חלל	320		begin,profane
	רשׁ	qal	impv	ms	ירשׁ	439		possess,inherit
	התגר	hith	impv	ms	גרה	173		excite oneself
2:25	אחל	hiph	impf	1cs	חלל	320		begin,profane
	תת	qal	infc		נתן	678		give,set
	ישׁמעון	qal	impf	3mp	שׁמע	1033		hear
	רגזו	qal	wcp	3cp	רגז	919		quake
	חלו	qal	wcp	3cp	חול	296		dance,writhe
2:26	אשׁלח	qal	wci	1cs	שׁלח	1018		send

ChVs	Form	Stem	Tnse	PGN	Root	BDB	Sfx	Meaning
2:26	אמר	qal	infc		אמר	55		say
2:27	אעברה	qal	coh	1cs	עבר	716		pass over
	אלך	qal	impf	1cs	הלך	229		walk,go
	אסור	qal	impf	1cs	סור	693		turn aside
2:28	תשברני	hiph	impf	2ms	שבר	991	1cs	sell grain
	אכלתי	qal	wcp	1cs	אכל	37		eat,devour
	תתן	qal	impf	2ms	נתן	678		give,set
	שתיתי	qal	wcp	1cs	שתה	1059		drink
	אעברה	qal	coh	1cs	עבר	716		pass over
2:29	עשו	qal	pft	3cp	עשה	793		do,make
	ישבים	qal	ptc	mp	ישב	442		sit,dwell
	ישבים	qal	ptc	mp	ישב	442		sit,dwell
	אעבר	qal	impf	1cs	עבר	716		pass over
	נתן	qal	ptc	ms	נתן	678		give,set
2:30	אבה	qal	pft	3ms	אבה	2		be willing
	העברנו	hiph	infc		עבר	716	1cp	cause to pass
	הקשה	hiph	pft	3ms	קשה	904		harden
	אמץ	piel	pft	3ms	אמץ	54		make firm
	תתו	qal	infc		נתן	678	3ms	give,set
2:31	יאמר	qal	wci	3ms	אמר	55		say
	ראה	qal	impv	ms	ראה	906		see
	החלתי	hiph	pft	1cs	חלל	320		begin,profane
	תת	qal	infc		נתן	678		give,set
	החל	hiph	impv	ms	חלל	320		begin,profane
	רש	qal	impv	ms	ירש	439		possess,inherit
	רשת	qal	infc		ירש	439		possess,inherit
2:32	יצא	qal	wci	3ms	יצא	422		go out
	קראתנו	qal	infc		קרא	896	1cp	meet,encounter
2:33	יתנהו	qal	wci	3ms	נתן	678	3ms	give,set
	נך	hiph	wci	1cp	נכה	645		smite
2:34	נלכד	qal	wci	1cp	לכד	539		capture
	נחרם	hiph	wci	1cp	חרם	355		ban,destroy
	השארנו	hiph	pft	1cp	שאר	983		leave,spare
2:35	בזזנו	qal	pft	1cp	בזז	102		plunder
	לכדנו	qal	pft	1cp	לכד	539		capture
2:36	היתה	qal	pft	3fs	היה	224		be,become
	שגבה	qal	pft	3fs	שגב	960		be high
	נתן	qal	pft	3ms	נתן	678		give,set
2:37	קרבת	qal	pft	2ms	קרב	897		approach
	צוה	piel	pft	3ms	צוה	845		command
3:1	נפן	qal	wci	1cp	פנה	815		turn
	נעל	qal	wci	1cp	עלה	748		go up
	יצא	qal	wci	3ms	יצא	422		go out
	קראתנו	qal	infc		קרא	896	1cp	meet,encounter
3:2	יאמר	qal	wci	3ms	אמר	55		say
	תירא	qal	jusm	2ms	ירא	431		fear
	נתתי	qal	pft	1cs	נתן	678		give,set
	עשית	qal	wcp	2ms	עשה	793		do,make
	עשית	qal	pft	2ms	עשה	793		do,make
	יושב	qal	ptc	ms	ישב	442		sit,dwell
3:3	יתן	qal	wci	3ms	נתן	678		give,set
	נכהו	hiph	wci	1cp	נכה	645	3ms	smite
	השאיר	hiph	pft	3ms	שאר	983		leave,spare
3:4	נלכד	qal	wci	1cp	לכד	539		capture
3:4	היתה	qal	pft	3fs	היה	224		be,become
	לקחנו	qal	pft	1cp	לקח	542		take
3:5	בצרות	qal	pptc	fp	בצר	130		cut off
	הרבה	hiph	infa		רבה	915		make many
3:6	נחרם	hiph	wci	1cp	חרם	355		ban,destroy
	עשינו	qal	pft	1cp	עשה	793		do,make
	החרם	hiph	infa		חרם	355		ban,destroy
3:7	בזונו	qal	pft	1cp	בזז	102		plunder
3:8	נקח	qal	wci	1cp	לקח	542		take
3:9	יקראו	qal	impf	3mp	קרא	894		call,proclaim
	יקראו	qal	impf	3mp	קרא	894		call,proclaim
3:11	נשאר	niph	pft	3ms	שאר	983		be left
3:12	ירשנו	qal	pft	1cp	ירש	439		possess,inherit
	נתתי	qal	pft	1cs	נתן	678		give,set
3:13	נתתי	qal	pft	1cs	נתן	678		give,set
	יקרא	niph	impf	3ms	קרא	894		be called
3:14	לקח	qal	pft	3ms	לקח	542		take
	יקרא	qal	wci	3ms	קרא	894		call,proclaim
3:15	נתתי	qal	pft	1cs	נתן	678		give,set
3:16	נתתי	qal	pft	1cs	נתן	678		give,set
3:18	אצו	piel	wci	1cs	צוה	845		command
	אמר	qal	infc		אמר	55		say
	נתן	qal	pft	3ms	נתן	678		give,set
	רשתה	qal	infc		ירש	439	3fs	possess,inherit
	חלוצים	qal	pptc	mp	חלץ	323		equipped
	תעברו	qal	impf	2mp	עבר	716		pass over
3:19	ידעתי	qal	pft	1cs	ידע	393		know
	ישבו	qal	impf	3mp	ישב	442		sit,dwell
	נתתי	qal	pft	1cs	נתן	678		give,set
3:20	יניח	hiph	impf	3ms	נוח	628		give rest,put
	ירשו	qal	wcp	3cp	ירש	439		possess,inherit
	נתן	qal	ptc	ms	נתן	678		give,set
	שבתם	qal	wcp	2mp	שוב	996		turn,return
	נתתי	qal	pft	1cs	נתן	678		give,set
3:21	צויתי	piel	pft	1cs	צוה	845		command
	אמר	qal	infc		אמר	55		say
	ראת	qal	ptc	fp	ראה	906		see
	עשה	qal	pft	3ms	עשה	793		do,make
	יעשה	qal	impf	3ms	עשה	793		do,make
	עבר	qal	ptc	ms	עבר	716		pass over
3:22	תיראום	qal	impf	2mp	ירא	431	3mp	fear
	נלחם	niph	ptc	ms	לחם	535		wage war
3:23	אתחנן	hith	wci	1cs	חנן	335		seek favor
	אמר	qal	infc		אמר	55		say
3:24	החלות	hiph	pft	2ms	חלל	320		begin,profane
	הראות	hiph	infc		ראה	906		show,exhibit
	יעשה	qal	impf	3ms	עשה	793		do,make
3:25	אעברה	qal	coh	1cs	עבר	716		pass over
	אראה	qal	cohm	1cs	ראה	906		see
3:26	יתעבר	hith	wci	3ms	עבר	720		be arrogant
	שמע	qal	pft	3ms	שמע	1033		hear
	יאמר	qal	wci	3ms	אמר	55		say
	תוסף	hiph	jus	2ms	יסף	414		add,do again
	דבר	piel	infc		דבר	180		speak

ChVs	Form	Stem	Tnse	PGN	Root	BDB	Sfx	Meaning
3:27	עלה	qal	impv	ms	עלה	748		go up
	שׂא	qal	impv	ms	נשׂא	669		lift,carry
	ראה	qal	impv	ms	ראה	906		see
	תעבר	qal	impf	2ms	עבר	716		pass over
3:28	צו	piel	impv	ms	צוה	845		command
	חזקהו	piel	impv	ms	חזק	304	3ms	make strong
	אמצהו	piel	impv	ms	אמץ	54	3ms	make firm
	יעבר	qal	impf	3ms	עבר	716		pass over
	ינחיל	hiph	impf	3ms	נחל	635		c. to inherit
	תראה	qal	impf	2ms	ראה	906		see
3:29	נשׁב	qal	wci	1cp	ישׁב	442		sit,dwell
4:1	שׁמע	qal	impv	ms	שׁמע	1033		hear
	מלמד	piel	ptc	ms	למד	540		teach
	עשׂות	qal	infc		עשׂה	793		do,make
	תחיו	qal	impf	2mp	חיה	310		live
	באתם	qal	wcp	2mp	בוא	97		come in
	ירשׁתם	qal	wcp	2mp	ירשׁ	439		possess,inherit
	נתן	qal	ptc	ms	נתן	678		give,set
4:2	תספו	hiph	impf	2mp	יסף	414		add,do again
	מצוה	piel	ptc	ms	צוה	845		command
	תגרעו	qal	impf	2mp	גרע	175		diminish
	שׁמר	qal	infc		שׁמר	1036		keep,watch
	מצוה	piel	ptc	ms	צוה	845		command
4:3	ראת	qal	ptc	fp	ראה	906		see
	עשׂה	qal	pft	3ms	עשׂה	793		do,make
	הלך	qal	pft	3ms	הלך	229		walk,go
	השׁמידו	hiph	pft	3ms	שׁמד	1029	3ms	exterminate
4:5	ראה	qal	impv	ms	ראה	906		see
	למדתי	piel	pft	1cs	למד	540		teach
	צוני	piel	pft	3ms	צוה	845	1cs	command
	עשׂות	qal	infc		עשׂה	793		do,make
	באים	qal	ptc	mp	בוא	97		come in
	רשׁתה	qal	infc		ירשׁ	439	3fs	possess,inherit
4:6	שׁמרתם	qal	wcp	2mp	שׁמר	1036		keep,watch
	עשׂיתם	qal	wcp	2mp	עשׂה	793		do,make
	ישׁמעון	qal	impf	3mp	שׁמע	1033		hear
	אמרו	qal	wcp	3cp	אמר	55		say
	נבון	niph	ptc	ms	בין	106		be discerning
4:7	קראנו	qal	infc		קרא	894	1cp	call,proclaim
4:8	נתן	qal	ptc	ms	נתן	678		give,set
4:9	השׁמר	niph	impv	ms	שׁמר	1036		be kept,guarded
	שׁמר	qal	impv	ms	שׁמר	1036		keep,watch
	תשׁכח	qal	impf	2ms	שׁכח	1013		forget
	ראו	qal	pft	3cp	ראה	906		see
	יסורו	qal	impf	3mp	סור	693		turn aside
	הודעתם	hiph	wcp	2ms	ידע	393	3mp	declare
4:10	עמדת	qal	pft	2ms	עמד	763		stand,stop
	אמר	qal	infc		אמר	55		say
	הקהל	hiph	impv	ms	קהל	874		call assembly
	אשׁמעם	hiph	jusm	1cs	שׁמע	1033	3mp	cause to hear
	ילמדון	qal	impf	3mp	למד	540		learn
	יראה	qal	infc		ירא	431		fear
	ילמדון	piel	impf	3mp	למד	540		teach
4:11	תקרבון	qal	wci	2mp	קרב	897		approach
4:11	תעמדון	qal	wci	2mp	עמד	763		stand,stop
	בער	qal	ptc	ms	בער	128		burn
4:12	ידבר	piel	wci	3ms	דבר	180		speak
	שׁמעים	qal	ptc	mp	שׁמע	1033		hear
	ראים	qal	ptc	mp	ראה	906		see
4:13	יגד	hiph	wci	3ms	נגד	616		declare,tell
	צוה	piel	pft	3ms	צוה	845		command
	עשׂות	qal	infc		עשׂה	793		do,make
	יכתבם	qal	wci	3ms	כתב	507	3mp	write
4:14	צוה	piel	pft	3ms	צוה	845		command
	למד	piel	infc		למד	540		teach
	עשׂתכם	qal	infc		עשׂה	793	2mp	do,make
	עברים	qal	ptc	mp	עבר	716		pass over
	רשׁתה	qal	infc		ירשׁ	439	3fs	possess,inherit
4:15	נשׁמרתם	niph	wcp	2mp	שׁמר	1036		be kept,guarded
	ראיתם	qal	pft	2mp	ראה	906		see
	דבר	piel	pft	3ms	דבר	180		speak
4:16	תשׁחתון	hiph	impf	2mp	שׁחת	1007		spoil,ruin
	עשׂיתם	qal	wcp	2mp	עשׂה	793		do,make
4:17	תעוף	qal	impf	3fs	עוף	733		fly
4:18	רמשׂ	qal	ptc	ms	רמשׂ	942		creep
4:19	תשׂא	qal	impf	2ms	נשׂא	669		lift,carry
	ראית	qal	wcp	2ms	ראה	906		see
	נדחת	niph	wcp	2ms	נדח	623		be banished
	השׁתחוית	hish	wcp	2ms	חוה	1005		bow down
	עבדתם	qal	wcp	2ms	עבד	712	3mp	work,serve
	חלק	qal	pft	3ms	חלק	323		divide,share
4:20	לקח	qal	pft	3ms	לקח	542		take
	יוצא	hiph	wci	3ms	יצא	422		bring out
	היות	qal	infc		היה	224		be,become
4:21	התאנף	hith	pft	3ms	אנף	60		be angry
	ישׁבע	niph	wci	3ms	שׁבע	989		swear
	עברי	qal	infc		עבר	716	1cs	pass over
	בא	qal	infc		בוא	97		come in
	נתן	qal	ptc	ms	נתן	678		give,set
4:22	מת	qal	ptc	ms	מות	559		die
	עבר	qal	ptc	ms	עבר	716		pass over
	עברים	qal	ptc	mp	עבר	716		pass over
	ירשׁתם	qal	wcp	2mp	ירשׁ	439		possess,inherit
4:23	השׁמרו	niph	impv	mp	שׁמר	1036		be kept,guarded
	תשׁכחו	qal	impf	2mp	שׁכח	1013		forget
	כרת	qal	pft	3ms	כרת	503		cut,destroy
	עשׂיתם	qal	wcp	2mp	עשׂה	793		do,make
	צוך	piel	pft	3ms	צוה	845	2ms	command
4:24	אכלה	qal	ptc	fs	אכל	37		eat,devour
4:25	תוליד	hiph	impf	2ms	ילד	408		beget
	נושׁנתם	niph	wcp	2mp	ישׁן	445		be old
	השׁחתם	hiph	wcp	2mp	שׁחת	1007		spoil,ruin
	עשׂיתם	qal	wcp	2mp	עשׂה	793		do,make
	עשׂיתם	qal	wcp	2mp	עשׂה	793		do,make
	הכעיסו	hiph	infc		כעס	494	3ms	vex,provoke
4:26	העידתי	hiph	pft	1cs	עוד	729		testify,warn
	אבד	qal	infa		אבד	1		perish
	תאבדון	qal	impf	2mp	אבד	1		perish

ChVs	Form	Stem	Tnse	PGN	Root	BDB	Sfx	Meaning
4:26	עברים	qal	ptc	mp	עבר	716		pass over
	רשתה	qal	infc		ירשׁ	439	3fs	possess,inherit
	תאריכן	hiph	impf	2mp	ארך	73		prolong
	השׁמד	niph	infa		שׁמד	1029		be exterminated
	תשׁמדון	niph	impf	2mp	שׁמד	1029		be exterminated
4:27	הפיץ	hiph	wcp	3ms	פוץ	806		scatter
	נשׁארתם	niph	wcp	2mp	שׁאר	983		be left
	ינהג	piel	impf	3ms	נהג	624		drive away,lead
4:28	עבדתם	qal	wcp	2mp	עבד	712		work,serve
	יראון	qal	impf	3mp	ראה	906		see
	ישׁמעון	qal	impf	3mp	שׁמע	1033		hear
	יאכלון	qal	impf	3mp	אכל	37		eat,devour
	יריחן	hiph	impf	3mp	ריח	926		smell
4:29	בקשׁתם	piel	wcp	2mp	בקשׁ	134		seek
	מצאת	qal	wcp	2ms	מצא	592		find
	תדרשׁנו	qal	impf	2ms	דרשׁ	205	3ms	resort to,seek
4:30	מצאוך	qal	wcp	3cp	מצא	592	2ms	find
	שׁבת	qal	wcp	2ms	שׁוב	996		turn,return
	שׁמעת	qal	wcp	2ms	שׁמע	1033		hear
4:31	ירפך	hiph	impf	3ms	רפה	951	2ms	slacken,abandon
	ישׁחיתך	hiph	impf	3ms	שׁחת	1007	2ms	spoil,ruin
	ישׁכח	qal	impf	3ms	שׁכח	1013		forget
	נשׁבע	niph	pft	3ms	שׁבע	989		swear
4:32	שׁאל	qal	impv	ms	שׁאל	981		ask,borrow
	היו	qal	pft	3cp	היה	224		be,become
	ברא	qal	pft	3ms	ברא	135		create
	נהיה	niph	pft	3ms	היה	224		be done
	נשׁמע	niph	pft	3ms	שׁמע	1033		be heard
4:33	שׁמע	qal	pft	3ms	שׁמע	1033		hear
	מדבר	piel	ptc	ms	דבר	180		speak
	שׁמעת	qal	pft	2ms	שׁמע	1033		hear
	יחי	qal	wci	3ms	חיה	310		live
4:34	נסה	piel	pft	3ms	נסה	650		test,try
	בוא	qal	infc		בוא	97		come in
	קחת	qal	infc		לקח	542		take
	נטויה	qal	pptc	fs	נטה	639		stretch,incline
	עשׂה	qal	pft	3ms	עשׂה	793		do,make
4:35	הראת	hoph	pft	2ms	ראה	906		be shown
	דעת	qal	infc		ידע	393		know
4:36	השׁמיעך	hiph	pft	3ms	שׁמע	1033	2ms	cause to hear
	יסרך	piel	infc		יסר	415	2ms	correct,chasten
	הראך	hiph	pft	3ms	ראה	906	2ms	show,exhibit
	שׁמעת	qal	pft	2ms	שׁמע	1033		hear
4:37	אהב	qal	pft	3ms	אהב	12		love
	יבחר	qal	wci	3ms	בחר	103		choose
	יוצאך	hiph	wci	3ms	יצא	422	2ms	bring out
4:38	הורישׁ	hiph	infc		ירשׁ	439		c. to possess
	הביאך	hiph	infc		בוא	97	2ms	bring in
	תת	qal	infc		נתן	678		give,set
4:39	ידעת	qal	wcp	2ms	ידע	393		know
	השׁבת	hiph	wcp	2ms	שׁוב	996		bring back
4:40	שׁמרת	qal	wcp	2ms	שׁמר	1036		keep,watch
	מצוך	piel	ptc	ms	צוה	845	2ms	command
	ייטב	qal	impf	3ms	יטב	405		be good
4:40	תאריך	hiph	impf	2ms	ארך	73		prolong
	נתן	qal	ptc	ms	נתן	678		give,set
4:41	יבדיל	hiph	impf	3ms	בדל	95		divide
4:42	נס	qal	infc		נוס	630		flee,escape
	רוצח	qal	ptc	ms	רצח	953		murder,slay
	ירצח	qal	impf	3ms	רצח	953		murder,slay
	שׂנא	qal	ptc	ms	שׂנא	971		hate
	נס	qal	wcp	3ms	נוס	630		flee,escape
	חי	qal	wcp	3ms	חיה	310		live
4:44	שׂם	qal	pft	3ms	שׂים	962		put,set
4:45	דבר	piel	pft	3ms	דבר	180		speak
	צאתם	qal	infc		יצא	422	3mp	go out
4:46	יושׁב	qal	ptc	ms	ישׁב	442		sit,dwell
	הכה	hiph	pft	3ms	נכה	645		smite
	צאתם	qal	infc		יצא	422	3mp	go out
4:47	יירשׁו	qal	wci	3mp	ירשׁ	439		possess,inherit
5:1	יקרא	qal	wci	3ms	קרא	894		call,proclaim
	יאמר	qal	wci	3ms	אמר	55		say
	שׁמע	qal	impv	ms	שׁמע	1033		hear
	דבר	qal	ptc	ms	דבר	180		speak
	למדתם	qal	wcp	2mp	למד	540		learn
	שׁמרתם	qal	wcp	2mp	שׁמר	1036		keep,watch
	עשׂתם	qal	infc		עשׂה	793	3mp	do,make
5:2	כרת	qal	pft	3ms	כרת	503		cut,destroy
5:3	כרת	qal	pft	3ms	כרת	503		cut,destroy
5:4	דבר	piel	pft	3ms	דבר	180		speak
5:5	עמד	qal	ptc	ms	עמד	763		stand,stop
	הגיד	hiph	infc		נגד	616		declare,tell
	יראתם	qal	pft	2mp	ירא	431		fear
	עליתם	qal	pft	2mp	עלה	748		go up
	אמר	qal	infc		אמר	55		say
5:6	הוצאתיך	hiph	pft	1cs	יצא	422	2ms	bring out
5:7	יהיה	qal	impf	3ms	היה	224		be,become
5:8	תעשׂה	qal	impf	2ms	עשׂה	793		do,make
5:9	תשׁתחוה	hish	impf	2ms	חוה	1005		bow down
	תעבדם	hoph	impf	2ms	עבד	712	3mp	be led to serve
	פקד	qal	ptc	ms	פקד	823		attend to,visit
	שׂנאי	qal	ptc	mp	שׂנא	971	1cs	hate
5:10	עשׂה	qal	ptc	ms	עשׂה	793		do,make
	אהבי	qal	ptc	mp	אהב	12	1cs	love
	שׁמרי	qal	ptc	mp	שׁמר	1036		keep,watch
5:11	תשׂא	qal	impf	2ms	נשׂא	669		lift,carry
	ינקה	piel	impf	3ms	נקה	667		acquit
	ישׂא	qal	impf	3ms	נשׂא	669		lift,carry
5:12	שׁמור	qal	infa		שׁמר	1036		keep,watch
	קדשׁו	piel	infc		קדשׁ	872	3ms	consecrate
	צוך	piel	pft	3ms	צוה	845	2ms	command
5:13	תעבד	qal	impf	2ms	עבד	712		work,serve
	עשׂית	qal	wcp	2ms	עשׂה	793		do,make
5:14	תעשׂה	qal	impf	2ms	עשׂה	793		do,make
	ינוח	qal	impf	3ms	נוח	628		rest
5:15	זכרת	qal	wcp	2ms	זכר	269		remember
	היית	qal	pft	2ms	היה	224		be,become
	יצאך	hiph	wci	3ms	יצא	422	2ms	bring out

ChVs	Form	Stem	Tnse	PGN	Root	BDB	Sfx	Meaning
5:15	נטויה	qal	pptc	fs	נטה	639		stretch,incline
	צוך	piel	pft	3ms	צוה	845	2ms	command
	עשׂות	qal	infc		עשׂה	793		do,make
5:16	כבד	piel	impv	ms	כבד	457		honor,make dull
	צוך	piel	pft	3ms	צוה	845	2ms	command
	יאריכן	hiph	impf	3mp	ארך	73		prolong
	ייטב	qal	impf	3ms	יטב	405		be good
	נתן	qal	ptc	ms	נתן	678		give,set
5:17	תרצח	qal	impf	2ms	רצח	953		murder,slay
5:18	תנאף	qal	impf	2ms	נאף	610		commit adultery
5:19	תגנב	qal	impf	2ms	גנב	170		steal
5:20	תענה	qal	impf	2ms	ענה	772		answer
5:21	תחמד	qal	impf	2ms	חמד	326		desire
	תתאוה	hith	impf	2ms	אוה	16		desire
5:22	דבר	piel	pft	3ms	דבר	180		speak
	יסף	qal	pft	3ms	יסף	414		add,increase
	יכתבם	qal	wci	3ms	כתב	507	3mp	write
	יתנם	qal	wci	3ms	נתן	678	3mp	give,set
5:23	יהי	qal	wci	3ms	היה	224		be,become
	שׁמעכם	qal	infc		שׁמע	1033	2mp	hear
	בער	qal	ptc	ms	בער	128		burn
	תקרבון	qal	wci	2mp	קרב	897		approach
5:24	תאמרו	qal	wci	2mp	אמר	55		say
	הראנו	hiph	pft	3ms	ראה	906	1cp	show,exhibit
	שׁמענו	qal	pft	1cp	שׁמע	1033		hear
	ראינו	qal	pft	1cp	ראה	906		see
	ידבר	piel	impf	3ms	דבר	180		speak
	חי	qal	wcp	3ms	חיה	310		live
5:25	נמות	qal	impf	1cp	מות	559		die
	תאכלנו	qal	impf	3fs	אכל	37	1cp	eat,devour
	יספים	qal	ptc	mp	יסף	414		add,increase
	שׁמע	qal	infc		שׁמע	1033		hear
	מתנו	qal	wcp	1cp	מות	559		die
5:26	שׁמע	qal	pft	3ms	שׁמע	1033		hear
	מדבר	piel	ptc	ms	דבר	180		speak
	יחי	qal	wci	3ms	חיה	310		live
5:27	קרב	qal	impv	ms	קרב	897		approach
	שׁמע	qal	impv	ms	שׁמע	1033		hear
	יאמר	qal	impf	3ms	אמר	55		say
	תדבר	piel	impf	2ms	דבר	180		speak
	ידבר	piel	impf	3ms	דבר	180		speak
	שׁמענו	qal	wcp	1cp	שׁמע	1033		hear
	עשׂינו	qal	wcp	1cp	עשׂה	793		do,make
5:28	ישׁמע	qal	wci	3ms	שׁמע	1033		hear
	דברכם	piel	infc		דבר	180	2mp	speak
	יאמר	qal	wci	3ms	אמר	55		say
	שׁמעתי	qal	pft	1cs	שׁמע	1033		hear
	דברו	piel	pft	3cp	דבר	180		speak
	היטיבו	hiph	pft	3cp	יטב	405		do good
	דברו	piel	pft	3cp	דבר	180		speak
5:29	יתן	qal	impf	3ms	נתן	678		give,set
	היה	qal	wcp	3ms	היה	224		be,become
	יראה	qal	infc		ירא	431		fear
	שׁמר	qal	infc		שׁמר	1036		keep,watch
5:29	ייטב	qal	impf	3ms	יטב	405		be good
5:30	לך	qal	impv	ms	הלך	229		walk,go
	אמר	qal	impv	ms	אמר	55		say
	שׁובו	qal	impv	mp	שׁוב	996		turn,return
5:31	עמד	qal	impv	ms	עמד	763		stand,stop
	אדברה	piel	coh	1cs	דבר	180		speak
	תלמדם	piel	impf	2ms	למד	540	3mp	teach
	עשׂו	qal	wcp	3cp	עשׂה	793		do,make
	נתן	qal	ptc	ms	נתן	678		give,set
	רשׁתה	qal	infc		ירשׁ	439	3fs	possess,inherit
5:32	שׁמרתם	qal	wcp	2mp	שׁמר	1036		keep,watch
	עשׂות	qal	infc		עשׂה	793		do,make
	צוה	piel	pft	3ms	צוה	845		command
	תסרו	qal	impf	2mp	סור	693		turn aside
5:33	צוה	piel	pft	3ms	צוה	845		command
	תלכו	qal	impf	2mp	הלך	229		walk,go
	תחיון	qal	impf	2mp	חיה	310		live
	טוב	qal	wcp	3ms	טוב	373		be pleasing
	הארכתם	hiph	wcp	2mp	ארך	73		prolong
	תירשׁון	qal	impf	2mp	ירשׁ	439		possess,inherit
6:1	צוה	piel	pft	3ms	צוה	845		command
	למד	piel	infc		למד	540		teach
	עשׂות	qal	infc		עשׂה	793		do,make
	עברים	qal	ptc	mp	עבר	716		pass over
	רשׁתה	qal	infc		ירשׁ	439	3fs	possess,inherit
6:2	תירא	qal	impf	2ms	ירא	431		fear
	שׁמר	qal	infc		שׁמר	1036		keep,watch
	מצוך	piel	ptc	ms	צוה	845	2ms	command
	יארכן	hiph	impf	3mp	ארך	73		prolong
6:3	שׁמעת	qal	wcp	2ms	שׁמע	1033		hear
	שׁמרת	qal	wcp	2ms	שׁמר	1036		keep,watch
	עשׂות	qal	infc		עשׂה	793		do,make
	ייטב	qal	impf	3ms	יטב	405		be good
	תרבון	qal	impf	2mp	רבה	915		be many,great
	דבר	piel	pft	3ms	דבר	180		speak
	זבת	qal	ptc	fs	זוב	264		flow,gush
6:4	שׁמע	qal	impv	ms	שׁמע	1033		hear
6:5	אהבת	qal	wcp	2ms	אהב	12		love
6:6	היו	qal	wcp	3cp	היה	224		be,become
	מצוך	piel	ptc	ms	צוה	845	2ms	command
6:7	שׁננתם	piel	wcp	2ms	שׁנן	1041	3mp	inculcate
	דברת	piel	wcp	2ms	דבר	180		speak
	שׁבתך	qal	infc		ישׁב	442	2ms	sit,dwell
	לכתך	qal	infc		הלך	229	2ms	walk,go
	שׁכבך	qal	infc		שׁכב	1011	2ms	lie,lie down
	קומך	qal	infc		קום	877	2ms	arise,stand
6:8	קשׁרתם	qal	wcp	2ms	קשׁר	905	3mp	bind
	היו	qal	wcp	3cp	היה	224		be,become
6:9	כתבתם	qal	wcp	2ms	כתב	507	3mp	write
6:10	היה	qal	wcp	3ms	היה	224		be,become
	יביאך	hiph	impf	3ms	בוא	97	2ms	bring in
	נשׁבע	niph	pft	3ms	שׁבע	989		swear
	תת	qal	infc		נתן	678		give,set
	בנית	qal	pft	2ms	בנה	124		build

ChVs	Form	Stem	Tnse	PGN	Root	BDB	Sfx	Meaning
6:11	מלאת	piel	pft	2ms	מלא	569		fill
	חצובים	qal	pptc	mp	חצב	345		hew out,dig
	חצבת	qal	pft	2ms	חצב	345		hew out,dig
	נטעת	qal	pft	2ms	נטע	642		plant
	אכלת	qal	wcp	2ms	אכל	37		eat,devour
	שׂבעת	qal	wcp	2ms	שׂבע	959		be sated
6:12	השמר	niph	impv	ms	שמר	1036		be kept,guarded
	תשכח	qal	impf	2ms	שכח	1013		forget
	הוציאך	hiph	pft	3ms	יצא	422	2ms	bring out
6:13	תירא	qal	impf	2ms	ירא	431		fear
	תעבד	qal	impf	2ms	עבד	712		work,serve
	תשבע	niph	impf	2ms	שבע	989		swear
6:14	תלכון	qal	impf	2mp	הלך	229		walk,go
6:15	יחרה	qal	impf	3ms	חרה	354		be kindled,burn
	השמידך	hiph	wcp	3ms	שמד	1029	2ms	exterminate
6:16	תנסו	piel	impf	2mp	נסה	650		test,try
	נסיתם	piel	pft	2mp	נסה	650		test,try
6:17	שמור	qal	infa		שמר	1036		keep,watch
	תשמרון	qal	impf	2mp	שמר	1036		keep,watch
	צוך	piel	pft	3ms	צוה	845	2ms	command
6:18	עשׂית	qal	wcp	2ms	עשׂה	793		do,make
	ייטב	qal	impf	3ms	יטב	405		be good
	באת	qal	wcp	2ms	בוא	97		come in
	ירשת	qal	wcp	2ms	ירשׁ	439		possess,inherit
	נשבע	niph	pft	3ms	שבע	989		swear
6:19	הדף	qal	infc		הדף	213		thrust,drive
	איביך	qal	ptc	mp	איב	33	2ms	be hostile to
	דבר	piel	pft	3ms	דבר	180		speak
6:20	ישאלך	qal	impf	3ms	שאל	981	2ms	ask,borrow
	אמר	qal	infc		אמר	55		say
	צוה	piel	pft	3ms	צוה	845		command
6:21	אמרת	qal	wcp	2ms	אמר	55		say
	היינו	qal	pft	1cp	היה	224		be,become
	יוציאנו	hiph	wci	3ms	יצא	422	1cp	bring out
6:22	יתן	qal	wci	3ms	נתן	678		give,set
6:23	הוציא	hiph	pft	3ms	יצא	422		bring out
	הביא	hiph	infc		בוא	97		bring in
	תת	qal	infc		נתן	678		give,set
	נשבע	niph	pft	3ms	שבע	989		swear
6:24	יצונו	piel	wci	3ms	צוה	845	1cp	command
	עשׂות	qal	infc		עשׂה	793		do,make
	יראה	qal	infc		ירא	431		fear
	חיתנו	piel	infc		חיה	310	1cp	preserve,revive
6:25	תהיה	qal	impf	3fs	היה	224		be,become
	נשמר	qal	impf	1cp	שמר	1036		keep,watch
	עשׂות	qal	infc		עשׂה	793		do,make
	צונו	piel	pft	3ms	צוה	845	1cp	command
7:1	יביאך	hiph	impf	3ms	בוא	97	2ms	bring in
	בא	qal	ptc	ms	בוא	97		come in
	רשתה	qal	infc		ירשׁ	439	3fs	possess,inherit
	נשל	qal	wcp	3ms	נשל	675		draw off
7:2	נתנם	qal	wcp	3ms	נתן	678	3mp	give,set
	הכיתם	hiph	wcp	2ms	נכה	645	3mp	smite
	החרם	hiph	infa		חרם	355		ban,destroy
7:2	תחרים	hiph	impf	2ms	חרם	355		ban,destroy
	תכרת	qal	impf	2ms	כרת	503		cut,destroy
	תחנם	qal	impf	2ms	חנן	335	3mp	show favor
7:3	תתחתן	hith	impf	2ms	חתן	368		be son-in-law
	תתן	qal	impf	2ms	נתן	678		give,set
	תקח	qal	impf	2ms	לקח	542		take
7:4	יסיר	hiph	impf	3ms	סור	693		take away
	עבדו	qal	wcp	3cp	עבד	712		work,serve
	חרה	qal	wcp	3ms	חרה	354		be kindled,burn
	השמידך	hiph	wcp	3ms	שמד	1029	2ms	exterminate
7:5	תעשׂו	qal	impf	2mp	עשׂה	793		do,make
	תתצו	qal	impf	2mp	נתץ	683		pull down
	תשברו	piel	impf	2mp	שבר	990		shatter
	תגדעון	piel	impf	2mp	גדע	154		hew off
	תשׂרפון	qal	impf	2mp	שׂרף	976		burn
7:6	בחר	qal	pft	3ms	בחר	103		choose
	היות	qal	infc		היה	224		be,become
7:7	רבכם	qal	infc		רבב	912	2mp	be many
	חשק	qal	pft	3ms	חשק	365		love
	יבחר	qal	wci	3ms	בחר	103		choose
7:8	שמרו	qal	infc		שמר	1036	3ms	keep,watch
	נשבע	niph	pft	3ms	שבע	989		swear
	הוציא	hiph	pft	3ms	יצא	422		bring out
	יפדך	qal	wci	3ms	פדה	804	2ms	ransom
7:9	ידעת	qal	wcp	2ms	ידע	393		know
	נאמן	niph	ptc	ms	אמן	52		be confirmed
	שמר	qal	ptc	ms	שמר	1036		keep,watch
	אהביו	qal	ptc	mp	אהב	12	3ms	love
	שמרי	qal	ptc	mp	שמר	1036		keep,watch
7:10	משלם	piel	ptc	ms	שלם	1022		finish,reward
	שׂנאיו	qal	ptc	mp	שׂנא	971	3ms	hate
	האבידו	hiph	infc		אבד	1	3ms	destroy
	יאחר	piel	impf	3ms	אחר	29		tarry,hinder
	שׂנאו	qal	ptc	ms	שׂנא	971	3ms	hate
	ישלם	piel	impf	3ms	שלם	1022		finish,reward
7:11	שמרת	qal	wcp	2ms	שמר	1036		keep,watch
	מצוך	piel	ptc	ms	צוה	845	2ms	command
	עשׂותם	qal	infc		עשׂה	793	3mp	do,make
7:12	היה	qal	wcp	3ms	היה	224		be,become
	תשמעון	qal	impf	2mp	שמע	1033		hear
	שמרתם	qal	wcp	2mp	שמר	1036		keep,watch
	עשׂיתם	qal	wcp	2mp	עשׂה	793		do,make
	שמר	qal	wcp	3ms	שמר	1036		keep,watch
	נשבע	niph	pft	3ms	שבע	989		swear
7:13	אהבך	qal	wcp	3ms	אהב	12	2ms	love
	ברכך	piel	wcp	3ms	ברך	138	2ms	bless
	הרבך	hiph	wcp	3ms	רבה	915	2ms	make many
	ברך	piel	wcp	3ms	ברך	138		bless
	נשבע	niph	pft	3ms	שבע	989		swear
	תת	qal	infc		נתן	678		give,set
7:14	ברוך	qal	pptc	ms	ברך	138		kneel,bless
	תהיה	qal	impf	2ms	היה	224		be,become
	יהיה	qal	impf	3ms	היה	224		be,become
7:15	הסיר	hiph	wcp	3ms	סור	693		take away

ChVs	Form	Stem	Tnse	PGN	Root	BDB	Sfx	Meaning
7:15	ידעת	qal	pft	2ms	ידע	393		know
	ישׂימם	qal	impf	3ms	שׂים	962	3mp	put,set
	נתנם	qal	wcp	3ms	נתן	678	3mp	give,set
	שׂנאיך	qal	ptc	mp	שׂנא	971	2ms	hate
7:16	אכלת	qal	wcp	2ms	אכל	37		eat,devour
	נתן	qal	ptc	ms	נתן	678		give,set
	תחס	qal	jusf	3fs	חוס	299?		pity
	תעבד	qal	impf	2ms	עבד	712		work,serve
7:17	תאמר	qal	impf	2ms	אמר	55		say
	אוכל	qal	impf	1cs	יכל	407		be able
	הורישׁם	hiph	infc		ירשׁ	439	3mp	c. to possess
7:18	תירא	qal	impf	2ms	ירא	431		fear
	זכר	qal	infa		זכר	269		remember
	תזכר	qal	impf	2ms	זכר	269		remember
	עשׂה	qal	pft	3ms	עשׂה	793		do,make
7:19	ראו	qal	pft	3cp	ראה	906		see
	נטויה	qal	pptc	fs	נטה	639		stretch,incline
	הוצאך	hiph	pft	3ms	יצא	422	2ms	bring out
	יעשׂה	qal	impf	3ms	עשׂה	793		do,make
	ירא	qal	ptc	ms	ירא	431		fear
7:20	ישׁלח	piel	impf	3ms	שׁלח	1018		send away,shoot
	אבד	qal	infc		אבד	1		perish
	נשׁארים	niph	ptc	mp	שׁאר	983		be left
	נסתרים	niph	ptc	mp	סתר	711		hide,be hid
7:21	תערץ	qal	impf	2ms	ערץ	791		frighten,fear
	נורא	niph	ptc	ms	ירא	431		be feared
7:22	נשׁל	qal	wcp	3ms	נשׁל	675		draw off
	תוכל	qal	impf	2ms	יכל	407		be able
	כלתם	piel	infc		כלה	477	3mp	complete,finish
	תרבה	qal	impf	3fs	רבה	915		be many,great
7:23	נתנם	qal	wcp	3ms	נתן	678	3mp	give,set
	המם	qal	wcp	3ms	הום	223	3mp	vex
	השׁמדם	niph	infc		שׁמד	1029	3mp	be exterminated
7:24	נתן	qal	wcp	3ms	נתן	678		give,set
	האבדת	hiph	wcp	2ms	אבד	1		destroy
	יתיצב	hith	impf	3ms	יצב	426		stand oneself
	השׁמדך	hiph	infc		שׁמד	1029	2ms	exterminate
7:25	תשׂרפון	qal	impf	2mp	שׂרף	976		burn
	תחמד	qal	impf	2ms	חמד	326		desire
	לקחת	qal	wcp	2ms	לקח	542		take
	תוקשׁ	niph	impf	2ms	יקשׁ	430		be ensnared
7:26	תביא	hiph	impf	2ms	בוא	97		bring in
	היית	qal	wcp	2ms	היה	224		be,become
	שׁקץ	piel	infa		שׁקץ	1055		detest
	תשׁקצנו	piel	impf	2ms	שׁקץ	1055	3ms	detest
	תעב	piel	infa		תעב	1073		abhor
	תתעבנו	piel	impf	2ms	תעב	1073	3ms	abhor
8:1	מצוך	piel	ptc	ms	צוה	845	2ms	command
	תשׁמרון	qal	impf	2mp	שׁמר	1036		keep,watch
	עשׂות	qal	infc		עשׂה	793		do,make
	תחיון	qal	impf	2mp	חיה	310		live
	רביתם	qal	wcp	2mp	רבה	915		be many,great
	באתם	qal	wcp	2mp	בוא	97		come in
	ירשׁתם	qal	wcp	2mp	ירשׁ	439		possess,inherit
8:1	נשׁבע	niph	pft	3ms	שׁבע	989		swear
8:2	זכרת	qal	wcp	2ms	זכר	269		remember
	הליכך	hiph	pft	3ms	הלך	229	2ms	lead,bring
	ענתך	piel	infc		ענה	776	2ms	humble
	נסתך	piel	infc		נסה	650	2ms	test,try
	דעת	qal	infc		ידע	393		know
	תשׁמר	qal	impf	2ms	שׁמר	1036		keep,watch
8:3	יענך	piel	wci	3ms	ענה	776	2ms	humble
	ירעבך	hiph	wci	3ms	רעב	944	2ms	cause to hunger
	יאכלך	hiph	wci	3ms	אכל	37	2ms	cause to eat
	ידעת	qal	pft	2ms	ידע	393		know
	ידעון	qal	pft	3cp	ידע	393		know
	הודעך	hiph	infc		ידע	393	2ms	declare
	יחיה	qal	impf	3ms	חיה	310		live
	יחיה	qal	impf	3ms	חיה	310		live
8:4	בלתה	qal	pft	3fs	בלה	115		wear out
	בצקה	qal	pft	3fs	בצק	130		swell
8:5	ידעת	qal	wcp	2ms	ידע	393		know
	ייסר	piel	impf	3ms	יסר	415		correct,chasten
	מיסרך	piel	ptc	ms	יסר	415	2ms	correct,chasten
8:6	שׁמרת	qal	wcp	2ms	שׁמר	1036		keep,watch
	לכת	qal	infc		הלך	229		walk,go
	יראה	qal	infc		ירא	431		fear
8:7	מביאך	hiph	ptc	ms	בוא	97	2ms	bring in
	יצאים	qal	ptc	mp	יצא	422		go out
8:9	תאכל	qal	impf	2ms	אכל	37		eat,devour
	תחסר	qal	impf	2ms	חסר	341		lack
	תחצב	qal	impf	2ms	חצב	345		hew out,dig
8:10	אכלת	qal	wcp	2ms	אכל	37		eat,devour
	שׂבעת	qal	wcp	2ms	שׂבע	959		be sated
	ברכת	piel	wcp	2ms	ברך	138		bless
	נתן	qal	pft	3ms	נתן	678		give,set
8:11	השׁמר	niph	impv	ms	שׁמר	1036		be kept,guarded
	תשׁכח	qal	impf	2ms	שׁכח	1013		forget
	שׁמר	qal	infc		שׁמר	1036		keep,watch
	מצוך	piel	ptc	ms	צוה	845	2ms	command
8:12	תאכל	qal	impf	2ms	אכל	37		eat,devour
	שׂבעת	qal	wcp	2ms	שׂבע	959		be sated
	תבנה	qal	impf	2ms	בנה	124		build
	ישׁבת	qal	wcp	2ms	ישׁב	442		sit,dwell
8:13	ירבין	qal	impf	3mp	רבה	915		be many,great
	ירבה	qal	impf	3ms	רבה	915		be many,great
	ירבה	qal	impf	3ms	רבה	915		be many,great
8:14	רם	qal	wcp	3ms	רום	926		be high
	שׁכחת	qal	wcp	2ms	שׁכח	1013		forget
	מוציאך	hiph	ptc	ms	יצא	422	2ms	bring out
8:15	מוליכך	hiph	ptc	ms	הלך	229	2ms	lead,bring
	נורא	niph	ptc	ms	ירא	431		be feared
	מוציא	hiph	ptc	ms	יצא	422		bring out
8:16	מאכלך	hiph	ptc	ms	אכל	37	2ms	cause to eat
	ידעון	qal	pft	3cp	ידע	393		know
	ענתך	piel	infc		ענה	776	2ms	humble
	נסתך	piel	infc		נסה	650	2ms	test,try
	היטבך	hiph	infc		יטב	405	2ms	do good

ChVs	Form	Stem	Tnse	PGN	Root	BDB	Sfx	Meaning
8: 17	אמרת	qal	wcp	2ms	אמר	55		say
	עשה	qal	pft	3ms	עשה	793		do,make
8: 18	זכרת	qal	wcp	2ms	זכר	269		remember
	נתן	qal	ptc	ms	נתן	678		give,set
	עשות	qal	infc		עשה	793		do,make
	הקים	hiph	infc		קום	877		raise,build,set
	נשבע	niph	pft	3ms	שבע	989		swear
8: 19	היה	qal	wcp	3ms	היה	224		be,become
	שכח	qal	infa		שכח	1013		forget
	תשכח	qal	impf	2ms	שכח	1013		forget
	הלכת	qal	wcp	2ms	הלך	229		walk,go
	עבדתם	qal	wcp	2ms	עבד	712	3mp	work,serve
	השתחוית	hish	wcp	2ms	חוה	1005		bow down
	העדתי	hiph	pft	1cs	עוד	729		testify,warn
	אבד	qal	infa		אבד	1		perish
	תאבדון	qal	impf	2mp	אבד	1		perish
8: 20	מאביד	hiph	ptc	ms	אבד	1		destroy
	תאבדון	qal	impf	2mp	אבד	1		perish
	תשמעון	qal	impf	2mp	שמע	1033		hear
9: 1	שמע	qal	impv	ms	שמע	1033		hear
	עבר	qal	ptc	ms	עבר	716		pass over
	בא	qal	infc		בוא	97		come in
	רשת	qal	infc		ירש	439		possess,inherit
	בצרת	qal	pptc	fp	בצר	130		cut off
9: 2	רם	qal	ptc	ms	רום	926		be high
	ידעת	qal	pft	2ms	ידע	393		know
	שמעת	qal	pft	2ms	שמע	1033		hear
	יתיצב	hith	impf	3ms	יצב	426		stand oneself
9: 3	ידעת	qal	wcp	2ms	ידע	393		know
	עבר	qal	ptc	ms	עבר	716		pass over
	אכלה	qal	ptc	fs	אכל	37		eat,devour
	ישמידם	hiph	impf	3ms	שמד	1029	3mp	exterminate
	יכניעם	hiph	impf	3ms	כנע	488	3mp	humble,subdue
	הורשתם	hiph	wcp	2ms	ירש	439	3mp	c. to possess
	האבדתם	hiph	wcp	2ms	אבד	1	3mp	destroy
	דבר	piel	pft	3ms	דבר	180		speak
9: 4	תאמר	qal	jusm	2ms	אמר	55		say
	הדף	qal	infc		הדף	213		thrust,drive
	אמר	qal	infc		אמר	55		say
	הביאני	hiph	pft	3ms	בוא	97	1cs	bring in
	רשת	qal	infc		ירש	439		possess,inherit
	מורישם	hiph	ptc	ms	ירש	439	3mp	c. to possess
9: 5	בא	qal	ptc	ms	בוא	97		come in
	רשת	qal	infc		ירש	439		possess,inherit
	מורישם	hiph	ptc	ms	ירש	439	3mp	c. to possess
	הקים	hiph	infc		קום	877		raise,build,set
	נשבע	niph	pft	3ms	שבע	989		swear
9: 6	ידעת	qal	wcp	2ms	ידע	393		know
	נתן	qal	ptc	ms	נתן	678		give,set
	רשתה	qal	infc		ירש	439	3fs	possess,inherit
9: 7	זכר	qal	impv	ms	זכר	269		remember
	תשכח	qal	jusm	2ms	שכח	1013		forget
	הקצפת	hiph	pft	2ms	קצף	893		provoke
	יצאת	qal	pft	2ms	יצא	422		go out
9: 7	באכם	qal	infc		בוא	97	2mp	come in
	ממרים	hiph	ptc	mp	מרה	598		rebel
	הייתם	qal	pft	2mp	היה	224		be,become
9: 8	הקצפתם	hiph	pft	2mp	קצף	893		provoke
	יתאנף	hith	wci	3ms	אנף	60		be angry
	השמיד	hiph	infc		שמד	1029		exterminate
9: 9	עלתי	qal	infc		עלה	748	1cs	go up
	קחת	qal	infc		לקח	542		take
	כרת	qal	pft	3ms	כרת	503		cut,destroy
	אשב	qal	wci	1cs	ישב	442		sit,dwell
	אכלתי	qal	pft	1cs	אכל	37		eat,devour
	שתיתי	qal	pft	1cs	שתה	1059		drink
9: 10	יתן	qal	wci	3ms	נתן	678		give,set
	כתבים	qal	pptc	mp	כתב	507		write
	דבר	piel	pft	3ms	דבר	180		speak
9: 11	יהי	qal	wci	3ms	היה	224		be,become
	נתן	qal	pft	3ms	נתן	678		give,set
9: 12	יאמר	qal	wci	3ms	אמר	55		say
	קום	qal	impv	ms	קום	877		arise,stand
	רד	qal	impv	ms	ירד	432		come down
	שחת	piel	pft	3ms	שחת	1007		spoil,ruin
	הוצאת	hiph	pft	2ms	יצא	422		bring out
	סרו	qal	pft	3cp	סור	693		turn aside
	צויתם	piel	pft	1cs	צוה	845	3mp	command
	עשו	qal	pft	3cp	עשה	793		do,make
9: 13	יאמר	qal	wci	3ms	אמר	55		say
	אמר	qal	infc		אמר	55		say
	ראיתי	qal	pft	1cs	ראה	906		see
9: 14	הרף	hiph	impv	ms	רפה	951		slacken,abandon
	אשמידם	hiph	cohm	1cs	שמד	1029	3mp	exterminate
	אמחה	qal	cohm	1cs	מחה	562		wipe, blot out
	אעשה	qal	impf	1cs	עשה	793		do,make
9: 15	אפן	qal	wci	1cs	פנה	815		turn
	ארד	qal	wci	1cs	ירד	432		come down
	בער	qal	ptc	ms	בער	128		burn
9: 16	ארא	qal	wci	1cs	ראה	906		see
	חטאתם	qal	pft	2mp	חטא	306		sin
	עשיתם	qal	pft	2mp	עשה	793		do,make
	סרתם	qal	pft	2mp	סור	693		turn aside
	צוה	piel	pft	3ms	צוה	845		command
9: 17	אתפש	qal	wci	1cs	תפש	1074		seize,grasp
	אשלכם	hiph	wci	1cs	שלך	1020	3mp	throw,cast
	אשברם	piel	wci	1cs	שבר	990	3mp	shatter
9: 18	אתנפל	hith	wci	1cs	נפל	656		throw oneself
	אכלתי	qal	pft	1cs	אכל	37		eat,devour
	שתיתי	qal	pft	1cs	שתה	1059		drink
	חטאתם	qal	pft	2mp	חטא	306		sin
	עשות	qal	infc		עשה	793		do,make
	הכעיסו	hiph	infc		כעס	494	3ms	vex,provoke
9: 19	יגרתי	qal	pft	1cs	יגר	388		be afraid
	קצף	qal	pft	3ms	קצף	893		be angry
	השמיד	hiph	infc		שמד	1029		exterminate
	ישמע	qal	wci	3ms	שמע	1033		hear
9: 20	התאנף	hith	pft	3ms	אנף	60		be angry

ChVs	Form	Stem	Tnse	PGN	Root	BDB	Sfx	Meaning
9: 20	השמידו	hiph	infc		שמד	1029	3ms	exterminate
	אתפלל	hith	wci	1cs	פלל	813		pray
9: 21	עשׂיתם	qal	pft	2mp	עשׂה	793		do,make
	לקחתי	qal	pft	1cs	לקח	542		take
	אשׂרף	qal	wci	1cs	שׂרף	976		burn
	אכת	qal	wci	1cs	כתת	510		beat,crush
	טחון	qal	infa		טחן	377		grind
	היטב	hiph	infa		יטב	405		do good
	דק	qal	pft	3ms	דקק	200		crush,be fine
	אשלך	hiph	wci	1cs	שלך	1020		throw,cast
	ירד	qal	ptc	ms	ירד	432		come down
9: 22	מקצפים	hiph	ptc	mp	קצף	893		provoke
	הייתם	qal	pft	2mp	היה	224		be,become
9: 23	שלח	qal	infc		שלח	1018		send
	אמר	qal	infc		אמר	55		say
	עלו	qal	impv	mp	עלה	748		go up
	רשו	qal	impv	mp	ירש	439		possess,inherit
	נתתי	qal	pft	1cs	נתן	678		give,set
	תמרו	hiph	wci	2mp	מרה	598		rebel
	האמנתם	hiph	pft	2mp	אמן	52		believe
	שמעתם	qal	pft	2mp	שמע	1033		hear
9: 24	ממרים	hiph	ptc	mp	מרה	598		rebel
	הייתם	qal	pft	2mp	היה	224		be,become
	דעתי	qal	infc		ידע	393	1cs	know
9: 25	אתנפל	hith	wci	1cs	נפל	656		throw oneself
	התנפלתי	hith	pft	1cs	נפל	656		throw oneself
	אמר	qal	pft	3ms	אמר	55		say
	השמיד	hiph	infc		שמד	1029		exterminate
9: 26	אתפלל	hith	wci	1cs	פלל	813		pray
	אמר	qal	wci	1cs	אמר	55		say
	תשחת	hiph	jus	2ms	שחת	1007		spoil,ruin
	פדית	qal	pft	2ms	פדה	804		ransom
	הוצאת	hiph	pft	2ms	יצא	422		bring out
9: 27	זכר	qal	impv	ms	זכר	269		remember
	תפן	qal	jus	2ms	פנה	815		turn
9: 28	יאמרו	qal	impf	3mp	אמר	55		say
	הוצאתנו	hiph	pft	2ms	יצא	422	1cp	bring out
	יכלת	qal	infc		יכל	407		be able
	הביאם	hiph	infc		בוא	97	3mp	bring in
	דבר	piel	pft	3ms	דבר	180		speak
	הוציאם	hiph	pft	3ms	יצא	422	3mp	bring out
	המתם	hiph	infc		מות	559	3mp	kill
9: 29	הוצאת	hiph	pft	2ms	יצא	422		bring out
	נטויה	qal	pptc	fs	נטה	639		stretch,incline
10: 1	אמר	qal	pft	3ms	אמר	55		say
	פסל	qal	impv	ms	פסל	820		hew out
	עלה	qal	impv	ms	עלה	748		go up
	עשׂית	qal	wcp	2ms	עשׂה	793		do,make
10: 2	אכתב	qal	impf	1cs	כתב	507		write
	היו	qal	pft	3cp	היה	224		be,become
	שברת	piel	pft	2ms	שבר	990		shatter
	שׂמתם	qal	wcp	2ms	שׂים	962	3mp	put,set
10: 3	אעשׂ	qal	wci	1cs	עשׂה	793		do,make
	אפסל	qal	wci	1cs	פסל	820		hew out
10: 3	אעל	qal	wci	1cs	עלה	748		go up
10: 4	יכתב	qal	wci	3ms	כתב	507		write
	דבר	piel	pft	3ms	דבר	180		speak
	יתנם	qal	wci	3ms	נתן	678	3mp	give,set
10: 5	אפן	qal	wci	1cs	פנה	815		turn
	ארד	qal	wci	1cs	ירד	432		come down
	אשׂם	qal	wci	1cs	שׂים	962		put,set
	עשׂיתי	qal	pft	1cs	עשׂה	793		do,make
	יהיו	qal	wci	3mp	היה	224		be,become
	צוני	piel	pft	3ms	צוה	845	1cs	command
10: 6	נסעו	qal	pft	3cp	נסע	652		pull up,set out
	מת	qal	pft	3ms	מות	559		die
	יקבר	niph	wci	3ms	קבר	868		be buried
	יכהן	piel	wci	3ms	כהן	464		act as priest
10: 7	נסעו	qal	pft	3cp	נסע	652		pull up,set out
10: 8	הבדיל	hiph	pft	3ms	בדל	95		divide
	שׂאת	qal	infc		נשׂא	669		lift,carry
	עמד	qal	infc		עמד	763		stand,stop
	שרתו	piel	infc		שרת	1058	3ms	minister,serve
	ברך	piel	infc		ברך	138		bless
10: 9	היה	qal	pft	3ms	היה	224		be,become
	דבר	piel	pft	3ms	דבר	180		speak
10: 10	עמדתי	qal	pft	1cs	עמד	763		stand,stop
	ישמע	qal	wci	3ms	שמע	1033		hear
	אבה	qal	pft	3ms	אבה	2		be willing
	השחיתך	hiph	infc		שחת	1007	2ms	spoil,ruin
10: 11	יאמר	qal	wci	3ms	אמר	55		say
	קום	qal	impv	ms	קום	877		arise,stand
	לך	qal	impv	ms	הלך	229		walk,go
	יבאו	qal	jusm	3mp	בוא	97		come in
	ירשו	qal	jusm	3mp	ירש	439		possess,inherit
	נשבעתי	niph	pft	1cs	שבע	989		swear
	תת	qal	infc		נתן	678		give,set
10: 12	שאל	qal	ptc	ms	שאל	981		ask,borrow
	יראה	qal	infc		ירא	431		fear
	לכת	qal	infc		הלך	229		walk,go
	אהבה	qal	infc		אהב	12		love
	עבד	qal	infc		עבד	712		work,serve
10: 13	שמר	qal	infc		שמר	1036		keep,watch
	מצוך	piel	ptc	ms	צוה	845	2ms	command
10: 15	חשק	qal	pft	3ms	חשק	365		love
	אהבה	qal	infc		אהב	12		love
	יבחר	qal	wci	3ms	בחר	103		choose
10: 16	מלתם	qal	wcp	2mp	מול	557		circumcise
	תקשו	hiph	impf	2mp	קשה	904		harden
10: 17	נורא	niph	ptc	ms	ירא	431		be feared
	ישׂא	qal	impf	3ms	נשׂא	669		lift,carry
	יקח	qal	impf	3ms	לקח	542		take
10: 18	עשׂה	qal	ptc	ms	עשׂה	793		do,make
	אהב	qal	ptc	ms	אהב	12		love
	תת	qal	infc		נתן	678		give,set
10: 19	אהבתם	qal	wcp	2mp	אהב	12		love
	הייתם	qal	pft	2mp	היה	224		be,become
10: 20	תירא	qal	impf	2ms	ירא	431		fear

ChVs	Form	Stem	Tnse	PGN	Root	BDB	Sfx	Meaning
10: 20	תעבד	qal	impf	2ms	עבד	712		work,serve
	תדבק	qal	impf	2ms	דבק	179		cling,cleave
	תשׁבע	niph	impf	2ms	שׁבע	989		swear
10: 21	עשׂה	qal	pft	3ms	עשׂה	793		do,make
	נוראת	niph	ptc	fp	ירא	431		be feared
	ראו	qal	pft	3cp	ראה	906		see
10: 22	ירדו	qal	pft	3cp	ירד	432		come down
	שׂמך	qal	pft	3ms	שׂים	962	2ms	put,set
11: 1	אהבת	qal	wcp	2ms	אהב	12		love
	שׁמרת	qal	wcp	2ms	שׁמר	1036		keep,watch
11: 2	ידעתם	qal	wcp	2mp	ידע	393		know
	ידעו	qal	pft	3cp	ידע	393		know
	ראו	qal	pft	3cp	ראה	906		see
	נטויה	qal	pptc	fs	נטה	639		stretch,incline
11: 3	עשׂה	qal	pft	3ms	עשׂה	793		do,make
11: 4	עשׂה	qal	pft	3ms	עשׂה	793		do,make
	הציף	hiph	pft	3ms	צוף	847		cause to flow
	רדפם	qal	infc		רדף	922	3mp	pursue
	יאבדם	piel	wci	3ms	אבד	1	3mp	destroy
11: 5	עשׂה	qal	pft	3ms	עשׂה	793		do,make
	באכם	qal	infc		בוא	97	2mp	come in
11: 6	עשׂה	qal	pft	3ms	עשׂה	793		do,make
	פצתה	qal	pft	3fs	פצה	822		open,set free
	תבלעם	qal	wci	3fs	בלע	118	3mp	swallow
11: 7	ראת	qal	ptc	fp	ראה	906		see
	עשׂה	qal	pft	3ms	עשׂה	793		do,make
11: 8	שׁמרתם	qal	wcp	2mp	שׁמר	1036		keep,watch
	מצוך	piel	ptc	ms	צוה	845	2ms	command
	תחזקו	qal	impf	2mp	חזק	304		be strong
	באתם	qal	wcp	2mp	בוא	97		come in
	ירשׁתם	qal	wcp	2mp	ירשׁ	439		possess,inherit
	עברים	qal	ptc	mp	עבר	716		pass over
	רשׁתה	qal	infc		ירשׁ	439	3fs	possess,inherit
11: 9	תאריכו	hiph	impf	2mp	ארך	73		prolong
	נשׁבע	niph	pft	3ms	שׁבע	989		swear
	תת	qal	infc		נתן	678		give,set
	זבת	qal	ptc	fs	זוב	264		flow,gush
11: 10	בא	qal	ptc	ms	בוא	97		come in
	רשׁתה	qal	infc		ירשׁ	439	3fs	possess,inherit
	יצאתם	qal	pft	2mp	יצא	422		go out
	תזרע	qal	impf	2ms	זרע	281		sow
	השׁקית	hiph	wcp	2ms	שׁקה	1052		give to drink
11: 11	עברים	qal	ptc	mp	עבר	716		pass over
	רשׁתה	qal	infc		ירשׁ	439	3fs	possess,inherit
	תשׁתה	qal	impf	3fs	שׁתה	1059		drink
11: 12	דרשׁ	qal	ptc	ms	דרשׁ	205		resort to,seek
11: 13	היה	qal	wcp	3ms	היה	224		be,become
	שׁמע	qal	infa		שׁמע	1033		hear
	תשׁמעו	qal	impf	2mp	שׁמע	1033		hear
	מצוה	piel	ptc	ms	צוה	845		command
	אהבה	qal	infc		אהב	12		love
	עבדו	qal	infc		עבד	712	3ms	work,serve
11: 14	נתתי	qal	wcp	1cs	נתן	678		give,set
	אספת	qal	wcp	2ms	אסף	62		gather
11: 15	נתתי	qal	wcp	1cs	נתן	678		give,set
	אכלת	qal	wcp	2ms	אכל	37		eat,devour
	שׂבעת	qal	wcp	2ms	שׂבע	959		be sated
11: 16	השׁמרו	niph	impv	mp	שׁמר	1036		be kept,guarded
	יפתה	qal	impf	3ms	פתה	834		be simple
	סרתם	qal	wcp	2mp	סור	693		turn aside
	עבדתם	qal	wcp	2mp	עבד	712		work,serve
	השׁתחויתם	hish	wcp	2mp	חוה	1005		bow down
11: 17	חרה	qal	wcp	3ms	חרה	354		be kindled, burn
	עצר	qal	wcp	3ms	עצר	783		restrain
	יהיה	qal	impf	3ms	היה	224		be, become
	תתן	qal	impf	3fs	נתן	678		give,set
	אבדתם	qal	wcp	2mp	אבד	1		perish
	נתן	qal	ptc	ms	נתן	678		give,set
11: 18	שׂמתם	qal	wcp	2mp	שׂים	962		put,set
	קשׁרתם	qal	wcp	2mp	קשׁר	905		bind
	היו	qal	wcp	3cp	היה	224		be, become
11: 19	למדתם	piel	wcp	2mp	למד	540		teach
	דבר	piel	infc		דבר	180		speak
	שׁבתך	qal	infc		ישׁב	442	2ms	sit,dwell
	לכתך	qal	infc		הלך	229	2ms	walk,go
	שׁכבך	qal	infc		שׁכב	1011	2ms	lie,lie down
	קומך	qal	infc		קום	877	2ms	arise,stand
11: 20	כתבתם	qal	wcp	2ms	כתב	507	3mp	write
11: 21	ירבו	qal	impf	3mp	רבה	915		be many, great
	נשׁבע	niph	pft	3ms	שׁבע	989		swear
	תת	qal	infc		נתן	678		give,set
11: 22	שׁמר	qal	infa		שׁמר	1036		keep,watch
	תשׁמרון	qal	impf	2mp	שׁמר	1036		keep,watch
	מצוה	piel	ptc	ms	צוה	845		command
	עשׂתה	qal	infc		עשׂה	793	3fs	do, make
	אהבה	qal	infc		אהב	12		love
	לכת	qal	infc		הלך	229		walk, go
	דבקה	qal	infc		דבק	179		cling,cleave
11: 23	הורישׁ	hiph	wcp	3ms	ירשׁ	439		c. to possess
	ירשׁתם	qal	wcp	2mp	ירשׁ	439		possess,inherit
11: 24	תדרך	qal	impf	3fs	דרך	201		tread, march
	יהיה	qal	impf	3ms	היה	224		be, become
	יהיה	qal	impf	3ms	היה	224		be, become
11: 25	יתיצב	hith	impf	3ms	יצב	426		stand oneself
	יתן	qal	impf	3ms	נתן	678		give,set
	תדרכו	qal	impf	2mp	דרך	201		tread, march
	דבר	piel	pft	3ms	דבר	180		speak
11: 26	ראה	qal	impv	ms	ראה	906		see
	נתן	qal	ptc	ms	נתן	678		give,set
11: 27	תשׁמעו	qal	impf	2mp	שׁמע	1033		hear
	מצוה	piel	ptc	ms	צוה	845		command
11: 28	תשׁמעו	qal	impf	2mp	שׁמע	1033		hear
	סרתם	qal	wcp	2mp	סור	693		turn aside
	מצוה	piel	ptc	ms	צוה	845		command
	לכת	qal	infc		הלך	229		walk, go
	ידעתם	qal	pft	2mp	ידע	393		know
11: 29	היה	qal	wcp	3ms	היה	224		be, become
	יביאך	hiph	impf	3ms	בוא	97	2ms	bring in

ChVs	Form	Stem	Tnse	PGN	Root	BDB	Sfx	Meaning
11:29	בא	qal	ptc	ms	בוא	97		come in
	רשתה	qal	infc		ירש	439	3fs	possess,inherit
	נתתה	qal	wcp	2ms	נתן	678		give,set
11:30	ישב	qal	ptc	ms	ישב	442		sit,dwell
11:31	עברים	qal	ptc	mp	עבר	716		pass over
	בא	qal	infc		בוא	97		come in
	רשת	qal	infc		ירש	439		possess,inherit
	נתן	qal	ptc	ms	נתן	678		give,set
	ירשתם	qal	wcp	2mp	ירש	439		possess,inherit
	ישבתם	qal	wcp	2mp	ישב	442		sit,dwell
11:32	שמרתם	qal	wcp	2mp	שמר	1036		keep,watch
	עשׂות	qal	infc		עשׂה	793		do,make
	נתן	qal	ptc	ms	נתן	678		give,set
12:1	תשמרון	qal	impf	2mp	שמר	1036		keep,watch
	עשׂות	qal	infc		עשׂה	793		do,make
	נתן	qal	pft	3ms	נתן	678		give,set
	רשתה	qal	infc		ירש	439	3fs	possess,inherit
12:2	אבד	piel	infa		אבד	1		destroy
	תאבדון	piel	impf	2mp	אבד	1		destroy
	עבדו	qal	pft	3cp	עבד	712		work,serve
	ירשים	qal	ptc	mp	ירש	439		possess,inherit
	רמים	qal	ptc	mp	רום	926		be high
12:3	נתצתם	piel	wcp	2mp	נתץ	683		tear down
	שברתם	piel	wcp	2mp	שבר	990		shatter
	תשׂרפון	qal	impf	2mp	שׂרף	976		burn
	תגדעון	piel	impf	2mp	גדע	154		hew off
	אבדתם	piel	wcp	2mp	אבד	1		destroy
12:4	תעשׂון	qal	impf	2mp	עשׂה	793		do,make
12:5	יבחר	qal	impf	3ms	בחר	103		choose
	שׂום	qal	infc		שׂים	962		put,set
	שכנו	qal	infc		שכן	1014	3ms	settle,dwell
	תדרשו	qal	impf	2mp	דרש	205		resort to,seek
	באת	qal	wcp	2ms	בוא	97		come in
12:6	הבאתם	hiph	wcp	2mp	בוא	97		bring in
12:7	אכלתם	qal	wcp	2mp	אכל	37		eat,devour
	שׂמחתם	qal	wcp	2mp	שׂמח	970		rejoice
	ברכך	piel	pft	3ms	ברך	138	2ms	bless
12:8	תעשׂון	qal	impf	2mp	עשׂה	793		do,make
	עשׂים	qal	ptc	mp	עשׂה	793		do,make
12:9	באתם	qal	pft	2mp	בוא	97		come in
	נתן	qal	ptc	ms	נתן	678		give,set
12:10	עברתם	qal	wcp	2mp	עבר	716		pass over
	ישבתם	qal	wcp	2mp	ישב	442		sit,dwell
	מנחיל	hiph	ptc	ms	נחל	635		c. to inherit
	הניח	hiph	wcp	3ms	נוח	628		give rest,put
	איביכם	qal	ptc	mp	איב	33	2mp	be hostile to
	ישבתם	qal	wcp	2mp	ישב	442		sit,dwell
12:11	היה	qal	wcp	3ms	היה	224		be,become
	יבחר	qal	impf	3ms	בחר	103		choose
	שכן	piel	infc		שכן	1014		establish
	תביאו	hiph	impf	2mp	בוא	97		bring in
	מצוה	piel	ptc	ms	צוה	845		command
	תדרו	qal	impf	2mp	נדר	623		vow
12:12	שׂמחתם	qal	wcp	2mp	שׂמח	970		rejoice

ChVs	Form	Stem	Tnse	PGN	Root	BDB	Sfx	Meaning
12:13	השמר	niph	impv	ms	שמר	1036		be kept,guarded
	תעלה	hiph	impf	2ms	עלה	748		bring up,offer
	תראה	qal	impf	2ms	ראה	906		see
12:14	יבחר	qal	impf	3ms	בחר	103		choose
	תעלה	hiph	impf	2ms	עלה	748		bring up,offer
	תעשׂה	qal	impf	2ms	עשׂה	793		do,make
	מצוך	piel	ptc	ms	צוה	845	2ms	command
12:15	תזבח	qal	impf	2ms	זבח	256		slaughter
	אכלת	qal	wcp	2ms	אכל	37		eat,devour
	נתן	qal	pft	3ms	נתן	678		give,set
	יאכלנו	qal	impf	3ms	אכל	37	3ms	eat,devour
12:16	תאכלו	qal	impf	2mp	אכל	37		eat,devour
	תשפכנו	qal	impf	2ms	שפך	1049	3ms	pour out
12:17	תוכל	qal	impf	2ms	יכל	407		be able
	אכל	qal	infc		אכל	37		eat,devour
	תדר	qal	impf	2ms	נדר	623		vow
12:18	תאכלנו	qal	impf	2ms	אכל	37	3ms	eat,devour
	יבחר	qal	impf	3ms	בחר	103		choose
	שׂמחת	qal	wcp	2ms	שׂמח	970		rejoice
12:19	השמר	niph	impv	ms	שמר	1036		be kept,guarded
	תעזב	qal	impf	2ms	עזב	736		leave,loose
12:20	ירחיב	hiph	impf	3ms	רחב	931		enlarge
	דבר	piel	pft	3ms	דבר	180		speak
	אמרת	qal	wcp	2ms	אמר	55		say
	אכלה	qal	coh	1cs	אכל	37		eat,devour
	תאוה	piel	impf	3fs	אוה	16		desire
	אכל	qal	infc		אכל	37		eat,devour
	תאכל	qal	impf	2ms	אכל	37		eat,devour
12:21	ירחק	qal	impf	3ms	רחק	934		be distant
	יבחר	qal	impf	3ms	בחר	103		choose
	שׂום	qal	infc		שׂים	962		put,set
	זבחת	qal	wcp	2ms	זבח	256		slaughter
	נתן	qal	pft	3ms	נתן	678		give,set
	צויתך	piel	pft	1cs	צוה	845	2ms	command
	אכלת	qal	wcp	2ms	אכל	37		eat,devour
12:22	יאכל	niph	impf	3ms	אכל	37		be eaten
	תאכלנו	qal	impf	2ms	אכל	37	3ms	eat,devour
	יאכלנו	qal	impf	3ms	אכל	37	3ms	eat,devour
12:23	חזק	qal	impv	ms	חזק	304		be strong
	אכל	qal	infc		אכל	37		eat,devour
	תאכל	qal	impf	2ms	אכל	37		eat,devour
12:24	תאכלנו	qal	impf	2ms	אכל	37	3ms	eat,devour
	תשפכנו	qal	impf	2ms	שפך	1049	3ms	pour out
12:25	תאכלנו	qal	impf	2ms	אכל	37	3ms	eat,devour
	ייטב	qal	impf	3ms	יטב	405		be good
	תעשׂה	qal	impf	2ms	עשׂה	793		do,make
12:26	יהיו	qal	impf	3mp	היה	224		be,become
	תשׂא	qal	impf	2ms	נשׂא	669		lift,carry
	באת	qal	wcp	2ms	בוא	97		come in
	יבחר	qal	impf	3ms	בחר	103		choose
12:27	עשׂית	qal	wcp	2ms	עשׂה	793		do,make
	ישפך	niph	impf	3ms	שפך	1049		be poured out
	תאכל	qal	impf	2ms	אכל	37		eat,devour
12:28	שמר	qal	impv	ms	שמר	1036		keep,watch

ChVs	Form	Stem	Tnse	PGN	Root	BDB	Sfx	Meaning
12:28	שמעת	qal	wcp	2ms	שמע	1033		hear
	מצוך	piel	ptc	ms	צוה	845	2ms	command
	ייטב	qal	impf	3ms	יטב	405		be good
	תעשה	qal	impf	2ms	עשה	793		do,make
12:29	יכרית	hiph	impf	3ms	כרת	503		cut off,destroy
	בא	qal	ptc	ms	בוא	97		come in
	רשת	qal	infc		ירש	439		possess,inherit
	ירשת	qal	wcp	2ms	ירש	439		possess,inherit
	ישבת	qal	wcp	2ms	ישב	442		sit,dwell
12:30	השמר	niph	impv	ms	שמר	1036		be kept,guarded
	תנקש	niph	impf	2ms	נקש	669		be thrust
	השמדם	niph	infc		שמד	1029	3mp	be exterminated
	תדרש	qal	impf	2ms	דרש	205		resort to,seek
	אמר	qal	infc		אמר	55		say
	יעבדו	qal	impf	3mp	עבד	712		work,serve
	אעשה	qal	impf	1cs	עשה	793		do,make
12:31	תעשה	qal	impf	2ms	עשה	793		do,make
	שנא	qal	pft	3ms	שנא	971		hate
	עשו	qal	pft	3cp	עשה	793		do,make
	ישרפו	qal	impf	3mp	שרף	976		burn
13:1	מצוה	piel	ptc	ms	צוה	845		command
	תשמרו	qal	impf	2mp	שמר	1036		keep,watch
	עשות	qal	infc		עשה	793		do,make
	תסף	hiph	jusf	2ms	יסף	414		add,do again
	תגרע	qal	impf	2ms	גרע	175		diminish
13:2	יקום	qal	impf	3ms	קום	877		arise,stand
	חלם	qal	ptc	ms	חלם	321		dream
	נתן	qal	wcp	3ms	נתן	678		give,set
13:3	בא	qal	wcp	3ms	בוא	97		come in
	דבר	piel	pft	3ms	דבר	180		speak
	אמר	qal	infc		אמר	55		say
	נלכה	qal	coh	1cp	הלך	229		walk,go
	ידעתם	qal	pft	2ms	ידע	393	3mp	know
	נעבדם	hoph	cohm	1cp	עבד	712	3mp	be led to serve
13:4	תשמע	qal	impf	2ms	שמע	1033		hear
	חולם	qal	ptc	ms	חלם	321		dream
	מנסה	piel	ptc	ms	נסה	650		test,try
	דעת	qal	infc		ידע	393		know
	אהבים	qal	ptc	mp	אהב	12		love
13:5	תלכו	qal	impf	2mp	הלך	229		walk,go
	תיראו	qal	impf	2mp	ירא	431		fear
	תשמרו	qal	impf	2mp	שמר	1036		keep,watch
	תשמעו	qal	impf	2mp	שמע	1033		hear
	תעבדו	qal	impf	2mp	עבד	712		work,serve
	תדבקון	qal	impf	2mp	דבק	179		cling,cleave
13:6	חלם	qal	ptc	ms	חלם	321		dream
	יומת	hoph	impf	3ms	מות	559		be killed
	דבר	piel	pft	3ms	דבר	180		speak
	מוציא	hiph	ptc	ms	יצא	422		bring out
	פדך	qal	ptc	ms	פדה	804	2ms	ransom
	הדיחך	hiph	infc		נדח	623	2ms	thrust out
	צוך	piel	pft	3ms	צוה	845	2ms	command
	לכת	qal	infc		הלך	229		walk,go
	בערת	piel	wcp	2ms	בער	128		burn,consume
13:7	יסיתך	hiph	impf	3ms	סות	694	2ms	incite,allure
	אמר	qal	infc		אמר	55		say
	נלכה	qal	coh	1cp	הלך	229		walk,go
	נעבדה	qal	coh	1cp	עבד	712		work,serve
	ידעת	qal	pft	2ms	ידע	393		know
13:9	תאבה	qal	impf	2ms	אבה	2		be willing
	תשמע	qal	impf	2ms	שמע	1033		hear
	תחוס	qal	jusf	3fs	חוס	299?		pity
	תחמל	qal	impf	2ms	חמל	328		spare
	תכסה	piel	impf	2ms	כסה	491		cover
13:10	הרג	qal	infa		הרג	246		kill
	תהרגנו	qal	impf	2ms	הרג	246	3ms	kill
	תהיה	qal	impf	3fs	היה	224		be,become
	המיתו	hiph	infc		מות	559	3ms	kill
13:11	סקלתו	qal	wcp	2ms	סקל	709	3ms	stone to death
	מת	qal	wcp	3ms	מות	559		die
	בקש	piel	pft	3ms	בקש	134		seek
	הדיחך	hiph	infc		נדח	623	2ms	thrust out
	מוציאך	hiph	ptc	ms	יצא	422	2ms	bring out
13:12	ישמעו	qal	impf	3mp	שמע	1033		hear
	יראון	qal	impf	3mp	ירא	431		fear
	יוספו	hiph	impf	3mp	יסף	414		add,do again
	עשות	qal	infc		עשה	793		do,make
13:13	תשמע	qal	impf	2ms	שמע	1033		hear
	נתן	qal	ptc	ms	נתן	678		give,set
	שבת	qal	infc		ישב	442		sit,dwell
	אמר	qal	infc		אמר	55		say
13:14	יצאו	qal	pft	3cp	יצא	422		go out
	ידיחו	hiph	wci	3mp	נדח	623		thrust out
	ישבי	qal	ptc	mp	ישב	442		sit,dwell
	אמר	qal	infc		אמר	55		say
	נלכה	qal	coh	1cp	הלך	229		walk,go
	נעבדה	qal	coh	1cp	עבד	712		work,serve
	ידעתם	qal	pft	2mp	ידע	393		know
13:15	דרשת	qal	wcp	2ms	דרש	205		resort to,seek
	חקרת	qal	wcp	2ms	חקר	350		search
	שאלת	qal	wcp	2ms	שאל	981		ask,borrow
	היטב	hiph	infa		יטב	405		do good
	נכון	niph	ptc	ms	כון	465		be established
	נעשתה	niph	pft	3fs	עשה	793		be done
13:16	הכה	hiph	infa		נכה	645		smite
	תכה	hiph	impf	2ms	נכה	645		smite
	ישבי	qal	ptc	mp	ישב	442		sit,dwell
	החרם	hiph	impv	ms	חרם	355		ban,destroy
13:17	תקבץ	qal	impf	2ms	קבץ	867		gather,collect
	שרפת	qal	wcp	2ms	שרף	976		burn
	היתה	qal	wcp	3fs	היה	224		be,become
	תבנה	niph	impf	3fs	בנה	124		be built
13:18	ידבק	qal	impf	3ms	דבק	179		cling,cleave
	ישוב	qal	impf	3ms	שוב	996		turn,return
	נתן	qal	wcp	3ms	נתן	678		give,set
	רחמך	piel	wcp	3ms	רחם	933	2ms	have compassion
	הרבך	hiph	wcp	3ms	רבה	915	2ms	make many
	נשבע	niph	pft	3ms	שבע	989		swear

ChVs	Form	Stem	Tnse	PGN	Root	BDB	Sfx	Meaning
13:19	תשמע	qal	impf	2ms	שמע	1033		hear
	שמר	qal	infc		שמר	1036		keep,watch
	מצוך	piel	ptc	ms	צוה	845	2ms	command
	עשות	qal	infc		עשה	793		do,make
14:1	תתגדדו	htpo	impf	2mp	גדד	151		cut self,throng
	תשימו	qal	impf	2mp	שים	962		put,set
	מת	qal	ptc	ms	מות	559		die
14:2	בחר	qal	pft	3ms	בחר	103		choose
	היות	qal	infc		היה	224		be,become
14:3	תאכל	qal	impf	2ms	אכל	37		eat,devour
14:4	תאכלו	qal	impf	2mp	אכל	37		eat,devour
14:6	מפרסת	hiph	ptc	fs	פרס	828		divide
	שסעת	qal	ptc	fs	שסע	1042		cleave,divide
	מעלת	hiph	ptc	fs	עלה	748		bring up,offer
	תאכלו	qal	impf	2mp	אכל	37		eat,devour
14:7	תאכלו	qal	impf	2mp	אכל	37		eat,devour
	מעלי	hiph	ptc	mp	עלה	748		bring up,offer
	מפריסי	hiph	ptc	mp	פרס	828		divide
	שסועה	qal	pptc	fs	שסע	1042		cleave,divide
	מעלה	hiph	ptc	ms	עלה	748		bring up,offer
	הפריסו	hiph	pft	3cp	פרס	828		divide
14:8	מפריס	hiph	ptc	ms	פרס	828		divide
	תאכלו	qal	impf	2mp	אכל	37		eat,devour
	תגעו	qal	impf	2mp	נגע	619		touch,strike
14:9	תאכלו	qal	impf	2mp	אכל	37		eat,devour
	תאכלו	qal	impf	2mp	אכל	37		eat,devour
14:10	תאכלו	qal	impf	2mp	אכל	37		eat,devour
14:11	תאכלו	qal	impf	2mp	אכל	37		eat,devour
14:12	תאכלו	qal	impf	2mp	אכל	37		eat,devour
14:19	יאכלו	niph	impf	3mp	אכל	37		be eaten
14:20	תאכלו	qal	impf	2mp	אכל	37		eat,devour
14:21	תאכלו	qal	impf	2mp	אכל	37		eat,devour
	תתננה	qal	impf	2ms	נתן	678	3fs	give,set
	אכלה	qal	wcp	3ms	אכל	37	3fs	eat,devour
	מכר	qal	infa		מכר	569		sell
	תבשל	piel	impf	2ms	בשל	143		boil,cook
14:22	עשר	piel	infa		עשר	797		give tenth
	תעשר	piel	impf	2ms	עשר	797		give tenth
	יצא	qal	ptc	ms	יצא	422		go out
14:23	אכלת	qal	wcp	2ms	אכל	37		eat,devour
	יבחר	qal	impf	3ms	בחר	103		choose
	שכן	piel	infc		שכן	1014		establish
	תלמד	qal	impf	2ms	למד	540		learn
	יראה	qal	infc		ירא	431		fear
14:24	ירבה	qal	impf	3ms	רבה	915		be many,great
	תוכל	qal	impf	2ms	יכל	407		be able
	שאתו	qal	infc		נשא	669	3ms	lift,carry
	ירחק	qal	impf	3ms	רחק	934		be distant
	יבחר	qal	impf	3ms	בחר	103		choose
	שום	qal	infc		שים	962		put,set
	יברכך	piel	impf	3ms	ברך	138	2ms	bless
14:25	נתתה	qal	wcp	2ms	נתן	678		give,set
	צרת	qal	wcp	2ms	צור	848		confine,shut in
	הלכת	qal	wcp	2ms	הלך	229		walk,go
14:25	יבחר	qal	impf	3ms	בחר	103		choose
14:26	נתתה	qal	wcp	2ms	נתן	678		give,set
	תאוה	piel	impf	3fs	אוה	16		desire
	תשאלך	qal	impf	3fs	שאל	981	2ms	ask,borrow
	אכלת	qal	wcp	2ms	אכל	37		eat,devour
	שמחת	qal	wcp	2ms	שמח	970		rejoice
14:27	תעזבנו	qal	impf	2ms	עזב	736	3ms	leave,loose
14:28	תוציא	hiph	impf	2ms	יצא	422		bring out
	הנחת	hiph	wcp	2ms	נוח	628		give rest,put
14:29	בא	qal	wcp	3ms	בוא	97		come in
	אכלו	qal	wcp	3cp	אכל	37		eat,devour
	שבעו	qal	wcp	3cp	שבע	959		be sated
	יברכך	piel	impf	3ms	ברך	138	2ms	bless
	תעשה	qal	impf	2ms	עשה	793		do,make
15:1	תעשה	qal	impf	2ms	עשה	793		do,make
15:2	שמוט	qal	infa		שמט	1030		let drop
	ישה	hiph	impf	3ms	נשה	674		lend
	יגש	qal	impf	3ms	נגש	620		press,exact
	קרא	qal	pft	3ms	קרא	894		call,proclaim
15:3	תגש	qal	impf	2ms	נגש	620		press,exact
	יהיה	qal	impf	3ms	היה	224		be,become
	תשמט	hiph	jus	3fs	שמט	1030		let loose
15:4	יהיה	qal	impf	3ms	היה	224		be,become
	ברך	piel	infa		ברך	138		bless
	יברכך	piel	impf	3ms	ברך	138	2ms	bless
	נתן	qal	ptc	ms	נתן	678		give,set
	רשתה	qal	infc		ירש	439	3fs	possess,inherit
15:5	שמוע	qal	infa		שמע	1033		hear
	תשמע	qal	impf	2ms	שמע	1033		hear
	שמר	qal	infc		שמר	1036		keep,watch
	עשות	qal	infc		עשה	793		do,make
	מצוך	piel	ptc	ms	צוה	845	2ms	command
15:6	ברכך	piel	pft	3ms	ברך	138	2ms	bless
	דבר	piel	pft	3ms	דבר	180		speak
	העבטת	hiph	wcp	2ms	עבט	716		lend on pledge
	תעבט	qal	impf	2ms	עבט	716		give a pledge
	משלת	qal	wcp	2ms	משל	605		rule
	ימשלו	qal	impf	3mp	משל	605		rule
15:7	יהיה	qal	impf	3ms	היה	224		be,become
	נתן	qal	ptc	ms	נתן	678		give,set
	תאמץ	piel	impf	2ms	אמץ	54		make firm
	תקפץ	qal	impf	2ms	קפץ	891		shut
15:8	פתח	qal	infa		פתח	834		open
	תפתח	qal	impf	2ms	פתח	834		open
	העבט	hiph	infa		עבט	716		lend on pledge
	תעביטנו	hiph	impf	2ms	עבט	716	3ms	lend on pledge
	יחסר	qal	impf	3ms	חסר	341		lack
15:9	השמר	niph	impv	ms	שמר	1036		be kept,guarded
	יהיה	qal	impf	3ms	היה	224		be,become
	אמר	qal	infc		אמר	55		say
	קרבה	qal	pft	3fs	קרב	897		approach
	רעה	qal	wcp	3fs	רעע	949		be evil
	תתן	qal	impf	2ms	נתן	678		give,set
	קרא	qal	wcp	3ms	קרא	894		call,proclaim

ChVs	Form	Stem	Tnse	PGN	Root	BDB	Sfx	Meaning
15: 9	היה	qal	wcp	3ms	היה	224		be, become
15: 10	נתון	qal	infa		נתן	678		give, set
	תתן	qal	impf	2ms	נתן	678		give, set
	ירע	qal	impf	3ms	רעע	949		be evil
	תתך	qal	infc		נתן	678	2ms	give, set
	יברכך	piel	impf	3ms	ברך	138	2ms	bless
15: 11	יחדל	qal	impf	3ms	חדל	292		cease
	מצוך	piel	ptc	ms	צוה	845	2ms	command
	אמר	qal	infc		אמר	55		say
	פתח	qal	infa		פתח	834		open
	תפתח	qal	impf	2ms	פתח	834		open
15: 12	ימכר	niph	impf	3ms	מכר	569		be sold
	עבדך	qal	wcp	3ms	עבד	712	2ms	work, serve
	תשלחנו	piel	impf	2ms	שלח	1018	3ms	send away, shoot
15: 13	תשלחנו	piel	impf	2ms	שלח	1018	3ms	send away, shoot
	תשלחנו	piel	impf	2ms	שלח	1018	3ms	send away, shoot
15: 14	העניק	hiph	infa		ענק	778		make necklace
	תעניק	hiph	impf	2ms	ענק	778		make necklace
	ברכך	piel	pft	3ms	ברך	138	2ms	bless
	תתן	qal	impf	2ms	נתן	678		give, set
15: 15	זכרת	qal	wcp	2ms	זכר	269		remember
	היית	qal	pft	2ms	היה	224		be, become
	יפדך	qal	wci	3ms	פדה	804	2ms	ransom
	מצוך	piel	ptc	ms	צוה	845	2ms	command
15: 16	היה	qal	wcp	3ms	היה	224		be, become
	יאמר	qal	impf	3ms	אמר	55		say
	אצא	qal	impf	1cs	יצא	422		go out
	אהבך	qal	pft	3ms	אהב	12	2ms	love
	טוב	qal	pft	3ms	טוב	373		be pleasing
15: 17	לקחת	qal	wcp	2ms	לקח	542		take
	נתתה	qal	wcp	2ms	נתן	678		give, set
	היה	qal	wcp	3ms	היה	224		be, become
	תעשׂה	qal	impf	2ms	עשׂה	793		do, make
15: 18	יקשׁה	qal	impf	3ms	קשׁה	904		be hard, severe
	שׁלחך	piel	infc		שׁלח	1018	2ms	send away, shoot
	עבדך	qal	pft	3ms	עבד	712	2ms	work, serve
	ברכך	piel	wcp	3ms	ברך	138	2ms	bless
	תעשׂה	qal	impf	2ms	עשׂה	793		do, make
15: 19	יולד	niph	impf	3ms	ילד	408		be born
	תקדישׁ	hiph	impf	2ms	קדשׁ	872		consecrate
	תעבד	qal	impf	2ms	עבד	712		work, serve
	תגז	qal	impf	2ms	גזז	159		shear
15: 20	תאכלנו	qal	impf	2ms	אכל	37	3ms	eat, devour
	יבחר	qal	impf	3ms	בחר	103		choose
15: 21	יהיה	qal	impf	3ms	היה	224		be, become
	תזבחנו	qal	impf	2ms	זבח	256	3ms	slaughter
15: 22	תאכלנו	qal	impf	2ms	אכל	37	3ms	eat, devour
15: 23	תאכל	qal	impf	2ms	אכל	37		eat, devour
	תשׁפכנו	qal	impf	2ms	שׁפך	1049	3ms	pour out
16: 1	שׁמור	qal	infa		שׁמר	1036		keep, watch
	עשׂית	qal	wcp	2ms	עשׂה	793		do, make
	הוציאך	hiph	pft	3ms	יצא	422	2ms	bring out
16: 2	זבחת	qal	wcp	2ms	זבח	256		slaughter
	יבחר	qal	impf	3ms	בחר	103		choose

ChVs	Form	Stem	Tnse	PGN	Root	BDB	Sfx	Meaning
16: 2	שׁכן	piel	infc		שׁכן	1014		establish
16: 3	תאכל	qal	impf	2ms	אכל	37		eat, devour
	תאכל	qal	impf	2ms	אכל	37		eat, devour
	יצאת	qal	pft	2ms	יצא	422		go out
	תזכר	qal	impf	2ms	זכר	269		remember
	צאתך	qal	infc		יצא	422	2ms	go out
16: 4	יראה	niph	impf	3ms	ראה	906		appear, be seen
	ילין	qal	impf	3ms	לון	533		lodge, remain
	תזבח	qal	impf	2ms	זבח	256		slaughter
16: 5	תוכל	qal	impf	2ms	יכל	407		be able
	זבח	qal	infc		זבח	256		slaughter
	נתן	qal	ptc	ms	נתן	678		give, set
16: 6	יבחר	qal	impf	3ms	בחר	103		choose
	שׁכן	piel	infc		שׁכן	1014		establish
	תזבח	qal	impf	2ms	זבח	256		slaughter
	בוא	qal	infc		בוא	97		come in
	צאתך	qal	infc		יצא	422	2ms	go out
16: 7	בשׁלת	piel	wcp	2ms	בשׁל	143		boil, cook
	אכלת	qal	wcp	2ms	אכל	37		eat, devour
	יבחר	qal	impf	3ms	בחר	103		choose
	פנית	qal	wcp	2ms	פנה	815		turn
	הלכת	qal	wcp	2ms	הלך	229		walk, go
16: 8	תאכל	qal	impf	2ms	אכל	37		eat, devour
	תעשׂה	qal	impf	2ms	עשׂה	793		do, make
16: 9	תספר	qal	impf	2ms	ספר	707		count
	החל	hiph	infc		חלל	320		begin, profane
	תחל	hiph	impf	2ms	חלל	320		begin, profane
	ספר	qal	infc		ספר	707		count
16: 10	עשׂית	qal	wcp	2ms	עשׂה	793		do, make
	תתן	qal	impf	2ms	נתן	678		give, set
	יברכך	piel	impf	3ms	ברך	138	2ms	bless
16: 11	שׂמחת	qal	wcp	2ms	שׂמח	970		rejoice
	יבחר	qal	impf	3ms	בחר	103		choose
	שׁכן	piel	infc		שׁכן	1014		establish
16: 12	זכרת	qal	wcp	2ms	זכר	269		remember
	היית	qal	pft	2ms	היה	224		be, become
	שׁמרת	qal	wcp	2ms	שׁמר	1036		keep, watch
	עשׂית	qal	wcp	2ms	עשׂה	793		do, make
16: 13	תעשׂה	qal	impf	2ms	עשׂה	793		do, make
	אספך	qal	infc		אסף	62	2ms	gather
16: 14	שׂמחת	qal	wcp	2ms	שׂמח	970		rejoice
16: 15	תחג	qal	impf	2ms	חגג	290		keep festival
	יבחר	qal	impf	3ms	בחר	103		choose
	יברכך	piel	impf	3ms	ברך	138	2ms	bless
	היית	qal	wcp	2ms	היה	224		be, become
16: 16	יראה	niph	impf	3ms	ראה	906		appear, be seen
	יבחר	qal	impf	3ms	בחר	103		choose
	יראה	niph	impf	3ms	ראה	906		appear, be seen
16: 17	נתן	qal	pft	3ms	נתן	678		give, set
16: 18	שׁפטים	qal	ptc	mp	שׁפט	1047		judge
	תתן	qal	impf	2ms	נתן	678		give, set
	נתן	qal	ptc	ms	נתן	678		give, set
	שׁפטו	qal	wcp	3cp	שׁפט	1047		judge
16: 19	תטה	hiph	impf	2ms	נטה	639		turn, incline

ChVs	Form	Stem	Tnse	PGN	Root	BDB	Sfx	Meaning
16:19	תכיר	hiph	impf	2ms	נכר	647		regard,notice
	תקח	qal	impf	2ms	לקח	542		take
	יעור	piel	impf	3ms	עור	734		make blind
	יסלף	piel	impf	3ms	סלף	701		pervert,turn
16:20	תרדף	qal	impf	2ms	רדף	922		pursue
	תחיה	qal	impf	2ms	חיה	310		live
	ירשת	qal	wcp	2ms	ירש	439		possess,inherit
	נתן	qal	ptc	ms	נתן	678		give,set
16:21	תטע	qal	impf	2ms	נטע	642		plant
	תעשה	qal	impf	2ms	עשה	793		do,make
16:22	תקים	hiph	impf	2ms	קום	877		raise,build,set
	שנא	qal	pft	3ms	שנא	971		hate
17:1	תזבח	qal	impf	2ms	זבח	256		slaughter
	יהיה	qal	impf	3ms	היה	224		be,become
17:2	ימצא	niph	impf	3ms	מצא	592		be found
	נתן	qal	ptc	ms	נתן	678		give,set
	יעשה	qal	impf	3ms	עשה	793		do,make
	עבר	qal	infc		עבר	716		pass over
17:3	ילך	qal	wci	3ms	הלך	229		walk,go
	יעבד	qal	wci	3ms	עבד	712		work,serve
	ישתחו	hish	wci	3ms	חוה	1005		bow down
	צויתי	piel	pft	1cs	צוה	845		command
17:4	הגד	hoph	wcp	3ms	נגד	616		be told
	שמעת	qal	wcp	2ms	שמע	1033		hear
	דרשת	qal	wcp	2ms	דרש	205		resort to,seek
	היטב	hiph	infa		יטב	405		do good
	נכון	niph	ptc	ms	כון	465		be established
	נעשתה	niph	pft	3fs	עשה	793		be done
17:5	הוצאת	hiph	wcp	2ms	יצא	422		bring out
	עשו	qal	pft	3cp	עשה	793		do,make
	סקלתם	qal	wcp	2ms	סקל	709	3mp	stone to death
	מתו	qal	wcp	3cp	מות	559		die
17:6	יומת	hoph	impf	3ms	מות	559		be killed
	מת	qal	ptc	ms	מות	559		die
	יומת	hoph	impf	3ms	מות	559		be killed
17:7	תהיה	qal	impf	3fs	היה	224		be,become
	המיתו	hiph	infc		מות	559	3ms	kill
	בערת	piel	wcp	2ms	בער	128		burn,consume
17:8	יפלא	niph	impf	3ms	פלא	810		be wonderful
	קמת	qal	wcp	2ms	קום	877		arise,stand
	עלית	qal	wcp	2ms	עלה	748		go up
	יבחר	qal	impf	3ms	בחר	103		choose
17:9	באת	qal	wcp	2ms	בוא	97		come in
	שפט	qal	ptc	ms	שפט	1047		judge
	יהיה	qal	impf	3ms	היה	224		be,become
	דרשת	qal	wcp	2ms	דרש	205		resort to,seek
	הגידו	hiph	wcp	3cp	נגד	616		declare,tell
17:10	עשית	qal	wcp	2ms	עשה	793		do,make
	יגידו	hiph	impf	3mp	נגד	616		declare,tell
	יבחר	qal	impf	3ms	בחר	103		choose
	שמרת	qal	wcp	2ms	שמר	1036		keep,watch
	עשות	qal	infc		עשה	793		do,make
	יורוך	hiph	impf	3mp	ירה	434	2ms	shoot,teach
17:11	יורוך	hiph	impf	3mp	ירה	434	2ms	shoot,teach
17:11	יאמרו	qal	impf	3mp	אמר	55		say
	תעשה	qal	impf	2ms	עשה	793		do,make
	תסור	qal	impf	2ms	סור	693		turn aside
	יגידו	hiph	impf	3mp	נגד	616		declare,tell
17:12	יעשה	qal	impf	3ms	עשה	793		do,make
	שמע	qal	infc		שמע	1033		hear
	עמד	qal	ptc	ms	עמד	763		stand,stop
	שרת	piel	infc		שרת	1058		minister,serve
	שפט	qal	ptc	ms	שפט	1047		judge
	מת	qal	wcp	3ms	מות	559		die
	בערת	piel	wcp	2ms	בער	128		burn,consume
17:13	ישמעו	qal	impf	3mp	שמע	1033		hear
	יראו	qal	impf	3mp	ירא	431		fear
	יזידון	hiph	impf	3mp	זיד	267		boil,presume
17:14	תבא	qal	impf	2ms	בוא	97		come in
	נתן	qal	ptc	ms	נתן	678		give,set
	ירשתה	qal	wcp	2ms	ירש	439	3fs	possess,inherit
	ישבתה	qal	wcp	2ms	ישב	442		sit,dwell
	אמרת	qal	wcp	2ms	אמר	55		say
	אשימה	qal	coh	1cs	שים	962		put,set
17:15	שום	qal	infa		שים	962		put,set
	תשים	qal	impf	2ms	שים	962		put,set
	יבחר	qal	impf	3ms	בחר	103		choose
	תשים	qal	impf	2ms	שים	962		put,set
	תוכל	qal	impf	2ms	יכל	407		be able
	תת	qal	infc		נתן	678		give,set
17:16	ירבה	hiph	impf	3ms	רבה	915		make many
	ישיב	hiph	impf	3ms	שוב	996		bring back
	הרבות	hiph	infc		רבה	915		make many
	אמר	qal	pft	3ms	אמר	55		say
	תספון	hiph	impf	2mp	יסף	414		add,do again
	שוב	qal	infc		שוב	996		turn,return
17:17	ירבה	hiph	impf	3ms	רבה	915		make many
	יסור	qal	impf	3ms	סור	693		turn aside
	ירבה	hiph	impf	3ms	רבה	915		make many
17:18	היה	qal	wcp	3ms	היה	224		be,become
	שבתו	qal	infc		ישב	442	3ms	sit,dwell
	כתב	qal	wcp	3ms	כתב	507		write
17:19	היתה	qal	wcp	3fs	היה	224		be,become
	קרא	qal	wcp	3ms	קרא	894		call,proclaim
	ילמד	qal	impf	3ms	למד	540		learn
	יראה	qal	infc		ירא	431		fear
	שמר	qal	infc		שמר	1036		keep,watch
	עשתם	qal	infc		עשה	793	3mp	do,make
17:20	רום	qal	infc		רום	926		be high
	סור	qal	infc		סור	693		turn aside
	יאריך	hiph	impf	3ms	ארך	73		prolong
18:1	יהיה	qal	impf	3ms	היה	224		be,become
	יאכלון	qal	impf	3mp	אכל	37		eat,devour
18:2	יהיה	qal	impf	3ms	היה	224		be,become
	דבר	piel	pft	3ms	דבר	180		speak
18:3	יהיה	qal	impf	3ms	היה	224		be,become
	זבחי	qal	ptc	mp	זבח	256		slaughter
	נתן	qal	wcp	3ms	נתן	678		give,set

ChVs	Form	Stem	Tnse	PGN	Root	BDB	Sfx	Meaning
18:4	תתן	qal	impf	2ms	נתן	678		give,set
18:5	בחר	qal	pft	3ms	בחר	103		choose
	עמד	qal	infc		עמד	763		stand,stop
	שרת	piel	infc		שרת	1058		minister,serve
18:6	יבא	qal	impf	3ms	בוא	97		come in
	גר	qal	ptc	ms	גור	157		sojourn
	בא	qal	wcp	3ms	בוא	97		come in
	יבחר	qal	impf	3ms	בחר	103		choose
18:7	שרת	piel	wcp	3ms	שרת	1058		minister,serve
	עמדים	qal	ptc	mp	עמד	763		stand,stop
18:8	יאכלו	qal	impf	3mp	אכל	37		eat,devour
18:9	בא	qal	ptc	ms	בוא	97		come in
	נתן	qal	ptc	ms	נתן	678		give,set
	תלמד	qal	impf	2ms	למד	540		learn
	עשות	qal	infc		עשה	793		do,make
18:10	ימצא	niph	impf	3ms	מצא	592		be found
	מעביר	hiph	ptc	ms	עבר	716		cause to pass
	קסם	qal	ptc	ms	קסם	890		divine
	מעונן	poel	ptc	ms	ענן	778		soothsay
	מנחש	piel	ptc	ms	נחש	638		divine
	מכשף	piel	ptc	ms	כשף	506		practice magic
18:11	חבר	qal	ptc	ms	חבר	287		unite
	שאל	qal	ptc	ms	שאל	981		ask,borrow
	דרש	qal	ptc	ms	דרש	205		resort to,seek
	מתים	qal	ptc	mp	מות	559		die
18:12	עשה	qal	ptc	ms	עשה	793		do,make
	מוריש	hiph	ptc	ms	ירש	439		c. to possess
18:13	תהיה	qal	impf	2ms	היה	224		be,become
18:14	יורש	qal	ptc	ms	ירש	439		possess,inherit
	מעננים	poel	ptc	mp	ענן	778		soothsay
	קסמים	qal	ptc	mp	קסם	890		divine
	ישמעו	qal	impf	3mp	שמע	1033		hear
	נתן	qal	pft	3ms	נתן	678		give,set
18:15	יקים	hiph	impf	3ms	קום	877		raise,build,set
	תשמעון	qal	impf	2mp	שמע	1033		hear
18:16	שאלת	qal	pft	2ms	שאל	981		ask,borrow
	אמר	qal	infc		אמר	55		say
	אסף	hiph	jus	1cs	יסף	414?		add,do again
	שמע	qal	infc		שמע	1033		hear
	אראה	qal	cohm	1cs	ראה	906		see
	אמות	qal	impf	1cs	מות	559		die
18:17	יאמר	qal	wci	3ms	אמר	55		say
	היטיבו	hiph	pft	3cp	יטב	405		do good
	דברו	piel	pft	3cp	דבר	180		speak
18:18	אקים	hiph	impf	1cs	קום	877		raise,build,set
	נתתי	qal	wcp	1cs	נתן	678		give,set
	דבר	piel	wcp	3ms	דבר	180		speak
	אצונו	piel	impf	1cs	צוה	845	3ms	command
18:19	היה	qal	wcp	3ms	היה	224		be,become
	ישמע	qal	impf	3ms	שמע	1033		hear
	ידבר	piel	impf	3ms	דבר	180		speak
	אדרש	qal	impf	1cs	דרש	205		resort to,seek
18:20	יזיד	hiph	impf	3ms	זיד	267		boil,presume
	דבר	piel	infc		דבר	180		speak
18:20	צויתיו	piel	pft	1cs	צוה	845	3ms	command
	דבר	piel	infc		דבר	180		speak
	ידבר	piel	impf	3ms	דבר	180		speak
	מת	qal	wcp	3ms	מות	559		die
18:21	תאמר	qal	impf	2ms	אמר	55		say
	נדע	qal	impf	1cp	ידע	393		know
	דברו	piel	pft	3ms	דבר	180	3ms	speak
18:22	ידבר	piel	impf	3ms	דבר	180		speak
	יהיה	qal	impf	3ms	היה	224		be,become
	יבוא	qal	impf	3ms	בוא	97		come in
	דברו	piel	pft	3ms	דבר	180	3ms	speak
	דברו	piel	pft	3ms	דבר	180	3ms	speak
	תגור	qal	impf	2ms	גור	158		dread
19:1	יכרית	hiph	impf	3ms	כרת	503		cut off,destroy
	נתן	qal	ptc	ms	נתן	678		give,set
	ירשתם	qal	wcp	2ms	ירש	439	3mp	possess,inherit
	ישבת	qal	wcp	2ms	ישב	442		sit,dwell
19:2	תבדיל	hiph	impf	2ms	בדל	95		divide
	נתן	qal	ptc	ms	נתן	678		give,set
	רשתה	qal	infc		ירש	439	3fs	possess,inherit
19:3	תכין	hiph	impf	2ms	כון	465		fix,prepare
	שלשת	piel	wcp	2ms	שלש	1026		divide into 3
	ינחילך	hiph	impf	3ms	נחל	635	2ms	c. to inherit
	היה	qal	wcp	3ms	היה	224		be,become
	נוס	qal	infc		נוס	630		flee,escape
	רצח	qal	ptc	ms	רצח	953		murder,slay
19:4	רצח	qal	ptc	ms	רצח	953		murder,slay
	ינוס	qal	impf	3ms	נוס	630		flee,escape
	חי	qal	wcp	3ms	חיה	310		live
	יכה	hiph	impf	3ms	נכה	645		smite
	שנא	qal	ptc	ms	שנא	971		hate
19:5	יבא	qal	impf	3ms	בוא	97		come in
	חטב	qal	infc		חטב	310		cut wood
	נדחה	niph	wcp	3fs	נדח	623		be banished
	כרת	qal	infc		כרת	503		cut,destroy
	נשל	qal	wcp	3ms	נשל	675		draw off
	מצא	qal	wcp	3ms	מצא	592		find
	מת	qal	wcp	3ms	מות	559		die
	ינוס	qal	impf	3ms	נוס	630		flee,escape
	חי	qal	wcp	3ms	חיה	310		live
19:6	ירדף	qal	impf	3ms	רדף	922		pursue
	גאל	qal	ptc	ms	גאל	145		redeem
	רצח	qal	ptc	ms	רצח	953		murder,slay
	יחם	qal	impf	3ms	חמם	328		be warm
	השיגו	hiph	wcp	3ms	נשג	673	3ms	reach,overtake
	ירבה	qal	impf	3ms	רבה	915		be many,great
	הכהו	hiph	wcp	3ms	נכה	645	3ms	smite
	שנא	qal	ptc	ms	שנא	971		hate
19:7	מצוך	piel	ptc	ms	צוה	845	2ms	command
	אמר	qal	infc		אמר	55		say
	תבדיל	hiph	impf	2ms	בדל	95		divide
19:8	ירחיב	hiph	impf	3ms	רחב	931		enlarge
	נשבע	niph	pft	3ms	שבע	989		swear
	נתן	qal	wcp	3ms	נתן	678		give,set

ChVs	Form	Stem	Tnse	PGN	Root	BDB	Sfx	Meaning
19:8	דבר	piel	pft	3ms	דבר	180		speak
	תת	qal	infc		נתן	678		give,set
19:9	תשמר	qal	impf	2ms	שמר	1036		keep,watch
	עשׂתה	qal	infc		עשׂה	793	3fs	do,make
	מצוך	piel	ptc	ms	צוה	845	2ms	command
	אהבה	qal	infc		אהב	12		love
	לכת	qal	infc		הלך	229		walk,go
	יספת	qal	wcp	2ms	יסף	414		add,increase
19:10	ישפך	niph	impf	3ms	שפך	1049		be poured out
	נתן	qal	ptc	ms	נתן	678		give,set
	היה	qal	wcp	3ms	היה	224		be,become
19:11	יהיה	qal	impf	3ms	היה	224		be,become
	שׂנא	qal	ptc	ms	שׂנא	971		hate
	ארב	qal	wcp	3ms	ארב	70		lie in wait
	קם	qal	wcp	3ms	קום	877		arise,stand
	הכהו	hiph	wcp	3ms	נכה	645	3ms	smite
	מת	qal	wcp	3ms	מות	559		die
	נס	qal	wcp	3ms	נוס	630		flee,escape
19:12	שלחו	qal	wcp	3cp	שלח	1018		send
	לקחו	qal	wcp	3cp	לקח	542		take
	נתנו	qal	wcp	3cp	נתן	678		give,set
	גאל	qal	ptc	ms	גאל	145		redeem
	מת	qal	wcp	3ms	מות	559		die
19:13	תחוס	qal	jusf	3fs	חוס	299?		pity
	בערת	piel	wcp	2ms	בער	128		burn,consume
	טוב	qal	wcp	3ms	טוב	373		be pleasing
19:14	תסיג	hiph	impf	2ms	סוג	690		displace
	גבלו	qal	pft	3cp	גבל	148		border
	תנחל	qal	impf	2ms	נחל	635		possess,inherit
	נתן	qal	ptc	ms	נתן	678		give,set
	רשתה	qal	infc		ירשׁ	439	3fs	possess,inherit
19:15	יקום	qal	impf	3ms	קום	877		arise,stand
	יחטא	qal	impf	3ms	חטא	306		sin
	יקום	qal	impf	3ms	קום	877		arise,stand
19:16	יקום	qal	impf	3ms	קום	877		arise,stand
	ענות	qal	infc		ענה	772		answer
19:17	עמדו	qal	wcp	3cp	עמד	763		stand,stop
	שׁפטים	qal	ptc	mp	שׁפט	1047		judge
	יהיו	qal	impf	3mp	היה	224		be,become
19:18	דרשׁו	qal	wcp	3cp	דרשׁ	205		resort to,seek
	שׁפטים	qal	ptc	mp	שׁפט	1047		judge
	היטב	hiph	infa		יטב	405		do good
	ענה	qal	pft	3ms	ענה	772		answer
19:19	עשׂיתם	qal	wcp	2mp	עשׂה	793		do,make
	זמם	qal	pft	3ms	זמם	273		consider,devise
	עשׂות	qal	infc		עשׂה	793		do,make
	בערת	piel	wcp	2ms	בער	128		burn,consume
19:20	נשׁארים	niph	ptc	mp	שׁאר	983		be left
	ישׁמעו	qal	impf	3mp	שׁמע	1033		hear
	יראו	qal	impf	3mp	ירא	431		fear
	יספו	hiph	impf	3mp	יסף	414		add,do again
	עשׂות	qal	infc		עשׂה	793		do,make
19:21	תחוס	qal	jusf	3fs	חוס	299?		pity
20:1	תצא	qal	impf	2ms	יצא	422		go out

ChVs	Form	Stem	Tnse	PGN	Root	BDB	Sfx	Meaning
20:1	איביך	qal	ptc	mp	איב	33	2ms	be hostile to
	ראית	qal	wcp	2ms	ראה	906		see
	תירא	qal	impf	2ms	ירא	431		fear
	מעלך	hiph	ptc	ms	עלה	748	2ms	bring up,offer
20:2	היה	qal	wcp	3ms	היה	224		be,become
	קרבכם	qal	infc		קרב	897	2mp	approach
	נגשׁ	niph	wcp	3ms	נגשׁ	620		draw near
	דבר	piel	wcp	3ms	דבר	180		speak
20:3	אמר	qal	wcp	3ms	אמר	55		say
	שׁמע	qal	impv	ms	שׁמע	1033		hear
	איביכם	qal	ptc	mp	איב	33	2mp	be hostile to
	ירך	qal	jusm	3ms	רכך	939		be tender,timid
	תיראו	qal	jusm	2mp	ירא	431		fear
	תחפזו	qal	jusm	2mp	חפז	342		be alarmed
	תערצו	qal	jusm	2mp	ערץ	791		frighten,fear
20:4	הלך	qal	ptc	ms	הלך	229		walk,go
	הלחם	niph	infc		לחם	535		wage war
	איביכם	qal	ptc	mp	איב	33	2mp	be hostile to
	הושׁיע	hiph	infc		ישׁע	446		deliver,save
20:5	דברו	piel	wcp	3cp	דבר	180		speak
	אמר	qal	infc		אמר	55		say
	בנה	qal	pft	3ms	בנה	124		build
	חנכו	qal	pft	3ms	חנך	335	3ms	train,dedicate
	ילך	qal	jusm	3ms	הלך	229		walk,go
	ישׁב	qal	jus	3ms	שׁוב	996		turn,return
	ימות	qal	impf	3ms	מות	559		die
	יחנכנו	qal	impf	3ms	חנך	335	3ms	train,dedicate
20:6	נטע	qal	pft	3ms	נטע	642		plant
	חללו	piel	pft	3ms	חלל	320	3ms	pollute
	ילך	qal	jusm	3ms	הלך	229		walk,go
	ישׁב	qal	jus	3ms	שׁוב	996		turn,return
	ימות	qal	impf	3ms	מות	559		die
	יחללנו	piel	impf	3ms	חלל	320	3ms	pollute
20:7	ארשׂ	piel	pft	3ms	ארשׂ	76		betroth
	לקחה	qal	pft	3ms	לקח	542	3fs	take
	ילך	qal	jusm	3ms	הלך	229		walk,go
	ישׁב	qal	jus	3ms	שׁוב	996		turn,return
	ימות	qal	impf	3ms	מות	559		die
	יקחנה	qal	impf	3ms	לקח	542	3fs	take
20:8	יספו	qal	wcp	3cp	יסף	414		add,increase
	דבר	piel	infc		דבר	180		speak
	אמרו	qal	wcp	3cp	אמר	55		say
	ירא	qal	ptc	ms	ירא	431		fear
	ילך	qal	jusm	3ms	הלך	229		walk,go
	ישׁב	qal	jus	3ms	שׁוב	996		turn,return
	ימס	niph	impf	3ms	מסס	587		melt,despair
20:9	היה	qal	wcp	3ms	היה	224		be,become
	כלת	piel	infc		כלה	477		complete,finish
	דבר	piel	infc		דבר	180		speak
	פקדו	qal	wcp	3cp	פקד	823		attend to,visit
20:10	תקרב	qal	impf	2ms	קרב	897		approach
	הלחם	niph	infc		לחם	535		wage war
	קראת	qal	wcp	2ms	קרא	894		call,proclaim
20:11	היה	qal	wcp	3ms	היה	224		be,become

ChVs	Form	Stem	Tnse	PGN	Root	BDB	Sfx	Meaning
20:11	תענך	qal	impf	3fs	ענה	772	2ms	answer
	פתחה	qal	wcp	3fs	פתח	834		open
	היה	qal	wcp	3ms	היה	224		be,become
	נמצא	niph	ptc	ms	מצא	592		be found
	יהיו	qal	impf	3mp	היה	224		be,become
	עבדוך	qal	wcp	3cp	עבד	712	2ms	work,serve
20:12	תשלים	hiph	impf	3fs	שלם	1022		complete
	עשׂתה	qal	wcp	3fs	עשׂה	793		do,make
	צרת	qal	wcp	2ms	צור	848		confine,shut in
20:13	נתנה	qal	wcp	3ms	נתן	678	3fs	give,set
	הכית	hiph	wcp	2ms	נכה	645		smite
20:14	יהיה	qal	impf	3ms	היה	224		be,become
	תבז	qal	impf	2ms	בזז	102		plunder
	אכלת	qal	wcp	2ms	אכל	37		eat,devour
	איביך	qal	ptc	mp	איב	33	2ms	be hostile to
	נתן	qal	pft	3ms	נתן	678		give,set
20:15	תעשׂה	qal	impf	2ms	עשׂה	793		do,make
20:16	נתן	qal	ptc	ms	נתן	678		give,set
	תחיה	piel	impf	2ms	חיה	310		preserve,revive
20:17	החרם	hiph	infa		חרם	355		ban,destroy
	תחרימם	hiph	impf	2ms	חרם	355	3mp	ban,destroy
	צוך	piel	pft	3ms	צוה	845	2ms	command
20:18	ילמדו	piel	impf	3mp	למד	540		teach
	עשׂות	qal	infc		עשׂה	793		do,make
	עשׂו	qal	pft	3cp	עשׂה	793		do,make
	חטאתם	qal	wcp	2mp	חטא	306		sin
20:19	תצור	qal	impf	2ms	צור	848		confine,shut in
	הלחם	niph	infc		לחם	535		wage war
	תפשׂה	qal	infc		תפשׂ	1074	3fs	seize,grasp
	תשחית	hiph	impf	2ms	שחת	1007		spoil,ruin
	נדח	qal	infc		נדח	623		impel,banish
	תאכל	qal	impf	2ms	אכל	37		eat,devour
	תכרת	qal	impf	2ms	כרת	503		cut,destroy
	בא	qal	infc		בוא	97		come in
20:20	תדע	qal	impf	2ms	ידע	393		know
	תשחית	hiph	impf	2ms	שחת	1007		spoil,ruin
	כרת	qal	wcp	2ms	כרת	503		cut,destroy
	בנית	qal	wcp	2ms	בנה	124		build
	עשׂה	qal	ptc	fs	עשׂה	793		do,make
	רדתה	qal	infc		ירד	432	3fs	come down
21:1	ימצא	niph	impf	3ms	מצא	592		be found
	נתן	qal	ptc	ms	נתן	678		give,set
	רשתה	qal	infc		ירשׁ	439	3fs	possess,inherit
	נפל	qal	ptc	ms	נפל	656		fall
	נודע	niph	pft	3ms	ידע	393		be made known
	הכהו	hiph	pft	3ms	נכה	645	3ms	smite
21:2	יצאו	qal	wcp	3cp	יצא	422		go out
	שׁפטיך	qal	ptc	mp	שׁפט	1047	2ms	judge
	מדדו	qal	wcp	3cp	מדד	551		measure
21:3	היה	qal	wcp	3ms	היה	224		be,become
	לקחו	qal	wcp	3cp	לקח	542		take
	עבד	qalp	pft	3ms	עבד	712		be worked
	משׁכה	qal	pft	3fs	משׁך	604		draw,pull
21:4	הורדו	hiph	wcp	3cp	ירד	432		bring down
21:4	יעבד	niph	impf	3ms	עבד	712		be tilled
	יזרע	niph	impf	3ms	זרע	281		be sown
	ערפו	qal	wcp	3cp	ערף	791		break neck
21:5	נגשׁו	niph	wcp	3cp	נגשׁ	620		draw near
	בחר	qal	pft	3ms	בחר	103		choose
	שׁרתו	piel	infc		שׁרת	1058	3ms	minister,serve
	ברך	piel	infc		ברך	138		bless
	יהיה	qal	impf	3ms	היה	224		be,become
21:6	ירחצו	qal	impf	3mp	רחץ	934		wash,bathe
	ערופה	qal	pptc	fs	ערף	791		break neck
21:7	ענו	qal	wcp	3cp	ענה	772		answer
	אמרו	qal	wcp	3cp	אמר	55		say
	שׁפכהk	qal	pft	3fs	שׁפך	1049		pour out
	שׁפכוq	qal	pft	3cp	שׁפך	1049		pour out
	ראו	qal	pft	3cp	ראה	906		see
21:8	כפר	piel	impv	ms	כפר	497		cover,atone
	פדית	qal	pft	2ms	פדה	804		ransom
	תתן	qal	jusm	2ms	נתן	678		give,set
	נכפר	nith	wcp	3ms	כפר	497?		be covered
21:9	תבער	piel	impf	2ms	בער	128		burn,consume
	תעשׂה	qal	impf	2ms	עשׂה	793		do,make
21:10	תצא	qal	impf	2ms	יצא	422		go out
	איביך	qal	ptc	mp	איב	33	2ms	be hostile to
	נתנו	qal	wcp	3ms	נתן	678	3ms	give,set
	שׁבית	qal	wcp	2ms	שׁבה	985		take captive
21:11	ראית	qal	wcp	2ms	ראה	906		see
	חשׁקת	qal	wcp	2ms	חשׁק	365		love
	לקחת	qal	wcp	2ms	לקח	542		take
21:12	הבאתה	hiph	wcp	2ms	בוא	97	3fs	bring in
	גלחה	piel	wcp	3fs	גלח	164		shave
	עשׂתה	qal	wcp	3fs	עשׂה	793		do,make
21:13	הסירה	hiph	wcp	3fs	סור	693		take away
	ישׁבה	qal	wcp	3fs	ישׁב	442		sit,dwell
	בכתה	qal	wcp	3fs	בכה	113		weep
	תבוא	qal	impf	2ms	בוא	97		come in
	בעלתה	qal	wcp	2ms	בעל	127	3fs	marry,rule over
	היתה	qal	wcp	3fs	היה	224		be,become
21:14	היה	qal	wcp	3ms	היה	224		be,become
	חפצת	qal	pft	2ms	חפץ	342		delight in
	שׁלחתה	piel	wcp	2ms	שׁלח	1018	3fs	send away,shoot
	מכר	qal	infa		מכר	569		sell
	תמכרנה	qal	impf	2ms	מכר	569	3fs	sell
	תתעמר	hith	impf	2ms	עמר	771		deal harshly
	עניתה	piel	pft	2ms	ענה	776	3fs	humble
21:15	תהיין	qal	impf	3fp	היה	224		be,become
	אהובה	qal	pptc	fs	אהב	12		love
	שׂנואה	qal	pptc	fs	שׂנא	971		hate
	ילדו	qal	wcp	3cp	ילד	408		bear,beget
	אהובה	qal	pptc	fs	אהב	12		love
	שׂנואה	qal	pptc	fs	שׂנא	971		hate
	היה	qal	wcp	3ms	היה	224		be,become
21:16	היה	qal	wcp	3ms	היה	224		be,become
	הנחילו	hiph	infc		נחל	635	3ms	c. to inherit
	יהיה	qal	impf	3ms	היה	224		be,become

ChVs	Form	Stem	Tnse	PGN	Root	BDB	Sfx	Meaning
21:16	יוכל	qal	impf	3ms	יכל	407		be able
	בכר	piel	infc		בכר	114		bear 1st fruit
	אהובה	qal	pptc	fs	אהב	12		love
	שׂנואה	qal	pptc	fs	שׂנא	971		hate
21:17	שׂנואה	qal	pptc	fs	שׂנא	971		hate
	יכיר	hiph	impf	3ms	נכר	647		regard,notice
	תת	qal	infc		נתן	678		give,set
	ימצא	niph	impf	3ms	מצא	592		be found
21:18	יהיה	qal	impf	3ms	היה	224		be,become
	סורר	qal	ptc	ms	סרר	710		be stubborn
	מורה	qal	ptc	ms	מרה	598		be disobedient
	שׁמע	qal	ptc	ms	שׁמע	1033		hear
	יסרו	piel	wcp	3cp	יסר	415		correct,chasten
	ישׁמע	qal	impf	3ms	שׁמע	1033		hear
21:19	תפשׂו	qal	wcp	3cp	תפשׂ	1074		seize,grasp
	הוציאו	hiph	wcp	3cp	יצא	422		bring out
21:20	אמרו	qal	wcp	3cp	אמר	55		say
	סורר	qal	ptc	ms	סרר	710		be stubborn
	מרה	qal	ptc	ms	מרה	598		be disobedient
	שׁמע	qal	ptc	ms	שׁמע	1033		hear
	זולל	qal	ptc	ms	זלל	272		be worthless
	סבא	qal	ptc	ms	סבא	684		imbibe
21:21	רגמהו	qal	wcp	3cp	רגם	920	3ms	stone
	מת	qal	wcp	3ms	מות	559		die
	בערת	piel	wcp	2ms	בער	128		burn,consume
	ישׁמעו	qal	impf	3mp	שׁמע	1033		hear
	יראו	qal	impf	3mp	ירא	431		fear
21:22	יהיה	qal	impf	3ms	היה	224		be,become
	הומת	hoph	wcp	3ms	מות	559		be killed
	תלית	qal	wcp	2ms	תלה	1067		hang
21:23	תלין	qal	impf	2ms	לון	533		lodge,remain
	קבור	qal	infa		קבר	868		bury
	תקברנו	qal	impf	2ms	קבר	868	3ms	bury
	תלוי	qal	pptc	ms	תלה	1067		hang
	תטמא	piel	impf	2ms	טמא	379		defile
	נתן	qal	ptc	ms	נתן	678		give,set
22:1	תראה	qal	impf	2ms	ראה	906		see
	נדחים	niph	ptc	mp	נדח	623		be banished
	התעלמת	hith	wcp	2ms	עלם	761		hide oneself
	השׁב	hiph	infa		שׁוב	996		bring back
	תשׁיבם	hiph	impf	2ms	שׁוב	996	3mp	bring back
22:2	ידעתו	qal	pft	2ms	ידע	393	3ms	know
	אספתו	qal	wcp	2ms	אסף	62	3ms	gather
	היה	qal	wcp	3ms	היה	224		be,become
	דרשׁ	qal	infc		דרשׁ	205		resort to,seek
	השׁבתו	hiph	wcp	2ms	שׁוב	996	3ms	bring back
22:3	תעשׂה	qal	impf	2ms	עשׂה	793		do,make
	תעשׂה	qal	impf	2ms	עשׂה	793		do,make
	תעשׂה	qal	impf	2ms	עשׂה	793		do,make
	תאבד	qal	impf	3fs	אבד	1		perish
	מצאתה	qal	wcp	2ms	מצא	592	3fs	find
	תוכל	qal	impf	2ms	יכל	407		be able
	התעלם	hith	infc		עלם	761		hide oneself
22:4	תראה	qal	impf	2ms	ראה	906		see
22:4	נפלים	qal	ptc	mp	נפל	656		fall
	התעלמת	hith	wcp	2ms	עלם	761		hide oneself
	הקם	hiph	infa		קום	877		raise,build,set
	תקים	hiph	impf	2ms	קום	877		raise,build,set
22:5	יהיה	qal	impf	3ms	היה	224		be,become
	ילבשׁ	qal	impf	3ms	לבשׁ	527		put on,clothe
	עשׂה	qal	ptc	ms	עשׂה	793		do,make
22:6	יקרא	niph	impf	3ms	קרא	896		meet
	רבצת	qal	ptc	fs	רבץ	918		lie down
	תקח	qal	impf	2ms	לקח	542		take
22:7	שׁלח	piel	infa		שׁלח	1018		send away,shoot
	תשׁלח	piel	impf	2ms	שׁלח	1018		send away,shoot
	תקח	qal	impf	2ms	לקח	542		take
	ייטב	qal	impf	3ms	יטב	405		be good
	הארכת	hiph	wcp	2ms	ארך	73		prolong
22:8	תבנה	qal	impf	2ms	בנה	124		build
	עשׂית	qal	wcp	2ms	עשׂה	793		do,make
	תשׂים	qal	impf	2ms	שׂים	962		put,set
	יפל	qal	impf	3ms	נפל	656		fall
	נפל	qal	ptc	ms	נפל	656		fall
22:9	תזרע	qal	impf	2ms	זרע	281		sow
	תקדשׁ	qal	impf	3fs	קדשׁ	872		be set apart
	תזרע	qal	impf	2ms	זרע	281		sow
22:10	תחרשׁ	qal	impf	2ms	חרשׁ	360		engrave,plough
22:11	תלבשׁ	qal	impf	2ms	לבשׁ	527		put on,clothe
22:12	תעשׂה	qal	impf	2ms	עשׂה	793		do,make
	תכסה	piel	impf	2ms	כסה	491		cover
22:13	יקח	qal	impf	3ms	לקח	542		take
	בא	qal	wcp	3ms	בוא	97		come in
	שׂנאה	qal	wcp	3ms	שׂנא	971	3fs	hate
22:14	שׂם	qal	wcp	3ms	שׂים	962		put,set
	הוציא	hiph	wcp	3ms	יצא	422		bring out
	אמר	qal	wcp	3ms	אמר	55		say
	לקחתי	qal	pft	1cs	לקח	542		take
	אקרב	qal	wci	1cs	קרב	897		approach
	מצאתי	qal	pft	1cs	מצא	592		find
22:15	לקח	qal	wcp	3ms	לקח	542		take
	הוציאו	hiph	wcp	3cp	יצא	422		bring out
22:16	אמר	qal	wcp	3ms	אמר	55		say
	נתתי	qal	pft	1cs	נתן	678		give,set
	ישׂנאה	qal	wci	3ms	שׂנא	971	3fs	hate
22:17	שׂם	qal	pft	3ms	שׂים	962		put,set
	אמר	qal	infc		אמר	55		say
	מצאתי	qal	pft	1cs	מצא	592		find
	פרשׂו	qal	wcp	3cp	פרשׂ	831		spread out
22:18	לקחו	qal	wcp	3cp	לקח	542		take
	יסרו	piel	wcp	3cp	יסר	415		correct,chasten
22:19	ענשׁו	qal	wcp	3cp	ענשׁ	778		punish,fine
	נתנו	qal	wcp	3cp	נתן	678		give,set
	הוציא	hiph	pft	3ms	יצא	422		bring out
	תהיה	qal	impf	3fs	היה	224		be,become
	יוכל	qal	impf	3ms	יכל	407		be able
	שׁלחה	piel	infc		שׁלח	1018	3fs	send away,shoot
22:20	היה	qal	pft	3ms	היה	224		be,become

ChVs	Form	Stem	Tnse	PGN	Root	BDB	Sfx	Meaning
22:20	נמצאו	niph	pft	3cp	מצא	592		be found
22:21	הוציאו	hiph	wcp	3cp	יצא	422		bring out
	סקלוה	qal	wcp	3cp	סקל	709	3fs	stone to death
	מתה	qal	wcp	3fs	מות	559		die
	עשׂתה	qal	pft	3fs	עשׂה	793		do,make
	זנות	qal	infc		זנה	275		act a harlot
	בערת	piel	wcp	2ms	בער	128		burn,consume
22:22	ימצא	niph	impf	3ms	מצא	592		be found
	שׁכב	qal	ptc	ms	שׁכב	1011		lie,lie down
	בעלת	qal	pptc	fs	בעל	127		marry,rule over
	מתו	qal	wcp	3cp	מות	559		die
	שׁכב	qal	ptc	ms	שׁכב	1011		lie,lie down
	בערת	piel	wcp	2ms	בער	128		burn,consume
22:23	יהיה	qal	impf	3ms	היה	224		be,become
	מארשׂה	pual	ptc	fs	ארשׂ	76		be betrothed
	מצאה	qal	wcp	3ms	מצא	592	3fs	find
	שׁכב	qal	wcp	3ms	שׁכב	1011		lie,lie down
22:24	הוצאתם	hiph	wcp	2mp	יצא	422		bring out
	סקלתם	qal	wcp	2mp	סקל	709		stone to death
	מתו	qal	wcp	3cp	מות	559		die
	צעקה	qal	pft	3fs	צעק	858		cry out
	ענה	piel	pft	3ms	ענה	776		humble
	בערת	piel	wcp	2ms	בער	128		burn,consume
22:25	ימצא	qal	impf	3ms	מצא	592		find
	מארשׂה	pual	ptc	fs	ארשׂ	76		be betrothed
	החזיק	hiph	wcp	3ms	חזק	304		make firm,seize
	שׁכב	qal	wcp	3ms	שׁכב	1011		lie,lie down
	מת	qal	wcp	3ms	מות	559		die
	שׁכב	qal	pft	3ms	שׁכב	1011		lie,lie down
22:26	תעשׂה	qal	impf	2ms	עשׂה	793		do,make
	יקום	qal	impf	3ms	קום	877		arise,stand
	רצחו	qal	wcp	3ms	רצח	953	3ms	murder,slay
22:27	מצאה	qal	pft	3ms	מצא	592	3fs	find
	צעקה	qal	pft	3fs	צעק	858		cry out
	מארשׂה	pual	ptc	fs	ארשׂ	76		be betrothed
	מושׁיע	hiph	ptc	ms	ישׁע	446		deliver,save
22:28	ימצא	qal	impf	3ms	מצא	592		find
	ארשׂה	pual	pft	3fs	ארשׂ	76		be betrothed
	תפשׂה	qal	wcp	3ms	תפשׂ	1074	3fs	seize,grasp
	שׁכב	qal	wcp	3ms	שׁכב	1011		lie,lie down
	נמצאו	niph	wcp	3cp	מצא	592		be found
22:29	נתן	qal	wcp	3ms	נתן	678		give,set
	שׁכב	qal	ptc	ms	שׁכב	1011		lie,lie down
	תהיה	qal	impf	3fs	היה	224		be,become
	ענה	piel	pft	3ms	ענה	776	3fs	humble
	יוכל	qal	impf	3ms	יכל	407		be able
	שׁלחה	piel	infc		שׁלח	1018	3fs	send away,shoot
23:1	יקח	qal	impf	3ms	לקח	542		take
	יגלה	piel	impf	3ms	גלה	162		uncover
23:2	יבא	qal	impf	3ms	בוא	97		come in
	פצוע	qal	pptc	ms	פצע	822		bruise
	כרות	qal	pptc	ms	כרת	503		cut,destroy
23:3	יבא	qal	impf	3ms	בוא	97		come in
	יבא	qal	impf	3ms	בוא	97		come in
23:4	יבא	qal	impf	3ms	בוא	97		come in
	יבא	qal	impf	3ms	בוא	97		come in
23:5	קדמו	piel	pft	3cp	קדם	869		meet,confront
	צאתכם	qal	infc		יצא	422	2mp	go out
	שׂכר	qal	pft	3ms	שׂכר	968		hire
	קללך	piel	infc		קלל	886	2ms	curse
23:6	אבה	qal	pft	3ms	אבה	2		be willing
	שׁמע	qal	infc		שׁמע	1033		hear
	יהפך	qal	wci	3ms	הפך	245		turn,overturn
	אהבך	qal	pft	3ms	אהב	12	2ms	love
23:7	תדרשׁ	qal	impf	2ms	דרשׁ	205		resort to,seek
23:8	תתעב	piel	impf	2ms	תעב	1073		abhor
	תתעב	piel	impf	2ms	תעב	1073		abhor
	היית	qal	pft	2ms	היה	224		be,become
23:9	יולדו	niph	impf	3mp	ילד	408		be born
	יבא	qal	impf	3ms	בוא	97		come in
23:10	תצא	qal	impf	2ms	יצא	422		go out
	איביך	qal	ptc	mp	איב	33	2ms	be hostile to
	נשׁמרת	niph	wcp	2ms	שׁמר	1036		be kept,guarded
23:11	יהיה	qal	impf	3ms	היה	224		be,become
	יהיה	qal	impf	3ms	היה	224		be,become
	יצא	qal	wcp	3ms	יצא	422		go out
	יבא	qal	impf	3ms	בוא	97		come in
23:12	היה	qal	wcp	3ms	היה	224		be,become
	פנות	qal	infc		פנה	815		turn
	ירחץ	qal	impf	3ms	רחץ	934		wash,bathe
	בא	qal	infc		בוא	97		come in
	יבא	qal	impf	3ms	בוא	97		come in
23:13	תהיה	qal	impf	3fs	היה	224		be,become
	יצאת	qal	wcp	2ms	יצא	422		go out
23:14	תהיה	qal	impf	3fs	היה	224		be,become
	היה	qal	wcp	3ms	היה	224		be,become
	שׁבתך	qal	infc		ישׁב	442	2ms	sit,dwell
	חפרתה	qal	wcp	2ms	חפר	343		dig,search
	שׁבת	qal	wcp	2ms	שׁוב	996		turn,return
	כסית	piel	wcp	2ms	כסה	491		cover
23:15	מתהלך	hith	ptc	ms	הלך	229		walk to and fro
	הצילך	hiph	infc		נצל	664	2ms	snatch,deliver
	תת	qal	infc		נתן	678		give,set
	איביך	qal	ptc	mp	איב	33	2ms	be hostile to
	היה	qal	wcp	3ms	היה	224		be,become
	יראה	qal	impf	3ms	ראה	906		see
	שׁב	qal	wcp	3ms	שׁוב	996		turn,return
23:16	תסגיר	hiph	impf	2ms	סגר	688		shut up,deliver
	ינצל	niph	impf	3ms	נצל	664		be delivered
23:17	ישׁב	qal	jusm	3ms	ישׁב	442		sit,dwell
	יבחר	qal	impf	3ms	בחר	103		choose
	תוננו	hiph	impf	2ms	ינה	413	3ms	oppress
23:18	תהיה	qal	impf	3fs	היה	224		be,become
	יהיה	qal	impf	3ms	היה	224		be,become
23:19	תביא	hiph	impf	2ms	בוא	97		bring in
	זונה	qal	ptc	fs	זנה	275		act a harlot
23:20	תשׁיך	hiph	impf	2ms	נשׁך	675		lend w/interest
	ישׁך	qal	impf	3ms	נשׁך	675		give interest

ChVs	Form	Stem	Tnse	PGN	Root	BDB	Sfx	Meaning
23:21	תשיך	hiph	impf	2ms	נשך	675		lend w/interest
	תשיך	hiph	impf	2ms	נשך	675		lend w/interest
	יברכך	piel	impf	3ms	ברך	138	2ms	bless
	בא	qal	ptc	ms	בוא	97		come in
	רשתה	qal	infc		ירש	439	3fs	possess,inherit
23:22	תדר	qal	impf	2ms	נדר	623		vow
	תאחר	piel	impf	2ms	אחר	29		tarry,hinder
	שלמו	piel	infc		שלם	1022	3ms	finish,reward
	דרש	qal	infa		דרש	205		resort to,seek
	ידרשנו	qal	impf	3ms	דרש	205	3ms	resort to,seek
	היה	qal	wcp	3ms	היה	224		be,become
23:23	תחדל	qal	impf	2ms	חדל	292		cease
	נדר	qal	infc		נדר	623		vow
	יהיה	qal	impf	3ms	היה	224		be,become
23:24	תשמר	qal	impf	2ms	שמר	1036		keep,watch
	עשית	qal	wcp	2ms	עשה	793		do,make
	נדרת	qal	pft	2ms	נדר	623		vow
	דברת	piel	pft	2ms	דבר	180		speak
23:25	תבא	qal	impf	2ms	בוא	97		come in
	אכלת	qal	wcp	2ms	אכל	37		eat,devour
	תתן	qal	impf	2ms	נתן	678		give,set
23:26	תבא	qal	impf	2ms	בוא	97		come in
	קטפת	qal	wcp	2ms	קטף	882		pluck off
	תניף	hiph	impf	2ms	נוף	631		swing,wave
24:1	יקח	qal	impf	3ms	לקח	542		take
	בעלה	qal	wcp	3ms	בעל	127	3fs	marry,rule over
	היה	qal	wcp	3ms	היה	224		be,become
	תמצא	qal	impf	3fs	מצא	592		find
	מצא	qal	pft	3ms	מצא	592		find
	כתב	qal	wcp	3ms	כתב	507		write
	נתן	qal	wcp	3ms	נתן	678		give,set
	שלחה	piel	wcp	3ms	שלח	1018	3fs	send away,shoot
24:2	יצאה	qal	wcp	3fs	יצא	422		go out
	הלכה	qal	wcp	3fs	הלך	229		walk,go
	היתה	qal	wcp	3fs	היה	224		be,become
24:3	שנאה	qal	wcp	3ms	שנא	971	3fs	hate
	כתב	qal	wcp	3ms	כתב	507		write
	נתן	qal	wcp	3ms	נתן	678		give,set
	שלחה	piel	wcp	3ms	שלח	1018	3fs	send away,shoot
	ימות	qal	impf	3ms	מות	559		die
	לקחה	qal	pft	3ms	לקח	542	3fs	take
24:4	יוכל	qal	impf	3ms	יכל	407		be able
	שלחה	piel	pft	3ms	שלח	1018	3fs	send away,shoot
	שוב	qal	infc		שוב	996		turn,return
	קחתה	qal	infc		לקח	542	3fs	take
	היות	qal	infc		היה	224		be,become
	הטמאה	hoth	pft	3fs	טמא	379		be defiled
	תחטיא	hiph	impf	2ms	חטא	306		cause to sin
	נתן	qal	ptc	ms	נתן	678		give,set
24:5	יקח	qal	impf	3ms	לקח	542		take
	יצא	qal	impf	3ms	יצא	422		go out
	יעבר	qal	impf	3ms	עבר	716		pass over
	יהיה	qal	impf	3ms	היה	224		be,become
	שמח	piel	wcp	3ms	שמח	970		gladden
24:5	לקח	qal	pft	3ms	לקח	542		take
24:6	יחבל	qal	impf	3ms	חבל	286		bind
	חבל	qal	ptc	ms	חבל	286		bind
24:7	ימצא	niph	impf	3ms	מצא	592		be found
	גנב	qal	ptc	ms	גנב	170		steal
	התעמר	hith	wcp	3ms	עמר	771		deal harshly
	מכרו	qal	wcp	3ms	מכר	569	3ms	sell
	מת	qal	wcp	3ms	מות	559		die
	בערת	piel	wcp	2ms	בער	128		burn,consume
24:8	השמר	niph	impv	ms	שמר	1036		be kept,guarded
	שמר	qal	infc		שמר	1036		keep,watch
	עשות	qal	infc		עשה	793		do,make
	יורו	hiph	impf	3mp	ירה	434		shoot,teach
	צויתם	piel	pft	1cs	צוה	845	3mp	command
	תשמרו	qal	impf	2mp	שמר	1036		keep,watch
	עשות	qal	infc		עשה	793		do,make
24:9	זכור	qal	infa		זכר	269		remember
	עשה	qal	pft	3ms	עשה	793		do,make
	צאתכם	qal	infc		יצא	422	2mp	go out
24:10	תשה	hiph	impf	2ms	נשה	674		lend
	תבא	qal	impf	2ms	בוא	97		come in
	עבט	qal	infc		עבט	716		give a pledge
24:11	תעמד	qal	impf	2ms	עמד	763		stand,stop
	נשה	qal	ptc	ms	נשה	674		lend
	יוציא	hiph	impf	3ms	יצא	422		bring out
24:12	תשכב	qal	impf	2ms	שכב	1011		lie,lie down
24:13	השב	hiph	infa		שוב	996		bring back
	תשיב	hiph	impf	2ms	שוב	996		bring back
	בא	qal	infc		בוא	97		come in
	שכב	qal	wcp	3ms	שכב	1011		lie,lie down
	ברכך	piel	wcp	3ms	ברך	138	2ms	bless
	תהיה	qal	impf	3fs	היה	224		be,become
24:14	תעשק	qal	impf	2ms	עשק	798		oppress,extort
24:15	תתן	qal	impf	2ms	נתן	678		give,set
	תבוא	qal	impf	3fs	בוא	97		come in
	נשא	qal	ptc	ms	נשא	669		lift,carry
	יקרא	qal	impf	3ms	קרא	894		call,proclaim
	היה	qal	wcp	3ms	היה	224		be,become
24:16	יומתו	hoph	impf	3mp	מות	559		be killed
	יומתו	hoph	impf	3mp	מות	559		be killed
	יומתו	hoph	impf	3mp	מות	559		be killed
24:17	תטה	hiph	impf	2ms	נטה	639		turn,incline
	תחבל	qal	impf	2ms	חבל	286		bind
24:18	זכרת	qal	wcp	2ms	זכר	269		remember
	היית	qal	pft	2ms	היה	224		be,become
	יפדך	qal	wci	3ms	פדה	804	2ms	ransom
	מצוך	piel	ptc	ms	צוה	845	2ms	command
	עשות	qal	infc		עשה	793		do,make
24:19	תקצר	qal	impf	2ms	קצר	894		reap,harvest
	שכחת	qal	wcp	2ms	שכח	1013		forget
	תשוב	qal	impf	2ms	שוב	996		turn,return
	קחתו	qal	infc		לקח	542	3ms	take
	יהיה	qal	impf	3ms	היה	224		be,become
	יברכך	piel	impf	3ms	ברך	138	2ms	bless

ChVs	Form	Stem	Tnse	PGN	Root	BDB	Sfx	Meaning
24:20	תחבט	qal	impf	2ms	חבט	286		beat out
	תפאר	piel	impf	2ms	פאר	802		go over boughs
	יהיה	qal	impf	3ms	היה	224		be,become
24:21	תבצר	qal	impf	2ms	בצר	130		cut off
	תעולל	poel	impf	2ms	עלל	760		glean
	יהיה	qal	impf	3ms	היה	224		be,become
24:22	זכרת	qal	wcp	2ms	זכר	269		remember
	היית	qal	pft	2ms	היה	224		be,become
	מצוך	piel	ptc	ms	צוה	845	2ms	command
	עשות	qal	infc		עשה	793		do,make
25:1	יהיה	qal	impf	3ms	היה	224		be,become
	נגשו	niph	wcp	3cp	נגש	620		draw near
	שפטום	qal	wcp	3cp	שפט	1047	3mp	judge
	הצדיקו	hiph	wcp	3cp	צדק	842		make righteous
	הרשיעו	hiph	wcp	3cp	רשע	957		condemn, be evil
25:2	היה	qal	wcp	3ms	היה	224		be,become
	הכות	hiph	infc		נכה	645		smite
	הפילו	hiph	wcp	3ms	נפל	656	3ms	cause to fall
	שפט	qal	ptc	ms	שפט	1047		judge
	הכהו	hiph	wcp	3ms	נכה	645	3ms	smite
25:3	יכנו	hiph	impf	3ms	נכה	645	3ms	smite
	יסיף	hiph	impf	3ms	יסף	414		add,do again
	יסיף	hiph	impf	3ms	יסף	414		add,do again
	הכתו	hiph	infc		נכה	645	3ms	smite
	נקלה	niph	wcp	3ms	קלה	885		be dishonored
25:4	תחסם	qal	impf	2ms	חסם	340		muzzle
	דישו	qal	infc		דוש	190	3ms	tread
25:5	ישבו	qal	impf	3mp	ישב	442		sit,dwell
	מת	qal	wcp	3ms	מות	559		die
	תהיה	qal	impf	3fs	היה	224		be,become
	מת	qal	ptc	ms	מות	559		die
	יבא	qal	impf	3ms	בוא	97		come in
	לקחה	qal	wcp	3ms	לקח	542	3fs	take
	יבמה	piel	wcp	3ms	יבם	386	3fs	be levirate
25:6	היה	qal	wcp	3ms	היה	224		be,become
	תלד	qal	impf	3fs	ילד	408		bear,beget
	יקום	qal	impf	3ms	קום	877		arise,stand
	מת	qal	ptc	ms	מות	559		die
	ימחה	niph	impf	3ms	מחה	562		be wiped out
25:7	יחפץ	qal	impf	3ms	חפץ	342		delight in
	קחת	qal	infc		לקח	542		take
	עלתה	qal	wcp	3fs	עלה	748		go up
	אמרה	qal	wcp	3fs	אמר	55		say
	מאין	piel	pft	3ms	מאן	549		refuse
	הקים	hiph	infc		קום	877		raise,build,set
	אבה	qal	pft	3ms	אבה	2		be willing
	יבמי	piel	infc		יבם	386	1cs	be levirate
25:8	קראו	qal	wcp	3cp	קרא	894		call,proclaim
	דברו	piel	wcp	3cp	דבר	180		speak
	עמד	qal	wcp	3ms	עמד	763		stand,stop
	אמר	qal	wcp	3ms	אמר	55		say
	חפצתי	qal	pft	1cs	חפץ	342		delight in
	קחתה	qal	infc		לקח	542	3fs	take
25:9	נגשה	niph	wcp	3fs	נגש	620		draw near
25:9	חלצה	qal	wcp	3fs	חלץ	322		draw off
	ירקה	qal	wcp	3fs	ירק	439		spit
	ענתה	qal	wcp	3fs	ענה	772		answer
	אמרה	qal	wcp	3fs	אמר	55		say
	יעשה	niph	impf	3ms	עשה	793		be done
	יבנה	qal	impf	3ms	בנה	124		build
25:10	נקרא	niph	wcp	3ms	קרא	894		be called
	חלוץ	qal	pptc	ms	חלץ	322		draw off
25:11	ינצו	niph	impf	3mp	נצה	663		struggle
	קרבה	qal	wcp	3fs	קרב	897		approach
	הציל	hiph	infc		נצל	664		snatch,deliver
	מכהו	hiph	ptc	ms	נכה	645	3ms	smite
	שלחה	qal	wcp	3fs	שלח	1018		send
	החזיקה	hiph	wcp	3fs	חזק	304		make firm,seize
25:12	קצתה	qal	wcp	2ms	קצץ	893		cut off
	תחוס	qal	jusf	3fs	חוס	299?		pity
25:13	יהיה	qal	impf	3ms	היה	224		be,become
25:14	יהיה	qal	impf	3ms	היה	224		be,become
25:15	יהיה	qal	impf	3ms	היה	224		be,become
	יהיה	qal	impf	3ms	היה	224		be,become
	יאריכו	hiph	impf	3mp	ארך	73		prolong
	נתן	qal	ptc	ms	נתן	678		give,set
25:16	עשה	qal	ptc	ms	עשה	793		do,make
	עשה	qal	ptc	ms	עשה	793		do,make
25:17	זכור	qal	infa		זכר	269		remember
	עשה	qal	pft	3ms	עשה	793		do,make
	צאתכם	qal	infc		יצא	422	2mp	go out
25:18	קרך	qal	pft	3ms	קרה	899	2ms	encounter,meet
	יזנב	piel	wci	3ms	זנב	275		cut off,smite
	נחשלים	niph	ptc	mp	חשל	365		be shattered
	ירא	qal	pft	3ms	ירא	431		fear
25:19	היה	qal	wcp	3ms	היה	224		be,become
	הניח	hiph	infc		נוח	628		give rest,put
	איביך	qal	ptc	mp	איב	33	2ms	be hostile to
	נתן	qal	ptc	ms	נתן	678		give,set
	רשתה	qal	infc		ירש	439	3fs	possess,inherit
	תמחה	qal	impf	2ms	מחה	562		wipe, blot out
	תשכח	qal	impf	2ms	שכח	1013		forget
26:1	היה	qal	wcp	3ms	היה	224		be,become
	תבוא	qal	impf	2ms	בוא	97		come in
	נתן	qal	ptc	ms	נתן	678		give,set
	ירשתה	qal	wcp	2ms	ירש	439	3fs	possess,inherit
	ישבת	qal	wcp	2ms	ישב	442		sit,dwell
26:2	לקחת	qal	wcp	2ms	לקח	542		take
	תביא	hiph	impf	2ms	בוא	97		bring in
	נתן	qal	ptc	ms	נתן	678		give,set
	שמת	qal	wcp	2ms	שים	962		put,set
	הלכת	qal	wcp	2ms	הלך	229		walk,go
	יבחר	qal	impf	3ms	בחר	103		choose
	שכן	piel	infc		שכן	1014		establish
26:3	באת	qal	wcp	2ms	בוא	97		come in
	יהיה	qal	impf	3ms	היה	224		be,become
	אמרת	qal	wcp	2ms	אמר	55		say
	הגדתי	hiph	pft	1cs	נגד	616		declare,tell

ChVs	Form	Stem	Tnse	PGN	Root	BDB	Sfx	Meaning
26:3	באתי	qal	pft	1cs	בוא	97		come in
	נשבע	niph	pft	3ms	שבע	989		swear
	תת	qal	infc		נתן	678		give,set
26:4	לקח	qal	wcp	3ms	לקח	542		take
	הניחו	hiph	wcp	3ms	נוח	628	3ms	give rest,put
26:5	ענית	qal	wcp	2ms	ענה	772		answer
	אמרת	qal	wcp	2ms	אמר	55		say
	אבד	qal	ptc	ms	אבד	1		perish
	ירד	qal	wci	3ms	ירד	432		come down
	יגר	qal	wci	3ms	גור	157		sojourn
	יהי	qal	wci	3ms	היה	224		be,become
26:6	ירעו	hiph	wci	3mp	רעע	949		hurt,do evil
	יענונו	piel	wci	3mp	ענה	776	1cp	humble
	יתנו	qal	wci	3mp	נתן	678		give,set
26:7	נצעק	qal	wci	1cp	צעק	858		cry out
	ישׁמע	qal	wci	3ms	שׁמע	1033		hear
	ירא	qal	wci	3ms	ראה	906		see
26:8	יוצאנו	hiph	wci	3ms	יצא	422	1cp	bring out
	נטויה	qal	pptc	fs	נטה	639		stretch,incline
26:9	יבאנו	hiph	wci	3ms	בוא	97	1cp	bring in
	יתן	qal	wci	3ms	נתן	678		give,set
	זבת	qal	ptc	fs	זוב	264		flow,gush
26:10	הבאתי	hiph	pft	1cs	בוא	97		bring in
	נתתה	qal	pft	2ms	נתן	678		give,set
	הנחתו	hiph	wcp	2ms	נוח	628	3ms	give rest,put
	השתחוית	hish	wcp	2ms	חוה	1005		bow down
26:11	שׂמחת	qal	wcp	2ms	שׂמח	970		rejoice
	נתן	qal	pft	3ms	נתן	678		give,set
26:12	תכלה	piel	impf	2ms	כלה	477		complete,finish
	עשׂר	hiph	infc		עשׂר	797		take tithe
	נתתה	qal	wcp	2ms	נתן	678		give,set
	אכלו	qal	wcp	3cp	אכל	37		eat,devour
	שׂבעו	qal	wcp	3cp	שׂבע	959		be sated
26:13	אמרת	qal	wcp	2ms	אמר	55		say
	בערתי	piel	pft	1cs	בער	128		burn,consume
	נתתיו	qal	pft	1cs	נתן	678	3ms	give,set
	צויתני	piel	pft	2ms	צוה	845	1cs	command
	עברתי	qal	pft	1cs	עבר	716		pass over
	שׁכחתי	qal	pft	1cs	שׁכח	1013		forget
26:14	אכלתי	qal	pft	1cs	אכל	37		eat,devour
	בערתי	piel	pft	1cs	בער	128		burn,consume
	נתתי	qal	pft	1cs	נתן	678		give,set
	מת	qal	ptc	ms	מות	559		die
	שׁמעתי	qal	pft	1cs	שׁמע	1033		hear
	עשׂיתי	qal	pft	1cs	עשׂה	793		do,make
	צויתני	piel	pft	2ms	צוה	845	1cs	command
26:15	השקיפה	hiph	impv	ms	שקף	1054		look down
	ברך	piel	impv	ms	ברך	138		bless
	נתתה	qal	pft	2ms	נתן	678		give,set
	נשבעת	niph	pft	2ms	שבע	989		swear
	זבת	qal	ptc	fs	זוב	264		flow,gush
26:16	מצוך	piel	ptc	ms	צוה	845	2ms	command
	עשׂות	qal	infc		עשׂה	793		do,make
	שׁמרת	qal	wcp	2ms	שׁמר	1036		keep,watch
26:16	עשׂית	qal	wcp	2ms	עשׂה	793		do,make
26:17	האמרת	hiph	pft	2ms	אמר	55		avow
	היות	qal	infc		היה	224		be,become
	לכת	qal	infc		הלך	229		walk,go
	שׁמר	qal	infc		שׁמר	1036		keep,watch
	שׁמע	qal	infc		שׁמע	1033		hear
26:18	האמירך	hiph	pft	3ms	אמר	55	2ms	avow
	היות	qal	infc		היה	224		be,become
	דבר	piel	pft	3ms	דבר	180		speak
	שׁמר	qal	infc		שׁמר	1036		keep,watch
26:19	תתך	qal	infc		נתן	678	2ms	give,set
	עשׂה	qal	pft	3ms	עשׂה	793		do,make
	היתך	qal	infc		היה	224	2ms	be,become
	דבר	piel	pft	3ms	דבר	180		speak
27:1	יצו	piel	wci	3ms	צוה	845		command
	אמר	qal	infc		אמר	55		say
	שׁמר	qal	infa		שׁמר	1036		keep,watch
	מצוה	piel	ptc	ms	צוה	845		command
27:2	היה	qal	wcp	3ms	היה	224		be,become
	תעברו	qal	impf	2mp	עבר	716		pass over
	נתן	qal	ptc	ms	נתן	678		give,set
	הקמת	hiph	wcp	2ms	קום	877		raise,build,set
	שׂדת	qal	wcp	2ms	שׂיד	966		whitewash
27:3	כתבת	qal	wcp	2ms	כתב	507		write
	עברך	qal	infc		עבר	716	2ms	pass over
	תבא	qal	impf	2ms	בוא	97		come in
	נתן	qal	ptc	ms	נתן	678		give,set
	זבת	qal	ptc	fs	זוב	264		flow,gush
	דבר	piel	pft	3ms	דבר	180		speak
27:4	היה	qal	wcp	3ms	היה	224		be,become
	עברכם	qal	infc		עבר	716	2mp	pass over
	תקימו	hiph	impf	2mp	קום	877		raise,build,set
	מצוה	piel	ptc	ms	צוה	845		command
	שׂדת	qal	wcp	2ms	שׂיד	966		whitewash
27:5	בנית	qal	wcp	2ms	בנה	124		build
	תניף	hiph	impf	2ms	נוף	631		swing,wave
27:6	תבנה	qal	impf	2ms	בנה	124		build
	העלית	hiph	wcp	2ms	עלה	748		bring up,offer
27:7	זבחת	qal	wcp	2ms	זבח	256		slaughter
	אכלת	qal	wcp	2ms	אכל	37		eat,devour
	שׂמחת	qal	wcp	2ms	שׂמח	970		rejoice
27:8	כתבת	qal	wcp	2ms	כתב	507		write
	באר	piel	infa		באר	91		make plain
	היטב	hiph	infa		יטב	405		do good
27:9	ידבר	piel	wci	3ms	דבר	180		speak
	אמר	qal	infc		אמר	55		say
	הסכת	hiph	impv	ms	סכת	698		keep silence
	שׁמע	qal	impv	ms	שׁמע	1033		hear
	נהיית	niph	pft	2ms	היה	224		be done
27:10	שׁמעת	qal	wcp	2ms	שׁמע	1033		hear
	עשׂית	qal	wcp	2ms	עשׂה	793		do,make
	מצוך	piel	ptc	ms	צוה	845	2ms	command
27:11	יצו	piel	wci	3ms	צוה	845		command
	אמר	qal	infc		אמר	55		say

ChVs	Form	Stem	Tnse	PGN	Root	BDB	Sfx	Meaning
27: 12	יעמדו	qal	impf	3mp	עמד	763		stand,stop
	ברך	piel	infc		ברך	138		bless
	עברכם	qal	infc		עבר	716	2mp	pass over
27: 13	יעמדו	qal	impf	3mp	עמד	763		stand,stop
27: 14	ענו	qal	wcp	3cp	ענה	772		answer
	אמרו	qal	wcp	3cp	אמר	55		say
	רם	qal	ptc	ms	רום	926		be high
27: 15	ארור	qal	pptc	ms	ארר	76		curse
	יעשׂה	qal	impf	3ms	עשׂה	793		do,make
	שׂם	qal	wcp	3ms	שׂים	962		put,set
	ענו	qal	wcp	3cp	ענה	772		answer
	אמרו	qal	wcp	3cp	אמר	55		say
27: 16	ארור	qal	pptc	ms	ארר	76		curse
	מקלה	hiph	ptc	ms	קלה	885		dishonor
	אמר	qal	wcp	3ms	אמר	55		say
27: 17	ארור	qal	pptc	ms	ארר	76		curse
	מסיג	hiph	ptc	ms	סוג	690		displace
	אמר	qal	wcp	3ms	אמר	55		say
27: 18	ארור	qal	pptc	ms	ארר	76		curse
	משׁגה	hiph	ptc	ms	שׁגה	993		lead astray
	אמר	qal	wcp	3ms	אמר	55		say
27: 19	ארור	qal	pptc	ms	ארר	76		curse
	מטה	hiph	ptc	ms	נטה	639		turn,incline
	אמר	qal	wcp	3ms	אמר	55		say
27: 20	ארור	qal	pptc	ms	ארר	76		curse
	שׁכב	qal	ptc	ms	שׁכב	1011		lie,lie down
	גלה	piel	pft	3ms	גלה	162		uncover
	אמר	qal	wcp	3ms	אמר	55		say
27: 21	ארור	qal	pptc	ms	ארר	76		curse
	שׁכב	qal	ptc	ms	שׁכב	1011		lie,lie down
	אמר	qal	wcp	3ms	אמר	55		say
27: 22	ארור	qal	pptc	ms	ארר	76		curse
	שׁכב	qal	ptc	ms	שׁכב	1011		lie,lie down
	אמר	qal	wcp	3ms	אמר	55		say
27: 23	ארור	qal	pptc	ms	ארר	76		curse
	שׁכב	qal	ptc	ms	שׁכב	1011		lie,lie down
	אמר	qal	wcp	3ms	אמר	55		say
27: 24	ארור	qal	pptc	ms	ארר	76		curse
	מכה	hiph	ptc	ms	נכה	645		smite
	אמר	qal	wcp	3ms	אמר	55		say
27: 25	ארור	qal	pptc	ms	ארר	76		curse
	לקח	qal	ptc	ms	לקח	542		take
	הכות	hiph	infc		נכה	645		smite
	אמר	qal	wcp	3ms	אמר	55		say
27: 26	ארור	qal	pptc	ms	ארר	76		curse
	יקים	hiph	impf	3ms	קום	877		raise,build,set
	עשׂות	qal	infc		עשׂה	793		do,make
	אמר	qal	wcp	3ms	אמר	55		say
28: 1	היה	qal	wcp	3ms	היה	224		be,become
	שׁמוע	qal	infa		שׁמע	1033		hear
	תשׁמע	qal	impf	2ms	שׁמע	1033		hear
	שׁמר	qal	infc		שׁמר	1036		keep,watch
	עשׂות	qal	infc		עשׂה	793		do,make
	מצוך	piel	ptc	ms	צוה	845	2ms	command
28: 1	נתנך	qal	wcp	3ms	נתן	678	2ms	give,set
28: 2	באו	qal	wcp	3cp	בוא	97		come in
	השׂיגך	hiph	wcp	3cp	נשׂג	673	2ms	reach,overtake
	תשׁמע	qal	impf	2ms	שׁמע	1033		hear
28: 3	ברוך	qal	pptc	ms	ברך	138		kneel,bless
	ברוך	qal	pptc	ms	ברך	138		kneel,bless
28: 4	ברוך	qal	pptc	ms	ברך	138		kneel,bless
28: 5	ברוך	qal	pptc	ms	ברך	138		kneel,bless
28: 6	ברוך	qal	pptc	ms	ברך	138		kneel,bless
	באך	qal	infc		בוא	97	2ms	come in
	ברוך	qal	pptc	ms	ברך	138		kneel,bless
	צאתך	qal	infc		יצא	422	2ms	go out
28: 7	יתן	qal	impf	3ms	נתן	678		give,set
	איביך	qal	ptc	mp	איב	33	2ms	be hostile to
	קמים	qal	ptc	mp	קום	877		arise,stand
	נגפים	niph	ptc	mp	נגף	619		be smitten
	יצאו	qal	impf	3mp	יצא	422		go out
	ינוסו	qal	impf	3mp	נוס	630		flee,escape
28: 8	יצו	piel	jusf	3ms	צוה	845		command
	ברכך	piel	wcp	3ms	ברך	138	2ms	bless
	נתן	qal	ptc	ms	נתן	678		give,set
28: 9	יקימך	hiph	impf	3ms	קום	877	2ms	raise,build,set
	נשׁבע	niph	pft	3ms	שׁבע	989		swear
	תשׁמר	qal	impf	2ms	שׁמר	1036		keep,watch
	הלכת	qal	wcp	2ms	הלך	229		walk,go
28: 10	ראו	qal	wcp	3cp	ראה	906		see
	נקרא	niph	pft	3ms	קרא	894		be called
	יראו	qal	wcp	3cp	ירא	431		fear
28: 11	הותרך	hiph	wcp	3ms	יתר	451	2ms	leave,spare
	נשׁבע	niph	pft	3ms	שׁבע	989		swear
	תת	qal	infc		נתן	678		give,set
28: 12	יפתח	qal	impf	3ms	פתח	834		open
	תת	qal	infc		נתן	678		give,set
	ברך	piel	infc		ברך	138		bless
	הלוית	hiph	wcp	2ms	לוה	531		lend
	תלוה	qal	impf	2ms	לוה	531		borrow
28: 13	נתנך	qal	wcp	3ms	נתן	678	2ms	give,set
	היית	qal	wcp	2ms	היה	224		be,become
	תהיה	qal	impf	2ms	היה	224		be,become
	תשׁמע	qal	impf	2ms	שׁמע	1033		hear
	מצוך	piel	ptc	ms	צוה	845	2ms	command
	שׁמר	qal	infc		שׁמר	1036		keep,watch
	עשׂות	qal	infc		עשׂה	793		do,make
28: 14	תסור	qal	impf	2ms	סור	693		turn aside
	מצוה	piel	ptc	ms	צוה	845		command
	לכת	qal	infc		הלך	229		walk,go
	עבדם	qal	infc		עבד	712	3mp	work,serve
28: 15	היה	qal	wcp	3ms	היה	224		be,become
	תשׁמע	qal	impf	2ms	שׁמע	1033		hear
	שׁמר	qal	infc		שׁמר	1036		keep,watch
	עשׂות	qal	infc		עשׂה	793		do,make
	מצוך	piel	ptc	ms	צוה	845	2ms	command
	באו	qal	wcp	3cp	בוא	97		come in
	השׂיגוך	hiph	wcp	3cp	נשׂג	673	2ms	reach,overtake

ChVs	Form	Stem	Tnse	PGN	Root	BDB	Sfx	Meaning
28:16	ארור	qal	pptc	ms	ארר	76		curse
	ארור	qal	pptc	ms	ארר	76		curse
28:17	ארור	qal	pptc	ms	ארר	76		curse
28:18	ארור	qal	pptc	ms	ארר	76		curse
28:19	ארור	qal	pptc	ms	ארר	76		curse
	באך	qal	infc		בוא	97	2ms	come in
	ארור	qal	pptc	ms	ארר	76		curse
	צאתך	qal	infc		יצא	422	2ms	go out
28:20	ישלח	piel	impf	3ms	שלח	1018		send away,shoot
	תעשה	qal	impf	2ms	עשה	793		do,make
	השמדך	niph	infc		שמד	1029	2ms	be exterminated
	אבדך	qal	infc		אבד	1	2ms	perish
	עזבתני	qal	pft	2ms	עזב	736	1cs	leave,loose
28:21	ידבק	hiph	jusf	3ms	דבק	179		cause to cling
	כלתו	piel	infc		כלה	477	3ms	complete,finish
	בא	qal	ptc	ms	בוא	97		come in
	רשתה	qal	infc		ירש	439	3fs	possess,inherit
28:22	יככה	hiph	impf	3ms	נכה	645	2ms	smite
	רדפוך	qal	wcp	3cp	רדף	922	2ms	pursue
	אבדך	qal	infc		אבד	1	2ms	perish
28:23	היו	qal	wcp	3cp	היה	224		be,become
28:24	יתן	qal	impf	3ms	נתן	678		give,set
	ירד	qal	impf	3ms	ירד	432		come down
	השמדך	niph	infc		שמד	1029	2ms	be exterminated
28:25	יתנך	qal	impf	3ms	נתן	678	2ms	give,set
	נגף	niph	ptc	ms	נגף	619		be smitten
	איביך	qal	ptc	mp	איב	33	2ms	be hostile to
	תצא	qal	impf	2ms	יצא	422		go out
	תנוס	qal	impf	2ms	נוס	630		flee,escape
	היית	qal	wcp	2ms	היה	224		be,become
28:26	היתה	qal	wcp	3fs	היה	224		be,become
	מחריד	hiph	ptc	ms	חרד	353		terrify
28:27	יככה	hiph	impf	3ms	נכה	645	2ms	smite
	תוכל	qal	impf	2ms	יכל	407		be able
	הרפא	niph	infc		רפא	950		be healed
28:28	יככה	hiph	impf	3ms	נכה	645	2ms	smite
28:29	היית	qal	wcp	2ms	היה	224		be,become
	ממשש	piel	ptc	ms	משש	606		grope
	ימשש	piel	impf	3ms	משש	606		grope
	תצליח	hiph	impf	2ms	צלח	852		cause to thrive
	היית	qal	wcp	2ms	היה	224		be,become
	עשוק	qal	pptc	ms	עשק	798		oppress,extort
	גזול	qal	pptc	ms	גזל	159		tear away,rob
	מושיע	hiph	ptc	ms	ישע	446		deliver,save
28:30	תארש	piel	impf	2ms	ארש	76		betroth
	ישגלנה k	qal	impf	3ms	שגל	993	3fs	violate,ravish
	ישכבנה q	qal	impf	3ms	שכב	1011	3fs	lie,lie down
	תבנה	qal	impf	2ms	בנה	124		build
	תשב	qal	impf	2ms	ישב	442		sit,dwell
	תטע	qal	impf	2ms	נטע	642		plant
	תחללנו	piel	impf	2ms	חלל	320	3ms	pollute
28:31	טבוח	qal	pptc	ms	טבח	370		slaughter
	תאכל	qal	impf	2ms	אכל	37		eat,devour
	גזול	qal	pptc	ms	גזל	159		tear away,rob
28:31	ישוב	qal	impf	3ms	שוב	996		turn,return
	נתנות	qal	pptc	fp	נתן	678		give,set
	איביך	qal	ptc	mp	איב	33	2ms	be hostile to
	מושיע	hiph	ptc	ms	ישע	446		deliver,save
28:32	נתנים	qal	pptc	mp	נתן	678		give,set
	ראות	qal	ptc	fp	ראה	906		see
28:33	יאכל	qal	impf	3ms	אכל	37		eat,devour
	ידעת	qal	pft	2ms	ידע	393		know
	היית	qal	wcp	2ms	היה	224		be,become
	עשוק	qal	pptc	ms	עשק	798		oppress,extort
	רצוץ	qal	pptc	ms	רצץ	954		crush
28:34	היית	qal	wcp	2ms	היה	224		be,become
	משגע	pual	ptc	ms	שגע	993		be mad
	תראה	qal	impf	2ms	ראה	906		see
28:35	יככה	hiph	impf	3ms	נכה	645	2ms	smite
	תוכל	qal	impf	2ms	יכל	407		be able
	הרפא	niph	infc		רפא	950		be healed
28:36	יולך	hiph	jusf	3ms	הלך	229		lead,bring
	תקים	hiph	impf	2ms	קום	877		raise,build,set
	ידעת	qal	pft	2ms	ידע	393		know
	עבדת	qal	wcp	2ms	עבד	712		work,serve
28:37	היית	qal	wcp	2ms	היה	224		be,become
	ינהגך	piel	impf	3ms	נהג	624	2ms	drive away,lead
28:38	תוציא	hiph	impf	2ms	יצא	422		bring out
	תאסף	qal	impf	2ms	אסף	62		gather
	יחסלנו	qal	impf	3ms	חסל	340	3ms	consume
28:39	תטע	qal	impf	2ms	נטע	642		plant
	עבדת	qal	wcp	2ms	עבד	712		work,serve
	תשתה	qal	impf	2ms	שתה	1059		drink
	תאגר	qal	impf	2ms	אגר	8		gather
	תאכלנו	qal	impf	3fs	אכל	37	3ms	eat,devour
28:40	יהיו	qal	impf	3mp	היה	224		be,become
	תסוך	qal	impf	2ms	סוך	691		anoint,pour
	ישל	qal	impf	3ms	נשל	675		draw off
28:41	תוליד	hiph	impf	2ms	ילד	408		beget
	יהיו	qal	impf	3mp	היה	224		be,become
	ילכו	qal	impf	3mp	הלך	229		walk,go
28:42	יירש	piel	impf	3ms	ירש	439		possess
28:43	יעלה	qal	impf	3ms	עלה	748		go up
	תרד	qal	impf	2ms	ירד	432		come down
28:44	ילוך	hiph	impf	3ms	לוה	531	2ms	lend
	תלונו	hiph	impf	2ms	לוה	531	3ms	lend
	יהיה	qal	impf	3ms	היה	224		be,become
	תהיה	qal	impf	2ms	היה	224		be,become
28:45	באו	qal	wcp	3cp	בוא	97		come in
	רדפוך	qal	wcp	3cp	רדף	922	2ms	pursue
	השיגוך	hiph	wcp	3cp	נשג	673	2ms	reach,overtake
	השמדך	niph	infc		שמד	1029	2ms	be exterminated
	שמעת	qal	pft	2ms	שמע	1033		hear
	שמר	qal	infc		שמר	1036		keep,watch
	צוך	piel	pft	3ms	צוה	845	2ms	command
28:46	היו	qal	wcp	3cp	היה	224		be,become
28:47	עבדת	qal	pft	2ms	עבד	712		work,serve
28:48	עבדת	qal	wcp	2ms	עבד	712		work,serve

ChVs	Form	Stem	Tnse	PGN	Root	BDB	Sfx	Meaning
28:48	איביך	qal	ptc	mp	איב	33	2ms	be hostile to
	ישלחנו	piel	impf	3ms	שלח	1018	3ms	send away,shoot
	נתן	qal	wcp	3ms	נתן	678		give,set
	השמידו	hiph	infc		שמד	1029	3ms	exterminate
28:49	ישא	qal	impf	3ms	נשא	669		lift,carry
	ידאה	qal	impf	3ms	דאה	178		fly swiftly
	תשמע	qal	impf	2ms	שמע	1033		hear
28:50	ישא	qal	impf	3ms	נשא	669		lift,carry
	יחן	qal	impf	3ms	חנן	335		show favor
28:51	אכל	qal	wcp	3ms	אכל	37		eat,devour
	השמדך	niph	infc		שמד	1029	2ms	be exterminated
	ישאיר	hiph	impf	3ms	שאר	983		leave,spare
	האבידו	hiph	infc		אבד	1	3ms	destroy
28:52	הצר	hiph	wcp	3ms	צרר	864		distress,cramp
	רדת	qal	infc		ירד	432		come down
	בצרות	qal	pptc	fp	בצר	130		cut off
	בטח	qal	ptc	ms	בטח	105		trust
	הצר	hiph	wcp	3ms	צרר	864		distress,cramp
	נתן	qal	pft	3ms	נתן	678		give,set
28:53	אכלת	qal	wcp	2ms	אכל	37		eat,devour
	נתן	qal	pft	3ms	נתן	678		give,set
	יציק	hiph	impf	3ms	צוק	847		constrain
	איבך	qal	ptc	ms	איב	33	2ms	be hostile to
28:54	תרע	qal	impf	3fs	רעע	949		be evil
	יותיר	hiph	impf	3ms	יתר	451		leave,spare
28:55	תת	qal	infc		נתן	678		give,set
	יאכל	qal	impf	3ms	אכל	37		eat,devour
	השאיר	hiph	pft	3ms	שאר	983		leave,spare
	יציק	hiph	impf	3ms	צוק	847		constrain
	איבך	qal	ptc	ms	איב	33	2ms	be hostile to
28:56	נסתה	piel	pft	3fs	נסה	650		test,try
	הצג	hiph	infc		יצג	426		place,establish
	התענג	hith	infc		ענג	772		enjoy oneself
	תרע	qal	impf	3fs	רעע	949		be evil
28:57	יוצת	qal	ptc	fs	יצא	422		go out
	תלד	qal	impf	3fs	ילד	408		bear,beget
	תאכלם	qal	impf	3fs	אכל	37	3mp	eat,devour
	יציק	hiph	impf	3ms	צוק	847		constrain
	איבך	qal	ptc	ms	איב	33	2ms	be hostile to
28:58	תשמר	qal	impf	2ms	שמר	1036		keep,watch
	עשות	qal	infc		עשה	793		do,make
	כתובים	qal	pptc	mp	כתב	507		write
	יראה	qal	infc		ירא	431		fear
	נכבד	niph	ptc	ms	כבד	457		be honored
	נורא	niph	ptc	ms	ירא	431		be feared
28:59	הפלא	hiph	wcp	3ms	פלא	810		do wondrously
	נאמנות	niph	ptc	fp	אמן	52		be confirmed
	נאמנים	niph	ptc	mp	אמן	52		be confirmed
28:60	השיב	hiph	wcp	3ms	שוב	996		bring back
	יגרת	qal	pft	2ms	יגר	388		be afraid
	דבקו	qal	wcp	3cp	דבק	179		cling,cleave
28:61	כתוב	qal	pptc	ms	כתב	507		write
	יעלם	hiph	impf	3ms	עלה	748	3mp	bring up,offer
	השמדך	niph	infc		שמד	1029	2ms	be exterminated
28:62	נשארתם	niph	wcp	2mp	שאר	983		be left
	הייתם	qal	pft	2mp	היה	224		be,become
	שמעת	qal	pft	2ms	שמע	1033		hear
28:63	היה	qal	wcp	3ms	היה	224		be,become
	שש	qal	pft	3ms	שוש	965		exult
	היטיב	hiph	infc		יטב	405		do good
	הרבות	hiph	infc		רבה	915		make many
	ישיש	qal	impf	3ms	שוש	965		exult
	האביד	hiph	infc		אבד	1		destroy
	השמיד	hiph	infc		שמד	1029		exterminate
	נסחתם	niph	wcp	2mp	נסח	650		be torn away
	בא	qal	ptc	ms	בוא	97		come in
	רשתה	qal	infc		ירש	439	3fs	possess,inherit
28:64	הפיצך	hiph	wcp	3ms	פוץ	806	2ms	scatter
	עבדת	qal	wcp	2ms	עבד	712		work,serve
	ידעת	qal	pft	2ms	ידע	393		know
28:65	תרגיע	hiph	impf	2ms	רגע	921		give rest
	יהיה	qal	impf	3ms	היה	224		be,become
	נתן	qal	wcp	3ms	נתן	678		give,set
28:66	היו	qal	wcp	3cp	היה	224		be,become
	תלאים	qal	pptc	mp	תלא	1067		hang
	פחדת	qal	wcp	2ms	פחד	808		be in dread
	תאמין	hiph	impf	2ms	אמן	52		believe
28:67	תאמר	qal	impf	2ms	אמר	55		say
	יתן	qal	impf	3ms	נתן	678		give,set
	תאמר	qal	impf	2ms	אמר	55		say
	יתן	qal	impf	3ms	נתן	678		give,set
	תפחד	qal	impf	2ms	פחד	808		be in dread
	תראה	qal	impf	2ms	ראה	906		see
28:68	השיבך	hiph	wcp	3ms	שוב	996	2ms	bring back
	אמרתי	qal	pft	1cs	אמר	55		say
	תסיף	hiph	impf	2ms	יסף	414		add,do again
	ראתה	qal	infc		ראה	906	3fs	see
	התמכרתם	hith	wcp	2mp	מכר	569		sell oneself
	איביך	qal	ptc	mp	איב	33	2ms	be hostile to
	קנה	qal	ptc	ms	קנה	888		get,buy
28:69	צוה	piel	pft	3ms	צוה	845		command
	כרת	qal	infc		כרת	503		cut,destroy
	כרת	qal	pft	3ms	כרת	503		cut,destroy
29:1	יקרא	qal	wci	3ms	קרא	894		call,proclaim
	יאמר	qal	wci	3ms	אמר	55		say
	ראיתם	qal	pft	2mp	ראה	906		see
	עשה	qal	pft	3ms	עשה	793		do,make
29:2	ראו	qal	pft	3cp	ראה	906		see
29:3	נתן	qal	pft	3ms	נתן	678		give,set
	דעת	qal	infc		ידע	393		know
	ראות	qal	infc		ראה	906		see
	שמע	qal	infc		שמע	1033		hear
29:4	אולך	hiph	wci	1cs	הלך	229		lead,bring
	בלו	qal	pft	3cp	בלה	115		wear out
	בלתה	qal	pft	3fs	בלה	115		wear out
29:5	אכלתם	qal	pft	2mp	אכל	37		eat,devour
	שתיתם	qal	pft	2mp	שתה	1059		drink
	תדעו	qal	impf	2mp	ידע	393		know

ChVs	Form	Stem	Tnse	PGN	Root	BDB	Sfx	Meaning
29:6	תבאו	qal	wci	2mp	בוא	97		come in
	יצא	qal	wci	3ms	יצא	422		go out
	קראתנו	qal	infc		קרא	896	1cp	meet,encounter
	נכם	hiph	wci	1cp	נכה	645	3mp	smite
29:7	נקח	qal	wci	1cp	לקח	542		take
	נתנה	qal	wci	1cp	נתן	678	3fs	give,set
29:8	שמרתם	qal	wcp	2mp	שמר	1036		keep,watch
	עשיתם	qal	wcp	2mp	עשה	793		do,make
	תשכילו	hiph	impf	2mp	שכל	968		look at,prosper
	תעשון	qal	impf	2mp	עשה	793		do,make
29:9	נצבים	niph	ptc	mp	נצב	662		stand
29:10	חטב	qal	ptc	ms	חטב	310		cut wood
	שאב	qal	ptc	ms	שאב	980		draw (water)
29:11	עברך	qal	infc		עבר	716	2ms	pass over
	כרת	qal	ptc	ms	כרת	503		cut,destroy
29:12	הקים	hiph	infc		קום	877		raise,build,set
	יהיה	qal	impf	3ms	היה	224		be,become
	דבר	piel	pft	3ms	דבר	180		speak
	נשבע	niph	pft	3ms	שבע	989		swear
29:13	כרת	qal	ptc	ms	כרת	503		cut,destroy
29:14	עמד	qal	ptc	ms	עמד	763		stand,stop
29:15	ידעתם	qal	pft	2mp	ידע	393		know
	ישבנו	qal	pft	1cp	ישב	442		sit,dwell
	עברנו	qal	pft	1cp	עבר	716		pass over
	עברתם	qal	pft	2mp	עבר	716		pass over
29:16	תראו	qal	wci	2mp	ראה	906		see
29:17	פנה	qal	ptc	ms	פנה	815		turn
	לכת	qal	infc		הלך	229		walk,go
	עבד	qal	infc		עבד	712		work,serve
	פרה	qal	ptc	ms	פרה	826		bear fruit
29:18	היה	qal	wcp	3ms	היה	224		be,become
	שמעו	qal	infc		שמע	1033	3ms	hear
	התברך	hith	wcp	3ms	ברך	138		bless oneself
	אמר	qal	infc		אמר	55		say
	יהיה	qal	impf	3ms	היה	224		be,become
	אלך	qal	impf	1cs	הלך	229		walk,go
	ספות	qal	infc		ספה	705		sweep away
29:19	יאבה	qal	impf	3ms	אבה	2		be willing
	סלח	qal	infc		סלח	699		forgive,pardon
	יעשן	qal	impf	3ms	עשן	798		smoke,fume
	רבצה	qal	wcp	3fs	רבץ	918		lie down
	כתובה	qal	pptc	fs	כתב	507		write
	מחה	qal	wcp	3ms	מחה	562		wipe,blot out
29:20	הבדילו	hiph	wcp	3ms	בדל	95	3ms	divide
	כתובה	qal	pptc	fs	כתב	507		write
29:21	אמר	qal	wcp	3ms	אמר	55		say
	יקומו	qal	impf	3mp	קום	877		arise,stand
	יבא	qal	impf	3ms	בוא	97		come in
	ראו	qal	wcp	3cp	ראה	906		see
	חלה	piel	pft	3ms	חלה	317		make sick
29:22	תזרע	niph	impf	3fs	זרע	281		be sown
	תצמח	hiph	impf	3fs	צמח	855		cause to grow
	יעלה	qal	impf	3ms	עלה	748		go up
	הפך	qal	pft	3ms	הפך	245		turn,overturn
29:23	אמרו	qal	wcp	3cp	אמר	55		say
	עשה	qal	pft	3ms	עשה	793		do,make
29:24	אמרו	qal	wcp	3cp	אמר	55		say
	עזבו	qal	pft	3cp	עזב	736		leave,loose
	כרת	qal	pft	3ms	כרת	503		cut,destroy
	הוציאו	hiph	infc		יצא	422	3ms	bring out
29:25	ילכו	qal	wci	3mp	הלך	229		walk,go
	יעבדו	qal	wci	3mp	עבד	712		work,serve
	ישתחוו	hish	wci	3mp	חוה	1005		bow down
	ידעום	qal	pft	3cp	ידע	393	3mp	know
	חלק	qal	pft	3ms	חלק	323		divide,share
29:26	יחר	qal	wci	3ms	חרה	354		be kindled,burn
	הביא	hiph	infc		בוא	97		bring in
	כתובה	qal	pptc	fs	כתב	507		write
29:27	יתשם	qal	wci	3ms	נתש	684	3mp	pull up
	ישלכם	hiph	wci	3ms	שלך	1020	3mp	throw,cast
29:28	נסתרת	niph	ptc	fp	סתר	711		hide,be hid
	נגלת	niph	ptc	fp	גלה	162		uncover self
	עשות	qal	infc		עשה	793		do,make
30:1	היה	qal	wcp	3ms	היה	224		be,become
	יבאו	qal	impf	3mp	בוא	97		come in
	נתתי	qal	pft	1cs	נתן	678		give,set
	השבת	hiph	wcp	2ms	שוב	996		bring back
	הדיחך	hiph	pft	3ms	נדח	623	2ms	thrust out
30:2	שבת	qal	wcp	2ms	שוב	996		turn,return
	שמעת	qal	wcp	2ms	שמע	1033		hear
	מצוך	piel	ptc	ms	צוה	845	2ms	command
30:3	שב	qal	wcp	3ms	שוב	996		turn,return
	רחמך	piel	wcp	3ms	רחם	933	2ms	have compassion
	שב	qal	wcp	3ms	שוב	996		turn,return
	קבצך	piel	wcp	3ms	קבץ	867	2ms	gather together
	הפיצך	hiph	pft	3ms	פוץ	806	2ms	scatter
30:4	יהיה	qal	impf	3ms	היה	224		be,become
	נדחך	niph	ptc	ms	נדח	623	2ms	be banished
	יקבצך	piel	impf	3ms	קבץ	867	2ms	gather together
	יקחך	qal	impf	3ms	לקח	542	2ms	take
30:5	הביאך	hiph	wcp	3ms	בוא	97	2ms	bring in
	ירשו	qal	pft	3cp	ירש	439		possess,inherit
	ירשתה	qal	wcp	2ms	ירש	439	3fs	possess,inherit
	היטבך	hiph	wcp	3ms	יטב	405	2ms	do good
	הרבך	hiph	wcp	3ms	רבה	915	2ms	make many
30:6	מל	qal	wcp	3ms	מול	557		circumcise
	אהבה	qal	infc		אהב	12		love
30:7	נתן	qal	wcp	3ms	נתן	678		give,set
	איביך	qal	ptc	mp	איב	33	2ms	be hostile to
	שנאיך	qal	ptc	mp	שנא	971	2ms	hate
	רדפוך	qal	pft	3cp	רדף	922	2ms	pursue
30:8	תשוב	qal	impf	2ms	שוב	996		turn,return
	שמעת	qal	wcp	2ms	שמע	1033		hear
	עשית	qal	wcp	2ms	עשה	793		do,make
	מצוך	piel	ptc	ms	צוה	845	2ms	command
30:9	הותירך	hiph	wcp	3ms	יתר	451	2ms	leave,spare
	ישוב	qal	impf	3ms	שוב	996		turn,return
	שוש	qal	infc		שוש	965		exult

ChVs	Form	Stem	Tnse	PGN	Root	BDB	Sfx	Meaning
30:9	שׂשׂ	qal	pft	3ms	שׂושׂ	965		exult
30:10	תשׁמע	qal	impf	2ms	שׁמע	1033		hear
	שׁמר	qal	infc		שׁמר	1036		keep,watch
	כתובה	qal	pptc	fs	כתב	507		write
	תשׁוב	qal	impf	2ms	שׁוב	996		turn,return
30:11	מצוך	piel	ptc	ms	צוה	845	2ms	command
	נפלאת	niph	ptc	fs	פלא	810		be wonderful
30:12	אמר	qal	infc		אמר	55		say
	יעלה	qal	impf	3ms	עלה	748		go up
	יקחה	qal	jusm	3ms	לקח	542	3fs	take
	ישׁמענו	hiph	jusm	3ms	שׁמע	1033	1cp	cause to hear
	נעשׂנה	qal	cohm	1cp	עשׂה	793	3fs	do,make
30:13	אמר	qal	infc		אמר	55		say
	יעבר	qal	impf	3ms	עבר	716		pass over
	יקחה	qal	impf	3ms	לקח	542	3fs	take
	ישׁמענו	hiph	impf	3ms	שׁמע	1033	1cp	cause to hear
	נעשׂנה	qal	impf	1cp	עשׂה	793	3fs	do,make
30:14	עשׂתו	qal	infc		עשׂה	793	3ms	do,make
30:15	ראה	qal	impv	ms	ראה	906		see
	נתתי	qal	pft	1cs	נתן	678		give,set
30:16	מצוך	piel	ptc	ms	צוה	845	2ms	command
	אהבה	qal	infc		אהב	12		love
	לכת	qal	infc		הלך	229		walk,go
	שׁמר	qal	infc		שׁמר	1036		keep,watch
	חיית	qal	wcp	2ms	חיה	310		live
	רבית	qal	wcp	2ms	רבה	915		be many,great
	ברכך	piel	wcp	3ms	ברך	138	2ms	bless
	בא	qal	ptc	ms	בוא	97		come in
	רשׁתה	qal	infc		ירשׁ	439	3fs	possess,inherit
30:17	יפנה	qal	impf	3ms	פנה	815		turn
	תשׁמע	qal	impf	2ms	שׁמע	1033		hear
	נדחת	niph	wcp	2ms	נדח	623		be banished
	השׁתחוית	hish	wcp	2ms	חוה	1005		bow down
	עבדתם	qal	wcp	2ms	עבד	712	3mp	work,serve
30:18	הגדתי	hiph	pft	1cs	נגד	616		declare,tell
	אבד	qal	infa		אבד	1		perish
	תאבדון	qal	impf	2mp	אבד	1		perish
	תאריכן	hiph	impf	2mp	ארך	73		prolong
	עבר	qal	ptc	ms	עבר	716		pass over
	בא	qal	infc		בוא	97		come in
	רשׁתה	qal	infc		ירשׁ	439	3fs	possess,inherit
30:19	העידתי	hiph	pft	1cs	עוד	729		testify,warn
	נתתי	qal	pft	1cs	נתן	678		give,set
	בחרת	qal	wcp	2ms	בחר	103		choose
	תחיה	qal	impf	2ms	חיה	310		live
30:20	אהבה	qal	infc		אהב	12		love
	שׁמע	qal	infc		שׁמע	1033		hear
	דבקה	qal	infc		דבק	179		cling,cleave
	שׁבת	qal	infc		ישׁב	442		sit,dwell
	נשׁבע	niph	pft	3ms	שׁבע	989		swear
	תת	qal	infc		נתן	678		give,set
31:1	ילך	qal	wci	3ms	הלך	229		walk,go
	ידבר	piel	wci	3ms	דבר	180		speak
31:2	יאמר	qal	wci	3ms	אמר	55		say
31:2	אוכל	qal	impf	1cs	יכל	407		be able
	צאת	qal	infc		יצא	422		go out
	בוא	qal	infc		בוא	97		come in
	אמר	qal	pft	3ms	אמר	55		say
	תעבר	qal	impf	2ms	עבר	716		pass over
31:3	עבר	qal	ptc	ms	עבר	716		pass over
	ישׁמיד	hiph	impf	3ms	שׁמד	1029		exterminate
	ירשׁתם	qal	wcp	2ms	ירשׁ	439	3mp	possess,inherit
	עבר	qal	ptc	ms	עבר	716		pass over
	דבר	piel	pft	3ms	דבר	180		speak
31:4	עשׂה	qal	wcp	3ms	עשׂה	793		do,make
	עשׂה	qal	pft	3ms	עשׂה	793		do,make
	השׁמיד	hiph	pft	3ms	שׁמד	1029		exterminate
31:5	נתנם	qal	wcp	3ms	נתן	678	3mp	give,set
	עשׂיתם	qal	wcp	2mp	עשׂה	793		do,make
	צויתי	piel	pft	1cs	צוה	845		command
31:6	חזקו	qal	impv	mp	חזק	304		be strong
	אמצו	qal	impv	mp	אמץ	54		be strong
	תיראו	qal	jusm	2mp	ירא	431		fear
	תערצו	qal	jusm	2mp	ערץ	791		frighten,fear
	הלך	qal	ptc	ms	הלך	229		walk,go
	ירפך	hiph	impf	3ms	רפה	951	2ms	slacken,abandon
	יעזבך	qal	impf	3ms	עזב	736	2ms	leave,loose
31:7	יקרא	qal	wci	3ms	קרא	894		call,proclaim
	יאמר	qal	wci	3ms	אמר	55		say
	חזק	qal	impv	ms	חזק	304		be strong
	אמץ	qal	impv	ms	אמץ	54		be strong
	תבוא	qal	impf	2ms	בוא	97		come in
	נשׁבע	niph	pft	3ms	שׁבע	989		swear
	תת	qal	infc		נתן	678		give,set
	תנחילנה	hiph	impf	2ms	נחל	635	3fs	c. to inherit
31:8	הלך	qal	ptc	ms	הלך	229		walk,go
	יהיה	qal	impf	3ms	היה	224		be,become
	ירפך	hiph	impf	3ms	רפה	951	2ms	slacken,abandon
	יעזבך	qal	impf	3ms	עזב	736	2ms	leave,loose
	תירא	qal	impf	2ms	ירא	431		fear
	תחת	qal	impf	2ms	חתת	369		be shattered
31:9	יכתב	qal	wci	3ms	כתב	507		write
	יתנה	qal	wci	3ms	נתן	678	3fs	give,set
	נשׂאים	qal	ptc	mp	נשׂא	669		lift,carry
31:10	יצו	piel	wci	3ms	צוה	845		command
	אמר	qal	infc		אמר	55		say
31:11	בוא	qal	infc		בוא	97		come in
	ראות	niph	infc		ראה	906		appear,be seen
	יבחר	qal	impf	3ms	בחר	103		choose
	תקרא	qal	impf	2ms	קרא	894		call,proclaim
31:12	הקהל	hiph	impv	ms	קהל	874		call assembly
	ישׁמעו	qal	impf	3mp	שׁמע	1033		hear
	ילמדו	qal	impf	3mp	למד	540		learn
	יראו	qal	wcp	3cp	ירא	431		fear
	שׁמרו	qal	wcp	3cp	שׁמר	1036		keep,watch
	עשׂות	qal	infc		עשׂה	793		do,make
31:13	ידעו	qal	pft	3cp	ידע	393		know
	ישׁמעו	qal	impf	3mp	שׁמע	1033		hear

ChVs	Form	Stem	Tnse	PGN	Root	BDB	Sfx	Meaning
31:13	למדו	qal	wcp	3cp	למד	540		learn
	יראה	qal	infc		ירא	431		fear
	עברים	qal	ptc	mp	עבר	716		pass over
	רשתה	qal	infc		ירש	439	3fs	possess,inherit
31:14	יאמר	qal	wci	3ms	אמר	55		say
	קרבו	qal	pft	3cp	קרב	897		approach
	מות	qal	infc		מות	559		die
	קרא	qal	impv	ms	קרא	894		call,proclaim
	התיצבו	hith	impv	mp	יצב	426		stand oneself
	אצונו	piel	wci	1cs	צוה	845	3ms	command
	ילך	qal	wci	3ms	הלך	229		walk,go
	יתיצבו	hith	wci	3mp	יצב	426		stand oneself
31:15	ירא	niph	wci	3ms	ראה	906		appear,be seen
	יעמד	qal	wci	3ms	עמד	763		stand,stop
31:16	יאמר	qal	wci	3ms	אמר	55		say
	שׁכב	qal	ptc	ms	שׁכב	1011		lie,lie down
	קם	qal	wcp	3ms	קום	877		arise,stand
	זנה	qal	wcp	3ms	זנה	275		act a harlot
	בא	qal	ptc	ms	בוא	97		come in
	עזבני	qal	wcp	3ms	עזב	736	1cs	leave,loose
	הפר	hiph	wcp	3ms	פרר	830		break,frustrate
	כרתי	qal	pft	1cs	כרת	503		cut,destroy
31:17	חרה	qal	wcp	3ms	חרה	354		be kindled,burn
	עזבתים	qal	wcp	1cs	עזב	736	3mp	leave,loose
	הסתרתי	hiph	wcp	1cs	סתר	711		hide
	היה	qal	wcp	3ms	היה	224		be,become
	אכל	qal	infc		אכל	37		eat,devour
	מצאהו	qal	wcp	3cp	מצא	592	3ms	find
	אמר	qal	wcp	3ms	אמר	55		say
	מצאוני	qal	pft	3cp	מצא	592	1cs	find
31:18	הסתר	hiph	infa		סתר	711		hide
	אסתיר	hiph	impf	1cs	סתר	711		hide
	עשׂה	qal	pft	3ms	עשׂה	793		do,make
	פנה	qal	pft	3ms	פנה	815		turn
31:19	כתבו	qal	impv	mp	כתב	507		write
	למדה	piel	impv	ms	למד	540	3fs	teach
	שׂימה	qal	impv	ms	שׂים	962	3fs	put,set
	תהיה	qal	impf	3fs	היה	224		be,become
31:20	אביאנו	hiph	impf	1cs	בוא	97	3ms	bring in
	נשׁבעתי	niph	pft	1cs	שׁבע	989		swear
	זבת	qal	ptc	fs	זוב	264		flow,gush
	אכל	qal	wcp	3ms	אכל	37		eat,devour
	שׂבע	qal	wcp	3ms	שׂבע	959		be sated
	דשׁן	qal	wcp	3ms	דשׁן	206		be fat
	פנה	qal	wcp	3ms	פנה	815		turn
	עבדום	qal	wcp	3cp	עבד	712	3mp	work,serve
	נאצוני	piel	wcp	3cp	נאץ	610	1cs	spurn
	הפר	hiph	wcp	3ms	פרר	830		break,frustrate
31:21	היה	qal	wcp	3ms	היה	224		be,become
	תמצאן	qal	impf	3fp	מצא	592		find
	ענתה	qal	wcp	3fs	ענה	772		answer
	תשׁכח	niph	impf	3fs	שׁכח	1013		be forgotten
	ידעתי	qal	pft	1cs	ידע	393		know
	עשׂה	qal	ptc	ms	עשׂה	793		do,make
31:21	אביאנו	hiph	impf	1cs	בוא	97	3ms	bring in
	נשׁבעתי	niph	pft	1cs	שׁבע	989		swear
31:22	יכתב	qal	wci	3ms	כתב	507		write
	ילמדה	piel	wci	3ms	למד	540	3fs	teach
31:23	יצו	piel	wci	3ms	צוה	845		command
	יאמר	qal	wci	3ms	אמר	55		say
	חזק	qal	impv	ms	חזק	304		be strong
	אמץ	qal	impv	ms	אמץ	54		be strong
	תביא	hiph	impf	2ms	בוא	97		bring in
	נשׁבעתי	niph	pft	1cs	שׁבע	989		swear
	אהיה	qal	impf	1cs	היה	224		be,become
31:24	יהי	qal	wci	3ms	היה	224		be,become
	כלות	piel	infc		כלה	477		complete,finish
	כתב	qal	infc		כתב	507		write
	תמם	qal	infc		תמם	1070	3mp	be finished
31:25	יצו	piel	wci	3ms	צוה	845		command
	נשׂאי	qal	ptc	mp	נשׂא	669		lift,carry
	אמר	qal	infc		אמר	55		say
31:26	לקח	qal	infa		לקח	542		take
	שׂמתם	qal	wcp	2mp	שׂים	962		put,set
	היה	qal	wcp	3ms	היה	224		be,become
31:27	ידעתי	qal	pft	1cs	ידע	393		know
	ממרים	hiph	ptc	mp	מרה	598		rebel
	היתם	qal	pft	2mp	היה	224		be,become
31:28	הקהילו	hiph	impv	mp	קהל	874		call assembly
	אדברה	piel	coh	1cs	דבר	180		speak
	אעידה	hiph	coh	1cs	עוד	729		testify,warn
31:29	ידעתי	qal	pft	1cs	ידע	393		know
	השׁחת	hiph	infa		שׁחת	1007		spoil,ruin
	תשׁחתון	hiph	impf	2mp	שׁחת	1007		spoil,ruin
	סרתם	qal	wcp	2mp	סור	693		turn aside
	צויתי	piel	pft	1cs	צוה	845		command
	קראת	qal	wcp	3fs	קרא	896		meet,encounter
	תעשׂו	qal	impf	2mp	עשׂה	793		do,make
	הכעיסו	hiph	infc		כעס	494	3ms	vex,provoke
31:30	ידבר	piel	wci	3ms	דבר	180		speak
	תמם	qal	infc		תמם	1070	3mp	be finished
32:1	האזינו	hiph	impv	mp	אזן	24		hear
	אדברה	piel	coh	1cs	דבר	180		speak
	תשׁמע	qal	jusm	3fs	שׁמע	1033		hear
32:2	יערף	qal	jusm	3ms	ערף	791		drip,drop
	תזל	qal	jusm	3fs	נזל	633		flow
32:3	אקרא	qal	impf	1cs	קרא	894		call,proclaim
	הבו	qal	impv	mp	יהב	396		give
32:5	שׁחת	piel	pft	3ms	שׁחת	1007		spoil,ruin
32:6	תגמלו	qal	impf	2mp	גמל	168		deal out,ripen
	קנך	qal	pft	3ms	קנה	888	2ms	get,buy
	עשׂך	qal	pft	3ms	עשׂה	793	2ms	do,make
	יכננך	pol	wci	3ms	כון	465	2ms	establish
32:7	זכר	qal	impv	ms	זכר	269		remember
	בינו	qal	impv	mp	בין	106		discern
	שׁאל	qal	impv	ms	שׁאל	981		ask,borrow
	יגדך	hiph	jus	3ms	נגד	616	2ms	declare,tell
	יאמרו	qal	impf	3mp	אמר	55		say

ChVs	Form	Stem	Tnse	PGN	Root	BDB	Sfx	Meaning
32: 8	הנחל	hiph	infc		נחל	635		c. to inherit
	הפרידו	hiph	infc		פרד	825	3ms	divide
	יצב	hiph	jusf	3ms	נצב	662		cause to stand
32: 10	ימצאהו	qal	impf	3ms	מצא	592	3ms	find
	יסבבנהו	poel	impf	3ms	סבב	685	3ms	encompass
	יבוננהו	pol	impf	3ms	בין	106	3ms	onsider
	יצרנהו	qal	impf	3ms	נצר	665	3ms	watch,guard
32: 11	יעיר	hiph	impf	3ms	עור	734		rouse,stir up
	ירחף	piel	impf	3ms	רחף	934		hover
	יפרש	qal	impf	3ms	פרש	831		spread out
	יקחהו	qal	impf	3ms	לקח	542	3ms	take
	ישאהו	qal	impf	3ms	נשא	669	3ms	lift,carry
32: 12	ינחנו	hiph	impf	3ms	נחה	634	3ms	lead,guide
32: 13	ירכבהו	hiph	impf	3ms	רכב	938	3ms	cause to ride
	יאכל	qal	wci	3ms	אכל	37		eat,devour
	ינקהו	hiph	wci	3ms	ינק	413	3ms	nurse
32: 14	תשתה	qal	impf	2ms	שתה	1059		drink
32: 15	ישמן	qal	wci	3ms	שמן	1031		be fat
	יבעט	qal	wci	3ms	בעט	127		kick
	שמנת	qal	pft	2ms	שמן	1031		be fat
	עבית	qal	pft	2ms	עבה	716		be thick
	כשית	qal	pft	2ms	כשה	505		be gorged
	יטש	qal	wci	3ms	נטש	643		leave,forsake
	עשהו	qal	pft	3ms	עשה	793	3ms	do,make
	ינבל	piel	wci	3ms	נבל	614		esteem lightly
32: 16	יקנאהו	hiph	impf	3mp	קנא	888	3ms	make jealous
	יכעיסהו	hiph	impf	3mp	כעס	494	3ms	vex,provoke
32: 17	יזבחו	qal	impf	3mp	זבח	256		slaughter
	ידעום	qal	pft	3cp	ידע	393	3mp	know
	באו	qal	pft	3cp	בוא	97		come in
	שערום	qal	pft	3cp	שער	973	3mp	be acquainted
32: 18	ילדך	qal	pft	3ms	ילד	408	2ms	bear,beget
	תשי	qal	jusf	2ms	שיה	1009		forget
	תשכח	qal	wci	2ms	שכח	1013		forget
	מחללך	pol	ptc	ms	חול	296	2ms	dance,writhe
32: 19	ירא	qal	wci	3ms	ראה	906		see
	ינאץ	qal	wci	3ms	נאץ	610		spurn
32: 20	יאמר	qal	wci	3ms	אמר	55		say
	אסתירה	hiph	coh	1cs	סתר	711		hide
	אראה	qal	impf	1cs	ראה	906		see
32: 21	קנאוני	piel	pft	3cp	קנא	888	1cs	be jealous
	כעסוני	piel	pft	3cp	כעס	494	1cs	irritate
	אקניאם	hiph	impf	1cs	קנא	888	3mp	make jealous
	אכעיסם	hiph	impf	1cs	כעס	494	3mp	vex,provoke
32: 22	קדחה	qal	pft	3fs	קדח	869		be kindled
	תיקד	qal	wci	3fs	יקד	428		be kindled
	תאכל	qal	wci	3fs	אכל	37		eat,devour
	תלהט	piel	wci	3fs	להט	529		set ablaze
32: 23	אספה	hiph	impf	1cs	ספה	705		gather up
	אכלה	piel	impf	1cs	כלה	477		complete,finish
32: 24	לחמי	qal	pptc	mp	לחם	536		eat,consume
	אשלח	piel	impf	1cs	שלח	1018		send away,shoot
	זחלי	qal	ptc	mp	זחל	267		crawl
32: 25	תשכל	piel	impf	3fs	שכל	1013		make childless
32: 25	יונק	qal	ptc	ms	ינק	413		suck
32: 26	אמרתי	qal	pft	1cs	אמר	55		say
	אפאיהם	hiph	cohm	1cs	פאה	802	3mp	cut in pieces
	אשביתה	hiph	coh	1cs	שבת	991		destroy,remove
32: 27	אויב	qal	ptc	ms	איב	33		be hostile to
	אגור	qal	impf	1cs	גור	158		dread
	ינכרו	piel	impf	3mp	נכר	649		treat strange
	יאמרו	qal	impf	3mp	אמר	55		say
	רמה	qal	pft	3fs	רום	926		be high
	פעל	qal	pft	3ms	פעל	821		do,make
32: 28	אבד	qal	ptc	ms	אבד	1		perish
32: 29	חכמו	qal	pft	3cp	חכם	314		be wise
	ישכילו	hiph	impf	3mp	שכל	968		look at,prosper
	יבינו	qal	impf	3mp	בין	106		discern
32: 30	ירדף	qal	impf	3ms	רדף	922		pursue
	יניסו	hiph	impf	3mp	נוס	630		put to flight
	מכרם	qal	pft	3ms	מכר	569	3mp	sell
	הסגירם	hiph	pft	3ms	סגר	688	3mp	shut up,deliver
32: 31	איבינו	qal	ptc	mp	איב	33	1cp	be hostile to
32: 34	כמס	qal	pptc	ms	כמס	485		store up
	חתם	qal	pptc	ms	חתם	367		seal
32: 35	תמוט	qal	impf	3fs	מוט	556		totter
	חש	qal	wcp	3ms	חוש	301		make haste
32: 36	ידין	qal	impf	3ms	דין	192		judge
	יתנחם	hith	impf	3ms	נחם	636		have compassion
	יראה	qal	impf	3ms	ראה	906		see
	אזלת	qal	pft	3fs	אזל	23		go
	עצור	qal	pptc	ms	עצר	783		restrain
	עזוב	qal	pptc	ms	עזב	736		leave,loose
32: 37	אמר	qal	wcp	3ms	אמר	55		say
	חסיו	qal	pft	3cp	חסה	340		seek refuge
32: 38	יאכלו	qal	impf	3mp	אכל	37		eat,devour
	ישתו	qal	impf	3mp	שתה	1059		drink
	יקומו	qal	jusm	3mp	קום	877		arise,stand
	יעזרכם	qal	jusm	3mp	עזר	740	2mp	help,aid
	יהי	qal	jus	3ms	היה	224		be,become
32: 39	ראו	qal	impv	mp	ראה	906		see
	אמית	hiph	impf	1cs	מות	559		kill
	אחיה	piel	impf	1cs	חיה	310		preserve,revive
	מחצתי	qal	pft	1cs	מחץ	563		smite through
	ארפא	qal	impf	1cs	רפא	950		heal
	מציל	hiph	ptc	ms	נצל	664		snatch,deliver
32: 40	אשא	qal	impf	1cs	נשא	669		lift,carry
	אמרתי	qal	wcp	1cs	אמר	55		say
32: 41	שנותי	qal	pft	1cs	שנן	1041		whet,sharpen
	תאחז	qal	impf	3fs	אחז	28		grasp
	אשיב	hiph	impf	1cs	שוב	996		bring back
	משנאי	piel	ptc	mp	שנא	971	1cs	hate
	אשלם	piel	impf	1cs	שלם	1022		finish,reward
32: 42	אשכיר	hiph	impf	1cs	שכר	1016		make drunk
	תאכל	qal	impf	3fs	אכל	37		eat,devour
	אויב	qal	ptc	ms	איב	33		be hostile to
32: 43	הרנינו	hiph	impv	mp	רנן	943		cause to shout
	יקום	qal	impf	3ms	נקם	667		avenge

ChVs	Form	Stem	Tnse	PGN	Root	BDB	Sfx	Meaning
32: 43	ישיב	hiph	impf	3ms	שוב	996		bring back
	כפר	piel	wcp	3ms	כפר	497		cover,atone
32: 44	יבא	qal	wci	3ms	בוא	97		come in
	ידבר	piel	wci	3ms	דבר	180		speak
32: 45	יכל	piel	wci	3ms	כלה	477		complete,finish
	דבר	piel	infc		דבר	180		speak
32: 46	יאמר	qal	wci	3ms	אמר	55		say
	שימו	qal	impv	mp	שים	962		put,set
	מעיד	hiph	ptc	ms	עוד	729		testify,warn
	תצום	piel	impf	2mp	צוה	845	3mp	command
	שמר	qal	infc		שמר	1036		keep,watch
	עשות	qal	infc		עשה	793		do,make
32: 47	תאריכו	hiph	impf	2mp	ארך	73		prolong
	עברים	qal	ptc	mp	עבר	716		pass over
	רשתה	qal	infc		ירש	439	3fs	possess,inherit
32: 48	ידבר	piel	wci	3ms	דבר	180		speak
	אמר	qal	infc		אמר	55		say
32: 49	עלה	qal	impv	ms	עלה	748		go up
	ראה	qal	impv	ms	ראה	906		see
	נתן	qal	ptc	ms	נתן	678		give,set
32: 50	מת	qal	impv	ms	מות	559		die
	עלה	qal	ptc	ms	עלה	748		go up
	האסף	niph	impv	ms	אסף	62		assemble
	מת	qal	pft	3ms	מות	559		die
	יאסף	niph	wci	3ms	אסף	62		assemble
32: 51	מעלתם	qal	pft	2mp	מעל	591		act faithlessly
	קדשתם	piel	pft	2mp	קדש	872		consecrate
32: 52	תראה	qal	impf	2ms	ראה	906		see
	תבוא	qal	impf	2ms	בוא	97		come in
	נתן	qal	ptc	ms	נתן	678		give,set
33: 1	ברך	piel	pft	3ms	ברך	138		bless
33: 2	יאמר	qal	wci	3ms	אמר	55		say
	בא	qal	pft	3ms	בוא	97		come in
	זרח	qal	pft	3ms	זרח	280		rise,appear
	הופיע	hiph	pft	3ms	יפע	422		shine forth
	אתה	qal	pft	3ms	אתה	87		come
33: 3	חבב	qal	ptc	ms	חבב	285		love
	תכו	pual	pft	3cp	תכה	1067		be led
	ישא	qal	impf	3ms	נשא	669		lift,carry
33: 4	צוה	piel	pft	3ms	צוה	845		command
33: 5	יהי	qal	wci	3ms	היה	224		be,become
	התאסף	hith	infc		אסף	62		gather selves
33: 6	יחי	qal	jus	3ms	חיה	310		live
	ימת	qal	jus	3ms	מות	559		die
	יהי	qal	jus	3ms	היה	224		be,become
33: 7	יאמר	qal	wci	3ms	אמר	55		say
	שמע	qal	impv	ms	שמע	1033		hear
	תביאנו	hiph	impf	2ms	בוא	97	3ms	bring in
	רב	qal	pft	3ms	ריב	936		strive,contend
	תהיה	qal	impf	2ms	היה	224		be,become
33: 8	אמר	qal	pft	3ms	אמר	55		say
	נסיתו	piel	pft	2ms	נסה	650	3ms	test,try
	תריבהו	qal	impf	2ms	ריב	936	3ms	strive,contend
33: 9	אמר	qal	ptc	ms	אמר	55		say

ChVs	Form	Stem	Tnse	PGN	Root	BDB	Sfx	Meaning
33: 9	ראיתיו	qal	pft	1cs	ראה	906	3ms	see
	הכיר	hiph	pft	3ms	נכר	647		regard,notice
	ידע	qal	pft	3ms	ידע	393		know
	שמרו	qal	pft	3cp	שמר	1036		keep,watch
	ינצרו	qal	impf	3mp	נצר	665		watch,guard
33: 10	יורו	hiph	impf	3mp	ירה	434		shoot,teach
	ישימו	qal	impf	3mp	שים	962		put,set
33: 11	ברך	piel	impv	ms	ברך	138		bless
	תרצה	qal	impf	2ms	רצה	953		be pleased
	מחץ	qal	impv	ms	מחץ	563		smite through
	קמיו	qal	ptc	mp	קום	877	3ms	arise,stand
	משנאיו	piel	ptc	mp	שנא	971	3ms	hate
	יקומון	qal	impf	3mp	קום	877		arise,stand
33: 12	אמר	qal	pft	3ms	אמר	55		say
	ישכן	qal	jusm	3ms	שכן	1014		settle,dwell
	חפף	qal	ptc	ms	חפף	342		enclose
	שכן	qal	pft	3ms	שכן	1014		settle,dwell
33: 13	אמר	qal	pft	3ms	אמר	55		say
	מברכת	pual	ptc	fs	ברך	138		be blessed
	רבצת	qal	ptc	fs	רבץ	918		lie down
33: 16	שכני	qal	ptc	ms	שכן	1014		settle,dwell
	תבואתה	qal	coh	3fs	בוא	97?3fs		come in
33: 17	ינגח	piel	impf	3ms	נגח	618		thrust at
33: 18	אמר	qal	pft	3ms	אמר	55		say
	שמח	qal	impv	ms	שמח	970		rejoice
	צאתך	qal	infc		יצא	422	2ms	go out
33: 19	יקראו	qal	impf	3mp	קרא	894		call,proclaim
	יזבחו	qal	impf	3mp	זבח	256		slaughter
	יינקו	qal	impf	3mp	ינק	413		suck
	שפוני	qal	pptc	mp	ספן	706		cover,panel
	טמוני	qal	pptc	mp	טמן	380		hide
33: 20	אמר	qal	pft	3ms	אמר	55		say
	ברוך	qal	pptc	ms	ברך	138		kneel,bless
	מרחיב	hiph	ptc	ms	רחב	931		enlarge
	שכן	qal	pft	3ms	שכן	1014		settle,dwell
	טרף	qal	wcp	3ms	טרף	382		tear,rend
33: 21	ירא	qal	wci	3ms	ראה	906		see
	מחקק	poel	ptc	ms	חקק	349		prescribe(r)
	ספון	qal	pptc	ms	ספן	706		cover,panel
	יתא	qal	wci	3ms	אתה	87		come
	עשה	qal	pft	3ms	עשה	793		do,make
33: 22	אמר	qal	pft	3ms	אמר	55		say
	יזנק	piel	impf	3ms	זנק	276		leap
33: 23	אמר	qal	pft	3ms	אמר	55		say
	ירשה	qal	impv	ms	ירש	439		possess,inherit
33: 24	אמר	qal	pft	3ms	אמר	55		say
	ברוך	qal	pptc	ms	ברך	138		kneel,bless
	יהי	qal	jus	3ms	היה	224		be,become
	רצוי	qal	pptc	ms	רצה	953		be pleased
	טבל	qal	ptc	ms	טבל	371		dip
33: 26	רכב	qal	ptc	ms	רכב	938		mount,ride
33: 27	יגרש	piel	wci	3ms	גרש	176		drive out
	אויב	qal	ptc	ms	איב	33		be hostile to
	יאמר	qal	wci	3ms	אמר	55		say

ChVs	Form	Stem	Tnse	PGN	Root	BDB	Sfx	Meaning
33: 27	השמד	hiph	impv	ms	שׁמד	1029		exterminate
33: 28	ישׁכן	qal	wci	3ms	שׁכן	1014		settle,dwell
	יערפו	qal	impf	3mp	ערף	791		drip,drop
33: 29	נושׁע	niph	pft	3ms	ישׁע	446		be saved
	יכחשׁו	niph	impf	3mp	כחשׁ	471		cringe
	איביך	qal	ptc	mp	איב	33	2ms	be hostile to
	תדרך	qal	impf	2ms	דרך	201		tread,march
34: 1	יעל	qal	wci	3ms	עלה	748		go up
	יראהו	hiph	wci	3ms	ראה	906	3ms	show,exhibit
34: 4	יאמר	qal	wci	3ms	אמר	55		say
	נשׁבעתי	niph	pft	1cs	שׁבע	989		swear
	אמר	qal	infc		אמר	55		say
	אתננה	qal	impf	1cs	נתן	678	3fs	give,set
	הראיתיך	hiph	pft	1cs	ראה	906	2ms	show,exhibit
	תעבר	qal	impf	2ms	עבר	716		pass over
34: 5	ימת	qal	wci	3ms	מות	559		die
34: 6	יקבר	qal	wci	3ms	קבר	868		bury
	ידע	qal	pft	3ms	ידע	393		know
34: 7	כהתה	qal	pft	3fs	כהה	462		grow dim
	נס	qal	pft	3ms	נוס	630		flee,escape
34: 8	יבכו	qal	wci	3mp	בכה	113		weep
	יתמו	qal	wci	3mp	תמם	1070		be finished
34: 9	מלא	qal	pft	3ms	מלא	569		be full,fill
	סמך	qal	pft	3ms	סמך	701		lean,support
	ישׁמעו	qal	wci	3mp	שׁמע	1033		hear
	יעשׂו	qal	wci	3mp	עשׂה	793		do,make
	צוה	piel	pft	3ms	צוה	845		command
34: 10	קם	qal	pft	3ms	קום	877		arise,stand
	ידעו	qal	pft	3ms	ידע	393	3ms	know
34: 11	שׁלחו	qal	pft	3ms	שׁלח	1018	3ms	send
	עשׂות	qal	infc		עשׂה	793		do,make
34: 12	עשׂה	qal	pft	3ms	עשׂה	793		do,make

JOSHUA

ChVs	Form	Stem	Tnse	PGN	Root	BDB	Sfx	Meaning
1: 1	יהי	qal	wci	3ms	היה	224		be,become
	יאמר	qal	wci	3ms	אמר	55		say
	משׁרת	piel	ptc	ms	שׁרת	1058		minister,serve
	אמר	qal	infc		אמר	55		say
1: 2	מת	qal	pft	3ms	מות	559		die
	קום	qal	impv	ms	קום	877		arise,stand
	עבר	qal	impv	ms	עבר	716		pass over
	נתן	qal	ptc	ms	נתן	678		give,set
1: 3	תדרך	qal	impf	3fs	דרך	201		tread,march
	נתתיו	qal	pft	1cs	נתן	678	3ms	give,set
	דברתי	piel	pft	1cs	דבר	180		speak
1: 4	יהיה	qal	impf	3ms	היה	224		be,become
1: 5	יתיצב	hith	impf	3ms	יצב	426		stand oneself
	הייתי	qal	pft	1cs	היה	224		be,become
	אהיה	qal	impf	1cs	היה	224		be,become
	ארפך	hiph	impf	1cs	רפה	951	2ms	slacken,abandon
	אעזבך	qal	impf	1cs	עזב	736	2ms	leave,loose
1: 6	חזק	qal	impv	ms	חזק	304		be strong
	אמץ	qal	impv	ms	אמץ	54		be strong
	תנחיל	hiph	impf	2ms	נחל	635		c. to inherit
1: 6	נשׁבעתי	niph	pft	1cs	שׁבע	989		swear
	תת	qal	infc		נתן	678		give,set
1: 7	חזק	qal	impv	ms	חזק	304		be strong
	אמץ	qal	impv	ms	אמץ	54		be strong
	שׁמר	qal	infc		שׁמר	1036		keep,watch
	עשׂות	qal	infc		עשׂה	793		do,make
	צוך	piel	pft	3ms	צוה	845	2ms	command
	תסור	qal	jusm	2ms	סור	693		turn aside
	תשׂכיל	hiph	impf	2ms	שׂכל	968		look at,prosper
	תלך	qal	impf	2ms	הלך	229		walk,go
1: 8	ימושׁ	qal	impf	3ms	מושׁ	559		depart,remove
	הגית	qal	wcp	2ms	הגה	211		groan,utter
	תשׁמר	qal	impf	2ms	שׁמר	1036		keep,watch
	עשׂות	qal	infc		עשׂה	793		do,make
	כתוב	qal	pptc	ms	כתב	507		write
	תצליח	hiph	impf	2ms	צלח	852		cause to thrive
	תשׂכיל	hiph	impf	2ms	שׂכל	968		look at,prosper
1: 9	צויתיך	piel	pft	1cs	צוה	845	2ms	command
	חזק	qal	impv	ms	חזק	304		be strong
	אמץ	qal	impv	ms	אמץ	54		be strong
	תערץ	qal	jusm	2ms	ערץ	791		frighten,fear
	תחת	qal	jusm	2ms	חתת	369		be shattered
	תלך	qal	impf	2ms	הלך	229		walk,go
1: 10	יצו	piel	wci	3ms	צוה	845		command
	אמר	qal	infc		אמר	55		say
1: 11	עברו	qal	impv	mp	עבר	716		pass over
	צוו	piel	impv	mp	צוה	845		command
	אמר	qal	infc		אמר	55		say
	הכינו	hiph	impv	mp	כון	465		fix,prepare
	עברים	qal	ptc	mp	עבר	716		pass over
	בוא	qal	infc		בוא	97		come in
	רשׁת	qal	infc		ירשׁ	439		possess,inherit
	נתן	qal	ptc	ms	נתן	678		give,set
	רשׁתה	qal	infc		ירשׁ	439	3fs	possess,inherit
1: 12	אמר	qal	pft	3ms	אמר	55		say
	אמר	qal	infc		אמר	55		say
1: 13	זכור	qal	infa		זכר	269		remember
	צוה	piel	pft	3ms	צוה	845		command
	אמר	qal	infc		אמר	55		say
	מניח	hiph	ptc	ms	נוח	628		give rest,put
	נתן	qal	wcp	3ms	נתן	678		give,set
1: 14	ישׁבו	qal	impf	3mp	ישׁב	442		sit,dwell
	נתן	qal	pft	3ms	נתן	678		give,set
	תעברו	qal	impf	2mp	עבר	716		pass over
	עזרתם	qal	wcp	2mp	עזר	740		help,aid
1: 15	יניח	hiph	impf	3ms	נוח	628		give rest,put
	ירשׁו	qal	wcp	3cp	ירשׁ	439		possess,inherit
	נתן	qal	ptc	ms	נתן	678		give,set
	שׁבתם	qal	wcp	2mp	שׁוב	996		turn,return
	ירשׁתם	qal	wcp	2mp	ירשׁ	439		possess,inherit
	נתן	qal	pft	3ms	נתן	678		give,set
1: 16	יענו	qal	wci	3mp	ענה	772		answer
	אמר	qal	infc		אמר	55		say
	צויתנו	piel	pft	2ms	צוה	845	1cp	command

ChVs	Form	Stem	Tnse	PGN	Root	BDB	Sfx	Meaning
1:16	נעשׂה	qal	impf	1cp	עשׂה	793		do,make
	תשׁלחנו	qal	impf	2ms	שׁלח	1018	1cp	send
	נלך	qal	impf	1cp	הלך	229		walk,go
1:17	שׁמענו	qal	pft	1cp	שׁמע	1033		hear
	נשׁמע	qal	impf	1cp	שׁמע	1033		hear
	יהיה	qal	jusm	3ms	היה	224		be,become
	היה	qal	pft	3ms	היה	224		be,become
1:18	ימרה	hiph	impf	3ms	מרה	598		rebel
	ישׁמע	qal	impf	3ms	שׁמע	1033		hear
	תצונו	piel	impf	2ms	צוה	845	3ms	command
	יומת	hoph	impf	3ms	מות	559		be killed
	חזק	qal	impv	ms	חזק	304		be strong
	אמץ	qal	impv	ms	אמץ	54		be strong
2:1	ישׁלח	qal	wci	3ms	שׁלח	1018		send
	מרגלים	piel	ptc	mp	רגל	920		slander,spy
	אמר	qal	infc		אמר	55		say
	לכו	qal	impv	mp	הלך	229		walk,go
	ראו	qal	impv	mp	ראה	906		see
	ילכו	qal	wci	3mp	הלך	229		walk,go
	יבאו	qal	wci	3mp	בוא	97		come in
	זונה	qal	ptc	fs	זנה	275		act a harlot
	ישׁכבו	qal	wci	3mp	שׁכב	1011		lie,lie down
2:2	יאמר	niph	wci	3ms	אמר	55		be said,called
	אמר	qal	infc		אמר	55		say
	באו	qal	pft	3cp	בוא	97		come in
	חפר	qal	infc		חפר	343		dig,search
2:3	ישׁלח	qal	wci	3ms	שׁלח	1018		send
	אמר	qal	infc		אמר	55		say
	הוציאי	hiph	impv	fs	יצא	422		bring out
	באים	qal	ptc	mp	בוא	97		come in
	באו	qal	pft	3cp	בוא	97		come in
	חפר	qal	infc		חפר	343		dig,search
	באו	qal	pft	3cp	בוא	97		come in
2:4	תקח	qal	wci	3fs	לקח	542		take
	תצפנו	qal	wci	3fs	צפן	860	3ms	hide
	תאמר	qal	wci	3fs	אמר	55		say
	באו	qal	pft	3cp	בוא	97		come in
	ידעתי	qal	pft	1cs	ידע	393		know
2:5	יהי	qal	wci	3ms	היה	224		be,become
	סגור	qal	infc		סגר	688		shut
	יצאו	qal	pft	3cp	יצא	422		go out
	ידעתי	qal	pft	1cs	ידע	393		know
	הלכו	qal	pft	3cp	הלך	229		walk,go
	רדפו	qal	impv	mp	רדף	922		pursue
	תשׂיגום	hiph	impf	2mp	נשׂג	673	3mp	reach,overtake
2:6	העלתם	hiph	pft	3fs	עלה	748	3mp	bring up,offer
	תטמנם	qal	wci	3fs	טמן	380	3mp	hide
	ערכות	qal	pptc	fp	ערך	789		set in order
2:7	רדפו	qal	pft	3cp	רדף	922		pursue
	סגרו	qal	pft	3cp	סגר	688		shut
	יצאו	qal	pft	3cp	יצא	422		go out
	רדפים	qal	ptc	mp	רדף	922		pursue
2:8	ישׁכבון	qal	impf	3mp	שׁכב	1011		lie,lie down
	עלתה	qal	pft	3fs	עלה	748		go up
2:9	תאמר	qal	wci	3fs	אמר	55		say
	ידעתי	qal	pft	1cs	ידע	393		know
	נתן	qal	pft	3ms	נתן	678		give,set
	נפלה	qal	pft	3fs	נפל	656		fall
	נמגו	niph	pft	3cp	מוג	556		melt away
	ישׁבי	qal	ptc	mp	ישׁב	442		sit,dwell
2:10	שׁמענו	qal	pft	1cp	שׁמע	1033		hear
	הוביש	hiph	pft	3ms	יבשׁ	386		make dry
	צאתכם	qal	infc		יצא	422	2mp	go out
	עשׂיתם	qal	pft	2mp	עשׂה	793		do,make
	החרמתם	hiph	pft	2mp	חרם	355		ban,destroy
2:11	נשׁמע	qal	wci	1cp	שׁמע	1033		hear
	ימס	niph	wci	3ms	מסס	587		melt,despair
	קמה	qal	pft	3fs	קום	877		arise,stand
2:12	השׁבעו	niph	impv	mp	שׁבע	989		swear
	עשׂיתי	qal	pft	1cs	עשׂה	793		do,make
	עשׂיתם	qal	wcp	2mp	עשׂה	793		do,make
	נתתם	qal	wcp	2mp	נתן	678		give,set
2:13	החיתם	hiph	wcp	2mp	חיה	310		preserve
	הצלתם	hiph	wcp	2mp	נצל	664		snatch,deliver
2:14	יאמרו	qal	wci	3mp	אמר	55		say
	מות	qal	infc		מות	559		die
	תגידו	hiph	impf	2mp	נגד	616		declare,tell
	היה	qal	wcp	3ms	היה	224		be,become
	תת	qal	infc		נתן	678		give,set
	עשׂינו	qal	wcp	1cp	עשׂה	793		do,make
2:15	תורדם	hiph	wci	3fs	ירד	432	3mp	bring down
	יושׁבת	qal	ptc	fs	ישׁב	442		sit,dwell
2:16	תאמר	qal	wci	3fs	אמר	55		say
	לכו	qal	impv	mp	הלך	229		walk,go
	יפגעו	qal	impf	3mp	פגע	803		meet,encounter
	רדפים	qal	ptc	mp	רדף	922		pursue
	נחבתם	niph	wcp	2mp	חבא	285		hide oneself
	שׁוב	qal	infc		שׁוב	996		turn,return
	רדפים	qal	ptc	mp	רדף	922		pursue
	תלכו	qal	impf	2mp	הלך	229		walk,go
2:17	יאמרו	qal	wci	3mp	אמר	55		say
	השׁבעתנו	hiph	pft	2fs	שׁבע	989	1cp	cause to swear
2:18	באים	qal	ptc	mp	בוא	97		come in
	תקשׁרי	qal	impf	2fs	קשׁר	905		bind
	הורדתנו	hiph	pft	2fs	ירד	432	1cp	bring down
	תאספי	qal	impf	2fs	אסף	62		gather
2:19	היה	qal	wcp	3ms	היה	224		be,become
	יצא	qal	impf	3ms	יצא	422		go out
	יהיה	qal	impf	3ms	היה	224		be,become
	תהיה	qal	impf	3fs	היה	224		be,become
2:20	תגידי	hiph	impf	2fs	נגד	616		declare,tell
	היינו	qal	wcp	1cp	היה	224		be,become
	השׁבעתנו	hiph	pft	2fs	שׁבע	989	1cp	cause to swear
2:21	תאמר	qal	wci	3fs	אמר	55		say
	תשׁלחם	piel	wci	3fs	שׁלח	1018	3mp	send away,shoot
	ילכו	qal	wci	3mp	הלך	229		walk,go
	תקשׁר	qal	wci	3fs	קשׁר	905		bind
2:22	ילכו	qal	wci	3mp	הלך	229		walk,go

ChVs	Form	Stem	Tnse	PGN	Root	BDB	Sfx	Meaning
2: 22	יבאו	qal	wci	3mp	בוא	97		come in
	ישבו	qal	wci	3mp	ישב	442		sit,dwell
	שבו	qal	pft	3cp	שוב	996		turn,return
	רדפים	qal	ptc	mp	רדף	922		pursue
	יבקשו	piel	wci	3mp	בקש	134		seek
	רדפים	qal	ptc	mp	רדף	922		pursue
	מצאו	qal	pft	3cp	מצא	592		find
2: 23	ישבו	qal	wci	3mp	שוב	996		turn,return
	ירדו	qal	wci	3mp	ירד	432		come down
	יעברו	qal	wci	3mp	עבר	716		pass over
	יבאו	qal	wci	3mp	בוא	97		come in
	יספרו	piel	wci	3mp	ספר	707		recount
	מצאות	qal	ptc	fp	מצא	592		find
2: 24	יאמרו	qal	wci	3mp	אמר	55		say
	נתן	qal	pft	3ms	נתן	678		give,set
	נמגו	niph	pft	3cp	מוג	556		melt away
	ישבי	qal	ptc	mp	ישב	442		sit,dwell
3: 1	ישכם	hiph	wci	3ms	שכם	1014		rise early
	יסעו	qal	wci	3mp	נסע	652		pull up,set out
	יבאו	qal	wci	3mp	בוא	97		come in
	ילנו	qal	wci	3mp	לון	533		lodge,remain
	יעברו	qal	impf	3mp	עבר	716		pass over
3: 2	יהי	qal	wci	3ms	היה	224		be,become
	יעברו	qal	wci	3mp	עבר	716		pass over
3: 3	יצוו	piel	wci	3mp	צוה	845		command
	אמר	qal	infc		אמר	55		say
	ראותכם	qal	infc		ראה	906	2mp	see
	נשאים	qal	ptc	mp	נשא	669		lift,carry
	תסעו	qal	impf	2mp	נסע	652		pull up,set out
	הלכתם	qal	wcp	2mp	הלך	229		walk,go
3: 4	יהיה	qal	impf	3ms	היה	224		be,become
	תקרבו	qal	jusm	2mp	קרב	897		approach
	תדעו	qal	impf	2mp	ידע	393		know
	תלכו	qal	impf	2mp	הלך	229		walk,go
	עברתם	qal	pft	2mp	עבר	716		pass over
3: 5	יאמר	qal	wci	3ms	אמר	55		say
	התקדשו	hith	impv	mp	קדש	872		consecrate self
	יעשה	qal	impf	3ms	עשה	793		do,make
	נפלאות	niph	ptc	fp	פלא	810		be wonderful
3: 6	יאמר	qal	wci	3ms	אמר	55		say
	אמר	qal	infc		אמר	55		say
	שאו	qal	impv	mp	נשא	669		lift,carry
	עברו	qal	impv	mp	עבר	716		pass over
	ישאו	qal	wci	3mp	נשא	669		lift,carry
	ילכו	qal	wci	3mp	הלך	229		walk,go
3: 7	יאמר	qal	wci	3ms	אמר	55		say
	אחל	hiph	impf	1cs	חלל	320		begin,profane
	גדלך	piel	infc		גדל	152	2ms	cause to grow
	ידעון	qal	impf	3mp	ידע	393		know
	הייתי	qal	pft	1cs	היה	224		be,become
	אהיה	qal	impf	1cs	היה	224		be,become
3: 8	תצוה	piel	impf	2ms	צוה	845		command
	נשאי	qal	ptc	mp	נשא	669		lift,carry
	אמר	qal	infc		אמר	55		say

ChVs	Form	Stem	Tnse	PGN	Root	BDB	Sfx	Meaning
3: 8	באכם	qal	infc		בוא	97	2mp	come in
	תעמדו	qal	impf	2mp	עמד	763		stand,stop
3: 9	יאמר	qal	wci	3ms	אמר	55		say
	גשו	qal	impv	mp	נגש	620		draw near
	שמעו	qal	impv	mp	שמע	1033		hear
3: 10	יאמר	qal	wci	3ms	אמר	55		say
	תדעון	qal	impf	2mp	ידע	393		know
	הורש	hiph	infa		ירש	439		c. to possess
	יוריש	hiph	impf	3ms	ירש	439		c. to possess
3: 11	עבר	qal	ptc	ms	עבר	716		pass over
3: 12	קחו	qal	impv	mp	לקח	542		take
3: 13	היה	qal	wcp	3ms	היה	224		be,become
	נוח	qal	infc		נוח	628		rest
	נשאי	qal	ptc	mp	נשא	669		lift,carry
	יכרתון	niph	impf	3mp	כרת	503		be cut off
	ירדים	qal	ptc	mp	ירד	432		come down
	יעמדו	qal	impf	3mp	עמד	763		stand,stop
3: 14	יהי	qal	wci	3ms	היה	224		be,become
	נסע	qal	infc		נסע	652		pull up,set out
	עבר	qal	infc		עבר	716		pass over
	נשאי	qal	ptc	mp	נשא	669		lift,carry
3: 15	בוא	qal	infc		בוא	97		come in
	נשאי	qal	ptc	mp	נשא	669		lift,carry
	נשאי	qal	ptc	mp	נשא	669		lift,carry
	נטבלו	niph	pft	3cp	טבל	371		be dipped
	מלא	qal	pft	3ms	מלא	569		be full,fill
3: 16	יעמדו	qal	wci	3mp	עמד	763		stand,stop
	ירדים	qal	ptc	mp	ירד	432		come down
	קמו	qal	pft	3cp	קום	877		arise,stand
	הרחק	hiph	infa		רחק	934		put far away
	ירדים	qal	ptc	mp	ירד	432		come down
	תמו	qal	pft	3cp	תמם	1070		be finished
	נכרתו	niph	pft	3cp	כרת	503		be cut off
	עברו	qal	pft	3cp	עבר	716		pass over
3: 17	יעמדו	qal	wci	3mp	עמד	763		stand,stop
	נשאי	qal	ptc	mp	נשא	669		lift,carry
	הכן	hiph	infa		כון	465		fix,prepare
	עברים	qal	ptc	mp	עבר	716		pass over
	תמו	qal	pft	3cp	תמם	1070		be finished
	עבר	qal	infc		עבר	716		pass over
4: 1	יהי	qal	wci	3ms	היה	224		be,become
	תמו	qal	pft	3cp	תמם	1070		be finished
	עבור	qal	infc		עבר	716		pass over
	יאמר	qal	wci	3ms	אמר	55		say
	אמר	qal	infc		אמר	55		say
4: 2	קחו	qal	impv	mp	לקח	542		take
4: 3	צוו	piel	impv	mp	צוה	845		command
	אמר	qal	infc		אמר	55		say
	שאו	qal	impv	mp	נשא	669		lift,carry
	הכין	hiph	infa		כון	465		fix,prepare
	העברתם	hiph	wcp	2mp	עבר	716		cause to pass
	הנחתם	hiph	wcp	2mp	נוח	628		give rest,put
	תלינו	qal	impf	2mp	לון	533		lodge,remain
4: 4	יקרא	qal	wci	3ms	קרא	894		call,proclaim

ChVs	Form	Stem	Tnse	PGN	Root	BDB	Sfx	Meaning
4:4	הכין	hiph	pft	3ms	כון	465		fix,prepare
4:5	יאמר	qal	wci	3ms	אמר	55		say
	עברו	qal	impv	mp	עבר	716		pass over
	הרימו	hiph	impv	mp	רום	926		raise,lift
4:6	תהיה	qal	impf	3fs	היה	224		be,become
	ישאלון	qal	impf	3mp	שׁאל	981		ask,borrow
	אמר	qal	infc		אמר	55		say
4:7	אמרתם	qal	wcp	2mp	אמר	55		say
	נכרתו	niph	pft	3cp	כרת	503		be cut off
	עברו	qal	infc		עבר	716	3ms	pass over
	נכרתו	niph	pft	3cp	כרת	503		be cut off
	היו	qal	wcp	3cp	היה	224		be,become
4:8	יעשׂו	qal	wci	3mp	עשׂה	793		do,make
	צוה	piel	pft	3ms	צוה	845		command
	ישׂאו	qal	wci	3mp	נשׂא	669		lift,carry
	דבר	piel	pft	3ms	דבר	180		speak
	יעברום	hiph	wci	3mp	עבר	716	3mp	cause to pass
	ינחום	hiph	wci	3mp	נוח	628	3mp	give rest,put
4:9	הקים	hiph	pft	3ms	קום	877		raise,build,set
	נשׂאי	qal	ptc	mp	נשׂא	669		lift,carry
	יהיו	qal	wci	3mp	היה	224		be,become
4:10	נשׂאי	qal	ptc	mp	נשׂא	669		lift,carry
	עמדים	qal	ptc	mp	עמד	763		stand,stop
	תם	qal	infc		תמם	1070		be finished
	צוה	piel	pft	3ms	צוה	845		command
	דבר	piel	infc		דבר	180		speak
	צוה	piel	pft	3ms	צוה	845		command
	ימהרו	piel	wci	3mp	מהר	554		hasten
	יעברו	qal	wci	3mp	עבר	716		pass over
4:11	יהי	qal	wci	3ms	היה	224		be,become
	תם	qal	pft	3ms	תמם	1070		be finished
	עבור	qal	infc		עבר	716		pass over
	יעבר	qal	wci	3ms	עבר	716		pass over
4:12	יעברו	qal	wci	3mp	עבר	716		pass over
	דבר	piel	pft	3ms	דבר	180		speak
4:13	חלוצי	qal	pptc	mp	חלץ	323		equipped
	עברו	qal	pft	3cp	עבר	716		pass over
4:14	גדל	piel	pft	3ms	גדל	152		cause to grow
	יראו	qal	wci	3mp	ירא	431		fear
	יראו	qal	pft	3cp	ירא	431		fear
4:15	יאמר	qal	wci	3ms	אמר	55		say
	אמר	qal	infc		אמר	55		say
4:16	צוה	piel	impv	ms	צוה	845		command
	נשׂאי	qal	ptc	mp	נשׂא	669		lift,carry
	יעלו	qal	jusm	3mp	עלה	748		go up
4:17	יצו	piel	wci	3ms	צוה	845		command
	אמר	qal	infc		אמר	55		say
	עלו	qal	impv	mp	עלה	748		go up
4:18	יהי	qal	wci	3ms	היה	224		be,become
	עלות	qal	infc		עלה	748		go up
	נשׂאי	qal	ptc	mp	נשׂא	669		lift,carry
	נתקו	niph	pft	3cp	נתק	683		be drawn,torn
	ישׁבו	qal	wci	3mp	שׁוב	996		turn,return
	ילכו	qal	wci	3mp	הלך	229		walk,go

ChVs	Form	Stem	Tnse	PGN	Root	BDB	Sfx	Meaning
4:19	עלו	qal	pft	3cp	עלה	748		go up
	יחנו	qal	wci	3mp	חנה	333		decline,encamp
4:20	לקחו	qal	pft	3cp	לקח	542		take
	הקים	hiph	pft	3ms	קום	877		raise,build,set
4:21	יאמר	qal	wci	3ms	אמר	55		say
	אמר	qal	infc		אמר	55		say
	ישאלון	qal	impf	3mp	שׁאל	981		ask,borrow
	אמר	qal	infc		אמר	55		say
4:22	הודעתם	hiph	wcp	2mp	ידע	393		declare
	אמר	qal	infc		אמר	55		say
	עבר	qal	pft	3ms	עבר	716		pass over
4:23	הוביש	hiph	pft	3ms	יבשׁ	386		make dry
	עברכם	qal	infc		עבר	716	2mp	pass over
	עשׂה	qal	pft	3ms	עשׂה	793		do,make
	הוביש	hiph	pft	3ms	יבשׁ	386		make dry
	עברנו	qal	infc		עבר	716	1cp	pass over
4:24	דעת	qal	infc		ידע	393		know
	יראתם	qal	pft	2mp	ירא	431		fear
5:1	יהי	qal	wci	3ms	היה	224		be,become
	שׁמע	qal	infc		שׁמע	1033		hear
	הוביש	hiph	pft	3ms	יבשׁ	386		make dry
	עברנוk	qal	infc		עבר	716	1cp	pass over
	עברםq	qal	infc		עבר	716	3mp	pass over
	ימס	niph	wci	3ms	מסס	587		melt,despair
	היה	qal	pft	3ms	היה	224		be,become
5:2	אמר	qal	pft	3ms	אמר	55		say
	עשׂה	qal	impv	ms	עשׂה	793		do,make
	שׁוב	qal	impv	ms	שׁוב	996		turn,return
	מל	qal	impv	ms	מול	557		circumcise
5:3	יעשׂ	qal	wci	3ms	עשׂה	793		do,make
	ימל	qal	wci	3ms	מול	557		circumcise
5:4	מל	qal	pft	3ms	מול	557		circumcise
	יצא	qal	ptc	ms	יצא	422		go out
	מתו	qal	pft	3cp	מות	559		die
	צאתם	qal	infc		יצא	422	3mp	go out
5:5	מלים	qal	pptc	mp	מול	557		circumcise
	היו	qal	pft	3cp	היה	224		be,become
	יצאים	qal	ptc	mp	יצא	422		go out
	צאתם	qal	infc		יצא	422	3mp	go out
	מלו	qal	pft	3cp	מול	557		circumcise
5:6	הלכו	qal	pft	3cp	הלך	229		walk,go
	תם	qal	infc		תמם	1070		be finished
	יצאים	qal	ptc	mp	יצא	422		go out
	שׁמעו	qal	pft	3cp	שׁמע	1033		hear
	נשׁבע	niph	pft	3ms	שׁבע	989		swear
	הראותם	hiph	infc		ראה	906	3mp	show,exhibit
	נשׁבע	niph	pft	3ms	שׁבע	989		swear
	תת	qal	infc		נתן	678		give,set
	זבת	qal	ptc	fs	זוב	264		flow,gush
5:7	הקים	hiph	pft	3ms	קום	877		raise,build,set
	מל	qal	pft	3ms	מול	557		circumcise
	היו	qal	pft	3cp	היה	224		be,become
	מלו	qal	pft	3cp	מול	557		circumcise
5:8	יהי	qal	wci	3ms	היה	224		be,become

ChVs	Form	Stem	Tnse	PGN	Root	BDB	Sfx	Meaning
5:8	תמו	qal	pft	3cp	תמם	1070		be finished
	המול	niph	infc		מול	557		be circumcised
	ישבו	qal	wci	3mp	ישב	442		sit,dwell
	חיותם	qal	infc		חיה	310	3mp	live
5:9	יאמר	qal	wci	3ms	אמר	55		say
	גלותי	qal	pft	1cs	גלל	164		roll away
	יקרא	qal	wci	3ms	קרא	894		call,proclaim
5:10	יחנו	qal	wci	3mp	חנה	333		decline,encamp
	יעשׂו	qal	wci	3mp	עשׂה	793		do,make
5:11	יאכלו	qal	wci	3mp	אכל	37		eat,devour
	קלוי	qal	pptc	ms	קלה	885		roast
5:12	ישבת	qal	wci	3ms	שבת	991		cease,desist
	אכלם	qal	infc		אכל	37	3mp	eat,devour
	היה	qal	pft	3ms	היה	224		be,become
	יאכלו	qal	wci	3mp	אכל	37		eat,devour
5:13	יהי	qal	wci	3ms	היה	224		be,become
	היות	qal	infc		היה	224		be,become
	ישׂא	qal	wci	3ms	נשׂא	669		lift,carry
	ירא	qal	wci	3ms	ראה	906		see
	עמד	qal	ptc	ms	עמד	763		stand,stop
	שׁלופה	qal	pptc	fs	שׁלף	1025		draw out,off
	ילך	qal	wci	3ms	הלך	229		walk,go
	יאמר	qal	wci	3ms	אמר	55		say
5:14	יאמר	qal	wci	3ms	אמר	55		say
	באתי	qal	pft	1cs	בוא	97		come in
	יפל	qal	wci	3ms	נפל	656		fall
	ישתחו	hish	wci	3ms	חוה	1005		bow down
	יאמר	qal	wci	3ms	אמר	55		say
	מדבר	piel	ptc	ms	דבר	180		speak
5:15	יאמר	qal	wci	3ms	אמר	55		say
	שׁל	qal	impv	ms	נשׁל	675		draw off
	עמד	qal	ptc	ms	עמד	763		stand,stop
	יעשׂ	qal	wci	3ms	עשׂה	793		do,make
6:1	סגרת	qal	ptc	fs	סגר	688		shut
	מסגרת	pual	ptc	fs	סגר	688		be shut up
	יוצא	qal	ptc	ms	יצא	422		go out
	בא	qal	ptc	ms	בוא	97		come in
6:2	יאמר	qal	wci	3ms	אמר	55		say
	ראה	qal	impv	ms	ראה	906		see
	נתתי	qal	pft	1cs	נתן	678		give,set
6:3	סבתם	qal	wcp	2mp	סבב	685		surround
	הקיף	hiph	infa		נקף	668		surround
	תעשׂה	qal	impf	2ms	עשׂה	793		do,make
6:4	ישׂאו	qal	impf	3mp	נשׂא	669		lift,carry
	תסבו	qal	impf	2mp	סבב	685		surround
	יתקעו	qal	impf	3mp	תקע	1075		thrust,clap
6:5	היה	qal	wcp	3ms	היה	224		be,become
	משׁך	qal	infc		משׁך	604		draw,pull
	שׁמעכם	qal	infc		שׁמע	1033	2mp	hear
	יריעו	hiph	impf	3mp	רוע	929		raise a shout
	נפלה	qal	wcp	3fs	נפל	656		fall
	עלו	qal	wcp	3cp	עלה	748		go up
6:6	יקרא	qal	wci	3ms	קרא	894		call,proclaim
	יאמר	qal	wci	3ms	אמר	55		say

ChVs	Form	Stem	Tnse	PGN	Root	BDB	Sfx	Meaning
6:6	שׂאו	qal	impv	mp	נשׂא	669		lift,carry
	ישׂאו	qal	impf	3mp	נשׂא	669		lift,carry
6:7	יאמרוk	qal	wci	3mp	אמר	55		say
	יאמרq	qal	wci	3ms	אמר	55		say
	עברו	qal	impv	mp	עבר	716		pass over
	סבו	qal	impv	mp	סבב	685		surround
	חלוץ	qal	pptc	ms	חלץ	323		equipped
	יעבר	qal	impf	3ms	עבר	716		pass over
6:8	יהי	qal	wci	3ms	היה	224		be,become
	אמר	qal	infc		אמר	55		say
	נשׂאים	qal	ptc	mp	נשׂא	669		lift,carry
	עברו	qal	pft	3cp	עבר	716		pass over
	תקעו	qal	pft	3cp	תקע	1075		thrust,clap
	הלך	qal	ptc	ms	הלך	229		walk,go
6:9	חלוץ	qal	pptc	ms	חלץ	323		equipped
	הלך	qal	ptc	ms	הלך	229		walk,go
	תקעוk	qal	wcp	3cp	תקע	1075		thrust,clap
	תקעיq	qal	ptc	mp	תקע	1075		thrust,clap
	מאסף	piel	ptc	ms	אסף	62		gather
	הלך	qal	ptc	ms	הלך	229		walk,go
	הלוך	qal	infa		הלך	229		walk,go
	תקוע	qal	infa		תקע	1075		thrust,clap
6:10	צוה	piel	pft	3ms	צוה	845		command
	אמר	qal	infc		אמר	55		say
	תריעו	hiph	impf	2mp	רוע	929		raise a shout
	תשׁמיעו	hiph	impf	2mp	שׁמע	1033		cause to hear
	יצא	qal	impf	3ms	יצא	422		go out
	אמרי	qal	infc		אמר	55	1cs	say
	הריעו	hiph	impv	mp	רוע	929		raise a shout
	הריעתם	hiph	wcp	2mp	רוע	929		raise a shout
6:11	יסב	hiph	wci	3ms	סבב	685		cause to turn
	הקף	hiph	infa		נקף	668		surround
	יבאו	qal	wci	3mp	בוא	97		come in
	ילינו	qal	wci	3mp	לון	533		lodge,remain
6:12	ישׁכם	hiph	wci	3ms	שׁכם	1014		rise early
	ישׂאו	qal	wci	3mp	נשׂא	669		lift,carry
6:13	נשׂאים	qal	ptc	mp	נשׂא	669		lift,carry
	הלכים	qal	ptc	mp	הלך	229		walk,go
	הלוך	qal	infa		הלך	229		walk,go
	תקעו	qal	wcp	3cp	תקע	1075		thrust,clap
	חלוץ	qal	pptc	ms	חלץ	323		equipped
	הלך	qal	ptc	ms	הלך	229		walk,go
	מאסף	piel	ptc	ms	אסף	62		gather
	הלך	qal	ptc	ms	הלך	229		walk,go
	הולךk	qal	ptc	ms	הלך	229		walk,go
	הלוךq	qal	infa		הלך	229		walk,go
	תקוע	qal	infa		תקע	1075		thrust,clap
6:14	יסבו	qal	wci	3mp	סבב	685		surround
	ישׁבו	qal	wci	3mp	שׁוב	996		turn,return
	עשׂו	qal	pft	3cp	עשׂה	793		do,make
6:15	יהי	qal	wci	3ms	היה	224		be,become
	ישׁכמו	hiph	wci	3mp	שׁכם	1014		rise early
	עלות	qal	infc		עלה	748		go up
	יסבו	qal	wci	3mp	סבב	685		surround

ChVs	Form	Stem	Tnse	PGN	Root	BDB	Sfx	Meaning
6:15	סבבו	qal	pft	3cp	סבב	685		surround
6:16	יהי	qal	wci	3ms	היה	224		be,become
	תקעו	qal	pft	3cp	תקע	1075		thrust,clap
	יאמר	qal	wci	3ms	אמר	55		say
	הריעו	hiph	impv	mp	רוע	929		raise a shout
	נתן	qal	pft	3ms	נתן	678		give,set
6:17	היתה	qal	wcp	3fs	היה	224		be,become
	זונה	qal	ptc	fs	זנה	275		act a harlot
	תחיה	qal	impf	3fs	חיה	310		live
	החבאתה	hiph	pft	3fs	חבא	285		hide
	שׁלחנו	qal	pft	1cp	שׁלח	1018		send
6:18	שׁמרו	qal	impv	mp	שׁמר	1036		keep,watch
	תחרימו	hiph	impf	2mp	חרם	355		ban,destroy
	לקחתם	qal	wcp	2mp	לקח	542		take
	שׂמתם	qal	wcp	2mp	שׂים	962		put,set
	עכרתם	qal	wcp	2mp	עכר	747		trouble
6:19	יבוא	qal	impf	3ms	בוא	97		come in
6:20	ירע	hiph	wci	3ms	רוע	929		raise a shout
	יתקעו	qal	wci	3mp	תקע	1075		thrust,clap
	יהי	qal	wci	3ms	היה	224		be,become
	שׁמע	qal	infc		שׁמע	1033		hear
	יריעו	hiph	wci	3mp	רוע	929		raise a shout
	תפל	qal	wci	3fs	נפל	656		fall
	יעל	qal	wci	3ms	עלה	748		go up
	ילכדו	qal	wci	3mp	לכד	539		capture
6:21	יחרימו	hiph	wci	3mp	חרם	355		ban,destroy
6:22	מרגלים	piel	ptc	mp	רגל	920		slander,spy
	אמר	qal	pft	3ms	אמר	55		say
	באו	qal	impv	mp	בוא	97		come in
	זונה	qal	ptc	fs	זנה	275		act a harlot
	הוציאו	hiph	impv	mp	יצא	422		bring out
	נשׁבעתם	niph	pft	2mp	שׁבע	989		swear
6:23	יבאו	qal	wci	3mp	בוא	97		come in
	מרגלים	piel	ptc	mp	רגל	920		slander,spy
	יציאו	hiph	wci	3mp	יצא	422		bring out
	הוציאו	hiph	pft	3cp	יצא	422		bring out
	יניחום	hiph	wci	3mp	נוח	628	3mp	give rest,put
6:24	שׂרפו	qal	pft	3cp	שׂרף	976		burn
	נתנו	qal	pft	3cp	נתן	678		give,set
6:25	זונה	qal	ptc	fs	זנה	275		act a harlot
	החיה	hiph	pft	3ms	חיה	310		preserve
	תשׁב	qal	wci	3fs	ישׁב	442		sit,dwell
	החביאה	hiph	pft	3fs	חבא	285		hide
	שׁלח	qal	pft	3ms	שׁלח	1018		send
	רגל	piel	infc		רגל	920		slander,spy
6:26	ישׁבע	hiph	wci	3ms	שׁבע	989		cause to swear
	אמר	qal	infc		אמר	55		say
	ארור	qal	pptc	ms	ארר	76		curse
	יקום	qal	impf	3ms	קום	877		arise,stand
	בנה	qal	wcp	3ms	בנה	124		build
	ייסדנה	piel	impf	3ms	יסד	413	3fs	found,establish
	יציב	hiph	impf	3ms	נצב	662		cause to stand
6:27	יהי	qal	wci	3ms	היה	224		be,become
	יהי	qal	wci	3ms	היה	224		be,become

ChVs	Form	Stem	Tnse	PGN	Root	BDB	Sfx	Meaning
7:1	ימעלו	qal	wci	3mp	מעל	591		act faithlessly
	יקח	qal	wci	3ms	לקח	542		take
	יחר	qal	wci	3ms	חרה	354		be kindled,burn
7:2	ישׁלח	qal	wci	3ms	שׁלח	1018		send
	יאמר	qal	wci	3ms	אמר	55		say
	אמר	qal	infc		אמר	55		say
	עלו	qal	impv	mp	עלה	748		go up
	רגלו	piel	impv	mp	רגל	920		slander,spy
	יעלו	qal	wci	3mp	עלה	748		go up
	ירגלו	piel	wci	3mp	רגל	920		slander,spy
7:3	ישׁבו	qal	wci	3mp	שׁוב	996		turn,return
	יאמרו	qal	wci	3mp	אמר	55		say
	יעל	qal	jus	3ms	עלה	748		go up
	יעלו	qal	jusm	3mp	עלה	748		go up
	יכו	hiph	jusm	3mp	נכה	645		smite
	תיגע	piel	jusm	2ms	יגע	388		make weary
7:4	יעלו	qal	wci	3mp	עלה	748		go up
	ינסו	qal	wci	3mp	נוס	630		flee,escape
7:5	יכו	hiph	wci	3mp	נכה	645		smite
	ירדפום	qal	wci	3mp	רדף	922	3mp	pursue
	יכום	hiph	wci	3mp	נכה	645	3mp	smite
	ימס	niph	wci	3ms	מסס	587		melt,despair
	יהי	qal	wci	3ms	היה	224		be,become
7:6	יקרע	qal	wci	3ms	קרע	902		tear,rend
	יפל	qal	wci	3ms	נפל	656		fall
	יעלו	hiph	wci	3mp	עלה	748		bring up,offer
7:7	יאמר	qal	wci	3ms	אמר	55		say
	העברת	hiph	pft	2ms	עבר	716		cause to pass
	העביר	hiph	infa		עבר	716		cause to pass
	תת	qal	infc		נתן	678		give,set
	האבידנו	hiph	infc		אבד	1	1cp	destroy
	הואלנו	hiph	pft	1cp	יאל	383		be willing
	נשׁב	qal	wci	1cp	ישׁב	442		sit,dwell
7:8	אמר	qal	impf	1cs	אמר	55		say
	הפך	qal	pft	3ms	הפך	245		turn,overturn
	איביו	qal	ptc	mp	איב	33	3ms	be hostile to
7:9	ישׁמעו	qal	impf	3mp	שׁמע	1033		hear
	ישׁבי	qal	ptc	mp	ישׁב	442		sit,dwell
	נסבו	niph	wcp	3cp	סבב	685		turn round
	הכריתו	hiph	wcp	3cp	כרת	503		cut off,destroy
	תעשׂה	qal	impf	2ms	עשׂה	793		do,make
7:10	יאמר	qal	wci	3ms	אמר	55		say
	קם	qal	impv	ms	קום	877		arise,stand
	נפל	qal	ptc	ms	נפל	656		fall
7:11	חטא	qal	pft	3ms	חטא	306		sin
	עברו	qal	pft	3cp	עבר	716		pass over
	צויתי	piel	pft	1cs	צוה	845		command
	לקחו	qal	pft	3cp	לקח	542		take
	גנבו	qal	pft	3cp	גנב	170		steal
	כחשׁו	piel	pft	3cp	כחשׁ	471		deceive
	שׂמו	qal	pft	3cp	שׂים	962		put,set
7:12	יכלו	qal	impf	3mp	יכל	407		be able
	קום	qal	infc		קום	877		arise,stand
	איביהם	qal	ptc	mp	איב	33	3mp	be hostile to

ChVs	Form	Stem	Tnse	PGN	Root	BDB	Sfx	Meaning
7:12	יפנו	qal	impf	3mp	פנה	815		turn
	איביהם	qal	ptc	mp	איב	33	3mp	be hostile to
	היו	qal	pft	3cp	היה	224		be,become
	אוסיף	hiph	impf	1cs	יסף	414		add,do again
	היות	qal	infc		היה	224		be,become
	תשׁמידו	hiph	impf	2mp	שׁמד	1029		exterminate
7:13	קם	qal	impv	ms	קום	877		arise,stand
	קדשׁ	piel	impv	ms	קדשׁ	872		consecrate
	אמרת	qal	wcp	2ms	אמר	55		say
	התקדשׁו	hith	impv	mp	קדשׁ	872		consecrate self
	אמר	qal	pft	3ms	אמר	55		say
	תוכל	qal	impf	2ms	יכל	407		be able
	קום	qal	infc		קום	877		arise,stand
	איביך	qal	ptc	mp	איב	33	2ms	be hostile to
	הסירכם	hiph	infc		סור	693	2mp	take away
7:14	נקרבתם	niph	wcp	2mp	קרב	897		be brought
	היה	qal	wcp	3ms	היה	224		be,become
	ילכדנו	qal	impf	3ms	לכד	539	3ms	capture
	יקרב	qal	impf	3ms	קרב	897		approach
	ילכדנה	qal	impf	3ms	לכד	539	3fs	capture
	תקרב	qal	impf	3fs	קרב	897		approach
	ילכדנו	qal	impf	3ms	לכד	539	3ms	capture
	יקרב	qal	impf	3ms	קרב	897		approach
7:15	היה	qal	wcp	3ms	היה	224		be,become
	נלכד	niph	ptc	ms	לכד	539		be captured
	ישׂרף	niph	impf	3ms	שׂרף	976		be burned
	עבר	qal	pft	3ms	עבר	716		pass over
	עשׂה	qal	pft	3ms	עשׂה	793		do,make
7:16	ישׁכם	hiph	wci	3ms	שׁכם	1014		rise early
	יקרב	hiph	wci	3ms	קרב	897		bring near
	ילכד	niph	wci	3ms	לכד	539		be captured
7:17	יקרב	hiph	wci	3ms	קרב	897		bring near
	ילכד	qal	wci	3ms	לכד	539		capture
	יקרב	hiph	wci	3ms	קרב	897		bring near
	ילכד	niph	wci	3ms	לכד	539		be captured
7:18	יקרב	hiph	wci	3ms	קרב	897		bring near
	ילכד	niph	wci	3ms	לכד	539		be captured
7:19	יאמר	qal	wci	3ms	אמר	55		say
	שׂים	qal	impv	ms	שׂים	962		put,set
	תן	qal	impv	ms	נתן	678		give,set
	הגד	hiph	impv	ms	נגד	616		declare,tell
	עשׂית	qal	pft	2ms	עשׂה	793		do,make
	תכחד	piel	jusm	2ms	כחד	470		hide
7:20	יען	qal	wci	3ms	ענה	772		answer
	יאמר	qal	wci	3ms	אמר	55		say
	חטאתי	qal	pft	1cs	חטא	306		sin
	עשׂיתי	qal	pft	1cs	עשׂה	793		do,make
7:21	אראהk	qal	wci	1cs	ראה	906		see
	אראq	qal	wci	1cs	ראה	906		see
	אחמדם	qal	wci	1cs	חמד	326	3mp	desire
	אקחם	qal	wci	1cs	לקח	542	3mp	take
	טמונים	qal	pptc	mp	טמן	380		hide
7:22	ישׁלח	qal	wci	3ms	שׁלח	1018		send
	ירצו	qal	wci	3mp	רוץ	930		run

ChVs	Form	Stem	Tnse	PGN	Root	BDB	Sfx	Meaning
7:22	טמונה	qal	pptc	fs	טמן	380		hide
7:23	יקחום	qal	wci	3mp	לקח	542	3mp	take
	יבאום	hiph	wci	3mp	בוא	97	3mp	bring in
	יצקם	hiph	wci	3mp	יצק	427	3mp	pour
7:24	יקח	qal	wci	3ms	לקח	542		take
	יעלו	hiph	wci	3mp	עלה	748		bring up,offer
7:25	יאמר	qal	wci	3ms	אמר	55		say
	עכרתנו	qal	pft	2ms	עכר	747	1cp	trouble
	יעכרך	qal	impf	3ms	עכר	747	2ms	trouble
	ירגמו	qal	wci	3mp	רגם	920		stone
	ישׂרפו	qal	wci	3mp	שׂרף	976		burn
	יסקלו	qal	wci	3mp	סקל	709		stone to death
7:26	יקימו	hiph	wci	3mp	קום	877		raise,build,set
	ישׁב	qal	wci	3ms	שׁוב	996		turn,return
	קרא	qal	pft	3ms	קרא	894		call,proclaim
8:1	יאמר	qal	wci	3ms	אמר	55		say
	תירא	qal	jusm	2ms	ירא	431		fear
	תחת	qal	jusm	2ms	חתת	369		be shattered
	קח	qal	impv	ms	לקח	542		take
	קום	qal	impv	ms	קום	877		arise,stand
	עלה	qal	impv	ms	עלה	748		go up
	ראה	qal	impv	ms	ראה	906		see
	נתתי	qal	pft	1cs	נתן	678		give,set
8:2	עשׂית	qal	wcp	2ms	עשׂה	793		do,make
	עשׂית	qal	pft	2ms	עשׂה	793		do,make
	תבזו	qal	impf	2mp	בזז	102		plunder
	שׂים	qal	impv	ms	שׂים	962		put,set
	ארב	qal	ptc	ms	ארב	70		lie in wait
8:3	יקם	qal	wci	3ms	קום	877		arise,stand
	עלות	qal	infc		עלה	748		go up
	יבחר	qal	wci	3ms	בחר	103		choose
	ישׁלחם	qal	wci	3ms	שׁלח	1018	3mp	send
8:4	יצו	piel	wci	3ms	צוה	845		command
	אמר	qal	infc		אמר	55		say
	ראו	qal	impv	mp	ראה	906		see
	ארבים	qal	ptc	mp	ארב	70		lie in wait
	תרחיקו	hiph	jusm	2mp	רחק	934		put far away
	הייתם	qal	wcp	2mp	היה	224		be,become
	נכנים	niph	ptc	mp	כון	465		be established
8:5	נקרב	qal	impf	1cp	קרב	897		approach
	היה	qal	wcp	3ms	היה	224		be,become
	יצאו	qal	impf	3mp	יצא	422		go out
	קראתנו	qal	infc		קרא	896	1cp	meet,encounter
	נסנו	qal	wcp	1cp	נוס	630		flee,escape
8:6	יצאו	qal	wcp	3cp	יצא	422		go out
	התיקנו	hiph	infc		נתק	683	1cp	draw away
	יאמרו	qal	impf	3mp	אמר	55		say
	נסים	qal	ptc	mp	נוס	630		flee,escape
	נסנו	qal	wcp	1cp	נוס	630		flee,escape
8:7	תקמו	qal	impf	2mp	קום	877		arise,stand
	אורב	qal	ptc	ms	ארב	70		lie in wait
	הורשׁתם	hiph	wcp	2mp	ירשׁ	439		c. to possess
	נתנה	qal	wcp	3ms	נתן	678	3fs	give,set
8:8	היה	qal	wcp	3ms	היה	224		be,become

ChVs	Form	Stem	Tnse	PGN	Root	BDB	Sfx	Meaning
8: 8	תפשׂכם	qal	infc		תפשׂ	1074	2mp	seize,grasp
	תציתו	hiph	impf	2mp	יצת	428		kindle
	תעשׂו	qal	impf	2mp	עשׂה	793		do,make
	ראו	qal	impv	mp	ראה	906		see
	צויתי	piel	pft	1cs	צוה	845		command
8: 9	ישׁלחם	qal	wci	3ms	שׁלח	1018	3mp	send
	ילכו	qal	wci	3mp	הלך	229		walk,go
	ישׁבו	qal	wci	3mp	ישׁב	442		sit,dwell
	ילן	qal	wci	3ms	לון	533		lodge,remain
8: 10	ישׁכם	hiph	wci	3ms	שׁכם	1014		rise early
	יפקד	qal	wci	3ms	פקד	823		attend to,visit
	יעל	qal	wci	3ms	עלה	748		go up
8: 11	עלו	qal	pft	3cp	עלה	748		go up
	ינשׁו	qal	wci	3mp	נגשׁ	620		draw near
	יבאו	qal	wci	3mp	בוא	97		come in
	יחנו	qal	wci	3mp	חנה	333		decline,encamp
8: 12	יקח	qal	wci	3ms	לקח	542		take
	ישׂם	qal	wci	3ms	שׂים	962		put,set
	ארב	qal	ptc	ms	ארב	70		lie in wait
8: 13	ישׂימו	qal	wci	3mp	שׂים	962		put,set
	ילך	qal	wci	3ms	הלך	229		walk,go
8: 14	יהי	qal	wci	3ms	היה	224		be,become
	ראות	qal	infc		ראה	906		see
	ימהרו	piel	wci	3mp	מהר	554		hasten
	ישׁכימו	hiph	wci	3mp	שׁכם	1014		rise early
	יצאו	qal	wci	3mp	יצא	422		go out
	קראת	qal	infc		קרא	896		meet,encounter
	ידע	qal	pft	3ms	ידע	393		know
	ארב	qal	ptc	ms	ארב	70		lie in wait
8: 15	ינגעו	niph	wci	3mp	נגע	619		be smitten
	ינסו	qal	wci	3mp	נוס	630		flee,escape
8: 16	יזעקו	niph	wci	3mp	זעק	277		assemble
	רדף	qal	infc		רדף	922		pursue
	ירדפו	qal	wci	3mp	רדף	922		pursue
	ינתקו	niph	wci	3mp	נתק	683		be drawn,torn
8: 17	נשׁאר	niph	pft	3ms	שׁאר	983		be left
	יצאו	qal	pft	3cp	יצא	422		go out
	יעזבו	qal	wci	3mp	עזב	736		leave,loose
	פתוחה	qal	pptc	fs	פתח	834		open
	ירדפו	qal	wci	3mp	רדף	922		pursue
8: 18	יאמר	qal	wci	3ms	אמר	55		say
	נטה	qal	impv	ms	נטה	639		stretch,incline
	אתננה	qal	impf	1cs	נתן	678	3fs	give,set
	יט	qal	wci	3ms	נטה	639		stretch,incline
8: 19	אורב	qal	ptc	ms	ארב	70		lie in wait
	קם	qal	pft	3ms	קום	877		arise,stand
	ירוצו	qal	wci	3mp	רוץ	930		run
	נטות	qal	infc		נטה	639		stretch,incline
	יבאו	qal	wci	3mp	בוא	97		come in
	ילכדוה	qal	wci	3mp	לכד	539	3fs	capture
	ימהרו	piel	wci	3mp	מהר	554		hasten
	יציתו	hiph	wci	3mp	יצת	428		kindle
8: 20	יפנו	qal	wci	3mp	פנה	815		turn
	יראו	qal	wci	3mp	ראה	906		see
8: 20	עלה	qal	pft	3ms	עלה	748		go up
	היה	qal	pft	3ms	היה	224		be,become
	נוס	qal	infc		נוס	630		flee,escape
	נס	qal	ptc	ms	נוס	630		flee,escape
	נהפך	niph	pft	3ms	הפך	245		turn oneself
	רודף	qal	ptc	ms	רדף	922		pursue
8: 21	ראו	qal	pft	3cp	ראה	906		see
	לכד	qal	pft	3ms	לכד	539		capture
	ארב	qal	ptc	ms	ארב	70		lie in wait
	עלה	qal	pft	3ms	עלה	748		go up
	ישׁבו	qal	wci	3mp	שׁוב	996		turn,return
	יכו	hiph	wci	3mp	נכה	645		smite
8: 22	יצאו	qal	pft	3cp	יצא	422		go out
	קראתם	qal	infc		קרא	896	3mp	meet,encounter
	יהיו	qal	wci	3mp	היה	224		be,become
	יכו	hiph	wci	3mp	נכה	645		smite
	השׁאיר	hiph	pft	3ms	שׁאר	983		leave,spare
8: 23	תפשׂו	qal	pft	3cp	תפשׂ	1074		seize,grasp
	יקרבו	hiph	wci	3mp	קרב	897		bring near
8: 24	יהי	qal	wci	3ms	היה	224		be,become
	כלות	piel	infc		כלה	477		complete,finish
	הרג	qal	infc		הרג	246		kill
	ישׁבי	qal	ptc	mp	ישׁב	442		sit,dwell
	רדפום	qal	pft	3cp	רדף	922	3mp	pursue
	יפלו	qal	wci	3mp	נפל	656		fall
	תמם	qal	infc		תמם	1070	3mp	be finished
	ישׁבו	qal	wci	3mp	שׁוב	996		turn,return
	יכו	hiph	wci	3mp	נכה	645		smite
8: 25	יהי	qal	wci	3ms	היה	224		be,become
	נפלים	qal	ptc	mp	נפל	656		fall
8: 26	השׁיב	hiph	pft	3ms	שׁוב	996		bring back
	נטה	qal	pft	3ms	נטה	639		stretch,incline
	החרים	hiph	pft	3ms	חרם	355		ban,destroy
	ישׁבי	qal	ptc	mp	ישׁב	442		sit,dwell
8: 27	בזזו	qal	pft	3cp	בזז	102		plunder
	צוה	piel	pft	3ms	צוה	845		command
8: 28	ישׂרף	qal	wci	3ms	שׂרף	976		burn
	ישׂימה	qal	wci	3ms	שׂים	962	3fs	put,set
8: 29	תלה	qal	pft	3ms	תלה	1067		hang
	בוא	qal	infc		בוא	97		come in
	צוה	piel	pft	3ms	צוה	845		command
	ירידו	hiph	wci	3mp	ירד	432		bring down
	ישׁליכו	hiph	wci	3mp	שׁלך	1020		throw,cast
	יקימו	hiph	wci	3mp	קום	877		raise,build,set
8: 30	יבנה	qal	impf	3ms	בנה	124		build
8: 31	צוה	piel	pft	3ms	צוה	845		command
	כתוב	qal	pptc	ms	כתב	507		write
	הניף	hiph	pft	3ms	נוף	631		swing,wave
	יעלו	hiph	wci	3mp	עלה	748		bring up,offer
	יזבחו	qal	wci	3mp	זבח	256		slaughter
8: 32	יכתב	qal	wci	3ms	כתב	507		write
	כתב	qal	pft	3ms	כתב	507		write
8: 33	שׁפטיו	qal	ptc	mp	שׁפט	1047	3ms	judge
	עמדים	qal	ptc	mp	עמד	763		stand,stop

ChVs	Form	Stem	Tnse	PGN	Root	BDB	Sfx	Meaning
8:33	נשׂאי	qal	ptc	mp	נשׂא	669		lift,carry
	צוה	piel	pft	3ms	צוה	845		command
	ברך	piel	infc		ברך	138		bless
8:34	קרא	qal	pft	3ms	קרא	894		call,proclaim
	כתוב	qal	pptc	ms	כתב	507		write
8:35	היה	qal	pft	3ms	היה	224		be,become
	צוה	piel	pft	3ms	צוה	845		command
	קרא	qal	pft	3ms	קרא	894		call,proclaim
	הלך	qal	ptc	ms	הלך	229		walk,go
9:1	יהי	qal	wci	3ms	היה	224		be,become
	שׁמע	qal	infc		שׁמע	1033		hear
9:2	יתקבצו	hith	wci	3mp	קבץ	867		gather together
	הלחם	niph	infc		לחם	535		wage war
9:3	ישׁבי	qal	ptc	mp	ישׁב	442		sit,dwell
	שׁמעו	qal	pft	3cp	שׁמע	1033		hear
	עשׂה	qal	pft	3ms	עשׂה	793		do,make
9:4	יעשׂו	qal	wci	3mp	עשׂה	793		do,make
	ילכו	qal	wci	3mp	הלך	229		walk,go
	יצטירו	hith	wci	3mp	ציר	851		go as messenger
	יקחו	qal	wci	3mp	לקח	542		take
	מבקעים	pual	ptc	mp	בקע	131		be ripped open
	מצררים	pual	ptc	mp	צרר	864		be tied up
9:5	מטלאות	pual	ptc	fp	טלא	378		patched
	יבשׁ	qal	pft	3ms	יבשׁ	386		be dry
	היה	qal	pft	3ms	היה	224		be,become
9:6	ילכו	qal	wci	3mp	הלך	229		walk,go
	יאמרו	qal	wci	3mp	אמר	55		say
	באנו	qal	pft	1cp	בוא	97		come in
	כרתו	qal	impv	mp	כרת	503		cut,destroy
9:7	יאמרוk	qal	wci	3mp	אמר	55		say
	יאמרq	qal	wci	3ms	אמר	55		say
	יושׁב	qal	ptc	ms	ישׁב	442		sit,dwell
	אכרותk	qal	impf	1cs	כרת	503		cut,destroy
	אכרתq	qal	impf	1cs	כרת	503		cut,destroy
9:8	יאמרו	qal	wci	3mp	אמר	55		say
	יאמר	qal	wci	3ms	אמר	55		say
	תבאו	qal	impf	2mp	בוא	97		come in
9:9	יאמרו	qal	wci	3mp	אמר	55		say
	באו	qal	pft	3cp	בוא	97		come in
	שׁמענו	qal	pft	1cp	שׁמע	1033		hear
	עשׂה	qal	pft	3ms	עשׂה	793		do,make
9:10	עשׂה	qal	pft	3ms	עשׂה	793		do,make
9:11	יאמרו	qal	wci	3mp	אמר	55		say
	ישׁבי	qal	ptc	mp	ישׁב	442		sit,dwell
	אמר	qal	infc		אמר	55		say
	קחו	qal	impv	mp	לקח	542		take
	לכו	qal	impv	mp	הלך	229		walk,go
	קראתם	qal	infc		קרא	896	3mp	meet,encounter
	אמרתם	qal	wcp	2mp	אמר	55		say
	כרתו	qal	impv	mp	כרת	503		cut,destroy
9:12	הצטידנו	hith	pft	1cp	ציד	845		supply self
	צאתנו	qal	infc		יצא	422	1cp	go out
	לכת	qal	infc		הלך	229		walk,go
	יבשׁ	qal	pft	3ms	יבשׁ	386		be dry

ChVs	Form	Stem	Tnse	PGN	Root	BDB	Sfx	Meaning
9:12	היה	qal	pft	3ms	היה	224		be,become
9:13	מלאנו	piel	pft	1cp	מלא	569		fill
	התבקעו	hith	pft	3cp	בקע	131		burst open
	בלו	qal	pft	3cp	בלה	115		wear out
	רב	qal	infc		רבב	912		be many
9:14	יקחו	qal	wci	3mp	לקח	542		take
	שׁאלו	qal	pft	3cp	שׁאל	981		ask,borrow
9:15	יעשׂ	qal	wci	3ms	עשׂה	793		do,make
	יכרת	qal	wci	3ms	כרת	503		cut,destroy
	חיותם	piel	infc		חיה	310	3mp	preserve,revive
	ישׁבעו	niph	wci	3mp	שׁבע	989		swear
9:16	יהי	qal	wci	3ms	היה	224		be,become
	כרתו	qal	pft	3cp	כרת	503		cut,destroy
	ישׁמעו	qal	wci	3mp	שׁמע	1033		hear
	ישׁבים	qal	ptc	mp	ישׁב	442		sit,dwell
9:17	יסעו	qal	wci	3mp	נסע	652		pull up,set out
	יבאו	qal	wci	3mp	בוא	97		come in
9:18	הכום	hiph	pft	3cp	נכה	645	3mp	smite
	נשׁבעו	niph	pft	3cp	שׁבע	989		swear
	ילנו	niph	wci	3mp	לון	534		murmur
9:19	יאמרו	qal	wci	3mp	אמר	55		say
	נשׁבענו	niph	pft	1cp	שׁבע	989		swear
	נוכל	qal	impf	1cp	יכל	407		be able
	נגע	qal	infc		נגע	619		touch,strike
9:20	נעשׂה	qal	impf	1cp	עשׂה	793		do,make
	החיה	hiph	infa		חיה	310		preserve
	יהיה	qal	impf	3ms	היה	224		be,become
	נשׁבענו	niph	pft	1cp	שׁבע	989		swear
9:21	יאמרו	qal	wci	3mp	אמר	55		say
	יחיו	qal	jusm	3mp	חיה	310		live
	יהיו	qal	wci	3mp	היה	224		be,become
	חטבי	qal	ptc	mp	חטב	310		cut wood
	שׁאבי	qal	ptc	mp	שׁאב	980		draw (water)
	דברו	piel	pft	3cp	דבר	180		speak
9:22	יקרא	qal	wci	3ms	קרא	894		call,proclaim
	ידבר	piel	wci	3ms	דבר	180		speak
	אמר	qal	infc		אמר	55		say
	רמיתם	piel	pft	2mp	רמה	941		beguile
	אמר	qal	infc		אמר	55		say
	ישׁבים	qal	ptc	mp	ישׁב	442		sit,dwell
9:23	ארורים	qal	pptc	mp	ארר	76		curse
	יכרת	niph	impf	3ms	כרת	503		be cut off
	חטבי	qal	ptc	mp	חטב	310		cut wood
	שׁאבי	qal	ptc	mp	שׁאב	980		draw (water)
9:24	יענו	qal	wci	3mp	ענה	772		answer
	יאמרו	qal	wci	3mp	אמר	55		say
	הגד	hoph	infa		נגד	616		be told
	הגד	hoph	pft	3ms	נגד	616		be told
	צוה	piel	pft	3ms	צוה	845		command
	תת	qal	infc		נתן	678		give,set
	השׁמיד	hiph	infc		שׁמד	1029		exterminate
	ישׁבי	qal	ptc	mp	ישׁב	442		sit,dwell
	נירא	qal	wci	1cp	ירא	431		fear
	נעשׂה	qal	wci	1cp	עשׂה	793		do,make

ChVs	Form	Stem	Tnse	PGN	Root	BDB	Sfx	Meaning
9:25	עשׂות	qal	infc		עשׂה	793		do,make
	עשׂה	qal	impv	ms	עשׂה	793		do,make
9:26	יעשׂ	qal	wci	3ms	עשׂה	793		do,make
	יצל	hiph	wci	3ms	נצל	664		snatch,deliver
	הרגום	qal	pft	3cp	הרג	246	3mp	kill
9:27	יתנם	qal	wci	3ms	נתן	678	3mp	give,set
	חטבי	qal	ptc	mp	חטב	310		cut wood
	שׁאבי	qal	ptc	mp	שׁאב	980		draw (water)
	יבחר	qal	impf	3ms	בחר	103		choose
10:1	יהי	qal	wci	3ms	היה	224		be,become
	שׁמע	qal	infc		שׁמע	1033		hear
	לכד	qal	pft	3ms	לכד	539		capture
	יחרימה	hiph	wci	3ms	חרם	355	3fs	ban,destroy
	עשׂה	qal	pft	3ms	עשׂה	793		do,make
	עשׂה	qal	pft	3ms	עשׂה	793		do,make
	השׁלימו	hiph	pft	3cp	שׁלם	1023		make peace
	ישׁבי	qal	ptc	mp	ישׁב	442		sit,dwell
	יהיו	qal	wci	3mp	היה	224		be,become
10:2	ייראו	qal	wci	3mp	ירא	431		fear
10:3	ישׁלח	qal	wci	3ms	שׁלח	1018		send
	אמר	qal	infc		אמר	55		say
10:4	עלו	qal	impv	mp	עלה	748		go up
	עזרני	qal	impv	mp	עזר	740	1cs	help,aid
	נכה	hiph	cohm	1cp	נכה	645		smite
	השׁלימה	hiph	pft	3fs	שׁלם	1023		make peace
10:5	יאספו	niph	wci	3mp	אסף	62		assemble
	יעלו	qal	wci	3mp	עלה	748		go up
	יחנו	qal	wci	3mp	חנה	333		decline,encamp
	ילחמו	niph	wci	3mp	לחם	535		wage war
10:6	ישׁלחו	qal	wci	3mp	שׁלח	1018		send
	אמר	qal	infc		אמר	55		say
	תרף	hiph	jus	2ms	רפה	951		slacken,abandon
	עלה	qal	impv	ms	עלה	748		go up
	הושׁיעה	hiph	impv	ms	ישׁע	446		deliver,save
	עזרנו	qal	impv	ms	עזר	740	1cp	help,aid
	נקבצו	niph	pft	3cp	קבץ	867		assemble,gather
	ישׁבי	qal	ptc	mp	ישׁב	442		sit,dwell
10:7	יעל	qal	wci	3ms	עלה	748		go up
10:8	יאמר	qal	wci	3ms	אמר	55		say
	תירא	qal	jusm	2ms	ירא	431		fear
	נתתים	qal	pft	1cs	נתן	678	3mp	give,set
	יעמד	qal	impf	3ms	עמד	763		stand,stop
10:9	יבא	qal	wci	3ms	בוא	97		come in
	עלה	qal	pft	3ms	עלה	748		go up
10:10	יהמם	qal	wci	3ms	המם	243	3mp	confuse,vex
	יכם	hiph	wci	3ms	נכה	645	3mp	smite
	ירדפם	qal	wci	3ms	רדף	922	3mp	pursue
	יכם	hiph	wci	3ms	נכה	645	3mp	smite
10:11	יהי	qal	wci	3ms	היה	224		be,become
	נסם	qal	infc		נוס	630	3mp	flee,escape
	השׁליך	hiph	pft	3ms	שׁלך	1020		throw,cast
	ימתו	qal	wci	3mp	מות	559		die
	מתו	qal	pft	3cp	מות	559		die
	הרגו	qal	pft	3cp	הרג	246		kill
10:12	ידבר	piel	impf	3ms	דבר	180		speak
	תת	qal	infc		נתן	678		give,set
	יאמר	qal	wci	3ms	אמר	55		say
	דום	qal	impv	ms	דמם	198		be silent
10:13	ידם	qal	wci	3ms	דמם	198		be silent
	עמד	qal	pft	3ms	עמד	763		stand,stop
	יקם	qal	impf	3ms	נקם	667		avenge
	איביו	qal	ptc	mp	איב	33	3ms	be hostile to
	כתובה	qal	pptc	fs	כתב	507		write
	יעמד	qal	wci	3ms	עמד	763		stand,stop
	אץ	qal	pft	3ms	אוץ	21		press,hasten
	בוא	qal	infc		בוא	97		come in
10:14	היה	qal	pft	3ms	היה	224		be,become
	שׁמע	qal	infc		שׁמע	1033		hear
	נלחם	niph	ptc	ms	לחם	535		wage war
10:15	ישׁב	qal	wci	3ms	שׁוב	996		turn,return
10:16	ינסו	qal	wci	3mp	נוס	630		flee,escape
	יחבאו	niph	wci	3mp	חבא	285		hide oneself
10:17	יגד	hoph	wci	3ms	נגד	616		be told
	אמר	qal	infc		אמר	55		say
	נמצאו	niph	pft	3cp	מצא	592		be found
	נחבאים	niph	ptc	mp	חבא	285		hide oneself
10:18	יאמר	qal	wci	3ms	אמר	55		say
	גלו	qal	impv	mp	גלל	164		roll away
	הפקידו	hiph	impv	mp	פקד	823		set,entrust
	שׁמרם	qal	infc		שׁמר	1036	3mp	keep,watch
10:19	תעמדו	qal	jusm	2mp	עמד	763		stand,stop
	רדפו	qal	impv	mp	רדף	922		pursue
	איביכם	qal	ptc	mp	איב	33	2mp	be hostile to
	זנבתם	piel	wcp	2mp	זנב	275		cut off,smite
	תתנום	qal	jusm	2mp	נתן	678	3mp	give,set
	בוא	qal	infc		בוא	97		come in
	נתנם	qal	pft	3ms	נתן	678	3mp	give,set
10:20	יהי	qal	wci	3ms	היה	224		be,become
	כלות	piel	infc		כלה	477		complete,finish
	הכותם	hiph	infc		נכה	645	3mp	smite
	תמם	qal	infc		תמם	1070	3mp	be finished
	שׂרדו	qal	pft	3cp	שׂרד	974		escape
	יבאו	qal	wci	3mp	בוא	97		come in
10:21	ישׁבו	qal	wci	3mp	שׁוב	996		turn,return
	חרץ	qal	pft	3ms	חרץ	358		cut,decide
10:22	יאמר	qal	wci	3ms	אמר	55		say
	פתחו	qal	impv	mp	פתח	834		open
	הוציאו	hiph	impv	mp	יצא	422		bring out
10:23	יעשׂו	qal	wci	3mp	עשׂה	793		do,make
	יציאו	hiph	wci	3mp	יצא	422		bring out
10:24	יהי	qal	wci	3ms	היה	224		be,become
	הוציאם	hiph	infc		יצא	422	3mp	bring out
	יקרא	qal	wci	3ms	קרא	894		call,proclaim
	יאמר	qal	wci	3ms	אמר	55		say
	הלכוא	qal	pft	3cp	הלך	229		walk,go
	קרבו	qal	impv	mp	קרב	897		approach
	שׂימו	qal	impv	mp	שׂים	962		put,set
	יקרבו	qal	wci	3mp	קרב	897		approach

ChVs	Form	Stem	Tnse	PGN	Root	BDB	Sfx	Meaning
10:24	ישׂימו	qal	wci	3mp	שׂים	962		put,set
10:25	יאמר	qal	wci	3ms	אמר	55		say
	תיראו	qal	jusm	2mp	ירא	431		fear
	תחתו	qal	jusm	2mp	חתת	369		be shattered
	חזקו	qal	impv	mp	חזק	304		be strong
	אמצו	qal	impv	mp	אמץ	54		be strong
	יעשׂה	qal	impf	3ms	עשׂה	793		do,make
	איביכם	qal	ptc	mp	איב	33	2mp	be hostile to
	נלחמים	niph	ptc	mp	לחם	535		wage war
10:26	יכם	hiph	wci	3ms	נכה	645	3mp	smite
	ימיתם	hiph	wci	3ms	מות	559	3mp	kill
	יתלם	qal	wci	3ms	תלה	1067	3mp	hang
	יהיו	qal	wci	3mp	היה	224		be,become
	תלוים	qal	pptc	mp	תלה	1067		hang
10:27	יהי	qal	wci	3ms	היה	224		be,become
	בוא	qal	infc		בוא	97		come in
	צוה	piel	pft	3ms	צוה	845		command
	ירידום	hiph	wci	3mp	ירד	432	3mp	bring down
	ישׁלכם	hiph	wci	3mp	שׁלך	1020	3mp	throw,cast
	נחבאו	niph	pft	3cp	חבא	285		hide oneself
	ישׂמו	qal	wci	3mp	שׂים	962		put,set
10:28	לכד	qal	pft	3ms	לכד	539		capture
	יכה	hiph	wci	3ms	נכה	645	3fs	smite
	החרם	hiph	pft	3ms	חרם	355		ban,destroy
	השׁאיר	hiph	pft	3ms	שׁאר	983		leave,spare
	יעשׂ	qal	wci	3ms	עשׂה	793		do,make
	עשׂה	qal	pft	3ms	עשׂה	793		do,make
10:29	יעבר	qal	wci	3ms	עבר	716		pass over
	ילחם	niph	wci	3ms	לחם	535		wage war
10:30	יתן	qal	wci	3ms	נתן	678		give,set
	יכה	hiph	wci	3ms	נכה	645	3fs	smite
	השׁאיר	hiph	pft	3ms	שׁאר	983		leave,spare
	יעשׂ	qal	wci	3ms	עשׂה	793		do,make
	עשׂה	qal	pft	3ms	עשׂה	793		do,make
10:31	יעבר	qal	wci	3ms	עבר	716		pass over
	יחן	qal	wci	3ms	חנה	333		decline,encamp
	ילחם	niph	wci	3ms	לחם	535		wage war
10:32	יתן	qal	wci	3ms	נתן	678		give,set
	ילכדה	qal	wci	3ms	לכד	539	3fs	capture
	יכה	hiph	wci	3ms	נכה	645	3fs	smite
	עשׂה	qal	pft	3ms	עשׂה	793		do,make
10:33	עלה	qal	pft	3ms	עלה	748		go up
	עזר	qal	infc		עזר	740		help,aid
	יכהו	hiph	wci	3ms	נכה	645	3ms	smite
	השׁאיר	hiph	pft	3ms	שׁאר	983		leave,spare
10:34	יעבר	qal	wci	3ms	עבר	716		pass over
	יחנו	qal	wci	3mp	חנה	333		decline,encamp
	ילחמו	niph	wci	3mp	לחם	535		wage war
10:35	ילכדוה	qal	wci	3mp	לכד	539	3fs	capture
	יכוה	hiph	wci	3mp	נכה	645	3fs	smite
	החרים	hiph	pft	3ms	חרם	355		ban,destroy
	עשׂה	qal	pft	3ms	עשׂה	793		do,make
10:36	יעל	qal	wci	3ms	עלה	748		go up
	ילחמו	niph	wci	3mp	לחם	535		wage war
10:37	ילכדוה	qal	wci	3mp	לכד	539	3fs	capture
	יכוה	hiph	wci	3mp	נכה	645	3fs	smite
	השׁאיר	hiph	pft	3ms	שׁאר	983		leave,spare
	עשׂה	qal	pft	3ms	עשׂה	793		do,make
	יחרם	hiph	wci	3ms	חרם	355		ban,destroy
10:38	ישׁב	qal	wci	3ms	שׁוב	996		turn,return
	ילחם	niph	wci	3ms	לחם	535		wage war
10:39	ילכדה	qal	wci	3ms	לכד	539	3fs	capture
	יכום	hiph	wci	3mp	נכה	645	3mp	smite
	יחרימו	hiph	wci	3mp	חרם	355		ban,destroy
	השׁאיר	hiph	pft	3ms	שׁאר	983		leave,spare
	עשׂה	qal	pft	3ms	עשׂה	793		do,make
	עשׂה	qal	pft	3ms	עשׂה	793		do,make
	עשׂה	qal	pft	3ms	עשׂה	793		do,make
10:40	יכה	hiph	wci	3ms	נכה	645		smite
	השׁאיר	hiph	pft	3ms	שׁאר	983		leave,spare
	החרים	hiph	pft	3ms	חרם	355		ban,destroy
	צוה	piel	pft	3ms	צוה	845		command
10:41	יכם	hiph	wci	3ms	נכה	645	3mp	smite
10:42	לכד	qal	pft	3ms	לכד	539		capture
	נלחם	niph	ptc	ms	לחם	535		wage war
10:43	ישׁב	qal	wci	3ms	שׁוב	996		turn,return
11:1	יהי	qal	wci	3ms	היה	224		be,become
	שׁמע	qal	infc		שׁמע	1033		hear
	ישׁלח	qal	wci	3ms	שׁלח	1018		send
11:4	יצאו	qal	wci	3mp	יצא	422		go out
11:5	יועדו	niph	wci	3mp	יעד	416		gather
	יבאו	qal	wci	3mp	בוא	97		come in
	יחנו	qal	wci	3mp	חנה	333		decline,encamp
	הלחם	niph	infc		לחם	535		wage war
11:6	יאמר	qal	wci	3ms	אמר	55		say
	תירא	qal	jusm	2ms	ירא	431		fear
	נתן	qal	ptc	ms	נתן	678		give,set
	תעקר	piel	impf	2ms	עקר	785		hamstring
	תשׂרף	qal	impf	2ms	שׂרף	976		burn
11:7	יבא	qal	wci	3ms	בוא	97		come in
	יפלו	qal	wci	3mp	נפל	656		fall
11:8	יתנם	qal	wci	3ms	נתן	678	3mp	give,set
	יכום	hiph	wci	3mp	נכה	645	3mp	smite
	ירדפום	qal	wci	3mp	רדף	922	3mp	pursue
	יכם	hiph	wci	3mp	נכה	645	3mp	smite
	השׁאיר	hiph	pft	3ms	שׁאר	983		leave,spare
11:9	יעשׂ	qal	wci	3ms	עשׂה	793		do,make
	אמר	qal	pft	3ms	אמר	55		say
	עקר	piel	pft	3ms	עקר	785		hamstring
	שׂרף	qal	pft	3ms	שׂרף	976		burn
11:10	ישׁב	qal	wci	3ms	שׁוב	996		turn,return
	ילכד	qal	wci	3ms	לכד	539		capture
	הכה	hiph	pft	3ms	נכה	645		smite
11:11	יכו	hiph	wci	3mp	נכה	645		smite
	החרם	hiph	infa		חרם	355		ban,destroy
	נותר	niph	pft	3ms	יתר	451		be left,remain
	שׂרף	qal	pft	3ms	שׂרף	976		burn
11:12	לכד	qal	pft	3ms	לכד	539		capture

ChVs	Form	Stem	Tnse	PGN	Root	BDB	Sfx	Meaning
11:12	יכם	hiph	wci	3ms	נכה	645	3mp	smite
	החרים	hiph	pft	3ms	חרם	355		ban,destroy
	צוה	piel	pft	3ms	צוה	845		command
11:13	עמדות	qal	ptc	fp	עמד	763		stand,stop
	שרפם	qal	pft	3ms	שרף	976	3mp	burn
	שרף	qal	pft	3ms	שרף	976		burn
11:14	בזזו	qal	pft	3cp	בזז	102		plunder
	הכו	hiph	pft	3cp	נכה	645		smite
	השמדם	hiph	infc		שמד	1029	3mp	exterminate
	השאירו	hiph	pft	3cp	שאר	983		leave,spare
11:15	צוה	piel	pft	3ms	צוה	845		command
	צוה	piel	pft	3ms	צוה	845		command
	עשה	qal	pft	3ms	עשה	793		do,make
	הסיר	hiph	pft	3ms	סור	693		take away
	צוה	piel	pft	3ms	צוה	845		command
11:16	יקח	qal	wci	3ms	לקח	542		take
11:17	עולה	qal	ptc	ms	עלה	748		go up
	לכד	qal	pft	3ms	לכד	539		capture
	יכם	hiph	wci	3ms	נכה	645	3mp	smite
	ימיתם	hiph	wci	3ms	מות	559	3mp	kill
11:18	עשה	qal	pft	3ms	עשה	793		do,make
11:19	היתה	qal	pft	3fs	היה	224		be,become
	השלימה	hiph	pft	3fs	שלם	1023		make peace
	ישבי	qal	ptc	mp	ישב	442		sit,dwell
	לקחו	qal	pft	3cp	לקח	542		take
11:20	היתה	qal	pft	3fs	היה	224		be,become
	חזק	piel	infc		חזק	304		make strong
	קראת	qal	infc		קרא	896		meet,encounter
	החרימם	hiph	infc		חרם	355	3mp	ban,destroy
	היות	qal	infc		היה	224		be,become
	השמידם	hiph	infc		שמד	1029	3mp	exterminate
	צוה	piel	pft	3ms	צוה	845		command
11:21	יבא	qal	wci	3ms	בוא	97		come in
	יכרת	hiph	wci	3ms	כרת	503		cut off,destroy
	החרימם	hiph	pft	3ms	חרם	355	3mp	ban,destroy
11:22	נותר	niph	pft	3ms	יתר	451		be left,remain
	נשארו	niph	pft	3cp	שאר	983		be left
11:23	יקח	qal	wci	3ms	לקח	542		take
	דבר	piel	pft	3ms	דבר	180		speak
	יתנה	qal	wci	3ms	נתן	678	3fs	give,set
	שקטה	qal	pft	3fs	שקט	1052		be quiet
12:1	הכו	hiph	pft	3cp	נכה	645		smite
	ירשו	qal	wci	3mp	ירש	439		possess,inherit
12:2	יושב	qal	ptc	ms	ישב	442		sit,dwell
	משל	qal	ptc	ms	משל	605		rule
12:4	יושב	qal	ptc	ms	ישב	442		sit,dwell
12:5	משל	qal	ptc	ms	משל	605		rule
12:6	הכום	hiph	pft	3cp	נכה	645	3mp	smite
	יתנה	qal	wci	3ms	נתן	678	3fs	give,set
12:7	הכה	hiph	pft	3ms	נכה	645		smite
	עלה	qal	ptc	ms	עלה	748		go up
	יתנה	qal	wci	3ms	נתן	678	3fs	give,set
13:1	זקן	qal	pft	3ms	זקן	278		be old
	בא	qal	pft	3ms	בוא	97		come in
13:1	יאמר	qal	wci	3ms	אמר	55		say
	זקנתה	qal	pft	2ms	זקן	278		be old
	באת	qal	pft	2ms	בוא	97		come in
	נשארה	niph	pft	3fs	שאר	983		be left
	הרבה	hiph	infa		רבה	915		make many
	רשתה	qal	infc		ירש	439	3fs	possess,inherit
13:2	נשארת	niph	ptc	fs	שאר	983		be left
13:3	תחשב	niph	impf	3fs	חשב	362		be thought
13:5	בוא	qal	infc		בוא	97		come in
13:6	ישבי	qal	ptc	mp	ישב	442		sit,dwell
	אורישם	hiph	impf	1cs	ירש	439	3mp	c. to possess
	הפלה	hiph	impv	ms	נפל	656	3fs	cause to fall
	צויתיך	piel	pft	1cs	צוה	845	2ms	command
13:7	חלק	piel	impv	ms	חלק	323		divide
13:8	לקחו	qal	pft	3cp	לקח	542		take
	נתן	qal	pft	3ms	נתן	678		give,set
	נתן	qal	pft	3ms	נתן	678		give,set
13:10	מלך	qal	pft	3ms	מלך	573		be king,reign
13:12	מלך	qal	pft	3ms	מלך	573		be king,reign
	נשאר	niph	pft	3ms	שאר	983		be left
	יכם	hiph	wci	3ms	נכה	645	3mp	smite
	ירשם	hiph	wci	3ms	ירש	439	3mp	c. to possess
13:13	הורישו	hiph	pft	3cp	ירש	439		c. to possess
	ישב	qal	wci	3ms	ישב	442		sit,dwell
13:14	נתן	qal	pft	3ms	נתן	678		give,set
	דבר	piel	pft	3ms	דבר	180		speak
13:15	יתן	qal	wci	3ms	נתן	678		give,set
13:16	יהי	qal	wci	3ms	היה	224		be,become
13:21	מלך	qal	pft	3ms	מלך	573		be king,reign
	הכה	hiph	pft	3ms	נכה	645		smite
	ישבי	qal	ptc	mp	ישב	442		sit,dwell
13:22	קוסם	qal	ptc	ms	קסם	890		divine
	הרגו	qal	pft	3cp	הרג	246		kill
13:23	יהי	qal	wci	3ms	היה	224		be,become
13:24	יתן	qal	wci	3ms	נתן	678		give,set
13:25	יהי	qal	wci	3ms	היה	224		be,become
13:29	יתן	qal	wci	3ms	נתן	678		give,set
	יהי	qal	wci	3ms	היה	224		be,become
13:30	יהי	qal	wci	3ms	היה	224		be,become
13:32	נחל	piel	pft	3ms	נחל	635		allot
13:33	נתן	qal	pft	3ms	נתן	678		give,set
	דבר	piel	pft	3ms	דבר	180		speak
14:1	נחלו	qal	pft	3cp	נחל	635		possess,inherit
	נחלו	piel	pft	3cp	נחל	635		allot
14:2	צוה	piel	pft	3ms	צוה	845		command
14:3	נתן	qal	pft	3ms	נתן	678		give,set
	נתן	qal	pft	3ms	נתן	678		give,set
14:4	היו	qal	pft	3cp	היה	224		be,become
	נתנו	qal	pft	3cp	נתן	678		give,set
	שבת	qal	infc		ישב	442		sit,dwell
14:5	צוה	piel	pft	3ms	צוה	845		command
	עשו	qal	pft	3cp	עשה	793		do,make
	יחלקו	qal	wci	3mp	חלק	323		divide,share
14:6	יגשו	qal	wci	3mp	נגש	620		draw near

ChVs	Form	Stem	Tnse	PGN	Root	BDB	Sfx	Meaning
14:6	יאמר	qal	wci	3ms	אמר	55		say
	ידעת	qal	pft	2ms	ידע	393		know
	דבר	piel	pft	3ms	דבר	180		speak
14:7	שלח	qal	infc		שלח	1018		send
	רגל	piel	infc		רגל	920		slander,spy
	אשב	hiph	wci	1cs	שוב	996		bring back
14:8	עלו	qal	pft	3cp	עלה	748		go up
	המסיו	hiph	pft	3cp	מסה	587		melt,dissolve
	מלאתי	piel	pft	1cs	מלא	569		fill
14:9	ישבע	niph	wci	3ms	שבע	989		swear
	אמר	qal	infc		אמר	55		say
	דרכה	qal	pft	3fs	דרך	201		tread,march
	תהיה	qal	impf	3fs	היה	224		be,become
	מלאת	piel	pft	2ms	מלא	569		fill
14:10	החיה	hiph	pft	3ms	חיה	310		preserve
	דבר	piel	pft	3ms	דבר	180		speak
	דבר	piel	pft	3ms	דבר	180		speak
	הלך	qal	pft	3ms	הלך	229		walk,go
14:11	שלח	qal	infc		שלח	1018		send
	צאת	qal	infc		יצא	422		go out
	בוא	qal	infc		בוא	97		come in
14:12	תנה	qal	impv	ms	נתן	678		give,set
	דבר	piel	pft	3ms	דבר	180		speak
	שמעת	qal	pft	2ms	שמע	1033		hear
	בצרות	qal	pptc	fp	בצר	130		cut off
	הורשתים	hiph	pft	1cs	ירש	439	3mp	c. to possess
	דבר	piel	pft	3ms	דבר	180		speak
14:13	יברכהו	piel	wci	3ms	ברך	138	3ms	bless
	יתן	qal	wci	3ms	נתן	678		give,set
14:14	היתה	qal	pft	3fs	היה	224		be,become
	מלא	piel	pft	3ms	מלא	569		fill
14:15	שקטה	qal	pft	3fs	שקט	1052		be quiet
15:1	יהי	qal	wci	3ms	היה	224		be,become
15:2	יהי	qal	wci	3ms	היה	224		be,become
	פנה	qal	ptc	ms	פנה	815		turn
15:3	יצא	qal	wcp	3ms	יצא	422		go out
	עבר	qal	wcp	3ms	עבר	716		pass over
	עלה	qal	wcp	3ms	עלה	748		go up
	עבר	qal	wcp	3ms	עבר	716		pass over
	עלה	qal	wcp	3ms	עלה	748		go up
	נסב	niph	wcp	3ms	סבב	685		turn round
15:4	עבר	qal	wcp	3ms	עבר	716		pass over
	יצא	qal	wcp	3ms	יצא	422		go out
	היהk	qal	wcp	3ms	היה	224		be,become
	היוq	qal	wcp	3cp	היה	224		be,become
	יהיה	qal	impf	3ms	היה	224		be,become
15:6	עלה	qal	wcp	3ms	עלה	748		go up
	עבר	qal	wcp	3ms	עבר	716		pass over
	עלה	qal	wcp	3ms	עלה	748		go up
15:7	עלה	qal	wcp	3ms	עלה	748		go up
	פנה	qal	ptc	ms	פנה	815		turn
	עבר	qal	wcp	3ms	עבר	716		pass over
	היו	qal	wcp	3cp	היה	224		be,become
15:8	עלה	qal	wcp	3ms	עלה	748		go up
15:8	עלה	qal	wcp	3ms	עלה	748		go up
15:9	תאר	qal	wcp	3ms	תאר	1061		incline
	יצא	qal	wcp	3ms	יצא	422		go out
	תאר	qal	wcp	3ms	תאר	1061		incline
15:10	נסב	niph	wcp	3ms	סבב	685		turn round
	עבר	qal	wcp	3ms	עבר	716		pass over
	ירד	qal	wcp	3ms	ירד	432		come down
	עבר	qal	wcp	3ms	עבר	716		pass over
15:11	יצא	qal	wcp	3ms	יצא	422		go out
	תאר	qal	wcp	3ms	תאר	1061		incline
	עבר	qal	wcp	3ms	עבר	716		pass over
	יצא	qal	wcp	3ms	יצא	422		go out
	היו	qal	wcp	3cp	היה	224		be,become
15:13	נתן	qal	pft	3ms	נתן	678		give,set
15:14	ירש	hiph	wci	3ms	ירש	439		c. to possess
15:15	יעל	qal	wci	3ms	עלה	748		go up
	ישבי	qal	ptc	mp	ישב	442		sit,dwell
15:16	יאמר	qal	wci	3ms	אמר	55		say
	יכה	hiph	impf	3ms	נכה	645		smite
	לכדה	qal	wcp	3ms	לכד	539	3fs	capture
	נתתי	qal	wcp	1cs	נתן	678		give,set
15:17	ילכדה	qal	wci	3ms	לכד	539	3fs	capture
	יתן	qal	wci	3ms	נתן	678		give,set
15:18	יהי	qal	wci	3ms	היה	224		be,become
	בואה	qal	infc		בוא	97	3fs	come in
	תסיתהו	hiph	wci	3fs	סות	694	3ms	incite,allure
	שאול	qal	infc		שאל	981		ask,borrow
	תצנח	qal	wci	3fs	צנח	856		descend
	יאמר	qal	wci	3ms	אמר	55		say
15:19	תאמר	qal	wci	3fs	אמר	55		say
	תנה	qal	impv	ms	נתן	678		give,set
	נתתני	qal	pft	2ms	נתן	678	1cs	give,set
	נתתה	qal	wcp	2ms	נתן	678		give,set
	יתן	qal	wci	3ms	נתן	678		give,set
15:21	יהיו	qal	wci	3mp	היה	224		be,become
15:63	יושבי	qal	ptc	mp	ישב	442		sit,dwell
	יוכלוk	qal	impf	3cp	יכל	407		be able
	יכלוq	qal	pft	3cp	יכל	407		be able
	הורישם	hiph	infc		ירש	439	3mp	c. to possess
	ישב	qal	wci	3ms	ישב	442		sit,dwell
16:1	יצא	qal	wci	3ms	יצא	422		go out
	עלה	qal	ptc	ms	עלה	748		go up
16:2	יצא	qal	wcp	3ms	יצא	422		go out
	עבר	qal	wcp	3ms	עבר	716		pass over
16:3	ירד	qal	wcp	3ms	ירד	432		come down
	היו	qal	wcp	3cp	היה	224		be,become
16:4	ינחלו	qal	wci	3mp	נחל	635		possess,inherit
16:5	יהי	qal	wci	3ms	היה	224		be,become
	יהי	qal	wci	3ms	היה	224		be,become
16:6	יצא	qal	wcp	3ms	יצא	422		go out
	נסב	niph	wcp	3ms	סבב	685		turn round
	עבר	qal	wcp	3ms	עבר	716		pass over
16:7	ירד	qal	wcp	3ms	ירד	432		come down
	פגע	qal	wcp	3ms	פגע	803		meet,encounter

ChVs	Form	Stem	Tnse	PGN	Root	BDB	Sfx	Meaning
16:7	יצא	qal	wcp	3ms	יצא	422		go out
16:8	ילך	qal	impf	3ms	הלך	229		walk,go
	היו	qal	wcp	3cp	היה	224		be,become
16:10	הורישו	hiph	pft	3cp	ירש	439		c. to possess
	יושב	qal	ptc	ms	ישב	442		sit,dwell
	ישב	qal	wci	3ms	ישב	442		sit,dwell
	יהי	qal	wci	3ms	היה	224		be,become
	עבד	qal	ptc	ms	עבד	712		work,serve
17:1	יהי	qal	wci	3ms	היה	224		be,become
	היה	qal	pft	3ms	היה	224		be,become
	יהי	qal	wci	3ms	היה	224		be,become
17:2	יהי	qal	wci	3ms	היה	224		be,become
	נותרים	niph	ptc	mp	יתר	451		be left,remain
17:3	היו	qal	pft	3cp	היה	224		be,become
17:4	תקרבנה	qal	wci	3fp	קרב	897		approach
	אמר	qal	infc		אמר	55		say
	צוה	piel	pft	3ms	צוה	845		command
	תת	qal	infc		נתן	678		give,set
	יתן	qal	wci	3ms	נתן	678		give,set
17:5	יפלו	qal	wci	3mp	נפל	656		fall
17:6	נחלו	qal	pft	3cp	נחל	635		possess,inherit
	היתה	qal	pft	3fs	היה	224		be,become
	נותרים	niph	ptc	mp	יתר	451		be left,remain
17:7	יהי	qal	wci	3ms	היה	224		be,become
	הלך	qal	wcp	3ms	הלך	229		walk,go
	ישבי	qal	ptc	mp	ישב	442		sit,dwell
17:8	היתה	qal	pft	3fs	היה	224		be,become
17:9	ירד	qal	wcp	3ms	ירד	432		come down
	יהי	qal	wci	3ms	היה	224		be,become
17:10	יהי	qal	wci	3ms	היה	224		be,become
	יפגעון	qal	impf	3mp	פגע	803		meet,encounter
17:11	יהי	qal	wci	3ms	היה	224		be,become
	ישבי	qal	ptc	mp	ישב	442		sit,dwell
	ישבי	qal	ptc	mp	ישב	442		sit,dwell
	ישבי	qal	ptc	mp	ישב	442		sit,dwell
	ישבי	qal	ptc	mp	ישב	442		sit,dwell
17:12	יכלו	qal	pft	3cp	יכל	407		be able
	הוריש	hiph	infc		ירש	439		c. to possess
	יואל	hiph	wci	3ms	יאל	383		be willing
	שבת	qal	infc		ישב	442		sit,dwell
17:13	יהי	qal	wci	3ms	היה	224		be,become
	חזקו	qal	pft	3cp	חזק	304		be strong
	יתנו	qal	wci	3mp	נתן	678		give,set
	הורש	hiph	infa		ירש	439		c. to possess
	הורישו	hiph	pft	3ms	ירש	439	3ms	c. to possess
17:14	ידברו	piel	wci	3mp	דבר	180		speak
	אמר	qal	infc		אמר	55		say
	נתתה	qal	pft	2ms	נתן	678		give,set
	ברכני	piel	pft	3ms	ברך	138	1cs	bless
17:15	יאמר	qal	wci	3ms	אמר	55		say
	עלה	qal	impv	ms	עלה	748		go up
	בראת	piel	wcp	2ms	ברא	135		cut down
	אץ	qal	pft	3ms	אוץ	21		press,hasten
17:16	יאמרו	qal	wci	3mp	אמר	55		say
17:16	ימצא	niph	impf	3ms	מצא	592		be found
	ישב	qal	ptc	ms	ישב	442		sit,dwell
17:17	יאמר	qal	wci	3ms	אמר	55		say
	אמר	qal	infc		אמר	55		say
	יהיה	qal	impf	3ms	היה	224		be,become
17:18	יהיה	qal	impf	3ms	היה	224		be,become
	בראתו	piel	wcp	2ms	ברא	135	3ms	cut down
	היה	qal	wcp	3ms	היה	224		be,become
	תוריש	hiph	impf	2ms	ירש	439		c. to possess
18:1	יקהלו	niph	wci	3mp	קהל	874		assemble
	ישכינו	hiph	wci	3mp	שכן	1014		cause to dwell
	נכבשה	niph	pft	3fs	כבש	461		be subdued
18:2	יותרו	niph	wci	3mp	יתר	451		be left,remain
	חלקו	qal	pft	3cp	חלק	323		divide,share
18:3	יאמר	qal	wci	3ms	אמר	55		say
	מתרפים	hith	ptc	mp	רפה	951		show self lazy
	בוא	qal	infc		בוא	97		come in
	רשת	qal	infc		ירש	439		possess,inherit
	נתן	qal	pft	3ms	נתן	678		give,set
18:4	הבו	qal	impv	mp	יהב	396		give
	אשלחם	qal	cohm	1cs	שלח	1018	3mp	send
	יקמו	qal	jusm	3mp	קום	877		arise,stand
	יתהלכו	hith	jusm	3mp	הלך	229		walk to and fro
	יכתבו	qal	jusm	3mp	כתב	507		write
	יבאו	qal	jusm	3mp	בוא	97		come in
18:5	התחלקו	hith	wcp	3cp	חלק	323		divide for self
	יעמד	qal	impf	3ms	עמד	763		stand,stop
	יעמדו	qal	impf	3mp	עמד	763		stand,stop
18:6	תכתבו	qal	impf	2mp	כתב	507		write
	הבאתם	hiph	wcp	2mp	בוא	97		bring in
	יריתי	qal	wcp	1cs	ירה	434		throw,shoot
18:7	לקחו	qal	pft	3cp	לקח	542		take
	נתן	qal	pft	3ms	נתן	678		give,set
18:8	יקמו	qal	wci	3mp	קום	877		arise,stand
	ילכו	qal	wci	3mp	הלך	229		walk,go
	יצו	piel	wci	3ms	צוה	845		command
	הלכים	qal	ptc	mp	הלך	229		walk,go
	כתב	qal	infc		כתב	507		write
	אמר	qal	infc		אמר	55		say
	לכו	qal	impv	mp	הלך	229		walk,go
	התהלכו	hith	impv	mp	הלך	229		walk to and fro
	כתבו	qal	impv	mp	כתב	507		write
	שובו	qal	impv	mp	שוב	996		turn,return
	אשליך	hiph	impf	1cs	שלך	1020		throw,cast
18:9	ילכו	qal	wci	3mp	הלך	229		walk,go
	יעברו	qal	wci	3mp	עבר	716		pass over
	יכתבוה	qal	wci	3mp	כתב	507	3fs	write
	יבאו	qal	wci	3mp	בוא	97		come in
18:10	ישלך	hiph	wci	3ms	שלך	1020		throw,cast
	יחלק	piel	wci	3ms	חלק	323		divide
18:11	יעל	qal	wci	3ms	עלה	748		go up
	יצא	qal	wci	3ms	יצא	422		go out
18:12	יהי	qal	wci	3ms	היה	224		be,become
	עלה	qal	wcp	3ms	עלה	748		go up

ChVs	Form	Stem	Tnse	PGN	Root	BDB	Sfx	Meaning
18:12	עלה	qal	wcp	3ms	עלה	748		go up
	היהk	qal	wcp	3ms	היה	224		be,become
	היוq	qal	wcp	3cp	היה	224		be,become
18:13	עבר	qal	wcp	3ms	עבר	716		pass over
	ירד	qal	wcp	3ms	ירד	432		come down
18:14	תאר	qal	wcp	3ms	תאר	1061		incline
	נסב	niph	wcp	3ms	סבב	685		turn round
	היהk	qal	wcp	3ms	היה	224		be,become
	היוq	qal	wcp	3cp	היה	224		be,become
18:15	יצא	qal	wcp	3ms	יצא	422		go out
	יצא	qal	wcp	3ms	יצא	422		go out
18:16	ירד	qal	wcp	3ms	ירד	432		come down
	ירד	qal	wcp	3ms	ירד	432		come down
	ירד	qal	wcp	3ms	ירד	432		come down
18:17	תאר	qal	wcp	3ms	תאר	1061		incline
	יצא	qal	wcp	3ms	יצא	422		go out
	יצא	qal	wcp	3ms	יצא	422		go out
	ירד	qal	wcp	3ms	ירד	432		come down
18:18	עבר	qal	wcp	3ms	עבר	716		pass over
	ירד	qal	wcp	3ms	ירד	432		come down
18:19	עבר	qal	wcp	3ms	עבר	716		pass over
	היהk	qal	wcp	3ms	היה	224		be,become
	היוq	qal	wcp	3cp	היה	224		be,become
18:20	יגבל	qal	impf	3ms	גבל	148		border
18:21	היו	qal	pft	3cp	היה	224		be,become
19:1	יצא	qal	wci	3ms	יצא	422		go out
	יהי	qal	wci	3ms	היה	224		be,become
19:2	יהי	qal	wci	3ms	היה	224		be,become
19:9	היה	qal	pft	3ms	היה	224		be,become
	ינחלו	qal	wci	3mp	נחל	635		possess,inherit
19:10	יעל	qal	wci	3ms	עלה	748		go up
	יהי	qal	wci	3ms	היה	224		be,become
19:11	עלה	qal	wcp	3ms	עלה	748		go up
	פגע	qal	wcp	3ms	פגע	803		meet,encounter
	פגע	qal	wcp	3ms	פגע	803		meet,encounter
19:12	שׁב	qal	wcp	3ms	שׁוב	996		turn,return
	יצא	qal	wcp	3ms	יצא	422		go out
	עלה	qal	wcp	3ms	עלה	748		go up
19:13	עבר	qal	pft	3ms	עבר	716		pass over
	יצא	qal	wcp	3ms	יצא	422		go out
	מתאר	pual	ptc	ms	תאר	1061		be turned
19:14	נסב	niph	wcp	3ms	סבב	685		turn round
	היו	qal	wcp	3cp	היה	224		be,become
19:17	יצא	qal	pft	3ms	יצא	422		go out
19:18	יהי	qal	wci	3ms	היה	224		be,become
19:22	פגע	qal	wcp	3ms	פגע	803		meet,encounter
	היו	qal	wcp	3cp	היה	224		be,become
19:24	יצא	qal	wci	3ms	יצא	422		go out
19:25	יהי	qal	wci	3ms	היה	224		be,become
19:26	פגע	qal	wcp	3ms	פגע	803		meet,encounter
19:27	שׁב	qal	wcp	3ms	שׁוב	996		turn,return
	פגע	qal	wcp	3ms	פגע	803		meet,encounter
	יצא	qal	wcp	3ms	יצא	422		go out
19:29	שׁב	qal	wcp	3ms	שׁוב	996		turn,return

ChVs	Form	Stem	Tnse	PGN	Root	BDB	Sfx	Meaning
19:29	שׁב	qal	wcp	3ms	שׁוב	996		turn,return
	יהיוk	qal	wci	3mp	היה	224		be,become
	היוq	qal	wcp	3cp	היה	224		be,become
19:32	יצא	qal	pft	3ms	יצא	422		go out
19:33	יהי	qal	wci	3ms	היה	224		be,become
	יהי	qal	wci	3ms	היה	224		be,become
19:34	שׁב	qal	wcp	3ms	שׁוב	996		turn,return
	יצא	qal	wcp	3ms	יצא	422		go out
	פגע	qal	wcp	3ms	פגע	803		meet,encounter
	פגע	qal	pft	3ms	פגע	803		meet,encounter
19:40	יצא	qal	pft	3ms	יצא	422		go out
19:41	יהי	qal	wci	3ms	היה	224		be,become
19:47	יצא	qal	wci	3ms	יצא	422		go out
	יעלו	qal	wci	3mp	עלה	748		go up
	ילחמו	niph	wci	3mp	לחם	535		wage war
	ילכדו	qal	wci	3mp	לכד	539		capture
	יכו	hiph	wci	3mp	נכה	645		smite
	ירשׁו	qal	wci	3mp	ירשׁ	439		possess,inherit
	ישׁבו	qal	wci	3mp	ישׁב	442		sit,dwell
	יקראו	qal	wci	3mp	קרא	894		call,proclaim
19:49	יכלו	piel	wci	3mp	כלה	477		complete,finish
	נחל	qal	infc		נחל	635		possess,inherit
	יתנו	qal	wci	3mp	נתן	678		give,set
19:50	נתנו	qal	pft	3cp	נתן	678		give,set
	שׁאל	qal	pft	3ms	שׁאל	981		ask,borrow
	יבנה	qal	wci	3ms	בנה	124		build
	ישׁב	qal	wci	3ms	ישׁב	442		sit,dwell
19:51	נחלו	piel	pft	3cp	נחל	635		allot
	יכלו	piel	wci	3mp	כלה	477		complete,finish
	חלק	piel	infc		חלק	323		divide
20:1	ידבר	piel	wci	3ms	דבר	180		speak
	אמר	qal	infc		אמר	55		say
20:2	דבר	piel	impv	ms	דבר	180		speak
	אמר	qal	infc		אמר	55		say
	תנו	qal	impv	mp	נתן	678		give,set
	דברתי	piel	pft	1cs	דבר	180		speak
20:3	נוס	qal	infc		נוס	630		flee,escape
	רוצח	qal	ptc	ms	רצח	953		murder,slay
	מכה	hiph	ptc	ms	נכה	645		smite
	היו	qal	wcp	3cp	היה	224		be,become
	גאל	qal	ptc	ms	גאל	145		redeem
20:4	נס	qal	wcp	3ms	נוס	630		flee,escape
	עמד	qal	wcp	3ms	עמד	763		stand,stop
	דבר	piel	wcp	3ms	דבר	180		speak
	אספו	qal	wcp	3cp	אסף	62		gather
	נתנו	qal	wcp	3cp	נתן	678		give,set
	ישׁב	qal	wcp	3ms	ישׁב	442		sit,dwell
20:5	ירדף	qal	impf	3ms	רדף	922		pursue
	גאל	qal	ptc	ms	גאל	145		redeem
	יסגרו	hiph	impf	3mp	סגר	688		shut up,deliver
	רצח	qal	ptc	ms	רצח	953		murder,slay
	הכה	hiph	pft	3ms	נכה	645		smite
	שׂנא	qal	ptc	ms	שׂנא	971		hate
20:6	ישׁב	qal	wcp	3ms	ישׁב	442		sit,dwell

ChVs	Form	Stem	Tnse	PGN	Root	BDB	Sfx	Meaning
20:6	עמדו	qal	infc		עמד	763	3ms	stand,stop
	יהיה	qal	impf	3ms	היה	224		be,become
	ישוב	qal	impf	3ms	שוב	996		turn,return
	רוצח	qal	ptc	ms	רצח	953		murder,slay
	בא	qal	wcp	3ms	בוא	97		come in
	נס	qal	pft	3ms	נוס	630		flee,escape
20:7	יקדשו	hiph	wci	3mp	קדש	872		consecrate
20:8	נתנו	qal	pft	3cp	נתן	678		give,set
20:9	היו	qal	pft	3cp	היה	224		be,become
	גר	qal	ptc	ms	גור	157		sojourn
	נוס	qal	infc		נוס	630		flee,escape
	מכה	hiph	ptc	ms	נכה	645		smite
	ימות	qal	impf	3ms	מות	559		die
	גאל	qal	ptc	ms	גאל	145		redeem
	עמדו	qal	infc		עמד	763	3ms	stand,stop
21:1	יגשו	qal	wci	3mp	נגש	620		draw near
21:2	ידברו	piel	wci	3mp	דבר	180		speak
	אמר	qal	infc		אמר	55		say
	צוה	piel	pft	3ms	צוה	845		command
	תת	qal	infc		נתן	678		give,set
	שבת	qal	infc		ישב	442		sit,dwell
21:3	יתנו	qal	wci	3mp	נתן	678		give,set
21:4	יצא	qal	wci	3ms	יצא	422		go out
	יהי	qal	wci	3ms	היה	224		be,become
21:5	נותרים	niph	ptc	mp	יתר	451		be left,remain
21:8	יתנו	qal	wci	3mp	נתן	678		give,set
	צוה	piel	pft	3ms	צוה	845		command
21:9	יתנו	qal	wci	3mp	נתן	678		give,set
	יקרא	qal	impf	3ms	קרא	894		call,proclaim
21:10	יהי	qal	wci	3ms	היה	224		be,become
	היה	qal	pft	3ms	היה	224		be,become
21:11	יתנו	qal	wci	3mp	נתן	678		give,set
21:12	נתנו	qal	pft	3cp	נתן	678		give,set
21:13	נתנו	qal	pft	3cp	נתן	678		give,set
	רצח	qal	ptc	ms	רצח	953		murder,slay
21:20	נותרים	niph	ptc	mp	יתר	451		be left,remain
	יהי	qal	wci	3ms	היה	224		be,become
21:21	יתנו	qal	wci	3mp	נתן	678		give,set
	רצח	qal	ptc	ms	רצח	953		murder,slay
21:26	נותרים	niph	ptc	mp	יתר	451		be left,remain
21:27	רצח	qal	ptc	ms	רצח	953		murder,slay
21:32	רצח	qal	ptc	ms	רצח	953		murder,slay
21:34	נותרים	niph	ptc	mp	יתר	451		be left,remain
21:38	רצח	qal	ptc	ms	רצח	953		murder,slay
21:40	נותרים	niph	ptc	mp	יתר	451		be left,remain
	יהי	qal	wci	3ms	היה	224		be,become
21:42	תהיינה	qal	impf	3fp	היה	224		be,become
21:43	יתן	qal	wci	3ms	נתן	678		give,set
	נשבע	niph	pft	3ms	שבע	989		swear
	תת	qal	infc		נתן	678		give,set
	ירשוה	qal	wci	3mp	ירש	439	3fs	possess,inherit
	ישבו	qal	wci	3mp	ישב	442		sit,dwell
21:44	ינח	hiph	wci	3ms	נוח	628		give rest,put
	נשבע	niph	pft	3ms	שבע	989		swear
21:44	עמד	qal	pft	3ms	עמד	763		stand,stop
	איביהם	qal	ptc	mp	איב	33	3mp	be hostile to
	איביהם	qal	ptc	mp	איב	33	3mp	be hostile to
	נתן	qal	pft	3ms	נתן	678		give,set
21:45	נפל	qal	pft	3ms	נפל	656		fall
	דבר	piel	pft	3ms	דבר	180		speak
	בא	qal	pft	3ms	בוא	97		come in
22:1	יקרא	qal	impf	3ms	קרא	894		call,proclaim
22:2	יאמר	qal	wci	3ms	אמר	55		say
	שמרתם	qal	pft	2mp	שמר	1036		keep,watch
	צוה	piel	pft	3ms	צוה	845		command
	תשמעו	qal	wci	2mp	שמע	1033		hear
	צויתי	piel	pft	1cs	צוה	845		command
22:3	עזבתם	qal	pft	2mp	עזב	736		leave,loose
	שמרתם	qal	pft	2mp	שמר	1036		keep,watch
22:4	הניח	hiph	pft	3ms	נוח	628		give rest,put
	דבר	piel	pft	3ms	דבר	180		speak
	פנו	qal	impv	mp	פנה	815		turn
	לכו	qal	impv	mp	הלך	229		walk,go
	נתן	qal	pft	3ms	נתן	678		give,set
22:5	שמרו	qal	impv	mp	שמר	1036		keep,watch
	עשות	qal	infc		עשה	793		do,make
	צוה	piel	pft	3ms	צוה	845		command
	אהבה	qal	infc		אהב	12		love
	לכת	qal	infc		הלך	229		walk,go
	שמר	qal	infc		שמר	1036		keep,watch
	דבקה	qal	infc		דבק	179		cling,cleave
	עבדו	qal	infc		עבד	712	3ms	work,serve
22:6	יברכם	piel	wci	3ms	ברך	138	3mp	bless
	ישלחם	piel	wci	3ms	שלח	1018	3mp	send away,shoot
	ילכו	qal	wci	3mp	הלך	229		walk,go
22:7	נתן	qal	pft	3ms	נתן	678		give,set
	נתן	qal	pft	3ms	נתן	678		give,set
	שלחם	piel	pft	3ms	שלח	1018	3mp	send away,shoot
	יברכם	piel	wci	3ms	ברך	138	3mp	bless
22:8	יאמר	qal	wci	3ms	אמר	55		say
	אמר	qal	infc		אמר	55		say
	שובו	qal	impv	mp	שוב	996		turn,return
	הרבה	hiph	infa		רבה	915		make many
	חלקו	qal	impv	mp	חלק	323		divide,share
	איביכם	qal	ptc	mp	איב	33	2mp	be hostile to
22:9	ישבו	qal	wci	3mp	שוב	996		turn,return
	ילכו	qal	wci	3mp	הלך	229		walk,go
	לכת	qal	infc		הלך	229		walk,go
	נאחזו	niph	pft	3cp	אחז	28		possess,caught
22:10	יבאו	qal	wci	3mp	בוא	97		come in
	יבנו	qal	wci	3mp	בנה	124		build
22:11	ישמעו	qal	wci	3mp	שמע	1033		hear
	אמר	qal	infc		אמר	55		say
	בנו	qal	pft	3cp	בנה	124		build
22:12	ישמעו	qal	wci	3mp	שמע	1033		hear
	יקהלו	niph	wci	3mp	קהל	874		assemble
	עלות	qal	infc		עלה	748		go up
22:13	ישלחו	qal	wci	3mp	שלח	1018		send

ChVs	Form	Stem	Tnse	PGN	Root	BDB	Sfx	Meaning
22:15	יבאו	qal	wci	3mp	בוא	97		come in
	ידברו	piel	wci	3mp	דבר	180		speak
	אמר	qal	infc		אמר	55		say
22:16	אמרו	qal	pft	3cp	אמר	55		say
	מעלתם	qal	pft	2mp	מעל	591		act faithlessly
	שׁוב	qal	infc		שׁוב	996		turn,return
	בנותכם	qal	infc		בנה	124	2mp	build
	מרדכם	qal	infc		מרד	597	2mp	rebel
22:17	הטהרנו	hith	pft	1cp	טהר	372		purify oneself
	יהי	qal	wci	3ms	היה	224		be,become
22:18	תשׁבו	qal	impf	2mp	שׁוב	996		turn,return
	היה	qal	wcp	3ms	היה	224		be,become
	תמרדו	qal	impf	2mp	מרד	597		rebel
	יקצף	qal	impf	3ms	קצף	893		be angry
22:19	עברו	qal	impv	mp	עבר	716		pass over
	שׁכן	qal	pft	3ms	שׁכן	1014		settle,dwell
	האחזו	niph	impv	mp	אחז	28		possess,caught
	תמרדו	qal	jusm	2mp	מרד	597		rebel
	תמרדו	qal	jusm	2mp	מרד	597		rebel
	בנתכם	qal	infc		בנה	124	2mp	build
22:20	מעל	qal	pft	3ms	מעל	591		act faithlessly
	היה	qal	pft	3ms	היה	224		be,become
	גוע	qal	pft	3ms	גוע	157		expire,die
22:21	יענו	qal	wci	3mp	ענה	772		answer
	ידברו	piel	wci	3mp	דבר	180		speak
22:22	ידע	qal	ptc	ms	ידע	393		know
	ידע	qal	jusm	3ms	ידע	393		know
	תושׁיענו	hiph	jusm	2ms	ישׁע	446	1cp	deliver,save
22:23	בנות	qal	infc		בנה	124		build
	שׁוב	qal	infc		שׁוב	996		turn,return
	העלות	hiph	infc		עלה	748		bring up,offer
	עשׂות	qal	infc		עשׂה	793		do,make
	יבקשׁ	piel	jusm	3ms	בקשׁ	134		seek
22:24	עשׂינו	qal	pft	1cp	עשׂה	793		do,make
	אמר	qal	infc		אמר	55		say
	יאמרו	qal	impf	3mp	אמר	55		say
	אמר	qal	infc		אמר	55		say
22:25	נתן	qal	pft	3ms	נתן	678		give,set
	השׁביתו	hiph	wcp	3cp	שׁבת	991		destroy,remove
	ירא	qal	infc		ירא	431		fear
22:26	נאמר	qal	wci	1cp	אמר	55		say
	נעשׂה	qal	cohm	1cp	עשׂה	793		do,make
	בנות	qal	infc		בנה	124		build
22:27	עבד	qal	infc		עבד	712		work,serve
	יאמרו	qal	impf	3mp	אמר	55		say
22:28	נאמר	qal	wci	1cp	אמר	55		say
	היה	qal	wcp	3ms	היה	224		be,become
	יאמרו	qal	impf	3mp	אמר	55		say
	אמרנו	qal	wcp	1cp	אמר	55		say
	ראו	qal	impv	mp	ראה	906		see
	עשׂו	qal	pft	3cp	עשׂה	793		do,make
22:29	מרד	qal	infc		מרד	597		rebel
	שׁוב	qal	infc		שׁוב	996		turn,return
	בנות	qal	infc		בנה	124		build
22:30	ישׁמע	qal	wci	3ms	שׁמע	1033		hear
	דברו	piel	pft	3cp	דבר	180		speak
	ייטב	qal	wci	3ms	יטב	405		be good
22:31	יאמר	qal	wci	3ms	אמר	55		say
	ידענו	qal	pft	1cp	ידע	393		know
	מעלתם	qal	pft	2mp	מעל	591		act faithlessly
	הצלתם	hiph	pft	2mp	נצל	664		snatch,deliver
22:32	ישׁב	qal	wci	3ms	שׁוב	996		turn,return
	ישׁבו	hiph	wci	3mp	שׁוב	996		bring back
22:33	ייטב	qal	wci	3ms	יטב	405		be good
	יברכו	piel	wci	3mp	ברך	138		bless
	אמרו	qal	pft	3cp	אמר	55		say
	עלות	qal	infc		עלה	748		go up
	שׁחת	piel	infc		שׁחת	1007		spoil,ruin
	ישׁבים	qal	ptc	mp	ישׁב	442		sit,dwell
22:34	יקראו	qal	wci	3mp	קרא	894		call,proclaim
23:1	יהי	qal	wci	3ms	היה	224		be,become
	הניח	hiph	pft	3ms	נוח	628		give rest,put
	איביהם	qal	ptc	mp	איב	33	3mp	be hostile to
	זקן	qal	pft	3ms	זקן	278		be old
	בא	qal	pft	3ms	בוא	97		come in
23:2	יקרא	qal	wci	3ms	קרא	894		call,proclaim
	שׁפטיו	qal	ptc	mp	שׁפט	1047	3ms	judge
	יאמר	qal	wci	3ms	אמר	55		say
	זקנתי	qal	pft	1cs	זקן	278		be old
	באתי	qal	pft	1cs	בוא	97		come in
23:3	ראיתם	qal	pft	2mp	ראה	906		see
	עשׂה	qal	pft	3ms	עשׂה	793		do,make
	נלחם	niph	ptc	ms	לחם	535		wage war
23:4	ראו	qal	impv	mp	ראה	906		see
	הפלתי	hiph	pft	1cs	נפל	656		cause to fall
	נשׁארים	niph	ptc	mp	שׁאר	983		be left
	הכרתי	hiph	pft	1cs	כרת	503		cut off,destroy
23:5	יהדפם	qal	impf	3ms	הדף	213	3mp	thrust,drive
	הורישׁ	hiph	wcp	3ms	ירשׁ	439		c. to possess
	ירשׁתם	qal	wcp	2mp	ירשׁ	439		possess,inherit
	דבר	piel	pft	3ms	דבר	180		speak
23:6	חזקתם	qal	wcp	2mp	חזק	304		be strong
	שׁמר	qal	infc		שׁמר	1036		keep,watch
	עשׂות	qal	infc		עשׂה	793		do,make
	כתוב	qal	pptc	ms	כתב	507		write
	סור	qal	infc		סור	693		turn aside
23:7	בוא	qal	infc		בוא	97		come in
	נשׁארים	niph	ptc	mp	שׁאר	983		be left
	תזכירו	hiph	impf	2mp	זכר	269		c. to remember
	תשׁביעו	hiph	impf	2mp	שׁבע	989		cause to swear
	תעבדום	qal	impf	2mp	עבד	712	3mp	work,serve
	תשׁתחוו	hish	impf	2mp	חוה	1005		bow down
23:8	תדבקו	qal	impf	2mp	דבק	179		cling,cleave
	עשׂיתם	qal	pft	2mp	עשׂה	793		do,make
23:9	יורשׁ	hiph	wci	3ms	ירשׁ	439		c. to possess
	עמד	qal	pft	3ms	עמד	763		stand,stop
23:10	ירדף	qal	impf	3ms	רדף	922		pursue
	נלחם	niph	ptc	ms	לחם	535		wage war

ChVs	Form	Stem	Tnse	PGN	Root	BDB	Sfx	Meaning
23:10	דבר	piel	pft	3ms	דבר	180		speak
23:11	נשמרתם	niph	wcp	2mp	שמר	1036		be kept, guarded
	אהבה	qal	infc		אהב	12		love
23:12	שׁוב	qal	infa		שׁוב	996		turn, return
	תשובו	qal	impf	2mp	שׁוב	996		turn, return
	דבקתם	qal	wcp	2mp	דבק	179		cling, cleave
	נשארים	niph	ptc	mp	שאר	983		be left
	התחתנתם	hith	wcp	2mp	חתן	368		be son-in-law
	באתם	qal	wcp	2mp	בוא	97		come in
23:13	ידוע	qal	infa		ידע	393		know
	תדעו	qal	impf	2mp	ידע	393		know
	יוסיף	hiph	impf	3ms	יסף	414		add, do again
	הוריש	hiph	infc		ירש	439		c. to possess
	היו	qal	wcp	3cp	היה	224		be, become
	אבדכם	qal	infc		אבד	1	2mp	perish
	נתן	qal	pft	3ms	נתן	678		give, set
23:14	הולך	qal	ptc	ms	הלך	229		walk, go
	ידעתם	qal	wcp	2mp	ידע	393		know
	נפל	qal	pft	3ms	נפל	656		fall
	דבר	piel	pft	3ms	דבר	180		speak
	באו	qal	pft	3cp	בוא	97		come in
	נפל	qal	pft	3ms	נפל	656		fall
23:15	היה	qal	wcp	3ms	היה	224		be, become
	בא	qal	pft	3ms	בוא	97		come in
	דבר	piel	pft	3ms	דבר	180		speak
	יביא	hiph	impf	3ms	בוא	97		bring in
	השמידו	hiph	infc		שמד	1029	3ms	exterminate
	נתן	qal	pft	3ms	נתן	678		give, set
23:16	עברכם	qal	infc		עבר	716	2mp	pass over
	צוה	piel	pft	3ms	צוה	845		command
	הלכתם	qal	wcp	2mp	הלך	229		walk, go
	עבדתם	qal	wcp	2mp	עבד	712		work, serve
	השתחויתם	hish	wcp	2mp	חוה	1005		bow down
	חרה	qal	wcp	3ms	חרה	354		be kindled, burn
	אבדתם	qal	wcp	2mp	אבד	1		perish
	נתן	qal	pft	3ms	נתן	678		give, set
24:1	יאסף	qal	wci	3ms	אסף	62		gather
	יקרא	qal	wci	3ms	קרא	894		call, proclaim
	שפטיו	qal	ptc	mp	שפט	1047	3ms	judge
	יתיצבו	hith	wci	3mp	יצב	426		stand oneself
24:2	יאמר	qal	wci	3ms	אמר	55		say
	אמר	qal	pft	3ms	אמר	55		say
	ישבו	qal	pft	3cp	ישב	442		sit, dwell
	יעבדו	qal	wci	3mp	עבד	712		work, serve
24:3	אקח	qal	wci	1cs	לקח	542		take
	אולך	hiph	wci	1cs	הלך	229		lead, bring
	ארבk	hiph	wci	1cs	רבה	915		make many
	ארבהq	hiph	wci	1cs	רבה	915		make many
	אתן	qal	wci	1cs	נתן	678		give, set
24:4	אתן	qal	wci	1cs	נתן	678		give, set
	אתן	qal	wci	1cs	נתן	678		give, set
	רשת	qal	infc		ירש	439		possess, inherit
	ירדו	qal	pft	3cp	ירד	432		come down
24:5	אשלח	qal	wci	1cs	שלח	1018		send
24:5	אגף	qal	wci	1cs	נגף	619		smite, strike
	עשׂיתי	qal	pft	1cs	עשׂה	793		do, make
	הוצאתי	hiph	pft	1cs	יצא	422		bring out
24:6	אוציא	hiph	wci	1cs	יצא	422		bring out
	תבאו	qal	wci	2mp	בוא	97		come in
	ירדפו	qal	wci	3mp	רדף	922		pursue
24:7	יצעקו	qal	wci	3mp	צעק	858		cry out
	ישם	qal	wci	3ms	שׂים	962		put, set
	יבא	hiph	wci	3ms	בוא	97		bring in
	יכסהו	piel	wci	3ms	כסה	491	3ms	cover
	תראינה	qal	wci	3fp	ראה	906		see
	עשׂיתי	qal	pft	1cs	עשׂה	793		do, make
	תשבו	qal	wci	2mp	ישב	442		sit, dwell
24:8	אבאהk	hiph	wci	1cs	בוא	97		bring in
	אביאq	hiph	wci	1cs	בוא	97		bring in
	יושב	qal	ptc	ms	ישב	442		sit, dwell
	ילחמו	niph	wci	3mp	לחם	535		wage war
	אתן	qal	wci	1cs	נתן	678		give, set
	תירשו	qal	wci	2mp	ירש	439		possess, inherit
	אשמידם	hiph	wci	1cs	שמד	1029	3mp	exterminate
24:9	יקם	qal	wci	3ms	קום	877		arise, stand
	ילחם	niph	wci	3ms	לחם	535		wage war
	ישלח	qal	wci	3ms	שלח	1018		send
	יקרא	qal	wci	3ms	קרא	894		call, proclaim
	קלל	piel	infc		קלל	886		curse
24:10	אביתי	qal	pft	1cs	אבה	2		be willing
	שמע	qal	infc		שמע	1033		hear
	יברך	piel	wci	3ms	ברך	138		bless
	ברוך	piel	infa		ברך	138		bless
	אצל	hiph	wci	1cs	נצל	664		snatch, deliver
24:11	תעברו	qal	wci	2mp	עבר	716		pass over
	תבאו	qal	wci	2mp	בוא	97		come in
	ילחמו	niph	wci	3mp	לחם	535		wage war
	אתן	qal	wci	1cs	נתן	678		give, set
24:12	אשלח	qal	wci	1cs	שלח	1018		send
	תגרש	piel	wci	3fs	גרש	176		drive out
24:13	אתן	qal	wci	1cs	נתן	678		give, set
	יגעת	qal	pft	2ms	יגע	388		toil, grow weary
	בניתם	qal	pft	2mp	בנה	124		build
	תשבו	qal	wci	2mp	ישב	442		sit, dwell
	נטעתם	qal	pft	2mp	נטע	642		plant
	אכלים	qal	ptc	mp	אכל	37		eat, devour
24:14	יראו	qal	impv	mp	ירא	431		fear
	עבדו	qal	impv	mp	עבד	712		work, serve
	הסירו	hiph	impv	mp	סור	693		take away
	עבדו	qal	pft	3cp	עבד	712		work, serve
	עבדו	qal	impv	mp	עבד	712		work, serve
24:15	עבד	qal	infc		עבד	712		work, serve
	בחרו	qal	impv	mp	בחר	103		choose
	תעבדון	qal	impf	2mp	עבד	712		work, serve
	עבדו	qal	pft	3cp	עבד	712		work, serve
	ישבים	qal	ptc	mp	ישב	442		sit, dwell
	נעבד	qal	impf	1cp	עבד	712		work, serve
24:16	יען	qal	wci	3ms	ענה	772		answer

ChVs	Form	Stem	Tnse	PGN	Root	BDB	Sfx	Meaning
24:16	יאמר	qal	wci	3ms	אמר	55		say
	עזב	qal	infc		עזב	736		leave,loose
	עבד	qal	infc		עבד	712		work,serve
24:17	מעלה	hiph	ptc	ms	עלה	748		bring up,offer
	עשׂה	qal	pft	3ms	עשׂה	793		do,make
	ישׁמרנו	qal	wci	3ms	שׁמר	1036	1cp	keep,watch
	הלכנו	qal	pft	1cp	הלך	229		walk,go
	עברנו	qal	pft	1cp	עבר	716		pass over
24:18	יגרשׁ	piel	wci	3ms	גרשׁ	176		drive out
	ישׁב	qal	ptc	ms	ישׁב	442		sit,dwell
	נעבד	qal	impf	1cp	עבד	712		work,serve
24:19	יאמר	qal	wci	3ms	אמר	55		say
	תוכלו	qal	impf	2mp	יכל	407		be able
	עבד	qal	infc		עבד	712		work,serve
	ישׂא	qal	impf	3ms	נשׂא	669		lift,carry
24:20	תעזבו	qal	impf	2mp	עזב	736		leave,loose
	עבדתם	qal	wcp	2mp	עבד	712		work,serve
	שׁב	qal	wcp	3ms	שׁוב	996		turn,return
	הרע	hiph	wcp	3ms	רעע	949		hurt,do evil
	כלה	piel	wcp	3ms	כלה	477		complete,finish
	היטיב	hiph	pft	3ms	יטב	405		do good
24:21	יאמר	qal	wci	3ms	אמר	55		say
	נעבד	qal	impf	1cp	עבד	712		work,serve
24:22	יאמר	qal	wci	3ms	אמר	55		say
	בחרתם	qal	pft	2mp	בחר	103		choose
	עבד	qal	infc		עבד	712		work,serve
	יאמרו	qal	wci	3mp	אמר	55		say
24:23	הסירו	hiph	impv	mp	סור	693		take away
	הטו	hiph	impv	mp	נטה	639		turn,incline
24:24	יאמרו	qal	wci	3mp	אמר	55		say
	נעבד	qal	impf	1cp	עבד	712		work,serve
	נשׁמע	qal	impf	1cp	שׁמע	1033		hear
24:25	יכרת	qal	wci	3ms	כרת	503		cut,destroy
	ישׂם	qal	wci	3ms	שׂים	962		put,set
24:26	יכתב	qal	wci	3ms	כתב	507		write
	יקח	qal	wci	3ms	לקח	542		take
	יקימה	hiph	wci	3ms	קום	877	3fs	raise,build,set
24:27	יאמר	qal	wci	3ms	אמר	55		say
	תהיה	qal	impf	3fs	היה	224		be,become
	שׁמעה	qal	pft	3fs	שׁמע	1033		hear
	דבר	piel	pft	3ms	דבר	180		speak
	היתה	qal	wcp	3fs	היה	224		be,become
	תכחשׁון	piel	impf	2mp	כחשׁ	471		deceive
24:28	ישׁלח	piel	wci	3ms	שׁלח	1018		send away,shoot
24:29	יהי	qal	wci	3ms	היה	224		be,become
	ימת	qal	wci	3ms	מות	559		die
24:30	יקברו	qal	wci	3mp	קבר	868		bury
24:31	יעבד	qal	wci	3ms	עבד	712		work,serve
	האריכו	hiph	pft	3cp	ארך	73		prolong
	ידעו	qal	pft	3cp	ידע	393		know
	עשׂה	qal	pft	3ms	עשׂה	793		do,make
24:32	העלו	hiph	pft	3cp	עלה	748		bring up,offer
	קברו	qal	pft	3cp	קבר	868		bury
	קנה	qal	pft	3ms	קנה	888		get,buy

ChVs	Form	Stem	Tnse	PGN	Root	BDB	Sfx	Meaning
24:32	יהיו	qal	wci	3mp	היה	224		be,become
24:33	מת	qal	pft	3ms	מות	559		die
	יקברו	qal	wci	3mp	קבר	868		bury
	נתן	niph	pft	3ms	נתן	678		be given
JUDGES								
1:1	יהי	qal	wci	3ms	היה	224		be,become
	ישׁאלו	qal	wci	3mp	שׁאל	981		ask,borrow
	אמר	qal	infc		אמר	55		say
	יעלה	qal	impf	3ms	עלה	748		go up
	הלחם	niph	infc		לחם	535		wage war
1:2	יאמר	qal	wci	3ms	אמר	55		say
	יעלה	qal	impf	3ms	עלה	748		go up
	נתתי	qal	pft	1cs	נתן	678		give,set
1:3	יאמר	qal	wci	3ms	אמר	55		say
	עלה	qal	impv	ms	עלה	748		go up
	נלחמה	niph	coh	1cp	לחם	535		wage war
	הלכתי	qal	wcp	1cs	הלך	229		walk,go
	ילך	qal	wci	3ms	הלך	229		walk,go
1:4	יעל	qal	wci	3ms	עלה	748		go up
	יתן	qal	wci	3ms	נתן	678		give,set
	יכום	hiph	wci	3mp	נכה	645	3mp	smite
1:5	ימצאו	qal	wci	3mp	מצא	592		find
	ילחמו	niph	wci	3mp	לחם	535		wage war
	יכו	hiph	wci	3mp	נכה	645		smite
1:6	ינס	qal	wci	3ms	נוס	630		flee,escape
	ירדפו	qal	wci	3mp	רדף	922		pursue
	יאחזו	qal	wci	3mp	אחז	28		grasp
	יקצצו	piel	wci	3mp	קצץ	893		cut off
1:7	יאמר	qal	wci	3ms	אמר	55		say
	מקצצים	pual	ptc	mp	קצץ	893		be cut off
	היו	qal	pft	3cp	היה	224		be,become
	מלקטים	piel	ptc	mp	לקט	544		gather
	עשׂיתי	qal	pft	1cs	עשׂה	793		do,make
	שׁלם	piel	pft	3ms	שׁלם	1022		finish,reward
	יביאהו	hiph	wci	3mp	בוא	97	3ms	bring in
	ימת	qal	wci	3ms	מות	559		die
1:8	ילחמו	niph	wci	3mp	לחם	535		wage war
	ילכדו	qal	wci	3mp	לכד	539		capture
	יכוה	hiph	wci	3mp	נכה	645	3fs	smite
	שׁלחו	piel	pft	3cp	שׁלח	1018		send away,shoot
1:9	ירדו	qal	pft	3cp	ירד	432		come down
	הלחם	niph	infc		לחם	535		wage war
	יושׁב	qal	ptc	ms	ישׁב	442		sit,dwell
1:10	ילך	qal	wci	3ms	הלך	229		walk,go
	יושׁב	qal	ptc	ms	ישׁב	442		sit,dwell
	יכו	hiph	wci	3mp	נכה	645		smite
1:11	ילך	qal	wci	3ms	הלך	229		walk,go
	יושׁבי	qal	ptc	mp	ישׁב	442		sit,dwell
1:12	יאמר	qal	wci	3ms	אמר	55		say
	יכה	hiph	impf	3ms	נכה	645		smite
	לכדה	qal	wcp	3ms	לכד	539	3fs	capture
	נתתי	qal	wcp	1cs	נתן	678		give,set
1:13	ילכדה	qal	wci	3ms	לכד	539	3fs	capture

ChVs	Form	Stem	Tnse	PGN	Root	BDB	Sfx	Meaning
1:13	יתן	qal	wci	3ms	נתן	678		give,set
1:14	יהי	qal	wci	3ms	היה	224		be,become
	בואה	qal	infc		בוא	97	3fs	come in
	תסיתהו	hiph	wci	3fs	סות	694	3ms	incite,allure
	שׁאול	qal	infc		שׁאל	981		ask,borrow
	תצנח	qal	wci	3fs	צנח	856		descend
	יאמר	qal	wci	3ms	אמר	55		say
1:15	תאמר	qal	wci	3fs	אמר	55		say
	הבה	qal	impv	ms	יהב	396		give
	נתתני	qal	pft	2ms	נתן	678	1cs	give,set
	נתתה	qal	wcp	2ms	נתן	678		give,set
	יתן	qal	wci	3ms	נתן	678		give,set
1:16	עלו	qal	pft	3cp	עלה	748		go up
	ילך	qal	wci	3ms	הלך	229		walk,go
	ישׁב	qal	wci	3ms	ישׁב	442		sit,dwell
1:17	ילך	qal	wci	3ms	הלך	229		walk,go
	יכו	hiph	wci	3mp	נכה	645		smite
	יושׁב	qal	ptc	ms	ישׁב	442		sit,dwell
	יחרימו	hiph	wci	3mp	חרם	355		ban,destroy
	יקרא	qal	wci	3ms	קרא	894		call,proclaim
1:18	ילכד	qal	wci	3ms	לכד	539		capture
1:19	יהי	qal	wci	3ms	היה	224		be,become
	ירשׁ	hiph	wci	3ms	ירשׁ	439		c. to possess
	הורישׁ	hiph	infc		ירשׁ	439		c. to possess
	ישׁבי	qal	ptc	mp	ישׁב	442		sit,dwell
1:20	יתנו	qal	wci	3mp	נתן	678		give,set
	דבר	piel	pft	3ms	דבר	180		speak
	יורשׁ	hiph	wci	3ms	ירשׁ	439		c. to possess
1:21	ישׁב	qal	ptc	ms	ישׁב	442		sit,dwell
	הורישׁו	hiph	pft	3cp	ירשׁ	439		c. to possess
	ישׁב	qal	wci	3ms	ישׁב	442		sit,dwell
1:22	יעלו	qal	wci	3mp	עלה	748		go up
1:23	יתירו	hiph	wci	3mp	תור	1064		spy out
1:24	יראו	qal	wci	3mp	ראה	906		see
	שׁמרים	qal	ptc	mp	שׁמר	1036		keep,watch
	יוצא	qal	ptc	ms	יצא	422		go out
	יאמרו	qal	wci	3mp	אמר	55		say
	הראנו	hiph	impv	ms	ראה	906	1cp	show,exhibit
	עשׂינו	qal	wcp	1cp	עשׂה	793		do,make
1:25	יראם	hiph	wci	3ms	ראה	906	3mp	show,exhibit
	יכו	hiph	wci	3mp	נכה	645		smite
	שׁלחו	piel	pft	3cp	שׁלח	1018		send away,shoot
1:26	ילך	qal	wci	3ms	הלך	229		walk,go
	יבן	qal	wci	3ms	בנה	124		build
	יקרא	qal	wci	3ms	קרא	894		call,proclaim
1:27	הורישׁ	hiph	pft	3ms	ירשׁ	439		c. to possess
	ישׁבk	qal	ptc	ms	ישׁב	442		sit,dwell
	ישׁביq	qal	ptc	mp	ישׁב	442		sit,dwell
	יושׁבי	qal	ptc	mp	ישׁב	442		sit,dwell
	יושׁבי	qal	ptc	mp	ישׁב	442		sit,dwell
	יואל	hiph	wci	3ms	יאל	383		be willing
	שׁבת	qal	infc		ישׁב	442		sit,dwell
1:28	יהי	qal	wci	3ms	היה	224		be,become
	חזק	qal	pft	3ms	חזק	304		be strong
1:28	ישׂם	qal	wci	3ms	שׂים	962		put,set
	הורישׁ	hiph	infa		ירשׁ	439		c. to possess
	הורישׁו	hiph	pft	3ms	ירשׁ	439	3ms	c. to possess
1:29	הורישׁ	hiph	pft	3ms	ירשׁ	439		c. to possess
	יושׁב	qal	ptc	ms	ישׁב	442		sit,dwell
	ישׁב	qal	wci	3ms	ישׁב	442		sit,dwell
1:30	הורישׁ	hiph	pft	3ms	ירשׁ	439		c. to possess
	יושׁבי	qal	ptc	mp	ישׁב	442		sit,dwell
	יושׁבי	qal	ptc	mp	ישׁב	442		sit,dwell
	ישׁב	qal	wci	3ms	ישׁב	442		sit,dwell
	יהיו	qal	wci	3mp	היה	224		be,become
1:31	הורישׁ	hiph	pft	3ms	ירשׁ	439		c. to possess
	ישׁבי	qal	ptc	mp	ישׁב	442		sit,dwell
	יושׁבי	qal	ptc	mp	ישׁב	442		sit,dwell
1:32	ישׁב	qal	wci	3ms	ישׁב	442		sit,dwell
	ישׁבי	qal	ptc	mp	ישׁב	442		sit,dwell
	הורישׁו	hiph	pft	3ms	ירשׁ	439	3ms	c. to possess
1:33	הורישׁ	hiph	pft	3ms	ירשׁ	439		c. to possess
	ישׁבי	qal	ptc	mp	ישׁב	442		sit,dwell
	ישׁבי	qal	ptc	mp	ישׁב	442		sit,dwell
	ישׁב	qal	wci	3ms	ישׁב	442		sit,dwell
	ישׁבי	qal	ptc	mp	ישׁב	442		sit,dwell
	ישׁבי	qal	ptc	mp	ישׁב	442		sit,dwell
	היו	qal	pft	3cp	היה	224		be,become
1:34	ילחצו	qal	wci	3mp	לחץ	537		press,oppress
	נתנו	qal	pft	3ms	נתן	678	3ms	give,set
	רדת	qal	infc		ירד	432		come down
1:35	יואל	hiph	wci	3ms	יאל	383		be willing
	שׁבת	qal	infc		ישׁב	442		sit,dwell
	תכבד	qal	wci	3fs	כבד	457		be heavy
	יהיו	qal	wci	3mp	היה	224		be,become
2:1	יעל	qal	wci	3ms	עלה	748		go up
	יאמר	qal	wci	3ms	אמר	55		say
	אעלה	hiph	impf	1cs	עלה	748		bring up,offer
	אביא	hiph	wci	1cs	בוא	97		bring in
	נשׁבעתי	niph	pft	1cs	שׁבע	989		swear
	אמר	qal	wci	1cs	אמר	55		say
	אפר	hiph	impf	1cs	פרר	830		break,frustrate
2:2	תכרתו	qal	impf	2mp	כרת	503		cut,destroy
	יושׁבי	qal	ptc	mp	ישׁב	442		sit,dwell
	תתצון	qal	impf	2mp	נתץ	683		pull down
	שׁמעתם	qal	pft	2mp	שׁמע	1033		hear
	עשׂיתם	qal	pft	2mp	עשׂה	793		do,make
2:3	אמרתי	qal	pft	1cs	אמר	55		say
	אגרשׁ	piel	impf	1cs	גרשׁ	176		drive out
	היו	qal	wcp	3cp	היה	224		be,become
	יהיו	qal	impf	3mp	היה	224		be,become
2:4	יהי	qal	wci	3ms	היה	224		be,become
	דבר	piel	infc		דבר	180		speak
	ישׂאו	qal	wci	3mp	נשׂא	669		lift,carry
	יבכו	qal	wci	3mp	בכה	113		weep
2:5	יקראו	qal	wci	3mp	קרא	894		call,proclaim
	יזבחו	qal	wci	3mp	זבח	256		slaughter
2:6	ישׁלח	piel	wci	3ms	שׁלח	1018		send away,shoot

ChVs	Form	Stem	Tnse	PGN	Root	BDB	Sfx	Meaning
2: 6	ילכו	qal	wci	3mp	הלך	229		walk,go
	רשת	qal	infc		ירשׁ	439		possess,inherit
2: 7	יעבדו	qal	wci	3mp	עבד	712		work,serve
	האריכו	hiph	pft	3cp	ארך	73		prolong
	ראו	qal	pft	3cp	ראה	906		see
	עשׂה	qal	pft	3ms	עשׂה	793		do,make
2: 8	ימת	qal	wci	3ms	מות	559		die
2: 9	יקברו	qal	wci	3mp	קבר	868		bury
2: 10	נאספו	niph	pft	3cp	אסף	62		assemble
	יקם	qal	wci	3ms	קום	877		arise,stand
	ידעו	qal	pft	3cp	ידע	393		know
	עשׂה	qal	pft	3ms	עשׂה	793		do,make
2: 11	יעשׂו	qal	wci	3mp	עשׂה	793		do,make
	יעבדו	qal	wci	3mp	עבד	712		work,serve
2: 12	יעזבו	qal	wci	3mp	עזב	736		leave,loose
	מוציא	hiph	ptc	ms	יצא	422		bring out
	ילכו	qal	wci	3mp	הלך	229		walk,go
	ישׁתחוו	hish	wci	3mp	חוה	1005		bow down
	יכעסו	hiph	wci	3mp	כעס	494		vex,provoke
2: 13	יעזבו	qal	wci	3mp	עזב	736		leave,loose
	יעבדו	qal	wci	3mp	עבד	712		work,serve
2: 14	יחר	qal	wci	3ms	חרה	354		be kindled,burn
	יתנם	qal	wci	3ms	נתן	678	3mp	give,set
	שׂסים	qal	ptc	mp	שׂסה	1042		plunder
	ישׂסו	qal	wci	3mp	שׂסס	1042		plunder
	ימכרם	qal	wci	3ms	מכר	569	3mp	sell
	אויביהם	qal	ptc	mp	איב	33	3mp	be hostile to
	יכלו	qal	pft	3cp	יכל	407		be able
	עמד	qal	infc		עמד	763		stand,stop
	אויביהם	qal	ptc	mp	איב	33	3mp	be hostile to
2: 15	יצאו	qal	pft	3cp	יצא	422		go out
	היתה	qal	pft	3fs	היה	224		be,become
	דבר	piel	pft	3ms	דבר	180		speak
	נשׁבע	niph	pft	3ms	שׁבע	989		swear
	יצר	qal	wci	3ms	צרר	864		bind,be cramped
2: 16	יקם	hiph	wci	3ms	קום	877		raise,build,set
	שׁפטים	qal	ptc	mp	שׁפט	1047		judge
	יושׁיעום	hiph	wci	3mp	ישׁע	446	3mp	deliver,save
	שׁסיהם	qal	ptc	mp	שׁסה	1042	3mp	plunder
2: 17	שׁפטיהם	qal	ptc	mp	שׁפט	1047	3mp	judge
	שׁמעו	qal	pft	3cp	שׁמע	1033		hear
	זנו	qal	pft	3cp	זנה	275		act a harlot
	ישׁתחוו	hish	wci	3mp	חוה	1005		bow down
	סרו	qal	pft	3cp	סור	693		turn aside
	הלכו	qal	pft	3cp	הלך	229		walk,go
	שׁמע	qal	infc		שׁמע	1033		hear
	עשׂו	qal	pft	3cp	עשׂה	793		do,make
2: 18	הקים	hiph	pft	3ms	קום	877		raise,build,set
	שׁפטים	qal	ptc	mp	שׁפט	1047		judge
	היה	qal	wcp	3ms	היה	224		be,become
	שׁפט	qal	ptc	ms	שׁפט	1047		judge
	הושׁיעם	hiph	wcp	3ms	ישׁע	446	3mp	deliver,save
	איביהם	qal	ptc	mp	איב	33	3mp	be hostile to
	שׁופט	qal	ptc	ms	שׁפט	1047		judge
2: 18	ינחם	niph	impf	3ms	נחם	636		be sorry
	לחציהם	qal	ptc	mp	לחץ	537	3mp	press,oppress
	דחקיהם	qal	ptc	mp	דחק	191	3mp	thrust,crowd
2: 19	היה	qal	wcp	3ms	היה	224		be,become
	מות	qal	infc		מות	559		die
	שׁופט	qal	ptc	ms	שׁפט	1047		judge
	ישׁבו	qal	impf	3mp	שׁוב	996		turn,return
	השׁחיתו	hiph	wcp	3cp	שׁחת	1007		spoil,ruin
	לכת	qal	infc		הלך	229		walk,go
	עבדם	qal	infc		עבד	712	3mp	work,serve
	השׁתחות	hish	infc		חוה	1005		bow down
	הפילו	hiph	pft	3cp	נפל	656		cause to fall
2: 20	יחר	qal	wci	3ms	חרה	354		be kindled,burn
	יאמר	qal	wci	3ms	אמר	55		say
	עברו	qal	pft	3cp	עבר	716		pass over
	צויתי	piel	pft	1cs	צוה	845		command
	שׁמעו	qal	pft	3cp	שׁמע	1033		hear
2: 21	אוסיף	hiph	impf	1cs	יסף	414		add,do again
	הורישׁ	hiph	infc		ירשׁ	439		c. to possess
	עזב	qal	pft	3ms	עזב	736		leave,loose
	ימת	qal	wci	3ms	מות	559		die
2: 22	נסות	piel	infc		נסה	650		test,try
	שׁמרים	qal	ptc	mp	שׁמר	1036		keep,watch
	לכת	qal	infc		הלך	229		walk,go
	שׁמרו	qal	pft	3cp	שׁמר	1036		keep,watch
2: 23	ינח	hiph	wci	3ms	נוח	628		give rest,put
	הורישׁם	hiph	infc		ירשׁ	439	3mp	c. to possess
	נתנם	qal	pft	3ms	נתן	678	3mp	give,set
3: 1	הניח	hiph	pft	3ms	נוח	628		give rest,put
	נסות	piel	infc		נסה	650		test,try
	ידעו	qal	pft	3cp	ידע	393		know
3: 2	דעת	qal	infc		ידע	393		know
	למדם	piel	infc		למד	540	3mp	teach
	ידעום	qal	pft	3cp	ידע	393	3mp	know
3: 3	ישׁב	qal	ptc	ms	ישׁב	442		sit,dwell
	בוא	qal	infc		בוא	97		come in
3: 4	יהיו	qal	wci	3mp	היה	224		be,become
	נסות	piel	infc		נסה	650		test,try
	דעת	qal	infc		ידע	393		know
	ישׁמעו	qal	impf	3mp	שׁמע	1033		hear
	צוה	piel	pft	3ms	צוה	845		command
3: 5	ישׁבו	qal	pft	3cp	ישׁב	442		sit,dwell
3: 6	יקחו	qal	wci	3mp	לקח	542		take
	נתנו	qal	pft	3cp	נתן	678		give,set
	יעבדו	qal	wci	3mp	עבד	712		work,serve
3: 7	יעשׂו	qal	wci	3mp	עשׂה	793		do,make
	ישׁכחו	qal	wci	3mp	שׁכח	1013		forget
	יעבדו	qal	wci	3mp	עבד	712		work,serve
3: 8	יחר	qal	wci	3ms	חרה	354		be kindled,burn
	ימכרם	qal	wci	3ms	מכר	569	3mp	sell
	יעבדו	qal	wci	3mp	עבד	712		work,serve
3: 9	יזעקו	qal	wci	3mp	זעק	277		call,cry out
	יקם	hiph	wci	3ms	קום	877		raise,build,set
	מושׁיע	hiph	ptc	ms	ישׁע	446		deliver,save

ChVs	Form	Stem	Tnse	PGN	Root	BDB	Sfx	Meaning
3:9	יושיעם	hiph	wci	3ms	ישע	446	3mp	deliver,save
3:10	תהי	qal	wci	3fs	היה	224		be,become
	ישפט	qal	wci	3ms	שפט	1047		judge
	יצא	qal	wci	3ms	יצא	422		go out
	יתן	qal	wci	3ms	נתן	678		give,set
	תעז	qal	wci	3fs	עזז	738		be strong
3:11	תשקט	qal	wci	3fs	שקט	1052		be quiet
	ימת	qal	wci	3ms	מות	559		die
3:12	יספו	hiph	wci	3mp	יסף	414		add,do again
	עשות	qal	infc		עשה	793		do,make
	יחזק	piel	wci	3ms	חזק	304		make strong
	עשו	qal	pft	3cp	עשה	793		do,make
3:13	יאסף	qal	wci	3ms	אסף	62		gather
	ילך	qal	wci	3ms	הלך	229		walk,go
	יך	hiph	wci	3ms	נכה	645		smite
	יירשו	qal	wci	3mp	ירש	439		possess,inherit
3:14	יעבדו	qal	wci	3mp	עבד	712		work,serve
3:15	יזעקו	qal	wci	3mp	זעק	277		call,cry out
	יקם	hiph	wci	3ms	קום	877		raise,build,set
	מושיע	hiph	ptc	ms	ישע	446		deliver,save
	ישלחו	qal	wci	3mp	שלח	1018		send
3:16	יעש	qal	wci	3ms	עשה	793		do,make
	יחגר	qal	wci	3ms	חגר	291		gird
3:17	יקרב	hiph	wci	3ms	קרב	897		bring near
3:18	יהי	qal	wci	3ms	היה	224		be,become
	כלה	piel	pft	3ms	כלה	477		complete,finish
	הקריב	hiph	infc		קרב	897		bring near
	ישלח	piel	wci	3ms	שלח	1018		send away,shoot
	נשאי	qal	ptc	mp	נשא	669		lift,carry
3:19	שב	qal	pft	3ms	שוב	996		turn,return
	יאמר	qal	wci	3ms	אמר	55		say
	יאמר	qal	wci	3ms	אמר	55		say
	יצאו	qal	wci	3mp	יצא	422		go out
	עמדים	qal	ptc	mp	עמד	763		stand,stop
3:20	בא	qal	pft	3ms	בוא	97		come in
	ישב	qal	ptc	ms	ישב	442		sit,dwell
	יאמר	qal	wci	3ms	אמר	55		say
	יקם	qal	wci	3ms	קום	877		arise,stand
3:21	ישלח	qal	wci	3ms	שלח	1018		send
	יקח	qal	wci	3ms	לקח	542		take
	יתקעה	qal	wci	3ms	תקע	1075	3fs	thrust,clap
3:22	יבא	qal	wci	3ms	בוא	97		come in
	יסגר	qal	wci	3ms	סגר	688		shut
	שלף	qal	pft	3ms	שלף	1025		draw out,off
	יצא	qal	wci	3ms	יצא	422		go out
3:23	יצא	qal	wci	3ms	יצא	422		go out
	יסגר	qal	wci	3ms	סגר	688		shut
	נעל	qal	pft	3ms	נעל	653		bar,bolt
3:24	יצא	qal	pft	3ms	יצא	422		go out
	באו	qal	pft	3cp	בוא	97		come in
	יראו	qal	wci	3mp	ראה	906		see
	נעלות	qal	pptc	fp	נעל	653		bar,bolt
	יאמרו	qal	wci	3mp	אמר	55		say
	מסיך	hiph	ptc	ms	סכך	696		cover
3:25	יחילו	qal	wci	3mp	חול	296		dance,writhe
	בוש	qal	infc		בוש	101		be ashamed
	פתח	qal	ptc	ms	פתח	834		open
	יקחו	qal	wci	3mp	לקח	542		take
	יפתחו	qal	wci	3mp	פתח	834		open
	נפל	qal	ptc	ms	נפל	656		fall
	מת	qal	ptc	ms	מות	559		die
3:26	נמלט	niph	pft	3ms	מלט	572		escape
	התמהמהם	htpp	infc		מהה	554	3mp	tarry
	עבר	qal	pft	3ms	עבר	716		pass over
	ימלט	niph	wci	3ms	מלט	572		escape
3:27	יהי	qal	wci	3ms	היה	224		be,become
	בואו	qal	infc		בוא	97	3ms	come in
	יתקע	qal	wci	3ms	תקע	1075		thrust,clap
	ירדו	qal	wci	3mp	ירד	432		come down
3:28	יאמר	qal	wci	3ms	אמר	55		say
	רדפו	qal	impv	mp	רדף	922		pursue
	נתן	qal	pft	3ms	נתן	678		give,set
	איביכם	qal	ptc	mp	איב	33	2mp	be hostile to
	ירדו	qal	wci	3mp	ירד	432		come down
	ילכדו	qal	wci	3mp	לכד	539		capture
	נתנו	qal	pft	3cp	נתן	678		give,set
	עבר	qal	infc		עבר	716		pass over
3:29	יכו	hiph	wci	3mp	נכה	645		smite
	נמלט	niph	pft	3ms	מלט	572		escape
3:30	תכנע	niph	wci	3fs	כנע	488		humble self
	תשקט	qal	wci	3fs	שקט	1052		be quiet
3:31	היה	qal	pft	3ms	היה	224		be,become
	יך	hiph	wci	3ms	נכה	645		smite
	ישע	hiph	wci	3ms	ישע	446		deliver,save
4:1	יספו	hiph	wci	3mp	יסף	414		add,do again
	עשות	qal	infc		עשה	793		do,make
	מת	qal	pft	3ms	מות	559		die
4:2	ימכרם	qal	wci	3ms	מכר	569	3mp	sell
	מלך	qal	pft	3ms	מלך	573		be king,reign
	יושב	qal	ptc	ms	ישב	442		sit,dwell
4:3	יצעקו	qal	wci	3mp	צעק	858		cry out
	לחץ	qal	pft	3ms	לחץ	537		press,oppress
4:4	שפטה	qal	ptc	fs	שפט	1047		judge
4:5	יושבת	qal	ptc	fs	ישב	442		sit,dwell
	יעלו	qal	wci	3mp	עלה	748		go up
4:6	תשלח	qal	wci	3fs	שלח	1018		send
	תקרא	qal	wci	3fs	קרא	894		call,proclaim
	תאמר	qal	wci	3fs	אמר	55		say
	צוה	piel	pft	3ms	צוה	845		command
	לך	qal	impv	ms	הלך	229		walk,go
	משכת	qal	wcp	2ms	משך	604		draw,pull
	לקחת	qal	wcp	2ms	לקח	542		take
4:7	משכתי	qal	wcp	1cs	משך	604		draw,pull
	נתתיהו	qal	wcp	1cs	נתן	678	3ms	give,set
4:8	יאמר	qal	wci	3ms	אמר	55		say
	תלכי	qal	impf	2fs	הלך	229		walk,go
	הלכתי	qal	wcp	1cs	הלך	229		walk,go
	תלכי	qal	impf	2fs	הלך	229		walk,go

ChVs	Form	Stem	Tnse	PGN	Root	BDB	Sfx	Meaning
4:8	אלך	qal	impf	1cs	הלך	229		walk,go
4:9	תאמר	qal	wci	3fs	אמר	55		say
	הלך	qal	infa		הלך	229		walk,go
	אלך	qal	impf	1cs	הלך	229		walk,go
	תהיה	qal	impf	3fs	היה	224		be,become
	הולך	qal	ptc	ms	הלך	229		walk,go
	ימכר	qal	impf	3ms	מכר	569		sell
	תקם	qal	wci	3fs	קום	877		arise,stand
	תלך	qal	wci	3fs	הלך	229		walk,go
4:10	יזעק	hiph	wci	3ms	זעק	277		call together
	יעל	qal	wci	3ms	עלה	748		go up
	תעל	qal	wci	3fs	עלה	748		go up
4:11	נפרד	niph	ptc	ms	פרד	825		divide
	יט	qal	wci	3ms	נטה	639		stretch,incline
4:12	יגדו	hiph	wci	3mp	נגד	616		declare,tell
	עלה	qal	pft	3ms	עלה	748		go up
4:13	יזעק	hiph	wci	3ms	זעק	277		call together
4:14	תאמר	qal	wci	3fs	אמר	55		say
	קום	qal	impv	ms	קום	877		arise,stand
	נתן	qal	pft	3ms	נתן	678		give,set
	יצא	qal	pft	3ms	יצא	422		go out
	ירד	qal	wci	3ms	ירד	432		come down
4:15	יהם	qal	wci	3ms	המם	243		confuse,vex
	ירד	qal	wci	3ms	ירד	432		come down
	ינס	qal	wci	3ms	נוס	630		flee,escape
4:16	רדף	qal	pft	3ms	רדף	922		pursue
	יפל	qal	wci	3ms	נפל	656		fall
	נשאר	niph	pft	3ms	שאר	983		be left
4:17	נס	qal	pft	3ms	נוס	630		flee,escape
4:18	תצא	qal	wci	3fs	יצא	422		go out
	קראת	qal	infc		קרא	896		meet,encounter
	תאמר	qal	wci	3fs	אמר	55		say
	סורה	qal	impv	ms	סור	693		turn aside
	סורה	qal	impv	ms	סור	693		turn aside
	תירא	qal	jusm	2ms	ירא	431		fear
	יסר	qal	wci	3ms	סור	693		turn aside
	תכסהו	piel	wci	3fs	כסה	491	3ms	cover
4:19	יאמר	qal	wci	3ms	אמר	55		say
	השקיני	hiph	impv	fs	שקה	1052	1cs	give to drink
	צמאתי	qal	pft	1cs	צמא	854		be thirsty
	תפתח	qal	wci	3fs	פתח	834		open
	תשקהו	hiph	wci	3fs	שקה	1052	3ms	give to drink
	תכסהו	piel	wci	3fs	כסה	491	3ms	cover
4:20	יאמר	qal	wci	3ms	אמר	55		say
	עמד	qal	impv	ms	עמד	763		stand,stop
	היה	qal	wcp	3ms	היה	224		be,become
	יבוא	qal	impf	3ms	בוא	97		come in
	שאלך	qal	wcp	3ms	שאל	981	2fs	ask,borrow
	אמר	qal	wcp	3ms	אמר	55		say
	אמרת	qal	wcp	2fs	אמר	55		say
4:21	תקח	qal	wci	3fs	לקח	542		take
	תשם	qal	wci	3fs	שים	962		put,set
	תבוא	qal	wci	3fs	בוא	97		come in
	תתקע	qal	wci	3fs	תקע	1075		thrust,clap
4:21	תצנח	qal	wci	3fs	צנח	856		descend
	נרדם	niph	ptc	ms	רדם	922		be fast asleep
	יעף	qal	wci	3ms	עיף	746		be faint
	ימת	qal	wci	3ms	מות	559		die
4:22	רדף	qal	ptc	ms	רדף	922		pursue
	תצא	qal	wci	3fs	יצא	422		go out
	קראתו	qal	infc		קרא	896	3ms	meet,encounter
	תאמר	qal	wci	3fs	אמר	55		say
	לך	qal	impv	ms	הלך	229		walk,go
	אראך	hiph	cohm	1cs	ראה	906	2ms	show,exhibit
	מבקש	piel	ptc	ms	בקש	134		seek
	יבא	qal	wci	3ms	בוא	97		come in
	נפל	qal	ptc	ms	נפל	656		fall
	מת	qal	ptc	ms	מות	559		die
4:23	יכנע	hiph	wci	3ms	כנע	488		humble,subdue
4:24	תלך	qal	wci	3fs	הלך	229		walk,go
	הלוך	qal	infa		הלך	229		walk,go
	הכריתו	hiph	pft	3cp	כרת	503		cut off,destroy
5:1	תשר	qal	wci	3fs	שיר	1010		sing
	אמר	qal	infc		אמר	55		say
5:2	פרע	qal	infc		פרע	828		act as leader
	התנדב	hith	infc		נדב	621		offer freely
	ברכו	piel	impv	mp	ברך	138		bless
5:3	שמעו	qal	impv	mp	שמע	1033		hear
	האזינו	hiph	impv	mp	אזן	24		hear
	אשירה	qal	coh	1cs	שיר	1010		sing
	אזמר	piel	impf	1cs	זמר	274		make music
5:4	צאתך	qal	infc		יצא	422	2ms	go out
	צעדך	qal	infc		צעד	857	2ms	step,march
	רעשה	qal	pft	3fs	רעש	950		quake
	נטפו	qal	pft	3cp	נטף	642		drop,drip
	נטפו	qal	pft	3cp	נטף	642		drop,drip
5:5	נזלו	qal	pft	3cp	נזל	633		flow
5:6	חדלו	qal	pft	3cp	חדל	292		cease
	הלכי	qal	ptc	mp	הלך	229		walk,go
	ילכו	qal	impf	3mp	הלך	229		walk,go
5:7	חדלו	qal	pft	3cp	חדל	292		cease
	חדלו	qal	pft	3cp	חדל	292		cease
	קמתי	qal	pft	1cs	קום	877		arise,stand
	קמתי	qal	pft	1cs	קום	877		arise,stand
5:8	יבחר	qal	impf	3ms	בחר	103		choose
	יראה	niph	impf	3ms	ראה	906		appear,be seen
5:9	חוקקי	qal	ptc	mp	חקק	349		cut in,inscribe
	מתנדבים	hith	ptc	mp	נדב	621		offer freely
	ברכו	piel	impv	mp	ברך	138		bless
5:10	רכבי	qal	ptc	mp	רכב	938		mount,ride
	ישבי	qal	ptc	mp	ישב	442		sit,dwell
	הלכי	qal	ptc	mp	הלך	229		walk,go
	שיחו	qal	impv	mp	שיח	967		muse,complain
5:11	מחצצים	piel	ptc	mp	חצץ	346		archers
	יתנו	piel	impf	3mp	תנה	1072		recount
	ירדו	qal	pft	3cp	ירד	432		come down
5:12	עורי	qal	impv	fs	עור	734		rouse self
	עורי	qal	impv	fs	עור	734		rouse self

ChVs	Form	Stem	Tnse	PGN	Root	BDB	Sfx	Meaning
5:12	עורי	qal	impv	fs	עור	734		rouse self
	עורי	qal	impv	fs	עור	734		rouse self
	דברי	piel	impv	fs	דבר	180		speak
	קום	qal	impv	ms	קום	877		arise,stand
	שבה	qal	impv	ms	שבה	985		take captive
5:13	ירד	qal	pft	3ms	ירד	432?		come down
	ירד	qal	pft	3ms	ירד	432?		come down
5:14	ירדו	qal	pft	3cp	ירד	432		come down
	מחקקים	poel	ptc	mp	חקק	349		prescribe(r)
	משכים	qal	ptc	mp	משך	604		draw,pull
5:15	שלח	pual	pft	3ms	שלח	1018		be sent off
5:16	ישבת	qal	pft	2ms	ישב	442		sit,dwell
	שמע	qal	infc		שמע	1033		hear
5:17	שכן	qal	pft	3ms	שכן	1014		settle,dwell
	יגור	qal	impf	3ms	גור	157		sojourn
	ישב	qal	pft	3ms	ישב	442		sit,dwell
	ישכון	qal	impf	3ms	שכן	1014		settle,dwell
5:18	חרף	piel	pft	3ms	חרף	357		reproach
	מות	qal	infc		מות	559		die
5:19	באו	qal	pft	3cp	בוא	97		come in
	נלחמו	niph	pft	3cp	לחם	535		wage war
	נלחמו	niph	pft	3cp	לחם	535		wage war
	לקחו	qal	pft	3cp	לקח	542		take
5:20	נלחמו	niph	pft	3cp	לחם	535		wage war
	נלחמו	niph	pft	3cp	לחם	535		wage war
5:21	גרפם	qal	pft	3ms	גרף	175	3mp	sweep away
	תדרכי	qal	impf	2fs	דרך	201		tread,march
5:22	הלמו	qal	pft	3cp	הלם	240		smite
5:23	אורו	qal	impv	mp	ארר	76		curse
	אמר	qal	pft	3ms	אמר	55		say
	ארו	qal	impv	mp	ארר	76		curse
	ארור	qal	infa		ארר	76		curse
	ישביה	qal	ptc	mp	ישב	442	3fs	sit,dwell
	באו	qal	pft	3cp	בוא	97		come in
5:24	תברך	pual	impf	3fs	ברך	138		be blessed
	תברך	pual	impf	3fs	ברך	138		be blessed
5:25	שאל	qal	pft	3ms	שאל	981		ask, borrow
	נתנה	qal	pft	3fs	נתן	678		give,set
	הקריבה	hiph	pft	3fs	קרב	897		bring near
5:26	תשלחנה	qal	impf	3fp	שלח	1018		send
	הלמה	qal	pft	3fs	הלם	240		smite
	מחקה	qal	pft	3fs	מחק	563		annihilate
	מחצה	qal	pft	3fs	מחץ	563		smite through
	חלפה	qal	pft	3fs	חלף	322		pass on
5:27	כרע	qal	pft	3ms	כרע	502		bow down
	נפל	qal	pft	3ms	נפל	656		fall
	שכב	qal	pft	3ms	שכב	1011		lie,lie down
	כרע	qal	pft	3ms	כרע	502		bow down
	נפל	qal	pft	3ms	נפל	656		fall
	כרע	qal	pft	3ms	כרע	502		bow down
	נפל	qal	pft	3ms	נפל	656		fall
	שדוד	qal	pptc	ms	שדד	994		destroy,oppress
5:28	נשקפה	niph	pft	3fs	שקף	1054		look down
	תיבב	piel	wci	3fs	יבב	384		cry shrilly
5:28	בשש	pol	pft	3ms	בוש	101		delay
	בוא	qal	infc		בוא	97		come in
	אחרו	piel	pft	3cp	אחר	29		tarry,hinder
5:29	תענינה	qal	impf	3fp	ענה	772	3fs	answer
	תשיב	hiph	impf	3fs	שוב	996		bring back
5:30	ימצאו	qal	impf	3mp	מצא	592		find
	יחלקו	piel	impf	3mp	חלק	323		divide
5:31	יאבדו	qal	jusm	3mp	אבד	1		perish
	אויביך	qal	ptc	mp	איב	33	2ms	be hostile to
	אהביו	qal	ptc	mp	אהב	12	3ms	love
	צאת	qal	infc		יצא	422		go out
	תשקט	qal	wci	3fs	שקט	1052		be quiet
6:1	יעשו	qal	wci	3mp	עשה	793		do,make
	יתנם	qal	wci	3ms	נתן	678	3mp	give,set
6:2	תעז	qal	wci	3fs	עזז	738		be strong
	עשו	qal	pft	3cp	עשה	793		do,make
6:3	היה	qal	wcp	3ms	היה	224		be,become
	זרע	qal	pft	3ms	זרע	281		sow
	עלה	qal	wcp	3ms	עלה	748		go up
	עלו	qal	wcp	3cp	עלה	748		go up
6:4	יחנו	qal	wci	3mp	חנה	333		decline,encamp
	ישחיתו	hiph	wci	3mp	שחת	1007		spoil,ruin
	בואך	qal	infc		בוא	97	2ms	come in
	ישאירו	hiph	impf	3mp	שאר	983		leave,spare
6:5	יעלו	qal	impf	3mp	עלה	748		go up
	יבאוk	qal	impf	3mp	בוא	97		come in
	באוq	qal	wcp	3cp	בוא	97		come in
	יבאו	qal	wci	3mp	בוא	97		come in
	שחתה	piel	infc		שחת	1007	3fs	spoil,ruin
6:6	ידל	niph	wci	3ms	דלל	195		be brought low
	יזעקו	qal	wci	3mp	זעק	277		call,cry out
6:7	יהי	qal	wci	3ms	היה	224		be,become
	זעקו	qal	pft	3cp	זעק	277		call,cry out
6:8	ישלח	qal	wci	3ms	שלח	1018		send
	יאמר	qal	wci	3ms	אמר	55		say
	אמר	qal	pft	3ms	אמר	55		say
	העליתי	hiph	pft	1cs	עלה	748		bring up,offer
	אציא	hiph	wci	1cs	יצא	422		bring out
6:9	אצל	hiph	wci	1cs	נצל	664		snatch,deliver
	לחציכם	qal	ptc	mp	לחץ	537	2mp	press,oppress
	אגרש	piel	wci	1cs	גרש	176		drive out
	אתנה	qal	wci	1cs	נתן	678		give,set
6:10	אמרה	qal	wci	1cs	אמר	55		say
	תיראו	qal	impf	2mp	ירא	431		fear
	יושבים	qal	ptc	mp	ישב	442		sit,dwell
	שמעתם	qal	pft	2mp	שמע	1033		hear
6:11	יבא	qal	wci	3ms	בוא	97		come in
	ישב	qal	wci	3ms	ישב	442		sit,dwell
	חבט	qal	ptc	ms	חבט	286		beat out
	הניס	hiph	infc		נוס	630		put to flight
6:12	ירא	niph	wci	3ms	ראה	906		appear, be seen
	יאמר	qal	wci	3ms	אמר	55		say
6:13	יאמר	qal	wci	3ms	אמר	55		say
	מצאתנו	qal	pft	3fs	מצא	592	1cp	find

ChVs	Form	Stem	Tnse	PGN	Root	BDB	Sfx	Meaning
6:13	נפלאתיו	niph	ptc	fp	פלא	810	3ms	be wonderful
	ספרו	piel	pft	3cp	ספר	707		recount
	אמר	qal	infc		אמר	55		say
	העלנו	hiph	pft	3ms	עלה	748	1cp	bring up,offer
	נטשנו	qal	pft	3ms	נטש	643	1cp	leave,forsake
	יתננו	qal	wci	3ms	נתן	678	1cp	give,set
6:14	יפן	qal	wci	3ms	פנה	815		turn
	יאמר	qal	wci	3ms	אמר	55		say
	לך	qal	impv	ms	הלך	229		walk,go
	הושעת	hiph	wcp	2ms	ישע	446		deliver,save
	שלחתיך	qal	pft	1cs	שלח	1018	2ms	send
6:15	יאמר	qal	wci	3ms	אמר	55		say
	אושיע	hiph	impf	1cs	ישע	446		deliver,save
6:16	יאמר	qal	wci	3ms	אמר	55		say
	אהיה	qal	impf	1cs	היה	224		be,become
	הכית	hiph	wcp	2ms	נכה	645		smite
6:17	יאמר	qal	wci	3ms	אמר	55		say
	מצאתי	qal	pft	1cs	מצא	592		find
	עשית	qal	wcp	2ms	עשה	793		do,make
	מדבר	piel	ptc	ms	דבר	180		speak
6:18	תמש	qal	jusm	2ms	מוש	559		depart,remove
	באי	qal	infc		בוא	97	1cs	come in
	הצאתי	hiph	wcp	1cs	יצא	422		bring out
	הנחתי	hiph	wcp	1cs	נוח	628		give rest,put
	יאמר	qal	wci	3ms	אמר	55		say
	אשב	qal	impf	1cs	ישב	442		sit,dwell
	שובך	qal	infc		שוב	996	2ms	turn,return
6:19	בא	qal	pft	3ms	בוא	97		come in
	יעש	qal	wci	3ms	עשה	793		do,make
	שם	qal	pft	3ms	שים	962		put,set
	שם	qal	pft	3ms	שים	962		put,set
	יוצא	hiph	wci	3ms	יצא	422		bring out
	יגש	hiph	wci	3ms	נגש	620		bring near
6:20	יאמר	qal	wci	3ms	אמר	55		say
	קח	qal	impv	ms	לקח	542		take
	הנח	hiph	impv	ms	נוח	628		give rest,put
	שפוך	qal	impv	ms	שפך	1049		pour out
	יעש	qal	wci	3ms	עשה	793		do,make
6:21	ישלח	qal	wci	3ms	שלח	1018		send
	יגע	qal	wci	3ms	נגע	619		touch,strike
	תעל	qal	wci	3fs	עלה	748		go up
	תאכל	qal	wci	3fs	אכל	37		eat,devour
	הלך	qal	pft	3ms	הלך	229		walk,go
6:22	ירא	qal	wci	3ms	ראה	906		see
	יאמר	qal	wci	3ms	אמר	55		say
	ראיתי	qal	pft	1cs	ראה	906		see
6:23	יאמר	qal	wci	3ms	אמר	55		say
	תירא	qal	jusm	2ms	ירא	431		fear
	תמות	qal	impf	2ms	מות	559		die
6:24	יבן	qal	wci	3ms	בנה	124		build
	יקרא	qal	wci	3ms	קרא	894		call,proclaim
6:25	יהי	qal	wci	3ms	היה	224		be,become
	יאמר	qal	wci	3ms	אמר	55		say
	קח	qal	impv	ms	לקח	542		take
6:25	הרסת	qal	wcp	2ms	הרס	248		throw down
	תכרת	qal	impf	2ms	כרת	503		cut,destroy
6:26	בנית	qal	wcp	2ms	בנה	124		build
	לקחת	qal	wcp	2ms	לקח	542		take
	העלית	hiph	wcp	2ms	עלה	748		bring up,offer
	תכרת	qal	impf	2ms	כרת	503		cut,destroy
6:27	יקח	qal	wci	3ms	לקח	542		take
	יעש	qal	wci	3ms	עשה	793		do,make
	דבר	piel	pft	3ms	דבר	180		speak
	יהי	qal	wci	3ms	היה	224		be,become
	ירא	qal	pft	3ms	ירא	431		fear
	עשות	qal	infc		עשה	793		do,make
	יעש	qal	wci	3ms	עשה	793		do,make
6:28	ישכימו	hiph	wci	3mp	שכם	1014		rise early
	נתץ	pual	pft	3ms	נתץ	683		be torn down
	כרתה	qalp	pft	3fs	כרת	503		be cut off
	העלה	hoph	pft	3ms	עלה	748		be taken up
	בנוי	qal	pptc	ms	בנה	124		build
6:29	יאמרו	qal	wci	3mp	אמר	55		say
	עשה	qal	pft	3ms	עשה	793		do,make
	ידרשו	qal	wci	3mp	דרש	205		resort to,seek
	יבקשו	piel	wci	3mp	בקש	134		seek
	יאמרו	qal	wci	3mp	אמר	55		say
	עשה	qal	pft	3ms	עשה	793		do,make
6:30	יאמרו	qal	wci	3mp	אמר	55		say
	הוצא	hiph	impv	ms	יצא	422		bring out
	ימת	qal	jus	3ms	מות	559		die
	נתץ	qal	pft	3ms	נתץ	683		pull down
	כרת	qal	pft	3ms	כרת	503		cut,destroy
6:31	יאמר	qal	wci	3ms	אמר	55		say
	עמדו	qal	pft	3cp	עמד	763		stand,stop
	תריבון	qal	impf	2mp	ריב	936		strive,contend
	תושיעון	hiph	impf	2mp	ישע	446		deliver,save
	יריב	qal	impf	3ms	ריב	936		strive,contend
	יומת	hoph	impf	3ms	מות	559		be killed
	ירב	qal	jus	3ms	ריב	936		strive,contend
	נתץ	qal	pft	3ms	נתץ	683		pull down
6:32	יקרא	qal	wci	3ms	קרא	894		call,proclaim
	אמר	qal	infc		אמר	55		say
	ירב	qal	jus	3ms	ריב	936		strive,contend
	נתץ	qal	pft	3ms	נתץ	683		pull down
6:33	נאספו	niph	pft	3cp	אסף	62		assemble
	יעברו	qal	wci	3mp	עבר	716		pass over
	יחנו	qal	wci	3mp	חנה	333		decline,encamp
6:34	לבשה	qal	pft	3fs	לבש	527		put on,clothe
	יתקע	qal	wci	3ms	תקע	1075		thrust,clap
	יזעק	niph	wci	3ms	זעק	277		assemble
6:35	שלח	qal	pft	3ms	שלח	1018		send
	יזעק	niph	wci	3ms	זעק	277		assemble
	שלח	qal	pft	3ms	שלח	1018		send
	יעלו	qal	wci	3mp	עלה	748		go up
	קראתם	qal	infc		קרא	896	3mp	meet,encounter
6:36	יאמר	qal	wci	3ms	אמר	55		say
	מושיע	hiph	ptc	ms	ישע	446		deliver,save

ChVs	Form	Stem	Tnse	PGN	Root	BDB	Sfx	Meaning
6:36	דברת	piel	pft	2ms	דבר	180		speak
6:37	מציג	hiph	ptc	ms	יצג	426		place,establish
	יהיה	qal	impf	3ms	היה	224		be,become
	ידעתי	qal	wcp	1cs	ידע	393		know
	תושיע	hiph	impf	2ms	ישע	446		deliver,save
	דברת	piel	pft	2ms	דבר	180		speak
6:38	יהי	qal	wci	3ms	היה	224		be,become
	ישכם	hiph	wci	3ms	שכם	1014		rise early
	יזר	qal	wci	3ms	זור	266		press down
	ימץ	qal	wci	3ms	מצה	594		drain out
6:39	יאמר	qal	wci	3ms	אמר	55		say
	יחר	qal	jus	3ms	חרה	354		be kindled,burn
	אדברה	piel	coh	1cs	דבר	180		speak
	אנסה	piel	cohm	1cs	נסה	650		test,try
	יהי	qal	jus	3ms	היה	224		be,become
	יהיה	qal	jusm	3ms	היה	224		be,become
6:40	יעש	qal	wci	3ms	עשה	793		do,make
	יהי	qal	wci	3ms	היה	224		be,become
	היה	qal	pft	3ms	היה	224		be,become
7:1	ישכם	hiph	wci	3ms	שכם	1014		rise early
	יחנו	qal	wci	3mp	חנה	333		decline,encamp
	היה	qal	pft	3ms	היה	224		be,become
7:2	יאמר	qal	wci	3ms	אמר	55		say
	תתי	qal	infc		נתן	678	1cs	give,set
	יתפאר	hith	impf	3ms	פאר	802		glorify self
	אמר	qal	infc		אמר	55		say
	הושיעה	hiph	pft	3fs	ישע	446		deliver,save
7:3	קרא	qal	impv	ms	קרא	894		call,proclaim
	אמר	qal	infc		אמר	55		say
	ירא	qal	ptc	ms	ירא	431		fear
	ישב	qal	jus	3ms	שוב	996		turn,return
	יצפר	qal	jusm	3ms	צפר	861		turn away
	ישב	qal	wci	3ms	שוב	996		turn,return
	נשארו	niph	pft	3cp	שאר	983		be left
7:4	יאמר	qal	wci	3ms	אמר	55		say
	הורד	hiph	impv	ms	ירד	432		bring down
	אצרפנו	qal	cohm	1cs	צרף	864	3ms	refine,test
	היה	qal	wcp	3ms	היה	224		be,become
	אמר	qal	impf	1cs	אמר	55		say
	ילך	qal	impf	3ms	הלך	229		walk,go
	ילך	qal	impf	3ms	הלך	229		walk,go
	אמר	qal	impf	1cs	אמר	55		say
	ילך	qal	impf	3ms	הלך	229		walk,go
	ילך	qal	impf	3ms	הלך	229		walk,go
7:5	יורד	hiph	wci	3ms	ירד	432		bring down
	יאמר	qal	wci	3ms	אמר	55		say
	ילק	qal	impf	3ms	לקק	545		lap,lick
	ילק	qal	impf	3ms	לקק	545		lap,lick
	תציג	hiph	impf	2ms	יצג	426		place,establish
	יכרע	qal	impf	3ms	כרע	502		bow down
	שתות	qal	infc		שתה	1059		drink
7:6	יהי	qal	wci	3ms	היה	224		be,become
	מלקקים	piel	ptc	mp	לקק	545		lap up
	כרעו	qal	pft	3cp	כרע	502		bow down
7:6	שתות	qal	infc		שתה	1059		drink
7:7	יאמר	qal	wci	3ms	אמר	55		say
	מלקקים	piel	ptc	mp	לקק	545		lap up
	אושיע	hiph	impf	1cs	ישע	446		deliver,save
	נתתי	qal	wcp	1cs	נתן	678		give,set
	ילכו	qal	jusm	3mp	הלך	229		walk,go
7:8	יקחו	qal	wci	3mp	לקח	542		take
	שלח	piel	pft	3ms	שלח	1018		send away,shoot
	החזיק	hiph	pft	3ms	חזק	304		make firm,seize
	היה	qal	pft	3ms	היה	224		be,become
7:9	יהי	qal	wci	3ms	היה	224		be,become
	יאמר	qal	wci	3ms	אמר	55		say
	קום	qal	impv	ms	קום	877		arise,stand
	רד	qal	impv	ms	ירד	432		come down
	נתתיו	qal	pft	1cs	נתן	678	3ms	give,set
7:10	ירא	qal	ptc	ms	ירא	431		fear
	רדת	qal	infc		ירד	432		come down
	רד	qal	impv	ms	ירד	432		come down
7:11	שמעת	qal	wcp	2ms	שמע	1033		hear
	ידברו	piel	impf	3mp	דבר	180		speak
	תחזקנה	qal	impf	3fp	חזק	304		be strong
	ירדת	qal	wcp	2ms	ירד	432		come down
	ירד	qal	wci	3ms	ירד	432		come down
7:12	נפלים	qal	ptc	mp	נפל	656		fall
7:13	יבא	qal	wci	3ms	בוא	97		come in
	מספר	piel	ptc	ms	ספר	707		recount
	יאמר	qal	wci	3ms	אמר	55		say
	חלמתי	qal	pft	1cs	חלם	321		dream
	מתהפך	hith	ptc	ms	הפך	245		turn every way
	יבא	qal	wci	3ms	בוא	97		come in
	יכהו	hiph	wci	3ms	נכה	645	3ms	smite
	יפל	qal	wci	3ms	נפל	656		fall
	יהפכהו	qal	wci	3ms	הפך	245	3ms	turn,overturn
	נפל	qal	pft	3ms	נפל	656		fall
7:14	יען	qal	wci	3ms	ענה	772		answer
	יאמר	qal	wci	3ms	אמר	55		say
	נתן	qal	pft	3ms	נתן	678		give,set
7:15	יהי	qal	wci	3ms	היה	224		be,become
	שמע	qal	infc		שמע	1033		hear
	ישתחו	hish	wci	3ms	חוה	1005		bow down
	ישב	qal	wci	3ms	שוב	996		turn,return
	יאמר	qal	wci	3ms	אמר	55		say
	קומו	qal	impv	mp	קום	877		arise,stand
	נתן	qal	pft	3ms	נתן	678		give,set
7:16	יחץ	qal	wci	3ms	חצה	345		divide
	יתן	qal	wci	3ms	נתן	678		give,set
7:17	יאמר	qal	wci	3ms	אמר	55		say
	תראו	qal	impf	2mp	ראה	906		see
	תעשו	qal	impf	2mp	עשה	793		do,make
	בא	qal	ptc	ms	בוא	97		come in
	היה	qal	wcp	3ms	היה	224		be,become
	אעשה	qal	impf	1cs	עשה	793		do,make
	תעשון	qal	impf	2mp	עשה	793		do,make
7:18	תקעתי	qal	wcp	1cs	תקע	1075		thrust,clap

ChVs	Form	Stem	Tnse	PGN	Root	BDB	Sfx	Meaning
7: 18	תקעתם	qal	wcp	2mp	תקע	1075		thrust,clap
	אמרתם	qal	wcp	2mp	אמר	55		say
7: 19	יבא	qal	wci	3ms	בוא	97		come in
	הקם	hiph	infa		קום	877		raise,build,set
	הקימו	hiph	pft	3cp	קום	877		raise,build,set
	שׁמרים	qal	ptc	mp	שׁמר	1036		keep,watch
	יתקעו	qal	wci	3mp	תקע	1075		thrust,clap
	נפוץ	qal	infa		נפץ	658		shatter
7: 20	יתקעו	qal	wci	3mp	תקע	1075		thrust,clap
	ישׁברו	qal	wci	3mp	שׁבר	990		break
	יחזיקו	hiph	wci	3mp	חזק	304		make firm,seize
	תקוע	qal	infc		תקע	1075		thrust,clap
	יקראו	qal	wci	3mp	קרא	894		call,proclaim
7: 21	יעמדו	qal	wci	3mp	עמד	763		stand,stop
	ירץ	qal	wci	3ms	רוץ	930		run
	יריעו	hiph	wci	3mp	רוע	929		raise a shout
	יניסוk	hiph	wci	3mp	נוס	630		put to flight
	ינוסוq	qal	wci	3mp	נוס	630		flee,escape
7: 22	יתקעו	qal	wci	3mp	תקע	1075		thrust,clap
	ישׂם	qal	wci	3ms	שׂים	962		put,set
	ינס	qal	wci	3ms	נוס	630		flee,escape
7: 23	יצעק	niph	wci	3ms	צעק	858		be summoned
	ירדפו	qal	wci	3mp	רדף	922		pursue
7: 24	שׁלח	qal	pft	3ms	שׁלח	1018		send
	אמר	qal	infc		אמר	55		say
	רדו	qal	impv	mp	ירד	432		come down
	קראת	qal	infc		קרא	896		meet,encounter
	לכדו	qal	impv	mp	לכד	539		capture
	יצעק	niph	wci	3ms	צעק	858		be summoned
	ילכדו	qal	wci	3mp	לכד	539		capture
7: 25	ילכדו	qal	wci	3mp	לכד	539		capture
	יהרגו	qal	wci	3mp	הרג	246		kill
	הרגו	qal	pft	3cp	הרג	246		kill
	ירדפו	qal	wci	3mp	רדף	922		pursue
	הביאו	hiph	pft	3cp	בוא	97		bring in
8: 1	יאמרו	qal	wci	3mp	אמר	55		say
	עשׂית	qal	pft	2ms	עשׂה	793		do,make
	קראות	qal	infc		קרא	894		call,proclaim
	הלכת	qal	pft	2ms	הלך	229		walk,go
	הלחם	niph	infc		לחם	535		wage war
	יריבון	qal	wci	3mp	ריב	936		strive,contend
8: 2	יאמר	qal	wci	3ms	אמר	55		say
	עשׂיתי	qal	pft	1cs	עשׂה	793		do,make
8: 3	נתן	qal	pft	3ms	נתן	678		give,set
	יכלתי	qal	pft	1cs	יכל	407		be able
	עשׂות	qal	infc		עשׂה	793		do,make
	רפתה	qal	pft	3fs	רפה	951		sink,relax
	דברו	piel	infc		דבר	180	3ms	speak
8: 4	יבא	qal	wci	3ms	בוא	97		come in
	עבר	qal	ptc	ms	עבר	716		pass over
	רדפים	qal	ptc	mp	רדף	922		pursue
8: 5	יאמר	qal	wci	3ms	אמר	55		say
	תנו	qal	impv	mp	נתן	678		give,set
	רדף	qal	ptc	ms	רדף	922		pursue
8: 6	יאמר	qal	wci	3ms	אמר	55		say
	נתן	qal	impf	1cp	נתן	678		give,set
8: 7	יאמר	qal	wci	3ms	אמר	55		say
	תת	qal	infc		נתן	678		give,set
	דשׁתי	qal	wcp	1cs	דושׁ	190		tread
8: 8	יעל	qal	wci	3ms	עלה	748		go up
	ידבר	piel	wci	3ms	דבר	180		speak
	יענו	qal	wci	3mp	ענה	772		answer
	ענו	qal	pft	3cp	ענה	772		answer
8: 9	יאמר	qal	wci	3ms	אמר	55		say
	אמר	qal	infc		אמר	55		say
	שׁובי	qal	infc		שׁוב	996	1cs	turn,return
	אתץ	qal	impf	1cs	נתץ	683		pull down
8: 10	נותרים	niph	ptc	mp	יתר	451		be left,remain
	נפלים	qal	ptc	mp	נפל	656		fall
	שׁלף	qal	ptc	ms	שׁלף	1025		draw out,off
8: 11	יעל	qal	wci	3ms	עלה	748		go up
	שׁכוני	qal	pptc	mp	שׁכן	1014		settle,dwell
	יך	hiph	wci	3ms	נכה	645		smite
	היה	qal	pft	3ms	היה	224		be,become
8: 12	ינוסו	qal	wci	3mp	נוס	630		flee,escape
	ירדף	qal	wci	3ms	רדף	922		pursue
	ילכד	qal	wci	3ms	לכד	539		capture
	החריד	hiph	pft	3ms	חרד	353		terrify
8: 13	ישׁב	qal	wci	3ms	שׁוב	996		turn,return
8: 14	ילכד	qal	wci	3ms	לכד	539		capture
	ישׁאלהו	qal	wci	3ms	שׁאל	981	3ms	ask,borrow
	יכתב	qal	wci	3ms	כתב	507		write
8: 15	יבא	qal	wci	3ms	בוא	97		come in
	יאמר	qal	wci	3ms	אמר	55		say
	חרפתם	piel	pft	2mp	חרף	357		reproach
	אמר	qal	infc		אמר	55		say
	נתן	qal	impf	1cp	נתן	678		give,set
8: 16	יקח	qal	wci	3ms	לקח	542		take
	ידע	hiph	wci	3ms	ידע	393		declare
8: 17	נתץ	qal	pft	3ms	נתץ	683		pull down
	יהרג	qal	wci	3ms	הרג	246		kill
8: 18	יאמר	qal	wci	3ms	אמר	55		say
	הרגתם	qal	pft	2mp	הרג	246		kill
	יאמרו	qal	wci	3mp	אמר	55		say
8: 19	יאמר	qal	wci	3ms	אמר	55		say
	החיתם	hiph	pft	2mp	חיה	310		preserve
	הרגתי	qal	pft	1cs	הרג	246		kill
8: 20	יאמר	qal	wci	3ms	אמר	55		say
	קום	qal	impv	ms	קום	877		arise,stand
	הרג	qal	impv	ms	הרג	246		kill
	שׁלף	qal	pft	3ms	שׁלף	1025		draw out,off
	ירא	qal	pft	3ms	ירא	431		fear
8: 21	יאמר	qal	wci	3ms	אמר	55		say
	קום	qal	impv	ms	קום	877		arise,stand
	פגע	qal	impv	ms	פגע	803		meet,encounter
	יקם	qal	wci	3ms	קום	877		arise,stand
	יהרג	qal	wci	3ms	הרג	246		kill
	יקח	qal	wci	3ms	לקח	542		take

ChVs	Form	Stem	Tnse	PGN	Root	BDB	Sfx	Meaning
8:22	יאמרו	qal	wci	3mp	אמר	55		say
	משׁל	qal	impv	ms	משׁל	605		rule
	הושׁעתנו	hiph	pft	2ms	ישׁע	446	1cp	deliver,save
8:23	יאמר	qal	wci	3ms	אמר	55		say
	אמשׁל	qal	impf	1cs	משׁל	605		rule
	ימשׁל	qal	impf	3ms	משׁל	605		rule
	ימשׁל	qal	impf	3ms	משׁל	605		rule
8:24	יאמר	qal	wci	3ms	אמר	55		say
	אשׁאלה	qal	coh	1cs	שׁאל	981		ask,borrow
	תנו	qal	impv	mp	נתן	678		give,set
8:25	יאמרו	qal	wci	3mp	אמר	55		say
	נתון	qal	infa		נתן	678		give,set
	נתן	qal	impf	1cp	נתן	678		give,set
	יפרשׂו	qal	wci	3mp	פרשׂ	831		spread out
	ישׁליכו	hiph	wci	3mp	שׁלך	1020		throw,cast
8:26	יהי	qal	wci	3ms	היה	224		be,become
	שׁאל	qal	pft	3ms	שׁאל	981		ask,borrow
8:27	יעשׂ	qal	wci	3ms	עשׂה	793		do,make
	יצג	hiph	wci	3ms	יצג	426		place,establish
	יזנו	qal	wci	3mp	זנה	275		act a harlot
	יהי	qal	wci	3ms	היה	224		be,become
8:28	יכנע	niph	wci	3ms	כנע	488		humble self
	יספו	qal	pft	3cp	יסף	414		add,increase
	שׂאת	qal	infc		נשׂא	669		lift,carry
	תשׁקט	qal	wci	3fs	שׁקט	1052		be quiet
8:29	ילך	qal	wci	3ms	הלך	229		walk,go
	ישׁב	qal	wci	3ms	ישׁב	442		sit,dwell
8:30	היו	qal	pft	3cp	היה	224		be,become
	יצאי	qal	ptc	mp	יצא	422		go out
	היו	qal	pft	3cp	היה	224		be,become
8:31	ילדה	qal	pft	3fs	ילד	408		bear,beget
	ישׂם	qal	wci	3ms	שׂים	962		put,set
8:32	ימת	qal	wci	3ms	מות	559		die
	יקבר	niph	wci	3ms	קבר	868		be buried
8:33	יהי	qal	wci	3ms	היה	224		be,become
	מת	qal	pft	3ms	מות	559		die
	ישׁובו	qal	wci	3mp	שׁוב	996		turn,return
	יזנו	qal	wci	3mp	זנה	275		act a harlot
	ישׂימו	qal	wci	3mp	שׂים	962		put,set
8:34	זכרו	qal	pft	3cp	זכר	269		remember
	מציל	hiph	ptc	ms	נצל	664		snatch,deliver
	איביהם	qal	ptc	mp	איב	33	3mp	be hostile to
8:35	עשׂו	qal	pft	3cp	עשׂה	793		do,make
	עשׂה	qal	pft	3ms	עשׂה	793		do,make
9:1	ילך	qal	wci	3ms	הלך	229		walk,go
	ידבר	piel	wci	3ms	דבר	180		speak
	אמר	qal	infc		אמר	55		say
9:2	דברו	piel	impv	mp	דבר	180		speak
	משׁל	qal	infc		משׁל	605		rule
	משׁל	qal	infc		משׁל	605		rule
	זכרתם	qal	wcp	2mp	זכר	269		remember
9:3	ידברו	piel	wci	3mp	דבר	180		speak
	יט	qal	wci	3ms	נטה	639		stretch,incline
	אמרו	qal	pft	3cp	אמר	55		say
9:4	יתנו	qal	wci	3mp	נתן	678		give,set
	ישׂכר	qal	wci	3ms	שׂכר	968		hire
	פחזים	qal	ptc	mp	פחז	808		be reckless
	ילכו	qal	wci	3mp	הלך	229		walk,go
9:5	יבא	qal	wci	3ms	בוא	97		come in
	יהרג	qal	wci	3ms	הרג	246		kill
	יותר	niph	wci	3ms	יתר	451		be left,remain
	נחבא	niph	pft	3ms	חבא	285		hide oneself
9:6	יאספו	niph	wci	3mp	אסף	62		assemble
	ילכו	qal	wci	3mp	הלך	229		walk,go
	ימליכו	hiph	wci	3mp	מלך	573		cause to reign
	מצב	hoph	ptc	ms	נצב	662		be fixed
9:7	יגדו	hiph	wci	3mp	נגד	616		declare,tell
	ילך	qal	wci	3ms	הלך	229		walk,go
	יעמד	qal	wci	3ms	עמד	763		stand,stop
	ישׂא	qal	wci	3ms	נשׂא	669		lift,carry
	יקרא	qal	wci	3ms	קרא	894		call,proclaim
	יאמר	qal	wci	3ms	אמר	55		say
	שׁמעו	qal	impv	mp	שׁמע	1033		hear
	ישׁמע	qal	jusm	3ms	שׁמע	1033		hear
9:8	הלוך	qal	infa		הלך	229		walk,go
	הלכו	qal	pft	3cp	הלך	229		walk,go
	משׁח	qal	infc		משׁח	602		smear,anoint
	יאמרו	qal	wci	3mp	אמר	55		say
	מלוכהk	qal	impv	ms	מלך	573		be king,reign
	מלכהq	qal	impv	ms	מלך	573		be king,reign
9:9	יאמר	qal	wci	3ms	אמר	55		say
	חדלתי	qal	pft	1cs	חדל	292		cease
	יכבדו	piel	impf	3mp	כבד	457		honor,make dull
	הלכתי	qal	wcp	1cs	הלך	229		walk,go
	נוע	qal	infc		נוע	631		totter,wave
9:10	יאמרו	qal	wci	3mp	אמר	55		say
	לכי	qal	impv	fs	הלך	229		walk,go
	מלכי	qal	impv	fs	מלך	573		be king,reign
9:11	תאמר	qal	wci	3fs	אמר	55		say
	חדלתי	qal	pft	1cs	חדל	292		cease
	הלכתי	qal	wcp	1cs	הלך	229		walk,go
	נוע	qal	infc		נוע	631		totter,wave
9:12	יאמרו	qal	wci	3mp	אמר	55		say
	לכי	qal	impv	fs	הלך	229		walk,go
	מלוכיk	qal	impv	fs	מלך	573		be king,reign
	מלכיq	qal	impv	fs	מלך	573		be king,reign
9:13	תאמר	qal	wci	3fs	אמר	55		say
	חדלתי	qal	pft	1cs	חדל	292		cease
	משׂמח	piel	ptc	ms	שׂמח	970		gladden
	הלכתי	qal	wcp	1cs	הלך	229		walk,go
	נוע	qal	infc		נוע	631		totter,wave
9:14	יאמרו	qal	wci	3mp	אמר	55		say
	לך	qal	impv	ms	הלך	229		walk,go
	מלך	qal	impv	ms	מלך	573		be king,reign
9:15	יאמר	qal	wci	3ms	אמר	55		say
	משׁחים	qal	ptc	mp	משׁח	602		smear,anoint
	באו	qal	impv	mp	בוא	97		come in
	חסו	qal	impv	mp	חסה	340		seek refuge

ChVs	Form	Stem	Tnse	PGN	Root	BDB	Sfx	Meaning
9:15	תצא	qal	jusm	3fs	יצא	422		go out
	תאכל	qal	jusm	3fs	אכל	37		eat,devour
9:16	עשׂיתם	qal	pft	2mp	עשׂה	793		do,make
	תמליכו	hiph	wci	2mp	מלך	573		cause to reign
	עשׂיתם	qal	pft	2mp	עשׂה	793		do,make
	עשׂיתם	qal	pft	2mp	עשׂה	793		do,make
9:17	נלחם	niph	pft	3ms	לחם	535		wage war
	ישׁלך	hiph	wci	3ms	שׁלך	1020		throw,cast
	יצל	hiph	wci	3ms	נצל	664		snatch,deliver
9:18	קמתם	qal	pft	2mp	קום	877		arise,stand
	תהרגו	qal	wci	2mp	הרג	246		kill
	תמליכו	hiph	wci	2mp	מלך	573		cause to reign
9:19	עשׂיתם	qal	pft	2mp	עשׂה	793		do,make
	שׂמחו	qal	impv	mp	שׂמח	970		rejoice
	ישׂמח	qal	jusm	3ms	שׂמח	970		rejoice
9:20	תצא	qal	jusm	3fs	יצא	422		go out
	תאכל	qal	jusm	3fs	אכל	37		eat,devour
	תצא	qal	jusm	3fs	יצא	422		go out
	תאכל	qal	jusm	3fs	אכל	37		eat,devour
9:21	ינס	qal	wci	3ms	נוס	630		flee,escape
	יברח	qal	wci	3ms	ברח	137		go thru,flee
	ילך	qal	wci	3ms	הלך	229		walk,go
	ישׁב	qal	wci	3ms	ישׁב	442		sit,dwell
9:22	ישׂר	qal	wci	3ms	שׂרר	979		rule
9:23	ישׁלח	qal	wci	3ms	שׁלח	1018		send
	יבגדו	qal	wci	3mp	בגד	93		act faithlessly
9:24	בוא	qal	infc		בוא	97		come in
	שׂום	qal	infc		שׂים	962		put,set
	הרג	qal	pft	3ms	הרג	246		kill
	חזקו	piel	pft	3cp	חזק	304		make strong
	הרג	qal	infc		הרג	246		kill
9:25	ישׂימו	qal	wci	3mp	שׂים	962		put,set
	מארבים	piel	ptc	mp	ארב	70		liers-in-wait
	יגזלו	qal	wci	3mp	גזל	159		tear away,rob
	יעבר	qal	impf	3ms	עבר	716		pass over
	יגד	hoph	wci	3ms	נגד	616		be told
9:26	יבא	qal	wci	3ms	בוא	97		come in
	יעברו	qal	wci	3mp	עבר	716		pass over
	יבטחו	qal	wci	3mp	בטח	105		trust
9:27	יצאו	qal	wci	3mp	יצא	422		go out
	יבצרו	qal	wci	3mp	בצר	130		cut off
	ידרכו	qal	wci	3mp	דרך	201		tread,march
	יעשׂו	qal	wci	3mp	עשׂה	793		do,make
	יבאו	qal	wci	3mp	בוא	97		come in
	יאכלו	qal	wci	3mp	אכל	37		eat,devour
	ישׁתו	qal	wci	3mp	שׁתה	1059		drink
	יקללו	piel	wci	3mp	קלל	886		curse
9:28	יאמר	qal	wci	3ms	אמר	55		say
	נעבדנו	qal	impf	1cp	עבד	712	3ms	work,serve
	עבדו	qal	impv	mp	עבד	712		work,serve
	נעבדנו	qal	impf	1cp	עבד	712	3ms	work,serve
9:29	יתן	qal	impf	3ms	נתן	678		give,set
	אסירה	hiph	coh	1cs	סור	693		take away
	יאמר	qal	wci	3ms	אמר	55		say

ChVs	Form	Stem	Tnse	PGN	Root	BDB	Sfx	Meaning
9:29	רבה	piel	impv	ms	רבה	915		make large
	צאה	qal	impv	ms	יצא	422		go out
9:30	ישׁמע	qal	wci	3ms	שׁמע	1033		hear
	יחר	qal	wci	3ms	חרה	354		be kindled,burn
9:31	ישׁלח	qal	wci	3ms	שׁלח	1018		send
	אמר	qal	infc		אמר	55		say
	באים	qal	ptc	mp	בוא	97		come in
	צרים	qal	ptc	mp	צור	848		confine,shut in
9:32	קום	qal	impv	ms	קום	877		arise,stand
	ארב	qal	impv	ms	ארב	70		lie in wait
9:33	היה	qal	wcp	3ms	היה	224		be,become
	זרח	qal	infc		זרח	280		rise,appear
	תשׁכים	hiph	impf	2ms	שׁכם	1014		rise early
	פשׁטת	qal	wcp	2ms	פשׁט	832		strip off
	יצאים	qal	ptc	mp	יצא	422		go out
	עשׂית	qal	wcp	2ms	עשׂה	793		do,make
	תמצא	qal	impf	3fs	מצא	592		find
9:34	יקם	qal	wci	3ms	קום	877		arise,stand
	יארבו	qal	wci	3mp	ארב	70		lie in wait
9:35	יצא	qal	wci	3ms	יצא	422		go out
	יעמד	qal	wci	3ms	עמד	763		stand,stop
	יקם	qal	wci	3ms	קום	877		arise,stand
9:36	ירא	qal	wci	3ms	ראה	906		see
	יאמר	qal	wci	3ms	אמר	55		say
	יורד	qal	ptc	ms	ירד	432		come down
	יאמר	qal	wci	3ms	אמר	55		say
	ראה	qal	ptc	ms	ראה	906		see
9:37	יסף	hiph	wci	3ms	יסף	414		add,do again
	דבר	piel	infc		דבר	180		speak
	יאמר	qal	wci	3ms	אמר	55		say
	יורדים	qal	ptc	mp	ירד	432		come down
	בא	qal	ptc	ms	בוא	97		come in
	מעוננים	poel	ptc	mp	ענן	778		soothsay
9:38	יאמר	qal	wci	3ms	אמר	55		say
	תאמר	qal	impf	2ms	אמר	55		say
	נעבדנו	qal	impf	1cp	עבד	712	3ms	work,serve
	מאסתה	qal	pft	2ms	מאס	549		reject,refuse
	צא	qal	impv	ms	יצא	422		go out
	הלחם	niph	impv	ms	לחם	535		wage war
9:39	יצא	qal	wci	3ms	יצא	422		go out
	ילחם	niph	wci	3ms	לחם	535		wage war
9:40	ירדפהו	qal	wci	3ms	רדף	922	3ms	pursue
	ינס	qal	wci	3ms	נוס	630		flee,escape
	יפלו	qal	wci	3mp	נפל	656		fall
9:41	ישׁב	qal	wci	3ms	ישׁב	442		sit,dwell
	יגרשׁ	piel	wci	3ms	גרשׁ	176		drive out
	שׁבת	qal	infc		ישׁב	442		sit,dwell
9:42	יהי	qal	wci	3ms	היה	224		be,become
	יצא	qal	wci	3ms	יצא	422		go out
	יגדו	hiph	wci	3mp	נגד	616		declare,tell
9:43	יקח	qal	wci	3ms	לקח	542		take
	יחצם	qal	wci	3ms	חצה	345	3mp	divide
	יארב	qal	wci	3ms	ארב	70		lie in wait
	ירא	qal	wci	3ms	ראה	906		see

ChVs	Form	Stem	Tnse	PGN	Root	BDB	Sfx	Meaning
9: 43	יצא	qal	ptc	ms	יצא	422		go out
	יקם	qal	wci	3ms	קום	877		arise,stand
	יכם	hiph	wci	3ms	נכה	645	3mp	smite
9: 44	פשטו	qal	pft	3cp	פשט	832		strip off
	יעמדו	qal	wci	3mp	עמד	763		stand,stop
	פשטו	qal	pft	3cp	פשט	832		strip off
	יכום	hiph	wci	3mp	נכה	645	3mp	smite
9: 45	נלחם	niph	ptc	ms	לחם	535		wage war
	ילכד	qal	wci	3ms	לכד	539		capture
	הרג	qal	pft	3ms	הרג	246		kill
	יתץ	qal	wci	3ms	נתץ	683		pull down
	יזרעה	qal	wci	3ms	זרע	281	3fs	sow
9: 46	ישמעו	qal	wci	3mp	שמע	1033		hear
	יבאו	qal	wci	3mp	בוא	97		come in
9: 47	יגד	hoph	wci	3ms	נגד	616		be told
	התקבצו	hith	pft	3cp	קבץ	867		gather together
9: 48	יעל	qal	wci	3ms	עלה	748		go up
	יקח	qal	wci	3ms	לקח	542		take
	יכרת	qal	wci	3ms	כרת	503		cut,destroy
	ישׂאה	qal	wci	3ms	נשׂא	669	3fs	lift,carry
	ישׂם	qal	wci	3ms	שׂים	962		put,set
	יאמר	qal	wci	3ms	אמר	55		say
	ראיתם	qal	pft	2mp	ראה	906		see
	עשׂיתי	qal	pft	1cs	עשׂה	793		do,make
	מהרו	piel	impv	mp	מהר	554		hasten
	עשׂו	qal	impv	mp	עשׂה	793		do,make
9: 49	יכרתו	qal	wci	3mp	כרת	503		cut,destroy
	ילכו	qal	wci	3mp	הלך	229		walk,go
	ישׂימו	qal	wci	3mp	שׂים	962		put,set
	יציתו	hiph	wci	3mp	יצת	428		kindle
	ימתו	qal	wci	3mp	מות	559		die
9: 50	ילך	qal	wci	3ms	הלך	229		walk,go
	יחן	qal	wci	3ms	חנה	333		decline,encamp
	ילכדה	qal	wci	3ms	לכד	539	3fs	capture
9: 51	היה	qal	pft	3ms	היה	224		be,become
	ינסו	qal	wci	3mp	נוס	630		flee,escape
	יסגרו	qal	wci	3mp	סגר	688		shut
	יעלו	qal	wci	3mp	עלה	748		go up
9: 52	יבא	qal	wci	3ms	בוא	97		come in
	ילחם	niph	wci	3ms	לחם	535		wage war
	יגשׁ	qal	wci	3ms	נגשׁ	620		draw near
	שׂרפו	qal	infc		שׂרף	976	3ms	burn
9: 53	תשלך	hiph	wci	3fs	שלך	1020		throw,cast
	תרץ	hiph	wci	3fs	רצץ	954		crush
9: 54	יקרא	qal	wci	3ms	קרא	894		call,proclaim
	נשׂא	qal	ptc	ms	נשׂא	669		lift,carry
	יאמר	qal	wci	3ms	אמר	55		say
	שׁלף	qal	impv	ms	שׁלף	1025		draw out,off
	מותתני	pol	impv	ms	מות	559	1cs	kill
	יאמרו	qal	impf	3mp	אמר	55		say
	הרגתהו	qal	pft	3fs	הרג	246	3ms	kill
	ידקרהו	qal	wci	3ms	דקר	201	3ms	pierce
	ימת	qal	wci	3ms	מות	559		die
9: 55	יראו	qal	wci	3mp	ראה	906		see
9: 55	מת	qal	pft	3ms	מות	559		die
	ילכו	qal	wci	3mp	הלך	229		walk,go
9: 56	ישׁב	hiph	wci	3ms	שׁוב	996		bring back
	עשׂה	qal	pft	3ms	עשׂה	793		do,make
	הרג	qal	infc		הרג	246		kill
9: 57	השׁיב	hiph	pft	3ms	שׁוב	996		bring back
	תבא	qal	wci	3fs	בוא	97		come in
10: 1	יקם	qal	wci	3ms	קום	877		arise,stand
	הושׁיע	hiph	infc		ישׁע	446		deliver,save
	ישׁב	qal	ptc	ms	ישׁב	442		sit,dwell
10: 2	ישׁפט	qal	wci	3ms	שׁפט	1047		judge
	ימת	qal	wci	3ms	מות	559		die
	יקבר	niph	wci	3ms	קבר	868		be buried
10: 3	יקם	qal	wci	3ms	קום	877		arise,stand
	ישׁפט	qal	wci	3ms	שׁפט	1047		judge
10: 4	יהי	qal	wci	3ms	היה	224		be,become
	רכבים	qal	ptc	mp	רכב	938		mount,ride
	יקראו	qal	impf	3mp	קרא	894		call,proclaim
10: 5	ימת	qal	wci	3ms	מות	559		die
	יקבר	niph	wci	3ms	קבר	868		be buried
10: 6	יספו	hiph	wci	3mp	יסף	414		add,do again
	עשׂות	qal	infc		עשׂה	793		do,make
	יעבדו	qal	wci	3mp	עבד	712		work,serve
	יעזבו	qal	wci	3mp	עזב	736		leave,loose
	עבדוהו	qal	pft	3cp	עבד	712	3ms	work,serve
10: 7	יחר	qal	wci	3ms	חרה	354		be kindled,burn
	ימכרם	qal	wci	3ms	מכר	569	3mp	sell
10: 8	ירעצו	qal	wci	3mp	רעץ	950		shatter
	ירצצו	poel	wci	3mp	רצץ	954		crush
10: 9	יעברו	qal	wci	3mp	עבר	716		pass over
	הלחם	niph	infc		לחם	535		wage war
	תצר	qal	wci	3fs	צרר	864		bind,be cramped
10: 10	יזעקו	qal	wci	3mp	זעק	277		call,cry out
	אמר	qal	infc		אמר	55		say
	חטאנו	qal	pft	1cp	חטא	306		sin
	עזבנו	qal	pft	1cp	עזב	736		leave,loose
	נעבד	qal	wci	1cp	עבד	712		work,serve
10: 11	יאמר	qal	wci	3ms	אמר	55		say
10: 12	לחצו	qal	pft	3cp	לחץ	537		press,oppress
	תצעקו	qal	wci	2mp	צעק	858		cry out
	אושׁיעה	hiph	wci	1cs	ישׁע	446		deliver,save
10: 13	עזבתם	qal	pft	2mp	עזב	736		leave,loose
	תעבדו	qal	wci	2mp	עבד	712		work,serve
	אוסיף	hiph	impf	1cs	יסף	414		add,do again
	הושׁיע	hiph	infc		ישׁע	446		deliver,save
10: 14	לכו	qal	impv	mp	הלך	229		walk,go
	זעקו	qal	impv	mp	זעק	277		call,cry out
	בחרתם	qal	pft	2mp	בחר	103		choose
	יושׁיעו	hiph	jusm	3mp	ישׁע	446		deliver,save
10: 15	יאמרו	qal	wci	3mp	אמר	55		say
	חטאנו	qal	pft	1cp	חטא	306		sin
	עשׂה	qal	impv	ms	עשׂה	793		do,make
	הצילנו	hiph	impv	ms	נצל	664	1cp	snatch,deliver
10: 16	יסירו	hiph	wci	3mp	סור	693		take away

ChVs	Form	Stem	Tnse	PGN	Root	BDB	Sfx	Meaning
10:16	יעבדו	qal	wci	3mp	עבד	712		work,serve
	תקצר	qal	wci	3fs	קצר	894		be short
10:17	יצעקו	niph	wci	3mp	צעק	858		be summoned
	יחנו	qal	wci	3mp	חנה	333		decline,encamp
	יאספו	niph	wci	3mp	אסף	62		assemble
	יחנו	qal	wci	3mp	חנה	333		decline,encamp
10:18	יאמרו	qal	wci	3mp	אמר	55		say
	יחל	hiph	impf	3ms	חלל	320		begin,profane
	הלחם	niph	infc		לחם	535		wage war
	יהיה	qal	impf	3ms	היה	224		be,become
	ישבי	qal	ptc	mp	ישב	442		sit,dwell
11:1	היה	qal	pft	3ms	היה	224		be,become
	זונה	qal	ptc	fs	זנה	275		act a harlot
	יולד	hiph	wci	3ms	ילד	408		beget
11:2	תלד	qal	wci	3fs	ילד	408		bear,beget
	יגדלו	qal	wci	3mp	גדל	152		be great,grow
	יגרשו	piel	wci	3mp	גרש	176		drive out
	יאמרו	qal	wci	3mp	אמר	55		say
	תנחל	qal	impf	2ms	נחל	635		possess,inherit
11:3	יברח	qal	wci	3ms	ברח	137		go thru,flee
	ישב	qal	wci	3ms	ישב	442		sit,dwell
	יתלקטו	hith	wci	3mp	לקט	544		gather self
	יצאו	qal	wci	3mp	יצא	422		go out
11:4	יהי	qal	wci	3ms	היה	224		be,become
	ילחמו	niph	wci	3mp	לחם	535		wage war
11:5	יהי	qal	wci	3ms	היה	224		be,become
	נלחמו	niph	pft	3cp	לחם	535		wage war
	ילכו	qal	wci	3mp	הלך	229		walk,go
	קחת	qal	infc		לקח	542		take
11:6	יאמרו	qal	wci	3mp	אמר	55		say
	לכה	qal	impv	ms	הלך	229		walk,go
	הייתה	qal	wcp	2ms	היה	224		be,become
	נלחמה	niph	coh	1cp	לחם	535		wage war
11:7	יאמר	qal	wci	3ms	אמר	55		say
	שנאתם	qal	pft	2mp	שנא	971		hate
	תגרשוני	piel	wci	2mp	גרש	176	1cs	drive out
	באתם	qal	pft	2mp	בוא	97		come in
11:8	יאמרו	qal	wci	3mp	אמר	55		say
	שבנו	qal	pft	1cp	שוב	996		turn,return
	הלכת	qal	wcp	2ms	הלך	229		walk,go
	נלחמת	niph	wcp	2ms	לחם	535		wage war
	היית	qal	wcp	2ms	היה	224		be,become
	ישבי	qal	ptc	mp	ישב	442		sit,dwell
11:9	יאמר	qal	wci	3ms	אמר	55		say
	משיבים	hiph	ptc	mp	שוב	996		bring back
	הלחם	niph	infc		לחם	535		wage war
	נתן	qal	wcp	3ms	נתן	678		give,set
	אהיה	qal	impf	1cs	היה	224		be,become
11:10	יאמרו	qal	wci	3mp	אמר	55		say
	יהיה	qal	impf	3ms	היה	224		be,become
	שמע	qal	ptc	ms	שמע	1033		hear
	נעשה	qal	impf	1cp	עשה	793		do,make
11:11	ילך	qal	wci	3ms	הלך	229		walk,go
	ישימו	qal	wci	3mp	שים	962		put,set
11:11	ידבר	piel	wci	3ms	דבר	180		speak
11:12	ישלח	qal	wci	3ms	שלח	1018		send
	אמר	qal	infc		אמר	55		say
	באת	qal	pft	2ms	בוא	97		come in
	הלחם	niph	infc		לחם	535		wage war
11:13	יאמר	qal	wci	3ms	אמר	55		say
	לקח	qal	pft	3ms	לקח	542		take
	עלותו	qal	infc		עלה	748	3ms	go up
	השיבה	hiph	impv	ms	שוב	996		bring back
11:14	יוסף	hiph	wci	3ms	יסף	414		add,do again
	ישלח	qal	wci	3ms	שלח	1018		send
11:15	יאמר	qal	wci	3ms	אמר	55		say
	אמר	qal	pft	3ms	אמר	55		say
	לקח	qal	pft	3ms	לקח	542		take
11:16	עלותם	qal	infc		עלה	748	3mp	go up
	ילך	qal	wci	3ms	הלך	229		walk,go
	יבא	qal	wci	3ms	בוא	97		come in
11:17	ישלח	qal	wci	3ms	שלח	1018		send
	אמר	qal	infc		אמר	55		say
	אעברה	qal	coh	1cs	עבר	716		pass over
	שמע	qal	pft	3ms	שמע	1033		hear
	שלח	qal	pft	3ms	שלח	1018		send
	אבה	qal	pft	3ms	אבה	2		be willing
	ישב	qal	wci	3ms	ישב	442		sit,dwell
11:18	ילך	qal	wci	3ms	הלך	229		walk,go
	יסב	qal	wci	3ms	סבב	685		surround
	יבא	qal	wci	3ms	בוא	97		come in
	יחנון	qal	wci	3mp	חנה	333		decline,encamp
	באו	qal	pft	3cp	בוא	97		come in
11:19	ישלח	qal	wci	3ms	שלח	1018		send
	יאמר	qal	wci	3ms	אמר	55		say
	נעברה	qal	coh	1cp	עבר	716		pass over
11:20	האמין	hiph	pft	3ms	אמן	52		believe
	עבר	qal	infc		עבר	716		pass over
	יאסף	qal	wci	3ms	אסף	62		gather
	יחנו	qal	wci	3mp	חנה	333		decline,encamp
	ילחם	niph	wci	3ms	לחם	535		wage war
11:21	יתן	qal	wci	3ms	נתן	678		give,set
	יכום	hiph	wci	3mp	נכה	645	3mp	smite
	יירש	qal	wci	3ms	ירש	439		possess,inherit
	יושב	qal	ptc	ms	ישב	442		sit,dwell
11:22	יירשו	qal	wci	3mp	ירש	439		possess,inherit
11:23	הוריש	hiph	pft	3ms	ירש	439		c. to possess
	תירשנו	qal	impf	2ms	ירש	439	3ms	possess,inherit
11:24	יורישך	hiph	impf	3ms	ירש	439	2ms	c. to possess
	תירש	qal	impf	2ms	ירש	439		possess,inherit
	הוריש	hiph	pft	3ms	ירש	439		c. to possess
	נירש	qal	impf	1cp	ירש	439		possess,inherit
11:25	טוב	qal	infa		טוב	373		be pleasing
	טוב	qal	ptc	ms	טוב	373		be pleasing
	רוב	qal	infa		ריב	936		strive,contend
	רב	qal	pft	3ms	ריב	936		strive,contend
	נלחם	niph	infa		לחם	535		wage war
	נלחם	niph	pft	3ms	לחם	535		wage war

ChVs	Form	Stem	Tnse	PGN	Root	BDB	Sfx	Meaning
11:26	שבת	qal	infc		ישב	442		sit,dwell
	הצלתם	hiph	pft	2mp	נצל	664		snatch,deliver
11:27	חטאתי	qal	pft	1cs	חטא	306		sin
	עשה	qal	ptc	ms	עשה	793		do,make
	הלחם	niph	infc		לחם	535		wage war
	ישפט	qal	jusm	3ms	שפט	1047		judge
	שפט	qal	ptc	ms	שפט	1047		judge
11:28	שמע	qal	pft	3ms	שמע	1033		hear
	שלח	qal	pft	3ms	שלח	1018		send
11:29	תהי	qal	wci	3fs	היה	224		be,become
	יעבר	qal	wci	3ms	עבר	716		pass over
	יעבר	qal	wci	3ms	עבר	716		pass over
	עבר	qal	pft	3ms	עבר	716		pass over
11:30	ידר	qal	wci	3ms	נדר	623		vow
	יאמר	qal	wci	3ms	אמר	55		say
	נתון	qal	infa		נתן	678		give,set
	תתן	qal	impf	2ms	נתן	678		give,set
11:31	היה	qal	wcp	3ms	היה	224		be,become
	יוצא	qal	ptc	ms	יצא	422		go out
	יצא	qal	impf	3ms	יצא	422		go out
	קראתי	qal	infc		קרא	896	1cs	meet,encounter
	שובי	qal	infc		שוב	996	1cs	turn,return
	היה	qal	wcp	3ms	היה	224		be,become
	העליתהו	hiph	wcp	1cs	עלה	748	3ms	bring up,offer
11:32	יעבר	qal	wci	3ms	עבר	716		pass over
	הלחם	niph	infc		לחם	535		wage war
	יתנם	qal	wci	3ms	נתן	678	3mp	give,set
11:33	יכם	hiph	wci	3ms	נכה	645	3mp	smite
	בואך	qal	infc		בוא	97	2ms	come in
	יכנעו	niph	wci	3mp	כנע	488		humble self
11:34	יבא	qal	wci	3ms	בוא	97		come in
	יצאת	qal	ptc	fs	יצא	422		go out
	קראתו	qal	infc		קרא	896	3ms	meet,encounter
11:35	יהי	qal	wci	3ms	היה	224		be,become
	ראותו	qal	infc		ראה	906	3ms	see
	יקרע	qal	wci	3ms	קרע	902		tear,rend
	יאמר	qal	wci	3ms	אמר	55		say
	הכרע	hiph	infa		כרע	502		cause to bow
	הכרעתני	hiph	pft	2fs	כרע	502	1cs	cause to bow
	היית	qal	pft	2fs	היה	224		be,become
	עכרי	qal	ptc	mp	עכר	747	1cs	trouble
	פציתי	qal	pft	1cs	פצה	822		open,set free
	אוכל	qal	impf	1cs	יכל	407		be able
	שוב	qal	infc		שוב	996		turn,return
11:36	תאמר	qal	wci	3fs	אמר	55		say
	פציתה	qal	pft	2ms	פצה	822		open,set free
	עשה	qal	impv	ms	עשה	793		do,make
	יצא	qal	pft	3ms	יצא	422		go out
	עשה	qal	pft	3ms	עשה	793		do,make
	איביך	qal	ptc	mp	איב	33	2ms	be hostile to
11:37	תאמר	qal	wci	3fs	אמר	55		say
	יעשה	niph	jusm	3ms	עשה	793		be done
	הרפה	hiph	impv	ms	רפה	951		slacken,abandon
	אלכה	qal	coh	1cs	הלך	229		walk,go

ChVs	Form	Stem	Tnse	PGN	Root	BDB	Sfx	Meaning
11:37	ירדתי	qal	wcp	1cs	ירד	432		come down
	אבכה	qal	cohm	1cs	בכה	113		weep
11:38	יאמר	qal	wci	3ms	אמר	55		say
	לכי	qal	impv	fs	הלך	229		walk,go
	ישלח	qal	wci	3ms	שלח	1018		send
	תלך	qal	wci	3fs	הלך	229		walk,go
	תבך	qal	wci	3fs	בכה	113		weep
11:39	יהי	qal	wci	3ms	היה	224		be,become
	תשב	qal	wci	3fs	שוב	996		turn,return
	יעש	qal	wci	3ms	עשה	793		do,make
	נדר	qal	pft	3ms	נדר	623		vow
	ידעה	qal	pft	3fs	ידע	393		know
	תהי	qal	wci	3fs	היה	224		be,become
11:40	תלכנה	qal	impf	3fp	הלך	229		walk,go
	תנות	piel	infc		תנה	1072		recount
12:1	יצעק	niph	wci	3ms	צעק	858		be summoned
	יעבר	qal	wci	3ms	עבר	716		pass over
	יאמרו	qal	wci	3mp	אמר	55		say
	עברת	qal	pft	2ms	עבר	716		pass over
	הלחם	niph	infc		לחם	535		wage war
	קראת	qal	pft	2ms	קרא	894		call,proclaim
	לכת	qal	infc		הלך	229		walk,go
	נשרף	qal	impf	1cp	שרף	976		burn
12:2	יאמר	qal	wci	3ms	אמר	55		say
	הייתי	qal	pft	1cs	היה	224		be,become
	אזעק	qal	wci	1cs	זעק	277		call,cry out
	הושעתם	hiph	pft	2mp	ישע	446		deliver,save
12:3	אראה	qal	wci	1cs	ראה	906		see
	מושיע	hiph	ptc	ms	ישע	446		deliver,save
	אשימה	qal	wci	1cs	שים	962		put,set
	אעברה	qal	wci	1cs	עבר	716		pass over
	יתנם	qal	wci	3ms	נתן	678	3mp	give,set
	עליתם	qal	pft	2mp	עלה	748		go up
	הלחם	niph	infc		לחם	535		wage war
12:4	יקבץ	qal	wci	3ms	קבץ	867		gather,collect
	ילחם	niph	wci	3ms	לחם	535		wage war
	יכו	hiph	wci	3mp	נכה	645		smite
	אמרו	qal	pft	3cp	אמר	55		say
12:5	ילכד	qal	wci	3ms	לכד	539		capture
	היה	qal	wcp	3ms	היה	224		be,become
	יאמרו	qal	impf	3mp	אמר	55		say
	אעברה	qal	coh	1cs	עבר	716		pass over
	יאמרו	qal	wci	3mp	אמר	55		say
	יאמר	qal	wci	3ms	אמר	55		say
12:6	יאמרו	qal	wci	3mp	אמר	55		say
	אמר	qal	impv	ms	אמר	55		say
	יאמר	qal	wci	3ms	אמר	55		say
	יכין	hiph	impf	3ms	כון	465		fix,prepare
	דבר	piel	infc		דבר	180		speak
	יאחזו	qal	wci	3mp	אחז	28		grasp
	ישחטוהו	qal	wci	3mp	שחט	1006	3ms	slaughter
	יפל	qal	wci	3ms	נפל	656		fall
12:7	ישפט	qal	wci	3ms	שפט	1047		judge
	ימת	qal	wci	3ms	מות	559		die

ChVs	Form	Stem	Tnse	PGN	Root	BDB	Sfx	Meaning
12:7	יקבר	niph	wci	3ms	קבר	868		be buried
12:8	ישפט	qal	wci	3ms	שפט	1047		judge
12:9	יהי	qal	wci	3ms	היה	224		be,become
	שלח	piel	pft	3ms	שלח	1018		send away,shoot
	הביא	hiph	pft	3ms	בוא	97		bring in
	ישפט	qal	wci	3ms	שפט	1047		judge
12:10	ימת	qal	wci	3ms	מות	559		die
	יקבר	niph	wci	3ms	קבר	868		be buried
12:11	ישפט	qal	wci	3ms	שפט	1047		judge
	ישפט	qal	wci	3ms	שפט	1047		judge
12:12	ימת	qal	wci	3ms	מות	559		die
	יקבר	niph	wci	3ms	קבר	868		be buried
12:13	ישפט	qal	wci	3ms	שפט	1047		judge
12:14	יהי	qal	wci	3ms	היה	224		be,become
	רכבים	qal	ptc	mp	רכב	938		mount,ride
	ישפט	qal	wci	3ms	שפט	1047		judge
12:15	ימת	qal	wci	3ms	מות	559		die
	יקבר	niph	wci	3ms	קבר	868		be buried
13:1	יספו	hiph	wci	3mp	יסף	414		add,do again
	עשות	qal	infc		עשה	793		do,make
	יתנם	qal	wci	3ms	נתן	678	3mp	give,set
13:2	יהי	qal	wci	3ms	היה	224		be,become
	ילדה	qal	pft	3fs	ילד	408		bear,beget
13:3	ירא	niph	wci	3ms	ראה	906		appear,be seen
	יאמר	qal	wci	3ms	אמר	55		say
	ילדת	qal	pft	2fs	ילד	408		bear,beget
	הרית	qal	wcp	2fs	הרה	247		conceive
	ילדת	qal	wcp	2fs	ילד	408		bear,beget
13:4	השמרי	niph	impv	fs	שמר	1036		be kept,guarded
	תשתי	qal	jusm	2fs	שתה	1059		drink
	תאכלי	qal	jusm	2fs	אכל	37		eat,devour
13:5	ילדת	qal	wcp	2fs	ילד	408?		bear,beget
	יעלה	qal	impf	3ms	עלה	748		go up
	יהיה	qal	impf	3ms	היה	224		be,become
	יחל	hiph	impf	3ms	חלל	320		begin,profane
	הושיע	hiph	infc		ישע	446		deliver,save
13:6	תבא	qal	wci	3fs	בוא	97		come in
	תאמר	qal	wci	3fs	אמר	55		say
	אמר	qal	infc		אמר	55		say
	בא	qal	pft	3ms	בוא	97		come in
	נורא	niph	ptc	ms	ירא	431		be feared
	שאלתיהו	qal	pft	1cs	שאל	981	3ms	ask,borrow
	הגיד	hiph	pft	3ms	נגד	616		declare,tell
13:7	יאמר	qal	wci	3ms	אמר	55		say
	ילדת	qal	wcp	2fs	ילד	408?		bear,beget
	תשתי	qal	jusm	2fs	שתה	1059		drink
	תאכלי	qal	jusm	2fs	אכל	37		eat,devour
	יהיה	qal	impf	3ms	היה	224		be,become
13:8	יעתר	qal	wci	3ms	עתר	801		pray
	יאמר	qal	wci	3ms	אמר	55		say
	שלחת	qal	pft	2ms	שלח	1018		send
	יבוא	qal	jusm	3ms	בוא	97		come in
	יורנו	hiph	jusm	3ms	ירה	434	1cp	shoot,teach
	נעשה	qal	impf	1cp	עשה	793		do,make
13:8	יולד	qalp	ptc	ms	ילד	408		be born
13:9	ישמע	qal	wci	3ms	שמע	1033		hear
	יבא	qal	wci	3ms	בוא	97		come in
	יושבת	qal	ptc	fs	ישב	442		sit,dwell
13:10	תמהר	piel	wci	3fs	מהר	554		hasten
	תרץ	qal	wci	3fs	רוץ	930		run
	תגד	hiph	wci	3fs	נגד	616		declare,tell
	תאמר	qal	wci	3fs	אמר	55		say
	נראה	niph	pft	3ms	ראה	906		appear,be seen
	בא	qal	pft	3ms	בוא	97		come in
13:11	יקם	qal	wci	3ms	קום	877		arise,stand
	ילך	qal	wci	3ms	הלך	229		walk,go
	יבא	qal	wci	3ms	בוא	97		come in
	יאמר	qal	wci	3ms	אמר	55		say
	דברת	piel	pft	2ms	דבר	180		speak
	יאמר	qal	wci	3ms	אמר	55		say
13:12	יאמר	qal	wci	3ms	אמר	55		say
	יבא	qal	impf	3ms	בוא	97		come in
	יהיה	qal	impf	3ms	היה	224		be,become
13:13	יאמר	qal	wci	3ms	אמר	55		say
	אמרתי	qal	pft	1cs	אמר	55		say
	תשמר	niph	impf	3fs	שמר	1036		be kept,guarded
13:14	יצא	qal	impf	3ms	יצא	422		go out
	תאכל	qal	impf	3fs	אכל	37		eat,devour
	תשת	qal	jus	3fs	שתה	1059		drink
	תאכל	qal	jusm	3fs	אכל	37		eat,devour
	צויתיה	piel	pft	1cs	צוה	845	3fs	command
	תשמר	qal	impf	3fs	שמר	1036		keep,watch
13:15	יאמר	qal	wci	3ms	אמר	55		say
	נעצרה	qal	coh	1cp	עצר	783		restrain
	נעשה	qal	cohm	1cp	עשה	793		do,make
13:16	יאמר	qal	wci	3ms	אמר	55		say
	תעצרני	qal	impf	2ms	עצר	783	1cs	restrain
	אכל	qal	impf	1cs	אכל	37		eat,devour
	תעשה	qal	impf	2ms	עשה	793		do,make
	תעלנה	hiph	impf	2ms	עלה	748	3fs	bring up,offer
	ידע	qal	pft	3ms	ידע	393		know
13:17	יאמר	qal	wci	3ms	אמר	55		say
	יבא	qal	impf	3ms	בוא	97		come in
	כבדנוך	piel	wcp	1cp	כבד	457	2ms	honor,make dull
13:18	יאמר	qal	wci	3ms	אמר	55		say
	תשאל	qal	impf	2ms	שאל	981		ask,borrow
13:19	יקח	qal	wci	3ms	לקח	542		take
	יעל	hiph	wci	3ms	עלה	748		bring up,offer
	מפלא	hiph	ptc	ms	פלא	810		do wondrously
	עשות	qal	infc		עשה	793		do,make
	ראים	qal	ptc	mp	ראה	906		see
13:20	יהי	qal	wci	3ms	היה	224		be,become
	עלות	qal	infc		עלה	748		go up
	יעל	qal	wci	3ms	עלה	748		go up
	ראים	qal	ptc	mp	ראה	906		see
	יפלו	qal	wci	3mp	נפל	656		fall
13:21	יסף	qal	pft	3ms	יסף	414		add,increase
	הראה	niph	infc		ראה	906		appear,be seen

ChVs	Form	Stem	Tnse	PGN	Root	BDB	Sfx	Meaning
13:21	ידע	qal	pft	3ms	ידע	393		know
13:22	יאמר	qal	wci	3ms	אמר	55		say
	מות	qal	infa		מות	559		die
	נמות	qal	impf	1cp	מות	559		die
	ראינו	qal	pft	1cp	ראה	906		see
13:23	תאמר	qal	wci	3fs	אמר	55		say
	חפץ	qal	pft	3ms	חפץ	342		delight in
	המיתנו	hiph	infc		מות	559	1cp	kill
	לקח	qal	pft	3ms	לקח	542		take
	הראנו	hiph	pft	3ms	ראה	906	1cp	show,exhibit
	השמיענו	hiph	pft	3ms	שמע	1033	1cp	cause to hear
13:24	תלד	qal	wci	3fs	ילד	408		bear,beget
	תקרא	qal	wci	3fs	קרא	894		call,proclaim
	יגדל	qal	wci	3ms	גדל	152		be great,grow
	יברכהו	piel	wci	3ms	ברך	138	3ms	bless
13:25	תחל	hiph	wci	3fs	חלל	320		begin,profane
	פעמו	qal	infc		פעם	821	3ms	impel
14:1	ירד	qal	wci	3ms	ירד	432		come down
	ירא	qal	wci	3ms	ראה	906		see
14:2	יעל	qal	wci	3ms	עלה	748		go up
	יגד	hiph	wci	3ms	נגד	616		declare,tell
	יאמר	qal	wci	3ms	אמר	55		say
	ראיתי	qal	pft	1cs	ראה	906		see
	קחו	qal	impv	mp	לקח	542		take
14:3	יאמר	qal	wci	3ms	אמר	55		say
	הולך	qal	ptc	ms	הלך	229		walk,go
	קחת	qal	infc		לקח	542		take
	יאמר	qal	wci	3ms	אמר	55		say
	קח	qal	impv	ms	לקח	542		take
	ישרה	qal	pft	3fs	ישר	448		be straight
14:4	ידעו	qal	pft	3cp	ידע	393		know
	מבקש	piel	ptc	ms	בקש	134		seek
	משלים	qal	ptc	mp	משל	605		rule
14:5	ירד	qal	wci	3ms	ירד	432		come down
	יבאו	qal	wci	3mp	בוא	97		come in
	שאג	qal	ptc	ms	שאג	980		roar
	קראתו	qal	infc		קרא	896	3ms	meet,encounter
14:6	תצלח	qal	wci	3fs	צלח	852		rush
	ישסעהו	piel	wci	3ms	שסע	1042	3ms	tear in two
	שסע	piel	infc		שסע	1042		tear in two
	הגיד	hiph	pft	3ms	נגד	616		declare,tell
	עשה	qal	pft	3ms	עשה	793		do,make
14:7	ירד	qal	wci	3ms	ירד	432		come down
	ידבר	piel	wci	3ms	דבר	180		speak
	תישר	qal	wci	3fs	ישר	448		be straight
14:8	ישב	qal	wci	3ms	שוב	996		turn,return
	קחתה	qal	infc		לקח	542	3fs	take
	יסר	qal	wci	3ms	סור	693		turn aside
	ראות	qal	infc		ראה	906		see
14:9	ירדהו	qal	wci	3ms	רדה	922	3ms	scrape out
	ילך	qal	wci	3ms	הלך	229		walk,go
	הלוך	qal	infa		הלך	229		walk,go
	אכל	qal	infa		אכל	37		eat,devour
	ילך	qal	wci	3ms	הלך	229		walk,go
14:9	יתן	qal	wci	3ms	נתן	678		give,set
	יאכלו	qal	wci	3mp	אכל	37		eat,devour
	הגיד	hiph	pft	3ms	נגד	616		declare,tell
	רדה	qal	pft	3ms	רדה	922		scrape out
14:10	ירד	qal	wci	3ms	ירד	432		come down
	יעש	qal	wci	3ms	עשה	793		do,make
	יעשו	qal	impf	3mp	עשה	793		do,make
14:11	יהי	qal	wci	3ms	היה	224		be,become
	ראותם	qal	infc		ראה	906	3mp	see
	יקחו	qal	wci	3mp	לקח	542		take
	יהיו	qal	wci	3mp	היה	224		be,become
14:12	יאמר	qal	wci	3ms	אמר	55		say
	אחודה	qal	coh	1cs	חוד	295		make a riddle
	הגד	hiph	infa		נגד	616		declare,tell
	תגידו	hiph	impf	2mp	נגד	616		declare,tell
	מצאתם	qal	wcp	2mp	מצא	592		find
	נתתי	qal	wcp	1cs	נתן	678		give,set
14:13	תוכלו	qal	impf	2mp	יכל	407		be able
	הגיד	hiph	infc		נגד	616		declare,tell
	נתתם	qal	wcp	2mp	נתן	678		give,set
	יאמרו	qal	wci	3mp	אמר	55		say
	חודה	qal	impv	ms	חוד	295		make a riddle
	נשמענה	qal	cohm	1cp	שמע	1033	3fs	hear
14:14	יאמר	qal	wci	3ms	אמר	55		say
	אכל	qal	ptc	ms	אכל	37		eat,devour
	יצא	qal	pft	3ms	יצא	422		go out
	יצא	qal	pft	3ms	יצא	422		go out
	יכלו	qal	pft	3cp	יכל	407		be able
	הגיד	hiph	infc		נגד	616		declare,tell
14:15	יהי	qal	wci	3ms	היה	224		be,become
	יאמרו	qal	wci	3mp	אמר	55		say
	פתי	piel	impv	fs	פתה	834		entice
	יגד	hiph	jus	3ms	נגד	616		declare,tell
	נשרף	qal	impf	1cp	שרף	976		burn
	ירשנו	qal	infc		ירש	439	1cp	possess,inherit
	קראתם	qal	pft	2mp	קרא	894		call,proclaim
14:16	תבך	qal	wci	3fs	בכה	113		weep
	תאמר	qal	wci	3fs	אמר	55		say
	שנאתני	qal	pft	2ms	שנא	971	1cs	hate
	אהבתני	qal	pft	2ms	אהב	12	1cs	love
	חדת	qal	pft	2ms	חוד	295		make a riddle
	הגדתה	hiph	pft	2ms	נגד	616		declare,tell
	יאמר	qal	wci	3ms	אמר	55		say
	הגדתי	hiph	pft	1cs	נגד	616		declare,tell
	אגיד	hiph	impf	1cs	נגד	616		declare,tell
14:17	תבך	qal	wci	3fs	בכה	113		weep
	היה	qal	pft	3ms	היה	224		be,become
	יהי	qal	wci	3ms	היה	224		be,become
	יגד	hiph	wci	3ms	נגד	616		declare,tell
	הציקתהו	hiph	pft	3fs	צוק	847	3ms	constrain
	תגד	hiph	wci	3fs	נגד	616		declare,tell
14:18	יאמרו	qal	wci	3mp	אמר	55		say
	יבא	qal	impf	3ms	בוא	97		come in
	יאמר	qal	wci	3ms	אמר	55		say

ChVs	Form	Stem	Tnse	PGN	Root	BDB	Sfx	Meaning
14:18	חרשתם	qal	pft	2mp	חרש	360		engrave,plough
	מצאתם	qal	pft	2mp	מצא	592		find
14:19	תצלח	qal	wci	3fs	צלח	852		rush
	ירד	qal	wci	3ms	ירד	432		come down
	יך	hiph	wci	3ms	נכה	645		smite
	יקח	qal	wci	3ms	לקח	542		take
	יתן	qal	wci	3ms	נתן	678		give,set
	מגידי	hiph	ptc	mp	נגד	616		declare,tell
	יחר	qal	wci	3ms	חרה	354		be kindled,burn
	יעל	qal	wci	3ms	עלה	748		go up
14:20	תהי	qal	wci	3fs	היה	224		be,become
	רעה	piel	pft	3ms	רעה	946		be friend
15:1	יהי	qal	wci	3ms	היה	224		be,become
	יפקד	qal	wci	3ms	פקד	823		attend to,visit
	יאמר	qal	wci	3ms	אמר	55		say
	אבאה	qal	coh	1cs	בוא	97		come in
	נתנו	qal	pft	3ms	נתן	678	3ms	give,set
	בוא	qal	infc		בוא	97		come in
15:2	יאמר	qal	wci	3ms	אמר	55		say
	אמר	qal	infa		אמר	55		say
	אמרתי	qal	pft	1cs	אמר	55		say
	שׂנא	qal	infa		שׂנא	971		hate
	שׂנאתה	qal	pft	2ms	שׂנא	971	3fs	hate
	אתננה	qal	wci	1cs	נתן	678	3fs	give,set
	תהי	qal	jus	3fs	היה	224		be,become
15:3	יאמר	qal	wci	3ms	אמר	55		say
	נקיתי	niph	pft	1cs	נקה	667		be clean,free
	עשׂה	qal	ptc	ms	עשׂה	793		do,make
15:4	ילך	qal	wci	3ms	הלך	229		walk,go
	ילכד	qal	wci	3ms	לכד	539		capture
	יקח	qal	wci	3ms	לקח	542		take
	יפן	hiph	wci	3ms	פנה	815		turn
	ישׂם	qal	wci	3ms	שׂים	962		put,set
15:5	יבער	hiph	wci	3ms	בער	128		cause to burn
	ישׁלח	piel	wci	3ms	שׁלח	1018		send away,shoot
	יבער	hiph	wci	3ms	בער	128		cause to burn
15:6	יאמרו	qal	wci	3mp	אמר	55		say
	עשׂה	qal	pft	3ms	עשׂה	793		do,make
	יאמרו	qal	wci	3mp	אמר	55		say
	לקח	qal	pft	3ms	לקח	542		take
	יתנה	qal	wci	3ms	נתן	678	3fs	give,set
	יעלו	qal	wci	3mp	עלה	748		go up
	ישׂרפו	qal	wci	3mp	שׂרף	976		burn
15:7	יאמר	qal	wci	3ms	אמר	55		say
	תעשׂון	qal	impf	2mp	עשׂה	793		do,make
	נקמתי	niph	pft	1cs	נקם	667		avenge oneself
	אחדל	qal	impf	1cs	חדל	292		cease
15:8	יך	hiph	wci	3ms	נכה	645		smite
	ירד	qal	wci	3ms	ירד	432		come down
	ישׁב	qal	wci	3ms	ישׁב	442		sit,dwell
15:9	יעלו	qal	wci	3mp	עלה	748		go up
	יחנו	qal	wci	3mp	חנה	333		decline,encamp
	ינטשׁו	niph	wci	3mp	נטשׁ	643		be forsaken
15:10	יאמרו	qal	wci	3mp	אמר	55		say
15:10	עליתם	qal	pft	2mp	עלה	748		go up
	יאמרו	qal	wci	3mp	אמר	55		say
	אסור	qal	infc		אסר	63		tie,bind
	עלינו	qal	pft	1cp	עלה	748		go up
	עשׂות	qal	infc		עשׂה	793		do,make
	עשׂה	qal	pft	3ms	עשׂה	793		do,make
15:11	ירדו	qal	wci	3mp	ירד	432		come down
	יאמרו	qal	wci	3mp	אמר	55		say
	ידעת	qal	pft	2ms	ידע	393		know
	משׁלים	qal	ptc	mp	משׁל	605		rule
	עשׂית	qal	pft	2ms	עשׂה	793		do,make
	יאמר	qal	wci	3ms	אמר	55		say
	עשׂו	qal	pft	3cp	עשׂה	793		do,make
	עשׂיתי	qal	pft	1cs	עשׂה	793		do,make
15:12	יאמרו	qal	wci	3mp	אמר	55		say
	אסרך	qal	infc		אסר	63	2ms	tie,bind
	ירדנו	qal	pft	1cp	ירד	432		come down
	תתך	qal	infc		נתן	678	2ms	give,set
	יאמר	qal	wci	3ms	אמר	55		say
	השׁבעו	niph	impv	mp	שׁבע	989		swear
	תפגעון	qal	impf	2mp	פגע	803		meet,encounter
15:13	יאמרו	qal	wci	3mp	אמר	55		say
	אמר	qal	infc		אמר	55		say
	אסר	qal	infa		אסר	63		tie,bind
	נאסרך	qal	impf	1cp	אסר	63	2ms	tie,bind
	נתנוך	qal	wcp	1cp	נתן	678	2ms	give,set
	המת	hiph	infa		מות	559		kill
	נמיתך	hiph	impf	1cp	מות	559	2ms	kill
	יאסרהו	qal	wci	3mp	אסר	63	3ms	tie,bind
	יעלוהו	hiph	wci	3mp	עלה	748	3ms	bring up,offer
15:14	בא	qal	ptc	ms	בוא	97		come in
	הריעו	hiph	pft	3cp	רוע	929		raise a shout
	קראתו	qal	infc		קרא	896	3ms	meet,encounter
	תצלח	qal	wci	3fs	צלח	852		rush
	תהיינה	qal	wci	3fp	היה	224		be,become
	בערו	qal	pft	3cp	בער	128		burn
	ימסו	niph	wci	3mp	מסס	587		melt,despair
15:15	ימצא	qal	wci	3ms	מצא	592		find
	ישׁלח	qal	wci	3ms	שׁלח	1018		send
	יקחה	qal	wci	3ms	לקח	542	3fs	take
	יך	hiph	wci	3ms	נכה	645		smite
15:16	יאמר	qal	wci	3ms	אמר	55		say
	הכיתי	hiph	pft	1cs	נכה	645		smite
15:17	יהי	qal	wci	3ms	היה	224		be,become
	כלתו	piel	infc		כלה	477	3ms	complete,finish
	דבר	piel	infc		דבר	180		speak
	ישׁלך	hiph	wci	3ms	שׁלך	1020		throw,cast
	יקרא	qal	wci	3ms	קרא	894		call,proclaim
15:18	יצמא	qal	wci	3ms	צמא	854		be thirsty
	יקרא	qal	wci	3ms	קרא	894		call,proclaim
	יאמר	qal	wci	3ms	אמר	55		say
	נתת	qal	pft	2ms	נתן	678		give,set
	אמות	qal	impf	1cs	מות	559		die
	נפלתי	qal	wcp	1cs	נפל	656		fall

ChVs	Form	Stem	Tnse	PGN	Root	BDB	Sfx	Meaning
15:19	יבקע	qal	wci	3ms	בקע	131		cleave, break
	יצאו	qal	wci	3mp	יצא	422		go out
	ישת	qal	wci	3ms	שתה	1059		drink
	תשב	qal	wci	3fs	שוב	996		turn, return
	יחי	qal	wci	3ms	חיה	310		live
	קרא	qal	pft	3ms	קרא	894		call, proclaim
15:20	ישפט	qal	wci	3ms	שפט	1047		judge
16:1	ילך	qal	wci	3ms	הלך	229		walk, go
	ירא	qal	wci	3ms	ראה	906		see
	זונה	qal	ptc	fs	זנה	275		act a harlot
	יבא	qal	wci	3ms	בוא	97		come in
16:2	אמר	qal	infc		אמר	55		say
	בא	qal	pft	3ms	בוא	97		come in
	יסבו	qal	wci	3mp	סבב	685		surround
	יארבו	qal	wci	3mp	ארב	70		lie in wait
	יתחרשו	hith	wci	3mp	חרש	361		keep quiet
	אמר	qal	infc		אמר	55		say
	הרגנהו	qal	wcp	1cp	הרג	246	3ms	kill
16:3	ישכב	qal	wci	3ms	שכב	1011		lie, lie down
	יקם	qal	wci	3ms	קום	877		arise, stand
	יאחז	qal	wci	3ms	אחז	28		grasp
	יסעם	qal	wci	3ms	נסע	652	3mp	pull up, set out
	ישם	qal	wci	3ms	שים	962		put, set
	יעלם	hiph	wci	3ms	עלה	748	3mp	bring up, offer
16:4	יהי	qal	wci	3ms	היה	224		be, become
	יאהב	qal	wci	3ms	אהב	12		love
16:5	יעלו	qal	wci	3mp	עלה	748		go up
	יאמרו	qal	wci	3mp	אמר	55		say
	פתי	piel	impv	fs	פתה	834		entice
	ראי	qal	impv	fs	ראה	906		see
	נוכל	qal	impf	1cp	יכל	407		be able
	אסרנהו	qal	wcp	1cp	אסר	63	3ms	tie, bind
	ענתו	piel	infc		ענה	776	3ms	humble
	נתן	qal	impf	1cp	נתן	678		give, set
16:6	תאמר	qal	wci	3fs	אמר	55		say
	הגידה	hiph	impv	ms	נגד	616		declare, tell
	תאסר	niph	impf	2ms	אסר	63		be bound
	ענותך	piel	infc		ענה	776	2ms	humble
16:7	יאמר	qal	wci	3ms	אמר	55		say
	יאסרני	qal	impf	3mp	אסר	63	1cs	tie, bind
	חרבו	pual	pft	3cp	חרב	351		be dried
	חליתי	qal	wcp	1cs	חלה	317		be weak, sick
	הייתי	qal	wcp	1cs	היה	224		be, become
16:8	יעלו	hiph	wci	3mp	עלה	748		bring up, offer
	חרבו	pual	pft	3cp	חרב	351		be dried
	תאסרהו	qal	wci	3fs	אסר	63	3ms	tie, bind
16:9	ארב	qal	ptc	ms	ארב	70		lie in wait
	ישב	qal	ptc	ms	ישב	442		sit, dwell
	תאמר	qal	wci	3fs	אמר	55		say
	ינתק	piel	wci	3ms	נתק	683		tear apart
	ינתק	niph	impf	3ms	נתק	683		be drawn, torn
	הריחו	hiph	infc		ריח	926	3ms	smell
	נודע	niph	pft	3ms	ידע	393		be made known
16:10	תאמר	qal	wci	3fs	אמר	55		say
16:10	התלת	hiph	pft	2ms	תלל	1068		mock, deceive
	תדבר	piel	wci	2ms	דבר	180		speak
	הגידה	hiph	impv	ms	נגד	616		declare, tell
	תאסר	niph	impf	2ms	אסר	63		be bound
16:11	יאמר	qal	wci	3ms	אמר	55		say
	אסור	qal	infa		אסר	63		tie, bind
	יאסרוני	qal	impf	3mp	אסר	63	1cs	tie, bind
	נעשה	niph	pft	3ms	עשה	793		be done
	חליתי	qal	wcp	1cs	חלה	317		be weak, sick
	הייתי	qal	wcp	1cs	היה	224		be, become
16:12	תקח	qal	wci	3fs	לקח	542		take
	תאסרהו	qal	wci	3fs	אסר	63	3ms	tie, bind
	תאמר	qal	wci	3fs	אמר	55		say
	ארב	qal	ptc	ms	ארב	70		lie in wait
	ישב	qal	ptc	ms	ישב	442		sit, dwell
	ינתקם	piel	wci	3ms	נתק	683	3mp	tear apart
16:13	תאמר	qal	wci	3fs	אמר	55		say
	התלת	hiph	pft	2ms	תלל	1068		mock, deceive
	תדבר	piel	wci	2ms	דבר	180		speak
	הגידה	hiph	impv	ms	נגד	616		declare, tell
	תאסר	niph	impf	2ms	אסר	63		be bound
	יאמר	qal	wci	3ms	אמר	55		say
	תארגי	qal	impf	2fs	ארג	70		weave
16:14	תתקע	qal	wci	3fs	תקע	1075		thrust, clap
	תאמר	qal	wci	3fs	אמר	55		say
	ייקץ	qal	wci	3ms	יקץ	429		awake
	יסע	qal	wci	3ms	נסע	652		pull up, set out
16:15	תאמר	qal	wci	3fs	אמר	55		say
	תאמר	qal	impf	2ms	אמר	55		say
	אהבתיך	qal	pft	1cs	אהב	12	2ms	love
	התלת	hiph	pft	2ms	תלל	1068		mock, deceive
	הגדת	hiph	pft	2ms	נגד	616		declare, tell
16:16	יהי	qal	wci	3ms	היה	224		be, become
	הציקה	hiph	pft	3fs	צוק	847		constrain
	תאלצהו	piel	wci	3fs	אלץ	49	3ms	urge
	תקצר	qal	wci	3fs	קצר	894		be short
	מות	qal	infc		מות	559		die
16:17	יגד	hiph	wci	3ms	נגד	616		declare, tell
	יאמר	qal	wci	3ms	אמר	55		say
	עלה	qal	pft	3ms	עלה	748		go up
	גלחתי	pual	pft	1cs	גלח	164		be shaven
	סר	qal	wcp	3ms	סור	693		turn aside
	חליתי	qal	wcp	1cs	חלה	317		be weak, sick
	הייתי	qal	wcp	1cs	היה	224		be, become
16:18	תרא	qal	wci	3fs	ראה	906		see
	הגיד	hiph	pft	3ms	נגד	616		declare, tell
	תשלח	qal	wci	3fs	שלח	1018		send
	תקרא	qal	wci	3fs	קרא	894		call, proclaim
	אמר	qal	infc		אמר	55		say
	עלו	qal	impv	mp	עלה	748		go up
	הגיד	hiph	pft	3ms	נגד	616		declare, tell
	עלו	qal	pft	3cp	עלה	748		go up
	יעלו	hiph	wci	3mp	עלה	748		bring up, offer
16:19	תישנהו	piel	wci	3fs	ישן	445	3ms	cause to sleep

ChVs	Form	Stem	Tnse	PGN	Root	BDB	Sfx	Meaning
16:19	תקרא	qal	wci	3fs	קרא	894		call,proclaim
	תגלח	piel	wci	3fs	גלח	164		shave
	תחל	hiph	wci	3fs	חלל	320		begin,profane
	ענותו	piel	infc		ענה	776	3ms	humble
	יסר	qal	wci	3ms	סור	693		turn aside
16:20	תאמר	qal	wci	3fs	אמר	55		say
	יקץ	qal	wci	3ms	יקץ	429		awake
	יאמר	qal	wci	3ms	אמר	55		say
	אצא	qal	impf	1cs	יצא	422		go out
	אנער	niph	impf	1cs	נער	654		be shaken out
	ידע	qal	pft	3ms	ידע	393		know
	סר	qal	pft	3ms	סור	693		turn aside
16:21	יאחזוהו	qal	wci	3mp	אחז	28	3ms	grasp
	ינקרו	piel	wci	3mp	נקר	669		bore out
	יורידו	hiph	wci	3mp	ירד	432		bring down
	יאסרוהו	qal	wci	3mp	אסר	63	3ms	tie,bind
	יהי	qal	wci	3ms	היה	224		be,become
	טוחן	qal	ptc	ms	טחן	377		grind
16:22	יחל	hiph	wci	3ms	חלל	320		begin,profane
	צמח	piel	infc		צמח	855		grow abundantly
	גלח	pual	pft	3ms	גלח	164		be shaven
16:23	נאספו	niph	pft	3cp	אסף	62		assemble
	זבח	qal	infc		זבח	256		slaughter
	יאמרו	qal	wci	3mp	אמר	55		say
	נתן	qal	pft	3ms	נתן	678		give,set
	אויבינו	qal	ptc	mp	איב	33	1cp	be hostile to
16:24	יראו	qal	wci	3mp	ראה	906		see
	יהללו	piel	wci	3mp	הלל	237		praise
	אמרו	qal	pft	3cp	אמר	55		say
	נתן	qal	pft	3ms	נתן	678		give,set
	אויבנו	qal	ptc	ms	איב	33	1cp	be hostile to
	מחריב	hiph	ptc	ms	חרב	351		make desolate
	הרבה	hiph	pft	3ms	רבה	915		make many
16:25	יהי	qal	wci	3ms	היה	224		be,become
	טובk	qal	pft	3ms	טוב	373		be pleasing
	טובq	qal	infc		טוב	373		be pleasing
	יאמרו	qal	wci	3mp	אמר	55		say
	קראו	qal	impv	mp	קרא	894		call,proclaim
	ישחק	piel	jusm	3ms	שחק	965		make sport
	יקראו	qal	wci	3mp	קרא	894		call,proclaim
	יצחק	piel	wci	3ms	צחק	850		jest,make sport
	יעמידו	hiph	wci	3mp	עמד	763		set up,raise
16:26	יאמר	qal	wci	3ms	אמר	55		say
	מחזיק	hiph	ptc	ms	חזק	304		make firm,seize
	הניחה	hiph	impv	ms	נוח	628		give rest,put
	הימשניk	hiph	impv	ms	ימש	413	1cs	touch
	המשניq	hiph	impv	ms	מוש	559	1cs	feel
	נכון	niph	ptc	ms	כון	465		be established
	אשען	niph	cohm	1cs	שען	1043		lean,support
16:27	מלא	qal	pft	3ms	מלא	569		be full,fill
	ראים	qal	ptc	mp	ראה	906		see
	שחוק	qal	infc		שחק	965		laugh
16:28	יקרא	qal	wci	3ms	קרא	894		call,proclaim
	יאמר	qal	wci	3ms	אמר	55		say
16:28	זכרני	qal	impv	ms	זכר	269	1cs	remember
	חזקני	piel	impv	ms	חזק	304	1cs	make strong
	אנקמה	niph	coh	1cs	נקם	667		avenge oneself
16:29	ילפת	qal	wci	3ms	לפת	542		grasp
	נכון	niph	ptc	ms	כון	465		be established
	יסמך	niph	wci	3ms	סמך	701		support oneself
16:30	יאמר	qal	wci	3ms	אמר	55		say
	תמות	qal	jusm	3fs	מות	559		die
	יט	qal	wci	3ms	נטה	639		stretch,incline
	יפל	qal	wci	3ms	נפל	656		fall
	יהיו	qal	wci	3mp	היה	224		be,become
	מתים	qal	ptc	mp	מות	559		die
	המית	hiph	pft	3ms	מות	559		kill
	המית	hiph	pft	3ms	מות	559		kill
16:31	ירדו	qal	wci	3mp	ירד	432		come down
	ישאו	qal	wci	3mp	נשא	669		lift,carry
	יעלו	hiph	wci	3mp	עלה	748		bring up,offer
	יקברו	qal	wci	3mp	קבר	868		bury
	שפט	qal	pft	3ms	שפט	1047		judge
17:1	יהי	qal	wci	3ms	היה	224		be,become
17:2	יאמר	qal	wci	3ms	אמר	55		say
	לקח	qalp	pft	3ms	לקח	542		be taken
	אלית	qal	pft	2fs	אלה	46		swear
	אמרת	qal	pft	2fs	אמר	55		say
	לקחתיו	qal	pft	1cs	לקח	542	3ms	take
	תאמר	qal	wci	3fs	אמר	55		say
	ברוך	qal	pptc	ms	ברך	138		kneel,bless
17:3	ישב	hiph	wci	3ms	שוב	996		bring back
	תאמר	qal	wci	3fs	אמר	55		say
	הקדש	hiph	infa		קדש	872		consecrate
	הקדשתי	hiph	pft	1cs	קדש	872		consecrate
	עשות	qal	infc		עשה	793		do,make
	אשיבנו	hiph	impf	1cs	שוב	996	3ms	bring back
17:4	ישב	hiph	wci	3ms	שוב	996		bring back
	תקח	qal	wci	3fs	לקח	542		take
	תתנהו	qal	wci	3fs	נתן	678	3ms	give,set
	צורף	qal	ptc	ms	צרף	864		refine,test
	יעשהו	qal	wci	3ms	עשה	793	3ms	do,make
	יהי	qal	wci	3ms	היה	224		be,become
17:5	יעש	qal	wci	3ms	עשה	793		do,make
	ימלא	piel	wci	3ms	מלא	569		fill
	יהי	qal	wci	3ms	היה	224		be,become
17:6	יעשה	qal	impf	3ms	עשה	793		do,make
17:7	יהי	qal	wci	3ms	היה	224		be,become
	גר	qal	ptc	ms	גור	157		sojourn
17:8	ילך	qal	wci	3ms	הלך	229		walk,go
	גור	qal	infc		גור	157		sojourn
	ימצא	qal	impf	3ms	מצא	592		find
	יבא	qal	wci	3ms	בוא	97		come in
	עשות	qal	infc		עשה	793		do,make
17:9	יאמר	qal	wci	3ms	אמר	55		say
	תבוא	qal	impf	2ms	בוא	97		come in
	יאמר	qal	wci	3ms	אמר	55		say
	הלך	qal	ptc	ms	הלך	229		walk,go

ChVs	Form	Stem	Tnse	PGN	Root	BDB	Sfx	Meaning
17:9	גור	qal	infc		גור	157		sojourn
	אמצא	qal	impf	1cs	מצא	592		find
17:10	יאמר	qal	wci	3ms	אמר	55		say
	שׁבה	qal	impv	ms	ישׁב	442		sit,dwell
	היה	qal	impv	ms	היה	224		be,become
	אתן	qal	impf	1cs	נתן	678		give,set
	ילך	qal	wci	3ms	הלך	229		walk,go
17:11	יואל	hiph	wci	3ms	יאל	383		be willing
	שׁבת	qal	infc		ישׁב	442		sit,dwell
	יהי	qal	wci	3ms	היה	224		be,become
17:12	ימלא	piel	wci	3ms	מלא	569		fill
	יהי	qal	wci	3ms	היה	224		be,become
	יהי	qal	wci	3ms	היה	224		be,become
17:13	יאמר	qal	wci	3ms	אמר	55		say
	ידעתי	qal	pft	1cs	ידע	393		know
	ייטיב	hiph	impf	3ms	יטב	405		do good
	היה	qal	pft	3ms	היה	224		be,become
18:1	מבקשׁ	piel	ptc	ms	בקשׁ	134		seek
	שׁבת	qal	infc		ישׁב	442		sit,dwell
	נפלה	qal	pft	3fs	נפל	656		fall
18:2	ישׁלחו	qal	wci	3mp	שׁלח	1018		send
	רגל	piel	infc		רגל	920		slander,spy
	חקרה	qal	infc		חקר	350	3fs	search
	יאמרו	qal	wci	3mp	אמר	55		say
	לכו	qal	impv	mp	הלך	229		walk,go
	חקרו	qal	impv	mp	חקר	350		search
	יבאו	qal	wci	3mp	בוא	97		come in
	ילינו	qal	wci	3mp	לון	533		lodge,remain
18:3	הכירו	hiph	pft	3cp	נכר	647		regard,notice
	יסורו	qal	wci	3mp	סור	693		turn aside
	יאמרו	qal	wci	3mp	אמר	55		say
	הביאך	hiph	pft	3ms	בוא	97	2ms	bring in
	עשׂה	qal	ptc	ms	עשׂה	793		do,make
18:4	יאמר	qal	wci	3ms	אמר	55		say
	עשׂה	qal	pft	3ms	עשׂה	793		do,make
	ישׂכרני	qal	wci	3ms	שׂכר	968	1cs	hire
	אהי	qal	wci	1cs	היה	224		be,become
18:5	יאמרו	qal	wci	3mp	אמר	55		say
	שׁאל	qal	impv	ms	שׁאל	981		ask, borrow
	נדעה	qal	coh	1cp	ידע	393		know
	תצליח	hiph	impf	3fs	צלח	852		cause to thrive
	הלכים	qal	ptc	mp	הלך	229		walk,go
18:6	יאמר	qal	wci	3ms	אמר	55		say
	לכו	qal	impv	mp	הלך	229		walk,go
	תלכו	qal	impf	2mp	הלך	229		walk,go
18:7	ילכו	qal	wci	3mp	הלך	229		walk,go
	יבאו	qal	wci	3mp	בוא	97		come in
	יראו	qal	wci	3mp	ראה	906		see
	יושׁבת	qal	ptc	fs	ישׁב	442		sit,dwell
	שׁקט	qal	ptc	ms	שׁקט	1052		be quiet
	בטח	qal	ptc	ms	בטח	105		trust
	מכלים	hiph	ptc	ms	כלם	483		humiliate
	יורשׁ	qal	ptc	ms	ירשׁ	439		possess,inherit
18:8	יבאו	qal	wci	3mp	בוא	97		come in
18:8	יאמרו	qal	wci	3mp	אמר	55		say
18:9	יאמרו	qal	wci	3mp	אמר	55		say
	קומה	qal	impv	ms	קום	877		arise,stand
	נעלה	qal	cohm	1cp	עלה	748		go up
	ראינו	qal	pft	1cp	ראה	906		see
	מחשׁים	hiph	ptc	mp	חשׁה	364		show silence
	תעצלו	niph	jusm	2mp	עצל	782		be sluggish
	לכת	qal	infc		הלך	229		walk,go
	בא	qal	infc		בוא	97		come in
	רשׁת	qal	infc		ירשׁ	439		possess,inherit
18:10	באכם	qal	infc		בוא	97	2mp	come in
	תבאו	qal	impf	2mp	בוא	97		come in
	בטח	qal	ptc	ms	בטח	105		trust
	נתנה	qal	pft	3ms	נתן	678	3fs	give,set
18:11	יסעו	qal	wci	3mp	נסע	652		pull up,set out
	חגור	qal	pptc	ms	חגר	291		gird
18:12	יעלו	qal	wci	3mp	עלה	748		go up
	יחנו	qal	wci	3mp	חנה	333		decline,encamp
	קראו	qal	pft	3cp	קרא	894		call,proclaim
18:13	יעברו	qal	wci	3mp	עבר	716		pass over
	יבאו	qal	wci	3mp	בוא	97		come in
18:14	יענו	qal	wci	3mp	ענה	772		answer
	הלכים	qal	ptc	mp	הלך	229		walk,go
	רגל	piel	infc		רגל	920		slander,spy
	יאמרו	qal	wci	3mp	אמר	55		say
	ידעתם	qal	pft	2mp	ידע	393		know
	דעו	qal	impv	mp	ידע	393		know
	תעשׂו	qal	impf	2mp	עשׂה	793		do,make
18:15	יסורו	qal	wci	3mp	סור	693		turn aside
	יבאו	qal	wci	3mp	בוא	97		come in
	ישׁאלו	qal	wci	3mp	שׁאל	981		ask, borrow
18:16	חגורים	qal	pptc	mp	חגר	291		gird
	נצבים	niph	ptc	mp	נצב	662		stand
18:17	יעלו	qal	wci	3mp	עלה	748		go up
	הלכים	qal	ptc	mp	הלך	229		walk,go
	רגל	piel	infc		רגל	920		slander,spy
	באו	qal	pft	3cp	בוא	97		come in
	לקחו	qal	pft	3cp	לקח	542		take
	נצב	niph	ptc	ms	נצב	662		stand
	חגור	qal	pptc	ms	חגר	291		gird
18:18	באו	qal	pft	3cp	בוא	97		come in
	יקחו	qal	wci	3mp	לקח	542		take
	יאמר	qal	wci	3ms	אמר	55		say
	עשׂים	qal	ptc	mp	עשׂה	793		do,make
18:19	יאמרו	qal	wci	3mp	אמר	55		say
	החרשׁ	hiph	impv	ms	חרשׁ	361		be silent
	שׂים	qal	impv	ms	שׂים	962		put,set
	לך	qal	impv	ms	הלך	229		walk,go
	היה	qal	impv	ms	היה	224		be,become
	היותך	qal	infc		היה	224	2ms	be,become
	היותך	qal	infc		היה	224	2ms	be,become
18:20	ייטב	qal	wci	3ms	יטב	405		be good
	יקח	qal	wci	3ms	לקח	542		take
	יבא	qal	wci	3ms	בוא	97		come in

ChVs	Form	Stem	Tnse	PGN	Root	BDB	Sfx	Meaning
18: 21	יפנו	qal	wci	3mp	פנה	815		turn
	ילכו	qal	wci	3mp	הלך	229		walk,go
	ישׂימו	qal	wci	3mp	שׂים	962		put,set
18: 22	הרחיקו	hiph	pft	3cp	רחק	934		put far away
	נזעקו	niph	pft	3cp	זעק	277		assemble
	ידביקו	hiph	wci	3mp	דבק	179		cause to cling
18: 23	יקראו	qal	wci	3mp	קרא	894		call,proclaim
	יסבו	hiph	wci	3mp	סבב	685		cause to turn
	יאמרו	qal	wci	3mp	אמר	55		say
	נזעקת	niph	pft	2ms	זעק	277		assemble
18: 24	יאמר	qal	wci	3ms	אמר	55		say
	עשׂיתי	qal	pft	1cs	עשׂה	793		do,make
	לקחתם	qal	pft	2mp	לקח	542		take
	תלכו	qal	wci	2mp	הלך	229		walk,go
	תאמרו	qal	impf	2mp	אמר	55		say
18: 25	יאמרו	qal	wci	3mp	אמר	55		say
	תשמע	hiph	jus	2ms	שמע	1033		cause to hear
	יפגעו	qal	impf	3mp	פגע	803		meet,encounter
	אספתה	qal	wcp	2ms	אסף	62		gather
18: 26	ילכו	qal	wci	3mp	הלך	229		walk,go
	ירא	qal	wci	3ms	ראה	906		see
	יפן	qal	wci	3ms	פנה	815		turn
	ישב	qal	wci	3ms	שׁוב	996		turn,return
18: 27	לקחו	qal	pft	3cp	לקח	542		take
	עשׂה	qal	pft	3ms	עשׂה	793		do,make
	היה	qal	pft	3ms	היה	224		be,become
	יבאו	qal	wci	3mp	בוא	97		come in
	שׁקט	qal	ptc	ms	שׁקט	1052		be quiet
	בטח	qal	ptc	ms	בטח	105		trust
	יכו	hiph	wci	3mp	נכה	645		smite
	שׂרפו	qal	pft	3cp	שׂרף	976		burn
18: 28	מציל	hiph	ptc	ms	נצל	664		snatch,deliver
	יבנו	qal	wci	3mp	בנה	124		build
	ישׁבו	qal	wci	3mp	ישׁב	442		sit,dwell
18: 29	יקראו	qal	wci	3mp	קרא	894		call,proclaim
	יולד	qalp	pft	3ms	ילד	408		be born
18: 30	יקימו	hiph	wci	3mp	קום	877		raise,build,set
	היו	qal	pft	3cp	היה	224		be,become
	גלות	qal	infc		גלה	162		uncover
18: 31	ישׂימו	qal	wci	3mp	שׂים	962		put,set
	עשׂה	qal	pft	3ms	עשׂה	793		do,make
	היות	qal	infc		היה	224		be,become
19: 1	יהי	qal	wci	3ms	היה	224		be,become
	יהי	qal	wci	3ms	היה	224		be,become
	גר	qal	ptc	ms	גור	157		sojourn
	יקח	qal	wci	3ms	לקח	542		take
19: 2	תזנה	qal	wci	3fs	זנה	275		act a harlot
	תלך	qal	wci	3fs	הלך	229		walk,go
	תהי	qal	wci	3fs	היה	224		be,become
19: 3	יקם	qal	wci	3ms	קום	877		arise,stand
	ילך	qal	wci	3ms	הלך	229		walk,go
	דבר	piel	infc		דבר	180		speak
	kהשׁיבו	hiph	infc		שׁוב	996	3ms	bring back
	qהשׁיבה	hiph	infc		שׁוב	996	3fs	bring back
19: 3	תביאהו	hiph	wci	3fs	בוא	97	3ms	bring in
	יראהו	qal	wci	3ms	ראה	906	3ms	see
	ישׂמח	qal	wci	3ms	שׂמח	970		rejoice
	קראתו	qal	infc		קרא	896	3ms	meet,encounter
19: 4	יחזק	qal	wci	3ms	חזק	304		be strong
	ישׁב	qal	wci	3ms	ישׁב	442		sit,dwell
	יאכלו	qal	wci	3mp	אכל	37		eat,devour
	ישׁתו	qal	wci	3mp	שׁתה	1059		drink
	ילינו	qal	wci	3mp	לון	533		lodge,remain
19: 5	יהי	qal	wci	3ms	היה	224		be,become
	ישׁכימו	hiph	wci	3mp	שׁכם	1014		rise early
	יקם	qal	wci	3ms	קום	877		arise,stand
	לכת	qal	infc		הלך	229		walk,go
	יאמר	qal	wci	3ms	אמר	55		say
	סעד	qal	impv	ms	סעד	703		support
	תלכו	qal	impf	2mp	הלך	229		walk,go
19: 6	ישׁבו	qal	wci	3mp	ישׁב	442		sit,dwell
	יאכלו	qal	wci	3mp	אכל	37		eat,devour
	ישׁתו	qal	wci	3mp	שׁתה	1059		drink
	יאמר	qal	wci	3ms	אמר	55		say
	הואל	hiph	impv	ms	יאל	383		be willing
	לין	qal	impv	ms	לון	533		lodge,remain
	יטב	qal	jusm	3ms	יטב	405		be good
19: 7	יקם	qal	wci	3ms	קום	877		arise,stand
	לכת	qal	infc		הלך	229		walk,go
	יפצר	qal	wci	3ms	פצר	823		push
	ישׁב	qal	wci	3ms	שׁוב	996		turn,return
	ילן	qal	wci	3ms	לון	533		lodge,remain
19: 8	ישׁכם	hiph	wci	3ms	שׁכם	1014		rise early
	לכת	qal	infc		הלך	229		walk,go
	יאמר	qal	wci	3ms	אמר	55		say
	סעד	qal	impv	ms	סעד	703		support
	התמהמהו	htpp	impv	mp	מהה	554		tarry
	נטות	qal	infc		נטה	639		stretch,incline
	יאכלו	qal	wci	3mp	אכל	37		eat,devour
19: 9	יקם	qal	wci	3ms	קום	877		arise,stand
	לכת	qal	infc		הלך	229		walk,go
	יאמר	qal	wci	3ms	אמר	55		say
	רפה	qal	pft	3ms	רפה	951		sink,relax
	ערב	qal	infc		ערב	788		grow dark
	לינו	qal	impv	mp	לון	533		lodge,remain
	חנות	qal	infc		חנה	333		decline,encamp
	לין	qal	impv	ms	לון	533		lodge,remain
	ייטב	qal	jusm	3ms	יטב	405		be good
	השׁכמתם	hiph	wcp	2mp	שׁכם	1014		rise early
	הלכת	qal	wcp	2ms	הלך	229		walk,go
19: 10	אבה	qal	pft	3ms	אבה	2		be willing
	לון	qal	infc		לון	533		lodge,remain
	יקם	qal	wci	3ms	קום	877		arise,stand
	ילך	qal	wci	3ms	הלך	229		walk,go
	יבא	qal	wci	3ms	בוא	97		come in
	חבושׁים	qal	pptc	mp	חבשׁ	289		bind
19: 11	רד	qal	pft	3ms	ירד	432		come down
	יאמר	qal	wci	3ms	אמר	55		say

ChVs	Form	Stem	Tnse	PGN	Root	BDB	Sfx	Meaning
19:11	לכה	qal	impv	ms	הלך	229		walk,go
	נסורה	qal	coh	1cp	סור	693		turn aside
	נלין	qal	cohm	1cp	לון	533		lodge,remain
19:12	יאמר	qal	wci	3ms	אמר	55		say
	נסור	qal	impf	1cp	סור	693		turn aside
	עברנו	qal	wcp	1cp	עבר	716		pass over
19:13	יאמר	qal	wci	3ms	אמר	55		say
	לךk	qal	impv	ms	הלך	229		walk,go
	לכהq	qal	impv	ms	הלך	229		walk,go
	נקרבה	qal	coh	1cp	קרב	897		approach
	לנו	qal	wcp	1cp	לון	533		lodge,remain
19:14	יעברו	qal	wci	3mp	עבר	716		pass over
	ילכו	qal	wci	3mp	הלך	229		walk,go
	תבא	qal	wci	3fs	בוא	97		come in
19:15	יסרו	qal	wci	3mp	סור	693		turn aside
	בוא	qal	infc		בוא	97		come in
	לון	qal	infc		לון	533		lodge,remain
	יבא	qal	wci	3ms	בוא	97		come in
	ישב	qal	wci	3ms	ישב	442		sit,dwell
	מאסף	piel	ptc	ms	אסף	62		gather
	לון	qal	infc		לון	533		lodge,remain
19:16	בא	qal	ptc	ms	בוא	97		come in
	גר	qal	ptc	ms	גור	157		sojourn
19:17	ישׂא	qal	wci	3ms	נשׂא	669		lift,carry
	ירא	qal	wci	3ms	ראה	906		see
	ארח	qal	ptc	ms	ארח	72		wander,go
	יאמר	qal	wci	3ms	אמר	55		say
	תלך	qal	impf	2ms	הלך	229		walk,go
	תבוא	qal	impf	2ms	בוא	97		come in
19:18	יאמר	qal	wci	3ms	אמר	55		say
	עברים	qal	ptc	mp	עבר	716		pass over
	אלך	qal	wci	1cs	הלך	229		walk,go
	הלך	qal	ptc	ms	הלך	229		walk,go
	מאסף	piel	ptc	ms	אסף	62		gather
19:20	יאמר	qal	wci	3ms	אמר	55		say
	תלן	qal	jus	2ms	לון	533		lodge,remain
19:21	יביאהו	hiph	wci	3ms	בוא	97	3ms	bring in
	יבולk	qal	wci	3ms	בלל	117		give provender
	יבלq	qal	wci	3ms	בלל	117		give provender
	ירחצו	qal	wci	3mp	רחץ	934		wash,bathe
	יאכלו	qal	wci	3mp	אכל	37		eat,devour
	ישתו	qal	wci	3mp	שתה	1059		drink
19:22	מיטיבים	hiph	ptc	mp	יטב	405		do good
	נסבו	niph	pft	3cp	סבב	685		turn round
	מתדפקים	hith	ptc	mp	דפק	200		beat violently
	יאמרו	qal	wci	3mp	אמר	55		say
	אמר	qal	infc		אמר	55		say
	הוצא	hiph	impv	ms	יצא	422		bring out
	בא	qal	pft	3ms	בוא	97		come in
	נדענו	qal	cohm	1cp	ידע	393	3ms	know
19:23	יצא	qal	wci	3ms	יצא	422		go out
	יאמר	qal	wci	3ms	אמר	55		say
	תרעו	hiph	jusm	2mp	רעע	949		hurt,do evil
	בא	qal	pft	3ms	בוא	97		come in
19:23	תעשׂו	qal	jusm	2mp	עשׂה	793		do,make
19:24	אוציאה	hiph	coh	1cs	יצא	422		bring out
	ענו	qal	impv	mp	ענה	776		be bowed down
	עשׂו	qal	impv	mp	עשׂה	793		do,make
	תעשׂו	qal	impf	2mp	עשׂה	793		do,make
19:25	אבו	qal	pft	3cp	אבה	2		be willing
	שמע	qal	infc		שמע	1033		hear
	יחזק	hiph	wci	3ms	חזק	304		make firm,seize
	יצא	hiph	wci	3ms	יצא	422		bring out
	ידעו	qal	wci	3mp	ידע	393		know
	יתעללו	hith	wci	3mp	עלל	759		busy,vex
	ישלחוה	piel	wci	3mp	שלח	1018	3fs	send away,shoot
	עלות	qal	infc		עלה	748		go up
19:26	תבא	qal	wci	3fs	בוא	97		come in
	פנות	qal	infc		פנה	815		turn
	תפל	qal	wci	3fs	נפל	656		fall
19:27	יקם	qal	wci	3ms	קום	877		arise,stand
	יפתח	qal	wci	3ms	פתח	834		open
	יצא	qal	wci	3ms	יצא	422		go out
	לכת	qal	infc		הלך	229		walk,go
	נפלת	qal	ptc	fs	נפל	656		fall
19:28	יאמר	qal	wci	3ms	אמר	55		say
	קומי	qal	impv	fs	קום	877		arise,stand
	נלכה	qal	coh	1cp	הלך	229		walk,go
	ענה	qal	ptc	ms	ענה	772		answer
	יקחה	qal	wci	3ms	לקח	542	3fs	take
	יקם	qal	wci	3ms	קום	877		arise,stand
	ילך	qal	wci	3ms	הלך	229		walk,go
19:29	יבא	qal	wci	3ms	בוא	97		come in
	יקח	qal	wci	3ms	לקח	542		take
	יחזק	hiph	wci	3ms	חזק	304		make firm,seize
	ינתחה	piel	wci	3ms	נתח	677	3fs	cut in pieces
	ישלחה	piel	wci	3ms	שלח	1018	3fs	send away,shoot
19:30	היה	qal	wcp	3ms	היה	224		be,become
	ראה	qal	ptc	ms	ראה	906		see
	אמר	qal	wcp	3ms	אמר	55		say
	נהיתה	niph	pft	3fs	היה	224		be done
	נראתה	niph	pft	3fs	ראה	906		appear,be seen
	עלות	qal	infc		עלה	748		go up
	שׂימו	qal	impv	mp	שׂים	962		put,set
	עצו	qal	impv	mp	עוץ	734		counsel
	דברו	piel	impv	mp	דבר	180		speak
20:1	יצאו	qal	wci	3mp	יצא	422		go out
	תקהל	niph	wci	3fs	קהל	874		assemble
20:2	יתיצבו	hith	wci	3mp	יצב	426		stand oneself
	שׁלף	qal	ptc	ms	שׁלף	1025		draw out,off
20:3	ישמעו	qal	wci	3mp	שמע	1033		hear
	עלו	qal	pft	3cp	עלה	748		go up
	יאמרו	qal	wci	3mp	אמר	55		say
	דברו	piel	impv	mp	דבר	180		speak
	נהיתה	niph	pft	3fs	היה	224		be done
20:4	יען	qal	wci	3ms	ענה	772		answer
	נרצחה	niph	ptc	fs	רצח	953		be slain
	יאמר	qal	wci	3ms	אמר	55		say

ChVs	Form	Stem	Tnse	PGN	Root	BDB	Sfx	Meaning
20: 4	באתי	qal	pft	1cs	בוא	97		come in
	לון	qal	infc		לון	533		lodge,remain
20: 5	יקמו	qal	wci	3mp	קום	877		arise,stand
	יסבו	qal	wci	3mp	סבב	685		surround
	דמו	piel	pft	3cp	דמה	197		liken,think
	הרג	qal	infc		הרג	246		kill
	ענו	piel	pft	3cp	ענה	776		humble
	תמת	qal	wci	3fs	מות	559		die
20: 6	אחז	qal	wci	1cs	אחז	28		grasp
	אנתחה	piel	wci	1cs	נתח	677	3fs	cut in pieces
	אשלחה	piel	wci	1cs	שלח	1018	3fs	send away,shoot
	עשׂו	qal	pft	3cp	עשׂה	793		do,make
20: 7	הבו	qal	impv	mp	יהב	396		give
20: 8	יקם	qal	wci	3ms	קום	877		arise,stand
	אמר	qal	infc		אמר	55		say
	נלך	qal	impf	1cp	הלך	229		walk,go
	נסור	qal	impf	1cp	סור	693		turn aside
20: 9	נעשׂה	qal	impf	1cp	עשׂה	793		do,make
20: 10	לקחנו	qal	wcp	1cp	לקח	542		take
	קחת	qal	infc		לקח	542		take
	עשׂות	qal	infc		עשׂה	793		do,make
	בואם	qal	infc		בוא	97	3mp	come in
	עשׂה	qal	pft	3ms	עשׂה	793		do,make
20: 11	יאסף	niph	wci	3ms	אסף	62		assemble
20: 12	ישלחו	qal	wci	3mp	שלח	1018		send
	אמר	qal	infc		אמר	55		say
	נהיתה	niph	pft	3fs	היה	224		be done
20: 13	תנו	qal	impv	mp	נתן	678		give,set
	נמיתם	hiph	cohm	1cp	מות	559	3mp	kill
	נבערה	piel	coh	1cp	בער	128		burn,consume
	אבו	qal	pft	3cp	אבה	2		be willing
	שמע	qal	infc		שמע	1033		hear
20: 14	יאספו	niph	wci	3mp	אסף	62		assemble
	צאת	qal	infc		יצא	422		go out
20: 15	יתפקדו	hith	wci	3mp	פקד	823		be mustered
	שלף	qal	ptc	ms	שלף	1025		draw out,off
	ישבי	qal	ptc	mp	ישב	442		sit,dwell
	התפקדו	hith	pft	3cp	פקד	823		be mustered
	בחור	qal	pptc	ms	בחר	103		choose
20: 16	בחור	qal	pptc	ms	בחר	103		choose
	קלע	qal	ptc	ms	קלע	887		sling,hurl
	יחטא	hiph	impf	3ms	חטא	306		cause to sin
20: 17	התפקדו	hith	pft	3cp	פקד	823		be mustered
	שלף	qal	ptc	ms	שלף	1025		draw out,off
20: 18	יקמו	qal	wci	3mp	קום	877		arise,stand
	יעלו	qal	wci	3mp	עלה	748		go up
	ישאלו	qal	wci	3mp	שאל	981		ask,borrow
	יאמרו	qal	wci	3mp	אמר	55		say
	יעלה	qal	impf	3ms	עלה	748		go up
	יאמר	qal	wci	3ms	אמר	55		say
20: 19	יקומו	qal	wci	3mp	קום	877		arise,stand
	יחנו	qal	wci	3mp	חנה	333		decline,encamp
20: 20	יצא	qal	wci	3ms	יצא	422		go out
	יערכו	qal	wci	3mp	ערך	789		set in order
20: 21	יצאו	qal	wci	3mp	יצא	422		go out
	ישחיתו	hiph	wci	3mp	שחת	1007		spoil,ruin
20: 22	יתחזק	hith	wci	3ms	חזק	304		strengthen self
	יספו	hiph	wci	3mp	יסף	414		add,do again
	ערך	qal	infc		ערך	789		set in order
	ערכו	qal	pft	3cp	ערך	789		set in order
20: 23	יעלו	qal	wci	3mp	עלה	748		go up
	יבכו	qal	wci	3mp	בכה	113		weep
	ישאלו	qal	wci	3mp	שאל	981		ask,borrow
	אמר	qal	infc		אמר	55		say
	אוסיף	hiph	impf	1cs	יסף	414		add,do again
	גשת	qal	infc		נגש	620		draw near
	יאמר	qal	wci	3ms	אמר	55		say
	עלו	qal	impv	mp	עלה	748		go up
20: 24	יקרבו	qal	wci	3mp	קרב	897		approach
20: 25	יצא	qal	wci	3ms	יצא	422		go out
	קראתם	qal	infc		קרא	896	3mp	meet,encounter
	ישחיתו	hiph	wci	3mp	שחת	1007		spoil,ruin
	שלפי	qal	ptc	mp	שלף	1025		draw out,off
20: 26	יעלו	qal	wci	3mp	עלה	748		go up
	יבאו	qal	wci	3mp	בוא	97		come in
	יבכו	qal	wci	3mp	בכה	113		weep
	ישבו	qal	wci	3mp	ישב	442		sit,dwell
	יצומו	qal	wci	3mp	צום	847		fast
	יעלו	hiph	wci	3mp	עלה	748		bring up,offer
20: 27	ישאלו	qal	wci	3mp	שאל	981		ask,borrow
20: 28	עמד	qal	ptc	ms	עמד	763		stand,stop
	אמר	qal	infc		אמר	55		say
	אוסף	hiph	impf	1cs	יסף	414		add,do again
	צאת	qal	infc		יצא	422		go out
	אחדל	qal	impf	1cs	חדל	292		cease
	יאמר	qal	wci	3ms	אמר	55		say
	עלו	qal	impv	mp	עלה	748		go up
	אתננו	qal	impf	1cs	נתן	678	3ms	give,set
20: 29	ישׂם	qal	wci	3ms	שׂים	962		put,set
	ארבים	qal	ptc	mp	ארב	70		lie in wait
20: 30	יעלו	qal	wci	3mp	עלה	748		go up
	יערכו	qal	wci	3mp	ערך	789		set in order
20: 31	יצאו	qal	wci	3mp	יצא	422		go out
	קראת	qal	infc		קרא	896		meet,encounter
	הנתקו	hoph	pft	3cp	נתק	683		be drawn away
	יחלו	hiph	wci	3mp	חלל	320		begin,profane
	הכות	hiph	infc		נכה	645		smite
	עלה	qal	ptc	fs	עלה	748		go up
20: 32	יאמרו	qal	wci	3mp	אמר	55		say
	נגפים	niph	ptc	mp	נגף	619		be smitten
	אמרו	qal	pft	3cp	אמר	55		say
	ננוסה	qal	coh	1cp	נוס	630		flee,escape
	נתקנהו	qal	wcp	1cp	נתק	683	3ms	draw away,pull
20: 33	קמו	qal	pft	3cp	קום	877		arise,stand
	יערכו	qal	wci	3mp	ערך	789		set in order
	ארב	qal	ptc	ms	ארב	70		lie in wait
	מגיח	hiph	ptc	ms	גיח	161		burst forth
20: 34	יבאו	qal	wci	3mp	בוא	97		come in

ChVs	Form	Stem	Tnse	PGN	Root	BDB	Sfx	Meaning
20:34	בחור	qal	pptc	ms	בחר	103		choose
	כבדה	qal	pft	3fs	כבד	457		be heavy
	ידעו	qal	pft	3cp	ידע	393		know
	נגעת	qal	ptc	fs	נגע	619		touch,strike
20:35	יגף	qal	wci	3ms	נגף	619		smite,strike
	ישחיתו	hiph	wci	3mp	שחת	1007		spoil,ruin
	שלף	qal	ptc	ms	שלף	1025		draw out,off
20:36	יראו	qal	wci	3mp	ראה	906		see
	נגפו	niph	pft	3cp	נגף	619		be smitten
	יתנו	qal	wci	3mp	נתן	678		give,set
	בטחו	qal	pft	3cp	בטח	105		trust
	ארב	qal	ptc	ms	ארב	70		lie in wait
	שמו	qal	pft	3cp	שים	962		put,set
20:37	ארב	qal	ptc	ms	ארב	70		lie in wait
	החישו	hiph	pft	3cp	חוש	301		show haste
	יפשטו	qal	wci	3mp	פשט	832		strip off
	ימשך	qal	wci	3ms	משך	604		draw,pull
	ארב	qal	ptc	ms	ארב	70		lie in wait
	יך	hiph	wci	3ms	נכה	645		smite
20:38	היה	qal	pft	3ms	היה	224		be,become
	ארב	qal	ptc	ms	ארב	70		lie in wait
	הרב	hiph	impv	ms	רבה	915		make many
	העלותם	hiph	infc		עלה	748	3mp	bring up,offer
20:39	יהפך	qal	wci	3ms	הפך	245		turn,overturn
	החל	hiph	pft	3ms	חלל	320		begin,profane
	הכות	hiph	infc		נכה	645		smite
	אמרו	qal	pft	3cp	אמר	55		say
	נגוף	niph	infa		נגף	619		be smitten
	נגף	niph	ptc	ms	נגף	619		be smitten
20:40	החלה	hiph	pft	3fs	חלל	320		begin,profane
	עלות	qal	infc		עלה	748		go up
	יפן	qal	wci	3ms	פנה	815		turn
	עלה	qal	pft	3ms	עלה	748		go up
20:41	הפך	qal	pft	3ms	הפך	245		turn,overturn
	יבהל	niph	wci	3ms	בהל	96		be disturbed
	ראה	qal	pft	3ms	ראה	906		see
	נגעה	qal	pft	3fs	נגע	619		touch,strike
20:42	יפנו	qal	wci	3mp	פנה	815		turn
	הדביקתהו	hiph	pft	3fs	דבק	179	3ms	cause to cling
	משחיתים	hiph	ptc	mp	שחת	1007		spoil,ruin
20:43	כתרו	piel	pft	3cp	כתר	509		surround,wait
	הרדיפהו	hiph	pft	3cp	רדף	922	3ms	chase
	הדריכהו	hiph	pft	3cp	דרך	201	3ms	tread,lead
20:44	יפלו	qal	wci	3mp	נפל	656		fall
20:45	יפנו	qal	wci	3mp	פנה	815		turn
	ינסו	qal	wci	3mp	נוס	630		flee,escape
	יעללהו	poel	wci	3mp	עלל	759	3ms	vex
	ידביקו	hiph	wci	3mp	דבק	179		cause to cling
	יכו	hiph	wci	3mp	נכה	645		smite
20:46	יהי	qal	wci	3ms	היה	224		be,become
	נפלים	qal	ptc	mp	נפל	656		fall
	שלף	qal	ptc	ms	שלף	1025		draw out,off
20:47	יפנו	qal	wci	3mp	פנה	815		turn
	ינסו	qal	wci	3mp	נוס	630		flee,escape
20:47	ישבו	qal	wci	3mp	ישב	442		sit,dwell
20:48	שבו	qal	pft	3cp	שוב	996		turn,return
	יכום	hiph	wci	3mp	נכה	645	3mp	smite
	נמצא	niph	ptc	ms	מצא	592		be found
	נמצאות	niph	ptc	fp	מצא	592		be found
	שלחו	piel	pft	3cp	שלח	1018		send away,shoot
21:1	נשבע	niph	pft	3ms	שבע	989		swear
	אמר	qal	infc		אמר	55		say
	יתן	qal	impf	3ms	נתן	678		give,set
21:2	יבא	qal	wci	3ms	בוא	97		come in
	ישבו	qal	wci	3mp	ישב	442		sit,dwell
	ישאו	qal	wci	3mp	נשא	669		lift,carry
	יבכו	qal	wci	3mp	בכה	113		weep
21:3	יאמרו	qal	wci	3mp	אמר	55		say
	היתה	qal	pft	3fs	היה	224		be,become
	הפקד	niph	infc		פקד	823		be visited
21:4	יהי	qal	wci	3ms	היה	224		be,become
	ישכימו	hiph	wci	3mp	שכם	1014		rise early
	יבנו	qal	wci	3mp	בנה	124		build
	יעלו	hiph	wci	3mp	עלה	748		bring up,offer
21:5	יאמרו	qal	wci	3mp	אמר	55		say
	עלה	qal	pft	3ms	עלה	748		go up
	היתה	qal	pft	3fs	היה	224		be,become
	עלה	qal	pft	3ms	עלה	748		go up
	אמר	qal	infc		אמר	55		say
	מות	qal	infa		מות	559		die
	יומת	hoph	impf	3ms	מות	559		be killed
21:6	ינחמו	niph	wci	3mp	נחם	636		be sorry
	יאמרו	qal	wci	3mp	אמר	55		say
	נגדע	niph	pft	3ms	גדע	154		be hewn off
21:7	נעשה	qal	impf	1cp	עשה	793		do,make
	נותרים	niph	ptc	mp	יתר	451		be left,remain
	נשבענו	niph	pft	1cp	שבע	989		swear
	תת	qal	infc		נתן	678		give,set
21:8	יאמרו	qal	wci	3mp	אמר	55		say
	עלה	qal	pft	3ms	עלה	748		go up
	בא	qal	pft	3ms	בוא	97		come in
21:9	יתפקד	hith	wci	3ms	פקד	823		be mustered
	יושבי	qal	ptc	mp	ישב	442		sit,dwell
21:10	ישלחו	qal	wci	3mp	שלח	1018		send
	יצוו	piel	wci	3mp	צוה	845		command
	אמר	qal	infc		אמר	55		say
	לכו	qal	impv	mp	הלך	229		walk,go
	הכיתם	hiph	wcp	2mp	נכה	645		smite
	יושבי	qal	ptc	mp	ישב	442		sit,dwell
21:11	תעשו	qal	impf	2mp	עשה	793		do,make
	ידעת	qal	ptc	fs	ידע	393		know
	תחרימו	hiph	impf	2mp	חרם	355		ban,destroy
21:12	ימצאו	qal	wci	3mp	מצא	592		find
	יושבי	qal	ptc	mp	ישב	442		sit,dwell
	ידעה	qal	pft	3fs	ידע	393		know
	יביאו	hiph	wci	3mp	בוא	97		bring in
21:13	ישלחו	qal	wci	3mp	שלח	1018		send
	ידברו	piel	wci	3mp	דבר	180		speak

ChVs	Form	Stem	Tnse	PGN	Root	BDB	Sfx	Meaning
21:13	יקראו	qal	wci	3mp	קרא	894		call,proclaim
21:14	ישב	qal	wci	3ms	שׁוב	996		turn,return
	יתנו	qal	wci	3mp	נתן	678		give,set
	חיו	piel	pft	3cp	חיה	310		preserve,revive
	מצאו	qal	pft	3cp	מצא	592		find
21:15	נחם	niph	pft	3ms	נחם	636		be sorry
	עשׂה	qal	pft	3ms	עשׂה	793		do,make
21:16	יאמרו	qal	wci	3mp	אמר	55		say
	נעשׂה	qal	impf	1cp	עשׂה	793		do,make
	נותרים	niph	ptc	mp	יתר	451		be left,remain
	נשמדה	niph	pft	3fs	שׁמד	1029		be exterminated
21:17	יאמרו	qal	wci	3mp	אמר	55		say
	ימחה	niph	impf	3ms	מחה	562		be wiped out
21:18	נוכל	qal	impf	1cp	יכל	407		be able
	תת	qal	infc		נתן	678		give,set
	נשבעו	niph	pft	3cp	שׁבע	989		swear
	אמר	qal	infc		אמר	55		say
	ארור	qal	pptc	ms	ארר	76		curse
	נתן	qal	ptc	ms	נתן	678		give,set
21:19	יאמרו	qal	wci	3mp	אמר	55		say
	עלה	qal	ptc	fs	עלה	748		go up
21:20	יצוk	piel	wci	3ms	צוה	845		command
	יצווq	piel	wci	3mp	צוה	845		command
	אמר	qal	infc		אמר	55		say
	לכו	qal	impv	mp	הלך	229		walk,go
	ארבתם	qal	wcp	2mp	ארב	70		lie in wait
21:21	ראיתם	qal	wcp	2mp	ראה	906		see
	יצאו	qal	impf	3mp	יצא	422		go out
	חול	qal	infc		חול	296		dance,writhe
	יצאתם	qal	wcp	2mp	יצא	422		go out
	חטפתם	qal	wcp	2mp	חטף	310		seize
	הלכתם	qal	wcp	2mp	הלך	229		walk,go
21:22	היה	qal	wcp	3ms	היה	224		be,become
	יבאו	qal	impf	3mp	בוא	97		come in
	רובk	qal	infc		ריב	936		strive,contend
	ריבq	qal	infc		ריב	936		strive,contend
	אמרנו	qal	wcp	1cp	אמר	55		say
	חנונו	qal	impv	mp	חנן	335	1cp	show favor
	לקחנו	qal	pft	1cp	לקח	542		take
	נתתם	qal	pft	2mp	נתן	678		give,set
	תאשמו	qal	impf	2mp	אשׁם	79		offend
21:23	יעשׂו	qal	wci	3mp	עשׂה	793		do,make
	ישׂאו	qal	wci	3mp	נשׂא	669		lift,carry
	מחללות	pol	ptc	fp	חול	296		dance,writhe
	גזלו	qal	pft	3cp	גזל	159		tear away,rob
	ילכו	qal	wci	3mp	הלך	229		walk,go
	ישובו	qal	wci	3mp	שׁוב	996		turn,return
	יבנו	qal	wci	3mp	בנה	124		build
	ישבו	qal	wci	3mp	ישׁב	442		sit,dwell
21:24	יתהלכו	hith	wci	3mp	הלך	229		walk to and fro
	יצאו	qal	wci	3mp	יצא	422		go out
21:25	יעשׂה	qal	impf	3ms	עשׂה	793		do,make

RUTH

ChVs	Form	Stem	Tnse	PGN	Root	BDB	Sfx	Meaning
1:1	יהי	qal	wci	3ms	היה	224		be,become
	שׁפט	qal	infc		שׁפט	1047		judge
	שׁפטים	qal	ptc	mp	שׁפט	1047		judge
	יהי	qal	wci	3ms	היה	224		be,become
	ילך	qal	wci	3ms	הלך	229		walk,go
	גור	qal	infc		גור	157		sojourn
1:2	יבאו	qal	wci	3mp	בוא	97		come in
	יהיו	qal	wci	3mp	היה	224		be,become
1:3	ימת	qal	wci	3ms	מות	559		die
	תשאר	niph	wci	3fs	שׁאר	983		be left
1:4	ישׂאו	qal	wci	3mp	נשׂא	669		lift,carry
	ישבו	qal	wci	3mp	ישׁב	442		sit,dwell
1:5	ימותו	qal	wci	3mp	מות	559		die
	תשאר	niph	wci	3fs	שׁאר	983		be left
1:6	תקם	qal	wci	3fs	קום	877		arise,stand
	תשב	qal	wci	3fs	שׁוב	996		turn,return
	שׁמעה	qal	pft	3fs	שׁמע	1033		hear
	פקד	qal	pft	3ms	פקד	823		attend to,visit
	תת	qal	infc		נתן	678		give,set
1:7	תצא	qal	wci	3fs	יצא	422		go out
	היתה	qal	pft	3fs	היה	224		be,become
	תלכנה	qal	wci	3fp	הלך	229		walk,go
	שׁוב	qal	infc		שׁוב	996		turn,return
1:8	תאמר	qal	wci	3fs	אמר	55		say
	לכנה	qal	impv	fp	הלך	229		walk,go
	שׁבנה	qal	impv	fp	שׁוב	996		turn,return
	יעשׂהk	qal	jusm	3ms	עשׂה	793		do,make
	יעשׂq	qal	jus	3ms	עשׂה	793		do,make
	עשׂיתם	qal	pft	2mp	עשׂה	793		do,make
	מתים	qal	ptc	mp	מות	559		die
1:9	יתן	qal	jusm	3ms	נתן	678		give,set
	מצאן	qal	impv	fp	מצא	592		find
	תשק	qal	wci	3fs	נשׁק	676		kiss
	תשׂאנה	qal	wci	3fp	נשׂא	669		lift,carry
	תבכינה	qal	wci	3fp	בכה	113		weep
1:10	תאמרנה	qal	wci	3fp	אמר	55		say
	נשוב	qal	impf	1cp	שׁוב	996		turn,return
1:11	תאמר	qal	wci	3fs	אמר	55		say
	שׁבנה	qal	impv	fp	שׁוב	996		turn,return
	תלכנה	qal	impf	2fp	הלך	229		walk,go
	היו	qal	wcp	3cp	היה	224		be,become
1:12	שׁבנה	qal	impv	fp	שׁוב	996		turn,return
	לכן	qal	impv	fp	הלך	229		walk,go
	זקנתי	qal	pft	1cs	זקן	278		be old
	היות	qal	infc		היה	224		be,become
	אמרתי	qal	pft	1cs	אמר	55		say
	הייתי	qal	pft	1cs	היה	224		be,become
	ילדתי	qal	pft	1cs	ילד	408		bear,beget
1:13	תשׂברנה	piel	impf	2fp	שׂבר	960		wait,hope
	יגדלו	qal	impf	3mp	גדל	152		be great,grow
	תעגנה	niph	impf	2fp	עגן	723		shut oneself of
	היות	qal	infc		היה	224		be,become
	יצאה	qal	pft	3fs	יצא	422		go out
1:14	תשׂנה	qal	wci	3fp	נשׂא	669		lift,carry

ChVs	Form	Stem	Tnse	PGN	Root	BDB	Sfx	Meaning
1:14	תבכינה	qal	wci	3fp	בכה	113		weep
	תשק	qal	wci	3fs	נשק	676		kiss
	דבקה	qal	pft	3fs	דבק	179		cling,cleave
1:15	תאמר	qal	wci	3fs	אמר	55		say
	שׁבה	qal	pft	3fs	שׁוב	996		turn,return
	שׁובי	qal	impv	fs	שׁוב	996		turn,return
1:16	תאמר	qal	wci	3fs	אמר	55		say
	תפגעי	qal	jusm	2fs	פגע	803		meet,encounter
	עזבך	qal	infc		עזב	736	2fs	leave,loose
	שׁוב	qal	infc		שׁוב	996		turn,return
	תלכי	qal	impf	2fs	הלך	229		walk,go
	אלך	qal	impf	1cs	הלך	229		walk,go
	תליני	qal	impf	2fs	לון	533		lodge,remain
	אלין	qal	impf	1cs	לון	533		lodge,remain
1:17	תמותי	qal	impf	2fs	מות	559		die
	אמות	qal	impf	1cs	מות	559		die
	אקבר	niph	impf	1cs	קבר	868		be buried
	יעשׂה	qal	jusm	3ms	עשׂה	793		do,make
	יסיף	hiph	jusm	3ms	יסף	414		add,do again
	יפריד	hiph	impf	3ms	פרד	825		divide
1:18	תרא	qal	wci	3fs	ראה	906		see
	מתאמצת	hith	ptc	fs	אמץ	54		strengthen self
	לכת	qal	infc		הלך	229		walk,go
	תחדל	qal	wci	3fs	חדל	292		cease
	דבר	piel	infc		דבר	180		speak
1:19	תלכנה	qal	wci	3fp	הלך	229		walk,go
	באנה	qal	infc		בוא	97	3fp	come in
	יהי	qal	wci	3ms	היה	224		be,become
	באנה	qal	infc		בוא	97	3fp	come in
	תהם	niph	wci	3fs	הום	223		be agitated
	תאמרנה	qal	wci	3fp	אמר	55		say
1:20	תאמר	qal	wci	3fs	אמר	55		say
	תקראנה	qal	jusm	2fp	קרא	894		call,proclaim
	קראן	qal	impv	fp	קרא	894		call,proclaim
	המר	hiph	pft	3ms	מרר	600		make bitter
1:21	הלכתי	qal	pft	1cs	הלך	229		walk,go
	השׁיבני	hiph	pft	3ms	שׁוב	996	1cs	bring back
	תקראנה	qal	impf	2fp	קרא	894		call,proclaim
	ענה	qal	pft	3ms	ענה	776		be bowed down
	הרע	hiph	pft	3ms	רעע	949		hurt,do evil
1:22	תשׁב	qal	wci	3fs	שׁוב	996		turn,return
	שׁבה	qal	pft	3fs	שׁוב	996		turn,return
	באו	qal	pft	3cp	בוא	97		come in
2:1	מידעk	pual	ptc	ms	ידע	393		be known
2:2	תאמר	qal	wci	3fs	אמר	55		say
	אלכה	qal	coh	1cs	הלך	229		walk,go
	אלקטה	piel	coh	1cs	לקט	544		gather
	אמצא	qal	impf	1cs	מצא	592		find
	תאמר	qal	wci	3fs	אמר	55		say
	לכי	qal	impv	fs	הלך	229		walk,go
2:3	תלך	qal	wci	3fs	הלך	229		walk,go
	תבוא	qal	wci	3fs	בוא	97		come in
	תלקט	piel	wci	3fs	לקט	544		gather
	קצרים	qal	ptc	mp	קצר	894		reap,harvest
2:3	יקר	qal	wci	3ms	קרה	899		encounter,meet
2:4	בא	qal	ptc	ms	בוא	97		come in
	יאמר	qal	wci	3ms	אמר	55		say
	קוצרים	qal	ptc	mp	קצר	894		reap,harvest
	יאמרו	qal	wci	3mp	אמר	55		say
	יברכך	piel	jusm	3ms	ברך	138	2ms	bless
2:5	יאמר	qal	wci	3ms	אמר	55		say
	נצב	niph	ptc	ms	נצב	662		stand
	קוצרים	qal	ptc	mp	קצר	894		reap,harvest
2:6	יען	qal	wci	3ms	ענה	772		answer
	נצב	niph	ptc	ms	נצב	662		stand
	קוצרים	qal	ptc	mp	קצר	894		reap,harvest
	יאמר	qal	wci	3ms	אמר	55		say
	שׁבה	qal	pft	3fs	שׁוב	996		turn,return
2:7	תאמר	qal	wci	3fs	אמר	55		say
	אלקטה	piel	coh	1cs	לקט	544		gather
	אספתי	qal	wcp	1cs	אסף	62		gather
	קוצרים	qal	ptc	mp	קצר	894		reap,harvest
	תבוא	qal	wci	3fs	בוא	97		come in
	תעמוד	qal	wci	3fs	עמד	763		stand,stop
	שׁבתה	qal	infc		ישׁב	442	3fs	sit,dwell
2:8	יאמר	qal	wci	3ms	אמר	55		say
	שׁמעת	qal	pft	2fs	שׁמע	1033		hear
	תלכי	qal	jusm	2fs	הלך	229		walk,go
	לקט	qal	infc		לקט	544		pick,gather
	תעבורי	qal	impf	2fs	עבר	716		pass over
	תדבקין	qal	impf	2fs	דבק	179		cling,cleave
2:9	יקצרון	qal	impf	3mp	קצר	894		reap,harvest
	הלכת	qal	wcp	2fs	הלך	229		walk,go
	צויתי	piel	pft	1cs	צוה	845		command
	נגעך	qal	infc		נגע	619	2fs	touch,strike
	צמת	qal	wcp	2fs	צמא	854		be thirsty
	הלכת	qal	wcp	2fs	הלך	229		walk,go
	שׁתית	qal	wcp	2fs	שׁתה	1059		drink
	ישׁאבון	qal	impf	3mp	שׁאב	980		draw (water)
2:10	תפל	qal	wci	3fs	נפל	656		fall
	תשׁתחו	hish	wci	3fs	חוה	1005		bow down
	תאמר	qal	wci	3fs	אמר	55		say
	מצאתי	qal	pft	1cs	מצא	592		find
	הכירני	hiph	infc		נכר	647	1cs	regard,notice
2:11	יען	qal	wci	3ms	ענה	772		answer
	יאמר	qal	wci	3ms	אמר	55		say
	הגד	hoph	infa		נגד	616		be told
	הגד	hoph	pft	3ms	נגד	616		be told
	עשׂית	qal	pft	2fs	עשׂה	793		do,make
	תעזבי	qal	wci	2fs	עזב	736		leave,loose
	תלכי	qal	wci	2fs	הלך	229		walk,go
	ידעת	qal	pft	2fs	ידע	393		know
2:12	ישׁלם	piel	jusm	3ms	שׁלם	1022		finish,reward
	תהי	qal	jus	3fs	היה	224		be,become
	באת	qal	pft	2fs	בוא	97		come in
	חסות	qal	infc		חסה	340		seek refuge
2:13	תאמר	qal	wci	3fs	אמר	55		say
	אמצא	qal	impf	1cs	מצא	592		find

ChVs	Form	Stem	Tnse	PGN	Root	BDB	Sfx	Meaning
2:13	נחמתני	piel	pft	2ms	נחם	636	1cs	comfort
	דברת	piel	pft	2ms	דבר	180		speak
	אהיה	qal	impf	1cs	היה	224		be,become
2:14	יאמר	qal	wci	3ms	אמר	55		say
	גשי	qal	impv	fs	נגשׁ	620		draw near
	אכלת	qal	wcp	2fs	אכל	37		eat,devour
	טבלת	qal	wcp	2fs	טבל	371		dip
	תשב	qal	wci	3fs	ישׁב	442		sit,dwell
	קוצרים	qal	ptc	mp	קצר	894		reap,harvest
	יצבט	qal	wci	3ms	צבט	840		reach,hold out
	תאכל	qal	wci	3fs	אכל	37		eat,devour
	תשׂבע	qal	wci	3fs	שׂבע	959		be sated
	תתר	hiph	wci	3fs	יתר	451		leave,spare
2:15	תקם	qal	wci	3fs	קום	877		arise,stand
	לקט	piel	infc		לקט	544		gather
	יצו	piel	wci	3ms	צוה	845		command
	אמר	qal	infc		אמר	55		say
	תלקט	piel	impf	3fs	לקט	544		gather
	תכלימוה	hiph	impf	2mp	כלם	483	3fs	humiliate
2:16	שׁל	qal	infa		שׁלל	1021		draw out
	תשׁלו	qal	impf	2mp	שׁלל	1021		draw out
	עזבתם	qal	wcp	2mp	עזב	736		leave,loose
	לקטה	piel	wcp	3fs	לקט	544		gather
	תגערו	qal	impf	2mp	גער	172		rebuke
2:17	תלקט	piel	wci	3fs	לקט	544		gather
	תחבט	qal	wci	3fs	חבט	286		beat out
	לקטה	piel	pft	3fs	לקט	544		gather
	יהי	qal	wci	3ms	היה	224		be,become
2:18	תשׂא	qal	wci	3fs	נשׂא	669		lift,carry
	תבוא	qal	wci	3fs	בוא	97		come in
	תרא	qal	wci	3fs	ראה	906		see
	לקטה	piel	pft	3fs	לקט	544		gather
	תוצא	hiph	wci	3fs	יצא	422		bring out
	תתן	qal	wci	3fs	נתן	678		give,set
	הותרה	hiph	pft	3fs	יתר	451		leave,spare
2:19	תאמר	qal	wci	3fs	אמר	55		say
	לקטת	piel	pft	2fs	לקט	544		gather
	עשׂית	qal	pft	2fs	עשׂה	793		do,make
	יהי	qal	jus	3ms	היה	224		be,become
	מכירך	hiph	ptc	ms	נכר	647	2fs	regard,notice
	ברוך	qal	pptc	ms	ברך	138		kneel,bless
	תגד	hiph	wci	3fs	נגד	616		declare,tell
	עשׂתה	qal	pft	3fs	עשׂה	793		do,make
	תאמר	qal	wci	3fs	אמר	55		say
	עשׂיתי	qal	pft	1cs	עשׂה	793		do,make
2:20	תאמר	qal	wci	3fs	אמר	55		say
	ברוך	qal	pptc	ms	ברך	138		kneel,bless
	עזב	qal	pft	3ms	עזב	736		leave,loose
	מתים	qal	ptc	mp	מות	559		die
	תאמר	qal	wci	3fs	אמר	55		say
	גאלנו	qal	ptc	ms	גאל	145	1cp	redeem
2:21	תאמר	qal	wci	3fs	אמר	55		say
	אמר	qal	pft	3ms	אמר	55		say
	תדבקין	qal	impf	2fs	דבק	179		cling,cleave
2:21	כלו	piel	pft	3cp	כלה	477		complete,finish
2:22	תאמר	qal	wci	3fs	אמר	55		say
	תצאי	qal	impf	2fs	יצא	422		go out
	יפגעו	qal	impf	3mp	פגע	803		meet,encounter
2:23	תדבק	qal	wci	3fs	דבק	179		cling,cleave
	לקט	piel	infc		לקט	544		gather
	כלות	qal	infc		כלה	477		finished,spent
	תשב	qal	wci	3fs	ישׁב	442		sit,dwell
3:1	תאמר	qal	wci	3fs	אמר	55		say
	אבקשׁ	piel	impf	1cs	בקשׁ	134		seek
	ייטב	qal	impf	3ms	יטב	405		be good
3:2	היית	qal	pft	2fs	היה	224		be,become
	זרה	qal	ptc	ms	זרה	279		scatter
3:3	רחצת	qal	wcp	2fs	רחץ	934		wash,bathe
	סכת	qal	wcp	2fs	סוך	691		anoint,pour
	שׂמת	qal	wcp	2fs	שׂים	962		put,set
	ירדתיk	qal	wcp	2fs	ירד	432		come down
	ירדתq	qal	wcp	2fs	ירד	432		come down
	תודעי	niph	jusm	2fs	ידע	393		be made known
	כלתו	piel	infc		כלה	477	3ms	complete,finish
	אכל	qal	infc		אכל	37		eat,devour
	שׁתות	qal	infc		שׁתה	1059		drink
3:4	יהי	qal	jus	3ms	היה	224		be,become
	שׁכבו	qal	infc		שׁכב	1011	3ms	lie,lie down
	ידעת	qal	wcp	2fs	ידע	393		know
	ישׁכב	qal	impf	3ms	שׁכב	1011		lie,lie down
	באת	qal	wcp	2fs	בוא	97		come in
	גלית	piel	wcp	2fs	גלה	162		uncover
	שׁכבתיk	qal	wcp	2fs	שׁכב	1011		lie,lie down
	שׁכבתq	qal	wcp	2fs	שׁכב	1011		lie,lie down
	יגיד	hiph	impf	3ms	נגד	616		declare,tell
	תעשׂין	qal	impf	2fs	עשׂה	793		do,make
3:5	תאמר	qal	wci	3fs	אמר	55		say
	תאמרי	qal	impf	2fs	אמר	55		say
	אעשׂה	qal	impf	1cs	עשׂה	793		do,make
3:6	תרד	qal	wci	3fs	ירד	432		come down
	תעשׂ	qal	wci	3fs	עשׂה	793		do,make
	צותה	piel	pft	3fs	צוה	845	3fs	command
3:7	יאכל	qal	wci	3ms	אכל	37		eat,devour
	ישׁת	qal	wci	3ms	שׁתה	1059		drink
	ייטב	qal	wci	3ms	יטב	405		be good
	יבא	qal	wci	3ms	בוא	97		come in
	שׁכב	qal	infc		שׁכב	1011		lie,lie down
	תבא	qal	wci	3fs	בוא	97		come in
	תגל	piel	wci	3fs	גלה	162		uncover
	תשׁכב	qal	wci	3fs	שׁכב	1011		lie,lie down
3:8	יהי	qal	wci	3ms	היה	224		be,become
	יחרד	qal	wci	3ms	חרד	353		tremble
	ילפת	niph	wci	3ms	לפת	542		turn oneself
	שׁכבת	qal	ptc	fs	שׁכב	1011		lie,lie down
3:9	יאמר	qal	wci	3ms	אמר	55		say
	תאמר	qal	wci	3fs	אמר	55		say
	פרשׂת	qal	wcp	2ms	פרשׂ	831		spread out
	גאל	qal	ptc	ms	גאל	145		redeem

ChVs	Form	Stem	Tnse	PGN	Root	BDB	Sfx	Meaning
3:10	יאמר	qal	wci	3ms	אמר	55		say
	ברוכה	qal	pptc	fs	ברך	138		kneel,bless
	היטבת	hiph	pft	2fs	יטב	405		do good
	לכת	qal	infc		הלך	229		walk,go
3:11	תיראי	qal	jusm	2fs	ירא	431		fear
	תאמרי	qal	impf	2fs	אמר	55		say
	אעשה	qal	impf	1cs	עשה	793		do,make
	יודע	qal	ptc	ms	ידע	393		know
3:12	גאל	qal	ptc	ms	גאל	145		redeem
	גאל	qal	ptc	ms	גאל	145		redeem
3:13	ליני	qal	impv	fs	לון	533		lodge,remain
	היה	qal	wcp	3ms	היה	224		be,become
	יגאלך	qal	impf	3ms	גאל	145	2fs	redeem
	יגאל	qal	jusm	3ms	גאל	145		redeem
	יחפץ	qal	impf	3ms	חפץ	342		delight in
	גאלך	qal	infc		גאל	145	2fs	redeem
	גאלתיך	qal	wcp	1cs	גאל	145	2fs	redeem
	שכבי	qal	impv	fs	שכב	1011		lie,lie down
3:14	תשכב	qal	wci	3fs	שכב	1011		lie,lie down
	תקם	qal	wci	3fs	קום	877		arise,stand
	יכיר	hiph	impf	3ms	נכר	647		regard,notice
	יאמר	qal	wci	3ms	אמר	55		say
	יודע	niph	jusm	3ms	ידע	393		be made known
	באה	qal	pft	3fs	בוא	97		come in
3:15	יאמר	qal	wci	3ms	אמר	55		say
	הבי	qal	impv	fs	יהב	396		give
	אחזי	qal	impv	fs	אחז	28		grasp
	תאחז	qal	wci	3fs	אחז	28		grasp
	ימד	qal	wci	3ms	מדד	551		measure
	ישת	qal	wci	3ms	שית	1011		put,set
	יבא	qal	wci	3ms	בוא	97		come in
3:16	תבוא	qal	wci	3fs	בוא	97		come in
	תאמר	qal	wci	3fs	אמר	55		say
	תגד	hiph	wci	3fs	נגד	616		declare,tell
	עשה	qal	pft	3ms	עשה	793		do,make
3:17	תאמר	qal	wci	3fs	אמר	55		say
	נתן	qal	pft	3ms	נתן	678		give,set
	אמר	qal	pft	3ms	אמר	55		say
	תבואי	qal	jusm	2fs	בוא	97		come in
3:18	תאמר	qal	wci	3fs	אמר	55		say
	שבי	qal	impv	fs	ישב	442		sit,dwell
	תדעין	qal	impf	2fs	ידע	393		know
	יפל	qal	impf	3ms	נפל	656		fall
	ישקט	qal	impf	3ms	שקט	1052		be quiet
	כלה	piel	pft	3ms	כלה	477		complete,finish
4:1	עלה	qal	pft	3ms	עלה	748		go up
	ישב	qal	wci	3ms	ישב	442		sit,dwell
	גאל	qal	ptc	ms	גאל	145		redeem
	עבר	qal	ptc	ms	עבר	716		pass over
	דבר	piel	pft	3ms	דבר	180		speak
	יאמר	qal	wci	3ms	אמר	55		say
	סורה	qal	impv	ms	סור	693		turn aside
	שבה	qal	impv	ms	ישב	442		sit,dwell
	יסר	qal	wci	3ms	סור	693		turn aside

ChVs	Form	Stem	Tnse	PGN	Root	BDB	Sfx	Meaning
4:1	ישב	qal	wci	3ms	ישב	442		sit,dwell
4:2	יקח	qal	wci	3ms	לקח	542		take
	יאמר	qal	wci	3ms	אמר	55		say
	שבו	qal	impv	mp	ישב	442		sit,dwell
	ישבו	qal	wci	3mp	ישב	442		sit,dwell
4:3	יאמר	qal	wci	3ms	אמר	55		say
	גאל	qal	ptc	ms	גאל	145		redeem
	מכרה	qal	pft	3fs	מכר	569		sell
	שבה	qal	pft	3fs	שוב	996		turn,return
4:4	אמרתי	qal	pft	1cs	אמר	55		say
	אגלה	qal	impf	1cs	גלה	162		uncover
	אמר	qal	infc		אמר	55		say
	קנה	qal	impv	ms	קנה	888		get,buy
	ישבים	qal	ptc	mp	ישב	442		sit,dwell
	תגאל	qal	impf	2ms	גאל	145		redeem
	גאל	qal	impv	ms	גאל	145		redeem
	יגאל	qal	impf	3ms	גאל	145		redeem
	הגידה	hiph	impv	ms	נגד	616		declare,tell
	אדעk	qal	cohm	1cs	ידע	393		know
	אדעהq	qal	coh	1cs	ידע	393		know
	גאול	qal	infc		גאל	145		redeem
	יאמר	qal	wci	3ms	אמר	55		say
	אגאל	qal	impf	1cs	גאל	145		redeem
4:5	יאמר	qal	wci	3ms	אמר	55		say
	קנותך	qal	infc		קנה	888	2ms	get,buy
	מת	qal	ptc	ms	מות	559		die
	קניתיk	qal	pft	1cs	קנה	888		get,buy
	קניתהq	qal	pft	2ms	קנה	888		get,buy
	הקים	hiph	infc		קום	877		raise,build,set
	מת	qal	ptc	ms	מות	559		die
4:6	יאמר	qal	wci	3ms	אמר	55		say
	גאל	qal	ptc	ms	גאל	145		redeem
	אוכל	qal	impf	1cs	יכל	407		be able
	גאולk	qal	infc		גאל	145		redeem
	גאלq	qal	infc		גאל	145		redeem
	אשחית	hiph	impf	1cs	שחת	1007		spoil,ruin
	גאל	qal	impv	ms	גאל	145		redeem
	אוכל	qal	impf	1cs	יכל	407		be able
	גאל	qal	infc		גאל	145		redeem
4:7	קים	piel	infc		קום	877		confirm
	שלף	qal	pft	3ms	שלף	1025		draw out,off
	נתן	qal	wcp	3ms	נתן	678		give,set
4:8	יאמר	qal	wci	3ms	אמר	55		say
	גאל	qal	ptc	ms	גאל	145		redeem
	קנה	qal	impv	ms	קנה	888		get,buy
	ישלף	qal	wci	3ms	שלף	1025		draw out,off
4:9	יאמר	qal	wci	3ms	אמר	55		say
	קניתי	qal	pft	1cs	קנה	888		get,buy
4:10	קניתי	qal	pft	1cs	קנה	888		get,buy
	הקים	hiph	infc		קום	877		raise,build,set
	מת	qal	ptc	ms	מות	559		die
	יכרת	niph	impf	3ms	כרת	503		be cut off
	מת	qal	ptc	ms	מות	559		die
4:11	יאמרו	qal	wci	3mp	אמר	55		say

ChVs	Form	Stem	Tnse	PGN	Root	BDB	Sfx	Meaning
4:11	יתן	qal	jusm	3ms	נתן	678		give,set
	באה	qal	ptc	fs	בוא	97		come in
	בנו	qal	pft	3cp	בנה	124		build
	עשׂה	qal	impv	ms	עשׂה	793		do,make
	קרא	qal	impv	ms	קרא	894		call,proclaim
4:12	יהי	qal	jus	3ms	היה	224		be,become
	ילדה	qal	pft	3fs	ילד	408		bear,beget
	יתן	qal	impf	3ms	נתן	678		give,set
4:13	יקח	qal	wci	3ms	לקח	542		take
	תהי	qal	wci	3fs	היה	224		be,become
	יבא	qal	wci	3ms	בוא	97		come in
	יתן	qal	wci	3ms	נתן	678		give,set
	תלד	qal	wci	3fs	ילד	408		bear,beget
4:14	תאמרנה	qal	wci	3fp	אמר	55		say
	ברוך	qal	pptc	ms	ברך	138		kneel,bless
	השבית	hiph	pft	3ms	שׁבת	991		destroy,remove
	גאל	qal	ptc	ms	גאל	145		redeem
	יקרא	niph	jusm	3ms	קרא	894		be called
4:15	היה	qal	wcp	3ms	היה	224		be,become
	משׁיב	hiph	ptc	ms	שׁוב	996		bring back
	כלכל	pilp	infc		כול	465		support
	אהבתך	qal	pft	3fs	אהב	12	2fs	love
	ילדתו	qal	pft	3fs	ילד	408	3ms	bear,beget
4:16	תקח	qal	wci	3fs	לקח	542		take
	תשׁתהו	qal	wci	3fs	שׂית	1011	3ms	put,set
	תהי	qal	wci	3fs	היה	224		be,become
	אמנת	qal	ptc	fs	אמן	52		nourish
4:17	תקראנה	qal	wci	3fp	קרא	894		call,proclaim
	אמר	qal	infc		אמר	55		say
	ילד	qalp	pft	3ms	ילד	408		be born
	תקראנה	qal	wci	3fp	קרא	894		call,proclaim
4:18	הוליד	hiph	pft	3ms	ילד	408		beget
4:19	הוליד	hiph	pft	3ms	ילד	408		beget
	הוליד	hiph	pft	3ms	ילד	408		beget
4:20	הוליד	hiph	pft	3ms	ילד	408		beget
	הוליד	hiph	pft	3ms	ילד	408		beget
4:21	הוליד	hiph	pft	3ms	ילד	408		beget
	הוליד	hiph	pft	3ms	ילד	408		beget
4:22	הוליד	hiph	pft	3ms	ילד	408		beget
	הוליד	hiph	pft	3ms	ילד	408		beget

1 SAMUEL

ChVs	Form	Stem	Tnse	PGN	Root	BDB	Sfx	Meaning
1:1	יהי	qal	wci	3ms	היה	224		be,become
1:2	יהי	qal	wci	3ms	היה	224		be,become
1:3	עלה	qal	wcp	3ms	עלה	748		go up
	השתחוות	hish	infc		חוה	1005		bow down
	זבח	qal	infc		זבח	256		slaughter
1:4	יהי	qal	wci	3ms	היה	224		be,become
	יזבח	qal	wci	3ms	זבח	256		slaughter
	נתן	qal	wcp	3ms	נתן	678		give,set
1:5	יתן	qal	impf	3ms	נתן	678		give,set
	אהב	qal	pft	3ms	אהב	12		love
	סגר	qal	pft	3ms	סגר	688		shut
1:6	כעסתה	piel	wcp	3fs	כעס	494	3fs	irritate
1:6	הרעמה	hiph	infc		רעם	947	3fs	thunder
	סגר	qal	pft	3ms	סגר	688		shut
1:7	יעשׂה	qal	impf	3ms	עשׂה	793		do,make
	עלתה	qal	infc		עלה	748	3fs	go up
	תכעסנה	hiph	impf	3fs	כעס	494	3fs	vex,provoke
	תבכה	qal	wci	3fs	בכה	113		weep
	תאכל	qal	impf	3fs	אכל	37		eat,devour
1:8	יאמר	qal	wci	3ms	אמר	55		say
	תבכי	qal	impf	2fs	בכה	113		weep
	תאכלי	qal	impf	2fs	אכל	37		eat,devour
	ירע	qal	impf	3ms	רעע	949		be evil
1:9	תקם	qal	wci	3fs	קום	877		arise,stand
	אכלה	qal	infc		אכל	37		eat,devour
	שׁתה	qal	infa		שׁתה	1059		drink
	ישׁב	qal	ptc	ms	ישׁב	442		sit,dwell
1:10	תתפלל	hith	wci	3fs	פלל	813		pray
	בכה	qal	infa		בכה	113		weep
	תבכה	qal	impf	3fs	בכה	113		weep
1:11	תדר	qal	wci	3fs	נדר	623		vow
	תאמר	qal	wci	3fs	אמר	55		say
	ראה	qal	infa		ראה	906		see
	תראה	qal	impf	2ms	ראה	906		see
	זכרתני	qal	wcp	2ms	זכר	269	1cs	remember
	תשׁכח	qal	impf	2ms	שׁכח	1013		forget
	נתתה	qal	wcp	2ms	נתן	678		give,set
	נתתיו	qal	wcp	1cs	נתן	678	3ms	give,set
	יעלה	qal	impf	3ms	עלה	748		go up
1:12	היה	qal	pft	3ms	היה	224		be,become
	הרבתה	hiph	pft	3fs	רבה	915		make many
	התפלל	hith	infc		פלל	813		pray
	שׁמר	qal	ptc	ms	שׁמר	1036		keep,watch
1:13	מדברת	piel	ptc	fs	דבר	180		speak
	נעות	qal	ptc	fp	נוע	631		totter,wave
	ישׁמע	niph	impf	3ms	שׁמע	1033		be heard
	יחשׁבה	qal	wci	3ms	חשׁב	362	3fs	think,devise
1:14	יאמר	qal	wci	3ms	אמר	55		say
	תשׁתכרין	hith	impf	2fs	שׁכר	1016		make self drunk
	הסירי	hiph	impv	fs	סור	693		take away
1:15	תען	qal	wci	3fs	ענה	772		answer
	תאמר	qal	wci	3fs	אמר	55		say
	שׁתיתי	qal	pft	1cs	שׁתה	1059		drink
	אשׁפך	qal	wci	1cs	שׁפך	1049		pour out
1:16	תתן	qal	jusm	2ms	נתן	678		give,set
	דברתי	piel	pft	1cs	דבר	180		speak
1:17	יען	qal	wci	3ms	ענה	772		answer
	יאמר	qal	wci	3ms	אמר	55		say
	לכי	qal	impv	fs	הלך	229		walk,go
	יתן	qal	jusm	3ms	נתן	678		give,set
	שׁאלת	qal	pft	2fs	שׁאל	981		ask,borrow
1:18	תאמר	qal	wci	3fs	אמר	55		say
	תמצא	qal	jusm	3fs	מצא	592		find
	תלך	qal	wci	3fs	הלך	229		walk,go
	תאכל	qal	wci	3fs	אכל	37		eat,devour
	היו	qal	pft	3cp	היה	224		be,become

ChVs	Form	Stem	Tnse	PGN	Root	BDB	Sfx	Meaning
1:19	ישכמו	hiph	wci	3mp	שכם	1014		rise early
	ישתחוו	hish	wci	3mp	חוה	1005		bow down
	ישבו	qal	wci	3mp	שוב	996		turn,return
	יבאו	qal	wci	3mp	בוא	97		come in
	ידע	qal	wci	3ms	ידע	393		know
	יזכרה	qal	wci	3ms	זכר	269	3fs	remember
1:20	יהי	qal	wci	3ms	היה	224		be,become
	תהר	qal	wci	3fs	הרה	247		conceive
	תלד	qal	wci	3fs	ילד	408		bear,beget
	תקרא	qal	wci	3fs	קרא	894		call,proclaim
	שאלתיו	qal	pft	1cs	שאל	981	3ms	ask,borrow
1:21	יעל	qal	wci	3ms	עלה	748		go up
	זבח	qal	infc		זבח	256		slaughter
1:22	עלתה	qal	pft	3fs	עלה	748		go up
	אמרה	qal	pft	3fs	אמר	55		say
	יגמל	niph	impf	3ms	גמל	168		be weaned
	הבאתיו	hiph	wcp	1cs	בוא	97	3ms	bring in
	נראה	niph	wcp	3ms	ראה	906		appear,be seen
	ישב	qal	wcp	3ms	ישב	442		sit,dwell
1:23	יאמר	qal	wci	3ms	אמר	55		say
	עשי	qal	impv	fs	עשה	793		do,make
	שבי	qal	impv	fs	ישב	442		sit,dwell
	גמלך	qal	infc		גמל	168	2fs	deal out,ripen
	יקם	hiph	jus	3ms	קום	877		raise,build,set
	תשב	qal	wci	3fs	ישב	442		sit,dwell
	תינק	hiph	wci	3fs	ינק	413		nurse
	גמלה	qal	infc		גמל	168	3fs	deal out,ripen
1:24	תעלהו	hiph	wci	3fs	עלה	748	3ms	bring up,offer
	גמלתו	qal	pft	3fs	גמל	168	3ms	deal out,ripen
	תבאהו	hiph	wci	3fs	בוא	97	3ms	bring in
1:25	ישחטו	qal	wci	3mp	שחט	1006		slaughter
	יביאו	hiph	wci	3mp	בוא	97		bring in
1:26	תאמר	qal	wci	3fs	אמר	55		say
	נצבת	niph	ptc	fs	נצב	662		stand
	התפלל	hith	infc		פלל	813		pray
1:27	התפללתי	hith	pft	1cs	פלל	813		pray
	יתן	qal	wci	3ms	נתן	678		give,set
	שאלתי	qal	pft	1cs	שאל	981		ask,borrow
1:28	השאלתהו	hiph	pft	1cs	שאל	981	3ms	give,lend
	היה	qal	pft	3ms	היה	224		be,become
	שאול	qal	pptc	ms	שאל	981		ask,borrow
	ישתחו	hish	wci	3ms	חוה	1005		bow down
2:1	תתפלל	hith	wci	3fs	פלל	813		pray
	תאמר	qal	wci	3fs	אמר	55		say
	עלץ	qal	pft	3ms	עלץ	763		rejoice,exult
	רמה	qal	pft	3fs	רום	926		be high
	רחב	qal	pft	3ms	רחב	931		be wide
	אויבי	qal	ptc	mp	איב	33	1cs	be hostile to
	שמחתי	qal	pft	1cs	שמח	970		rejoice
2:3	תרבו	hiph	jusm	2mp	רבה	915		make many
	תדברו	piel	impf	2mp	דבר	180		speak
	יצא	qal	impf	3ms	יצא	422		go out
	נתכנו	niph	pft	3cp	תכן	1067		be estimated
2:4	נכשלים	niph	ptc	mp	כשל	505		stumble

ChVs	Form	Stem	Tnse	PGN	Root	BDB	Sfx	Meaning
2:4	אזרו	qal	pft	3cp	אזר	25		gird
2:5	נשכרו	niph	pft	3cp	שכר	968		hire self out
	חדלו	qal	pft	3cp	חדל	292		cease
	ילדה	qal	pft	3fs	ילד	408		bear,beget
	אמללה	pul	pft	3fs	אמל	51		be feeble
2:6	ממית	hiph	ptc	ms	מות	559		kill
	מחיה	piel	ptc	ms	חיה	310		preserve,revive
	מוריד	hiph	ptc	ms	ירד	432		bring down
	יעל	hiph	wci	3ms	עלה	748		bring up,offer
2:7	מוריש	hiph	ptc	ms	ירש	439		c. to possess
	מעשיר	hiph	ptc	ms	עשר	799		make rich
	משפיל	hiph	ptc	ms	שפל	1050		make low,abase
	מרומם	pol	ptc	ms	רום	926		raise,rear
2:8	מקים	hiph	ptc	ms	קום	877		raise,build,set
	ירים	hiph	impf	3ms	רום	926		raise,lift
	הושיב	hiph	infc		ישב	442		cause to dwell
	ינחלם	hiph	impf	3ms	נחל	635	3mp	c. to inherit
	ישת	qal	wci	3ms	שית	1011		put,set
2:9	ישמר	qal	impf	3ms	שמר	1036		keep,watch
	ידמו	niph	impf	3mp	דמם	198		be made silent
	יגבר	qal	impf	3ms	גבר	149		be strong
2:10	יחתו	qal	impf	3mp	חתת	369		be shattered
	מריבוk	hiph	ptc	ms	ריב	936	3ms	strive,contend
	מריביוq	hiph	ptc	mp	ריב	936	3ms	strive,contend
	ירעם	hiph	impf	3ms	רעם	947		thunder
	ידין	qal	impf	3ms	דין	192		judge
	יתן	qal	impf	3ms	נתן	678		give,set
	ירם	hiph	impf	3ms	רום	926		raise,lift
2:11	ילך	qal	wci	3ms	הלך	229		walk,go
	היה	qal	pft	3ms	היה	224		be,become
	משרת	piel	ptc	ms	שרת	1058		minister,serve
2:12	ידעו	qal	pft	3cp	ידע	393		know
2:13	זבח	qal	ptc	ms	זבח	256		slaughter
	בא	qal	wcp	3ms	בוא	97		come in
	בשל	piel	infc		בשל	143		boil,cook
2:14	הכה	hiph	wcp	3ms	נכה	645		smite
	יעלה	hiph	impf	3ms	עלה	748		bring up,offer
	יקח	qal	impf	3ms	לקח	542		take
	יעשו	qal	impf	3mp	עשה	793		do,make
	באים	qal	ptc	mp	בוא	97		come in
2:15	יקטרון	hiph	impf	3mp	קטר	882		make sacrifices
	בא	qal	wcp	3ms	בוא	97		come in
	אמר	qal	wcp	3ms	אמר	55		say
	זבח	qal	ptc	ms	זבח	256		slaughter
	תנה	qal	impv	ms	נתן	678		give,set
	צלות	qal	infc		צלה	852		roast
	יקח	qal	impf	3ms	לקח	542		take
	מבשל	pual	ptc	ms	בשל	143		be boiled
2:16	יאמר	qal	wci	3ms	אמר	55		say
	קטר	piel	infa		קטר	882		make sacrifices
	יקטירון	hiph	jusm	3mp	קטר	882		make sacrifices
	קח	qal	impv	ms	לקח	542		take
	תאוה	piel	impf	3fs	אוה	16		desire
	אמר	qal	wcp	3ms	אמר	55		say

ChVs	Form	Stem	Tnse	PGN	Root	BDB	Sfx	Meaning
2:16	תתן	qal	impf	2ms	נתן	678		give,set
	לקחתי	qal	pft	1cs	לקח	542		take
2:17	תהי	qal	wci	3fs	היה	224		be,become
	נאצו	piel	pft	3cp	נאץ	610		spurn
2:18	משרת	piel	ptc	ms	שרת	1058		minister,serve
	חגור	qal	pptc	ms	חגר	291		gird
2:19	תעשה	qal	impf	3fs	עשה	793		do,make
	העלתה	hiph	pft	3fs	עלה	748		bring up,offer
	עלותה	qal	infc		עלה	748	3fs	go up
	זבח	qal	infc		זבח	256		slaughter
2:20	ברך	piel	wcp	3ms	ברך	138		bless
	אמר	qal	wcp	3ms	אמר	55		say
	ישם	qal	jus	3ms	שים	962		put,set
	שאל	qal	pft	3ms	שאל	981		ask,borrow
	הלכו	qal	wcp	3cp	הלך	229		walk,go
2:21	פקד	qal	pft	3ms	פקד	823		attend to,visit
	תהר	qal	wci	3fs	הרה	247		conceive
	תלד	qal	wci	3fs	ילד	408		bear,beget
	יגדל	qal	wci	3ms	גדל	152		be great,grow
2:22	זקן	qal	pft	3ms	זקן	278		be old
	שמע	qal	wcp	3ms	שמע	1033		hear
	יעשון	qal	impf	3mp	עשה	793		do,make
	ישכבון	qal	impf	3mp	שכב	1011		lie,lie down
	צבאות	qal	ptc	fp	צבא	838		wage war
2:23	יאמר	qal	wci	3ms	אמר	55		say
	תעשון	qal	impf	2mp	עשה	793		do,make
	שמע	qal	ptc	ms	שמע	1033		hear
2:24	שמע	qal	ptc	ms	שמע	1033		hear
	מעברים	hiph	ptc	mp	עבר	716		cause to pass
2:25	יחטא	qal	impf	3ms	חטא	306		sin
	פללו	piel	wcp	3ms	פלל	813	3ms	mediate,judge
	יחטא	qal	impf	3ms	חטא	306		sin
	יתפלל	hith	impf	3ms	פלל	813		pray
	ישמעו	qal	impf	3mp	שמע	1033		hear
	חפץ	qal	pft	3ms	חפץ	342		delight in
	המיתם	hiph	infc		מות	559	3mp	kill
2:26	הלך	qal	ptc	ms	הלך	229		walk,go
2:27	יבא	qal	wci	3ms	בוא	97		come in
	יאמר	qal	wci	3ms	אמר	55		say
	אמר	qal	pft	3ms	אמר	55		say
	נגלה	niph	infa		גלה	162		uncover self
	נגליתי	niph	pft	1cs	גלה	162		uncover self
	היותם	qal	infc		היה	224	3mp	be,become
2:28	בחר	qal	infa		בחר	103		choose
	עלות	qal	infc		עלה	748		go up
	הקטיר	hiph	infc		קטר	882		make sacrifices
	שאת	qal	infc		נשא	669		lift,carry
	אתנה	qal	wci	1cs	נתן	678		give,set
2:29	תבעטו	qal	impf	2mp	בעט	127		kick
	צויתי	piel	pft	1cs	צוה	845		command
	תכבד	piel	wci	2ms	כבד	457		honor,make dull
	הבריאכם	hiph	infc		ברא	135	2mp	make fat
2:30	אמור	qal	infa		אמר	55		say
	אמרתי	qal	pft	1cs	אמר	55		say
2:30	יתהלכו	hith	impf	3mp	הלך	229		walk to and fro
	מכבדי	piel	ptc	mp	כבד	457	1cs	honor,make dull
	אכבד	piel	impf	1cs	כבד	457		honor,make dull
	בזי	qal	ptc	mp	בזה	102	1cs	despise
	יקלו	qal	impf	3mp	קלל	886		be slight,swift
2:31	באים	qal	ptc	mp	בוא	97		come in
	גדעתי	qal	wcp	1cs	גדע	154		cut in two
	היות	qal	infc		היה	224		be,become
2:32	הבטת	hiph	wcp	2ms	נבט	613		look,regard
	ייטיב	hiph	impf	3ms	יטב	405		do good
	יהיה	qal	impf	3ms	היה	224		be,become
2:33	אכרית	hiph	impf	1cs	כרת	503		cut off,destroy
	כלות	piel	infc		כלה	477		complete,finish
	אדיב	hiph	infc		אדב	9		grieve
	ימותו	qal	impf	3mp	מות	559		die
2:34	יבא	qal	impf	3ms	בוא	97		come in
	ימותו	qal	impf	3mp	מות	559		die
2:35	הקימתי	hiph	wcp	1cs	קום	877		raise,build,set
	נאמן	niph	ptc	ms	אמן	52		be confirmed
	יעשה	qal	impf	3ms	עשה	793		do,make
	בניתי	qal	wcp	1cs	בנה	124		build
	נאמן	niph	ptc	ms	אמן	52		be confirmed
	התהלך	hith	wcp	3ms	הלך	229		walk to and fro
2:36	היה	qal	wcp	3ms	היה	224		be,become
	נותר	niph	ptc	ms	יתר	451		be left,remain
	יבוא	qal	impf	3ms	בוא	97		come in
	השתחות	hish	infc		חוה	1005		bow down
	אמר	qal	wcp	3ms	אמר	55		say
	ספחני	qal	impv	ms	ספח	705	1cs	attach to
	אכל	qal	infc		אכל	37		eat,devour
3:1	משרת	piel	ptc	ms	שרת	1058		minister,serve
	היה	qal	pft	3ms	היה	224		be,become
	נפרץ	niph	ptc	ms	פרץ	829		be spread
3:2	יהי	qal	wci	3ms	היה	224		be,become
	שכב	qal	ptc	ms	שכב	1011		lie,lie down
	החלו	hiph	pft	3cp	חלל	320		begin,profane
	יוכל	qal	impf	3ms	יכל	407		be able
	ראות	qal	infc		ראה	906		see
3:3	יכבה	qal	impf	3ms	כבה	459		be quenched
	שכב	qal	ptc	ms	שכב	1011		lie,lie down
3:4	יקרא	qal	wci	3ms	קרא	894		call,proclaim
	יאמר	qal	wci	3ms	אמר	55		say
3:5	ירץ	qal	wci	3ms	רוץ	930		run
	יאמר	qal	wci	3ms	אמר	55		say
	קראת	qal	pft	2ms	קרא	894		call,proclaim
	יאמר	qal	wci	3ms	אמר	55		say
	קראתי	qal	pft	1cs	קרא	894		call,proclaim
	שוב	qal	impv	ms	שוב	996		turn,return
	שכב	qal	impv	ms	שכב	1011		lie,lie down
	ילך	qal	wci	3ms	הלך	229		walk,go
	ישכב	qal	wci	3ms	שכב	1011		lie,lie down
3:6	יסף	hiph	wci	3ms	יסף	414		add,do again
	קרא	qal	infc		קרא	894		call,proclaim
	יקם	qal	wci	3ms	קום	877		arise,stand

ChVs	Form	Stem	Tnse	PGN	Root	BDB	Sfx	Meaning
3:6	ילך	qal	wci	3ms	הלך	229		walk,go
	יאמר	qal	wci	3ms	אמר	55		say
	קראת	qal	pft	2ms	קרא	894		call,proclaim
	יאמר	qal	wci	3ms	אמר	55		say
	קראתי	qal	pft	1cs	קרא	894		call,proclaim
	שוב	qal	impv	ms	שוב	996		turn,return
	שכב	qal	impv	ms	שכב	1011		lie,lie down
3:7	ידע	qal	pft	3ms	ידע	393		know
	יגלה	niph	impf	3ms	גלה	162		uncover self
3:8	יסף	hiph	wci	3ms	יסף	414		add,do again
	קרא	qal	infc		קרא	894		call,proclaim
	יקם	qal	wci	3ms	קום	877		arise,stand
	ילך	qal	wci	3ms	הלך	229		walk,go
	יאמר	qal	wci	3ms	אמר	55		say
	קראת	qal	pft	2ms	קרא	894		call,proclaim
	יבן	qal	wci	3ms	בין	106		discern
	קרא	qal	ptc	ms	קרא	894		call,proclaim
3:9	יאמר	qal	wci	3ms	אמר	55		say
	לך	qal	impv	ms	הלך	229		walk,go
	שכב	qal	impv	ms	שכב	1011		lie,lie down
	היה	qal	wcp	3ms	היה	224		be,become
	יקרא	qal	impf	3ms	קרא	894		call,proclaim
	אמרת	qal	wcp	2ms	אמר	55		say
	דבר	piel	impv	ms	דבר	180		speak
	שמע	qal	ptc	ms	שמע	1033		hear
	ילך	qal	wci	3ms	הלך	229		walk,go
	ישכב	qal	wci	3ms	שכב	1011		lie,lie down
3:10	יבא	qal	wci	3ms	בוא	97		come in
	יתיצב	hith	wci	3ms	יצב	426		stand oneself
	יקרא	qal	wci	3ms	קרא	894		call,proclaim
	יאמר	qal	wci	3ms	אמר	55		say
	דבר	piel	impv	ms	דבר	180		speak
	שמע	qal	ptc	ms	שמע	1033		hear
3:11	יאמר	qal	wci	3ms	אמר	55		say
	עשה	qal	ptc	ms	עשה	793		do,make
	שמעו	qal	ptc	ms	שמע	1033	3ms	hear
	תצלינה	qal	impf	3fp	צלל	852		tingle
3:12	אקים	hiph	impf	1cs	קום	877		raise,build,set
	דברתי	piel	pft	1cs	דבר	180		speak
	החל	hiph	infa		חלל	320		begin,profane
	כלה	piel	infa		כלה	477		complete,finish
3:13	הגדתי	hiph	pft	1cs	נגד	616		declare,tell
	שפט	qal	ptc	ms	שפט	1047		judge
	ידע	qal	pft	3ms	ידע	393		know
	מקללים	piel	ptc	mp	קלל	886		curse
	כהה	piel	pft	3ms	כהה	462		rebuke
3:14	נשבעתי	niph	pft	1cs	שבע	989		swear
	יתכפר	hith	impf	3ms	כפר	497		be covered
3:15	ישכב	qal	wci	3ms	שכב	1011		lie,lie down
	יפתח	qal	wci	3ms	פתח	834		open
	ירא	qal	pft	3ms	ירא	431		fear
	הגיד	hiph	infc		נגד	616		declare,tell
3:16	יקרא	qal	wci	3ms	קרא	894		call,proclaim
	יאמר	qal	wci	3ms	אמר	55		say
3:16	יאמר	qal	wci	3ms	אמר	55		say
3:17	יאמר	qal	wci	3ms	אמר	55		say
	דבר	piel	pft	3ms	דבר	180		speak
	תכחד	piel	jusm	2ms	כחד	470		hide
	יעשה	qal	jusm	3ms	עשה	793		do,make
	יוסיף	hiph	jusm	3ms	יסף	414		add,do again
	תכחד	piel	impf	2ms	כחד	470		hide
	דבר	piel	pft	3ms	דבר	180		speak
3:18	יגד	hiph	wci	3ms	נגד	616		declare,tell
	כחד	piel	pft	3ms	כחד	470		hide
	יאמר	qal	wci	3ms	אמר	55		say
	יעשה	qal	jusm	3ms	עשה	793		do,make
3:19	יגדל	qal	wci	3ms	גדל	152		be great,grow
	היה	qal	pft	3ms	היה	224		be,become
	הפיל	hiph	pft	3ms	נפל	656		cause to fall
3:20	ידע	qal	wci	3ms	ידע	393		know
	נאמן	niph	ptc	ms	אמן	52		be confirmed
3:21	יסף	hiph	wci	3ms	יסף	414		add,do again
	הראה	niph	infc		ראה	906		appear,be seen
	נגלה	niph	pft	3ms	גלה	162		uncover self
4:1	יהי	qal	wci	3ms	היה	224		be,become
	יצא	qal	wci	3ms	יצא	422		go out
	קראת	qal	infc		קרא	896		meet,encounter
	יחנו	qal	wci	3mp	חנה	333		decline,encamp
	חנו	qal	pft	3cp	חנה	333		decline,encamp
4:2	יערכו	qal	wci	3mp	ערך	789		set in order
	קראת	qal	infc		קרא	896		meet,encounter
	תטש	qal	wci	3fs	נטש	643		leave,forsake
	ינגף	niph	wci	3ms	נגף	619		be smitten
	יכו	hiph	wci	3mp	נכה	645		smite
4:3	יבא	qal	wci	3ms	בוא	97		come in
	יאמרו	qal	wci	3mp	אמר	55		say
	נגפנו	qal	pft	3ms	נגף	619	1cp	smite,strike
	נקחה	qal	coh	1cp	לקח	542		take
	יבא	qal	jus	3ms	בוא	97		come in
	ישענו	hiph	jusm	3ms	ישע	446	1cp	deliver,save
	איבינו	qal	ptc	mp	איב	33	1cp	be hostile to
4:4	ישלח	qal	wci	3ms	שלח	1018		send
	ישאו	qal	wci	3mp	נשא	669		lift,carry
	ישב	qal	ptc	ms	ישב	442		sit,dwell
4:5	יהי	qal	wci	3ms	היה	224		be,become
	בוא	qal	infc		בוא	97		come in
	ירעו	hiph	wci	3mp	רוע	929		raise a shout
	תהם	niph	wci	3fs	הום	223		be agitated
4:6	ישמעו	qal	wci	3mp	שמע	1033		hear
	יאמרו	qal	wci	3mp	אמר	55		say
	ידעו	qal	wci	3mp	ידע	393		know
	בא	qal	pft	3ms	בוא	97		come in
4:7	יראו	qal	wci	3mp	ירא	431		fear
	אמרו	qal	pft	3cp	אמר	55		say
	בא	qal	pft	3ms	בוא	97		come in
	יאמרו	qal	wci	3mp	אמר	55		say
	היתה	qal	pft	3fs	היה	224		be,become
4:8	יצילנו	hiph	impf	3ms	נצל	664	1cp	snatch,deliver

ChVs	Form	Stem	Tnse	PGN	Root	BDB	Sfx	Meaning
4:8	מכים	hiph	ptc	mp	נכה	645		smite
4:9	התחזקו	hith	impv	mp	חזק	304		strengthen self
	היו	qal	impv	mp	היה	224		be,become
	תעבדו	qal	impf	2mp	עבד	712		work,serve
	עבדו	qal	pft	3cp	עבד	712		work,serve
	הייתם	qal	wcp	2mp	היה	224		be,become
	נלחמתם	niph	wcp	2mp	לחם	535		wage war
4:10	ילחמו	niph	wci	3mp	לחם	535		wage war
	ינגף	niph	wci	3ms	נגף	619		be smitten
	ינסו	qal	wci	3mp	נוס	630		flee,escape
	תהי	qal	wci	3fs	היה	224		be,become
	יפל	qal	wci	3ms	נפל	656		fall
4:11	נלקח	niph	pft	3ms	לקח	542		be taken
	מתו	qal	pft	3cp	מות	559		die
4:12	ירץ	qal	wci	3ms	רוץ	930		run
	יבא	qal	wci	3ms	בוא	97		come in
	קרעים	qal	pptc	mp	קרע	902		tear,rend
4:13	יבוא	qal	wci	3ms	בוא	97		come in
	ישב	qal	ptc	ms	ישב	442		sit,dwell
	מצפה	piel	ptc	ms	צפה	859		watch closely
	היה	qal	pft	3ms	היה	224		be,become
	בא	qal	pft	3ms	בוא	97		come in
	הגיד	hiph	infc		נגד	616		declare,tell
	תזעק	qal	wci	3fs	זעק	277		call,cry out
4:14	ישמע	qal	wci	3ms	שמע	1033		hear
	יאמר	qal	wci	3ms	אמר	55		say
	מהר	piel	pft	3ms	מהר	554		hasten
	יבא	qal	wci	3ms	בוא	97		come in
	יגד	hiph	wci	3ms	נגד	616		declare,tell
4:15	קמה	qal	pft	3fs	קום	877		arise,stand
	יכול	qal	pft	3ms	יכל	407		be able
	ראות	qal	infc		ראה	906		see
4:16	יאמר	qal	wci	3ms	אמר	55		say
	בא	qal	ptc	ms	בוא	97		come in
	נסתי	qal	pft	1cs	נוס	630		flee,escape
	יאמר	qal	wci	3ms	אמר	55		say
	היה	qal	pft	3ms	היה	224		be,become
4:17	יען	qal	wci	3ms	ענה	772		answer
	מבשר	piel	ptc	ms	בשר	142		bear tidings
	יאמר	qal	wci	3ms	אמר	55		say
	נס	qal	pft	3ms	נוס	630		flee,escape
	היתה	qal	pft	3fs	היה	224		be,become
	מתו	qal	pft	3cp	מות	559		die
	נלקחה	niph	pft	3fs	לקח	542		be taken
4:18	יהי	qal	wci	3ms	היה	224		be,become
	הזכירו	hiph	infc		זכר	269	3ms	c. to remember
	יפל	qal	wci	3ms	נפל	656		fall
	תשבר	niph	wci	3fs	שבר	990		be broken
	ימת	qal	wci	3ms	מות	559		die
	זקן	qal	pft	3ms	זקן	278		be old
	שפט	qal	pft	3ms	שפט	1047		judge
4:19	לת	qal	infc		ילד	408		bear,beget
	תשמע	qal	wci	3fs	שמע	1033		hear
	הלקח	niph	infc		לקח	542		be taken

ChVs	Form	Stem	Tnse	PGN	Root	BDB	Sfx	Meaning
4:19	מת	qal	pft	3ms	מות	559		die
	תכרע	qal	wci	3fs	כרע	502		bow down
	תלד	qal	wci	3fs	ילד	408		bear,beget
	נהפכו	niph	pft	3cp	הפך	245		turn oneself
4:20	מותה	qal	infc		מות	559	3fs	die
	תדברנה	piel	wci	3fp	דבר	180		speak
	נצבות	niph	ptc	fp	נצב	662		stand
	תיראי	qal	jusm	2fs	ירא	431		fear
	ילדת	qal	pft	2fs	ילד	408		bear,beget
	ענתה	qal	pft	3fs	ענה	772		answer
	שתה	qal	pft	3fs	שית	1011		put,set
4:21	תקרא	qal	wci	3fs	קרא	894		call,proclaim
	אמר	qal	infc		אמר	55		say
	גלה	qal	pft	3ms	גלה	162		uncover
	הלקח	niph	infc		לקח	542		be taken
4:22	תאמר	qal	wci	3fs	אמר	55		say
	גלה	qal	pft	3ms	גלה	162		uncover
	נלקח	niph	pft	3ms	לקח	542		be taken
5:1	לקחו	qal	pft	3cp	לקח	542		take
	יבאהו	hiph	wci	3mp	בוא	97	3ms	bring in
5:2	יקחו	qal	wci	3mp	לקח	542		take
	יביאו	hiph	wci	3mp	בוא	97		bring in
	יציגו	hiph	wci	3mp	יצג	426		place,establish
5:3	ישכמו	hiph	wci	3mp	שכם	1014		rise early
	נפל	qal	ptc	ms	נפל	656		fall
	יקחו	qal	wci	3mp	לקח	542		take
	ישבו	hiph	wci	3mp	שוב	996		bring back
5:4	ישכמו	hiph	wci	3mp	שכם	1014		rise early
	נפל	qal	ptc	ms	נפל	656		fall
	כרתות	qal	pptc	fp	כרת	503		cut,destroy
	נשאר	niph	pft	3ms	שאר	983		be left
5:5	ידרכו	qal	impf	3mp	דרך	201		tread,march
	באים	qal	ptc	mp	בוא	97		come in
5:6	תכבד	qal	wci	3fs	כבד	457		be heavy
	ישמם	hiph	wci	3ms	שמם	1030		ravage,appall
	יך	hiph	wci	3ms	נכה	645		smite
5:7	יראו	qal	wci	3mp	ראה	906		see
	אמרו	qal	wcp	3cp	אמר	55		say
	ישב	qal	impf	3ms	ישב	442		sit,dwell
	קשתה	qal	pft	3fs	קשה	904		be hard,severe
5:8	ישלחו	qal	wci	3mp	שלח	1018		send
	יאספו	qal	wci	3mp	אסף	62		gather
	יאמרו	qal	wci	3mp	אמר	55		say
	נעשה	qal	impf	1cp	עשה	793		do,make
	יאמרו	qal	wci	3mp	אמר	55		say
	יסב	qal	jusm	3ms	סבב	685		surround
	יסבו	hiph	wci	3mp	סבב	685		cause to turn
5:9	יהי	qal	wci	3ms	היה	224		be,become
	הסבו	hiph	pft	3cp	סבב	685		cause to turn
	תהי	qal	wci	3fs	היה	224		be,become
	יך	hiph	wci	3ms	נכה	645		smite
	ישתרו	niph	wci	3mp	שתר	979		break out
5:10	ישלחו	piel	wci	3mp	שלח	1018		send away,shoot
	יהי	qal	wci	3ms	היה	224		be,become

ChVs	Form	Stem	Tnse	PGN	Root	BDB	Sfx	Meaning
5:10	בוא	qal	infc		בוא	97		come in
	יזעקו	qal	wci	3mp	זעק	277		call,cry out
	אמר	qal	infc		אמר	55		say
	הסבו	hiph	pft	3cp	סבב	685		cause to turn
	המיתני	hiph	infc		מות	559	1cs	kill
5:11	ישלחו	qal	wci	3mp	שלח	1018		send
	יאספו	qal	wci	3mp	אסף	62		gather
	יאמרו	qal	wci	3mp	אמר	55		say
	שלחו	piel	impv	mp	שלח	1018		send away,shoot
	ישב	qal	jus	3ms	שוב	996		turn,return
	ימית	hiph	impf	3ms	מות	559		kill
	היתה	qal	pft	3fs	היה	224		be,become
	כבדה	qal	pft	3fs	כבד	457		be heavy
5:12	מתו	qal	pft	3cp	מות	559		die
	הכו	hoph	pft	3cp	נכה	645		be smitten
	תעל	qal	wci	3fs	עלה	748		go up
6:1	יהי	qal	wci	3ms	היה	224		be,become
6:2	יקראו	qal	wci	3mp	קרא	894		call,proclaim
	קסמים	qal	ptc	mp	קסם	890		divine
	אמר	qal	infc		אמר	55		say
	נעשׂה	qal	impf	1cp	עשׂה	793		do,make
	הודענו	hiph	impv	mp	ידע	393	1cp	declare
	נשלחנו	piel	impf	1cp	שלח	1018	3ms	send away,shoot
6:3	יאמרו	qal	wci	3mp	אמר	55		say
	משלחים	piel	ptc	mp	שלח	1018		send away,shoot
	תשלחו	piel	jusm	2mp	שלח	1018		send away,shoot
	השב	hiph	infa		שוב	996		bring back
	תשיבו	hiph	impf	2mp	שוב	996		bring back
	תרפאו	niph	impf	2mp	רפא	950		be healed
	נודע	niph	wcp	3ms	ידע	393		be made known
	תסור	qal	impf	3fs	סור	693		turn aside
6:4	יאמרו	qal	wci	3mp	אמר	55		say
	נשיב	hiph	impf	1cp	שוב	996		bring back
	יאמרו	qal	wci	3mp	אמר	55		say
6:5	עשׂיתם	qal	wcp	2mp	עשׂה	793		do,make
	משחיתם	hiph	ptc	mp	שחת	1007		spoil,ruin
	נתתם	qal	wcp	2mp	נתן	678		give,set
	יקל	hiph	impf	3ms	קלל	886		make light
6:6	תכבדו	piel	impf	2mp	כבד	457		honor,make dull
	כבדו	piel	pft	3cp	כבד	457		honor,make dull
	התעלל	hith	pft	3ms	עלל	759		busy,vex
	ישלחום	piel	wci	3mp	שלח	1018	3mp	send away,shoot
	ילכו	qal	wci	3mp	הלך	229		walk,go
6:7	קחו	qal	impv	mp	לקח	542		take
	עשׂו	qal	impv	mp	עשׂה	793		do,make
	עלות	qal	ptc	fp	עול	732		give suck
	עלה	qal	pft	3ms	עלה	748		go up
	אסרתם	qal	wcp	2mp	אסר	63		tie,bind
	השיבתם	hiph	wcp	2mp	שוב	996		bring back
6:8	לקחתם	qal	wcp	2mp	לקח	542		take
	נתתם	qal	wcp	2mp	נתן	678		give,set
	השבתם	hiph	pft	2mp	שוב	996		bring back
	תשׂימו	qal	impf	2mp	שׂים	962		put,set
	שלחתם	piel	wcp	2mp	שלח	1018		send away,shoot
6:8	הלך	qal	wcp	3ms	הלך	229		walk,go
6:9	ראיתם	qal	wcp	2mp	ראה	906		see
	יעלה	qal	impf	3ms	עלה	748		go up
	עשׂה	qal	pft	3ms	עשׂה	793		do,make
	ידענו	qal	wcp	1cp	ידע	393		know
	נגעה	qal	pft	3fs	נגע	619		touch,strike
	היה	qal	pft	3ms	היה	224		be,become
6:10	יעשׂו	qal	wci	3mp	עשׂה	793		do,make
	יקחו	qal	wci	3mp	לקח	542		take
	עלות	qal	ptc	fp	עול	732		give suck
	יאסרום	qal	wci	3mp	אסר	63	3mp	tie,bind
	כלו	qal	pft	3cp	כלא	476		shut up
6:11	ישׂמו	qal	wci	3mp	שׂים	962		put,set
6:12	ישרנה	qal	wci	3fp	ישר	448		be straight
	הלכו	qal	pft	3cp	הלך	229		walk,go
	הלך	qal	infa		הלך	229		walk,go
	געו	qal	infa		געה	171		low (of cattle)
	סרו	qal	pft	3cp	סור	693		turn aside
	הלכים	qal	ptc	mp	הלך	229		walk,go
6:13	קצרים	qal	ptc	mp	קצר	894		reap,harvest
	ישׂאו	qal	wci	3mp	נשׂא	669		lift,carry
	יראו	qal	wci	3mp	ראה	906		see
	ישׂמחו	qal	wci	3mp	שׂמח	970		rejoice
	ראות	qal	infc		ראה	906		see
6:14	באה	qal	pft	3fs	בוא	97		come in
	תעמד	qal	wci	3fs	עמד	763		stand,stop
	יבקעו	piel	wci	3mp	בקע	131		cut to pieces
	העלו	hiph	pft	3cp	עלה	748		bring up,offer
6:15	הורידו	hiph	pft	3cp	ירד	432		bring down
	ישׂמו	qal	wci	3mp	שׂים	962		put,set
	העלו	hiph	pft	3cp	עלה	748		bring up,offer
	יזבחו	qal	wci	3mp	זבח	256		slaughter
6:16	ראו	qal	pft	3cp	ראה	906		see
	ישבו	qal	wci	3mp	שוב	996		turn,return
6:17	השיבו	hiph	pft	3cp	שוב	996		bring back
6:18	הניחו	hiph	pft	3cp	נוח	628		give rest,put
6:19	יך	hiph	wci	3ms	נכה	645		smite
	ראו	qal	pft	3cp	ראה	906		see
	יך	hiph	wci	3ms	נכה	645		smite
	יתאבלו	hith	wci	3mp	אבל	5		mourn
	הכה	hiph	pft	3ms	נכה	645		smite
6:20	יאמרו	qal	wci	3mp	אמר	55		say
	יוכל	qal	impf	3ms	יכל	407		be able
	עמד	qal	infc		עמד	763		stand,stop
	יעלה	qal	impf	3ms	עלה	748		go up
6:21	ישלחו	qal	wci	3mp	שלח	1018		send
	יושבי	qal	ptc	mp	ישב	442		sit,dwell
	אמר	qal	infc		אמר	55		say
	השבו	hiph	pft	3cp	שוב	996		bring back
	רדו	qal	impv	mp	ירד	432		come down
	העלו	hiph	impv	mp	עלה	748		bring up,offer
7:1	יבאו	qal	wci	3mp	בוא	97		come in
	יעלו	hiph	wci	3mp	עלה	748		bring up,offer
	יבאו	hiph	wci	3mp	בוא	97		bring in

ChVs	Form	Stem	Tnse	PGN	Root	BDB	Sfx	Meaning
7:1	קדשׁו	piel	pft	3cp	קדשׁ	872		consecrate
	שׁמר	qal	infc		שׁמר	1036		keep,watch
7:2	יהי	qal	wci	3ms	היה	224		be,become
	שׁבת	qal	infc		ישׁב	442		sit,dwell
	ירבו	qal	wci	3mp	רבה	915		be many,great
	יהיו	qal	wci	3mp	היה	224		be,become
	ינהו	niph	wci	3mp	נהה	624		lament,gather
7:3	יאמר	qal	wci	3ms	אמר	55		say
	אמר	qal	infc		אמר	55		say
	שׁבים	qal	ptc	mp	שׁוב	996		turn,return
	הסירו	hiph	impv	mp	סור	693		take away
	הכינו	hiph	impv	mp	כון	465		fix,prepare
	עבדהו	qal	impv	mp	עבד	712	3ms	work,serve
	יצל	hiph	jus	3ms	נצל	664		snatch,deliver
7:4	יסירו	hiph	wci	3mp	סור	693		take away
	יעבדו	qal	wci	3mp	עבד	712		work,serve
7:5	יאמר	qal	wci	3ms	אמר	55		say
	קבצו	qal	impv	mp	קבץ	867		gather,collect
	אתפלל	hith	cohm	1cs	פלל	813		pray
7:6	יקבצו	niph	wci	3mp	קבץ	867		assemble,gather
	ישׁאבו	qal	wci	3mp	שׁאב	980		draw (water)
	ישׁפכו	qal	wci	3mp	שׁפך	1049		pour out
	יצומו	qal	wci	3mp	צום	847		fast
	יאמרו	qal	wci	3mp	אמר	55		say
	חטאנו	qal	pft	1cp	חטא	306		sin
	ישׁפט	qal	wci	3ms	שׁפט	1047		judge
7:7	ישׁמעו	qal	wci	3mp	שׁמע	1033		hear
	התקבצו	hith	pft	3cp	קבץ	867		gather together
	יעלו	qal	wci	3mp	עלה	748		go up
	ישׁמעו	qal	wci	3mp	שׁמע	1033		hear
	יראו	qal	wci	3mp	ירא	431		fear
7:8	יאמרו	qal	wci	3mp	אמר	55		say
	תחרשׁ	hiph	jus	2ms	חרשׁ	361		be silent
	זעק	qal	infc		זעק	277		call,cry out
	ישׁענו	hiph	jusm	3ms	ישׁע	446	1cp	deliver,save
7:9	יקח	qal	wci	3ms	לקח	542		take
	יעלהk	hiph	wci	3ms	עלה	748		bring up,offer
	יעלהוq	hiph	wci	3ms	עלה	748	3ms	bring up,offer
	יזעק	qal	wci	3ms	זעק	277		call,cry out
	יענהו	qal	wci	3ms	ענה	772		answer
7:10	יהי	qal	wci	3ms	היה	224		be,become
	מעלה	hiph	ptc	ms	עלה	748		bring up,offer
	נגשׁו	niph	pft	3cp	נגשׁ	620		draw near
	ירעם	hiph	wci	3ms	רעם	947		thunder
	יהמם	qal	wci	3ms	המם	243	3mp	confuse,vex
	ינגפו	niph	wci	3mp	נגף	619		be smitten
7:11	יצאו	qal	wci	3mp	יצא	422		go out
	ירדפו	qal	wci	3mp	רדף	922		pursue
	יכום	hiph	wci	3mp	נכה	645	3mp	smite
7:12	יקח	qal	wci	3ms	לקח	542		take
	ישׂם	qal	wci	3ms	שׂים	962		put,set
	יקרא	qal	wci	3ms	קרא	894		call,proclaim
	יאמר	qal	wci	3ms	אמר	55		say
	עזרנו	qal	pft	3ms	עזר	740	1cp	help,aid
7:13	יכנעו	niph	wci	3mp	כנע	488		humble self
	יספו	qal	pft	3cp	יסף	414		add,increase
	בוא	qal	infc		בוא	97		come in
	תהי	qal	wci	3fs	היה	224		be,become
7:14	תשׁבנה	qal	wci	3fp	שׁוב	996		turn,return
	לקחו	qal	pft	3cp	לקח	542		take
	הציל	hiph	pft	3ms	נצל	664		snatch,deliver
	יהי	qal	wci	3ms	היה	224		be,become
7:15	ישׁפט	qal	wci	3ms	שׁפט	1047		judge
7:16	הלך	qal	wcp	3ms	הלך	229		walk,go
	סבב	qal	wcp	3ms	סבב	685		surround
	שׁפט	qal	wcp	3ms	שׁפט	1047		judge
7:17	שׁפט	qal	pft	3ms	שׁפט	1047		judge
	יבן	qal	wci	3ms	בנה	124		build
8:1	יהי	qal	wci	3ms	היה	224		be,become
	זקן	qal	pft	3ms	זקן	278		be old
	ישׂם	qal	wci	3ms	שׂים	962		put,set
	שׁפטים	qal	ptc	mp	שׁפט	1047		judge
8:2	יהי	qal	wci	3ms	היה	224		be,become
	שׁפטים	qal	ptc	mp	שׁפט	1047		judge
8:3	הלכו	qal	pft	3cp	הלך	229		walk,go
	יטו	qal	wci	3mp	נטה	639		stretch,incline
	יקחו	qal	wci	3mp	לקח	542		take
	יטו	hiph	wci	3mp	נטה	639		turn,incline
8:4	יתקבצו	hith	wci	3mp	קבץ	867		gather together
	יבאו	qal	wci	3mp	בוא	97		come in
8:5	יאמרו	qal	wci	3mp	אמר	55		say
	זקנת	qal	pft	2ms	זקן	278		be old
	הלכו	qal	pft	3cp	הלך	229		walk,go
	שׂימה	qal	impv	ms	שׂים	962		put,set
	שׁפטנו	qal	infc		שׁפט	1047	1cp	judge
8:6	ירע	qal	wci	3ms	רעע	949		be evil
	אמרו	qal	pft	3cp	אמר	55		say
	תנה	qal	impv	ms	נתן	678		give,set
	שׁפטנו	qal	infc		שׁפט	1047	1cp	judge
	יתפלל	hith	wci	3ms	פלל	813		pray
8:7	יאמר	qal	wci	3ms	אמר	55		say
	שׁמע	qal	impv	ms	שׁמע	1033		hear
	יאמרו	qal	impf	3mp	אמר	55		say
	מאסו	qal	pft	3cp	מאס	549		reject,refuse
	מאסו	qal	pft	3cp	מאס	549		reject,refuse
	מלך	qal	infc		מלך	573		be king,reign
8:8	עשׂו	qal	pft	3cp	עשׂה	793		do,make
	העלתי	hiph	infc		עלה	748	1cs	bring up,offer
	יעזבני	qal	wci	3mp	עזב	736	1cs	leave,loose
	יעבדו	qal	wci	3mp	עבד	712		work,serve
	עשׂים	qal	ptc	mp	עשׂה	793		do,make
8:9	שׁמע	qal	impv	ms	שׁמע	1033		hear
	העד	hiph	infa		עוד	729		testify,warn
	תעיד	hiph	impf	2ms	עוד	729		testify,warn
	הגדת	hiph	wcp	2ms	נגד	616		declare,tell
	ימלך	qal	impf	3ms	מלך	573		be king,reign
8:10	יאמר	qal	wci	3ms	אמר	55		say
	שׁאלים	qal	ptc	mp	שׁאל	981		ask,borrow

ChVs	Form	Stem	Tnse	PGN	Root	BDB	Sfx	Meaning
8:11	יאמר	qal	wci	3ms	אמר	55		say
	יהיה	qal	impf	3ms	היה	224		be,become
	ימלך	qal	impf	3ms	מלך	573		be king,reign
	יקח	qal	impf	3ms	לקח	542		take
	שׂם	qal	wcp	3ms	שׂים	962		put,set
	רצו	qal	wcp	3cp	רוץ	930		run
8:12	שׂום	qal	infc		שׂים	962		put,set
	חרשׁ	qal	infc		חרשׁ	360		engrave,plough
	קצר	qal	infc		קצר	894		reap,harvest
	עשׂות	qal	infc		עשׂה	793		do,make
8:13	יקח	qal	impf	3ms	לקח	542		take
	אפות	qal	ptc	fp	אפה	66		bake
8:14	יקח	qal	impf	3ms	לקח	542		take
	נתן	qal	wcp	3ms	נתן	678		give,set
8:15	יעשׂר	qal	impf	3ms	עשׂר	797		tithe
	נתן	qal	wcp	3ms	נתן	678		give,set
8:16	יקח	qal	impf	3ms	לקח	542		take
	עשׂה	qal	wcp	3ms	עשׂה	793		do,make
8:17	יעשׂר	qal	impf	3ms	עשׂר	797		tithe
	תהיו	qal	impf	2mp	היה	224		be,become
8:18	זעקתם	qal	wcp	2mp	זעק	277		call,cry out
	בחרתם	qal	pft	2mp	בחר	103		choose
	יענה	qal	impf	3ms	ענה	772		answer
8:19	ימאנו	piel	wci	3mp	מאן	549		refuse
	שׁמע	qal	infc		שׁמע	1033		hear
	יאמרו	qal	wci	3mp	אמר	55		say
	יהיה	qal	impf	3ms	היה	224		be,become
8:20	היינו	qal	wcp	1cp	היה	224		be,become
	שׁפטנו	qal	wcp	3ms	שׁפט	1047	1cp	judge
	יצא	qal	wcp	3ms	יצא	422		go out
	נלחם	niph	wcp	3ms	לחם	535		wage war
8:21	ישׁמע	qal	wci	3ms	שׁמע	1033		hear
	ידברם	piel	wci	3ms	דבר	180	3mp	speak
8:22	יאמר	qal	wci	3ms	אמר	55		say
	שׁמע	qal	impv	ms	שׁמע	1033		hear
	המלכת	hiph	wcp	2ms	מלך	573		cause to reign
	יאמר	qal	wci	3ms	אמר	55		say
	לכו	qal	impv	mp	הלך	229		walk,go
9:1	יהי	qal	wci	3ms	היה	224		be,become
9:2	היה	qal	pft	3ms	היה	224		be,become
9:3	תאבדנה	qal	wci	3fp	אבד	1		perish
	יאמר	qal	wci	3ms	אמר	55		say
	קח	qal	impv	ms	לקח	542		take
	קום	qal	impv	ms	קום	877		arise,stand
	לך	qal	impv	ms	הלך	229		walk,go
	בקשׁ	piel	impv	ms	בקשׁ	134		seek
9:4	יעבר	qal	wci	3ms	עבר	716		pass over
	יעבר	qal	wci	3ms	עבר	716		pass over
	מצאו	qal	pft	3cp	מצא	592		find
	יעברו	qal	wci	3mp	עבר	716		pass over
	יעבר	qal	wci	3ms	עבר	716		pass over
	מצאו	qal	pft	3cp	מצא	592		find
9:5	באו	qal	pft	3cp	בוא	97		come in
	אמר	qal	pft	3ms	אמר	55		say
9:5	לכה	qal	impv	ms	הלך	229		walk,go
	נשׁובה	qal	coh	1cp	שׁוב	996		turn,return
	יחדל	qal	impf	3ms	חדל	292		cease
	דאג	qal	wcp	3ms	דאג	178		be anxious
9:6	יאמר	qal	wci	3ms	אמר	55		say
	נכבד	niph	ptc	ms	כבד	457		be honored
	ידבר	piel	impf	3ms	דבר	180		speak
	בוא	qal	infa		בוא	97		come in
	יבוא	qal	impf	3ms	בוא	97		come in
	נלכה	qal	coh	1cp	הלך	229		walk,go
	יגיד	hiph	impf	3ms	נגד	616		declare,tell
	הלכנו	qal	pft	1cp	הלך	229		walk,go
9:7	יאמר	qal	wci	3ms	אמר	55		say
	נלך	qal	impf	1cp	הלך	229		walk,go
	נביא	hiph	impf	1cp	בוא	97		bring in
	אזל	qal	pft	3ms	אזל	23		go
	הביא	hiph	infc		בוא	97		bring in
9:8	יסף	hiph	wci	3ms	יסף	414		add,do again
	ענות	qal	infc		ענה	772		answer
	יאמר	qal	wci	3ms	אמר	55		say
	נמצא	niph	ptc	ms	מצא	592		be found
	נתתי	qal	wcp	1cs	נתן	678		give,set
	הגיד	hiph	wcp	3ms	נגד	616		declare,tell
9:9	אמר	qal	pft	3ms	אמר	55		say
	לכתו	qal	infc		הלך	229	3ms	walk,go
	דרושׁ	qal	infc		דרשׁ	205		resort to,seek
	לכו	qal	impv	mp	הלך	229		walk,go
	נלכה	qal	coh	1cp	הלך	229		walk,go
	יקרא	niph	impf	3ms	קרא	894		be called
9:10	יאמר	qal	wci	3ms	אמר	55		say
	לכה	qal	impv	ms	הלך	229		walk,go
	נלכה	qal	coh	1cp	הלך	229		walk,go
	ילכו	qal	wci	3mp	הלך	229		walk,go
9:11	עלים	qal	ptc	mp	עלה	748		go up
	מצאו	qal	pft	3cp	מצא	592		find
	יצאות	qal	ptc	fp	יצא	422		go out
	שׁאב	qal	infc		שׁאב	980		draw (water)
	יאמרו	qal	wci	3mp	אמר	55		say
9:12	תענינה	qal	wci	3fp	ענה	772		answer
	תאמרנה	qal	wci	3fp	אמר	55		say
	מהר	piel	impv	ms	מהר	554		hasten
	בא	qal	pft	3ms	בוא	97		come in
9:13	באכם	qal	infc		בוא	97	2mp	come in
	תמצאון	qal	impf	2mp	מצא	592		find
	יעלה	qal	impf	3ms	עלה	748		go up
	אכל	qal	infc		אכל	37		eat,devour
	יאכל	qal	impf	3ms	אכל	37		eat,devour
	באו	qal	infc		בוא	97	3ms	come in
	יברך	piel	impf	3ms	ברך	138		bless
	יאכלו	qal	impf	3mp	אכל	37		eat,devour
	קראים	qal	pptc	mp	קרא	894		call,proclaim
	עלו	qal	impv	mp	עלה	748		go up
	תמצאון	qal	impf	2mp	מצא	592		find
9:14	יעלו	qal	wci	3mp	עלה	748		go up

ChVs	Form	Stem	Tnse	PGN	Root	BDB	Sfx	Meaning
9:14	באים	qal	ptc	mp	בוא	97		come in
	יצא	qal	ptc	ms	יצא	422		go out
	קראתם	qal	infc		קרא	896	3mp	meet,encounter
	עלות	qal	infc		עלה	748		go up
9:15	גלה	qal	pft	3ms	גלה	162		uncover
	בוא	qal	infc		בוא	97		come in
	אמר	qal	infc		אמר	55		say
9:16	אשלח	qal	impf	1cs	שלח	1018		send
	משחתו	qal	wcp	2ms	משח	602	3ms	smear,anoint
	הושיע	hiph	wcp	3ms	ישע	446		deliver,save
	ראיתי	qal	pft	1cs	ראה	906		see
	באה	qal	pft	3fs	בוא	97		come in
9:17	ראה	qal	pft	3ms	ראה	906		see
	ענהו	qal	pft	3ms	ענה	772	3ms	answer
	אמרתי	qal	pft	1cs	אמר	55		say
	יעצר	qal	impf	3ms	עצר	783		restrain
9:18	יגש	qal	wci	3ms	נגש	620		draw near
	יאמר	qal	wci	3ms	אמר	55		say
	הגידה	hiph	impv	ms	נגד	616		declare,tell
9:19	יען	qal	wci	3ms	ענה	772		answer
	יאמר	qal	wci	3ms	אמר	55		say
	עלה	qal	impv	ms	עלה	748		go up
	אכלתם	qal	wcp	2mp	אכל	37		eat,devour
	שלחתיך	piel	wcp	1cs	שלח	1018	2ms	send away,shoot
	אגיד	hiph	impf	1cs	נגד	616		declare,tell
9:20	אבדות	qal	ptc	fp	אבד	1		perish
	תשם	qal	jus	2ms	שים	962		put,set
	נמצאו	niph	pft	3cp	מצא	592		be found
9:21	יען	qal	wci	3ms	ענה	772		answer
	יאמר	qal	wci	3ms	אמר	55		say
	דברת	piel	pft	2ms	דבר	180		speak
9:22	יקח	qal	wci	3ms	לקח	542		take
	יביאם	hiph	wci	3ms	בוא	97	3mp	bring in
	יתן	qal	wci	3ms	נתן	678		give,set
	קרואים	qal	pptc	mp	קרא	894		call,proclaim
9:23	יאמר	qal	wci	3ms	אמר	55		say
	תנה	qal	impv	ms	נתן	678		give,set
	נתתי	qal	pft	1cs	נתן	678		give,set
	אמרתי	qal	pft	1cs	אמר	55		say
	שים	qal	impv	ms	שים	962		put,set
9:24	ירם	hiph	wci	3ms	רום	926		raise,lift
	ישם	qal	wci	3ms	שים	962		put,set
	יאמר	qal	wci	3ms	אמר	55		say
	נשאר	niph	ptc	ms	שאר	983		be left
	שים	qal	impv	ms	שים	962		put,set
	אכל	qal	impv	ms	אכל	37		eat,devour
	שמור	qal	pptc	ms	שמר	1036		keep,watch
	אמר	qal	infc		אמר	55		say
	קראתי	qal	pft	1cs	קרא	894		call,proclaim
	יאכל	qal	wci	3ms	אכל	37		eat,devour
9:25	ירדו	qal	wci	3mp	ירד	432		come down
	ידבר	piel	wci	3ms	דבר	180		speak
9:26	ישכמו	hiph	wci	3mp	שכם	1014		rise early
	יהי	qal	wci	3ms	היה	224		be,become
9:26	עלות	qal	infc		עלה	748		go up
	יקרא	qal	wci	3ms	קרא	894		call,proclaim
	אמר	qal	infc		אמר	55		say
	קומה	qal	impv	ms	קום	877		arise,stand
	אשלחך	piel	cohm	1cs	שלח	1018	2ms	send away,shoot
	יקם	qal	wci	3ms	קום	877		arise,stand
	יצאו	qal	wci	3mp	יצא	422		go out
9:27	יורדים	qal	ptc	mp	ירד	432		come down
	אמר	qal	pft	3ms	אמר	55		say
	אמר	qal	impv	ms	אמר	55		say
	יעבר	qal	jusm	3ms	עבר	716		pass over
	יעבר	qal	wci	3ms	עבר	716		pass over
	עמד	qal	impv	ms	עמד	763		stand,stop
	אשמיעך	hiph	cohm	1cs	שמע	1033	2ms	cause to hear
10:1	יקח	qal	wci	3ms	לקח	542		take
	יצק	qal	wci	3ms	יצק	427		pour out,cast
	ישקהו	qal	wci	3ms	נשק	676	3ms	kiss
	יאמר	qal	wci	3ms	אמר	55		say
	משחך	qal	pft	3ms	משח	602	2ms	smear,anoint
10:2	לכתך	qal	infc		הלך	229	2ms	walk,go
	מצאת	qal	wcp	2ms	מצא	592		find
	אמרו	qal	wcp	3cp	אמר	55		say
	נמצאו	niph	pft	3cp	מצא	592		be found
	הלכת	qal	pft	2ms	הלך	229		walk,go
	בקש	piel	infc		בקש	134		seek
	נטש	qal	pft	3ms	נטש	643		leave,forsake
	דאג	qal	wcp	3ms	דאג	178		be anxious
	אמר	qal	infc		אמר	55		say
	אעשה	qal	impf	1cs	עשה	793		do,make
10:3	חלפת	qal	wcp	2ms	חלף	322		pass on
	באת	qal	wcp	2ms	בוא	97		come in
	מצאוך	qal	wcp	3cp	מצא	592	2ms	find
	עלים	qal	ptc	mp	עלה	748		go up
	נשא	qal	ptc	ms	נשא	669		lift,carry
	נשא	qal	ptc	ms	נשא	669		lift,carry
	נשא	qal	ptc	ms	נשא	669		lift,carry
10:4	שאלו	qal	wcp	3cp	שאל	981		ask,borrow
	נתנו	qal	wcp	3cp	נתן	678		give,set
	לקחת	qal	wcp	2ms	לקח	542		take
10:5	תבוא	qal	impf	2ms	בוא	97		come in
	יהי	qal	jusf	3ms	היה	224		be,become
	באך	qal	infc		בוא	97	2ms	come in
	פגעת	qal	wcp	2ms	פגע	803		meet,encounter
	ירדים	qal	ptc	mp	ירד	432		come down
	מתנבאים	hith	ptc	mp	נבא	612		prophesy
10:6	צלחה	qal	wcp	3fs	צלח	852		rush
	התנבית	hith	wcp	2ms	נבא	612		prophesy
	נהפכת	niph	wcp	2ms	הפך	245		turn oneself
10:7	היה	qal	wcp	3ms	היה	224		be,become
	תבאינה k	qal	impf	3fp	בוא	97		come in
	תבאנה q	qal	impf	3fp	בוא	97		come in
	עשה	qal	impv	ms	עשה	793		do,make
	תמצא	qal	impf	3fs	מצא	592		find
10:8	ירדת	qal	wcp	2ms	ירד	432		come down

ChVs	Form	Stem	Tnse	PGN	Root	BDB	Sfx	Meaning
10: 8	ירד	qal	ptc	ms	ירד	432		come down
	העלות	hiph	infc		עלה	748		bring up,offer
	זבח	qal	infc		זבח	256		slaughter
	תוחל	hiph	jus	2ms	יחל	403		wait
	בואי	qal	infc		בוא	97	1cs	come in
	הודעתי	hiph	wcp	1cs	ידע	393		declare
	תעשׂה	qal	impf	2ms	עשׂה	793		do,make
10: 9	היה	qal	pft	3ms	היה	224		be,become
	הפנתו	hiph	infc		פנה	815	3ms	turn
	לכת	qal	infc		הלך	229		walk,go
	יהפך	qal	wci	3ms	הפך	245		turn,overturn
	יבאו	qal	wci	3mp	בוא	97		come in
10: 10	יבאו	qal	wci	3mp	בוא	97		come in
	קראתו	qal	infc		קרא	896	3ms	meet,encounter
	תצלח	qal	wci	3fs	צלח	852		rush
	יתנבא	hith	wci	3ms	נבא	612		prophesy
10: 11	יהי	qal	wci	3ms	היה	224		be,become
	יודעו	qal	ptc	ms	ידע	393	3ms	know
	יראו	qal	wci	3mp	ראה	906		see
	נבא	niph	ptc	ms	נבא	612		prophesy
	יאמר	qal	wci	3ms	אמר	55		say
	היה	qal	pft	3ms	היה	224		be,become
10: 12	יען	qal	wci	3ms	ענה	772		answer
	יאמר	qal	wci	3ms	אמר	55		say
	היתה	qal	pft	3fs	היה	224		be,become
10: 13	יכל	piel	wci	3ms	כלה	477		complete,finish
	התנבות	hith	infc		נבא	612		prophesy
	יבא	qal	wci	3ms	בוא	97		come in
10: 14	יאמר	qal	wci	3ms	אמר	55		say
	הלכתם	qal	pft	2mp	הלך	229		walk,go
	יאמר	qal	wci	3ms	אמר	55		say
	בקשׁ	piel	infc		בקשׁ	134		seek
	נראה	qal	wci	1cp	ראה	906		see
	נבוא	qal	wci	1cp	בוא	97		come in
10: 15	יאמר	qal	wci	3ms	אמר	55		say
	הגידה	hiph	impv	ms	נגד	616		declare,tell
	אמר	qal	pft	3ms	אמר	55		say
10: 16	יאמר	qal	wci	3ms	אמר	55		say
	הגד	hiph	infa		נגד	616		declare,tell
	הגיד	hiph	pft	3ms	נגד	616		declare,tell
	נמצאו	niph	pft	3cp	מצא	592		be found
	הגיד	hiph	pft	3ms	נגד	616		declare,tell
	אמר	qal	pft	3ms	אמר	55		say
10: 17	יצעק	hiph	wci	3ms	צעק	858		call together
10: 18	יאמר	qal	wci	3ms	אמר	55		say
	אמר	qal	pft	3ms	אמר	55		say
	העליתי	hiph	pft	1cs	עלה	748		bring up,offer
	אציל	hiph	wci	1cs	נצל	664		snatch,deliver
	לחצים	qal	ptc	mp	לחץ	537		press,oppress
10: 19	מאסתם	qal	pft	2mp	מאס	549		reject,refuse
	מושׁיע	hiph	ptc	ms	ישׁע	446		deliver,save
	תאמרו	qal	wci	2mp	אמר	55		say
	תשׂים	qal	impf	2ms	שׂים	962		put,set
	התיצבו	hith	impv	mp	יצב	426		stand oneself
10: 20	יקרב	hiph	wci	3ms	קרב	897		bring near
	ילכד	niph	wci	3ms	לכד	539		be captured
10: 21	יקרב	hiph	wci	3ms	קרב	897		bring near
	תלכד	niph	wci	3fs	לכד	539		be captured
	ילכד	niph	wci	3ms	לכד	539		be captured
	יבקשׁהו	piel	wci	3mp	בקשׁ	134	3ms	seek
	נמצא	niph	pft	3ms	מצא	592		be found
10: 22	ישׁאלו	qal	wci	3mp	שׁאל	981		ask,borrow
	בא	qal	pft	3ms	בוא	97		come in
	יאמר	qal	wci	3ms	אמר	55		say
	נחבא	niph	ptc	ms	חבא	285		hide oneself
10: 23	ירצו	qal	wci	3mp	רוץ	930		run
	יקחהו	qal	wci	3mp	לקח	542	3ms	take
	יתיצב	hith	wci	3ms	יצב	426		stand oneself
	יגבה	qal	wci	3ms	גבה	146		be high
10: 24	יאמר	qal	wci	3ms	אמר	55		say
	ראיתם	qal	pft	2mp	ראה	906		see
	בחר	qal	pft	3ms	בחר	103		choose
	ירעו	hiph	wci	3mp	רוע	929		raise a shout
	יאמרו	qal	wci	3mp	אמר	55		say
	יחי	qal	jus	3ms	חיה	310		live
10: 25	ידבר	piel	wci	3ms	דבר	180		speak
	יכתב	qal	wci	3ms	כתב	507		write
	ינח	hiph	wci	3ms	נוח	628		give rest,put
	ישׁלח	piel	wci	3ms	שׁלח	1018		send away,shoot
10: 26	הלך	qal	pft	3ms	הלך	229		walk,go
	ילכו	qal	wci	3mp	הלך	229		walk,go
	נגע	qal	pft	3ms	נגע	619		touch,strike
10: 27	אמרו	qal	pft	3cp	אמר	55		say
	ישׁענו	hiph	impf	3ms	ישׁע	446	1cp	deliver,save
	יבזהו	qal	wci	3mp	בזה	102	3ms	despise
	הביאו	hiph	pft	3cp	בוא	97		bring in
	יהי	qal	wci	3ms	היה	224		be,become
	מחרישׁ	hiph	ptc	ms	חרשׁ	361		be silent
11: 1	יעל	qal	wci	3ms	עלה	748		go up
	יחן	qal	wci	3ms	חנה	333		decline,encamp
	יאמרו	qal	wci	3mp	אמר	55		say
	כרת	qal	impv	ms	כרת	503		cut,destroy
	נעבדך	qal	cohm	1cp	עבד	712	2ms	work,serve
11: 2	יאמר	qal	wci	3ms	אמר	55		say
	אכרת	qal	impf	1cs	כרת	503		cut,destroy
	נקור	qal	infc		נקר	669		bore
	שׂמתיה	qal	wcp	1cs	שׂים	962	3fs	put,set
11: 3	יאמרו	qal	wci	3mp	אמר	55		say
	הרף	hiph	impv	ms	רפה	951		slacken,abandon
	נשׁלחה	qal	coh	1cp	שׁלח	1018		send
	מושׁיע	hiph	ptc	ms	ישׁע	446		deliver,save
	יצאנו	qal	wcp	1cp	יצא	422		go out
11: 4	יבאו	qal	wci	3mp	בוא	97		come in
	ידברו	piel	wci	3mp	דבר	180		speak
	ישׂאו	qal	wci	3mp	נשׂא	669		lift,carry
	יבכו	qal	wci	3mp	בכה	113		weep
11: 5	בא	qal	ptc	ms	בוא	97		come in
	יאמר	qal	wci	3ms	אמר	55		say

ChVs	Form	Stem	Tnse	PGN	Root	BDB	Sfx	Meaning
11:5	יבכו	qal	impf	3mp	בכה	113		weep
	יספרו	piel	wci	3mp	ספר	707		recount
11:6	תצלח	qal	wci	3fs	צלח	852		rush
	שמעו	qal	infc		שמע	1033	3ms	hear
	יחר	qal	wci	3ms	חרה	354		be kindled,burn
11:7	יקח	qal	wci	3ms	לקח	542		take
	ינתחהו	piel	wci	3ms	נתח	677	3ms	cut in pieces
	ישלח	piel	wci	3ms	שלח	1018		send away,shoot
	אמר	qal	infc		אמר	55		say
	יצא	qal	ptc	ms	יצא	422		go out
	יעשה	niph	impf	3ms	עשה	793		be done
	יפל	qal	wci	3ms	נפל	656		fall
	יצאו	qal	wci	3mp	יצא	422		go out
11:8	יפקדם	qal	wci	3ms	פקד	823	3mp	attend to,visit
	יהיו	qal	wci	3mp	היה	224		be,become
11:9	יאמרו	qal	wci	3mp	אמר	55		say
	באים	qal	ptc	mp	בוא	97		come in
	תאמרון	qal	impf	2mp	אמר	55		say
	תהיה	qal	impf	3fs	היה	224		be,become
	חם	qal	infc		חמם	328		be warm
	יבאו	qal	wci	3mp	בוא	97		come in
	יגידו	hiph	wci	3mp	נגד	616		declare,tell
	ישמחו	qal	wci	3mp	שמח	970		rejoice
11:10	יאמרו	qal	wci	3mp	אמר	55		say
	נצא	qal	impf	1cp	יצא	422		go out
	עשיתם	qal	wcp	2mp	עשה	793		do,make
11:11	יהי	qal	wci	3ms	היה	224		be,become
	ישם	qal	wci	3ms	שים	962		put,set
	יבאו	qal	wci	3mp	בוא	97		come in
	יכו	hiph	wci	3mp	נכה	645		smite
	יהי	qal	wci	3ms	היה	224		be,become
	נשארים	niph	ptc	mp	שאר	983		be left
	יפצו	qal	wci	3mp	פוץ	806		be scattered
	נשארו	niph	pft	3cp	שאר	983		be left
11:12	יאמר	qal	wci	3ms	אמר	55		say
	אמר	qal	ptc	ms	אמר	55		say
	ימלך	qal	impf	3ms	מלך	573		be king,reign
	תנו	qal	impv	mp	נתן	678		give,set
	נמיתם	hiph	cohm	1cp	מות	559	3mp	kill
11:13	יאמר	qal	wci	3ms	אמר	55		say
	יומת	hoph	impf	3ms	מות	559		be killed
	עשה	qal	pft	3ms	עשה	793		do,make
11:14	יאמר	qal	wci	3ms	אמר	55		say
	לכו	qal	impv	mp	הלך	229		walk,go
	נלכה	qal	coh	1cp	הלך	229		walk,go
	נחדש	piel	cohm	1cp	חדש	293		renew,repair
11:15	ילכו	qal	wci	3mp	הלך	229		walk,go
	ימלכו	hiph	wci	3mp	מלך	573		cause to reign
	יזבחו	qal	wci	3mp	זבח	256		slaughter
	ישמח	qal	wci	3ms	שמח	970		rejoice
12:1	יאמר	qal	wci	3ms	אמר	55		say
	שמעתי	qal	pft	1cs	שמע	1033		hear
	אמרתם	qal	pft	2mp	אמר	55		say
	אמליך	hiph	wci	1cs	מלך	573		cause to reign

ChVs	Form	Stem	Tnse	PGN	Root	BDB	Sfx	Meaning
12:2	מתהלך	hith	ptc	ms	הלך	229		walk to and fro
	זקנתי	qal	pft	1cs	זקן	278		be old
	שבתי	qal	pft	1cs	שיב	966		be hoary
	התהלכתי	hith	pft	1cs	הלך	229		walk to and fro
12:3	ענו	qal	impv	mp	ענה	772		answer
	לקחתי	qal	pft	1cs	לקח	542		take
	לקחתי	qal	pft	1cs	לקח	542		take
	עשקתי	qal	pft	1cs	עשק	798		oppress,extort
	רצותי	qal	pft	1cs	רצץ	954		crush
	לקחתי	qal	pft	1cs	לקח	542		take
	אעלים	hiph	impf	1cs	עלם	761		conceal,hide
	אשיב	hiph	impf	1cs	שוב	996		bring back
12:4	יאמרו	qal	wci	3mp	אמר	55		say
	עשקתנו	qal	pft	2ms	עשק	798	1cp	oppress,extort
	רצותנו	qal	pft	2ms	רצץ	954	1cp	crush
	לקחת	qal	pft	2ms	לקח	542		take
12:5	יאמר	qal	wci	3ms	אמר	55		say
	מצאתם	qal	pft	2mp	מצא	592		find
	יאמר	qal	wci	3ms	אמר	55		say
12:6	יאמר	qal	wci	3ms	אמר	55		say
	עשה	qal	pft	3ms	עשה	793		do,make
	העלה	hiph	pft	3ms	עלה	748		bring up,offer
12:7	התיצבו	hith	impv	mp	יצב	426		stand oneself
	אשפטה	niph	coh	1cs	שפט	1047		plead
	עשה	qal	pft	3ms	עשה	793		do,make
12:8	בא	qal	pft	3ms	בוא	97		come in
	יזעקו	qal	wci	3mp	זעק	277		call,cry out
	ישלח	qal	wci	3ms	שלח	1018		send
	יוציאו	hiph	wci	3mp	יצא	422		bring out
	ישבום	hiph	wci	3mp	ישב	442	3mp	cause to dwell
12:9	ישכחו	qal	wci	3mp	שכח	1013		forget
	ימכר	qal	wci	3ms	מכר	569		sell
	ילחמו	niph	wci	3mp	לחם	535		wage war
12:10	יזעקו	qal	wci	3mp	זעק	277		call,cry out
	יאמרk	qal	wci	3ms	אמר	55		say
	יאמרוq	qal	wci	3mp	אמר	55		say
	חטאנו	qal	pft	1cp	חטא	306		sin
	עזבנו	qal	pft	1cp	עזב	736		leave,loose
	נעבד	qal	wci	1cp	עבד	712		work,serve
	הצילנו	hiph	impv	mp	נצל	664	1cp	snatch,deliver
	איבינו	qal	ptc	mp	איב	33	1cp	be hostile to
	נעבדך	qal	cohm	1cp	עבד	712	2ms	work,serve
12:11	ישלח	qal	wci	3ms	שלח	1018		send
	יצל	hiph	wci	3ms	נצל	664		snatch,deliver
	איביכם	qal	ptc	mp	איב	33	2mp	be hostile to
	תשבו	qal	wci	2mp	ישב	442		sit,dwell
12:12	תראו	qal	wci	2mp	ראה	906		see
	בא	qal	ptc	ms	בוא	97		come in
	תאמרו	qal	wci	2mp	אמר	55		say
	ימלך	qal	impf	3ms	מלך	573		be king,reign
12:13	בחרתם	qal	pft	2mp	בחר	103		choose
	שאלתם	qal	pft	2mp	שאל	981		ask,borrow
	נתן	qal	pft	3ms	נתן	678		give,set
12:14	תיראו	qal	impf	2mp	ירא	431		fear

ChVs	Form	Stem	Tnse	PGN	Root	BDB	Sfx	Meaning
12:14	עבדתם	qal	wcp	2mp	עבד	712		work,serve
	שמעתם	qal	wcp	2mp	שמע	1033		hear
	תמרו	hiph	impf	2mp	מרה	598		rebel
	היתם	qal	wcp	2mp	היה	224		be,become
	מלך	qal	pft	3ms	מלך	573		be king,reign
12:15	תשמעו	qal	impf	2mp	שמע	1033		hear
	מריתם	qal	wcp	2mp	מרה	598		be disobedient
	היתה	qal	wcp	3fs	היה	224		be,become
12:16	התיצבו	hith	impv	mp	יצב	426		stand oneself
	ראו	qal	impv	mp	ראה	906		see
	עשה	qal	ptc	ms	עשה	793		do,make
12:17	אקרא	qal	cohm	1cs	קרא	894		call,proclaim
	יתן	qal	jusm	3ms	נתן	678		give,set
	דעו	qal	impv	mp	ידע	393		know
	ראו	qal	impv	mp	ראה	906		see
	עשיתם	qal	pft	2mp	עשה	793		do,make
	שאול	qal	infc		שאל	981		ask,borrow
12:18	יקרא	qal	wci	3ms	קרא	894		call,proclaim
	יתן	qal	wci	3ms	נתן	678		give,set
	יירא	qal	wci	3ms	ירא	431		fear
12:19	יאמרו	qal	wci	3mp	אמר	55		say
	התפלל	hith	impv	ms	פלל	813		pray
	נמות	qal	cohm	1cp	מות	559		die
	יספנו	qal	pft	1cp	יסף	414		add,increase
	שאל	qal	infc		שאל	981		ask,borrow
12:20	יאמר	qal	wci	3ms	אמר	55		say
	תיראו	qal	jusm	2mp	ירא	431		fear
	עשיתם	qal	pft	2mp	עשה	793		do,make
	תסורו	qal	jusm	2mp	סור	693		turn aside
	עבדתם	qal	wcp	2mp	עבד	712		work,serve
12:21	תסורו	qal	impf	2mp	סור	693		turn aside
	יועילו	hiph	impf	3mp	יעל	418		profit,benefit
	יצילו	hiph	impf	3mp	נצל	664		snatch,deliver
12:22	יטש	qal	impf	3ms	נטש	643		leave,forsake
	הואיל	hiph	pft	3ms	יאל	383		be willing
	עשות	qal	infc		עשה	793		do,make
12:23	חטא	qal	infc		חטא	306		sin
	חדל	qal	infc		חדל	292		cease
	התפלל	hith	infc		פלל	813		pray
	הוריתי	hiph	wcp	1cs	ירה	434		shoot,teach
12:24	יראו	qal	impv	mp	ירא	431		fear
	עבדתם	qal	wcp	2mp	עבד	712		work,serve
	ראו	qal	impv	mp	ראה	906		see
	הגדל	hiph	pft	3ms	גדל	152		make great
12:25	הרע	hiph	infa		רעע	949		hurt,do evil
	תרעו	hiph	impf	2mp	רעע	949		hurt,do evil
	תספו	niph	impf	2mp	ספה	705		be swept away
13:1	מלכו	qal	infc		מלך	573	3ms	be king,reign
	מלך	qal	pft	3ms	מלך	573		be king,reign
13:2	יבחר	qal	wci	3ms	בחר	103		choose
	יהיו	qal	wci	3mp	היה	224		be,become
	היו	qal	pft	3cp	היה	224		be,become
	שלח	piel	pft	3ms	שלח	1018		send away,shoot
13:3	יך	hiph	wci	3ms	נכה	645		smite
13:3	ישמעו	qal	wci	3mp	שמע	1033		hear
	תקע	qal	pft	3ms	תקע	1075		thrust,clap
	אמר	qal	infc		אמר	55		say
	ישמעו	qal	jusm	3mp	שמע	1033		hear
13:4	שמעו	qal	pft	3cp	שמע	1033		hear
	אמר	qal	infc		אמר	55		say
	הכה	hiph	pft	3ms	נכה	645		smite
	נבאש	niph	pft	3ms	באש	92		make odious
	יצעקו	niph	wci	3mp	צעק	858		be summoned
13:5	נאספו	niph	pft	3cp	אסף	62		assemble
	הלחם	niph	infc		לחם	535		wage war
	יעלו	qal	wci	3mp	עלה	748		go up
	יחנו	qal	wci	3mp	חנה	333		decline,encamp
13:6	ראו	qal	pft	3cp	ראה	906		see
	צר	qal	pft	3ms	צרר	864		bind,be cramped
	נגש	niph	pft	3ms	נגש	620		be pressed
	יתחבאו	hith	wci	3mp	חבא	285		hide oneself
13:7	עברו	qal	pft	3cp	עבר	716		pass over
	חרדו	qal	pft	3cp	חרד	353		tremble
13:8	ייחל k	niph	wci	3ms	יחל	403		wait
	ויוחל q	hiph	wci	3ms	יחל	403		wait
	בא	qal	pft	3ms	בוא	97		come in
	יפץ	hiph	wci	3ms	פוץ	806		scatter
13:9	יאמר	qal	wci	3ms	אמר	55		say
	הגשו	hiph	impv	mp	נגש	620		bring near
	יעל	hiph	wci	3ms	עלה	748		bring up,offer
13:10	יהי	qal	wci	3ms	היה	224		be,become
	כלתו	piel	infc		כלה	477	3ms	complete,finish
	העלות	hiph	infc		עלה	748		bring up,offer
	בא	qal	ptc	ms	בוא	97		come in
	יצא	qal	wci	3ms	יצא	422		go out
	קראתו	qal	infc		קרא	896	3ms	meet,encounter
	ברכו	piel	infc		ברך	138	3ms	bless
13:11	יאמר	qal	wci	3ms	אמר	55		say
	עשית	qal	pft	2ms	עשה	793		do,make
	יאמר	qal	wci	3ms	אמר	55		say
	ראיתי	qal	pft	1cs	ראה	906		see
	נפץ	qal	pft	3ms	נפץ	659		disperse
	באת	qal	pft	2ms	בוא	97		come in
	נאספים	niph	ptc	mp	אסף	62		assemble
13:12	אמר	qal	wci	1cs	אמר	55		say
	ירדו	qal	impf	3mp	ירד	432		come down
	חליתי	piel	pft	1cs	חלה	318		pacify,appease
	אתאפק	hith	wci	1cs	אפק	67		restrain self
	אעלה	hiph	wci	1cs	עלה	748		bring up,offer
13:13	יאמר	qal	wci	3ms	אמר	55		say
	נסכלת	niph	pft	2ms	סכל	698		act foolishly
	שמרת	qal	pft	2ms	שמר	1036		keep,watch
	צוך	piel	pft	3ms	צוה	845	2ms	command
	הכין	hiph	pft	3ms	כון	465		fix,prepare
13:14	תקום	qal	impf	3fs	קום	877		arise,stand
	בקש	piel	pft	3ms	בקש	134		seek
	יצוהו	piel	wci	3ms	צוה	845	3ms	command
	שמרת	qal	pft	2ms	שמר	1036		keep,watch

ChVs	Form	Stem	Tnse	PGN	Root	BDB	Sfx	Meaning
13:14	צוך	piel	pft	3ms	צוה	845	2ms	command
13:15	יקם	qal	wci	3ms	קום	877		arise,stand
	יעל	qal	wci	3ms	עלה	748		go up
	יפקד	qal	wci	3ms	פקד	823		attend to,visit
	נמצאים	niph	ptc	mp	מצא	592		be found
13:16	נמצא	niph	ptc	ms	מצא	592		be found
	ישבים	qal	ptc	mp	ישב	442		sit,dwell
	חנו	qal	pft	3cp	חנה	333		decline,encamp
13:17	יצא	qal	wci	3ms	יצא	422		go out
	משחית	hiph	ptc	ms	שחת	1007		spoil,ruin
	יפנה	qal	impf	3ms	פנה	815		turn
13:18	יפנה	qal	impf	3ms	פנה	815		turn
	יפנה	qal	impf	3ms	פנה	815		turn
	נשקף	niph	ptc	ms	שקף	1054		look down
13:19	ימצא	niph	impf	3ms	מצא	592		be found
	אמרk	qal	pft	3ms	אמר	55		say
	אמרוq	qal	pft	3cp	אמר	55		say
	יעשו	qal	impf	3mp	עשה	793		do,make
13:20	ירדו	qal	wci	3mp	ירד	432		come down
	לטוש	qal	infc		לטש	538		hammer,sharpen
13:21	היתה	qal	wcp	3fs	היה	224		be,become
	הציב	hiph	infc		נצב	662		cause to stand
13:22	היה	qal	wcp	3ms	היה	224		be,become
	נמצא	niph	pft	3ms	מצא	592		be found
	תמצא	niph	wci	3fs	מצא	592		be found
13:23	יצא	qal	wci	3ms	יצא	422		go out
14:1	יהי	qal	wci	3ms	היה	224		be,become
	יאמר	qal	wci	3ms	אמר	55		say
	נשא	qal	ptc	ms	נשא	669		lift,carry
	לכה	qal	impv	ms	הלך	229		walk,go
	נעברה	qal	coh	1cp	עבר	716		pass over
	הגיד	hiph	pft	3ms	נגד	616		declare,tell
14:2	יושב	qal	ptc	ms	ישב	442		sit,dwell
14:3	נשא	qal	ptc	ms	נשא	669		lift,carry
	ידע	qal	pft	3ms	ידע	393		know
	הלך	qal	pft	3ms	הלך	229		walk,go
14:4	בקש	piel	pft	3ms	בקש	134		seek
	עבר	qal	infc		עבר	716		pass over
14:6	יאמר	qal	wci	3ms	אמר	55		say
	נשא	qal	ptc	ms	נשא	669		lift,carry
	לכה	qal	impv	ms	הלך	229		walk,go
	נעברה	qal	coh	1cp	עבר	716		pass over
	יעשה	qal	impf	3ms	עשה	793		do,make
	הושיע	hiph	infc		ישע	446		deliver,save
14:7	יאמר	qal	wci	3ms	אמר	55		say
	נשא	qal	ptc	ms	נשא	669		lift,carry
	עשה	qal	impv	ms	עשה	793		do,make
	נטה	qal	impv	ms	נטה	639		stretch,incline
14:8	יאמר	qal	wci	3ms	אמר	55		say
	עברים	qal	ptc	mp	עבר	716		pass over
	נגלינו	niph	wcp	1cp	גלה	162		uncover self
14:9	יאמרו	qal	impf	3mp	אמר	55		say
	דמו	qal	impv	mp	דמם	198		be silent
	הגיענו	hiph	infc		נגע	619	1cp	reach,arrive
14:9	עמדנו	qal	wcp	1cp	עמד	763		stand,stop
	נעלה	qal	impf	1cp	עלה	748		go up
14:10	יאמרו	qal	impf	3mp	אמר	55		say
	עלו	qal	impv	mp	עלה	748		go up
	עלינו	qal	wcp	1cp	עלה	748		go up
	נתנם	qal	pft	3ms	נתן	678	3mp	give,set
14:11	יגלו	niph	wci	3mp	גלה	162		uncover self
	יאמרו	qal	wci	3mp	אמר	55		say
	יצאים	qal	ptc	mp	יצא	422		go out
	התחבאו	hith	pft	3cp	חבא	285		hide oneself
14:12	יענו	qal	wci	3mp	ענה	772		answer
	נשא	qal	ptc	ms	נשא	669		lift,carry
	יאמרו	qal	wci	3mp	אמר	55		say
	עלו	qal	impv	mp	עלה	748		go up
	נודיעה	hiph	coh	1cp	ידע	393		declare
	יאמר	qal	wci	3ms	אמר	55		say
	נשא	qal	ptc	ms	נשא	669		lift,carry
	עלה	qal	impv	ms	עלה	748		go up
	נתנם	qal	pft	3ms	נתן	678	3mp	give,set
14:13	יעל	qal	wci	3ms	עלה	748		go up
	נשא	qal	ptc	ms	נשא	669		lift,carry
	יפלו	qal	wci	3mp	נפל	656		fall
	נשא	qal	ptc	ms	נשא	669		lift,carry
	ממותת	pol	ptc	ms	מות	559		kill
14:14	תהי	qal	wci	3fs	היה	224		be,become
	הכה	hiph	pft	3ms	נכה	645		smite
	נשא	qal	ptc	ms	נשא	669		lift,carry
14:15	תהי	qal	wci	3fs	היה	224		be,become
	משחית	hiph	ptc	ms	שחת	1007		spoil,ruin
	חרדו	qal	pft	3cp	חרד	353		tremble
	תרגז	qal	wci	3fs	רגז	919		quake
	תהי	qal	wci	3fs	היה	224		be,become
14:16	יראו	qal	wci	3mp	ראה	906		see
	צפים	qal	ptc	mp	צפה	859		keep watch
	נמוג	niph	pft	3ms	מוג	556		melt away
	ילך	qal	wci	3ms	הלך	229		walk,go
14:17	יאמר	qal	wci	3ms	אמר	55		say
	פקדו	qal	impv	mp	פקד	823		attend to,visit
	ראו	qal	impv	mp	ראה	906		see
	הלך	qal	pft	3ms	הלך	229		walk,go
	יפקדו	qal	wci	3mp	פקד	823		attend to,visit
	נשא	qal	ptc	ms	נשא	669		lift,carry
14:18	יאמר	qal	wci	3ms	אמר	55		say
	הגישה	hiph	impv	ms	נגש	620		bring near
	היה	qal	pft	3ms	היה	224		be,become
14:19	יהי	qal	wci	3ms	היה	224		be,become
	דבר	piel	pft	3ms	דבר	180		speak
	ילך	qal	wci	3ms	הלך	229		walk,go
	הלוך	qal	infa		הלך	229		walk,go
	יאמר	qal	wci	3ms	אמר	55		say
	אסף	qal	impv	ms	אסף	62		gather
14:20	יזעק	niph	wci	3ms	זעק	277		assemble
	יבאו	qal	wci	3mp	בוא	97		come in
	היתה	qal	pft	3fs	היה	224		be,become

ChVs	Form	Stem	Tnse	PGN	Root	BDB	Sfx	Meaning
14:21	היו	qal	pft	3cp	היה	224		be,become
	עלו	qal	pft	3cp	עלה	748		go up
	היות	qal	infc		היה	224		be,become
14:22	מתחבאים	hith	ptc	mp	חבא	285		hide oneself
	שמעו	qal	pft	3cp	שמע	1033		hear
	נסו	qal	pft	3cp	נוס	630		flee,escape
	ידבקו	hiph	wci	3mp	דבק	179		cause to cling
14:23	יושע	hiph	wci	3ms	ישע	446		deliver,save
	עברה	qal	pft	3fs	עבר	716		pass over
14:24	נגש	niph	pft	3ms	נגש	620		be pressed
	יאל	hiph	wci	3ms	אלה	46		put under oath
	אמר	qal	infc		אמר	55		say
	ארור	qal	pptc	ms	ארר	76		curse
	יאכל	qal	impf	3ms	אכל	37		eat,devour
	נקמתי	niph	wcp	1cs	נקם	667		avenge oneself
	איבי	qal	ptc	mp	איב	33	1cs	be hostile to
	טעם	qal	pft	3ms	טעם	380		taste
14:25	באו	qal	pft	3cp	בוא	97		come in
	יהי	qal	wci	3ms	היה	224		be,become
14:26	יבא	qal	wci	3ms	בוא	97		come in
	משיג	hiph	ptc	ms	נשג	673		reach,overtake
	ירא	qal	pft	3ms	ירא	431		fear
14:27	שמע	qal	pft	3ms	שמע	1033		hear
	השביע	hiph	infc		שבע	989		cause to swear
	ישלח	qal	wci	3ms	שלח	1018		send
	יטבל	qal	wci	3ms	טבל	371		dip
	ישב	hiph	wci	3ms	שוב	996		bring back
	תראנהk	qal	wci	3fp	ראה	906		see
	תארנהq	qal	wci	3fp	אור	21		become light
14:28	יען	qal	wci	3ms	ענה	772		answer
	יאמר	qal	wci	3ms	אמר	55		say
	השבע	hiph	infa		שבע	989		cause to swear
	השביע	hiph	pft	3ms	שבע	989		cause to swear
	אמר	qal	infc		אמר	55		say
	ארור	qal	pptc	ms	ארר	76		curse
	יאכל	qal	impf	3ms	אכל	37		eat,devour
	יעף	qal	wci	3ms	עיף	746		be faint
14:29	יאמר	qal	wci	3ms	אמר	55		say
	עכר	qal	pft	3ms	עכר	747		trouble
	ראו	qal	impv	mp	ראה	906		see
	ארו	qal	pft	3cp	אור	21		become light
	טעמתי	qal	pft	1cs	טעם	380		taste
14:30	אכל	qal	infa		אכל	37		eat,devour
	אכל	qal	pft	3ms	אכל	37		eat,devour
	איביו	qal	ptc	mp	איב	33	3ms	be hostile to
	מצא	qal	pft	3ms	מצא	592		find
	רבתה	qal	pft	3fs	רבה	915		be many,great
14:31	יכו	hiph	wci	3mp	נכה	645		smite
	יעף	qal	wci	3ms	עיף	746		be faint
14:32	יעשk	qal	wci	3ms	עשה	793		do,make
	יעטq	qal	wci	3ms	עיט	743		dart greedily
	יקחו	qal	wci	3mp	לקח	542		take
	ישחטו	qal	wci	3mp	שחט	1006		slaughter
	יאכל	qal	wci	3ms	אכל	37		eat,devour
14:33	יגידו	hiph	wci	3mp	נגד	616		declare,tell
	אמר	qal	infc		אמר	55		say
	חטאים	qal	ptc	mp	חטא	306		sin
	אכל	qal	infc		אכל	37		eat,devour
	יאמר	qal	wci	3ms	אמר	55		say
	בגדתם	qal	pft	2mp	בגד	93		act faithlessly
	גלו	qal	impv	mp	גלל	164		roll away
14:34	יאמר	qal	wci	3ms	אמר	55		say
	פצו	qal	impv	mp	פוץ	806		be scattered
	אמרתם	qal	wcp	2mp	אמר	55		say
	הגישו	hiph	impv	mp	נגש	620		bring near
	שחטתם	qal	wcp	2mp	שחט	1006		slaughter
	אכלתם	qal	wcp	2mp	אכל	37		eat,devour
	תחטאו	qal	impf	2mp	חטא	306		sin
	אכל	qal	infc		אכל	37		eat,devour
	יגשו	hiph	wci	3mp	נגש	620		bring near
	ישחטו	qal	wci	3mp	שחט	1006		slaughter
14:35	יבן	qal	wci	3ms	בנה	124		build
	החל	hiph	pft	3ms	חלל	320		begin,profane
	בנות	qal	infc		בנה	124		build
14:36	יאמר	qal	wci	3ms	אמר	55		say
	נרדה	qal	coh	1cp	ירד	432		come down
	נבזה	qal	coh	1cp	בזז	102		plunder
	נשאר	hiph	jus	1cp	שאר	983		leave,spare
	יאמרו	qal	wci	3mp	אמר	55		say
	עשה	qal	impv	ms	עשה	793		do,make
	יאמר	qal	wci	3ms	אמר	55		say
	נקרבה	qal	coh	1cp	קרב	897		approach
14:37	ישאל	qal	wci	3ms	שאל	981		ask,borrow
	ארד	qal	impf	1cs	ירד	432		come down
	תתנם	qal	impf	2ms	נתן	678	3mp	give,set
	ענהו	qal	pft	3ms	ענה	772	3ms	answer
14:38	יאמר	qal	wci	3ms	אמר	55		say
	גשו	qal	impv	mp	נגש	620		draw near
	דעו	qal	impv	mp	ידע	393		know
	ראו	qal	impv	mp	ראה	906		see
	היתה	qal	pft	3fs	היה	224		be,become
14:39	מושיע	hiph	ptc	ms	ישע	446		deliver,save
	מות	qal	infa		מות	559		die
	ימות	qal	impf	3ms	מות	559		die
	ענהו	qal	ptc	ms	ענה	772	3ms	answer
14:40	יאמר	qal	wci	3ms	אמר	55		say
	תהיו	qal	impf	2mp	היה	224		be,become
	נהיה	qal	impf	1cp	היה	224		be,become
	יאמרו	qal	wci	3mp	אמר	55		say
	עשה	qal	impv	ms	עשה	793		do,make
14:41	יאמר	qal	wci	3ms	אמר	55		say
	הבה	qal	impv	ms	יהב	396		give
	ילכד	niph	wci	3ms	לכד	539		be captured
	יצאו	qal	pft	3cp	יצא	422		go out
14:42	יאמר	qal	wci	3ms	אמר	55		say
	הפילו	hiph	impv	mp	נפל	656		cause to fall
	ילכד	niph	wci	3ms	לכד	539		be captured
14:43	יאמר	qal	wci	3ms	אמר	55		say

ChVs	Form	Stem	Tnse	PGN	Root	BDB	Sfx	Meaning
14:43	הגידה	hiph	impv	ms	נגד	616		declare,tell
	עשיתה	qal	pft	2ms	עשה	793		do,make
	יגד	hiph	wci	3ms	נגד	616		declare,tell
	יאמר	qal	wci	3ms	אמר	55		say
	טעם	qal	infa		טעם	380		taste
	טעמתי	qal	pft	1cs	טעם	380		taste
	אמות	qal	impf	1cs	מות	559		die
14:44	יאמר	qal	wci	3ms	אמר	55		say
	יעשה	qal	jusm	3ms	עשה	793		do,make
	יוסף	hiph	jusm	3ms	יסף	414		add,do again
	מות	qal	infa		מות	559		die
	תמות	qal	impf	2ms	מות	559		die
14:45	יאמר	qal	wci	3ms	אמר	55		say
	ימות	qal	impf	3ms	מות	559		die
	עשה	qal	pft	3ms	עשה	793		do,make
	יפל	qal	impf	3ms	נפל	656		fall
	עשה	qal	pft	3ms	עשה	793		do,make
	יפדו	qal	wci	3mp	פדה	804		ransom
	מת	qal	pft	3ms	מות	559		die
14:46	יעל	qal	wci	3ms	עלה	748		go up
	הלכו	qal	pft	3cp	הלך	229		walk,go
14:47	לכד	qal	pft	3ms	לכד	539		capture
	ילחם	niph	wci	3ms	לחם	535		wage war
	איביו	qal	ptc	mp	איב	33	3ms	be hostile to
	יפנה	qal	impf	3ms	פנה	815		turn
	ירשיע	hiph	impf	3ms	רשע	957		condemn, be evil
14:48	יעש	qal	wci	3ms	עשה	793		do,make
	יך	hiph	wci	3ms	נכה	645		smite
	יצל	hiph	wci	3ms	נצל	664		snatch,deliver
	שסהו	qal	ptc	ms	שסה	1042	3ms	plunder
14:49	יהיו	qal	wci	3mp	היה	224		be,become
14:52	תהי	qal	wci	3fs	היה	224		be,become
	ראה	qal	wcp	3ms	ראה	906		see
	יאספהו	qal	wci	3ms	אסף	62	3ms	gather
15:1	יאמר	qal	wci	3ms	אמר	55		say
	שלח	qal	pft	3ms	שלח	1018		send
	משחך	qal	infc		משח	602	2ms	smear,anoint
	שמע	qal	impv	ms	שמע	1033		hear
15:2	אמר	qal	pft	3ms	אמר	55		say
	פקדתי	qal	pft	1cs	פקד	823		attend to,visit
	עשה	qal	pft	3ms	עשה	793		do,make
	שם	qal	pft	3ms	שים	962		put,set
	עלתו	qal	infc		עלה	748	3ms	go up
15:3	לך	qal	impv	ms	הלך	229		walk,go
	הכיתה	hiph	wcp	2ms	נכה	645		smite
	החרמתם	hiph	wcp	2mp	חרם	355		ban,destroy
	תחמל	qal	impf	2ms	חמל	328		spare
	המתה	hiph	wcp	2ms	מות	559		kill
	יונק	qal	ptc	ms	ינק	413		suck
15:4	ישמע	piel	wci	3ms	שמע	1033		cause to hear
	יפקדם	qal	wci	3ms	פקד	823	3mp	attend to,visit
15:5	יבא	qal	wci	3ms	בוא	97		come in
	ירב	hiph	wci	3ms	ארב	70		lie in wait
15:6	יאמר	qal	wci	3ms	אמר	55		say
15:6	לכו	qal	impv	mp	הלך	229		walk,go
	סרו	qal	impv	mp	סור	693		turn aside
	רדו	qal	impv	mp	ירד	432		come down
	אספך	qal	impf	1cs	אסף	62	2ms	gather
	עשיתה	qal	pft	2ms	עשה	793		do,make
	עלותם	qal	infc		עלה	748	3mp	go up
	יסר	qal	wci	3ms	סור	693		turn aside
15:7	יך	hiph	wci	3ms	נכה	645		smite
	בואך	qal	infc		בוא	97	2ms	come in
15:8	יתפש	qal	wci	3ms	תפש	1074		seize,grasp
	החרים	hiph	pft	3ms	חרם	355		ban,destroy
15:9	יחמל	qal	wci	3ms	חמל	328		spare
	אבו	qal	pft	3cp	אבה	2		be willing
	החרימם	hiph	infc		חרם	355	3mp	ban,destroy
	נמבזה	niph	ptc	fs	בזה	102?		despised
	נמס	niph	ptc	ms	מסס	587		melt,despair
	החרימו	hiph	pft	3cp	חרם	355		ban,destroy
15:10	יהי	qal	wci	3ms	היה	224		be,become
	אמר	qal	infc		אמר	55		say
15:11	נחמתי	niph	pft	1cs	נחם	636		be sorry
	המלכתי	hiph	pft	1cs	מלך	573		cause to reign
	שב	qal	pft	3ms	שוב	996		turn,return
	הקים	hiph	pft	3ms	קום	877		raise,build,set
	יחר	qal	wci	3ms	חרה	354		be kindled,burn
	יזעק	qal	wci	3ms	זעק	277		call,cry out
15:12	ישכם	hiph	wci	3ms	שכם	1014		rise early
	קראת	qal	infc		קרא	896		meet,encounter
	יגד	hoph	wci	3ms	נגד	616		be told
	אמר	qal	infc		אמר	55		say
	בא	qal	pft	3ms	בוא	97		come in
	מציב	hiph	ptc	ms	נצב	662		cause to stand
	יסב	qal	wci	3ms	סבב	685		surround
	יעבר	qal	wci	3ms	עבר	716		pass over
	ירד	qal	wci	3ms	ירד	432		come down
15:13	יבא	qal	wci	3ms	בוא	97		come in
	יאמר	qal	wci	3ms	אמר	55		say
	ברוך	qal	pptc	ms	ברך	138		kneel,bless
	הקימתי	hiph	pft	1cs	קום	877		raise,build,set
15:14	יאמר	qal	wci	3ms	אמר	55		say
	שמע	qal	ptc	ms	שמע	1033		hear
15:15	יאמר	qal	wci	3ms	אמר	55		say
	הביאום	hiph	pft	3cp	בוא	97	3mp	bring in
	חמל	qal	pft	3ms	חמל	328		spare
	זבח	qal	infc		זבח	256		slaughter
	החרמנו	hiph	pft	1cp	חרם	355		ban,destroy
15:16	יאמר	qal	wci	3ms	אמר	55		say
	הרף	hiph	impv	ms	רפה	951		slacken,abandon
	אגידה	hiph	coh	1cs	נגד	616		declare,tell
	דבר	piel	pft	3ms	דבר	180		speak
	יאמרוk	qal	wci	3mp	אמר	55		say
	יאמרq	qal	wci	3ms	אמר	55		say
	דבר	piel	impv	ms	דבר	180		speak
15:17	יאמר	qal	wci	3ms	אמר	55		say
	ימשחך	qal	wci	3ms	משח	602	2ms	smear,anoint

ChVs	Form	Stem	Tnse	PGN	Root	BDB	Sfx	Meaning
15:18	ישלחך	qal	wci	3ms	שלח	1018	2ms	send
	יאמר	qal	wci	3ms	אמר	55		say
	לך	qal	impv	ms	הלך	229		walk,go
	החרמתה	hiph	wcp	2ms	חרם	355		ban,destroy
	נלחמת	niph	wcp	2ms	לחם	535		wage war
	כלותם	piel	infc		כלה	477	3mp	complete,finish
15:19	שמעת	qal	pft	2ms	שמע	1033		hear
	תעט	qal	wci	2ms	עיט	743		dart greedily
	תעש	qal	wci	2ms	עשה	793		do,make
15:20	יאמר	qal	wci	3ms	אמר	55		say
	שמעתי	qal	pft	1cs	שמע	1033		hear
	אלך	qal	wci	1cs	הלך	229		walk,go
	שלחני	qal	pft	3ms	שלח	1018	1cs	send
	אביא	hiph	wci	1cs	בוא	97		bring in
	החרמתי	hiph	pft	1cs	חרם	355		ban,destroy
15:21	יקח	qal	wci	3ms	לקח	542		take
	זבח	qal	infc		זבח	256		slaughter
15:22	יאמר	qal	wci	3ms	אמר	55		say
	שמע	qal	infc		שמע	1033		hear
	שמע	qal	infc		שמע	1033		hear
	הקשיב	hiph	infc		קשב	904		give attention
15:23	הפצר	hiph	infa		פצר	823		be obstinate
	מאסת	qal	pft	2ms	מאס	549		reject,refuse
	ימאסך	qal	wci	3ms	מאס	549	2ms	reject,refuse
15:24	יאמר	qal	wci	3ms	אמר	55		say
	חטאתי	qal	pft	1cs	חטא	306		sin
	עברתי	qal	pft	1cs	עבר	716		pass over
	יראתי	qal	pft	1cs	ירא	431		fear
	אשמע	qal	wci	1cs	שמע	1033		hear
15:25	שא	qal	impv	ms	נשא	669		lift,carry
	שוב	qal	impv	ms	שוב	996		turn,return
	אשתחוה	hish	cohm	1cs	חוה	1005		bow down
15:26	יאמר	qal	wci	3ms	אמר	55		say
	אשוב	qal	impf	1cs	שוב	996		turn,return
	מאסתה	qal	pft	2ms	מאס	549		reject,refuse
	ימאסך	qal	wci	3ms	מאס	549	2ms	reject,refuse
	היות	qal	infc		היה	224		be,become
15:27	יסב	qal	wci	3ms	סבב	685		surround
	לכת	qal	infc		הלך	229		walk,go
	יחזק	hiph	wci	3ms	חזק	304		make firm,seize
	יקרע	niph	wci	3ms	קרע	902		be rent,split
15:28	יאמר	qal	wci	3ms	אמר	55		say
	קרע	qal	pft	3ms	קרע	902		tear,rend
	נתנה	qal	wcp	3ms	נתן	678	3fs	give,set
15:29	ישקר	piel	impf	3ms	שקר	1055		deal falsely
	ינחם	niph	impf	3ms	נחם	636		be sorry
	הנחם	niph	infc		נחם	636		be sorry
15:30	יאמר	qal	wci	3ms	אמר	55		say
	חטאתי	qal	pft	1cs	חטא	306		sin
	כבדני	piel	impv	ms	כבד	457	1cs	honor,make dull
	שוב	qal	impv	ms	שוב	996		turn,return
	השתחויתי	hish	wcp	1cs	חוה	1005		bow down
15:31	ישב	qal	wci	3ms	שוב	996		turn,return
	ישתחו	hish	wci	3ms	חוה	1005		bow down
15:32	יאמר	qal	wci	3ms	אמר	55		say
	הגישו	hiph	impv	mp	נגש	620		bring near
	ילך	qal	wci	3ms	הלך	229		walk,go
	יאמר	qal	wci	3ms	אמר	55		say
	סר	qal	pft	3ms	סור	693		turn aside
15:33	יאמר	qal	wci	3ms	אמר	55		say
	שכלה	piel	pft	3fs	שכל	1013		make childless
	תשכל	qal	impf	3fs	שכל	1013		be bereaved
	ישסף	piel	wci	3ms	שסף	1043		hew in pieces
15:34	ילך	qal	wci	3ms	הלך	229		walk,go
	עלה	qal	pft	3ms	עלה	748		go up
15:35	יסף	qal	pft	3ms	יסף	414		add,increase
	ראות	qal	infc		ראה	906		see
	התאבל	hith	pft	3ms	אבל	5		mourn
	נחם	niph	pft	3ms	נחם	636		be sorry
	המליך	hiph	pft	3ms	מלך	573		cause to reign
16:1	יאמר	qal	wci	3ms	אמר	55		say
	מתאבל	hith	ptc	ms	אבל	5		mourn
	מאסתיו	qal	pft	1cs	מאס	549	3ms	reject,refuse
	מלך	qal	infc		מלך	573		be king,reign
	מלא	piel	impv	ms	מלא	569		fill
	לך	qal	impv	ms	הלך	229		walk,go
	אשלחך	qal	impf	1cs	שלח	1018	2ms	send
	ראיתי	qal	pft	1cs	ראה	906		see
16:2	יאמר	qal	wci	3ms	אמר	55		say
	אלך	qal	impf	1cs	הלך	229		walk,go
	שמע	qal	wcp	3ms	שמע	1033		hear
	הרגני	qal	wcp	3ms	הרג	246	1cs	kill
	יאמר	qal	wci	3ms	אמר	55		say
	תקח	qal	impf	2ms	לקח	542		take
	אמרת	qal	wcp	2ms	אמר	55		say
	זבח	qal	infc		זבח	256		slaughter
	באתי	qal	pft	1cs	בוא	97		come in
16:3	קראת	qal	wcp	2ms	קרא	894		call,proclaim
	אודיעך	hiph	impf	1cs	ידע	393	2ms	declare
	תעשה	qal	impf	2ms	עשה	793		do,make
	משחת	qal	wcp	2ms	משח	602		smear,anoint
	אמר	qal	impf	1cs	אמר	55		say
16:4	יעש	qal	wci	3ms	עשה	793		do,make
	דבר	piel	pft	3ms	דבר	180		speak
	יבא	qal	wci	3ms	בוא	97		come in
	יחרדו	qal	wci	3mp	חרד	353		tremble
	קראתו	qal	infc		קרא	896	3ms	meet,encounter
	יאמר	qal	wci	3ms	אמר	55		say
	בואך	qal	infc		בוא	97	2ms	come in
16:5	יאמר	qal	wci	3ms	אמר	55		say
	זבח	qal	infc		זבח	256		slaughter
	באתי	qal	pft	1cs	בוא	97		come in
	התקדשו	hith	impv	mp	קדש	872		consecrate self
	באתם	qal	wcp	2mp	בוא	97		come in
	יקדש	piel	wci	3ms	קדש	872		consecrate
	יקרא	qal	wci	3ms	קרא	894		call,proclaim
16:6	יהי	qal	wci	3ms	היה	224		be,become
	בואם	qal	infc		בוא	97	3mp	come in

ChVs	Form	Stem	Tnse	PGN	Root	BDB	Sfx	Meaning
16:6	ירא	qal	wci	3ms	ראה	906		see
	יאמר	qal	wci	3ms	אמר	55		say
16:7	יאמר	qal	wci	3ms	אמר	55		say
	תבט	hiph	jus	2ms	נבט	613		look,regard
	מאסתיהו	qal	pft	1cs	מאס	549	3ms	reject,refuse
	יראה	qal	impf	3ms	ראה	906		see
	יראה	qal	impf	3ms	ראה	906		see
	יראה	qal	impf	3ms	ראה	906		see
16:8	יקרא	qal	wci	3ms	קרא	894		call,proclaim
	יעברהו	hiph	wci	3ms	עבר	716	3ms	cause to pass
	יאמר	qal	wci	3ms	אמר	55		say
	בחר	qal	pft	3ms	בחר	103		choose
16:9	יעבר	hiph	wci	3ms	עבר	716		cause to pass
	יאמר	qal	wci	3ms	אמר	55		say
	בחר	qal	pft	3ms	בחר	103		choose
16:10	יעבר	hiph	wci	3ms	עבר	716		cause to pass
	יאמר	qal	wci	3ms	אמר	55		say
	בחר	qal	pft	3ms	בחר	103		choose
16:11	יאמר	qal	wci	3ms	אמר	55		say
	תמו	qal	pft	3cp	תמם	1070		be finished
	יאמר	qal	wci	3ms	אמר	55		say
	שׁאר	qal	pft	3ms	שׁאר	983		remain
	רעה	qal	ptc	ms	רעה	944		pasture,tend
	יאמר	qal	wci	3ms	אמר	55		say
	שׁלחה	qal	impv	ms	שׁלח	1018		send
	קחנו	qal	impv	ms	לקח	542	3ms	take
	נסב	qal	impf	1cp	סבב	685		surround
	באו	qal	infc		בוא	97	3ms	come in
16:12	ישׁלח	qal	wci	3ms	שׁלח	1018		send
	יביאהו	hiph	wci	3ms	בוא	97	3ms	bring in
	יאמר	qal	wci	3ms	אמר	55		say
	קום	qal	impv	ms	קום	877		arise,stand
	משׁחהו	qal	impv	ms	משׁח	602	3ms	smear,anoint
16:13	יקח	qal	wci	3ms	לקח	542		take
	ימשׁח	qal	wci	3ms	משׁח	602		smear,anoint
	תצלח	qal	wci	3fs	צלח	852		rush
	יקם	qal	wci	3ms	קום	877		arise,stand
	ילך	qal	wci	3ms	הלך	229		walk,go
16:14	סרה	qal	pft	3fs	סור	693		turn aside
	בעתתו	piel	wcp	3fs	בעת	129	3ms	terrify
16:15	יאמרו	qal	wci	3mp	אמר	55		say
	מבעתך	piel	ptc	fs	בעת	129	2ms	terrify
16:16	יאמר	qal	jusm	3ms	אמר	55		say
	יבקשׁו	piel	jusm	3mp	בקשׁ	134		seek
	ידע	qal	ptc	ms	ידע	393		know
	מנגן	piel	ptc	ms	נגן	618		play (strings)
	היה	qal	wcp	3ms	היה	224		be,become
	היות	qal	infc		היה	224		be,become
	נגן	piel	wcp	3ms	נגן	618		play (strings)
	טוב	qal	wcp	3ms	טוב	373		be pleasing
16:17	יאמר	qal	wci	3ms	אמר	55		say
	ראו	qal	impv	mp	ראה	906		see
	מיטיב	hiph	ptc	ms	יטב	405		do good
	נגן	piel	infc		נגן	618		play (strings)
16:17	הביאותם	hiph	wcp	2mp	בוא	97		bring in
16:18	יען	qal	wci	3ms	ענה	772		answer
	יאמר	qal	wci	3ms	אמר	55		say
	ראיתי	qal	pft	1cs	ראה	906		see
	ידע	qal	ptc	ms	ידע	393		know
	נגן	piel	infc		נגן	618		play (strings)
	נבון	niph	ptc	ms	בין	106		be discerning
16:19	ישׁלח	qal	wci	3ms	שׁלח	1018		send
	יאמר	qal	wci	3ms	אמר	55		say
	שׁלחה	qal	impv	ms	שׁלח	1018		send
16:20	יקח	qal	wci	3ms	לקח	542		take
	ישׁלח	qal	wci	3ms	שׁלח	1018		send
16:21	יבא	qal	wci	3ms	בוא	97		come in
	יעמד	qal	wci	3ms	עמד	763		stand,stop
	יאהבהו	qal	wci	3ms	אהב	12	3ms	love
	יהי	qal	wci	3ms	היה	224		be,become
	נשׂא	qal	ptc	ms	נשׂא	669		lift,carry
16:22	ישׁלח	qal	wci	3ms	שׁלח	1018		send
	אמר	qal	infc		אמר	55		say
	יעמד	qal	jusm	3ms	עמד	763		stand,stop
	מצא	qal	pft	3ms	מצא	592		find
16:23	היה	qal	wcp	3ms	היה	224		be,become
	היות	qal	infc		היה	224		be,become
	לקח	qal	wcp	3ms	לקח	542		take
	נגן	piel	wcp	3ms	נגן	618		play (strings)
	רוח	qal	wcp	3ms	רוח	926		be wide
	טוב	qal	wcp	3ms	טוב	373		be pleasing
	סרה	qal	wcp	3fs	סור	693		turn aside
17:1	יאספו	qal	wci	3mp	אסף	62		gather
	יאספו	niph	wci	3mp	אסף	62		assemble
	יחנו	qal	wci	3mp	חנה	333		decline,encamp
17:2	נאספו	niph	pft	3cp	אסף	62		assemble
	יחנו	qal	wci	3mp	חנה	333		decline,encamp
	יערכו	qal	wci	3mp	ערך	789		set in order
	קראת	qal	infc		קרא	896		meet,encounter
17:3	עמדים	qal	ptc	mp	עמד	763		stand,stop
	עמדים	qal	ptc	mp	עמד	763		stand,stop
17:4	יצא	qal	wci	3ms	יצא	422		go out
17:5	לבושׁ	qal	pptc	ms	לבשׁ	527		put on,clothe
17:7	ארגים	qal	ptc	mp	ארג	70		weave
	נשׂא	qal	ptc	ms	נשׂא	669		lift,carry
	הלך	qal	ptc	ms	הלך	229		walk,go
17:8	יעמד	qal	wci	3ms	עמד	763		stand,stop
	יקרא	qal	wci	3ms	קרא	894		call,proclaim
	יאמר	qal	wci	3ms	אמר	55		say
	תצאו	qal	impf	2mp	יצא	422		go out
	ערך	qal	infc		ערך	789		set in order
	ברו	qal	impv	mp	ברה	136		eat
	ירד	qal	jusm	3ms	ירד	432		come down
17:9	יוכל	qal	impf	3ms	יכל	407		be able
	הלחם	niph	infc		לחם	535		wage war
	הכני	hiph	wcp	3ms	נכה	645	1cs	smite
	היינו	qal	wcp	1cp	היה	224		be,become
	אוכל	qal	impf	1cs	יכל	407		be able

ChVs	Form	Stem	Tnse	PGN	Root	BDB	Sfx	Meaning
17:9	הכיתיו	hiph	wcp	1cs	נכה	645	3ms	smite
	הייתם	qal	wcp	2mp	היה	224		be,become
	עבדתם	qal	wcp	2mp	עבד	712		work,serve
17:10	יאמר	qal	wci	3ms	אמר	55		say
	חרפתי	piel	pft	1cs	חרף	357		reproach
	תנו	qal	impv	mp	נתן	678		give,set
	נלחמה	niph	coh	1cp	לחם	535		wage war
17:11	ישמע	qal	wci	3ms	שמע	1033		hear
	יחתו	qal	wci	3mp	חתת	369		be shattered
	יראו	qal	wci	3mp	ירא	431		fear
17:12	זקן	qal	pft	3ms	זקן	278		be old
	בא	qal	pft	3ms	בוא	97		come in
17:13	ילכו	qal	wci	3mp	הלך	229		walk,go
	הלכו	qal	pft	3cp	הלך	229		walk,go
	הלכו	qal	pft	3cp	הלך	229		walk,go
17:14	הלכו	qal	pft	3cp	הלך	229		walk,go
17:15	הלך	qal	ptc	ms	הלך	229		walk,go
	שב	qal	ptc	ms	שוב	996		turn,return
	רעות	qal	infc		רעה	944		pasture,tend
17:16	יגש	qal	wci	3ms	נגש	620		draw near
	השכם	hiph	infa		שכם	1014		rise early
	הערב	hiph	infa		ערב	788		grow dark
	יתיצב	hith	wci	3ms	יצב	426		stand oneself
17:17	יאמר	qal	wci	3ms	אמר	55		say
	קח	qal	impv	ms	לקח	542		take
	הרץ	hiph	impv	ms	רוץ	930		bring quickly
17:18	תביא	hiph	impf	2ms	בוא	97		bring in
	תפקד	qal	impf	2ms	פקד	823		attend to,visit
	תקח	qal	impf	2ms	לקח	542		take
17:19	נלחמים	niph	ptc	mp	לחם	535		wage war
17:20	ישכם	hiph	wci	3ms	שכם	1014		rise early
	יטש	qal	wci	3ms	נטש	643		leave,forsake
	שמר	qal	ptc	ms	שמר	1036		keep,watch
	ישא	qal	wci	3ms	נשא	669		lift,carry
	ילך	qal	wci	3ms	הלך	229		walk,go
	צוהו	piel	pft	3ms	צוה	845	3ms	command
	יבא	qal	wci	3ms	בוא	97		come in
	יצא	qal	ptc	ms	יצא	422		go out
	הרעו	hiph	wcp	3cp	רוע	929		raise a shout
17:21	תערך	qal	wci	3fs	ערך	789		set in order
	קראת	qal	infc		קרא	896		meet,encounter
17:22	יטש	qal	wci	3ms	נטש	643		leave,forsake
	שומר	qal	ptc	ms	שמר	1036		keep,watch
	ירץ	qal	wci	3ms	רוץ	930		run
	יבא	qal	wci	3ms	בוא	97		come in
	ישאל	qal	wci	3ms	שאל	981		ask,borrow
17:23	מדבר	piel	ptc	ms	דבר	180		speak
	עולה	qal	ptc	ms	עלה	748		go up
	ידבר	piel	wci	3ms	דבר	180		speak
	ישמע	qal	wci	3ms	שמע	1033		hear
17:24	ראותם	qal	infc		ראה	906	3mp	see
	ינסו	qal	wci	3mp	נוס	630		flee,escape
	ייראו	qal	wci	3mp	ירא	431		fear
17:25	יאמר	qal	wci	3ms	אמר	55		say
17:25	ראיתם	qal	pft	2mp	ראה	906		see
	עלה	qal	ptc	ms	עלה	748		go up
	חרף	piel	infc		חרף	357		reproach
	עלה	qal	ptc	ms	עלה	748		go up
	היה	qal	wcp	3ms	היה	224		be,become
	יכנו	hiph	impf	3ms	נכה	645	3ms	smite
	יעשרנו	hiph	impf	3ms	עשר	799	3ms	make rich
	יתן	qal	impf	3ms	נתן	678		give,set
	יעשה	qal	impf	3ms	עשה	793		do,make
17:26	יאמר	qal	wci	3ms	אמר	55		say
	עמדים	qal	ptc	mp	עמד	763		stand,stop
	אמר	qal	infc		אמר	55		say
	יעשה	niph	impf	3ms	עשה	793		be done
	יכה	hiph	impf	3ms	נכה	645		smite
	הסיר	hiph	wcp	3ms	סור	693		take away
	חרף	piel	pft	3ms	חרף	357		reproach
17:27	יאמר	qal	wci	3ms	אמר	55		say
	אמר	qal	infc		אמר	55		say
	יעשה	niph	impf	3ms	עשה	793		be done
	יכנו	hiph	impf	3ms	נכה	645	3ms	smite
17:28	ישמע	qal	wci	3ms	שמע	1033		hear
	דברו	piel	infc		דבר	180	3ms	speak
	יחר	qal	wci	3ms	חרה	354		be kindled,burn
	יאמר	qal	wci	3ms	אמר	55		say
	ירדת	qal	pft	2ms	ירד	432		come down
	נטשת	qal	pft	2ms	נטש	643		leave,forsake
	ידעתי	qal	pft	1cs	ידע	393		know
	ראות	qal	infc		ראה	906		see
	ירדת	qal	pft	2ms	ירד	432		come down
17:29	יאמר	qal	wci	3ms	אמר	55		say
	עשיתי	qal	pft	1cs	עשה	793		do,make
17:30	יסב	qal	wci	3ms	סבב	685		surround
	יאמר	qal	wci	3ms	אמר	55		say
	ישבהו	hiph	wci	3mp	שוב	996	3ms	bring back
17:31	ישמעו	niph	wci	3mp	שמע	1033		be heard
	דבר	piel	pft	3ms	דבר	180		speak
	יגדו	hiph	wci	3mp	נגד	616		declare,tell
	יקחהו	qal	wci	3ms	לקח	542	3ms	take
17:32	יאמר	qal	wci	3ms	אמר	55		say
	יפל	qal	jusm	3ms	נפל	656		fall
	ילך	qal	impf	3ms	הלך	229		walk,go
	נלחם	niph	wcp	3ms	לחם	535		wage war
17:33	יאמר	qal	wci	3ms	אמר	55		say
	תוכל	qal	impf	2ms	יכל	407		be able
	לכת	qal	infc		הלך	229		walk,go
	הלחם	niph	infc		לחם	535		wage war
17:34	יאמר	qal	wci	3ms	אמר	55		say
	רעה	qal	ptc	ms	רעה	944		pasture,tend
	היה	qal	pft	3ms	היה	224		be,become
	בא	qal	wcp	3ms	בוא	97		come in
	נשא	qal	wcp	3ms	נשא	669		lift,carry
17:35	יצאתי	qal	wcp	1cs	יצא	422		go out
	הכתיו	hiph	wcp	1cs	נכה	645	3ms	smite
	הצלתי	hiph	wcp	1cs	נצל	664		snatch,deliver

ChVs	Form	Stem	Tnse	PGN	Root	BDB	Sfx	Meaning
17:35	יקם	qal	wci	3ms	קום	877		arise,stand
	החזקתי	hiph	wcp	1cs	חזק	304		make firm,seize
	הכתיו	hiph	wcp	1cs	נכה	645	3ms	smite
	המיתיו	hiph	wcp	1cs	מות	559	3ms	kill
17:36	הכה	hiph	pft	3ms	נכה	645		smite
	היה	qal	wcp	3ms	היה	224		be,become
	חרף	piel	pft	3ms	חרף	357		reproach
17:37	יאמר	qal	wci	3ms	אמר	55		say
	הצלני	hiph	pft	3ms	נצל	664	1cs	snatch,deliver
	יצילני	hiph	impf	3ms	נצל	664	1cs	snatch,deliver
	יאמר	qal	wci	3ms	אמר	55		say
	לך	qal	impv	ms	הלך	229		walk,go
	יהיה	qal	jusm	3ms	היה	224		be,become
17:38	ילבש	hiph	wci	3ms	לבש	527		clothe
	נתן	qal	pft	3ms	נתן	678		give,set
	ילבש	hiph	wci	3ms	לבש	527		clothe
17:39	יחגר	qal	wci	3ms	חגר	291		gird
	יאל	hiph	wci	3ms	יאל	383		be willing
	לכת	qal	infc		הלך	229		walk,go
	נסה	piel	pft	3ms	נסה	650		test,try
	יאמר	qal	wci	3ms	אמר	55		say
	אוכל	qal	impf	1cs	יכל	407		be able
	לכת	qal	infc		הלך	229		walk,go
	נסיתי	piel	pft	1cs	נסה	650		test,try
	יסרם	hiph	wci	3ms	סור	693	3mp	take away
17:40	יקח	qal	wci	3ms	לקח	542		take
	יבחר	qal	wci	3ms	בחר	103		choose
	ישם	qal	wci	3ms	שים	962		put,set
	רעים	qal	ptc	mp	רעה	944		pasture,tend
	ינש	qal	wci	3ms	נגש	620		draw near
17:41	ילך	qal	wci	3ms	הלך	229		walk,go
	הלך	qal	ptc	ms	הלך	229		walk,go
	נשא	qal	ptc	ms	נשא	669		lift,carry
17:42	יבט	hiph	wci	3ms	נבט	613		look,regard
	יראה	qal	wci	3ms	ראה	906		see
	יבזהו	qal	wci	3ms	בזה	102	3ms	despise
	היה	qal	pft	3ms	היה	224		be,become
17:43	יאמר	qal	wci	3ms	אמר	55		say
	בא	qal	ptc	ms	בוא	97		come in
	יקלל	piel	wci	3ms	קלל	886		curse
17:44	יאמר	qal	wci	3ms	אמר	55		say
	לכה	qal	impv	ms	הלך	229		walk,go
	אתנה	qal	coh	1cs	נתן	678		give,set
17:45	יאמר	qal	wci	3ms	אמר	55		say
	בא	qal	ptc	ms	בוא	97		come in
	בא	qal	ptc	ms	בוא	97		come in
	חרפת	piel	pft	2ms	חרף	357		reproach
17:46	יסגרך	piel	impf	3ms	סגר	688	2ms	deliver
	הכיתך	hiph	wcp	1cs	נכה	645	2ms	smite
	הסרתי	hiph	wcp	1cs	סור	693		take away
	נתתי	qal	wcp	1cs	נתן	678		give,set
	ידעו	qal	impf	3mp	ידע	393		know
17:47	ידעו	qal	impf	3mp	ידע	393		know
	יהושיע	hiph	impf	3ms	ישע	446		deliver,save
17:47	נתן	qal	wcp	3ms	נתן	678		give,set
17:48	היה	qal	pft	3ms	היה	224		be,become
	קם	qal	pft	3ms	קום	877		arise,stand
	ילך	qal	wci	3ms	הלך	229		walk,go
	יקרב	qal	wci	3ms	קרב	897		approach
	קראת	qal	infc		קרא	896		meet,encounter
	ימהר	piel	wci	3ms	מהר	554		hasten
	ירץ	qal	wci	3ms	רוץ	930		run
	קראת	qal	infc		קרא	896		meet,encounter
17:49	ישלח	qal	wci	3ms	שלח	1018		send
	יקח	qal	wci	3ms	לקח	542		take
	יקלע	piel	wci	3ms	קלע	887		sling,hurl
	יך	hiph	wci	3ms	נכה	645		smite
	תטבע	qal	wci	3fs	טבע	371		sink
	יפל	qal	wci	3ms	נפל	656		fall
17:50	יחזק	qal	wci	3ms	חזק	304		be strong
	יך	hiph	wci	3ms	נכה	645		smite
	ימיתהו	hiph	wci	3ms	מות	559	3ms	kill
17:51	ירץ	qal	wci	3ms	רוץ	930		run
	יעמד	qal	wci	3ms	עמד	763		stand,stop
	יקח	qal	wci	3ms	לקח	542		take
	ישלפה	qal	wci	3ms	שלף	1025	3fs	draw out,off
	ימתתהו	pol	wci	3ms	מות	559	3ms	kill
	יכרת	qal	wci	3ms	כרת	503		cut,destroy
	יראו	qal	wci	3mp	ראה	906		see
	מת	qal	pft	3ms	מות	559		die
	ינסו	qal	wci	3mp	נוס	630		flee,escape
17:52	יקמו	qal	wci	3mp	קום	877		arise,stand
	ירעו	hiph	wci	3mp	רוע	929		raise a shout
	ירדפו	qal	wci	3mp	רדף	922		pursue
	בואך	qal	infc		בוא	97	2ms	come in
	יפלו	qal	wci	3mp	נפל	656		fall
17:53	ישבו	qal	wci	3mp	שוב	996		turn,return
	דלק	qal	infc		דלק	196		burn,pursue
	ישסו	qal	wci	3mp	שסס	1042		plunder
17:54	יקח	qal	wci	3ms	לקח	542		take
	יבאהו	hiph	wci	3ms	בוא	97	3ms	bring in
	שם	qal	pft	3ms	שים	962		put,set
17:55	ראות	qal	infc		ראה	906		see
	יצא	qal	ptc	ms	יצא	422		go out
	קראת	qal	infc		קרא	896		meet,encounter
	אמר	qal	pft	3ms	אמר	55		say
	יאמר	qal	wci	3ms	אמר	55		say
	ידעתי	qal	pft	1cs	ידע	393		know
17:56	יאמר	qal	wci	3ms	אמר	55		say
	שאל	qal	impv	ms	שאל	981		ask,borrow
17:57	שוב	qal	infc		שוב	996		turn,return
	הכות	hiph	infc		נכה	645		smite
	יקח	qal	wci	3ms	לקח	542		take
	יבאהו	hiph	wci	3ms	בוא	97	3ms	bring in
17:58	יאמר	qal	wci	3ms	אמר	55		say
	יאמר	qal	wci	3ms	אמר	55		say
18:1	יהי	qal	wci	3ms	היה	224		be,become
	כלתו	piel	infc		כלה	477	3ms	complete,finish

ChVs	Form	Stem	Tnse	PGN	Root	BDB	Sfx	Meaning
18:1	דבר	piel	infc		דבר	180		speak
	נקשרה	niph	pft	3fs	קשר	905		be bound
	יאהבוk	qal	wci	3mp	אהב	12		love
	יאהבהוq	qal	wci	3ms	אהב	12	3ms	love
18:2	יקחהו	qal	wci	3ms	לקח	542	3ms	take
	נתנו	qal	pft	3ms	נתן	678	3ms	give,set
	שׁוב	qal	infc		שׁוב	996		turn,return
18:3	יכרת	qal	wci	3ms	כרת	503		cut,destroy
	אהבתו	qal	infc		אהב	12	3ms	love
18:4	יתפשׁט	hith	wci	3ms	פשׁט	832		strip oneself
	יתנהו	qal	wci	3ms	נתן	678	3ms	give,set
18:5	יצא	qal	wci	3ms	יצא	422		go out
	ישׁלחנו	qal	impf	3ms	שׁלח	1018	3ms	send
	ישׂכיל	hiph	impf	3ms	שׂכל	968		look at,prosper
	ישׂמהו	qal	wci	3ms	שׂים	962	3ms	put,set
	ייטב	qal	wci	3ms	יטב	405		be good
18:6	יהי	qal	wci	3ms	היה	224		be,become
	בואם	qal	infc		בוא	97	3mp	come in
	שׁוב	qal	infc		שׁוב	996		turn,return
	הכות	hiph	infc		נכה	645		smite
	תצאנה	qal	wci	3fp	יצא	422		go out
	שׁורk	qal	infc		שׁיר	1010		sing
	שׁירq	qal	infc		שׁיר	1010		sing
	קראת	qal	infc		קרא	896		meet,encounter
18:7	תענינה	qal	wci	3fp	ענה	777		sing
	משׂחקות	piel	ptc	fp	שׂחק	965		make sport
	תאמרן	qal	wci	3fp	אמר	55		say
	הכה	hiph	pft	3ms	נכה	645		smite
18:8	יחר	qal	wci	3ms	חרה	354		be kindled,burn
	ירע	qal	wci	3ms	רעע	949		be evil
	יאמר	qal	wci	3ms	אמר	55		say
	נתנו	qal	pft	3cp	נתן	678		give,set
	נתנו	qal	pft	3cp	נתן	678		give,set
18:9	יהי	qal	wci	3ms	היה	224		be,become
	עוןk	qal	ptc	ms	עין	745		eye (enviously)
	עוין q	qal	ptc	ms	עין	745		eye (enviously)
18:10	יהי	qal	wci	3ms	היה	224		be,become
	תצלח	qal	wci	3fs	צלח	852		rush
	יתנבא	hith	wci	3ms	נבא	612		prophesy
	מנגן	piel	ptc	ms	נגן	618		play (strings)
18:11	יטל	hiph	wci	3ms	טול	376		cast
	יאמר	qal	wci	3ms	אמר	55		say
	אכה	hiph	impf	1cs	נכה	645		smite
	יסב	qal	wci	3ms	סבב	685		surround
18:12	ירא	qal	wci	3ms	ירא	431		fear
	היה	qal	pft	3ms	היה	224		be,become
	סר	qal	pft	3ms	סור	693		turn aside
18:13	יסרהו	hiph	wci	3ms	סור	693	3ms	take away
	ישׂמהו	qal	wci	3ms	שׂים	962	3ms	put,set
	יצא	qal	wci	3ms	יצא	422		go out
	יבא	qal	wci	3ms	בוא	97		come in
18:14	יהי	qal	wci	3ms	היה	224		be,become
	משׂכיל	hiph	ptc	ms	שׂכל	968		look at,prosper
18:15	ירא	qal	wci	3ms	ראה	906		see
18:15	משׂכיל	hiph	ptc	ms	שׂכל	968		look at,prosper
	יגר	qal	wci	3ms	גור	158		dread
18:16	אהב	qal	ptc	ms	אהב	12		love
	יוצא	qal	ptc	ms	יצא	422		go out
	בא	qal	ptc	ms	בוא	97		come in
18:17	יאמר	qal	wci	3ms	אמר	55		say
	אתן	qal	impf	1cs	נתן	678		give,set
	היה	qal	impv	ms	היה	224		be,become
	הלחם	niph	impv	ms	לחם	535		wage war
	אמר	qal	pft	3ms	אמר	55		say
	תהי	qal	jus	3fs	היה	224		be,become
	תהי	qal	jus	3fs	היה	224		be,become
18:18	יאמר	qal	wci	3ms	אמר	55		say
	אהיה	qal	impf	1cs	היה	224		be,become
18:19	יהי	qal	wci	3ms	היה	224		be,become
	תת	qal	infc		נתן	678		give,set
	נתנה	niph	pft	3fs	נתן	678		be given
18:20	תאהב	qal	wci	3fs	אהב	12		love
	יגדו	hiph	wci	3mp	נגד	616		declare,tell
	ישׁר	qal	wci	3ms	ישׁר	448		be straight
18:21	יאמר	qal	wci	3ms	אמר	55		say
	אתננה	qal	cohm	1cs	נתן	678	3fs	give,set
	תהי	qal	jus	3fs	היה	224		be,become
	תהי	qal	jus	3fs	היה	224		be,become
	יאמר	qal	wci	3ms	אמר	55		say
	תתחתן	hith	impf	2ms	חתן	368		be son-in-law
18:22	יצו	piel	wci	3ms	צוה	845		command
	דברו	piel	impv	mp	דבר	180		speak
	אמר	qal	infc		אמר	55		say
	חפץ	qal	pft	3ms	חפץ	342		delight in
	אהבוך	qal	pft	3cp	אהב	12	2ms	love
	התחתן	hith	impv	ms	חתן	368		be son-in-law
18:23	ידברו	piel	wci	3mp	דבר	180		speak
	יאמר	qal	wci	3ms	אמר	55		say
	נקלה	niph	ptc	fs	קלל	886		be trifling
	התחתן	hith	infc		חתן	368		be son-in-law
	רשׁ	qal	ptc	ms	רושׁ	930		be in want
	נקלה	niph	ptc	ms	קלה	885		be dishonored
18:24	יגדו	hiph	wci	3mp	נגד	616		declare,tell
	אמר	qal	infc		אמר	55		say
	דבר	piel	pft	3ms	דבר	180		speak
18:25	יאמר	qal	wci	3ms	אמר	55		say
	תאמרו	qal	impf	2mp	אמר	55		say
	הנקם	niph	infc		נקם	667		avenge oneself
	איבי	qal	ptc	mp	איב	33		be hostile to
	חשׁב	qal	pft	3ms	חשׁב	362		think,devise
	הפיל	hiph	infc		נפל	656		cause to fall
18:26	יגדו	hiph	wci	3mp	נגד	616		declare,tell
	ישׁר	qal	wci	3ms	ישׁר	448		be straight
	התחתן	hith	infc		חתן	368		be son-in-law
	מלאו	qal	pft	3cp	מלא	569		be full,fill
18:27	יקם	qal	wci	3ms	קום	877		arise,stand
	ילך	qal	wci	3ms	הלך	229		walk,go
	יך	hiph	wci	3ms	נכה	645		smite

ChVs	Form	Stem	Tnse	PGN	Root	BDB	Sfx	Meaning
18:27	יבא	hiph	wci	3ms	בוא	97		bring in
	ימלאום	piel	wci	3mp	מלא	569	3mp	fill
	התחתן	hith	infc		חתן	368		be son-in-law
	יתן	qal	wci	3ms	נתן	678		give,set
18:28	ירא	qal	wci	3ms	ראה	906		see
	ידע	qal	wci	3ms	ידע	393		know
	אהבתהו	qal	pft	3fs	אהב	12	3ms	love
18:29	יאסף	hiph	wci	3ms	יסף	414		add,do again
	רא	qal	infc		ירא	431		fear
	יהי	qal	wci	3ms	היה	224		be,become
	איב	qal	ptc	ms	איב	33		be hostile to
18:30	יצאו	qal	wci	3mp	יצא	422		go out
	יהי	qal	wci	3ms	היה	224		be,become
	צאתם	qal	infc		יצא	422	3mp	go out
	שׂכל	qal	pft	3ms	שׂכל	968		be prudent
	ייקר	qal	wci	3ms	יקר	429		be precious
19:1	ידבר	piel	wci	3ms	דבר	180		speak
	המית	hiph	infc		מות	559		kill
	חפץ	qal	pft	3ms	חפץ	342		delight in
19:2	יגד	hiph	wci	3ms	נגד	616		declare,tell
	אמר	qal	infc		אמר	55		say
	מבקשׁ	piel	ptc	ms	בקשׁ	134		seek
	המיתך	hiph	infc		מות	559	2ms	kill
	השׁמר	niph	impv	ms	שׁמר	1036		be kept,guarded
	ישׁבת	qal	wcp	2ms	ישׁב	442		sit,dwell
	נחבאת	niph	wcp	2ms	חבא	285		hide oneself
19:3	אצא	qal	impf	1cs	יצא	422		go out
	עמדתי	qal	wcp	1cs	עמד	763		stand,stop
	אדבר	piel	impf	1cs	דבר	180		speak
	ראיתי	qal	wcp	1cs	ראה	906		see
	הגדתי	hiph	wcp	1cs	נגד	616		declare,tell
19:4	ידבר	piel	wci	3ms	דבר	180		speak
	יאמר	qal	wci	3ms	אמר	55		say
	יחטא	qal	jusm	3ms	חטא	306		sin
	חטא	qal	pft	3ms	חטא	306		sin
19:5	ישׂם	qal	wci	3ms	שׂים	962		put,set
	יך	hiph	wci	3ms	נכה	645		smite
	יעשׂ	qal	wci	3ms	עשׂה	793		do,make
	ראית	qal	pft	2ms	ראה	906		see
	תשׂמח	qal	wci	2ms	שׂמח	970		rejoice
	תחטא	qal	impf	2ms	חטא	306		sin
	המית	hiph	infc		מות	559		kill
19:6	ישׁמע	qal	wci	3ms	שׁמע	1033		hear
	ישׁבע	niph	wci	3ms	שׁבע	989		swear
	יומת	hoph	impf	3ms	מות	559		be killed
19:7	יקרא	qal	wci	3ms	קרא	894		call,proclaim
	יגד	hiph	wci	3ms	נגד	616		declare,tell
	יבא	hiph	wci	3ms	בוא	97		bring in
	יהי	qal	wci	3ms	היה	224		be,become
19:8	תוסף	hiph	wci	3fs	יסף	414		add,do again
	היות	qal	infc		היה	224		be,become
	יצא	qal	wci	3ms	יצא	422		go out
	ילחם	niph	wci	3ms	לחם	535		wage war
	יך	hiph	wci	3ms	נכה	645		smite
19:8	ינסו	qal	wci	3mp	נוס	630		flee,escape
19:9	תהי	qal	wci	3fs	היה	224		be,become
	יושׁב	qal	ptc	ms	ישׁב	442		sit,dwell
	מנגן	piel	ptc	ms	נגן	618		play (strings)
19:10	יבקשׁ	piel	wci	3ms	בקשׁ	134		seek
	הכות	hiph	infc		נכה	645		smite
	יפטר	qal	wci	3ms	פטר	809		remove,set free
	יך	hiph	wci	3ms	נכה	645		smite
	נס	qal	pft	3ms	נוס	630		flee,escape
	ימלט	niph	wci	3ms	מלט	572		escape
19:11	ישׁלח	qal	wci	3ms	שׁלח	1018		send
	שׁמרו	qal	infc		שׁמר	1036	3ms	keep,watch
	המיתו	hiph	infc		מות	559	3ms	kill
	תגד	hiph	wci	3fs	נגד	616		declare,tell
	אמר	qal	infc		אמר	55		say
	ממלט	piel	ptc	ms	מלט	572		deliver
	מומת	hoph	ptc	ms	מות	559		be killed
19:12	תרד	hiph	wci	3fs	ירד	432		bring down
	ילך	qal	wci	3ms	הלך	229		walk,go
	יברח	qal	wci	3ms	ברח	137		go thru,flee
	ימלט	niph	wci	3ms	מלט	572		escape
19:13	תקח	qal	wci	3fs	לקח	542		take
	תשׂם	qal	wci	3fs	שׂים	962		put,set
	שׂמה	qal	pft	3fs	שׂים	962		put,set
	תכס	piel	wci	3fs	כסה	491		cover
19:14	ישׁלח	qal	wci	3ms	שׁלח	1018		send
	קחת	qal	infc		לקח	542		take
	תאמר	qal	wci	3fs	אמר	55		say
	חלה	qal	ptc	ms	חלה	317		be weak,sick
19:15	ישׁלח	qal	wci	3ms	שׁלח	1018		send
	ראות	qal	infc		ראה	906		see
	אמר	qal	infc		אמר	55		say
	העלו	hiph	impv	mp	עלה	748		bring up,offer
	המתו	hiph	infc		מות	559	3ms	kill
19:16	יבאו	qal	wci	3mp	בוא	97		come in
19:17	יאמר	qal	wci	3ms	אמר	55		say
	רמיתני	piel	pft	2fs	רמה	941	1cs	beguile
	תשׁלחי	piel	wci	2fs	שׁלח	1018	1cs	send away,shoot
	איבי	qal	ptc	ms	איב	33	1cs	be hostile to
	ימלט	niph	wci	3ms	מלט	572		escape
	תאמר	qal	wci	3fs	אמר	55		say
	אמר	qal	pft	3ms	אמר	55		say
	שׁלחני	piel	impv	ms	שׁלח	1018	1cs	send away,shoot
	אמיתך	hiph	impf	1cs	מות	559	2fs	kill
19:18	ברח	qal	pft	3ms	ברח	137		go thru,flee
	ימלט	niph	wci	3ms	מלט	572		escape
	יבא	qal	wci	3ms	בוא	97		come in
	יגד	hiph	wci	3ms	נגד	616		declare,tell
	עשׂה	qal	pft	3ms	עשׂה	793		do,make
	ילך	qal	wci	3ms	הלך	229		walk,go
	ישׁבו	qal	wci	3mp	ישׁב	442		sit,dwell
19:19	יגד	hoph	wci	3ms	נגד	616		be told
	אמר	qal	infc		אמר	55		say
19:20	ישׁלח	qal	wci	3ms	שׁלח	1018		send

ChVs	Form	Stem	Tnse	PGN	Root	BDB	Sfx	Meaning
19: 20	קחת	qal	infc		לקח	542		take
	ירא	qal	wci	3ms	ראה	906		see
	נבאים	niph	ptc	mp	נבא	612		prophesy
	עמד	qal	ptc	ms	עמד	763		stand,stop
	נצב	niph	ptc	ms	נצב	662		stand
	תהי	qal	wci	3fs	היה	224		be,become
	יתנבאו	hith	wci	3mp	נבא	612		prophesy
19: 21	יגדו	hiph	wci	3mp	נגד	616		declare,tell
	ישלח	qal	wci	3ms	שׁלח	1018		send
	יתנבאו	hith	wci	3mp	נבא	612		prophesy
	יסף	hiph	wci	3ms	יסף	414		add,do again
	ישלח	qal	wci	3ms	שׁלח	1018		send
	יתנבאו	hith	wci	3mp	נבא	612		prophesy
19: 22	ילך	qal	wci	3ms	הלך	229		walk,go
	יבא	qal	wci	3ms	בוא	97		come in
	ישאל	qal	wci	3ms	שׁאל	981		ask,borrow
	יאמר	qal	wci	3ms	אמר	55		say
	יאמר	qal	wci	3ms	אמר	55		say
19: 23	ילך	qal	wci	3ms	הלך	229		walk,go
	תהי	qal	wci	3fs	היה	224		be,become
	ילך	qal	wci	3ms	הלך	229		walk,go
	הלוך	qal	infa		הלך	229		walk,go
	יתנבא	hith	wci	3ms	נבא	612		prophesy
	באו	qal	infc		בוא	97	3ms	come in
19: 24	יפשט	qal	wci	3ms	פשׁט	832		strip off
	יתנבא	hith	wci	3ms	נבא	612		prophesy
	יפל	qal	wci	3ms	נפל	656		fall
	יאמרו	qal	impf	3mp	אמר	55		say
20: 1	יברח	qal	wci	3ms	ברח	137		go thru,flee
	יבא	qal	wci	3ms	בוא	97		come in
	יאמר	qal	wci	3ms	אמר	55		say
	עשיתי	qal	pft	1cs	עשׂה	793		do,make
	מבקש	piel	ptc	ms	בקשׁ	134		seek
20: 2	יאמר	qal	wci	3ms	אמר	55		say
	תמות	qal	impf	2ms	מות	559		die
	עשהk	qal	pft	3ms	עשׂה	793		do,make
	יעשהq	qal	impf	3ms	עשׂה	793		do,make
	יגלה	qal	impf	3ms	גלה	162		uncover
	יסתיר	hiph	impf	3ms	סתר	711		hide
20: 3	ישבע	niph	wci	3ms	שׁבע	989		swear
	יאמר	qal	wci	3ms	אמר	55		say
	ידע	qal	infa		ידע	393		know
	ידע	qal	pft	3ms	ידע	393		know
	מצאתי	qal	pft	1cs	מצא	592		find
	יאמר	qal	wci	3ms	אמר	55		say
	ידע	qal	jusm	3ms	ידע	393		know
	יעצב	niph	impf	3ms	עצב	780		be pained
20: 4	יאמר	qal	wci	3ms	אמר	55		say
	תאמר	qal	impf	3fs	אמר	55		say
	אעשה	qal	cohm	1cs	עשׂה	793		do,make
20: 5	יאמר	qal	wci	3ms	אמר	55		say
	ישב	qal	infa		ישׁב	442		sit,dwell
	אשב	qal	impf	1cs	ישׁב	442		sit,dwell
	אכול	qal	infc		אכל	37		eat,devour
20: 5	שלחתני	piel	wcp	2ms	שׁלח	1018	1cs	send away,shoot
	נסתרתי	niph	wcp	1cs	סתר	711		hide,be hid
20: 6	פקד	qal	infa		פקד	823		attend to,visit
	יפקדני	qal	impf	3ms	פקד	823	1cs	attend to,visit
	אמרת	qal	wcp	2ms	אמר	55		say
	נשאל	niph	infa		שׁאל	981		ask for self
	נשאל	niph	pft	3ms	שׁאל	981		ask for self
	רוץ	qal	infc		רוץ	930		run
20: 7	יאמר	qal	impf	3ms	אמר	55		say
	חרה	qal	infa		חרה	354		be kindled,burn
	יחרה	qal	impf	3ms	חרה	354		be kindled,burn
	דע	qal	impv	ms	ידע	393		know
	כלתה	qal	pft	3fs	כלה	477		finished,spent
20: 8	עשית	qal	wcp	2ms	עשׂה	793		do,make
	הבאת	hiph	pft	2ms	בוא	97		bring in
	המיתני	hiph	impv	ms	מות	559	1cs	kill
	תביאני	hiph	impf	2ms	בוא	97	1cs	bring in
20: 9	יאמר	qal	wci	3ms	אמר	55		say
	ידע	qal	infa		ידע	393		know
	אדע	qal	impf	1cs	ידע	393		know
	כלתה	qal	pft	3fs	כלה	477		finished,spent
	בוא	qal	infc		בוא	97		come in
	אגיד	hiph	impf	1cs	נגד	616		declare,tell
20: 10	יאמר	qal	wci	3ms	אמר	55		say
	יגיד	hiph	impf	3ms	נגד	616		declare,tell
	יענך	qal	impf	3ms	ענה	772	2ms	answer
20: 11	יאמר	qal	wci	3ms	אמר	55		say
	לכה	qal	impv	ms	הלך	229		walk,go
	נצא	qal	cohm	1cp	יצא	422		go out
	יצאו	qal	wci	3mp	יצא	422		go out
20: 12	יאמר	qal	wci	3ms	אמר	55		say
	אחקר	qal	impf	1cs	חקר	350		search
	טוב	qal	pft	3ms	טוב	373		be pleasing
	אשלח	qal	impf	1cs	שׁלח	1018		send
	גליתי	qal	wcp	1cs	גלה	162		uncover
20: 13	יעשה	qal	jusm	3ms	עשׂה	793		do,make
	יסיף	hiph	jusm	3ms	יסף	414		add,do again
	ייטב	hiph	impf	3ms	יטב	405		do good
	גליתי	qal	wcp	1cs	גלה	162		uncover
	שלחתיך	piel	wcp	1cs	שׁלח	1018	2ms	send away,shoot
	הלכת	qal	wcp	2ms	הלך	229		walk,go
	יהי	qal	jus	3ms	היה	224		be,become
	היה	qal	pft	3ms	היה	224		be,become
20: 14	תעשה	qal	impf	2ms	עשׂה	793		do,make
	אמות	qal	impf	1cs	מות	559		die
20: 15	תכרת	hiph	impf	2ms	כרת	503		cut off,destroy
	הכרת	hiph	infc		כרת	503		cut off,destroy
	איבי	qal	ptc	mp	איב	33		be hostile to
20: 16	יכרת	qal	wci	3ms	כרת	503		cut,destroy
	בקש	piel	wcp	3ms	בקשׁ	134		seek
	איבי	qal	ptc	mp	איב	33		be hostile to
20: 17	יוסף	hiph	wci	3ms	יסף	414		add,do again
	השביע	hiph	infc		שׁבע	989		cause to swear
	אהבו	qal	pft	3ms	אהב	12	3ms	love

ChVs	Form	Stem	Tnse	PGN	Root	BDB	Sfx	Meaning
20:18	יאמר	qal	wci	3ms	אמר	55		say
	נפקדת	niph	wcp	2ms	פקד	823		be visited
	יפקד	niph	impf	3ms	פקד	823		be visited
20:19	שׁלשׁת	piel	wcp	2ms	שׁלשׁ	1026		divide into 3
	תרד	qal	impf	2ms	ירד	432		come down
	באת	qal	wcp	2ms	בוא	97		come in
	נסתרת	niph	pft	2ms	סתר	711		hide, be hid
	ישׁבת	qal	wcp	2ms	ישׁב	442		sit, dwell
20:20	אורה	hiph	impf	1cs	ירה	434		shoot, teach
	שׁלח	piel	infc		שׁלח	1018		send away, shoot
20:21	אשׁלח	qal	impf	1cs	שׁלח	1018		send
	לך	qal	impv	ms	הלך	229		walk, go
	מצא	qal	impv	ms	מצא	592		find
	אמר	qal	infa		אמר	55		say
	אמר	qal	impf	1cs	אמר	55		say
	קחנו	qal	impv	ms	לקח	542	3ms	take
	באה	qal	impv	ms	בוא	97		come in
20:22	אמר	qal	impf	1cs	אמר	55		say
	לך	qal	impv	ms	הלך	229		walk, go
	שׁלחך	piel	pft	3ms	שׁלח	1018	2ms	send away, shoot
20:23	דברנו	piel	pft	1cp	דבר	180		speak
20:24	יסתר	niph	wci	3ms	סתר	711		hide, be hid
	יהי	qal	wci	3ms	היה	224		be, become
	ישׁב	qal	wci	3ms	ישׁב	442		sit, dwell
	אכול	qal	infc		אכל	37		eat, devour
20:25	ישׁב	qal	wci	3ms	ישׁב	442		sit, dwell
	יקם	qal	wci	3ms	קום	877		arise, stand
	ישׁב	qal	wci	3ms	ישׁב	442		sit, dwell
	יפקד	niph	wci	3ms	פקד	823		be visited
20:26	דבר	piel	pft	3ms	דבר	180		speak
	אמר	qal	pft	3ms	אמר	55		say
20:27	יהי	qal	wci	3ms	היה	224		be, become
	יפקד	niph	wci	3ms	פקד	823		be visited
	יאמר	qal	wci	3ms	אמר	55		say
	בא	qal	pft	3ms	בוא	97		come in
20:28	יען	qal	wci	3ms	ענה	772		answer
	נשׁאל	niph	infa		שׁאל	981		ask for self
	נשׁאל	niph	pft	3ms	שׁאל	981		ask for self
20:29	יאמר	qal	wci	3ms	אמר	55		say
	שׁלחני	piel	impv	ms	שׁלח	1018	1cs	send away, shoot
	צוה	piel	pft	3ms	צוה	845		command
	מצאתי	qal	pft	1cs	מצא	592		find
	אמלטה	niph	coh	1cs	מלט	572		escape
	אראה	qal	cohm	1cs	ראה	906		see
	בא	qal	pft	3ms	בוא	97		come in
20:30	יחר	qal	wci	3ms	חרה	354		be kindled, burn
	יאמר	qal	wci	3ms	אמר	55		say
	נעות	niph	ptc	fs	עוה	730		be bent
	ידעתי	qal	pft	1cs	ידע	393		know
	בחר	qal	ptc	ms	בחר	103		choose
20:31	תכון	niph	impf	2ms	כון	465		be established
	שׁלח	qal	impv	ms	שׁלח	1018		send
	קח	qal	impv	ms	לקח	542		take
20:32	יען	qal	wci	3ms	ענה	772		answer
20:32	יאמר	qal	wci	3ms	אמר	55		say
	יומת	hoph	impf	3ms	מות	559		be killed
	עשׂה	qal	pft	3ms	עשׂה	793		do, make
20:33	יטל	hiph	wci	3ms	טול	376		cast
	הכתו	hiph	infc		נכה	645	3ms	smite
	ידע	qal	wci	3ms	ידע	393		know
	כלה	qal	pft	3ms	כלה	477		finished, spent
	המית	hiph	infc		מות	559		kill
20:34	יקם	qal	wci	3ms	קום	877		arise, stand
	אכל	qal	pft	3ms	אכל	37		eat, devour
	נעצב	niph	pft	3ms	עצב	780		be pained
	הכלמו	hiph	pft	3ms	כלם	483	3ms	humiliate
20:35	יהי	qal	wci	3ms	היה	224		be, become
	יצא	qal	wci	3ms	יצא	422		go out
20:36	יאמר	qal	wci	3ms	אמר	55		say
	רץ	qal	impv	ms	רוץ	930		run
	מצא	qal	impv	ms	מצא	592		find
	מורה	hiph	ptc	ms	ירה	434		shoot, teach
	רץ	qal	pft	3ms	רוץ	930		run
	ירה	qal	pft	3ms	ירה	434		throw, shoot
	העברו	hiph	infc		עבר	716	3ms	cause to pass
20:37	יבא	qal	wci	3ms	בוא	97		come in
	ירה	qal	pft	3ms	ירה	434		throw, shoot
	יקרא	qal	wci	3ms	קרא	894		call, proclaim
	יאמר	qal	wci	3ms	אמר	55		say
20:38	יקרא	qal	wci	3ms	קרא	894		call, proclaim
	חושׁה	qal	impv	ms	חושׁ	301		make haste
	תעמד	qal	jusm	2ms	עמד	763		stand, stop
	ילקט	piel	wci	3ms	לקט	544		gather
	יבא	qal	wci	3ms	בוא	97		come in
20:39	ידע	qal	pft	3ms	ידע	393		know
	ידעו	qal	pft	3cp	ידע	393		know
20:40	יתן	qal	wci	3ms	נתן	678		give, set
	יאמר	qal	wci	3ms	אמר	55		say
	לך	qal	impv	ms	הלך	229		walk, go
	הביא	hiph	impv	ms	בוא	97		bring in
20:41	בא	qal	pft	3ms	בוא	97		come in
	קם	qal	pft	3ms	קום	877		arise, stand
	יפל	qal	wci	3ms	נפל	656		fall
	ישׁתחו	hish	wci	3ms	חוה	1005		bow down
	ישׁקו	qal	wci	3mp	נשׁק	676		kiss
	יבכו	qal	wci	3mp	בכה	113		weep
	הגדיל	hiph	pft	3ms	גדל	152		make great
20:42	יאמר	qal	wci	3ms	אמר	55		say
	לך	qal	impv	ms	הלך	229		walk, go
	נשׁבענו	niph	pft	1cp	שׁבע	989		swear
	אמר	qal	infc		אמר	55		say
	יהיה	qal	impf	3ms	היה	224		be, become
21:1	יקם	qal	wci	3ms	קום	877		arise, stand
	ילך	qal	wci	3ms	הלך	229		walk, go
	בא	qal	pft	3ms	בוא	97		come in
21:2	יבא	qal	wci	3ms	בוא	97		come in
	יחרד	qal	wci	3ms	חרד	353		tremble
	קראת	qal	infc		קרא	896		meet, encounter

ChVs	Form	Stem	Tnse	PGN	Root	BDB	Sfx	Meaning
21:2	יאמר	qal	wci	3ms	אמר	55		say
21:3	יאמר	qal	wci	3ms	אמר	55		say
	צוני	piel	pft	3ms	צוה	845	1cs	command
	יאמר	qal	wci	3ms	אמר	55		say
	ידע	qal	jusm	3ms	ידע	393		know
	שלחך	qal	ptc	ms	שלח	1018	2ms	send
	צויתך	piel	pft	1cs	צוה	845	2ms	command
	יודעתי	poel	pft	1cs	ידע	393		cause to know
21:4	תנה	qal	impv	ms	נתן	678		give,set
	נמצא	niph	ptc	ms	מצא	592		be found
21:5	יען	qal	wci	3ms	ענה	772		answer
	יאמר	qal	wci	3ms	אמר	55		say
	נשמרו	niph	pft	3cp	שמר	1036		be kept,guarded
21:6	יען	qal	wci	3ms	ענה	772		answer
	יאמר	qal	wci	3ms	אמר	55		say
	עצרה	qal	pptc	fs	עצר	783		restrain
	צאתי	qal	infc		יצא	422	1cs	go out
	יהיו	qal	wci	3mp	היה	224		be,become
	יקדש	qal	impf	3ms	קדש	872		be set apart
21:7	יתן	qal	wci	3ms	נתן	678		give,set
	היה	qal	pft	3ms	היה	224		be,become
	מוסרים	hoph	ptc	mp	סור	693		be taken away
	שום	qal	infc		שים	962		put,set
	הלקחו	niph	infc		לקח	542	3ms	be taken
21:8	נעצר	niph	ptc	ms	עצר	783		be restrained
	רעים	qal	ptc	mp	רעה	944		pasture,tend
21:9	יאמר	qal	wci	3ms	אמר	55		say
	לקחתי	qal	pft	1cs	לקח	542		take
	היה	qal	pft	3ms	היה	224		be,become
	נחוץ	qal	pptc	ms	נחץ	637		urge
21:10	יאמר	qal	wci	3ms	אמר	55		say
	הכית	hiph	pft	2ms	נכה	645		smite
	לוטה	qal	pptc	fs	לוט	532		wrap
	תקח	qal	impf	2ms	לקח	542		take
	קח	qal	impv	ms	לקח	542		take
	יאמר	qal	wci	3ms	אמר	55		say
	תננה	qal	impv	ms	נתן	678	3fs	give,set
21:11	יקם	qal	wci	3ms	קום	877		arise,stand
	יברח	qal	wci	3ms	ברח	137		go thru,flee
	יבא	qal	wci	3ms	בוא	97		come in
21:12	יאמרו	qal	wci	3mp	אמר	55		say
	יענו	qal	impf	3mp	ענה	777		sing
	אמר	qal	infc		אמר	55		say
	הכה	hiph	pft	3ms	נכה	645		smite
21:13	ישם	qal	wci	3ms	שים	962		put,set
	ירא	qal	wci	3ms	ירא	431		fear
21:14	ישנו	piel	wci	3ms	שנה	1039	3ms	change,alter
	יתהלל	htpo	wci	3ms	הלל	237		act madly
	ויתו k	piel	wci	3ms	תוה	1063		make mark
	ויתיו q	piel	wci	3ms	תוה	1063		make mark
	יורד	hiph	wci	3ms	ירד	432		bring down
21:15	יאמר	qal	wci	3ms	אמר	55		say
	תראו	qal	impf	2mp	ראה	906		see
	משתגע	hith	ptc	ms	שגע	993		show madness
21:15	תביאו	hiph	impf	2mp	בוא	97		bring in
21:16	משגעים	pual	ptc	mp	שגע	993		be mad
	הבאתם	hiph	pft	2mp	בוא	97		bring in
	השתגע	hith	infc		שגע	993		show madness
	יבוא	qal	impf	3ms	בוא	97		come in
22:1	ילך	qal	wci	3ms	הלך	229		walk,go
	ימלט	niph	wci	3ms	מלט	572		escape
	ישמעו	qal	wci	3mp	שמע	1033		hear
	ירדו	qal	wci	3mp	ירד	432		come down
22:2	יתקבצו	hith	wci	3mp	קבץ	867		gather together
	נשא	qal	ptc	ms	נשא	673		be creditor
	יהי	qal	wci	3ms	היה	224		be,become
	יהיו	qal	wci	3mp	היה	224		be,become
22:3	ילך	qal	wci	3ms	הלך	229		walk,go
	יאמר	qal	wci	3ms	אמר	55		say
	יצא	qal	jusm	3ms	יצא	422		go out
	אדע	qal	impf	1cs	ידע	393		know
	יעשה	qal	impf	3ms	עשה	793		do,make
22:4	ינחם	hiph	wci	3ms	נחה	634	3mp	lead,guide
	ישבו	qal	wci	3mp	ישב	442		sit,dwell
	היות	qal	infc		היה	224		be,become
22:5	יאמר	qal	wci	3ms	אמר	55		say
	תשב	qal	impf	2ms	ישב	442		sit,dwell
	לך	qal	impv	ms	הלך	229		walk,go
	באת	qal	wcp	2ms	בוא	97		come in
	ילך	qal	wci	3ms	הלך	229		walk,go
	יבא	qal	wci	3ms	בוא	97		come in
22:6	ישמע	qal	wci	3ms	שמע	1033		hear
	נודע	niph	pft	3ms	ידע	393		be made known
	יושב	qal	ptc	ms	ישב	442		sit,dwell
	נצבים	niph	ptc	mp	נצב	662		stand
22:7	יאמר	qal	wci	3ms	אמר	55		say
	נצבים	niph	ptc	mp	נצב	662		stand
	שמעו	qal	impv	mp	שמע	1033		hear
	יתן	qal	impf	3ms	נתן	678		give,set
	ישים	qal	impf	3ms	שים	962		put,set
22:8	קשרתם	qal	pft	2mp	קשר	905		bind
	גלה	qal	ptc	ms	גלה	162		uncover
	כרת	qal	infc		כרת	503		cut,destroy
	חלה	qal	ptc	ms	חלה	317		be weak,sick
	גלה	qal	ptc	ms	גלה	162		uncover
	הקים	hiph	pft	3ms	קום	877		raise,build,set
	ארב	qal	ptc	ms	ארב	70		lie in wait
22:9	יען	qal	wci	3ms	ענה	772		answer
	נצב	niph	ptc	ms	נצב	662		stand
	יאמר	qal	wci	3ms	אמר	55		say
	ראיתי	qal	pft	1cs	ראה	906		see
	בא	qal	ptc	ms	בוא	97		come in
22:10	ישאל	qal	wci	3ms	שאל	981		ask,borrow
	נתן	qal	pft	3ms	נתן	678		give,set
	נתן	qal	pft	3ms	נתן	678		give,set
22:11	ישלח	qal	wci	3ms	שלח	1018		send
	קרא	qal	infc		קרא	894		call,proclaim
	יבאו	qal	wci	3mp	בוא	97		come in

ChVs	Form	Stem	Tnse	PGN	Root	BDB	Sfx	Meaning
22:12	יאמר	qal	wci	3ms	אמר	55		say
	שמע	qal	impv	ms	שמע	1033		hear
	יאמר	qal	wci	3ms	אמר	55		say
22:13	יאמר	qal	wci	3ms	אמר	55		say
	קשרתם	qal	pft	2mp	קשר	905		bind
	תתך	qal	infc		נתן	678	2ms	give,set
	שאול	qal	infa		שאל	981		ask,borrow
	קום	qal	infc		קום	877		arise,stand
	ארב	qal	ptc	ms	ארב	70		lie in wait
22:14	יען	qal	wci	3ms	ענה	772		answer
	יאמר	qal	wci	3ms	אמר	55		say
	נאמן	niph	ptc	ms	אמן	52		be confirmed
	סר	qal	ptc	ms	סור	693?		turn aside
	נכבד	niph	ptc	ms	כבד	457		be honored
22:15	החלתי	hiph	pft	1cs	חלל	320		begin,profane
	שאולk	qal	infc		שאל	981		ask,borrow
	שאלq	qal	infc		שאל	981		ask,borrow
	ישם	qal	jus	3ms	שים	962		put,set
	ידע	qal	pft	3ms	ידע	393		know
22:16	יאמר	qal	wci	3ms	אמר	55		say
	מות	qal	infa		מות	559		die
	תמות	qal	impf	2ms	מות	559		die
22:17	יאמר	qal	wci	3ms	אמר	55		say
	רצים	qal	ptc	mp	רוץ	930		run
	נצבים	niph	ptc	mp	נצב	662		stand
	סבו	qal	impv	mp	סבב	685		surround
	המיתו	hiph	impv	mp	מות	559		kill
	ידעו	qal	pft	3cp	ידע	393		know
	ברח	qal	ptc	ms	ברח	137		go thru,flee
	גלו	qal	pft	3cp	גלה	162		uncover
	אבו	qal	pft	3cp	אבה	2		be willing
	שלח	qal	infc		שלח	1018		send
	פגע	qal	infc		פגע	803		meet,encounter
22:18	יאמר	qal	wci	3ms	אמר	55		say
	סב	qal	impv	ms	סבב	685		surround
	פגע	qal	impv	ms	פגע	803		meet,encounter
	יסב	qal	wci	3ms	סבב	685		surround
	יפגע	qal	wci	3ms	פגע	803		meet,encounter
	ימת	hiph	wci	3ms	מות	559		kill
	נשא	qal	ptc	ms	נשא	669		lift,carry
22:19	הכה	hiph	pft	3ms	נכה	645		smite
	יונק	qal	ptc	ms	ינק	413		suck
22:20	ימלט	niph	wci	3ms	מלט	572		escape
	יברח	qal	wci	3ms	ברח	137		go thru,flee
22:21	יגד	hiph	wci	3ms	נגד	616		declare,tell
	הרג	qal	pft	3ms	הרג	246		kill
22:22	יאמר	qal	wci	3ms	אמר	55		say
	ידעתי	qal	pft	1cs	ידע	393		know
	הגד	hiph	infa		נגד	616		declare,tell
	יגיד	hiph	impf	3ms	נגד	616		declare,tell
	סבתי	qal	pft	1cs	סבב	685		surround
22:23	שבה	qal	impv	ms	ישב	442		sit,dwell
	תירא	qal	jusm	2ms	ירא	431		fear
	יבקש	piel	impf	3ms	בקש	134		seek

ChVs	Form	Stem	Tnse	PGN	Root	BDB	Sfx	Meaning
22:23	יבקש	piel	impf	3ms	בקש	134		seek
23:1	יגדו	hiph	wci	3mp	נגד	616		declare,tell
	אמר	qal	infc		אמר	55		say
	נלחמים	niph	ptc	mp	לחם	535		wage war
	שסים	qal	ptc	mp	שסה	1042		plunder
23:2	ישאל	qal	wci	3ms	שאל	981		ask,borrow
	אמר	qal	infc		אמר	55		say
	אלך	qal	impf	1cs	הלך	229		walk,go
	הכיתי	hiph	wcp	1cs	נכה	645		smite
	יאמר	qal	wci	3ms	אמר	55		say
	לך	qal	impv	ms	הלך	229		walk,go
	הכית	hiph	wcp	2ms	נכה	645		smite
	הושעת	hiph	wcp	2ms	ישע	446		deliver,save
23:3	יאמרו	qal	wci	3mp	אמר	55		say
	יראים	qal	ptc	mp	ירא	431		fear
	נלך	qal	impf	1cp	הלך	229		walk,go
23:4	יוסף	hiph	wci	3ms	יסף	414		add,do again
	שאל	qal	infc		שאל	981		ask,borrow
	יענהו	qal	wci	3ms	ענה	772	3ms	answer
	יאמר	qal	wci	3ms	אמר	55		say
	קום	qal	impv	ms	קום	877		arise,stand
	רד	qal	impv	ms	ירד	432		come down
	נתן	qal	ptc	ms	נתן	678		give,set
23:5	ילך	qal	wci	3ms	הלך	229		walk,go
	ילחם	niph	wci	3ms	לחם	535		wage war
	ינהג	qal	wci	3ms	נהג	624		drive
	יך	hiph	wci	3ms	נכה	645		smite
	ישע	hiph	wci	3ms	ישע	446		deliver,save
	ישבי	qal	ptc	mp	ישב	442		sit,dwell
23:6	יהי	qal	wci	3ms	היה	224		be,become
	ברח	qal	infc		ברח	137		go thru,flee
	ירד	qal	pft	3ms	ירד	432		come down
23:7	יגד	hoph	wci	3ms	נגד	616		be told
	בא	qal	pft	3ms	בוא	97		come in
	יאמר	qal	wci	3ms	אמר	55		say
	נכר	piel	pft	3ms	נכר	649		treat strange
	נסגר	niph	pft	3ms	סגר	688		be shut
	בוא	qal	infc		בוא	97		come in
23:8	ישמע	piel	wci	3ms	שמע	1033		cause to hear
	רדת	qal	infc		ירד	432		come down
	צור	qal	infc		צור	848		confine,shut in
23:9	ידע	qal	wci	3ms	ידע	393		know
	מחריש	hiph	ptc	ms	חרש	360		contrive
	יאמר	qal	wci	3ms	אמר	55		say
	הגישה	hiph	impv	ms	נגש	620		bring near
23:10	יאמר	qal	wci	3ms	אמר	55		say
	שמע	qal	infa		שמע	1033		hear
	שמע	qal	pft	3ms	שמע	1033		hear
	מבקש	piel	ptc	ms	בקש	134		seek
	בוא	qal	infc		בוא	97		come in
	שחת	piel	infc		שחת	1007		spoil,ruin
23:11	יסגרני	hiph	impf	3mp	סגר	688	1cs	shut up,deliver
	ירד	qal	impf	3ms	ירד	432		come down
	שמע	qal	pft	3ms	שמע	1033		hear

ChVs	Form	Stem	Tnse	PGN	Root	BDB	Sfx	Meaning
23:11	הגד	hiph	impv	ms	נגד	616		declare,tell
	יאמר	qal	wci	3ms	אמר	55		say
	ירד	qal	impf	3ms	ירד	432		come down
23:12	יאמר	qal	wci	3ms	אמר	55		say
	יסגרו	hiph	impf	3mp	סגר	688		shut up,deliver
	יאמר	qal	wci	3ms	אמר	55		say
	יסגירו	hiph	impf	3mp	סגר	688		shut up,deliver
23:13	יקם	qal	wci	3ms	קום	877		arise,stand
	יצאו	qal	wci	3mp	יצא	422		go out
	יתהלכו	hith	wci	3mp	הלך	229		walk to and fro
	יתהלכו	hith	impf	3mp	הלך	229		walk to and fro
	הגד	hoph	pft	3ms	נגד	616		be told
	נמלט	niph	pft	3ms	מלט	572		escape
	יחדל	qal	wci	3ms	חדל	292		cease
	צאת	qal	infc		יצא	422		go out
23:14	ישב	qal	wci	3ms	ישב	442		sit,dwell
	ישב	qal	wci	3ms	ישב	442		sit,dwell
	יבקשהו	piel	wci	3ms	בקש	134	3ms	seek
	נתנו	qal	pft	3ms	נתן	678	3ms	give,set
23:15	ירא	qal	wci	3ms	ראה	906		see
	יצא	qal	pft	3ms	יצא	422		go out
	בקש	piel	infc		בקש	134		seek
23:16	יקם	qal	wci	3ms	קום	877		arise,stand
	ילך	qal	wci	3ms	הלך	229		walk,go
	יחזק	piel	wci	3ms	חזק	304		make strong
23:17	יאמר	qal	wci	3ms	אמר	55		say
	תירא	qal	jusm	2ms	ירא	431		fear
	תמצאך	qal	impf	3fs	מצא	592	2ms	find
	תמלך	qal	impf	2ms	מלך	573		be king,reign
	אהיה	qal	impf	1cs	היה	224		be,become
	ידע	qal	ptc	ms	ידע	393		know
23:18	יכרתו	qal	wci	3mp	כרת	503		cut,destroy
	ישב	qal	wci	3ms	ישב	442		sit,dwell
	הלך	qal	pft	3ms	הלך	229		walk,go
23:19	יעלו	qal	wci	3mp	עלה	748		go up
	אמר	qal	infc		אמר	55		say
	מסתתר	hith	ptc	ms	סתר	711		hide self
23:20	רדת	qal	infc		ירד	432		come down
	רד	qal	impv	ms	ירד	432		come down
	הסגירו	hiph	infc		סגר	688	3ms	shut up,deliver
23:21	יאמר	qal	wci	3ms	אמר	55		say
	ברוכים	qal	pptc	mp	ברך	138		kneel,bless
	חמלתם	qal	pft	2mp	חמל	328		spare
23:22	לכו	qal	impv	mp	הלך	229		walk,go
	הכינו	hiph	impv	mp	כון	465		fix,prepare
	דעו	qal	impv	mp	ידע	393		know
	ראו	qal	impv	mp	ראה	906		see
	תהיה	qal	impf	3fs	היה	224		be,become
	ראהו	qal	pft	3ms	ראה	906	3ms	see
	אמר	qal	pft	3ms	אמר	55		say
	ערום	qal	infa		ערם	791		be crafty
	יערם	hiph	impf	3ms	ערם	791		act craftily
23:23	ראו	qal	impv	mp	ראה	906		see
	דעו	qal	impv	mp	ידע	393		know
23:23	יתחבא	hith	impf	3ms	חבא	285		hide oneself
	שבתם	qal	wcp	2mp	שוב	996		turn,return
	נכון	niph	ptc	ms	כון	465		be established
	הלכתי	qal	wcp	1cs	הלך	229		walk,go
	היה	qal	wcp	3ms	היה	224		be,become
	חפשתי	piel	wcp	1cs	חפש	344		search for
23:24	יקומו	qal	wci	3mp	קום	877		arise,stand
	ילכו	qal	wci	3mp	הלך	229		walk,go
23:25	ילך	qal	wci	3ms	הלך	229		walk,go
	בקש	piel	infc		בקש	134		seek
	יגדו	hiph	wci	3mp	נגד	616		declare,tell
	ירד	qal	wci	3ms	ירד	432		come down
	ישב	qal	wci	3ms	ישב	442		sit,dwell
	ישמע	qal	wci	3ms	שמע	1033		hear
	ירדף	qal	wci	3ms	רדף	922		pursue
23:26	ילך	qal	wci	3ms	הלך	229		walk,go
	יהי	qal	wci	3ms	היה	224		be,become
	נחפז	niph	ptc	ms	חפז	342		hurry in alarm
	לכת	qal	infc		הלך	229		walk,go
	עטרים	qal	ptc	mp	עטר	742		surround
	תפשם	qal	infc		תפש	1074	3mp	seize,grasp
23:27	בא	qal	pft	3ms	בוא	97		come in
	אמר	qal	infc		אמר	55		say
	מהרה	piel	impv	ms	מהר	554		hasten
	לכה	qal	impv	ms	הלך	229		walk,go
	פשטו	qal	pft	3cp	פשט	832		strip off
23:28	ישב	qal	wci	3ms	שוב	996		turn,return
	רדף	qal	infc		רדף	922		pursue
	ילך	qal	wci	3ms	הלך	229		walk,go
	קראת	qal	infc		קרא	896		meet,encounter
	קראו	qal	pft	3cp	קרא	894		call,proclaim
24:1	יעל	qal	wci	3ms	עלה	748		go up
	ישב	qal	wci	3ms	ישב	442		sit,dwell
24:2	יהי	qal	wci	3ms	היה	224		be,become
	שב	qal	pft	3ms	שוב	996		turn,return
	יגדו	hiph	wci	3mp	נגד	616		declare,tell
	אמר	qal	infc		אמר	55		say
24:3	יקח	qal	wci	3ms	לקח	542		take
	בחור	qal	pptc	ms	בחר	103		choose
	ילך	qal	wci	3ms	הלך	229		walk,go
	בקש	piel	infc		בקש	134		seek
24:4	יבא	qal	wci	3ms	בוא	97		come in
	יבא	qal	wci	3ms	בוא	97		come in
	הסך	hiph	infc		סכך	696		cover
	ישבים	qal	ptc	mp	ישב	442		sit,dwell
24:5	יאמרו	qal	wci	3mp	אמר	55		say
	אמר	qal	pft	3ms	אמר	55		say
	נתן	qal	ptc	ms	נתן	678		give,set
	איביך k	qal	ptc	mp	איב	33	2ms	be hostile to
	איבך q	qal	ptc	ms	איב	33	2ms	be hostile to
	עשית	qal	wcp	2ms	עשה	793		do,make
	יטב	qal	impf	3ms	יטב	405		be good
	יקם	qal	wci	3ms	קום	877		arise,stand
	יכרת	qal	wci	3ms	כרת	503		cut,destroy

ChVs	Form	Stem	Tnse	PGN	Root	BDB	Sfx	Meaning
24: 6	יהי	qal	wci	3ms	היה	224		be,become
	יך	hiph	wci	3ms	נכה	645		smite
	כרת	qal	pft	3ms	כרת	503		cut,destroy
24: 7	יאמר	qal	wci	3ms	אמר	55		say
	אעשׂה	qal	impf	1cs	עשׂה	793		do,make
	שׁלח	qal	infc		שׁלח	1018		send
24: 8	ישׁסע	piel	wci	3ms	שׁסע	1042		tear in two
	נתנם	qal	pft	3ms	נתן	678	3mp	give,set
	קום	qal	infc		קום	877		arise,stand
	קם	qal	pft	3ms	קום	877		arise,stand
	ילך	qal	wci	3ms	הלך	229		walk,go
24: 9	יקם	qal	wci	3ms	קום	877		arise,stand
	יצא	qal	wci	3ms	יצא	422		go out
	יקרא	qal	wci	3ms	קרא	894		call,proclaim
	אמר	qal	infc		אמר	55		say
	יבט	hiph	wci	3ms	נבט	613		look,regard
	יקד	qal	wci	3ms	קדד	869		bow down
	ישׁתחו	hish	wci	3ms	חוה	1005		bow down
24: 10	יאמר	qal	wci	3ms	אמר	55		say
	תשׁמע	qal	impf	2ms	שׁמע	1033		hear
	אמר	qal	infc		אמר	55		say
	מבקשׁ	piel	ptc	ms	בקשׁ	134		seek
24: 11	ראו	qal	pft	3cp	ראה	906		see
	נתנך	qal	pft	3ms	נתן	678	2ms	give,set
	אמר	qal	wcp	3ms	אמר	55		say
	הרגך	qal	infc		הרג	246	2ms	kill
	תחס	qal	wci	3fs	חוס	299		pity
	אמר	qal	wci	1cs	אמר	55		say
	אשׁלח	qal	impf	1cs	שׁלח	1018		send
24: 12	ראה	qal	impv	ms	ראה	906		see
	ראה	qal	impv	ms	ראה	906		see
	כרתי	qal	infc		כרת	503	1cs	cut,destroy
	הרגתיך	qal	pft	1cs	הרג	246	2ms	kill
	דע	qal	impv	ms	ידע	393		know
	ראה	qal	impv	ms	ראה	906		see
	חטאתי	qal	pft	1cs	חטא	306		sin
	צדה	qal	ptc	ms	צדה	841		lie in wait
	קחתה	qal	infc		לקח	542	3fs	take
24: 13	ישׁפט	qal	jusm	3ms	שׁפט	1047		judge
	נקמני	qal	wcp	3ms	נקם	667	1cs	avenge
	תהיה	qal	impf	3fs	היה	224		be,become
24: 14	יאמר	qal	impf	3ms	אמר	55		say
	יצא	qal	impf	3ms	יצא	422		go out
	תהיה	qal	impf	3fs	היה	224		be,become
24: 15	יצא	qal	pft	3ms	יצא	422		go out
	רדף	qal	ptc	ms	רדף	922		pursue
	מת	qal	ptc	ms	מות	559		die
24: 16	היה	qal	wcp	3ms	היה	224		be,become
	שׁפט	qal	wcp	3ms	שׁפט	1047		judge
	ירא	qal	jus	3ms	ראה	906		see
	ירב	qal	jus	3ms	ריב	936		strive,contend
	ישׁפטני	qal	jusm	3ms	שׁפט	1047	1cs	judge
24: 17	יהי	qal	wci	3ms	היה	224		be,become
	כלות	piel	infc		כלה	477		complete,finish
24: 17	דבר	piel	infc		דבר	180		speak
	יאמר	qal	wci	3ms	אמר	55		say
	ישׂא	qal	wci	3ms	נשׂא	669		lift,carry
	יבך	qal	wci	3ms	בכה	113		weep
24: 18	יאמר	qal	wci	3ms	אמר	55		say
	גמלתני	qal	pft	2ms	גמל	168	1cs	deal out,ripen
	גמלתיך	qal	pft	1cs	גמל	168	2ms	deal out,ripen
24: 19	הגדת	hiph	pft	2ms	נגד	616		declare,tell
	עשׂיתה	qal	pft	2ms	עשׂה	793		do,make
	סגרני	piel	pft	3ms	סגר	688	1cs	deliver
	הרגתני	qal	pft	2ms	הרג	246	1cs	kill
24: 20	ימצא	qal	impf	3ms	מצא	592		find
	איבו	qal	ptc	ms	איב	33	3ms	be hostile to
	שׁלחו	piel	wcp	3ms	שׁלח	1018	3ms	send away,shoot
	ישׁלמך	piel	jusm	3ms	שׁלם	1022	2ms	finish,reward
	עשׂיתה	qal	pft	2ms	עשׂה	793		do,make
24: 21	ידעתי	qal	pft	1cs	ידע	393		know
	מלך	qal	infa		מלך	573		be king,reign
	תמלוך	qal	impf	2ms	מלך	573		be king,reign
	קמה	qal	wcp	3fs	קום	877		arise,stand
24: 22	השׁבעה	niph	impv	ms	שׁבע	989		swear
	תכרית	hiph	impf	2ms	כרת	503		cut off,destroy
	תשׁמיד	hiph	impf	2ms	שׁמד	1029		exterminate
24: 23	ישׁבע	niph	wci	3ms	שׁבע	989		swear
	ילך	qal	wci	3ms	הלך	229		walk,go
	עלו	qal	pft	3cp	עלה	748		go up
25: 1	ימת	qal	wci	3ms	מות	559		die
	יקבצו	niph	wci	3mp	קבץ	867		assemble,gather
	יספדו	qal	wci	3mp	ספד	704		wail,lament
	יקברהו	qal	wci	3mp	קבר	868	3ms	bury
	יקם	qal	wci	3ms	קום	877		arise,stand
	ירד	qal	wci	3ms	ירד	432		come down
25: 2	יהי	qal	wci	3ms	היה	224		be,become
	גזז	qal	infc		גזז	159		shear
25: 4	ישׁמע	qal	wci	3ms	שׁמע	1033		hear
	גזז	qal	ptc	ms	גזז	159		shear
25: 5	ישׁלח	qal	wci	3ms	שׁלח	1018		send
	יאמר	qal	wci	3ms	אמר	55		say
	עלו	qal	impv	mp	עלה	748		go up
	באתם	qal	wcp	2mp	בוא	97		come in
	שׁאלתם	qal	wcp	2mp	שׁאל	981		ask,borrow
25: 6	אמרתם	qal	wcp	2mp	אמר	55		say
25: 7	שׁמעתי	qal	pft	1cs	שׁמע	1033		hear
	גזזים	qal	ptc	mp	גזז	159		shear
	רעים	qal	ptc	mp	רעה	944		pasture,tend
	היו	qal	pft	3cp	היה	224		be,become
	הכלמנום	hiph	pft	1cp	כלם	483	3mp	humiliate
	נפקד	niph	pft	3ms	פקד	823		be visited
	היותם	qal	infc		היה	224	3mp	be,become
25: 8	שׁאל	qal	impv	ms	שׁאל	981		ask,borrow
	יגידו	hiph	impf	3mp	נגד	616		declare,tell
	ימצאו	qal	jusm	3mp	מצא	592		find
	בנו	qal	pft	1cp	בוא	97		come in
	תנה	qal	impv	ms	נתן	678		give,set

ChVs	Form	Stem	Tnse	PGN	Root	BDB	Sfx	Meaning
25:8	תמצא	qal	impf	3fs	מצא	592		find
25:9	יבאו	qal	wci	3mp	בוא	97		come in
	ידברו	piel	wci	3mp	דבר	180		speak
	ינוחו	qal	wci	3mp	נוח	628		rest
25:10	יען	qal	wci	3ms	ענה	772		answer
	יאמר	qal	wci	3ms	אמר	55		say
	רבו	qal	pft	3cp	רבב	912		be many
	מתפרצים	hith	ptc	mp	פרץ	829		break away
25:11	לקחתי	qal	wcp	1cs	לקח	542		take
	טבחתי	qal	pft	1cs	טבח	370		slaughter
	גזזי	qal	ptc	mp	גזז	159	1cs	shear
	נתתי	qal	wcp	1cs	נתן	678		give,set
	ידעתי	qal	pft	1cs	ידע	393		know
25:12	יהפכו	qal	wci	3mp	הפך	245		turn,overturn
	ישׁבו	qal	wci	3mp	שׁוב	996		turn,return
	יבאו	qal	wci	3mp	בוא	97		come in
	יגדו	hiph	wci	3mp	נגד	616		declare,tell
25:13	יאמר	qal	wci	3ms	אמר	55		say
	חגרו	qal	impv	mp	חגר	291		gird
	יחגרו	qal	wci	3mp	חגר	291		gird
	יחגר	qal	wci	3ms	חגר	291		gird
	יעלו	qal	wci	3mp	עלה	748		go up
	ישׁבו	qal	pft	3cp	ישׁב	442		sit,dwell
25:14	הגיד	hiph	pft	3ms	נגד	616		declare,tell
	אמר	qal	infc		אמר	55		say
	שׁלח	qal	pft	3ms	שׁלח	1018		send
	ברך	piel	infc		ברך	138		bless
	יעט	qal	wci	3ms	עיט	743		scream
25:15	הכלמנו	hoph	pft	1cp	כלם	483		be humiliated
	פקדנו	qal	pft	1cp	פקד	823		attend to,visit
	התהלכנו	hith	pft	1cp	הלך	229		walk to and fro
	היותנו	qal	infc		היה	224	1cp	be,become
25:16	היו	qal	pft	3cp	היה	224		be,become
	היותנו	qal	infc		היה	224	1cp	be,become
	רעים	qal	ptc	mp	רעה	944		pasture,tend
25:17	דעי	qal	impv	fs	ידע	393		know
	ראי	qal	impv	fs	ראה	906		see
	תעשׂי	qal	impf	2fs	עשׂה	793		do,make
	כלתה	qal	pft	3fs	כלה	477		finished,spent
	דבר	piel	infc		דבר	180		speak
25:18	תמהר	piel	wci	3fs	מהר	554		hasten
	תקח	qal	wci	3fs	לקח	542		take
	עשׂוותk	qal	pptc	fp	עשׂה	793		do,make
	עשׂויותq	qal	pptc	fp	עשׂה	793		do,make
	תשׂם	qal	wci	3fs	שׂים	962		put,set
25:19	תאמר	qal	wci	3fs	אמר	55		say
	עברו	qal	impv	mp	עבר	716		pass over
	באה	qal	ptc	fs	בוא	97		come in
	הגידה	hiph	pft	3fs	נגד	616		declare,tell
25:20	היה	qal	pft	3ms	היה	224		be,become
	רכבת	qal	ptc	fs	רכב	938		mount,ride
	ירדת	qal	ptc	fs	ירד	432		come down
	ירדים	qal	ptc	mp	ירד	432		come down
	קראתה	qal	infc		קרא	896	3fs	meet,encounter
25:20	תפגשׁ	qal	wci	3fs	פגשׁ	803		meet
25:21	אמר	qal	pft	3ms	אמר	55		say
	שׁמרתי	qal	pft	1cs	שׁמר	1036		keep,watch
	נפקד	niph	pft	3ms	פקד	823		be visited
	ישׁב	hiph	wci	3ms	שׁוב	996		bring back
25:22	יעשׂה	qal	jusm	3ms	עשׂה	793		do,make
	איבי	qal	ptc	mp	איב	33		be hostile to
	יסיף	hiph	jusm	3ms	יסף	414		add,do again
	אשׁאיר	hiph	impf	1cs	שׁאר	983		leave,spare
	משׁתין	hiph	ptc	ms	שׁתן	1010		urinate
25:23	תרא	qal	wci	3fs	ראה	906		see
	תמהר	piel	wci	3fs	מהר	554		hasten
	תרד	qal	wci	3fs	ירד	432		come down
	תפל	qal	wci	3fs	נפל	656		fall
	תשׁתחו	hish	wci	3fs	חוה	1005		bow down
25:24	תפל	qal	wci	3fs	נפל	656		fall
	תאמר	qal	wci	3fs	אמר	55		say
	תדבר	piel	jusm	3fs	דבר	180		speak
	שׁמע	qal	impv	ms	שׁמע	1033		hear
25:25	ישׂים	qal	jusm	3ms	שׂים	962		put,set
	ראיתי	qal	pft	1cs	ראה	906		see
	שׁלחת	qal	pft	2ms	שׁלח	1018		send
25:26	מנעך	qal	pft	3ms	מנע	586	2ms	withhold
	בוא	qal	infc		בוא	97		come in
	הושׁע	hiph	infa		ישׁע	446		deliver,save
	יהיו	qal	jusm	3mp	היה	224		be,become
	איביך	qal	ptc	mp	איב	33	2ms	be hostile to
	מבקשׁים	piel	ptc	mp	בקשׁ	134		seek
25:27	הביא	hiph	pft	3ms	בוא	97		bring in
	נתנה	niph	wcp	3fs	נתן	678		be given
	מתהלכים	hith	ptc	mp	הלך	229		walk to and fro
25:28	שׂא	qal	impv	ms	נשׂא	669		lift,carry
	עשׂה	qal	infa		עשׂה	793		do,make
	יעשׂה	qal	impf	3ms	עשׂה	793		do,make
	נאמן	niph	ptc	ms	אמן	52		be confirmed
	נלחם	niph	ptc	ms	לחם	535		wage war
	תמצא	niph	impf	3fs	מצא	592		be found
25:29	יקם	qal	wci	3ms	קום	877		arise,stand
	רדפך	qal	infc		רדף	922	2ms	pursue
	בקשׁ	piel	infc		בקשׁ	134		seek
	היתה	qal	wcp	3fs	היה	224		be,become
	צרורה	qal	pptc	fs	צרר	864		bind,be cramped
	איביך	qal	ptc	mp	איב	33	2ms	be hostile to
	יקלענה	piel	impf	3ms	קלע	887	3fs	sling,hurl
25:30	היה	qal	wcp	3ms	היה	224		be,become
	יעשׂה	qal	impf	3ms	עשׂה	793		do,make
	דבר	piel	pft	3ms	דבר	180		speak
	צוך	piel	wcp	3ms	צוה	845	2ms	command
25:31	תהיה	qal	impf	3fs	היה	224		be,become
	שׁפך	qal	infc		שׁפך	1049		pour out
	הושׁיע	hiph	infc		ישׁע	446		deliver,save
	היטב	hiph	wcp	3ms	יטב	405		do good
	זכרת	qal	wcp	2ms	זכר	269		remember
25:32	יאמר	qal	wci	3ms	אמר	55		say

ChVs	Form	Stem	Tnse	PGN	Root	BDB	Sfx	Meaning
25:32	ברוך	qal	pptc	ms	ברך	138		kneel, bless
	שׁלחך	qal	pft	3ms	שׁלח	1018	2fs	send
	קראתי	qal	infc		קרא	896	1cs	meet, encounter
25:33	ברוך	qal	pptc	ms	ברך	138		kneel, bless
	ברוכה	qal	pptc	fs	ברך	138		kneel, bless
	כלתני	qal	pft	2fs	כלא	476	1cs	shut up
	בוא	qal	infc		בוא	97		come in
	השׁע	hiph	infa		ישׁע	446		deliver, save
25:34	מנעני	qal	pft	3ms	מנע	586	1cs	withhold
	הרע	hiph	infc		רעע	949		hurt, do evil
	מהרת	piel	pft	2fs	מהר	554		hasten
	תבאתיk	qal	wci	2fs	בוא	97?		come in
	תבאתq	qal	wci	2fs	בוא	97?		come in
	קראתי	qal	infc		קרא	896	1cs	meet, encounter
	נותר	niph	pft	3ms	יתר	451		be left, remain
	משׁתין	hiph	ptc	ms	שׁתן	1010		urinate
25:35	יקח	qal	wci	3ms	לקח	542		take
	הביאה	hiph	pft	3fs	בוא	97		bring in
	אמר	qal	pft	3ms	אמר	55		say
	עלי	qal	impv	fs	עלה	748		go up
	ראי	qal	impv	fs	ראה	906		see
	שׁמעתי	qal	pft	1cs	שׁמע	1033		hear
	אשׂא	qal	wci	1cs	נשׂא	669		lift, carry
25:36	תבא	qal	wci	3fs	בוא	97		come in
	טוב	qal	pft	3ms	טוב	373		be pleasing
	הגידה	hiph	pft	3fs	נגד	616		declare, tell
25:37	יהי	qal	wci	3ms	היה	224		be, become
	צאת	qal	infc		יצא	422		go out
	תגד	hiph	wci	3fs	נגד	616		declare, tell
	ימת	qal	wci	3ms	מות	559		die
	היה	qal	pft	3ms	היה	224		be, become
25:38	יהי	qal	wci	3ms	היה	224		be, become
	יגף	qal	wci	3ms	נגף	619		smite, strike
	ימת	qal	wci	3ms	מות	559		die
25:39	ישׁמע	qal	wci	3ms	שׁמע	1033		hear
	מת	qal	pft	3ms	מות	559		die
	יאמר	qal	wci	3ms	אמר	55		say
	ברוך	qal	pptc	ms	ברך	138		kneel, bless
	רב	qal	pft	3ms	ריב	936		strive, contend
	חשׂך	qal	pft	3ms	חשׂך	362		withhold
	השׁיב	hiph	pft	3ms	שׁוב	996		bring back
	ישׁלח	qal	wci	3ms	שׁלח	1018		send
	ידבר	piel	wci	3ms	דבר	180		speak
	קחתה	qal	infc		לקח	542	3fs	take
25:40	יבאו	qal	wci	3mp	בוא	97		come in
	ידברו	piel	wci	3mp	דבר	180		speak
	אמר	qal	infc		אמר	55		say
	שׁלחנו	qal	pft	3ms	שׁלח	1018	1cp	send
	קחתך	qal	infc		לקח	542	2fs	take
25:41	תקם	qal	wci	3fs	קום	877		arise, stand
	תשׁתחו	hish	wci	3fs	חוה	1005		bow down
	תאמר	qal	wci	3fs	אמר	55		say
	רחץ	qal	infc		רחץ	934		wash, bathe
25:42	תמהר	piel	wci	3fs	מהר	554		hasten
25:42	תקם	qal	wci	3fs	קום	877		arise, stand
	תרכב	qal	wci	3fs	רכב	938		mount, ride
	הלכות	qal	ptc	fp	הלך	229		walk, go
	תלך	qal	wci	3fs	הלך	229		walk, go
	תהי	qal	wci	3fs	היה	224		be, become
25:43	לקח	qal	pft	3ms	לקח	542		take
	תהיין	qal	wci	3fp	היה	224		be, become
25:44	נתן	qal	pft	3ms	נתן	678		give, set
26:1	יבאו	qal	wci	3mp	בוא	97		come in
	אמר	qal	infc		אמר	55		say
	מסתתר	hith	ptc	ms	סתר	711		hide self
26:2	יקם	qal	wci	3ms	קום	877		arise, stand
	ירד	qal	wci	3ms	ירד	432		come down
	בחורי	qal	pptc	mp	בחר	103		choose
	בקשׁ	piel	infc		בקשׁ	134		seek
26:3	יחן	qal	wci	3ms	חנה	333		decline, encamp
	ישׁב	qal	ptc	ms	ישׁב	442		sit, dwell
	ירא	qal	wci	3ms	ראה	906		see
	בא	qal	pft	3ms	בוא	97		come in
26:4	ישׁלח	qal	wci	3ms	שׁלח	1018		send
	מרגלים	piel	ptc	mp	רגל	920		slander, spy
	ידע	qal	wci	3ms	ידע	393		know
	בא	qal	pft	3ms	בוא	97		come in
	נכון	niph	ptc	ms	כון	465		be established
26:5	יקם	qal	wci	3ms	קום	877		arise, stand
	יבא	qal	wci	3ms	בוא	97		come in
	חנה	qal	pft	3ms	חנה	333		decline, encamp
	ירא	qal	wci	3ms	ראה	906		see
	שׁכב	qal	pft	3ms	שׁכב	1011		lie, lie down
	שׁכב	qal	ptc	ms	שׁכב	1011		lie, lie down
	חנים	qal	ptc	mp	חנה	333		decline, encamp
26:6	יען	qal	wci	3ms	ענה	772		answer
	יאמר	qal	wci	3ms	אמר	55		say
	אמר	qal	infc		אמר	55		say
	ירד	qal	impf	3ms	ירד	432		come down
	יאמר	qal	wci	3ms	אמר	55		say
	ארד	qal	impf	1cs	ירד	432		come down
26:7	יבא	qal	wci	3ms	בוא	97		come in
	שׁכב	qal	ptc	ms	שׁכב	1011		lie, lie down
	מעוכה	qal	pptc	fs	מעך	590		press
	שׁכבים	qal	ptc	mp	שׁכב	1011		lie, lie down
26:8	יאמר	qal	wci	3ms	אמר	55		say
	סגר	piel	pft	3ms	סגר	688		deliver
	אויבך	qal	ptc	ms	איב	33	2ms	be hostile to
	אכנו	hiph	cohm	1cs	נכה	645	3ms	smite
	אשׁנה	qal	impf	1cs	שׁנה	1040		do again, repeat
26:9	יאמר	qal	wci	3ms	אמר	55		say
	תשׁחיתהו	hiph	jusm	2ms	שׁחת	1007	3ms	spoil, ruin
	שׁלח	qal	pft	3ms	שׁלח	1018		send
	נקה	niph	wcp	3ms	נקה	667		be clean, free
26:10	יאמר	qal	wci	3ms	אמר	55		say
	יגפנו	qal	impf	3ms	נגף	619	3ms	smite, strike
	יבוא	qal	impf	3ms	בוא	97		come in
	מת	qal	wcp	3ms	מות	559		die

ChVs	Form	Stem	Tnse	PGN	Root	BDB	Sfx	Meaning
26:10	ירד	qal	impf	3ms	ירד	432		come down
	נספה	niph	wcp	3ms	ספה	705		be swept away
26:11	שׁלח	qal	infc		שׁלח	1018		send
	קח	qal	impv	ms	לקח	542		take
	נלכה	qal	coh	1cp	הלך	229		walk,go
26:12	יקח	qal	wci	3ms	לקח	542		take
	ילכו	qal	wci	3mp	הלך	229		walk,go
	ראה	qal	ptc	ms	ראה	906		see
	יודע	qal	ptc	ms	ידע	393		know
	מקיץ	hiph	ptc	ms	קיץ	884		awake
	נפלה	qal	pft	3fs	נפל	656		fall
26:13	יעבר	qal	wci	3ms	עבר	716		pass over
	יעמד	qal	wci	3ms	עמד	763		stand,stop
26:14	יקרא	qal	wci	3ms	קרא	894		call,proclaim
	אמר	qal	infc		אמר	55		say
	תענה	qal	impf	2ms	ענה	772		answer
	יען	qal	wci	3ms	ענה	772		answer
	יאמר	qal	wci	3ms	אמר	55		say
	קראת	qal	pft	2ms	קרא	894		call,proclaim
26:15	יאמר	qal	wci	3ms	אמר	55		say
	שׁמרת	qal	pft	2ms	שׁמר	1036		keep,watch
	בא	qal	pft	3ms	בוא	97		come in
	השׁחית	hiph	infc		שׁחת	1007		spoil,ruin
26:16	עשׂית	qal	pft	2ms	עשׂה	793		do,make
	שׁמרתם	qal	pft	2mp	שׁמר	1036		keep,watch
	ראה	qal	impv	ms	ראה	906		see
26:17	יכר	hiph	wci	3ms	נכר	647		regard,notice
	יאמר	qal	wci	3ms	אמר	55		say
	יאמר	qal	wci	3ms	אמר	55		say
26:18	יאמר	qal	wci	3ms	אמר	55		say
	רדף	qal	ptc	ms	רדף	922		pursue
	עשׂיתי	qal	pft	1cs	עשׂה	793		do,make
26:19	ישׁמע	qal	jusm	3ms	שׁמע	1033		hear
	הסיתך	hiph	pft	3ms	סות	694	2ms	incite,allure
	ירח	hiph	jus	3ms	ריח	926		smell
	ארורים	qal	pptc	mp	ארר	76		curse
	גרשׁוני	piel	pft	3cp	גרשׁ	176	1cs	drive out
	הסתפח	hith	infc		ספח	705		join oneself
	אמר	qal	infc		אמר	55		say
	לך	qal	impv	ms	הלך	229		walk,go
	עבד	qal	impv	ms	עבד	712		work,serve
26:20	יפל	qal	jusm	3ms	נפל	656		fall
	יצא	qal	pft	3ms	יצא	422		go out
	בקשׁ	piel	infc		בקשׁ	134		seek
	ירדף	qal	impf	3ms	רדף	922		pursue
26:21	יאמר	qal	wci	3ms	אמר	55		say
	חטאתי	qal	pft	1cs	חטא	306		sin
	שׁוב	qal	impv	ms	שׁוב	996		turn,return
	ארע	hiph	impf	1cs	רעע	949		hurt,do evil
	יקרה	qal	pft	3fs	יקר	429		be precious
	הסכלתי	hiph	pft	1cs	סכל	698		do foolishly
	אשׁגה	qal	wci	1cs	שׁגה	993		err,go astray
	הרבה	hiph	infa		רבה	915		make many
26:22	יען	qal	wci	3ms	ענה	772		answer
26:22	יאמר	qal	wci	3ms	אמר	55		say
	יעבר	qal	jusm	3ms	עבר	716		pass over
	יקחה	qal	jusm	3ms	לקח	542	3fs	take
26:23	ישׁיב	hiph	impf	3ms	שׁוב	996		bring back
	נתנך	qal	pft	3ms	נתן	678	2ms	give,set
	אביתי	qal	pft	1cs	אבה	2		be willing
	שׁלח	qal	infc		שׁלח	1018		send
26:24	גדלה	qal	pft	3fs	גדל	152		be great,grow
	תגדל	qal	jusm	3fs	גדל	152		be great,grow
	יצלני	hiph	jus	3ms	נצל	664	1cs	snatch,deliver
26:25	יאמר	qal	wci	3ms	אמר	55		say
	ברוך	qal	pptc	ms	ברך	138		kneel,bless
	עשׂה	qal	infa		עשׂה	793		do,make
	תעשׂה	qal	impf	2ms	עשׂה	793		do,make
	יכל	qal	infa		יכל	407		be able
	תוכל	qal	impf	2ms	יכל	407		be able
	ילך	qal	wci	3ms	הלך	229		walk,go
	שׁב	qal	pft	3ms	שׁוב	996		turn,return
27:1	יאמר	qal	wci	3ms	אמר	55		say
	אספה	niph	impf	1cs	ספה	705		be swept away
	המלט	niph	infa		מלט	572		escape
	אמלט	niph	impf	1cs	מלט	572		escape
	נואשׁ	niph	wcp	3ms	יאשׁ	384		despair
	בקשׁני	piel	infc		בקשׁ	134	1cs	seek
	נמלטתי	niph	wcp	1cs	מלט	572		escape
27:2	יקם	qal	wci	3ms	קום	877		arise,stand
	יעבר	qal	wci	3ms	עבר	716		pass over
27:3	ישׁב	qal	wci	3ms	ישׁב	442		sit,dwell
27:4	יגד	hoph	wci	3ms	נגד	616		be told
	ברח	qal	pft	3ms	ברח	137		go thru,flee
	יוסףk	hiph	impf	3ms	יסף	414		add,do again
	יסףq	qal	pft	3ms	יסף	414		add,increase
	בקשׁו	piel	infc		בקשׁ	134	3ms	seek
27:5	יאמר	qal	wci	3ms	אמר	55		say
	מצאתי	qal	pft	1cs	מצא	592		find
	יתנו	qal	jusm	3mp	נתן	678		give,set
	אשׁבה	qal	coh	1cs	ישׁב	442		sit,dwell
	ישׁב	qal	impf	3ms	ישׁב	442		sit,dwell
27:6	יתן	qal	wci	3ms	נתן	678		give,set
	היתה	qal	pft	3fs	היה	224		be,become
27:7	יהי	qal	wci	3ms	היה	224		be,become
	ישׁב	qal	pft	3ms	ישׁב	442		sit,dwell
27:8	יעל	qal	wci	3ms	עלה	748		go up
	יפשׁטו	qal	wci	3mp	פשׁט	832		strip off
	ישׁבות	qal	ptc	fp	ישׁב	442		sit,dwell
	בואך	qal	infc		בוא	97	2ms	come in
27:9	הכה	hiph	wcp	3ms	נכה	645		smite
	יחיה	piel	impf	3ms	חיה	310		preserve,revive
	לקח	qal	wcp	3ms	לקח	542		take
	ישׁב	qal	wci	3ms	שׁוב	996		turn,return
	יבא	qal	wci	3ms	בוא	97		come in
27:10	יאמר	qal	wci	3ms	אמר	55		say
	פשׁטתם	qal	pft	2mp	פשׁט	832		strip off
	יאמר	qal	wci	3ms	אמר	55		say

ChVs	Form	Stem	Tnse	PGN	Root	BDB	Sfx	Meaning
27:11	יחיה	piel	impf	3ms	חיה	310		preserve,revive
	הביא	hiph	infc		בוא	97		bring in
	אמר	qal	infc		אמר	55		say
	יגדו	hiph	impf	3mp	נגד	616		declare,tell
	אמר	qal	infc		אמר	55		say
	עשׂה	qal	pft	3ms	עשׂה	793		do,make
	ישׁב	qal	pft	3ms	ישׁב	442		sit,dwell
27:12	יאמן	hiph	wci	3ms	אמן	52		believe
	אמר	qal	infc		אמר	55		say
	הבאשׁ	hiph	infa		באשׁ	92		cause to stink
	הבאישׁ	hiph	pft	3ms	באשׁ	92		cause to stink
	היה	qal	wcp	3ms	היה	224		be,become
28:1	יהי	qal	wci	3ms	היה	224		be,become
	יקבצו	qal	wci	3mp	קבץ	867		gather,collect
	הלחם	niph	infc		לחם	535		wage war
	יאמר	qal	wci	3ms	אמר	55		say
	ידע	qal	infa		ידע	393		know
	תדע	qal	impf	2ms	ידע	393		know
	תצא	qal	impf	2ms	יצא	422		go out
28:2	יאמר	qal	wci	3ms	אמר	55		say
	תדע	qal	impf	2ms	ידע	393		know
	יעשׂה	qal	impf	3ms	עשׂה	793		do,make
	יאמר	qal	wci	3ms	אמר	55		say
	שׁמר	qal	ptc	ms	שׁמר	1036		keep,watch
	אשׂימך	qal	impf	1cs	שׂים	962	2ms	put,set
28:3	מת	qal	pft	3ms	מות	559		die
	יספדו	qal	wci	3mp	ספד	704		wail,lament
	יקברהו	qal	wci	3mp	קבר	868	3ms	bury
	הסיר	hiph	pft	3ms	סור	693		take away
28:4	יקבצו	niph	wci	3mp	קבץ	867		assemble,gather
	יבאו	qal	wci	3mp	בוא	97		come in
	יחנו	qal	wci	3mp	חנה	333		decline,encamp
	יקבץ	qal	wci	3ms	קבץ	867		gather,collect
	יחנו	qal	wci	3mp	חנה	333		decline,encamp
28:5	ירא	qal	wci	3ms	ראה	906		see
	ירא	qal	wci	3ms	ירא	431		fear
	יחרד	qal	wci	3ms	חרד	353		tremble
28:6	ישׁאל	qal	wci	3ms	שׁאל	981		ask,borrow
	ענהו	qal	pft	3ms	ענה	772	3ms	answer
28:7	יאמר	qal	wci	3ms	אמר	55		say
	בקשׁו	piel	impv	mp	בקשׁ	134		seek
	אלכה	qal	coh	1cs	הלך	229		walk,go
	אדרשׁה	qal	coh	1cs	דרשׁ	205		resort to,seek
	יאמרו	qal	wci	3mp	אמר	55		say
28:8	יתחפשׂ	hith	wci	3ms	חפשׂ	344		disguise self
	ילבשׁ	qal	wci	3ms	לבשׁ	527		put on,clothe
	ילך	qal	wci	3ms	הלך	229		walk,go
	יבאו	qal	wci	3mp	בוא	97		come in
	יאמר	qal	wci	3ms	אמר	55		say
	קסומיk	qal	impv	fs	קסם	890		divine
	קסמיq	qal	impv	fs	קסם	890		divine
	העלי	hiph	impv	fs	עלה	748		bring up,offer
	אמר	qal	impf	1cs	אמר	55		say
28:9	תאמר	qal	wci	3fs	אמר	55		say
28:9	ידעת	qal	pft	2ms	ידע	393		know
	עשׂה	qal	pft	3ms	עשׂה	793		do,make
	הכרית	hiph	pft	3ms	כרת	503		cut off,destroy
	מתנקשׁ	hith	ptc	ms	נקשׁ	669		strike
	המיתני	hiph	infc		מות	559	1cs	kill
28:10	ישׁבע	niph	wci	3ms	שׁבע	989		swear
	אמר	qal	infc		אמר	55		say
	יקרך	qal	impf	3ms	קרה	899	2fs	encounter,meet
28:11	תאמר	qal	wci	3fs	אמר	55		say
	אעלה	hiph	impf	1cs	עלה	748		bring up,offer
	יאמר	qal	wci	3ms	אמר	55		say
	העלי	hiph	impv	fs	עלה	748		bring up,offer
28:12	תרא	qal	wci	3fs	ראה	906		see
	תזעק	qal	wci	3fs	זעק	277		call,cry out
	תאמר	qal	wci	3fs	אמר	55		say
	אמר	qal	infc		אמר	55		say
	רמיתני	piel	pft	2ms	רמה	941	1cs	beguile
28:13	יאמר	qal	wci	3ms	אמר	55		say
	תיראי	qal	jusm	2fs	ירא	431		fear
	ראית	qal	pft	2fs	ראה	906		see
	תאמר	qal	wci	3fs	אמר	55		say
	ראיתי	qal	pft	1cs	ראה	906		see
	עלים	qal	ptc	mp	עלה	748		go up
28:14	יאמר	qal	wci	3ms	אמר	55		say
	תאמר	qal	wci	3fs	אמר	55		say
	עלה	qal	ptc	ms	עלה	748		go up
	עטה	qal	ptc	ms	עטה	741		wrap oneself
	ידע	qal	wci	3ms	ידע	393		know
	יקד	qal	wci	3ms	קדד	869		bow down
	ישׁתחו	hish	wci	3ms	חוה	1005		bow down
28:15	יאמר	qal	wci	3ms	אמר	55		say
	הרגזתני	hiph	pft	2ms	רגז	919	1cs	cause to quake
	העלות	hiph	infc		עלה	748		bring up,offer
	יאמר	qal	wci	3ms	אמר	55		say
	צר	qal	pft	3ms	צרר	864		bind,be cramped
	נלחמים	niph	ptc	mp	לחם	535		wage war
	סר	qal	pft	3ms	סור	693		turn aside
	ענני	qal	pft	3ms	ענה	772	1cs	answer
	אקראה	qal	wci	1cs	קרא	894		call,proclaim
	הודיעני	hiph	infc		ידע	393	1cs	declare
	אעשׂה	qal	impf	1cs	עשׂה	793		do,make
28:16	יאמר	qal	wci	3ms	אמר	55		say
	תשׁאלני	qal	impf	2ms	שׁאל	981	1cs	ask,borrow
	סר	qal	pft	3ms	סור	693		turn aside
	יהי	qal	wci	3ms	היה	224		be,become
28:17	יעשׂ	qal	wci	3ms	עשׂה	793		do,make
	דבר	piel	pft	3ms	דבר	180		speak
	יקרע	qal	wci	3ms	קרע	902		tear,rend
	יתנה	qal	wci	3ms	נתן	678	3fs	give,set
28:18	שׁמעת	qal	pft	2ms	שׁמע	1033		hear
	עשׂית	qal	pft	2ms	עשׂה	793		do,make
	עשׂה	qal	pft	3ms	עשׂה	793		do,make
28:19	יתן	qal	impf	3ms	נתן	678		give,set
	יתן	qal	impf	3ms	נתן	678		give,set

ChVs	Form	Stem	Tnse	PGN	Root	BDB	Sfx	Meaning
28: 20	ימהר	piel	wci	3ms	מהר	554		hasten
	יפל	qal	wci	3ms	נפל	656		fall
	ירא	qal	wci	3ms	ירא	431		fear
	היה	qal	pft	3ms	היה	224		be, become
	אכל	qal	pft	3ms	אכל	37		eat, devour
28: 21	תבוא	qal	wci	3fs	בוא	97		come in
	תרא	qal	wci	3fs	ראה	906		see
	נבהל	niph	pft	3ms	בהל	96		be disturbed
	תאמר	qal	wci	3fs	אמר	55		say
	שמעה	qal	pft	3fs	שמע	1033		hear
	אשים	qal	wci	1cs	שים	962		put, set
	אשמע	qal	wci	1cs	שמע	1033		hear
	דברת	piel	pft	2ms	דבר	180		speak
28: 22	שמע	qal	impv	ms	שמע	1033		hear
	אשמה	qal	coh	1cs	שים	962		put, set
	אכול	qal	impv	ms	אכל	37		eat, devour
	יהי	qal	jus	3ms	היה	224		be, become
	תלך	qal	impf	2ms	הלך	229		walk, go
28: 23	ימאן	piel	wci	3ms	מאן	549		refuse
	יאמר	qal	wci	3ms	אמר	55		say
	אכל	qal	impf	1cs	אכל	37		eat, devour
	יפרצו	qal	wci	3mp	פרץ	829		break through
	ישמע	qal	wci	3ms	שמע	1033		hear
	יקם	qal	wci	3ms	קום	877		arise, stand
	ישב	qal	wci	3ms	ישב	442		sit, dwell
28: 24	תמהר	piel	wci	3fs	מהר	554		hasten
	תזבחהו	qal	wci	3fs	זבח	256	3ms	slaughter
	תקח	qal	wci	3fs	לקח	542		take
	תלש	qal	wci	3fs	לוש	534		knead
	תפהו	qal	wci	3fs	אפה	66	3ms	bake
28: 25	תגש	hiph	wci	3fs	נגש	620		bring near
	יאכלו	qal	wci	3mp	אכל	37		eat, devour
	יקמו	qal	wci	3mp	קום	877		arise, stand
	ילכו	qal	wci	3mp	הלך	229		walk, go
29: 1	יקבצו	qal	wci	3mp	קבץ	867		gather, collect
	חנים	qal	ptc	mp	חנה	333		decline, encamp
29: 2	עברים	qal	ptc	mp	עבר	716		pass over
	עברים	qal	ptc	mp	עבר	716		pass over
29: 3	יאמרו	qal	wci	3mp	אמר	55		say
	יאמר	qal	wci	3ms	אמר	55		say
	היה	qal	pft	3ms	היה	224		be, become
	מצאתי	qal	pft	1cs	מצא	592		find
	נפלו	qal	infc		נפל	656	3ms	fall
29: 4	יקצפו	qal	wci	3mp	קצף	893		be angry
	יאמרו	qal	wci	3mp	אמר	55		say
	השב	hiph	impv	ms	שוב	996		bring back
	ישב	qal	jus	3ms	שוב	996		turn, return
	הפקדתו	hiph	pft	2ms	פקד	823	3ms	set, entrust
	ירד	qal	impf	3ms	ירד	432		come down
	יהיה	qal	impf	3ms	היה	224		be, become
	יתרצה	hith	impf	3ms	רצה	953		make pleasing
29: 5	יענו	qal	impf	3mp	ענה	777		sing
	אמר	qal	infc		אמר	55		say
	הכה	hiph	pft	3ms	נכה	645		smite
29: 6	יקרא	qal	wci	3ms	קרא	894		call, proclaim
	יאמר	qal	wci	3ms	אמר	55		say
	צאתך	qal	infc		יצא	422	2ms	go out
	באך	qal	infc		בוא	97	2ms	come in
	מצאתי	qal	pft	1cs	מצא	592		find
	באך	qal	infc		בוא	97	2ms	come in
29: 7	שוב	qal	impv	ms	שוב	996		turn, return
	לך	qal	impv	ms	הלך	229		walk, go
	תעשה	qal	impf	2ms	עשה	793		do, make
29: 8	יאמר	qal	wci	3ms	אמר	55		say
	עשיתי	qal	pft	1cs	עשה	793		do, make
	מצאת	qal	pft	2ms	מצא	592		find
	הייתי	qal	pft	1cs	היה	224		be, become
	אבוא	qal	impf	1cs	בוא	97		come in
	נלחמתי	niph	wcp	1cs	לחם	535		wage war
	איבי	qal	ptc	mp	איב	33		be hostile to
29: 9	יען	qal	wci	3ms	ענה	772		answer
	יאמר	qal	wci	3ms	אמר	55		say
	ידעתי	qal	pft	1cs	ידע	393		know
	אמרו	qal	pft	3cp	אמר	55		say
	יעלה	qal	impf	3ms	עלה	748		go up
29: 10	השכם	hiph	impv	ms	שכם	1014		rise early
	באו	qal	pft	3cp	בוא	97		come in
	השכמתם	hiph	wcp	2mp	שכם	1014		rise early
	אור	qal	wcp	3ms	אור	21		become light
	לכו	qal	impv	mp	הלך	229		walk, go
29: 11	ישכם	hiph	wci	3ms	שכם	1014		rise early
	לכת	qal	infc		הלך	229		walk, go
	שוב	qal	infc		שוב	996		turn, return
	עלו	qal	pft	3cp	עלה	748		go up
30: 1	יהי	qal	wci	3ms	היה	224		be, become
	בא	qal	infc		בוא	97		come in
	פשטו	qal	pft	3cp	פשט	832		strip off
	יכו	hiph	wci	3mp	נכה	645		smite
	ישרפו	qal	wci	3mp	שרף	976		burn
30: 2	ישבו	qal	wci	3mp	שבה	985		take captive
	המיתו	hiph	pft	3cp	מות	559		kill
	ינהגו	qal	wci	3mp	נהג	624		drive
	ילכו	qal	wci	3mp	הלך	229		walk, go
30: 3	יבא	qal	wci	3ms	בוא	97		come in
	שרופה	qal	pptc	fs	שרף	976		burn
	נשבו	niph	pft	3cp	שבה	985		be held captive
30: 4	ישא	qal	wci	3ms	נשא	669		lift, carry
	יבכו	qal	wci	3mp	בכה	113		weep
	בכות	qal	infc		בכה	113		weep
30: 5	נשבו	niph	pft	3cp	שבה	985		be held captive
30: 6	תצר	qal	wci	3fs	צרר	864		bind, be cramped
	אמרו	qal	pft	3cp	אמר	55		say
	סקלו	qal	infc		סקל	709	3ms	stone to death
	מרה	qal	pft	3fs	מרר	600		be bitter
	יתחזק	hith	wci	3ms	חזק	304		strengthen self
30: 7	יאמר	qal	wci	3ms	אמר	55		say
	הגישה	hiph	impv	ms	נגש	620		bring near
	יגש	hiph	wci	3ms	נגש	620		bring near

ChVs	Form	Stem	Tnse	PGN	Root	BDB	Sfx	Meaning
30: 8	ישאל	qal	wci	3ms	שאל	981		ask, borrow
	אמר	qal	infc		אמר	55		say
	ארדף	qal	impf	1cs	רדף	922		pursue
	אשׂגנו	hiph	impf	1cs	נשׂג	673	3ms	reach, overtake
	יאמר	qal	wci	3ms	אמר	55		say
	רדף	qal	impv	ms	רדף	922		pursue
	השׂג	hiph	infa		נשׂג	673		reach, overtake
	תשׂיג	hiph	impf	2ms	נשׂג	673		reach, overtake
	הצל	hiph	infa		נצל	664		snatch, deliver
	תציל	hiph	impf	2ms	נצל	664		snatch, deliver
30: 9	ילך	qal	wci	3ms	הלך	229		walk, go
	יבאו	qal	wci	3mp	בוא	97		come in
	נותרים	niph	ptc	mp	יתר	451		be left, remain
	עמדו	qal	pft	3cp	עמד	763		stand, stop
30: 10	ירדף	qal	wci	3ms	רדף	922		pursue
	יעמדו	qal	wci	3mp	עמד	763		stand, stop
	פגרו	piel	pft	3cp	פגר	803		be faint
	עבר	qal	infc		עבר	716		pass over
30: 11	ימצאו	qal	wci	3mp	מצא	592		find
	יקחו	qal	wci	3mp	לקח	542		take
	יתנו	qal	wci	3mp	נתן	678		give, set
	יאכל	qal	wci	3ms	אכל	37		eat, devour
	ישקהו	hiph	wci	3mp	שקה	1052	3ms	give to drink
30: 12	יתנו	qal	wci	3mp	נתן	678		give, set
	יאכל	qal	wci	3ms	אכל	37		eat, devour
	תשב	qal	wci	3fs	שוב	996		turn, return
	אכל	qal	pft	3ms	אכל	37		eat, devour
	שתה	qal	pft	3ms	שתה	1059		drink
30: 13	יאמר	qal	wci	3ms	אמר	55		say
	יאמר	qal	wci	3ms	אמר	55		say
	יעזבני	qal	wci	3ms	עזב	736	1cs	leave, loose
	חליתי	qal	pft	1cs	חלה	317		be weak, sick
30: 14	פשטנו	qal	pft	1cp	פשט	832		strip off
	שׂרפנו	qal	pft	1cp	שׂרף	976		burn
30: 15	יאמר	qal	wci	3ms	אמר	55		say
	תורדני	hiph	impf	2ms	ירד	432	1cs	bring down
	יאמר	qal	wci	3ms	אמר	55		say
	השבעה	niph	impv	ms	שבע	989		swear
	תמיתני	hiph	impf	2ms	מות	559	1cs	kill
	תסגרני	hiph	impf	2ms	סגר	688	1cs	shut up, deliver
	אורדך	hiph	cohm	1cs	ירד	432	2ms	bring down
30: 16	ירדהו	hiph	wci	3ms	ירד	432	3ms	bring down
	נטשים	qal	pptc	mp	נטש	643		leave, forsake
	אכלים	qal	ptc	mp	אכל	37		eat, devour
	שתים	qal	ptc	mp	שתה	1059		drink
	חגגים	qal	ptc	mp	חגג	290		keep festival
	לקחו	qal	pft	3cp	לקח	542		take
30: 17	יכם	hiph	wci	3ms	נכה	645	3mp	smite
	נמלט	niph	pft	3ms	מלט	572		escape
	רכבו	qal	pft	3cp	רכב	938		mount, ride
	ינסו	qal	wci	3mp	נוס	630		flee, escape
30: 18	יצל	hiph	wci	3ms	נצל	664		snatch, deliver
	לקחו	qal	pft	3cp	לקח	542		take
	הציל	hiph	pft	3ms	נצל	664		snatch, deliver

ChVs	Form	Stem	Tnse	PGN	Root	BDB	Sfx	Meaning
30: 19	נעדר	niph	pft	3ms	עדר	727		be lacking, fail
	לקחו	qal	pft	3cp	לקח	542		take
	השיב	hiph	pft	3ms	שוב	996		bring back
30: 20	יקח	qal	wci	3ms	לקח	542		take
	נהגו	qal	pft	3cp	נהג	624		drive
	יאמרו	qal	wci	3mp	אמר	55		say
30: 21	יבא	qal	wci	3ms	בוא	97		come in
	פגרו	piel	pft	3cp	פגר	803		be faint
	לכת	qal	infc		הלך	229		walk, go
	ישיבם	hiph	wci	3mp	ישב	442	3mp	cause to dwell
	יצאו	qal	wci	3mp	יצא	422		go out
	קראת	qal	infc		קרא	896		meet, encounter
	קראת	qal	infc		קרא	896		meet, encounter
	יגש	qal	wci	3ms	נגש	620		draw near
	ישאל	qal	wci	3ms	שאל	981		ask, borrow
30: 22	יען	qal	wci	3ms	ענה	772		answer
	הלכו	qal	pft	3cp	הלך	229		walk, go
	יאמרו	qal	wci	3mp	אמר	55		say
	הלכו	qal	pft	3cp	הלך	229		walk, go
	נתן	qal	impf	1cp	נתן	678		give, set
	הצלנו	hiph	pft	1cp	נצל	664		snatch, deliver
	ינהגו	qal	impf	3mp	נהג	624		drive
	ילכו	qal	impf	3mp	הלך	229		walk, go
30: 23	יאמר	qal	wci	3ms	אמר	55		say
	תעשׂו	qal	impf	2mp	עשׂה	793		do, make
	נתן	qal	pft	3ms	נתן	678		give, set
	ישמר	qal	wci	3ms	שמר	1036		keep, watch
	יתן	qal	wci	3ms	נתן	678		give, set
	בא	qal	ptc	ms	בוא	97		come in
30: 24	ישמע	qal	impf	3ms	שמע	1033		hear
	ירד	qal	ptc	ms	ירד	432		come down
	ישב	qal	ptc	ms	ישב	442		sit, dwell
	יחלקו	qal	impf	3mp	חלק	323		divide, share
30: 25	יהי	qal	wci	3ms	היה	224		be, become
	ישׂמה	qal	wci	3ms	שׂים	962	3fs	put, set
30: 26	יבא	qal	wci	3ms	בוא	97		come in
	ישלח	piel	wci	3ms	שלח	1018		send away, shoot
	אמר	qal	infc		אמר	55		say
	איבי	qal	ptc	mp	איב	33		be hostile to
30: 31	התהלך	hith	pft	3ms	הלך	229		walk to and fro
31: 1	נלחמים	niph	ptc	mp	לחם	535		wage war
	ינסו	qal	wci	3mp	נוס	630		flee, escape
	יפלו	qal	wci	3mp	נפל	656		fall
31: 2	ידבקו	hiph	wci	3mp	דבק	179		cause to cling
	יכו	hiph	wci	3mp	נכה	645		smite
31: 3	תכבד	qal	wci	3fs	כבד	457		be heavy
	ימצאהו	qal	wci	3mp	מצא	592	3ms	find
	מורים	hiph	ptc	mp	ירה	434		shoot, teach
	יחל	qal	wci	3ms	חול	296		dance, writhe
	מורים	hiph	ptc	mp	ירה	434		shoot, teach
31: 4	יאמר	qal	wci	3ms	אמר	55		say
	נשׂא	qal	ptc	ms	נשׂא	669		lift, carry
	שׁלף	qal	impv	ms	שׁלף	1025		draw out, off
	דקרני	qal	impv	ms	דקר	201	1cs	pierce

ChVs	Form	Stem	Tnse	PGN	Root	BDB	Sfx	Meaning
31:4	יבואו	qal	impf	3mp	בוא	97		come in
	דקרני	qal	wcp	3cp	דקר	201	1cs	pierce
	התעללו	hith	wcp	3cp	עלל	759		busy,vex
	אבה	qal	pft	3ms	אבה	2		be willing
	נשׂא	qal	ptc	ms	נשׂא	669		lift,carry
	ירא	qal	pft	3ms	ירא	431		fear
	יקח	qal	wci	3ms	לקח	542		take
	יפל	qal	wci	3ms	נפל	656		fall
31:5	ירא	qal	wci	3ms	ראה	906		see
	נשׂא	qal	ptc	ms	נשׂא	669		lift,carry
	מת	qal	pft	3ms	מות	559		die
	יפל	qal	wci	3ms	נפל	656		fall
	ימת	qal	wci	3ms	מות	559		die
31:6	ימת	qal	wci	3ms	מות	559		die
	נשׂא	qal	ptc	ms	נשׂא	669		lift,carry
31:7	יראו	qal	wci	3mp	ראה	906		see
	נסו	qal	pft	3cp	נוס	630		flee,escape
	מתו	qal	pft	3cp	מות	559		die
	יעזבו	qal	wci	3mp	עזב	736		leave,loose
	ינסו	qal	wci	3mp	נוס	630		flee,escape
	יבאו	qal	wci	3mp	בוא	97		come in
	ישׁבו	qal	wci	3mp	ישׁב	442		sit,dwell
31:8	יהי	qal	wci	3ms	היה	224		be,become
	יבאו	qal	wci	3mp	בוא	97		come in
	פשׁט	piel	infc		פשׁט	832		strip
	ימצאו	qal	wci	3mp	מצא	592		find
	נפלים	qal	ptc	mp	נפל	656		fall
31:9	יכרתו	qal	wci	3mp	כרת	503		cut,destroy
	יפשׁיטו	hiph	wci	3mp	פשׁט	832		strip off
	ישׁלחו	piel	wci	3mp	שׁלח	1018		send away,shoot
	בשׂר	piel	infc		בשׂר	142		bear tidings
31:10	ישׂמו	qal	wci	3mp	שׂים	962		put,set
	תקעו	qal	pft	3cp	תקע	1075		thrust,clap
31:11	ישׁמעו	qal	wci	3mp	שׁמע	1033		hear
	ישׁבי	qal	ptc	mp	ישׁב	442		sit,dwell
	עשׂו	qal	pft	3cp	עשׂה	793		do,make
31:12	יקומו	qal	wci	3mp	קום	877		arise,stand
	ילכו	qal	wci	3mp	הלך	229		walk,go
	יקחו	qal	wci	3mp	לקח	542		take
	יבאו	qal	wci	3mp	בוא	97		come in
	ישׂרפו	qal	wci	3mp	שׂרף	976		burn
31:13	יקחו	qal	wci	3mp	לקח	542		take
	יקברו	qal	wci	3mp	קבר	868		bury
	יצמו	qal	wci	3mp	צום	847		fast

2 SAMUEL

ChVs	Form	Stem	Tnse	PGN	Root	BDB	Sfx	Meaning
1:1	יהי	qal	wci	3ms	היה	224		be,become
	שׁב	qal	pft	3ms	שׁוב	996		turn,return
	הכות	hiph	infc		נכה	645		smite
	ישׁב	qal	wci	3ms	ישׁב	442		sit,dwell
1:2	יהי	qal	wci	3ms	היה	224		be,become
	בא	qal	ptc	ms	בוא	97		come in
	קרעים	qal	pptc	mp	קרע	902		tear,rend
	יהי	qal	wci	3ms	היה	224		be,become
1:2	באו	qal	infc		בוא	97	3ms	come in
	יפל	qal	wci	3ms	נפל	656		fall
	ישׁתחו	hish	wci	3ms	חוה	1005		bow down
1:3	יאמר	qal	wci	3ms	אמר	55		say
	תבוא	qal	impf	2ms	בוא	97		come in
	יאמר	qal	wci	3ms	אמר	55		say
	נמלטתי	niph	pft	1cs	מלט	572		escape
1:4	יאמר	qal	wci	3ms	אמר	55		say
	היה	qal	pft	3ms	היה	224		be,become
	הגד	hiph	impv	ms	נגד	616		declare,tell
	יאמר	qal	wci	3ms	אמר	55		say
	נס	qal	pft	3ms	נוס	630		flee,escape
	הרבה	hiph	infa		רבה	915		make many
	נפל	qal	pft	3ms	נפל	656		fall
	ימתו	qal	wci	3mp	מות	559		die
	מתו	qal	pft	3cp	מות	559		die
1:5	יאמר	qal	wci	3ms	אמר	55		say
	מגיד	hiph	ptc	ms	נגד	616		declare,tell
	ידעת	qal	pft	2ms	ידע	393		know
	מת	qal	pft	3ms	מות	559		die
1:6	יאמר	qal	wci	3ms	אמר	55		say
	מגיד	hiph	ptc	ms	נגד	616		declare,tell
	נקרא	niph	infa		קרא	896		meet
	נקריתי	niph	pft	1cs	קרה	899		encounter
	נשׁען	niph	ptc	ms	שׁען	1043		lean,support
	הדבקהו	hiph	pft	3cp	דבק	179	3ms	cause to cling
1:7	יפן	qal	wci	3ms	פנה	815		turn
	יראני	qal	wci	3ms	ראה	906	1cs	see
	יקרא	qal	wci	3ms	קרא	894		call,proclaim
	אמר	qal	wci	1cs	אמר	55		say
1:8	יאמר	qal	wci	3ms	אמר	55		say
	יאמרk	qal	wci	3ms	אמר	55		say
	אמרq	qal	wci	1cs	אמר	55		say
1:9	יאמר	qal	wci	3ms	אמר	55		say
	עמד	qal	impv	ms	עמד	763		stand,stop
	מתתני	pol	impv	ms	מות	559	1cs	kill
	אחזני	qal	pft	3ms	אחז	28	1cs	grasp
1:10	אעמד	qal	wci	1cs	עמד	763		stand,stop
	אמתתהו	pol	wci	1cs	מות	559	3ms	kill
	ידעתי	qal	pft	1cs	ידע	393		know
	יחיה	qal	impf	3ms	חיה	310		live
	נפלו	qal	infc		נפל	656	3ms	fall
	אקח	qal	wci	1cs	לקח	542		take
	אביאם	hiph	wci	1cs	בוא	97	3mp	bring in
1:11	יחזק	hiph	wci	3ms	חזק	304		make firm,seize
	יקרעם	qal	wci	3ms	קרע	902	3mp	tear,rend
1:12	יספדו	qal	wci	3mp	ספד	704		wail,lament
	יבכו	qal	wci	3mp	בכה	113		weep
	יצמו	qal	wci	3mp	צום	847		fast
	נפלו	qal	pft	3cp	נפל	656		fall
1:13	יאמר	qal	wci	3ms	אמר	55		say
	מגיד	hiph	ptc	ms	נגד	616		declare,tell
	יאמר	qal	wci	3ms	אמר	55		say
1:14	יאמר	qal	wci	3ms	אמר	55		say

ChVs	Form	Stem	Tnse	PGN	Root	BDB	Sfx	Meaning
1:14	יראת	qal	pft	2ms	ירא	431		fear
	שלח	qal	infc		שלח	1018		send
	שחת	piel	infc		שחת	1007		spoil,ruin
1:15	יקרא	qal	wci	3ms	קרא	894		call,proclaim
	יאמר	qal	wci	3ms	אמר	55		say
	גש	qal	impv	ms	נגש	620		draw near
	פגע	qal	impv	ms	פגע	803		meet,encounter
	יכהו	hiph	wci	3ms	נכה	645	3ms	smite
	ימת	qal	wci	3ms	מות	559		die
1:16	יאמר	qal	wci	3ms	אמר	55		say
	ענה	qal	pft	3ms	ענה	772		answer
	אמר	qal	infc		אמר	55		say
	מתתי	pol	pft	1cs	מות	559		kill
1:17	יקנן	pol	wci	3ms	קין	884		hant a dirge
1:18	יאמר	qal	wci	3ms	אמר	55		say
	למד	piel	infc		למד	540		teach
	כתובה	qal	pptc	fs	כתב	507		write
1:19	נפלו	qal	pft	3cp	נפל	656		fall
1:20	תגידו	hiph	jusm	2mp	נגד	616		declare,tell
	תבשרו	piel	jusm	2mp	בשר	142		bear tidings
	תשמחנה	qal	impf	3fp	שמח	970		rejoice
	תעלזנה	qal	impf	3fp	עלז	759		exult,triumph
1:21	נגעל	niph	pft	3ms	געל	171		be rejected
	משיח	qal	pptc	ms	משח	602		smear,anoint
1:22	נשוג	niph	pft	3ms	סוג	690		turn away
	תשוב	qal	impf	3fs	שוב	996		turn,return
1:23	נאהבים	niph	ptc	mp	אהב	12		beloved
	נפרדו	niph	pft	3cp	פרד	825		divide
	קלו	qal	pft	3cp	קלל	886		be slight,swift
	גברו	qal	pft	3cp	גבר	149		be strong
1:24	בכינה	qal	impv	fp	בכה	113		weep
	מלבשכם	hiph	ptc	ms	לבש	527	2mp	clothe
	מעלה	hiph	ptc	ms	עלה	748		bring up,offer
1:25	נפלו	qal	pft	3cp	נפל	656		fall
1:26	צר	qal	pft	3ms	צרר	864		bind,be cramped
	נעמת	qal	pft	2ms	נעם	653		be delightful
	נפלאתה	niph	pft	3fs	פלא	810		be wonderful
1:27	נפלו	qal	pft	3cp	נפל	656		fall
	יאבדו	qal	wci	3mp	אבד	1		perish
2:1	יהי	qal	wci	3ms	היה	224		be,become
	ישאל	qal	wci	3ms	שאל	981		ask,borrow
	אמר	qal	infc		אמר	55		say
	אעלה	qal	impf	1cs	עלה	748		go up
	יאמר	qal	wci	3ms	אמר	55		say
	עלה	qal	impv	ms	עלה	748		go up
	יאמר	qal	wci	3ms	אמר	55		say
	אעלה	qal	impf	1cs	עלה	748		go up
	יאמר	qal	wci	3ms	אמר	55		say
2:2	יעל	qal	wci	3ms	עלה	748		go up
2:3	העלה	hiph	pft	3ms	עלה	748		bring up,offer
	ישבו	qal	wci	3mp	ישב	442		sit,dwell
2:4	יבאו	qal	wci	3mp	בוא	97		come in
	ימשחו	qal	wci	3mp	משח	602		smear,anoint
	יגדו	hiph	wci	3mp	נגד	616		declare,tell
2:4	אמר	qal	infc		אמר	55		say
	קברו	qal	pft	3cp	קבר	868		bury
2:5	ישלח	qal	wci	3ms	שלח	1018		send
	יאמר	qal	wci	3ms	אמר	55		say
	ברכים	qal	pptc	mp	ברך	138		kneel,bless
	עשיתם	qal	pft	2mp	עשה	793		do,make
	תקברו	qal	wci	2mp	קבר	868		bury
2:6	יעש	qal	jus	3ms	עשה	793		do,make
	אעשה	qal	impf	1cs	עשה	793		do,make
	עשיתם	qal	pft	2mp	עשה	793		do,make
2:7	תחזקנה	qal	jusm	3fp	חזק	304		be strong
	היו	qal	impv	mp	היה	224		be,become
	מת	qal	pft	3ms	מות	559		die
	משחו	qal	pft	3cp	משח	602		smear,anoint
2:8	לקח	qal	pft	3ms	לקח	542		take
	יעברהו	hiph	wci	3ms	עבר	716	3ms	cause to pass
2:9	ימלכהו	hiph	wci	3ms	מלך	573	3ms	cause to reign
2:10	מלכו	qal	infc		מלך	573	3ms	be king,reign
	מלך	qal	pft	3ms	מלך	573		be king,reign
	היו	qal	pft	3cp	היה	224		be,become
2:11	יהי	qal	wci	3ms	היה	224		be,become
	היה	qal	pft	3ms	היה	224		be,become
2:12	יצא	qal	wci	3ms	יצא	422		go out
2:13	יצאו	qal	pft	3cp	יצא	422		go out
	יפגשום	qal	wci	3mp	פגש	803	3mp	meet
	ישבו	qal	wci	3mp	ישב	442		sit,dwell
2:14	יאמר	qal	wci	3ms	אמר	55		say
	יקומו	qal	jusm	3mp	קום	877		arise,stand
	ישחקו	piel	jusm	3mp	שחק	965		make sport
	יאמר	qal	wci	3ms	אמר	55		say
	יקמו	qal	jusm	3mp	קום	877		arise,stand
2:15	יקמו	qal	wci	3mp	קום	877		arise,stand
	יעברו	qal	wci	3mp	עבר	716		pass over
2:16	יחזקו	hiph	wci	3mp	חזק	304		make firm,seize
	יפלו	qal	wci	3mp	נפל	656		fall
	יקרא	qal	wci	3ms	קרא	894		call,proclaim
2:17	תהי	qal	wci	3fs	היה	224		be,become
	ינגף	niph	wci	3ms	נגף	619		be smitten
2:18	יהיו	qal	wci	3mp	היה	224		be,become
2:19	ירדף	qal	wci	3ms	רדף	922		pursue
	נטה	qal	pft	3ms	נטה	639		stretch,incline
	לכת	qal	infc		הלך	229		walk,go
2:20	יפן	qal	wci	3ms	פנה	815		turn
	יאמר	qal	wci	3ms	אמר	55		say
	יאמר	qal	wci	3ms	אמר	55		say
2:21	יאמר	qal	wci	3ms	אמר	55		say
	נטה	qal	impv	ms	נטה	639		stretch,incline
	אחז	qal	impv	ms	אחז	28		grasp
	קח	qal	impv	ms	לקח	542		take
	אבה	qal	pft	3ms	אבה	2		be willing
	סור	qal	infc		סור	693		turn aside
2:22	יסף	hiph	wci	3ms	יסף	414		add,do again
	אמר	qal	infc		אמר	55		say
	סור	qal	impv	ms	סור	693		turn aside

ChVs	Form	Stem	Tnse	PGN	Root	BDB	Sfx	Meaning
2:22	אכּכּה	hiph	impf	1cs	נכה	645	2ms	smite
	אשׂא	qal	impf	1cs	נשׂא	669		lift,carry
2:23	ימאן	piel	wci	3ms	מאן	549		refuse
	סור	qal	infc		סור	693		turn aside
	יכּהו	hiph	wci	3ms	נכה	645	3ms	smite
	תצא	qal	wci	3fs	יצא	422		go out
	יפּל	qal	wci	3ms	נפל	656		fall
	ימת	qal	wci	3ms	מות	559		die
	יהי	qal	wci	3ms	היה	224		be,become
	בא	qal	ptc	ms	בוא	97		come in
	נפל	qal	pft	3ms	נפל	656		fall
	ימת	qal	wci	3ms	מות	559		die
	יעמדו	qal	wci	3mp	עמד	763		stand,stop
2:24	ירדפו	qal	wci	3mp	רדף	922		pursue
	באה	qal	pft	3fs	בוא	97		come in
	באו	qal	pft	3cp	בוא	97		come in
2:25	יתקבצו	hith	wci	3mp	קבץ	867		gather together
	יהיו	qal	wci	3mp	היה	224		be,become
	יעמדו	qal	wci	3mp	עמד	763		stand,stop
2:26	יקרא	qal	wci	3ms	קרא	894		call,proclaim
	יאמר	qal	wci	3ms	אמר	55		say
	תאכל	qal	impf	3fs	אכל	37		eat,devour
	ידעתה	qal	pft	2ms	ידע	393		know
	תהיה	qal	impf	3fs	היה	224		be,become
	תאמר	qal	impf	2ms	אמר	55		say
	שׁוב	qal	infc		שׁוב	996		turn,return
2:27	יאמר	qal	wci	3ms	אמר	55		say
	דברת	piel	pft	2ms	דבר	180		speak
	נעלה	niph	pft	3ms	עלה	748		be brought up
2:28	יתקע	qal	wci	3ms	תקע	1075		thrust,clap
	יעמדו	qal	wci	3mp	עמד	763		stand,stop
	ירדפו	qal	impf	3mp	רדף	922		pursue
	יספו	qal	pft	3cp	יסף	414		add,increase
	הלחם	niph	infc		לחם	535		wage war
2:29	הלכו	qal	pft	3cp	הלך	229		walk,go
	יעברו	qal	wci	3mp	עבר	716		pass over
	ילכו	qal	wci	3mp	הלך	229		walk,go
	יבאו	qal	wci	3mp	בוא	97		come in
2:30	שׁב	qal	pft	3ms	שׁוב	996		turn,return
	יקבץ	qal	wci	3ms	קבץ	867		gather,collect
	יפקדו	niph	wci	3mp	פקד	823		be visited
2:31	הכו	hiph	pft	3cp	נכה	645		smite
	מתו	qal	pft	3cp	מות	559		die
2:32	ישׂאו	qal	wci	3mp	נשׂא	669		lift,carry
	יקברהו	qal	wci	3mp	קבר	868	3ms	bury
	ילכו	qal	wci	3mp	הלך	229		walk,go
	יאר	niph	wci	3ms	אור	21		be lit
3:1	תהי	qal	wci	3fs	היה	224		be,become
	הלך	qal	ptc	ms	הלך	229		walk,go
	חזק	qal	ptc	ms	חזק	304		be strong
	הלכים	qal	ptc	mp	הלך	229		walk,go
3:2	ילדוk	qalp	wci	3mp	ילד	408		be born
	יולדוq	niph	wci	3mp	ילד	408		be born
	יהי	qal	wci	3ms	היה	224		be,become
3:5	ילדו	qalp	pft	3cp	ילד	408		be born
3:6	יהי	qal	wci	3ms	היה	224		be,become
	היות	qal	infc		היה	224		be,become
	היה	qal	pft	3ms	היה	224		be,become
	מתחזק	hith	ptc	ms	חזק	304		strengthen self
3:7	יאמר	qal	wci	3ms	אמר	55		say
	באתה	qal	pft	2ms	בוא	97		come in
3:8	יחר	qal	wci	3ms	חרה	354		be kindled,burn
	יאמר	qal	wci	3ms	אמר	55		say
	אעשׂה	qal	impf	1cs	עשׂה	793		do,make
	המציתך	hiph	pft	1cs	מצא	592	2ms	cause to find
	תפקד	qal	wci	2ms	פקד	823		attend to,visit
3:9	יעשׂה	qal	jusm	3ms	עשׂה	793		do,make
	יסיף	hiph	jusm	3ms	יסף	414		add,do again
	נשׁבע	niph	pft	3ms	שׁבע	989		swear
	אעשׂה	qal	impf	1cs	עשׂה	793		do,make
3:10	העביר	hiph	infc		עבר	716		cause to pass
	הקים	hiph	infc		קום	877		raise,build,set
3:11	יכל	qal	pft	3ms	יכל	407		be able
	השׁיב	hiph	infc		שׁוב	996		bring back
	יראתו	qal	infc		ירא	431	3ms	fear
3:12	ישׁלח	qal	wci	3ms	שׁלח	1018		send
	אמר	qal	infc		אמר	55		say
	אמר	qal	infc		אמר	55		say
	כרתה	qal	impv	ms	כרת	503		cut,destroy
	הסב	hiph	infc		סבב	685		cause to turn
3:13	יאמר	qal	wci	3ms	אמר	55		say
	אכרת	qal	impf	1cs	כרת	503		cut,destroy
	שׁאל	qal	ptc	ms	שׁאל	981		ask,borrow
	אמר	qal	infc		אמר	55		say
	תראה	qal	impf	2ms	ראה	906		see
	הביאך	hiph	infc		בוא	97	2ms	bring in
	באך	qal	infc		בוא	97	2ms	come in
	ראות	qal	infc		ראה	906		see
3:14	ישׁלח	qal	wci	3ms	שׁלח	1018		send
	אמר	qal	infc		אמר	55		say
	תנה	qal	impv	ms	נתן	678		give,set
	ארשׂתי	piel	pft	1cs	ארשׂ	76		betroth
3:15	ישׁלח	qal	wci	3ms	שׁלח	1018		send
	יקחה	qal	wci	3ms	לקח	542	3fs	take
3:16	ילך	qal	wci	3ms	הלך	229		walk,go
	הלוך	qal	infa		הלך	229		walk,go
	בכה	qal	infa		בכה	113		weep
	יאמר	qal	wci	3ms	אמר	55		say
	לך	qal	impv	ms	הלך	229		walk,go
	שׁוב	qal	impv	ms	שׁוב	996		turn,return
	ישׁב	qal	wci	3ms	שׁוב	996		turn,return
3:17	היה	qal	pft	3ms	היה	224		be,become
	אמר	qal	infc		אמר	55		say
	הייתם	qal	pft	2mp	היה	224		be,become
	מבקשׁים	piel	ptc	mp	בקשׁ	134		seek
3:18	עשׂו	qal	impv	mp	עשׂה	793		do,make
	אמר	qal	pft	3ms	אמר	55		say
	אמר	qal	infc		אמר	55		say

ChVs	Form	Stem	Tnse	PGN	Root	BDB	Sfx	Meaning
3: 18	הושיע	hiph	infc		ישע	446		deliver,save
	איביהם	qal	ptc	mp	איב	33	3mp	be hostile to
3: 19	ידבר	piel	wci	3ms	דבר	180		speak
	ילך	qal	wci	3ms	הלך	229		walk,go
	דבר	piel	infc		דבר	180		speak
	טוב	qal	pft	3ms	טוב	373		be pleasing
3: 20	יבא	qal	wci	3ms	בוא	97		come in
	יעשׂ	qal	wci	3ms	עשׂה	793		do,make
3: 21	יאמר	qal	wci	3ms	אמר	55		say
	אקומה	qal	coh	1cs	קום	877		arise,stand
	אלכה	qal	coh	1cs	הלך	229		walk,go
	אקבצה	qal	coh	1cs	קבץ	867		gather,collect
	יכרתו	qal	jusm	3mp	כרת	503		cut,destroy
	מלכת	qal	wcp	2ms	מלך	573		be king,reign
	תאוה	piel	impf	3fs	אוה	16		desire
	ישׁלח	piel	wci	3ms	שׁלח	1018		send away,shoot
	ילך	qal	wci	3ms	הלך	229		walk,go
3: 22	בא	qal	ptc	ms	בוא	97		come in
	הביאו	hiph	pft	3cp	בוא	97		bring in
	שׁלחו	piel	pft	3ms	שׁלח	1018	3ms	send away,shoot
	ילך	qal	wci	3ms	הלך	229		walk,go
3: 23	באו	qal	pft	3cp	בוא	97		come in
	יגדו	hiph	wci	3mp	נגד	616		declare,tell
	אמר	qal	infc		אמר	55		say
	בא	qal	pft	3ms	בוא	97		come in
	ישׁלחהו	piel	wci	3ms	שׁלח	1018	3ms	send away,shoot
	ילך	qal	wci	3ms	הלך	229		walk,go
3: 24	יבא	qal	wci	3ms	בוא	97		come in
	יאמר	qal	wci	3ms	אמר	55		say
	עשׂיתה	qal	pft	2ms	עשׂה	793		do,make
	בא	qal	pft	3ms	בוא	97		come in
	שׁלחתו	piel	pft	2ms	שׁלח	1018	3ms	send away,shoot
	ילך	qal	wci	3ms	הלך	229		walk,go
	הלוך	qal	infa		הלך	229		walk,go
3: 25	ידעת	qal	pft	2ms	ידע	393		know
	פתתך	piel	infc		פתה	834	2ms	entice
	בא	qal	pft	3ms	בוא	97		come in
	דעת	qal	infc		ידע	393		know
	דעת	qal	infc		ידע	393		know
	עשׂה	qal	ptc	ms	עשׂה	793		do,make
3: 26	יצא	qal	wci	3ms	יצא	422		go out
	ישׁלח	qal	wci	3ms	שׁלח	1018		send
	ישׁבו	hiph	wci	3mp	שׁוב	996		bring back
	ידע	qal	pft	3ms	ידע	393		know
3: 27	ישׁב	qal	wci	3ms	שׁוב	996		turn,return
	יטהו	hiph	wci	3ms	נטה	639	3ms	turn,incline
	דבר	piel	infc		דבר	180		speak
	יכהו	hiph	wci	3ms	נכה	645	3ms	smite
	ימת	qal	wci	3ms	מות	559		die
3: 28	ישׁמע	qal	wci	3ms	שׁמע	1033		hear
	יאמר	qal	wci	3ms	אמר	55		say
3: 29	יחלו	qal	jusm	3mp	חול	296		dance,writhe
	יכרת	niph	jusm	3ms	כרת	503		be cut off
	זב	qal	ptc	ms	זוב	264		flow,gush
3: 29	מצרע	pual	ptc	ms	צרע	863		be leprous
	מחזיק	hiph	ptc	ms	חזק	304		make firm,seize
	נפל	qal	ptc	ms	נפל	656		fall
3: 30	הרגו	qal	pft	3cp	הרג	246		kill
	המית	hiph	pft	3ms	מות	559		kill
3: 31	יאמר	qal	wci	3ms	אמר	55		say
	קרעו	qal	impv	mp	קרע	902		tear,rend
	חגרו	qal	impv	mp	חגר	291		gird
	ספדו	qal	impv	mp	ספד	704		wail,lament
	הלך	qal	ptc	ms	הלך	229		walk,go
3: 32	יקברו	qal	wci	3mp	קבר	868		bury
	ישׂא	qal	wci	3ms	נשׂא	669		lift,carry
	יבך	qal	wci	3ms	בכה	113		weep
	יבכו	qal	wci	3mp	בכה	113		weep
3: 33	יקנן	pol	wci	3ms	קין	884		hant a dirge
	יאמר	qal	wci	3ms	אמר	55		say
	ימות	qal	impf	3ms	מות	559		die
3: 34	אסרות	qal	ptc	fp	אסר	63		tie,bind
	הגשׁו	hoph	pft	3cp	נגשׁ	620		be brought near
	נפול	qal	infc		נפל	656		fall
	נפלת	qal	pft	2ms	נפל	656		fall
	יספו	hiph	wci	3mp	יסף	414		add,do again
	בכות	qal	infc		בכה	113		weep
3: 35	יבא	qal	wci	3ms	בוא	97		come in
	הברות	hiph	infc		ברה	136		cause to eat
	ישׁבע	niph	wci	3ms	שׁבע	989		swear
	אמר	qal	infc		אמר	55		say
	יעשׂה	qal	jusm	3ms	עשׂה	793		do,make
	יסיף	hiph	jusm	3ms	יסף	414		add,do again
	בוא	qal	infc		בוא	97		come in
	אטעם	qal	impf	1cs	טעם	380		taste
3: 36	הכירו	hiph	pft	3cp	נכר	647		regard,notice
	ייטב	qal	wci	3ms	יטב	405		be good
	עשׂה	qal	pft	3ms	עשׂה	793		do,make
	טוב	qal	pft	3ms	טוב	373		be pleasing
3: 37	ידעו	qal	wci	3mp	ידע	393		know
	היתה	qal	pft	3fs	היה	224		be,become
	המית	hiph	infc		מות	559		kill
3: 38	יאמר	qal	wci	3ms	אמר	55		say
	תדעו	qal	impf	2mp	ידע	393		know
	נפל	qal	pft	3ms	נפל	656		fall
3: 39	משׁוח	qal	pptc	ms	משׁח	602		smear,anoint
	ישׁלם	piel	jusm	3ms	שׁלם	1022		finish,reward
	עשׂה	qal	ptc	ms	עשׂה	793		do,make
4: 1	ישׁמע	qal	wci	3ms	שׁמע	1033		hear
	מת	qal	pft	3ms	מות	559		die
	ירפו	qal	wci	3mp	רפה	951		sink,relax
	נבהלו	niph	pft	3cp	בהל	96		be disturbed
4: 2	היו	qal	pft	3cp	היה	224		be,become
	תחשׁב	niph	impf	3fs	חשׁב	362		be thought
4: 3	יברחו	qal	wci	3mp	ברח	137		go thru,flee
	יהיו	qal	wci	3mp	היה	224		be,become
	גרים	qal	ptc	mp	גור	157		sojourn
4: 4	היה	qal	pft	3ms	היה	224		be,become

ChVs	Form	Stem	Tnse	PGN	Root	BDB	Sfx	Meaning
4:4	בא	qal	infc		בוא	97		come in
	תשׂאהו	qal	wci	3fs	נשׂא	669	3ms	lift,carry
	אמנתו	qal	ptc	fs	אמן	52	3ms	nourish
	תנס	qal	wci	3fs	נוס	630		flee,escape
	יהי	qal	wci	3ms	היה	224		be,become
	חפזה	qal	infc		חפז	342	3fs	be alarmed
	נוס	qal	infc		נוס	630		flee,escape
	יפל	qal	wci	3ms	נפל	656		fall
	יפסח	niph	wci	3ms	פסח	820		be lame
4:5	ילכו	qal	wci	3mp	הלך	229		walk,go
	יבאו	qal	wci	3mp	בוא	97		come in
	שׁכב	qal	ptc	ms	שׁכב	1011		lie,lie down
4:6	באו	qal	pft	3cp	בוא	97		come in
	לקחי	qal	ptc	mp	לקח	542		take
	יכהו	hiph	wci	3mp	נכה	645	3ms	smite
	נמלטו	niph	pft	3cp	מלט	572		escape
4:7	יבאו	qal	wci	3mp	בוא	97		come in
	שׁכב	qal	ptc	ms	שׁכב	1011		lie,lie down
	יכהו	hiph	wci	3mp	נכה	645	3ms	smite
	ימתהו	hiph	wci	3mp	מות	559	3ms	kill
	יסירו	hiph	wci	3mp	סור	693		take away
	יקחו	qal	wci	3mp	לקח	542		take
	ילכו	qal	wci	3mp	הלך	229		walk,go
4:8	יבאו	hiph	wci	3mp	בוא	97		bring in
	יאמרו	qal	wci	3mp	אמר	55		say
	איבך	qal	ptc	ms	איב	33	2ms	be hostile to
	בקשׁ	piel	pft	3ms	בקשׁ	134		seek
	יתן	qal	wci	3ms	נתן	678		give,set
4:9	יען	qal	wci	3ms	ענה	772		answer
	יאמר	qal	wci	3ms	אמר	55		say
	פדה	qal	pft	3ms	פדה	804		ransom
4:10	מגיד	hiph	ptc	ms	נגד	616		declare,tell
	אמר	qal	infc		אמר	55		say
	מת	qal	pft	3ms	מות	559		die
	היה	qal	pft	3ms	היה	224		be,become
	מבשׂר	piel	ptc	ms	בשׂר	142		bear tidings
	אחזה	qal	wci	1cs	אחז	28		grasp
	אהרגהו	qal	wci	1cs	הרג	246	3ms	kill
	תתי	qal	infc		נתן	678	1cs	give,set
4:11	הרגו	qal	pft	3cp	הרג	246		kill
	אבקשׁ	piel	impf	1cs	בקשׁ	134		seek
	בערתי	piel	wcp	1cs	בער	128		burn,consume
4:12	יצו	piel	wci	3ms	צוה	845		command
	יהרגום	qal	wci	3mp	הרג	246	3mp	kill
	יקצצו	piel	wci	3mp	קצץ	893		cut off
	יתלו	qal	wci	3mp	תלה	1067		hang
	לקחו	qal	pft	3cp	לקח	542		take
	יקברו	qal	wci	3mp	קבר	868		bury
5:1	יבאו	qal	wci	3mp	בוא	97		come in
	יאמרו	qal	wci	3mp	אמר	55		say
	אמר	qal	infc		אמר	55		say
5:2	היות	qal	infc		היה	224		be,become
	kהייתה	qal	pft	2ms	היה	224		be,become
	qהיית	qal	pft	2ms	היה	224		be,become
5:2	מוציא	hiph	ptc	ms	יצא	422		bring out
	kמבי	hiph	ptc	ms	בוא	97		bring in
	qמביא	hiph	ptc	ms	בוא	97		bring in
	יאמר	qal	wci	3ms	אמר	55		say
	תרעה	qal	impf	2ms	רעה	944		pasture,tend
	תהיה	qal	impf	2ms	היה	224		be,become
5:3	יבאו	qal	wci	3mp	בוא	97		come in
	יכרת	qal	wci	3ms	כרת	503		cut,destroy
	ימשׁחו	qal	wci	3mp	משׁח	602		smear,anoint
5:4	מלכו	qal	infc		מלך	573	3ms	be king,reign
	מלך	qal	pft	3ms	מלך	573		be king,reign
5:5	מלך	qal	pft	3ms	מלך	573		be king,reign
	מלך	qal	pft	3ms	מלך	573		be king,reign
5:6	ילך	qal	wci	3ms	הלך	229		walk,go
	יושׁב	qal	ptc	ms	ישׁב	442		sit,dwell
	יאמר	qal	wci	3ms	אמר	55		say
	אמר	qal	infc		אמר	55		say
	תבוא	qal	impf	2ms	בוא	97		come in
	הסירך	hiph	pft	3ms	סור	693	2ms	take away
	אמר	qal	infc		אמר	55		say
	יבוא	qal	impf	3ms	בוא	97		come in
5:7	ילכד	qal	wci	3ms	לכד	539		capture
5:8	יאמר	qal	wci	3ms	אמר	55		say
	מכה	hiph	ptc	ms	נכה	645		smite
	יגע	qal	jusm	3ms	נגע	619		touch,strike
	kשׂנאו	qal	pft	3cp	שׂנא	971		hate
	qשׂנאי	qal	pptc	mp	שׂנא	971		hate
	יאמרו	qal	impf	3mp	אמר	55		say
	יבוא	qal	impf	3ms	בוא	97		come in
5:9	ישׁב	qal	wci	3ms	ישׁב	442		sit,dwell
	יקרא	qal	wci	3ms	קרא	894		call,proclaim
	יבן	qal	wci	3ms	בנה	124		build
5:10	ילך	qal	wci	3ms	הלך	229		walk,go
	הלוך	qal	infa		הלך	229		walk,go
5:11	ישׁלח	qal	wci	3ms	שׁלח	1018		send
	יבנו	qal	wci	3mp	בנה	124		build
5:12	ידע	qal	wci	3ms	ידע	393		know
	הכינו	hiph	pft	3ms	כון	465	3ms	fix,prepare
	נשׂא	piel	pft	3ms	נשׂא	669		lift up
5:13	יקח	qal	wci	3ms	לקח	542		take
	באו	qal	infc		בוא	97	3ms	come in
	יולדו	niph	wci	3mp	ילד	408		be born
5:17	ישׁמעו	qal	wci	3mp	שׁמע	1033		hear
	משׁחו	qal	pft	3cp	משׁח	602		smear,anoint
	יעלו	qal	wci	3mp	עלה	748		go up
	בקשׁ	piel	infc		בקשׁ	134		seek
	ישׁמע	qal	wci	3ms	שׁמע	1033		hear
	ירד	qal	wci	3ms	ירד	432		come down
5:18	באו	qal	pft	3cp	בוא	97		come in
	ינטשׁו	niph	wci	3mp	נטשׁ	643		be forsaken
5:19	ישׁאל	qal	wci	3ms	שׁאל	981		ask,borrow
	אמר	qal	infc		אמר	55		say
	אעלה	qal	impf	1cs	עלה	748		go up
	תתנם	qal	impf	2ms	נתן	678	3mp	give,set

ChVs	Form	Stem	Tnse	PGN	Root	BDB	Sfx	Meaning
5:19	יאמר	qal	wci	3ms	אמר	55		say
	עלה	qal	impv	ms	עלה	748		go up
	נתן	qal	infa		נתן	678		give,set
	אתן	qal	impf	1cs	נתן	678		give,set
5:20	יבא	qal	wci	3ms	בוא	97		come in
	יכם	hiph	wci	3ms	נכה	645	3mp	smite
	יאמר	qal	wci	3ms	אמר	55		say
	פרץ	qal	pft	3ms	פרץ	829		break through
	איבי	qal	ptc	mp	איב	33	1cs	be hostile to
	קרא	qal	pft	3ms	קרא	894		call,proclaim
5:21	יעזבו	qal	wci	3mp	עזב	736		leave,loose
	ישׂאם	qal	wci	3ms	נשׂא	669	3mp	lift,carry
5:22	יספו	hiph	wci	3mp	יסף	414		add,do again
	עלות	qal	infc		עלה	748		go up
	ינטשו	niph	wci	3mp	נטשׁ	643		be forsaken
5:23	ישׁאל	qal	wci	3ms	שׁאל	981		ask,borrow
	יאמר	qal	wci	3ms	אמר	55		say
	תעלה	qal	impf	2ms	עלה	748		go up
	הסב	hiph	impv	ms	סבב	685		cause to turn
	באת	qal	wcp	2ms	בוא	97		come in
5:24	יהי	qal	jus	3ms	היה	224		be,become
	שׁמעך	qal	infc		שׁמע	1033	2ms	hear
	תחרץ	qal	impf	2ms	חרץ	358		cut,decide
	יצא	qal	pft	3ms	יצא	422		go out
	הכות	hiph	infc		נכה	645		smite
5:25	יעשׂ	qal	wci	3ms	עשׂה	793		do,make
	צוהו	piel	pft	3ms	צוה	845	3ms	command
	יך	hiph	wci	3ms	נכה	645		smite
	באך	qal	infc		בוא	97	2ms	come in
6:1	יסף	qal	wci	3ms	אסף	62		gather
	בחור	qal	pptc	ms	בחר	103		choose
6:2	יקם	qal	wci	3ms	קום	877		arise,stand
	ילך	qal	wci	3ms	הלך	229		walk,go
	העלות	hiph	infc		עלה	748		bring up,offer
	נקרא	niph	pft	3ms	קרא	894		be called
	ישׁב	qal	ptc	ms	ישׁב	442		sit,dwell
6:3	ירכבו	hiph	wci	3mp	רכב	938		cause to ride
	ישׂאהו	qal	wci	3mp	נשׂא	669	3ms	lift,carry
	נהגים	qal	ptc	mp	נהג	624		drive
6:4	ישׂאהו	qal	wci	3mp	נשׂא	669	3ms	lift,carry
	הלך	qal	ptc	ms	הלך	229		walk,go
6:5	משׂחקים	piel	ptc	mp	שׂחק	965		make sport
6:6	יבאו	qal	wci	3mp	בוא	97		come in
	ישׁלח	qal	wci	3ms	שׁלח	1018		send
	יאחז	qal	wci	3ms	אחז	28		grasp
	שׁמטו	qal	pft	3cp	שׁמט	1030		let drop
6:7	יחר	qal	wci	3ms	חרה	354		be kindled, burn
	יכהו	hiph	wci	3ms	נכה	645	3ms	smite
	ימת	qal	wci	3ms	מות	559		die
6:8	יחר	qal	wci	3ms	חרה	354		be kindled, burn
	פרץ	qal	pft	3ms	פרץ	829		break through
	יקרא	qal	wci	3ms	קרא	894		call,proclaim
6:9	ירא	qal	wci	3ms	ירא	431		fear
	יאמר	qal	wci	3ms	אמר	55		say
6:9	יבוא	qal	impf	3ms	בוא	97		come in
6:10	אבה	qal	pft	3ms	אבה	2		be willing
	הסיר	hiph	infc		סור	693		take away
	יטהו	hiph	wci	3ms	נטה	639	3ms	turn,incline
6:11	ישׁב	qal	wci	3ms	ישׁב	442		sit,dwell
	יברך	piel	wci	3ms	ברך	138		bless
6:12	יגד	hoph	wci	3ms	נגד	616		be told
	אמר	qal	infc		אמר	55		say
	ברך	piel	pft	3ms	ברך	138		bless
	ילך	qal	wci	3ms	הלך	229		walk,go
	יעל	hiph	wci	3ms	עלה	748		bring up,offer
6:13	יהי	qal	wci	3ms	היה	224		be,become
	צעדו	qal	pft	3cp	צעד	857		step,march
	נשׂאי	qal	ptc	mp	נשׂא	669		lift,carry
	יזבח	qal	wci	3ms	זבח	256		slaughter
6:14	מכרכר	pilp	ptc	ms	כרר	502		dance,whirl
	חגור	qal	pptc	ms	חגר	291		gird
6:15	מעלים	hiph	ptc	mp	עלה	748		bring up,offer
6:16	היה	qal	pft	3ms	היה	224		be,become
	בא	qal	ptc	ms	בוא	97		come in
	נשׁקפה	niph	pft	3fs	שׁקף	1054		look down
	תרא	qal	wci	3fs	ראה	906		see
	מפזז	piel	ptc	ms	פזז	808		show agility
	מכרכר	pilp	ptc	ms	כרר	502		dance,whirl
	תבז	qal	wci	3fs	בזה	102		despise
6:17	יבאו	hiph	wci	3mp	בוא	97		bring in
	יצגו	hiph	wci	3mp	יצג	426		place,establish
	נטה	qal	pft	3ms	נטה	639		stretch,incline
	יעל	hiph	wci	3ms	עלה	748		bring up,offer
6:18	יכל	piel	wci	3ms	כלה	477		complete,finish
	העלות	hiph	infc		עלה	748		bring up,offer
	יברך	piel	wci	3ms	ברך	138		bless
6:19	יחלק	piel	wci	3ms	חלק	323		divide
	ילך	qal	wci	3ms	הלך	229		walk,go
6:20	ישׁב	qal	wci	3ms	שׁוב	996		turn,return
	ברך	piel	infc		ברך	138		bless
	תצא	qal	wci	3fs	יצא	422		go out
	קראת	qal	infc		קרא	896		meet,encounter
	תאמר	qal	wci	3fs	אמר	55		say
	נכבד	niph	pft	3ms	כבד	457		be honored
	נגלה	niph	pft	3ms	גלה	162		uncover self
	הגלות	niph	infc		גלה	162		uncover self
	נגלות	niph	infc		גלה	162		uncover self
6:21	יאמר	qal	wci	3ms	אמר	55		say
	בחר	qal	pft	3ms	בחר	103		choose
	צות	piel	infc		צוה	845		command
	שׂחקתי	piel	wcp	1cs	שׂחק	965		make sport
6:22	נקלתי	niph	wcp	1cs	קלל	886		be trifling
	הייתי	qal	wcp	1cs	היה	224		be,become
	אמרת	qal	pft	2fs	אמר	55		say
	אכבדה	niph	coh	1cs	כבד	457		be honored
6:23	היה	qal	pft	3ms	היה	224		be,become
7:1	יהי	qal	wci	3ms	היה	224		be,become
	ישׁב	qal	pft	3ms	ישׁב	442		sit,dwell

ChVs	Form	Stem	Tnse	PGN	Root	BDB	Sfx	Meaning
7:1	הניח	hiph	pft	3ms	נוח	628		give rest,put
	איביו	qal	ptc	mp	איב	33	3ms	be hostile to
7:2	יאמר	qal	wci	3ms	אמר	55		say
	ראה	qal	impv	ms	ראה	906		see
	יושב	qal	ptc	ms	ישב	442		sit,dwell
	ישב	qal	ptc	ms	ישב	442		sit,dwell
7:3	יאמר	qal	wci	3ms	אמר	55		say
	לך	qal	impv	ms	הלך	229		walk,go
	עשה	qal	impv	ms	עשה	793		do,make
7:4	יהי	qal	wci	3ms	היה	224		be,become
	יהי	qal	wci	3ms	היה	224		be,become
	אמר	qal	infc		אמר	55		say
7:5	לך	qal	impv	ms	הלך	229		walk,go
	אמרת	qal	wcp	2ms	אמר	55		say
	אמר	qal	pft	3ms	אמר	55		say
	תבנה	qal	impf	2ms	בנה	124		build
	שבתי	qal	infc		ישב	442	1cs	sit,dwell
7:6	ישבתי	qal	pft	1cs	ישב	442		sit,dwell
	העלתי	hiph	infc		עלה	748	1cs	bring up,offer
	אהיה	qal	wci	1cs	היה	224		be,become
	מתהלך	hith	ptc	ms	הלך	229		walk to and fro
7:7	התהלכתי	hith	pft	1cs	הלך	229		walk to and fro
	דברתי	piel	pft	1cs	דבר	180		speak
	צויתי	piel	pft	1cs	צוה	845		command
	רעות	qal	infc		רעה	944		pasture,tend
	אמר	qal	infc		אמר	55		say
	בניתם	qal	pft	2mp	בנה	124		build
7:8	תאמר	qal	impf	2ms	אמר	55		say
	אמר	qal	pft	3ms	אמר	55		say
	לקחתיך	qal	pft	1cs	לקח	542	2ms	take
	היות	qal	infc		היה	224		be,become
7:9	אהיה	qal	wci	1cs	היה	224		be,become
	הלכת	qal	pft	2ms	הלך	229		walk,go
	אכרתה	hiph	wci	1cs	כרת	503		cut off,destroy
	איביך	qal	ptc	mp	איב	33	2ms	be hostile to
	עשתי	qal	wcp	1cs	עשה	793		do,make
7:10	שמתי	qal	wcp	1cs	שים	962		put,set
	נטעתיו	qal	wcp	1cs	נטע	642	3ms	plant
	שכן	qal	wcp	3ms	שכן	1014		settle,dwell
	ירגז	qal	impf	3ms	רגז	919		quake
	יסיפו	hiph	impf	3mp	יסף	414		add,do again
	ענותו	piel	infc		ענה	776	3ms	humble
7:11	צויתי	piel	pft	1cs	צוה	845		command
	שפטים	qal	ptc	mp	שפט	1047		judge
	הניחתי	hiph	wcp	1cs	נוח	628		give rest,put
	איביך	qal	ptc	mp	איב	33	2ms	be hostile to
	הגיד	hiph	pft	3ms	נגד	616		declare,tell
	יעשה	qal	impf	3ms	עשה	793		do,make
7:12	ימלאו	qal	impf	3mp	מלא	569		be full,fill
	שכבת	qal	wcp	2ms	שכב	1011		lie,lie down
	הקימתי	hiph	wcp	1cs	קום	877		raise,build,set
	יצא	qal	impf	3ms	יצא	422		go out
	הכינתי	hiph	wcp	1cs	כון	465		fix,prepare
7:13	יבנה	qal	impf	3ms	בנה	124		build
7:13	כננתי	pol	wcp	1cs	כון	465		establish
7:14	אהיה	qal	impf	1cs	היה	224		be,become
	יהיה	qal	impf	3ms	היה	224		be,become
	העותו	hiph	infc		עוה	731	3ms	commit iniquity
	הכחתיו	hiph	wcp	1cs	יכח	406	3ms	decide,reprove
7:15	יסור	qal	impf	3ms	סור	693		turn aside
	הסרתי	hiph	pft	1cs	סור	693		take away
	הסרתי	hiph	pft	1cs	סור	693		take away
7:16	נאמן	niph	wcp	3ms	אמן	52		be confirmed
	יהיה	qal	impf	3ms	היה	224		be,become
	נכון	niph	ptc	ms	כון	465		be established
7:17	דבר	piel	pft	3ms	דבר	180		speak
7:18	יבא	qal	wci	3ms	בוא	97		come in
	ישב	qal	wci	3ms	ישב	442		sit,dwell
	יאמר	qal	wci	3ms	אמר	55		say
	הביאתני	hiph	pft	2ms	בוא	97	1cs	bring in
7:19	תקטן	qal	wci	3fs	קטן	881		be little
	ותדבר	piel	wci	2ms	דבר	180		speak
7:20	יוסיף	hiph	impf	3ms	יסף	414		add,do again
	דבר	piel	infc		דבר	180		speak
	ידעת	qal	pft	2ms	ידע	393		know
7:21	עשית	qal	pft	2ms	עשה	793		do,make
	הודיע	hiph	infc		ידע	393		declare
7:22	גדלת	qal	pft	2ms	גדל	152		be great,grow
	שמענו	qal	pft	1cp	שמע	1033		hear
7:23	הלכו	qal	pft	3cp	הלך	229		walk,go
	פדות	qal	infc		פדה	804		ransom
	שום	qal	infc		שים	962		put,set
	עשות	qal	infc		עשה	793		do,make
	נראות	niph	ptc	fp	ירא	431		be feared
	פדית	qal	pft	2ms	פדה	804		ransom
7:24	תכונן	pol	wci	2ms	כון	465		establish
	היית	qal	pft	2ms	היה	224		be,become
7:25	דברת	piel	pft	2ms	דבר	180		speak
	הקם	hiph	impv	ms	קום	877		raise,build,set
	עשה	qal	impv	ms	עשה	793		do,make
	דברת	piel	pft	2ms	דבר	180		speak
7:26	יגדל	qal	jusm	3ms	גדל	152		be great,grow
	אמר	qal	infc		אמר	55		say
	יהיה	qal	impf	3ms	היה	224		be,become
	נכון	niph	ptc	ms	כון	465		be established
7:27	גליתה	qal	pft	2ms	גלה	162		uncover
	אמר	qal	infc		אמר	55		say
	אבנה	qal	impf	1cs	בנה	124		build
	מצא	qal	pft	3ms	מצא	592		find
	התפלל	hith	infc		פלל	813		pray
7:28	יהיו	qal	impf	3mp	היה	224		be,become
	תדבר	piel	wci	2ms	דבר	180		speak
7:29	הואל	hiph	impv	ms	יאל	383		be willing
	ברך	piel	impv	ms	ברך	138		bless
	היות	qal	infc		היה	224		be,become
	דברת	piel	pft	2ms	דבר	180		speak
	יברך	pual	impf	3ms	ברך	138		be blessed
8:1	יהי	qal	wci	3ms	היה	224		be,become

ChVs	Form	Stem	Tnse	PGN	Root	BDB	Sfx	Meaning
8: 1	יך	hiph	wci	3ms	נכה	645		smite
	יכניעם	hiph	wci	3ms	כנע	488	3mp	humble,subdue
	יקח	qal	wci	3ms	לקח	542		take
8: 2	יך	hiph	wci	3ms	נכה	645		smite
	ימדדם	piel	wci	3ms	מדד	551	3mp	measure
	השכב	hiph	infa		שכב	1011		lay
	ימדד	piel	wci	3ms	מדד	551		measure
	המית	hiph	infc		מות	559		kill
	החיות	hiph	infc		חיה	310		preserve
	תהי	qal	wci	3fs	היה	224		be,become
	נשאי	qal	ptc	mp	נשא	669		lift,carry
8: 3	יך	hiph	wci	3ms	נכה	645		smite
	לכתו	qal	infc		הלך	229	3ms	walk,go
	השיב	hiph	infc		שוב	996		bring back
8: 4	ילכד	qal	wci	3ms	לכד	539		capture
	יעקר	piel	wci	3ms	עקר	785		hamstring
	יותר	hiph	wci	3ms	יתר	451		leave,spare
8: 5	תבא	qal	wci	3fs	בוא	97		come in
	עזר	qal	infc		עזר	740		help,aid
	יך	hiph	wci	3ms	נכה	645		smite
8: 6	ישם	qal	wci	3ms	שים	962		put,set
	תהי	qal	wci	3fs	היה	224		be,become
	נושאי	qal	ptc	mp	נשא	669		lift,carry
	ישע	hiph	wci	3ms	ישע	446		deliver,save
	הלך	qal	pft	3ms	הלך	229		walk,go
8: 7	יקח	qal	wci	3ms	לקח	542		take
	היו	qal	pft	3cp	היה	224		be,become
	יביאם	hiph	wci	3ms	בוא	97	3mp	bring in
8: 8	לקח	qal	pft	3ms	לקח	542		take
	הרבה	hiph	infa		רבה	915		make many
8: 9	ישמע	qal	wci	3ms	שמע	1033		hear
	הכה	hiph	pft	3ms	נכה	645		smite
8: 10	ישלח	qal	wci	3ms	שלח	1018		send
	שאל	qal	infc		שאל	981		ask,borrow
	ברכו	piel	infc		ברך	138	3ms	bless
	נלחם	niph	pft	3ms	לחם	535		wage war
	יכהו	hiph	wci	3ms	נכה	645	3ms	smite
	היה	qal	pft	3ms	היה	224		be,become
	היו	qal	pft	3cp	היה	224		be,become
8: 11	הקדיש	hiph	pft	3ms	קדש	872		consecrate
	הקדיש	hiph	pft	3ms	קדש	872		consecrate
	כבש	piel	pft	3ms	כבש	461		subdue
8: 13	יעש	qal	wci	3ms	עשה	793		do,make
	שבו	qal	infc		שוב	996	3ms	turn,return
	הכותו	hiph	infc		נכה	645	3ms	smite
8: 14	ישם	qal	wci	3ms	שים	962		put,set
	שם	qal	pft	3ms	שים	962		put,set
	יהי	qal	wci	3ms	היה	224		be,become
	יושע	hiph	wci	3ms	ישע	446		deliver,save
	הלך	qal	pft	3ms	הלך	229		walk,go
8: 15	ימלך	qal	wci	3ms	מלך	573		be king,reign
	יהי	qal	wci	3ms	היה	224		be,become
	עשה	qal	ptc	ms	עשה	793		do,make
8: 16	מזכיר	hiph	ptc	ms	זכר	269		c. to remember

ChVs	Form	Stem	Tnse	PGN	Root	BDB	Sfx	Meaning
8: 18	היו	qal	pft	3cp	היה	224		be,become
9: 1	יאמר	qal	wci	3ms	אמר	55		say
	נותר	niph	pft	3ms	יתר	451		be left,remain
	אעשה	qal	impf	1cs	עשה	793		do,make
9: 2	יקראו	qal	wci	3mp	קרא	894		call,proclaim
	יאמר	qal	wci	3ms	אמר	55		say
	יאמר	qal	wci	3ms	אמר	55		say
9: 3	יאמר	qal	wci	3ms	אמר	55		say
	אעשה	qal	impf	1cs	עשה	793		do,make
	יאמר	qal	wci	3ms	אמר	55		say
9: 4	יאמר	qal	wci	3ms	אמר	55		say
	יאמר	qal	wci	3ms	אמר	55		say
9: 5	ישלח	qal	wci	3ms	שלח	1018		send
	יקחהו	qal	wci	3ms	לקח	542	3ms	take
9: 6	יבא	qal	wci	3ms	בוא	97		come in
	יפל	qal	wci	3ms	נפל	656		fall
	ישתחו	hish	wci	3ms	חוה	1005		bow down
	יאמר	qal	wci	3ms	אמר	55		say
	יאמר	qal	wci	3ms	אמר	55		say
9: 7	יאמר	qal	wci	3ms	אמר	55		say
	תירא	qal	jusm	2ms	ירא	431		fear
	עשה	qal	infa		עשה	793		do,make
	אעשה	qal	impf	1cs	עשה	793		do,make
	השבתי	hiph	wcp	1cs	שוב	996		bring back
	תאכל	qal	impf	2ms	אכל	37		eat,devour
9: 8	ישתחו	hish	wci	3ms	חוה	1005		bow down
	יאמר	qal	wci	3ms	אמר	55		say
	פנית	qal	pft	2ms	פנה	815		turn
	מת	qal	ptc	ms	מות	559		die
9: 9	יקרא	qal	wci	3ms	קרא	894		call,proclaim
	יאמר	qal	wci	3ms	אמר	55		say
	היה	qal	pft	3ms	היה	224		be,become
	נתתי	qal	pft	1cs	נתן	678		give,set
9: 10	עבדת	qal	wcp	2ms	עבד	712		work,serve
	הבאת	hiph	wcp	2ms	בוא	97		bring in
	היה	qal	wcp	3ms	היה	224		be,become
	אכלו	qal	wcp	3ms	אכל	37	3ms	eat,devour
	יאכל	qal	impf	3ms	אכל	37		eat,devour
9: 11	יאמר	qal	wci	3ms	אמר	55		say
	יצוה	piel	impf	3ms	צוה	845		command
	יעשה	qal	impf	3ms	עשה	793		do,make
	אכל	qal	ptc	ms	אכל	37		eat,devour
9: 13	ישב	qal	ptc	ms	ישב	442		sit,dwell
	אכל	qal	ptc	ms	אכל	37		eat,devour
10: 1	יהי	qal	wci	3ms	היה	224		be,become
	ימת	qal	wci	3ms	מות	559		die
	ימלך	qal	wci	3ms	מלך	573		be king,reign
10: 2	יאמר	qal	wci	3ms	אמר	55		say
	אעשה	qal	impf	1cs	עשה	793		do,make
	עשה	qal	pft	3ms	עשה	793		do,make
	ישלח	qal	wci	3ms	שלח	1018		send
	נחמו	piel	infc		נחם	636	3ms	comfort
	יבאו	qal	wci	3mp	בוא	97		come in
10: 3	יאמרו	qal	wci	3mp	אמר	55		say

ChVs	Form	Stem	Tnse	PGN	Root	BDB	Sfx	Meaning
10:3	מכבד	piel	ptc	ms	כבד	457		honor,make dull
	שלח	qal	pft	3ms	שלח	1018		send
	מנחמים	piel	ptc	mp	נחם	636		comfort
	חקור	qal	infc		חקר	350		search
	רגלה	piel	infc		רגל	920	3fs	slander,spy
	הפכה	qal	infc		הפך	245	3fs	turn,overturn
	שלח	qal	pft	3ms	שלח	1018		send
10:4	יקח	qal	wci	3ms	לקח	542		take
	יגלח	piel	wci	3ms	גלח	164		shave
	יכרת	qal	wci	3ms	כרת	503		cut,destroy
	ישלחם	piel	wci	3ms	שלח	1018	3mp	send away,shoot
10:5	יגדו	hiph	wci	3mp	נגד	616		declare,tell
	ישלח	qal	wci	3ms	שלח	1018		send
	קראתם	qal	infc		קרא	896	3mp	meet,encounter
	היו	qal	pft	3cp	היה	224		be,become
	נכלמים	niph	ptc	mp	כלם	483		be humiliated
	יאמר	qal	wci	3ms	אמר	55		say
	שבו	qal	impv	mp	ישב	442		sit,dwell
	יצמח	piel	impf	3ms	צמח	855		grow abundantly
	שבתם	qal	wcp	2mp	שוב	996		turn,return
10:6	יראו	qal	wci	3mp	ראה	906		see
	נבאשו	niph	pft	3cp	באש	92		make odious
	ישלחו	qal	wci	3mp	שלח	1018		send
	ישכרו	qal	wci	3mp	שכר	968		hire
10:7	ישמע	qal	wci	3ms	שמע	1033		hear
	ישלח	qal	wci	3ms	שלח	1018		send
10:8	יצאו	qal	wci	3mp	יצא	422		go out
	יערכו	qal	wci	3mp	ערך	789		set in order
10:9	ירא	qal	wci	3ms	ראה	906		see
	היתה	qal	pft	3fs	היה	224		be,become
	יבחר	qal	wci	3ms	בחר	103		choose
	בחורי	qal	pptc	mp	בחר	103		choose
	יערך	qal	wci	3ms	ערך	789		set in order
	קראת	qal	infc		קרא	896		meet,encounter
10:10	נתן	qal	pft	3ms	נתן	678		give,set
	יערך	qal	wci	3ms	ערך	789		set in order
	קראת	qal	infc		קרא	896		meet,encounter
10:11	יאמר	qal	wci	3ms	אמר	55		say
	תחזק	qal	impf	3fs	חזק	304		be strong
	היתה	qal	wcp	2ms	היה	224		be,become
	יחזקו	qal	impf	3mp	חזק	304		be strong
	הלכתי	qal	wcp	1cs	הלך	229		walk,go
	הושיע	hiph	infc		ישע	446		deliver,save
10:12	חזק	qal	impv	ms	חזק	304		be strong
	נתחזק	hith	cohm	1cp	חזק	304		strengthen self
	יעשה	qal	impf	3ms	עשה	793		do,make
10:13	יגש	qal	wci	3ms	נגש	620		draw near
	ינסו	qal	wci	3mp	נוס	630		flee,escape
10:14	ראו	qal	pft	3cp	ראה	906		see
	נס	qal	pft	3ms	נוס	630		flee,escape
	ינסו	qal	wci	3mp	נוס	630		flee,escape
	יבאו	qal	wci	3mp	בוא	97		come in
	ישב	qal	wci	3ms	שוב	996		turn,return
	יבא	qal	wci	3ms	בוא	97		come in
10:15	ירא	qal	wci	3ms	ראה	906		see
	נגף	niph	pft	3ms	נגף	619		be smitten
	יאספו	niph	wci	3mp	אסף	62		assemble
10:16	ישלח	qal	wci	3ms	שלח	1018		send
	יצא	hiph	wci	3ms	יצא	422		bring out
	יבאו	qal	wci	3mp	בוא	97		come in
10:17	יגד	hoph	wci	3ms	נגד	616		be told
	יאסף	qal	wci	3ms	אסף	62		gather
	יעבר	qal	wci	3ms	עבר	716		pass over
	יבא	qal	wci	3ms	בוא	97		come in
	יערכו	qal	wci	3mp	ערך	789		set in order
	קראת	qal	infc		קרא	896		meet,encounter
	ילחמו	niph	wci	3mp	לחם	535		wage war
10:18	ינס	qal	wci	3ms	נוס	630		flee,escape
	יהרג	qal	wci	3ms	הרג	246		kill
	הכה	hiph	pft	3ms	נכה	645		smite
	ימת	qal	wci	3ms	מות	559		die
10:19	יראו	qal	wci	3mp	ראה	906		see
	נגפו	niph	pft	3cp	נגף	619		be smitten
	ישלמו	hiph	wci	3mp	שלם	1023		make peace
	יעבדום	qal	wci	3mp	עבד	712	3mp	work,serve
	יראו	qal	wci	3mp	ירא	431		fear
	הושיע	hiph	infc		ישע	446		deliver,save
11:1	יהי	qal	wci	3ms	היה	224		be,become
	צאת	qal	infc		יצא	422		go out
	ישלח	qal	wci	3ms	שלח	1018		send
	ישחתו	hiph	wci	3mp	שחת	1007		spoil,ruin
	יצרו	qal	wci	3mp	צור	848		confine,shut in
	יושב	qal	ptc	ms	ישב	442		sit,dwell
11:2	יהי	qal	wci	3ms	היה	224		be,become
	יקם	qal	wci	3ms	קום	877		arise,stand
	יתהלך	hith	wci	3ms	הלך	229		walk to and fro
	ירא	qal	wci	3ms	ראה	906		see
	רחצת	qal	ptc	fs	רחץ	934		wash,bathe
11:3	ישלח	qal	wci	3ms	שלח	1018		send
	ידרש	qal	wci	3ms	דרש	205		resort to,seek
	יאמר	qal	wci	3ms	אמר	55		say
11:4	ישלח	qal	wci	3ms	שלח	1018		send
	יקחה	qal	wci	3ms	לקח	542	3fs	take
	תבוא	qal	wci	3fs	בוא	97		come in
	ישכב	qal	wci	3ms	שכב	1011		lie,lie down
	מתקדשת	hith	ptc	fs	קדש	872		consecrate self
	תשב	qal	wci	3fs	שוב	996		turn,return
11:5	תהר	qal	wci	3fs	הרה	247		conceive
	תשלח	qal	wci	3fs	שלח	1018		send
	תגד	hiph	wci	3fs	נגד	616		declare,tell
	תאמר	qal	wci	3fs	אמר	55		say
11:6	ישלח	qal	wci	3ms	שלח	1018		send
	שלח	qal	impv	ms	שלח	1018		send
	ישלח	qal	wci	3ms	שלח	1018		send
11:7	יבא	qal	wci	3ms	בוא	97		come in
	ישאל	qal	wci	3ms	שאל	981		ask,borrow
11:8	יאמר	qal	wci	3ms	אמר	55		say
	רד	qal	impv	ms	ירד	432		come down

ChVs	Form	Stem	Tnse	PGN	Root	BDB	Sfx	Meaning
11:8	רחץ	qal	impv	ms	רחץ	934		wash,bathe
	יצא	qal	wci	3ms	יצא	422		go out
	תצא	qal	wci	3fs	יצא	422		go out
11:9	ישׁכב	qal	wci	3ms	שׁכב	1011		lie,lie down
	ירד	qal	pft	3ms	ירד	432		come down
11:10	יגדו	hiph	wci	3mp	נגד	616		declare,tell
	אמר	qal	infc		אמר	55		say
	ירד	qal	pft	3ms	ירד	432		come down
	יאמר	qal	wci	3ms	אמר	55		say
	בא	qal	ptc	ms	בוא	97		come in
	ירדת	qal	pft	2ms	ירד	432		come down
11:11	יאמר	qal	wci	3ms	אמר	55		say
	ישׁבים	qal	ptc	mp	ישׁב	442		sit,dwell
	חנים	qal	ptc	mp	חנה	333		decline,encamp
	אבוא	qal	impf	1cs	בוא	97		come in
	אכל	qal	infc		אכל	37		eat,devour
	שׁתות	qal	infc		שׁתה	1059		drink
	שׁכב	qal	infc		שׁכב	1011		lie,lie down
	אעשׂה	qal	impf	1cs	עשׂה	793		do,make
11:12	יאמר	qal	wci	3ms	אמר	55		say
	שׁב	qal	impv	ms	ישׁב	442		sit,dwell
	אשׁלחך	piel	impf	1cs	שׁלח	1018	2ms	send away,shoot
	ישׁב	qal	wci	3ms	ישׁב	442		sit,dwell
11:13	יקרא	qal	wci	3ms	קרא	894		call,proclaim
	יאכל	qal	wci	3ms	אכל	37		eat,devour
	ישׁת	qal	wci	3ms	שׁתה	1059		drink
	ישׁכרהו	piel	wci	3ms	שׁכר	1016	3ms	make drunk
	יצא	qal	wci	3ms	יצא	422		go out
	שׁכב	qal	infc		שׁכב	1011		lie,lie down
	ירד	qal	pft	3ms	ירד	432		come down
11:14	יהי	qal	wci	3ms	היה	224		be,become
	יכתב	qal	wci	3ms	כתב	507		write
	ישׁלח	qal	wci	3ms	שׁלח	1018		send
11:15	יכתב	qal	wci	3ms	כתב	507		write
	אמר	qal	infc		אמר	55		say
	הבו	qal	impv	mp	יהב	396		give
	שׁבתם	qal	wcp	2mp	שׁוב	996		turn,return
	נכה	niph	wcp	3ms	נכה	645		be smitten
	מת	qal	wcp	3ms	מות	559		die
11:16	יהי	qal	wci	3ms	היה	224		be,become
	שׁמור	qal	infc		שׁמר	1036		keep,watch
	יתן	qal	wci	3ms	נתן	678		give,set
	ידע	qal	pft	3ms	ידע	393		know
11:17	יצאו	qal	wci	3mp	יצא	422		go out
	ילחמו	niph	wci	3mp	לחם	535		wage war
	יפל	qal	wci	3ms	נפל	656		fall
	ימת	qal	wci	3ms	מות	559		die
11:18	ישׁלח	qal	wci	3ms	שׁלח	1018		send
	יגד	hiph	wci	3ms	נגד	616		declare,tell
11:19	יצו	piel	wci	3ms	צוה	845		command
	אמר	qal	infc		אמר	55		say
	כלותך	piel	infc		כלה	477	2ms	complete,finish
	דבר	piel	infc		דבר	180		speak
11:20	היה	qal	wcp	3ms	היה	224		be,become
11:20	תעלה	qal	impf	3fs	עלה	748		go up
	אמר	qal	wcp	3ms	אמר	55		say
	נגשׁתם	niph	pft	2mp	נגשׁ	620		draw near
	הלחם	niph	infc		לחם	535		wage war
	ידעתם	qal	pft	2mp	ידע	393		know
	ירו	hiph	impf	3cp	ירה	434		shoot,teach
11:21	הכה	hiph	pft	3ms	נכה	645		smite
	השׁליכה	hiph	pft	3fs	שׁלך	1020		throw,cast
	ימת	qal	wci	3ms	מות	559		die
	נגשׁתם	niph	pft	2mp	נגשׁ	620		draw near
	אמרת	qal	wcp	2ms	אמר	55		say
	מת	qal	pft	3ms	מות	559		die
11:22	ילך	qal	wci	3ms	הלך	229		walk,go
	יבא	qal	wci	3ms	בוא	97		come in
	יגד	hiph	wci	3ms	נגד	616		declare,tell
	שׁלחו	qal	pft	3ms	שׁלח	1018	3ms	send
11:23	יאמר	qal	wci	3ms	אמר	55		say
	גברו	qal	pft	3cp	גבר	149		be strong
	יצאו	qal	wci	3mp	יצא	422		go out
	נהיה	qal	wci	1cp	היה	224		be,become
11:24	יראוk	hiph	wci	3mp	ירא	432		shoot
	ירוq	hiph	wci	3mp	ירה	434		shoot,teach
	מוראיםk	hiph	ptc	mp	ירא	432		shoot
	מוריםq	hiph	ptc	mp	ירה	434		shoot,teach
	ימותו	qal	wci	3mp	מות	559		die
	מת	qal	pft	3ms	מות	559		die
11:25	יאמר	qal	wci	3ms	אמר	55		say
	תאמר	qal	impf	2ms	אמר	55		say
	ירע	qal	jusm	3ms	רעע	949		be evil
	תאכל	qal	impf	3fs	אכל	37		eat,devour
	החזק	hiph	impv	ms	חזק	304		make firm,seize
	הרסה	qal	impv	ms	הרס	248	3fs	throw down
	חזקהו	piel	impv	ms	חזק	304	3ms	make strong
11:26	תשׁמע	qal	wci	3fs	שׁמע	1033		hear
	מת	qal	pft	3ms	מות	559		die
	תספד	qal	wci	3fs	ספד	704		wail,lament
11:27	יעבר	qal	wci	3ms	עבר	716		pass over
	ישׁלח	qal	wci	3ms	שׁלח	1018		send
	יאספה	qal	wci	3ms	אסף	62	3fs	gather
	תהי	qal	wci	3fs	היה	224		be,become
	תלד	qal	wci	3fs	ילד	408		bear,beget
	ירע	qal	wci	3ms	רעע	949		be evil
	עשׂה	qal	pft	3ms	עשׂה	793		do,make
12:1	ישׁלח	qal	wci	3ms	שׁלח	1018		send
	יבא	qal	wci	3ms	בוא	97		come in
	יאמר	qal	wci	3ms	אמר	55		say
	היו	qal	pft	3cp	היה	224		be,become
	ראשׁ	qal	ptc	ms	רושׁ	930		be in want
12:2	היה	qal	pft	3ms	היה	224		be,become
	הרבה	hiph	infa		רבה	915		make many
12:3	רשׁ	qal	ptc	ms	רושׁ	930		be in want
	קנה	qal	pft	3ms	קנה	888		get,buy
	יחיה	piel	wci	3ms	חיה	310	3fs	preserve,revive
	תגדל	qal	wci	3fs	גדל	152		be great,grow

ChVs	Form	Stem	Tnse	PGN	Root	BDB	Sfx	Meaning
12: 3	תאכל	qal	impf	3fs	אכל	37		eat,devour
	תשתה	qal	impf	3fs	שתה	1059		drink
	תשכב	qal	impf	3fs	שכב	1011		lie,lie down
	תהי	qal	wci	3fs	היה	224		be,become
12: 4	יבא	qal	wci	3ms	בוא	97		come in
	יחמל	qal	wci	3ms	חמל	328		spare
	קחת	qal	infc		לקח	542		take
	עשׂות	qal	infc		עשׂה	793		do,make
	ארח	qal	ptc	ms	ארח	72		wander,go
	בא	qal	ptc	ms	בוא	97		come in
	יקח	qal	wci	3ms	לקח	542		take
	ראשׁ	qal	ptc	ms	רושׁ	930		be in want
	יעשׂה	qal	wci	3ms	עשׂה	793	3fs	do,make
	בא	qal	ptc	ms	בוא	97		come in
12: 5	יחר	qal	wci	3ms	חרה	354		be kindled,burn
	יאמר	qal	wci	3ms	אמר	55		say
	עשׂה	qal	ptc	ms	עשׂה	793		do,make
12: 6	ישׁלם	piel	impf	3ms	שׁלם	1022		finish,reward
	עשׂה	qal	pft	3ms	עשׂה	793		do,make
	חמל	qal	pft	3ms	חמל	328		spare
12: 7	יאמר	qal	wci	3ms	אמר	55		say
	אמר	qal	pft	3ms	אמר	55		say
	משׁחתיך	qal	pft	1cs	משׁח	602	2ms	smear,anoint
	הצלתיך	hiph	pft	1cs	נצל	664	2ms	snatch,deliver
12: 8	אתנה	qal	wci	1cs	נתן	678		give,set
	אתנה	qal	wci	1cs	נתן	678		give,set
	אספה	hiph	coh	1cs	יסף	414		add,do again
12: 9	בזית	qal	pft	2ms	בזה	102		despise
	עשׂות	qal	infc		עשׂה	793		do,make
	הכית	hiph	pft	2ms	נכה	645		smite
	לקחת	qal	pft	2ms	לקח	542		take
	הרגת	qal	pft	2ms	הרג	246		kill
12: 10	תסור	qal	impf	3fs	סור	693		turn aside
	בזתני	qal	pft	2ms	בזה	102	1cs	despise
	תקח	qal	wci	2ms	לקח	542		take
	היות	qal	infc		היה	224		be,become
12: 11	אמר	qal	pft	3ms	אמר	55		say
	מקים	hiph	ptc	ms	קום	877		raise,build,set
	לקחתי	qal	wcp	1cs	לקח	542		take
	נתתי	qal	wcp	1cs	נתן	678		give,set
	שׁכב	qal	wcp	3ms	שׁכב	1011		lie,lie down
12: 12	עשׂית	qal	pft	2ms	עשׂה	793		do,make
	אעשׂה	qal	impf	1cs	עשׂה	793		do,make
12: 13	יאמר	qal	wci	3ms	אמר	55		say
	חטאתי	qal	pft	1cs	חטא	306		sin
	יאמר	qal	wci	3ms	אמר	55		say
	העביר	hiph	pft	3ms	עבר	716		cause to pass
	תמות	qal	impf	2ms	מות	559		die
12: 14	נאץ	piel	infa		נאץ	610		spurn
	נאצת	piel	pft	2ms	נאץ	610		spurn
	איבי	qal	ptc	mp	איב	33		be hostile to
	מות	qal	infa		מות	559		die
	ימות	qal	impf	3ms	מות	559		die
12: 15	ילך	qal	wci	3ms	הלך	229		walk,go
12: 15	יגף	qal	wci	3ms	נגף	619		smite,strike
	ילדה	qal	pft	3fs	ילד	408		bear,beget
	יאנשׁ	niph	wci	3ms	אנשׁ	60		be sick
12: 16	יבקשׁ	piel	wci	3ms	בקשׁ	134		seek
	יצם	qal	wci	3ms	צום	847		fast
	בא	qal	wcp	3ms	בוא	97		come in
	לן	qal	wcp	3ms	לון	533		lodge,remain
	שׁכב	qal	wcp	3ms	שׁכב	1011		lie,lie down
12: 17	יקמו	qal	wci	3mp	קום	877		arise,stand
	הקימו	hiph	infc		קום	877	3ms	raise,build,set
	אבה	qal	pft	3ms	אבה	2		be willing
	ברא	qal	pft	3ms	ברה	136		eat
12: 18	יהי	qal	wci	3ms	היה	224		be,become
	ימת	qal	wci	3ms	מות	559		die
	יראו	qal	wci	3mp	ירא	431		fear
	הגיד	hiph	infc		נגד	616		declare,tell
	מת	qal	pft	3ms	מות	559		die
	אמרו	qal	pft	3cp	אמר	55		say
	היות	qal	infc		היה	224		be,become
	דברנו	piel	pft	1cp	דבר	180		speak
	שׁמע	qal	pft	3ms	שׁמע	1033		hear
	נאמר	qal	impf	1cp	אמר	55		say
	מת	qal	pft	3ms	מות	559		die
	עשׂה	qal	wcp	3ms	עשׂה	793		do,make
12: 19	ירא	qal	wci	3ms	ראה	906		see
	מתלחשׁים	hith	ptc	mp	לחשׁ	538		whisper
	יבן	qal	wci	3ms	בין	106		discern
	מת	qal	pft	3ms	מות	559		die
	יאמר	qal	wci	3ms	אמר	55		say
	מת	qal	pft	3ms	מות	559		die
	יאמרו	qal	wci	3mp	אמר	55		say
	מת	qal	pft	3ms	מות	559		die
12: 20	יקם	qal	wci	3ms	קום	877		arise,stand
	ירחץ	qal	wci	3ms	רחץ	934		wash,bathe
	יסך	qal	wci	3ms	סוך	691		anoint,pour
	יחלף	piel	wci	3ms	חלף	322		change
	יבא	qal	wci	3ms	בוא	97		come in
	ישׁתחו	hish	wci	3ms	חוה	1005		bow down
	יבא	qal	wci	3ms	בוא	97		come in
	ישׁאל	qal	wci	3ms	שׁאל	981		ask,borrow
	ישׂימו	qal	wci	3mp	שׂים	962		put,set
	יאכל	qal	wci	3ms	אכל	37		eat,devour
12: 21	יאמרו	qal	wci	3mp	אמר	55		say
	עשׂיתה	qal	pft	2ms	עשׂה	793		do,make
	צמת	qal	pft	2ms	צום	847		fast
	תבך	qal	wci	2ms	בכה	113		weep
	מת	qal	pft	3ms	מות	559		die
	קמת	qal	pft	2ms	קום	877		arise,stand
	תאכל	qal	wci	2ms	אכל	37		eat,devour
12: 22	יאמר	qal	wci	3ms	אמר	55		say
	צמתי	qal	pft	1cs	צום	847		fast
	אבכה	qal	wci	1cs	בכה	113		weep
	אמרתי	qal	pft	1cs	אמר	55		say
	יודע	qal	ptc	ms	ידע	393		know

ChVs	Form	Stem	Tnse	PGN	Root	BDB	Sfx	Meaning
12: 22	איחנני k	qal	jusm	3ms	חנן	335	1cs	show favor
	חנני q	qal	wcp	3ms	חנן	335	1cs	show favor
	חי	qal	wcp	3ms	חיה	310		live
12: 23	מת	qal	pft	3ms	מות	559		die
	צם	qal	ptc	ms	צום	847		fast
	אוכל	qal	impf	1cs	יכל	407		be able
	השׁיבו	hiph	infc		שׁוב	996	3ms	bring back
	הלך	qal	ptc	ms	הלך	229		walk, go
	ישׁוב	qal	impf	3ms	שׁוב	996		turn, return
12: 24	ינחם	piel	wci	3ms	נחם	636		comfort
	יבא	qal	wci	3ms	בוא	97		come in
	ישׁכב	qal	wci	3ms	שׁכב	1011		lie, lie down
	תלד	qal	wci	3fs	ילד	408		bear, beget
	איקרא k	qal	wci	3ms	קרא	894		call, proclaim
	תקרא q	qal	wci	3fs	קרא	894		call, proclaim
	אהבו	qal	pft	3ms	אהב	12	3ms	love
12: 25	ישׁלח	qal	wci	3ms	שׁלח	1018		send
	יקרא	qal	wci	3ms	קרא	894		call, proclaim
12: 26	ילחם	niph	wci	3ms	לחם	535		wage war
	ילכד	qal	wci	3ms	לכד	539		capture
12: 27	ישׁלח	qal	wci	3ms	שׁלח	1018		send
	יאמר	qal	wci	3ms	אמר	55		say
	נלחמתי	niph	pft	1cs	לחם	535		wage war
	לכדתי	qal	pft	1cs	לכד	539		capture
12: 28	אסף	qal	impv	ms	אסף	62		gather
	חנה	qal	impv	ms	חנה	333		decline, encamp
	לכדה	qal	impv	ms	לכד	539	3fs	capture
	אלכד	qal	impf	1cs	לכד	539		capture
	נקרא	niph	wcp	3ms	קרא	894		be called
12: 29	יאסף	qal	wci	3ms	אסף	62		gather
	ילך	qal	wci	3ms	הלך	229		walk, go
	ילחם	niph	wci	3ms	לחם	535		wage war
	ילכדה	qal	wci	3ms	לכד	539	3fs	capture
12: 30	יקח	qal	wci	3ms	לקח	542		take
	תהי	qal	wci	3fs	היה	224		be, become
	הוציא	hiph	pft	3ms	יצא	422		bring out
	הרבה	hiph	infa		רבה	915		make many
12: 31	הוציא	hiph	pft	3ms	יצא	422		bring out
	ישׂם	qal	wci	3ms	שׂים	962		put, set
	העביר	hiph	wcp	3ms	עבר	716		cause to pass
	יעשׂה	qal	impf	3ms	עשׂה	793		do, make
	ישׁב	qal	wci	3ms	שׁוב	996		turn, return
13: 1	יהי	qal	wci	3ms	היה	224		be, become
	יאהבה	qal	wci	3ms	אהב	12	3fs	love
13: 2	יצר	qal	wci	3ms	צרר	864		bind, be cramped
	התחלות	hith	infc		חלה	317		make self sick
	יפלא	niph	wci	3ms	פלא	810		be wonderful
	עשׂות	qal	infc		עשׂה	793		do, make
13: 4	יאמר	qal	wci	3ms	אמר	55		say
	תגיד	hiph	impf	2ms	נגד	616		declare, tell
	יאמר	qal	wci	3ms	אמר	55		say
	אהב	qal	ptc	ms	אהב	12		love
13: 5	יאמר	qal	wci	3ms	אמר	55		say
	שׁכב	qal	impv	ms	שׁכב	1011		lie, lie down
13: 5	התחל	hith	impv	ms	חלה	317		make self sick
	בא	qal	wcp	3ms	בוא	97		come in
	ראותך	qal	infc		ראה	906	2ms	see
	אמרת	qal	wcp	2ms	אמר	55		say
	תבא	qal	jusm	3fs	בוא	97		come in
	תברני	hiph	jusm	3fs	ברה	136	1cs	cause to eat
	עשׂתה	qal	wcp	3fs	עשׂה	793		do, make
	אראה	qal	impf	1cs	ראה	906		see
	אכלתי	qal	wcp	1cs	אכל	37		eat, devour
13: 6	ישׁכב	qal	wci	3ms	שׁכב	1011		lie, lie down
	יתחל	hith	wci	3ms	חלה	317		make self sick
	יבא	qal	wci	3ms	בוא	97		come in
	ראתו	qal	infc		ראה	906	3ms	see
	יאמר	qal	wci	3ms	אמר	55		say
	תבוא	qal	jusm	3fs	בוא	97		come in
	תלבב	piel	jusm	3fs	לבב	525		encourage
	אברה	qal	cohm	1cs	ברה	136		eat
13: 7	ישׁלח	qal	wci	3ms	שׁלח	1018		send
	אמר	qal	infc		אמר	55		say
	לכי	qal	impv	fs	הלך	229		walk, go
	עשׂי	qal	impv	fs	עשׂה	793		do, make
13: 8	תלך	qal	wci	3fs	הלך	229		walk, go
	שׁכב	qal	ptc	ms	שׁכב	1011		lie, lie down
	תקח	qal	wci	3fs	לקח	542		take
	תלושׁ k	qal	wci	3fs	לושׁ	534		knead
	תלשׁ q	qal	wci	3fs	לושׁ	534		knead
	תלבב	piel	wci	3fs	לבב	525		encourage
	תבשׁל	piel	wci	3fs	בשׁל	143		boil, cook
13: 9	תקח	qal	wci	3fs	לקח	542		take
	תצק	qal	wci	3fs	יצק	427		pour out, cast
	ימאן	piel	wci	3ms	מאן	549		refuse
	אכול	qal	infc		אכל	37		eat, devour
	יאמר	qal	wci	3ms	אמר	55		say
	הוציאו	hiph	impv	mp	יצא	422		bring out
	יצאו	qal	wci	3mp	יצא	422		go out
13: 10	יאמר	qal	wci	3ms	אמר	55		say
	הביאי	hiph	impv	fs	בוא	97		bring in
	אברה	qal	cohm	1cs	ברה	136		eat
	תקח	qal	wci	3fs	לקח	542		take
	עשׂתה	qal	pft	3fs	עשׂה	793		do, make
	תבא	hiph	wci	3fs	בוא	97		bring in
13: 11	תגשׁ	hiph	wci	3fs	נגשׁ	620		bring near
	אכל	qal	infc		אכל	37		eat, devour
	יחזק	hiph	wci	3ms	חזק	304		make firm, seize
	יאמר	qal	wci	3ms	אמר	55		say
	בואי	qal	impv	fs	בוא	97		come in
	שׁכבי	qal	impv	fs	שׁכב	1011		lie, lie down
13: 12	תאמר	qal	wci	3fs	אמר	55		say
	תענני	piel	jusm	2ms	ענה	776	1cs	humble
	יעשׂה	niph	impf	3ms	עשׂה	793		be done
	תעשׂה	qal	jusm	2ms	עשׂה	793		do, make
13: 13	אוליך	hiph	impf	1cs	הלך	229		lead, bring
	תהיה	qal	impf	2ms	היה	224		be, become
	דבר	piel	impv	ms	דבר	180		speak

ChVs	Form	Stem	Tnse	PGN	Root	BDB	Sfx	Meaning
13:13	ימנעני	qal	impf	3ms	מנע	586	1cs	withhold
13:14	אבה	qal	pft	3ms	אבה	2		be willing
	שמע	qal	infc		שמע	1033		hear
	יחזק	qal	wci	3ms	חזק	304		be strong
	יענה	piel	wci	3ms	ענה	776	3fs	humble
	ישכב	qal	wci	3ms	שכב	1011		lie,lie down
13:15	ישנאה	qal	wci	3ms	שנא	971	3fs	hate
	שנאה	qal	pft	3ms	שנא	971	3fs	hate
	אהבה	qal	pft	3ms	אהב	12	3fs	love
	יאמר	qal	wci	3ms	אמר	55		say
	קומי	qal	impv	fs	קום	877		arise,stand
	לכי	qal	impv	fs	הלך	229		walk,go
13:16	תאמר	qal	wci	3fs	אמר	55		say
	עשית	qal	pft	2ms	עשה	793		do,make
	שלחני	piel	infc		שלח	1018	1cs	send away,shoot
	אבה	qal	pft	3ms	אבה	2		be willing
	שמע	qal	infc		שמע	1033		hear
13:17	יקרא	qal	wci	3ms	קרא	894		call,proclaim
	משרתו	piel	ptc	ms	שרת	1058	3ms	minister,serve
	יאמר	qal	wci	3ms	אמר	55		say
	שלחו	qal	impv	mp	שלח	1018		send
	נעל	qal	impv	ms	נעל	653		bar,bolt
13:18	תלבשן	qal	impf	3fp	לבש	527		put on,clothe
	יצא	hiph	wci	3ms	יצא	422		bring out
	משרתו	piel	ptc	ms	שרת	1058	3ms	minister,serve
	נעל	qal	pft	3ms	נעל	653		bar,bolt
13:19	תקח	qal	wci	3fs	לקח	542		take
	קרעה	qal	pft	3fs	קרע	902		tear,rend
	תשם	qal	wci	3fs	שים	962		put,set
	תלך	qal	wci	3fs	הלך	229		walk,go
	הלוך	qal	infa		הלך	229		walk,go
	זעקה	qal	wcp	3fs	זעק	277		call,cry out
13:20	יאמר	qal	wci	3ms	אמר	55		say
	היה	qal	pft	3ms	היה	224		be,become
	החרישי	hiph	impv	fs	חרש	361		be silent
	תשיתי	qal	jusm	2fs	שית	1011		put,set
	תשב	qal	wci	3fs	ישב	442		sit,dwell
	שממה	qal	ptc	fs	שמם	1030		be desolate
13:21	שמע	qal	pft	3ms	שמע	1033		hear
	יחר	qal	wci	3ms	חרה	354		be kindled,burn
13:22	דבר	piel	pft	3ms	דבר	180		speak
	שנא	qal	pft	3ms	שנא	971		hate
	ענה	piel	pft	3ms	ענה	776		humble
13:23	יהי	qal	wci	3ms	היה	224		be,become
	יהיו	qal	wci	3mp	היה	224		be,become
	גזזים	qal	ptc	mp	גזז	159		shear
	יקרא	qal	wci	3ms	קרא	894		call,proclaim
13:24	יבא	qal	wci	3ms	בוא	97		come in
	יאמר	qal	wci	3ms	אמר	55		say
	גזזים	qal	ptc	mp	גזז	159		shear
	ילך	qal	jusm	3ms	הלך	229		walk,go
13:25	יאמר	qal	wci	3ms	אמר	55		say
	נלך	qal	cohm	1cp	הלך	229		walk,go
	נכבד	qal	impf	1cp	כבד	457		be heavy
13:25	יפרץ	qal	wci	3ms	פרץ	829		break through
	אבה	qal	pft	3ms	אבה	2		be willing
	לכת	qal	infc		הלך	229		walk,go
	יברכהו	piel	wci	3ms	ברך	138	3ms	bless
13:26	יאמר	qal	wci	3ms	אמר	55		say
	ילך	qal	jusm	3ms	הלך	229		walk,go
	יאמר	qal	wci	3ms	אמר	55		say
	ילך	qal	impf	3ms	הלך	229		walk,go
13:27	יפרץ	qal	wci	3ms	פרץ	829		break through
	ישלח	qal	wci	3ms	שלח	1018		send
13:28	יצו	piel	wci	3ms	צוה	845		command
	אמר	qal	infc		אמר	55		say
	ראו	qal	impv	mp	ראה	906		see
	טוב	qal	infc		טוב	373		be pleasing
	אמרתי	qal	wcp	1cs	אמר	55		say
	הכו	hiph	impv	mp	נכה	645		smite
	המתם	hiph	wcp	2mp	מות	559		kill
	תיראו	qal	jusm	2mp	ירא	431		fear
	צויתי	piel	pft	1cs	צוה	845		command
	חזקו	qal	impv	mp	חזק	304		be strong
	היו	qal	impv	mp	היה	224		be,become
13:29	יעשו	qal	wci	3mp	עשה	793		do,make
	צוה	piel	pft	3ms	צוה	845		command
	יקמו	qal	wci	3mp	קום	877		arise,stand
	ירכבו	qal	wci	3mp	רכב	938		mount,ride
	ינסו	qal	wci	3mp	נוס	630		flee,escape
13:30	יהי	qal	wci	3ms	היה	224		be,become
	באה	qal	pft	3fs	בוא	97		come in
	אמר	qal	infc		אמר	55		say
	הכה	hiph	pft	3ms	נכה	645		smite
	נותר	niph	pft	3ms	יתר	451		be left,remain
13:31	יקם	qal	wci	3ms	קום	877		arise,stand
	יקרע	qal	wci	3ms	קרע	902		tear,rend
	ישכב	qal	wci	3ms	שכב	1011		lie,lie down
	נצבים	niph	ptc	mp	נצב	662		stand
	קרעי	qal	pptc	mp	קרע	902		tear,rend
13:32	יען	qal	wci	3ms	ענה	772		answer
	יאמר	qal	wci	3ms	אמר	55		say
	יאמר	qal	jusm	3ms	אמר	55		say
	המיתו	hiph	pft	3cp	מות	559		kill
	מת	qal	pft	3ms	מות	559		die
	היתה	qal	pft	3fs	היה	224		be,become
	ענתו	piel	infc		ענה	776	3ms	humble
13:33	ישם	qal	jus	3ms	שים	962		put,set
	אמר	qal	infc		אמר	55		say
	מתו	qal	pft	3cp	מות	559		die
	מת	qal	pft	3ms	מות	559		die
13:34	יברח	qal	wci	3ms	ברח	137		go thru,flee
	ישא	qal	wci	3ms	נשא	669		lift,carry
	צפה	qal	ptc	ms	צפה	859		keep watch
	ירא	qal	wci	3ms	ראה	906		see
	הלכים	qal	ptc	mp	הלך	229		walk,go
13:35	יאמר	qal	wci	3ms	אמר	55		say
	באו	qal	pft	3cp	בוא	97		come in

ChVs	Form	Stem	Tnse	PGN	Root	BDB	Sfx	Meaning
13:35	היה	qal	pft	3ms	היה	224		be,become
13:36	יהי	qal	wci	3ms	היה	224		be,become
	כלתו	piel	infc		כלה	477	3ms	complete,finish
	דבר	piel	infc		דבר	180		speak
	באו	qal	pft	3cp	בוא	97		come in
	ישׂאו	qal	wci	3mp	נשׂא	669		lift,carry
	יבכו	qal	wci	3mp	בכה	113		weep
	בכו	qal	pft	3cp	בכה	113		weep
13:37	ברח	qal	pft	3ms	ברח	137		go thru,flee
	ילך	qal	wci	3ms	הלך	229		walk,go
	יתאבל	hith	wci	3ms	אבל	5		mourn
13:38	ברח	qal	pft	3ms	ברח	137		go thru,flee
	ילך	qal	wci	3ms	הלך	229		walk,go
	יהי	qal	wci	3ms	היה	224		be,become
13:39	תכל	piel	wci	3fs	כלה	477		complete,finish
	צאת	qal	infc		יצא	422		go out
	נחם	niph	pft	3ms	נחם	636		be sorry
	מת	qal	pft	3ms	מות	559		die
14:1	ידע	qal	wci	3ms	ידע	393		know
14:2	ישׁלח	qal	wci	3ms	שׁלח	1018		send
	יקח	qal	wci	3ms	לקח	542		take
	יאמר	qal	wci	3ms	אמר	55		say
	התאבלי	hith	impv	fs	אבל	5		mourn
	לבשׁי	qal	impv	fs	לבשׁ	527		put on,clothe
	תסוכי	qal	jusm	2fs	סוך	691		anoint,pour
	היית	qal	wcp	2fs	היה	224		be,become
	מתאבלת	hith	ptc	fs	אבל	5		mourn
	מת	qal	ptc	ms	מות	559		die
14:3	באת	qal	wcp	2fs	בוא	97		come in
	דברת	piel	wcp	2fs	דבר	180		speak
	ישׂם	qal	wci	3ms	שׂים	962		put,set
14:4	תאמר	qal	wci	3fs	אמר	55		say
	תפל	qal	wci	3fs	נפל	656		fall
	תשתחו	hish	wci	3fs	חוה	1005		bow down
	תאמר	qal	wci	3fs	אמר	55		say
	הושׁעה	hiph	impv	ms	ישׁע	446		deliver,save
14:5	יאמר	qal	wci	3ms	אמר	55		say
	תאמר	qal	wci	3fs	אמר	55		say
	ימת	qal	wci	3ms	מות	559		die
14:6	ינצו	niph	wci	3mp	נצה	663		struggle
	מציל	hiph	ptc	ms	נצל	664		snatch,deliver
	יכו	hiph	wci	3ms	נכה	645	3ms	smite
	ימת	hiph	wci	3ms	מות	559		kill
14:7	קמה	qal	pft	3fs	קום	877		arise,stand
	יאמרו	qal	wci	3mp	אמר	55		say
	תני	qal	impv	fs	נתן	678		give,set
	מכה	hiph	ptc	ms	נכה	645		smite
	נמתהו	hiph	cohm	1cp	מות	559	3ms	kill
	הרג	qal	pft	3ms	הרג	246		kill
	נשׁמידה	hiph	coh	1cp	שׁמד	1029		exterminate
	יורשׁ	qal	ptc	ms	ירשׁ	439		possess,inherit
	כבו	piel	wcp	3cp	כבה	459		extinguish
	נשׁארה	niph	pft	3fs	שׁאר	983		be left
	שׂוםk	qal	infc		שׂים	962		put,set
14:7	שׂיםq	qal	infc		שׂים	962		put,set
14:8	יאמר	qal	wci	3ms	אמר	55		say
	לכי	qal	impv	fs	הלך	229		walk,go
	אצוה	piel	impf	1cs	צוה	845		command
14:9	תאמר	qal	wci	3fs	אמר	55		say
14:10	יאמר	qal	wci	3ms	אמר	55		say
	מדבר	piel	ptc	ms	דבר	180		speak
	הבאתו	hiph	wcp	2fs	בוא	97	3ms	bring in
	יסיף	hiph	impf	3ms	יסף	414		add,do again
	געת	qal	infc		נגע	619		touch,strike
14:11	תאמר	qal	wci	3fs	אמר	55		say
	יזכר	qal	jusm	3ms	זכר	269		remember
	הרביתk	hiph	infc		רבה	915		make many
	הרבתq	hiph	infc		רבה	915		make many
	גאל	qal	ptc	ms	גאל	145		redeem
	שׁחת	piel	infc		שׁחת	1007		spoil,ruin
	ישׁמידו	hiph	impf	3mp	שׁמד	1029		exterminate
	יאמר	qal	wci	3ms	אמר	55		say
	יפל	qal	impf	3ms	נפל	656		fall
14:12	תאמר	qal	wci	3fs	אמר	55		say
	תדבר	piel	jusm	3fs	דבר	180		speak
	יאמר	qal	wci	3ms	אמר	55		say
	דברי	piel	impv	fs	דבר	180		speak
14:13	תאמר	qal	wci	3fs	אמר	55		say
	חשׁבתה	qal	pft	2ms	חשׁב	362		think,devise
	מדבר	hith	ptc	ms	דבר	180		speak
	השׁיב	hiph	infc		שׁוב	996		bring back
	נדחו	niph	ptc	ms	נדח	623	3ms	be banished
14:14	מות	qal	infa		מות	559		die
	נמות	qal	impf	1cp	מות	559		die
	נגרים	niph	ptc	mp	נגר	620		be poured
	יאספו	niph	impf	3mp	אסף	62		assemble
	ישׂא	qal	impf	3ms	נשׂא	669		lift,carry
	חשׁב	qal	wcp	3ms	חשׁב	362		think,devise
	ידח	qal	impf	3ms	נדח	623		impel,banish
	נדח	niph	ptc	ms	נדח	623		be banished
14:15	באתי	qal	pft	1cs	בוא	97		come in
	דבר	piel	infc		דבר	180		speak
	יראני	piel	impf	3mp	ירא	431	1cs	terrify
	תאמר	qal	wci	3fs	אמר	55		say
	אדברה	piel	coh	1cs	דבר	180		speak
	יעשׂה	qal	impf	3ms	עשׂה	793		do,make
14:16	ישׁמע	qal	impf	3ms	שׁמע	1033		hear
	הציל	hiph	infc		נצל	664		snatch,deliver
	השׁמיד	hiph	infc		שׁמד	1029		exterminate
14:17	תאמר	qal	wci	3fs	אמר	55		say
	יהיה	qal	jusm	3ms	היה	224		be,become
	שׁמע	qal	infc		שׁמע	1033		hear
	יהי	qal	jus	3ms	היה	224		be,become
14:18	יען	qal	wci	3ms	ענה	772		answer
	יאמר	qal	wci	3ms	אמר	55		say
	תכחדי	piel	jusm	2fs	כחד	470		hide
	שׁאל	qal	ptc	ms	שׁאל	981		ask,borrow
	תאמר	qal	wci	3fs	אמר	55		say

ChVs	Form	Stem	Tnse	PGN	Root	BDB	Sfx	Meaning
14:18	ידבר	piel	jusm	3ms	דבר	180		speak
14:19	יאמר	qal	wci	3ms	אמר	55		say
	תען	qal	wci	3fs	ענה	772		answer
	תאמר	qal	wci	3fs	אמר	55		say
	המין	hiph	infc		ימן	412		go to right
	השׂמיל	hiph	infc		שׂמאל	970		go to left
	דבר	piel	pft	3ms	דבר	180		speak
	צוני	piel	pft	3ms	צוה	845	1cs	command
	שׂם	qal	pft	3ms	שׂים	962		put,set
14:20	סבב	piel	infc		סבב	685		change
	עשׂה	qal	pft	3ms	עשׂה	793		do,make
	דעת	qal	infc		ידע	393		know
14:21	יאמר	qal	wci	3ms	אמר	55		say
	עשׂיתי	qal	pft	1cs	עשׂה	793		do,make
	לך	qal	impv	ms	הלך	229		walk,go
	השב	hiph	impv	ms	שׁוב	996		bring back
14:22	יפל	qal	wci	3ms	נפל	656		fall
	ישׁתחו	hish	wci	3ms	חוה	1005		bow down
	יברך	piel	wci	3ms	ברך	138		bless
	יאמר	qal	wci	3ms	אמר	55		say
	ידע	qal	pft	3ms	ידע	393		know
	מצאתי	qal	pft	1cs	מצא	592		find
	עשׂה	qal	pft	3ms	עשׂה	793		do,make
14:23	יקם	qal	wci	3ms	קום	877		arise,stand
	ילך	qal	wci	3ms	הלך	229		walk,go
	יבא	hiph	wci	3ms	בוא	97		bring in
14:24	יאמר	qal	wci	3ms	אמר	55		say
	יסב	qal	impf	3ms	סבב	685		surround
	יראה	qal	impf	3ms	ראה	906		see
	יסב	qal	wci	3ms	סבב	685		surround
	ראה	qal	pft	3ms	ראה	906		see
14:25	היה	qal	pft	3ms	היה	224		be,become
	הלל	piel	infc		הלל	237		praise
	היה	qal	pft	3ms	היה	224		be,become
14:26	גלחו	piel	infc		גלח	164	3ms	shave
	היה	qal	wcp	3ms	היה	224		be,become
	יגלח	piel	impf	3ms	גלח	164		shave
	גלחו	piel	wcp	3ms	גלח	164	3ms	shave
	שׁקל	qal	wcp	3ms	שׁקל	1053		weigh
14:27	יולדו	niph	wci	3mp	ילד	408		be born
	היתה	qal	pft	3fs	היה	224		be,become
14:28	ישׁב	qal	wci	3ms	ישׁב	442		sit,dwell
	ראה	qal	pft	3ms	ראה	906		see
14:29	ישׁלח	qal	wci	3ms	שׁלח	1018		send
	שׁלח	qal	infc		שׁלח	1018		send
	אבה	qal	pft	3ms	אבה	2		be willing
	בוא	qal	infc		בוא	97		come in
	ישׁלח	qal	wci	3ms	שׁלח	1018		send
	אבה	qal	pft	3ms	אבה	2		be willing
	בוא	qal	infc		בוא	97		come in
14:30	יאמר	qal	wci	3ms	אמר	55		say
	ראו	qal	impv	mp	ראה	906		see
	לכו	qal	impv	mp	הלך	229		walk,go
	kהוצתיה	hiph	wcp	1cs	יצת	428	3fs	kindle

ChVs	Form	Stem	Tnse	PGN	Root	BDB	Sfx	Meaning
14:30	qהציתוה	hiph	impv	mp	יצת	428	3fs	kindle
	יצתו	hiph	wci	3mp	יצת	428		kindle
14:31	יקם	qal	wci	3ms	קום	877		arise,stand
	יבא	qal	wci	3ms	בוא	97		come in
	יאמר	qal	wci	3ms	אמר	55		say
	הציתו	hiph	pft	3cp	יצת	428		kindle
14:32	יאמר	qal	wci	3ms	אמר	55		say
	שׁלחתי	qal	pft	1cs	שׁלח	1018		send
	אמר	qal	infc		אמר	55		say
	בא	qal	impv	ms	בוא	97		come in
	אשׁלחה	qal	coh	1cs	שׁלח	1018		send
	אמר	qal	infc		אמר	55		say
	באתי	qal	pft	1cs	בוא	97		come in
	טוב	qal	pft	3ms	טוב	373		be pleasing
	אראה	qal	cohm	1cs	ראה	906		see
	המתני	hiph	wcp	3ms	מות	559	1cs	kill
14:33	יבא	qal	wci	3ms	בוא	97		come in
	יגד	hiph	wci	3ms	נגד	616		declare,tell
	יקרא	qal	wci	3ms	קרא	894		call,proclaim
	יבא	qal	wci	3ms	בוא	97		come in
	ישׁתחו	hish	wci	3ms	חוה	1005		bow down
	ישׁק	qal	wci	3ms	נשׁק	676		kiss
15:1	יהי	qal	wci	3ms	היה	224		be,become
	יעשׂ	qal	wci	3ms	עשׂה	793		do,make
	רצים	qal	ptc	mp	רוץ	930		run
15:2	השׁכים	hiph	wcp	3ms	שׁכם	1014		rise early
	עמד	qal	wcp	3ms	עמד	763		stand,stop
	יהי	qal	wci	3ms	היה	224		be,become
	יהיה	qal	impf	3ms	היה	224		be,become
	בוא	qal	infc		בוא	97		come in
	יקרא	qal	wci	3ms	קרא	894		call,proclaim
	יאמר	qal	wci	3ms	אמר	55		say
	יאמר	qal	wci	3ms	אמר	55		say
15:3	יאמר	qal	wci	3ms	אמר	55		say
	ראה	qal	impv	ms	ראה	906		see
	שׁמע	qal	ptc	ms	שׁמע	1033		hear
15:4	יאמר	qal	wci	3ms	אמר	55		say
	ישׂמני	qal	impf	3ms	שׂים	962	1cs	put,set
	שׁפט	qal	ptc	ms	שׁפט	1047		judge
	יבוא	qal	impf	3ms	בוא	97		come in
	יהיה	qal	impf	3ms	היה	224		be,become
	הצדקתיו	hiph	wcp	1cs	צדק	842	3ms	make righteous
15:5	היה	qal	wcp	3ms	היה	224		be,become
	קרב	qal	infc		קרב	897		approach
	השׁתחות	hish	infc		חוה	1005		bow down
	שׁלח	qal	wcp	3ms	שׁלח	1018		send
	החזיק	hiph	wcp	3ms	חזק	304		make firm,seize
	נשׁק	qal	wcp	3ms	נשׁק	676		kiss
15:6	יעשׂ	qal	wci	3ms	עשׂה	793		do,make
	יבאו	qal	impf	3mp	בוא	97		come in
	יגנב	piel	wci	3ms	גנב	170		steal away
15:7	יהי	qal	wci	3ms	היה	224		be,become
	יאמר	qal	wci	3ms	אמר	55		say
	אלכה	qal	coh	1cs	הלך	229		walk,go

ChVs	Form	Stem	Tnse	PGN	Root	BDB	Sfx	Meaning
15:7	אשׁלם	piel	cohm	1cs	שׁלם	1022		finish,reward
	נדרתי	qal	pft	1cs	נדר	623		vow
15:8	נדר	qal	pft	3ms	נדר	623		vow
	שׁבתי	qal	infc		ישׁב	442	1cs	sit,dwell
	אמר	qal	infc		אמר	55		say
	ישׁיבk	hiph	impf	3ms	שׁוב	996?		bring back
	ישׁובq	qal	infa		ישׁב	442?		sit,dwell
	ישׁיבני	hiph	impf	3ms	שׁוב	996	1cs	bring back
	עבדתי	qal	wcp	1cs	עבד	712		work,serve
15:9	יאמר	qal	wci	3ms	אמר	55		say
	לך	qal	impv	ms	הלך	229		walk,go
	יקם	qal	wci	3ms	קום	877		arise,stand
	ילך	qal	wci	3ms	הלך	229		walk,go
15:10	ישׁלח	qal	wci	3ms	שׁלח	1018		send
	מרגלים	piel	ptc	mp	רגל	920		slander,spy
	אמר	qal	infc		אמר	55		say
	שׁמעכם	qal	infc		שׁמע	1033	2mp	hear
	אמרתם	qal	wcp	2mp	אמר	55		say
	מלך	qal	pft	3ms	מלך	573		be king,reign
15:11	הלכו	qal	pft	3cp	הלך	229		walk,go
	קראים	qal	pptc	mp	קרא	894		call,proclaim
	הלכים	qal	ptc	mp	הלך	229		walk,go
	ידעו	qal	pft	3cp	ידע	393		know
15:12	ישׁלח	qal	wci	3ms	שׁלח	1018		send
	יועץ	qal	ptc	ms	יעץ	419		advise,counsel
	זבחו	qal	infc		זבח	256	3ms	slaughter
	יהי	qal	wci	3ms	היה	224		be,become
	הולך	qal	ptc	ms	הלך	229		walk,go
15:13	יבא	qal	wci	3ms	בוא	97		come in
	מגיד	hiph	ptc	ms	נגד	616		declare,tell
	אמר	qal	infc		אמר	55		say
	היה	qal	pft	3ms	היה	224		be,become
15:14	יאמר	qal	wci	3ms	אמר	55		say
	קומו	qal	impv	mp	קום	877		arise,stand
	נברחה	qal	coh	1cp	ברח	137		go thru,flee
	תהיה	qal	impf	3fs	היה	224		be,become
	מהרו	piel	impv	mp	מהר	554		hasten
	לכת	qal	infc		הלך	229		walk,go
	ימהר	piel	impf	3ms	מהר	554		hasten
	השׂגנו	hiph	wcp	3ms	נשׂג	673	1cp	reach,overtake
	הדיח	hiph	wcp	3ms	נדח	623		thrust out
	הכה	hiph	wcp	3ms	נכה	645		smite
15:15	יאמרו	qal	wci	3mp	אמר	55		say
	יבחר	qal	impf	3ms	בחר	103		choose
15:16	יצא	qal	wci	3ms	יצא	422		go out
	יעזב	qal	wci	3ms	עזב	736		leave,loose
	שׁמר	qal	infc		שׁמר	1036		keep,watch
15:17	יצא	qal	wci	3ms	יצא	422		go out
	יעמדו	qal	wci	3mp	עמד	763		stand,stop
15:18	עברים	qal	ptc	mp	עבר	716		pass over
	באו	qal	pft	3cp	בוא	97		come in
	עברים	qal	ptc	mp	עבר	716		pass over
15:19	יאמר	qal	wci	3ms	אמר	55		say
	תלך	qal	impf	2ms	הלך	229		walk,go
15:19	שׁוב	qal	impv	ms	שׁוב	996		turn,return
	שׁב	qal	impv	ms	ישׁב	442		sit,dwell
	גלה	qal	ptc	ms	גלה	162		uncover
15:20	בואך	qal	infc		בוא	97	2ms	come in
	אנועךk	qal	impf	1cs	נוע	631?	2ms	totter,wave
	אניעךq	hiph	impf	1cs	נוע	631	2ms	shake,disturb
	לכת	qal	infc		הלך	229		walk,go
	הולך	qal	ptc	ms	הלך	229		walk,go
	הולך	qal	ptc	ms	הלך	229		walk,go
	שׁוב	qal	impv	ms	שׁוב	996		turn,return
	השׁב	hiph	impv	ms	שׁוב	996		bring back
15:21	יען	qal	wci	3ms	ענה	772		answer
	יאמר	qal	wci	3ms	אמר	55		say
	יהיה	qal	impf	3ms	היה	224		be,become
	יהיה	qal	impf	3ms	היה	224		be,become
15:22	יאמר	qal	wci	3ms	אמר	55		say
	לך	qal	impv	ms	הלך	229		walk,go
	עבר	qal	impv	ms	עבר	716		pass over
	יעבר	qal	wci	3ms	עבר	716		pass over
15:23	בוכים	qal	ptc	mp	בכה	113		weep
	עברים	qal	ptc	mp	עבר	716		pass over
	עבר	qal	ptc	ms	עבר	716		pass over
	עברים	qal	ptc	mp	עבר	716		pass over
15:24	נשׂאים	qal	ptc	mp	נשׂא	669		lift,carry
	יצקו	hiph	wci	3mp	יצק	427		pour
	יעל	qal	wci	3ms	עלה	748		go up
	תם	qal	infc		תמם	1070		be finished
	עבור	qal	infc		עבר	716		pass over
15:25	יאמר	qal	wci	3ms	אמר	55		say
	השׁב	hiph	impv	ms	שׁוב	996		bring back
	אמצא	qal	impf	1cs	מצא	592		find
	השׁבני	hiph	wcp	3ms	שׁוב	996	1cs	bring back
	הראני	hiph	wcp	3ms	ראה	906	1cs	show,exhibit
15:26	יאמר	qal	impf	3ms	אמר	55		say
	חפצתי	qal	pft	1cs	חפץ	342		delight in
	יעשׂה	qal	jusm	3ms	עשׂה	793		do,make
	טוב	qal	pft	3ms	טוב	373		be pleasing
15:27	יאמר	qal	wci	3ms	אמר	55		say
	שׁבה	qal	impv	ms	שׁוב	996		turn,return
15:28	ראו	qal	impv	mp	ראה	906		see
	מתמהמה	htpp	ptc	ms	מהה	554		tarry
	בוא	qal	infc		בוא	97		come in
	הגיד	hiph	infc		נגד	616		declare,tell
15:29	ישׁב	hiph	wci	3ms	שׁוב	996		bring back
	ישׁבו	qal	wci	3mp	ישׁב	442		sit,dwell
15:30	עלה	qal	ptc	ms	עלה	748		go up
	עלה	qal	ptc	ms	עלה	748		go up
	בוכה	qal	ptc	ms	בכה	113		weep
	חפוי	qal	pptc	ms	חפה	341		cover
	הלך	qal	ptc	ms	הלך	229		walk,go
	חפו	qal	pft	3cp	חפה	341		cover
	עלו	qal	wcp	3cp	עלה	748		go up
	עלה	qal	infa		עלה	748		go up
	בכה	qal	infa		בכה	113		weep

ChVs	Form	Stem	Tnse	PGN	Root	BDB	Sfx	Meaning
15:31	הגיד	hiph	pft	3ms	נגד	616		declare,tell
	אמר	qal	infc		אמר	55		say
	קשרים	qal	ptc	mp	קשר	905		bind
	יאמר	qal	wci	3ms	אמר	55		say
	סכל	piel	impv	ms	סכל	698		make foolish
15:32	יהי	qal	wci	3ms	היה	224		be,become
	בא	qal	ptc	ms	בוא	97		come in
	ישתחוה	hish	impf	3ms	חוה	1005		bow down
	קראתו	qal	infc		קרא	896	3ms	meet,encounter
	קרוע	qal	pptc	ms	קרע	902		tear,rend
15:33	יאמר	qal	wci	3ms	אמר	55		say
	עברת	qal	pft	2ms	עבר	716		pass over
	הית	qal	wcp	2ms	היה	224		be,become
15:34	תשוב	qal	impf	2ms	שוב	996		turn,return
	אמרת	qal	wcp	2ms	אמר	55		say
	אהיה	qal	impf	1cs	היה	224		be,become
	הפרתה	hiph	wcp	2ms	פרר	830		break,frustrate
15:35	היה	qal	wcp	3ms	היה	224		be,become
	תשמע	qal	impf	2ms	שמע	1033		hear
	תגיד	hiph	impf	2ms	נגד	616		declare,tell
15:36	שלחתם	qal	wcp	2mp	שלח	1018		send
	תשמעו	qal	impf	2mp	שמע	1033		hear
15:37	יבא	qal	wci	3ms	בוא	97		come in
	יבא	qal	impf	3ms	בוא	97		come in
16:1	עבר	qal	pft	3ms	עבר	716		pass over
	קראתו	qal	infc		קרא	896	3ms	meet,encounter
	חבשים	qal	pptc	mp	חבש	289		bind
16:2	יאמר	qal	wci	3ms	אמר	55		say
	יאמר	qal	wci	3ms	אמר	55		say
	רכב	qal	infc		רכב	938		mount,ride
	אכול	qal	infc		אכל	37		eat,devour
	שתות	qal	infc		שתה	1059		drink
16:3	יאמר	qal	wci	3ms	אמר	55		say
	יאמר	qal	wci	3ms	אמר	55		say
	יושב	qal	ptc	ms	ישב	442		sit,dwell
	אמר	qal	pft	3ms	אמר	55		say
	ישיבו	hiph	impf	3mp	שוב	996		bring back
16:4	יאמר	qal	wci	3ms	אמר	55		say
	יאמר	qal	wci	3ms	אמר	55		say
	השתחויתי	hish	pft	1cs	חוה	1005		bow down
	אמצא	qal	cohm	1cs	מצא	592		find
16:5	בא	qal	pft	3ms	בוא	97		come in
	יוצא	qal	ptc	ms	יצא	422		go out
	יצא	qal	ptc	ms	יצא	422		go out
	יצוא	qal	infa		יצא	422		go out
	מקלל	piel	ptc	ms	קלל	886		curse
16:6	יסקל	piel	wci	3ms	סקל	709		stone,destone
16:7	אמר	qal	pft	3ms	אמר	55		say
	קללו	piel	infc		קלל	886	3ms	curse
	צא	qal	impv	ms	יצא	422		go out
	צא	qal	impv	ms	יצא	422		go out
16:8	השיב	hiph	pft	3ms	שוב	996		bring back
	מלכת	qal	pft	2ms	מלך	573		be king,reign
	יתן	qal	wci	3ms	נתן	678		give,set
16:9	יאמר	qal	wci	3ms	אמר	55		say
	יקלל	piel	impf	3ms	קלל	886		curse
	מת	qal	ptc	ms	מות	559		die
	אעברה	qal	coh	1cs	עבר	716		pass over
	אסירה	hiph	coh	1cs	סור	693		take away
16:10	יאמר	qal	wci	3ms	אמר	55		say
	יקלל	piel	impf	3ms	קלל	886		curse
	אמר	qal	pft	3ms	אמר	55		say
	קלל	piel	impv	ms	קלל	886		curse
	יאמר	qal	impf	3ms	אמר	55		say
	עשיתה	qal	pft	2ms	עשה	793		do,make
16:11	יאמר	qal	wci	3ms	אמר	55		say
	יצא	qal	pft	3ms	יצא	422		go out
	מבקש	piel	ptc	ms	בקש	134		seek
	הנחו	hiph	impv	mp	נוח	628		give rest,put
	יקלל	piel	jusm	3ms	קלל	886		curse
	אמר	qal	pft	3ms	אמר	55		say
16:12	יראה	qal	impf	3ms	ראה	906		see
	השיב	hiph	wcp	3ms	שוב	996		bring back
16:13	ילך	qal	wci	3ms	הלך	229		walk,go
	הלך	qal	ptc	ms	הלך	229		walk,go
	הלוך	qal	infa		הלך	229		walk,go
	יקלל	piel	wci	3ms	קלל	886		curse
	יסקל	piel	wci	3ms	סקל	709		stone,destone
	עפר	piel	wcp	3ms	עפר	780		pelt with dust
16:14	יבא	qal	wci	3ms	בוא	97		come in
	ינפש	niph	wci	3ms	נפש	661		refresh oneself
16:15	באו	qal	pft	3cp	בוא	97		come in
16:16	יהי	qal	wci	3ms	היה	224		be,become
	בא	qal	pft	3ms	בוא	97		come in
	יאמר	qal	wci	3ms	אמר	55		say
	יחי	qal	jus	3ms	חיה	310		live
	יחי	qal	jus	3ms	חיה	310		live
16:17	יאמר	qal	wci	3ms	אמר	55		say
	הלכת	qal	pft	2ms	הלך	229		walk,go
16:18	יאמר	qal	wci	3ms	אמר	55		say
	בחר	qal	pft	3ms	בחר	103		choose
	אהיה	qal	impf	1cs	היה	224		be,become
	אשב	qal	impf	1cs	ישב	442		sit,dwell
16:19	אעבד	qal	impf	1cs	עבד	712		work,serve
	עבדתי	qal	pft	1cs	עבד	712		work,serve
	אהיה	qal	impf	1cs	היה	224		be,become
16:20	יאמר	qal	wci	3ms	אמר	55		say
	הבו	qal	impv	mp	יהב	396		give
	נעשה	qal	impf	1cp	עשה	793		do,make
16:21	יאמר	qal	wci	3ms	אמר	55		say
	בוא	qal	impv	ms	בוא	97		come in
	הניח	hiph	pft	3ms	נוח	628		give rest,put
	שמור	qal	infc		שמר	1036		keep,watch
	שמע	qal	wcp	3ms	שמע	1033		hear
	נבאשת	niph	pft	2ms	באש	92		make odious
	חזקו	qal	wcp	3cp	חזק	304		be strong
16:22	יטו	hiph	wci	3mp	נטה	639		turn,incline
	יבא	qal	wci	3ms	בוא	97		come in

ChVs	Form	Stem	Tnse	PGN	Root	BDB	Sfx	Meaning
16:23	יעץ	qal	pft	3ms	יעץ	419		advise,counsel
	ישאל	qal	impf	3ms	שאל	981		ask,borrow
17:1	יאמר	qal	wci	3ms	אמר	55		say
	אבחרה	qal	coh	1cs	בחר	103		choose
	אקומה	qal	coh	1cs	קום	877		arise,stand
	ארדפה	qal	coh	1cs	רדף	922		pursue
17:2	אבוא	qal	cohm	1cs	בוא	97		come in
	החרדתי	hiph	wcp	1cs	חרד	353		terrify
	נס	qal	wcp	3ms	נוס	630		flee,escape
	הכיתי	hiph	wcp	1cs	נכה	645		smite
17:3	אשיבה	hiph	coh	1cs	שוב	996		bring back
	שוב	qal	infc		שוב	996		turn,return
	מבקש	piel	ptc	ms	בקש	134		seek
	יהיה	qal	impf	3ms	היה	224		be,become
17:4	יישר	qal	wci	3ms	ישר	448		be straight
17:5	יאמר	qal	wci	3ms	אמר	55		say
	קרא	qal	impv	ms	קרא	894		call,proclaim
	נשמעה	qal	coh	1cp	שמע	1033		hear
17:6	יבא	qal	wci	3ms	בוא	97		come in
	יאמר	qal	wci	3ms	אמר	55		say
	אמר	qal	infc		אמר	55		say
	דבר	piel	pft	3ms	דבר	180		speak
	נעשה	qal	impf	1cp	עשה	793		do,make
	דבר	piel	impv	ms	דבר	180		speak
17:7	יאמר	qal	wci	3ms	אמר	55		say
	יעץ	qal	pft	3ms	יעץ	419		advise,counsel
17:8	יאמר	qal	wci	3ms	אמר	55		say
	ידעת	qal	pft	2ms	ידע	393		know
	ילין	qal	impf	3ms	לון	533		lodge,remain
17:9	נחבא	niph	ptc	ms	חבא	285		hide oneself
	היה	qal	wcp	3ms	היה	224		be,become
	נפל	qal	infc		נפל	656		fall
	שמע	qal	wcp	3ms	שמע	1033		hear
	שמע	qal	ptc	ms	שמע	1033		hear
	אמר	qal	wcp	3ms	אמר	55		say
	היתה	qal	pft	3fs	היה	224		be,become
17:10	המס	niph	infa		מסס	587		melt,despair
	ימס	niph	impf	3ms	מסס	587		melt,despair
	ידע	qal	ptc	ms	ידע	393		know
17:11	יעצתי	qal	pft	1cs	יעץ	419		advise,counsel
	האסף	niph	infa		אסף	62		assemble
	יאסף	niph	jusm	3ms	אסף	62		assemble
	הלכים	qal	ptc	mp	הלך	229		walk,go
17:12	באנו	qal	wcp	1cp	בוא	97		come in
	נמצא	niph	pft	3ms	מצא	592		be found
	יפל	qal	impf	3ms	נפל	656		fall
	נותר	hiph	jus	1cp	יתר	451		leave,spare
17:13	יאסף	niph	impf	3ms	אסף	62		assemble
	השיאו	hiph	wcp	3cp	נשא	669		cause to bring
	סחבנו	qal	wcp	1cp	סחב	694		drag
	נמצא	niph	pft	3ms	מצא	592		be found
17:14	יאמר	qal	wci	3ms	אמר	55		say
	צוה	piel	pft	3ms	צוה	845		command
	הפר	hiph	infc		פרר	830		break,frustrate
17:14	הביא	hiph	infc		בוא	97		bring in
17:15	יאמר	qal	wci	3ms	אמר	55		say
	יעץ	qal	pft	3ms	יעץ	419		advise,counsel
	יעצתי	qal	pft	1cs	יעץ	419		advise,counsel
17:16	שלחו	qal	impv	mp	שלח	1018		send
	הגידו	hiph	impv	mp	נגד	616		declare,tell
	אמר	qal	infc		אמר	55		say
	תלן	qal	jus	2ms	לון	533		lodge,remain
	עבור	qal	infa		עבר	716		pass over
	תעבור	qal	impf	2ms	עבר	716		pass over
	יבלע	pual	impf	3ms	בלע	118		be swallowed up
17:17	עמדים	qal	ptc	mp	עמד	763		stand,stop
	הלכה	qal	wcp	3fs	הלך	229		walk,go
	הגידה	hiph	wcp	3fs	נגד	616		declare,tell
	ילכו	qal	impf	3mp	הלך	229		walk,go
	הגידו	hiph	wcp	3cp	נגד	616		declare,tell
	יוכלו	qal	impf	3mp	יכל	407		be able
	הראות	niph	infc		ראה	906		appear,be seen
	בוא	qal	infc		בוא	97		come in
17:18	ירא	qal	wci	3ms	ראה	906		see
	יגד	hiph	wci	3ms	נגד	616		declare,tell
	ילכו	qal	wci	3mp	הלך	229		walk,go
	יבאו	qal	wci	3mp	בוא	97		come in
	ירדו	qal	wci	3mp	ירד	432		come down
17:19	תקח	qal	wci	3fs	לקח	542		take
	תפרש	qal	wci	3fs	פרש	831		spread out
	תשטח	qal	wci	3fs	שטח	1008		spread abroad
	נודע	niph	pft	3ms	ידע	393		be made known
17:20	יבאו	qal	wci	3mp	בוא	97		come in
	יאמרו	qal	wci	3mp	אמר	55		say
	תאמר	qal	wci	3fs	אמר	55		say
	עברו	qal	pft	3cp	עבר	716		pass over
	יבקשו	piel	wci	3mp	בקש	134		seek
	מצאו	qal	pft	3cp	מצא	592		find
	ישבו	qal	wci	3mp	שוב	996		turn,return
17:21	יהי	qal	wci	3ms	היה	224		be,become
	לכתם	qal	infc		הלך	229	3mp	walk,go
	יעלו	qal	wci	3mp	עלה	748		go up
	ילכו	qal	wci	3mp	הלך	229		walk,go
	יגדו	hiph	wci	3mp	נגד	616		declare,tell
	יאמרו	qal	wci	3mp	אמר	55		say
	קומו	qal	impv	mp	קום	877		arise,stand
	עברו	qal	impv	mp	עבר	716		pass over
	יעץ	qal	pft	3ms	יעץ	419		advise,counsel
17:22	יקם	qal	wci	3ms	קום	877		arise,stand
	יעברו	qal	wci	3mp	עבר	716		pass over
	נעדר	niph	pft	3ms	עדר	727		be lacking,fail
	עבר	qal	pft	3ms	עבר	716		pass over
17:23	ראה	qal	pft	3ms	ראה	906		see
	נעשתה	niph	pft	3fs	עשה	793		be done
	יחבש	qal	wci	3ms	חבש	289		bind
	יקם	qal	wci	3ms	קום	877		arise,stand
	ילך	qal	wci	3ms	הלך	229		walk,go
	יצו	piel	wci	3ms	צוה	845		command

ChVs	Form	Stem	Tnse	PGN	Root	BDB	Sfx	Meaning
17:23	יחנק	niph	wci	3ms	חנק	338		strangle self
	ימת	qal	wci	3ms	מות	559		die
	יקבר	niph	wci	3ms	קבר	868		be buried
17:24	בא	qal	pft	3ms	בוא	97		come in
	עבר	qal	pft	3ms	עבר	716		pass over
17:25	שׂם	qal	pft	3ms	שׂים	962		put,set
	בא	qal	pft	3ms	בוא	97		come in
17:26	יחן	qal	wci	3ms	חנה	333		decline,encamp
17:27	יהי	qal	wci	3ms	היה	224		be,become
	בוא	qal	infc		בוא	97		come in
17:28	יוצר	qal	ptc	ms	יצר	427		form,create
17:29	הגישׁו	hiph	pft	3cp	נגשׁ	620		bring near
	אכול	qal	infc		אכל	37		eat,devour
	אמרו	qal	pft	3cp	אמר	55		say
18:1	יפקד	qal	wci	3ms	פקד	823		attend to,visit
	ישׂם	qal	wci	3ms	שׂים	962		put,set
18:2	ישׁלח	piel	wci	3ms	שׁלח	1018		send away,shoot
	יאמר	qal	wci	3ms	אמר	55		say
	יצא	qal	infa		יצא	422		go out
	אצא	qal	impf	1cs	יצא	422		go out
18:3	יאמר	qal	wci	3ms	אמר	55		say
	תצא	qal	impf	2ms	יצא	422		go out
	נס	qal	infa		נוס	630		flee,escape
	ננוס	qal	impf	1cp	נוס	630		flee,escape
	ישׂימו	qal	impf	3mp	שׂים	962		put,set
	ימתו	qal	impf	3mp	מות	559		die
	ישׂימו	qal	impf	3mp	שׂים	962		put,set
	תהיה	qal	impf	2ms	היה	224		be,become
	עזירk	hiph	infc		עזר	740		help
	עזורq	qal	infc		עזר	740		help,aid
18:4	יאמר	qal	wci	3ms	אמר	55		say
	ייטב	qal	impf	3ms	יטב	405		be good
	אעשׂה	qal	impf	1cs	עשׂה	793		do,make
	יעמד	qal	wci	3ms	עמד	763		stand,stop
	יצאו	qal	pft	3cp	יצא	422		go out
18:5	יצו	piel	wci	3ms	צוה	845		command
	אמר	qal	infc		אמר	55		say
	שׁמעו	qal	pft	3cp	שׁמע	1033		hear
	צות	piel	infc		צוה	845		command
18:6	יצא	qal	wci	3ms	יצא	422		go out
	קראת	qal	infc		קרא	896		meet,encounter
	תהי	qal	wci	3fs	היה	224		be,become
18:7	ינגפו	niph	wci	3mp	נגף	619		be smitten
	תהי	qal	wci	3fs	היה	224		be,become
18:8	תהי	qal	wci	3fs	היה	224		be,become
	נפציתk	niph	ptc	fp	פוץ	806?		be scattered
	נפוצתq	niph	ptc	fs	פוץ	806		be scattered
	ירב	hiph	wci	3ms	רבה	915		make many
	אכל	qal	infc		אכל	37		eat,devour
	אכלה	qal	pft	3fs	אכל	37		eat,devour
18:9	יקרא	niph	wci	3ms	קרא	896		meet
	רכב	qal	ptc	ms	רכב	938		mount,ride
	יבא	qal	wci	3ms	בוא	97		come in
	יחזק	qal	wci	3ms	חזק	304		be strong
18:9	יתן	qalp	wci	3ms	נתן	678		be given
	עבר	qal	pft	3ms	עבר	716		pass over
18:10	ירא	qal	wci	3ms	ראה	906		see
	יגד	hiph	wci	3ms	נגד	616		declare,tell
	יאמר	qal	wci	3ms	אמר	55		say
	ראיתי	qal	pft	1cs	ראה	906		see
	תלוי	qal	pptc	ms	תלה	1067		hang
18:11	יאמר	qal	wci	3ms	אמר	55		say
	מגיד	hiph	ptc	ms	נגד	616		declare,tell
	ראית	qal	pft	2ms	ראה	906		see
	הכיתו	hiph	pft	2ms	נכה	645	3ms	smite
	תת	qal	infc		נתן	678		give,set
18:12	יאמר	qal	wci	3ms	אמר	55		say
	שׁקל	qal	ptc	ms	שׁקל	1053		weigh
	אשׁלח	qal	impf	1cs	שׁלח	1018		send
	צוה	piel	pft	3ms	צוה	845		command
	אמר	qal	infc		אמר	55		say
	שׁמרו	qal	impv	mp	שׁמר	1036		keep,watch
18:13	עשׂיתי	qal	pft	1cs	עשׂה	793		do,make
	יכחד	niph	impf	3ms	כחד	470		be hid,effaced
	תתיצב	hith	impf	2ms	יצב	426		stand oneself
18:14	יאמר	qal	wci	3ms	אמר	55		say
	אחילה	hiph	coh	1cs	יחל	403		wait
	יקח	qal	wci	3ms	לקח	542		take
	יתקעם	qal	wci	3ms	תקע	1075	3mp	thrust,clap
18:15	יסבו	qal	wci	3mp	סבב	685		surround
	נשׂאי	qal	ptc	mp	נשׂא	669		lift,carry
	יכו	hiph	wci	3mp	נכה	645		smite
	ימיתהו	hiph	wci	3mp	מות	559	3ms	kill
18:16	יתקע	qal	wci	3ms	תקע	1075		thrust,clap
	ישׁב	qal	wci	3ms	שׁוב	996		turn,return
	רדף	qal	infc		רדף	922		pursue
	חשׂך	qal	pft	3ms	חשׂך	362		withhold
18:17	יקחו	qal	wci	3mp	לקח	542		take
	ישׁליכו	hiph	wci	3mp	שׁלך	1020		throw,cast
	יצבו	hiph	wci	3mp	נצב	662		cause to stand
	נסו	qal	pft	3cp	נוס	630		flee,escape
18:18	לקח	qal	pft	3ms	לקח	542		take
	יצב	hiph	wci	3ms	נצב	662		cause to stand
	אמר	qal	pft	3ms	אמר	55		say
	הזכיר	hiph	infc		זכר	269		c. to remember
	יקרא	qal	wci	3ms	קרא	894		call,proclaim
	יקרא	niph	wci	3ms	קרא	894		be called
18:19	אמר	qal	pft	3ms	אמר	55		say
	ארוצה	qal	coh	1cs	רוץ	930		run
	אבשׂרה	piel	coh	1cs	בשׂר	142		bear tidings
	שׁפטו	qal	pft	3ms	שׁפט	1047	3ms	judge
	איביו	qal	ptc	mp	איב	33	3ms	be hostile to
18:20	יאמר	qal	wci	3ms	אמר	55		say
	בשׂרת	piel	wcp	2ms	בשׂר	142		bear tidings
	תבשׂר	piel	impf	2ms	בשׂר	142		bear tidings
	מת	qal	pft	3ms	מות	559		die
18:21	יאמר	qal	wci	3ms	אמר	55		say
	לך	qal	impv	ms	הלך	229		walk,go

ChVs	Form	Stem	Tnse	PGN	Root	BDB	Sfx	Meaning
18:21	הגד	hiph	impv	ms	נגד	616		declare,tell
	ראיתה	qal	pft	2ms	ראה	906		see
	ישתחו	hish	wci	3ms	חוה	1005		bow down
	ירץ	qal	wci	3ms	רוץ	930		run
18:22	יסף	hiph	wci	3ms	יסף	414		add,do again
	יאמר	qal	wci	3ms	אמר	55		say
	יהי	qal	jus	3ms	היה	224		be,become
	ארצה	qal	coh	1cs	רוץ	930		run
	יאמר	qal	wci	3ms	אמר	55		say
	רץ	qal	ptc	ms	רוץ	930		run
	מצאת	qal	ptc	fs	מצא	592		find
18:23	יהי	qal	jus	3ms	היה	224		be,become
	ארוץ	qal	impf	1cs	רוץ	930		run
	יאמר	qal	wci	3ms	אמר	55		say
	רוץ	qal	impv	ms	רוץ	930		run
	ירץ	qal	wci	3ms	רוץ	930		run
	יעבר	qal	wci	3ms	עבר	716		pass over
18:24	יושב	qal	ptc	ms	ישב	442		sit,dwell
	ילך	qal	wci	3ms	הלך	229		walk,go
	צפה	qal	ptc	ms	צפה	859		keep watch
	ישׂא	qal	wci	3ms	נשׂא	669		lift,carry
	ירא	qal	wci	3ms	ראה	906		see
	רץ	qal	ptc	ms	רוץ	930		run
18:25	יקרא	qal	wci	3ms	קרא	894		call,proclaim
	צפה	qal	ptc	ms	צפה	859		keep watch
	יגד	hiph	wci	3ms	נגד	616		declare,tell
	יאמר	qal	wci	3ms	אמר	55		say
	ילך	qal	wci	3ms	הלך	229		walk,go
	הלוך	qal	infa		הלך	229		walk,go
18:26	ירא	qal	wci	3ms	ראה	906		see
	צפה	qal	ptc	ms	צפה	859		keep watch
	רץ	qal	ptc	ms	רוץ	930		run
	יקרא	qal	wci	3ms	קרא	894		call,proclaim
	צפה	qal	ptc	ms	צפה	859		keep watch
	יאמר	qal	wci	3ms	אמר	55		say
	רץ	qal	ptc	ms	רוץ	930		run
	יאמר	qal	wci	3ms	אמר	55		say
	מבשׂר	piel	ptc	ms	בשׂר	142		bear tidings
18:27	יאמר	qal	wci	3ms	אמר	55		say
	צפה	qal	ptc	ms	צפה	859		keep watch
	ראה	qal	ptc	ms	ראה	906		see
	יאמר	qal	wci	3ms	אמר	55		say
	יבוא	qal	impf	3ms	בוא	97		come in
18:28	יקרא	qal	wci	3ms	קרא	894		call,proclaim
	יאמר	qal	wci	3ms	אמר	55		say
	ישתחו	hish	wci	3ms	חוה	1005		bow down
	יאמר	qal	wci	3ms	אמר	55		say
	ברוך	qal	pptc	ms	ברך	138		kneel,bless
	סגר	piel	pft	3ms	סגר	688		deliver
	נשׂאו	qal	pft	3cp	נשׂא	669		lift,carry
18:29	יאמר	qal	wci	3ms	אמר	55		say
	יאמר	qal	wci	3ms	אמר	55		say
	ראיתי	qal	pft	1cs	ראה	906		see
	שׁלח	qal	infc		שׁלח	1018		send
18:29	ידעתי	qal	pft	1cs	ידע	393		know
18:30	יאמר	qal	wci	3ms	אמר	55		say
	סב	qal	impv	ms	סבב	685		surround
	התיצב	hith	impv	ms	יצב	426		stand oneself
	יסב	qal	wci	3ms	סבב	685		surround
	יעמד	qal	wci	3ms	עמד	763		stand,stop
18:31	בא	qal	ptc	ms	בוא	97		come in
	יאמר	qal	wci	3ms	אמר	55		say
	יתבשׂר	hith	jusm	3ms	בשׂר	142		receive tidings
	שׁפטך	qal	pft	3ms	שׁפט	1047	2ms	judge
	קמים	qal	ptc	mp	קום	877		arise,stand
18:32	יאמר	qal	wci	3ms	אמר	55		say
	יאמר	qal	wci	3ms	אמר	55		say
	יהיו	qal	jusm	3mp	היה	224		be,become
	איבי	qal	ptc	mp	איב	33		be hostile to
	קמו	qal	pft	3cp	קום	877		arise,stand
19:1	ירגז	qal	wci	3ms	רגז	919		quake
	יעל	qal	wci	3ms	עלה	748		go up
	יבך	qal	wci	3ms	בכה	113		weep
	אמר	qal	pft	3ms	אמר	55		say
	לכתו	qal	infc		הלך	229	3ms	walk,go
	יתן	qal	impf	3ms	נתן	678		give,set
	מותי	qal	infc		מות	559	1cs	die
19:2	יגד	hoph	wci	3ms	נגד	616		be told
	בכה	qal	ptc	ms	בכה	113		weep
	יתאבל	hith	wci	3ms	אבל	5		mourn
19:3	תהי	qal	wci	3fs	היה	224		be,become
	שׁמע	qal	pft	3ms	שׁמע	1033		hear
	אמר	qal	infc		אמר	55		say
	נעצב	niph	pft	3ms	עצב	780		be pained
19:4	יתגנב	hith	wci	3ms	גנב	170		steal away
	בוא	qal	infc		בוא	97		come in
	יתגנב	hith	impf	3ms	גנב	170		steal away
	נכלמים	niph	ptc	mp	כלם	483		be humiliated
	נוסם	qal	infc		נוס	630	3mp	flee,escape
19:5	לאט	qal	pft	3ms	לאט	521		cover
	יזעק	qal	wci	3ms	זעק	277		call,cry out
19:6	יבא	qal	wci	3ms	בוא	97		come in
	יאמר	qal	wci	3ms	אמר	55		say
	הבשׁת	hiph	pft	2ms	בושׁ	101		put to shame
	ממלטים	piel	ptc	mp	מלט	572		deliver
19:7	אהבה	qal	infc		אהב	12		love
	שׂנאיך	qal	ptc	mp	שׂנא	971	2ms	hate
	שׂנא	qal	infc		שׂנא	971		hate
	אהביך	qal	ptc	mp	אהב	12	2ms	love
	הגדת	hiph	pft	2ms	נגד	616		declare,tell
	ידעתי	qal	pft	1cs	ידע	393		know
	מתים	qal	ptc	mp	מות	559		die
19:8	קום	qal	impv	ms	קום	877		arise,stand
	צא	qal	impv	ms	יצא	422		go out
	דבר	piel	impv	ms	דבר	180		speak
	נשׁבעתי	niph	pft	1cs	שׁבע	989		swear
	יוצא	qal	ptc	ms	יצא	422		go out
	ילין	qal	impf	3ms	לון	533		lodge,remain

ChVs	Form	Stem	Tnse	PGN	Root	BDB	Sfx	Meaning
19:8	באה	qal	pft	3fs	בוא	97		come in
19:9	יקם	qal	wci	3ms	קום	877		arise,stand
	ישב	qal	wci	3ms	ישב	442		sit,dwell
	הגידו	hiph	pft	3cp	נגד	616		declare,tell
	אמר	qal	infc		אמר	55		say
	יושב	qal	ptc	ms	ישב	442		sit,dwell
	יבא	qal	wci	3ms	בוא	97		come in
	נס	qal	pft	3ms	נוס	630		flee,escape
19:10	יהי	qal	wci	3ms	היה	224		be,become
	נדון	niph	ptc	ms	דין	192		be at strife
	אמר	qal	infc		אמר	55		say
	הצילנו	hiph	pft	3ms	נצל	664	1cp	snatch,deliver
	איבינו	qal	ptc	mp	איב	33	1cp	be hostile to
	מלטנו	piel	pft	3ms	מלט	572	1cp	deliver
	ברח	qal	pft	3ms	ברח	137		go thru,flee
19:11	משחנו	qal	pft	1cp	משח	602		smear,anoint
	מת	qal	pft	3ms	מות	559		die
	מחרשים	hiph	ptc	mp	חרש	361		be silent
	השיב	hiph	infc		שוב	996		bring back
19:12	שלח	qal	pft	3ms	שלח	1018		send
	אמר	qal	infc		אמר	55		say
	דברו	piel	impv	mp	דבר	180		speak
	אמר	qal	infc		אמר	55		say
	תהיו	qal	impf	2mp	היה	224		be,become
	השיב	hiph	infc		שוב	996		bring back
	בא	qal	pft	3ms	בוא	97		come in
19:13	תהיו	qal	impf	2mp	היה	224		be,become
	השיב	hiph	infc		שוב	996		bring back
19:14	תמרו	qal	impf	2mp	אמר	55		say
	יעשה	qal	jusm	3ms	עשה	793		do,make
	יוסיף	hiph	jusm	3ms	יסף	414		add,do again
	תהיה	qal	impf	2ms	היה	224		be,become
19:15	יט	hiph	wci	3ms	נטה	639		turn,incline
	ישלחו	qal	wci	3mp	שלח	1018		send
	שוב	qal	impv	ms	שוב	996		turn,return
19:16	ישב	qal	wci	3ms	שוב	996		turn,return
	יבא	qal	wci	3ms	בוא	97		come in
	בא	qal	pft	3ms	בוא	97		come in
	לכת	qal	infc		הלך	229		walk,go
	קראת	qal	infc		קרא	896		meet,encounter
	העביר	hiph	infc		עבר	716		cause to pass
19:17	ימהר	piel	wci	3ms	מהר	554		hasten
	ירד	qal	wci	3ms	ירד	432		come down
	קראת	qal	infc		קרא	896		meet,encounter
19:18	צלחו	qal	pft	3cp	צלח	852		rush
19:19	עברה	qal	pft	3fs	עבר	716		pass over
	עביר	hiph	infc		עבר	716		cause to pass
	עשות	qal	infc		עשה	793		do,make
	נפל	qal	pft	3ms	נפל	656		fall
	עברו	qal	infc		עבר	716	3ms	pass over
19:20	יאמר	qal	wci	3ms	אמר	55		say
	יחשב	qal	jus	3ms	חשב	362		think,devise
	תזכר	qal	jusm	2ms	זכר	269		remember
	העוה	hiph	pft	3ms	עוה	731		commit iniquity
19:20	יצא	qal	pft	3ms	יצא	422		go out
	שום	qal	infc		שים	962		put,set
19:21	ידע	qal	pft	3ms	ידע	393		know
	חטאתי	qal	pft	1cs	חטא	306		sin
	באתי	qal	pft	1cs	בוא	97		come in
	רדת	qal	infc		ירד	432		come down
	קראת	qal	infc		קרא	896		meet,encounter
19:22	יען	qal	wci	3ms	ענה	772		answer
	יאמר	qal	wci	3ms	אמר	55		say
	יומת	hoph	impf	3ms	מות	559		be killed
	קלל	piel	pft	3ms	קלל	886		curse
19:23	יאמר	qal	wci	3ms	אמר	55		say
	תהיו	qal	impf	2mp	היה	224		be,become
	יומת	hoph	impf	3ms	מות	559		be killed
	ידעתי	qal	pft	1cs	ידע	393		know
19:24	יאמר	qal	wci	3ms	אמר	55		say
	תמות	qal	impf	2ms	מות	559		die
	ישבע	niph	wci	3ms	שבע	989		swear
19:25	ירד	qal	pft	3ms	ירד	432		come down
	קראת	qal	infc		קרא	896		meet,encounter
	עשה	qal	pft	3ms	עשה	793		do,make
	עשה	qal	pft	3ms	עשה	793		do,make
	כבס	piel	pft	3ms	כבס	460		wash
	לכת	qal	infc		הלך	229		walk,go
	בא	qal	pft	3ms	בוא	97		come in
19:26	יהי	qal	wci	3ms	היה	224		be,become
	בא	qal	pft	3ms	בוא	97		come in
	קראת	qal	infc		קרא	896		meet,encounter
	יאמר	qal	wci	3ms	אמר	55		say
	הלכת	qal	pft	2ms	הלך	229		walk,go
19:27	יאמר	qal	wci	3ms	אמר	55		say
	רמני	piel	pft	3ms	רמה	941	1cs	beguile
	אמר	qal	pft	3ms	אמר	55		say
	אחבשה	qal	coh	1cs	חבש	289		bind
	ארכב	qal	cohm	1cs	רכב	938		mount,ride
	אלך	qal	cohm	1cs	הלך	229		walk,go
19:28	ירגל	piel	wci	3ms	רגל	920		slander,spy
	עשה	qal	impv	ms	עשה	793		do,make
19:29	היה	qal	pft	3ms	היה	224		be,become
	תשת	qal	wci	2ms	שית	1011		put,set
	אכלי	qal	ptc	mp	אכל	37		eat,devour
	זעק	qal	infc		זעק	277		call,cry out
19:30	יאמר	qal	wci	3ms	אמר	55		say
	תדבר	piel	impf	2ms	דבר	180		speak
	אמרתי	qal	pft	1cs	אמר	55		say
	תחלקו	qal	impf	2mp	חלק	323		divide,share
19:31	יאמר	qal	wci	3ms	אמר	55		say
	יקח	qal	jusm	3ms	לקח	542		take
	בא	qal	pft	3ms	בוא	97		come in
19:32	ירד	qal	pft	3ms	ירד	432		come down
	יעבר	qal	wci	3ms	עבר	716		pass over
	שלחו	piel	infc		שלח	1018	3ms	send away,shoot
19:33	זקן	qal	pft	3ms	זקן	278		be old
	כלכל	pilp	pft	3ms	כול	465		support

ChVs	Form	Stem	Tnse	PGN	Root	BDB	Sfx	Meaning
19:34	יאמר	qal	wci	3ms	אמר	55		say
	עבר	qal	impv	ms	עבר	716		pass over
	כלכלתי	pilp	wcp	1cs	כול	465		support
19:35	יאמר	qal	wci	3ms	אמר	55		say
	אעלה	qal	impf	1cs	עלה	748		go up
19:36	אדע	qal	impf	1cs	ידע	393		know
	יטעם	qal	impf	3ms	טעם	380		taste
	אכל	qal	impf	1cs	אכל	37		eat,devour
	אשתה	qal	impf	1cs	שתה	1059		drink
	אשמע	qal	impf	1cs	שמע	1033		hear
	שרים	qal	ptc	mp	שיר	1010		sing
	שרות	qal	ptc	fp	שיר	1010		sing
	יהיה	qal	impf	3ms	היה	224		be,become
19:37	יעבר	qal	impf	3ms	עבר	716		pass over
	יגמלני	qal	impf	3ms	גמל	168	1cs	deal out,ripen
19:38	ישב	qal	jus	3ms	שוב	996		turn,return
	אמת	qal	cohm	1cs	מות	559		die
	יעבר	qal	jusm	3ms	עבר	716		pass over
	עשה	qal	impv	ms	עשה	793		do,make
	טוב	qal	pft	3ms	טוב	373		be pleasing
19:39	יאמר	qal	wci	3ms	אמר	55		say
	יעבר	qal	impf	3ms	עבר	716		pass over
	אעשה	qal	impf	1cs	עשה	793		do,make
	תבחר	qal	impf	2ms	בחר	103		choose
	אעשה	qal	impf	1cs	עשה	793		do,make
19:40	יעבר	qal	wci	3ms	עבר	716		pass over
	עבר	qal	pft	3ms	עבר	716		pass over
	ישק	qal	wci	3ms	נשק	676		kiss
	יברכהו	piel	wci	3ms	ברך	138	3ms	bless
	ישב	qal	wci	3ms	שוב	996		turn,return
19:41	יעבר	qal	wci	3ms	עבר	716		pass over
	עבר	qal	pft	3ms	עבר	716		pass over
	יעברוk	hiph	wci	3mp	עבר	716		cause to pass
	העבירוq	hiph	pft	3cp	עבר	716		cause to pass
19:42	באים	qal	ptc	mp	בוא	97		come in
	יאמרו	qal	wci	3mp	אמר	55		say
	גנבוך	qal	pft	3cp	גנב	170	2ms	steal
	יעברו	hiph	wci	3mp	עבר	716		cause to pass
19:43	יען	qal	wci	3ms	ענה	772		answer
	חרה	qal	pft	3ms	חרה	354		be kindled,burn
	אכול	qal	infa		אכל	37		eat,devour
	אכלנו	qal	pft	1cp	אכל	37		eat,devour
	נשאת	niph	infa		נשא	669?		be lifted up
	נשא	piel	pft	3ms	נשא	669		lift up
19:44	יען	qal	wci	3ms	ענה	772		answer
	יאמר	qal	wci	3ms	אמר	55		say
	הקלתני	hiph	pft	2ms	קלל	886	1cs	make light
	היה	qal	pft	3ms	היה	224		be,become
	השיב	hiph	infc		שוב	996		bring back
	יקש	qal	wci	3ms	קשה	904		be hard,severe
20:1	נקרא	niph	pft	3ms	קרא	896		meet
	יתקע	qal	wci	3ms	תקע	1075		thrust,clap
	יאמר	qal	wci	3ms	אמר	55		say
20:2	יעל	qal	wci	3ms	עלה	748		go up
20:2	דבקו	qal	pft	3cp	דבק	179		cling,cleave
20:3	יבא	qal	wci	3ms	בוא	97		come in
	יקח	qal	wci	3ms	לקח	542		take
	הניח	hiph	pft	3ms	נוח	628		give rest,put
	שמר	qal	infc		שמר	1036		keep,watch
	יתנם	qal	wci	3ms	נתן	678	3mp	give,set
	יכלכלם	pilp	wci	3ms	כול	465	3mp	support
	בא	qal	pft	3ms	בוא	97		come in
	תהיינה	qal	wci	3fp	היה	224		be,become
	צררות	qal	pptc	fp	צרר	864		bind,be cramped
	מתן	qal	infc		מות	559	3fp	die
20:4	יאמר	qal	wci	3ms	אמר	55		say
	הזעק	hiph	impv	ms	זעק	277		call together
	עמד	qal	impv	ms	עמד	763		stand,stop
20:5	ילך	qal	wci	3ms	הלך	229		walk,go
	הזעיק	hiph	infc		זעק	277		call together
	ייחרk	piel	wci	3ms	אחר	29?		tarry,hinder
	יוחרq	hiph	wci	3ms	אחר	29		delay
	יעדו	qal	pft	3ms	יעד	416	3ms	appoint
20:6	יאמר	qal	wci	3ms	אמר	55		say
	ירע	qal	impf	3ms	רעע	949		be evil
	קח	qal	impv	ms	לקח	542		take
	רדף	qal	impv	ms	רדף	922		pursue
	מצא	qal	pft	3ms	מצא	592		find
	בצרות	qal	pptc	fp	בצר	130		cut off
	הציל	hiph	wcp	3ms	נצל	664		snatch,deliver
20:7	יצאו	qal	wci	3mp	יצא	422		go out
	יצאו	qal	wci	3mp	יצא	422		go out
	רדף	qal	infc		רדף	922		pursue
20:8	בא	qal	pft	3ms	בוא	97		come in
	חגור	qal	pptc	ms	חגר	291		gird
	מצמדת	pual	ptc	fs	צמד	855		be bound
	יצא	qal	pft	3ms	יצא	422		go out
	תפל	qal	wci	3fs	נפל	656		fall
20:9	יאמר	qal	wci	3ms	אמר	55		say
	תחז	qal	wci	3fs	אחז	28		grasp
	נשק	qal	infc		נשק	676		kiss
20:10	נשמר	niph	pft	3ms	שמר	1036		be kept,guarded
	יכהו	hiph	wci	3ms	נכה	645	3ms	smite
	ישפך	qal	wci	3ms	שפך	1049		pour out
	שנה	qal	pft	3ms	שנה	1040		do again,repeat
	ימת	qal	wci	3ms	מות	559		die
	רדף	qal	pft	3ms	רדף	922		pursue
20:11	עמד	qal	pft	3ms	עמד	763		stand,stop
	יאמר	qal	wci	3ms	אמר	55		say
	חפץ	qal	pft	3ms	חפץ	342		delight in
20:12	מתגלל	htpo	ptc	ms	גלל	164		roll oneself
	ירא	qal	wci	3ms	ראה	906		see
	עמד	qal	pft	3ms	עמד	763		stand,stop
	יסב	hiph	wci	3ms	סבב	685		cause to turn
	ישלך	hiph	wci	3ms	שלך	1020		throw,cast
	ראה	qal	pft	3ms	ראה	906		see
	בא	qal	ptc	ms	בוא	97		come in
	עמד	qal	pft	3ms	עמד	763		stand,stop

ChVs	Form	Stem	Tnse	PGN	Root	BDB	Sfx	Meaning
20:13	הנה	hiph	pft	3ms	יגה	387		remove
	עבר	qal	pft	3ms	עבר	716		pass over
	רדף	qal	infc		רדף	922		pursue
20:14	יעבר	qal	wci	3ms	עבר	716		pass over
	יקלהוk	niph	wci	3mp	קהל	874		assemble
	יקהלוq	niph	wci	3mp	קהל	874		assemble
	יבאו	qal	wci	3mp	בוא	97		come in
20:15	יבאו	qal	wci	3mp	בוא	97		come in
	יצרו	qal	wci	3mp	צור	848		confine,shut in
	ישפכו	qal	wci	3mp	שפך	1049		pour out
	תעמד	qal	wci	3fs	עמד	763		stand,stop
	משחיתם	hiph	ptc	mp	שחת	1007		spoil,ruin
	הפיל	hiph	infc		נפל	656		cause to fall
20:16	תקרא	qal	wci	3fs	קרא	894		call,proclaim
	שמעו	qal	impv	mp	שמע	1033		hear
	שמעו	qal	impv	mp	שמע	1033		hear
	אמרו	qal	impv	mp	אמר	55		say
	קרב	qal	impv	ms	קרב	897		approach
	אדברה	piel	coh	1cs	דבר	180		speak
20:17	יקרב	qal	wci	3ms	קרב	897		approach
	תאמר	qal	wci	3fs	אמר	55		say
	יאמר	qal	wci	3ms	אמר	55		say
	תאמר	qal	wci	3fs	אמר	55		say
	שמע	qal	impv	ms	שמע	1033		hear
	יאמר	qal	wci	3ms	אמר	55		say
	שמע	qal	ptc	ms	שמע	1033		hear
20:18	תאמר	qal	wci	3fs	אמר	55		say
	אמר	qal	infc		אמר	55		say
	דבר	piel	infa		דבר	180		speak
	ידברו	piel	impf	3mp	דבר	180		speak
	אמר	qal	infc		אמר	55		say
	שאל	qal	infa		שאל	981		ask,borrow
	ישאלו	piel	impf	3mp	שאל	981		inquire,beg
	התמו	hiph	pft	3cp	תמם	1070		finish
20:19	שלמי	qal	pptc	mp	שלם	1023		be at peace
	אמוני	qal	pptc	mp	אמן	52		nourish
	מבקש	piel	ptc	ms	בקש	134		seek
	המית	hiph	infc		מות	559		kill
	תבלע	piel	impf	2ms	בלע	118		swallow up
20:20	יען	qal	wci	3ms	ענה	772		answer
	יאמר	qal	wci	3ms	אמר	55		say
	אבלע	piel	impf	1cs	בלע	118		swallow up
	אשחית	hiph	impf	1cs	שחת	1007		spoil,ruin
20:21	נשא	qal	pft	3ms	נשא	669		lift,carry
	תנו	qal	impv	mp	נתן	678		give,set
	אלכה	qal	coh	1cs	הלך	229		walk,go
	תאמר	qal	wci	3fs	אמר	55		say
	משלך	hoph	ptc	ms	שלך	1020		be cast
20:22	תבוא	qal	wci	3fs	בוא	97		come in
	יכרתו	qal	wci	3mp	כרת	503		cut,destroy
	ישלכו	hiph	wci	3mp	שלך	1020		throw,cast
	יתקע	qal	wci	3ms	תקע	1075		thrust,clap
	יפצו	qal	wci	3mp	פוץ	806		be scattered
	שב	qal	pft	3ms	שוב	996		turn,return
20:24	מזכיר	hiph	ptc	ms	זכר	269		c. to remember
20:26	היה	qal	pft	3ms	היה	224		be,become
21:1	יהי	qal	wci	3ms	היה	224		be,become
	יבקש	piel	wci	3ms	בקש	134		seek
	יאמר	qal	wci	3ms	אמר	55		say
	המית	hiph	pft	3ms	מות	559		kill
21:2	יקרא	qal	wci	3ms	קרא	894		call,proclaim
	יאמר	qal	wci	3ms	אמר	55		say
	נשבעו	niph	pft	3cp	שבע	989		swear
	יבקש	piel	wci	3ms	בקש	134		seek
	הכתם	hiph	infc		נכה	645	3mp	smite
	קנאתו	piel	infc		קנא	888	3ms	be jealous
21:3	יאמר	qal	wci	3ms	אמר	55		say
	אעשה	qal	impf	1cs	עשה	793		do,make
	אכפר	piel	impf	1cs	כפר	497		cover,atone
	ברכו	piel	impv	mp	ברך	138		bless
21:4	יאמרו	qal	wci	3mp	אמר	55		say
	המית	hiph	infc		מות	559		kill
	יאמר	qal	wci	3ms	אמר	55		say
	אמרים	qal	ptc	mp	אמר	55		say
	אעשה	qal	impf	1cs	עשה	793		do,make
21:5	יאמרו	qal	wci	3mp	אמר	55		say
	כלנו	piel	pft	3ms	כלה	477	1cp	complete,finish
	דמה	piel	pft	3ms	דמה	197		liken,think
	נשמדנו	niph	pft	3ms	שמד	1029	1cp	be exterminated
	התיצב	hith	infc		יצב	426		stand oneself
21:6	ינתןk	niph	jusm	3ms	נתן	678		be given
	יתןq	qalp	jusm	3ms	נתן	678		be given
	הוקענום	hiph	wcp	1cp	יקע	429	3mp	hang
	יאמר	qal	wci	3ms	אמר	55		say
	אתן	qal	impf	1cs	נתן	678		give,set
21:7	יחמל	qal	wci	3ms	חמל	328		spare
21:8	יקח	qal	wci	3ms	לקח	542		take
	ילדה	qal	pft	3fs	ילד	408		bear,beget
	ילדה	qal	pft	3fs	ילד	408		bear,beget
21:9	יתנם	qal	wci	3ms	נתן	678	3mp	give,set
	יקיעם	hiph	wci	3mp	יקע	429	3mp	hang
	יפלו	qal	wci	3mp	נפל	656		fall
	המתו	hoph	pft	3cp	מות	559		be killed
21:10	תקח	qal	wci	3fs	לקח	542		take
	תטהו	hiph	wci	3fs	נטה	639	3ms	turn,incline
	נתך	niph	pft	3ms	נתך	677		be poured
	נתנה	qal	pft	3fs	נתן	678		give,set
	נוח	qal	infc		נוח	628		rest
21:11	יגד	hoph	wci	3ms	נגד	616		be told
	עשתה	qal	pft	3fs	עשה	793		do,make
21:12	ילך	qal	wci	3ms	הלך	229		walk,go
	יקח	qal	wci	3ms	לקח	542		take
	גנבו	qal	pft	3cp	גנב	170		steal
	תלוםk	qal	pft	3cp	תלה	1067	3mp	hang
	תלאוםq	qal	pft	3cp	תלא	1067	3mp	hang
	הכות	hiph	infc		נכה	645		smite
21:13	יעל	hiph	wci	3ms	עלה	748		bring up,offer
	יאספו	qal	wci	3mp	אסף	62		gather

ChVs	Form	Stem	Tnse	PGN	Root	BDB	Sfx	Meaning
21:13	מוקעים	hoph	ptc	mp	יקע	429		be hanged
21:14	יקברו	qal	wci	3mp	קבר	868		bury
	יעשׂו	qal	wci	3mp	עשׂה	793		do,make
	צוה	piel	pft	3ms	צוה	845		command
	יעתר	niph	wci	3ms	עתר	801		be supplicated
21:15	תהי	qal	wci	3fs	היה	224		be,become
	ירד	qal	wci	3ms	ירד	432		come down
	ילחמו	niph	wci	3mp	לחם	535		wage war
	יעף	qal	wci	3ms	עיף	746		be faint
21:16	חגור	qal	pptc	ms	חגר	291		gird
	יאמר	qal	wci	3ms	אמר	55		say
	הכות	hiph	infc		נכה	645		smite
21:17	יעזר	qal	wci	3ms	עזר	740		help,aid
	יך	hiph	wci	3ms	נכה	645		smite
	ימיתהו	hiph	wci	3ms	מות	559	3ms	kill
	נשׁבעו	niph	pft	3cp	שׁבע	989		swear
	אמר	qal	infc		אמר	55		say
	תצא	qal	impf	2ms	יצא	422		go out
	תכבה	piel	impf	2ms	כבה	459		extinguish
21:18	יהי	qal	wci	3ms	היה	224		be,become
	תהי	qal	wci	3fs	היה	224		be,become
	הכה	hiph	pft	3ms	נכה	645		smite
21:19	תהי	qal	wci	3fs	היה	224		be,become
	יך	hiph	wci	3ms	נכה	645		smite
	ארגים	qal	ptc	mp	ארג	70		weave
21:20	תהי	qal	wci	3fs	היה	224		be,become
	יהי	qal	wci	3ms	היה	224		be,become
	ילד	qalp	pft	3ms	ילד	408		be born
21:21	יחרף	piel	wci	3ms	חרף	357		reproach
	יכהו	hiph	wci	3ms	נכה	645	3ms	smite
21:22	ילדו	qalp	pft	3cp	ילד	408		be born
	יפלו	qal	wci	3mp	נפל	656		fall
22:1	ידבר	piel	wci	3ms	דבר	180		speak
	הציל	hiph	pft	3ms	נצל	664		snatch,deliver
	איביו	qal	ptc	mp	איב	33	3ms	be hostile to
22:2	יאמר	qal	wci	3ms	אמר	55		say
	מפלטי	piel	ptc	ms	פלט	812	1cs	deliver
22:3	אחסה	qal	impf	1cs	חסה	340		seek refuge
	משׁעי	hiph	ptc	ms	ישׁע	446	1cs	deliver,save
	תשׁעני	hiph	impf	2ms	ישׁע	446	1cs	deliver,save
22:4	מהלל	pual	ptc	ms	הלל	237		be praised
	אקרא	qal	impf	1cs	קרא	894		call,proclaim
	איבי	qal	ptc	mp	איב	33	1cs	be hostile to
	אושׁע	niph	impf	1cs	ישׁע	446		be saved
22:5	אפפני	qal	pft	3cp	אפף	67	1cs	encompass
	יבעתני	piel	impf	3mp	בעת	129	1cs	terrify
22:6	סבני	qal	pft	3cp	סבב	685	1cs	surround
	קדמני	piel	pft	3cp	קדם	869	1cs	meet,confront
22:7	אקרא	qal	impf	1cs	קרא	894		call,proclaim
	אקרא	qal	impf	1cs	קרא	894		call,proclaim
	ישׁמע	qal	wci	3ms	שׁמע	1033		hear
22:8	תגעשׁk	qal	wci	3fs	געשׁ	172		quake
	יתגעשׁq	hith	wci	3fs	געשׁ	172		toss to and fro
	תרעשׁ	qal	wci	3fs	רעשׁ	950		quake
22:8	ירגזו	qal	impf	3mp	רגז	919		quake
	יתגעשׁו	hith	wci	3mp	געשׁ	172		toss to and fro
	חרה	qal	pft	3ms	חרה	354		be kindled,burn
22:9	עלה	qal	pft	3ms	עלה	748		go up
	תאכל	qal	impf	3fs	אכל	37		eat,devour
	בערו	qal	pft	3cp	בער	128		burn
22:10	יט	qal	wci	3ms	נטה	639		stretch,incline
	ירד	qal	wci	3ms	ירד	432		come down
22:11	ירכב	qal	wci	3ms	רכב	938		mount,ride
	יעף	qal	wci	3ms	עוף	733		fly
	ירא	niph	wci	3ms	ראה	906		appear,be seen
22:12	ישׁת	qal	wci	3ms	שׁית	1011		put,set
22:13	בערו	qal	pft	3cp	בער	128		burn
22:14	ירעם	hiph	impf	3ms	רעם	947		thunder
	יתן	qal	impf	3ms	נתן	678		give,set
22:15	ישׁלח	qal	wci	3ms	שׁלח	1018		send
	יפיצם	hiph	wci	3ms	פוץ	806	3mp	scatter
	יהמםk	qal	wci	3ms	המם	243	3mp	confuse,vex
	יהםq	qal	wci	3ms	המם	243		confuse,vex
22:16	יראו	niph	wci	3mp	ראה	906		appear,be seen
	יגלו	niph	wci	3mp	גלה	162		uncover self
22:17	ישׁלח	qal	impf	3ms	שׁלח	1018		send
	יקחני	qal	impf	3ms	לקח	542	1cs	take
	ימשׁני	hiph	impf	3ms	משׁה	602	1cs	draw out,save
22:18	יצילני	hiph	impf	3ms	נצל	664	1cs	snatch,deliver
	איבי	qal	ptc	ms	איב	33	1cs	be hostile to
	שׂנאי	qal	ptc	mp	שׂנא	971	1cs	hate
	אמצו	qal	pft	3cp	אמץ	54		be strong
22:19	יקדמני	piel	impf	3mp	קדם	869	1cs	meet,confront
	יהי	qal	wci	3ms	היה	224		be,become
22:20	יצא	hiph	wci	3ms	יצא	422		bring out
	יחלצני	piel	impf	3ms	חלץ	322	1cs	deliver
	חפץ	qal	pft	3ms	חפץ	342		delight in
22:21	יגמלני	qal	impf	3ms	גמל	168	1cs	deal out,ripen
	ישׁיב	hiph	impf	3ms	שׁוב	996		bring back
22:22	שׁמרתי	qal	pft	1cs	שׁמר	1036		keep,watch
	רשׁעתי	qal	pft	1cs	רשׁע	957		be wicked
22:23	אסור	qal	impf	1cs	סור	693		turn aside
22:24	אהיה	qal	wci	1cs	היה	224		be,become
	אשׁתמרה	hith	wci	1cs	שׁמר	1036		keep oneself
22:25	ישׁב	hiph	wci	3ms	שׁוב	996		bring back
22:26	תתחסד	hith	impf	2ms	חסד	338		show self kind
	תתמם	hith	impf	2ms	תמם	1070		act honestly
22:27	נבר	niph	ptc	ms	ברר	140		purify oneself
	תתבר	hith	impf	2ms	ברר	140		purify oneself
	תתפל	hith	impf	2ms	פתל	836		deal perversely
22:28	תושׁיע	hiph	impf	2ms	ישׁע	446		deliver,save
	רמים	qal	ptc	mp	רום	926		be high
	תשׁפיל	hiph	impf	2ms	שׁפל	1050		make low,abase
22:29	יגיה	hiph	impf	3ms	נגה	618		cause to shine
22:30	ארוץ	qal	impf	1cs	רוץ	930		run
	אדלג	piel	impf	1cs	דלג	194		leap over
22:31	צרופה	qal	pptc	fs	צרף	864		refine,test
	חסים	qal	ptc	mp	חסה	340		seek refuge

ChVs	Form	Stem	Tnse	PGN	Root	BDB	Sfx	Meaning
22:33	יתר	hiph	wci	3ms	נתר	684		loosen,set free
22:34	משוה	piel	ptc	ms	שוה	1001		set,place
	יעמדני	hiph	impf	3ms	עמד	763	1cs	set up,raise
22:35	מלמד	piel	ptc	ms	למד	540		teach
	נחת	piel	wcp	3ms	נחת	639		press down
22:36	תתן	qal	wci	2ms	נתן	678		give,set
	תרבני	hiph	impf	2ms	רבה	915	1cs	make many
22:37	תרחיב	hiph	impf	2ms	רחב	931		enlarge
	מעדו	qal	pft	3cp	מעד	588		slip,waver
22:38	ארדפה	qal	coh	1cs	רדף	922		pursue
	איבי	qal	ptc	mp	איב	33	1cs	be hostile to
	אשמידם	hiph	wci	1cs	שמד	1029	3mp	exterminate
	אשוב	qal	impf	1cs	שוב	996		turn,return
	כלותם	piel	infc		כלה	477	3mp	complete,finish
22:39	אכלם	piel	wci	1cs	כלה	477	3mp	complete,finish
	אמחצם	qal	wci	1cs	מחץ	563	3mp	smite through
	יקומון	qal	impf	3mp	קום	877		arise,stand
	יפלו	qal	wci	3mp	נפל	656		fall
22:40	תזרני	piel	wci	2ms	אזר	25	1cs	gird
	תכריע	hiph	impf	2ms	כרע	502		cause to bow
	קמי	qal	ptc	mp	קום	877	1cs	arise,stand
22:41	איבי	qal	ptc	mp	איב	33	1cs	be hostile to
	תתה	qal	pft	2ms	נתן	678		give,set
	משנאי	piel	ptc	mp	שנא	971	1cs	hate
	אצמיתם	hiph	wci	1cs	צמת	856	3mp	annihilate
22:42	ישעו	qal	impf	3mp	שעה	1043		gaze,regard
	משיע	hiph	ptc	ms	ישע	446		deliver,save
	ענם	qal	pft	3ms	ענה	772	3mp	answer
22:43	אשחקם	qal	impf	1cs	שחק	1006	3mp	rub away
	אדקם	hiph	impf	1cs	דקק	200	3mp	pulverize
	ארקעם	qal	impf	1cs	רקע	955	3mp	stamp,beat
22:44	תפלטני	piel	wci	2ms	פלט	812	1cs	deliver
	תשמרני	qal	impf	2ms	שמר	1036	1cs	keep,watch
	ידעתי	qal	pft	1cs	ידע	393		know
	יעבדני	qal	impf	3mp	עבד	712	1cs	work,serve
22:45	יתכחשו	hith	impf	3mp	כחש	471		cringe
	שמוע	qal	infc		שמע	1033		hear
	ישמעו	niph	impf	3mp	שמע	1033		be heard
22:46	יבלו	qal	impf	3mp	נבל	615		sink,droop
	יחגרו	qal	impf	3mp	חגר	291		gird
22:47	ברוך	qal	pptc	ms	ברך	138		kneel,bless
	ירם	qal	jus	3ms	רום	926		be high
22:48	נתן	qal	ptc	ms	נתן	678		give,set
	מוריד	hiph	ptc	ms	ירד	432		bring down
22:49	מוציאי	hiph	ptc	ms	יצא	422	1cs	bring out
	איבי	qal	ptc	mp	איב	33	1cs	be hostile to
	קמי	qal	ptc	mp	קום	877	1cs	arise,stand
	תרוממני	pol	impf	2ms	רום	926	1cs	raise,rear
	תצילני	hiph	impf	2ms	נצל	664	1cs	snatch,deliver
22:50	אודך	hiph	impf	1cs	ידה	392	2ms	praise
	אזמר	piel	impf	1cs	זמר	274		make music
22:51	עשה	qal	ptc	ms	עשה	793		do,make
23:1	הקם	hoph	pft	3ms	קום	877		be raised up
23:2	דבר	piel	pft	3ms	דבר	180		speak
23:3	אמר	qal	pft	3ms	אמר	55		say
	דבר	piel	pft	3ms	דבר	180		speak
	מושל	qal	ptc	ms	משל	605		rule
	מושל	qal	ptc	ms	משל	605		rule
23:4	יזרח	qal	impf	3ms	זרח	280		rise,appear
23:5	שם	qal	pft	3ms	שים	962		put,set
	ערוכה	qal	pptc	fs	ערך	789		set in order
	שמרה	qal	pptc	fs	שמר	1036		keep,watch
	יצמיח	hiph	impf	3ms	צמח	855		cause to grow
23:6	מנד	hoph	ptc	ms	נדד	622		be chased away
	יקחו	niph	impf	3mp	לקח	542		be taken
23:7	יגע	qal	impf	3ms	נגע	619		touch,strike
	ימלא	niph	impf	3ms	מלא	569		be filled
	שרוף	qal	infa		שרף	976		burn
	ישרפו	niph	impf	3mp	שרף	976		be burned
23:9	חרפם	piel	infc		חרף	357	3mp	reproach
	נאספו	niph	pft	3cp	אסף	62		assemble
	יעלו	qal	wci	3mp	עלה	748		go up
23:10	קם	qal	pft	3ms	קום	877		arise,stand
	יך	hiph	wci	3ms	נכה	645		smite
	יגעה	qal	pft	3fs	יגע	388		toil,grow weary
	תדבק	qal	wci	3fs	דבק	179		cling,cleave
	יעש	qal	wci	3ms	עשה	793		do,make
	ישבו	qal	impf	3mp	שוב	996		turn,return
	פשט	piel	infc		פשט	832		strip
23:11	יאספו	niph	wci	3mp	אסף	62		assemble
	תהי	qal	wci	3fs	היה	224		be,become
	נס	qal	pft	3ms	נוס	630		flee,escape
23:12	יתיצב	hith	wci	3ms	יצב	426		stand oneself
	יצילה	hiph	wci	3ms	נצל	664	3fs	snatch,deliver
	יך	hiph	wci	3ms	נכה	645		smite
	יעש	qal	wci	3ms	עשה	793		do,make
23:13	ירדו	qal	wci	3mp	ירד	432		come down
	יבאו	qal	wci	3mp	בוא	97		come in
	חנה	qal	ptc	fs	חנה	333		decline,encamp
23:15	יתאוה	hith	wci	3ms	אוה	16		desire
	יאמר	qal	wci	3ms	אמר	55		say
	ישקני	hiph	impf	3ms	שקה	1052	1cs	give to drink
23:16	יבקעו	qal	wci	3mp	בקע	131		cleave,break
	ישאבו	qal	wci	3mp	שאב	980		draw (water)
	ישאו	qal	wci	3mp	נשא	669		lift,carry
	יבאו	hiph	wci	3mp	בוא	97		bring in
	אבה	qal	pft	3ms	אבה	2		be willing
	שתותם	qal	infc		שתה	1059	3mp	drink
	יסך	hiph	wci	3ms	נסך	650		pour out
23:17	יאמר	qal	wci	3ms	אמר	55		say
	עשתי	qal	infc		עשה	793	1cs	do,make
	הלכים	qal	ptc	mp	הלך	229		walk,go
	אבה	qal	pft	3ms	אבה	2		be willing
	שתותם	qal	infc		שתה	1059	3mp	drink
	עשו	qal	pft	3cp	עשה	793		do,make
23:18	עורר	pol	pft	3ms	עור	734		rouse,incite
23:19	נכבד	niph	ptc	ms	כבד	457		be honored
	יהי	qal	wci	3ms	היה	224		be,become

ChVs	Form	Stem	Tnse	PGN	Root	BDB	Sfx	Meaning
23:19	בא	qal	pft	3ms	בוא	97		come in
23:20	הכה	hiph	pft	3ms	נכה	645		smite
	ירד	qal	pft	3ms	ירד	432		come down
	הכה	hiph	pft	3ms	נכה	645		smite
23:21	הכה	hiph	pft	3ms	נכה	645		smite
	ירד	qal	wci	3ms	ירד	432		come down
	יגזל	qal	wci	3ms	גזל	159		tear away, rob
	יהרגהו	qal	wci	3ms	הרג	246	3ms	kill
23:22	עשׂה	qal	pft	3ms	עשׂה	793		do, make
23:23	נכבד	niph	ptc	ms	כבד	457		be honored
	בא	qal	pft	3ms	בוא	97		come in
	ישׂמהו	qal	wci	3ms	שׂים	962	3ms	put, set
23:37	נשׂאיk	qal	ptc	mp	נשׂא	669		lift, carry
	נשׂאq	qal	ptc	ms	נשׂא	669		lift, carry
24:1	יסף	hiph	wci	3ms	יסף	414		add, do again
	חרות	qal	infc		חרה	354		be kindled, burn
	יסת	hiph	wci	3ms	סות	694		incite, allure
	אמר	qal	infc		אמר	55		say
	לך	qal	impv	ms	הלך	229		walk, go
	מנה	qal	impv	ms	מנה	584		count, allot
24:2	יאמר	qal	wci	3ms	אמר	55		say
	שׁוט	qal	impv	ms	שׁוט	1001		go about
	פקדו	qal	impv	mp	פקד	823		attend to, visit
	ידעתי	qal	wcp	1cs	ידע	393		know
24:3	יאמר	qal	wci	3ms	אמר	55		say
	יוסף	hiph	jus	3ms	יסף	414		add, do again
	ראות	qal	ptc	fp	ראה	906		see
	חפץ	qal	pft	3ms	חפץ	342		delight in
24:4	יחזק	qal	wci	3ms	חזק	304		be strong
	יצא	qal	wci	3ms	יצא	422		go out
	פקד	qal	infc		פקד	823		attend to, visit
24:5	יעברו	qal	wci	3mp	עבר	716		pass over
	יחנו	qal	wci	3mp	חנה	333		decline, encamp
24:6	יבאו	qal	wci	3mp	בוא	97		come in
	יבאו	qal	wci	3mp	בוא	97		come in
24:7	יבאו	qal	wci	3mp	בוא	97		come in
	יצאו	qal	wci	3mp	יצא	422		go out
24:8	ישׁטו	qal	wci	3mp	שׁוט	1001		go about
	יבאו	qal	wci	3mp	בוא	97		come in
24:9	יתן	qal	wci	3ms	נתן	678		give, set
	תהי	qal	wci	3fs	היה	224		be, become
	שׁלף	qal	ptc	ms	שׁלף	1025		draw out, off
24:10	יך	hiph	wci	3ms	נכה	645		smite
	ספר	qal	pft	3ms	ספר	707		count
	יאמר	qal	wci	3ms	אמר	55		say
	חטאתי	qal	pft	1cs	חטא	306		sin
	עשׂיתי	qal	pft	1cs	עשׂה	793		do, make
	העבר	hiph	impv	ms	עבר	716		cause to pass
	נסכלתי	niph	pft	1cs	סכל	698		act foolishly
24:11	יקם	qal	wci	3ms	קום	877		arise, stand
	היה	qal	pft	3ms	היה	224		be, become
	אמר	qal	infc		אמר	55		say
24:12	הלוך	qal	infa		הלך	229		walk, go
	דברת	piel	wcp	2ms	דבר	180		speak
24:12	אמר	qal	pft	3ms	אמר	55		say
	נוטל	qal	ptc	ms	נטל	642		lift, bear
	בחר	qal	impv	ms	בחר	103		choose
	אעשׂה	qal	cohm	1cs	עשׂה	793		do, make
24:13	יבא	qal	wci	3ms	בוא	97		come in
	יגד	hiph	wci	3ms	נגד	616		declare, tell
	יאמר	qal	wci	3ms	אמר	55		say
	תבוא	qal	impf	3fs	בוא	97		come in
	נסך	qal	infc		נוס	630	2ms	flee, escape
	רדפך	qal	ptc	ms	רדף	922	2ms	pursue
	היות	qal	infc		היה	224		be, become
	דע	qal	impv	ms	ידע	393		know
	ראה	qal	impv	ms	ראה	906		see
	אשׁיב	hiph	impf	1cs	שׁוב	996		bring back
	שׁלחי	qal	ptc	ms	שׁלח	1018	1cs	send
24:14	יאמר	qal	wci	3ms	אמר	55		say
	נפלה	qal	coh	1cp	נפל	656		fall
	אפלה	qal	coh	1cs	נפל	656		fall
24:15	יתן	qal	wci	3ms	נתן	678		give, set
	ימת	qal	wci	3ms	מות	559		die
24:16	ישׁלח	qal	wci	3ms	שׁלח	1018		send
	שׁחתה	piel	infc		שׁחת	1007	3fs	spoil, ruin
	ינחם	niph	wci	3ms	נחם	636		be sorry
	יאמר	qal	wci	3ms	אמר	55		say
	משׁחית	hiph	ptc	ms	שׁחת	1007		spoil, ruin
	הרף	hiph	impv	ms	רפה	951		slacken, abandon
	היה	qal	pft	3ms	היה	224		be, become
24:17	יאמר	qal	wci	3ms	אמר	55		say
	ראתו	qal	infc		ראה	906	3ms	see
	מכה	hiph	ptc	ms	נכה	645		smite
	יאמר	qal	wci	3ms	אמר	55		say
	חטאתי	qal	pft	1cs	חטא	306		sin
	העויתי	hiph	pft	1cs	עוה	731		commit iniquity
	עשׂו	qal	pft	3cp	עשׂה	793		do, make
	תהי	qal	jus	3fs	היה	224		be, become
24:18	יבא	qal	wci	3ms	בוא	97		come in
	יאמר	qal	wci	3ms	אמר	55		say
	עלה	qal	impv	ms	עלה	748		go up
	הקם	hiph	impv	ms	קום	877		raise, build, set
24:19	יעל	qal	wci	3ms	עלה	748		go up
	צוה	piel	pft	3ms	צוה	845		command
24:20	ישׁקף	hiph	wci	3ms	שׁקף	1054		look down
	ירא	qal	wci	3ms	ראה	906		see
	עברים	qal	ptc	mp	עבר	716		pass over
	יצא	qal	wci	3ms	יצא	422		go out
	ישׁתחו	hish	wci	3ms	חוה	1005		bow down
24:21	יאמר	qal	wci	3ms	אמר	55		say
	בא	qal	pft	3ms	בוא	97		come in
	יאמר	qal	wci	3ms	אמר	55		say
	קנות	qal	infc		קנה	888		get, buy
	בנות	qal	infc		בנה	124		build
	תעצר	niph	impf	3fs	עצר	783		be restrained
24:22	יאמר	qal	wci	3ms	אמר	55		say
	יקח	qal	jusm	3ms	לקח	542		take

ChVs	Form	Stem	Tnse	PGN	Root	BDB	Sfx	Meaning
24:22	יעל	hiph	jus	3ms	עלה	748		bring up,offer
	ראה	qal	impv	ms	ראה	906		see
24:23	נתן	qal	pft	3ms	נתן	678		give,set
	יאמר	qal	wci	3ms	אמר	55		say
	ירצך	qal	jusm	3ms	רצה	953	2ms	be pleased
24:24	יאמר	qal	wci	3ms	אמר	55		say
	קנו	qal	infa		קנה	888		get,buy
	אקנה	qal	impf	1cs	קנה	888		get,buy
	אעלה	hiph	impf	1cs	עלה	748		bring up,offer
	יקן	qal	wci	3ms	קנה	888		get,buy
24:25	יבן	qal	wci	3ms	בנה	124		build
	יעל	hiph	wci	3ms	עלה	748		bring up,offer
	יעתר	niph	wci	3ms	עתר	801		be supplicated
	תעצר	niph	wci	3fs	עצר	783		be restrained

1 KINGS

ChVs	Form	Stem	Tnse	PGN	Root	BDB	Sfx	Meaning
1:1	זקן	qal	pft	3ms	זקן	278		be old
	בא	qal	pft	3ms	בוא	97		come in
	יכסהו	piel	wci	3mp	כסה	491	3ms	cover
	יחם	qal	impf	3ms	חמם	328		be warm
1:2	יאמרו	qal	wci	3mp	אמר	55		say
	יבקשו	piel	jusm	3mp	בקש	134		seek
	עמדה	qal	wcp	3fs	עמד	763		stand,stop
	תהי	qal	jus	3fs	היה	224		be,become
	סכנת	qal	ptc	fs	סכן	698		be of use
	שכבה	qal	wcp	3fs	שכב	1011		lie,lie down
	חם	qal	wcp	3ms	חמם	328		be warm
1:3	יבקשו	piel	wci	3mp	בקש	134		seek
	ימצאו	qal	wci	3mp	מצא	592		find
	יבאו	hiph	wci	3mp	בוא	97		bring in
1:4	תהי	qal	wci	3fs	היה	224		be,become
	סכנת	qal	ptc	fs	סכן	698		be of use
	תשרתהו	piel	wci	3fs	שרת	1058	3ms	minister,serve
	ידעה	qal	pft	3ms	ידע	393	3fs	know
1:5	מתנשא	hith	ptc	ms	נשא	669		lift self up
	אמר	qal	infc		אמר	55		say
	אמלך	qal	impf	1cs	מלך	573		be king,reign
	יעש	qal	wci	3ms	עשה	793		do,make
	רצים	qal	ptc	mp	רוץ	930		run
1:6	עצבו	qal	pft	3ms	עצב	780	3ms	hurt,pain
	אמר	qal	infc		אמר	55		say
	עשית	qal	pft	2ms	עשה	793		do,make
	ילדה	qal	pft	3fs	ילד	408		bear,beget
1:7	יהיו	qal	wci	3mp	היה	224		be,become
	יעזרו	qal	wci	3mp	עזר	740		help,aid
1:8	היו	qal	pft	3cp	היה	224		be,become
1:9	יזבח	qal	wci	3ms	זבח	256		slaughter
	יקרא	qal	wci	3ms	קרא	894		call,proclaim
1:10	קרא	qal	pft	3ms	קרא	894		call,proclaim
1:11	יאמר	qal	wci	3ms	אמר	55		say
	אמר	qal	infc		אמר	55		say
	שמעת	qal	pft	2fs	שמע	1033		hear
	מלך	qal	pft	3ms	מלך	573		be king,reign
	ידע	qal	pft	3ms	ידע	393		know
1:12	לכי	qal	impv	fs	הלך	229		walk,go
	איעצך	qal	cohm	1cs	יעץ	419	2fs	advise,counsel
	מלטי	piel	impv	fs	מלט	572		deliver
1:13	לכי	qal	impv	fs	הלך	229		walk,go
	באי	qal	impv	fs	בוא	97		come in
	אמרת	qal	wcp	2fs	אמר	55		say
	נשבעת	niph	pft	2ms	שבע	989		swear
	אמר	qal	infc		אמר	55		say
	ימלך	qal	impf	3ms	מלך	573		be king,reign
	ישב	qal	impf	3ms	ישב	442		sit,dwell
	מלך	qal	pft	3ms	מלך	573		be king,reign
1:14	מדברת	piel	ptc	fs	דבר	180		speak
	אבוא	qal	impf	1cs	בוא	97		come in
	מלאתי	piel	wcp	1cs	מלא	569		fill
1:15	תבא	qal	wci	3fs	בוא	97		come in
	זקן	qal	pft	3ms	זקן	278		be old
	משרת	piel	ptc	fs	שרת	1058		minister,serve
1:16	תקד	qal	wci	3fs	קדד	869		bow down
	תשתחו	hish	wci	3fs	חוה	1005		bow down
	יאמר	qal	wci	3ms	אמר	55		say
1:17	תאמר	qal	wci	3fs	אמר	55		say
	נשבעת	niph	pft	2ms	שבע	989		swear
	ימלך	qal	impf	3ms	מלך	573		be king,reign
	ישב	qal	impf	3ms	ישב	442		sit,dwell
1:18	מלך	qal	pft	3ms	מלך	573		be king,reign
	ידעת	qal	pft	2ms	ידע	393		know
1:19	יזבח	qal	wci	3ms	זבח	256		slaughter
	יקרא	qal	wci	3ms	קרא	894		call,proclaim
	קרא	qal	pft	3ms	קרא	894		call,proclaim
1:20	הגיד	hiph	infc		נגד	616		declare,tell
	ישב	qal	impf	3ms	ישב	442		sit,dwell
1:21	היה	qal	wcp	3ms	היה	224		be,become
	שכב	qal	infc		שכב	1011		lie,lie down
	הייתי	qal	wcp	1cs	היה	224		be,become
1:22	מדברת	piel	ptc	fs	דבר	180		speak
	בא	qal	pft	3ms	בוא	97		come in
1:23	יגידו	hiph	wci	3mp	נגד	616		declare,tell
	אמר	qal	infc		אמר	55		say
	יבא	qal	wci	3ms	בוא	97		come in
	ישתחו	hish	wci	3ms	חוה	1005		bow down
1:24	יאמר	qal	wci	3ms	אמר	55		say
	אמרת	qal	pft	2ms	אמר	55		say
	ימלך	qal	impf	3ms	מלך	573		be king,reign
	ישב	qal	impf	3ms	ישב	442		sit,dwell
1:25	ירד	qal	pft	3ms	ירד	432		come down
	יזבח	qal	wci	3ms	זבח	256		slaughter
	יקרא	qal	wci	3ms	קרא	894		call,proclaim
	אכלים	qal	ptc	mp	אכל	37		eat,devour
	שתים	qal	ptc	mp	שתה	1059		drink
	יאמרו	qal	wci	3mp	אמר	55		say
	יחי	qal	jus	3ms	חיה	310		live
1:26	קרא	qal	pft	3ms	קרא	894		call,proclaim
1:27	נהיה	niph	pft	3ms	היה	224		be done
	הודעת	hiph	pft	2ms	ידע	393		declare

ChVs	Form	Stem	Tnse	PGN	Root	BDB	Sfx	Meaning
1:27	ישב	qal	impf	3ms	ישב	442		sit,dwell
1:28	יען	qal	wci	3ms	ענה	772		answer
	יאמר	qal	wci	3ms	אמר	55		say
	קראו	qal	impv	mp	קרא	894		call,proclaim
	תבא	qal	wci	3fs	בוא	97		come in
	תעמד	qal	wci	3fs	עמד	763		stand,stop
1:29	ישבע	niph	wci	3ms	שבע	989		swear
	יאמר	qal	wci	3ms	אמר	55		say
	פדה	qal	pft	3ms	פדה	804		ransom
1:30	נשבעתי	niph	pft	1cs	שבע	989		swear
	אמר	qal	infc		אמר	55		say
	ימלך	qal	impf	3ms	מלך	573		be king,reign
	ישב	qal	impf	3ms	ישב	442		sit,dwell
	אעשה	qal	impf	1cs	עשה	793		do,make
1:31	תקד	qal	wci	3fs	קדד	869		bow down
	תשתחו	hish	wci	3fs	חוה	1005		bow down
	תאמר	qal	wci	3fs	אמר	55		say
	יחי	qal	jus	3ms	חיה	310		live
1:32	יאמר	qal	wci	3ms	אמר	55		say
	קראו	qal	impv	mp	קרא	894		call,proclaim
	יבאו	qal	wci	3mp	בוא	97		come in
1:33	יאמר	qal	wci	3ms	אמר	55		say
	קחו	qal	impv	mp	לקח	542		take
	הרכבתם	hiph	wcp	2mp	רכב	938		cause to ride
	הורדתם	hiph	wcp	2mp	ירד	432		bring down
1:34	משח	qal	wcp	3ms	משח	602		smear,anoint
	תקעתם	qal	wcp	2mp	תקע	1075		thrust,clap
	אמרתם	qal	wcp	2mp	אמר	55		say
	יחי	qal	jus	3ms	חיה	310		live
1:35	עליתם	qal	wcp	2mp	עלה	748		go up
	בא	qal	wcp	3ms	בוא	97		come in
	ישב	qal	wcp	3ms	ישב	442		sit,dwell
	ימלך	qal	impf	3ms	מלך	573		be king,reign
	צויתי	piel	pft	1cs	צוה	845		command
	היות	qal	infc		היה	224		be,become
1:36	יען	qal	wci	3ms	ענה	772		answer
	יאמר	qal	wci	3ms	אמר	55		say
	יאמר	qal	jusm	3ms	אמר	55		say
1:37	היה	qal	pft	3ms	היה	224		be,become
	יהיk	qal	jus	3ms	היה	224		be,become
	יהיהq	qal	impf	3ms	היה	224		be,become
	יגדל	piel	jusm	3ms	גדל	152		cause to grow
1:38	ירד	qal	wci	3ms	ירד	432		come down
	ירכבו	hiph	wci	3mp	רכב	938		cause to ride
	ילכו	hiph	wci	3mp	הלך	229		lead,bring
1:39	יקח	qal	wci	3ms	לקח	542		take
	ימשח	qal	wci	3ms	משח	602		smear,anoint
	יתקעו	qal	wci	3mp	תקע	1075		thrust,clap
	יאמרו	qal	wci	3mp	אמר	55		say
	יחי	qal	jus	3ms	חיה	310		live
1:40	יעלו	qal	wci	3mp	עלה	748		go up
	מחללים	piel	ptc	mp	חלל	320		play pipe
	תבקע	niph	wci	3fs	בקע	131		be cleft
1:41	ישמע	qal	wci	3ms	שמע	1033		hear
1:41	קראים	qal	pptc	mp	קרא	894		call,proclaim
	כלו	piel	pft	3cp	כלה	477		complete,finish
	אכל	qal	infc		אכל	37		eat,devour
	ישמע	qal	wci	3ms	שמע	1033		hear
	יאמר	qal	wci	3ms	אמר	55		say
	הומה	qal	ptc	fs	המה	242		growl,murmur
1:42	מדבר	piel	ptc	ms	דבר	180		speak
	בא	qal	pft	3ms	בוא	97		come in
	יאמר	qal	wci	3ms	אמר	55		say
	בא	qal	impv	ms	בוא	97		come in
	תבשר	piel	impf	2ms	בשר	142		bear tidings
1:43	יען	qal	wci	3ms	ענה	772		answer
	יאמר	qal	wci	3ms	אמר	55		say
	המליך	hiph	pft	3ms	מלך	573		cause to reign
1:44	ישלח	qal	wci	3ms	שלח	1018		send
	ירכבו	hiph	wci	3mp	רכב	938		cause to ride
1:45	ימשחו	qal	wci	3mp	משח	602		smear,anoint
	יעלו	qal	wci	3mp	עלה	748		go up
	תהם	niph	wci	3fs	הום	223		be agitated
	שמעתם	qal	pft	2mp	שמע	1033		hear
1:46	ישב	qal	pft	3ms	ישב	442		sit,dwell
1:47	באו	qal	pft	3cp	בוא	97		come in
	ברך	piel	infc		ברך	138		bless
	אמר	qal	infc		אמר	55		say
	ייטב	hiph	jus	3ms	יטב	405		do good
	יגדל	piel	jusm	3ms	גדל	152		cause to grow
	ישתחו	hish	wci	3ms	חוה	1005		bow down
1:48	אמר	qal	pft	3ms	אמר	55		say
	ברוך	qal	pptc	ms	ברך	138		kneel,bless
	נתן	qal	pft	3ms	נתן	678		give,set
	ישב	qal	ptc	ms	ישב	442		sit,dwell
	ראות	qal	ptc	fp	ראה	906		see
1:49	יחרדו	qal	wci	3mp	חרד	353		tremble
	יקמו	qal	wci	3mp	קום	877		arise,stand
	קראים	qal	pptc	mp	קרא	894		call,proclaim
	ילכו	qal	wci	3mp	הלך	229		walk,go
1:50	ירא	qal	pft	3ms	ירא	431		fear
	יקם	qal	wci	3ms	קום	877		arise,stand
	ילך	qal	wci	3ms	הלך	229		walk,go
	יחזק	hiph	wci	3ms	חזק	304		make firm,seize
1:51	יגד	hoph	wci	3ms	נגד	616		be told
	אמר	qal	infc		אמר	55		say
	ירא	qal	pft	3ms	ירא	431		fear
	אחז	qal	pft	3ms	אחז	28		grasp
	אמר	qal	infc		אמר	55		say
	ישבע	niph	jusm	3ms	שבע	989		swear
	ימית	hiph	impf	3ms	מות	559		kill
1:52	יאמר	qal	wci	3ms	אמר	55		say
	יהיה	qal	impf	3ms	היה	224		be,become
	יפל	qal	impf	3ms	נפל	656		fall
	תמצא	niph	impf	3fs	מצא	592		be found
	מת	qal	wcp	3ms	מות	559		die
1:53	ישלח	qal	wci	3ms	שלח	1018		send
	ירדהו	hiph	wci	3mp	ירד	432	3ms	bring down

ChVs	Form	Stem	Tnse	PGN	Root	BDB	Sfx	Meaning
1:53	יבא	qal	wci	3ms	בוא	97		come in
	ישתחו	hish	wci	3ms	חוה	1005		bow down
	יאמר	qal	wci	3ms	אמר	55		say
	לך	qal	impv	ms	הלך	229		walk,go
2:1	יקרבו	qal	wci	3mp	קרב	897		approach
	מות	qal	infc		מות	559		die
	יצו	piel	wci	3ms	צוה	845		command
	אמר	qal	infc		אמר	55		say
2:2	הלך	qal	ptc	ms	הלך	229		walk,go
	חזקת	qal	wcp	2ms	חזק	304		be strong
	היית	qal	wcp	2ms	היה	224		be,become
2:3	שׁמרת	qal	wcp	2ms	שׁמר	1036		keep,watch
	לכת	qal	infc		הלך	229		walk,go
	שׁמר	qal	infc		שׁמר	1036		keep,watch
	כתוב	qal	pptc	ms	כתב	507		write
	תשׂכיל	hiph	impf	2ms	שׂכל	968		look at,prosper
	תעשׂה	qal	impf	2ms	עשׂה	793		do,make
	תפנה	qal	impf	2ms	פנה	815		turn
2:4	יקים	hiph	impf	3ms	קום	877		raise,build,set
	דבר	piel	pft	3ms	דבר	180		speak
	אמר	qal	infc		אמר	55		say
	ישׁמרו	qal	impf	3mp	שׁמר	1036		keep,watch
	לכת	qal	infc		הלך	229		walk,go
	אמר	qal	infc		אמר	55		say
	יכרת	niph	impf	3ms	כרת	503		be cut off
2:5	ידעת	qal	pft	2ms	ידע	393		know
	עשׂה	qal	pft	3ms	עשׂה	793		do,make
	עשׂה	qal	pft	3ms	עשׂה	793		do,make
	יהרגם	qal	wci	3ms	הרג	246	3mp	kill
	ישׂם	qal	wci	3ms	שׂים	962		put,set
	יתן	qal	wci	3ms	נתן	678		give,set
2:6	עשׂית	qal	wcp	2ms	עשׂה	793		do,make
	תורד	hiph	jusf	2ms	ירד	432		bring down
2:7	תעשׂה	qal	impf	2ms	עשׂה	793		do,make
	היו	qal	wcp	3cp	היה	224		be,become
	אכלי	qal	ptc	mp	אכל	37		eat,devour
	קרבו	qal	pft	3cp	קרב	897		approach
	ברחי	qal	infc		ברח	137	1cs	go thru,flee
2:8	קללני	piel	pft	3ms	קלל	886	1cs	curse
	נמרצת	niph	ptc	fs	מרץ	599		be grievous
	לכתי	qal	infc		הלך	229	1cs	walk,go
	ירד	qal	pft	3ms	ירד	432		come down
	קראתי	qal	infc		קרא	896	1cs	meet,encounter
	אשׁבע	niph	wci	1cs	שׁבע	989		swear
	אמר	qal	infc		אמר	55		say
	אמיתך	hiph	impf	1cs	מות	559	2ms	kill
2:9	תנקהו	piel	jusm	2ms	נקה	667	3ms	acquit
	ידעת	qal	wcp	2ms	ידע	393		know
	תעשׂה	qal	impf	2ms	עשׂה	793		do,make
	הורדת	hiph	wcp	2ms	ירד	432		bring down
2:10	ישׁכב	qal	wci	3ms	שׁכב	1011		lie,lie down
	יקבר	niph	wci	3ms	קבר	868		be buried
2:11	מלך	qal	pft	3ms	מלך	573		be king,reign
	מלך	qal	pft	3ms	מלך	573		be king,reign
2:11	מלך	qal	pft	3ms	מלך	573		be king,reign
2:12	ישׁב	qal	pft	3ms	ישׁב	442		sit,dwell
	תכן	niph	wci	3fs	כון	465		be established
2:13	יבא	qal	wci	3ms	בוא	97		come in
	תאמר	qal	wci	3fs	אמר	55		say
	באך	qal	infc		בוא	97	2ms	come in
	יאמר	qal	wci	3ms	אמר	55		say
2:14	יאמר	qal	wci	3ms	אמר	55		say
	תאמר	qal	wci	3fs	אמר	55		say
	דבר	piel	impv	ms	דבר	180		speak
2:15	יאמר	qal	wci	3ms	אמר	55		say
	ידעת	qal	pft	2fs	ידע	393		know
	היתה	qal	pft	3fs	היה	224		be,become
	שׂמו	qal	pft	3cp	שׂים	962		put,set
	מלך	qal	infc		מלך	573		be king,reign
	תסב	qal	wci	3fs	סבב	685		surround
	תהי	qal	wci	3fs	היה	224		be,become
	היתה	qal	pft	3fs	היה	224		be,become
2:16	שׁאל	qal	ptc	ms	שׁאל	981		ask,borrow
	תשׁבי	hiph	jusm	2fs	שׁוב	996		bring back
	תאמר	qal	wci	3fs	אמר	55		say
	דבר	piel	impv	ms	דבר	180		speak
2:17	יאמר	qal	wci	3ms	אמר	55		say
	אמרי	qal	impv	fs	אמר	55		say
	ישׁיב	hiph	impf	3ms	שׁוב	996		bring back
	יתן	qal	jusm	3ms	נתן	678		give,set
2:18	תאמר	qal	wci	3fs	אמר	55		say
	אדבר	piel	impf	1cs	דבר	180		speak
2:19	תבא	qal	wci	3fs	בוא	97		come in
	דבר	piel	infc		דבר	180		speak
	יקם	qal	wci	3ms	קום	877		arise,stand
	קראתה	qal	infc		קרא	896	3fs	meet,encounter
	ישׁתחו	hish	wci	3ms	חוה	1005		bow down
	ישׁב	qal	wci	3ms	ישׁב	442		sit,dwell
	ישׂם	qal	wci	3ms	שׂים	962		put,set
	תשׁב	qal	wci	3fs	ישׁב	442		sit,dwell
2:20	תאמר	qal	wci	3fs	אמר	55		say
	שׁאלת	qal	ptc	fs	שׁאל	981		ask,borrow
	תשׁב	hiph	jus	2ms	שׁוב	996		bring back
	יאמר	qal	wci	3ms	אמר	55		say
	שׁאלי	qal	impv	fs	שׁאל	981		ask,borrow
	אשׁיב	hiph	impf	1cs	שׁוב	996		bring back
2:21	תאמר	qal	wci	3fs	אמר	55		say
	יתן	qalp	jusm	3ms	נתן	678		be given
2:22	יען	qal	wci	3ms	ענה	772		answer
	יאמר	qal	wci	3ms	אמר	55		say
	שׁאלת	qal	ptc	fs	שׁאל	981		ask,borrow
	שׁאלי	qal	impv	fs	שׁאל	981		ask,borrow
2:23	ישׁבע	niph	wci	3ms	שׁבע	989		swear
	אמר	qal	infc		אמר	55		say
	יעשׂה	qal	jusm	3ms	עשׂה	793		do,make
	יוסיף	hiph	jusm	3ms	יסף	414		add,do again
	דבר	piel	pft	3ms	דבר	180		speak
2:24	הכינני	hiph	pft	3ms	כון	465	1cs	fix,prepare

ChVs	Form	Stem	Tnse	PGN	Root	BDB	Sfx	Meaning
2:24	יושיביני	hiph	wci	3ms	ישב	442	1cs	cause to dwell
	יושיבניq	hiph	wci	3ms	ישב	442	1cs	cause to dwell
	עשה	qal	pft	3ms	עשה	793		do,make
	דבר	piel	pft	3ms	דבר	180		speak
	יומת	hoph	impf	3ms	מות	559		be killed
2:25	ישלח	qal	wci	3ms	שלח	1018		send
	יפגע	qal	wci	3ms	פגע	803		meet,encounter
	ימת	qal	wci	3ms	מות	559		die
2:26	אמר	qal	pft	3ms	אמר	55		say
	לך	qal	impv	ms	הלך	229		walk,go
	אמיתך	hiph	impf	1cs	מות	559	2ms	kill
	נשאת	qal	pft	2ms	נשא	669		lift,carry
	התענית	hith	pft	2ms	ענה	776		humble oneself
	התענה	hith	pft	3ms	ענה	776		humble oneself
2:27	יגרש	piel	wci	3ms	גרש	176		drive out
	היות	qal	infc		היה	224		be,become
	מלא	piel	infc		מלא	569		fill
	דבר	piel	pft	3ms	דבר	180		speak
2:28	באה	qal	pft	3fs	בוא	97		come in
	נטה	qal	pft	3ms	נטה	639		stretch,incline
	נטה	qal	pft	3ms	נטה	639		stretch,incline
	ינס	qal	wci	3ms	נוס	630		flee,escape
	יחזק	hiph	wci	3ms	חזק	304		make firm,seize
2:29	יגד	hoph	wci	3ms	נגד	616		be told
	נס	qal	pft	3ms	נוס	630		flee,escape
	ישלח	qal	wci	3ms	שלח	1018		send
	אמר	qal	infc		אמר	55		say
	לך	qal	impv	ms	הלך	229		walk,go
	פגע	qal	impv	ms	פגע	803		meet,encounter
2:30	יבא	qal	wci	3ms	בוא	97		come in
	יאמר	qal	wci	3ms	אמר	55		say
	אמר	qal	pft	3ms	אמר	55		say
	צא	qal	impv	ms	יצא	422		go out
	יאמר	qal	wci	3ms	אמר	55		say
	אמות	qal	impf	1cs	מות	559		die
	ישב	hiph	wci	3ms	שוב	996		bring back
	אמר	qal	infc		אמר	55		say
	דבר	piel	pft	3ms	דבר	180		speak
	ענני	qal	pft	3ms	ענה	772	1cs	answer
2:31	יאמר	qal	wci	3ms	אמר	55		say
	עשה	qal	impv	ms	עשה	793		do,make
	דבר	piel	pft	3ms	דבר	180		speak
	פגע	qal	impv	ms	פגע	803		meet,encounter
	קברתו	qal	wcp	2ms	קבר	868	3ms	bury
	הסירת	hiph	wcp	2ms	סור	693		take away
	שפך	qal	pft	3ms	שפך	1049		pour out
2:32	השיב	hiph	wcp	3ms	שוב	996		bring back
	פגע	qal	pft	3ms	פגע	803		meet,encounter
	יהרגם	qal	wci	3ms	הרג	246	3mp	kill
	ידע	qal	pft	3ms	ידע	393		know
2:33	שבו	qal	wcp	3cp	שוב	996		turn,return
	יהיה	qal	jusm	3ms	היה	224		be,become
2:34	יעל	qal	wci	3ms	עלה	748		go up
	יפגע	qal	wci	3ms	פגע	803		meet,encounter
2:34	ימתהו	hiph	wci	3ms	מות	559	3ms	kill
	יקבר	niph	wci	3ms	קבר	868		be buried
2:35	יתן	qal	wci	3ms	נתן	678		give,set
	נתן	qal	pft	3ms	נתן	678		give,set
2:36	ישלח	qal	wci	3ms	שלח	1018		send
	יקרא	qal	wci	3ms	קרא	894		call,proclaim
	יאמר	qal	wci	3ms	אמר	55		say
	בנה	qal	impv	ms	בנה	124		build
	ישבת	qal	wcp	2ms	ישב	442		sit,dwell
	תצא	qal	impf	2ms	יצא	422		go out
2:37	היה	qal	wcp	3ms	היה	224		be,become
	צאתך	qal	infc		יצא	422	2ms	go out
	עברת	qal	wcp	2ms	עבר	716		pass over
	ידע	qal	infa		ידע	393		know
	תדע	qal	impf	2ms	ידע	393		know
	מות	qal	infa		מות	559		die
	תמות	qal	impf	2ms	מות	559		die
	יהיה	qal	impf	3ms	היה	224		be,become
2:38	יאמר	qal	wci	3ms	אמר	55		say
	דבר	piel	pft	3ms	דבר	180		speak
	יעשה	qal	impf	3ms	עשה	793		do,make
	ישב	qal	wci	3ms	ישב	442		sit,dwell
2:39	יהי	qal	wci	3ms	היה	224		be,become
	יברחו	qal	wci	3mp	ברח	137		go thru,flee
	יגידו	hiph	wci	3mp	נגד	616		declare,tell
	אמר	qal	infc		אמר	55		say
2:40	יקם	qal	wci	3ms	קום	877		arise,stand
	יחבש	qal	wci	3ms	חבש	289		bind
	ילך	qal	wci	3ms	הלך	229		walk,go
	בקש	piel	infc		בקש	134		seek
	ילך	qal	wci	3ms	הלך	229		walk,go
	יבא	hiph	wci	3ms	בוא	97		bring in
2:41	יגד	hoph	wci	3ms	נגד	616		be told
	הלך	qal	pft	3ms	הלך	229		walk,go
	ישב	qal	wci	3ms	שוב	996		turn,return
2:42	ישלח	qal	wci	3ms	שלח	1018		send
	יקרא	qal	wci	3ms	קרא	894		call,proclaim
	יאמר	qal	wci	3ms	אמר	55		say
	השבעתיך	hiph	pft	1cs	שבע	989	2ms	cause to swear
	אעד	hiph	wci	1cs	עוד	729		testify,warn
	אמר	qal	infc		אמר	55		say
	צאתך	qal	infc		יצא	422	2ms	go out
	הלכת	qal	wcp	2ms	הלך	229		walk,go
	ידע	qal	infa		ידע	393		know
	תדע	qal	impf	2ms	ידע	393		know
	מות	qal	infa		מות	559		die
	תמות	qal	impf	2ms	מות	559		die
	תאמר	qal	wci	2ms	אמר	55		say
	שמעתי	qal	pft	1cs	שמע	1033		hear
2:43	שמרת	qal	pft	2ms	שמר	1036		keep,watch
	צויתי	piel	pft	1cs	צוה	845		command
2:44	יאמר	qal	wci	3ms	אמר	55		say
	ידעת	qal	pft	2ms	ידע	393		know
	ידע	qal	pft	3ms	ידע	393		know

ChVs	Form	Stem	Tnse	PGN	Root	BDB	Sfx	Meaning
2: 44	עשית	qal	pft	2ms	עשה	793		do, make
	השיב	hiph	wcp	3ms	שוב	996		bring back
2: 45	ברוך	qal	pptc	ms	ברך	138		kneel, bless
	יהיה	qal	impf	3ms	היה	224		be, become
	נכון	niph	ptc	ms	כון	465		be established
2: 46	יצו	piel	wci	3ms	צוה	845		command
	יצא	qal	wci	3ms	יצא	422		go out
	יפגע	qal	wci	3ms	פגע	803		meet, encounter
	ימת	qal	wci	3ms	מות	559		die
	נכונה	niph	pft	3fs	כון	465		be established
3: 1	יתחתן	hith	wci	3ms	חתן	368		be son-in-law
	יקח	qal	wci	3ms	לקח	542		take
	יביאה	hiph	wci	3ms	בוא	97	3fs	bring in
	כלתו	piel	infc		כלה	477	3ms	complete, finish
	בנות	qal	infc		בנה	124		build
3: 2	מזבחים	piel	ptc	mp	זבח	256		sacrifice
	נבנה	niph	pft	3ms	בנה	124		be built
3: 3	יאהב	qal	wci	3ms	אהב	12		love
	לכת	qal	infc		הלך	229		walk, go
	מזבח	piel	ptc	ms	זבח	256		sacrifice
	מקטיר	hiph	ptc	ms	קטר	882		make sacrifices
3: 4	ילך	qal	wci	3ms	הלך	229		walk, go
	זבח	qal	infc		זבח	256		slaughter
	יעלה	hiph	impf	3ms	עלה	748		bring up, offer
3: 5	נראה	niph	pft	3ms	ראה	906		appear, be seen
	יאמר	qal	wci	3ms	אמר	55		say
	שאל	qal	impv	ms	שאל	981		ask, borrow
	אתן	qal	impf	1cs	נתן	678		give, set
3: 6	יאמר	qal	wci	3ms	אמר	55		say
	עשית	qal	pft	2ms	עשה	793		do, make
	הלך	qal	pft	3ms	הלך	229		walk, go
	תשמר	qal	wci	2ms	שמר	1036		keep, watch
	תתן	qal	wci	2ms	נתן	678		give, set
	ישב	qal	ptc	ms	ישב	442		sit, dwell
3: 7	המלכת	hiph	pft	2ms	מלך	573		cause to reign
	אדע	qal	impf	1cs	ידע	393		know
	צאת	qal	infc		יצא	422		go out
	בא	qal	infc		בוא	97		come in
3: 8	בחרת	qal	pft	2ms	בחר	103		choose
	ימנה	niph	impf	3ms	מנה	584		be counted
	יספר	niph	impf	3ms	ספר	707		be counted
3: 9	נתת	qal	wcp	2ms	נתן	678		give, set
	שמע	qal	ptc	ms	שמע	1033		hear
	שפט	qal	infc		שפט	1047		judge
	הבין	hiph	infc		בין	106		understand
	יוכל	qal	impf	3ms	יכל	407		be able
	שפט	qal	infc		שפט	1047		judge
3: 10	ייטב	qal	wci	3ms	יטב	405		be good
	שאל	qal	pft	3ms	שאל	981		ask, borrow
3: 11	יאמר	qal	wci	3ms	אמר	55		say
	שאלת	qal	pft	2ms	שאל	981		ask, borrow
	שאלת	qal	pft	2ms	שאל	981		ask, borrow
	שאלת	qal	pft	2ms	שאל	981		ask, borrow
	שאלת	qal	pft	2ms	שאל	981		ask, borrow
3: 11	איביך	qal	ptc	mp	איב	33	2ms	be hostile to
	שאלת	qal	pft	2ms	שאל	981		ask, borrow
	הבין	hiph	infc		בין	106		understand
	שמע	qal	infc		שמע	1033		hear
3: 12	עשיתי	qal	pft	1cs	עשה	793		do, make
	נתתי	qal	pft	1cs	נתן	678		give, set
	נבון	niph	ptc	ms	בין	106		be discerning
	היה	qal	pft	3ms	היה	224		be, become
	יקום	qal	impf	3ms	קום	877		arise, stand
3: 13	שאלת	qal	pft	2ms	שאל	981		ask, borrow
	נתתי	qal	pft	1cs	נתן	678		give, set
	היה	qal	pft	3ms	היה	224		be, become
3: 14	תלך	qal	impf	2ms	הלך	229		walk, go
	שמר	qal	infc		שמר	1036		keep, watch
	הלך	qal	pft	3ms	הלך	229		walk, go
	הארכתי	hiph	wcp	1cs	ארך	73		prolong
3: 15	יקץ	qal	wci	3ms	יקץ	429		awake
	יבוא	qal	wci	3ms	בוא	97		come in
	יעמד	qal	wci	3ms	עמד	763		stand, stop
	יעל	hiph	wci	3ms	עלה	748		bring up, offer
	יעש	qal	wci	3ms	עשה	793		do, make
	יעש	qal	wci	3ms	עשה	793		do, make
3: 16	תבאנה	qal	impf	3fp	בוא	97		come in
	זנות	qal	ptc	fp	זנה	275		act a harlot
	תעמדנה	qal	wci	3fp	עמד	763		stand, stop
3: 17	תאמר	qal	wci	3fs	אמר	55		say
	ישבת	qal	ptc	fp	ישב	442		sit, dwell
	אלד	qal	wci	1cs	ילד	408		bear, beget
3: 18	יהי	qal	wci	3ms	היה	224		be, become
	לדתי	qal	infc		ילד	408	1cs	bear, beget
	תלד	qal	wci	3fs	ילד	408		bear, beget
	זר	qal	ptc	ms	זור	266		be stranger
3: 19	ימת	qal	wci	3ms	מות	559		die
	שכבה	qal	pft	3fs	שכב	1011		lie, lie down
3: 20	תקם	qal	wci	3fs	קום	877		arise, stand
	תקח	qal	wci	3fs	לקח	542		take
	תשכיבהו	hiph	wci	3fs	שכב	1011	3ms	lay
	מת	qal	ptc	ms	מות	559		die
	השכיבה	hiph	pft	3fs	שכב	1011		lay
3: 21	אקם	qal	wci	1cs	קום	877		arise, stand
	היניק	hiph	infc		ינק	413		nurse
	מת	qal	pft	3ms	מות	559		die
	אתבונן	htpo	wci	1cs	בין	106		understand
	היה	qal	pft	3ms	היה	224		be, become
	ילדתי	qal	pft	1cs	ילד	408		bear, beget
3: 22	תאמר	qal	wci	3fs	אמר	55		say
	מת	qal	ptc	ms	מות	559		die
	אמרת	qal	ptc	fs	אמר	55		say
	מת	qal	ptc	ms	מות	559		die
	תדברנה	piel	wci	3fp	דבר	180		speak
3: 23	יאמר	qal	wci	3ms	אמר	55		say
	אמרת	qal	ptc	fs	אמר	55		say
	מת	qal	ptc	ms	מות	559		die
	אמרת	qal	ptc	fs	אמר	55		say

ChVs	Form	Stem	Tnse	PGN	Root	BDB	Sfx	Meaning
3:23	מת	qal	ptc	ms	מות	559		die
3:24	יאמר	qal	wci	3ms	אמר	55		say
	קחו	qal	impv	mp	לקח	542		take
	יבאו	hiph	wci	3mp	בוא	97		bring in
3:25	יאמר	qal	wci	3ms	אמר	55		say
	גזרו	qal	impv	mp	גזר	160		divide
	תנו	qal	impv	mp	נתן	678		give,set
3:26	תאמר	qal	wci	3fs	אמר	55		say
	נכמרו	niph	pft	3cp	כמר	485		grow warm
	תאמר	qal	wci	3fs	אמר	55		say
	תנו	qal	impv	mp	נתן	678		give,set
	ילוד	qal	pptc	ms	ילד	408		bear,beget
	המת	hiph	infa		מות	559		kill
	תמיתהו	hiph	jusm	2mp	מות	559	3ms	kill
	אמרת	qal	ptc	fs	אמר	55		say
	יהיה	qal	impf	3ms	היה	224		be,become
	גזרו	qal	impv	mp	גזר	160		divide
3:27	יען	qal	wci	3ms	ענה	772		answer
	יאמר	qal	wci	3ms	אמר	55		say
	תנו	qal	impv	mp	נתן	678		give,set
	ילוד	qal	pptc	ms	ילד	408		bear,beget
	המת	hiph	infa		מות	559		kill
	תמיתהו	hiph	impf	2mp	מות	559	3ms	kill
3:28	ישמעו	qal	wci	3mp	שמע	1033		hear
	שפט	qal	pft	3ms	שפט	1047		judge
	יראו	qal	wci	3mp	ירא	431		fear
	ראו	qal	pft	3cp	ראה	906		see
	עשות	qal	infc		עשה	793		do,make
4:1	יהי	qal	wci	3ms	היה	224		be,become
4:3	מזכיר	hiph	ptc	ms	זכר	269		c. to remember
4:5	נצבים	niph	ptc	mp	נצב	662		stand
4:7	נצבים	niph	ptc	mp	נצב	662		stand
	כלכלו	pilp	wcp	3cp	כול	465		support
	יהיה	qal	impf	3ms	היה	224		be,become
	כלכל	pilp	infc		כול	465		support
4:11	היתה	qal	pft	3fs	היה	224		be,become
4:15	לקח	qal	pft	3ms	לקח	542		take
4:20	אכלים	qal	ptc	mp	אכל	37		eat,devour
	שתים	qal	ptc	mp	שתה	1059		drink
5:1	היה	qal	pft	3ms	היה	224		be,become
	מושל	qal	ptc	ms	משל	605		rule
	מגשים	hiph	ptc	mp	נגש	620		bring near
	עבדים	qal	ptc	mp	עבד	712		work,serve
5:2	יהי	qal	wci	3ms	היה	224		be,become
5:3	אבוסים	qal	pptc	mp	אבס	7		fatten
5:4	רדה	qal	ptc	ms	רדה	921		rule
	היה	qal	pft	3ms	היה	224		be,become
5:5	ישב	qal	wci	3ms	ישב	442		sit,dwell
5:6	יהי	qal	wci	3ms	היה	224		be,become
5:7	כלכלו	pilp	wcp	3cp	כול	465		support
	נצבים	niph	ptc	mp	נצב	662		stand
	יעדרו	piel	impf	3mp	עדר	727		leave lacking
5:8	יבאו	hiph	impf	3mp	בוא	97		bring in
	יהיה	qal	impf	3ms	היה	224		be,become
5:9	יתן	qal	wci	3ms	נתן	678		give,set
	הרבה	hiph	infa		רבה	915		make many
5:10	תרב	qal	wci	3fs	רבה	915		be many,great
5:11	יחכם	qal	wci	3ms	חכם	314		be wise
	יהי	qal	wci	3ms	היה	224		be,become
5:12	ידבר	piel	wci	3ms	דבר	180		speak
	יהי	qal	wci	3ms	היה	224		be,become
5:13	ידבר	piel	wci	3ms	דבר	180		speak
	יצא	qal	ptc	ms	יצא	422		go out
	ידבר	piel	wci	3ms	דבר	180		speak
5:14	יבאו	qal	wci	3mp	בוא	97		come in
	שמע	qal	infc		שמע	1033		hear
	שמעו	qal	pft	3cp	שמע	1033		hear
5:15	ישלח	qal	wci	3ms	שלח	1018		send
	שמע	qal	pft	3ms	שמע	1033		hear
	משחו	qal	pft	3cp	משח	602		smear,anoint
	אהב	qal	ptc	ms	אהב	12		love
	היה	qal	pft	3ms	היה	224		be,become
5:16	ישלח	qal	wci	3ms	שלח	1018		send
	אמר	qal	infc		אמר	55		say
5:17	ידעת	qal	pft	2ms	ידע	393		know
	יכל	qal	pft	3ms	יכל	407		be able
	בנות	qal	infc		בנה	124		build
	סבבהו	qal	pft	3cp	סבב	685	3ms	surround
	תת	qal	infc		נתן	678		give,set
5:18	הניח	hiph	pft	3ms	נוח	628		give rest,put
5:19	אמר	qal	ptc	ms	אמר	55		say
	בנות	qal	infc		בנה	124		build
	דבר	piel	pft	3ms	דבר	180		speak
	אמר	qal	infc		אמר	55		say
	אתן	qal	impf	1cs	נתן	678		give,set
	יבנה	qal	impf	3ms	בנה	124		build
5:20	צוה	piel	impv	ms	צוה	845		command
	יכרתו	qal	jusm	3mp	כרת	503		cut,destroy
	יהיו	qal	impf	3mp	היה	224		be,become
	אתן	qal	impf	1cs	נתן	678		give,set
	תאמר	qal	impf	2ms	אמר	55		say
	ידעת	qal	pft	2ms	ידע	393		know
	ידע	qal	ptc	ms	ידע	393		know
	כרת	qal	infc		כרת	503		cut,destroy
5:21	יהי	qal	wci	3ms	היה	224		be,become
	שמע	qal	infc		שמע	1033		hear
	ישמח	qal	wci	3ms	שמח	970		rejoice
	יאמר	qal	wci	3ms	אמר	55		say
	ברוך	qal	pptc	ms	ברך	138		kneel,bless
	נתן	qal	pft	3ms	נתן	678		give,set
5:22	ישלח	qal	wci	3ms	שלח	1018		send
	אמר	qal	infc		אמר	55		say
	שמעתי	qal	pft	1cs	שמע	1033		hear
	שלחת	qal	pft	2ms	שלח	1018		send
	אעשה	qal	impf	1cs	עשה	793		do,make
5:23	ירדו	hiph	impf	3mp	ירד	432		bring down
	אשימם	qal	impf	1cs	שים	962	3mp	put,set
	תשלח	qal	impf	2ms	שלח	1018		send

ChVs	Form	Stem	Tnse	PGN	Root	BDB	Sfx	Meaning
5:23	נפצתים	piel	wcp	1cs	נפץ	658	3mp	dash to pieces
	תשׂא	qal	impf	2ms	נשׂא	669		lift,carry
	תעשׂה	qal	impf	2ms	עשׂה	793		do,make
	תת	qal	infc		נתן	678		give,set
5:24	יהי	qal	wci	3ms	היה	224		be,become
	נתן	qal	ptc	ms	נתן	678		give,set
5:25	נתן	qal	pft	3ms	נתן	678		give,set
	יתן	qal	impf	3ms	נתן	678		give,set
5:26	נתן	qal	pft	3ms	נתן	678		give,set
	דבר	piel	pft	3ms	דבר	180		speak
	יהי	qal	wci	3ms	היה	224		be,become
	יכרתו	qal	wci	3mp	כרת	503		cut,destroy
5:27	יעל	hiph	wci	3ms	עלה	748		bring up,offer
	יהי	qal	wci	3ms	היה	224		be,become
5:28	ישׁלחם	qal	wci	3ms	שׁלח	1018	3mp	send
	יהיו	qal	impf	3mp	היה	224		be,become
5:29	יהי	qal	wci	3ms	היה	224		be,become
	נשׂא	qal	ptc	ms	נשׂא	669		lift,carry
	חצב	qal	ptc	ms	חצב	345		hew out,dig
5:30	נצבים	niph	ptc	mp	נצב	662		stand
	רדים	qal	ptc	mp	רדה	921		rule
	עשׂים	qal	ptc	mp	עשׂה	793		do,make
5:31	יצו	piel	wci	3ms	צוה	845		command
	יסעו	hiph	wci	3mp	נסע	652		lead out,remove
	יסד	piel	infc		יסד	413		found,establish
5:32	יפסלו	qal	wci	3mp	פסל	820		hew out
	בני	qal	ptc	mp	בנה	124		build
	בני	qal	ptc	mp	בנה	124		build
	יכינו	hiph	wci	3mp	כון	465		fix,prepare
	בנות	qal	infc		בנה	124		build
6:1	יהי	qal	wci	3ms	היה	224		be,become
	צאת	qal	infc		יצא	422		go out
	מלך	qal	infc		מלך	573		be king,reign
	יבן	qal	wci	3ms	בנה	124		build
6:2	בנה	qal	pft	3ms	בנה	124		build
6:4	יעשׂ	qal	wci	3ms	עשׂה	793		do,make
	אטמים	qal	pptc	mp	אטם	31		shut
6:5	יבן	qal	wci	3ms	בנה	124		build
	יעשׂ	qal	wci	3ms	עשׂה	793		do,make
6:6	נתן	qal	pft	3ms	נתן	678		give,set
	אחז	qal	infc		אחז	28		grasp
6:7	הבנתו	niph	infc		בנה	124	3ms	be built
	נבנה	niph	pft	3ms	בנה	124		be built
	נשמע	niph	pft	3ms	שׁמע	1033		be heard
	הבנתו	niph	infc		בנה	124	3ms	be built
6:8	יעלו	qal	impf	3mp	עלה	748		go up
6:9	יבן	qal	wci	3ms	בנה	124		build
	יכלהו	piel	wci	3ms	כלה	477	3ms	complete,finish
	יספן	qal	wci	3ms	ספן	706		cover,panel
6:10	יבן	qal	wci	3ms	בנה	124		build
	יאחז	qal	wci	3ms	אחז	28		grasp
6:11	יהי	qal	wci	3ms	היה	224		be,become
	אמר	qal	infc		אמר	55		say
6:12	בנה	qal	ptc	ms	בנה	124		build
6:12	תלך	qal	impf	2ms	הלך	229		walk,go
	תעשׂה	qal	impf	2ms	עשׂה	793		do,make
	שׁמרת	qal	wcp	2ms	שׁמר	1036		keep,watch
	לכת	qal	infc		הלך	229		walk,go
	הקמתי	hiph	wcp	1cs	קום	877		raise,build,set
	דברתי	piel	pft	1cs	דבר	180		speak
6:13	שׁכנתי	qal	wcp	1cs	שׁכן	1014		settle,dwell
	אעזב	qal	impf	1cs	עזב	736		leave,loose
6:14	יבן	qal	wci	3ms	בנה	124		build
	יכלהו	piel	wci	3ms	כלה	477	3ms	complete,finish
6:15	יבן	qal	wci	3ms	בנה	124		build
	צפה	piel	pft	3ms	צפה	860		overlay
	יצף	piel	wci	3ms	צפה	860		overlay
6:16	יבן	qal	wci	3ms	בנה	124		build
	יבן	qal	wci	3ms	בנה	124		build
6:17	היה	qal	pft	3ms	היה	224		be,become
6:18	פטורי	qal	pptc	mp	פטר	809		remove,set free
	נראה	niph	ptc	fs	ראה	906		appear,be seen
6:19	הכין	hiph	pft	3ms	כון	465		fix,prepare
	תתן	qal	infc		נתן	678?		give,set
6:20	יצפהו	piel	wci	3ms	צפה	860	3ms	overlay
	סגור	qal	pptc	ms	סגר	688		shut
	יצף	piel	wci	3ms	צפה	860		overlay
6:21	יצף	piel	wci	3ms	צפה	860		overlay
	סגור	qal	pptc	ms	סגר	688		shut
	יעבר	piel	wci	3ms	עבר	716		spread over
	יצפהו	piel	wci	3ms	צפה	860	3ms	overlay
6:22	צפה	piel	pft	3ms	צפה	860		overlay
	תם	qal	infc		תמם	1070		be finished
	צפה	piel	pft	3ms	צפה	860		overlay
6:23	יעשׂ	qal	wci	3ms	עשׂה	793		do,make
6:27	יתן	qal	wci	3ms	נתן	678		give,set
	יפרשׂו	qal	wci	3mp	פרשׂ	831		spread out
	תגע	qal	wci	3fs	נגע	619		touch,strike
	נגעת	qal	ptc	fs	נגע	619		touch,strike
	נגעת	qal	ptc	fp	נגע	619		touch,strike
6:28	יצף	piel	wci	3ms	צפה	860		overlay
6:29	קלע	qal	pft	3ms	קלע	887		carve
	פטורי	qal	pptc	mp	פטר	809		remove,set free
6:30	צפה	piel	pft	3ms	צפה	860		overlay
6:31	עשׂה	qal	pft	3ms	עשׂה	793		do,make
6:32	קלע	qal	pft	3ms	קלע	887		carve
	פטורי	qal	pptc	mp	פטר	809		remove,set free
	צפה	piel	pft	3ms	צפה	860		overlay
	ירד	hiph	wci	3ms	רדד	921		beat out
6:33	עשׂה	qal	pft	3ms	עשׂה	793		do,make
6:35	קלע	qal	pft	3ms	קלע	887		carve
	פטרי	qal	pptc	mp	פטר	809		remove,set free
	צפה	piel	pft	3ms	צפה	860		overlay
	מישׁר	pual	ptc	ms	ישׁר	448		be made even
6:36	יבן	qal	wci	3ms	בנה	124		build
	כרתת	qal	pptc	fp	כרת	503		cut,destroy
6:37	יסד	pual	pft	3ms	יסד	413		be founded
6:38	כלה	qal	pft	3ms	כלה	477		finished,spent

ChVs	Form	Stem	Tnse	PGN	Root	BDB	Sfx	Meaning
6:38	יבנהו	qal	wci	3ms	בנה	124	3ms	build
7:1	בנה	qal	pft	3ms	בנה	124		build
	יכל	piel	wci	3ms	כלה	477		complete,finish
7:2	יבן	qal	wci	3ms	בנה	124		build
	כרתות	qal	pptc	fp	כרת	503		cut,destroy
7:3	ספן	qal	pptc	ms	ספן	706		cover,panel
7:5	רבעים	qal	pptc	mp	רבע	917		be square
7:6	עשׂה	qal	pft	3ms	עשׂה	793		do,make
7:7	ישׁפט	qal	impf	3ms	שׁפט	1047		judge
	עשׂה	qal	pft	3ms	עשׂה	793		do,make
	ספון	qal	pptc	ms	ספן	706		cover,panel
7:8	ישׁב	qal	impf	3ms	ישׁב	442		sit,dwell
	היה	qal	pft	3ms	היה	224		be,become
	יעשׂה	qal	impf	3ms	עשׂה	793		do,make
	לקח	qal	pft	3ms	לקח	542		take
7:9	מגררות	poal	ptc	fp	גרר	176		be sawed
7:10	מיסד	pual	ptc	ms	יסד	413		be founded
7:12	כרתת	qal	pptc	fp	כרת	503		cut,destroy
7:13	ישׁלח	qal	wci	3ms	שׁלח	1018		send
	יקח	qal	wci	3ms	לקח	542		take
7:14	חרשׁ	qal	ptc	ms	חרשׁ	360		engrave,plough
	ימלא	niph	wci	3ms	מלא	569		be filled
	עשׂות	qal	infc		עשׂה	793		do,make
	יבוא	qal	wci	3ms	בוא	97		come in
	יעשׂ	qal	wci	3ms	עשׂה	793		do,make
7:15	יצר	qal	wci	3ms	צור	849		fashion
	יסב	qal	impf	3ms	סבב	685		surround
7:16	עשׂה	qal	pft	3ms	עשׂה	793		do,make
	תת	qal	infc		נתן	678		give,set
	מצק	hoph	ptc	ms	יצק	427		be poured,firm
7:18	יעשׂ	qal	wci	3ms	עשׂה	793		do,make
	כסות	piel	infc		כסה	491		cover
	עשׂה	qal	pft	3ms	עשׂה	793		do,make
7:21	יקם	hiph	wci	3ms	קום	877		raise,build,set
	יקם	hiph	wci	3ms	קום	877		raise,build,set
	יקרא	qal	wci	3ms	קרא	894		call,proclaim
	יקם	hiph	wci	3ms	קום	877		raise,build,set
	יקרא	qal	wci	3ms	קרא	894		call,proclaim
7:22	תתם	qal	wci	3fs	תמם	1070		be finished
7:23	יעשׂ	qal	wci	3ms	עשׂה	793		do,make
	מוצק	hoph	ptc	ms	יצק	427		be poured,firm
	יסב	qal	impf	3ms	סבב	685		surround
7:24	סבבים	qal	ptc	mp	סבב	685		surround
	מקפים	hiph	ptc	mp	נקף	668		surround
	יצקים	qal	pptc	mp	יצק	427		pour out,cast
7:25	עמד	qal	ptc	ms	עמד	763		stand,stop
	פנים	qal	ptc	mp	פנה	815		turn
	פנים	qal	ptc	mp	פנה	815		turn
	פנים	qal	ptc	mp	פנה	815		turn
	פנים	qal	ptc	mp	פנה	815		turn
7:26	יכיל	hiph	impf	3ms	כול	465		contain
7:27	יעשׂ	qal	wci	3ms	עשׂה	793		do,make
7:30	יצקות	qal	pptc	fp	יצק	427		pour out,cast
7:31	מרבעות	pual	ptc	fp	רבע	917		be square
7:33	מוצק	hoph	ptc	ms	יצק	427		be poured,firm
7:36	יפתח	piel	wci	3ms	פתח	836		engrave
7:37	עשׂה	qal	pft	3ms	עשׂה	793		do,make
7:38	יעשׂ	qal	wci	3ms	עשׂה	793		do,make
	יכיל	hiph	impf	3ms	כול	465		contain
7:39	יתן	qal	wci	3ms	נתן	678		give,set
	נתן	qal	pft	3ms	נתן	678		give,set
7:40	יעשׂ	qal	wci	3ms	עשׂה	793		do,make
	יכל	piel	wci	3ms	כלה	477		complete,finish
	עשׂות	qal	infc		עשׂה	793		do,make
	עשׂה	qal	pft	3ms	עשׂה	793		do,make
7:41	כסות	piel	infc		כסה	491		cover
7:42	כסות	piel	infc		כסה	491		cover
7:45	עשׂה	qal	pft	3ms	עשׂה	793		do,make
	ממרט	pual	ptc	ms	מרט	598		smooth,polished
7:46	יצקם	qal	pft	3ms	יצק	427	3ms	pour out,cast
7:47	ינח	hiph	wci	3ms	נוח	628		give rest,put
	נחקר	niph	pft	3ms	חקר	350		be searched out
7:48	יעשׂ	qal	wci	3ms	עשׂה	793		do,make
7:49	סגור	qal	pptc	ms	סגר	688		shut
7:50	סגור	qal	pptc	ms	סגר	688		shut
7:51	תשׁלם	qal	wci	3fs	שׁלם	1022		be complete
	עשׂה	qal	pft	3ms	עשׂה	793		do,make
	יבא	hiph	wci	3ms	בוא	97		bring in
	נתן	qal	pft	3ms	נתן	678		give,set
8:1	יקהל	hiph	jusf	3ms	קהל	874		call assembly
	העלות	hiph	infc		עלה	748		bring up,offer
8:2	יקהלו	niph	wci	3mp	קהל	874		assemble
8:3	יבאו	qal	wci	3mp	בוא	97		come in
	ישׂאו	qal	wci	3mp	נשׂא	669		lift,carry
8:4	יעלו	hiph	wci	3mp	עלה	748		bring up,offer
	יעלו	hiph	wci	3mp	עלה	748		bring up,offer
8:5	נועדים	niph	ptc	mp	יעד	416		gather
	מזבחים	piel	ptc	mp	זבח	256		sacrifice
	יספרו	niph	impf	3mp	ספר	707		be counted
	ימנו	niph	impf	3mp	מנה	584		be counted
8:6	יבאו	hiph	wci	3mp	בוא	97		bring in
8:7	פרשׂים	qal	ptc	mp	פרשׂ	831		spread out
	יסכו	qal	wci	3mp	סכך	696		cover
8:8	יארכו	hiph	wci	3mp	ארך	73		prolong
	יראו	niph	wci	3mp	ראה	906		appear,be seen
	יראו	niph	impf	3mp	ראה	906		appear,be seen
	יהיו	qal	wci	3mp	היה	224		be,become
8:9	הנח	hiph	pft	3ms	נוח	628		give rest,put
	כרת	qal	pft	3ms	כרת	503		cut,destroy
	צאתם	qal	infc		יצא	422	3mp	go out
8:10	יהי	qal	wci	3ms	היה	224		be,become
	צאת	qal	infc		יצא	422		go out
	מלא	qal	pft	3ms	מלא	569		be full,fill
8:11	יכלו	qal	pft	3cp	יכל	407		be able
	עמד	qal	infc		עמד	763		stand,stop
	שׁרת	piel	infc		שׁרת	1058		minister,serve
	מלא	qal	pft	3ms	מלא	569		be full,fill
8:12	אמר	qal	pft	3ms	אמר	55		say

ChVs	Form	Stem	Tnse	PGN	Root	BDB	Sfx	Meaning
8:12	אמר	qal	pft	3ms	אמר	55		say
	שכן	qal	infc		שכן	1014		settle,dwell
8:13	בנה	qal	infa		בנה	124		build
	בניתי	qal	pft	1cs	בנה	124		build
	שבתך	qal	infc		ישב	442	2ms	sit,dwell
8:14	יסב	hiph	wci	3ms	סבב	685		cause to turn
	יברך	piel	wci	3ms	ברך	138		bless
	עמד	qal	ptc	ms	עמד	763		stand,stop
8:15	יאמר	qal	wci	3ms	אמר	55		say
	ברוך	qal	pptc	ms	ברך	138		kneel,bless
	דבר	piel	pft	3ms	דבר	180		speak
	מלא	piel	pft	3ms	מלא	569		fill
	אמר	qal	infc		אמר	55		say
8:16	הוצאתי	hiph	pft	1cs	יצא	422		bring out
	בחרתי	qal	pft	1cs	בחר	103		choose
	בנות	qal	infc		בנה	124		build
	היות	qal	infc		היה	224		be,become
	אבחר	qal	wci	1cs	בחר	103		choose
	היות	qal	infc		היה	224		be,become
8:17	יהי	qal	wci	3ms	היה	224		be,become
	בנות	qal	infc		בנה	124		build
8:18	יאמר	qal	wci	3ms	אמר	55		say
	היה	qal	pft	3ms	היה	224		be,become
	בנות	qal	infc		בנה	124		build
	הטיבת	hiph	pft	2ms	טוב	373		do well
	היה	qal	pft	3ms	היה	224		be,become
8:19	תבנה	qal	impf	2ms	בנה	124		build
	יצא	qal	ptc	ms	יצא	422		go out
	יבנה	qal	impf	3ms	בנה	124		build
8:20	יקם	hiph	wci	3ms	קום	877		raise,build,set
	דבר	piel	pft	3ms	דבר	180		speak
	אקם	qal	wci	1cs	קום	877		arise,stand
	אשב	qal	wci	1cs	ישב	442		sit,dwell
	דבר	piel	pft	3ms	דבר	180		speak
	אבנה	qal	wci	1cs	בנה	124		build
8:21	אשם	qal	wci	1cs	שים	962		put,set
	כרת	qal	pft	3ms	כרת	503		cut,destroy
	הוציאו	hiph	infc		יצא	422	3ms	bring out
8:22	יעמד	qal	wci	3ms	עמד	763		stand,stop
	יפרש	qal	wci	3ms	פרש	831		spread out
8:23	יאמר	qal	wci	3ms	אמר	55		say
	שמר	qal	ptc	ms	שמר	1036		keep,watch
	הלכים	qal	ptc	mp	הלך	229		walk,go
8:24	שמרת	qal	pft	2ms	שמר	1036		keep,watch
	דברת	piel	pft	2ms	דבר	180		speak
	תדבר	piel	wci	2ms	דבר	180		speak
	מלאת	piel	pft	2ms	מלא	569		fill
8:25	שמר	qal	impv	ms	שמר	1036		keep,watch
	דברת	piel	pft	2ms	דבר	180		speak
	אמר	qal	infc		אמר	55		say
	יכרת	niph	impf	3ms	כרת	503		be cut off
	ישב	qal	ptc	ms	ישב	442		sit,dwell
	ישמרו	qal	impf	3mp	שמר	1036		keep,watch
	לכת	qal	infc		הלך	229		walk,go
8:25	הלכת	qal	pft	2ms	הלך	229		walk,go
8:26	יאמן	niph	jusm	3ms	אמן	52		be confirmed
	דברת	piel	pft	2ms	דבר	180		speak
8:27	ישב	qal	impf	3ms	ישב	442		sit,dwell
	יכלכלוך	pilp	impf	3mp	כול	465	2ms	support
	בניתי	qal	pft	1cs	בנה	124		build
8:28	פנית	qal	wcp	2ms	פנה	815		turn
	שמע	qal	infc		שמע	1033		hear
	מתפלל	hith	ptc	ms	פלל	813		pray
8:29	היות	qal	infc		היה	224		be,become
	פתחות	qal	pptc	fp	פתח	834		open
	אמרת	qal	pft	2ms	אמר	55		say
	יהיה	qal	impf	3ms	היה	224		be,become
	שמע	qal	infc		שמע	1033		hear
	יתפלל	hith	impf	3ms	פלל	813		pray
8:30	שמעת	qal	wcp	2ms	שמע	1033		hear
	יתפללו	hith	impf	3mp	פלל	813		pray
	תשמע	qal	impf	2ms	שמע	1033		hear
	שבתך	qal	infc		ישב	442	2ms	sit,dwell
	שמעת	qal	wcp	2ms	שמע	1033		hear
	סלחת	qal	wcp	2ms	סלח	699		forgive,pardon
8:31	יחטא	qal	impf	3ms	חטא	306		sin
	נשא	qal	wcp	3ms	נשא	673?		be creditor
	האלתו	hiph	infc		אלה	46	3ms	put under oath
	בא	qal	wcp	3ms	בוא	97		come in
	אלה	qal	pft	3ms	אלה	46		swear
8:32	תשמע	qal	impf	2ms	שמע	1033		hear
	עשית	qal	wcp	2ms	עשה	793		do,make
	שפטת	qal	wcp	2ms	שפט	1047		judge
	הרשיע	hiph	infc		רשע	957		condemn, be evil
	תת	qal	infc		נתן	678		give,set
	הצדיק	hiph	infc		צדק	842		make righteous
	תת	qal	infc		נתן	678		give,set
8:33	הנגף	niph	infc		נגף	619		be smitten
	אויב	qal	ptc	ms	איב	33		be hostile to
	יחטאו	qal	impf	3mp	חטא	306		sin
	שבו	qal	wcp	3cp	שוב	996		turn,return
	הודו	hiph	wcp	3cp	ידה	392		praise
	התפללו	hith	wcp	3cp	פלל	813		pray
	התחננו	hith	wcp	3cp	חנן	335		seek favor
8:34	תשמע	qal	impf	2ms	שמע	1033		hear
	סלחת	qal	wcp	2ms	סלח	699		forgive,pardon
	השבתם	hiph	wcp	2ms	שוב	996	3mp	bring back
	נתת	qal	pft	2ms	נתן	678		give,set
8:35	העצר	niph	infc		עצר	783		be restrained
	יהיה	qal	impf	3ms	היה	224		be,become
	יחטאו	qal	impf	3mp	חטא	306		sin
	התפללו	hith	wcp	3cp	פלל	813		pray
	הודו	hiph	wcp	3cp	ידה	392		praise
	ישובון	qal	impf	3mp	שוב	996		turn,return
	תענם	hiph	impf	2ms	ענה	776	3mp	afflict
8:36	תשמע	qal	impf	2ms	שמע	1033		hear
	סלחת	qal	wcp	2ms	סלח	699		forgive,pardon
	תורם	hiph	impf	2ms	ירה	434	3mp	shoot,teach

ChVs	Form	Stem	Tnse	PGN	Root	BDB	Sfx	Meaning
8:36	ילכו	qal	impf	3mp	הלך	229		walk,go
	נתתה	qal	wcp	2ms	נתן	678		give,set
	נתתה	qal	pft	2ms	נתן	678		give,set
8:37	יהיה	qal	impf	3ms	היה	224		be,become
	יהיה	qal	impf	3ms	היה	224		be,become
	יהיה	qal	impf	3ms	היה	224		be,become
	יצר	hiph	impf	3ms	צרר	864		distress,cramp
	איבו	qal	ptc	ms	איב	33	3ms	be hostile to
8:38	תהיה	qal	impf	3fs	היה	224		be,become
	ידעון	qal	impf	3mp	ידע	393		know
	פרשׂ	qal	wcp	3ms	פרשׂ	831		spread out
8:39	תשמע	qal	impf	2ms	שמע	1033		hear
	שבתך	qal	infc		ישב	442	2ms	sit,dwell
	סלחת	qal	wcp	2ms	סלח	699		forgive,pardon
	עשׂית	qal	wcp	2ms	עשׂה	793		do,make
	נתת	qal	wcp	2ms	נתן	678		give,set
	תדע	qal	impf	2ms	ידע	393		know
	ידעת	qal	pft	2ms	ידע	393		know
8:40	יראוך	qal	impf	3mp	ירא	431	2ms	fear
	נתתה	qal	pft	2ms	נתן	678		give,set
8:41	בא	qal	wcp	3ms	בוא	97		come in
8:42	ישמעון	qal	impf	3mp	שמע	1033		hear
	נטויה	qal	pptc	fs	נטה	639		stretch,incline
	בא	qal	wcp	3ms	בוא	97		come in
	התפלל	hith	wcp	3ms	פלל	813		pray
8:43	תשמע	qal	impf	2ms	שמע	1033		hear
	שבתך	qal	infc		ישב	442	2ms	sit,dwell
	עשׂית	qal	wcp	2ms	עשׂה	793		do,make
	יקרא	qal	impf	3ms	קרא	894		call,proclaim
	ידעון	qal	impf	3mp	ידע	393		know
	יראה	qal	infc		ירא	431		fear
	דעת	qal	infc		ידע	393		know
	נקרא	niph	pft	3ms	קרא	894		be called
	בניתי	qal	pft	1cs	בנה	124		build
8:44	יצא	qal	impf	3ms	יצא	422		go out
	איבו	qal	ptc	ms	איב	33	3ms	be hostile to
	תשלחם	qal	impf	2ms	שלח	1018	3mp	send
	התפללו	hith	wcp	3cp	פלל	813		pray
	בחרת	qal	pft	2ms	בחר	103		choose
	בנתי	qal	pft	1cs	בנה	124		build
8:45	שמעת	qal	wcp	2ms	שמע	1033		hear
	עשׂית	qal	wcp	2ms	עשׂה	793		do,make
8:46	יחטאו	qal	impf	3mp	חטא	306		sin
	יחטא	qal	impf	3ms	חטא	306		sin
	אנפת	qal	wcp	2ms	אנף	60		be angry
	נתתם	qal	wcp	2ms	נתן	678	3mp	give,set
	אויב	qal	ptc	ms	איב	33		be hostile to
	שבום	qal	wcp	3cp	שבה	985	3mp	take captive
	שביהם	qal	ptc	mp	שבה	985	3mp	take captive
	אויב	qal	ptc	ms	איב	33		be hostile to
8:47	השיבו	hiph	wcp	3cp	שוב	996		bring back
	נשבו	niph	pft	3cp	שבה	985		be held captive
	שבו	qal	wcp	3cp	שוב	996		turn,return
	התחננו	hith	wcp	3cp	חנן	335		seek favor
8:47	שביהם	qal	ptc	mp	שבה	985	3mp	take captive
	אמר	qal	infc		אמר	55		say
	חטאנו	qal	pft	1cp	חטא	306		sin
	העוינו	hiph	pft	1cp	עוה	731		commit iniquity
	רשענו	qal	pft	1cp	רשע	957		be wicked
8:48	שבו	qal	wcp	3cp	שוב	996		turn,return
	איביהם	qal	ptc	mp	איב	33	3mp	be hostile to
	שבו	qal	pft	3cp	שבה	985		take captive
	התפללו	hith	wcp	3cp	פלל	813		pray
	נתתה	qal	pft	2ms	נתן	678		give,set
	בחרת	qal	pft	2ms	בחר	103		choose
	בניתk	qal	pft	1cs	בנה	124		build
	בניתיq	qal	pft	1cs	בנה	124		build
8:49	שמעת	qal	wcp	2ms	שמע	1033		hear
	שבתך	qal	infc		ישב	442	2ms	sit,dwell
	עשׂית	qal	wcp	2ms	עשׂה	793		do,make
8:50	סלחת	qal	wcp	2ms	סלח	699		forgive,pardon
	חטאו	qal	pft	3cp	חטא	306		sin
	פשעו	qal	pft	3cp	פשע	833		rebel,sin
	נתתם	qal	wcp	2ms	נתן	678	3mp	give,set
	שביהם	qal	ptc	mp	שבה	985	3mp	take captive
	רחמום	piel	wcp	3cp	רחם	933	3mp	have compassion
8:51	הוצאת	hiph	pft	2ms	יצא	422		bring out
8:52	היות	qal	infc		היה	224		be,become
	פתחות	qal	pptc	fp	פתח	834		open
	שמע	qal	infc		שמע	1033		hear
	קראם	qal	infc		קרא	894	3mp	call,proclaim
8:53	הבדלתם	hiph	pft	2ms	בדל	95	3mp	divide
	דברת	piel	pft	2ms	דבר	180		speak
	הוציאך	hiph	infc		יצא	422	2ms	bring out
8:54	יהי	qal	wci	3ms	היה	224		be,become
	כלות	piel	infc		כלה	477		complete,finish
	התפלל	hith	infc		פלל	813		pray
	קם	qal	pft	3ms	קום	877		arise,stand
	כרע	qal	infc		כרע	502		bow down
	פרשׂות	qal	pptc	fp	פרשׂ	831		spread out
8:55	יעמד	qal	wci	3ms	עמד	763		stand,stop
	יברך	piel	wci	3ms	ברך	138		bless
	אמר	qal	infc		אמר	55		say
8:56	ברוך	qal	pptc	ms	ברך	138		kneel,bless
	נתן	qal	pft	3ms	נתן	678		give,set
	דבר	piel	pft	3ms	דבר	180		speak
	נפל	qal	pft	3ms	נפל	656		fall
	דבר	piel	pft	3ms	דבר	180		speak
8:57	יהי	qal	jus	3ms	היה	224		be,become
	היה	qal	pft	3ms	היה	224		be,become
	יעזבנו	qal	jusm	3ms	עזב	736	1cp	leave,loose
	יטשנו	qal	jusm	3ms	נטשׁ	643	1cp	leave,forsake
8:58	הטות	hiph	infc		נטה	639		turn,incline
	לכת	qal	infc		הלך	229		walk,go
	שמר	qal	infc		שמר	1036		keep,watch
	צוה	piel	pft	3ms	צוה	845		command
8:59	יהיו	qal	jusm	3mp	היה	224		be,become
	התחננתי	hith	pft	1cs	חנן	335		seek favor

ChVs	Form	Stem	Tnse	PGN	Root	BDB	Sfx	Meaning
8:59	עשות	qal	infc		עשה	793		do,make
8:60	דעת	qal	infc		ידע	393		know
8:61	היה	qal	wcp	3ms	היה	224		be,become
	לכת	qal	infc		הלך	229		walk,go
	שמר	qal	infc		שמר	1036		keep,watch
8:62	זבחים	qal	ptc	mp	זבח	256		slaughter
8:63	יזבח	qal	wci	3ms	זבח	256		slaughter
	זבח	qal	pft	3ms	זבח	256		slaughter
	יחנכו	qal	wci	3mp	חנך	335		train,dedicate
8:64	קדש	piel	pft	3ms	קדש	872		consecrate
	עשה	qal	pft	3ms	עשה	793		do,make
	הכיל	hiph	infc		כול	465		contain
8:65	יעש	qal	wci	3ms	עשה	793		do,make
	בוא	qal	infc		בוא	97		come in
8:66	שלח	piel	pft	3ms	שלח	1018		send away,shoot
	יברכו	piel	wci	3mp	ברך	138		bless
	ילכו	qal	wci	3mp	הלך	229		walk,go
	עשה	qal	pft	3ms	עשה	793		do,make
9:1	יהי	qal	wci	3ms	היה	224		be,become
	כלות	piel	infc		כלה	477		complete,finish
	בנות	qal	infc		בנה	124		build
	חפץ	qal	pft	3ms	חפץ	342		delight in
	עשות	qal	infc		עשה	793		do,make
9:2	ירא	niph	wci	3ms	ראה	906		appear,be seen
	נראה	niph	pft	3ms	ראה	906		appear,be seen
9:3	יאמר	qal	wci	3ms	אמר	55		say
	שמעתי	qal	pft	1cs	שמע	1033		hear
	התחננתה	hith	pft	2ms	חנן	335		seek favor
	הקדשתי	hiph	pft	1cs	קדש	872		consecrate
	בנתה	qal	pft	2ms	בנה	124		build
	שום	qal	infc		שים	962		put,set
	היו	qal	wcp	3cp	היה	224		be,become
9:4	תלך	qal	impf	2ms	הלך	229		walk,go
	הלך	qal	pft	3ms	הלך	229		walk,go
	עשות	qal	infc		עשה	793		do,make
	צויתיך	piel	pft	1cs	צוה	845	2ms	command
	תשמר	qal	impf	2ms	שמר	1036		keep,watch
9:5	הקמתי	hiph	wcp	1cs	קום	877		raise,build,set
	דברתי	piel	pft	1cs	דבר	180		speak
	אמר	qal	infc		אמר	55		say
	יכרת	niph	impf	3ms	כרת	503		be cut off
9:6	שוב	qal	infa		שוב	996		turn,return
	תשבון	qal	impf	2mp	שוב	996		turn,return
	תשמרו	qal	impf	2mp	שמר	1036		keep,watch
	נתתי	qal	pft	1cs	נתן	678		give,set
	הלכתם	qal	wcp	2mp	הלך	229		walk,go
	עבדתם	qal	wcp	2mp	עבד	712		work,serve
	השתחויתם	hish	wcp	2mp	חוה	1005		bow down
9:7	הכרתי	hiph	wcp	1cs	כרת	503		cut off,destroy
	נתתי	qal	pft	1cs	נתן	678		give,set
	הקדשתי	hiph	pft	1cs	קדש	872		consecrate
	אשלח	piel	impf	1cs	שלח	1018		send away,shoot
	היה	qal	wcp	3ms	היה	224		be,become
9:8	יהיה	qal	impf	3ms	היה	224		be,become
9:8	עבר	qal	ptc	ms	עבר	716		pass over
	ישם	qal	impf	3ms	שמם	1030		be desolate
	שרק	qal	wcp	3ms	שרק	1056		hiss
	אמרו	qal	wcp	3cp	אמר	55		say
	עשה	qal	pft	3ms	עשה	793		do,make
9:9	אמרו	qal	wcp	3cp	אמר	55		say
	עזבו	qal	pft	3cp	עזב	736		leave,loose
	הוציא	hiph	pft	3ms	יצא	422		bring out
	יחזקו	hiph	wci	3mp	חזק	304		make firm,seize
	kישתחו	hish	wci	3ms	חוה	1005		bow down
	qישתחוו	hish	wci	3mp	חוה	1005		bow down
	יעבדם	qal	wci	3mp	עבד	712	3mp	work,serve
	הביא	hiph	pft	3ms	בוא	97		bring in
9:10	יהי	qal	wci	3ms	היה	224		be,become
	בנה	qal	pft	3ms	בנה	124		build
9:11	נשא	piel	pft	3ms	נשא	669		lift up
	יתן	qal	impf	3ms	נתן	678		give,set
9:12	יצא	qal	wci	3ms	יצא	422		go out
	ראות	qal	infc		ראה	906		see
	נתן	qal	pft	3ms	נתן	678		give,set
	ישרו	qal	pft	3cp	ישר	448		be straight
9:13	יאמר	qal	wci	3ms	אמר	55		say
	נתתה	qal	pft	2ms	נתן	678		give,set
	יקרא	qal	wci	3ms	קרא	894		call,proclaim
9:14	ישלח	qal	wci	3ms	שלח	1018		send
9:15	העלה	hiph	pft	3ms	עלה	748		bring up,offer
	בנות	qal	infc		בנה	124		build
9:16	עלה	qal	pft	3ms	עלה	748		go up
	ילכד	qal	wci	3ms	לכד	539		capture
	ישרפה	qal	wci	3ms	שרף	976	3fs	burn
	ישב	qal	ptc	ms	ישב	442		sit,dwell
	הרג	qal	pft	3ms	הרג	246		kill
	יתנה	qal	wci	3ms	נתן	678	3fs	give,set
9:17	יבן	qal	wci	3ms	בנה	124		build
9:19	היו	qal	pft	3cp	היה	224		be,become
	חשק	qal	pft	3ms	חשק	365		love
	בנות	qal	infc		בנה	124		build
9:20	נותר	niph	ptc	ms	יתר	451		be left,remain
9:21	נתרו	niph	pft	3cp	יתר	451		be left,remain
	יכלו	qal	pft	3cp	יכל	407		be able
	החרימם	hiph	infc		חרם	355	3mp	ban,destroy
	יעלם	hiph	wci	3ms	עלה	748	3mp	bring up,offer
	עבד	qal	ptc	ms	עבד	712		work,serve
9:22	נתן	qal	pft	3ms	נתן	678		give,set
9:23	נצבים	niph	ptc	mp	נצב	662		stand
	רדים	qal	ptc	mp	רדה	921		rule
	עשים	qal	ptc	mp	עשה	793		do,make
9:24	עלתה	qal	pft	3fs	עלה	748		go up
	בנה	qal	pft	3ms	בנה	124		build
	בנה	qal	pft	3ms	בנה	124		build
9:25	העלה	hiph	wcp	3ms	עלה	748		bring up,offer
	בנה	qal	pft	3ms	בנה	124		build
	הקטיר	hiph	infa		קטר	882		make sacrifices
	שלם	piel	pft	3ms	שלם	1022		finish,reward

ChVs	Form	Stem	Tnse	PGN	Root	BDB	Sfx	Meaning
9: 26	עשׂה	qal	pft	3ms	עשׂה	793		do,make
9: 27	ישׁלח	qal	wci	3ms	שׁלח	1018		send
	ידעי	qal	ptc	mp	ידע	393		know
9: 28	יבאו	qal	wci	3mp	בוא	97		come in
	יקחו	qal	wci	3mp	לקח	542		take
	יבאו	qal	wci	3mp	בוא	97		come in
10: 1	שׁמעת	qal	ptc	fs	שׁמע	1033		hear
	תבא	qal	wci	3fs	בוא	97		come in
	נסתו	piel	infc		נסה	650	3ms	test,try
10: 2	תבא	qal	wci	3fs	בוא	97		come in
	נשׂאים	qal	ptc	mp	נשׂא	669		lift,carry
	תבא	qal	wci	3fs	בוא	97		come in
	תדבר	piel	wci	3fs	דבר	180		speak
	היה	qal	pft	3ms	היה	224		be,become
10: 3	יגד	hiph	wci	3ms	נגד	616		declare,tell
	היה	qal	pft	3ms	היה	224		be,become
	נעלם	niph	ptc	ms	עלם	761		be concealed
	הגיד	hiph	pft	3ms	נגד	616		declare,tell
10: 4	תרא	qal	wci	3fs	ראה	906		see
	בנה	qal	pft	3ms	בנה	124		build
10: 5	משׁרתוk	piel	ptc	ms	שׁרת	1058	3ms	minister,serve
	משׁרתיוq	piel	ptc	mp	שׁרת	1058	3ms	minister,serve
	יעלה	hiph	impf	3ms	עלה	748		bring up,offer
	היה	qal	pft	3ms	היה	224		be,become
10: 6	תאמר	qal	wci	3fs	אמר	55		say
	היה	qal	pft	3ms	היה	224		be,become
	שׁמעתי	qal	pft	1cs	שׁמע	1033		hear
10: 7	האמנתי	hiph	pft	1cs	אמן	52		believe
	באתי	qal	pft	1cs	בוא	97		come in
	תראינה	qal	wci	3fp	ראה	906		see
	הגד	hoph	pft	3ms	נגד	616		be told
	הוספת	hiph	pft	2ms	יסף	414		add,do again
	שׁמעתי	qal	pft	1cs	שׁמע	1033		hear
10: 8	עמדים	qal	ptc	mp	עמד	763		stand,stop
	שׁמעים	qal	ptc	mp	שׁמע	1033		hear
10: 9	יהי	qal	jus	3ms	היה	224		be,become
	ברוך	qal	pptc	ms	ברך	138		kneel,bless
	חפץ	qal	pft	3ms	חפץ	342		delight in
	תתך	qal	infc		נתן	678	2ms	give,set
	אהבת	qal	infc		אהב	12		love
	ישׂימך	qal	wci	3ms	שׂים	962	2ms	put,set
	עשׂות	qal	infc		עשׂה	793		do,make
10: 10	תתן	qal	wci	3fs	נתן	678		give,set
	הרבה	hiph	infa		רבה	915		make many
	בא	qal	pft	3ms	בוא	97		come in
	נתנה	qal	pft	3fs	נתן	678		give,set
10: 11	נשׂא	qal	pft	3ms	נשׂא	669		lift,carry
	הביא	hiph	pft	3ms	בוא	97		bring in
	הרבה	hiph	infa		רבה	915		make many
10: 12	יעשׂ	qal	wci	3ms	עשׂה	793		do,make
	שׁרים	qal	ptc	mp	שׁיר	1010		sing
	בא	qal	pft	3ms	בוא	97		come in
	נראה	niph	pft	3ms	ראה	906		appear,be seen
10: 13	נתן	qal	pft	3ms	נתן	678		give,set
10: 13	שׁאלה	qal	pft	3fs	שׁאל	981		ask,borrow
	נתן	qal	pft	3ms	נתן	678		give,set
	תפן	qal	wci	3fs	פנה	815		turn
	תלך	qal	wci	3fs	הלך	229		walk,go
10: 14	יהי	qal	wci	3ms	היה	224		be,become
	בא	qal	pft	3ms	בוא	97		come in
10: 15	תרים	qal	ptc	mp	תור	1064		seek out,spy
	רכלים	qal	ptc	mp	רכל	940		trade,gossip
10: 16	יעשׂ	qal	wci	3ms	עשׂה	793		do,make
	שׁחוט	qal	pptc	ms	שׁחט	1006		slaughter
	יעלה	hiph	impf	3ms	עלה	748		bring up,offer
10: 17	שׁחוט	qal	pptc	ms	שׁחט	1006		slaughter
	יעלה	hiph	impf	3ms	עלה	748		bring up,offer
	יתנם	qal	wci	3ms	נתן	678	3mp	give,set
10: 18	יעשׂ	qal	wci	3ms	עשׂה	793		do,make
	יצפהו	piel	wci	3ms	צפה	860	3ms	overlay
	מופז	hoph	ptc	ms	פזז	808		be refined
10: 19	עמדים	qal	ptc	mp	עמד	763		stand,stop
10: 20	עמדים	qal	ptc	mp	עמד	763		stand,stop
	נעשׂה	niph	pft	3ms	עשׂה	793		be done
10: 21	סגור	qal	pptc	ms	סגר	688		shut
	נחשׁב	niph	ptc	ms	חשׁב	362		be thought
10: 22	תבוא	qal	impf	3fs	בוא	97		come in
	נשׂאת	qal	ptc	fs	נשׂא	669		lift,carry
10: 23	יגדל	qal	wci	3ms	גדל	152		be great,grow
10: 24	מבקשׁים	piel	ptc	mp	בקשׁ	134		seek
	שׁמע	qal	infc		שׁמע	1033		hear
	נתן	qal	pft	3ms	נתן	678		give,set
10: 25	מבאים	hiph	ptc	mp	בוא	97		bring in
10: 26	יאסף	qal	wci	3ms	אסף	62		gather
	יהי	qal	wci	3ms	היה	224		be,become
	ינחם	hiph	wci	3ms	נחה	634	3mp	lead,guide
10: 27	יתן	qal	wci	3ms	נתן	678		give,set
	נתן	qal	pft	3ms	נתן	678		give,set
10: 28	סחרי	qal	ptc	mp	סחר	695		go around
	יקחו	qal	impf	3mp	לקח	542		take
10: 29	תעלה	qal	wci	3fs	עלה	748		go up
	תצא	qal	wci	3fs	יצא	422		go out
	יצאו	hiph	impf	3mp	יצא	422		bring out
11: 1	אהב	qal	pft	3ms	אהב	12		love
11: 2	אמר	qal	pft	3ms	אמר	55		say
	תבאו	qal	impf	2mp	בוא	97		come in
	יבאו	qal	impf	3mp	בוא	97		come in
	יטו	hiph	impf	3mp	נטה	639		turn,incline
	דבק	qal	pft	3ms	דבק	179		cling,cleave
	אהבה	qal	infc		אהב	12		love
11: 3	יהי	qal	wci	3ms	היה	224		be,become
	יטו	hiph	wci	3mp	נטה	639		turn,incline
11: 4	יהי	qal	wci	3ms	היה	224		be,become
	הטו	hiph	pft	3cp	נטה	639		turn,incline
	היה	qal	pft	3ms	היה	224		be,become
11: 5	ילך	qal	wci	3ms	הלך	229		walk,go
11: 6	יעשׂ	qal	wci	3ms	עשׂה	793		do,make
	מלא	piel	pft	3ms	מלא	569		fill

ChVs	Form	Stem	Tnse	PGN	Root	BDB	Sfx	Meaning
11:7	יבנה	qal	impf	3ms	בנה	124		build
11:8	עשׂה	qal	pft	3ms	עשׂה	793		do,make
	מקטירות	hiph	ptc	fp	קטר	882		make sacrifices
	מזבחות	piel	ptc	fp	זבח	256		sacrifice
11:9	יתאנף	hith	wci	3ms	אנף	60		be angry
	נטה	qal	pft	3ms	נטה	639		stretch,incline
	נראה	niph	pft	3ms	ראה	906		appear,be seen
11:10	צוה	piel	wcp	3ms	צוה	845		command
	לכת	qal	infc		הלך	229		walk,go
	שׁמר	qal	pft	3ms	שׁמר	1036		keep,watch
	צוה	piel	pft	3ms	צוה	845		command
11:11	יאמר	qal	wci	3ms	אמר	55		say
	היתה	qal	pft	3fs	היה	224		be,become
	שׁמרת	qal	pft	2ms	שׁמר	1036		keep,watch
	צויתי	piel	pft	1cs	צוה	845		command
	קרע	qal	infa		קרע	902		tear,rend
	אקרע	qal	impf	1cs	קרע	902		tear,rend
	נתתיה	qal	wcp	1cs	נתן	678	3fs	give,set
11:12	אעשׂנה	qal	impf	1cs	עשׂה	793	3fs	do,make
	אקרענה	qal	impf	1cs	קרע	902	3fs	tear,rend
11:13	אקרע	qal	impf	1cs	קרע	902		tear,rend
	אתן	qal	impf	1cs	נתן	678		give,set
	בחרתי	qal	pft	1cs	בחר	103		choose
11:14	יקם	hiph	wci	3ms	קום	877		raise,build,set
11:15	יהי	qal	wci	3ms	היה	224		be,become
	היות	qal	infc		היה	224		be,become
	עלות	qal	infc		עלה	748		go up
	קבר	piel	infc		קבר	868		bury
	יך	hiph	wci	3ms	נכה	645		smite
11:16	ישׁב	qal	pft	3ms	ישׁב	442		sit,dwell
	הכרית	hiph	pft	3ms	כרת	503		cut off,destroy
11:17	יברח	qal	wci	3ms	ברח	137		go thru,flee
	בוא	qal	infc		בוא	97		come in
11:18	יקמו	qal	wci	3mp	קום	877		arise,stand
	יבאו	qal	wci	3mp	בוא	97		come in
	יקחו	qal	wci	3mp	לקח	542		take
	יבאו	qal	wci	3mp	בוא	97		come in
	יתן	qal	wci	3ms	נתן	678		give,set
	אמר	qal	pft	3ms	אמר	55		say
	נתן	qal	pft	3ms	נתן	678		give,set
11:19	ימצא	qal	wci	3ms	מצא	592		find
	יתן	qal	wci	3ms	נתן	678		give,set
11:20	תלד	qal	wci	3fs	ילד	408		bear,beget
	תגמלהו	qal	wci	3fs	גמל	168	3ms	deal out,ripen
	יהי	qal	wci	3ms	היה	224		be,become
11:21	שׁמע	qal	pft	3ms	שׁמע	1033		hear
	שׁכב	qal	pft	3ms	שׁכב	1011		lie,lie down
	מת	qal	pft	3ms	מות	559		die
	יאמר	qal	wci	3ms	אמר	55		say
	שׁלחני	piel	impv	ms	שׁלח	1018	1cs	send away,shoot
	אלך	qal	cohm	1cs	הלך	229		walk,go
11:22	יאמר	qal	wci	3ms	אמר	55		say
	חסר	qal	ptc	ms	חסר	341		lack
	מבקשׁ	piel	ptc	ms	בקשׁ	134		seek
11:22	לכת	qal	infc		הלך	229		walk,go
	יאמר	qal	wci	3ms	אמר	55		say
	שׁלח	piel	infa		שׁלח	1018		send away,shoot
	תשׁלחני	piel	impf	2ms	שׁלח	1018	1cs	send away,shoot
11:23	יקם	hiph	wci	3ms	קום	877		raise,build,set
	ברח	qal	pft	3ms	ברח	137		go thru,flee
11:24	יקבץ	qal	wci	3ms	קבץ	867		gather,collect
	יהי	qal	wci	3ms	היה	224		be,become
	הרג	qal	infc		הרג	246		kill
	ילכו	qal	wci	3mp	הלך	229		walk,go
	ישׁבו	qal	wci	3mp	ישׁב	442		sit,dwell
	ימלכו	qal	wci	3mp	מלך	573		be king,reign
11:25	יהי	qal	wci	3ms	היה	224		be,become
	יקץ	qal	wci	3ms	קוץ	880		loathe,abhor
	ימלך	qal	wci	3ms	מלך	573		be king,reign
11:26	ירם	hiph	wci	3ms	רום	926		raise,lift
11:27	הרים	hiph	pft	3ms	רום	926		raise,lift
	בנה	qal	pft	3ms	בנה	124		build
	סגר	qal	pft	3ms	סגר	688		shut
11:28	ירא	qal	wci	3ms	ראה	906		see
	עשׂה	qal	ptc	ms	עשׂה	793		do,make
	יפקד	hiph	wci	3ms	פקד	823		set,entrust
11:29	יהי	qal	wci	3ms	היה	224		be,become
	יצא	qal	pft	3ms	יצא	422		go out
	ימצא	qal	wci	3ms	מצא	592		find
	מתכסה	hith	ptc	ms	כסה	491		cover oneself
11:30	יתפשׂ	qal	wci	3ms	תפשׂ	1074		seize,grasp
	יקרעה	qal	wci	3ms	קרע	902	3fs	tear,rend
11:31	יאמר	qal	wci	3ms	אמר	55		say
	קח	qal	impv	ms	לקח	542		take
	אמר	qal	pft	3ms	אמר	55		say
	קרע	qal	ptc	ms	קרע	902		tear,rend
	נתתי	qal	wcp	1cs	נתן	678		give,set
11:32	יהיה	qal	impf	3ms	היה	224		be,become
	בחרתי	qal	pft	1cs	בחר	103		choose
11:33	עזבוני	qal	pft	3cp	עזב	736	1cs	leave,loose
	ישׁתחוו	hish	wci	3mp	חוה	1005		bow down
	הלכו	qal	pft	3cp	הלך	229		walk,go
	עשׂות	qal	infc		עשׂה	793		do,make
11:34	אקח	qal	impf	1cs	לקח	542		take
	אשׁתנו	qal	impf	1cs	שׁית	1011	3ms	put,set
	בחרתי	qal	pft	1cs	בחר	103		choose
	שׁמר	qal	pft	3ms	שׁמר	1036		keep,watch
11:35	לקחתי	qal	wcp	1cs	לקח	542		take
	נתתיה	qal	wcp	1cs	נתן	678	3fs	give,set
11:36	אתן	qal	impf	1cs	נתן	678		give,set
	היות	qal	infc		היה	224		be,become
	בחרתי	qal	pft	1cs	בחר	103		choose
	שׂום	qal	infc		שׂים	962		put,set
11:37	אקח	qal	impf	1cs	לקח	542		take
	מלכת	qal	wcp	2ms	מלך	573		be king,reign
	תאוה	piel	impf	3fs	אוה	16		desire
	היית	qal	wcp	2ms	היה	224		be,become
11:38	היה	qal	wcp	3ms	היה	224		be,become

ChVs	Form	Stem	Tnse	PGN	Root	BDB	Sfx	Meaning
11:38	תשמע	qal	impf	2ms	שמע	1033		hear
	אצוך	piel	impf	1cs	צוה	845	2ms	command
	הלכת	qal	wcp	2ms	הלך	229		walk,go
	עשית	qal	wcp	2ms	עשה	793		do,make
	שמור	qal	infc		שמר	1036		keep,watch
	עשה	qal	pft	3ms	עשה	793		do,make
	הייתי	qal	wcp	1cs	היה	224		be,become
	בניתי	qal	wcp	1cs	בנה	124		build
	נאמן	niph	ptc	ms	אמן	52		be confirmed
	בניתי	qal	pft	1cs	בנה	124		build
	נתתי	qal	wcp	1cs	נתן	678		give,set
11:39	אענה	piel	wci	1cs	ענה	776		humble
11:40	יבקש	piel	wci	3ms	בקש	134		seek
	המית	hiph	infc		מות	559		kill
	יקם	qal	wci	3ms	קום	877		arise,stand
	יברח	qal	wci	3ms	ברח	137		go thru,flee
	יהי	qal	wci	3ms	היה	224		be,become
11:41	עשה	qal	pft	3ms	עשה	793		do,make
	כתבים	qal	pptc	mp	כתב	507		write
11:42	מלך	qal	pft	3ms	מלך	573		be king,reign
11:43	ישכב	qal	wci	3ms	שכב	1011		lie,lie down
	יקבר	niph	wci	3ms	קבר	868		be buried
	ימלך	qal	wci	3ms	מלך	573		be king,reign
12:1	ילך	qal	wci	3ms	הלך	229		walk,go
	בא	qal	pft	3ms	בוא	97		come in
	המליך	hiph	infc		מלך	573		cause to reign
12:2	יהי	qal	wci	3ms	היה	224		be,become
	שמע	qal	infc		שמע	1033		hear
	ברח	qal	pft	3ms	ברח	137		go thru,flee
	ישב	qal	wci	3ms	ישב	442		sit,dwell
12:3	ישלחו	qal	wci	3mp	שלח	1018		send
	יקראו	qal	wci	3mp	קרא	894		call,proclaim
	יבאוk	qal	wci	3mp	בוא	97		come in
	יבאq	qal	wci	3ms	בוא	97		come in
	ידברו	piel	wci	3mp	דבר	180		speak
	אמר	qal	infc		אמר	55		say
12:4	הקשה	hiph	pft	3ms	קשה	904		harden
	הקל	hiph	impv	ms	קלל	886		make light
	נתן	qal	pft	3ms	נתן	678		give,set
	נעבדך	qal	cohm	1cp	עבד	712	2ms	work,serve
12:5	יאמר	qal	wci	3ms	אמר	55		say
	לכו	qal	impv	mp	הלך	229		walk,go
	שובו	qal	impv	mp	שוב	996		turn,return
	ילכו	qal	wci	3mp	הלך	229		walk,go
12:6	יועץ	niph	wci	3ms	יעץ	419		consult
	היו	qal	pft	3cp	היה	224		be,become
	עמדים	qal	ptc	mp	עמד	763		stand,stop
	היתו	qal	infc		היה	224	3ms	be,become
	אמר	qal	infc		אמר	55		say
	נועצים	niph	ptc	mp	יעץ	419		consult
	השיב	hiph	infc		שוב	996		bring back
12:7	ידברk	piel	wci	3ms	דבר	180		speak
	ידברוq	piel	wci	3mp	דבר	180		speak
	אמר	qal	infc		אמר	55		say
12:7	תהיה	qal	impf	2ms	היה	224		be,become
	עבדתם	qal	wcp	2ms	עבד	712	3mp	work,serve
	עניתם	qal	wcp	2ms	ענה	772	3mp	answer
	דברת	piel	wcp	2ms	דבר	180		speak
	היו	qal	wcp	3cp	היה	224		be,become
12:8	יעזב	qal	wci	3ms	עזב	736		leave,loose
	יעצהו	qal	pft	3cp	יעץ	419	3ms	advise,counsel
	יועץ	niph	wci	3ms	יעץ	419		consult
	גדלו	qal	pft	3cp	גדל	152		be great,grow
	עמדים	qal	ptc	mp	עמד	763		stand,stop
12:9	יאמר	qal	wci	3ms	אמר	55		say
	נועצים	niph	ptc	mp	יעץ	419		consult
	נשיב	hiph	impf	1cp	שוב	996		bring back
	דברו	piel	pft	3cp	דבר	180		speak
	אמר	qal	infc		אמר	55		say
	הקל	hiph	impv	ms	קלל	886		make light
	נתן	qal	pft	3ms	נתן	678		give,set
12:10	ידברו	piel	wci	3mp	דבר	180		speak
	גדלו	qal	pft	3cp	גדל	152		be great,grow
	אמר	qal	infc		אמר	55		say
	תאמר	qal	impf	2ms	אמר	55		say
	דברו	piel	pft	3cp	דבר	180		speak
	אמר	qal	infc		אמר	55		say
	הכביד	hiph	pft	3ms	כבד	457		make heavy
	הקל	hiph	impv	ms	קלל	886		make light
	תדבר	piel	impf	2ms	דבר	180		speak
	עבה	qal	pft	3ms	עבה	716		be thick
12:11	העמים	hiph	pft	3ms	עמס	770		load
	אוסיף	hiph	impf	1cs	יסף	414		add,do again
	יסר	piel	pft	3ms	יסר	415		correct,chasten
	איסר	piel	impf	1cs	יסר	415		correct,chasten
12:12	יבוk	qal	wci	3ms	בוא	97		come in
	יבואq	qal	wci	3ms	בוא	97		come in
	דבר	piel	pft	3ms	דבר	180		speak
	אמר	qal	infc		אמר	55		say
	שובו	qal	impv	mp	שוב	996		turn,return
12:13	יען	qal	wci	3ms	ענה	772		answer
	יעזב	qal	wci	3ms	עזב	736		leave,loose
	יעצהו	qal	pft	3cp	יעץ	419	3ms	advise,counsel
12:14	ידבר	piel	wci	3ms	דבר	180		speak
	אמר	qal	infc		אמר	55		say
	הכביד	hiph	pft	3ms	כבד	457		make heavy
	אסיף	hiph	impf	1cs	יסף	414		add,do again
	יסר	piel	pft	3ms	יסר	415		correct,chasten
	איסר	piel	impf	1cs	יסר	415		correct,chasten
12:15	שמע	qal	pft	3ms	שמע	1033		hear
	היתה	qal	pft	3fs	היה	224		be,become
	הקים	hiph	infc		קום	877		raise,build,set
	דבר	piel	pft	3ms	דבר	180		speak
12:16	ירא	qal	wci	3ms	ראה	906		see
	שמע	qal	pft	3ms	שמע	1033		hear
	ישבו	hiph	wci	3mp	שוב	996		bring back
	אמר	qal	infc		אמר	55		say
	ראה	qal	impv	ms	ראה	906		see

ChVs	Form	Stem	Tnse	PGN	Root	BDB	Sfx	Meaning
12: 16	ילך	qal	wci	3ms	הלך	229		walk,go
12: 17	ישׁבים	qal	ptc	mp	ישׁב	442		sit,dwell
	ימלך	qal	wci	3ms	מלך	573		be king,reign
12: 18	ישׁלח	qal	wci	3ms	שׁלח	1018		send
	ירגמו	qal	wci	3mp	רגם	920		stone
	ימת	qal	wci	3ms	מות	559		die
	התאמץ	hith	pft	3ms	אמץ	54		strengthen self
	עלות	qal	infc		עלה	748		go up
	נוס	qal	infc		נוס	630		flee,escape
12: 19	יפשׁעו	qal	wci	3mp	פשׁע	833		rebel,sin
12: 20	יהי	qal	wci	3ms	היה	224		be,become
	שׁמע	qal	infc		שׁמע	1033		hear
	שׁב	qal	pft	3ms	שׁוב	996		turn,return
	ישׁלחו	qal	wci	3mp	שׁלח	1018		send
	יקראו	qal	wci	3mp	קרא	894		call,proclaim
	ימליכו	hiph	wci	3mp	מלך	573		cause to reign
	היה	qal	pft	3ms	היה	224		be,become
12: 21	יבאוk	qal	wci	3mp	בוא	97		come in
	יבאq	qal	wci	3ms	בוא	97		come in
	יקהל	hiph	wci	3ms	קהל	874		call assembly
	בחור	qal	pptc	ms	בחר	103		choose
	עשׂה	qal	ptc	ms	עשׂה	793		do,make
	הלחם	niph	infc		לחם	535		wage war
	השׁיב	hiph	infc		שׁוב	996		bring back
12: 22	יהי	qal	wci	3ms	היה	224		be,become
	אמר	qal	infc		אמר	55		say
12: 23	אמר	qal	impv	ms	אמר	55		say
	אמר	qal	infc		אמר	55		say
12: 24	אמר	qal	pft	3ms	אמר	55		say
	תעלו	qal	impf	2mp	עלה	748		go up
	תלחמון	niph	impf	2mp	לחם	535		wage war
	שׁובו	qal	impv	mp	שׁוב	996		turn,return
	נהיה	niph	pft	3ms	היה	224		be done
	ישׁמעו	qal	wci	3mp	שׁמע	1033		hear
	ישׁבו	qal	wci	3mp	שׁוב	996		turn,return
	לכת	qal	infc		הלך	229		walk,go
12: 25	יבן	qal	wci	3ms	בנה	124		build
	ישׁב	qal	wci	3ms	ישׁב	442		sit,dwell
	יצא	qal	wci	3ms	יצא	422		go out
	יבן	qal	wci	3ms	בנה	124		build
12: 26	יאמר	qal	wci	3ms	אמר	55		say
	תשׁוב	qal	impf	3fs	שׁוב	996		turn,return
12: 27	יעלה	qal	impf	3ms	עלה	748		go up
	עשׂות	qal	infc		עשׂה	793		do,make
	שׁב	qal	wcp	3ms	שׁוב	996		turn,return
	הרגני	qal	wcp	3cp	הרג	246	1cs	kill
	שׁבו	qal	wcp	3cp	שׁוב	996		turn,return
12: 28	יועץ	niph	wci	3ms	יעץ	419		consult
	יעשׂ	qal	wci	3ms	עשׂה	793		do,make
	יאמר	qal	wci	3ms	אמר	55		say
	עלות	qal	infc		עלה	748		go up
	העלוך	hiph	pft	3cp	עלה	748	2ms	bring up,offer
12: 29	ישׂם	qal	wci	3ms	שׂים	962		put,set
	נתן	qal	pft	3ms	נתן	678		give,set
12: 30	יהי	qal	wci	3ms	היה	224		be,become
	ילכו	qal	wci	3mp	הלך	229		walk,go
12: 31	יעשׂ	qal	wci	3ms	עשׂה	793		do,make
	יעשׂ	qal	wci	3ms	עשׂה	793		do,make
	היו	qal	pft	3cp	היה	224		be,become
12: 32	יעשׂ	qal	wci	3ms	עשׂה	793		do,make
	יעל	hiph	wci	3ms	עלה	748		bring up,offer
	עשׂה	qal	pft	3ms	עשׂה	793		do,make
	זבח	piel	infc		זבח	256		sacrifice
	עשׂה	qal	pft	3ms	עשׂה	793		do,make
	העמיד	hiph	pft	3ms	עמד	763		set up,raise
	עשׂה	qal	pft	3ms	עשׂה	793		do,make
12: 33	יעל	hiph	wci	3ms	עלה	748		bring up,offer
	עשׂה	qal	pft	3ms	עשׂה	793		do,make
	בדא	qal	pft	3ms	בדא	94		devise
	יעשׂ	qal	wci	3ms	עשׂה	793		do,make
	יעל	hiph	wci	3ms	עלה	748		bring up,offer
	הקטיר	hiph	infc		קטר	882		make sacrifices
13: 1	בא	qal	pft	3ms	בוא	97		come in
	עמד	qal	ptc	ms	עמד	763		stand,stop
	הקטיר	hiph	infc		קטר	882		make sacrifices
13: 2	יקרא	qal	wci	3ms	קרא	894		call,proclaim
	יאמר	qal	wci	3ms	אמר	55		say
	אמר	qal	pft	3ms	אמר	55		say
	נולד	niph	ptc	ms	ילד	408		be born
	זבח	qal	wcp	3ms	זבח	256		slaughter
	מקטרים	hiph	ptc	mp	קטר	882		make sacrifices
	ישׂרפו	qal	impf	3mp	שׂרף	976		burn
13: 3	נתן	qal	pft	3ms	נתן	678		give,set
	אמר	qal	infc		אמר	55		say
	דבר	piel	pft	3ms	דבר	180		speak
	נקרע	niph	ptc	ms	קרע	902		be rent,split
	נשׁפך	niph	wcp	3ms	שׁפך	1049		be poured out
13: 4	יהי	qal	wci	3ms	היה	224		be,become
	שׁמע	qal	infc		שׁמע	1033		hear
	קרא	qal	pft	3ms	קרא	894		call,proclaim
	ישׁלח	qal	wci	3ms	שׁלח	1018		send
	אמר	qal	infc		אמר	55		say
	תפשׂהו	qal	impv	mp	תפשׂ	1074	3ms	seize,grasp
	תיבשׁ	qal	wci	3fs	יבשׁ	386		be dry
	שׁלח	qal	pft	3ms	שׁלח	1018		send
	יכל	qal	pft	3ms	יכל	407		be able
	השׁיבה	hiph	infc		שׁוב	996	3fs	bring back
13: 5	נקרע	niph	pft	3ms	קרע	902		be rent,split
	ישׁפך	niph	wci	3ms	שׁפך	1049		be poured out
	נתן	qal	pft	3ms	נתן	678		give,set
13: 6	יען	qal	wci	3ms	ענה	772		answer
	יאמר	qal	wci	3ms	אמר	55		say
	חל	piel	impv	ms	חלה	318		pacify,appease
	התפלל	hith	impv	ms	פלל	813		pray
	תשׁב	qal	jus	3fs	שׁוב	996		turn,return
	יחל	piel	wci	3ms	חלה	318		pacify,appease
	תשׁב	qal	wci	3fs	שׁוב	996		turn,return
	תהי	qal	wci	3fs	היה	224		be,become

ChVs	Form	Stem	Tnse	PGN	Root	BDB	Sfx	Meaning
13:7	ידבר	piel	wci	3ms	דבר	180		speak
	באה	qal	impv	ms	בוא	97		come in
	סעדה	qal	impv	ms	סעד	703		support
	אתנה	qal	coh	1cs	נתן	678		give,set
13:8	יאמר	qal	wci	3ms	אמר	55		say
	תתן	qal	impf	2ms	נתן	678		give,set
	אבא	qal	impf	1cs	בוא	97		come in
	אכל	qal	impf	1cs	אכל	37		eat,devour
	אשתה	qal	impf	1cs	שתה	1059		drink
13:9	צוה	piel	pft	3ms	צוה	845		command
	אמר	qal	infc		אמר	55		say
	תאכל	qal	impf	2ms	אכל	37		eat,devour
	תשתה	qal	impf	2ms	שתה	1059		drink
	תשוב	qal	impf	2ms	שוב	996		turn,return
	הלכת	qal	pft	2ms	הלך	229		walk,go
13:10	ילך	qal	wci	3ms	הלך	229		walk,go
	שב	qal	pft	3ms	שוב	996		turn,return
	בא	qal	pft	3ms	בוא	97		come in
13:11	ישב	qal	ptc	ms	ישב	442		sit,dwell
	יבוא	qal	wci	3ms	בוא	97		come in
	יספר	piel	wci	3ms	ספר	707		recount
	עשה	qal	pft	3ms	עשה	793		do,make
	דבר	piel	pft	3ms	דבר	180		speak
	יספרום	piel	wci	3mp	ספר	707	3mp	recount
13:12	ידבר	piel	wci	3ms	דבר	180		speak
	הלך	qal	pft	3ms	הלך	229		walk,go
	יראו	qal	wci	3mp	ראה	906		see
	הלך	qal	pft	3ms	הלך	229		walk,go
	בא	qal	pft	3ms	בוא	97		come in
13:13	יאמר	qal	wci	3ms	אמר	55		say
	חבשו	qal	impv	mp	חבש	289		bind
	יחבשו	qal	wci	3mp	חבש	289		bind
	ירכב	qal	wci	3ms	רכב	938		mount,ride
13:14	ילך	qal	wci	3ms	הלך	229		walk,go
	ימצאהו	qal	wci	3ms	מצא	592	3ms	find
	ישב	qal	ptc	ms	ישב	442		sit,dwell
	יאמר	qal	wci	3ms	אמר	55		say
	באת	qal	pft	2ms	בוא	97		come in
	יאמר	qal	wci	3ms	אמר	55		say
13:15	יאמר	qal	wci	3ms	אמר	55		say
	לך	qal	impv	ms	הלך	229		walk,go
	אכל	qal	impv	ms	אכל	37		eat,devour
13:16	יאמר	qal	wci	3ms	אמר	55		say
	אוכל	qal	impf	1cs	יכל	407		be able
	שוב	qal	infc		שוב	996		turn,return
	בוא	qal	infc		בוא	97		come in
	אכל	qal	impf	1cs	אכל	37		eat,devour
	אשתה	qal	impf	1cs	שתה	1059		drink
13:17	תאכל	qal	impf	2ms	אכל	37		eat,devour
	תשתה	qal	impf	2ms	שתה	1059		drink
	תשוב	qal	impf	2ms	שוב	996		turn,return
	לכת	qal	infc		הלך	229		walk,go
	הלכת	qal	pft	2ms	הלך	229		walk,go
13:18	יאמר	qal	wci	3ms	אמר	55		say
13:18	דבר	piel	pft	3ms	דבר	180		speak
	אמר	qal	infc		אמר	55		say
	השבהו	hiph	impv	ms	שוב	996	3ms	bring back
	יאכל	qal	jusm	3ms	אכל	37		eat,devour
	ישת	qal	jus	3ms	שתה	1059		drink
	כחש	piel	pft	3ms	כחש	471		deceive
13:19	ישב	qal	wci	3ms	שוב	996		turn,return
	יאכל	qal	wci	3ms	אכל	37		eat,devour
	ישת	qal	wci	3ms	שתה	1059		drink
13:20	יהי	qal	wci	3ms	היה	224		be,become
	ישבים	qal	ptc	mp	ישב	442		sit,dwell
	יהי	qal	wci	3ms	היה	224		be,become
	השיבו	hiph	pft	3ms	שוב	996	3ms	bring back
13:21	יקרא	qal	wci	3ms	קרא	894		call,proclaim
	בא	qal	pft	3ms	בוא	97		come in
	אמר	qal	infc		אמר	55		say
	אמר	qal	pft	3ms	אמר	55		say
	מרית	qal	pft	2ms	מרה	598		be disobedient
	שמרת	qal	pft	2ms	שמר	1036		keep,watch
	צוך	piel	pft	3ms	צוה	845	2ms	command
13:22	תשב	qal	wci	2ms	שוב	996		turn,return
	תאכל	qal	wci	2ms	אכל	37		eat,devour
	תשת	qal	wci	2ms	שתה	1059		drink
	דבר	piel	pft	3ms	דבר	180		speak
	תאכל	qal	jusm	2ms	אכל	37		eat,devour
	תשת	qal	jus	2ms	שתה	1059		drink
	תבוא	qal	impf	3fs	בוא	97		come in
13:23	יהי	qal	wci	3ms	היה	224		be,become
	אכלו	qal	infc		אכל	37	3ms	eat,devour
	שתותו	qal	infc		שתה	1059	3ms	drink
	יחבש	qal	wci	3ms	חבש	289		bind
	השיבו	hiph	pft	3ms	שוב	996	3ms	bring back
13:24	ילך	qal	wci	3ms	הלך	229		walk,go
	ימצאהו	qal	wci	3ms	מצא	592	3ms	find
	ימיתהו	hiph	wci	3ms	מות	559	3ms	kill
	תהי	qal	wci	3fs	היה	224		be,become
	משלכת	hoph	ptc	fs	שלך	1020		be cast
	עמד	qal	ptc	ms	עמד	763		stand,stop
	עמד	qal	ptc	ms	עמד	763		stand,stop
13:25	עברים	qal	ptc	mp	עבר	716		pass over
	יראו	qal	wci	3mp	ראה	906		see
	משלכת	hoph	ptc	fs	שלך	1020		be cast
	עמד	qal	ptc	ms	עמד	763		stand,stop
	יבאו	qal	wci	3mp	בוא	97		come in
	ידברו	piel	wci	3mp	דבר	180		speak
	ישב	qal	ptc	ms	ישב	442		sit,dwell
13:26	ישמע	qal	wci	3ms	שמע	1033		hear
	השיבו	hiph	pft	3ms	שוב	996	3ms	bring back
	יאמר	qal	wci	3ms	אמר	55		say
	מרה	qal	pft	3ms	מרה	598		be disobedient
	יתנהו	qal	wci	3ms	נתן	678	3ms	give,set
	ישברהו	qal	wci	3ms	שבר	990	3ms	break
	ימתהו	hiph	wci	3ms	מות	559	3ms	kill
	דבר	piel	pft	3ms	דבר	180		speak

ChVs	Form	Stem	Tnse	PGN	Root	BDB	Sfx	Meaning
13:27	ידבר	piel	wci	3ms	דבר	180		speak
	אמר	qal	infc		אמר	55		say
	חבשו	qal	impv	mp	חבש	289		bind
	יחבשו	qal	wci	3mp	חבש	289		bind
13:28	ילך	qal	wci	3ms	הלך	229		walk,go
	ימצא	qal	wci	3ms	מצא	592		find
	משלכת	hoph	ptc	fs	שלך	1020		be cast
	עמדים	qal	ptc	mp	עמד	763		stand,stop
	אכל	qal	pft	3ms	אכל	37		eat,devour
	שבר	qal	pft	3ms	שבר	990		break
13:29	ישׂא	qal	wci	3ms	נשׂא	669		lift,carry
	ינחהו	hiph	wci	3ms	נוח	628	3ms	give rest,put
	ישיבהו	hiph	wci	3ms	שוב	996	3ms	bring back
	יבא	qal	wci	3ms	בוא	97		come in
	ספד	qal	infc		ספד	704		wail,lament
	קברו	qal	infc		קבר	868	3ms	bury
13:30	ינח	hiph	wci	3ms	נוח	628		give rest,put
	יספדו	qal	wci	3mp	ספד	704		wail,lament
13:31	יהי	qal	wci	3ms	היה	224		be,become
	קברו	qal	infc		קבר	868	3ms	bury
	יאמר	qal	wci	3ms	אמר	55		say
	אמר	qal	infc		אמר	55		say
	מותי	qal	infc		מות	559	1cs	die
	קברתם	qal	wcp	2mp	קבר	868		bury
	קבור	qal	pptc	ms	קבר	868		bury
	הניחו	hiph	impv	mp	נוח	628		give rest,put
13:32	היה	qal	infa		היה	224		be,become
	יהיה	qal	impf	3ms	היה	224		be,become
	קרא	qal	pft	3ms	קרא	894		call,proclaim
13:33	שב	qal	pft	3ms	שוב	996		turn,return
	ישב	qal	wci	3ms	שוב	996		turn,return
	יעשׂ	qal	wci	3ms	עשׂה	793		do,make
	חפץ	qal	ptc	ms	חפץ	342		delight in
	ימלא	piel	impf	3ms	מלא	569		fill
	יהי	qal	jus	3ms	היה	224		be,become
13:34	יהי	qal	wci	3ms	היה	224		be,become
	הכחיד	hiph	infc		כחד	470		hide,efface
	השמיד	hiph	infc		שמד	1029		exterminate
14:1	חלה	qal	pft	3ms	חלה	317		be weak,sick
14:2	יאמר	qal	wci	3ms	אמר	55		say
	קומי	qal	impv	fs	קום	877		arise,stand
	השתנית	hith	wcp	2fs	שנה	1039		disguise self
	ידעו	qal	impf	3mp	ידע	393		know
	הלכת	qal	wcp	2fs	הלך	229		walk,go
	דבר	piel	pft	3ms	דבר	180		speak
14:3	לקחת	qal	wcp	2fs	לקח	542		take
	באת	qal	wcp	2fs	בוא	97		come in
	יגיד	hiph	impf	3ms	נגד	616		declare,tell
	יהיה	qal	impf	3ms	היה	224		be,become
14:4	תעשׂ	qal	wci	3fs	עשׂה	793		do,make
	תקם	qal	wci	3fs	קום	877		arise,stand
	תלך	qal	wci	3fs	הלך	229		walk,go
	תבא	qal	wci	3fs	בוא	97		come in
	יכל	qal	pft	3ms	יכל	407		be able
14:4	ראות	qal	infc		ראה	906		see
	קמו	qal	pft	3cp	קום	877		arise,stand
14:5	אמר	qal	pft	3ms	אמר	55		say
	באה	qal	ptc	fs	בוא	97		come in
	דרש	qal	infc		דרש	205		resort to,seek
	חלה	qal	ptc	ms	חלה	317		be weak,sick
	תדבר	piel	impf	2ms	דבר	180		speak
	יהי	qal	jus	3ms	היה	224		be,become
	באה	qal	infc		בוא	97	3fs	come in
	מתנכרה	hith	ptc	fs	נכר	647		be recognized
14:6	יהי	qal	wci	3ms	היה	224		be,become
	שמע	qal	infc		שמע	1033		hear
	באה	qal	ptc	fs	בוא	97		come in
	יאמר	qal	wci	3ms	אמר	55		say
	באי	qal	impv	fs	בוא	97		come in
	מתנכרה	hith	ptc	fs	נכר	647		be recognized
	שלוח	qal	pptc	ms	שלח	1018		send
14:7	לכי	qal	impv	fs	הלך	229		walk,go
	אמרי	qal	impv	fs	אמר	55		say
	אמר	qal	pft	3ms	אמר	55		say
	הרימתיך	hiph	pft	1cs	רום	926	2ms	raise,lift
	אתנך	qal	wci	1cs	נתן	678	2ms	give,set
14:8	אקרע	qal	wci	1cs	קרע	902		tear,rend
	אתנה	qal	wci	1cs	נתן	678	3fs	give,set
	היית	qal	pft	2ms	היה	224		be,become
	שמר	qal	pft	3ms	שמר	1036		keep,watch
	הלך	qal	pft	3ms	הלך	229		walk,go
	עשׂות	qal	infc		עשׂה	793		do,make
14:9	תרע	hiph	wci	2ms	רעע	949		hurt,do evil
	עשׂות	qal	infc		עשׂה	793		do,make
	היו	qal	pft	3cp	היה	224		be,become
	תלך	qal	wci	2ms	הלך	229		walk,go
	תעשׂה	qal	wci	2ms	עשׂה	793		do,make
	הכעיסני	hiph	infc		כעס	494	1cs	vex,provoke
	השלכת	hiph	pft	2ms	שלך	1020		throw,cast
14:10	מביא	hiph	ptc	ms	בוא	97		bring in
	הכרתי	hiph	wcp	1cs	כרת	503		cut off,destroy
	משתין	hiph	ptc	ms	שתן	1010		urinate
	עצור	qal	pptc	ms	עצר	783		restrain
	עזוב	qal	pptc	ms	עזב	736		leave,loose
	בערתי	piel	wcp	1cs	בער	128		burn,consume
	יבער	piel	impf	3ms	בער	128		burn,consume
	תמו	qal	infc		תמם	1070	3ms	be finished
14:11	מת	qal	ptc	ms	מות	559		die
	יאכלו	qal	impf	3mp	אכל	37		eat,devour
	מת	qal	ptc	ms	מות	559		die
	יאכלו	qal	impf	3mp	אכל	37		eat,devour
	דבר	piel	pft	3ms	דבר	180		speak
14:12	קומי	qal	impv	fs	קום	877		arise,stand
	לכי	qal	impv	fs	הלך	229		walk,go
	באה	qal	infc		בוא	97		come in
	מת	qal	wcp	3ms	מות	559		die
14:13	ספדו	qal	wcp	3cp	ספד	704		wail,lament
	קברו	qal	wcp	3cp	קבר	868		bury

ChVs	Form	Stem	Tnse	PGN	Root	BDB	Sfx	Meaning
14:13	יבא	qal	impf	3ms	בוא	97		come in
	נמצא	niph	pft	3ms	מצא	592		be found
14:14	הקים	hiph	wcp	3ms	קום	877		raise,build,set
	יכרית	hiph	impf	3ms	כרת	503		cut off,destroy
14:15	הכה	hiph	wcp	3ms	נכה	645		smite
	ינוד	qal	impf	3ms	נוד	626		wander,lament
	נתשׁ	qal	wcp	3ms	נתשׁ	684		pull up
	נתן	qal	pft	3ms	נתן	678		give,set
	זרם	piel	wcp	3ms	זרה	279	3mp	scatter
	עשׂו	qal	pft	3cp	עשׂה	793		do,make
	מכעיסים	hiph	ptc	mp	כעס	494		vex,provoke
14:16	יתן	qal	impf	3ms	נתן	678		give,set
	חטא	qal	pft	3ms	חטא	306		sin
	החטיא	hiph	pft	3ms	חטא	306		cause to sin
14:17	תקם	qal	wci	3fs	קום	877		arise,stand
	תלך	qal	wci	3fs	הלך	229		walk,go
	תבא	qal	wci	3fs	בוא	97		come in
	באה	qal	ptc	fs	בוא	97		come in
	מת	qal	pft	3ms	מות	559		die
14:18	יקברו	qal	wci	3mp	קבר	868		bury
	יספדו	qal	wci	3mp	ספד	704		wail,lament
	דבר	piel	pft	3ms	דבר	180		speak
14:19	נלחם	niph	pft	3ms	לחם	535		wage war
	מלך	qal	pft	3ms	מלך	573		be king,reign
	כתובים	qal	pptc	mp	כתב	507		write
14:20	מלך	qal	pft	3ms	מלך	573		be king,reign
	ישׁכב	qal	wci	3ms	שׁכב	1011		lie,lie down
	ימלך	qal	wci	3ms	מלך	573		be king,reign
14:21	מלך	qal	pft	3ms	מלך	573		be king,reign
	מלכו	qal	infc		מלך	573	3ms	be king,reign
	מלך	qal	pft	3ms	מלך	573		be king,reign
	בחר	qal	pft	3ms	בחר	103		choose
	שׂום	qal	infc		שׂים	962		put,set
14:22	יעשׂ	qal	wci	3ms	עשׂה	793		do,make
	יקנאו	piel	wci	3mp	קנא	888		be jealous
	עשׂו	qal	pft	3cp	עשׂה	793		do,make
	חטאו	qal	pft	3cp	חטא	306		sin
14:23	יבנו	qal	wci	3mp	בנה	124		build
14:24	היה	qal	pft	3ms	היה	224		be,become
	עשׂו	qal	pft	3cp	עשׂה	793		do,make
	הורישׁ	hiph	pft	3ms	ירשׁ	439		c. to possess
14:25	יהי	qal	wci	3ms	היה	224		be,become
	עלה	qal	pft	3ms	עלה	748		go up
14:26	יקח	qal	wci	3ms	לקח	542		take
	לקח	qal	pft	3ms	לקח	542		take
	יקח	qal	wci	3ms	לקח	542		take
	עשׂה	qal	pft	3ms	עשׂה	793		do,make
14:27	יעשׂ	qal	wci	3ms	עשׂה	793		do,make
	הפקיד	hiph	wcp	3ms	פקד	823		set,entrust
	רצים	qal	ptc	mp	רוץ	930		run
	שׁמרים	qal	ptc	mp	שׁמר	1036		keep,watch
14:28	יהי	qal	wci	3ms	היה	224		be,become
	בא	qal	infc		בוא	97		come in
	ישׂאום	qal	impf	3mp	נשׂא	669	3mp	lift,carry
14:28	רצים	qal	ptc	mp	רוץ	930		run
	השׁיבום	hiph	wcp	3cp	שׁוב	996	3mp	bring back
	רצים	qal	ptc	mp	רוץ	930		run
14:29	עשׂה	qal	pft	3ms	עשׂה	793		do,make
	כתובים	qal	pptc	mp	כתב	507		write
14:30	היתה	qal	pft	3fs	היה	224		be,become
14:31	ישׁכב	qal	wci	3ms	שׁכב	1011		lie,lie down
	יקבר	niph	wci	3ms	קבר	868		be buried
	ימלך	qal	wci	3ms	מלך	573		be king,reign
15:1	מלך	qal	pft	3ms	מלך	573		be king,reign
15:2	מלך	qal	pft	3ms	מלך	573		be king,reign
15:3	ילך	qal	wci	3ms	הלך	229		walk,go
	עשׂה	qal	pft	3ms	עשׂה	793		do,make
	היה	qal	pft	3ms	היה	224		be,become
15:4	נתן	qal	pft	3ms	נתן	678		give,set
	הקים	hiph	infc		קום	877		raise,build,set
	העמיד	hiph	infc		עמד	763		set up,raise
15:5	עשׂה	qal	pft	3ms	עשׂה	793		do,make
	סר	qal	pft	3ms	סור	693		turn aside
	צוהו	piel	pft	3ms	צוה	845	3ms	command
15:6	היתה	qal	pft	3fs	היה	224		be,become
15:7	עשׂה	qal	pft	3ms	עשׂה	793		do,make
	כתובים	qal	pptc	mp	כתב	507		write
	היתה	qal	pft	3fs	היה	224		be,become
15:8	ישׁכב	qal	wci	3ms	שׁכב	1011		lie,lie down
	יקברו	qal	wci	3mp	קבר	868		bury
	ימלך	qal	wci	3ms	מלך	573		be king,reign
15:9	מלך	qal	pft	3ms	מלך	573		be king,reign
15:10	מלך	qal	pft	3ms	מלך	573		be king,reign
15:11	יעשׂ	qal	wci	3ms	עשׂה	793		do,make
15:12	יעבר	hiph	wci	3ms	עבר	716		cause to pass
	יסר	hiph	wci	3ms	סור	693		take away
	עשׂו	qal	pft	3cp	עשׂה	793		do,make
15:13	יסרה	hiph	wci	3ms	סור	693	3fs	take away
	עשׂתה	qal	pft	3fs	עשׂה	793		do,make
	יכרת	qal	wci	3ms	כרת	503		cut,destroy
	ישׂרף	qal	wci	3ms	שׂרף	976		burn
15:14	סרו	qal	pft	3cp	סור	693		turn aside
	היה	qal	pft	3ms	היה	224		be,become
15:15	יבא	hiph	wci	3ms	בוא	97		bring in
15:16	היתה	qal	pft	3fs	היה	224		be,become
15:17	יעל	qal	wci	3ms	עלה	748		go up
	יבן	qal	wci	3ms	בנה	124		build
	תת	qal	infc		נתן	678		give,set
	יצא	qal	ptc	ms	יצא	422		go out
	בא	qal	ptc	ms	בוא	97		come in
15:18	יקח	qal	wci	3ms	לקח	542		take
	נותרים	niph	ptc	mp	יתר	451		be left,remain
	יתנם	qal	wci	3ms	נתן	678	3mp	give,set
	ישׁלחם	qal	wci	3ms	שׁלח	1018	3mp	send
	ישׁב	qal	ptc	ms	ישׁב	442		sit,dwell
	אמר	qal	infc		אמר	55		say
15:19	שׁלחתי	qal	pft	1cs	שׁלח	1018		send
	לך	qal	impv	ms	הלך	229		walk,go

ChVs	Form	Stem	Tnse	PGN	Root	BDB	Sfx	Meaning
15:19	הפרה	hiph	impv	ms	פרר	830		break,frustrate
	יעלה	qal	jusm	3ms	עלה	748		go up
15:20	ישמע	qal	wci	3ms	שמע	1033		hear
	ישלח	qal	wci	3ms	שלח	1018		send
	יך	hiph	wci	3ms	נכה	645		smite
15:21	יהי	qal	wci	3ms	היה	224		be,become
	שמע	qal	infc		שמע	1033		hear
	יחדל	qal	wci	3ms	חדל	292		cease
	בנות	qal	infc		בנה	124		build
	ישב	qal	wci	3ms	ישב	442		sit,dwell
15:22	השמיע	hiph	pft	3ms	שמע	1033		cause to hear
	ישאו	qal	wci	3mp	נשא	669		lift,carry
	בנה	qal	pft	3ms	בנה	124		build
	יבן	qal	wci	3ms	בנה	124		build
15:23	עשה	qal	pft	3ms	עשה	793		do,make
	בנה	qal	pft	3ms	בנה	124		build
	כתובים	qal	pptc	mp	כתב	507		write
	חלה	qal	pft	3ms	חלה	317		be weak,sick
15:24	ישכב	qal	wci	3ms	שכב	1011		lie,lie down
	יקבר	niph	wci	3ms	קבר	868		be buried
	ימלך	qal	wci	3ms	מלך	573		be king,reign
15:25	מלך	qal	pft	3ms	מלך	573		be king,reign
	ימלך	qal	wci	3ms	מלך	573		be king,reign
15:26	יעש	qal	wci	3ms	עשה	793		do,make
	ילך	qal	wci	3ms	הלך	229		walk,go
	החטיא	hiph	pft	3ms	חטא	306		cause to sin
15:27	יקשר	qal	wci	3ms	קשר	905		bind
	יכהו	hiph	wci	3ms	נכה	645	3ms	smite
	צרים	qal	ptc	mp	צור	848		confine,shut in
15:28	ימתהו	hiph	wci	3ms	מות	559	3ms	kill
	ימלך	qal	wci	3ms	מלך	573		be king,reign
15:29	יהי	qal	wci	3ms	היה	224		be,become
	מלכו	qal	infc		מלך	573	3ms	be king,reign
	הכה	hiph	pft	3ms	נכה	645		smite
	השאיר	hiph	pft	3ms	שאר	983		leave,spare
	השמדו	hiph	pft	3ms	שמד	1029	3ms	exterminate
	דבר	piel	pft	3ms	דבר	180		speak
15:30	חטא	qal	pft	3ms	חטא	306		sin
	החטיא	hiph	pft	3ms	חטא	306		cause to sin
	הכעיס	hiph	pft	3ms	כעס	494		vex,provoke
15:31	עשה	qal	pft	3ms	עשה	793		do,make
	כתובים	qal	pptc	mp	כתב	507		write
15:32	היתה	qal	pft	3fs	היה	224		be,become
15:33	מלך	qal	pft	3ms	מלך	573		be king,reign
15:34	יעש	qal	wci	3ms	עשה	793		do,make
	ילך	qal	wci	3ms	הלך	229		walk,go
	החטיא	hiph	pft	3ms	חטא	306		cause to sin
16:1	יהי	qal	wci	3ms	היה	224		be,become
	אמר	qal	infc		אמר	55		say
16:2	הרימתיך	hiph	pft	1cs	רום	926	2ms	raise,lift
	אתנך	qal	wci	1cs	נתן	678	2ms	give,set
	תלך	qal	wci	2ms	הלך	229		walk,go
	תחטא	hiph	wci	2ms	חטא	306		cause to sin
	הכעיסני	hiph	infc		כעס	494	1cs	vex,provoke
16:3	מבעיר	hiph	ptc	ms	בער	128		cause to burn
	נתתי	qal	wcp	1cs	נתן	678		give,set
16:4	מת	qal	ptc	ms	מות	559		die
	יאכלו	qal	impf	3mp	אכל	37		eat,devour
	מת	qal	ptc	ms	מות	559		die
	יאכלו	qal	impf	3mp	אכל	37		eat,devour
16:5	עשה	qal	pft	3ms	עשה	793		do,make
	כתובים	qal	pptc	mp	כתב	507		write
16:6	ישכב	qal	wci	3ms	שכב	1011		lie,lie down
	יקבר	niph	wci	3ms	קבר	868		be buried
	ימלך	qal	wci	3ms	מלך	573		be king,reign
16:7	היה	qal	pft	3ms	היה	224		be,become
	עשה	qal	pft	3ms	עשה	793		do,make
	הכעיסו	hiph	infc		כעס	494	3ms	vex,provoke
	היות	qal	infc		היה	224		be,become
	הכה	hiph	pft	3ms	נכה	645		smite
16:8	מלך	qal	pft	3ms	מלך	573		be king,reign
16:9	יקשר	qal	wci	3ms	קשר	905		bind
	שתה	qal	ptc	ms	שתה	1059		drink
16:10	יבא	qal	wci	3ms	בוא	97		come in
	יכהו	hiph	wci	3ms	נכה	645	3ms	smite
	ימיתהו	hiph	wci	3ms	מות	559	3ms	kill
	ימלך	qal	wci	3ms	מלך	573		be king,reign
16:11	יהי	qal	wci	3ms	היה	224		be,become
	מלכו	qal	infc		מלך	573	3ms	be king,reign
	שבתו	qal	infc		ישב	442	3ms	sit,dwell
	הכה	hiph	pft	3ms	נכה	645		smite
	השאיר	hiph	pft	3ms	שאר	983		leave,spare
	משתין	hiph	ptc	ms	שתן	1010		urinate
	גאליו	qal	ptc	mp	גאל	145	3ms	redeem
16:12	ישמד	hiph	wci	3ms	שמד	1029		exterminate
	דבר	piel	pft	3ms	דבר	180		speak
16:13	חטאו	qal	pft	3cp	חטא	306		sin
	החטיאו	hiph	pft	3cp	חטא	306		cause to sin
	הכעיס	hiph	infc		כעס	494		vex,provoke
16:14	עשה	qal	pft	3ms	עשה	793		do,make
	כתובים	qal	pptc	mp	כתב	507		write
16:15	מלך	qal	pft	3ms	מלך	573		be king,reign
	חנים	qal	ptc	mp	חנה	333		decline,encamp
16:16	ישמע	qal	wci	3ms	שמע	1033		hear
	חנים	qal	ptc	mp	חנה	333		decline,encamp
	אמר	qal	infc		אמר	55		say
	קשר	qal	pft	3ms	קשר	905		bind
	הכה	hiph	pft	3ms	נכה	645		smite
	ימלכו	hiph	wci	3mp	מלך	573		cause to reign
16:17	יעלה	qal	wci	3ms	עלה	748		go up
	יצרו	qal	wci	3mp	צור	848		confine,shut in
16:18	יהי	qal	wci	3ms	היה	224		be,become
	ראות	qal	infc		ראה	906		see
	נלכדה	niph	pft	3fs	לכד	539		be captured
	יבא	qal	wci	3ms	בוא	97		come in
	ישרף	qal	wci	3ms	שרף	976		burn
	ימת	qal	wci	3ms	מות	559		die
16:19	חטא	qal	pft	3ms	חטא	306		sin

ChVs	Form	Stem	Tnse	PGN	Root	BDB	Sfx	Meaning
16:19	עשׂות	qal	infc		עשׂה	793		do,make
	לכת	qal	infc		הלך	229		walk,go
	עשׂה	qal	pft	3ms	עשׂה	793		do,make
	החטיא	hiph	infc		חטא	306		cause to sin
16:20	קשׁר	qal	pft	3ms	קשׁר	905		bind
	כתובים	qal	pptc	mp	כתב	507		write
16:21	יחלק	niph	impf	3ms	חלק	323		be divided
	היה	qal	pft	3ms	היה	224		be,become
	המליכו	hiph	infc		מלך	573	3ms	cause to reign
16:22	יחזק	qal	wci	3ms	חזק	304		be strong
	ימת	qal	wci	3ms	מות	559		die
	ימלך	qal	wci	3ms	מלך	573		be king,reign
16:23	מלך	qal	pft	3ms	מלך	573		be king,reign
	מלך	qal	pft	3ms	מלך	573		be king,reign
16:24	יקן	qal	wci	3ms	קנה	888		get,buy
	יבן	qal	wci	3ms	בנה	124		build
	יקרא	qal	wci	3ms	קרא	894		call,proclaim
	בנה	qal	pft	3ms	בנה	124		build
16:25	יעשׂה	qal	wci	3ms	עשׂה	793		do,make
	ירע	hiph	wci	3ms	רעע	949		hurt,do evil
16:26	ילך	qal	wci	3ms	הלך	229		walk,go
	החטיא	hiph	pft	3ms	חטא	306		cause to sin
	הכעיס	hiph	infc		כעס	494		vex,provoke
16:27	עשׂה	qal	pft	3ms	עשׂה	793		do,make
	עשׂה	qal	pft	3ms	עשׂה	793		do,make
	כתובים	qal	pptc	mp	כתב	507		write
16:28	ישׁכב	qal	wci	3ms	שׁכב	1011		lie,lie down
	יקבר	niph	wci	3ms	קבר	868		be buried
	ימלך	qal	wci	3ms	מלך	573		be king,reign
16:29	מלך	qal	pft	3ms	מלך	573		be king,reign
	ימלך	qal	wci	3ms	מלך	573		be king,reign
16:30	יעשׂ	qal	wci	3ms	עשׂה	793		do,make
16:31	יהי	qal	wci	3ms	היה	224		be,become
	נקל	niph	pft	3ms	קלל	886		be trifling
	לכתו	qal	infc		הלך	229	3ms	walk,go
	יקח	qal	wci	3ms	לקח	542		take
	ילך	qal	wci	3ms	הלך	229		walk,go
	יעבד	qal	wci	3ms	עבד	712		work,serve
	ישׁתחו	hish	wci	3ms	חוה	1005		bow down
16:32	יקם	hiph	wci	3ms	קום	877		raise,build,set
	בנה	qal	pft	3ms	בנה	124		build
16:33	יעשׂ	qal	wci	3ms	עשׂה	793		do,make
	יוסף	hiph	wci	3ms	יסף	414		add,do again
	עשׂות	qal	infc		עשׂה	793		do,make
	הכעיס	hiph	infc		כעס	494		vex,provoke
	היו	qal	pft	3cp	היה	224		be,become
16:34	בנה	qal	pft	3ms	בנה	124		build
	יסדה	piel	pft	3ms	יסד	413	3fs	found,establish
	הציב	hiph	pft	3ms	נצב	662		cause to stand
	דבר	piel	pft	3ms	דבר	180		speak
17:1	יאמר	qal	wci	3ms	אמר	55		say
	עמדתי	qal	pft	1cs	עמד	763		stand,stop
	יהיה	qal	impf	3ms	היה	224		be,become
17:2	יהי	qal	wci	3ms	היה	224		be,become
17:2	אמר	qal	infc		אמר	55		say
17:3	לך	qal	impv	ms	הלך	229		walk,go
	פנית	qal	wcp	2ms	פנה	815		turn
	נסתרת	niph	wcp	2ms	סתר	711		hide,be hid
17:4	היה	qal	wcp	3ms	היה	224		be,become
	תשׁתה	qal	impf	2ms	שׁתה	1059		drink
	צויתי	piel	pft	1cs	צוה	845		command
	כלכלך	pilp	infc		כול	465	2ms	support
17:5	ילך	qal	wci	3ms	הלך	229		walk,go
	יעשׂ	qal	wci	3ms	עשׂה	793		do,make
	ילך	qal	wci	3ms	הלך	229		walk,go
	ישׁב	qal	wci	3ms	ישׁב	442		sit,dwell
17:6	מביאים	hiph	ptc	mp	בוא	97		bring in
	ישׁתה	qal	impf	3ms	שׁתה	1059		drink
17:7	יהי	qal	wci	3ms	היה	224		be,become
	ייבשׁ	qal	wci	3ms	יבשׁ	386		be dry
	היה	qal	pft	3ms	היה	224		be,become
17:8	יהי	qal	wci	3ms	היה	224		be,become
	אמר	qal	infc		אמר	55		say
17:9	קום	qal	impv	ms	קום	877		arise,stand
	לך	qal	impv	ms	הלך	229		walk,go
	ישׁבת	qal	wcp	2ms	ישׁב	442		sit,dwell
	צויתי	piel	pft	1cs	צוה	845		command
	כלכלך	pilp	infc		כול	465	2ms	support
17:10	יקם	qal	wci	3ms	קום	877		arise,stand
	ילך	qal	wci	3ms	הלך	229		walk,go
	יבא	qal	wci	3ms	בוא	97		come in
	מקשׁשׁת	poel	ptc	fs	קשׁשׁ	905		gather stubble
	יקרא	qal	wci	3ms	קרא	894		call,proclaim
	יאמר	qal	wci	3ms	אמר	55		say
	קחי	qal	impv	fs	לקח	542		take
	אשׁתה	qal	cohm	1cs	שׁתה	1059		drink
17:11	תלך	qal	wci	3fs	הלך	229		walk,go
	קחת	qal	infc		לקח	542		take
	יקרא	qal	wci	3ms	קרא	894		call,proclaim
	יאמר	qal	wci	3ms	אמר	55		say
	לקחי	qal	impv	fs	לקח	542		take
17:12	תאמר	qal	wci	3fs	אמר	55		say
	מקשׁשׁת	poel	ptc	fs	קשׁשׁ	905		gather stubble
	באתי	qal	wcp	1cs	בוא	97		come in
	עשׂיתיהו	qal	wcp	1cs	עשׂה	793	3ms	do,make
	אכלנהו	qal	wcp	1cp	אכל	37	3ms	eat,devour
	מתנו	qal	wcp	1cp	מות	559		die
17:13	יאמר	qal	wci	3ms	אמר	55		say
	תיראי	qal	jusm	2fs	ירא	431		fear
	באי	qal	impv	fs	בוא	97		come in
	עשׂי	qal	impv	fs	עשׂה	793		do,make
	עשׂי	qal	impv	fs	עשׂה	793		do,make
	הוצאת	hiph	wcp	2fs	יצא	422		bring out
	תעשׂי	qal	impf	2fs	עשׂה	793		do,make
17:14	אמר	qal	pft	3ms	אמר	55		say
	תכלה	qal	impf	3fs	כלה	477		finished,spent
	תחסר	qal	impf	3fs	חסר	341		lack
	תתןk	qal	infc		נתן	678		give,set

ChVs	Form	Stem	Tnse	PGN	Root	BDB	Sfx	Meaning
17:14	תתq	qal	infc		נתן	678		give,set
17:15	תלך	qal	wci	3fs	הלך	229		walk,go
	תעשׂה	qal	wci	3fs	עשׂה	793		do,make
	תאכל	qal	wci	3fs	אכל	37		eat,devour
17:16	כלתה	qal	pft	3fs	כלה	477		finished,spent
	חסר	qal	pft	3ms	חסר	341		lack
	דבר	piel	pft	3ms	דבר	180		speak
17:17	יהי	qal	wci	3ms	היה	224		be,become
	חלה	qal	pft	3ms	חלה	317		be weak,sick
	יהי	qal	wci	3ms	היה	224		be,become
	נותרה	niph	pft	3fs	יתר	451		be left,remain
17:18	תאמר	qal	wci	3fs	אמר	55		say
	באת	qal	pft	2ms	בוא	97		come in
	הזכיר	hiph	infc		זכר	269		c. to remember
	המית	hiph	infc		מות	559		kill
17:19	יאמר	qal	wci	3ms	אמר	55		say
	תני	qal	impv	fs	נתן	678		give,set
	יקחהו	qal	wci	3ms	לקח	542	3ms	take
	יעלהו	hiph	wci	3ms	עלה	748	3ms	bring up,offer
	ישׁב	qal	ptc	ms	ישׁב	442		sit,dwell
	ישׁכבהו	hiph	wci	3ms	שׁכב	1011	3ms	lay
17:20	יקרא	qal	wci	3ms	קרא	894		call,proclaim
	יאמר	qal	wci	3ms	אמר	55		say
	מתגורר	htpo	ptc	ms	גור	157		sojourn
	הרעות	hiph	pft	2ms	רעע	949		hurt,do evil
	המית	hiph	infc		מות	559		kill
17:21	יתמדד	htpo	wci	3ms	מדד	551		measure self
	יקרא	qal	wci	3ms	קרא	894		call,proclaim
	יאמר	qal	wci	3ms	אמר	55		say
	תשׁב	qal	jus	3fs	שׁוב	996		turn,return
17:22	ישׁמע	qal	wci	3ms	שׁמע	1033		hear
	תשׁב	qal	wci	3fs	שׁוב	996		turn,return
	יחי	qal	wci	3ms	חיה	310		live
17:23	יקח	qal	wci	3ms	לקח	542		take
	ירדהו	hiph	wci	3ms	ירד	432	3ms	bring down
	יתנהו	qal	wci	3ms	נתן	678	3ms	give,set
	יאמר	qal	wci	3ms	אמר	55		say
	ראי	qal	impv	fs	ראה	906		see
17:24	תאמר	qal	wci	3fs	אמר	55		say
	ידעתי	qal	pft	1cs	ידע	393		know
18:1	יהי	qal	wci	3ms	היה	224		be,become
	היה	qal	pft	3ms	היה	224		be,become
	אמר	qal	infc		אמר	55		say
	לך	qal	impv	ms	הלך	229		walk,go
	הראה	niph	impv	ms	ראה	906		appear,be seen
	אתנה	qal	coh	1cs	נתן	678		give,set
18:2	ילך	qal	wci	3ms	הלך	229		walk,go
	הראות	niph	infc		ראה	906		appear,be seen
18:3	יקרא	qal	wci	3ms	קרא	894		call,proclaim
	היה	qal	pft	3ms	היה	224		be,become
	ירא	qal	ptc	ms	ירא	431		fear
18:4	יהי	qal	wci	3ms	היה	224		be,become
	הכרית	hiph	infc		כרת	503		cut off,destroy
	יקח	qal	wci	3ms	לקח	542		take
18:4	יחביאם	hiph	wci	3ms	חבא	285	3mp	hide
	כלכלם	pilp	wcp	3ms	כול	465	3mp	support
18:5	יאמר	qal	wci	3ms	אמר	55		say
	לך	qal	impv	ms	הלך	229		walk,go
	נמצא	qal	impf	1cp	מצא	592		find
	נחיה	piel	impf	1cp	חיה	310		preserve,revive
	נכרית	hiph	impf	1cp	כרת	503		cut off,destroy
18:6	יחלקו	piel	wci	3mp	חלק	323		divide
	עבר	qal	infc		עבר	716		pass over
	הלך	qal	pft	3ms	הלך	229		walk,go
	הלך	qal	pft	3ms	הלך	229		walk,go
18:7	יהי	qal	wci	3ms	היה	224		be,become
	קראתו	qal	infc		קרא	896	3ms	meet,encounter
	יכרהו	hiph	wci	3ms	נכר	647	3ms	regard,notice
	יפל	qal	wci	3ms	נפל	656		fall
	יאמר	qal	wci	3ms	אמר	55		say
18:8	יאמר	qal	wci	3ms	אמר	55		say
	לך	qal	impv	ms	הלך	229		walk,go
	אמר	qal	impv	ms	אמר	55		say
18:9	יאמר	qal	wci	3ms	אמר	55		say
	חטאתי	qal	pft	1cs	חטא	306		sin
	נתן	qal	ptc	ms	נתן	678		give,set
	המיתני	hiph	infc		מות	559	1cs	kill
18:10	שׁלח	qal	pft	3ms	שׁלח	1018		send
	בקשׁך	piel	infc		בקשׁ	134	2ms	seek
	אמרו	qal	wcp	3cp	אמר	55		say
	השׁביע	hiph	wcp	3ms	שׁבע	989		cause to swear
	ימצאכה	qal	impf	3ms	מצא	592	2ms	find
18:11	אמר	qal	ptc	ms	אמר	55		say
	לך	qal	impv	ms	הלך	229		walk,go
	אמר	qal	impv	ms	אמר	55		say
18:12	היה	qal	wcp	3ms	היה	224		be,become
	אלך	qal	impf	1cs	הלך	229		walk,go
	ישׂאך	qal	impf	3ms	נשׂא	669	2ms	lift,carry
	אדע	qal	impf	1cs	ידע	393		know
	באתי	qal	wcp	1cs	בוא	97		come in
	הגיד	hiph	infc		נגד	616		declare,tell
	ימצאך	qal	impf	3ms	מצא	592	2ms	find
	הרגני	qal	wcp	3ms	הרג	246	1cs	kill
	ירא	qal	ptc	ms	ירא	431		fear
18:13	הגד	hoph	pft	3ms	נגד	616		be told
	עשׂיתי	qal	pft	1cs	עשׂה	793		do,make
	הרג	qal	infc		הרג	246		kill
	אחבא	hiph	wci	1cs	חבא	285		hide
	אכלכלם	pilp	wci	1cs	כול	465	3mp	support
18:14	אמר	qal	ptc	ms	אמר	55		say
	לך	qal	impv	ms	הלך	229		walk,go
	אמר	qal	impv	ms	אמר	55		say
	הרגני	qal	wcp	3ms	הרג	246	1cs	kill
18:15	יאמר	qal	wci	3ms	אמר	55		say
	עמדתי	qal	pft	1cs	עמד	763		stand,stop
	אראה	niph	impf	1cs	ראה	906		appear,be seen
18:16	ילך	qal	wci	3ms	הלך	229		walk,go
	קראת	qal	infc		קרא	896		meet,encounter

ChVs	Form	Stem	Tnse	PGN	Root	BDB	Sfx	Meaning
18:16	ינד	hiph	wci	3ms	נגד	616		declare,tell
	ילך	qal	wci	3ms	הלך	229		walk,go
	קראת	qal	infc		קרא	896		meet,encounter
18:17	יהי	qal	wci	3ms	היה	224		be,become
	ראות	qal	infc		ראה	906		see
	יאמר	qal	wci	3ms	אמר	55		say
	עכר	qal	ptc	ms	עכר	747		trouble
18:18	יאמר	qal	wci	3ms	אמר	55		say
	עכרתי	qal	pft	1cs	עכר	747		trouble
	עזבכם	qal	infc		עזב	736	2mp	leave,loose
	תלך	qal	wci	2ms	הלך	229		walk,go
18:19	שׁלח	qal	impv	ms	שׁלח	1018		send
	קבץ	qal	impv	ms	קבץ	867		gather,collect
	אכלי	qal	ptc	mp	אכל	37		eat,devour
18:20	ישׁלח	qal	wci	3ms	שׁלח	1018		send
	יקבץ	qal	wci	3ms	קבץ	867		gather,collect
18:21	ינשׁ	qal	wci	3ms	נגשׁ	620		draw near
	יאמר	qal	wci	3ms	אמר	55		say
	פסחים	qal	ptc	mp	פסח	820		limp
	לכו	qal	impv	mp	הלך	229		walk,go
	לכו	qal	impv	mp	הלך	229		walk,go
	ענו	qal	pft	3cp	ענה	772		answer
18:22	יאמר	qal	wci	3ms	אמר	55		say
	נותרתי	niph	pft	1cs	יתר	451		be left,remain
18:23	יתנו	qal	jusm	3mp	נתן	678		give,set
	יבחרו	qal	jusm	3mp	בחר	103		choose
	ינתחהו	piel	jusm	3mp	נתח	677	3ms	cut in pieces
	ישׂימו	qal	jusm	3mp	שׂים	962		put,set
	ישׂימו	qal	impf	3mp	שׂים	962		put,set
	אעשׂה	qal	impf	1cs	עשׂה	793		do,make
	נתתי	qal	wcp	1cs	נתן	678		give,set
	אשׂים	qal	impf	1cs	שׂים	962		put,set
18:24	קראתם	qal	wcp	2mp	קרא	894		call,proclaim
	אקרא	qal	impf	1cs	קרא	894		call,proclaim
	היה	qal	wcp	3ms	היה	224		be,become
	יענה	qal	impf	3ms	ענה	772		answer
	יען	qal	wci	3ms	ענה	772		answer
	יאמרו	qal	wci	3mp	אמר	55		say
18:25	יאמר	qal	wci	3ms	אמר	55		say
	בחרו	qal	impv	mp	בחר	103		choose
	עשׂו	qal	impv	mp	עשׂה	793		do,make
	קראו	qal	impv	mp	קרא	894		call,proclaim
	תשׂימו	qal	impf	2mp	שׂים	962		put,set
18:26	יקחו	qal	wci	3mp	לקח	542		take
	נתן	qal	pft	3ms	נתן	678		give,set
	יעשׂו	qal	wci	3mp	עשׂה	793		do,make
	יקראו	qal	wci	3mp	קרא	894		call,proclaim
	אמר	qal	infc		אמר	55		say
	עננו	qal	impv	ms	ענה	772	1cp	answer
	ענה	qal	ptc	ms	ענה	772		answer
	יפסחו	piel	wci	3mp	פסח	820		go limp,leap
	עשׂה	qal	pft	3ms	עשׂה	793		do,make
18:27	יהי	qal	wci	3ms	היה	224		be,become
	יהתל	piel	wci	3ms	התל	251		deceive
18:27	יאמר	qal	wci	3ms	אמר	55		say
	קראו	qal	impv	mp	קרא	894		call,proclaim
	יקץ	qal	wcp	3ms	יקץ	429		awake
18:28	יקראו	qal	wci	3mp	קרא	894		call,proclaim
	יתגדדו	htpo	wci	3mp	גדד	151		cut self,throng
	שׁפך	qal	infc		שׁפך	1049		pour out
18:29	יהי	qal	wci	3ms	היה	224		be,become
	עבר	qal	infc		עבר	716		pass over
	יתנבאו	hith	wci	3mp	נבא	612		prophesy
	עלות	qal	infc		עלה	748		go up
	ענה	qal	ptc	ms	ענה	772		answer
18:30	יאמר	qal	wci	3ms	אמר	55		say
	גשׁו	qal	impv	mp	נגשׁ	620		draw near
	יגשׁו	qal	wci	3mp	נגשׁ	620		draw near
	ירפא	piel	wci	3ms	רפא	950		heal
	הרוס	qal	pptc	ms	הרס	248		throw down
18:31	יקח	qal	wci	3ms	לקח	542		take
	היה	qal	pft	3ms	היה	224		be,become
	אמר	qal	infc		אמר	55		say
	יהיה	qal	impf	3ms	היה	224		be,become
18:32	יבנה	qal	wci	3ms	בנה	124		build
	יעשׂ	qal	wci	3ms	עשׂה	793		do,make
18:33	יערך	qal	wci	3ms	ערך	789		set in order
	ינתח	piel	wci	3ms	נתח	677		cut in pieces
	ישׂם	qal	wci	3ms	שׂים	962		put,set
18:34	יאמר	qal	wci	3ms	אמר	55		say
	מלאו	qal	impv	mp	מלא	569		be full,fill
	יצקו	qal	impv	mp	יצק	427		pour out,cast
	יאמר	qal	wci	3ms	אמר	55		say
	שׁנו	qal	impv	mp	שׁנה	1040		do again,repeat
	ישׁנו	qal	wci	3mp	שׁנה	1040		do again,repeat
	יאמר	qal	wci	3ms	אמר	55		say
	שׁלשׁו	piel	impv	mp	שׁלשׁ	1026		divide into 3
	ישׁלשׁו	piel	wci	3mp	שׁלשׁ	1026		divide into 3
18:35	ילכו	qal	wci	3mp	הלך	229		walk,go
	מלא	piel	pft	3ms	מלא	569		fill
18:36	יהי	qal	wci	3ms	היה	224		be,become
	עלות	qal	infc		עלה	748		go up
	ינשׁ	qal	wci	3ms	נגשׁ	620		draw near
	יאמר	qal	wci	3ms	אמר	55		say
	יודע	niph	jusm	3ms	ידע	393		be made known
	עשׂיתי	qal	pft	1cs	עשׂה	793		do,make
18:37	עננִי	qal	impv	ms	ענה	772	1cs	answer
	עננִי	qal	impv	ms	ענה	772	1cs	answer
	ידעו	qal	jusm	3mp	ידע	393		know
	הסבת	hiph	pft	2ms	סבב	685		cause to turn
18:38	תפל	qal	wci	3fs	נפל	656		fall
	תאכל	qal	wci	3fs	אכל	37		eat,devour
	לחכה	piel	pft	3fs	לחך	535		lick up
18:39	ירא	qal	wci	3ms	ראה	906		see
	יפלו	qal	wci	3mp	נפל	656		fall
	יאמרו	qal	wci	3mp	אמר	55		say
18:40	יאמר	qal	wci	3ms	אמר	55		say
	תפשׂו	qal	impv	mp	תפשׂ	1074		seize,grasp

ChVs	Form	Stem	Tnse	PGN	Root	BDB	Sfx	Meaning
18:40	ימלט	niph	jusm	3ms	מלט	572		escape
	יתפשום	qal	wci	3mp	תפש	1074	3mp	seize,grasp
	יורדם	hiph	wci	3ms	ירד	432	3mp	bring down
	ישחטם	qal	wci	3ms	שחט	1006	3mp	slaughter
18:41	יאמר	qal	wci	3ms	אמר	55		say
	עלה	qal	impv	ms	עלה	748		go up
	אכל	qal	impv	ms	אכל	37		eat,devour
	שתה	qal	impv	ms	שתה	1059		drink
18:42	יעלה	qal	wci	3ms	עלה	748		go up
	אכל	qal	infc		אכל	37		eat,devour
	שתות	qal	infc		שתה	1059		drink
	עלה	qal	pft	3ms	עלה	748		go up
	יגהר	qal	wci	3ms	גהר	155		bend
	ישם	qal	wci	3ms	שים	962		put,set
18:43	יאמר	qal	wci	3ms	אמר	55		say
	עלה	qal	impv	ms	עלה	748		go up
	הבט	hiph	impv	ms	נבט	613		look,regard
	יעל	qal	wci	3ms	עלה	748		go up
	יבט	hiph	wci	3ms	נבט	613		look,regard
	יאמר	qal	wci	3ms	אמר	55		say
	יאמר	qal	wci	3ms	אמר	55		say
	שב	qal	impv	ms	שוב	996		turn,return
18:44	יהי	qal	wci	3ms	היה	224		be,become
	יאמר	qal	wci	3ms	אמר	55		say
	עלה	qal	ptc	fs	עלה	748		go up
	יאמר	qal	wci	3ms	אמר	55		say
	עלה	qal	impv	ms	עלה	748		go up
	אמר	qal	impv	ms	אמר	55		say
	אסר	qal	impv	ms	אסר	63		tie,bind
	רד	qal	impv	ms	ירד	432		come down
	יעצרכה	qal	impf	3ms	עצר	783	2ms	restrain
18:45	יהי	qal	wci	3ms	היה	224		be,become
	התקדרו	hith	pft	3cp	קדר	871		grow dark
	יהי	qal	wci	3ms	היה	224		be,become
	ירכב	qal	wci	3ms	רכב	938		mount,ride
	ילך	qal	wci	3ms	הלך	229		walk,go
18:46	היתה	qal	pft	3fs	היה	224		be,become
	ישנס	piel	wci	3ms	שנס	1042		gird up
	ירץ	qal	wci	3ms	רוץ	930		run
	באכה	qal	infc		בוא	97	2ms	come in
19:1	יגד	hiph	wci	3ms	נגד	616		declare,tell
	עשה	qal	pft	3ms	עשה	793		do,make
	הרג	qal	pft	3ms	הרג	246		kill
19:2	תשלח	qal	wci	3fs	שלח	1018		send
	אמר	qal	infc		אמר	55		say
	יעשון	qal	jusm	3mp	עשה	793		do,make
	יוספון	hiph	jusm	3mp	יסף	414		add,do again
	אשים	qal	impf	1cs	שים	962		put,set
19:3	ירא	qal	wci	3ms	ראה	906		see
	יקם	qal	wci	3ms	קום	877		arise,stand
	ילך	qal	wci	3ms	הלך	229		walk,go
	יבא	qal	wci	3ms	בוא	97		come in
	ינח	hiph	wci	3ms	נוח	628		give rest,put
19:4	הלך	qal	pft	3ms	הלך	229		walk,go
19:4	יבא	qal	wci	3ms	בוא	97		come in
	ישב	qal	wci	3ms	ישב	442		sit,dwell
	ישאל	qal	wci	3ms	שאל	981		ask,borrow
	מות	qal	infc		מות	559		die
	יאמר	qal	wci	3ms	אמר	55		say
	קח	qal	impv	ms	לקח	542		take
19:5	ישכב	qal	wci	3ms	שכב	1011		lie,lie down
	יישן	qal	wci	3ms	ישן	445		sleep
	נגע	qal	ptc	ms	נגע	619		touch,strike
	יאמר	qal	wci	3ms	אמר	55		say
	קום	qal	impv	ms	קום	877		arise,stand
	אכול	qal	impv	ms	אכל	37		eat,devour
19:6	יבט	hiph	wci	3ms	נבט	613		look,regard
	יאכל	qal	wci	3ms	אכל	37		eat,devour
	ישת	qal	wci	3ms	שתה	1059		drink
	ישב	qal	wci	3ms	שוב	996		turn,return
	ישכב	qal	wci	3ms	שכב	1011		lie,lie down
19:7	ישב	qal	wci	3ms	שוב	996		turn,return
	יגע	qal	wci	3ms	נגע	619		touch,strike
	יאמר	qal	wci	3ms	אמר	55		say
	קום	qal	impv	ms	קום	877		arise,stand
	אכל	qal	impv	ms	אכל	37		eat,devour
19:8	יקם	qal	wci	3ms	קום	877		arise,stand
	יאכל	qal	wci	3ms	אכל	37		eat,devour
	ישתה	qal	wci	3ms	שתה	1059		drink
	ילך	qal	wci	3ms	הלך	229		walk,go
19:9	יבא	qal	wci	3ms	בוא	97		come in
	ילן	qal	wci	3ms	לון	533		lodge,remain
	יאמר	qal	wci	3ms	אמר	55		say
19:10	יאמר	qal	wci	3ms	אמר	55		say
	קנא	piel	infa		קנא	888		be jealous
	קנאתי	piel	pft	1cs	קנא	888		be jealous
	עזבו	qal	pft	3cp	עזב	736		leave,loose
	הרסו	qal	pft	3cp	הרס	248		throw down
	הרגו	qal	pft	3cp	הרג	246		kill
	אותר	niph	wci	1cs	יתר	451		be left,remain
	יבקשו	piel	wci	3mp	בקש	134		seek
	קחתה	qal	infc		לקח	542	3fs	take
19:11	יאמר	qal	wci	3ms	אמר	55		say
	צא	qal	impv	ms	יצא	422		go out
	עמדת	qal	wcp	2ms	עמד	763		stand,stop
	עבר	qal	ptc	ms	עבר	716		pass over
	מפרק	piel	ptc	ms	פרק	830		tear off
	משבר	piel	ptc	ms	שבר	990		shatter
19:13	יהי	qal	wci	3ms	היה	224		be,become
	שמע	qal	infc		שמע	1033		hear
	ילט	hiph	wci	3ms	לוט	532		wrap
	יצא	qal	wci	3ms	יצא	422		go out
	יעמד	qal	wci	3ms	עמד	763		stand,stop
	יאמר	qal	wci	3ms	אמר	55		say
19:14	יאמר	qal	wci	3ms	אמר	55		say
	קנא	piel	infa		קנא	888		be jealous
	קנאתי	piel	pft	1cs	קנא	888		be jealous
	עזבו	qal	pft	3cp	עזב	736		leave,loose

ChVs	Form	Stem	Tnse	PGN	Root	BDB	Sfx	Meaning
19:14	הרסו	qal	pft	3cp	הרס	248		throw down
	הרגו	qal	pft	3cp	הרג	246		kill
	אותר	niph	wci	1cs	יתר	451		be left,remain
	יבקשו	piel	wci	3mp	בקש	134		seek
	קחתה	qal	infc		לקח	542	3fs	take
19:15	יאמר	qal	wci	3ms	אמר	55		say
	לך	qal	impv	ms	הלך	229		walk,go
	שוב	qal	impv	ms	שוב	996		turn,return
	באת	qal	wcp	2ms	בוא	97		come in
	משחת	qal	wcp	2ms	משח	602		smear,anoint
19:16	תמשח	qal	impf	2ms	משח	602		smear,anoint
	תמשח	qal	impf	2ms	משח	602		smear,anoint
19:17	היה	qal	wcp	3ms	היה	224		be,become
	נמלט	niph	ptc	ms	מלט	572		escape
	ימית	hiph	impf	3ms	מות	559		kill
	נמלט	niph	ptc	ms	מלט	572		escape
	ימית	hiph	impf	3ms	מות	559		kill
19:18	השארתי	hiph	wcp	1cs	שאר	983		leave,spare
	כרעו	qal	pft	3cp	כרע	502		bow down
	נשק	qal	pft	3ms	נשק	676		kiss
19:19	ילך	qal	wci	3ms	הלך	229		walk,go
	ימצא	qal	wci	3ms	מצא	592		find
	חרש	qal	ptc	ms	חרש	360		engrave,plough
	יעבר	qal	wci	3ms	עבר	716		pass over
	ישלך	hiph	wci	3ms	שלך	1020		throw,cast
19:20	יעזב	qal	wci	3ms	עזב	736		leave,loose
	ירץ	qal	wci	3ms	רוץ	930		run
	יאמר	qal	wci	3ms	אמר	55		say
	אשקה	qal	coh	1cs	נשק	676		kiss
	אלכה	qal	coh	1cs	הלך	229		walk,go
	יאמר	qal	wci	3ms	אמר	55		say
	לך	qal	impv	ms	הלך	229		walk,go
	שוב	qal	impv	ms	שוב	996		turn,return
	עשיתי	qal	pft	1cs	עשה	793		do,make
19:21	ישב	qal	wci	3ms	שוב	996		turn,return
	יקח	qal	wci	3ms	לקח	542		take
	יזבחהו	qal	wci	3ms	זבח	256	3ms	slaughter
	בשלם	piel	pft	3ms	בשל	143	3mp	boil,cook
	יתן	qal	wci	3ms	נתן	678		give,set
	יאכלו	qal	wci	3mp	אכל	37		eat,devour
	יקם	qal	wci	3ms	קום	877		arise,stand
	ילך	qal	wci	3ms	הלך	229		walk,go
	ישרתהו	piel	wci	3ms	שרת	1058	3ms	minister,serve
20:1	קבץ	qal	pft	3ms	קבץ	867		gather,collect
	יעל	qal	wci	3ms	עלה	748		go up
	יצר	qal	wci	3ms	צור	848		confine,shut in
	ילחם	niph	wci	3ms	לחם	535		wage war
20:2	ישלח	qal	wci	3ms	שלח	1018		send
20:3	יאמר	qal	wci	3ms	אמר	55		say
	אמר	qal	pft	3ms	אמר	55		say
20:4	יען	qal	wci	3ms	ענה	772		answer
	יאמר	qal	wci	3ms	אמר	55		say
20:5	ישבו	qal	wci	3mp	שוב	996		turn,return
	יאמרו	qal	wci	3mp	אמר	55		say
20:5	אמר	qal	pft	3ms	אמר	55		say
	אמר	qal	infc		אמר	55		say
	שלחתי	qal	pft	1cs	שלח	1018		send
	אמר	qal	infc		אמר	55		say
	תתן	qal	impf	2ms	נתן	678		give,set
20:6	אשלח	qal	impf	1cs	שלח	1018		send
	חפשו	piel	wcp	3cp	חפש	344		search for
	היה	qal	wcp	3ms	היה	224		be,become
	ישימו	qal	impf	3mp	שים	962		put,set
	לקחו	qal	wcp	3cp	לקח	542		take
20:7	יקרא	qal	wci	3ms	קרא	894		call,proclaim
	יאמר	qal	wci	3ms	אמר	55		say
	דעו	qal	impv	mp	ידע	393		know
	ראו	qal	impv	mp	ראה	906		see
	מבקש	piel	ptc	ms	בקש	134		seek
	שלח	qal	pft	3ms	שלח	1018		send
	מנעתי	qal	pft	1cs	מנע	586		withhold
20:8	יאמרו	qal	wci	3mp	אמר	55		say
	תשמע	qal	jusm	2ms	שמע	1033		hear
	תאבה	qal	impf	2ms	אבה	2		be willing
20:9	יאמר	qal	wci	3ms	אמר	55		say
	אמרו	qal	impv	mp	אמר	55		say
	שלחת	qal	pft	2ms	שלח	1018		send
	אעשה	qal	impf	1cs	עשה	793		do,make
	אוכל	qal	impf	1cs	יכל	407		be able
	עשות	qal	infc		עשה	793		do,make
	ילכו	qal	wci	3mp	הלך	229		walk,go
	ישבהו	hiph	wci	3mp	שוב	996	3ms	bring back
20:10	ישלח	qal	wci	3ms	שלח	1018		send
	יאמר	qal	wci	3ms	אמר	55		say
	יעשון	qal	jusm	3mp	עשה	793		do,make
	יוספו	hiph	jusm	3mp	יסף	414		add,do again
	ישפק	qal	impf	3ms	שפק	974		suffice
20:11	יען	qal	wci	3ms	ענה	772		answer
	יאמר	qal	wci	3ms	אמר	55		say
	דברו	piel	impv	mp	דבר	180		speak
	יתהלל	hith	jusm	3ms	הלל	237		glory
	חגר	qal	ptc	ms	חגר	291		gird
	מפתח	piel	ptc	ms	פתח	834		loose,free
20:12	יהי	qal	wci	3ms	היה	224		be,become
	שמע	qal	infc		שמע	1033		hear
	שתה	qal	ptc	ms	שתה	1059		drink
	יאמר	qal	wci	3ms	אמר	55		say
	שימו	qal	impv	mp	שים	962		put,set
	ישימו	qal	wci	3mp	שים	962		put,set
20:13	נגש	niph	pft	3ms	נגש	620		draw near
	יאמר	qal	wci	3ms	אמר	55		say
	אמר	qal	pft	3ms	אמר	55		say
	ראית	qal	pft	2ms	ראה	906		see
	נתנו	qal	ptc	ms	נתן	678	3ms	give,set
	ידעת	qal	wcp	2ms	ידע	393		know
20:14	יאמר	qal	wci	3ms	אמר	55		say
	יאמר	qal	wci	3ms	אמר	55		say
	אמר	qal	pft	3ms	אמר	55		say

ChVs	Form	Stem	Tnse	PGN	Root	BDB	Sfx	Meaning
20: 14	יאמר	qal	wci	3ms	אמר	55		say
	יאסר	qal	impf	3ms	אסר	63		tie, bind
	יאמר	qal	wci	3ms	אמר	55		say
20: 15	יפקד	qal	wci	3ms	פקד	823		attend to, visit
	יהיו	qal	wci	3mp	היה	224		be, become
	פקד	qal	pft	3ms	פקד	823		attend to, visit
20: 16	יצאו	qal	wci	3mp	יצא	422		go out
	שתה	qal	ptc	ms	שתה	1059		drink
	עזר	qal	ptc	ms	עזר	740		help, aid
20: 17	יצאו	qal	wci	3mp	יצא	422		go out
	ישלח	qal	wci	3ms	שלח	1018		send
	יגידו	hiph	wci	3mp	נגד	616		declare, tell
	אמר	qal	infc		אמר	55		say
	יצאו	qal	pft	3cp	יצא	422		go out
20: 18	יאמר	qal	wci	3ms	אמר	55		say
	יצאו	qal	pft	3cp	יצא	422		go out
	תפשום	qal	impv	mp	תפש	1074	3mp	seize, grasp
	יצאו	qal	pft	3cp	יצא	422		go out
	תפשום	qal	impv	mp	תפש	1074	3mp	seize, grasp
20: 19	יצאו	qal	pft	3cp	יצא	422		go out
20: 20	יכו	hiph	wci	3mp	נכה	645		smite
	ינסו	qal	wci	3mp	נוס	630		flee, escape
	ירדפם	qal	wci	3ms	רדף	922	3mp	pursue
	ימלט	niph	wci	3ms	מלט	572		escape
20: 21	יצא	qal	wci	3ms	יצא	422		go out
	יך	hiph	wci	3ms	נכה	645		smite
	הכה	hiph	pft	3ms	נכה	645		smite
20: 22	יגש	qal	wci	3ms	נגש	620		draw near
	יאמר	qal	wci	3ms	אמר	55		say
	לך	qal	impv	ms	הלך	229		walk, go
	התחזק	hith	impv	ms	חזק	304		strengthen self
	דע	qal	impv	ms	ידע	393		know
	ראה	qal	impv	ms	ראה	906		see
	תעשׂה	qal	impf	2ms	עשׂה	793		do, make
	עלה	qal	ptc	ms	עלה	748		go up
20: 23	אמרו	qal	pft	3cp	אמר	55		say
	חזקו	qal	pft	3cp	חזק	304		be strong
	נלחם	niph	impf	1cp	לחם	535		wage war
	נחזק	qal	impf	1cp	חזק	304		be strong
20: 24	עשׂה	qal	impv	ms	עשׂה	793		do, make
	הסר	hiph	impv	ms	סור	693		take away
	שׂים	qal	impv	ms	שׂים	962		put, set
20: 25	תמנה	qal	impf	2ms	מנה	584		count, allot
	נפל	qal	ptc	ms	נפל	656		fall
	נלחמה	niph	coh	1cp	לחם	535		wage war
	נחזק	qal	impf	1cp	חזק	304		be strong
	ישמע	qal	wci	3ms	שמע	1033		hear
	יעשׂ	qal	wci	3ms	עשׂה	793		do, make
20: 26	יהי	qal	wci	3ms	היה	224		be, become
	יפקד	qal	wci	3ms	פקד	823		attend to, visit
	יעל	qal	wci	3ms	עלה	748		go up
20: 27	התפקדו	hoth	pft	3cp	פקד	823		be mustered
	כלכלו	polp	pft	3cp	כול	465		be supplied
	ילכו	qal	wci	3mp	הלך	229		walk, go
20: 27	קראתם	qal	infc		קרא	896	3mp	meet, encounter
	יחנו	qal	wci	3mp	חנה	333		decline, encamp
	מלאו	piel	pft	3cp	מלא	569		fill
20: 28	יגש	qal	wci	3ms	נגש	620		draw near
	יאמר	qal	wci	3ms	אמר	55		say
	יאמר	qal	wci	3ms	אמר	55		say
	אמר	qal	pft	3ms	אמר	55		say
	אמרו	qal	pft	3cp	אמר	55		say
	נתתי	qal	wcp	1cs	נתן	678		give, set
	ידעתם	qal	wcp	2mp	ידע	393		know
20: 29	יחנו	qal	wci	3mp	חנה	333		decline, encamp
	יהי	qal	wci	3ms	היה	224		be, become
	תקרב	qal	wci	3fs	קרב	897		approach
	יכו	hiph	wci	3mp	נכה	645		smite
20: 30	ינסו	qal	wci	3mp	נוס	630		flee, escape
	נותרים	niph	ptc	mp	יתר	451		be left, remain
	תפל	qal	wci	3fs	נפל	656		fall
	נותרים	niph	ptc	mp	יתר	451		be left, remain
	נס	qal	pft	3ms	נוס	630		flee, escape
	יבא	qal	wci	3ms	בוא	97		come in
20: 31	יאמרו	qal	wci	3mp	אמר	55		say
	שמענו	qal	pft	1cp	שמע	1033		hear
	נשׂימה	qal	coh	1cp	שׂים	962		put, set
	נצא	qal	cohm	1cp	יצא	422		go out
	יחיה	piel	impf	3ms	חיה	310		preserve, revive
20: 32	יחגרו	qal	wci	3mp	חגר	291		gird
	יבאו	qal	wci	3mp	בוא	97		come in
	יאמרו	qal	wci	3mp	אמר	55		say
	אמר	qal	pft	3ms	אמר	55		say
	תחי	qal	jus	3fs	חיה	310		live
	יאמר	qal	wci	3ms	אמר	55		say
20: 33	ינחשו	piel	impf	3mp	נחש	638		divine
	ימהרו	piel	wci	3mp	מהר	554		hasten
	יחלטו	hiph	wci	3mp	חלט	319		snatch
	יאמרו	qal	wci	3mp	אמר	55		say
	יאמר	qal	wci	3ms	אמר	55		say
	באו	qal	impv	mp	בוא	97		come in
	קחהו	qal	impv	mp	לקח	542	3ms	take
	יצא	qal	wci	3ms	יצא	422		go out
	יעלהו	hiph	wci	3ms	עלה	748	3ms	bring up, offer
20: 34	יאמר	qal	wci	3ms	אמר	55		say
	לקח	qal	pft	3ms	לקח	542		take
	אשיב	hiph	impf	1cs	שוב	996		bring back
	תשׂים	qal	impf	2ms	שׂים	962		put, set
	שׂם	qal	pft	3ms	שׂים	962		put, set
	אשלחך	piel	impf	1cs	שלח	1018	2ms	send away, shoot
	יכרת	qal	wci	3ms	כרת	503		cut, destroy
	ישלחהו	piel	wci	3ms	שלח	1018	3ms	send away, shoot
20: 35	אמר	qal	pft	3ms	אמר	55		say
	הכיני	hiph	impv	ms	נכה	645	1cs	smite
	ימאן	piel	wci	3ms	מאן	549		refuse
	הכתו	hiph	infc		נכה	645	3ms	smite
20: 36	יאמר	qal	wci	3ms	אמר	55		say
	שמעת	qal	pft	2ms	שמע	1033		hear

ChVs	Form	Stem	Tnse	PGN	Root	BDB	Sfx	Meaning
20:36	הולך	qal	ptc	ms	הלך	229		walk,go
	הכך	hiph	wcp	3ms	נכה	645	2ms	smite
	ילך	qal	wci	3ms	הלך	229		walk,go
	ימצאהו	qal	wci	3ms	מצא	592	3ms	find
	יכהו	hiph	wci	3ms	נכה	645	3ms	smite
20:37	ימצא	qal	wci	3ms	מצא	592		find
	יאמר	qal	wci	3ms	אמר	55		say
	הכיני	hiph	impv	ms	נכה	645	1cs	smite
	יכהו	hiph	wci	3ms	נכה	645	3ms	smite
	הכה	hiph	infa		נכה	645		smite
	פצע	qal	infa		פצע	822		bruise
20:38	ילך	qal	wci	3ms	הלך	229		walk,go
	יעמד	qal	wci	3ms	עמד	763		stand,stop
	יתחפשׂ	hith	wci	3ms	חפשׂ	344		disguise self
20:39	יהי	qal	wci	3ms	היה	224		be,become
	עבר	qal	ptc	ms	עבר	716		pass over
	צעק	qal	pft	3ms	צעק	858		cry out
	יאמר	qal	wci	3ms	אמר	55		say
	יצא	qal	pft	3ms	יצא	422		go out
	סר	qal	pft	3ms	סור	693		turn aside
	יבא	hiph	wci	3ms	בוא	97		bring in
	יאמר	qal	wci	3ms	אמר	55		say
	שׁמר	qal	impv	ms	שׁמר	1036		keep,watch
	הפקד	niph	infa		פקד	823		be visited
	יפקד	niph	impf	3ms	פקד	823		be visited
	היתה	qal	wcp	3fs	היה	224		be,become
	תשקול	qal	impf	2ms	שׁקל	1053		weigh
20:40	יהי	qal	wci	3ms	היה	224		be,become
	עשׂה	qal	ptc	ms	עשׂה	793		do,make
	יאמר	qal	wci	3ms	אמר	55		say
	חרצת	qal	pft	2ms	חרץ	358		cut,decide
20:41	ימהר	piel	wci	3ms	מהר	554		hasten
	יסר	hiph	wci	3ms	סור	693		take away
	יכר	hiph	wci	3ms	נכר	647		regard,notice
20:42	יאמר	qal	wci	3ms	אמר	55		say
	אמר	qal	pft	3ms	אמר	55		say
	שׁלחת	piel	pft	2ms	שׁלח	1018		send away,shoot
	היתה	qal	wcp/	3fs	היה	224		be,become
20:43	ילך	qal	wci	3ms	הלך	229		walk,go
	יבא	qal	wci	3ms	בוא	97		come in
21:1	יהי	qal	wci	3ms	היה	224		be,become
	היה	qal	pft	3ms	היה	224		be,become
21:2	ידבר	piel	wci	3ms	דבר	180		speak
	אמר	qal	infc		אמר	55		say
	תנה	qal	impv	ms	נתן	678		give,set
	יהי	qal	jus	3ms	היה	224		be,become
	אתנה	qal	coh	1cs	נתן	678		give,set
	טוב	qal	pft	3ms	טוב	373		be pleasing
	אתנה	qal	coh	1cs	נתן	678		give,set
21:3	יאמר	qal	wci	3ms	אמר	55		say
	תתי	qal	infc		נתן	678	1cs	give,set
21:4	יבא	qal	wci	3ms	בוא	97		come in
	דבר	piel	pft	3ms	דבר	180		speak
	יאמר	qal	wci	3ms	אמר	55		say
21:4	אתן	qal	impf	1cs	נתן	678		give,set
	ישׁכב	qal	wci	3ms	שׁכב	1011		lie,lie down
	יסב	hiph	wci	3ms	סבב	685		cause to turn
	אכל	qal	pft	3ms	אכל	37		eat,devour
21:5	תבא	qal	wci	3fs	בוא	97		come in
	תדבר	piel	wci	3fs	דבר	180		speak
	אכל	qal	ptc	ms	אכל	37		eat,devour
21:6	ידבר	piel	wci	3ms	דבר	180		speak
	אדבר	piel	impf	1cs	דבר	180		speak
	אמר	qal	wci	1cs	אמר	55		say
	תנה	qal	impv	ms	נתן	678		give,set
	אתנה	qal	coh	1cs	נתן	678		give,set
	יאמר	qal	wci	3ms	אמר	55		say
	אתן	qal	impf	1cs	נתן	678		give,set
21:7	תאמר	qal	wci	3fs	אמר	55		say
	תעשׂה	qal	impf	2ms	עשׂה	793		do,make
	קום	qal	impv	ms	קום	877		arise,stand
	אכל	qal	impv	ms	אכל	37		eat,devour
	יטב	qal	jusm	3ms	יטב	405		be good
	אתן	qal	impf	1cs	נתן	678		give,set
21:8	תכתב	qal	wci	3fs	כתב	507		write
	תחתם	qal	wci	3fs	חתם	367		seal
	תשׁלח	qal	wci	3fs	שׁלח	1018		send
	ישׁבים	qal	ptc	mp	ישׁב	442		sit,dwell
21:9	תכתב	qal	wci	3fs	כתב	507		write
	אמר	qal	infc		אמר	55		say
	קראו	qal	impv	mp	קרא	894		call,proclaim
	הושׁיבו	hiph	impv	mp	ישׁב	442		cause to dwell
21:10	הושׁיבו	hiph	impv	mp	ישׁב	442		cause to dwell
	יעדהו	hiph	jusm	3mp	עוד	729	3ms	testify,warn
	אמר	qal	infc		אמר	55		say
	ברכת	piel	pft	2ms	ברך	138		bless
	הוציאהו	hiph	impv	mp	יצא	422	3ms	bring out
	סקלהו	qal	impv	mp	סקל	709	3ms	stone to death
	ימת	qal	jus	3ms	מות	559		die
21:11	יעשׂו	qal	wci	3mp	עשׂה	793		do,make
	ישׁבים	qal	ptc	mp	ישׁב	442		sit,dwell
	שׁלחה	qal	pft	3fs	שׁלח	1018		send
	כתוב	qal	pptc	ms	כתב	507		write
	שׁלחה	qal	pft	3fs	שׁלח	1018		send
21:12	קראו	qal	pft	3cp	קרא	894		call,proclaim
	השׁיבו	hiph	pft	3cp	ישׁב	442		cause to dwell
21:13	יבאו	qal	wci	3mp	בוא	97		come in
	ישׁבו	qal	wci	3mp	ישׁב	442		sit,dwell
	יעדהו	hiph	wci	3mp	עוד	729	3ms	testify,warn
	אמר	qal	infc		אמר	55		say
	ברך	piel	pft	3ms	ברך	138		bless
	יצאהו	hiph	wci	3mp	יצא	422	3ms	bring out
	יסקלהו	qal	wci	3mp	סקל	709	3ms	stone to death
	ימת	qal	wci	3ms	מות	559		die
21:14	ישׁלחו	qal	wci	3mp	שׁלח	1018		send
	אמר	qal	infc		אמר	55		say
	סקל	pual	pft	3ms	סקל	709		be stoned
	ימת	qal	wci	3ms	מות	559		die

ChVs	Form	Stem	Tnse	PGN	Root	BDB	Sfx	Meaning
21:15	יהי	qal	wci	3ms	היה	224		be,become
	שמע	qal	infc		שמע	1033		hear
	סקל	pual	pft	3ms	סקל	709		be stoned
	ימת	qal	wci	3ms	מות	559		die
	תאמר	qal	wci	3fs	אמר	55		say
	קום	qal	impv	ms	קום	877		arise,stand
	רש	qal	impv	ms	ירש	439		possess,inherit
	מאן	piel	pft	3ms	מאן	549		refuse
	תת	qal	infc		נתן	678		give,set
	מת	qal	pft	3ms	מות	559		die
21:16	יהי	qal	wci	3ms	היה	224		be,become
	שמע	qal	infc		שמע	1033		hear
	מת	qal	pft	3ms	מות	559		die
	יקם	qal	wci	3ms	קום	877		arise,stand
	רדת	qal	infc		ירד	432		come down
	רשתו	qal	infc		ירש	439	3ms	possess,inherit
21:17	יהי	qal	wci	3ms	היה	224		be,become
	אמר	qal	infc		אמר	55		say
21:18	קום	qal	impv	ms	קום	877		arise,stand
	רד	qal	impv	ms	ירד	432		come down
	קראת	qal	infc		קרא	896		meet,encounter
	ירד	qal	pft	3ms	ירד	432		come down
	רשתו	qal	infc		ירש	439	3ms	possess,inherit
21:19	דברת	piel	wcp	2ms	דבר	180		speak
	אמר	qal	infc		אמר	55		say
	אמר	qal	pft	3ms	אמר	55		say
	רצחת	qal	pft	2ms	רצח	953		murder,slay
	ירשת	qal	pft	2ms	ירש	439		possess,inherit
	דברת	piel	wcp	2ms	דבר	180		speak
	אמר	qal	infc		אמר	55		say
	אמר	qal	pft	3ms	אמר	55		say
	לקקו	qal	pft	3cp	לקק	545		lap,lick
	ילקו	qal	impf	3mp	לקק	545		lap,lick
21:20	יאמר	qal	wci	3ms	אמר	55		say
	מצאתני	qal	pft	2ms	מצא	592	1cs	find
	איבי	qal	ptc	ms	איב	33	1cs	be hostile to
	יאמר	qal	wci	3ms	אמר	55		say
	מצאתי	qal	pft	1cs	מצא	592		find
	התמכרך	hith	infc		מכר	569	2ms	sell oneself
	עשות	qal	infc		עשה	793		do,make
21:21	מביk	hiph	ptc	ms	בוא	97		bring in
	מביאq	hiph	ptc	ms	בוא	97		bring in
	בערתי	piel	wcp	1cs	בער	128		burn,consume
	הכרתי	hiph	wcp	1cs	כרת	503		cut off,destroy
	משתין	hiph	ptc	ms	שתן	1010		urinate
	עצור	qal	pptc	ms	עצר	783		restrain
	עזוב	qal	pptc	ms	עזב	736		leave,loose
21:22	נתתי	qal	wcp	1cs	נתן	678		give,set
	הכעסת	hiph	pft	2ms	כעס	494		vex,provoke
	תחטא	hiph	wci	2ms	חטא	306		cause to sin
21:23	דבר	piel	pft	3ms	דבר	180		speak
	אמר	qal	infc		אמר	55		say
	יאכלו	qal	impf	3mp	אכל	37		eat,devour
21:24	מת	qal	ptc	ms	מות	559		die
21:24	יאכלו	qal	impf	3mp	אכל	37		eat,devour
	מת	qal	ptc	ms	מות	559		die
	יאכלו	qal	impf	3mp	אכל	37		eat,devour
21:25	היה	qal	pft	3ms	היה	224		be,become
	התמכר	hith	pft	3ms	מכר	569		sell oneself
	עשות	qal	infc		עשה	793		do,make
	הסתה	hiph	pft	3fs	סות	694		incite,allure
21:26	יתעב	hiph	wci	3ms	תעב	1073		do abominably
	לכת	qal	infc		הלך	229		walk,go
	עשו	qal	pft	3cp	עשה	793		do,make
	הוריש	hiph	pft	3ms	ירש	439		c. to possess
21:27	יהי	qal	wci	3ms	היה	224		be,become
	שמע	qal	infc		שמע	1033		hear
	יקרע	qal	wci	3ms	קרע	902		tear,rend
	ישם	qal	wci	3ms	שים	962		put,set
	יצום	qal	wci	3ms	צום	847		fast
	ישכב	qal	wci	3ms	שכב	1011		lie,lie down
	יהלך	piel	wci	3ms	הלך	229		walk
21:28	יהי	qal	wci	3ms	היה	224		be,become
	אמר	qal	infc		אמר	55		say
21:29	ראית	qal	pft	2ms	ראה	906		see
	נכנע	niph	pft	3ms	כנע	488		humble self
	נכנע	niph	pft	3ms	כנע	488		humble self
	אביk	hiph	impf	1cs	בוא	97		bring in
	אביאq	hiph	impf	1cs	בוא	97		bring in
	אביא	hiph	impf	1cs	בוא	97		bring in
22:1	ישבו	qal	wci	3mp	ישב	442		sit,dwell
22:2	יהי	qal	wci	3ms	היה	224		be,become
	ירד	qal	wci	3ms	ירד	432		come down
22:3	יאמר	qal	wci	3ms	אמר	55		say
	ידעתם	qal	pft	2mp	ידע	393		know
	מחשים	hiph	ptc	mp	חשה	364		show silence
	קחת	qal	infc		לקח	542		take
22:4	יאמר	qal	wci	3ms	אמר	55		say
	תלך	qal	impf	2ms	הלך	229		walk,go
	יאמר	qal	wci	3ms	אמר	55		say
22:5	יאמר	qal	wci	3ms	אמר	55		say
	דרש	qal	impv	ms	דרש	205		resort to,seek
22:6	יקבץ	qal	wci	3ms	קבץ	867		gather,collect
	יאמר	qal	wci	3ms	אמר	55		say
	אלך	qal	impf	1cs	הלך	229		walk,go
	אחדל	qal	impf	1cs	חדל	292		cease
	יאמרו	qal	wci	3mp	אמר	55		say
	עלה	qal	impv	ms	עלה	748		go up
	יתן	qal	jusm	3ms	נתן	678		give,set
22:7	יאמר	qal	wci	3ms	אמר	55		say
	נדרשה	qal	coh	1cp	דרש	205		resort to,seek
22:8	יאמר	qal	wci	3ms	אמר	55		say
	דרש	qal	infc		דרש	205		resort to,seek
	שנאתיו	qal	pft	1cs	שנא	971	3ms	hate
	יתנבא	hith	impf	3ms	נבא	612		prophesy
	יאמר	qal	wci	3ms	אמר	55		say
	יאמר	qal	jusm	3ms	אמר	55		say
22:9	יקרא	qal	wci	3ms	קרא	894		call,proclaim

ChVs	Form	Stem	Tnse	PGN	Root	BDB	Sfx	Meaning
22: 9	יאמר	qal	wci	3ms	אמר	55		say
	מהרה	piel	impv	ms	מהר	554		hasten
22: 10	ישבים	qal	ptc	mp	ישב	442		sit,dwell
	מלבשים	pual	ptc	mp	לבש	527		be clothed
	מתנבאים	hith	ptc	mp	נבא	612		prophesy
22: 11	יעש	qal	wci	3ms	עשה	793		do,make
	יאמר	qal	wci	3ms	אמר	55		say
	אמר	qal	pft	3ms	אמר	55		say
	תנגח	piel	impf	2ms	נגח	618		thrust at
	כלתם	piel	infc		כלה	477	3mp	complete,finish
22: 12	נבאים	niph	ptc	mp	נבא	612		prophesy
	אמר	qal	infc		אמר	55		say
	עלה	qal	impv	ms	עלה	748		go up
	הצלח	hiph	impv	ms	צלח	852		cause to thrive
	נתן	qal	wcp	3ms	נתן	678		give,set
22: 13	הלך	qal	pft	3ms	הלך	229		walk,go
	קרא	qal	infc		קרא	894		call,proclaim
	דבר	piel	pft	3ms	דבר	180		speak
	אמר	qal	infc		אמר	55		say
	יהי	qal	jus	3ms	היה	224		be,become
	דברת	piel	wcp	2ms	דבר	180		speak
22: 14	יאמר	qal	wci	3ms	אמר	55		say
	יאמר	qal	impf	3ms	אמר	55		say
	אדבר	piel	impf	1cs	דבר	180		speak
22: 15	יבוא	qal	wci	3ms	בוא	97		come in
	יאמר	qal	wci	3ms	אמר	55		say
	נלך	qal	impf	1cp	הלך	229		walk,go
	נחדל	qal	impf	1cp	חדל	292		cease
	יאמר	qal	wci	3ms	אמר	55		say
	עלה	qal	impv	ms	עלה	748		go up
	הצלח	hiph	impv	ms	צלח	852		cause to thrive
	נתן	qal	wcp	3ms	נתן	678		give,set
22: 16	יאמר	qal	wci	3ms	אמר	55		say
	משבעך	hiph	ptc	ms	שבע	989	2ms	cause to swear
	תדבר	piel	impf	2ms	דבר	180		speak
22: 17	יאמר	qal	wci	3ms	אמר	55		say
	ראיתי	qal	pft	1cs	ראה	906		see
	נפצים	niph	ptc	mp	פוץ	806		be scattered
	רעה	qal	ptc	ms	רעה	944		pasture,tend
	יאמר	qal	wci	3ms	אמר	55		say
	ישובו	qal	jusm	3mp	שוב	996		turn,return
22: 18	יאמר	qal	wci	3ms	אמר	55		say
	אמרתי	qal	pft	1cs	אמר	55		say
	יתנבא	hith	impf	3ms	נבא	612		prophesy
22: 19	יאמר	qal	wci	3ms	אמר	55		say
	שמע	qal	impv	ms	שמע	1033		hear
	ראיתי	qal	pft	1cs	ראה	906		see
	ישב	qal	ptc	ms	ישב	442		sit,dwell
	עמד	qal	ptc	ms	עמד	763		stand,stop
22: 20	יאמר	qal	wci	3ms	אמר	55		say
	יפתה	piel	impf	3ms	פתה	834		entice
	יעל	qal	jus	3ms	עלה	748		go up
	יפל	qal	jusm	3ms	נפל	656		fall
	יאמר	qal	wci	3ms	אמר	55		say
22: 20	אמר	qal	ptc	ms	אמר	55		say
22: 21	יצא	qal	wci	3ms	יצא	422		go out
	יעמד	qal	wci	3ms	עמד	763		stand,stop
	יאמר	qal	wci	3ms	אמר	55		say
	אפתנו	piel	impf	1cs	פתה	834	3ms	entice
	יאמר	qal	wci	3ms	אמר	55		say
22: 22	יאמר	qal	wci	3ms	אמר	55		say
	אצא	qal	impf	1cs	יצא	422		go out
	הייתי	qal	wcp	1cs	היה	224		be,become
	יאמר	qal	wci	3ms	אמר	55		say
	תפתה	piel	impf	2ms	פתה	834		entice
	תוכל	qal	impf	2ms	יכל	407		be able
	צא	qal	impv	ms	יצא	422		go out
	עשה	qal	impv	ms	עשה	793		do,make
22: 23	נתן	qal	pft	3ms	נתן	678		give,set
	דבר	piel	pft	3ms	דבר	180		speak
22: 24	יגש	qal	wci	3ms	נגש	620		draw near
	יכה	hiph	wci	3ms	נכה	645		smite
	יאמר	qal	wci	3ms	אמר	55		say
	עבר	qal	pft	3ms	עבר	716		pass over
	דבר	piel	infc		דבר	180		speak
22: 25	יאמר	qal	wci	3ms	אמר	55		say
	ראה	qal	ptc	ms	ראה	906		see
	תבא	qal	impf	2ms	בוא	97		come in
	החבה	niph	infc		חבה	285		hide oneself
22: 26	יאמר	qal	wci	3ms	אמר	55		say
	קח	qal	impv	ms	לקח	542		take
	השיבהו	hiph	impv	ms	שוב	996	3ms	bring back
22: 27	אמרת	qal	wcp	2ms	אמר	55		say
	אמר	qal	pft	3ms	אמר	55		say
	שימו	qal	impv	mp	שים	962		put,set
	האכילהו	hiph	impv	mp	אכל	37	3ms	cause to eat
	באי	qal	infc		בוא	97	1cs	come in
22: 28	יאמר	qal	wci	3ms	אמר	55		say
	שוב	qal	infa		שוב	996		turn,return
	תשוב	qal	impf	2ms	שוב	996		turn,return
	דבר	piel	pft	3ms	דבר	180		speak
	יאמר	qal	wci	3ms	אמר	55		say
	שמעו	qal	impv	mp	שמע	1033		hear
22: 29	יעל	qal	wci	3ms	עלה	748		go up
22: 30	יאמר	qal	wci	3ms	אמר	55		say
	התחפש	hith	infa		חפש	344		disguise self
	בא	qal	infa		בוא	97		come in
	לבש	qal	impv	ms	לבש	527		put on,clothe
	יתחפש	hith	wci	3ms	חפש	344		disguise self
	יבוא	qal	wci	3ms	בוא	97		come in
22: 31	צוה	piel	pft	3ms	צוה	845		command
	אמר	qal	infc		אמר	55		say
	תלחמו	niph	impf	2mp	לחם	535		wage war
22: 32	יהי	qal	wci	3ms	היה	224		be,become
	ראות	qal	infc		ראה	906		see
	אמרו	qal	pft	3cp	אמר	55		say
	יסרו	qal	wci	3mp	סור	693		turn aside
	הלחם	niph	infc		לחם	535		wage war

ChVs	Form	Stem	Tnse	PGN	Root	BDB	Sfx	Meaning
22: 32	יזעק	qal	wci	3ms	זעק	277		call, cry out
22: 33	יהי	qal	wci	3ms	היה	224		be, become
	ראות	qal	infc		ראה	906		see
	ישׁובו	qal	wci	3mp	שׁוב	996		turn, return
22: 34	משׁך	qal	pft	3ms	משׁך	604		draw, pull
	יכה	hiph	wci	3ms	נכה	645		smite
	יאמר	qal	wci	3ms	אמר	55		say
	הפך	qal	impv	ms	הפך	245		turn, overturn
	הוציאני	hiph	impv	ms	יצא	422	1cs	bring out
	החליתי	hoph	pft	1cs	חלה	317		be made sick
22: 35	תעלה	qal	wci	3fs	עלה	748		go up
	היה	qal	pft	3ms	היה	224		be, become
	מעמד	hoph	ptc	ms	עמד	763		be placed
	ימת	qal	wci	3ms	מות	559		die
	יצק	qal	wci	3ms	יצק	427		pour out, cast
22: 36	יעבר	qal	wci	3ms	עבר	716		pass over
	בא	qal	infc		בוא	97		come in
	אמר	qal	infc		אמר	55		say
22: 37	ימת	qal	wci	3ms	מות	559		die
	יבוא	qal	wci	3ms	בוא	97		come in
	יקברו	qal	wci	3mp	קבר	868		bury
22: 38	ישׁטף	qal	wci	3ms	שׁטף	1009		overflow
	ילקו	qal	wci	3mp	לקק	545		lap, lick
	זנות	qal	ptc	fp	זנה	275		act a harlot
	רחצו	qal	pft	3cp	רחץ	934		wash, bathe
	דבר	piel	pft	3ms	דבר	180		speak
22: 39	עשׂה	qal	pft	3ms	עשׂה	793		do, make
	בנה	qal	pft	3ms	בנה	124		build
	בנה	qal	pft	3ms	בנה	124		build
	כתובים	qal	pptc	mp	כתב	507		write
22: 40	ישׁכב	qal	wci	3ms	שׁכב	1011		lie, lie down
	ימלך	qal	wci	3ms	מלך	573		be king, reign
22: 41	מלך	qal	pft	3ms	מלך	573		be king, reign
22: 42	מלכו	qal	infc		מלך	573	3ms	be king, reign
	מלך	qal	pft	3ms	מלך	573		be king, reign
22: 43	ילך	qal	wci	3ms	הלך	229		walk, go
	סר	qal	pft	3ms	סור	693		turn aside
	עשׂות	qal	infc		עשׂה	793		do, make
22: 44	סרו	qal	pft	3cp	סור	693		turn aside
	מזבחים	piel	ptc	mp	זבח	256		sacrifice
	מקטרים	piel	ptc	mp	קטר	882		make sacrifices
22: 45	ישׁלם	hiph	wci	3ms	שׁלם	1023		make peace
22: 46	עשׂה	qal	pft	3ms	עשׂה	793		do, make
	נלחם	niph	pft	3ms	לחם	535		wage war
	כתובים	qal	pptc	mp	כתב	507		write
22: 47	נשׁאר	niph	pft	3ms	שׁאר	983		be left
	בער	piel	pft	3ms	בער	128		burn, consume
22: 48	נצב	niph	ptc	ms	נצב	662		stand
22: 49	עשׂרk	qal	pft	3ms	עשׂר	797		tithe
	עשׂהq	qal	pft	3ms	עשׂה	793		do, make
	לכת	qal	infc		הלך	229		walk, go
	הלך	qal	pft	3ms	הלך	229		walk, go
	נשׁברהk	niph	pft	3fs	שׁבר	990		be broken
	נשׁברוq	niph	pft	3cp	שׁבר	990		be broken
22: 50	אמר	qal	pft	3ms	אמר	55		say
	ילכו	qal	jusm	3mp	הלך	229		walk, go
	אבה	qal	pft	3ms	אבה	2		be willing
22: 51	ישׁכב	qal	wci	3ms	שׁכב	1011		lie, lie down
	יקבר	niph	wci	3ms	קבר	868		be buried
	ימלך	qal	wci	3ms	מלך	573		be king, reign
22: 52	מלך	qal	pft	3ms	מלך	573		be king, reign
	ימלך	qal	wci	3ms	מלך	573		be king, reign
22: 53	יעשׂ	qal	wci	3ms	עשׂה	793		do, make
	ילך	qal	wci	3ms	הלך	229		walk, go
	החטיא	hiph	pft	3ms	חטא	306		cause to sin
22: 54	יעבד	qal	wci	3ms	עבד	712		work, serve
	ישׁתחוה	hish	wci	3ms	חוה	1005		bow down
	יכעס	hiph	wci	3ms	כעס	494		vex, provoke
	עשׂה	qal	pft	3ms	עשׂה	793		do, make
2 KINGS								
1: 1	יפשׁע	qal	wci	3ms	פשׁע	833		rebel, sin
1: 2	יפל	qal	wci	3ms	נפל	656		fall
	יחל	qal	wci	3ms	חלה	317		be weak, sick
	ישׁלח	qal	wci	3ms	שׁלח	1018		send
	יאמר	qal	wci	3ms	אמר	55		say
	לכו	qal	impv	mp	הלך	229		walk, go
	דרשׁו	qal	impv	mp	דרשׁ	205		resort to, seek
	אחיה	qal	impf	1cs	חיה	310		live
1: 3	דבר	piel	pft	3ms	דבר	180		speak
	קום	qal	impv	ms	קום	877		arise, stand
	עלה	qal	impv	ms	עלה	748		go up
	קראת	qal	infc		קרא	896		meet, encounter
	דבר	piel	impv	ms	דבר	180		speak
	הלכים	qal	ptc	mp	הלך	229		walk, go
	דרשׁ	qal	infc		דרשׁ	205		resort to, seek
1: 4	אמר	qal	pft	3ms	אמר	55		say
	עלית	qal	pft	2ms	עלה	748		go up
	תרד	qal	impf	2ms	ירד	432		come down
	מות	qal	infa		מות	559		die
	תמות	qal	impf	2ms	מות	559		die
	ילך	qal	wci	3ms	הלך	229		walk, go
1: 5	ישׁובו	qal	wci	3mp	שׁוב	996		turn, return
	יאמר	qal	wci	3ms	אמר	55		say
	שׁבתם	qal	pft	2mp	שׁוב	996		turn, return
1: 6	יאמרו	qal	wci	3mp	אמר	55		say
	עלה	qal	pft	3ms	עלה	748		go up
	קראתנו	qal	infc		קרא	896	1cp	meet, encounter
	יאמר	qal	wci	3ms	אמר	55		say
	לכו	qal	impv	mp	הלך	229		walk, go
	שׁובו	qal	impv	mp	שׁוב	996		turn, return
	שׁלח	qal	pft	3ms	שׁלח	1018		send
	דברתם	piel	wcp	2mp	דבר	180		speak
	אמר	qal	pft	3ms	אמר	55		say
	שׁלח	qal	ptc	ms	שׁלח	1018		send
	דרשׁ	qal	infc		דרשׁ	205		resort to, seek
	עלית	qal	pft	2ms	עלה	748		go up
	תרד	qal	impf	2ms	ירד	432		come down

ChVs	Form	Stem	Tnse	PGN	Root	BDB	Sfx	Meaning
1:6	מות	qal	infa		מות	559		die
	תמות	qal	impf	2ms	מות	559		die
1:7	ידבר	piel	wci	3ms	דבר	180		speak
	עלה	qal	pft	3ms	עלה	748		go up
	קראתכם	qal	infc		קרא	896	2mp	meet,encounter
	ידבר	piel	wci	3ms	דבר	180		speak
1:8	יאמרו	qal	wci	3mp	אמר	55		say
	אזור	qal	pptc	ms	אזר	25		gird
	יאמר	qal	wci	3ms	אמר	55		say
1:9	ישׁלח	qal	wci	3ms	שׁלח	1018		send
	יעל	qal	wci	3ms	עלה	748		go up
	ישׁב	qal	ptc	ms	ישׁב	442		sit,dwell
	ידבר	piel	wci	3ms	דבר	180		speak
	דבר	piel	pft	3ms	דבר	180		speak
	רדה	qal	impv	ms	ירד	432		come down
1:10	יענה	qal	wci	3ms	ענה	772		answer
	ידבר	piel	wci	3ms	דבר	180		speak
	תרד	qal	jus	3fs	ירד	432		come down
	תאכל	qal	jusm	3fs	אכל	37		eat,devour
	תרד	qal	wci	3fs	ירד	432		come down
	תאכל	qal	wci	3fs	אכל	37		eat,devour
1:11	ישׁב	qal	wci	3ms	שׁוב	996		turn,return
	ישׁלח	qal	wci	3ms	שׁלח	1018		send
	יען	qal	wci	3ms	ענה	772		answer
	ידבר	piel	wci	3ms	דבר	180		speak
	אמר	qal	pft	3ms	אמר	55		say
	רדה	qal	impv	ms	ירד	432		come down
1:12	יען	qal	wci	3ms	ענה	772		answer
	ידבר	piel	wci	3ms	דבר	180		speak
	תרד	qal	jus	3fs	ירד	432		come down
	תאכל	qal	jusm	3fs	אכל	37		eat,devour
	תרד	qal	wci	3fs	ירד	432		come down
	תאכל	qal	wci	3fs	אכל	37		eat,devour
1:13	ישׁב	qal	wci	3ms	שׁוב	996		turn,return
	ישׁלח	qal	wci	3ms	שׁלח	1018		send
	יעל	qal	wci	3ms	עלה	748		go up
	יבא	qal	wci	3ms	בוא	97		come in
	יכרע	qal	wci	3ms	כרע	502		bow down
	יתחנן	hith	wci	3ms	חנן	335		seek favor
	ידבר	piel	wci	3ms	דבר	180		speak
	תיקר	qal	jusm	3fs	יקר	429		be precious
1:14	ירדה	qal	pft	3fs	ירד	432		come down
	תאכל	qal	wci	3fs	אכל	37		eat,devour
	תיקר	qal	jusm	3fs	יקר	429		be precious
1:15	ידבר	piel	wci	3ms	דבר	180		speak
	רד	qal	impv	ms	ירד	432		come down
	תירא	qal	jusm	2ms	ירא	431		fear
	יקם	qal	wci	3ms	קום	877		arise,stand
	ירד	qal	wci	3ms	ירד	432		come down
1:16	ידבר	piel	wci	3ms	דבר	180		speak
	אמר	qal	pft	3ms	אמר	55		say
	שׁלחת	qal	pft	2ms	שׁלח	1018		send
	דרשׁ	qal	infc		דרשׁ	205		resort to,seek
	דרשׁ	qal	infc		דרשׁ	205		resort to,seek
1:16	עלית	qal	pft	2ms	עלה	748		go up
	תרד	qal	impf	2ms	ירד	432		come down
	מות	qal	infa		מות	559		die
	תמות	qal	impf	2ms	מות	559		die
1:17	ימת	qal	wci	3ms	מות	559		die
	דבר	piel	pft	3ms	דבר	180		speak
	ימלך	qal	wci	3ms	מלך	573		be king,reign
	היה	qal	pft	3ms	היה	224		be,become
1:18	עשׂה	qal	pft	3ms	עשׂה	793		do,make
	כתובים	qal	pptc	mp	כתב	507		write
2:1	יהי	qal	wci	3ms	היה	224		be,become
	העלות	hiph	infc		עלה	748		bring up,offer
	ילך	qal	wci	3ms	הלך	229		walk,go
2:2	יאמר	qal	wci	3ms	אמר	55		say
	שׁב	qal	impv	ms	ישׁב	442		sit,dwell
	שׁלחני	qal	pft	3ms	שׁלח	1018	1cs	send
	יאמר	qal	wci	3ms	אמר	55		say
	אעזבך	qal	impf	1cs	עזב	736	2ms	leave,loose
	ירדו	qal	wci	3mp	ירד	432		come down
2:3	יצאו	qal	wci	3mp	יצא	422		go out
	יאמרו	qal	wci	3mp	אמר	55		say
	ידעת	qal	pft	2ms	ידע	393		know
	לקח	qal	ptc	ms	לקח	542		take
	יאמר	qal	wci	3ms	אמר	55		say
	ידעתי	qal	pft	1cs	ידע	393		know
	החשו	hiph	impv	mp	חשה	364		show silence
2:4	יאמר	qal	wci	3ms	אמר	55		say
	שׁב	qal	impv	ms	ישׁב	442		sit,dwell
	שׁלחני	qal	pft	3ms	שׁלח	1018	1cs	send
	יאמר	qal	wci	3ms	אמר	55		say
	אעזבך	qal	impf	1cs	עזב	736	2ms	leave,loose
	יבאו	qal	wci	3mp	בוא	97		come in
2:5	יגשׁו	qal	wci	3mp	נגשׁ	620		draw near
	יאמרו	qal	wci	3mp	אמר	55		say
	ידעת	qal	pft	2ms	ידע	393		know
	לקח	qal	ptc	ms	לקח	542		take
	יאמר	qal	wci	3ms	אמר	55		say
	ידעתי	qal	pft	1cs	ידע	393		know
	החשו	hiph	impv	mp	חשה	364		show silence
2:6	יאמר	qal	wci	3ms	אמר	55		say
	שׁב	qal	impv	ms	ישׁב	442		sit,dwell
	שׁלחני	qal	pft	3ms	שׁלח	1018	1cs	send
	יאמר	qal	wci	3ms	אמר	55		say
	אעזבך	qal	impf	1cs	עזב	736	2ms	leave,loose
	ילכו	qal	wci	3mp	הלך	229		walk,go
2:7	הלכו	qal	pft	3cp	הלך	229		walk,go
	יעמדו	qal	wci	3mp	עמד	763		stand,stop
	עמדו	qal	pft	3cp	עמד	763		stand,stop
2:8	יקח	qal	wci	3ms	לקח	542		take
	יגלם	qal	wci	3ms	גלם	166		wrap up,fold
	יכה	hiph	wci	3ms	נכה	645		smite
	יחצו	niph	wci	3mp	חצה	345		be divided
	יעברו	qal	wci	3mp	עבר	716		pass over
2:9	יהי	qal	wci	3ms	היה	224		be,become

ChVs	Form	Stem	Tnse	PGN	Root	BDB	Sfx	Meaning
2: 9	עברם	qal	infc		עבר	716	3mp	pass over
	אמר	qal	pft	3ms	אמר	55		say
	שׁאל	qal	impv	ms	שׁאל	981		ask, borrow
	אעשׂה	qal	impf	1cs	עשׂה	793		do, make
	אלקח	niph	impf	1cs	לקח	542		be taken
	יאמר	qal	wci	3ms	אמר	55		say
	יהי	qal	jus	3ms	היה	224		be, become
2: 10	יאמר	qal	wci	3ms	אמר	55		say
	הקשׁית	hiph	pft	2ms	קשׁה	904		harden
	שׁאול	qal	infc		שׁאל	981		ask, borrow
	תראה	qal	impf	2ms	ראה	906		see
	לקח	qalp	pft	3ms	לקח	542		be taken
	יהי	qal	jus	3ms	היה	224		be, become
	יהיה	qal	impf	3ms	היה	224		be, become
2: 11	יהי	qal	wci	3ms	היה	224		be, become
	הלכים	qal	ptc	mp	הלך	229		walk, go
	הלוך	qal	infa		הלך	229		walk, go
	דבר	piel	infa		דבר	180		speak
	יפרדו	hiph	wci	3mp	פרד	825		divide
	יעל	qal	wci	3ms	עלה	748		go up
2: 12	ראה	qal	ptc	ms	ראה	906		see
	מצעק	piel	ptc	ms	צעק	858		cry aloud
	ראהו	qal	pft	3ms	ראה	906	3ms	see
	יחזק	hiph	wci	3ms	חזק	304		make firm, seize
	יקרעם	qal	wci	3ms	קרע	902	3mp	tear, rend
2: 13	ירם	hiph	wci	3ms	רום	926		raise, lift
	נפלה	qal	pft	3fs	נפל	656		fall
	ישׁב	qal	wci	3ms	שׁוב	996		turn, return
	יעמד	qal	wci	3ms	עמד	763		stand, stop
2: 14	יקח	qal	wci	3ms	לקח	542		take
	נפלה	qal	pft	3fs	נפל	656		fall
	יכה	hiph	wci	3ms	נכה	645		smite
	יאמר	qal	wci	3ms	אמר	55		say
	יכה	hiph	wci	3ms	נכה	645		smite
	יחצו	niph	wci	3mp	חצה	345		be divided
	יעבר	qal	wci	3ms	עבר	716		pass over
2: 15	יראהו	qal	wci	3mp	ראה	906	3ms	see
	יאמרו	qal	wci	3mp	אמר	55		say
	נחה	qal	pft	3fs	נוח	628		rest
	יבאו	qal	wci	3mp	בוא	97		come in
	קראתו	qal	infc		קרא	896	3ms	meet, encounter
	ישׁתחוו	hish	wci	3mp	חוה	1005		bow down
2: 16	יאמרו	qal	wci	3mp	אמר	55		say
	ילכו	qal	jusm	3mp	הלך	229		walk, go
	יבקשׁו	piel	jusm	3mp	בקשׁ	134		seek
	נשׂאו	qal	pft	3ms	נשׂא	669	3ms	lift, carry
	ישׁלכהו	hiph	wci	3ms	שׁלך	1020	3ms	throw, cast
	יאמר	qal	wci	3ms	אמר	55		say
	תשׁלחו	qal	impf	2mp	שׁלח	1018		send
2: 17	יפצרו	qal	wci	3mp	פצר	823		push
	בשׁ	qal	infc		בושׁ	101		be ashamed
	יאמר	qal	wci	3ms	אמר	55		say
	שׁלחו	qal	impv	mp	שׁלח	1018		send
	ישׁלחו	qal	wci	3mp	שׁלח	1018		send
2: 17	יבקשׁו	piel	wci	3mp	בקשׁ	134		seek
	מצאהו	qal	pft	3cp	מצא	592	3ms	find
2: 18	ישׁבו	qal	wci	3mp	שׁוב	996		turn, return
	ישׁב	qal	ptc	ms	ישׁב	442		sit, dwell
	יאמר	qal	wci	3ms	אמר	55		say
	אמרתי	qal	pft	1cs	אמר	55		say
	תלכו	qal	jusm	2mp	הלך	229		walk, go
2: 19	יאמרו	qal	wci	3mp	אמר	55		say
	ראה	qal	ptc	ms	ראה	906		see
	משׁכלת	piel	ptc	fs	שׁכל	1013		make childless
2: 20	יאמר	qal	wci	3ms	אמר	55		say
	קחו	qal	impv	mp	לקח	542		take
	שׂימו	qal	impv	mp	שׂים	962		put, set
	יקחו	qal	wci	3mp	לקח	542		take
2: 21	יצא	qal	wci	3ms	יצא	422		go out
	ישׁלך	hiph	wci	3ms	שׁלך	1020		throw, cast
	יאמר	qal	wci	3ms	אמר	55		say
	אמר	qal	pft	3ms	אמר	55		say
	רפאתי	piel	pft	1cs	רפא	950		heal
	יהיה	qal	impf	3ms	היה	224		be, become
	משׁכלת	piel	ptc	fs	שׁכל	1013		make childless
2: 22	ירפו	niph	wci	3mp	רפא	950		be healed
	דבר	piel	pft	3ms	דבר	180		speak
2: 23	יעל	qal	wci	3ms	עלה	748		go up
	עלה	qal	ptc	ms	עלה	748		go up
	יצאו	qal	pft	3cp	יצא	422		go out
	יתקלסו	hith	wci	3mp	קלס	887		mock, deride
	יאמרו	qal	wci	3mp	אמר	55		say
	עלה	qal	impv	ms	עלה	748		go up
	עלה	qal	impv	ms	עלה	748		go up
2: 24	יפן	qal	wci	3ms	פנה	815		turn
	יראם	qal	wci	3ms	ראה	906	3mp	see
	יקללם	piel	wci	3ms	קלל	886	3mp	curse
	תצאנה	qal	wci	3fp	יצא	422		go out
	תבקענה	piel	wci	3fp	בקע	131		cut to pieces
2: 25	ילך	qal	wci	3ms	הלך	229		walk, go
	שׁב	qal	pft	3ms	שׁוב	996		turn, return
3: 1	מלך	qal	pft	3ms	מלך	573		be king, reign
	ימלך	qal	wci	3ms	מלך	573		be king, reign
3: 2	יעשׂה	qal	wci	3ms	עשׂה	793		do, make
	יסר	hiph	wci	3ms	סור	693		take away
	עשׂה	qal	pft	3ms	עשׂה	793		do, make
3: 3	החטיא	hiph	pft	3ms	חטא	306		cause to sin
	דבק	qal	pft	3ms	דבק	179		cling, cleave
	סר	qal	pft	3ms	סור	693		turn aside
3: 4	היה	qal	pft	3ms	היה	224		be, become
	השׁיב	hiph	wcp	3ms	שׁוב	996		bring back
3: 5	יהי	qal	wci	3ms	היה	224		be, become
	מות	qal	infc		מות	559		die
	יפשׁע	qal	wci	3ms	פשׁע	833		rebel, sin
3: 6	יצא	qal	wci	3ms	יצא	422		go out
	יפקד	qal	wci	3ms	פקד	823		attend to, visit
3: 7	ילך	qal	wci	3ms	הלך	229		walk, go
	ישׁלח	qal	wci	3ms	שׁלח	1018		send

ChVs	Form	Stem	Tnse	PGN	Root	BDB	Sfx	Meaning
3: 7	אמר	qal	infc		אמר	55		say
	פשע	qal	pft	3ms	פשע	833		rebel,sin
	תלך	qal	impf	2ms	הלך	229		walk,go
	יאמר	qal	wci	3ms	אמר	55		say
	אעלה	qal	impf	1cs	עלה	748		go up
3: 8	יאמר	qal	wci	3ms	אמר	55		say
	נעלה	qal	impf	1cp	עלה	748		go up
	יאמר	qal	wci	3ms	אמר	55		say
3: 9	ילך	qal	wci	3ms	הלך	229		walk,go
	יסבו	qal	wci	3mp	סבב	685		surround
	היה	qal	pft	3ms	היה	224		be, become
3: 10	יאמר	qal	wci	3ms	אמר	55		say
	קרא	qal	pft	3ms	קרא	894		call,proclaim
	תת	qal	infc		נתן	678		give,set
3: 11	יאמר	qal	wci	3ms	אמר	55		say
	נדרשה	qal	coh	1cp	דרש	205		resort to,seek
	יען	qal	wci	3ms	ענה	772		answer
	יאמר	qal	wci	3ms	אמר	55		say
	יצק	qal	pft	3ms	יצק	427		pour out,cast
3: 12	יאמר	qal	wci	3ms	אמר	55		say
	ירדו	qal	wci	3mp	ירד	432		come down
3: 13	יאמר	qal	wci	3ms	אמר	55		say
	לך	qal	impv	ms	הלך	229		walk,go
	יאמר	qal	wci	3ms	אמר	55		say
	קרא	qal	pft	3ms	קרא	894		call,proclaim
	תת	qal	infc		נתן	678		give,set
3: 14	יאמר	qal	wci	3ms	אמר	55		say
	עמדתי	qal	pft	1cs	עמד	763		stand,stop
	נשא	qal	ptc	ms	נשא	669		lift,carry
	אביט	hiph	impf	1cs	נבט	613		look,regard
	אראך	qal	impf	1cs	ראה	906	2ms	see
3: 15	קחו	qal	impv	mp	לקח	542		take
	מנגן	piel	ptc	ms	נגן	618		play (strings)
	היה	qal	wcp	3ms	היה	224		be, become
	נגן	piel	infc		נגן	618		play (strings)
	מנגן	piel	ptc	ms	נגן	618		play (strings)
	תהי	qal	wci	3fs	היה	224		be, become
3: 16	יאמר	qal	wci	3ms	אמר	55		say
	אמר	qal	pft	3ms	אמר	55		say
	עשה	qal	infa		עשה	793		do,make
3: 17	אמר	qal	pft	3ms	אמר	55		say
	תראו	qal	impf	2mp	ראה	906		see
	תראו	qal	impf	2mp	ראה	906		see
	ימלא	niph	impf	3ms	מלא	569		be filled
	שתיתם	qal	wcp	2mp	שתה	1059		drink
3: 18	נקל	niph	wcp	3ms	קלל	886		be trifling
	נתן	qal	wcp	3ms	נתן	678		give,set
3: 19	הכיתם	hiph	wcp	2mp	נכה	645		smite
	תפילו	hiph	impf	2mp	נפל	656		cause to fall
	תסתמו	qal	impf	2mp	סתם	711		stop up
	תכאבו	hiph	impf	2mp	כאב	456		pain, mar
3: 20	יהי	qal	wci	3ms	היה	224		be, become
	עלות	qal	infc		עלה	748		go up
	באים	qal	ptc	mp	בוא	97		come in
3: 20	תמלא	niph	wci	3fs	מלא	569		be filled
3: 21	שמעו	qal	pft	3cp	שמע	1033		hear
	עלו	qal	pft	3cp	עלה	748		go up
	הלחם	niph	infc		לחם	535		wage war
	יצעקו	niph	wci	3mp	צעק	858		be summoned
	חגר	qal	ptc	ms	חגר	291		gird
	יעמדו	qal	wci	3mp	עמד	763		stand,stop
3: 22	ישכימו	hiph	wci	3mp	שכם	1014		rise early
	זרחה	qal	pft	3fs	זרח	280		rise,appear
	יראו	qal	wci	3mp	ראה	906		see
3: 23	יאמרו	qal	wci	3mp	אמר	55		say
	החרב	hoph	infa		חרב	352		be destroyed
	נחרבו	niph	pft	3cp	חרב	352		attack oneself
	יכו	hiph	wci	3mp	נכה	645		smite
3: 24	יבאו	qal	wci	3mp	בוא	97		come in
	יקמו	qal	wci	3mp	קום	877		arise,stand
	יכו	hiph	wci	3mp	נכה	645		smite
	ינסו	qal	wci	3mp	נוס	630		flee,escape
	יבוk	qal	wci	3mp	בוא	97		come in
	יכוq	hiph	wci	3mp	נכה	645		smite
	הכות	hiph	infc		נכה	645		smite
3: 25	יהרסו	qal	impf	3mp	הרס	248		throw down
	ישליכו	hiph	impf	3mp	שלך	1020		throw,cast
	מלאוה	piel	wcp	3cp	מלא	569	3fs	fill
	יסתמו	qal	impf	3mp	סתם	711		stop up
	יפילו	hiph	impf	3mp	נפל	656		cause to fall
	השאיר	hiph	pft	3ms	שאר	983		leave,spare
	יסבו	qal	wci	3mp	סבב	685		surround
	יכוה	hiph	wci	3mp	נכה	645	3fs	smite
3: 26	ירא	qal	wci	3ms	ראה	906		see
	חזק	qal	pft	3ms	חזק	304		be strong
	יקח	qal	wci	3ms	לקח	542		take
	שלף	qal	ptc	ms	שלף	1025		draw out,off
	הבקיע	hiph	infc		בקע	131		break into
	יכלו	qal	pft	3cp	יכל	407		be able
3: 27	יקח	qal	wci	3ms	לקח	542		take
	ימלך	qal	impf	3ms	מלך	573		be king,reign
	יעלהו	hiph	wci	3ms	עלה	748	3ms	bring up,offer
	יהי	qal	wci	3ms	היה	224		be, become
	יסעו	qal	wci	3mp	נסע	652		pull up,set out
	ישבו	qal	wci	3mp	שוב	996		turn,return
4: 1	צעקה	qal	pft	3fs	צעק	858		cry out
	אמר	qal	infc		אמר	55		say
	מת	qal	pft	3ms	מות	559		die
	ידעת	qal	pft	2ms	ידע	393		know
	היה	qal	pft	3ms	היה	224		be, become
	ירא	qal	ptc	ms	ירא	431		fear
	נשה	qal	ptc	ms	נשה	674		lend
	בא	qal	ptc	ms	בוא	97		come in
	קחת	qal	infc		לקח	542		take
4: 2	יאמר	qal	wci	3ms	אמר	55		say
	אעשה	qal	impf	1cs	עשה	793		do,make
	הגידי	hiph	impv	fs	נגד	616		declare,tell
	תאמר	qal	wci	3fs	אמר	55		say

ChVs	Form	Stem	Tnse	PGN	Root	BDB	Sfx	Meaning
4: 3	יאמר	qal	wci	3ms	אמר	55		say
	לכי	qal	impv	fs	הלך	229		walk,go
	שׁאלי	qal	impv	fs	שׁאל	981		ask,borrow
	תמעיטי	hiph	jusm	2fs	מעט	589		make small
4: 4	באת	qal	wcp	2fs	בוא	97		come in
	סגרת	qal	wcp	2fs	סגר	688		shut
	יצקת	qal	wcp	2fs	יצק	427		pour out,cast
	תסיעי	hiph	impf	2fs	נסע	652		lead out,remove
4: 5	תלך	qal	wci	3fs	הלך	229		walk,go
	תסגר	qal	wci	3fs	סגר	688		shut
	מגשׁים	hiph	ptc	mp	נגשׁ	620		bring near
	מיצקתk	hiph	ptc	fs	יצק	427		pour
	מוצקתq	hiph	ptc	fs	יצק	427		pour
4: 6	יהי	qal	wci	3ms	היה	224		be,become
	מלאת	qal	infc		מלא	569		be full,fill
	תאמר	qal	wci	3fs	אמר	55		say
	הגישׁה	hiph	impv	ms	נגשׁ	620		bring near
	יאמר	qal	wci	3ms	אמר	55		say
	יעמד	qal	wci	3ms	עמד	763		stand,stop
4: 7	תבא	qal	wci	3fs	בוא	97		come in
	תגד	hiph	wci	3fs	נגד	616		declare,tell
	יאמר	qal	wci	3ms	אמר	55		say
	לכי	qal	impv	fs	הלך	229		walk,go
	מכרי	qal	impv	fs	מכר	569		sell
	שׁלמי	piel	impv	fs	שׁלם	1022		finish,reward
	תחיי	qal	impf	2fs	חיה	310		live
	נותר	niph	ptc	ms	יתר	451		be left,remain
4: 8	יהי	qal	wci	3ms	היה	224		be,become
	יעבר	qal	wci	3ms	עבר	716		pass over
	תחזק	hiph	wci	3fs	חזק	304		make firm,seize
	אכל	qal	infc		אכל	37		eat,devour
	יהי	qal	wci	3ms	היה	224		be,become
	עברו	qal	infc		עבר	716	3ms	pass over
	יסר	qal	impf	3ms	סור	693		turn aside
	אכל	qal	infc		אכל	37		eat,devour
4: 9	תאמר	qal	wci	3fs	אמר	55		say
	ידעתי	qal	pft	1cs	ידע	393		know
	עבר	qal	ptc	ms	עבר	716		pass over
4: 10	נעשׂה	qal	cohm	1cp	עשׂה	793		do,make
	נשׂים	qal	cohm	1cp	שׂים	962		put,set
	היה	qal	wcp	3ms	היה	224		be,become
	באו	qal	infc		בוא	97	3ms	come in
	יסור	qal	impf	3ms	סור	693		turn aside
4: 11	יהי	qal	wci	3ms	היה	224		be,become
	יבא	qal	wci	3ms	בוא	97		come in
	יסר	qal	wci	3ms	סור	693		turn aside
	ישׁכב	qal	wci	3ms	שׁכב	1011		lie,lie down
4: 12	יאמר	qal	wci	3ms	אמר	55		say
	קרא	qal	impv	ms	קרא	894		call,proclaim
	יקרא	qal	wci	3ms	קרא	894		call,proclaim
	תעמד	qal	wci	3fs	עמד	763		stand,stop
4: 13	יאמר	qal	wci	3ms	אמר	55		say
	אמר	qal	impv	ms	אמר	55		say
	חרדת	qal	pft	2fs	חרד	353		tremble
4: 13	עשׂות	qal	infc		עשׂה	793		do,make
	דבר	piel	infc		דבר	180		speak
	תאמר	qal	wci	3fs	אמר	55		say
	ישׁבת	qal	ptc	fs	ישׁב	442		sit,dwell
4: 14	יאמר	qal	wci	3ms	אמר	55		say
	עשׂות	qal	infc		עשׂה	793		do,make
	יאמר	qal	wci	3ms	אמר	55		say
	זקן	qal	pft	3ms	זקן	278		be old
4: 15	יאמר	qal	wci	3ms	אמר	55		say
	קרא	qal	impv	ms	קרא	894		call,proclaim
	יקרא	qal	wci	3ms	קרא	894		call,proclaim
	תעמד	qal	wci	3fs	עמד	763		stand,stop
4: 16	יאמר	qal	wci	3ms	אמר	55		say
	חבקת	qal	ptc	fs	חבק	287		embrace
	תאמר	qal	wci	3fs	אמר	55		say
	תכזב	piel	jusm	2ms	כזב	469		lie,deceive
4: 17	תהר	qal	wci	3fs	הרה	247		conceive
	תלד	qal	wci	3fs	ילד	408		bear,beget
	דבר	piel	pft	3ms	דבר	180		speak
4: 18	יגדל	qal	wci	3ms	גדל	152		be great,grow
	יהי	qal	wci	3ms	היה	224		be,become
	יצא	qal	wci	3ms	יצא	422		go out
	קצרים	qal	ptc	mp	קצר	894		reap,harvest
4: 19	יאמר	qal	wci	3ms	אמר	55		say
	יאמר	qal	wci	3ms	אמר	55		say
	שׂאהו	qal	impv	ms	נשׂא	669	3ms	lift,carry
4: 20	ישׂאהו	qal	wci	3ms	נשׂא	669	3ms	lift,carry
	יביאהו	hiph	wci	3ms	בוא	97	3ms	bring in
	ישׁב	qal	wci	3ms	ישׁב	442		sit,dwell
	ימת	qal	wci	3ms	מות	559		die
4: 21	תעל	qal	wci	3fs	עלה	748		go up
	תשׁכבהו	hiph	wci	3fs	שׁכב	1011	3ms	lay
	תסגר	qal	wci	3fs	סגר	688		shut
	תצא	qal	wci	3fs	יצא	422		go out
4: 22	תקרא	qal	wci	3fs	קרא	894		call,proclaim
	תאמר	qal	wci	3fs	אמר	55		say
	שׁלחה	qal	impv	ms	שׁלח	1018		send
	ארוצה	qal	coh	1cs	רוץ	930		run
	אשׁובה	qal	coh	1cs	שׁוב	996		turn,return
4: 23	יאמר	qal	wci	3ms	אמר	55		say
	הלכתיk	qal	ptc	fs	הלך	229		walk,go
	הלכתq	qal	ptc	fs	הלך	229		walk,go
	תאמר	qal	wci	3fs	אמר	55		say
4: 24	תחבשׁ	qal	wci	3fs	חבשׁ	289		bind
	תאמר	qal	wci	3fs	אמר	55		say
	נהג	qal	impv	ms	נהג	624		drive
	לך	qal	impv	ms	הלך	229		walk,go
	תעצר	qal	jusm	2ms	עצר	783		restrain
	רכב	qal	infc		רכב	938		mount,ride
	אמרתי	qal	pft	1cs	אמר	55		say
4: 25	תלך	qal	wci	3fs	הלך	229		walk,go
	תבוא	qal	wci	3fs	בוא	97		come in
	יהי	qal	wci	3ms	היה	224		be,become
	ראות	qal	infc		ראה	906		see

ChVs	Form	Stem	Tnse	PGN	Root	BDB	Sfx	Meaning
4:25	יאמר	qal	wci	3ms	אמר	55		say
4:26	רוץ	qal	impv	ms	רוץ	930		run
	קראתה	qal	infc		קרא	896	3fs	meet,encounter
	אמר	qal	impv	ms	אמר	55		say
	תאמר	qal	wci	3fs	אמר	55		say
4:27	תבא	qal	wci	3fs	בוא	97		come in
	תחזק	hiph	wci	3fs	חזק	304		make firm,seize
	יגש	qal	wci	3ms	נגש	620		draw near
	הדפה	qal	infc		הדף	213	3fs	thrust,drive
	יאמר	qal	wci	3ms	אמר	55		say
	הרפה	hiph	impv	ms	רפה	951		slacken,abandon
	מרה	qal	pft	3fs	מרר	600		be bitter
	העלים	hiph	pft	3ms	עלם	761		conceal,hide
	הגיד	hiph	pft	3ms	נגד	616		declare,tell
4:28	תאמר	qal	wci	3fs	אמר	55		say
	שאלתי	qal	pft	1cs	שאל	981		ask,borrow
	אמרתי	qal	pft	1cs	אמר	55		say
	תשלה	hiph	impf	2ms	שלה	1017		mislead
4:29	יאמר	qal	wci	3ms	אמר	55		say
	חגר	qal	impv	ms	חגר	291		gird
	קח	qal	impv	ms	לקח	542		take
	לך	qal	impv	ms	הלך	229		walk,go
	תמצא	qal	impf	2ms	מצא	592		find
	תברכנו	piel	impf	2ms	ברך	138	3ms	bless
	יברכך	piel	impf	3ms	ברך	138	2ms	bless
	תעננו	qal	impf	2ms	ענה	772	3ms	answer
	שמת	qal	wcp	2ms	שים	962		put,set
4:30	תאמר	qal	wci	3fs	אמר	55		say
	אעזבך	qal	impf	1cs	עזב	736	2ms	leave,loose
	יקם	qal	wci	3ms	קום	877		arise,stand
	ילך	qal	wci	3ms	הלך	229		walk,go
4:31	עבר	qal	pft	3ms	עבר	716		pass over
	ישם	qal	wci	3ms	שים	962		put,set
	ישב	qal	wci	3ms	שוב	996		turn,return
	קראתו	qal	infc		קרא	896	3ms	meet,encounter
	יגד	hiph	wci	3ms	נגד	616		declare,tell
	אמר	qal	infc		אמר	55		say
	הקיץ	hiph	pft	3ms	קיץ	884		awake
4:32	יבא	qal	wci	3ms	בוא	97		come in
	מת	qal	ptc	ms	מות	559		die
	משכב	hoph	ptc	ms	שכב	1011		be laid
4:33	יבא	qal	wci	3ms	בוא	97		come in
	יסגר	qal	wci	3ms	סגר	688		shut
	יתפלל	hith	wci	3ms	פלל	813		pray
4:34	יעל	qal	wci	3ms	עלה	748		go up
	ישכב	qal	wci	3ms	שכב	1011		lie,lie down
	ישם	qal	wci	3ms	שים	962		put,set
	יגהר	qal	wci	3ms	גהר	155		bend
	יחם	qal	wci	3ms	חמם	328		be warm
4:35	ישב	qal	wci	3ms	שוב	996		turn,return
	ילך	qal	wci	3ms	הלך	229		walk,go
	יעל	qal	wci	3ms	עלה	748		go up
	יגהר	qal	wci	3ms	גהר	155		bend
	יזורר	poel	wci	3ms	זרר	284		sneeze
4:35	יפקח	qal	wci	3ms	פקח	824		open
4:36	יקרא	qal	wci	3ms	קרא	894		call,proclaim
	יאמר	qal	wci	3ms	אמר	55		say
	קרא	qal	impv	ms	קרא	894		call,proclaim
	יקראה	qal	wci	3ms	קרא	894	3fs	call,proclaim
	תבוא	qal	wci	3fs	בוא	97		come in
	יאמר	qal	wci	3ms	אמר	55		say
	שאי	qal	impv	fs	נשא	669		lift,carry
4:37	תבא	qal	wci	3fs	בוא	97		come in
	תפל	qal	wci	3fs	נפל	656		fall
	תשתחו	hish	wci	3fs	חוה	1005		bow down
	תשא	qal	wci	3fs	נשא	669		lift,carry
	תצא	qal	wci	3fs	יצא	422		go out
4:38	שב	qal	pft	3ms	שוב	996		turn,return
	ישבים	qal	ptc	mp	ישב	442		sit,dwell
	יאמר	qal	wci	3ms	אמר	55		say
	שפת	qal	impv	ms	שפת	1046		set,establish
	בשל	piel	impv	ms	בשל	143		boil,cook
4:39	יצא	qal	wci	3ms	יצא	422		go out
	לקט	piel	infc		לקט	544		gather
	ימצא	qal	wci	3ms	מצא	592		find
	ילקט	piel	wci	3ms	לקט	544		gather
	יבא	qal	wci	3ms	בוא	97		come in
	יפלח	piel	wci	3ms	פלח	812		cleave
	ידעו	qal	pft	3cp	ידע	393		know
4:40	יצקו	qal	wci	3mp	יצק	427		pour out,cast
	אכול	qal	infc		אכל	37		eat,devour
	יהי	qal	wci	3ms	היה	224		be,become
	אכלם	qal	infc		אכל	37	3mp	eat,devour
	צעקו	qal	pft	3cp	צעק	858		cry out
	יאמרו	qal	wci	3mp	אמר	55		say
	יכלו	qal	pft	3cp	יכל	407		be able
	אכל	qal	infc		אכל	37		eat,devour
4:41	יאמר	qal	wci	3ms	אמר	55		say
	קחו	qal	impv	mp	לקח	542		take
	ישלך	hiph	wci	3ms	שלך	1020		throw,cast
	יאמר	qal	wci	3ms	אמר	55		say
	צק	qal	impv	ms	יצק	427		pour out,cast
	יאכלו	qal	jusm	3mp	אכל	37		eat,devour
	היה	qal	pft	3ms	היה	224		be,become
4:42	בא	qal	pft	3ms	בוא	97		come in
	יבא	hiph	wci	3ms	בוא	97		bring in
	יאמר	qal	wci	3ms	אמר	55		say
	תן	qal	impv	ms	נתן	678		give,set
	יאכלו	qal	jusm	3mp	אכל	37		eat,devour
4:43	יאמר	qal	wci	3ms	אמר	55		say
	משרתו	piel	ptc	ms	שרת	1058	3ms	minister,serve
	אתן	qal	impf	1cs	נתן	678		give,set
	יאמר	qal	wci	3ms	אמר	55		say
	תן	qal	impv	ms	נתן	678		give,set
	יאכלו	qal	jusm	3mp	אכל	37		eat,devour
	אמר	qal	pft	3ms	אמר	55		say
	אכל	qal	infa		אכל	37		eat,devour
	הותר	hiph	infa		יתר	451		leave,spare

ChVs	Form	Stem	Tnse	PGN	Root	BDB	Sfx	Meaning
4:44	יתן	qal	wci	3ms	נתן	678		give,set
	יאכלו	qal	wci	3mp	אכל	37		eat,devour
	יותרו	hiph	wci	3mp	יתר	451		leave,spare
5:1	היה	qal	pft	3ms	היה	224		be,become
	נשא	qal	pptc	ms	נשא	669		lift,carry
	נתן	qal	pft	3ms	נתן	678		give,set
	היה	qal	pft	3ms	היה	224		be,become
	מצרע	pual	ptc	ms	צרע	863		be leprous
5:2	יצאו	qal	pft	3cp	יצא	422		go out
	ישבו	qal	wci	3mp	שבה	985		take captive
	תהי	qal	wci	3fs	היה	224		be,become
5:3	תאמר	qal	wci	3fs	אמר	55		say
	יאסף	qal	impf	3ms	אסף	62		gather
5:4	יבא	qal	wci	3ms	בוא	97		come in
	יגד	hiph	wci	3ms	נגד	616		declare,tell
	אמר	qal	infc		אמר	55		say
	דברה	piel	pft	3fs	דבר	180		speak
5:5	יאמר	qal	wci	3ms	אמר	55		say
	לך	qal	impv	ms	הלך	229		walk,go
	בא	qal	impv	ms	בוא	97		come in
	אשלחה	qal	coh	1cs	שלח	1018		send
	ילך	qal	wci	3ms	הלך	229		walk,go
	יקח	qal	wci	3ms	לקח	542		take
5:6	יבא	hiph	wci	3ms	בוא	97		bring in
	אמר	qal	infc		אמר	55		say
	בוא	qal	infc		בוא	97		come in
	שלחתי	qal	pft	1cs	שלח	1018		send
	אספתו	qal	wcp	2ms	אסף	62	3ms	gather
5:7	יהי	qal	wci	3ms	היה	224		be,become
	קרא	qal	infc		קרא	894		call,proclaim
	יקרע	qal	wci	3ms	קרע	902		tear,rend
	יאמר	qal	wci	3ms	אמר	55		say
	המית	hiph	infc		מות	559		kill
	החיות	hiph	infc		חיה	310		preserve
	שלח	qal	ptc	ms	שלח	1018		send
	אסף	qal	infc		אסף	62		gather
	דעו	qal	impv	mp	ידע	393		know
	ראו	qal	impv	mp	ראה	906		see
	מתאנה	hith	ptc	ms	אנה	58		seek occasion
5:8	יהי	qal	wci	3ms	היה	224		be,become
	שמע	qal	infc		שמע	1033		hear
	קרע	qal	pft	3ms	קרע	902		tear,rend
	ישלח	qal	wci	3ms	שלח	1018		send
	אמר	qal	infc		אמר	55		say
	קרעת	qal	pft	2ms	קרע	902		tear,rend
	יבא	qal	jus	3ms	בוא	97		come in
	ידע	qal	jusm	3ms	ידע	393		know
5:9	יבא	qal	wci	3ms	בוא	97		come in
	יעמד	qal	wci	3ms	עמד	763		stand,stop
5:10	ישלח	qal	wci	3ms	שלח	1018		send
	אמר	qal	infc		אמר	55		say
	הלוך	qal	infa		הלך	229		walk,go
	רחצת	qal	wcp	2ms	רחץ	934		wash,bathe
	ישב	qal	jus	3ms	שוב	996		turn,return
5:10	טהר	qal	impv	ms	טהר	372		be clean,pure
5:11	יקצף	qal	wci	3ms	קצף	893		be angry
	ילך	qal	wci	3ms	הלך	229		walk,go
	יאמר	qal	wci	3ms	אמר	55		say
	אמרתי	qal	pft	1cs	אמר	55		say
	יצא	qal	impf	3ms	יצא	422		go out
	יצוא	qal	infa		יצא	422		go out
	עמד	qal	wcp	3ms	עמד	763		stand,stop
	קרא	qal	wcp	3ms	קרא	894		call,proclaim
	הניף	hiph	wcp	3ms	נוף	631		swing,wave
	אסף	qal	wcp	3ms	אסף	62		gather
	מצרע	pual	ptc	ms	צרע	863		be leprous
5:12	ארחץ	qal	impf	1cs	רחץ	934		wash,bathe
	טהרתי	qal	wcp	1cs	טהר	372		be clean,pure
	יפן	qal	wci	3ms	פנה	815		turn
	ילך	qal	wci	3ms	הלך	229		walk,go
5:13	יגשו	qal	wci	3mp	נגש	620		draw near
	ידברו	piel	wci	3mp	דבר	180		speak
	יאמרו	qal	wci	3mp	אמר	55		say
	דבר	piel	pft	3ms	דבר	180		speak
	תעשה	qal	impf	2ms	עשה	793		do,make
	אמר	qal	pft	3ms	אמר	55		say
	רחץ	qal	impv	ms	רחץ	934		wash,bathe
	טהר	qal	impv	ms	טהר	372		be clean,pure
5:14	ירד	qal	wci	3ms	ירד	432		come down
	יטבל	qal	wci	3ms	טבל	371		dip
	ישב	qal	wci	3ms	שוב	996		turn,return
	יטהר	qal	wci	3ms	טהר	372		be clean,pure
5:15	ישב	qal	wci	3ms	שוב	996		turn,return
	יבא	qal	wci	3ms	בוא	97		come in
	יעמד	qal	wci	3ms	עמד	763		stand,stop
	יאמר	qal	wci	3ms	אמר	55		say
	ידעתי	qal	pft	1cs	ידע	393		know
	קח	qal	impv	ms	לקח	542		take
5:16	יאמר	qal	wci	3ms	אמר	55		say
	עמדתי	qal	pft	1cs	עמד	763		stand,stop
	אקח	qal	impf	1cs	לקח	542		take
	יפצר	qal	wci	3ms	פצר	823		push
	קחת	qal	infc		לקח	542		take
	ימאן	piel	wci	3ms	מאן	549		refuse
5:17	יאמר	qal	wci	3ms	אמר	55		say
	יתן	qalp	jusm	3ms	נתן	678		be given
	יעשה	qal	impf	3ms	עשה	793		do,make
5:18	יסלח	qal	jusm	3ms	סלח	699		forgive,pardon
	בוא	qal	infc		בוא	97		come in
	השתחות	hish	infc		חוה	1005		bow down
	נשען	niph	ptc	ms	שען	1043		lean,support
	השתחויתי	hish	wcp	1cs	חוה	1005		bow down
	השתחויתי	hish	infc		חוה	1005	1cs	bow down
	יסלח	qal	jusm	3ms	סלח	699		forgive,pardon
5:19	יאמר	qal	wci	3ms	אמר	55		say
	לך	qal	impv	ms	הלך	229		walk,go
	ילך	qal	wci	3ms	הלך	229		walk,go
5:20	יאמר	qal	wci	3ms	אמר	55		say

ChVs	Form	Stem	Tnse	PGN	Root	BDB	Sfx	Meaning
5: 20	חשׂך	qal	pft	3ms	חשׂך	362		withhold
	קחת	qal	infc		לקח	542		take
	הביא	hiph	pft	3ms	בוא	97		bring in
	רצתי	qal	pft	1cs	רוץ	930		run
	לקחתי	qal	wcp	1cs	לקח	542		take
5: 21	ירדף	qal	wci	3ms	רדף	922		pursue
	יראה	qal	wci	3ms	ראה	906		see
	רץ	qal	ptc	ms	רוץ	930		run
	יפל	qal	wci	3ms	נפל	656		fall
	קראתו	qal	infc		קרא	896	3ms	meet, encounter
	יאמר	qal	wci	3ms	אמר	55		say
5: 22	יאמר	qal	wci	3ms	אמר	55		say
	שׁלחני	qal	pft	3ms	שׁלח	1018	1cs	send
	אמר	qal	infc		אמר	55		say
	באו	qal	pft	3cp	בוא	97		come in
	תנה	qal	impv	ms	נתן	678		give, set
5: 23	יאמר	qal	wci	3ms	אמר	55		say
	הואל	hiph	impv	ms	יאל	383		be willing
	קח	qal	impv	ms	לקח	542		take
	יפרץ	qal	wci	3ms	פרץ	829		break through
	יצר	qal	wci	3ms	צור	848		confine, shut in
	יתן	qal	wci	3ms	נתן	678		give, set
	ישׂאו	qal	wci	3mp	נשׂא	669		lift, carry
5: 24	יבא	qal	wci	3ms	בוא	97		come in
	יקח	qal	wci	3ms	לקח	542		take
	יפקד	qal	wci	3ms	פקד	823		attend to, visit
	ישׁלח	piel	wci	3ms	שׁלח	1018		send away, shoot
	ילכו	qal	wci	3mp	הלך	229		walk, go
5: 25	בא	qal	pft	3ms	בוא	97		come in
	יעמד	qal	wci	3ms	עמד	763		stand, stop
	יאמר	qal	wci	3ms	אמר	55		say
	יאמר	qal	wci	3ms	אמר	55		say
	הלך	qal	pft	3ms	הלך	229		walk, go
5: 26	יאמר	qal	wci	3ms	אמר	55		say
	הלך	qal	pft	3ms	הלך	229		walk, go
	הפך	qal	pft	3ms	הפך	245		turn, overturn
	קראתך	qal	infc		קרא	896	2ms	meet, encounter
	קחת	qal	infc		לקח	542		take
	קחת	qal	infc		לקח	542		take
5: 27	תדבק	qal	impf	3fs	דבק	179		cling, cleave
	יצא	qal	wci	3ms	יצא	422		go out
	מצרע	pual	ptc	ms	צרע	863		be leprous
6: 1	יאמרו	qal	wci	3mp	אמר	55		say
	ישׁבים	qal	ptc	mp	ישׁב	442		sit, dwell
6: 2	נלכה	qal	coh	1cp	הלך	229		walk, go
	נקחה	qal	coh	1cp	לקח	542		take
	נעשׂה	qal	cohm	1cp	עשׂה	793		do, make
	שׁבת	qal	infc		ישׁב	442		sit, dwell
	יאמר	qal	wci	3ms	אמר	55		say
	לכו	qal	impv	mp	הלך	229		walk, go
6: 3	יאמר	qal	wci	3ms	אמר	55		say
	הואל	hiph	impv	ms	יאל	383		be willing
	לך	qal	impv	ms	הלך	229		walk, go
	יאמר	qal	wci	3ms	אמר	55		say
6: 3	אלך	qal	impf	1cs	הלך	229		walk, go
6: 4	ילך	qal	wci	3ms	הלך	229		walk, go
	יבאו	qal	wci	3mp	בוא	97		come in
	יגזרו	qal	wci	3mp	גזר	160		divide
6: 5	יהי	qal	wci	3ms	היה	224		be, become
	מפיל	hiph	ptc	ms	נפל	656		cause to fall
	נפל	qal	pft	3ms	נפל	656		fall
	יצעק	qal	wci	3ms	צעק	858		cry out
	יאמר	qal	wci	3ms	אמר	55		say
	שׁאול	qal	pptc	ms	שׁאל	981		ask, borrow
6: 6	יאמר	qal	wci	3ms	אמר	55		say
	נפל	qal	pft	3ms	נפל	656		fall
	יראהו	hiph	wci	3ms	ראה	906	3ms	show, exhibit
	יקצב	qal	wci	3ms	קצב	891		cut off, shear
	ישׁלך	hiph	wci	3ms	שׁלך	1020		throw, cast
	יצף	hiph	wci	3ms	צוף	847		cause to flow
6: 7	יאמר	qal	wci	3ms	אמר	55		say
	הרם	hiph	impv	ms	רום	926		raise, lift
	ישׁלח	qal	wci	3ms	שׁלח	1018		send
	יקחהו	qal	wci	3ms	לקח	542	3ms	take
6: 8	היה	qal	pft	3ms	היה	224		be, become
	נלחם	niph	ptc	ms	לחם	535		wage war
	יועץ	niph	wci	3ms	יעץ	419		consult
	אמר	qal	infc		אמר	55		say
6: 9	ישׁלח	qal	wci	3ms	שׁלח	1018		send
	אמר	qal	infc		אמר	55		say
	השׁמר	niph	impv	ms	שׁמר	1036		be kept, guarded
	עבר	qal	infc		עבר	716		pass over
6: 10	ישׁלח	qal	wci	3ms	שׁלח	1018		send
	אמר	qal	pft	3ms	אמר	55		say
	הזהירהk	hiph	wcp	3ms	זהר	264	3ms	teach
	הזהירוq	hiph	wcp	3ms	זהר	264	3ms	teach
	נשׁמר	niph	wcp	3ms	שׁמר	1036		be kept, guarded
6: 11	יסער	niph	wci	3ms	סער	704		be enraged
	יקרא	qal	wci	3ms	קרא	894		call, proclaim
	יאמר	qal	wci	3ms	אמר	55		say
	תגידו	hiph	impf	2mp	נגד	616		declare, tell
6: 12	יאמר	qal	wci	3ms	אמר	55		say
	יגיד	hiph	impf	3ms	נגד	616		declare, tell
	תדבר	piel	impf	2ms	דבר	180		speak
6: 13	יאמר	qal	wci	3ms	אמר	55		say
	לכו	qal	impv	mp	הלך	229		walk, go
	ראו	qal	impv	mp	ראה	906		see
	אשׁלח	qal	cohm	1cs	שׁלח	1018		send
	אקחהו	qal	cohm	1cs	לקח	542	3ms	take
	יגד	hoph	wci	3ms	נגד	616		be told
	אמר	qal	infc		אמר	55		say
6: 14	ישׁלח	qal	wci	3ms	שׁלח	1018		send
	יבאו	qal	wci	3mp	בוא	97		come in
	יקפו	hiph	wci	3mp	נקף	668		surround
6: 15	ישׁכם	hiph	wci	3ms	שׁכם	1014		rise early
	משׁרת	piel	ptc	ms	שׁרת	1058		minister, serve
	קום	qal	infc		קום	877		arise, stand
	יצא	qal	wci	3ms	יצא	422		go out

ChVs	Form	Stem	Tnse	PGN	Root	BDB	Sfx	Meaning
6:15	סובב	qal	ptc	ms	סבב	685		surround
	יאמר	qal	wci	3ms	אמר	55		say
	נעשׂה	qal	impf	1cp	עשׂה	793		do,make
6:16	יאמר	qal	wci	3ms	אמר	55		say
	תירא	qal	jusm	2ms	ירא	431		fear
6:17	יתפלל	hith	wci	3ms	פלל	813		pray
	יאמר	qal	wci	3ms	אמר	55		say
	פקח	qal	impv	ms	פקח	824		open
	יראה	qal	jusm	3ms	ראה	906		see
	יפקח	qal	wci	3ms	פקח	824		open
	ירא	qal	wci	3ms	ראה	906		see
	מלא	qal	pft	3ms	מלא	569		be full,fill
6:18	ירדו	qal	wci	3mp	ירד	432		come down
	יתפלל	hith	wci	3ms	פלל	813		pray
	יאמר	qal	wci	3ms	אמר	55		say
	הך	hiph	impv	ms	נכה	645		smite
	יכם	hiph	wci	3ms	נכה	645	3mp	smite
6:19	יאמר	qal	wci	3ms	אמר	55		say
	לכו	qal	impv	mp	הלך	229		walk,go
	אוליכה	hiph	coh	1cs	הלך	229		lead,bring
	תבקשׁון	piel	impf	2mp	בקשׁ	134		seek
	ילך	hiph	wci	3ms	הלך	229		lead,bring
6:20	יהי	qal	wci	3ms	היה	224		be,become
	באם	qal	infc		בוא	97	3mp	come in
	יאמר	qal	wci	3ms	אמר	55		say
	פקח	qal	impv	ms	פקח	824		open
	יראו	qal	jusm	3mp	ראה	906		see
	יפקח	qal	wci	3ms	פקח	824		open
	יראו	qal	wci	3mp	ראה	906		see
6:21	יאמר	qal	wci	3ms	אמר	55		say
	ראתו	qal	infc		ראה	906	3ms	see
	אכה	hiph	impf	1cs	נכה	645		smite
	אכה	hiph	impf	1cs	נכה	645		smite
6:22	יאמר	qal	wci	3ms	אמר	55		say
	תכה	hiph	impf	2ms	נכה	645		smite
	שׁבית	qal	pft	2ms	שׁבה	985		take captive
	מכה	hiph	ptc	ms	נכה	645		smite
	שׂים	qal	impv	ms	שׂים	962		put,set
	יאכלו	qal	jusm	3mp	אכל	37		eat,devour
	ישׁתו	qal	jusm	3mp	שׁתה	1059		drink
	ילכו	qal	jusm	3mp	הלך	229		walk,go
6:23	יכרה	qal	wci	3ms	כרה	500		give a feast
	יאכלו	qal	wci	3mp	אכל	37		eat,devour
	ישׁתו	qal	wci	3mp	שׁתה	1059		drink
	ישׁלחם	piel	wci	3ms	שׁלח	1018	3mp	send away,shoot
	ילכו	qal	wci	3mp	הלך	229		walk,go
	יספו	qal	pft	3cp	יסף	414		add,increase
	בוא	qal	infc		בוא	97		come in
6:24	יהי	qal	wci	3ms	היה	224		be,become
	יקבץ	qal	wci	3ms	קבץ	867		gather,collect
	יעל	qal	wci	3ms	עלה	748		go up
	יצר	qal	wci	3ms	צור	848		confine,shut in
6:25	יהי	qal	wci	3ms	היה	224		be,become
	צרים	qal	ptc	mp	צור	848		confine,shut in
6:25	היות	qal	infc		היה	224		be,become
6:26	יהי	qal	wci	3ms	היה	224		be,become
	עבר	qal	ptc	ms	עבר	716		pass over
	צעקה	qal	pft	3fs	צעק	858		cry out
	אמר	qal	infc		אמר	55		say
	הושׁיעה	hiph	impv	ms	ישׁע	446		deliver,save
6:27	יאמר	qal	wci	3ms	אמר	55		say
	יושׁעך	hiph	jusm	3ms	ישׁע	446	2ms	deliver,save
	אושׁיעך	hiph	impf	1cs	ישׁע	446	2ms	deliver,save
6:28	יאמר	qal	wci	3ms	אמר	55		say
	תאמר	qal	wci	3fs	אמר	55		say
	אמרה	qal	pft	3fs	אמר	55		say
	תני	qal	impv	fs	נתן	678		give,set
	נאכלנו	qal	cohm	1cp	אכל	37	3ms	eat,devour
	נאכל	qal	impf	1cp	אכל	37		eat,devour
6:29	נבשׁל	piel	wci	1cp	בשׁל	143		boil,cook
	נאכלהו	qal	wci	1cp	אכל	37	3ms	eat,devour
	אמר	qal	wci	1cs	אמר	55		say
	תני	qal	impv	fs	נתן	678		give,set
	נאכלנו	qal	cohm	1cp	אכל	37	3ms	eat,devour
	תחבא	hiph	wci	3fs	חבא	285		hide
6:30	יהי	qal	wci	3ms	היה	224		be,become
	שׁמע	qal	infc		שׁמע	1033		hear
	יקרע	qal	wci	3ms	קרע	902		tear,rend
	עבר	qal	ptc	ms	עבר	716		pass over
	ירא	qal	wci	3ms	ראה	906		see
6:31	יאמר	qal	wci	3ms	אמר	55		say
	יעשׂה	qal	jusm	3ms	עשׂה	793		do,make
	יוסף	hiph	jusm	3ms	יסף	414		add,do again
	יעמד	qal	impf	3ms	עמד	763		stand,stop
6:32	ישׁב	qal	ptc	ms	ישׁב	442		sit,dwell
	ישׁבים	qal	ptc	mp	ישׁב	442		sit,dwell
	ישׁלח	qal	wci	3ms	שׁלח	1018		send
	יבא	qal	impf	3ms	בוא	97		come in
	אמר	qal	pft	3ms	אמר	55		say
	ראיתם	qal	pft	2mp	ראה	906		see
	שׁלח	qal	pft	3ms	שׁלח	1018		send
	מרצח	piel	ptc	ms	רצח	953		murder
	הסיר	hiph	infc		סור	693		take away
	ראו	qal	impv	mp	ראה	906		see
	בא	qal	infc		בוא	97		come in
	סגרו	qal	impv	mp	סגר	688		shut
	לחצתם	qal	wcp	2mp	לחץ	537		press,oppress
6:33	מדבר	piel	ptc	ms	דבר	180		speak
	ירד	qal	ptc	ms	ירד	432		come down
	יאמר	qal	wci	3ms	אמר	55		say
	אוחיל	hiph	impf	1cs	יחל	403		wait
7:1	יאמר	qal	wci	3ms	אמר	55		say
	שׁמעו	qal	impv	mp	שׁמע	1033		hear
	אמר	qal	pft	3ms	אמר	55		say
7:2	יען	qal	wci	3ms	ענה	772		answer
	נשׁען	niph	ptc	ms	שׁען	1043		lean,support
	יאמר	qal	wci	3ms	אמר	55		say
	עשׂה	qal	ptc	ms	עשׂה	793		do,make

ChVs	Form	Stem	Tnse	PGN	Root	BDB	Sfx	Meaning
7:2	יהיה	qal	impf	3ms	היה	224		be,become
	יאמר	qal	wci	3ms	אמר	55		say
	ראה	qal	ptc	ms	ראה	906		see
	תאכל	qal	impf	2ms	אכל	37		eat,devour
7:3	היו	qal	pft	3cp	היה	224		be,become
	מצרעים	pual	ptc	mp	צרע	863		be leprous
	יאמרו	qal	wci	3mp	אמר	55		say
	ישבים	qal	ptc	mp	ישב	442		sit,dwell
	מתנו	qal	pft	1cp	מות	559		die
7:4	אמרנו	qal	pft	1cp	אמר	55		say
	נבוא	qal	impf	1cp	בוא	97		come in
	מתנו	qal	wcp	1cp	מות	559		die
	ישבנו	qal	pft	1cp	ישב	442		sit,dwell
	מתנו	qal	wcp	1cp	מות	559		die
	לכו	qal	impv	mp	הלך	229		walk,go
	נפלה	qal	coh	1cp	נפל	656		fall
	יחינו	piel	impf	3mp	חיה	310	1cp	preserve,revive
	נחיה	qal	impf	1cp	חיה	310		live
	ימיתנו	hiph	impf	3mp	מות	559	1cp	kill
	מתנו	qal	wcp	1cp	מות	559		die
7:5	יקומו	qal	wci	3mp	קום	877		arise,stand
	בוא	qal	infc		בוא	97		come in
	יבאו	qal	wci	3mp	בוא	97		come in
7:6	השמיע	hiph	pft	3ms	שמע	1033		cause to hear
	יאמרו	qal	wci	3mp	אמר	55		say
	שׂכר	qal	pft	3ms	שׂכר	968		hire
	בוא	qal	infc		בוא	97		come in
7:7	יקומו	qal	wci	3mp	קום	877		arise,stand
	ינוסו	qal	wci	3mp	נוס	630		flee,escape
	יעזבו	qal	wci	3mp	עזב	736		leave,loose
	ינסו	qal	wci	3mp	נוס	630		flee,escape
7:8	יבאו	qal	wci	3mp	בוא	97		come in
	מצרעים	pual	ptc	mp	צרע	863		be leprous
	יבאו	qal	wci	3mp	בוא	97		come in
	יאכלו	qal	wci	3mp	אכל	37		eat,devour
	ישתו	qal	wci	3mp	שתה	1059		drink
	ישׂאו	qal	wci	3mp	נשׂא	669		lift,carry
	ילכו	qal	wci	3mp	הלך	229		walk,go
	יטמנו	hiph	wci	3mp	טמן	380		hide
	ישבו	qal	wci	3mp	שוב	996		turn,return
	יבאו	qal	wci	3mp	בוא	97		come in
	ישׂאו	qal	wci	3mp	נשׂא	669		lift,carry
	ילכו	qal	wci	3mp	הלך	229		walk,go
	יטמנו	hiph	wci	3mp	טמן	380		hide
7:9	יאמרו	qal	wci	3mp	אמר	55		say
	עשׂים	qal	ptc	mp	עשׂה	793		do,make
	מחשים	hiph	ptc	mp	חשה	364		show silence
	חכינו	piel	wcp	1cp	חכה	314		wait
	מצאנו	qal	wcp	3ms	מצא	592	1cp	find
	לכו	qal	impv	mp	הלך	229		walk,go
	נבאה	qal	coh	1cp	בוא	97		come in
	נגידה	hiph	coh	1cp	נגד	616		declare,tell
7:10	יבאו	qal	wci	3mp	בוא	97		come in
	יקראו	qal	wci	3mp	קרא	894		call,proclaim
7:10	יגידו	hiph	wci	3mp	נגד	616		declare,tell
	אמר	qal	infc		אמר	55		say
	באנו	qal	pft	1cp	בוא	97		come in
	אסור	qal	pptc	ms	אסר	63		tie,bind
	אסור	qal	pptc	ms	אסר	63		tie,bind
7:11	יקרא	qal	wci	3ms	קרא	894		call,proclaim
	יגידו	hiph	wci	3mp	נגד	616		declare,tell
7:12	יקם	qal	wci	3ms	קום	877		arise,stand
	יאמר	qal	wci	3ms	אמר	55		say
	אגידה	hiph	coh	1cs	נגד	616		declare,tell
	עשׂו	qal	pft	3cp	עשׂה	793		do,make
	ידעו	qal	pft	3cp	ידע	393		know
	יצאו	qal	wci	3mp	יצא	422		go out
	החבה	niph	infc		חבה	285		hide oneself
	אמר	qal	infc		אמר	55		say
	יצאו	qal	impf	3mp	יצא	422		go out
	נתפשׂם	qal	impf	1cp	תפשׂ	1074	3mp	seize,grasp
	נבא	qal	impf	1cp	בוא	97		come in
7:13	יען	qal	wci	3ms	ענה	772		answer
	יאמר	qal	wci	3ms	אמר	55		say
	יקחו	qal	jusm	3mp	לקח	542		take
	נשארים	niph	ptc	mp	שאר	983		be left
	נשארו	niph	pft	3cp	שאר	983		be left
	נשארו	niph	pft	3cp	שאר	983		be left
	תמו	qal	pft	3cp	תמם	1070		be finished
	נשלחה	qal	coh	1cp	שלח	1018		send
	נראה	qal	cohm	1cp	ראה	906		see
7:14	יקחו	qal	wci	3mp	לקח	542		take
	ישלח	qal	wci	3ms	שלח	1018		send
	אמר	qal	infc		אמר	55		say
	לכו	qal	impv	mp	הלך	229		walk,go
	ראו	qal	impv	mp	ראה	906		see
7:15	ילכו	qal	wci	3mp	הלך	229		walk,go
	השליכו	hiph	pft	3cp	שלך	1020		throw,cast
	kהחפזם	niph	infc		חפז	342	3mp	hurry in alarm
	qחפזם	qal	infc		חפז	342	3mp	be alarmed
	ישבו	qal	wci	3mp	שוב	996		turn,return
	יגדו	hiph	wci	3mp	נגד	616		declare,tell
7:16	יצא	qal	wci	3ms	יצא	422		go out
	יבזו	qal	wci	3mp	בזז	102		plunder
	יהי	qal	wci	3ms	היה	224		be,become
7:17	הפקיד	hiph	pft	3ms	פקד	823		set,entrust
	נשען	niph	ptc	ms	שען	1043		lean,support
	ירמסהו	qal	wci	3mp	רמס	942	3ms	trample
	ימת	qal	wci	3ms	מות	559		die
	דבר	piel	pft	3ms	דבר	180		speak
	דבר	piel	pft	3ms	דבר	180		speak
	רדת	qal	infc		ירד	432		come down
7:18	יהי	qal	wci	3ms	היה	224		be,become
	דבר	piel	infc		דבר	180		speak
	אמר	qal	infc		אמר	55		say
	יהיה	qal	impf	3ms	היה	224		be,become
7:19	יען	qal	wci	3ms	ענה	772		answer
	יאמר	qal	wci	3ms	אמר	55		say

ChVs	Form	Stem	Tnse	PGN	Root	BDB	Sfx	Meaning
7:19	עשׂה	qal	ptc	ms	עשׂה	793		do,make
	יהיה	qal	impf	3ms	היה	224		be,become
	יאמר	qal	wci	3ms	אמר	55		say
	ראה	qal	ptc	ms	ראה	906		see
	תאכל	qal	impf	2ms	אכל	37		eat,devour
7:20	יהי	qal	wci	3ms	היה	224		be,become
	ירמסו	qal	wci	3mp	רמס	942		trample
	ימת	qal	wci	3ms	מות	559		die
8:1	דבר	piel	pft	3ms	דבר	180		speak
	החיה	hiph	pft	3ms	חיה	310		preserve
	אמר	qal	infc		אמר	55		say
	קומי	qal	impv	fs	קום	877		arise,stand
	לכי	qal	impv	fs	הלך	229		walk,go
	גורי	qal	impv	fs	גור	157		sojourn
	תגורי	qal	impf	2fs	גור	157		sojourn
	קרא	qal	pft	3ms	קרא	894		call,proclaim
	בא	qal	pft	3ms	בוא	97		come in
8:2	תקם	qal	wci	3fs	קום	877		arise,stand
	תעשׂ	qal	wci	3fs	עשׂה	793		do,make
	תלך	qal	wci	3fs	הלך	229		walk,go
	תגר	qal	wci	3fs	גור	157		sojourn
8:3	יהי	qal	wci	3ms	היה	224		be,become
	תשׁב	qal	wci	3fs	שׁוב	996		turn,return
	תצא	qal	wci	3fs	יצא	422		go out
	צעק	qal	infc		צעק	858		cry out
8:4	מדבר	piel	ptc	ms	דבר	180		speak
	אמר	qal	infc		אמר	55		say
	ספרה	piel	impv	ms	ספר	707		recount
	עשׂה	qal	pft	3ms	עשׂה	793		do,make
8:5	יהי	qal	wci	3ms	היה	224		be,become
	מספר	piel	ptc	ms	ספר	707		recount
	החיה	hiph	pft	3ms	חיה	310		preserve
	מת	qal	ptc	ms	מות	559		die
	החיה	hiph	pft	3ms	חיה	310		preserve
	צעקת	qal	ptc	fs	צעק	858		cry out
	יאמר	qal	wci	3ms	אמר	55		say
	החיה	hiph	pft	3ms	חיה	310		preserve
8:6	ישׁאל	qal	wci	3ms	שׁאל	981		ask,borrow
	תספר	piel	wci	3fs	ספר	707		recount
	יתן	qal	wci	3ms	נתן	678		give,set
	אמר	qal	infc		אמר	55		say
	השׁיב	hiph	impv	ms	שׁוב	996		bring back
	עזבה	qal	pft	3fs	עזב	736		leave,loose
8:7	יבא	qal	wci	3ms	בוא	97		come in
	חלה	qal	ptc	ms	חלה	317		be weak,sick
	יגד	hoph	wci	3ms	נגד	616		be told
	אמר	qal	infc		אמר	55		say
	בא	qal	pft	3ms	בוא	97		come in
8:8	יאמר	qal	wci	3ms	אמר	55		say
	קח	qal	impv	ms	לקח	542		take
	לך	qal	impv	ms	הלך	229		walk,go
	קראת	qal	infc		קרא	896		meet,encounter
	דרשׁת	qal	wcp	2ms	דרשׁ	205		resort to,seek
	אמר	qal	infc		אמר	55		say
8:8	אחיה	qal	impf	1cs	חיה	310		live
8:9	ילך	qal	wci	3ms	הלך	229		walk,go
	קראתו	qal	infc		קרא	896	3ms	meet,encounter
	יקח	qal	wci	3ms	לקח	542		take
	יבא	qal	wci	3ms	בוא	97		come in
	יעמד	qal	wci	3ms	עמד	763		stand,stop
	יאמר	qal	wci	3ms	אמר	55		say
	שׁלחני	qal	pft	3ms	שׁלח	1018	1cs	send
	אמר	qal	infc		אמר	55		say
	אחיה	qal	impf	1cs	חיה	310		live
8:10	יאמר	qal	wci	3ms	אמר	55		say
	לך	qal	impv	ms	הלך	229		walk,go
	אמר	qal	impv	ms	אמר	55		say
	חיה	qal	infa		חיה	310		live
	תחיה	qal	impf	2ms	חיה	310		live
	הראני	hiph	pft	3ms	ראה	906	1cs	show,exhibit
	מות	qal	infa		מות	559		die
	ימות	qal	impf	3ms	מות	559		die
8:11	יעמד	hiph	wci	3ms	עמד	763		set up,raise
	ישׂם	qal	wci	3ms	שׂים	962		put,set
	בשׁ	qal	infc		בושׁ	101		be ashamed
	יבך	qal	wci	3ms	בכה	113		weep
8:12	יאמר	qal	wci	3ms	אמר	55		say
	בכה	qal	ptc	ms	בכה	113		weep
	יאמר	qal	wci	3ms	אמר	55		say
	ידעתי	qal	pft	1cs	ידע	393		know
	תעשׂה	qal	impf	2ms	עשׂה	793		do,make
	תשׁלח	piel	impf	2ms	שׁלח	1018		send away,shoot
	תהרג	qal	impf	2ms	הרג	246		kill
	תרטשׁ	piel	impf	2ms	רטשׁ	936		dash in pieces
	תבקע	piel	impf	2ms	בקע	131		cut to pieces
8:13	יאמר	qal	wci	3ms	אמר	55		say
	יעשׂה	qal	impf	3ms	עשׂה	793		do,make
	יאמר	qal	wci	3ms	אמר	55		say
	הראני	hiph	pft	3ms	ראה	906	1cs	show,exhibit
8:14	ילך	qal	wci	3ms	הלך	229		walk,go
	יבא	qal	wci	3ms	בוא	97		come in
	יאמר	qal	wci	3ms	אמר	55		say
	אמר	qal	pft	3ms	אמר	55		say
	יאמר	qal	wci	3ms	אמר	55		say
	אמר	qal	pft	3ms	אמר	55		say
	חיה	qal	infa		חיה	310		live
	תחיה	qal	impf	2ms	חיה	310		live
8:15	יהי	qal	wci	3ms	היה	224		be,become
	יקח	qal	wci	3ms	לקח	542		take
	יטבל	qal	wci	3ms	טבל	371		dip
	יפרשׂ	qal	wci	3ms	פרשׂ	831		spread out
	ימת	qal	wci	3ms	מות	559		die
	ימלך	qal	wci	3ms	מלך	573		be king,reign
8:16	מלך	qal	pft	3ms	מלך	573		be king,reign
8:17	היה	qal	pft	3ms	היה	224		be,become
	מלכו	qal	infc		מלך	573	3ms	be king,reign
	מלך	qal	pft	3ms	מלך	573		be king,reign
8:18	ילך	qal	wci	3ms	הלך	229		walk,go

ChVs	Form	Stem	Tnse	PGN	Root	BDB	Sfx	Meaning
8: 18	עשׂו	qal	pft	3cp	עשׂה	793		do,make
	היתה	qal	pft	3fs	היה	224		be,become
	יעשׂ	qal	wci	3ms	עשׂה	793		do,make
8: 19	אבה	qal	pft	3ms	אבה	2		be willing
	השחית	hiph	infc		שחת	1007		spoil,ruin
	אמר	qal	pft	3ms	אמר	55		say
	תת	qal	infc		נתן	678		give,set
8: 20	פשע	qal	pft	3ms	פשע	833		rebel,sin
	ימלכו	hiph	wci	3mp	מלך	573		cause to reign
8: 21	יעבר	qal	wci	3ms	עבר	716		pass over
	יהי	qal	wci	3ms	היה	224		be,become
	קם	qal	pft	3ms	קום	877		arise,stand
	יכה	hiph	wci	3ms	נכה	645		smite
	סביב	qal	ptc	ms	סבב	685		surround
	ינס	qal	wci	3ms	נוס	630		flee,escape
8: 22	יפשע	qal	wci	3ms	פשע	833		rebel,sin
	תפשע	qal	impf	3fs	פשע	833		rebel,sin
8: 23	עשׂה	qal	pft	3ms	עשׂה	793		do,make
	כתובים	qal	pptc	mp	כתב	507		write
8: 24	ישׁכב	qal	wci	3ms	שׁכב	1011		lie,lie down
	יקבר	niph	wci	3ms	קבר	868		be buried
	ימלך	qal	wci	3ms	מלך	573		be king,reign
8: 25	מלך	qal	pft	3ms	מלך	573		be king,reign
8: 26	מלכו	qal	infc		מלך	573	3ms	be king,reign
	מלך	qal	pft	3ms	מלך	573		be king,reign
8: 27	ילך	qal	wci	3ms	הלך	229		walk,go
	יעשׂ	qal	wci	3ms	עשׂה	793		do,make
8: 28	ילך	qal	wci	3ms	הלך	229		walk,go
	יכו	hiph	wci	3mp	נכה	645		smite
8: 29	ישׁב	qal	wci	3ms	שׁוב	996		turn,return
	התרפא	hith	infc		רפא	950		get healed
	יכהו	hiph	impf	3mp	נכה	645	3ms	smite
	הלחמו	niph	infc		לחם	535	3ms	wage war
	ירד	qal	pft	3ms	ירד	432		come down
	ראות	qal	infc		ראה	906		see
	חלה	qal	ptc	ms	חלה	317		be weak,sick
9: 1	קרא	qal	pft	3ms	קרא	894		call,proclaim
	יאמר	qal	wci	3ms	אמר	55		say
	חגר	qal	impv	ms	חגר	291		gird
	קח	qal	impv	ms	לקח	542		take
	לך	qal	impv	ms	הלך	229		walk,go
9: 2	באת	qal	wcp	2ms	בוא	97		come in
	ראה	qal	impv	ms	ראה	906		see
	באת	qal	wcp	2ms	בוא	97		come in
	הקמתו	hiph	wcp	2ms	קום	877	3ms	raise,build,set
	הביאת	hiph	wcp	2ms	בוא	97		bring in
9: 3	לקחת	qal	wcp	2ms	לקח	542		take
	יצקת	qal	wcp	2ms	יצק	427		pour out,cast
	אמרת	qal	wcp	2ms	אמר	55		say
	אמר	qal	pft	3ms	אמר	55		say
	משחתיך	qal	pft	1cs	משח	602	2ms	smear,anoint
	פתחת	qal	wcp	2ms	פתח	834		open
	נסתה	qal	wcp	2ms	נוס	630		flee,escape
	תחכה	piel	impf	2ms	חכה	314		wait
9: 4	ילך	qal	wci	3ms	הלך	229		walk,go
9: 5	יבא	qal	wci	3ms	בוא	97		come in
	ישׁבים	qal	ptc	mp	ישׁב	442		sit,dwell
	יאמר	qal	wci	3ms	אמר	55		say
	יאמר	qal	wci	3ms	אמר	55		say
	יאמר	qal	wci	3ms	אמר	55		say
9: 6	יקם	qal	wci	3ms	קום	877		arise,stand
	יבא	qal	wci	3ms	בוא	97		come in
	יצק	qal	wci	3ms	יצק	427		pour out,cast
	יאמר	qal	wci	3ms	אמר	55		say
	אמר	qal	pft	3ms	אמר	55		say
	משחתיך	qal	pft	1cs	משח	602	2ms	smear,anoint
9: 7	הכיתה	hiph	wcp	2ms	נכה	645		smite
	נקמתי	piel	wcp	1cs	נקם	667		avenge
9: 8	אבד	qal	wcp	3ms	אבד	1		perish
	הכרתי	hiph	wcp	1cs	כרת	503		cut off,destroy
	משתין	hiph	ptc	ms	שתן	1010		urinate
	עצור	qal	pptc	ms	עצר	783		restrain
	עזוב	qal	pptc	ms	עזב	736		leave,loose
9: 9	נתתי	qal	wcp	1cs	נתן	678		give,set
9: 10	יאכלו	qal	impf	3mp	אכל	37		eat,devour
	קבר	qal	ptc	ms	קבר	868		bury
	יפתח	qal	wci	3ms	פתח	834		open
	ינס	qal	wci	3ms	נוס	630		flee,escape
9: 11	יצא	qal	pft	3ms	יצא	422		go out
	יאמר	qal	wci	3ms	אמר	55		say
	בא	qal	pft	3ms	בוא	97		come in
	משגע	pual	ptc	ms	שׁגע	993		be mad
	יאמר	qal	wci	3ms	אמר	55		say
	ידעתם	qal	pft	2mp	ידע	393		know
9: 12	יאמרו	qal	wci	3mp	אמר	55		say
	הגד	hiph	impv	ms	נגד	616		declare,tell
	יאמר	qal	wci	3ms	אמר	55		say
	אמר	qal	pft	3ms	אמר	55		say
	אמר	qal	infc		אמר	55		say
	אמר	qal	pft	3ms	אמר	55		say
	משחתיך	qal	pft	1cs	משח	602	2ms	smear,anoint
9: 13	ימהרו	piel	wci	3mp	מהר	554		hasten
	יקחו	qal	wci	3mp	לקח	542		take
	ישׂימו	qal	wci	3mp	שׂים	962		put,set
	יתקעו	qal	wci	3mp	תקע	1075		thrust,clap
	יאמרו	qal	wci	3mp	אמר	55		say
	מלך	qal	pft	3ms	מלך	573		be king,reign
9: 14	יתקשׁר	hith	wci	3ms	קשׁר	905		conspire
	היה	qal	pft	3ms	היה	224		be,become
	שׁמר	qal	ptc	ms	שׁמר	1036		keep,watch
9: 15	ישׁב	qal	wci	3ms	שׁוב	996		turn,return
	התרפא	hith	infc		רפא	950		get healed
	יכהו	hiph	impf	3mp	נכה	645	3ms	smite
	הלחמו	niph	infc		לחם	535	3ms	wage war
	יאמר	qal	wci	3ms	אמר	55		say
	יצא	qal	jusm	3ms	יצא	422		go out
	לכת	qal	infc		הלך	229		walk,go
	kגיד	hiph	infc		נגד	616		declare,tell

ChVs	Form	Stem	Tnse	PGN	Root	BDB	Sfx	Meaning
9:15	qהגיד	hiph	infc		נגד	616		declare,tell
9:16	ירכב	qal	wci	3ms	רכב	938		mount,ride
	ילך	qal	wci	3ms	הלך	229		walk,go
	שכב	qal	ptc	ms	שכב	1011		lie,lie down
	ירד	qal	pft	3ms	ירד	432		come down
	ראות	qal	infc		ראה	906		see
9:17	צפה	qal	ptc	ms	צפה	859		keep watch
	עמד	qal	ptc	ms	עמד	763		stand,stop
	ירא	qal	wci	3ms	ראה	906		see
	באו	qal	infc		בוא	97	3ms	come in
	יאמר	qal	wci	3ms	אמר	55		say
	ראה	qal	ptc	ms	ראה	906		see
	יאמר	qal	wci	3ms	אמר	55		say
	קח	qal	impv	ms	לקח	542		take
	שלח	qal	impv	ms	שלח	1018		send
	קראתם	qal	infc		קרא	896	3mp	meet,encounter
	יאמר	qal	impf	3ms	אמר	55		say
9:18	ילך	qal	wci	3ms	הלך	229		walk,go
	רכב	qal	ptc	ms	רכב	938		mount,ride
	קראתו	qal	infc		קרא	896	3ms	meet,encounter
	יאמר	qal	wci	3ms	אמר	55		say
	אמר	qal	pft	3ms	אמר	55		say
	יאמר	qal	wci	3ms	אמר	55		say
	סב	qal	impv	ms	סבב	685		surround
	יגד	hiph	wci	3ms	נגד	616		declare,tell
	צפה	qal	ptc	ms	צפה	859		keep watch
	אמר	qal	infc		אמר	55		say
	בא	qal	pft	3ms	בוא	97		come in
	שב	qal	pft	3ms	שוב	996		turn,return
9:19	ישלח	qal	wci	3ms	שלח	1018		send
	רכב	qal	ptc	ms	רכב	938		mount,ride
	יבא	qal	wci	3ms	בוא	97		come in
	יאמר	qal	wci	3ms	אמר	55		say
	אמר	qal	pft	3ms	אמר	55		say
	יאמר	qal	wci	3ms	אמר	55		say
	סב	qal	impv	ms	סבב	685		surround
9:20	יגד	hiph	wci	3ms	נגד	616		declare,tell
	צפה	qal	ptc	ms	צפה	859		keep watch
	אמר	qal	infc		אמר	55		say
	בא	qal	pft	3ms	בוא	97		come in
	שב	qal	pft	3ms	שוב	996		turn,return
	ינהג	qal	impf	3ms	נהג	624		drive
9:21	יאמר	qal	wci	3ms	אמר	55		say
	אסר	qal	impv	ms	אסר	63		tie,bind
	יאסר	qal	wci	3ms	אסר	63		tie,bind
	יצא	qal	wci	3ms	יצא	422		go out
	יצאו	qal	wci	3mp	יצא	422		go out
	קראת	qal	infc		קרא	896		meet,encounter
	ימצאהו	qal	wci	3mp	מצא	592	3ms	find
9:22	יהי	qal	wci	3ms	היה	224		be,become
	ראות	qal	infc		ראה	906		see
	יאמר	qal	wci	3ms	אמר	55		say
	יאמר	qal	wci	3ms	אמר	55		say
9:23	יהפך	qal	wci	3ms	הפך	245		turn,overturn
9:23	ינס	qal	wci	3ms	נוס	630		flee,escape
	יאמר	qal	wci	3ms	אמר	55		say
9:24	מלא	piel	pft	3ms	מלא	569		fill
	יך	hiph	wci	3ms	נכה	645		smite
	יצא	qal	wci	3ms	יצא	422		go out
	יכרע	qal	wci	3ms	כרע	502		bow down
9:25	יאמר	qal	wci	3ms	אמר	55		say
	שא	qal	impv	ms	נשא	669		lift,carry
	השלכהו	hiph	impv	ms	שלך	1020	3ms	throw,cast
	זכר	qal	impv	ms	זכר	269		remember
	רכבים	qal	ptc	mp	רכב	938		mount,ride
	נשא	qal	pft	3ms	נשא	669		lift,carry
9:26	ראיתי	qal	pft	1cs	ראה	906		see
	שלמתי	piel	wcp	1cs	שלם	1022		finish,reward
	שא	qal	impv	ms	נשא	669		lift,carry
	השלכהו	hiph	impv	ms	שלך	1020	3ms	throw,cast
9:27	ראה	qal	pft	3ms	ראה	906		see
	ינס	qal	wci	3ms	נוס	630		flee,escape
	ירדף	qal	wci	3ms	רדף	922		pursue
	יאמר	qal	wci	3ms	אמר	55		say
	הכהו	hiph	impv	mp	נכה	645	3ms	smite
	ינס	qal	wci	3ms	נוס	630		flee,escape
	ימת	qal	wci	3ms	מות	559		die
9:28	ירכבו	hiph	wci	3mp	רכב	938		cause to ride
	יקברו	qal	wci	3mp	קבר	868		bury
9:29	מלך	qal	pft	3ms	מלך	573		be king,reign
9:30	יבוא	qal	wci	3ms	בוא	97		come in
	שמעה	qal	pft	3fs	שמע	1033		hear
	תשם	qal	wci	3fs	שים	962		put,set
	תיטב	hiph	wci	3fs	יטב	405		do good
	תשקף	hiph	wci	3fs	שקף	1054		look down
9:31	בא	qal	pft	3ms	בוא	97		come in
	תאמר	qal	wci	3fs	אמר	55		say
	הרג	qal	ptc	ms	הרג	246		kill
9:32	ישא	qal	wci	3ms	נשא	669		lift,carry
	יאמר	qal	wci	3ms	אמר	55		say
	ישקיפו	hiph	wci	3mp	שקף	1054		look down
9:33	יאמר	qal	wci	3ms	אמר	55		say
	kשמטהו	qal	impv	mp	שמט	1030	3ms	let drop
	qשמטוה	qal	impv	mp	שמט	1030	3fs	let drop
	ישמטוה	qal	wci	3mp	שמט	1030	3fs	let drop
	יז	qal	wci	3ms	נזה	633		spatter
	ירמסנה	qal	wci	3ms	רמס	942	3fs	trample
9:34	יבא	qal	wci	3ms	בוא	97		come in
	יאכל	qal	wci	3ms	אכל	37		eat,devour
	ישת	qal	wci	3ms	שתה	1059		drink
	יאמר	qal	wci	3ms	אמר	55		say
	פקדו	qal	impv	mp	פקד	823		attend to,visit
	ארורה	qal	pptc	fs	ארר	76		curse
	קברוה	qal	impv	mp	קבר	868	3fs	bury
9:35	ילכו	qal	wci	3mp	הלך	229		walk,go
	קברה	qal	infc		קבר	868	3fs	bury
	מצאו	qal	pft	3cp	מצא	592		find
9:36	ישבו	qal	wci	3mp	שוב	996		turn,return

ChVs	Form	Stem	Tnse	PGN	Root	BDB	Sfx	Meaning
9:36	יגידו	hiph	wci	3mp	נגד	616		declare,tell
	יאמר	qal	wci	3ms	אמר	55		say
	דבר	piel	pft	3ms	דבר	180		speak
	אמר	qal	infc		אמר	55		say
	יאכלו	qal	impf	3mp	אכל	37		eat,devour
9:37	היתk	qal	wcp	3fs	היה	224		be,become
	היתהq	qal	wcp	3fs	היה	224		be,become
	יאמרו	qal	impf	3mp	אמר	55		say
10:1	יכתב	qal	wci	3ms	כתב	507		write
	ישלח	qal	wci	3ms	שלח	1018		send
	אמנים	qal	ptc	mp	אמן	52		nourish
	אמר	qal	infc		אמר	55		say
10:2	בא	qal	infc		בוא	97		come in
10:3	ראיתם	qal	wcp	2mp	ראה	906		see
	שׂמתם	qal	wcp	2mp	שׂים	962		put,set
	הלחמו	niph	impv	mp	לחם	535		wage war
10:4	יראו	qal	wci	3mp	ירא	431		fear
	יאמרו	qal	wci	3mp	אמר	55		say
	עמדו	qal	pft	3cp	עמד	763		stand,stop
	נעמד	qal	impf	1cp	עמד	763		stand,stop
10:5	ישלח	qal	wci	3ms	שלח	1018		send
	אמנים	qal	ptc	mp	אמן	52		nourish
	אמר	qal	infc		אמר	55		say
	תאמר	qal	impf	2ms	אמר	55		say
	נעשׂה	qal	impf	1cp	עשׂה	793		do,make
	נמליך	hiph	impf	1cp	מלך	573		cause to reign
	עשׂה	qal	impv	ms	עשׂה	793		do,make
10:6	יכתב	qal	wci	3ms	כתב	507		write
	אמר	qal	infc		אמר	55		say
	שׁמעים	qal	ptc	mp	שׁמע	1033		hear
	קחו	qal	impv	mp	לקח	542		take
	באו	qal	impv	mp	בוא	97		come in
	מגדלים	piel	ptc	mp	גדל	152		cause to grow
10:7	יהי	qal	wci	3ms	היה	224		be,become
	בא	qal	infc		בוא	97		come in
	יקחו	qal	wci	3mp	לקח	542		take
	ישׁחטו	qal	wci	3mp	שׁחט	1006		slaughter
	ישׂימו	qal	wci	3mp	שׂים	962		put,set
	ישׁלחו	qal	wci	3mp	שׁלח	1018		send
10:8	יבא	qal	wci	3ms	בוא	97		come in
	יגד	hiph	wci	3ms	נגד	616		declare,tell
	אמר	qal	infc		אמר	55		say
	הביאו	hiph	pft	3cp	בוא	97		bring in
	יאמר	qal	wci	3ms	אמר	55		say
	שׂימו	qal	impv	mp	שׂים	962		put,set
10:9	יהי	qal	wci	3ms	היה	224		be,become
	יצא	qal	wci	3ms	יצא	422		go out
	יעמד	qal	wci	3ms	עמד	763		stand,stop
	יאמר	qal	wci	3ms	אמר	55		say
	קשׁרתי	qal	pft	1cs	קשׁר	905		bind
	אהרגהו	qal	wci	1cs	הרג	246	3ms	kill
	הכה	hiph	pft	3ms	נכה	645		smite
10:10	דעו	qal	impv	mp	ידע	393		know
	יפל	qal	impf	3ms	נפל	656		fall
10:10	דבר	piel	pft	3ms	דבר	180		speak
	עשׂה	qal	pft	3ms	עשׂה	793		do,make
	דבר	piel	pft	3ms	דבר	180		speak
10:11	יך	hiph	wci	3ms	נכה	645		smite
	נשׁארים	niph	ptc	mp	שׁאר	983		be left
	מידעיו	pual	ptc	mp	ידע	393	3ms	be known
	השׁאיר	hiph	pft	3ms	שׁאר	983		leave,spare
10:12	יקם	qal	wci	3ms	קום	877		arise,stand
	יבא	qal	wci	3ms	בוא	97		come in
	ילך	qal	wci	3ms	הלך	229		walk,go
	רעים	qal	ptc	mp	רעה	944		pasture,tend
10:13	מצא	qal	pft	3ms	מצא	592		find
	יאמר	qal	wci	3ms	אמר	55		say
	יאמרו	qal	wci	3mp	אמר	55		say
	נרד	qal	wci	1cp	ירד	432		come down
10:14	יאמר	qal	wci	3ms	אמר	55		say
	תפשׂום	qal	impv	mp	תפשׂ	1074	3mp	seize,grasp
	יתפשׂום	qal	wci	3mp	תפשׂ	1074	3mp	seize,grasp
	ישׁחטום	qal	wci	3mp	שׁחט	1006	3mp	slaughter
	השׁאיר	hiph	pft	3ms	שׁאר	983		leave,spare
10:15	ילך	qal	wci	3ms	הלך	229		walk,go
	ימצא	qal	wci	3ms	מצא	592		find
	קראתו	qal	infc		קרא	896	3ms	meet,encounter
	יברכהו	piel	wci	3ms	ברך	138	3ms	bless
	יאמר	qal	wci	3ms	אמר	55		say
	יאמר	qal	wci	3ms	אמר	55		say
	תנה	qal	impv	ms	נתן	678		give,set
	יתן	qal	wci	3ms	נתן	678		give,set
	יעלהו	hiph	wci	3ms	עלה	748	3ms	bring up,offer
10:16	יאמר	qal	wci	3ms	אמר	55		say
	לכה	qal	impv	ms	הלך	229		walk,go
	ראה	qal	impv	ms	ראה	906		see
	ירכבו	hiph	wci	3mp	רכב	938		cause to ride
10:17	יבא	qal	wci	3ms	בוא	97		come in
	יך	hiph	wci	3ms	נכה	645		smite
	נשׁארים	niph	ptc	mp	שׁאר	983		be left
	השׁמידו	hiph	pft	3ms	שׁמד	1029	3ms	exterminate
	דבר	piel	pft	3ms	דבר	180		speak
10:18	יקבץ	qal	wci	3ms	קבץ	867		gather,collect
	יאמר	qal	wci	3ms	אמר	55		say
	עבד	qal	pft	3ms	עבד	712		work,serve
	יעבדנו	qal	impf	3ms	עבד	712	3ms	work,serve
	הרבה	hiph	infa		רבה	915		make many
10:19	עבדיו	qal	ptc	mp	עבד	712	3ms	work,serve
	קראו	qal	impv	mp	קרא	894		call,proclaim
	יפקד	niph	jusm	3ms	פקד	823		be visited
	יפקד	niph	impf	3ms	פקד	823		be visited
	יחיה	qal	impf	3ms	חיה	310		live
	עשׂה	qal	pft	3ms	עשׂה	793		do,make
	האביד	hiph	infc		אבד	1		destroy
	עבדי	qal	ptc	mp	עבד	712		work,serve
10:20	יאמר	qal	wci	3ms	אמר	55		say
	קדשׁו	piel	impv	mp	קדשׁ	872		consecrate
	יקראו	qal	wci	3mp	קרא	894		call,proclaim

ChVs	Form	Stem	Tnse	PGN	Root	BDB	Sfx	Meaning
10:21	ישלח	qal	wci	3ms	שלח	1018		send
	יבאו	qal	wci	3mp	בוא	97		come in
	עבדי	qal	ptc	mp	עבד	712		work,serve
	נשאר	niph	pft	3ms	שאר	983		be left
	בא	qal	pft	3ms	בוא	97		come in
	יבאו	qal	wci	3mp	בוא	97		come in
	ימלא	niph	wci	3ms	מלא	569		be filled
10:22	יאמר	qal	wci	3ms	אמר	55		say
	הוצא	hiph	impv	ms	יצא	422		bring out
	עבדי	qal	ptc	mp	עבד	712		work,serve
	יצא	hiph	wci	3ms	יצא	422		bring out
10:23	יבא	qal	wci	3ms	בוא	97		come in
	יאמר	qal	wci	3ms	אמר	55		say
	עבדי	qal	ptc	mp	עבד	712		work,serve
	חפשו	piel	impv	mp	חפש	344		search for
	ראו	qal	impv	mp	ראה	906		see
	עבדי	qal	ptc	mp	עבד	712		work,serve
10:24	יבאו	qal	wci	3mp	בוא	97		come in
	עשות	qal	infc		עשה	793		do,make
	שם	qal	pft	3ms	שים	962		put,set
	יאמר	qal	wci	3ms	אמר	55		say
	ימלט	niph	impf	3ms	מלט	572		escape
	מביא	hiph	ptc	ms	בוא	97		bring in
10:25	יהי	qal	wci	3ms	היה	224		be,become
	כלתו	piel	infc		כלה	477	3ms	complete,finish
	עשות	qal	infc		עשה	793		do,make
	יאמר	qal	wci	3ms	אמר	55		say
	רצים	qal	ptc	mp	רוץ	930		run
	באו	qal	impv	mp	בוא	97		come in
	הכום	hiph	impv	mp	נכה	645	3mp	smite
	יצא	qal	jusm	3ms	יצא	422		go out
	יכום	hiph	wci	3mp	נכה	645	3mp	smite
	ישלכו	hiph	wci	3mp	שלך	1020		throw,cast
	רצים	qal	ptc	mp	רוץ	930		run
	ילכו	qal	wci	3mp	הלך	229		walk,go
10:26	יצאו	hiph	wci	3mp	יצא	422		bring out
	ישרפוה	qal	wci	3mp	שרף	976	3fs	burn
10:27	יתצו	qal	wci	3mp	נתץ	683		pull down
	יתצו	qal	wci	3mp	נתץ	683		pull down
	ישמהו	qal	wci	3mp	שים	962	3ms	put,set
10:28	ישמד	hiph	wci	3ms	שמד	1029		exterminate
10:29	החטיא	hiph	pft	3ms	חטא	306		cause to sin
	סר	qal	pft	3ms	סור	693		turn aside
10:30	יאמר	qal	wci	3ms	אמר	55		say
	הטיבת	hiph	pft	2ms	טוב	373		do well
	עשות	qal	infc		עשה	793		do,make
	עשית	qal	pft	2ms	עשה	793		do,make
	ישבו	qal	impf	3mp	ישב	442		sit,dwell
10:31	שמר	qal	pft	3ms	שמר	1036		keep,watch
	לכת	qal	infc		הלך	229		walk,go
	סר	qal	pft	3ms	סור	693		turn aside
	החטיא	hiph	pft	3ms	חטא	306		cause to sin
10:32	החל	hiph	pft	3ms	חלל	320		begin,profane
	קצות	piel	infc		קצה	891		cut off

ChVs	Form	Stem	Tnse	PGN	Root	BDB	Sfx	Meaning
10:32	יכם	hiph	wci	3ms	נכה	645	3ms	smite
10:34	עשה	qal	pft	3ms	עשה	793		do,make
	כתובים	qal	pptc	mp	כתב	507		write
10:35	ישכב	qal	wci	3ms	שכב	1011		lie,lie down
	יקברו	qal	wci	3mp	קבר	868		bury
	ימלך	qal	wci	3ms	מלך	573		be king,reign
10:36	מלך	qal	pft	3ms	מלך	573		be king,reign
11:1	ראתה	qal	pft	3fs	ראה	906		see
	מת	qal	pft	3ms	מות	559		die
	תקם	qal	wci	3fs	קום	877		arise,stand
	תאבד	piel	wci	3fs	אבד	1		destroy
11:2	תקח	qal	wci	3fs	לקח	542		take
	תגנב	qal	wci	3fs	גנב	170		steal
	מומתים q	hoph	ptc	mp	מות	559		be killed
	מינקתו	hiph	ptc	fs	ינק	413	3ms	nurse
	יסתרו	hiph	wci	3mp	סתר	711		hide
	הומת	hoph	pft	3ms	מות	559		be killed
11:3	יהי	qal	wci	3ms	היה	224		be,become
	מתחבא	hith	ptc	ms	חבא	285		hide oneself
	מלכת	qal	ptc	fs	מלך	573		be king,reign
11:4	שלח	qal	pft	3ms	שלח	1018		send
	יקח	qal	wci	3ms	לקח	542		take
	רצים	qal	ptc	mp	רוץ	930		run
	יבא	hiph	wci	3ms	בוא	97		bring in
	יכרת	qal	wci	3ms	כרת	503		cut,destroy
	ישבע	hiph	wci	3ms	שבע	989		cause to swear
	ירא	hiph	wci	3ms	ראה	906		show,exhibit
11:5	יצום	piel	wci	3ms	צוה	845	3mp	command
	אמר	qal	infc		אמר	55		say
	תעשון	qal	impf	2mp	עשה	793		do,make
	באי	qal	ptc	mp	בוא	97		come in
	שמרי	qal	ptc	mp	שמר	1036		keep,watch
11:6	רצים	qal	ptc	mp	רוץ	930		run
	שמרתם	qal	wcp	2mp	שמר	1036		keep,watch
11:7	יצאי	qal	ptc	mp	יצא	422		go out
	שמרו	qal	wcp	3cp	שמר	1036		keep,watch
11:8	הקפתם	hiph	wcp	2mp	נקף	668		surround
	בא	qal	ptc	ms	בוא	97		come in
	יומת	hoph	impf	3ms	מות	559		be killed
	היו	qal	impv	mp	היה	224		be,become
	צאתו	qal	infc		יצא	422	3ms	go out
	באו	qal	infc		בוא	97	3ms	come in
11:9	יעשו	qal	wci	3mp	עשה	793		do,make
	צוה	piel	pft	3ms	צוה	845		command
	יקחו	qal	wci	3mp	לקח	542		take
	באי	qal	ptc	mp	בוא	97		come in
	יצאי	qal	ptc	mp	יצא	422		go out
	יבאו	qal	wci	3mp	בוא	97		come in
11:10	יתן	qal	wci	3ms	נתן	678		give,set
11:11	יעמדו	qal	wci	3mp	עמד	763		stand,stop
	רצים	qal	ptc	mp	רוץ	930		run
11:12	יוצא	hiph	wci	3ms	יצא	422		bring out
	יתן	qal	wci	3ms	נתן	678		give,set
	ימלכו	hiph	wci	3mp	מלך	573		cause to reign

ChVs	Form	Stem	Tnse	PGN	Root	BDB	Sfx	Meaning
11:12	ימשׁחהו	qal	wci	3mp	משׁח	602	3ms	smear,anoint
	יכו	hiph	wci	3mp	נכה	645		smite
	יאמרו	qal	wci	3mp	אמר	55		say
	יחי	qal	jus	3ms	חיה	310		live
11:13	תשׁמע	qal	wci	3fs	שׁמע	1033		hear
	רצין	qal	ptc	mp	רוץ	930		run
	תבא	qal	wci	3fs	בוא	97		come in
11:14	תרא	qal	wci	3fs	ראה	906		see
	עמד	qal	ptc	ms	עמד	763		stand,stop
	תקע	qal	ptc	ms	תקע	1075		thrust,clap
	תקרע	qal	wci	3fs	קרע	902		tear,rend
	תקרא	qal	wci	3fs	קרא	894		call,proclaim
11:15	יצו	piel	wci	3ms	צוה	845		command
	פקדי	qal	pptc	mp	פקד	823		attend to,visit
	יאמר	qal	wci	3ms	אמר	55		say
	הוציאו	hiph	impv	mp	יצא	422		bring out
	בא	qal	ptc	ms	בוא	97		come in
	המת	hiph	infa		מות	559		kill
	אמר	qal	pft	3ms	אמר	55		say
	תומת	hoph	jusm	3fs	מות	559		be killed
11:16	ישׂמו	qal	wci	3mp	שׂים	962		put,set
	תבוא	qal	wci	3fs	בוא	97		come in
	תומת	hoph	wci	3fs	מות	559		be killed
11:17	יכרת	qal	wci	3ms	כרת	503		cut,destroy
	היות	qal	infc		היה	224		be,become
11:18	יבאו	qal	wci	3mp	בוא	97		come in
	יתצהו	qal	wci	3mp	נתץ	683	3ms	pull down
	שׁברו	piel	pft	3cp	שׁבר	990		shatter
	היטב	hiph	infa		יטב	405		do good
	הרגו	qal	pft	3cp	הרג	246		kill
	ישׂם	qal	wci	3ms	שׂים	962		put,set
11:19	יקח	qal	wci	3ms	לקח	542		take
	רצים	qal	ptc	mp	רוץ	930		run
	ירידו	hiph	wci	3mp	ירד	432		bring down
	יבואו	qal	wci	3mp	בוא	97		come in
	רצים	qal	ptc	mp	רוץ	930		run
	ישׁב	qal	wci	3ms	ישׁב	442		sit,dwell
11:20	ישׂמח	qal	wci	3ms	שׂמח	970		rejoice
	שׁקטה	qal	pft	3fs	שׁקט	1052		be quiet
	המיתו	hiph	pft	3cp	מות	559		kill
12:1	מלכו	qal	infc		מלך	573	3ms	be king,reign
12:2	מלך	qal	pft	3ms	מלך	573		be king,reign
	מלך	qal	pft	3ms	מלך	573		be king,reign
12:3	יעשׂ	qal	wci	3ms	עשׂה	793		do,make
	הורהו	hiph	pft	3ms	ירה	434	3ms	shoot,teach
12:4	סרו	qal	pft	3cp	סור	693		turn aside
	מזבחים	piel	ptc	mp	זבח	256		sacrifice
	מקטרים	piel	ptc	mp	קטר	882		make sacrifices
12:5	יאמר	qal	wci	3ms	אמר	55		say
	יובא	hoph	impf	3ms	בוא	97		be brought
	עובר	qal	ptc	ms	עבר	716		pass over
	יעלה	qal	impf	3ms	עלה	748		go up
	הביא	hiph	infc		בוא	97		bring in
12:6	יקחו	qal	jusm	3mp	לקח	542		take
12:6	יחזקו	piel	impf	3mp	חזק	304		make strong
	ימצא	niph	impf	3ms	מצא	592		be found
12:7	יהי	qal	wci	3ms	היה	224		be,become
	חזקו	piel	pft	3cp	חזק	304		make strong
12:8	יקרא	qal	wci	3ms	קרא	894		call,proclaim
	יאמר	qal	wci	3ms	אמר	55		say
	מחזקים	piel	ptc	mp	חזק	304		make strong
	תקחו	qal	jusm	2mp	לקח	542		take
	תתנהו	qal	impf	2mp	נתן	678	3ms	give,set
12:9	יאתו	niph	wci	3mp	אות	22		consent
	קחת	qal	infc		לקח	542		take
	חזק	piel	infc		חזק	304		make strong
12:10	יקח	qal	wci	3ms	לקח	542		take
	יקב	qal	wci	3ms	נקב	666		pierce
	יתן	qal	wci	3ms	נתן	678		give,set
	בוא	qal	infc		בוא	97		come in
	נתנו	qal	wcp	3cp	נתן	678		give,set
	שׁמרי	qal	ptc	mp	שׁמר	1036		keep,watch
	מובא	hoph	ptc	ms	בוא	97		be brought
12:11	יהי	qal	wci	3ms	היה	224		be,become
	ראותם	qal	infc		ראה	906	3mp	see
	יעל	qal	wci	3ms	עלה	748		go up
	יצרו	qal	wci	3mp	צור	848		confine,shut in
	ימנו	qal	wci	3mp	מנה	584		count,allot
	נמצא	niph	ptc	ms	מצא	592		be found
12:12	נתנו	qal	wcp	3cp	נתן	678		give,set
	מתכן	pual	ptc	ms	תכן	1067		be measured out
	עשׂי	qal	ptc	mp	עשׂה	793		do,make
	פקדיםk	qal	ptc	mp	פקד	823		attend to,visit
	מפקדיםq	hoph	ptc	mp	פקד	823		be appointed
	יוציאהו	hiph	wci	3mp	יצא	422	3ms	bring out
	בנים	qal	ptc	mp	בנה	124		build
	עשׂים	qal	ptc	mp	עשׂה	793		do,make
12:13	גדרים	qal	ptc	mp	גדר	154		wall up
	חצבי	qal	ptc	mp	חצב	345		hew out,dig
	קנות	qal	infc		קנה	888		get,buy
	חזק	piel	infc		חזק	304		make strong
	יצא	qal	impf	3ms	יצא	422		go out
	חזקה	qal	infc		חזק	304		be strong
12:14	יעשׂה	niph	impf	3ms	עשׂה	793		be done
	מובא	hoph	ptc	ms	בוא	97		be brought
12:15	עשׂי	qal	ptc	mp	עשׂה	793		do,make
	יתנהו	qal	impf	3mp	נתן	678	3ms	give,set
	חזקו	piel	wcp	3cp	חזק	304		make strong
12:16	יחשׁבו	piel	impf	3mp	חשׁב	362		devise
	יתנו	qal	impf	3mp	נתן	678		give,set
	תת	qal	infc		נתן	678		give,set
	עשׂי	qal	ptc	mp	עשׂה	793		do,make
	עשׂים	qal	ptc	mp	עשׂה	793		do,make
12:17	יובא	hoph	impf	3ms	בוא	97		be brought
	יהיו	qal	impf	3mp	היה	224		be,become
12:18	יעלה	qal	impf	3ms	עלה	748		go up
	ילחם	niph	wci	3ms	לחם	535		wage war
	ילכדה	qal	wci	3ms	לכד	539	3fs	capture

ChVs	Form	Stem	Tnse	PGN	Root	BDB	Sfx	Meaning
12:18	ישׂם	qal	wci	3ms	שׂים	962		put,set
	עלות	qal	infc		עלה	748		go up
12:19	יקח	qal	wci	3ms	לקח	542		take
	הקדישׁו	hiph	pft	3cp	קדשׁ	872		consecrate
	נמצא	niph	ptc	ms	מצא	592		be found
	ישׁלח	qal	wci	3ms	שׁלח	1018		send
	יעל	qal	wci	3ms	עלה	748		go up
12:20	עשׂה	qal	pft	3ms	עשׂה	793		do,make
	כתובים	qal	pptc	mp	כתב	507		write
12:21	יקמו	qal	wci	3mp	קום	877		arise,stand
	יקשׁרו	qal	wci	3mp	קשׁר	905		bind
	יכו	hiph	wci	3mp	נכה	645		smite
	יורד	qal	ptc	ms	ירד	432		come down
12:22	הכהו	hiph	pft	3cp	נכה	645	3ms	smite
	ימת	qal	wci	3ms	מות	559		die
	יקברו	qal	wci	3mp	קבר	868		bury
	ימלך	qal	wci	3ms	מלך	573		be king,reign
13:1	מלך	qal	pft	3ms	מלך	573		be king,reign
13:2	יעשׂ	qal	wci	3ms	עשׂה	793		do,make
	ילך	qal	wci	3ms	הלך	229		walk,go
	החטיא	hiph	pft	3ms	חטא	306		cause to sin
	סר	qal	pft	3ms	סור	693		turn aside
13:3	יחר	qal	wci	3ms	חרה	354		be kindled,burn
	יתנם	qal	wci	3ms	נתן	678	3mp	give,set
13:4	יחל	piel	wci	3ms	חלה	318		pacify,appease
	ישׁמע	qal	wci	3ms	שׁמע	1033		hear
	ראה	qal	pft	3ms	ראה	906		see
	לחץ	qal	pft	3ms	לחץ	537		press,oppress
13:5	יתן	qal	wci	3ms	נתן	678		give,set
	מושׁיע	hiph	ptc	ms	ישׁע	446		deliver,save
	יצאו	qal	wci	3mp	יצא	422		go out
	ישׁבו	qal	wci	3mp	ישׁב	442		sit,dwell
13:6	סרו	qal	pft	3cp	סור	693		turn aside
	kהחטי	hiph	pft	3ms	חטא	306		cause to sin
	qהחטיא	hiph	pft	3ms	חטא	306		cause to sin
	הלך	qal	pft	3ms	הלך	229		walk,go
	עמדה	qal	pft	3fs	עמד	763		stand,stop
13:7	השׁאיר	hiph	pft	3ms	שׁאר	983		leave,spare
	אבדם	piel	pft	3ms	אבד	1	3mp	destroy
	ישׂמם	qal	wci	3ms	שׂים	962	3mp	put,set
	דשׁ	qal	infc		דושׁ	190		tread
13:8	עשׂה	qal	pft	3ms	עשׂה	793		do,make
	כתובים	qal	pptc	mp	כתב	507		write
13:9	ישׁכב	qal	wci	3ms	שׁכב	1011		lie,lie down
	יקברהו	qal	wci	3mp	קבר	868	3ms	bury
	ימלך	qal	wci	3ms	מלך	573		be king,reign
13:10	מלך	qal	pft	3ms	מלך	573		be king,reign
13:11	יעשׂה	qal	wci	3ms	עשׂה	793		do,make
	סר	qal	pft	3ms	סור	693		turn aside
	החטיא	hiph	pft	3ms	חטא	306		cause to sin
	הלך	qal	pft	3ms	הלך	229		walk,go
13:12	עשׂה	qal	pft	3ms	עשׂה	793		do,make
	נלחם	niph	pft	3ms	לחם	535		wage war
	כתובים	qal	pptc	mp	כתב	507		write
13:13	ישׁכב	qal	wci	3ms	שׁכב	1011		lie,lie down
	ישׁב	qal	pft	3ms	ישׁב	442		sit,dwell
	יקבר	niph	wci	3ms	קבר	868		be buried
13:14	חלה	qal	pft	3ms	חלה	317		be weak,sick
	ימות	qal	impf	3ms	מות	559		die
	ירד	qal	wci	3ms	ירד	432		come down
	יבך	qal	wci	3ms	בכה	113		weep
	יאמר	qal	wci	3ms	אמר	55		say
13:15	יאמר	qal	wci	3ms	אמר	55		say
	קח	qal	impv	ms	לקח	542		take
	יקח	qal	wci	3ms	לקח	542		take
13:16	יאמר	qal	wci	3ms	אמר	55		say
	הרכב	hiph	impv	ms	רכב	938		cause to ride
	ירכב	hiph	wci	3ms	רכב	938		cause to ride
	ישׂם	qal	wci	3ms	שׂים	962		put,set
13:17	יאמר	qal	wci	3ms	אמר	55		say
	פתח	qal	impv	ms	פתח	834		open
	יפתח	qal	wci	3ms	פתח	834		open
	יאמר	qal	wci	3ms	אמר	55		say
	ירה	qal	impv	ms	ירה	434		throw,shoot
	יור	hiph	wci	3ms	ירה	434		shoot,teach
	יאמר	qal	wci	3ms	אמר	55		say
	הכית	hiph	wcp	2ms	נכה	645		smite
	כלה	piel	infa		כלה	477		complete,finish
13:18	יאמר	qal	wci	3ms	אמר	55		say
	קח	qal	impv	ms	לקח	542		take
	יקח	qal	wci	3ms	לקח	542		take
	יאמר	qal	wci	3ms	אמר	55		say
	הך	hiph	impv	ms	נכה	645		smite
	יך	hiph	wci	3ms	נכה	645		smite
	יעמד	qal	wci	3ms	עמד	763		stand,stop
13:19	יקצף	qal	wci	3ms	קצף	893		be angry
	יאמר	qal	wci	3ms	אמר	55		say
	הכות	hiph	infc		נכה	645		smite
	הכית	hiph	pft	2ms	נכה	645		smite
	כלה	piel	infa		כלה	477		complete,finish
	תכה	hiph	impf	2ms	נכה	645		smite
13:20	ימת	qal	wci	3ms	מות	559		die
	יקברהו	qal	wci	3mp	קבר	868	3ms	bury
	יבאו	qal	impf	3mp	בוא	97		come in
	בא	qal	ptc	ms	בוא	97		come in
13:21	יהי	qal	wci	3ms	היה	224		be,become
	קברים	qal	ptc	mp	קבר	868		bury
	ראו	qal	pft	3cp	ראה	906		see
	ישׁליכו	hiph	wci	3mp	שׁלך	1020		throw,cast
	ילך	qal	wci	3ms	הלך	229		walk,go
	יגע	qal	wci	3ms	נגע	619		touch,strike
	יחי	qal	wci	3ms	חיה	310		live
	יקם	qal	wci	3ms	קום	877		arise,stand
13:22	לחץ	qal	pft	3ms	לחץ	537		press,oppress
13:23	יחן	qal	wci	3ms	חנן	335		show favor
	ירחמם	piel	wci	3ms	רחם	933	3mp	have compassion
	יפן	qal	wci	3ms	פנה	815		turn
	אבה	qal	pft	3ms	אבה	2		be willing

ChVs	Form	Stem	Tnse	PGN	Root	BDB	Sfx	Meaning
13:23	השחיתם	hiph	infc		שחת	1007	3mp	spoil,ruin
	השליכם	hiph	pft	3ms	שלך	1020	3mp	throw,cast
13:24	ימת	qal	wci	3ms	מות	559		die
	ימלך	qal	wci	3ms	מלך	573		be king,reign
13:25	ישב	qal	wci	3ms	שוב	996		turn,return
	יקח	qal	wci	3ms	לקח	542		take
	לקח	qal	pft	3ms	לקח	542		take
	הכהו	hiph	pft	3ms	נכה	645	3ms	smite
	ישב	hiph	wci	3ms	שוב	996		bring back
14:1	מלך	qal	pft	3ms	מלך	573		be king,reign
14:2	היה	qal	pft	3ms	היה	224		be,become
	מלכו	qal	infc		מלך	573	3ms	be king,reign
	מלך	qal	pft	3ms	מלך	573		be king,reign
14:3	יעש	qal	wci	3ms	עשה	793		do,make
	עשה	qal	pft	3ms	עשה	793		do,make
	עשה	qal	pft	3ms	עשה	793		do,make
14:4	סרו	qal	pft	3cp	סור	693		turn aside
	מזבחים	piel	ptc	mp	זבח	256		sacrifice
	מקטרים	piel	ptc	mp	קטר	882		make sacrifices
14:5	יהי	qal	wci	3ms	היה	224		be,become
	חזקה	qal	pft	3fs	חזק	304		be strong
	יך	hiph	wci	3ms	נכה	645		smite
	מכים	hiph	ptc	mp	נכה	645		smite
14:6	מכים	hiph	ptc	mp	נכה	645		smite
	המית	hiph	pft	3ms	מות	559		kill
	כתוב	qal	pptc	ms	כתב	507		write
	צוה	piel	pft	3ms	צוה	845		command
	אמר	qal	infc		אמר	55		say
	יומתו	hoph	impf	3mp	מות	559		be killed
	יומתו	hoph	impf	3mp	מות	559		be killed
	ימות k	qal	impf	3ms	מות	559		die
	יומת q	hoph	impf	3ms	מות	559		be killed
14:7	הכה	hiph	pft	3ms	נכה	645		smite
	תפש	qal	pft	3ms	תפש	1074		seize,grasp
	יקרא	qal	wci	3ms	קרא	894		call,proclaim
14:8	שלח	qal	pft	3ms	שלח	1018		send
	אמר	qal	infc		אמר	55		say
	לכה	qal	impv	ms	הלך	229		walk,go
	נתראה	hith	cohm	1cp	ראה	906		look at each
14:9	ישלח	qal	wci	3ms	שלח	1018		send
	אמר	qal	infc		אמר	55		say
	שלח	qal	pft	3ms	שלח	1018		send
	אמר	qal	infc		אמר	55		say
	תנה	qal	impv	ms	נתן	678		give,set
	תעבר	qal	wci	3fs	עבר	716		pass over
	תרמס	qal	wci	3fs	רמס	942		trample
14:10	הכה	hiph	infa		נכה	645		smite
	הכית	hiph	pft	2ms	נכה	645		smite
	נשאך	qal	wcp	3ms	נשא	669	2ms	lift,carry
	הכבד	niph	impv	ms	כבד	457		be honored
	שב	qal	impv	ms	ישב	442		sit,dwell
	תתגרה	hith	impf	2ms	גרה	173		excite oneself
	נפלתה	qal	wcp	2ms	נפל	656		fall
14:11	שמע	qal	pft	3ms	שמע	1033		hear
14:11	יעל	qal	wci	3ms	עלה	748		go up
	יתראו	hith	wci	3mp	ראה	906		look at each
14:12	ינגף	niph	wci	3ms	נגף	619		be smitten
	ינסו	qal	wci	3mp	נוס	630		flee,escape
14:13	תפש	qal	pft	3ms	תפש	1074		seize,grasp
	יבאו k	qal	wci	3mp	בוא	97		come in
	יבא q	qal	wci	3ms	בוא	97		come in
	יפרץ	qal	wci	3ms	פרץ	829		break through
14:14	לקח	qal	pft	3ms	לקח	542		take
	נמצאים	niph	ptc	mp	מצא	592		be found
	ישב	qal	wci	3ms	שוב	996		turn,return
14:15	עשה	qal	pft	3ms	עשה	793		do,make
	נלחם	niph	pft	3ms	לחם	535		wage war
	כתובים	qal	pptc	mp	כתב	507		write
14:16	ישכב	qal	wci	3ms	שכב	1011		lie,lie down
	יקבר	niph	wci	3ms	קבר	868		be buried
	ימלך	qal	wci	3ms	מלך	573		be king,reign
14:17	יחי	qal	wci	3ms	חיה	310		live
14:18	כתובים	qal	pptc	mp	כתב	507		write
14:19	יקשרו	qal	wci	3mp	קשר	905		bind
	ינס	qal	wci	3ms	נוס	630		flee,escape
	ישלחו	qal	wci	3mp	שלח	1018		send
	ימתהו	hiph	wci	3mp	מות	559	3ms	kill
14:20	ישאו	qal	wci	3mp	נשא	669		lift,carry
	יקבר	niph	wci	3ms	קבר	868		be buried
14:21	יקחו	qal	wci	3mp	לקח	542		take
	ימלכו	hiph	wci	3mp	מלך	573		cause to reign
14:22	בנה	qal	pft	3ms	בנה	124		build
	ישבה	hiph	wci	3ms	שוב	996	3fs	bring back
	שכב	qal	infc		שכב	1011		lie,lie down
14:23	מלך	qal	pft	3ms	מלך	573		be king,reign
14:24	יעש	qal	wci	3ms	עשה	793		do,make
	סר	qal	pft	3ms	סור	693		turn aside
	החטיא	hiph	pft	3ms	חטא	306		cause to sin
14:25	השיב	hiph	pft	3ms	שוב	996		bring back
	בוא	qal	infc		בוא	97		come in
	דבר	piel	pft	3ms	דבר	180		speak
14:26	ראה	qal	pft	3ms	ראה	906		see
	מרה	qal	ptc	ms	מרה	598		be disobedient
	עצור	qal	pptc	ms	עצר	783		restrain
	עזוב	qal	pptc	ms	עזב	736		leave,loose
	עזר	qal	ptc	ms	עזר	740		help,aid
14:27	דבר	piel	pft	3ms	דבר	180		speak
	מחות	qal	infc		מחה	562		wipe, blot out
	יושיעם	hiph	wci	3ms	ישע	446	3mp	deliver,save
14:28	עשה	qal	pft	3ms	עשה	793		do,make
	נלחם	niph	pft	3ms	לחם	535		wage war
	השיב	hiph	pft	3ms	שוב	996		bring back
	כתובים	qal	pptc	mp	כתב	507		write
14:29	ישכב	qal	wci	3ms	שכב	1011		lie,lie down
	ימלך	qal	wci	3ms	מלך	573		be king,reign
15:1	מלך	qal	pft	3ms	מלך	573		be king,reign
15:2	היה	qal	pft	3ms	היה	224		be,become
	מלכו	qal	infc		מלך	573	3ms	be king,reign

ChVs	Form	Stem	Tnse	PGN	Root	BDB	Sfx	Meaning
15:2	מלך	qal	pft	3ms	מלך	573		be king,reign
15:3	יעשׂ	qal	wci	3ms	עשׂה	793		do,make
	עשׂה	qal	pft	3ms	עשׂה	793		do,make
15:4	סרו	qal	pft	3cp	סור	693		turn aside
	מזבחים	piel	ptc	mp	זבח	256		sacrifice
	מקטרים	piel	ptc	mp	קטר	882		make sacrifices
15:5	ינגע	piel	wci	3ms	נגע	619		strike
	יהי	qal	wci	3ms	היה	224		be,become
	מצרע	pual	ptc	ms	צרע	863		be leprous
	ישׁב	qal	wci	3ms	ישׁב	442		sit,dwell
	שׁפט	qal	ptc	ms	שׁפט	1047		judge
15:6	עשׂה	qal	pft	3ms	עשׂה	793		do,make
	כתובים	qal	pptc	mp	כתב	507		write
15:7	ישׁכב	qal	wci	3ms	שׁכב	1011		lie,lie down
	יקברו	qal	wci	3mp	קבר	868		bury
	ימלך	qal	wci	3ms	מלך	573		be king,reign
15:8	מלך	qal	pft	3ms	מלך	573		be king,reign
15:9	יעשׂ	qal	wci	3ms	עשׂה	793		do,make
	עשׂו	qal	pft	3cp	עשׂה	793		do,make
	סר	qal	pft	3ms	סור	693		turn aside
	החטיא	hiph	pft	3ms	חטא	306		cause to sin
15:10	יקשׁר	qal	wci	3ms	קשׁר	905		bind
	יכהו	hiph	wci	3ms	נכה	645	3ms	smite
	ימיתהו	hiph	wci	3ms	מות	559	3ms	kill
	ימלך	qal	wci	3ms	מלך	573		be king,reign
15:11	כתובים	qal	pptc	mp	כתב	507		write
15:12	דבר	piel	pft	3ms	דבר	180		speak
	אמר	qal	infc		אמר	55		say
	ישׁבו	qal	impf	3mp	ישׁב	442		sit,dwell
	יהי	qal	wci	3ms	היה	224		be,become
15:13	מלך	qal	pft	3ms	מלך	573		be king,reign
	ימלך	qal	wci	3ms	מלך	573		be king,reign
15:14	יעל	qal	wci	3ms	עלה	748		go up
	יבא	qal	wci	3ms	בוא	97		come in
	יך	hiph	wci	3ms	נכה	645		smite
	ימיתהו	hiph	wci	3ms	מות	559	3ms	kill
	ימלך	qal	wci	3ms	מלך	573		be king,reign
15:15	קשׁר	qal	pft	3ms	קשׁר	905		bind
	כתבים	qal	pptc	mp	כתב	507		write
15:16	יכה	hiph	impf	3ms	נכה	645		smite
	פתח	qal	pft	3ms	פתח	834		open
	יך	hiph	wci	3ms	נכה	645		smite
	בקע	piel	pft	3ms	בקע	131		cut to pieces
15:17	מלך	qal	pft	3ms	מלך	573		be king,reign
15:18	יעשׂ	qal	wci	3ms	עשׂה	793		do,make
	סר	qal	pft	3ms	סור	693		turn aside
	החטיא	hiph	pft	3ms	חטא	306		cause to sin
15:19	בא	qal	pft	3ms	בוא	97		come in
	יתן	qal	wci	3ms	נתן	678		give,set
	היות	qal	infc		היה	224		be,become
	החזיק	hiph	infc		חזק	304		make firm,seize
15:20	יצא	hiph	wci	3ms	יצא	422		bring out
	תת	qal	infc		נתן	678		give,set
	ישׁב	qal	wci	3ms	שׁוב	996		turn,return
15:20	עמד	qal	pft	3ms	עמד	763		stand,stop
15:21	עשׂה	qal	pft	3ms	עשׂה	793		do,make
	כתובים	qal	pptc	mp	כתב	507		write
15:22	ישׁכב	qal	wci	3ms	שׁכב	1011		lie,lie down
	ימלך	qal	wci	3ms	מלך	573		be king,reign
15:23	מלך	qal	pft	3ms	מלך	573		be king,reign
15:24	יעשׂ	qal	wci	3ms	עשׂה	793		do,make
	סר	qal	pft	3ms	סור	693		turn aside
	החטיא	hiph	pft	3ms	חטא	306		cause to sin
15:25	יקשׁר	qal	wci	3ms	קשׁר	905		bind
	יכהו	hiph	wci	3ms	נכה	645	3ms	smite
	ימיתהו	hiph	wci	3ms	מות	559	3ms	kill
	ימלך	qal	wci	3ms	מלך	573		be king,reign
15:26	עשׂה	qal	pft	3ms	עשׂה	793		do,make
	כתובים	qal	pptc	mp	כתב	507		write
15:27	מלך	qal	pft	3ms	מלך	573		be king,reign
15:28	יעשׂ	qal	wci	3ms	עשׂה	793		do,make
	סר	qal	pft	3ms	סור	693		turn aside
	החטיא	hiph	pft	3ms	חטא	306		cause to sin
15:29	בא	qal	pft	3ms	בוא	97		come in
	יקח	qal	wci	3ms	לקח	542		take
	יגלם	hiph	wci	3ms	גלה	162	3mp	lead into exile
15:30	יקשׁר	qal	wci	3ms	קשׁר	905		bind
	יכהו	hiph	wci	3ms	נכה	645	3ms	smite
	ימיתהו	hiph	wci	3ms	מות	559	3ms	kill
	ימלך	qal	wci	3ms	מלך	573		be king,reign
15:31	עשׂה	qal	pft	3ms	עשׂה	793		do,make
	כתובים	qal	pptc	mp	כתב	507		write
15:32	מלך	qal	pft	3ms	מלך	573		be king,reign
15:33	היה	qal	pft	3ms	היה	224		be,become
	מלכו	qal	infc		מלך	573	3ms	be king,reign
	מלך	qal	pft	3ms	מלך	573		be king,reign
15:34	יעשׂ	qal	wci	3ms	עשׂה	793		do,make
	עשׂה	qal	pft	3ms	עשׂה	793		do,make
	עשׂה	qal	pft	3ms	עשׂה	793		do,make
15:35	סרו	qal	pft	3cp	סור	693		turn aside
	מזבחים	piel	ptc	mp	זבח	256		sacrifice
	מקטרים	piel	ptc	mp	קטר	882		make sacrifices
	בנה	qal	pft	3ms	בנה	124		build
15:36	עשׂה	qal	pft	3ms	עשׂה	793		do,make
	כתובים	qal	pptc	mp	כתב	507		write
15:37	החל	hiph	pft	3ms	חלל	320		begin,profane
	השׁליח	hiph	infc		שׁלח	1018		send
15:38	ישׁכב	qal	wci	3ms	שׁכב	1011		lie,lie down
	יקבר	niph	wci	3ms	קבר	868		be buried
	ימלך	qal	wci	3ms	מלך	573		be king,reign
16:1	מלך	qal	pft	3ms	מלך	573		be king,reign
16:2	מלכו	qal	infc		מלך	573	3ms	be king,reign
	מלך	qal	pft	3ms	מלך	573		be king,reign
	עשׂה	qal	pft	3ms	עשׂה	793		do,make
16:3	ילך	qal	wci	3ms	הלך	229		walk,go
	העביר	hiph	pft	3ms	עבר	716		cause to pass
	הוריש	hiph	pft	3ms	ירשׁ	439		c. to possess
16:4	יזבח	piel	wci	3ms	זבח	256		sacrifice

ChVs	Form	Stem	Tnse	PGN	Root	BDB	Sfx	Meaning
16:4	יקטר	piel	wci	3ms	קטר	882		make sacrifices
16:5	יעלה	qal	impf	3ms	עלה	748		go up
	יצרו	qal	wci	3mp	צור	848		confine,shut in
	יכלו	qal	pft	3cp	יכל	407		be able
	הלחם	niph	infc		לחם	535		wage war
16:6	השיב	hiph	pft	3ms	שוב	996		bring back
	ינשל	piel	wci	3ms	נשל	675		clear away
	באו	qal	pft	3cp	בוא	97		come in
	ישבו	qal	wci	3mp	ישב	442		sit,dwell
16:7	ישלח	qal	wci	3ms	שלח	1018		send
	אמר	qal	infc		אמר	55		say
	עלה	qal	impv	ms	עלה	748		go up
	הושעני	hiph	impv	ms	ישע	446	1cs	deliver,save
	קומים	qal	ptc	mp	קום	877		arise,stand
16:8	יקח	qal	wci	3ms	לקח	542		take
	נמצא	niph	ptc	ms	מצא	592		be found
	ישלח	qal	wci	3ms	שלח	1018		send
16:9	ישמע	qal	wci	3ms	שמע	1033		hear
	יעל	qal	wci	3ms	עלה	748		go up
	יתפשה	qal	wci	3ms	תפש	1074	3fs	seize,grasp
	יגלה	hiph	wci	3ms	גלה	162	3fs	lead into exile
	המית	hiph	pft	3ms	מות	559		kill
16:10	ילך	qal	wci	3ms	הלך	229		walk,go
	קראת	qal	infc		קרא	896		meet,encounter
	ירא	qal	wci	3ms	ראה	906		see
	ישלח	qal	wci	3ms	שלח	1018		send
16:11	יבן	qal	wci	3ms	בנה	124		build
	שלח	qal	pft	3ms	שלח	1018		send
	עשה	qal	pft	3ms	עשה	793		do,make
	בוא	qal	infc		בוא	97		come in
16:12	יבא	qal	wci	3ms	בוא	97		come in
	ירא	qal	wci	3ms	ראה	906		see
	יקרב	qal	wci	3ms	קרב	897		approach
	יעל	hiph	wci	3ms	עלה	748		bring up,offer
16:13	יקטר	hiph	wci	3ms	קטר	882		make sacrifices
	יסך	hiph	wci	3ms	נסך	650		pour out
	יזרק	qal	wci	3ms	זרק	284		toss,scatter
16:14	יקרב	hiph	wci	3ms	קרב	897		bring near
	יתן	qal	wci	3ms	נתן	678		give,set
16:15	יצוהוk	piel	wci	3ms	צוה	845	3ms	command
	יצוהq	piel	wci	3ms	צוה	845		command
	אמר	qal	infc		אמר	55		say
	הקטר	hiph	impv	ms	קטר	882		make sacrifices
	תזרק	qal	impf	2ms	זרק	284		toss,scatter
	יהיה	qal	impf	3ms	היה	224		be,become
	בקר	piel	infc		בקר	133		seek,inquire
16:16	יעש	qal	wci	3ms	עשה	793		do,make
	צוה	piel	pft	3ms	צוה	845		command
16:17	יקצץ	piel	wci	3ms	קצץ	893		cut off
	יסר	hiph	wci	3ms	סור	693		take away
	הורד	hiph	pft	3ms	ירד	432		bring down
	יתן	qal	wci	3ms	נתן	678		give,set
16:18	בנו	qal	pft	3cp	בנה	124		build
	הסב	hiph	pft	3ms	סבב	685		cause to turn
16:19	עשה	qal	pft	3ms	עשה	793		do,make
	כתובים	qal	pptc	mp	כתב	507		write
16:20	ישכב	qal	wci	3ms	שכב	1011		lie,lie down
	יקבר	niph	wci	3ms	קבר	868		be buried
	ימלך	qal	wci	3ms	מלך	573		be king,reign
17:1	מלך	qal	pft	3ms	מלך	573		be king,reign
17:2	יעש	qal	wci	3ms	עשה	793		do,make
	היו	qal	pft	3cp	היה	224		be,become
17:3	עלה	qal	pft	3ms	עלה	748		go up
	יהי	qal	wci	3ms	היה	224		be,become
	ישב	hiph	wci	3ms	שוב	996		bring back
17:4	ימצא	qal	wci	3ms	מצא	592		find
	שלח	qal	pft	3ms	שלח	1018		send
	העלה	hiph	pft	3ms	עלה	748		bring up,offer
	יעצרהו	qal	wci	3ms	עצר	783	3ms	restrain
	יאסרהו	qal	wci	3ms	אסר	63	3ms	tie,bind
17:5	יעל	qal	wci	3ms	עלה	748		go up
	יעל	qal	wci	3ms	עלה	748		go up
	יצר	qal	wci	3ms	צור	848		confine,shut in
17:6	לכד	qal	pft	3ms	לכד	539		capture
	יגל	hiph	wci	3ms	גלה	162		lead into exile
	ישב	hiph	wci	3ms	ישב	442		cause to dwell
17:7	יהי	qal	wci	3ms	היה	224		be,become
	חטאו	qal	pft	3cp	חטא	306		sin
	מעלה	hiph	ptc	ms	עלה	748		bring up,offer
	ייראו	qal	wci	3mp	ירא	431		fear
17:8	ילכו	qal	wci	3mp	הלך	229		walk,go
	הוריש	hiph	pft	3ms	ירש	439		c. to possess
	עשו	qal	pft	3cp	עשה	793		do,make
17:9	יחפאו	piel	wci	3mp	חפא	341		do secretly
	יבנו	qal	wci	3mp	בנה	124		build
	נוצרים	qal	ptc	mp	נצר	665		watch,guard
17:10	יצבו	hiph	wci	3mp	נצב	662		cause to stand
17:11	יקטרו	piel	wci	3mp	קטר	882		make sacrifices
	הגלה	hiph	pft	3ms	גלה	162		lead into exile
	יעשו	qal	wci	3mp	עשה	793		do,make
	הכעים	hiph	infc		כעס	494		vex,provoke
17:12	יעבדו	qal	wci	3mp	עבד	712		work,serve
	אמר	qal	pft	3ms	אמר	55		say
	תעשו	qal	impf	2mp	עשה	793		do,make
17:13	יעד	hiph	wci	3ms	עוד	729		testify,warn
	אמר	qal	infc		אמר	55		say
	שבו	qal	impv	mp	שוב	996		turn,return
	שמרו	qal	impv	mp	שמר	1036		keep,watch
	צויתי	piel	pft	1cs	צוה	845		command
	שלחתי	qal	pft	1cs	שלח	1018		send
17:14	שמעו	qal	pft	3cp	שמע	1033		hear
	יקשו	hiph	wci	3mp	קשה	904		harden
	האמינו	hiph	pft	3cp	אמן	52		believe
17:15	ימאסו	qal	wci	3mp	מאס	549		reject,refuse
	כרת	qal	pft	3ms	כרת	503		cut,destroy
	העיד	hiph	pft	3ms	עוד	729		testify,warn
	ילכו	qal	wci	3mp	הלך	229		walk,go
	יהבלו	qal	wci	3mp	הבל	211		be worthless

ChVs	Form	Stem	Tnse	PGN	Root	BDB	Sfx	Meaning
17:15	צוה	piel	pft	3ms	צוה	845		command
	עשׂות	qal	infc		עשׂה	793		do,make
17:16	יעזבו	qal	wci	3mp	עזב	736		leave,loose
	יעשׂו	qal	wci	3mp	עשׂה	793		do,make
	יעשׂו	qal	wci	3mp	עשׂה	793		do,make
	ישׁתחוו	hish	wci	3mp	חוה	1005		bow down
	יעבדו	qal	wci	3mp	עבד	712		work,serve
17:17	יעבירו	hiph	wci	3mp	עבר	716		cause to pass
	יקסמו	qal	wci	3mp	קסם	890		divine
	ינחשׁו	piel	wci	3mp	נחשׁ	638		divine
	יתמכרו	hith	wci	3mp	מכר	569		sell oneself
	עשׂות	qal	infc		עשׂה	793		do,make
	הכעיסו	hiph	infc		כעס	494	3ms	vex,provoke
17:18	יתאנף	hith	wci	3ms	אנף	60		be angry
	יסרם	hiph	wci	3ms	סור	693	3mp	take away
	נשׁאר	niph	pft	3ms	שׁאר	983		be left
17:19	שׁמר	qal	pft	3ms	שׁמר	1036		keep,watch
	ילכו	qal	wci	3mp	הלך	229		walk,go
	עשׂו	qal	pft	3cp	עשׂה	793		do,make
17:20	ימאס	qal	wci	3ms	מאס	549		reject,refuse
	יענם	piel	wci	3ms	ענה	776	3mp	humble
	יתנם	qal	wci	3ms	נתן	678	3mp	give,set
	שׁסים	qal	ptc	mp	שׁסה	1042		plunder
	השׁליכם	hiph	pft	3ms	שׁלך	1020	3mp	throw,cast
17:21	קרע	qal	pft	3ms	קרע	902		tear,rend
	ימליכו	hiph	wci	3mp	מלך	573		cause to reign
	ידאk	hiph	wci	3ms	נדא	621		drive away
	ידחq	hiph	wci	3ms	נדח	623		thrust out
	החטיאם	hiph	pft	3ms	חטא	306	3mp	cause to sin
17:22	ילכו	qal	wci	3mp	הלך	229		walk,go
	עשׂה	qal	pft	3ms	עשׂה	793		do,make
	סרו	qal	pft	3cp	סור	693		turn aside
17:23	הסיר	hiph	pft	3ms	סור	693		take away
	דבר	piel	pft	3ms	דבר	180		speak
	יגל	qal	wci	3ms	גלה	162		uncover
17:24	יבא	hiph	wci	3ms	בוא	97		bring in
	ישׁב	hiph	wci	3ms	ישׁב	442		cause to dwell
	ירשׁו	qal	wci	3mp	ירשׁ	439		possess,inherit
	ישׁבו	qal	wci	3mp	ישׁב	442		sit,dwell
17:25	יהי	qal	wci	3ms	היה	224		be,become
	שׁבתם	qal	infc		ישׁב	442	3mp	sit,dwell
	יראו	qal	pft	3cp	ירא	431		fear
	ישׁלח	piel	wci	3ms	שׁלח	1018		send away,shoot
	יהיו	qal	wci	3mp	היה	224		be,become
	הרגים	qal	ptc	mp	הרג	246		kill
17:26	יאמרו	qal	wci	3mp	אמר	55		say
	אמר	qal	infc		אמר	55		say
	הגלית	hiph	pft	2ms	גלה	162		lead into exile
	תושׁב	hiph	wci	2ms	ישׁב	442		cause to dwell
	ידעו	qal	pft	3cp	ידע	393		know
	ישׁלח	piel	wci	3ms	שׁלח	1018		send away,shoot
	ממיתים	hiph	ptc	mp	מות	559		kill
	ידעים	qal	ptc	mp	ידע	393		know
17:27	יצו	piel	wci	3ms	צוה	845		command
17:27	אמר	qal	infc		אמר	55		say
	הליכו	hiph	impv	mp	הלך	229		lead,bring
	הגליתם	hiph	pft	2mp	גלה	162		lead into exile
	ילכו	qal	jusm	3mp	הלך	229		walk,go
	ישׁבו	qal	jusm	3mp	ישׁב	442		sit,dwell
	ירם	hiph	jusm	3ms	ירה	434	3mp	shoot,teach
17:28	יבא	qal	wci	3ms	בוא	97		come in
	הגלו	hiph	pft	3cp	גלה	162		lead into exile
	ישׁב	qal	wci	3ms	ישׁב	442		sit,dwell
	יהי	qal	wci	3ms	היה	224		be,become
	מורה	hiph	ptc	ms	ירה	434		shoot,teach
	ייראו	qal	impf	3mp	ירא	431		fear
17:29	יהיו	qal	wci	3mp	היה	224		be,become
	עשׂים	qal	ptc	mp	עשׂה	793		do,make
	יניחו	hiph	wci	3mp	נוח	628		give rest,put
	עשׂו	qal	pft	3cp	עשׂה	793		do,make
	ישׁבים	qal	ptc	mp	ישׁב	442		sit,dwell
17:30	עשׂו	qal	pft	3cp	עשׂה	793		do,make
	עשׂו	qal	pft	3cp	עשׂה	793		do,make
	עשׂו	qal	pft	3cp	עשׂה	793		do,make
17:31	עשׂו	qal	pft	3cp	עשׂה	793		do,make
	שׂרפים	qal	ptc	mp	שׂרף	976		burn
17:32	יהיו	qal	wci	3mp	היה	224		be,become
	יראים	qal	ptc	mp	ירא	431		fear
	יעשׂו	qal	wci	3mp	עשׂה	793		do,make
	יהיו	qal	wci	3mp	היה	224		be,become
	עשׂים	qal	ptc	mp	עשׂה	793		do,make
17:33	היו	qal	pft	3cp	היה	224		be,become
	יראים	qal	ptc	mp	ירא	431		fear
	היו	qal	pft	3cp	היה	224		be,become
	עבדים	qal	ptc	mp	עבד	712		work,serve
	הגלו	hiph	pft	3cp	גלה	162		lead into exile
17:34	עשׂים	qal	ptc	mp	עשׂה	793		do,make
	יראים	qal	ptc	mp	ירא	431		fear
	עשׂים	qal	ptc	mp	עשׂה	793		do,make
	צוה	piel	pft	3ms	צוה	845		command
	שׂם	qal	pft	3ms	שׂים	962		put,set
17:35	יכרת	qal	wci	3ms	כרת	503		cut,destroy
	יצום	piel	wci	3ms	צוה	845	3mp	command
	אמר	qal	infc		אמר	55		say
	תיראו	qal	impf	2mp	ירא	431		fear
	תשׁתחוו	hish	impf	2mp	חוה	1005		bow down
	תעבדום	qal	impf	2mp	עבד	712	3mp	work,serve
	תזבחו	qal	impf	2mp	זבח	256		slaughter
17:36	העלה	hiph	pft	3ms	עלה	748		bring up,offer
	נטויה	qal	pptc	fs	נטה	639		stretch,incline
	תיראו	qal	impf	2mp	ירא	431		fear
	תשׁתחוו	hish	impf	2mp	חוה	1005		bow down
	תזבחו	qal	impf	2mp	זבח	256		slaughter
17:37	כתב	qal	pft	3ms	כתב	507		write
	תשׁמרון	qal	impf	2mp	שׁמר	1036		keep,watch
	עשׂות	qal	infc		עשׂה	793		do,make
	תיראו	qal	impf	2mp	ירא	431		fear
17:38	כרתי	qal	pft	1cs	כרת	503		cut,destroy

ChVs	Form	Stem	Tnse	PGN	Root	BDB	Sfx	Meaning
17:38	תשׁכחו	qal	impf	2mp	שׁכח	1013		forget
	תיראו	qal	impf	2mp	ירא	431		fear
17:39	תיראו	qal	impf	2mp	ירא	431		fear
	יציל	hiph	impf	3ms	נצל	664		snatch,deliver
	איביכם	qal	ptc	mp	איב	33	2mp	be hostile to
17:40	שׁמעו	qal	pft	3cp	שׁמע	1033		hear
	עשׂים	qal	ptc	mp	עשׂה	793		do,make
17:41	יהיו	qal	wci	3mp	היה	224		be,become
	יראים	qal	ptc	mp	ירא	431		fear
	היו	qal	pft	3cp	היה	224		be,become
	עבדים	qal	ptc	mp	עבד	712		work,serve
	עשׂו	qal	pft	3cp	עשׂה	793		do,make
	עשׂים	qal	ptc	mp	עשׂה	793		do,make
18:1	יהי	qal	wci	3ms	היה	224		be,become
	מלך	qal	pft	3ms	מלך	573		be king,reign
18:2	היה	qal	pft	3ms	היה	224		be,become
	מלכו	qal	infc		מלך	573	3ms	be king,reign
	מלך	qal	pft	3ms	מלך	573		be king,reign
18:3	יעשׂ	qal	wci	3ms	עשׂה	793		do,make
	עשׂה	qal	pft	3ms	עשׂה	793		do,make
18:4	הסיר	hiph	pft	3ms	סור	693		take away
	שׁבר	piel	pft	3ms	שׁבר	990		shatter
	כרת	qal	pft	3ms	כרת	503		cut,destroy
	כתת	piel	pft	3ms	כתת	510		beat to pieces
	עשׂה	qal	pft	3ms	עשׂה	793		do,make
	היו	qal	pft	3cp	היה	224		be,become
	מקטרים	piel	ptc	mp	קטר	882		make sacrifices
	יקרא	qal	wci	3ms	קרא	894		call,proclaim
18:5	בטח	qal	pft	3ms	בטח	105		trust
	היה	qal	pft	3ms	היה	224		be,become
	היו	qal	pft	3cp	היה	224		be,become
18:6	ידבק	qal	wci	3ms	דבק	179		cling,cleave
	סר	qal	pft	3ms	סור	693		turn aside
	ישׁמר	qal	wci	3ms	שׁמר	1036		keep,watch
	צוה	piel	pft	3ms	צוה	845		command
18:7	היה	qal	wcp	3ms	היה	224		be,become
	יצא	qal	impf	3ms	יצא	422		go out
	ישׂכיל	hiph	impf	3ms	שׂכל	968		look at,prosper
	ימרד	qal	wci	3ms	מרד	597		rebel
	עבדו	qal	pft	3ms	עבד	712	3ms	work,serve
18:8	הכה	hiph	pft	3ms	נכה	645		smite
	נוצרים	qal	ptc	mp	נצר	665		watch,guard
18:9	יהי	qal	wci	3ms	היה	224		be,become
	עלה	qal	pft	3ms	עלה	748		go up
	יצר	qal	wci	3ms	צור	848		confine,shut in
18:10	ילכדה	qal	wci	3mp	לכד	539	3fs	capture
	נלכדה	niph	pft	3fs	לכד	539		be captured
18:11	יגל	hiph	wci	3ms	גלה	162		lead into exile
	ינחם	hiph	wci	3ms	נחה	634	3mp	lead,guide
18:12	שׁמעו	qal	pft	3cp	שׁמע	1033		hear
	יעברו	qal	wci	3mp	עבר	716		pass over
	צוה	piel	pft	3ms	צוה	845		command
	שׁמעו	qal	pft	3cp	שׁמע	1033		hear
	עשׂו	qal	pft	3cp	עשׂה	793		do,make
18:13	עלה	qal	pft	3ms	עלה	748		go up
	בצרות	qal	pptc	fp	בצר	130		cut off
	יתפשׂם	qal	wci	3ms	תפשׂ	1074	3mp	seize,grasp
18:14	ישׁלח	qal	wci	3ms	שׁלח	1018		send
	אמר	qal	infc		אמר	55		say
	חטאתי	qal	pft	1cs	חטא	306		sin
	שׁוב	qal	impv	ms	שׁוב	996		turn,return
	תתן	qal	impf	2ms	נתן	678		give,set
	אשׂא	qal	impf	1cs	נשׂא	669		lift,carry
	ישׂם	qal	wci	3ms	שׂים	962		put,set
18:15	יתן	qal	wci	3ms	נתן	678		give,set
	נמצא	niph	ptc	ms	מצא	592		be found
18:16	קצץ	piel	pft	3ms	קצץ	893		cut off
	צפה	piel	pft	3ms	צפה	860		overlay
	יתנם	qal	wci	3ms	נתן	678	3mp	give,set
18:17	ישׁלח	qal	wci	3ms	שׁלח	1018		send
	יעלו	qal	wci	3mp	עלה	748		go up
	יבאו	qal	wci	3mp	בוא	97		come in
	יעלו	qal	wci	3mp	עלה	748		go up
	יבאו	qal	wci	3mp	בוא	97		come in
	יעמדו	qal	wci	3mp	עמד	763		stand,stop
	כובס	qal	ptc	ms	כבס	460		tread
18:18	יקראו	qal	wci	3mp	קרא	894		call,proclaim
	יצא	qal	wci	3ms	יצא	422		go out
	מזכיר	hiph	ptc	ms	זכר	269		c. to remember
18:19	יאמר	qal	wci	3ms	אמר	55		say
	אמרו	qal	impv	mp	אמר	55		say
	אמר	qal	pft	3ms	אמר	55		say
	בטחת	qal	pft	2ms	בטח	105		trust
18:20	אמרת	qal	pft	2ms	אמר	55		say
	בטחת	qal	pft	2ms	בטח	105		trust
	מרדת	qal	pft	2ms	מרד	597		rebel
18:21	בטחת	qal	pft	2ms	בטח	105		trust
	רצוץ	qal	pptc	ms	רצץ	954		crush
	יסמך	niph	impf	3ms	סמך	701		support oneself
	בא	qal	wcp	3ms	בוא	97		come in
	נקבה	qal	wcp	3ms	נקב	666	3fs	pierce
	בטחים	qal	ptc	mp	בטח	105		trust
18:22	תאמרון	qal	impf	2mp	אמר	55		say
	בטחנו	qal	pft	1cp	בטח	105		trust
	הסיר	hiph	pft	3ms	סור	693		take away
	יאמר	qal	wci	3ms	אמר	55		say
	תשׁתחוו	hish	impf	2mp	חוה	1005		bow down
18:23	התערב	hith	impv	ms	ערב	786		exchange,share
	אתנה	qal	coh	1cs	נתן	678		give,set
	תוכל	qal	impf	2ms	יכל	407		be able
	תת	qal	infc		נתן	678		give,set
	רכבים	qal	ptc	mp	רכב	938		mount,ride
18:24	תשׁיב	hiph	impf	2ms	שׁוב	996		bring back
	תבטח	qal	wci	2ms	בטח	105		trust
18:25	עליתי	qal	pft	1cs	עלה	748		go up
	השׁחתו	hiph	infc		שׁחת	1007	3ms	spoil,ruin
	אמר	qal	pft	3ms	אמר	55		say
	עלה	qal	impv	ms	עלה	748		go up

ChVs	Form	Stem	Tnse	PGN	Root	BDB	Sfx	Meaning
18: 25	השחיתה	hiph	impv	ms	שחת	1007	3fs	spoil,ruin
18: 26	יאמר	qal	wci	3ms	אמר	55		say
	דבר	piel	impv	ms	דבר	180		speak
	שמעים	qal	ptc	mp	שמע	1033		hear
	תדבר	piel	jusm	2ms	דבר	180		speak
18: 27	יאמר	qal	wci	3ms	אמר	55		say
	שלחני	qal	pft	3ms	שלח	1018	1cs	send
	דבר	piel	infc		דבר	180		speak
	ישבים	qal	ptc	mp	ישב	442		sit,dwell
	אכל	qal	infc		אכל	37		eat,devour
	שתות	qal	infc		שתה	1059		drink
18: 28	יעמד	qal	wci	3ms	עמד	763		stand,stop
	יקרא	qal	wci	3ms	קרא	894		call,proclaim
	ידבר	piel	wci	3ms	דבר	180		speak
	יאמר	qal	wci	3ms	אמר	55		say
	שמעו	qal	impv	mp	שמע	1033		hear
18: 29	אמר	qal	pft	3ms	אמר	55		say
	ישיא	hiph	jusm	3ms	נשא	674		beguile
	יוכל	qal	impf	3ms	יכל	407		be able
	הציל	hiph	infc		נצל	664		snatch,deliver
18: 30	יבטח	hiph	jusm	3ms	בטח	105		cause to trust
	אמר	qal	infc		אמר	55		say
	הצל	hiph	infa		נצל	664		snatch,deliver
	יצילנו	hiph	impf	3ms	נצל	664	1cp	snatch,deliver
	תנתן	niph	impf	3fs	נתן	678		be given
18: 31	תשמעו	qal	jusm	2mp	שמע	1033		hear
	אמר	qal	pft	3ms	אמר	55		say
	עשו	qal	impv	mp	עשה	793		do,make
	צאו	qal	impv	mp	יצא	422		go out
	אכלו	qal	impv	mp	אכל	37		eat,devour
	שתו	qal	impv	mp	שתה	1059		drink
18: 32	באי	qal	infc		בוא	97	1cs	come in
	לקחתי	qal	wcp	1cs	לקח	542		take
	חיו	qal	impv	mp	חיה	310		live
	תמתו	qal	impf	2mp	מות	559		die
	תשמעו	qal	jusm	2mp	שמע	1033		hear
	יסית	hiph	impf	3ms	סות	694		incite,allure
	אמר	qal	infc		אמר	55		say
	יצילנו	hiph	impf	3ms	נצל	664	1cp	snatch,deliver
18: 33	הצל	hiph	infa		נצל	664		snatch,deliver
	הצילו	hiph	pft	3cp	נצל	664		snatch,deliver
18: 34	הצילו	hiph	pft	3cp	נצל	664		snatch,deliver
18: 35	הצילו	hiph	pft	3cp	נצל	664		snatch,deliver
	יציל	hiph	impf	3ms	נצל	664		snatch,deliver
18: 36	החרישו	hiph	pft	3cp	חרש	361		be silent
	ענו	qal	pft	3cp	ענה	772		answer
	אמר	qal	infc		אמר	55		say
	תענהו	qal	impf	2mp	ענה	772	3ms	answer
18: 37	יבא	qal	wci	3ms	בוא	97		come in
	מזכיר	hiph	ptc	ms	זכר	269		c. to remember
	קרועי	qal	pptc	mp	קרע	902		tear,rend
	יגדו	hiph	wci	3mp	נגד	616		declare,tell
19: 1	יהי	qal	wci	3ms	היה	224		be,become
	שמע	qal	infc		שמע	1033		hear

ChVs	Form	Stem	Tnse	PGN	Root	BDB	Sfx	Meaning
19: 1	יקרע	qal	wci	3ms	קרע	902		tear,rend
	יתכס	hith	wci	3ms	כסה	491		cover oneself
	יבא	qal	wci	3ms	בוא	97		come in
19: 2	ישלח	qal	wci	3ms	שלח	1018		send
	מתכסים	hith	ptc	mp	כסה	491		cover oneself
19: 3	יאמרו	qal	wci	3mp	אמר	55		say
	אמר	qal	pft	3ms	אמר	55		say
	באו	qal	pft	3cp	בוא	97		come in
	לדה	qal	infc		ילד	408		bear,beget
19: 4	ישמע	qal	impf	3ms	שמע	1033		hear
	שלחו	qal	pft	3ms	שלח	1018	3ms	send
	חרף	piel	infc		חרף	357		reproach
	הוכיח	hiph	wcp	3ms	יכח	406		decide,reprove
	שמע	qal	pft	3ms	שמע	1033		hear
	נשאת	qal	wcp	2ms	נשא	669		lift,carry
	נמצאה	niph	ptc	fs	מצא	592		be found
19: 5	יבאו	qal	wci	3mp	בוא	97		come in
19: 6	יאמר	qal	wci	3ms	אמר	55		say
	תאמרון	qal	impf	2mp	אמר	55		say
	אמר	qal	pft	3ms	אמר	55		say
	תירא	qal	jusm	2ms	ירא	431		fear
	שמעת	qal	pft	2ms	שמע	1033		hear
	גדפו	piel	pft	3cp	גדף	154		revile
19: 7	נתן	qal	ptc	ms	נתן	678		give,set
	שמע	qal	wcp	3ms	שמע	1033		hear
	שב	qal	wcp	3ms	שוב	996		turn,return
	הפלתיו	hiph	wcp	1cs	נפל	656	3ms	cause to fall
19: 8	ישב	qal	wci	3ms	שוב	996		turn,return
	ימצא	qal	wci	3ms	מצא	592		find
	נלחם	niph	ptc	ms	לחם	535		wage war
	שמע	qal	pft	3ms	שמע	1033		hear
	נסע	qal	pft	3ms	נסע	652		pull up,set out
19: 9	ישמע	qal	wci	3ms	שמע	1033		hear
	אמר	qal	infc		אמר	55		say
	יצא	qal	pft	3ms	יצא	422		go out
	הלחם	niph	infc		לחם	535		wage war
	ישב	qal	wci	3ms	שוב	996		turn,return
	ישלח	qal	wci	3ms	שלח	1018		send
	אמר	qal	infc		אמר	55		say
19: 10	תאמרון	qal	impf	2mp	אמר	55		say
	אמר	qal	infc		אמר	55		say
	ישאך	hiph	jus	3ms	נשא	674	2ms	beguile
	בטח	qal	ptc	ms	בטח	105		trust
	אמר	qal	infc		אמר	55		say
	תנתן	niph	impf	3fs	נתן	678		be given
19: 11	שמעת	qal	pft	2ms	שמע	1033		hear
	עשו	qal	pft	3cp	עשה	793		do,make
	החרימם	hiph	infc		חרם	355	3mp	ban,destroy
	תנצל	niph	impf	2ms	נצל	664		be delivered
19: 12	הצילו	hiph	pft	3cp	נצל	664		snatch,deliver
	שחתו	piel	pft	3cp	שחת	1007		spoil,ruin
19: 14	יקח	qal	wci	3ms	לקח	542		take
	יקראם	qal	wci	3ms	קרא	894	3mp	call,proclaim
	יעל	qal	wci	3ms	עלה	748		go up

ChVs	Form	Stem	Tnse	PGN	Root	BDB	Sfx	Meaning
19:14	יפרשׂהו	qal	wci	3ms	פרשׂ	831	3ms	spread out
19:15	יתפלל	hith	wci	3ms	פלל	813		pray
	יאמר	qal	wci	3ms	אמר	55		say
	ישׁב	qal	ptc	ms	ישׁב	442		sit,dwell
	עשׂית	qal	pft	2ms	עשׂה	793		do,make
19:16	הטה	hiph	impv	ms	נטה	639		turn,incline
	שׁמע	qal	impv	ms	שׁמע	1033		hear
	פקח	qal	impv	ms	פקח	824		open
	ראה	qal	impv	ms	ראה	906		see
	שׁמע	qal	impv	ms	שׁמע	1033		hear
	שׁלחו	qal	pft	3ms	שׁלח	1018	3ms	send
	חרף	piel	infc		חרף	357		reproach
19:17	החריבו	hiph	pft	3cp	חרב	351		make desolate
19:18	נתנו	qal	pft	3cp	נתן	678		give,set
	יאבדום	piel	wci	3mp	אבד	1	3mp	destroy
19:19	הושׁיענו	hiph	impv	ms	ישׁע	446	1cp	deliver,save
	ידעו	qal	jusm	3mp	ידע	393		know
19:20	ישׁלח	qal	wci	3ms	שׁלח	1018		send
	אמר	qal	infc		אמר	55		say
	אמר	qal	pft	3ms	אמר	55		say
	התפללת	hith	pft	2ms	פלל	813		pray
	שׁמעתי	qal	pft	1cs	שׁמע	1033		hear
19:21	דבר	piel	pft	3ms	דבר	180		speak
	בזה	qal	pft	3fs	בוז	100		despise
	לעגה	qal	pft	3fs	לעג	541		mock,deride
	הניעה	hiph	pft	3fs	נוע	631		shake,disturb
19:22	חרפת	piel	pft	2ms	חרף	357		reproach
	גדפת	piel	pft	2ms	גדף	154		revile
	הרימות	hiph	pft	2ms	רום	926		raise,lift
	תשׂא	qal	wci	2ms	נשׂא	669		lift,carry
19:23	חרפת	piel	pft	2ms	חרף	357		reproach
	תאמר	qal	wci	2ms	אמר	55		say
	עליתי	qal	pft	1cs	עלה	748		go up
	אכרת	qal	impf	1cs	כרת	503		cut,destroy
	אבואה	qal	coh	1cs	בוא	97		come in
19:24	קרתי	qal	pft	1cs	קור	881		bore,dig
	שׁתיתי	qal	pft	1cs	שׁתה	1059		drink
	זרים	qal	ptc	mp	זור	266		be stranger
	אחרב	hiph	impf	1cs	חרב	351		dry up
19:25	שׁמעת	qal	pft	2ms	שׁמע	1033		hear
	עשׂיתי	qal	pft	1cs	עשׂה	793		do,make
	יצרתיה	qal	pft	1cs	יצר	427	3fs	form,create
	הביאתיה	hiph	pft	1cs	בוא	97	3fs	bring in
	תהי	qal	jus	2fs	היה	224		be,become
	השׁות	hiph	infc		שׁאה	980		lay waste
	נצים	niph	ptc	mp	נצה	663		be ruined
	בצרות	qal	pptc	fp	בצר	130		cut off
19:26	ישׁביהן	qal	ptc	mp	ישׁב	442	3fp	sit,dwell
	חתו	qal	pft	3cp	חתת	369		be shattered
	יבשׁו	qal	wci	3mp	בושׁ	101		be ashamed
	היו	qal	pft	3cp	היה	224		be,become
19:27	שׁבתך	qal	infc		ישׁב	442	2ms	sit,dwell
	צאתך	qal	infc		יצא	422	2ms	go out
	באך	qal	infc		בוא	97	2ms	come in
19:27	ידעתי	qal	pft	1cs	ידע	393		know
	התרגזך	hith	infc		רגז	919	2ms	excite oneself
19:28	התרגזך	hith	infc		רגז	919	2ms	excite oneself
	עלה	qal	pft	3ms	עלה	748		go up
	שׂמתי	qal	wcp	1cs	שׂים	962		put,set
	השׁבתיך	hiph	wcp	1cs	שׁוב	996	2ms	bring back
	באת	qal	pft	2ms	בוא	97		come in
19:29	אכול	qal	infa		אכל	37		eat,devour
	זרעו	qal	impv	mp	זרע	281		sow
	קצרו	qal	impv	mp	קצר	894		reap,harvest
	נטעו	qal	impv	mp	נטע	642		plant
	אכלו	qal	impv	mp	אכל	37		eat,devour
19:30	יספה	qal	wcp	3fs	יסף	414		add,increase
	נשׁארה	niph	ptc	fs	שׁאר	983		be left
	עשׂה	qal	wcp	3ms	עשׂה	793		do,make
19:31	תצא	qal	impf	3fs	יצא	422		go out
	תעשׂה	qal	impf	3fs	עשׂה	793		do,make
19:32	אמר	qal	pft	3ms	אמר	55		say
	יבא	qal	impf	3ms	בוא	97		come in
	יורה	hiph	impf	3ms	ירה	434		shoot,teach
	יקדמנה	piel	impf	3ms	קדם	869	3fs	meet,confront
	ישׁפך	qal	impf	3ms	שׁפך	1049		pour out
19:33	יבא	qal	impf	3ms	בוא	97		come in
	ישׁוב	qal	impf	3ms	שׁוב	996		turn,return
	יבא	qal	impf	3ms	בוא	97		come in
19:34	גנותי	qal	wcp	1cs	גנן	170		defend
	הושׁיעה	hiph	infc		ישׁע	446	3fs	deliver,save
19:35	יהי	qal	wci	3ms	היה	224		be,become
	יצא	qal	wci	3ms	יצא	422		go out
	יך	hiph	wci	3ms	נכה	645		smite
	ישׁכימו	hiph	wci	3mp	שׁכם	1014		rise early
	מתים	qal	ptc	mp	מות	559		die
19:36	יסע	qal	wci	3ms	נסע	652		pull up,set out
	ילך	qal	wci	3ms	הלך	229		walk,go
	ישׁב	qal	wci	3ms	שׁוב	996		turn,return
	ישׁב	qal	wci	3ms	ישׁב	442		sit,dwell
19:37	יהי	qal	wci	3ms	היה	224		be,become
	משׁתחוה	hish	ptc	ms	חוה	1005		bow down
	הכהו	hiph	pft	3cp	נכה	645	3ms	smite
	נמלטו	niph	pft	3cp	מלט	572		escape
	ימלך	qal	wci	3ms	מלך	573		be king,reign
20:1	חלה	qal	pft	3ms	חלה	317		be weak,sick
	מות	qal	infc		מות	559		die
	יבא	qal	wci	3ms	בוא	97		come in
	יאמר	qal	wci	3ms	אמר	55		say
	אמר	qal	pft	3ms	אמר	55		say
	צו	piel	impv	ms	צוה	845		command
	מת	qal	ptc	ms	מות	559		die
	תחיה	qal	impf	2ms	חיה	310		live
20:2	יסב	hiph	wci	3ms	סבב	685		cause to turn
	יתפלל	hith	wci	3ms	פלל	813		pray
	אמר	qal	infc		אמר	55		say
20:3	זכר	qal	impv	ms	זכר	269		remember
	התהלכתי	hith	pft	1cs	הלך	229		walk to and fro

ChVs	Form	Stem	Tnse	PGN	Root	BDB	Sfx	Meaning
20:3	עשׂיתי	qal	pft	1cs	עשׂה	793		do,make
	יבך	qal	wci	3ms	בכה	113		weep
20:4	יהי	qal	wci	3ms	היה	224		be,become
	יצא	qal	pft	3ms	יצא	422		go out
	היה	qal	pft	3ms	היה	224		be,become
	אמר	qal	infc		אמר	55		say
20:5	שׁוב	qal	impv	ms	שׁוב	996		turn,return
	אמרת	qal	wcp	2ms	אמר	55		say
	אמר	qal	pft	3ms	אמר	55		say
	שׁמעתי	qal	pft	1cs	שׁמע	1033		hear
	ראיתי	qal	pft	1cs	ראה	906		see
	רפא	qal	ptc	ms	רפא	950		heal
	תעלה	qal	impf	2ms	עלה	748		go up
20:6	הספתי	hiph	wcp	1cs	יסף	414		add,do again
	אצילך	hiph	impf	1cs	נצל	664	2ms	snatch,deliver
	גנותי	qal	wcp	1cs	גנן	170		defend
20:7	יאמר	qal	wci	3ms	אמר	55		say
	קחו	qal	impv	mp	לקח	542		take
	יקחו	qal	wci	3mp	לקח	542		take
	ישׂימו	qal	wci	3mp	שׂים	962		put,set
	יחי	qal	wci	3ms	חיה	310		live
20:8	יאמר	qal	wci	3ms	אמר	55		say
	ירפא	qal	impf	3ms	רפא	950		heal
	עליתי	qal	wcp	1cs	עלה	748		go up
20:9	יאמר	qal	wci	3ms	אמר	55		say
	יעשׂה	qal	impf	3ms	עשׂה	793		do,make
	דבר	piel	pft	3ms	דבר	180		speak
	הלך	qal	pft	3ms	הלך	229		walk,go
	ישׁוב	qal	impf	3ms	שׁוב	996		turn,return
20:10	יאמר	qal	wci	3ms	אמר	55		say
	נקל	niph	pft	3ms	קלל	886		be trifling
	נטות	qal	infc		נטה	639		stretch,incline
	ישׁוב	qal	jusm	3ms	שׁוב	996		turn,return
20:11	יקרא	qal	wci	3ms	קרא	894		call,proclaim
	ישׁב	hiph	wci	3ms	שׁוב	996		bring back
	ירדה	qal	pft	3fs	ירד	432		come down
20:12	שׁלח	qal	pft	3ms	שׁלח	1018		send
	שׁמע	qal	pft	3ms	שׁמע	1033		hear
	חלה	qal	pft	3ms	חלה	317		be weak,sick
20:13	ישׁמע	qal	wci	3ms	שׁמע	1033		hear
	יראם	hiph	wci	3ms	ראה	906	3mp	show,exhibit
	נמצא	niph	pft	3ms	מצא	592		be found
	היה	qal	pft	3ms	היה	224		be,become
	הראם	hiph	pft	3ms	ראה	906	3mp	show,exhibit
20:14	יבא	qal	wci	3ms	בוא	97		come in
	יאמר	qal	wci	3ms	אמר	55		say
	אמרו	qal	pft	3cp	אמר	55		say
	יבאו	qal	impf	3mp	בוא	97		come in
	יאמר	qal	wci	3ms	אמר	55		say
	באו	qal	pft	3cp	בוא	97		come in
20:15	יאמר	qal	wci	3ms	אמר	55		say
	ראו	qal	pft	3cp	ראה	906		see
	יאמר	qal	wci	3ms	אמר	55		say
	ראו	qal	pft	3cp	ראה	906		see
20:15	היה	qal	pft	3ms	היה	224		be,become
	הראיתם	hiph	pft	1cs	ראה	906	3mp	show,exhibit
20:16	יאמר	qal	wci	3ms	אמר	55		say
	שׁמע	qal	impv	ms	שׁמע	1033		hear
20:17	באים	qal	ptc	mp	בוא	97		come in
	נשׂא	niph	wcp	3ms	נשׂא	669		be lifted up
	אצרו	qal	pft	3cp	אצר	69		store up
	יותר	niph	impf	3ms	יתר	451		be left,remain
	אמר	qal	pft	3ms	אמר	55		say
20:18	יצאו	qal	impf	3mp	יצא	422		go out
	תוליד	hiph	impf	2ms	ילד	408		beget
	יקחk	qal	impf	3ms	לקח	542		take
	יקחוq	qal	impf	3mp	לקח	542		take
	היו	qal	wcp	3cp	היה	224		be,become
20:19	יאמר	qal	wci	3ms	אמר	55		say
	דברת	piel	pft	2ms	דבר	180		speak
	יאמר	qal	wci	3ms	אמר	55		say
	יהיה	qal	impf	3ms	היה	224		be,become
20:20	עשׂה	qal	pft	3ms	עשׂה	793		do,make
	יבא	hiph	wci	3ms	בוא	97		bring in
	כתובים	qal	pptc	mp	כתב	507		write
20:21	ישׁכב	qal	wci	3ms	שׁכב	1011		lie,lie down
	ימלך	qal	wci	3ms	מלך	573		be king,reign
21:1	מלכו	qal	infc		מלך	573	3ms	be king,reign
	מלך	qal	pft	3ms	מלך	573		be king,reign
21:2	יעשׂ	qal	wci	3ms	עשׂה	793		do,make
	הוריש	hiph	pft	3ms	ירשׁ	439		c. to possess
21:3	ישׁב	qal	wci	3ms	שׁוב	996		turn,return
	יבן	qal	wci	3ms	בנה	124		build
	אבד	piel	pft	3ms	אבד	1		destroy
	יקם	hiph	wci	3ms	קום	877		raise,build,set
	יעשׂ	qal	wci	3ms	עשׂה	793		do,make
	עשׂה	qal	pft	3ms	עשׂה	793		do,make
	ישׁתחו	hish	wci	3ms	חוה	1005		bow down
	יעבד	qal	wci	3ms	עבד	712		work,serve
21:4	בנה	qal	wcp	3ms	בנה	124		build
	אמר	qal	pft	3ms	אמר	55		say
	אשׂים	qal	impf	1cs	שׂים	962		put,set
21:5	יבן	qal	wci	3ms	בנה	124		build
21:6	העביר	hiph	wcp	3ms	עבר	716		cause to pass
	עונן	poel	wcp	3ms	ענן	778		soothsay
	נחשׁ	piel	wcp	3ms	נחשׁ	638		divine
	עשׂה	qal	wcp	3ms	עשׂה	793		do,make
	הרבה	hiph	pft	3ms	רבה	915		make many
	עשׂות	qal	infc		עשׂה	793		do,make
	הכעיס	hiph	infc		כעס	494		vex,provoke
21:7	ישׂם	qal	wci	3ms	שׂים	962		put,set
	עשׂה	qal	pft	3ms	עשׂה	793		do,make
	אמר	qal	pft	3ms	אמר	55		say
	בחרתי	qal	pft	1cs	בחר	103		choose
	אשׂים	qal	impf	1cs	שׂים	962		put,set
21:8	אסיף	hiph	impf	1cs	יסף	414		add,do again
	הניד	hiph	infc		נוד	626		cause to wander
	נתתי	qal	pft	1cs	נתן	678		give,set

ChVs	Form	Stem	Tnse	PGN	Root	BDB	Sfx	Meaning
21: 8	ישמרו	qal	impf	3mp	שמר	1036		keep,watch
	עשות	qal	infc		עשה	793		do,make
	צויתים	piel	pft	1cs	צוה	845	3mp	command
	צוה	piel	pft	3ms	צוה	845		command
21: 9	שמעו	qal	pft	3cp	שמע	1033		hear
	יתעם	hiph	wci	3ms	תעה	1073	3mp	cause to err
	עשות	qal	infc		עשה	793		do,make
	השמיד	hiph	pft	3ms	שמד	1029		exterminate
21: 10	ידבר	piel	wci	3ms	דבר	180		speak
	אמר	qal	infc		אמר	55		say
21: 11	עשה	qal	pft	3ms	עשה	793		do,make
	הרע	hiph	pft	3ms	רעע	949		hurt,do evil
	עשו	qal	pft	3cp	עשה	793		do,make
	יחטא	hiph	wci	3ms	חטא	306		cause to sin
21: 12	אמר	qal	pft	3ms	אמר	55		say
	מביא	hiph	ptc	ms	בוא	97		bring in
	שמעיוk	qal	ptc	mp	שמע	1033	3ms	hear
	שמעהq	qal	ptc	ms	שמע	1033	3fs	hear
	תצלנה	qal	impf	3fp	צלל	852		tingle
21: 13	נטיתי	qal	wcp	1cs	נטה	639		stretch,incline
	מחיתי	qal	wcp	1cs	מחה	562		wipe, blot out
	ימחה	qal	impf	3ms	מחה	562		wipe, blot out
	מחה	qal	pft	3ms	מחה	562		wipe, blot out
	הפך	qal	pft	3ms	הפך	245		turn,overturn
21: 14	נטשתי	qal	wcp	1cs	נטש	643		leave,forsake
	נתתים	qal	wcp	1cs	נתן	678	3mp	give,set
	איביהם	qal	ptc	mp	איב	33	3mp	be hostile to
	היו	qal	wcp	3cp	היה	224		be, become
	איביהם	qal	ptc	mp	איב	33	3mp	be hostile to
21: 15	עשו	qal	pft	3cp	עשה	793		do,make
	יהיו	qal	wci	3mp	היה	224		be, become
	מכעסים	hiph	ptc	mp	כעס	494		vex, provoke
	יצאו	qal	pft	3cp	יצא	422		go out
21: 16	שפך	qal	pft	3ms	שפך	1049		pour out
	הרבה	hiph	infa		רבה	915		make many
	מלא	piel	pft	3ms	מלא	569		fill
	החטיא	hiph	pft	3ms	חטא	306		cause to sin
	עשות	qal	infc		עשה	793		do,make
21: 17	עשה	qal	pft	3ms	עשה	793		do,make
	חטא	qal	pft	3ms	חטא	306		sin
	כתובים	qal	pptc	mp	כתב	507		write
21: 18	ישכב	qal	wci	3ms	שכב	1011		lie, lie down
	יקבר	niph	wci	3ms	קבר	868		be buried
	ימלך	qal	wci	3ms	מלך	573		be king,reign
21: 19	מלכו	qal	infc		מלך	573	3ms	be king,reign
	מלך	qal	pft	3ms	מלך	573		be king,reign
21: 20	יעש	qal	wci	3ms	עשה	793		do,make
	עשה	qal	pft	3ms	עשה	793		do,make
21: 21	ילך	qal	wci	3ms	הלך	229		walk,go
	הלך	qal	pft	3ms	הלך	229		walk,go
	יעבד	qal	wci	3ms	עבד	712		work,serve
	עבד	qal	pft	3ms	עבד	712		work,serve
	ישתחו	hish	wci	3ms	חוה	1005		bow down
21: 22	יעזב	qal	wci	3ms	עזב	736		leave,loose
21: 22	הלך	qal	pft	3ms	הלך	229		walk,go
21: 23	יקשרו	qal	wci	3mp	קשר	905		bind
	ימיתו	hiph	wci	3mp	מות	559		kill
21: 24	יך	hiph	wci	3ms	נכה	645		smite
	קשרים	qal	ptc	mp	קשר	905		bind
	ימליכו	hiph	wci	3mp	מלך	573		cause to reign
21: 25	עשה	qal	pft	3ms	עשה	793		do,make
	כתובים	qal	pptc	mp	כתב	507		write
21: 26	יקבר	qal	wci	3ms	קבר	868		bury
	ימלך	qal	wci	3ms	מלך	573		be king,reign
22: 1	מלכו	qal	infc		מלך	573	3ms	be king,reign
	מלך	qal	pft	3ms	מלך	573		be king,reign
22: 2	יעש	qal	wci	3ms	עשה	793		do,make
	ילך	qal	wci	3ms	הלך	229		walk,go
	סר	qal	pft	3ms	סור	693		turn aside
22: 3	יהי	qal	wci	3ms	היה	224		be, become
	שלח	qal	pft	3ms	שלח	1018		send
	אמר	qal	infc		אמר	55		say
22: 4	עלה	qal	impv	ms	עלה	748		go up
	יתם	hiph	jusm	3ms	תמם	1070		finish
	מובא	hoph	ptc	ms	בוא	97		be brought
	אספו	qal	pft	3cp	אסף	62		gather
	שמרי	qal	ptc	mp	שמר	1036		keep,watch
22: 5	יתנהk	qal	jusm	3mp	נתן	678	3ms	give,set
	יתנהוq	qal	jusm	3mp	נתן	678	3ms	give,set
	עשי	qal	ptc	mp	עשה	793		do,make
	מפקדים	hoph	ptc	mp	פקד	823		be appointed
	יתנו	qal	jusm	3mp	נתן	678		give,set
	עשי	qal	ptc	mp	עשה	793		do,make
	חזק	piel	infc		חזק	304		make strong
22: 6	בנים	qal	ptc	mp	בנה	124		build
	גדרים	qal	ptc	mp	גדר	154		wall up
	קנות	qal	infc		קנה	888		get,buy
	חזק	piel	infc		חזק	304		make strong
22: 7	יחשב	niph	impf	3ms	חשב	362		be thought
	נתן	niph	ptc	ms	נתן	678		be given
	עשים	qal	ptc	mp	עשה	793		do,make
22: 8	יאמר	qal	wci	3ms	אמר	55		say
	מצאתי	qal	pft	1cs	מצא	592		find
	יתן	qal	wci	3ms	נתן	678		give,set
	יקראהו	qal	wci	3ms	קרא	894	3ms	call,proclaim
22: 9	יבא	qal	wci	3ms	בוא	97		come in
	ישב	hiph	wci	3ms	שוב	996		bring back
	יאמר	qal	wci	3ms	אמר	55		say
	התיכו	hiph	pft	3cp	נתך	677		pour out
	נמצא	niph	ptc	ms	מצא	592		be found
	יתנהו	qal	wci	3mp	נתן	678	3ms	give,set
	עשי	qal	ptc	mp	עשה	793		do,make
	מפקדים	hoph	ptc	mp	פקד	823		be appointed
22: 10	יגד	hiph	wci	3ms	נגד	616		declare,tell
	אמר	qal	infc		אמר	55		say
	נתן	qal	pft	3ms	נתן	678		give,set
	יקראהו	qal	wci	3ms	קרא	894	3ms	call,proclaim
22: 11	יהי	qal	wci	3ms	היה	224		be, become

ChVs	Form	Stem	Tnse	PGN	Root	BDB	Sfx	Meaning
22:11	שׁמע	qal	infc		שׁמע	1033		hear
	יקרע	qal	wci	3ms	קרע	902		tear,rend
22:12	יצו	piel	wci	3ms	צוה	845		command
	אמר	qal	infc		אמר	55		say
22:13	לכו	qal	impv	mp	הלך	229		walk,go
	דרשׁו	qal	impv	mp	דרשׁ	205		resort to,seek
	נמצא	niph	ptc	ms	מצא	592		be found
	נצתה	niph	pft	3fs	יצת	428		be kindled
	שׁמעו	qal	pft	3cp	שׁמע	1033		hear
	עשׂות	qal	infc		עשׂה	793		do,make
	כתוב	qal	pptc	ms	כתב	507		write
22:14	ילך	qal	wci	3ms	הלך	229		walk,go
	שׁמר	qal	ptc	ms	שׁמר	1036		keep,watch
	ישׁבת	qal	ptc	fs	ישׁב	442		sit,dwell
	ידברו	piel	wci	3mp	דבר	180		speak
22:15	תאמר	qal	wci	3fs	אמר	55		say
	אמר	qal	pft	3ms	אמר	55		say
	אמרו	qal	impv	mp	אמר	55		say
	שׁלח	qal	pft	3ms	שׁלח	1018		send
22:16	אמר	qal	pft	3ms	אמר	55		say
	מביא	hiph	ptc	ms	בוא	97		bring in
	ישׁביו	qal	ptc	mp	ישׁב	442	3ms	sit,dwell
	קרא	qal	pft	3ms	קרא	894		call,proclaim
22:17	עזבוני	qal	pft	3cp	עזב	736	1cs	leave,loose
	יקטרו	piel	wci	3mp	קטר	882		make sacrifices
	הכעיסני	hiph	infc		כעס	494	1cs	vex,provoke
	נצתה	niph	wcp	3fs	יצת	428		be kindled
	תכבה	qal	impf	3fs	כבה	459		be quenched
22:18	שׁלח	qal	ptc	ms	שׁלח	1018		send
	דרשׁ	qal	infc		דרשׁ	205		resort to,seek
	תאמרו	qal	impf	2mp	אמר	55		say
	אמר	qal	pft	3ms	אמר	55		say
	שׁמעת	qal	pft	2ms	שׁמע	1033		hear
22:19	רך	qal	pft	3ms	רכך	939		be tender,timid
	תכנע	niph	wci	2ms	כנע	488		humble self
	שׁמעך	qal	infc		שׁמע	1033	2ms	hear
	דברתי	piel	pft	1cs	דבר	180		speak
	ישׁביו	qal	ptc	mp	ישׁב	442	3ms	sit,dwell
	היות	qal	infc		היה	224		be,become
	תקרע	qal	wci	2ms	קרע	902		tear,rend
	תבכה	qal	wci	2ms	בכה	113		weep
	שׁמעתי	qal	pft	1cs	שׁמע	1033		hear
22:20	אספך	qal	ptc	ms	אסף	62	2ms	gather
	נאספת	niph	wcp	2ms	אסף	62		assemble
	תראינה	qal	impf	3fp	ראה	906		see
	מביא	hiph	ptc	ms	בוא	97		bring in
	ישׁיבו	hiph	wci	3mp	שׁוב	996		bring back
23:1	ישׁלח	qal	wci	3ms	שׁלח	1018		send
	יאספו	qal	wci	3mp	אסף	62		gather
23:2	יעל	qal	wci	3ms	עלה	748		go up
	ישׁבי	qal	ptc	mp	ישׁב	442		sit,dwell
	יקרא	qal	wci	3ms	קרא	894		call,proclaim
	נמצא	niph	ptc	ms	מצא	592		be found
23:3	יעמד	qal	wci	3ms	עמד	763		stand,stop
23:3	יכרת	qal	wci	3ms	כרת	503		cut,destroy
	לכת	qal	infc		הלך	229		walk,go
	שׁמר	qal	infc		שׁמר	1036		keep,watch
	הקים	hiph	infc		קום	877		raise,build,set
	כתבים	qal	pptc	mp	כתב	507		write
	יעמד	qal	wci	3ms	עמד	763		stand,stop
23:4	יצו	piel	wci	3ms	צוה	845		command
	שׁמרי	qal	ptc	mp	שׁמר	1036		keep,watch
	הוציא	hiph	infc		יצא	422		bring out
	עשׂוים	qal	pptc	mp	עשׂה	793		do,make
	ישׂרפם	qal	wci	3ms	שׂרף	976	3mp	burn
	נשׂא	qal	pft	3ms	נשׂא	669		lift,carry
23:5	השׁבית	hiph	pft	3ms	שׁבת	991		destroy,remove
	נתנו	qal	pft	3cp	נתן	678		give,set
	יקטר	piel	wci	3ms	קטר	882		make sacrifices
	מקטרים	piel	ptc	mp	קטר	882		make sacrifices
23:6	יצא	hiph	wci	3ms	יצא	422		bring out
	ישׂרף	qal	wci	3ms	שׂרף	976		burn
	ידק	hiph	wci	3ms	דקק	200		pulverize
	ישׁלך	hiph	wci	3ms	שׁלך	1020		throw,cast
23:7	יתץ	qal	wci	3ms	נתץ	683		pull down
	ארגות	qal	ptc	fp	ארג	70		weave
23:8	יבא	hiph	wci	3ms	בוא	97		bring in
	יטמא	piel	wci	3ms	טמא	379		defile
	קטרו	piel	pft	3cp	קטר	882		make sacrifices
	נתץ	qal	pft	3ms	נתץ	683		pull down
23:9	יעלו	qal	impf	3mp	עלה	748		go up
	אכלו	qal	pft	3cp	אכל	37		eat,devour
23:10	טמא	piel	pft	3ms	טמא	379		defile
	העביר	hiph	infc		עבר	716		cause to pass
23:11	ישׁבת	hiph	wci	3ms	שׁבת	991		destroy,remove
	נתנו	qal	pft	3cp	נתן	678		give,set
	בא	qal	infc		בוא	97		come in
	שׂרף	qal	pft	3ms	שׂרף	976		burn
23:12	עשׂו	qal	pft	3cp	עשׂה	793		do,make
	עשׂה	qal	pft	3ms	עשׂה	793		do,make
	נתץ	qal	pft	3ms	נתץ	683		pull down
	ירץ	qal	wci	3ms	רוץ	930		run
	השׁליך	hiph	pft	3ms	שׁלך	1020		throw,cast
23:13	בנה	qal	pft	3ms	בנה	124		build
	טמא	piel	pft	3ms	טמא	379		defile
23:14	שׁבר	piel	pft	3ms	שׁבר	990		shatter
	יכרת	qal	wci	3ms	כרת	503		cut,destroy
	ימלא	piel	wci	3ms	מלא	569		fill
23:15	עשׂה	qal	pft	3ms	עשׂה	793		do,make
	החטיא	hiph	pft	3ms	חטא	306		cause to sin
	נתץ	qal	pft	3ms	נתץ	683		pull down
	ישׂרף	qal	wci	3ms	שׂרף	976		burn
	הדק	hiph	pft	3ms	דקק	200		pulverize
	שׂרף	qal	pft	3ms	שׂרף	976		burn
23:16	יפן	qal	wci	3ms	פנה	815		turn
	ירא	qal	wci	3ms	ראה	906		see
	ישׁלח	qal	wci	3ms	שׁלח	1018		send
	יקח	qal	wci	3ms	לקח	542		take

ChVs	Form	Stem	Tnse	PGN	Root	BDB	Sfx	Meaning
23:16	ישׂרף	qal	wci	3ms	שׂרף	976		burn
	יטמאהו	piel	wci	3ms	טמא	379	3ms	defile
	קרא	qal	pft	3ms	קרא	894		call,proclaim
	קרא	qal	pft	3ms	קרא	894		call,proclaim
23:17	יאמר	qal	wci	3ms	אמר	55		say
	ראה	qal	ptc	ms	ראה	906		see
	יאמרו	qal	wci	3mp	אמר	55		say
	בא	qal	pft	3ms	בוא	97		come in
	יקרא	qal	wci	3ms	קרא	894		call,proclaim
	עשׂית	qal	pft	2ms	עשׂה	793		do,make
23:18	יאמר	qal	wci	3ms	אמר	55		say
	הניחו	hiph	impv	mp	נוח	628		give rest,put
	ינע	hiph	jus	3ms	נוע	631		shake,disturb
	ימלטו	piel	wci	3mp	מלט	572		deliver
	בא	qal	pft	3ms	בוא	97		come in
23:19	עשׂו	qal	pft	3cp	עשׂה	793		do,make
	הכעיס	hiph	infc		כעס	494		vex,provoke
	הסיר	hiph	pft	3ms	סור	693		take away
	יעשׂ	qal	wci	3ms	עשׂה	793		do,make
	עשׂה	qal	pft	3ms	עשׂה	793		do,make
23:20	יזבח	qal	wci	3ms	זבח	256		slaughter
	ישׂרף	qal	wci	3ms	שׂרף	976		burn
	ישׁב	qal	wci	3ms	שׁוב	996		turn,return
23:21	יצו	piel	wci	3ms	צוה	845		command
	אמר	qal	infc		אמר	55		say
	עשׂו	qal	impv	mp	עשׂה	793		do,make
	כתוב	qal	pptc	ms	כתב	507		write
23:22	נעשׂה	niph	pft	3ms	עשׂה	793		be done
	שׁפטים	qal	ptc	mp	שׁפט	1047		judge
	שׁפטו	qal	pft	3cp	שׁפט	1047		judge
23:23	נעשׂה	niph	pft	3ms	עשׂה	793		be done
23:24	נראו	niph	pft	3cp	ראה	906		appear,be seen
	בער	piel	pft	3ms	בער	128		burn,consume
	הקים	hiph	infc		קום	877		raise,build,set
	כתבים	qal	pptc	mp	כתב	507		write
	מצא	qal	pft	3ms	מצא	592		find
23:25	היה	qal	pft	3ms	היה	224		be,become
	שׁב	qal	pft	3ms	שׁוב	996		turn,return
	קם	qal	pft	3ms	קום	877		arise,stand
23:26	שׁב	qal	pft	3ms	שׁוב	996		turn,return
	חרה	qal	pft	3ms	חרה	354		be kindled,burn
	הכעיסו	hiph	pft	3ms	כעס	494	3ms	vex,provoke
23:27	יאמר	qal	wci	3ms	אמר	55		say
	אסיר	hiph	impf	1cs	סור	693		take away
	הסרתי	hiph	pft	1cs	סור	693		take away
	מאסתי	qal	wcp	1cs	מאס	549		reject,refuse
	בחרתי	qal	pft	1cs	בחר	103		choose
	אמרתי	qal	pft	1cs	אמר	55		say
	יהיה	qal	impf	3ms	היה	224		be,become
23:28	עשׂה	qal	pft	3ms	עשׂה	793		do,make
	כתובים	qal	pptc	mp	כתב	507		write
23:29	עלה	qal	pft	3ms	עלה	748		go up
	ילך	qal	wci	3ms	הלך	229		walk,go
	קראתו	qal	infc		קרא	896	3ms	meet,encounter
23:29	ימיתהו	hiph	wci	3ms	מות	559	3ms	kill
	ראתו	qal	infc		ראה	906	3ms	see
23:30	ירכבהו	hiph	wci	3mp	רכב	938	3ms	cause to ride
	מת	qal	ptc	ms	מות	559		die
	יבאהו	hiph	wci	3mp	בוא	97	3ms	bring in
	יקברהו	qal	wci	3mp	קבר	868	3ms	bury
	יקח	qal	wci	3ms	לקח	542		take
	ימשׁחו	qal	wci	3mp	משׁח	602		smear,anoint
	ימליכו	hiph	wci	3mp	מלך	573		cause to reign
23:31	מלכו	qal	infc		מלך	573	3ms	be king,reign
	מלך	qal	pft	3ms	מלך	573		be king,reign
23:32	יעשׂ	qal	wci	3ms	עשׂה	793		do,make
	עשׂו	qal	pft	3cp	עשׂה	793		do,make
23:33	יאסרהו	qal	wci	3ms	אסר	63	3ms	tie,bind
	מלך	qal	infc		מלך	573		be king,reign
	יתן	qal	wci	3ms	נתן	678		give,set
23:34	ימלך	hiph	wci	3ms	מלך	573		cause to reign
	יסב	hiph	wci	3ms	סבב	685		cause to turn
	לקח	qal	pft	3ms	לקח	542		take
	יבא	qal	wci	3ms	בוא	97		come in
	ימת	qal	wci	3ms	מות	559		die
23:35	נתן	qal	pft	3ms	נתן	678		give,set
	העריך	hiph	pft	3ms	ערך	790		value,tax
	תת	qal	infc		נתן	678		give,set
	נגשׂ	qal	pft	3ms	נגשׂ	620		press,exact
	תת	qal	infc		נתן	678		give,set
23:36	מלכו	qal	infc		מלך	573	3ms	be king,reign
	מלך	qal	pft	3ms	מלך	573		be king,reign
23:37	יעשׂ	qal	wci	3ms	עשׂה	793		do,make
	עשׂו	qal	pft	3cp	עשׂה	793		do,make
24:1	עלה	qal	pft	3ms	עלה	748		go up
	יהי	qal	wci	3ms	היה	224		be,become
	ישׁב	qal	wci	3ms	שׁוב	996		turn,return
	ימרד	qal	wci	3ms	מרד	597		rebel
24:2	ישׁלח	piel	wci	3ms	שׁלח	1018		send away,shoot
	ישׁלחם	piel	wci	3ms	שׁלח	1018	3mp	send away,shoot
	האבידו	hiph	infc		אבד	1	3ms	destroy
	דבר	piel	pft	3ms	דבר	180		speak
24:3	היתה	qal	pft	3fs	היה	224		be,become
	הסיר	hiph	infc		סור	693		take away
	עשׂה	qal	pft	3ms	עשׂה	793		do,make
24:4	שׁפך	qal	pft	3ms	שׁפך	1049		pour out
	ימלא	piel	wci	3ms	מלא	569		fill
	אבה	qal	pft	3ms	אבה	2		be willing
	סלח	qal	infc		סלח	699		forgive,pardon
24:5	עשׂה	qal	pft	3ms	עשׂה	793		do,make
	כתובים	qal	pptc	mp	כתב	507		write
24:6	ישׁכב	qal	wci	3ms	שׁכב	1011		lie,lie down
	ימלך	qal	wci	3ms	מלך	573		be king,reign
24:7	הסיף	hiph	pft	3ms	יסף	414		add,do again
	צאת	qal	infc		יצא	422		go out
	לקח	qal	pft	3ms	לקח	542		take
	היתה	qal	pft	3fs	היה	224		be,become
24:8	מלכו	qal	infc		מלך	573	3ms	be king,reign

ChVs	Form	Stem	Tnse	PGN	Root	BDB	Sfx	Meaning
24: 8	מלך	qal	pft	3ms	מלך	573		be king,reign
24: 9	יעשׂ	qal	wci	3ms	עשׂה	793		do,make
	עשׂה	qal	pft	3ms	עשׂה	793		do,make
24: 10	עלהk	qal	pft	3ms	עלה	748		go up
	עלוq	qal	pft	3cp	עלה	748		go up
	תבא	qal	wci	3fs	בוא	97		come in
24: 11	יבא	qal	wci	3ms	בוא	97		come in
	צרים	qal	ptc	mp	צור	848		confine,shut in
24: 12	יצא	qal	wci	3ms	יצא	422		go out
	יקח	qal	wci	3ms	לקח	542		take
	מלכו	qal	infc		מלך	573	3ms	be king,reign
24: 13	יוצא	hiph	wci	3ms	יצא	422		bring out
	יקצץ	piel	wci	3ms	קצץ	893		cut off
	עשׂה	qal	pft	3ms	עשׂה	793		do,make
	דבר	piel	pft	3ms	דבר	180		speak
24: 14	הגלה	hiph	pft	3ms	גלה	162		lead into exile
	גולה	qal	ptc	ms	גלה	162		uncover
	נשׁאר	niph	pft	3ms	שׁאר	983		be left
24: 15	יגל	hiph	wci	3ms	גלה	162		lead into exile
	הוליך	hiph	pft	3ms	הלך	229		lead,bring
24: 16	עשׂי	qal	ptc	mp	עשׂה	793		do,make
	יביאם	hiph	wci	3ms	בוא	97	3mp	bring in
24: 17	ימלך	hiph	wci	3ms	מלך	573		cause to reign
	יסב	hiph	wci	3ms	סבב	685		cause to turn
24: 18	מלכו	qal	infc		מלך	573	3ms	be king,reign
	מלך	qal	pft	3ms	מלך	573		be king,reign
24: 19	יעשׂ	qal	wci	3ms	עשׂה	793		do,make
	עשׂה	qal	pft	3ms	עשׂה	793		do,make
24: 20	היתה	qal	pft	3fs	היה	224		be,become
	השׁלכו	hiph	infc		שׁלך	1020	3ms	throw,cast
	ימרד	qal	wci	3ms	מרד	597		rebel
25: 1	יהי	qal	wci	3ms	היה	224		be,become
	מלכו	qal	infc		מלך	573	3ms	be king,reign
	בא	qal	pft	3ms	בוא	97		come in
	יחן	qal	wci	3ms	חנה	333		decline,encamp
	יבנו	qal	wci	3mp	בנה	124		build
25: 2	תבא	qal	wci	3fs	בוא	97		come in
25: 3	יחזק	qal	wci	3ms	חזק	304		be strong
	היה	qal	pft	3ms	היה	224		be,become
25: 4	תבקע	niph	wci	3fs	בקע	131		be cleft
	ילך	qal	wci	3ms	הלך	229		walk,go
25: 5	ירדפו	qal	wci	3mp	רדף	922		pursue
	ישׂגו	hiph	wci	3mp	נשׂג	673		reach,overtake
	נפצו	niph	pft	3cp	פוץ	806		be scattered
25: 6	יתפשׂו	qal	wci	3mp	תפשׂ	1074		seize,grasp
	יעלו	hiph	wci	3mp	עלה	748		bring up,offer
	ידברו	piel	wci	3mp	דבר	180		speak
25: 7	שׁחטו	qal	pft	3cp	שׁחט	1006		slaughter
	עור	piel	pft	3ms	עור	734		make blind
	יאסרהו	qal	wci	3ms	אסר	63	3ms	tie,bind
	יבאהו	hiph	wci	3ms	בוא	97	3ms	bring in
25: 8	בא	qal	pft	3ms	בוא	97		come in
25: 9	ישׂרף	qal	wci	3ms	שׂרף	976		burn
	שׂרף	qal	pft	3ms	שׂרף	976		burn
25: 10	נתצו	qal	pft	3cp	נתץ	683		pull down
25: 11	נשׁארים	niph	ptc	mp	שׁאר	983		be left
	נפלים	qal	ptc	mp	נפל	656		fall
	נפלו	qal	pft	3cp	נפל	656		fall
	הגלה	hiph	pft	3ms	גלה	162		lead into exile
25: 12	השׁאיר	hiph	pft	3ms	שׁאר	983		leave,spare
	כרמים	qal	ptc	mp	כרם	501		tend vineyard
	יגבים	qal	ptc	mp	יגב	387		till
25: 13	שׁברו	piel	pft	3cp	שׁבר	990		shatter
	ישׂאו	qal	wci	3mp	נשׂא	669		lift,carry
25: 14	ישׁרתו	piel	impf	3mp	שׁרת	1058		minister,serve
	לקחו	qal	pft	3cp	לקח	542		take
25: 15	לקח	qal	pft	3ms	לקח	542		take
25: 16	עשׂה	qal	pft	3ms	עשׂה	793		do,make
	היה	qal	pft	3ms	היה	224		be,become
25: 18	יקח	qal	wci	3ms	לקח	542		take
	שׁמרי	qal	ptc	mp	שׁמר	1036		keep,watch
25: 19	לקח	qal	pft	3ms	לקח	542		take
	ראי	qal	ptc	mp	ראה	906		see
	נמצאו	niph	pft	3cp	מצא	592		be found
	מצבא	hiph	ptc	ms	צבא	838		muster
	נמצאים	niph	ptc	mp	מצא	592		be found
25: 20	יקח	qal	wci	3ms	לקח	542		take
	ילך	hiph	wci	3ms	הלך	229		lead,bring
25: 21	יך	hiph	wci	3ms	נכה	645		smite
	ימיתם	hiph	wci	3ms	מות	559	3mp	kill
	יגל	qal	wci	3ms	גלה	162		uncover
25: 22	נשׁאר	niph	ptc	ms	שׁאר	983		be left
	השׁאיר	hiph	pft	3ms	שׁאר	983		leave,spare
	יפקד	hiph	wci	3ms	פקד	823		set,entrust
25: 23	ישׁמעו	qal	wci	3mp	שׁמע	1033		hear
	הפקיד	hiph	pft	3ms	פקד	823		set,entrust
	יבאו	qal	wci	3mp	בוא	97		come in
25: 24	ישׁבע	niph	wci	3ms	שׁבע	989		swear
	יאמר	qal	wci	3ms	אמר	55		say
	תיראו	qal	jusm	2mp	ירא	431		fear
	שׁבו	qal	impv	mp	ישׁב	442		sit,dwell
	עבדו	qal	impv	mp	עבד	712		work,serve
	יטב	qal	jusm	3ms	יטב	405		be good
25: 25	יהי	qal	wci	3ms	היה	224		be,become
	בא	qal	pft	3ms	בוא	97		come in
	יכו	hiph	wci	3mp	נכה	645		smite
	ימת	qal	wci	3ms	מות	559		die
	היו	qal	pft	3cp	היה	224		be,become
25: 26	יקמו	qal	wci	3mp	קום	877		arise,stand
	יבאו	qal	wci	3mp	בוא	97		come in
	יראו	qal	pft	3cp	ירא	431		fear
25: 27	יהי	qal	wci	3ms	היה	224		be,become
	נשׂא	qal	pft	3ms	נשׂא	669		lift,carry
	מלכו	qal	infc		מלך	573	3ms	be king,reign
25: 28	ידבר	piel	wci	3ms	דבר	180		speak
	יתן	qal	wci	3ms	נתן	678		give,set
25: 29	שׁנא	piel	pft	3ms	שׁנה	1039		change,alter
	אכל	qal	wcp	3ms	אכל	37		eat,devour

ChVs	Form	Stem	Tnse	PGN	Root	BDB	Sfx	Meaning
25: 30	נתנה	niph	pft	3fs	נתן	678		be given
1 CHRONICLES								
1: 10	ילד	qal	pft	3ms	ילד	408		bear, beget
	החל	hiph	pft	3ms	חלל	320		begin, profane
	היות	qal	infc		היה	224		be, become
1: 11	ילד	qal	pft	3ms	ילד	408		bear, beget
1: 12	יצאו	qal	pft	3cp	יצא	422		go out
1: 13	ילד	qal	pft	3ms	ילד	408		bear, beget
1: 18	ילד	qal	pft	3ms	ילד	408		bear, beget
	ילד	qal	pft	3ms	ילד	408		bear, beget
1: 19	ילד	qalp	pft	3ms	ילד	408		be born
	נפלגה	niph	pft	3fs	פלג	811		be divided
1: 20	ילד	qal	pft	3ms	ילד	408		bear, beget
1: 32	ילדה	qal	pft	3fs	ילד	408		bear, beget
1: 34	יולד	hiph	wci	3ms	ילד	408		beget
1: 43	מלכו	qal	pft	3cp	מלך	573		be king, reign
	מלך	qal	infc		מלך	573		be king, reign
1: 44	ימת	qal	wci	3ms	מות	559		die
	ימלך	qal	wci	3ms	מלך	573		be king, reign
1: 45	ימת	qal	wci	3ms	מות	559		die
	ימלך	qal	wci	3ms	מלך	573		be king, reign
1: 46	ימת	qal	wci	3ms	מות	559		die
	ימלך	qal	wci	3ms	מלך	573		be king, reign
	מכה	hiph	ptc	ms	נכה	645		smite
1: 47	ימת	qal	wci	3ms	מות	559		die
	ימלך	qal	wci	3ms	מלך	573		be king, reign
1: 48	ימת	qal	wci	3ms	מות	559		die
	ימלך	qal	wci	3ms	מלך	573		be king, reign
1: 49	ימת	qal	wci	3ms	מות	559		die
	ימלך	qal	wci	3ms	מלך	573		be king, reign
1: 50	ימת	qal	wci	3ms	מות	559		die
	ימלך	qal	wci	3ms	מלך	573		be king, reign
1: 51	ימת	qal	wci	3ms	מות	559		die
	יהיו	qal	wci	3mp	היה	224		be, become
2: 3	נולד	niph	pft	3ms	ילד	408		be born
	יהי	qal	wci	3ms	היה	224		be, become
	ימיתהו	hiph	wci	3ms	מות	559	3ms	kill
2: 4	ילדה	qal	pft	3fs	ילד	408		bear, beget
2: 7	עוכר	qal	ptc	ms	עכר	747		trouble
	מעל	qal	pft	3ms	מעל	591		act faithlessly
2: 9	נולד	niph	pft	3ms	ילד	408		be born
2: 10	הוליד	hiph	pft	3ms	ילד	408		beget
	הוליד	hiph	pft	3ms	ילד	408		beget
2: 11	הוליד	hiph	pft	3ms	ילד	408		beget
	הוליד	hiph	pft	3ms	ילד	408		beget
2: 12	הוליד	hiph	pft	3ms	ילד	408		beget
	הוליד	hiph	pft	3ms	ילד	408		beget
2: 13	הוליד	hiph	pft	3ms	ילד	408		beget
2: 17	ילדה	qal	pft	3fs	ילד	408		bear, beget
2: 18	הוליד	hiph	pft	3ms	ילד	408		beget
2: 19	תמת	qal	wci	3fs	מות	559		die
	יקח	qal	wci	3ms	לקח	542		take
	תלד	qal	wci	3fs	ילד	408		bear, beget
2: 20	הוליד	hiph	pft	3ms	ילד	408		beget
	הוליד	hiph	pft	3ms	ילד	408		beget
2: 21	בא	qal	pft	3ms	בוא	97		come in
	לקחה	qal	pft	3ms	לקח	542	3fs	take
	תלד	qal	wci	3fs	ילד	408		bear, beget
2: 22	הוליד	hiph	pft	3ms	ילד	408		beget
	יהי	qal	wci	3ms	היה	224		be, become
2: 23	יקח	qal	wci	3ms	לקח	542		take
2: 24	תלד	qal	wci	3fs	ילד	408		bear, beget
2: 25	יהיו	qal	wci	3mp	היה	224		be, become
2: 26	תהי	qal	wci	3fs	היה	224		be, become
2: 27	יהיו	qal	wci	3mp	היה	224		be, become
2: 28	יהיו	qal	wci	3mp	היה	224		be, become
2: 29	תלד	qal	wci	3fs	ילד	408		bear, beget
2: 30	ימת	qal	wci	3ms	מות	559		die
2: 32	ימת	qal	wci	3ms	מות	559		die
2: 33	היו	qal	pft	3cp	היה	224		be, become
2: 34	היה	qal	pft	3ms	היה	224		be, become
2: 35	יתן	qal	wci	3ms	נתן	678		give, set
	תלד	qal	wci	3fs	ילד	408		bear, beget
2: 36	הליד	hiph	pft	3ms	ילד	408		beget
	הוליד	hiph	pft	3ms	ילד	408		beget
2: 37	הוליד	hiph	pft	3ms	ילד	408		beget
	הוליד	hiph	pft	3ms	ילד	408		beget
2: 38	הוליד	hiph	pft	3ms	ילד	408		beget
	הוליד	hiph	pft	3ms	ילד	408		beget
2: 39	הליד	hiph	pft	3ms	ילד	408		beget
	הליד	hiph	pft	3ms	ילד	408		beget
2: 40	הליד	hiph	pft	3ms	ילד	408		beget
	הליד	hiph	pft	3ms	ילד	408		beget
2: 41	הוליד	hiph	pft	3ms	ילד	408		beget
	הליד	hiph	pft	3ms	ילד	408		beget
2: 44	הוליד	hiph	pft	3ms	ילד	408		beget
	הוליד	hiph	pft	3ms	ילד	408		beget
2: 46	ילדה	qal	pft	3fs	ילד	408		bear, beget
	הליד	hiph	pft	3ms	ילד	408		beget
2: 48	ילד	qal	pft	3ms	ילד	408		bear, beget
2: 49	תלד	qal	wci	3fs	ילד	408		bear, beget
2: 50	היו	qal	pft	3cp	היה	224		be, become
2: 52	יהיו	qal	wci	3mp	היה	224		be, become
2: 53	יצאו	qal	pft	3cp	יצא	422		go out
2: 55	ישבוk	qal	pft	3cp	ישב	442		sit, dwell
	ישביq	qal	ptc	mp	ישב	442		sit, dwell
	באים	qal	ptc	mp	בוא	97		come in
3: 1	היו	qal	pft	3cp	היה	224		be, become
	נולד	niph	pft	3ms	ילד	408		be born
3: 4	נולד	niph	pft	3ms	ילד	408		be born
	ימלך	qal	wci	3ms	מלך	573		be king, reign
	מלך	qal	pft	3ms	מלך	573		be king, reign
3: 5	נולדו	niph	pft	3cp	ילד	408		be born
4: 2	הוליד	hiph	pft	3ms	ילד	408		beget
	הליד	hiph	pft	3ms	ילד	408		beget
4: 5	היו	qal	pft	3cp	היה	224		be, become
4: 6	תלד	qal	wci	3fs	ילד	408		bear, beget

ChVs	Form	Stem	Tnse	PGN	Root	BDB	Sfx	Meaning
4: 8	הוליד	hiph	pft	3ms	ילד	408		beget
4: 9	יהי	qal	wci	3ms	היה	224		be, become
	נכבד	niph	ptc	ms	כבד	457		be honored
	קראה	qal	pft	3fs	קרא	894		call, proclaim
	אמר	qal	infc		אמר	55		say
	ילדתי	qal	pft	1cs	ילד	408		bear, beget
4: 10	יקרא	qal	wci	3ms	קרא	894		call, proclaim
	אמר	qal	infc		אמר	55		say
	ברך	piel	infa		ברך	138		bless
	תברכני	piel	impf	2ms	ברך	138	1cs	bless
	הרבית	hiph	wcp	2ms	רבה	915		make many
	היתה	qal	wcp	3fs	היה	224		be, become
	עשית	qal	wcp	2ms	עשה	793		do, make
	עצבי	qal	infc		עצב	780	1cs	hurt, pain
	יבא	hiph	wci	3ms	בוא	97		bring in
	שאל	qal	pft	3ms	שאל	981		ask, borrow
4: 11	הוליד	hiph	pft	3ms	ילד	408		beget
4: 12	הוליד	hiph	pft	3ms	ילד	408		beget
4: 14	הוליד	hiph	pft	3ms	ילד	408		beget
	הוליד	hiph	pft	3ms	ילד	408		beget
	היו	qal	pft	3cp	היה	224		be, become
4: 17	תהר	qal	wci	3fs	הרה	247		conceive
4: 18	ילדה	qal	pft	3fs	ילד	408		bear, beget
	לקח	qal	pft	3ms	לקח	542		take
4: 22	בעלו	qal	pft	3cp	בעל	127		marry, rule over
4: 23	יוצרים	qal	ptc	mp	יצר	427		form, create
	ישבי	qal	ptc	mp	ישב	442		sit, dwell
	ישבו	qal	pft	3cp	ישב	442		sit, dwell
4: 27	הרבו	hiph	pft	3cp	רבה	915		make many
4: 28	ישבו	qal	wci	3mp	ישב	442		sit, dwell
4: 31	מלך	qal	infc		מלך	573		be king, reign
4: 33	התיחשם	hith	infc		יחש	405	3mp	be registered
4: 38	באים	qal	ptc	mp	בוא	97		come in
	פרצו	qal	pft	3cp	פרץ	829		break through
4: 39	ילכו	qal	wci	3mp	הלך	229		walk, go
	בקש	piel	infc		בקש	134		seek
4: 40	ימצאו	qal	wci	3mp	מצא	592		find
	שקטת	qal	ptc	fs	שקט	1052		be quiet
	ישבים	qal	ptc	mp	ישב	442		sit, dwell
4: 41	יבאו	qal	wci	3mp	בוא	97		come in
	כתובים	qal	pptc	mp	כתב	507		write
	יכו	hiph	wci	3mp	נכה	645		smite
	נמצאו	niph	pft	3cp	מצא	592		be found
	יחרימם	hiph	wci	3mp	חרם	355	3mp	ban, destroy
	ישבו	qal	wci	3mp	ישב	442		sit, dwell
4: 42	הלכו	qal	pft	3cp	הלך	229		walk, go
4: 43	יכו	hiph	wci	3mp	נכה	645		smite
	ישבו	qal	wci	3mp	ישב	442		sit, dwell
5: 1	חללו	piel	infc		חלל	320	3ms	pollute
	נתנה	niph	pft	3fs	נתן	678		be given
	התיחש	hith	infc		יחש	405		be registered
5: 2	גבר	qal	pft	3ms	גבר	149		be strong
5: 6	הגלה	hiph	pft	3ms	גלה	162		lead into exile
5: 7	התיחש	hith	infc		יחש	405		be registered

ChVs	Form	Stem	Tnse	PGN	Root	BDB	Sfx	Meaning
5: 8	יושב	qal	ptc	ms	ישב	442		sit, dwell
5: 9	ישב	qal	pft	3ms	ישב	442		sit, dwell
	בוא	qal	infc		בוא	97		come in
	רבו	qal	pft	3cp	רבה	915		be many, great
5: 10	עשו	qal	pft	3cp	עשה	793		do, make
	יפלו	qal	wci	3mp	נפל	656		fall
	ישבו	qal	wci	3mp	ישב	442		sit, dwell
5: 11	ישבו	qal	pft	3cp	ישב	442		sit, dwell
5: 16	ישבו	qal	wci	3mp	ישב	442		sit, dwell
5: 17	התיחשו	hith	pft	3cp	יחש	405		be registered
5: 18	נשאי	qal	ptc	mp	נשא	669		lift, carry
	דרכי	qal	ptc	mp	דרך	201		tread, march
	למודי	qal	pptc	mp	למד	540		learn
	יצאי	qal	ptc	mp	יצא	422		go out
5: 19	יעשו	qal	wci	3mp	עשה	793		do, make
5: 20	יעזרו	niph	wci	3mp	עזר	740		be helped
	ינתנו	niph	wci	3mp	נתן	678		be given
	זעקו	qal	pft	3cp	זעק	277		call, cry out
	נעתור	niph	infa		עתר	801		be supplicated
	בטחו	qal	pft	3cp	בטח	105		trust
5: 21	ישבו	qal	wci	3mp	שבה	985		take captive
5: 22	נפלו	qal	pft	3cp	נפל	656		fall
	ישבו	qal	wci	3mp	ישב	442		sit, dwell
5: 23	ישבו	qal	pft	3cp	ישב	442		sit, dwell
	רבו	qal	pft	3cp	רבה	915		be many, great
5: 25	ימעלו	qal	wci	3mp	מעל	591		act faithlessly
	יזנו	qal	wci	3mp	זנה	275		act a harlot
	השמיד	hiph	pft	3ms	שמד	1029		exterminate
5: 26	יער	hiph	wci	3ms	עור	734		rouse, stir up
	יגלם	hiph	wci	3ms	גלה	162	3mp	lead into exile
	יביאם	hiph	wci	3ms	בוא	97	3mp	bring in
5: 30	הוליד	hiph	pft	3ms	ילד	408		beget
	הליד	hiph	pft	3ms	ילד	408		beget
5: 31	הוליד	hiph	pft	3ms	ילד	408		beget
	הוליד	hiph	pft	3ms	ילד	408		beget
5: 32	הוליד	hiph	pft	3ms	ילד	408		beget
	הוליד	hiph	pft	3ms	ילד	408		beget
5: 33	הוליד	hiph	pft	3ms	ילד	408		beget
	הוליד	hiph	pft	3ms	ילד	408		beget
5: 34	הוליד	hiph	pft	3ms	ילד	408		beget
	הוליד	hiph	pft	3ms	ילד	408		beget
5: 35	הוליד	hiph	pft	3ms	ילד	408		beget
	הוליד	hiph	pft	3ms	ילד	408		beget
5: 36	הוליד	hiph	pft	3ms	ילד	408		beget
	כהן	piel	pft	3ms	כהן	464		act as priest
	בנה	qal	pft	3ms	בנה	124		build
5: 37	יולד	hiph	wci	3ms	ילד	408		beget
	הוליד	hiph	pft	3ms	ילד	408		beget
5: 38	הוליד	hiph	pft	3ms	ילד	408		beget
	הוליד	hiph	pft	3ms	ילד	408		beget
5: 39	הוליד	hiph	pft	3ms	ילד	408		beget
	הוליד	hiph	pft	3ms	ילד	408		beget
5: 40	הוליד	hiph	pft	3ms	ילד	408		beget
	הוליד	hiph	pft	3ms	ילד	408		beget

ChVs	Form	Stem	Tnse	PGN	Root	BDB	Sfx	Meaning
5: 41	הלך	qal	pft	3ms	הלך	229		walk,go
	הגלות	hiph	infc		גלה	162		lead into exile
6: 16	העמיד	hiph	pft	3ms	עמד	763		set up,raise
6: 17	יהיו	qal	wci	3mp	היה	224		be,become
	משׁרתים	piel	ptc	mp	שׁרת	1058		minister,serve
	בנות	qal	infc		בנה	124		build
	יעמדו	qal	wci	3mp	עמד	763		stand,stop
6: 18	עמדים	qal	ptc	mp	עמד	763		stand,stop
	משׁורר	pol	ptc	ms	שׁיר	1010		sing
6: 24	עמד	qal	ptc	ms	עמד	763		stand,stop
6: 33	נתונים	qal	pptc	mp	נתן	678		give,set
6: 34	מקטירים	hiph	ptc	mp	קטר	882		make sacrifices
	כפר	piel	infc		כפר	497		cover,atone
	צוה	piel	pft	3ms	צוה	845		command
6: 39	היה	qal	pft	3ms	היה	224		be,become
6: 40	יתנו	qal	wci	3mp	נתן	678		give,set
6: 41	נתנו	qal	pft	3cp	נתן	678		give,set
6: 42	נתנו	qal	pft	3cp	נתן	678		give,set
6: 46	נותרים	niph	ptc	mp	יתר	451		be left,remain
6: 49	יתנו	qal	wci	3mp	נתן	678		give,set
6: 50	יתנו	qal	wci	3mp	נתן	678		give,set
	יקראו	qal	impf	3mp	קרא	894		call,proclaim
6: 51	יהי	qal	wci	3ms	היה	224		be,become
6: 52	יתנו	qal	wci	3mp	נתן	678		give,set
6: 55	נותרים	niph	ptc	mp	יתר	451		be left,remain
6: 62	נותרים	niph	ptc	mp	יתר	451		be left,remain
7: 4	הרבו	hiph	pft	3cp	רבה	915		make many
7: 5	התיחשׂם	hith	infc		יחשׂ	405	3mp	be registered
7: 7	התיחשׂם	hith	infc		יחשׂ	405	3mp	be registered
7: 9	התיחשׂם	hith	infc		יחשׂ	405	3mp	be registered
7: 11	יצאי	qal	ptc	mp	יצא	422		go out
7: 14	ילדה	qal	pft	3fs	ילד	408		bear,beget
	ילדה	qal	pft	3fs	ילד	408		bear,beget
7: 15	לקח	qal	pft	3ms	לקח	542		take
	תהינה	qal	wci	3fp	היה	224		be,become
7: 16	תלד	qal	wci	3fs	ילד	408		bear,beget
	תקרא	qal	wci	3fs	קרא	894		call,proclaim
7: 18	ילדה	qal	pft	3fs	ילד	408		bear,beget
7: 19	יהיו	qal	wci	3mp	היה	224		be,become
7: 21	הרגום	qal	pft	3cp	הרג	246	3mp	kill
	נולדים	niph	ptc	mp	ילד	408		be born
	ירדו	qal	pft	3cp	ירד	432		come down
	קחת	qal	infc		לקח	542		take
7: 22	יתאבל	hith	wci	3ms	אבל	5		mourn
	יבאו	qal	wci	3mp	בוא	97		come in
	נחמו	piel	infc		נחם	636	3ms	comfort
7: 23	יבא	qal	wci	3ms	בוא	97		come in
	תהר	qal	wci	3fs	הרה	247		conceive
	תלד	qal	wci	3fs	ילד	408		bear,beget
	יקרא	qal	wci	3ms	קרא	894		call,proclaim
	היתה	qal	pft	3fs	היה	224		be,become
7: 24	תבן	qal	wci	3fs	בנה	124		build
7: 29	ישׁבו	qal	pft	3cp	ישׁב	442		sit,dwell
7: 32	הוליד	hiph	pft	3ms	ילד	408		beget
7: 40	ברורים	qal	pptc	mp	ברר	140		purify,polish
	התיחשׂם	hith	infc		יחשׂ	405	3mp	be registered
8: 1	הוליד	hiph	pft	3ms	ילד	408		beget
8: 3	יהיו	qal	wci	3mp	היה	224		be,become
8: 6	יושׁבי	qal	ptc	mp	ישׁב	442		sit,dwell
	יגלום	hiph	wci	3mp	גלה	162	3mp	lead into exile
8: 7	הגלם	hiph	pft	3ms	גלה	162	3mp	lead into exile
	הוליד	hiph	pft	3ms	ילד	408		beget
8: 8	הוליד	hiph	pft	3ms	ילד	408		beget
	שׁלחו	piel	infc		שׁלח	1018	3ms	send away,shoot
8: 9	יולד	hiph	wci	3ms	ילד	408		beget
8: 11	הוליד	hiph	pft	3ms	ילד	408		beget
8: 12	בנה	qal	pft	3ms	בנה	124		build
8: 13	יושׁבי	qal	ptc	mp	ישׁב	442		sit,dwell
	הבריחו	hiph	pft	3cp	ברח	137		cause to flee
	יושׁבי	qal	ptc	mp	ישׁב	442		sit,dwell
8: 28	ישׁבו	qal	pft	3cp	ישׁב	442		sit,dwell
8: 29	ישׁבו	qal	pft	3cp	ישׁב	442		sit,dwell
8: 32	הוליד	hiph	pft	3ms	ילד	408		beget
	ישׁבו	qal	pft	3cp	ישׁב	442		sit,dwell
8: 33	הוליד	hiph	pft	3ms	ילד	408		beget
	הוליד	hiph	pft	3ms	ילד	408		beget
	הוליד	hiph	pft	3ms	ילד	408		beget
8: 34	הוליד	hiph	pft	3ms	ילד	408		beget
8: 36	הוליד	hiph	pft	3ms	ילד	408		beget
	הוליד	hiph	pft	3ms	ילד	408		beget
	הוליד	hiph	pft	3ms	ילד	408		beget
8: 37	הוליד	hiph	pft	3ms	ילד	408		beget
8: 40	יהיו	qal	wci	3mp	היה	224		be,become
	דרכי	qal	ptc	mp	דרך	201		tread,march
	מרבים	hiph	ptc	mp	רבה	915		make many
9: 1	התיחשׂו	hith	pft	3cp	יחשׂ	405		be registered
	כתובים	qal	pptc	mp	כתב	507		write
	הגלו	hoph	pft	3cp	גלה	162		led into exile
9: 2	יושׁבים	qal	ptc	mp	ישׁב	442		sit,dwell
9: 3	ישׁבו	qal	pft	3cp	ישׁב	442		sit,dwell
9: 16	יושׁב	qal	ptc	ms	ישׁב	442		sit,dwell
9: 19	שׁמרי	qal	ptc	mp	שׁמר	1036		keep,watch
	שׁמרי	qal	ptc	mp	שׁמר	1036		keep,watch
9: 20	היה	qal	pft	3ms	היה	224		be,become
9: 22	ברורים	qal	pptc	mp	ברר	140		purify,polish
	התיחשׂם	hith	infc		יחשׂ	405	3mp	be registered
	יסד	piel	pft	3ms	יסד	413		found,establish
9: 24	יהיו	qal	impf	3mp	היה	224		be,become
9: 25	בוא	qal	infc		בוא	97		come in
9: 26	היו	qal	wcp	3cp	היה	224		be,become
9: 27	ילינו	qal	impf	3mp	לון	533		lodge,remain
9: 28	יביאום	hiph	impf	3mp	בוא	97	3mp	bring in
	יוציאום	hiph	impf	3mp	יצא	422	3mp	bring out
9: 29	ממנים	pual	ptc	mp	מנה	584		be appointed
9: 30	רקחי	qal	ptc	mp	רקח	955		mix,compound
9: 32	הכין	hiph	infc		כון	465		fix,prepare
9: 33	משׁררים	pol	ptc	mp	שׁיר	1010		sing
	פטוריםq	qal	pptc	mp	פטר	809		remove,set free

ChVs	Form	Stem	Tnse	PGN	Root	BDB	Sfx	Meaning
9:34	ישׁבו	qal	pft	3cp	ישׁב	442		sit,dwell
9:35	ישׁבו	qal	pft	3cp	ישׁב	442		sit,dwell
9:38	הוליד	hiph	pft	3ms	ילד	408		beget
	ישׁבו	qal	pft	3cp	ישׁב	442		sit,dwell
9:39	הוליד	hiph	pft	3ms	ילד	408		beget
	הוליד	hiph	pft	3ms	ילד	408		beget
	הוליד	hiph	pft	3ms	ילד	408		beget
9:40	הוליד	hiph	pft	3ms	ילד	408		beget
9:42	הוליד	hiph	pft	3ms	ילד	408		beget
	הוליד	hiph	pft	3ms	ילד	408		beget
	הוליד	hiph	pft	3ms	ילד	408		beget
9:43	הוליד	hiph	pft	3ms	ילד	408		beget
10:1	נלחמו	niph	pft	3cp	לחם	535		wage war
	ינס	qal	wci	3ms	נוס	630		flee,escape
	יפלו	qal	wci	3mp	נפל	656		fall
10:2	ידבקו	hiph	wci	3mp	דבק	179		cause to cling
	יכו	hiph	wci	3mp	נכה	645		smite
10:3	תכבד	qal	wci	3fs	כבד	457		be heavy
	ימצאהו	qal	wci	3mp	מצא	592	3ms	find
	מורים	hiph	ptc	mp	ירה	434		shoot,teach
	יחל	qal	wci	3ms	חול	296		dance,writhe
	יורים	qal	ptc	mp	ירה	434		throw,shoot
10:4	יאמר	qal	wci	3ms	אמר	55		say
	נשׂא	qal	ptc	ms	נשׂא	669		lift,carry
	שׁלף	qal	impv	ms	שׁלף	1025		draw out,off
	דקרני	qal	impv	ms	דקר	201	1cs	pierce
	יבאו	qal	impf	3mp	בוא	97		come in
	התעללו	hith	wcp	3cp	עלל	759		busy,vex
	אבה	qal	pft	3ms	אבה	2		be willing
	נשׂא	qal	ptc	ms	נשׂא	669		lift,carry
	ירא	qal	pft	3ms	ירא	431		fear
	יקח	qal	wci	3ms	לקח	542		take
	יפל	qal	wci	3ms	נפל	656		fall
10:5	ירא	qal	wci	3ms	ראה	906		see
	נשׂא	qal	ptc	ms	נשׂא	669		lift,carry
	מת	qal	pft	3ms	מות	559		die
	יפל	qal	wci	3ms	נפל	656		fall
	ימת	qal	wci	3ms	מות	559		die
10:6	ימת	qal	wci	3ms	מות	559		die
	מתו	qal	pft	3cp	מות	559		die
10:7	יראו	qal	wci	3mp	ראה	906		see
	נסו	qal	pft	3cp	נוס	630		flee,escape
	מתו	qal	pft	3cp	מות	559		die
	יעזבו	qal	wci	3mp	עזב	736		leave,loose
	ינסו	qal	wci	3mp	נוס	630		flee,escape
	יבאו	qal	wci	3mp	בוא	97		come in
	ישׁבו	qal	wci	3mp	ישׁב	442		sit,dwell
10:8	יהי	qal	wci	3ms	היה	224		be,become
	יבאו	qal	wci	3mp	בוא	97		come in
	פשׁט	piel	infc		פשׁט	832		strip
	ימצאו	qal	wci	3mp	מצא	592		find
	נפלים	qal	ptc	mp	נפל	656		fall
10:9	יפשׁיטהו	hiph	wci	3mp	פשׁט	832	3ms	strip off
	ישׂאו	qal	wci	3mp	נשׂא	669		lift,carry
10:9	ישׁלחו	piel	wci	3mp	שׁלח	1018		send away,shoot
	בשׂר	piel	infc		בשׂר	142		bear tidings
10:10	ישׂימו	qal	wci	3mp	שׂים	962		put,set
	תקעו	qal	pft	3cp	תקע	1075		thrust,clap
10:11	ישׁמעו	qal	wci	3mp	שׁמע	1033		hear
	עשׂו	qal	pft	3cp	עשׂה	793		do,make
10:12	יקומו	qal	wci	3mp	קום	877		arise,stand
	ישׂאו	qal	wci	3mp	נשׂא	669		lift,carry
	יביאום	hiph	wci	3mp	בוא	97	3mp	bring in
	יקברו	qal	wci	3mp	קבר	868		bury
	יצומו	qal	wci	3mp	צום	847		fast
10:13	ימת	qal	wci	3ms	מות	559		die
	מעל	qal	pft	3ms	מעל	591		act faithlessly
	שׁמר	qal	pft	3ms	שׁמר	1036		keep,watch
	שׁאול	qal	infc		שׁאל	981		ask,borrow
	דרושׁ	qal	infc		דרשׁ	205		resort to,seek
10:14	דרשׁ	qal	pft	3ms	דרשׁ	205		resort to,seek
	ימיתהו	hiph	wci	3ms	מות	559	3ms	kill
	יסב	hiph	wci	3ms	סבב	685		cause to turn
11:1	יקבצו	niph	wci	3mp	קבץ	867		assemble,gather
	אמר	qal	infc		אמר	55		say
11:2	היות	qal	infc		היה	224		be,become
	מוציא	hiph	ptc	ms	יצא	422		bring out
	מביא	hiph	ptc	ms	בוא	97		bring in
	יאמר	qal	wci	3ms	אמר	55		say
	תרעה	qal	impf	2ms	רעה	944		pasture,tend
	תהיה	qal	impf	2ms	היה	224		be,become
11:3	יבאו	qal	wci	3mp	בוא	97		come in
	יכרת	qal	wci	3ms	כרת	503		cut,destroy
	ימשׁחו	qal	wci	3mp	משׁח	602		smear,anoint
11:4	ילך	qal	wci	3ms	הלך	229		walk,go
	ישׁבי	qal	ptc	mp	ישׁב	442		sit,dwell
11:5	יאמרו	qal	wci	3mp	אמר	55		say
	ישׁבי	qal	ptc	mp	ישׁב	442		sit,dwell
	תבוא	qal	impf	2ms	בוא	97		come in
	ילכד	qal	wci	3ms	לכד	539		capture
11:6	יאמר	qal	wci	3ms	אמר	55		say
	מכה	hiph	ptc	ms	נכה	645		smite
	יהיה	qal	impf	3ms	היה	224		be,become
	יעל	qal	wci	3ms	עלה	748		go up
	יהי	qal	wci	3ms	היה	224		be,become
11:7	ישׁב	qal	wci	3ms	ישׁב	442		sit,dwell
	קראו	qal	pft	3cp	קרא	894		call,proclaim
11:8	יבן	qal	wci	3ms	בנה	124		build
	יחיה	piel	impf	3ms	חיה	310		preserve,revive
11:9	ילך	qal	wci	3ms	הלך	229		walk,go
	הלוך	qal	infa		הלך	229		walk,go
	גדול	qal	infa		גדל	152		be great,grow
11:10	מתחזקים	hith	ptc	mp	חזק	304		strengthen self
	המליכו	hiph	infc		מלך	573	3ms	cause to reign
11:11	עורר	pol	pft	3ms	עור	734		rouse,incite
11:13	היה	qal	pft	3ms	היה	224		be,become
	נאספו	niph	pft	3cp	אסף	62		assemble
	תהי	qal	wci	3fs	היה	224		be,become

ChVs	Form	Stem	Tnse	PGN	Root	BDB	Sfx	Meaning
11:13	נסו	qal	pft	3cp	נוס	630		flee,escape
11:14	יתיצבו	hith	wci	3mp	יצב	426		stand oneself
	יצילוה	hiph	wci	3mp	נצל	664	3fs	snatch,deliver
	יכו	hiph	wci	3mp	נכה	645		smite
	יושע	hiph	wci	3ms	ישע	446		deliver,save
11:15	ירדו	qal	wci	3mp	ירד	432		come down
	חנה	qal	ptc	fs	חנה	333		decline,encamp
11:17	איתאוk	hith	wci	3ms	אוה	16		desire
	יתאיוq	hith	wci	3ms	אוה	16?		desire
	יאמר	qal	wci	3ms	אמר	55		say
	ישקני	hiph	impf	3ms	שקה	1052	1cs	give to drink
11:18	יבקעו	qal	wci	3mp	בקע	131		cleave,break
	ישאבו	qal	wci	3mp	שאב	980		draw (water)
	ישאו	qal	wci	3mp	נשא	669		lift,carry
	יבאו	hiph	wci	3mp	בוא	97		bring in
	אבה	qal	pft	3ms	אבה	2		be willing
	שתותם	qal	infc		שתה	1059	3mp	drink
	ינסך	piel	wci	3ms	נסך	650		pour out
11:19	יאמר	qal	wci	3ms	אמר	55		say
	עשות	qal	infc		עשה	793		do,make
	אשתה	qal	impf	1cs	שתה	1059		drink
	הביאום	hiph	pft	3cp	בוא	97	3mp	bring in
	אבה	qal	pft	3ms	אבה	2		be willing
	שתותם	qal	infc		שתה	1059	3mp	drink
	עשו	qal	pft	3cp	עשה	793		do,make
11:20	היה	qal	pft	3ms	היה	224		be,become
	עורר	pol	pft	3ms	עור	734		rouse,incite
11:21	נכבד	niph	ptc	ms	כבד	457		be honored
	יהי	qal	wci	3ms	היה	224		be,become
	בא	qal	pft	3ms	בוא	97		come in
11:22	הכה	hiph	pft	3ms	נכה	645		smite
	ירד	qal	pft	3ms	ירד	432		come down
	הכה	hiph	pft	3ms	נכה	645		smite
11:23	הכה	hiph	pft	3ms	נכה	645		smite
	ארגים	qal	ptc	mp	ארג	70		weave
	ירד	qal	wci	3ms	ירד	432		come down
	יגזל	qal	wci	3ms	גזל	159		tear away,rob
	יהרגהו	qal	wci	3ms	הרג	246	3ms	kill
11:24	עשה	qal	pft	3ms	עשה	793		do,make
11:25	נכבד	niph	ptc	ms	כבד	457		be honored
	בא	qal	pft	3ms	בוא	97		come in
	ישימהו	qal	wci	3ms	שים	962	3ms	put,set
11:39	נשא	qal	ptc	ms	נשא	669		lift,carry
12:1	באים	qal	ptc	mp	בוא	97		come in
	עצור	qal	pptc	ms	עצר	783		restrain
	עזרי	qal	ptc	mp	עזר	740		help,aid
12:2	נשקי	qal	ptc	mp	נשק	676		be armed with
	מימינים	hiph	ptc	mp	ימן	412		go to right
	משמאלים	hiph	ptc	mp	שמאל	970		go to left
12:9	נבדלו	niph	pft	3cp	בדל	95		separate self
	ערכי	qal	ptc	mp	ערך	789		set in order
	מהר	piel	infc		מהר	554		hasten
12:16	עברו	qal	pft	3cp	עבר	716		pass over
	ממלא	piel	ptc	ms	מלא	569		fill
12:16	יבריחו	hiph	wci	3mp	ברח	137		cause to flee
12:17	יבאו	qal	wci	3mp	בוא	97		come in
12:18	יצא	qal	wci	3ms	יצא	422		go out
	יען	qal	wci	3ms	ענה	772		answer
	יאמר	qal	wci	3ms	אמר	55		say
	באתם	qal	pft	2mp	בוא	97		come in
	עזרני	qal	infc		עזר	740	1cs	help,aid
	יהיה	qal	impf	3ms	היה	224		be,become
	רמותני	piel	infc		רמה	941	1cs	beguile
	ירא	qal	jus	3ms	ראה	906		see
	יוכח	hiph	jus	3ms	יכח	406		decide,reprove
12:19	לבשה	qal	pft	3fs	לבש	527		put on,clothe
	עזרך	qal	ptc	ms	עזר	740	2ms	help,aid
	עזרך	qal	pft	3ms	עזר	740	2ms	help,aid
	יקבלם	piel	wci	3ms	קבל	867	3mp	take,receive
	יתנם	qal	wci	3ms	נתן	678	3mp	give,set
12:20	נפלו	qal	pft	3cp	נפל	656		fall
	באו	qal	infc		בוא	97	3ms	come in
	עזרם	qal	pft	3cp	עזר	740	3mp	help,aid
	שלחהו	piel	pft	3cp	שלח	1018	3ms	send away,shoot
	אמר	qal	infc		אמר	55		say
	יפול	qal	impf	3ms	נפל	656		fall
12:21	לכתו	qal	infc		הלך	229	3ms	walk,go
	נפלו	qal	pft	3cp	נפל	656		fall
12:22	עזרו	qal	pft	3cp	עזר	740		help,aid
	יהיו	qal	wci	3mp	היה	224		be,become
12:23	יבאו	qal	impf	3mp	בוא	97		come in
	עזרו	qal	infc		עזר	740	3ms	help,aid
12:24	חלוץ	qal	pptc	ms	חלץ	323		equipped
	באו	qal	pft	3cp	בוא	97		come in
	הסב	hiph	infc		סבב	685		cause to turn
12:25	נשאי	qal	ptc	mp	נשא	669		lift,carry
	חלוצי	qal	pptc	mp	חלץ	323		equipped
12:30	שמרים	qal	ptc	mp	שמר	1036		keep,watch
12:32	נקבו	niph	pft	3cp	נקב	666		be marked
	בוא	qal	infc		בוא	97		come in
	המליך	hiph	infc		מלך	573		cause to reign
12:33	יודעי	qal	ptc	mp	ידע	393		know
	דעת	qal	infc		ידע	393		know
	יעשה	qal	impf	3ms	עשה	793		do,make
12:34	יוצאי	qal	ptc	mp	יצא	422		go out
	ערכי	qal	ptc	mp	ערך	789		set in order
	עדר	qal	infc		עדר	727		help
12:36	ערכי	qal	ptc	mp	ערך	789		set in order
12:37	יוצאי	qal	ptc	mp	יצא	422		go out
	ערך	qal	infc		ערך	789		set in order
12:39	עדרי	qal	ptc	mp	עדר	727		help
	באו	qal	pft	3cp	בוא	97		come in
	המליך	hiph	infc		מלך	573		cause to reign
	המליך	hiph	infc		מלך	573		cause to reign
12:40	יהיו	qal	wci	3mp	היה	224		be,become
	אכלים	qal	ptc	mp	אכל	37		eat,devour
	שותים	qal	ptc	mp	שתה	1059		drink
	הכינו	hiph	pft	3cp	כון	465		fix,prepare

ChVs	Form	Stem	Tnse	PGN	Root	BDB	Sfx	Meaning
12:41	מביאים	hiph	ptc	mp	בוא	97		bring in
13:1	יועץ	niph	wci	3ms	יעץ	419		consult
13:2	יאמר	qal	wci	3ms	אמר	55		say
	טוב	qal	pft	3ms	טוב	373		be pleasing
	נפרצה	qal	coh	1cp	פרץ	829		break through
	נשלחה	qal	coh	1cp	שלח	1018		send
	נשארים	niph	ptc	mp	שאר	983		be left
	יקבצו	niph	jusm	3mp	קבץ	867		assemble, gather
13:3	נסבה	hiph	coh	1cp	סבב	685		cause to turn
	דרשנהו	qal	pft	1cp	דרש	205	3ms	resort to, seek
13:4	יאמרו	qal	wci	3mp	אמר	55		say
	עשות	qal	infc		עשה	793		do, make
	ישר	qal	pft	3ms	ישר	448		be straight
13:5	יקהל	hiph	wci	3ms	קהל	874		call assembly
	בוא	qal	infc		בוא	97		come in
	הביא	hiph	infc		בוא	97		bring in
13:6	יעל	qal	wci	3ms	עלה	748		go up
	העלות	hiph	infc		עלה	748		bring up, offer
	יושב	qal	ptc	ms	ישב	442		sit, dwell
	נקרא	niph	pft	3ms	קרא	894		be called
13:7	ירכיבו	hiph	wci	3mp	רכב	938		cause to ride
	נהגים	qal	ptc	mp	נהג	624		drive
13:8	משחקים	piel	ptc	mp	שחק	965		make sport
13:9	יבאו	qal	wci	3mp	בוא	97		come in
	ישלח	qal	wci	3ms	שלח	1018		send
	אחז	qal	infc		אחז	28		grasp
	שמטו	qal	pft	3cp	שמט	1030		let drop
13:10	יחר	qal	wci	3ms	חרה	354		be kindled, burn
	יכהו	hiph	wci	3ms	נכה	645	3ms	smite
	שלח	qal	pft	3ms	שלח	1018		send
	ימת	qal	wci	3ms	מות	559		die
13:11	יחר	qal	wci	3ms	חרה	354		be kindled, burn
	פרץ	qal	pft	3ms	פרץ	829		break through
	יקרא	qal	wci	3ms	קרא	894		call, proclaim
13:12	יירא	qal	wci	3ms	ירא	431		fear
	אמר	qal	infc		אמר	55		say
	אביא	hiph	impf	1cs	בוא	97		bring in
13:13	הסיר	hiph	pft	3ms	סור	693		take away
	יטהו	hiph	wci	3ms	נטה	639	3ms	turn, incline
13:14	ישב	qal	wci	3ms	ישב	442		sit, dwell
	יברך	piel	wci	3ms	ברך	138		bless
14:1	ישלח	qal	wci	3ms	שלח	1018		send
	בנות	qal	infc		בנה	124		build
14:2	ידע	qal	wci	3ms	ידע	393		know
	הכינו	hiph	pft	3ms	כון	465	3ms	fix, prepare
	נשאת	niph	pft	3fs	נשא	669		be lifted up
14:3	יקח	qal	wci	3ms	לקח	542		take
	יולד	hiph	wci	3ms	ילד	408		beget
14:4	ילודים	qal	pptc	mp	ילד	408		bear, beget
	היו	qal	pft	3cp	היה	224		be, become
14:8	ישמעו	qal	wci	3mp	שמע	1033		hear
	נמשח	niph	pft	3ms	משח	602		be anointed
	יעלו	qal	wci	3mp	עלה	748		go up
	בקש	piel	infc		בקש	134		seek
14:8	ישמע	qal	wci	3ms	שמע	1033		hear
	יצא	qal	wci	3ms	יצא	422		go out
14:9	באו	qal	pft	3cp	בוא	97		come in
	יפשטו	qal	wci	3mp	פשט	832		strip off
14:10	ישאל	qal	wci	3ms	שאל	981		ask, borrow
	אמר	qal	infc		אמר	55		say
	אעלה	qal	impf	1cs	עלה	748		go up
	נתתם	qal	wcp	2ms	נתן	678	3mp	give, set
	יאמר	qal	wci	3ms	אמר	55		say
	עלה	qal	impv	ms	עלה	748		go up
	נתתים	qal	wcp	1cs	נתן	678	3mp	give, set
14:11	יעלו	qal	wci	3mp	עלה	748		go up
	יכם	hiph	wci	3ms	נכה	645	3mp	smite
	יאמר	qal	wci	3ms	אמר	55		say
	פרץ	qal	pft	3ms	פרץ	829		break through
	אויבי	qal	ptc	mp	איב	33	1cs	be hostile to
	קראו	qal	pft	3cp	קרא	894		call, proclaim
14:12	יעזבו	qal	wci	3mp	עזב	736		leave, loose
	יאמר	qal	wci	3ms	אמר	55		say
	ישרפו	niph	wci	3mp	שרף	976		be burned
14:13	יסיפו	hiph	wci	3mp	יסף	414		add, do again
	יפשטו	qal	wci	3mp	פשט	832		strip off
14:14	ישאל	qal	wci	3ms	שאל	981		ask, borrow
	יאמר	qal	wci	3ms	אמר	55		say
	תעלה	qal	impf	2ms	עלה	748		go up
	הסב	hiph	impv	ms	סבב	685		cause to turn
	באת	qal	wcp	2ms	בוא	97		come in
14:15	יהי	qal	jus	3ms	היה	224		be, become
	שמעך	qal	infc		שמע	1033	2ms	hear
	תצא	qal	impf	2ms	יצא	422		go out
	יצא	qal	pft	3ms	יצא	422		go out
	הכות	hiph	infc		נכה	645		smite
14:16	יעש	qal	wci	3ms	עשה	793		do, make
	צוהו	piel	pft	3ms	צוה	845	3ms	command
	יכו	hiph	wci	3mp	נכה	645		smite
14:17	יצא	qal	wci	3ms	יצא	422		go out
	נתן	qal	pft	3ms	נתן	678		give, set
15:1	יעש	qal	wci	3ms	עשה	793		do, make
	יכן	hiph	wci	3ms	כון	465		fix, prepare
	יט	qal	wci	3ms	נטה	639		stretch, incline
15:2	אמר	qal	pft	3ms	אמר	55		say
	שאת	qal	infc		נשא	669		lift, carry
	בחר	qal	pft	3ms	בחר	103		choose
	שאת	qal	infc		נשא	669		lift, carry
	שרתו	piel	infc		שרת	1058	3ms	minister, serve
15:3	יקהל	hiph	wci	3ms	קהל	874		call assembly
	העלות	hiph	infc		עלה	748		bring up, offer
	הכין	hiph	pft	3ms	כון	465		fix, prepare
15:4	יאסף	qal	wci	3ms	אסף	62		gather
15:11	יקרא	qal	wci	3ms	קרא	894		call, proclaim
15:12	יאמר	qal	wci	3ms	אמר	55		say
	התקדשו	hith	impv	mp	קדש	872		consecrate self
	העליתם	hiph	wcp	2mp	עלה	748		bring up, offer
	הכינותי	hiph	pft	1cs	כון	465		fix, prepare

ChVs	Form	Stem	Tnse	PGN	Root	BDB	Sfx	Meaning
15:13	פרץ	qal	pft	3ms	פרץ	829		break through
	דרשנהו	qal	pft	1cp	דרש	205	3ms	resort to,seek
15:14	יתקדשו	hith	wci	3mp	קדש	872		consecrate self
	העלות	hiph	infc		עלה	748		bring up,offer
15:15	ישאו	qal	wci	3mp	נשא	669		lift,carry
	צוה	piel	pft	3ms	צוה	845		command
15:16	יאמר	qal	wci	3ms	אמר	55		say
	העמיד	hiph	infc		עמד	763		set up,raise
	משררים	pol	ptc	mp	שיר	1010		sing
	משמיעים	hiph	ptc	mp	שמע	1033		cause to hear
	הרים	hiph	infc		רום	926		raise,lift
15:17	יעמידו	hiph	wci	3mp	עמד	763		set up,raise
15:19	משררים	pol	ptc	mp	שיר	1010		sing
	השמיע	hiph	infc		שמע	1033		cause to hear
15:21	נצח	piel	infc		נצח	663		act as director
15:22	יסר	qal	infa		יסר	415		discipline
	מבין	hiph	ptc	ms	בין	106		understand
15:24	מחצצריםk	hiph	ptc	mp	חצצר	348		sound w/clarion
	qמחצרים	hiph	ptc	mp	חצר	348		sound w/clarion
15:25	יהי	qal	wci	3ms	היה	224		be,become
	הלכים	qal	ptc	mp	הלך	229		walk,go
	העלות	hiph	infc		עלה	748		bring up,offer
15:26	יהי	qal	wci	3ms	היה	224		be,become
	עזר	qal	infc		עזר	740		help,aid
	נשאי	qal	ptc	mp	נשא	669		lift,carry
	יזבחו	qal	wci	3mp	זבח	256		slaughter
15:27	מכרבל	pual	ptc	ms	כרבל	499		be clothed
	נשאים	qal	ptc	mp	נשא	669		lift,carry
	משררים	pol	ptc	mp	שיר	1010		sing
	משררים	pol	ptc	mp	שיר	1010		sing
15:28	מעלים	hiph	ptc	mp	עלה	748		bring up,offer
	משמעים	hiph	ptc	mp	שמע	1033		cause to hear
15:29	יהי	qal	wci	3ms	היה	224		be,become
	בא	qal	ptc	ms	בוא	97		come in
	נשקפה	niph	pft	3fs	שקף	1054		look down
	תרא	qal	wci	3fs	ראה	906		see
	מרקד	piel	ptc	ms	רקד	955		leap,dance
	משחק	piel	ptc	ms	שחק	965		make sport
	תבז	qal	wci	3fs	בזה	102		despise
16:1	יביאו	hiph	wci	3mp	בוא	97		bring in
	יציגו	hiph	wci	3mp	יצג	426		place,establish
	נטה	qal	pft	3ms	נטה	639		stretch,incline
	יקריבו	hiph	wci	3mp	קרב	897		bring near
16:2	יכל	piel	wci	3ms	כלה	477		complete,finish
	העלות	hiph	infc		עלה	748		bring up,offer
	יברך	piel	wci	3ms	ברך	138		bless
16:3	יחלק	piel	wci	3ms	חלק	323		divide
16:4	יתן	qal	wci	3ms	נתן	678		give,set
	משרתים	piel	ptc	mp	שרת	1058		minister,serve
	הזכיר	hiph	infc		זכר	269		c. to remember
	הודות	hiph	infc		ידה	392		praise
	הלל	piel	infc		הלל	237		praise
16:5	משמיע	hiph	ptc	ms	שמע	1033		cause to hear
16:7	נתן	qal	pft	3ms	נתן	678		give,set
16:7	הדות	hiph	infc		ידה	392		praise
16:8	הודו	hiph	impv	mp	ידה	392		praise
	קראו	qal	impv	mp	קרא	894		call,proclaim
	הודיעו	hiph	impv	mp	ידע	393		declare
16:9	שירו	qal	impv	mp	שיר	1010		sing
	זמרו	piel	impv	mp	זמר	274		make music
	שיחו	qal	impv	mp	שיח	967		muse,complain
	נפלאתיו	niph	ptc	fp	פלא	810	3ms	be wonderful
16:10	התהללו	hith	impv	mp	הלל	237		glory
	ישמח	qal	jusm	3ms	שמח	970		rejoice
	מבקשי	piel	ptc	mp	בקש	134		seek
16:11	דרשו	qal	impv	mp	דרש	205		resort to,seek
	בקשו	piel	impv	mp	בקש	134		seek
16:12	זכרו	qal	impv	mp	זכר	269		remember
	נפלאתיו	niph	ptc	fp	פלא	810	3ms	be wonderful
	עשה	qal	pft	3ms	עשה	793		do,make
16:15	זכרו	qal	impv	mp	זכר	269		remember
	צוה	piel	pft	3ms	צוה	845		command
16:16	כרת	qal	pft	3ms	כרת	503		cut,destroy
16:17	יעמידה	hiph	wci	3ms	עמד	763	3fs	set up,raise
16:18	אמר	qal	infc		אמר	55		say
	אתן	qal	impf	1cs	נתן	678		give,set
16:19	היותכם	qal	infc		היה	224	2mp	be,become
	גרים	qal	ptc	mp	גור	157		sojourn
16:20	יתהלכו	hith	wci	3mp	הלך	229		walk to and fro
16:21	הניח	hiph	pft	3ms	נוח	628		give rest,put
	עשקם	qal	infc		עשק	798	3mp	oppress,extort
	יוכח	hiph	wci	3ms	יכח	406		decide,reprove
16:22	תגעו	qal	jusm	2mp	נגע	619		touch,strike
	תרעו	hiph	jusm	2mp	רעע	949		hurt,do evil
16:23	שירו	qal	impv	mp	שיר	1010		sing
	בשרו	piel	impv	mp	בשר	142		bear tidings
16:24	ספרו	piel	impv	mp	ספר	707		recount
	נפלאתיו	niph	ptc	fp	פלא	810	3ms	be wonderful
16:25	מהלל	pual	ptc	ms	הלל	237		be praised
	נורא	niph	ptc	ms	ירא	431		be feared
16:26	עשה	qal	pft	3ms	עשה	793		do,make
16:28	הבו	qal	impv	mp	יהב	396		give
	הבו	qal	impv	mp	יהב	396		give
16:29	הבו	qal	impv	mp	יהב	396		give
	שאו	qal	impv	mp	נשא	669		lift,carry
	באו	qal	impv	mp	בוא	97		come in
	השתחוו	hish	impv	mp	חוה	1005		bow down
16:30	חילו	qal	impv	mp	חול	296		dance,writhe
	תכון	niph	impf	3fs	כון	465		be established
	תמוט	niph	impf	3fs	מוט	556		be shaken
16:31	ישמחו	qal	jusm	3mp	שמח	970		rejoice
	תגל	qal	jus	3fs	גיל	162		rejoice
	יאמרו	qal	jusm	3mp	אמר	55		say
	מלך	qal	pft	3ms	מלך	573		be king,reign
16:32	ירעם	qal	jusm	3ms	רעם	947		thunder
	יעלץ	qal	jusm	3ms	עלץ	763		rejoice,exult
16:33	ירננו	piel	impf	3mp	רנן	943		shout w/joy
	בא	qal	ptc	ms	בוא	97		come in

ChVs	Form	Stem	Tnse	PGN	Root	BDB	Sfx	Meaning
16:33	שפוט	qal	infc		שפט	1047		judge
16:34	הודו	hiph	impv	mp	ידה	392		praise
16:35	אמרו	qal	impv	mp	אמר	55		say
	הושיענו	hiph	impv	ms	ישע	446	1cp	deliver,save
	קבצנו	piel	impv	ms	קבץ	867	1cp	gather together
	הצילנו	hiph	impv	ms	נצל	664	1cp	snatch,deliver
	הדות	hiph	infc		ידה	392		praise
	השתבח	hith	infc		שבח	986		boast
16:36	ברוך	qal	pptc	ms	ברך	138		kneel,bless
	יאמרו	qal	wci	3mp	אמר	55		say
	הלל	piel	infa		הלל	237		praise
16:37	יעזב	qal	wci	3ms	עזב	736		leave,loose
	שרת	piel	infc		שרת	1058		minister,serve
16:40	העלות	hiph	infc		עלה	748		bring up,offer
	כתוב	qal	pptc	ms	כתב	507		write
	צוה	piel	pft	3ms	צוה	845		command
16:41	ברורים	qal	pptc	mp	ברר	140		purify,polish
	נקבו	niph	pft	3cp	נקב	666		be marked
	הדות	hiph	infc		ידה	392		praise
16:42	משמיעים	hiph	ptc	mp	שמע	1033		cause to hear
16:43	ילכו	qal	wci	3mp	הלך	229		walk,go
	יסב	qal	wci	3ms	סבב	685		surround
	ברך	piel	infc		ברך	138		bless
17:1	יהי	qal	wci	3ms	היה	224		be,become
	ישב	qal	pft	3ms	ישב	442		sit,dwell
	יאמר	qal	wci	3ms	אמר	55		say
	יושב	qal	ptc	ms	ישב	442		sit,dwell
17:2	יאמר	qal	wci	3ms	אמר	55		say
	עשה	qal	impv	ms	עשה	793		do,make
17:3	יהי	qal	wci	3ms	היה	224		be,become
	יהי	qal	wci	3ms	היה	224		be,become
	אמר	qal	infc		אמר	55		say
17:4	לך	qal	impv	ms	הלך	229		walk,go
	אמרת	qal	wcp	2ms	אמר	55		say
	אמר	qal	pft	3ms	אמר	55		say
	תבנה	qal	impf	2ms	בנה	124		build
	שבת	qal	infc		ישב	442		sit,dwell
17:5	ישבתי	qal	pft	1cs	ישב	442		sit,dwell
	העליתי	hiph	pft	1cs	עלה	748		bring up,offer
	אהיה	qal	wci	1cs	היה	224		be,become
17:6	התהלכתי	hith	pft	1cs	הלך	229		walk to and fro
	דברתי	piel	pft	1cs	דבר	180		speak
	שפטי	qal	ptc	mp	שפט	1047		judge
	צויתי	piel	pft	1cs	צוה	845		command
	רעות	qal	infc		רעה	944		pasture,tend
	אמר	qal	infc		אמר	55		say
	בניתם	qal	pft	2mp	בנה	124		build
17:7	תאמר	qal	impf	2ms	אמר	55		say
	אמר	qal	pft	3ms	אמר	55		say
	לקחתיך	qal	pft	1cs	לקח	542	2ms	take
	היות	qal	infc		היה	224		be,become
17:8	אהיה	qal	wci	1cs	היה	224		be,become
	הלכת	qal	pft	2ms	הלך	229		walk,go
	אכרית	hiph	wci	1cs	כרת	503		cut off,destroy
17:8	אויביך	qal	ptc	mp	איב	33	2ms	be hostile to
	עשיתי	qal	wcp	1cs	עשה	793		do,make
17:9	שמתי	qal	wcp	1cs	שים	962		put,set
	נטעתיהו	qal	wcp	1cs	נטע	642	3ms	plant
	שכן	qal	wcp	3ms	שכן	1014		settle,dwell
	ירגז	qal	impf	3ms	רגז	919		quake
	יוסיפו	hiph	impf	3mp	יסף	414		add,do again
	בלתו	piel	infc		בלה	115	3ms	wear out
17:10	צויתי	piel	pft	1cs	צוה	845		command
	שפטים	qal	ptc	mp	שפט	1047		judge
	הכנעתי	hiph	wcp	1cs	כנע	488		humble,subdue
	אויביך	qal	ptc	mp	איב	33	2ms	be hostile to
	אגד	hiph	wci	1cs	נגד	616		declare,tell
	יבנה	qal	impf	3ms	בנה	124		build
17:11	היה	qal	wcp	3ms	היה	224		be,become
	מלאו	qal	pft	3cp	מלא	569		be full,fill
	לכת	qal	infc		הלך	229		walk,go
	הקימותי	hiph	wcp	1cs	קום	877		raise,build,set
	יהיה	qal	impf	3ms	היה	224		be,become
	הכינותי	hiph	wcp	1cs	כון	465		fix,prepare
17:12	יבנה	qal	impf	3ms	בנה	124		build
	כננתי	pol	wcp	1cs	כון	465		establish
17:13	אהיה	qal	impf	1cs	היה	224		be,become
	יהיה	qal	impf	3ms	היה	224		be,become
	אסיר	hiph	impf	1cs	סור	693		take away
	הסירותי	hiph	pft	1cs	סור	693		take away
	היה	qal	pft	3ms	היה	224		be,become
17:14	העמדתיהו	hiph	wcp	1cs	עמד	763	3ms	set up,raise
	יהיה	qal	impf	3ms	היה	224		be,become
	נכון	niph	ptc	ms	כון	465		be established
17:15	דבר	piel	pft	3ms	דבר	180		speak
17:16	יבא	qal	wci	3ms	בוא	97		come in
	ישב	qal	wci	3ms	ישב	442		sit,dwell
	יאמר	qal	wci	3ms	אמר	55		say
	הביאתני	hiph	pft	2ms	בוא	97	1cs	bring in
17:17	תקטן	qal	wci	3fs	קטן	881		be little
	תדבר	piel	wci	2ms	דבר	180		speak
	ראיתני	qal	pft	2ms	ראה	906	1cs	see
17:18	יוסיף	hiph	impf	3ms	יסף	414		add,do again
	ידעת	qal	pft	2ms	ידע	393		know
17:19	עשית	qal	pft	2ms	עשה	793		do,make
	הדיע	hiph	infc		ידע	393		declare
17:20	שמענו	qal	pft	1cp	שמע	1033		hear
17:21	הלך	qal	pft	3ms	הלך	229		walk,go
	פדות	qal	infc		פדה	804		ransom
	שום	qal	infc		שים	962		put,set
	נראות	niph	ptc	fp	ירא	431		be feared
	גרש	piel	infc		גרש	176		drive out
	פדית	qal	pft	2ms	פדה	804		ransom
17:22	תתן	qal	wci	2ms	נתן	678		give,set
	היית	qal	pft	2ms	היה	224		be,become
17:23	דברת	piel	pft	2ms	דבר	180		speak
	יאמן	niph	jusm	3ms	אמן	52		be confirmed
	עשה	qal	impv	ms	עשה	793		do,make

ChVs	Form	Stem	Tnse	PGN	Root	BDB	Sfx	Meaning
17:23	דברת	piel	pft	2ms	דבר	180		speak
17:24	יאמן	niph	impf	3ms	אמן	52		be confirmed
	יגדל	qal	impf	3ms	גדל	152		be great, grow
	אמר	qal	infc		אמר	55		say
	נכון	niph	ptc	ms	כון	465		be established
17:25	גלית	qal	pft	2ms	גלה	162		uncover
	בנות	qal	infc		בנה	124		build
	מצא	qal	pft	3ms	מצא	592		find
	התפלל	hith	infc		פלל	813		pray
17:26	תדבר	piel	wci	2ms	דבר	180		speak
17:27	הואלת	hiph	pft	2ms	יאל	383		be willing
	ברך	piel	infc		ברך	138		bless
	היות	qal	infc		היה	224		be, become
	ברכת	piel	pft	2ms	ברך	138		bless
	מברך	pual	ptc	ms	ברך	138		be blessed
18:1	יהי	qal	wci	3ms	היה	224		be, become
	יך	hiph	wci	3ms	נכה	645		smite
	יכניעם	hiph	wci	3ms	כנע	488	3mp	humble, subdue
	יקח	qal	wci	3ms	לקח	542		take
18:2	יך	hiph	wci	3ms	נכה	645		smite
	יהיו	qal	wci	3mp	היה	224		be, become
	נשׂאי	qal	ptc	mp	נשׂא	669		lift, carry
18:3	יך	hiph	wci	3ms	נכה	645		smite
	לכתו	qal	infc		הלך	229	3ms	walk, go
	הציב	hiph	infc		נצב	662		cause to stand
18:4	ילכד	qal	wci	3ms	לכד	539		capture
	יעקר	piel	wci	3ms	עקר	785		hamstring
	יותר	hiph	wci	3ms	יתר	451		leave, spare
18:5	יבא	qal	wci	3ms	בוא	97		come in
	עזור	qal	infc		עזר	740		help, aid
	יך	hiph	wci	3ms	נכה	645		smite
18:6	ישׂם	qal	wci	3ms	שׂים	962		put, set
	יהי	qal	wci	3ms	היה	224		be, become
	נשׂאי	qal	ptc	mp	נשׂא	669		lift, carry
	יושׁע	hiph	wci	3ms	ישׁע	446		deliver, save
	הלך	qal	pft	3ms	הלך	229		walk, go
18:7	יקח	qal	wci	3ms	לקח	542		take
	היו	qal	pft	3cp	היה	224		be, become
	יביאם	hiph	wci	3ms	בוא	97	3mp	bring in
18:8	לקח	qal	pft	3ms	לקח	542		take
	עשׂה	qal	pft	3ms	עשׂה	793		do, make
18:9	ישׁמע	qal	wci	3ms	שׁמע	1033		hear
	הכה	hiph	pft	3ms	נכה	645		smite
18:10	ישׁלח	qal	wci	3ms	שׁלח	1018		send
	שׁאולk	qal	infc		שׁאל	981		ask, borrow
	שׁאלq	qal	infc		שׁאל	981		ask, borrow
	ברכו	piel	infc		ברך	138	3ms	bless
	נלחם	niph	pft	3ms	לחם	535		wage war
	יכהו	hiph	wci	3ms	נכה	645	3ms	smite
	היה	qal	pft	3ms	היה	224		be, become
18:11	הקדישׁ	hiph	pft	3ms	קדשׁ	872		consecrate
	נשׂא	qal	pft	3ms	נשׂא	669		lift, carry
18:12	הכה	hiph	pft	3ms	נכה	645		smite
18:13	ישׂם	qal	wci	3ms	שׂים	962		put, set
18:13	יהיו	qal	wci	3mp	היה	224		be, become
	יושׁע	hiph	wci	3ms	ישׁע	446		deliver, save
	הלך	qal	pft	3ms	הלך	229		walk, go
18:14	ימלך	qal	wci	3ms	מלך	573		be king, reign
	יהי	qal	wci	3ms	היה	224		be, become
	עשׂה	qal	ptc	ms	עשׂה	793		do, make
18:15	מזכיר	hiph	ptc	ms	זכר	269		c. to remember
19:1	יהי	qal	wci	3ms	היה	224		be, become
	ימת	qal	wci	3ms	מות	559		die
	ימלך	qal	wci	3ms	מלך	573		be king, reign
19:2	יאמר	qal	wci	3ms	אמר	55		say
	אעשׂה	qal	impf	1cs	עשׂה	793		do, make
	עשׂה	qal	pft	3ms	עשׂה	793		do, make
	ישׁלח	qal	wci	3ms	שׁלח	1018		send
	נחמו	piel	infc		נחם	636	3ms	comfort
	יבאו	qal	wci	3mp	בוא	97		come in
	נחמו	piel	infc		נחם	636	3ms	comfort
19:3	יאמרו	qal	wci	3mp	אמר	55		say
	מכבד	piel	ptc	ms	כבד	457		honor, make dull
	שׁלח	qal	pft	3ms	שׁלח	1018		send
	מנחמים	piel	ptc	mp	נחם	636		comfort
	חקר	qal	infc		חקר	350		search
	הפך	qal	infc		הפך	245		turn, overturn
	רגל	piel	infc		רגל	920		slander, spy
	באו	qal	pft	3cp	בוא	97		come in
19:4	יקח	qal	wci	3ms	לקח	542		take
	יגלחם	piel	wci	3ms	גלח	164	3mp	shave
	יכרת	qal	wci	3ms	כרת	503		cut, destroy
	ישׁלחם	piel	wci	3ms	שׁלח	1018	3mp	send away, shoot
19:5	ילכו	qal	wci	3mp	הלך	229		walk, go
	יגידו	hiph	wci	3mp	נגד	616		declare, tell
	ישׁלח	qal	wci	3ms	שׁלח	1018		send
	קראתם	qal	infc		קרא	896	3mp	meet, encounter
	היו	qal	pft	3cp	היה	224		be, become
	נכלמים	niph	ptc	mp	כלם	483		be humiliated
	יאמר	qal	wci	3ms	אמר	55		say
	שׁבו	qal	impv	mp	ישׁב	442		sit, dwell
	יצמח	piel	impf	3ms	צמח	855		grow abundantly
	שׁבתם	qal	wcp	2mp	שׁוב	996		turn, return
19:6	יראו	qal	wci	3mp	ראה	906		see
	התבאשׁו	hith	pft	3cp	באשׁ	92		be odious
	ישׁלח	qal	wci	3ms	שׁלח	1018		send
	שׂכר	qal	infc		שׂכר	968		hire
19:7	ישׂכרו	qal	wci	3mp	שׂכר	968		hire
	יבאו	qal	wci	3mp	בוא	97		come in
	יחנו	qal	wci	3mp	חנה	333		decline, encamp
	נאספו	niph	pft	3cp	אסף	62		assemble
	יבאו	qal	wci	3mp	בוא	97		come in
19:8	ישׁמע	qal	wci	3ms	שׁמע	1033		hear
	ישׁלח	qal	wci	3ms	שׁלח	1018		send
19:9	יצאו	qal	wci	3mp	יצא	422		go out
	יערכו	qal	wci	3mp	ערך	789		set in order
	באו	qal	pft	3cp	בוא	97		come in
19:10	ירא	qal	wci	3ms	ראה	906		see

ChVs	Form	Stem	Tnse	PGN	Root	BDB	Sfx	Meaning
19:10	היתה	qal	pft	3fs	היה	224		be,become
	יבחר	qal	wci	3ms	בחר	103		choose
	בחור	qal	pptc	ms	בחר	103		choose
	יערך	qal	wci	3ms	ערך	789		set in order
	קראת	qal	infc		קרא	896		meet,encounter
19:11	נתן	qal	pft	3ms	נתן	678		give,set
	יערכו	qal	wci	3mp	ערך	789		set in order
	קראת	qal	infc		קרא	896		meet,encounter
19:12	יאמר	qal	wci	3ms	אמר	55		say
	תחזק	qal	impf	3fs	חזק	304		be strong
	היית	qal	wcp	2ms	היה	224		be,become
	יחזקו	qal	impf	3mp	חזק	304		be strong
	הושעתיך	hiph	wcp	1cs	ישע	446	2ms	deliver,save
19:13	חזק	qal	impv	ms	חזק	304		be strong
	נתחזקה	hith	coh	1cp	חזק	304		strengthen self
	יעשה	qal	impf	3ms	עשה	793		do,make
19:14	יגש	qal	wci	3ms	נגש	620		draw near
	ינוסו	qal	wci	3mp	נוס	630		flee,escape
19:15	ראו	qal	pft	3cp	ראה	906		see
	נס	qal	pft	3ms	נוס	630		flee,escape
	ינוסו	qal	wci	3mp	נוס	630		flee,escape
	יבאו	qal	wci	3mp	בוא	97		come in
	יבא	qal	wci	3ms	בוא	97		come in
19:16	ירא	qal	wci	3ms	ראה	906		see
	נגפו	niph	pft	3cp	נגף	619		be smitten
	ישלחו	qal	wci	3mp	שלח	1018		send
	יוציאו	hiph	wci	3mp	יצא	422		bring out
19:17	יגד	hoph	wci	3ms	נגד	616		be told
	יאסף	qal	wci	3ms	אסף	62		gather
	יעבר	qal	wci	3ms	עבר	716		pass over
	יבא	qal	wci	3ms	בוא	97		come in
	יערך	qal	wci	3ms	ערך	789		set in order
	יערך	qal	wci	3ms	ערך	789		set in order
	קראת	qal	infc		קרא	896		meet,encounter
	ילחמו	niph	wci	3mp	לחם	535		wage war
19:18	ינס	qal	wci	3ms	נוס	630		flee,escape
	יהרג	qal	wci	3ms	הרג	246		kill
	המית	hiph	pft	3ms	מות	559		kill
19:19	יראו	qal	wci	3mp	ראה	906		see
	נגפו	niph	pft	3cp	נגף	619		be smitten
	ישלימו	hiph	wci	3mp	שלם	1023		make peace
	יעבדהו	qal	wci	3mp	עבד	712	3ms	work,serve
	אבה	qal	pft	3ms	אבה	2		be willing
	הושיע	hiph	infc		ישע	446		deliver,save
20:1	יהי	qal	wci	3ms	היה	224		be,become
	צאת	qal	infc		יצא	422		go out
	ינהג	qal	wci	3ms	נהג	624		drive
	ישחת	hiph	wci	3ms	שחת	1007		spoil,ruin
	יבא	qal	wci	3ms	בוא	97		come in
	יצר	qal	wci	3ms	צור	848		confine,shut in
	ישב	qal	ptc	ms	ישב	442		sit,dwell
	יך	hiph	wci	3ms	נכה	645		smite
	יהרסה	qal	wci	3ms	הרס	248	3fs	throw down
20:2	יקח	qal	wci	3ms	לקח	542		take
20:2	ימצאה	qal	wci	3ms	מצא	592	3fs	find
	תהי	qal	wci	3fs	היה	224		be,become
	הוציא	hiph	pft	3ms	יצא	422		bring out
	הרבה	hiph	infa		רבה	915		make many
20:3	הוציא	hiph	pft	3ms	יצא	422		bring out
	ישר	qal	wci	3ms	שור	965		saw
	יעשה	qal	impf	3ms	עשה	793		do,make
	ישב	qal	wci	3ms	שוב	996		turn,return
20:4	יהי	qal	wci	3ms	היה	224		be,become
	תעמד	qal	wci	3fs	עמד	763		stand,stop
	הכה	hiph	pft	3ms	נכה	645		smite
	יכנעו	niph	wci	3mp	כנע	488		humble self
20:5	תהי	qal	wci	3fs	היה	224		be,become
	יך	hiph	wci	3ms	נכה	645		smite
	ארגים	qal	ptc	mp	ארג	70		weave
20:6	תהי	qal	wci	3fs	היה	224		be,become
	יהי	qal	wci	3ms	היה	224		be,become
	נולד	niph	pft	3ms	ילד	408		be born
20:7	יחרף	piel	wci	3ms	חרף	357		reproach
	יכהו	hiph	wci	3ms	נכה	645	3ms	smite
20:8	נולדו	niph	pft	3cp	ילד	408		be born
	יפלו	qal	wci	3mp	נפל	656		fall
21:1	יעמד	qal	wci	3ms	עמד	763		stand,stop
	יסת	hiph	wci	3ms	סות	694		incite,allure
	מנות	qal	infc		מנה	584		count,allot
21:2	יאמר	qal	wci	3ms	אמר	55		say
	לכו	qal	impv	mp	הלך	229		walk,go
	ספרו	qal	impv	mp	ספר	707		count
	הביאו	hiph	impv	mp	בוא	97		bring in
	אדעה	qal	coh	1cs	ידע	393		know
21:3	יאמר	qal	wci	3ms	אמר	55		say
	יוסף	hiph	jus	3ms	יסף	414		add,do again
	יבקש	piel	impf	3ms	בקש	134		seek
	יהיה	qal	impf	3ms	היה	224		be,become
21:4	חזק	qal	pft	3ms	חזק	304		be strong
	יצא	qal	wci	3ms	יצא	422		go out
	יתהלך	hith	wci	3ms	הלך	229		walk to and fro
	יבא	qal	wci	3ms	בוא	97		come in
21:5	יתן	qal	wci	3ms	נתן	678		give,set
	יהי	qal	wci	3ms	היה	224		be,become
	שלף	qal	ptc	ms	שלף	1025		draw out,off
	שלף	qal	ptc	ms	שלף	1025		draw out,off
21:6	פקד	qal	pft	3ms	פקד	823		attend to,visit
	נתעב	niph	pft	3ms	תעב	1073		be abhorred
21:7	ירע	qal	wci	3ms	רעע	949		be evil
	יך	hiph	wci	3ms	נכה	645		smite
21:8	יאמר	qal	wci	3ms	אמר	55		say
	חטאתי	qal	pft	1cs	חטא	306		sin
	עשיתי	qal	pft	1cs	עשה	793		do,make
	העבר	hiph	impv	ms	עבר	716		cause to pass
	נסכלתי	niph	pft	1cs	סכל	698		act foolishly
21:9	ידבר	piel	wci	3ms	דבר	180		speak
	אמר	qal	infc		אמר	55		say
21:10	לך	qal	impv	ms	הלך	229		walk,go

ChVs	Form	Stem	Tnse	PGN	Root	BDB	Sfx	Meaning
21:10	דברת	piel	wcp	2ms	דבר	180		speak
	אמר	qal	infc		אמר	55		say
	אמר	qal	pft	3ms	אמר	55		say
	נטה	qal	ptc	ms	נטה	639		stretch,incline
	בחר	qal	impv	ms	בחר	103		choose
	אעשׂה	qal	cohm	1cs	עשׂה	793		do,make
21:11	יבא	qal	wci	3ms	בוא	97		come in
	יאמר	qal	wci	3ms	אמר	55		say
	אמר	qal	pft	3ms	אמר	55		say
	קבל	piel	impv	ms	קבל	867		take,receive
21:12	נספה	niph	ptc	ms	ספה	705		be swept away
	אויבך	qal	ptc	mp	איב	33	2ms	be hostile to
	משׂגת	hiph	ptc	fs	נשׂג	673		reach,overtake
	משחית	hiph	ptc	ms	שחת	1007		spoil,ruin
	ראה	qal	impv	ms	ראה	906		see
	אשׁיב	hiph	impf	1cs	שׁוב	996		bring back
	שׁלחי	qal	ptc	ms	שׁלח	1018	1cs	send
21:13	יאמר	qal	wci	3ms	אמר	55		say
	אפלה	qal	coh	1cs	נפל	656		fall
	אפל	qal	cohm	1cs	נפל	656		fall
21:14	יתן	qal	wci	3ms	נתן	678		give,set
	יפל	qal	wci	3ms	נפל	656		fall
21:15	ישׁלח	qal	wci	3ms	שׁלח	1018		send
	השחיתה	hiph	infc		שחת	1007	3fs	spoil,ruin
	השחית	hiph	infc		שחת	1007		spoil,ruin
	ראה	qal	pft	3ms	ראה	906		see
	ינחם	niph	wci	3ms	נחם	636		be sorry
	יאמר	qal	wci	3ms	אמר	55		say
	משחית	hiph	ptc	ms	שחת	1007		spoil,ruin
	הרף	hiph	impv	ms	רפה	951		slacken,abandon
	עמד	qal	ptc	ms	עמד	763		stand,stop
21:16	ישׂא	qal	wci	3ms	נשׂא	669		lift,carry
	ירא	qal	wci	3ms	ראה	906		see
	עמד	qal	ptc	ms	עמד	763		stand,stop
	שׁלופה	qal	pptc	fs	שׁלף	1025		draw out,off
	נטויה	qal	pptc	fs	נטה	639		stretch,incline
	יפל	qal	wci	3ms	נפל	656		fall
	מכסים	pual	ptc	mp	כסה	491		be covered
21:17	יאמר	qal	wci	3ms	אמר	55		say
	אמרתי	qal	pft	1cs	אמר	55		say
	מנות	qal	infc		מנה	584		count,allot
	חטאתי	qal	pft	1cs	חטא	306		sin
	הרע	hiph	infa		רעע	949		hurt,do evil
	הרעותי	hiph	pft	1cs	רעע	949		hurt,do evil
	עשׂו	qal	pft	3cp	עשׂה	793		do,make
	תהי	qal	jus	3fs	היה	224		be,become
21:18	אמר	qal	pft	3ms	אמר	55		say
	אמר	qal	infc		אמר	55		say
	יעלה	qal	impf	3ms	עלה	748		go up
	הקים	hiph	infc		קום	877		raise,build,set
21:19	יעל	qal	wci	3ms	עלה	748		go up
	דבר	piel	pft	3ms	דבר	180		speak
21:20	ישׁב	qal	wci	3ms	שׁוב	996		turn,return
	ירא	qal	wci	3ms	ראה	906		see
21:20	מתחבאים	hith	ptc	mp	חבא	285		hide oneself
	דשׁ	qal	pft	3ms	דושׁ	190		tread
21:21	יבא	qal	wci	3ms	בוא	97		come in
	יבט	hiph	wci	3ms	נבט	613		look,regard
	ירא	qal	wci	3ms	ראה	906		see
	יצא	qal	wci	3ms	יצא	422		go out
	ישׁתחו	hish	wci	3ms	חוה	1005		bow down
21:22	יאמר	qal	wci	3ms	אמר	55		say
	תנה	qal	impv	ms	נתן	678		give,set
	אבנה	qal	cohm	1cs	בנה	124		build
	תנהו	qal	impv	ms	נתן	678	3ms	give,set
	תעצר	niph	jusm	3fs	עצר	783		be restrained
21:23	יאמר	qal	wci	3ms	אמר	55		say
	קח	qal	impv	ms	לקח	542		take
	יעשׂ	qal	jus	3ms	עשׂה	793		do,make
	ראה	qal	impv	ms	ראה	906		see
	נתתי	qal	pft	1cs	נתן	678		give,set
	נתתי	qal	pft	1cs	נתן	678		give,set
21:24	יאמר	qal	wci	3ms	אמר	55		say
	קנה	qal	infa		קנה	888		get,buy
	אקנה	qal	impf	1cs	קנה	888		get,buy
	אשׂא	qal	impf	1cs	נשׂא	669		lift,carry
	העלות	hiph	infc		עלה	748		bring up,offer
21:25	יתן	qal	wci	3ms	נתן	678		give,set
21:26	יבן	qal	wci	3ms	בנה	124		build
	יעל	hiph	wci	3ms	עלה	748		bring up,offer
	יקרא	qal	wci	3ms	קרא	894		call,proclaim
	יענהו	qal	wci	3ms	ענה	772	3ms	answer
21:27	יאמר	qal	wci	3ms	אמר	55		say
	ישׁב	hiph	wci	3ms	שׁוב	996		bring back
21:28	ראות	qal	infc		ראה	906		see
	ענהו	qal	pft	3ms	ענה	772	3ms	answer
	יזבח	qal	wci	3ms	זבח	256		slaughter
21:29	עשׂה	qal	pft	3ms	עשׂה	793		do,make
21:30	יכל	qal	pft	3ms	יכל	407		be able
	לכת	qal	infc		הלך	229		walk,go
	דרשׁ	qal	infc		דרשׁ	205		resort to,seek
	נבעת	niph	pft	3ms	בעת	129		be terrified
22:1	יאמר	qal	wci	3ms	אמר	55		say
22:2	יאמר	qal	wci	3ms	אמר	55		say
	כנוס	qal	infc		כנס	488		collect
	יעמד	hiph	wci	3ms	עמד	763		set up,raise
	חצבים	qal	ptc	mp	חצב	345		hew out,dig
	חצוב	qal	infc		חצב	345		hew out,dig
	בנות	qal	infc		בנה	124		build
22:3	הכין	hiph	pft	3ms	כון	465		fix,prepare
22:4	הביאו	hiph	pft	3cp	בוא	97		bring in
22:5	יאמר	qal	wci	3ms	אמר	55		say
	בנות	qal	infc		בנה	124		build
	הגדיל	hiph	infc		גדל	152		make great
	אכינה	hiph	coh	1cs	כון	465		fix,prepare
	יכן	hiph	wci	3ms	כון	465		fix,prepare
22:6	יקרא	qal	wci	3ms	קרא	894		call,proclaim
	יצוהו	piel	wci	3ms	צוה	845	3ms	command

ChVs	Form	Stem	Tnse	PGN	Root	BDB	Sfx	Meaning
22: 6	בנות	qal	infc		בנה	124		build
22: 7	יאמר	qal	wci	3ms	אמר	55		say
	היה	qal	pft	3ms	היה	224		be, become
	בנות	qal	infc		בנה	124		build
22: 8	יהי	qal	wci	3ms	היה	224		be, become
	אמר	qal	infc		אמר	55		say
	שׁפכת	qal	pft	2ms	שׁפך	1049		pour out
	עשׂית	qal	pft	2ms	עשׂה	793		do, make
	תבנה	qal	impf	2ms	בנה	124		build
	שׁפכת	qal	pft	2ms	שׁפך	1049		pour out
22: 9	נולד	niph	ptc	ms	ילד	408		be born
	יהיה	qal	impf	3ms	היה	224		be, become
	הנחותי	hiph	wcp	1cs	נוח	628		give rest, put
	אויביו	qal	ptc	mp	איב	33	3ms	be hostile to
	יהיה	qal	impf	3ms	היה	224		be, become
	אתן	qal	impf	1cs	נתן	678		give, set
22: 10	יבנה	qal	impf	3ms	בנה	124		build
	יהיה	qal	impf	3ms	היה	224		be, become
	הכינותי	hiph	wcp	1cs	כון	465		fix, prepare
22: 11	יהי	qal	jus	3ms	היה	224		be, become
	הצלחת	hiph	wcp	2ms	צלח	852		cause to thrive
	בנית	qal	wcp	2ms	בנה	124		build
	דבר	piel	pft	3ms	דבר	180		speak
22: 12	יתן	qal	jusm	3ms	נתן	678		give, set
	יצוך	piel	impf	3ms	צוה	845	2ms	command
	שׁמור	qal	infc		שׁמר	1036		keep, watch
22: 13	תצליח	hiph	impf	2ms	צלח	852		cause to thrive
	תשׁמור	qal	impf	2ms	שׁמר	1036		keep, watch
	עשׂות	qal	infc		עשׂה	793		do, make
	צוה	piel	pft	3ms	צוה	845		command
	חזק	qal	impv	ms	חזק	304		be strong
	אמץ	qal	impv	ms	אמץ	54		be strong
	תירא	qal	jusm	2ms	ירא	431		fear
	תחת	qal	jusm	2ms	חתת	369		be shattered
22: 14	הכינותי	hiph	pft	1cs	כון	465		fix, prepare
	היה	qal	pft	3ms	היה	224		be, become
	הכינותי	hiph	pft	1cs	כון	465		fix, prepare
	תוסיף	hiph	impf	2ms	יסף	414		add, do again
22: 15	עשׂי	qal	ptc	mp	עשׂה	793		do, make
	חצבים	qal	ptc	mp	חצב	345		hew out, dig
22: 16	קום	qal	impv	ms	קום	877		arise, stand
	עשׂה	qal	impv	ms	עשׂה	793		do, make
	יהי	qal	jus	3ms	היה	224		be, become
22: 17	יצו	piel	wci	3ms	צוה	845		command
	עזר	qal	infc		עזר	740		help, aid
22: 18	הניח	hiph	wcp	3ms	נוח	628		give rest, put
	נתן	qal	pft	3ms	נתן	678		give, set
	ישׁבי	qal	ptc	mp	ישׁב	442		sit, dwell
	נכבשׁה	niph	wcp	3fs	כבשׁ	461		be subdued
22: 19	תנו	qal	impv	mp	נתן	678		give, set
	דרושׁ	qal	infc		דרשׁ	205		resort to, seek
	קומו	qal	impv	mp	קום	877		arise, stand
	בנו	qal	impv	mp	בנה	124		build
	הביא	hiph	infc		בוא	97		bring in
22: 19	נבנה	niph	ptc	ms	בנה	124		be built
23: 1	זקן	qal	pft	3ms	זקן	278		be old
	שׂבע	qal	pft	3ms	שׂבע	959		be sated
	ימלך	hiph	wci	3ms	מלך	573		cause to reign
23: 2	יאסף	qal	wci	3ms	אסף	62		gather
23: 3	יספרו	niph	wci	3mp	ספר	707		be counted
	יהי	qal	wci	3ms	היה	224		be, become
23: 4	נצח	piel	infc		נצח	663		act as director
	שׁפטים	qal	ptc	mp	שׁפט	1047		judge
23: 5	מהללים	piel	ptc	mp	הלל	237		praise
	עשׂיתי	qal	pft	1cs	עשׂה	793		do, make
	הלל	piel	infc		הלל	237		praise
23: 6	יחלקם	piel	wci	3ms	חלק	323	3mp	divide
23: 11	יהי	qal	wci	3ms	היה	224		be, become
	הרבו	hiph	pft	3cp	רבה	915		make many
	יהיו	qal	wci	3mp	היה	224		be, become
23: 13	יבדל	niph	wci	3ms	בדל	95		separate self
	הקדישׁו	hiph	infc		קדשׁ	872	3ms	consecrate
	הקטיר	hiph	infc		קטר	882		make sacrifices
	שׁרתו	piel	infc		שׁרת	1058	3ms	minister, serve
	ברך	piel	infc		ברך	138		bless
23: 14	יקראו	niph	impf	3mp	קרא	894		be called
23: 17	יהיו	qal	wci	3mp	היה	224		be, become
	היה	qal	pft	3ms	היה	224		be, become
	רבו	qal	pft	3cp	רבה	915		be many, great
23: 22	ימת	qal	wci	3ms	מות	559		die
	היו	qal	pft	3cp	היה	224		be, become
	ישׂאום	qal	wci	3mp	נשׂא	669	3mp	lift, carry
23: 24	פקודיהם	qal	pptc	mp	פקד	823	3mp	attend to, visit
	עשׂה	qal	ptc	ms	עשׂה	793		do, make
23: 25	אמר	qal	pft	3ms	אמר	55		say
	הניח	hiph	pft	3ms	נוח	628		give rest, put
	ישׁכן	qal	wci	3ms	שׁכן	1014		settle, dwell
23: 26	שׂאת	qal	infc		נשׂא	669		lift, carry
23: 29	מרבכת	hoph	ptc	fs	רבך	916		be mixed
23: 30	עמד	qal	infc		עמד	763		stand, stop
	הדות	hiph	infc		ידה	392		praise
	הלל	piel	infc		הלל	237		praise
23: 31	העלות	hiph	infc		עלה	748		bring up, offer
23: 32	שׁמרו	qal	wcp	3cp	שׁמר	1036		keep, watch
24: 2	ימת	qal	wci	3ms	מות	559		die
	היו	qal	pft	3cp	היה	224		be, become
	יכהנו	piel	wci	3mp	כהן	464		act as priest
24: 3	יחלקם	piel	wci	3ms	חלק	323	3mp	divide
24: 4	ימצאו	niph	wci	3mp	מצא	592		be found
	יחלקום	qal	wci	3mp	חלק	323	3mp	divide, share
24: 5	יחלקום	qal	wci	3mp	חלק	323	3mp	divide, share
	היו	qal	pft	3cp	היה	224		be, become
24: 6	יכתבם	qal	wci	3ms	כתב	507	3mp	write
	אחז	qal	pptc	ms	אחז	28		grasp
	אחז	qal	pptc	ms	אחז	28		grasp
	אחז	qal	pptc	ms	אחז	28		grasp
24: 7	יצא	qal	wci	3ms	יצא	422		go out
24: 19	בוא	qal	infc		בוא	97		come in

ChVs	Form	Stem	Tnse	PGN	Root	BDB	Sfx	Meaning
24:19	צוהו	piel	pft	3ms	צוה	845	3ms	command
24:20	נותרים	niph	ptc	mp	יתר	451		be left,remain
24:28	היה	qal	pft	3ms	היה	224		be,become
24:31	יפילו	hiph	wci	3mp	נפל	656		cause to fall
25:1	יבדל	hiph	wci	3ms	בדל	95		divide
	qנבאים	niph	ptc	mp	נבא	612		prophesy
	יהי	qal	wci	3ms	היה	224		be,become
25:2	נבא	niph	ptc	ms	נבא	612		prophesy
25:3	נבא	niph	ptc	ms	נבא	612		prophesy
	הדות	hiph	infc		ידה	392		praise
	הלל	piel	infc		הלל	237		praise
25:5	הרים	hiph	infc		רום	926		raise,lift
	יתן	qal	wci	3ms	נתן	678		give,set
25:7	יהי	qal	wci	3ms	היה	224		be,become
	מלמדי	pual	ptc	mp	למד	540		be taught
	מבין	hiph	ptc	ms	בין	106		understand
25:8	יפילו	hiph	wci	3mp	נפל	656		cause to fall
	מבין	hiph	ptc	ms	בין	106		understand
25:9	יצא	qal	wci	3ms	יצא	422		go out
26:5	ברכו	piel	pft	3ms	ברך	138	3ms	bless
26:6	נולד	niph	pft	3ms	ילד	408		be born
26:10	היה	qal	pft	3ms	היה	224		be,become
	ישׂימהו	qal	wci	3ms	שׂים	962	3ms	put,set
26:12	שׁרת	piel	infc		שׁרת	1058		minister,serve
26:13	יפילו	hiph	wci	3mp	נפל	656		cause to fall
26:14	יפל	qal	wci	3ms	נפל	656		fall
	יועץ	qal	ptc	ms	יעץ	419		advise,counsel
	הפילו	hiph	pft	3cp	נפל	656		cause to fall
	יצא	qal	wci	3ms	יצא	422		go out
26:16	עולה	qal	ptc	fs	עלה	748		go up
26:26	הקדישׁ	hiph	pft	3ms	קדשׁ	872		consecrate
26:27	הקדישׁו	hiph	pft	3cp	קדשׁ	872		consecrate
	חזק	piel	infc		חזק	304		make strong
26:28	הקדישׁ	hiph	pft	3ms	קדשׁ	872		consecrate
	מקדישׁ	hiph	ptc	ms	קדשׁ	872		consecrate
26:29	שׁפטים	qal	ptc	mp	שׁפט	1047		judge
26:31	נדרשׁו	niph	pft	3cp	דרשׁ	205		be sought out
	ימצא	niph	wci	3ms	מצא	592		be found
26:32	יפקידם	hiph	wci	3ms	פקד	823	3mp	set,entrust
27:1	משׁרתים	piel	ptc	mp	שׁרת	1058		minister,serve
	באה	qal	ptc	fs	בוא	97		come in
	יצאת	qal	ptc	fs	יצא	422		go out
27:23	נשׂא	qal	pft	3ms	נשׂא	669		lift,carry
	אמר	qal	pft	3ms	אמר	55		say
	הרבות	hiph	infc		רבה	915		make many
27:24	החל	hiph	pft	3ms	חלל	320		begin,profane
	מנות	qal	infc		מנה	584		count,allot
	כלה	piel	pft	3ms	כלה	477		complete,finish
	יהי	qal	wci	3ms	היה	224		be,become
	עלה	qal	pft	3ms	עלה	748		go up
27:26	עשׂי	qal	ptc	mp	עשׂה	793		do,make
27:29	רעים	qal	ptc	mp	רעה	944		pasture,tend
27:32	יועץ	qal	ptc	ms	יעץ	419		advise,counsel
	מבין	hiph	ptc	ms	בין	106		understand
27:33	יועץ	qal	ptc	ms	יעץ	419		advise,counsel
28:1	יקהל	hiph	wci	3ms	קהל	874		call assembly
	משׁרתים	piel	ptc	mp	שׁרת	1058		minister,serve
28:2	יקם	qal	wci	3ms	קום	877		arise,stand
	יאמר	qal	wci	3ms	אמר	55		say
	שׁמעוני	qal	impv	mp	שׁמע	1033	1cs	hear
	בנות	qal	infc		בנה	124		build
	הכינותי	hiph	pft	1cs	כון	465		fix,prepare
	בנות	qal	infc		בנה	124		build
28:3	אמר	qal	pft	3ms	אמר	55		say
	תבנה	qal	impf	2ms	בנה	124		build
	שׁפכת	qal	pft	2ms	שׁפך	1049		pour out
28:4	יבחר	qal	wci	3ms	בחר	103		choose
	היות	qal	infc		היה	224		be,become
	בחר	qal	pft	3ms	בחר	103		choose
	רצה	qal	pft	3ms	רצה	953		be pleased
	המליך	hiph	infc		מלך	573		cause to reign
28:5	נתן	qal	pft	3ms	נתן	678		give,set
	יבחר	qal	wci	3ms	בחר	103		choose
	שׁבת	qal	infc		ישׁב	442		sit,dwell
28:6	יאמר	qal	wci	3ms	אמר	55		say
	יבנה	qal	impf	3ms	בנה	124		build
	בחרתי	qal	pft	1cs	בחר	103		choose
	אהיה	qal	impf	1cs	היה	224		be,become
28:7	הכינותי	hiph	wcp	1cs	כון	465		fix,prepare
	יחזק	qal	impf	3ms	חזק	304		be strong
	עשׂות	qal	infc		עשׂה	793		do,make
28:8	שׁמרו	qal	impv	mp	שׁמר	1036		keep,watch
	דרשׁו	qal	impv	mp	דרשׁ	205		resort to,seek
	תירשׁו	qal	impf	2mp	ירשׁ	439		possess,inherit
	הנחלתם	hiph	wcp	2mp	נחל	635		c. to inherit
28:9	דע	qal	impv	ms	ידע	393		know
	עבדהו	qal	impv	ms	עבד	712	3ms	work,serve
	דורשׁ	qal	ptc	ms	דרשׁ	205		resort to,seek
	מבין	hiph	ptc	ms	בין	106		understand
	תדרשׁנו	qal	impf	2ms	דרשׁ	205	3ms	resort to,seek
	ימצא	niph	impf	3ms	מצא	592		be found
	תעזבנו	qal	impf	2ms	עזב	736	3ms	leave,loose
	יזניחך	hiph	impf	3ms	זנח	276	2ms	reject
28:10	ראה	qal	impv	ms	ראה	906		see
	בחר	qal	pft	3ms	בחר	103		choose
	בנות	qal	infc		בנה	124		build
	חזק	qal	impv	ms	חזק	304		be strong
	עשׂה	qal	impv	ms	עשׂה	793		do,make
28:11	יתן	qal	wci	3ms	נתן	678		give,set
28:12	היה	qal	pft	3ms	היה	224		be,become
28:18	מזקק	pual	ptc	ms	זקק	279		refined
	פרשׂים	qal	ptc	mp	פרשׂ	831		spread out
	סככים	qal	ptc	mp	סכך	696		cover
28:19	השׂכיל	hiph	pft	3ms	שׂכל	968		look at,prosper
28:20	יאמר	qal	wci	3ms	אמר	55		say
	חזק	qal	impv	ms	חזק	304		be strong
	אמץ	qal	impv	ms	אמץ	54		be strong
	עשׂה	qal	impv	ms	עשׂה	793		do,make

ChVs	Form	Stem	Tnse	PGN	Root	BDB	Sfx	Meaning
28:20	תירא	qal	jusm	2ms	ירא	431		fear
	תחת	qal	jusm	2ms	חתת	369		be shattered
	ירפך	hiph	impf	3ms	רפה	951	2ms	slacken,abandon
	יעזבך	qal	impf	3ms	עזב	736	2ms	leave,loose
	כלות	qal	infc		כלה	477		finished,spent
29:1	יאמר	qal	wci	3ms	אמר	55		say
	בחר	qal	pft	3ms	בחר	103		choose
29:2	הכינותי	hiph	pft	1cs	כון	465		fix,prepare
29:3	רצותי	qal	infc		רצה	953	1cs	be pleased
	נתתי	qal	pft	1cs	נתן	678		give,set
	הכינותי	hiph	pft	1cs	כון	465		fix,prepare
29:4	מזקק	pual	ptc	ms	זקק	279		refined
	טוח	qal	infc		טוח	376		overlay
29:5	מתנדב	hith	ptc	ms	נדב	621		offer freely
	מלאות	piel	infc		מלא	569		fill
29:6	יתנדבו	hith	wci	3mp	נדב	621		offer freely
29:7	יתנו	qal	wci	3mp	נתן	678		give,set
29:8	נמצא	niph	ptc	ms	מצא	592		be found
	נתנו	qal	pft	3cp	נתן	678		give,set
29:9	ישמחו	qal	wci	3mp	שמח	970		rejoice
	התנדבם	hith	infc		נדב	621	3mp	offer freely
	התנדבו	hith	pft	3cp	נדב	621		offer freely
	שמח	qal	pft	3ms	שמח	970		rejoice
29:10	יברך	piel	wci	3ms	ברך	138		bless
	יאמר	qal	wci	3ms	אמר	55		say
	ברוך	qal	pptc	ms	ברך	138		kneel,bless
29:11	מתנשא	hith	ptc	ms	נשא	669		lift self up
29:12	מושל	qal	ptc	ms	משל	605		rule
	גדל	piel	infc		גדל	152		cause to grow
	חזק	piel	infc		חזק	304		make strong
29:13	מודים	hiph	ptc	mp	ידה	392		praise
	מהללים	piel	ptc	mp	הלל	237		praise
29:14	נעצר	qal	impf	1cp	עצר	783		restrain
	התנדב	hith	infc		נדב	621		offer freely
	נתנו	qal	pft	1cp	נתן	678		give,set
29:16	הכינונו	hiph	pft	1cp	כון	465		fix,prepare
	בנות	qal	infc		בנה	124		build
29:17	ידעתי	qal	wcp	1cs	ידע	393		know
	בחן	qal	ptc	ms	בחן	103		examine,try
	תרצה	qal	impf	2ms	רצה	953		be pleased
	התנדבתי	hith	pft	1cs	נדב	621		offer freely
	נמצאו	niph	pft	3cp	מצא	592		be found
	ראיתי	qal	pft	1cs	ראה	906		see
	התנדב	hith	infc		נדב	621		offer freely
29:18	שמרה	qal	impv	ms	שמר	1036		keep,watch
	הכן	hiph	impv	ms	כון	465		fix,prepare
29:19	תן	qal	impv	ms	נתן	678		give,set
	שמור	qal	infc		שמר	1036		keep,watch
	עשות	qal	infc		עשה	793		do,make
	בנות	qal	infc		בנה	124		build
	הכינותי	hiph	pft	1cs	כון	465		fix,prepare
29:20	יאמר	qal	wci	3ms	אמר	55		say
	ברכו	piel	impv	mp	ברך	138		bless
	יברכו	piel	wci	3mp	ברך	138		bless
29:20	יקדו	qal	wci	3mp	קדד	869		bow down
	ישתחוו	hish	wci	3mp	חוה	1005		bow down
29:21	יזבחו	qal	wci	3mp	זבח	256		slaughter
	יעלו	hiph	wci	3mp	עלה	748		bring up,offer
29:22	יאכלו	qal	wci	3mp	אכל	37		eat,devour
	ישתו	qal	wci	3mp	שתה	1059		drink
	ימליכו	hiph	wci	3mp	מלך	573		cause to reign
	ימשחו	qal	wci	3mp	משח	602		smear,anoint
29:23	ישב	qal	wci	3ms	ישב	442		sit,dwell
	יצלח	hiph	wci	3ms	צלח	852		cause to thrive
	ישמעו	qal	wci	3mp	שמע	1033		hear
29:24	נתנו	qal	pft	3cp	נתן	678		give,set
29:25	יגדל	piel	wci	3ms	גדל	152		cause to grow
	יתן	qal	wci	3ms	נתן	678		give,set
	היה	qal	pft	3ms	היה	224		be,become
29:26	מלך	qal	pft	3ms	מלך	573		be king,reign
29:27	מלך	qal	pft	3ms	מלך	573		be king,reign
	מלך	qal	pft	3ms	מלך	573		be king,reign
	מלך	qal	pft	3ms	מלך	573		be king,reign
29:28	ימת	qal	wci	3ms	מות	559		die
	ימלך	qal	wci	3ms	מלך	573		be king,reign
29:29	כתובים	qal	pptc	mp	כתב	507		write
29:30	עברו	qal	pft	3cp	עבר	716		pass over
2 CHRONICLES								
1:1	יתחזק	hith	wci	3ms	חזק	304		strengthen self
	יגדלהו	piel	wci	3ms	גדל	152	3ms	cause to grow
1:2	יאמר	qal	wci	3ms	אמר	55		say
	שפטים	qal	ptc	mp	שפט	1047		judge
1:3	ילכו	qal	wci	3mp	הלך	229		walk,go
	היה	qal	pft	3ms	היה	224		be,become
	עשה	qal	pft	3ms	עשה	793		do,make
1:4	העלה	hiph	pft	3ms	עלה	748		bring up,offer
	הכין	hiph	pft	3ms	כון	465		fix,prepare
	נטה	qal	pft	3ms	נטה	639		stretch,incline
1:5	עשה	qal	pft	3ms	עשה	793		do,make
	שם	qal	pft	3ms	שים	962		put,set
	ידרשהו	qal	wci	3ms	דרש	205	3ms	resort to,seek
1:6	יעל	qal	wci	3ms	עלה	748		go up
	יעל	hiph	wci	3ms	עלה	748		bring up,offer
1:7	נראה	niph	pft	3ms	ראה	906		appear,be seen
	יאמר	qal	wci	3ms	אמר	55		say
	שאל	qal	impv	ms	שאל	981		ask,borrow
	אתן	qal	impf	1cs	נתן	678		give,set
1:8	יאמר	qal	wci	3ms	אמר	55		say
	עשית	qal	pft	2ms	עשה	793		do,make
	המלכתני	hiph	pft	2ms	מלך	573	1cs	cause to reign
1:9	יאמן	niph	jusm	3ms	אמן	52		be confirmed
	המלכתני	hiph	pft	2ms	מלך	573	1cs	cause to reign
1:10	תן	qal	impv	ms	נתן	678		give,set
	אצאה	qal	coh	1cs	יצא	422		go out
	אבואה	qal	coh	1cs	בוא	97		come in
	ישפט	qal	impf	3ms	שפט	1047		judge
1:11	יאמר	qal	wci	3ms	אמר	55		say

ChVs	Form	Stem	Tnse	PGN	Root	BDB	Sfx	Meaning
1: 11	היתה	qal	pft	3fs	היה	224		be,become
	שׁאלת	qal	pft	2ms	שׁאל	981		ask,borrow
	שׂנאיך	qal	ptc	mp	שׂנא	971	2ms	hate
	שׁאלת	qal	pft	2ms	שׁאל	981		ask,borrow
	תשׁאל	qal	wci	2ms	שׁאל	981		ask,borrow
	תשׁפוט	qal	impf	2ms	שׁפט	1047		judge
	המלכתיך	hiph	pft	1cs	מלך	573	2ms	cause to reign
1: 12	נתון	qal	pptc	ms	נתן	678		give,set
	אתן	qal	impf	1cs	נתן	678		give,set
	היה	qal	pft	3ms	היה	224		be,become
	יהיה	qal	impf	3ms	היה	224		be,become
1: 13	יבא	qal	wci	3ms	בוא	97		come in
	ימלך	qal	wci	3ms	מלך	573		be king,reign
1: 14	יאסף	qal	wci	3ms	אסף	62		gather
	יהי	qal	wci	3ms	היה	224		be,become
	יניחם	hiph	wci	3ms	נוח	628	3mp	give rest,put
1: 15	יתן	qal	wci	3ms	נתן	678		give,set
	נתן	qal	pft	3ms	נתן	678		give,set
1: 16	סחרי	qal	ptc	mp	סחר	695		go around
	יקחו	qal	impf	3mp	לקח	542		take
1: 17	יעלו	hiph	wci	3mp	עלה	748		bring up,offer
	יוציאו	hiph	wci	3mp	יצא	422		bring out
	יוציאו	hiph	impf	3mp	יצא	422		bring out
1: 18	יאמר	qal	wci	3ms	אמר	55		say
	בנות	qal	infc		בנה	124		build
2: 1	יספר	qal	wci	3ms	ספר	707		count
	חצב	qal	ptc	ms	חצב	345		hew out,dig
	מנצחים	piel	ptc	mp	נצח	663		act as director
2: 2	ישׁלח	qal	wci	3ms	שׁלח	1018		send
	אמר	qal	infc		אמר	55		say
	עשׂית	qal	pft	2ms	עשׂה	793		do,make
	תשׁלח	qal	wci	2ms	שׁלח	1018		send
	בנות	qal	infc		בנה	124		build
	שׁבת	qal	infc		ישׁב	442		sit,dwell
2: 3	בונה	qal	ptc	ms	בנה	124		build
	הקדישׁ	hiph	infc		קדשׁ	872		consecrate
	הקטיר	hiph	infc		קטר	882		make sacrifices
2: 4	בונה	qal	ptc	ms	בנה	124		build
2: 5	יעצר	qal	impf	3ms	עצר	783		restrain
	בנות	qal	infc		בנה	124		build
	יכלכלהו	pilp	impf	3mp	כול	465	3ms	support
	אבנה	qal	impf	1cs	בנה	124		build
	הקטיר	hiph	infc		קטר	882		make sacrifices
2: 6	שׁלח	qal	impv	ms	שׁלח	1018		send
	עשׂות	qal	infc		עשׂה	793		do,make
	ידע	qal	ptc	ms	ידע	393		know
	פתח	piel	infc		פתח	836		engrave
	הכין	hiph	pft	3ms	כון	465		fix,prepare
2: 7	שׁלח	qal	impv	ms	שׁלח	1018		send
	ידעתי	qal	pft	1cs	ידע	393		know
	יודעים	qal	ptc	mp	ידע	393		know
	כרות	qal	infc		כרת	503		cut,destroy
2: 8	הכין	hiph	infc		כון	465		fix,prepare
	בונה	qal	ptc	ms	בנה	124		build
2: 8	הפלא	hiph	infa		פלא	810		do wondrously
2: 9	חטבים	qal	ptc	mp	חטב	310		cut wood
	כרתי	qal	ptc	mp	כרת	503		cut,destroy
	נתתי	qal	pft	1cs	נתן	678		give,set
2: 10	יאמר	qal	wci	3ms	אמר	55		say
	ישׁלח	qal	wci	3ms	שׁלח	1018		send
	אהבת	qal	infc		אהב	12		love
	נתנך	qal	pft	3ms	נתן	678	2ms	give,set
2: 11	יאמר	qal	wci	3ms	אמר	55		say
	ברוך	qal	pptc	ms	ברך	138		kneel,bless
	עשׂה	qal	pft	3ms	עשׂה	793		do,make
	נתן	qal	pft	3ms	נתן	678		give,set
	יודע	qal	ptc	ms	ידע	393		know
	יבנה	qal	impf	3ms	בנה	124		build
2: 12	שׁלחתי	qal	pft	1cs	שׁלח	1018		send
	יודע	qal	ptc	ms	ידע	393		know
2: 13	יודע	qal	ptc	ms	ידע	393		know
	עשׂות	qal	infc		עשׂה	793		do,make
	פתח	piel	infc		פתח	836		engrave
	חשׁב	qal	infc		חשׁב	362		think,devise
	ינתן	niph	impf	3ms	נתן	678		be given
2: 14	אמר	qal	pft	3ms	אמר	55		say
	ישׁלח	qal	jusm	3ms	שׁלח	1018		send
2: 15	נכרת	qal	impf	1cp	כרת	503		cut,destroy
	נביאם	hiph	impf	1cp	בוא	97	3mp	bring in
	תעלה	hiph	impf	2ms	עלה	748		bring up,offer
2: 16	יספר	qal	wci	3ms	ספר	707		count
	ספרם	qal	pft	3ms	ספר	707	3mp	count
	ימצאו	niph	wci	3mp	מצא	592		be found
2: 17	יעשׂ	qal	wci	3ms	עשׂה	793		do,make
	חצב	qal	ptc	ms	חצב	345		hew out,dig
	מנצחים	piel	ptc	mp	נצח	663		act as director
	העביד	hiph	infc		עבד	712		cause to serve
3: 1	יחל	hiph	wci	3ms	חלל	320		begin,profane
	בנות	qal	infc		בנה	124		build
	נראה	niph	pft	3ms	ראה	906		appear,be seen
	הכין	hiph	pft	3ms	כון	465		fix,prepare
3: 2	יחל	hiph	wci	3ms	חלל	320		begin,profane
	בנות	qal	infc		בנה	124		build
3: 3	הוסד	hoph	infc		יסד	413		be founded
	בנות	qal	infc		בנה	124		build
3: 4	יצפהו	piel	wci	3ms	צפה	860	3ms	overlay
3: 5	חפה	piel	pft	3ms	חפה	341		overlay
	יחפהו	piel	wci	3ms	חפה	341	3ms	overlay
	יעל	hiph	wci	3ms	עלה	748		bring up,offer
3: 6	יצף	piel	wci	3ms	צפה	860		overlay
3: 7	יחף	piel	wci	3ms	חפה	341		overlay
	פתח	piel	pft	3ms	פתח	836		engrave
3: 8	יעשׂ	qal	wci	3ms	עשׂה	793		do,make
	יחפהו	piel	wci	3ms	חפה	341	3ms	overlay
3: 9	חפה	piel	pft	3ms	חפה	341		overlay
3: 10	יעשׂ	qal	wci	3ms	עשׂה	793		do,make
	יצפו	piel	wci	3mp	צפה	860		overlay
3: 11	מגעת	hiph	ptc	fs	נגע	619		reach,arrive

ChVs	Form	Stem	Tnse	PGN	Root	BDB	Sfx	Meaning
3:11	מגיע	hiph	ptc	ms	נגע	619		reach,arrive
3:12	מגיע	hiph	ptc	ms	נגע	619		reach,arrive
3:13	פרשׂים	qal	ptc	mp	פרשׂ	831		spread out
	עמדים	qal	ptc	mp	עמד	763		stand,stop
3:14	יעשׂ	qal	wci	3ms	עשׂה	793		do,make
	יעל	hiph	wci	3ms	עלה	748		bring up,offer
3:15	יעשׂ	qal	wci	3ms	עשׂה	793		do,make
3:16	יעשׂ	qal	wci	3ms	עשׂה	793		do,make
	יתן	qal	wci	3ms	נתן	678		give,set
	יעשׂ	qal	wci	3ms	עשׂה	793		do,make
	יתן	qal	wci	3ms	נתן	678		give,set
3:17	יקם	hiph	wci	3ms	קום	877		raise,build,set
	יקרא	qal	wci	3ms	קרא	894		call,proclaim
4:1	יעשׂ	qal	wci	3ms	עשׂה	793		do,make
4:2	יעשׂ	qal	wci	3ms	עשׂה	793		do,make
	מוצק	hoph	ptc	ms	יצק	427		be poured,firm
	יסב	qal	impf	3ms	סבב	685		surround
4:3	סובבים	qal	ptc	mp	סבב	685		surround
	מקיפים	hiph	ptc	mp	נקף	668		surround
	יצוקים	qal	pptc	mp	יצק	427		pour out,cast
4:4	עומד	qal	ptc	ms	עמד	763		stand,stop
	פנים	qal	ptc	mp	פנה	815		turn
	פנים	qal	ptc	mp	פנה	815		turn
	פנים	qal	ptc	mp	פנה	815		turn
	פנים	qal	ptc	mp	פנה	815		turn
4:5	מחזיק	hiph	ptc	ms	חזק	304		make firm,seize
	יכיל	hiph	impf	3ms	כול	465		contain
4:6	יעשׂ	qal	wci	3ms	עשׂה	793		do,make
	יתן	qal	wci	3ms	נתן	678		give,set
	רחצה	qal	infc		רחץ	934		wash,bathe
	ידיחו	hiph	impf	3mp	דוח	188		rinse
	רחצה	qal	infc		רחץ	934		wash,bathe
4:7	יעשׂ	qal	wci	3ms	עשׂה	793		do,make
	יתן	qal	wci	3ms	נתן	678		give,set
4:8	יעשׂ	qal	wci	3ms	עשׂה	793		do,make
	ינח	hiph	wci	3ms	נוח	628		give rest,put
	יעשׂ	qal	wci	3ms	עשׂה	793		do,make
4:9	יעשׂ	qal	wci	3ms	עשׂה	793		do,make
	צפה	piel	pft	3ms	צפה	860		overlay
4:10	נתן	qal	pft	3ms	נתן	678		give,set
4:11	יעשׂ	qal	wci	3ms	עשׂה	793		do,make
	יכל	piel	wci	3ms	כלה	477		complete,finish
	עשׂות	qal	infc		עשׂה	793		do,make
	עשׂה	qal	pft	3ms	עשׂה	793		do,make
4:12	כסות	piel	infc		כסה	491		cover
4:13	כסות	piel	infc		כסה	491		cover
4:14	עשׂה	qal	pft	3ms	עשׂה	793		do,make
	עשׂה	qal	pft	3ms	עשׂה	793		do,make
4:16	עשׂה	qal	pft	3ms	עשׂה	793		do,make
	מרוק	qal	pptc	ms	מרק	599		polish
4:17	יצקם	qal	pft	3ms	יצק	427	3mp	pour out,cast
4:18	יעשׂ	qal	wci	3ms	עשׂה	793		do,make
	נחקר	niph	pft	3ms	חקר	350		be searched out
4:19	יעשׂ	qal	wci	3ms	עשׂה	793		do,make
4:20	בערם	piel	infc		בער	128	3mp	burn,consume
	סגור	qal	pptc	ms	סגר	688		shut
4:22	סגור	qal	pptc	ms	סגר	688		shut
5:1	תשׁלם	qal	wci	3fs	שׁלם	1022		be complete
	עשׂה	qal	pft	3ms	עשׂה	793		do,make
	יבא	hiph	wci	3ms	בוא	97		bring in
	נתן	qal	pft	3ms	נתן	678		give,set
5:2	יקהיל	hiph	impf	3ms	קהל	874		call assembly
	העלות	hiph	infc		עלה	748		bring up,offer
5:3	יקהלו	niph	wci	3mp	קהל	874		assemble
5:4	יבאו	qal	wci	3mp	בוא	97		come in
	ישׂאו	qal	wci	3mp	נשׂא	669		lift,carry
5:5	יעלו	hiph	wci	3mp	עלה	748		bring up,offer
	העלו	hiph	pft	3cp	עלה	748		bring up,offer
5:6	נועדים	niph	ptc	mp	יעד	416		gather
	מזבחים	piel	ptc	mp	זבח	256		sacrifice
	יספרו	niph	impf	3mp	ספר	707		be counted
	ימנו	niph	impf	3mp	מנה	584		be counted
5:7	יביאו	hiph	wci	3mp	בוא	97		bring in
5:8	יהיו	qal	wci	3mp	היה	224		be,become
	פרשׂים	qal	ptc	mp	פרשׂ	831		spread out
	יכסו	piel	wci	3mp	כסה	491		cover
5:9	יאריכו	hiph	wci	3mp	ארך	73		prolong
	יראו	niph	wci	3mp	ראה	906		appear,be seen
	יראו	niph	impf	3mp	ראה	906		appear,be seen
	יהי	qal	wci	3ms	היה	224		be,become
5:10	נתן	qal	pft	3ms	נתן	678		give,set
	כרת	qal	pft	3ms	כרת	503		cut,destroy
	צאתם	qal	infc		יצא	422	3mp	go out
5:11	יהי	qal	wci	3ms	היה	224		be,become
	צאת	qal	infc		יצא	422		go out
	נמצאים	niph	ptc	mp	מצא	592		be found
	התקדשׁו	hith	pft	3cp	קדשׁ	872		consecrate self
	שׁמור	qal	infc		שׁמר	1036		keep,watch
5:12	משׁררים	pol	ptc	mp	שׁיר	1010		sing
	מלבשׁים	pual	ptc	mp	לבשׁ	527		be clothed
	עמדים	qal	ptc	mp	עמד	763		stand,stop
	מחצררים k	hiph	ptc	mp	חצצר	348		sound w/clarion
	מחצרים q	hiph	ptc	mp	חצר	348		sound w/clarion
5:13	יהי	qal	wci	3ms	היה	224		be,become
	מחצצרים k	piel	ptc	mp	חצצר	348		clarion players
	מחצרים q	piel	ptc	mp	חצר	348		clarion players
	משׁררים	pol	ptc	mp	שׁיר	1010		sing
	השׁמיע	hiph	infc		שׁמע	1033		cause to hear
	הלל	piel	infc		הלל	237		praise
	הדות	hiph	infc		ידה	392		praise
	הרים	hiph	infc		רום	926		raise,lift
	הלל	piel	infc		הלל	237		praise
	מלא	qal	pft	3ms	מלא	569		be full,fill
5:14	יכלו	qal	pft	3cp	יכל	407		be able
	עמוד	qal	infc		עמד	763		stand,stop
	שׁרת	piel	infc		שׁרת	1058		minister,serve
	מלא	qal	pft	3ms	מלא	569		be full,fill
6:1	אמר	qal	pft	3ms	אמר	55		say

ChVs	Form	Stem	Tnse	PGN	Root	BDB	Sfx	Meaning
6:1	אמר	qal	pft	3ms	אמר	55		say
	שׁכון	qal	infc		שׁכן	1014		settle,dwell
6:2	בניתי	qal	pft	1cs	בנה	124		build
	שׁבתך	qal	infc		ישׁב	442	2ms	sit,dwell
6:3	יסב	hiph	wci	3ms	סבב	685		cause to turn
	יברך	piel	wci	3ms	ברך	138		bless
	עומד	qal	ptc	ms	עמד	763		stand,stop
6:4	יאמר	qal	wci	3ms	אמר	55		say
	ברוך	qal	pptc	ms	ברך	138		kneel,bless
	דבר	piel	pft	3ms	דבר	180		speak
	מלא	piel	pft	3ms	מלא	569		fill
	אמר	qal	infc		אמר	55		say
6:5	הוצאתי	hiph	pft	1cs	יצא	422		bring out
	בחרתי	qal	pft	1cs	בחר	103		choose
	בנות	qal	infc		בנה	124		build
	היות	qal	infc		היה	224		be,become
	בחרתי	qal	pft	1cs	בחר	103		choose
	היות	qal	infc		היה	224		be,become
6:6	אבחר	qal	wci	1cs	בחר	103		choose
	היות	qal	infc		היה	224		be,become
	אבחר	qal	wci	1cs	בחר	103		choose
	היות	qal	infc		היה	224		be,become
6:7	יהי	qal	wci	3ms	היה	224		be,become
	בנות	qal	infc		בנה	124		build
6:8	יאמר	qal	wci	3ms	אמר	55		say
	היה	qal	pft	3ms	היה	224		be,become
	בנות	qal	infc		בנה	124		build
	הטיבות	hiph	pft	2ms	טוב	373		do well
	היה	qal	pft	3ms	היה	224		be,become
6:9	תבנה	qal	impf	2ms	בנה	124		build
	יוצא	qal	ptc	ms	יצא	422		go out
	יבנה	qal	impf	3ms	בנה	124		build
6:10	יקם	hiph	wci	3ms	קום	877		raise,build,set
	דבר	piel	pft	3ms	דבר	180		speak
	אקום	qal	wci	1cs	קום	877		arise,stand
	אשׁב	qal	wci	1cs	ישׁב	442		sit,dwell
	דבר	piel	pft	3ms	דבר	180		speak
	אבנה	qal	wci	1cs	בנה	124		build
6:11	אשׂים	qal	wci	1cs	שׂים	962		put,set
	כרת	qal	pft	3ms	כרת	503		cut,destroy
6:12	יעמד	qal	wci	3ms	עמד	763		stand,stop
	יפרשׂ	qal	wci	3ms	פרשׂ	831		spread out
6:13	עשׂה	qal	pft	3ms	עשׂה	793		do,make
	יתנהו	qal	wci	3ms	נתן	678	3ms	give,set
	יעמד	qal	wci	3ms	עמד	763		stand,stop
	יברך	qal	wci	3ms	ברך	138		kneel,bless
	יפרשׂ	qal	wci	3ms	פרשׂ	831		spread out
6:14	יאמר	qal	wci	3ms	אמר	55		say
	שׁמר	qal	ptc	ms	שׁמר	1036		keep,watch
	הלכים	qal	ptc	mp	הלך	229		walk,go
6:15	שׁמרת	qal	pft	2ms	שׁמר	1036		keep,watch
	דברת	piel	pft	2ms	דבר	180		speak
	תדבר	piel	wci	2ms	דבר	180		speak
	מלאת	piel	pft	2ms	מלא	569		fill
6:16	שׁמר	qal	impv	ms	שׁמר	1036		keep,watch
	דברת	piel	pft	2ms	דבר	180		speak
	אמר	qal	infc		אמר	55		say
	יכרת	niph	impf	3ms	כרת	503		be cut off
	יושׁב	qal	ptc	ms	ישׁב	442		sit,dwell
	ישׁמרו	qal	impf	3mp	שׁמר	1036		keep,watch
	לכת	qal	infc		הלך	229		walk,go
	הלכת	qal	pft	2ms	הלך	229		walk,go
6:17	יאמן	niph	jusm	3ms	אמן	52		be confirmed
	דברת	piel	pft	2ms	דבר	180		speak
6:18	ישׁב	qal	impf	3ms	ישׁב	442		sit,dwell
	יכלכלוך	pilp	impf	3mp	כול	465	2ms	support
	בניתי	qal	pft	1cs	בנה	124		build
6:19	פנית	qal	wcp	2ms	פנה	815		turn
	שׁמע	qal	infc		שׁמע	1033		hear
	מתפלל	hith	ptc	ms	פלל	813		pray
6:20	היות	qal	infc		היה	224		be,become
	פתחות	qal	pptc	fp	פתח	834		open
	אמרת	qal	pft	2ms	אמר	55		say
	שׂום	qal	infc		שׂים	962		put,set
	שׁמוע	qal	infc		שׁמע	1033		hear
	יתפלל	hith	impf	3ms	פלל	813		pray
6:21	שׁמעת	qal	wcp	2ms	שׁמע	1033		hear
	יתפללו	hith	impf	3mp	פלל	813		pray
	תשׁמע	qal	impf	2ms	שׁמע	1033		hear
	שׁבתך	qal	infc		ישׁב	442	2ms	sit,dwell
	שׁמעת	qal	wcp	2ms	שׁמע	1033		hear
	סלחת	qal	wcp	2ms	סלח	699		forgive,pardon
6:22	יחטא	qal	impf	3ms	חטא	306		sin
	נשׁא	qal	wcp	3ms	נשׁא	673?		be creditor
	האלתו	hiph	infc		אלה	46	3ms	put under oath
	בא	qal	wcp	3ms	בוא	97		come in
	אלה	qal	pft	3ms	אלה	46		swear
6:23	תשׁמע	qal	impf	2ms	שׁמע	1033		hear
	עשׂית	qal	wcp	2ms	עשׂה	793		do,make
	שׁפטת	qal	wcp	2ms	שׁפט	1047		judge
	השׁיב	hiph	infc		שׁוב	996		bring back
	תת	qal	infc		נתן	678		give,set
	הצדיק	hiph	infc		צדק	842		make righteous
	תת	qal	infc		נתן	678		give,set
6:24	ינגף	niph	impf	3ms	נגף	619		be smitten
	אויב	qal	ptc	ms	איב	33		be hostile to
	יחטאו	qal	impf	3mp	חטא	306		sin
	שׁבו	qal	wcp	3cp	שׁוב	996		turn,return
	הודו	hiph	wcp	3cp	ידה	392		praise
	התפללו	hith	wcp	3cp	פלל	813		pray
	התחננו	hith	wcp	3cp	חנן	335		seek favor
6:25	תשׁמע	qal	impf	2ms	שׁמע	1033		hear
	סלחת	qal	wcp	2ms	סלח	699		forgive,pardon
	השׁיבותם	hiph	wcp	2ms	שׁוב	996	3mp	bring back
	נתתה	qal	pft	2ms	נתן	678		give,set
6:26	העצר	niph	infc		עצר	783		be restrained
	יהיה	qal	impf	3ms	היה	224		be,become
	יחטאו	qal	impf	3mp	חטא	306		sin

ChVs	Form	Stem	Tnse	PGN	Root	BDB	Sfx	Meaning
6: 26	התפללו	hith	wcp	3cp	פלל	813		pray
	הודו	hiph	wcp	3cp	ידה	392		praise
	ישובון	qal	impf	3mp	שוב	996		turn, return
	תענם	hiph	impf	2ms	ענה	776	3mp	afflict
6: 27	תשמע	qal	impf	2ms	שמע	1033		hear
	סלחת	qal	wcp	2ms	סלח	699		forgive, pardon
	תורם	hiph	impf	2ms	ירה	434	3mp	shoot, teach
	ילכו	qal	impf	3mp	הלך	229		walk, go
	נתתה	qal	wcp	2ms	נתן	678		give, set
	נתתה	qal	pft	2ms	נתן	678		give, set
6: 28	יהיה	qal	impf	3ms	היה	224		be, become
	יהיה	qal	impf	3ms	היה	224		be, become
	יהיה	qal	impf	3ms	היה	224		be, become
	יצר	hiph	impf	3ms	צרר	864		distress, cramp
	אויביו	qal	ptc	mp	איב	33	3ms	be hostile to
6: 29	יהיה	qal	impf	3ms	היה	224		be, become
	ידעו	qal	impf	3mp	ידע	393		know
	פרש	qal	wcp	3ms	פרש	831		spread out
6: 30	תשמע	qal	impf	2ms	שמע	1033		hear
	שבתך	qal	infc		ישב	442	2ms	sit, dwell
	סלחת	qal	wcp	2ms	סלח	699		forgive, pardon
	נתתה	qal	wcp	2ms	נתן	678		give, set
	תדע	qal	impf	2ms	ידע	393		know
	ידעת	qal	pft	2ms	ידע	393		know
6: 31	ייראוך	qal	impf	3mp	ירא	431	2ms	fear
	לכת	qal	infc		הלך	229		walk, go
	נתתה	qal	pft	2ms	נתן	678		give, set
6: 32	בא	qal	wcp	3ms	בוא	97		come in
	נטויה	qal	pptc	fs	נטה	639		stretch, incline
	באו	qal	wcp	3cp	בוא	97		come in
	התפללו	hith	wcp	3cp	פלל	813		pray
6: 33	תשמע	qal	impf	2ms	שמע	1033		hear
	שבתך	qal	infc		ישב	442	2ms	sit, dwell
	עשית	qal	wcp	2ms	עשה	793		do, make
	יקרא	qal	impf	3ms	קרא	894		call, proclaim
	ידעו	qal	impf	3mp	ידע	393		know
	יראה	qal	infc		ירא	431		fear
	דעת	qal	infc		ידע	393		know
	נקרא	niph	pft	3ms	קרא	894		be called
	בניתי	qal	pft	1cs	בנה	124		build
6: 34	יצא	qal	impf	3ms	יצא	422		go out
	אויביו	qal	ptc	mp	איב	33	3ms	be hostile to
	תשלחם	qal	impf	2ms	שלח	1018	3mp	send
	התפללו	hith	wcp	3cp	פלל	813		pray
	בחרת	qal	pft	2ms	בחר	103		choose
	בניתי	qal	pft	1cs	בנה	124		build
6: 35	שמעת	qal	wcp	2ms	שמע	1033		hear
	עשית	qal	wcp	2ms	עשה	793		do, make
6: 36	יחטאו	qal	impf	3mp	חטא	306		sin
	יחטא	qal	impf	3ms	חטא	306		sin
	אנפת	qal	wcp	2ms	אנף	60		be angry
	נתתם	qal	wcp	2ms	נתן	678	3mp	give, set
	אויב	qal	ptc	ms	איב	33		be hostile to
	שבום	qal	wcp	3cp	שבה	985	3mp	take captive
6: 36	שוביהם	qal	ptc	mp	שבה	985	3mp	take captive
6: 37	השיבו	hiph	wcp	3cp	שוב	996		bring back
	נשבו	niph	pft	3cp	שבה	985		be held captive
	שבו	qal	wcp	3cp	שוב	996		turn, return
	התחננו	hith	wcp	3cp	חנן	335		seek favor
	אמר	qal	infc		אמר	55		say
	חטאנו	qal	pft	1cp	חטא	306		sin
	העוינו	hiph	pft	1cp	עוה	731		commit iniquity
	רשענו	qal	pft	1cp	רשע	957		be wicked
6: 38	שבו	qal	wcp	3cp	שוב	996		turn, return
	שבו	qal	pft	3cp	שבה	985		take captive
	התפללו	hith	wcp	3cp	פלל	813		pray
	נתתה	qal	pft	2ms	נתן	678		give, set
	בחרת	qal	pft	2ms	בחר	103		choose
	בניתי	qal	pft	1cs	בנה	124		build
6: 39	שמעת	qal	wcp	2ms	שמע	1033		hear
	שבתך	qal	infc		ישב	442	2ms	sit, dwell
	עשית	qal	wcp	2ms	עשה	793		do, make
	סלחת	qal	wcp	2ms	סלח	699		forgive, pardon
	חטאו	qal	pft	3cp	חטא	306		sin
6: 40	יהיו	qal	jusm	3mp	היה	224		be, become
	פתחות	qal	pptc	fp	פתח	834		open
6: 41	קומה	qal	impv	ms	קום	877		arise, stand
	ילבשו	qal	jusm	3mp	לבש	527		put on, clothe
	ישמחו	qal	jusm	3mp	שמח	970		rejoice
6: 42	תשב	hiph	jus	2ms	שוב	996		bring back
	זכרה	qal	impv	ms	זכר	269		remember
7: 1	כלות	piel	infc		כלה	477		complete, finish
	התפלל	hith	infc		פלל	813		pray
	ירדה	qal	pft	3fs	ירד	432		come down
	תאכל	qal	wci	3fs	אכל	37		eat, devour
	מלא	qal	pft	3ms	מלא	569		be full, fill
7: 2	יכלו	qal	pft	3cp	יכל	407		be able
	בוא	qal	infc		בוא	97		come in
	מלא	qal	pft	3ms	מלא	569		be full, fill
7: 3	ראים	qal	ptc	mp	ראה	906		see
	רדת	qal	infc		ירד	432		come down
	יכרעו	qal	wci	3mp	כרע	502		bow down
	ישתחוו	hish	wci	3mp	חוה	1005		bow down
	הודות	hiph	infc		ידה	392		praise
7: 4	זבחים	qal	ptc	mp	זבח	256		slaughter
7: 5	יזבח	qal	wci	3ms	זבח	256		slaughter
	יחנכו	qal	wci	3mp	חנך	335		train, dedicate
7: 6	עמדים	qal	ptc	mp	עמד	763		stand, stop
	עשה	qal	pft	3ms	עשה	793		do, make
	הדות	hiph	infc		ידה	392		praise
	הלל	piel	infc		הלל	237		praise
	מחצצרים k	hiph	ptc	mp	חצצר	348		sound w/clarion
	מחצרים q	hiph	ptc	mp	חצר	348		sound w/clarion
	עמדים	qal	ptc	mp	עמד	763		stand, stop
7: 7	יקדש	piel	wci	3ms	קדש	872		consecrate
	עשה	qal	pft	3ms	עשה	793		do, make
	עשה	qal	pft	3ms	עשה	793		do, make
	יכול	qal	pft	3ms	יכל	407		be able

ChVs	Form	Stem	Tnse	PGN	Root	BDB	Sfx	Meaning
7:7	הכיל	hiph	infc		כול	465		contain
7:8	יעשׂ	qal	wci	3ms	עשׂה	793		do,make
	בוא	qal	infc		בוא	97		come in
7:9	יעשׂו	qal	wci	3mp	עשׂה	793		do,make
	עשׂו	qal	pft	3cp	עשׂה	793		do,make
7:10	שׁלח	piel	pft	3ms	שׁלח	1018		send away,shoot
	עשׂה	qal	pft	3ms	עשׂה	793		do,make
7:11	יכל	piel	wci	3ms	כלה	477		complete,finish
	בא	qal	ptc	ms	בוא	97		come in
	עשׂות	qal	infc		עשׂה	793		do,make
	הצליח	hiph	pft	3ms	צלח	852		cause to thrive
7:12	ירא	niph	wci	3ms	ראה	906		appear,be seen
	יאמר	qal	wci	3ms	אמר	55		say
	שׁמעתי	qal	pft	1cs	שׁמע	1033		hear
	בחרתי	qal	wcp	1cs	בחר	103		choose
7:13	אעצר	qal	impf	1cs	עצר	783		restrain
	יהיה	qal	impf	3ms	היה	224		be,become
	אצוה	piel	impf	1cs	צוה	845		command
	אכול	qal	infc		אכל	37		eat,devour
	אשׁלח	piel	impf	1cs	שׁלח	1018		send away,shoot
7:14	יכנעו	niph	impf	3mp	כנע	488		humble self
	נקרא	niph	pft	3ms	קרא	894		be called
	יתפללו	hith	impf	3mp	פלל	813		pray
	יבקשׁו	piel	impf	3mp	בקשׁ	134		seek
	ישׁבו	qal	impf	3mp	שׁוב	996		turn,return
	אשׁמע	qal	impf	1cs	שׁמע	1033		hear
	אסלח	qal	impf	1cs	סלח	699		forgive,pardon
	ארפא	qal	impf	1cs	רפא	950		heal
7:15	יהיו	qal	impf	3mp	היה	224		be,become
	פתחות	qal	pptc	fp	פתח	834		open
7:16	בחרתי	qal	pft	1cs	בחר	103		choose
	הקדשׁתי	hiph	pft	1cs	קדשׁ	872		consecrate
	היות	qal	infc		היה	224		be,become
	היו	qal	wcp	3cp	היה	224		be,become
7:17	תלך	qal	impf	2ms	הלך	229		walk,go
	הלך	qal	pft	3ms	הלך	229		walk,go
	עשׂות	qal	infc		עשׂה	793		do,make
	צויתיך	piel	pft	1cs	צוה	845	2ms	command
	תשׁמור	qal	impf	2ms	שׁמר	1036		keep,watch
7:18	הקימותי	hiph	wcp	1cs	קום	877		raise,build,set
	כרתי	qal	pft	1cs	כרת	503		cut,destroy
	אמר	qal	infc		אמר	55		say
	יכרת	niph	impf	3ms	כרת	503		be cut off
	מושׁל	qal	ptc	ms	משׁל	605		rule
7:19	תשׁובון	qal	impf	2mp	שׁוב	996		turn,return
	עזבתם	qal	wcp	2mp	עזב	736		leave,loose
	נתתי	qal	pft	1cs	נתן	678		give,set
	הלכתם	qal	wcp	2mp	הלך	229		walk,go
	עבדתם	qal	wcp	2mp	עבד	712		work,serve
	השׁתחויתם	hish	wcp	2mp	חוה	1005		bow down
7:20	נתשׁתים	qal	wcp	1cs	נתשׁ	684	3mp	pull up
	נתתי	qal	pft	1cs	נתן	678		give,set
	הקדשׁתי	hiph	pft	1cs	קדשׁ	872		consecrate
	אשׁליך	hiph	impf	1cs	שׁלך	1020		throw,cast
7:20	אתננו	qal	impf	1cs	נתן	678	3ms	give,set
7:21	היה	qal	pft	3ms	היה	224		be,become
	עבר	qal	ptc	ms	עבר	716		pass over
	ישׁם	qal	impf	3ms	שׁמם	1030		be desolate
	אמר	qal	wcp	3ms	אמר	55		say
	עשׂה	qal	pft	3ms	עשׂה	793		do,make
7:22	אמרו	qal	wcp	3cp	אמר	55		say
	עזבו	qal	pft	3cp	עזב	736		leave,loose
	הוציאם	hiph	pft	3ms	יצא	422	3mp	bring out
	יחזיקו	hiph	wci	3mp	חזק	304		make firm,seize
	ישׁתחוו	hish	wci	3mp	חוה	1005		bow down
	יעבדום	qal	wci	3mp	עבד	712	3mp	work,serve
	הביא	hiph	pft	3ms	בוא	97		bring in
8:1	יהי	qal	wci	3ms	היה	224		be,become
	בנה	qal	pft	3ms	בנה	124		build
8:2	נתן	qal	pft	3ms	נתן	678		give,set
	בנה	qal	pft	3ms	בנה	124		build
	יושׁב	hiph	wci	3ms	ישׁב	442		cause to dwell
8:3	ילך	qal	wci	3ms	הלך	229		walk,go
	יחזק	qal	wci	3ms	חזק	304		be strong
8:4	יבן	qal	wci	3ms	בנה	124		build
	בנה	qal	pft	3ms	בנה	124		build
8:5	יבן	qal	wci	3ms	בנה	124		build
8:6	היו	qal	pft	3cp	היה	224		be,become
	חשׁק	qal	pft	3ms	חשׁק	365		love
	בנות	qal	infc		בנה	124		build
8:7	נותר	niph	ptc	ms	יתר	451		be left,remain
8:8	נותרו	niph	pft	3cp	יתר	451		be left,remain
	כלום	piel	pft	3cp	כלה	477	3mp	complete,finish
	יעלם	hiph	wci	3ms	עלה	748	3mp	bring up,offer
8:9	נתן	qal	pft	3ms	נתן	678		give,set
8:10	נצביםq	niph	ptc	mp	נצב	662		stand
	רדים	qal	ptc	mp	רדה	921		rule
8:11	העלה	hiph	pft	3ms	עלה	748		bring up,offer
	בנה	qal	pft	3ms	בנה	124		build
	אמר	qal	pft	3ms	אמר	55		say
	תשׁב	qal	impf	3fs	ישׁב	442		sit,dwell
	באה	qal	pft	3fs	בוא	97		come in
8:12	העלה	hiph	pft	3ms	עלה	748		bring up,offer
	בנה	qal	pft	3ms	בנה	124		build
8:13	העלות	hiph	infc		עלה	748		bring up,offer
8:14	יעמד	hiph	wci	3ms	עמד	763		set up,raise
	הלל	piel	infc		הלל	237		praise
	שׁרת	piel	infc		שׁרת	1058		minister,serve
8:15	סרו	qal	pft	3cp	סור	693		turn aside
8:16	תכן	niph	wci	3fs	כון	465		be established
	כלתו	qal	infc		כלה	477	3ms	finished,spent
8:17	הלך	qal	pft	3ms	הלך	229		walk,go
8:18	ישׁלח	qal	wci	3ms	שׁלח	1018		send
	יודעי	qal	ptc	mp	ידע	393		know
	יבאו	qal	wci	3mp	בוא	97		come in
	יקחו	qal	wci	3mp	לקח	542		take
	יביאו	hiph	wci	3mp	בוא	97		bring in
9:1	שׁמעה	qal	pft	3fs	שׁמע	1033		hear

ChVs	Form	Stem	Tnse	PGN	Root	BDB	Sfx	Meaning
9:1	תבוא	qal	wci	3fs	בוא	97		come in
	נסות	piel	infc		נסה	650		test,try
	נשׂאים	qal	ptc	mp	נשׂא	669		lift,carry
	תבוא	qal	wci	3fs	בוא	97		come in
	תדבר	piel	wci	3fs	דבר	180		speak
	היה	qal	pft	3ms	היה	224		be,become
9:2	יגד	hiph	wci	3ms	נגד	616		declare,tell
	נעלם	niph	pft	3ms	עלם	761		be concealed
	הגיד	hiph	pft	3ms	נגד	616		declare,tell
9:3	תרא	qal	wci	3fs	ראה	906		see
	בנה	qal	pft	3ms	בנה	124		build
9:4	משׁרתיו	piel	ptc	mp	שׁרת	1058	3ms	minister,serve
	יעלה	qal	impf	3ms	עלה	748		go up
	היה	qal	pft	3ms	היה	224		be,become
9:5	תאמר	qal	wci	3fs	אמר	55		say
	שׁמעתי	qal	pft	1cs	שׁמע	1033		hear
9:6	האמנתי	hiph	pft	1cs	אמן	52		believe
	באתי	qal	pft	1cs	בוא	97		come in
	תראינה	qal	wci	3fp	ראה	906		see
	הגד	hoph	pft	3ms	נגד	616		be told
	יספת	qal	pft	2ms	יסף	414		add,increase
	שׁמעתי	qal	pft	1cs	שׁמע	1033		hear
9:7	עמדים	qal	ptc	mp	עמד	763		stand,stop
	שׁמעים	qal	ptc	mp	שׁמע	1033		hear
9:8	יהי	qal	jus	3ms	היה	224		be,become
	ברוך	qal	pptc	ms	ברך	138		kneel,bless
	חפץ	qal	pft	3ms	חפץ	342		delight in
	תתך	qal	infc		נתן	678	2ms	give,set
	אהבת	qal	infc		אהב	12		love
	העמידו	hiph	infc		עמד	763	3ms	set up,raise
	יתנך	qal	wci	3ms	נתן	678	2ms	give,set
	עשׂות	qal	infc		עשׂה	793		do,make
9:9	תתן	qal	wci	3fs	נתן	678		give,set
	היה	qal	pft	3ms	היה	224		be,become
	נתנה	qal	pft	3fs	נתן	678		give,set
9:10	הביאו	hiph	pft	3cp	בוא	97		bring in
	הביאו	hiph	pft	3cp	בוא	97		bring in
9:11	יעשׂ	qal	wci	3ms	עשׂה	793		do,make
	שׁרים	qal	ptc	mp	שׁיר	1010		sing
	נראו	niph	pft	3cp	ראה	906		appear,be seen
9:12	נתן	qal	pft	3ms	נתן	678		give,set
	שׁאלה	qal	pft	3fs	שׁאל	981		ask,borrow
	הביאה	hiph	pft	3fs	בוא	97		bring in
	תהפך	qal	wci	3fs	הפך	245		turn,overturn
	תלך	qal	wci	3fs	הלך	229		walk,go
9:13	יהי	qal	wci	3ms	היה	224		be,become
	בא	qal	pft	3ms	בוא	97		come in
9:14	תרים	qal	ptc	mp	תור	1064		seek out,spy
	סחרים	qal	ptc	mp	סחר	695		go around
	מביאים	hiph	ptc	mp	בוא	97		bring in
	מביאים	hiph	ptc	mp	בוא	97		bring in
9:15	יעשׂ	qal	wci	3ms	עשׂה	793		do,make
	שׁחוט	qal	pptc	ms	שׁחט	1006		slaughter
	שׁחוט	qal	pptc	ms	שׁחט	1006		slaughter
9:15	יעלה	hiph	impf	3ms	עלה	748		bring up,offer
9:16	שׁחוט	qal	pptc	ms	שׁחט	1006		slaughter
	יעלה	hiph	impf	3ms	עלה	748		bring up,offer
	יתנם	qal	wci	3ms	נתן	678	3mp	give,set
9:17	יעשׂ	qal	wci	3ms	עשׂה	793		do,make
	יצפהו	piel	wci	3ms	צפה	860	3ms	overlay
9:18	מאחזים	hoph	ptc	mp	אחז	28		fastened
	עמדים	qal	ptc	mp	עמד	763		stand,stop
9:19	עמדים	qal	ptc	mp	עמד	763		stand,stop
	נעשׂה	niph	pft	3ms	עשׂה	793		be done
9:20	נחשׁב	niph	ptc	ms	חשׁב	362		be thought
9:21	הלכות	qal	ptc	fp	הלך	229		walk,go
	תבואנה	qal	impf	3fp	בוא	97		come in
	נשׂאות	qal	ptc	fp	נשׂא	669		lift,carry
9:22	יגדל	qal	wci	3ms	גדל	152		be great,grow
9:23	מבקשׁים	piel	ptc	mp	בקשׁ	134		seek
	שׁמע	qal	infc		שׁמע	1033		hear
	נתן	qal	pft	3ms	נתן	678		give,set
9:24	מביאים	hiph	ptc	mp	בוא	97		bring in
9:25	יהי	qal	wci	3ms	היה	224		be,become
	יניחם	hiph	wci	3ms	נוח	628	3mp	give rest,put
9:26	יהי	qal	wci	3ms	היה	224		be,become
	מושׁל	qal	ptc	ms	משׁל	605		rule
9:27	יתן	qal	wci	3ms	נתן	678		give,set
	נתן	qal	pft	3ms	נתן	678		give,set
9:28	מוציאים	hiph	ptc	mp	יצא	422		bring out
9:29	כתובים	qal	pptc	mp	כתב	507		write
9:30	ימלך	qal	wci	3ms	מלך	573		be king,reign
9:31	ישׁכב	qal	wci	3ms	שׁכב	1011		lie,lie down
	יקברהו	qal	wci	3mp	קבר	868	3ms	bury
	ימלך	qal	wci	3ms	מלך	573		be king,reign
10:1	ילך	qal	wci	3ms	הלך	229		walk,go
	באו	qal	pft	3cp	בוא	97		come in
	המליך	hiph	infc		מלך	573		cause to reign
10:2	יהי	qal	wci	3ms	היה	224		be,become
	שׁמע	qal	infc		שׁמע	1033		hear
	ברח	qal	pft	3ms	ברח	137		go thru,flee
	ישׁב	qal	wci	3ms	שׁוב	996		turn,return
10:3	ישׁלחו	qal	wci	3mp	שׁלח	1018		send
	יקראו	qal	wci	3mp	קרא	894		call,proclaim
	יבא	qal	wci	3ms	בוא	97		come in
	ידברו	piel	wci	3mp	דבר	180		speak
	אמר	qal	infc		אמר	55		say
10:4	הקשׁה	hiph	pft	3ms	קשׁה	904		harden
	הקל	hiph	impv	ms	קלל	886		make light
	נתן	qal	pft	3ms	נתן	678		give,set
	נעבדך	qal	cohm	1cp	עבד	712	2ms	work,serve
10:5	יאמר	qal	wci	3ms	אמר	55		say
	שׁובו	qal	impv	mp	שׁוב	996		turn,return
	ילך	qal	wci	3ms	הלך	229		walk,go
10:6	יועץ	niph	wci	3ms	יעץ	419		consult
	היו	qal	pft	3cp	היה	224		be,become
	עמדים	qal	ptc	mp	עמד	763		stand,stop
	היתו	qal	infc		היה	224	3ms	be,become

ChVs	Form	Stem	Tnse	PGN	Root	BDB	Sfx	Meaning
10: 6	אמר	qal	infc		אמר	55		say
	נועצים	niph	ptc	mp	יעץ	419		consult
	השיב	hiph	infc		שוב	996		bring back
10: 7	ידברו	piel	wci	3mp	דבר	180		speak
	אמר	qal	infc		אמר	55		say
	תהיה	qal	impf	2ms	היה	224		be,become
	רציתם	qal	wcp	2ms	רצה	953	3mp	be pleased
	דברת	piel	wcp	2ms	דבר	180		speak
	היו	qal	wcp	3cp	היה	224		be,become
10: 8	יעזב	qal	wci	3ms	עזב	736		leave,loose
	יעצהו	qal	pft	3cp	יעץ	419	3ms	advise,counsel
	יועץ	niph	wci	3ms	יעץ	419		consult
	גדלו	qal	pft	3cp	גדל	152		be great,grow
	עמדים	qal	ptc	mp	עמד	763		stand,stop
10: 9	יאמר	qal	wci	3ms	אמר	55		say
	נועצים	niph	ptc	mp	יעץ	419		consult
	נשיב	hiph	impf	1cp	שוב	996		bring back
	דברו	piel	pft	3cp	דבר	180		speak
	אמר	qal	infc		אמר	55		say
	הקל	hiph	impv	ms	קלל	886		make light
	נתן	qal	pft	3ms	נתן	678		give,set
10: 10	ידברו	piel	wci	3mp	דבר	180		speak
	גדלו	qal	pft	3cp	גדל	152		be great,grow
	אמר	qal	infc		אמר	55		say
	תאמר	qal	impf	2ms	אמר	55		say
	דברו	piel	pft	3cp	דבר	180		speak
	אמר	qal	infc		אמר	55		say
	הכביד	hiph	pft	3ms	כבד	457		make heavy
	הקל	hiph	impv	ms	קלל	886		make light
	תאמר	qal	impf	2ms	אמר	55		say
	עבה	qal	pft	3ms	עבה	716		be thick
10: 11	העמים	hiph	pft	3ms	עמס	770		load
	אסיף	hiph	impf	1cs	יסף	414		add,do again
	יסר	piel	pft	3ms	יסר	415		correct,chasten
10: 12	יבא	qal	wci	3ms	בוא	97		come in
	דבר	piel	pft	3ms	דבר	180		speak
	אמר	qal	infc		אמר	55		say
	שובו	qal	impv	mp	שוב	996		turn,return
10: 13	יענם	qal	wci	3ms	ענה	772	3mp	answer
	יעזב	qal	wci	3ms	עזב	736		leave,loose
10: 14	ידבר	piel	wci	3ms	דבר	180		speak
	אמר	qal	infc		אמר	55		say
	אכביד	hiph	impf	1cs	כבד	457		make heavy
	אסיף	hiph	impf	1cs	יסף	414		add,do again
	יסר	piel	pft	3ms	יסר	415		correct,chasten
10: 15	שמע	qal	pft	3ms	שמע	1033		hear
	היתה	qal	pft	3fs	היה	224		be,become
	הקים	hiph	infc		קום	877		raise,build,set
	דבר	piel	pft	3ms	דבר	180		speak
10: 16	שמע	qal	pft	3ms	שמע	1033		hear
	ישיבו	hiph	wci	3mp	שוב	996		bring back
	אמר	qal	infc		אמר	55		say
	ראה	qal	impv	ms	ראה	906		see
	ילך	qal	wci	3ms	הלך	229		walk,go

ChVs	Form	Stem	Tnse	PGN	Root	BDB	Sfx	Meaning
10: 17	ישבים	qal	ptc	mp	ישב	442		sit,dwell
	ימלך	qal	wci	3ms	מלך	573		be king,reign
10: 18	ישלח	qal	wci	3ms	שלח	1018		send
	ירגמו	qal	wci	3mp	רגם	920		stone
	ימת	qal	wci	3ms	מות	559		die
	התאמץ	hith	pft	3ms	אמץ	54		strengthen self
	עלות	qal	infc		עלה	748		go up
	נוס	qal	infc		נוס	630		flee,escape
10: 19	יפשעו	qal	wci	3mp	פשע	833		rebel,sin
11: 1	יבא	qal	wci	3ms	בוא	97		come in
	יקהל	hiph	wci	3ms	קהל	874		call assembly
	בחור	qal	pptc	ms	בחר	103		choose
	עשה	qal	ptc	ms	עשה	793		do,make
	הלחם	niph	infc		לחם	535		wage war
	השיב	hiph	infc		שוב	996		bring back
11: 2	יהי	qal	wci	3ms	היה	224		be,become
	אמר	qal	infc		אמר	55		say
11: 3	אמר	qal	impv	ms	אמר	55		say
	אמר	qal	infc		אמר	55		say
11: 4	אמר	qal	pft	3ms	אמר	55		say
	תעלו	qal	impf	2mp	עלה	748		go up
	תלחמו	niph	impf	2mp	לחם	535		wage war
	שובו	qal	impv	mp	שוב	996		turn,return
	נהיה	niph	pft	3ms	היה	224		be done
	ישמעו	qal	wci	3mp	שמע	1033		hear
	ישבו	qal	wci	3mp	שוב	996		turn,return
	לכת	qal	infc		הלך	229		walk,go
11: 5	ישב	qal	wci	3ms	ישב	442		sit,dwell
	יבן	qal	wci	3ms	בנה	124		build
11: 6	יבן	qal	wci	3ms	בנה	124		build
11: 11	יחזק	piel	wci	3ms	חזק	304		make strong
	יתן	qal	wci	3ms	נתן	678		give,set
11: 12	יחזקם	piel	wci	3ms	חזק	304	3mp	make strong
	הרבה	hiph	infa		רבה	915		make many
	יהי	qal	wci	3ms	היה	224		be,become
11: 13	התיצבו	hith	pft	3cp	יצב	426		stand oneself
11: 14	עזבו	qal	pft	3cp	עזב	736		leave,loose
	ילכו	qal	wci	3mp	הלך	229		walk,go
	הזניחם	hiph	pft	3ms	זנח	276	3mp	reject
	כהן	piel	infc		כהן	464		act as priest
11: 15	יעמד	hiph	wci	3ms	עמד	763		set up,raise
	עשה	qal	pft	3ms	עשה	793		do,make
11: 16	נתנים	qal	ptc	mp	נתן	678		give,set
	בקש	piel	infc		בקש	134		seek
	באו	qal	pft	3cp	בוא	97		come in
	זבוח	qal	infc		זבח	256		slaughter
11: 17	יחזקו	piel	wci	3mp	חזק	304		make strong
	יאמצו	piel	wci	3mp	אמץ	54		make firm
	הלכו	qal	pft	3cp	הלך	229		walk,go
11: 18	יקח	qal	wci	3ms	לקח	542		take
11: 19	תלד	qal	wci	3fs	ילד	408		bear,beget
11: 20	לקח	qal	pft	3ms	לקח	542		take
	תלד	qal	wci	3fs	ילד	408		bear,beget
11: 21	יאהב	qal	wci	3ms	אהב	12		love

ChVs	Form	Stem	Tnse	PGN	Root	BDB	Sfx	Meaning
11:21	נשא	qal	pft	3ms	נשא	669		lift,carry
	יולד	hiph	wci	3ms	ילד	408		beget
11:22	יעמד	hiph	wci	3ms	עמד	763		set up,raise
	המליכו	hiph	infc		מלך	573	3ms	cause to reign
11:23	יבן	hiph	wci	3ms	בין	106		understand
	יפרץ	qal	wci	3ms	פרץ	829		break through
	יתן	qal	wci	3ms	נתן	678		give,set
	ישאל	qal	wci	3ms	שאל	981		ask,borrow
12:1	יהי	qal	wci	3ms	היה	224		be,become
	הכין	hiph	infc		כון	465		fix,prepare
	עזב	qal	pft	3ms	עזב	736		leave,loose
12:2	יהי	qal	wci	3ms	היה	224		be,become
	עלה	qal	pft	3ms	עלה	748		go up
	מעלו	qal	pft	3cp	מעל	591		act faithlessly
12:3	באו	qal	pft	3cp	בוא	97		come in
12:4	ילכד	qal	wci	3ms	לכד	539		capture
	יבא	qal	wci	3ms	בוא	97		come in
12:5	בא	qal	pft	3ms	בוא	97		come in
	נאספו	niph	pft	3cp	אסף	62		assemble
	יאמר	qal	wci	3ms	אמר	55		say
	אמר	qal	pft	3ms	אמר	55		say
	עזבתם	qal	pft	2mp	עזב	736		leave,loose
	עזבתי	qal	pft	1cs	עזב	736		leave,loose
12:6	יכנעו	niph	wci	3mp	כנע	488		humble self
	יאמרו	qal	wci	3mp	אמר	55		say
12:7	ראות	qal	infc		ראה	906		see
	נכנעו	niph	pft	3cp	כנע	488		humble self
	היה	qal	pft	3ms	היה	224		be,become
	אמר	qal	infc		אמר	55		say
	נכנעו	niph	pft	3cp	כנע	488		humble self
	אשחיתם	hiph	impf	1cs	שחת	1007	3mp	spoil,ruin
	נתתי	qal	wcp	1cs	נתן	678		give,set
	תתך	qal	impf	3fs	נתך	677		pour forth
12:8	יהיו	qal	impf	3mp	היה	224		be,become
	ידעו	qal	impf	3mp	ידע	393		know
12:9	יעל	qal	wci	3ms	עלה	748		go up
	יקח	qal	wci	3ms	לקח	542		take
	לקח	qal	pft	3ms	לקח	542		take
	יקח	qal	wci	3ms	לקח	542		take
	עשה	qal	pft	3ms	עשה	793		do,make
12:10	יעש	qal	wci	3ms	עשה	793		do,make
	הפקיד	hiph	pft	3ms	פקד	823		set,entrust
	רצים	qal	ptc	mp	רוץ	930		run
	שמרים	qal	ptc	mp	שמר	1036		keep,watch
12:11	יהי	qal	wci	3ms	היה	224		be,become
	בוא	qal	infc		בוא	97		come in
	באו	qal	pft	3cp	בוא	97		come in
	רצים	qal	ptc	mp	רוץ	930		run
	נשאום	qal	wcp	3cp	נשא	669	3mp	lift,carry
	השבום	hiph	wcp	3cp	שוב	996	3mp	bring back
	רצים	qal	ptc	mp	רוץ	930		run
12:12	הכנעו	niph	infc		כנע	488	3ms	humble self
	שב	qal	pft	3ms	שוב	996		turn,return
	השחית	hiph	infc		שחת	1007		spoil,ruin
12:12	היה	qal	pft	3ms	היה	224		be,become
12:13	יתחזק	hith	wci	3ms	חזק	304		strengthen self
	ימלך	qal	wci	3ms	מלך	573		be king,reign
	מלכו	qal	infc		מלך	573	3ms	be king,reign
	מלך	qal	pft	3ms	מלך	573		be king,reign
	בחר	qal	pft	3ms	בחר	103		choose
	שום	qal	infc		שים	962		put,set
12:14	יעש	qal	wci	3ms	עשה	793		do,make
	הכין	hiph	pft	3ms	כון	465		fix,prepare
	דרוש	qal	infc		דרש	205		resort to,seek
12:15	כתובים	qal	pptc	mp	כתב	507		write
	התיחש	hith	infc		יחש	405		be registered
12:16	ישכב	qal	wci	3ms	שכב	1011		lie,lie down
	יקבר	niph	wci	3ms	קבר	868		be buried
	ימלך	qal	wci	3ms	מלך	573		be king,reign
13:1	ימלך	qal	wci	3ms	מלך	573		be king,reign
13:2	מלך	qal	pft	3ms	מלך	573		be king,reign
	היתה	qal	pft	3fs	היה	224		be,become
13:3	יאסר	qal	wci	3ms	אסר	63		tie,bind
	בחור	qal	pptc	ms	בחר	103		choose
	ערך	qal	pft	3ms	ערך	789		set in order
	בחור	qal	pptc	ms	בחר	103		choose
13:4	יקם	qal	wci	3ms	קום	877		arise,stand
	יאמר	qal	wci	3ms	אמר	55		say
	שמעוני	qal	impv	mp	שמע	1033	1cs	hear
13:5	דעת	qal	infc		ידע	393		know
	נתן	qal	pft	3ms	נתן	678		give,set
13:6	יקם	qal	wci	3ms	קום	877		arise,stand
	ימרד	qal	wci	3ms	מרד	597		rebel
13:7	יקבצו	niph	wci	3mp	קבץ	867		assemble,gather
	יתאמצו	hith	wci	3mp	אמץ	54		strengthen self
	היה	qal	pft	3ms	היה	224		be,become
	התחזק	hith	pft	3ms	חזק	304		strengthen self
13:8	אמרים	qal	ptc	mp	אמר	55		say
	התחזק	hith	infc		חזק	304		strengthen self
	עשה	qal	pft	3ms	עשה	793		do,make
13:9	הדחתם	hiph	pft	2mp	נדח	623		thrust out
	תעשו	qal	wci	2mp	עשה	793		do,make
	בא	qal	ptc	ms	בוא	97		come in
	מלא	piel	infc		מלא	569		fill
	היה	qal	wcp	3ms	היה	224		be,become
13:10	עזבנהו	qal	pft	1cp	עזב	736	3ms	leave,loose
	משרתים	piel	ptc	mp	שרת	1058		minister,serve
13:11	מקטרים	hiph	ptc	mp	קטר	882		make sacrifices
	בער	piel	infc		בער	128		burn,consume
	שמרים	qal	ptc	mp	שמר	1036		keep,watch
	עזבתם	qal	pft	2mp	עזב	736		leave,loose
13:12	הריע	hiph	infc		רוע	929		raise a shout
	תלחמו	niph	jusm	2mp	לחם	535		wage war
	תצליחו	hiph	impf	2mp	צלח	852		cause to thrive
13:13	הסב	hiph	pft	3ms	סבב	685		cause to turn
	בוא	qal	infc		בוא	97		come in
	יהיו	qal	wci	3mp	היה	224		be,become
13:14	יפנו	qal	wci	3mp	פנה	815		turn

ChVs	Form	Stem	Tnse	PGN	Root	BDB	Sfx	Meaning
13:14	יצעקו	qal	wci	3mp	צעק	858		cry out
	מחצצרים k	hiph	ptc	mp	חצצר	348		sound w/clarion
	מחצרים q	hiph	ptc	mp	חצר	348		sound w/clarion
13:15	יריעו	hiph	wci	3mp	רוע	929		raise a shout
	יהי	qal	wci	3ms	היה	224		be,become
	הריע	hiph	infc		רוע	929		raise a shout
	נגף	qal	pft	3ms	נגף	619		smite,strike
13:16	ינוסו	qal	wci	3mp	נוס	630		flee,escape
	יתנם	qal	wci	3ms	נתן	678	3mp	give,set
13:17	יכו	hiph	wci	3mp	נכה	645		smite
	יפלו	qal	wci	3mp	נפל	656		fall
	בחור	qal	pptc	ms	בחר	103		choose
13:18	יכנעו	niph	wci	3mp	כנע	488		humble self
	יאמצו	qal	wci	3mp	אמץ	54		be strong
	נשענו	niph	pft	3cp	שען	1043		lean,support
13:19	ירדף	qal	wci	3ms	רדף	922		pursue
	ילכד	qal	wci	3ms	לכד	539		capture
13:20	עצר	qal	pft	3ms	עצר	783		restrain
	יגפהו	qal	wci	3ms	נגף	619	3ms	smite,strike
	ימת	qal	wci	3ms	מות	559		die
13:21	יתחזק	hith	wci	3ms	חזק	304		strengthen self
	ישא	qal	wci	3ms	נשא	669		lift,carry
	יולד	hiph	wci	3ms	ילד	408		beget
13:22	כתובים	qal	pptc	mp	כתב	507		write
13:23	ישכב	qal	wci	3ms	שכב	1011		lie,lie down
	יקברו	qal	wci	3mp	קבר	868		bury
	ימלך	qal	wci	3ms	מלך	573		be king,reign
	שקטה	qal	pft	3fs	שקט	1052		be quiet
14:1	יעש	qal	wci	3ms	עשה	793		do,make
14:2	יסר	hiph	wci	3ms	סור	693		take away
	ישבר	piel	wci	3ms	שבר	990		shatter
	יגדע	piel	wci	3ms	גדע	154		hew off
14:3	יאמר	qal	wci	3ms	אמר	55		say
	דרוש	qal	infc		דרש	205		resort to,seek
	עשות	qal	infc		עשה	793		do,make
14:4	יסר	hiph	wci	3ms	סור	693		take away
	תשקט	qal	wci	3fs	שקט	1052		be quiet
14:5	יבן	qal	wci	3ms	בנה	124		build
	שקטה	qal	pft	3fs	שקט	1052		be quiet
	הניח	hiph	pft	3ms	נוח	628		give rest,put
14:6	יאמר	qal	wci	3ms	אמר	55		say
	נבנה	qal	cohm	1cp	בנה	124		build
	נסב	hiph	cohm	1cp	סבב	685		cause to turn
	דרשנו	qal	pft	1cp	דרש	205		resort to,seek
	דרשנו	qal	pft	1cp	דרש	205		resort to,seek
	ינח	hiph	wci	3ms	נוח	628		give rest,put
	יבנו	qal	wci	3mp	בנה	124		build
	יצליחו	hiph	wci	3mp	צלח	852		cause to thrive
14:7	יהי	qal	wci	3ms	היה	224		be,become
	נשא	qal	ptc	ms	נשא	669		lift,carry
	נשאי	qal	ptc	mp	נשא	669		lift,carry
	דרכי	qal	ptc	mp	דרך	201		tread,march
14:8	יצא	qal	wci	3ms	יצא	422		go out
	יבא	qal	wci	3ms	בוא	97		come in
14:9	יצא	qal	wci	3ms	יצא	422		go out
	יערכו	qal	wci	3mp	ערך	789		set in order
14:10	יקרא	qal	wci	3ms	קרא	894		call,proclaim
	יאמר	qal	wci	3ms	אמר	55		say
	עזור	qal	infc		עזר	740		help,aid
	עזרנו	qal	impv	ms	עזר	740	1cp	help,aid
	נשענו	niph	pft	1cp	שען	1043		lean,support
	באנו	qal	pft	1cp	בוא	97		come in
	יעצר	qal	jusm	3ms	עצר	783		restrain
14:11	יגף	qal	wci	3ms	נגף	619		smite,strike
	ינסו	qal	wci	3mp	נוס	630		flee,escape
14:12	ירדפם	qal	wci	3ms	רדף	922	3mp	pursue
	יפל	qal	wci	3ms	נפל	656		fall
	נשברו	niph	pft	3cp	שבר	990		be broken
	ישאו	qal	wci	3mp	נשא	669		lift,carry
	הרבה	hiph	infa		רבה	915		make many
14:13	יכו	hiph	wci	3mp	נכה	645		smite
	היה	qal	pft	3ms	היה	224		be,become
	יבזו	qal	wci	3mp	בזז	102		plunder
	היתה	qal	pft	3fs	היה	224		be,become
14:14	הכו	hiph	pft	3cp	נכה	645		smite
	ישבו	qal	wci	3mp	שבה	985		take captive
	ישבו	qal	wci	3mp	שוב	996		turn,return
15:1	היתה	qal	pft	3fs	היה	224		be,become
15:2	יצא	qal	wci	3ms	יצא	422		go out
	יאמר	qal	wci	3ms	אמר	55		say
	שמעוני	qal	impv	mp	שמע	1033	1cs	hear
	היותכם	qal	infc		היה	224	2mp	be,become
	תדרשהו	qal	impf	2mp	דרש	205	3ms	resort to,seek
	ימצא	niph	impf	3ms	מצא	592		be found
	תעזבהו	qal	impf	2mp	עזב	736	3ms	leave,loose
	יעזב	qal	impf	3ms	עזב	736		leave,loose
15:3	מורה	hiph	ptc	ms	ירה	434		shoot,teach
15:4	ישב	qal	wci	3ms	שוב	996		turn,return
	יבקשהו	piel	wci	3mp	בקש	134	3ms	seek
	ימצא	niph	wci	3ms	מצא	592		be found
15:5	יוצא	qal	ptc	ms	יצא	422		go out
	בא	qal	ptc	ms	בוא	97		come in
	יושבי	qal	ptc	mp	ישב	442		sit,dwell
15:6	כתתו	pual	wcp	3cp	כתת	510		be beaten
	הממם	qal	pft	3ms	המם	243	3mp	confuse,vex
15:7	חזקו	qal	impv	mp	חזק	304		be strong
	ירפו	qal	jusm	3mp	רפה	951		sink,relax
15:8	שמע	qal	infc		שמע	1033		hear
	התחזק	hith	pft	3ms	חזק	304		strengthen self
	יעבר	hiph	wci	3ms	עבר	716		cause to pass
	לכד	qal	pft	3ms	לכד	539		capture
	יחדש	piel	wci	3ms	חדש	293		renew,repair
15:9	יקבץ	qal	wci	3ms	קבץ	867		gather,collect
	גרים	qal	ptc	mp	גור	157		sojourn
	נפלו	qal	pft	3cp	נפל	656		fall
	ראתם	qal	infc		ראה	906	3mp	see
15:10	יקבצו	niph	wci	3mp	קבץ	867		assemble,gather
15:11	יזבחו	qal	wci	3mp	זבח	256		slaughter

ChVs	Form	Stem	Tnse	PGN	Root	BDB	Sfx	Meaning
15:11	הביאו	hiph	pft	3cp	בוא	97		bring in
15:12	יבאו	qal	wci	3mp	בוא	97		come in
	דרוש	qal	infc		דרש	205		resort to,seek
15:13	ידרש	qal	impf	3ms	דרש	205		resort to,seek
	יומת	hoph	impf	3ms	מות	559		be killed
15:14	ישבעו	niph	wci	3mp	שבע	989		swear
15:15	ישמחו	qal	wci	3mp	שמח	970		rejoice
	נשבעו	niph	pft	3cp	שבע	989		swear
	בקשהו	piel	pft	3cp	בקש	134	3ms	seek
	ימצא	niph	wci	3ms	מצא	592		be found
	ינח	hiph	wci	3ms	נוח	628		give rest,put
15:16	הסירה	hiph	pft	3ms	סור	693	3fs	take away
	עשתה	qal	pft	3fs	עשה	793		do,make
	יכרת	qal	wci	3ms	כרת	503		cut,destroy
	ידק	hiph	wci	3ms	דקק	200		pulverize
	ישרף	qal	wci	3ms	שרף	976		burn
15:17	סרו	qal	pft	3cp	סור	693		turn aside
	היה	qal	pft	3ms	היה	224		be,become
15:18	יבא	hiph	wci	3ms	בוא	97		bring in
15:19	היתה	qal	pft	3fs	היה	224		be,become
16:1	עלה	qal	pft	3ms	עלה	748		go up
	יבן	qal	wci	3ms	בנה	124		build
	תת	qal	infc		נתן	678		give,set
	יוצא	qal	ptc	ms	יצא	422		go out
	בא	qal	ptc	ms	בוא	97		come in
16:2	יצא	hiph	wci	3ms	יצא	422		bring out
	ישלח	qal	wci	3ms	שלח	1018		send
	יושב	qal	ptc	ms	ישב	442		sit,dwell
	אמר	qal	infc		אמר	55		say
16:3	שלחתי	qal	pft	1cs	שלח	1018		send
	לך	qal	impv	ms	הלך	229		walk,go
	הפר	hiph	impv	ms	פרר	830		break,frustrate
	יעלה	qal	jusm	3ms	עלה	748		go up
16:4	ישמע	qal	wci	3ms	שמע	1033		hear
	ישלח	qal	wci	3ms	שלח	1018		send
	יכו	hiph	wci	3mp	נכה	645		smite
16:5	יהי	qal	wci	3ms	היה	224		be,become
	שמע	qal	infc		שמע	1033		hear
	יחדל	qal	wci	3ms	חדל	292		cease
	בנות	qal	infc		בנה	124		build
	ישבת	hiph	wci	3ms	שבת	991		destroy,remove
16:6	לקח	qal	pft	3ms	לקח	542		take
	ישאו	qal	wci	3mp	נשא	669		lift,carry
	בנה	qal	pft	3ms	בנה	124		build
	יבן	qal	wci	3ms	בנה	124		build
16:7	בא	qal	pft	3ms	בוא	97		come in
	יאמר	qal	wci	3ms	אמר	55		say
	השענך	niph	infc		שען	1043	2ms	lean,support
	נשענת	niph	pft	2ms	שען	1043		lean,support
	נמלט	niph	pft	3ms	מלט	572		escape
16:8	היו	qal	pft	3cp	היה	224		be,become
	הרבה	hiph	infa		רבה	915		make many
	השענך	niph	infc		שען	1043	2ms	lean,support
	נתנם	qal	pft	3ms	נתן	678	3mp	give,set
16:9	משטטות	pol	ptc	fp	שוט	1001		go quickly
	התחזק	hith	infc		חזק	304		strengthen self
	נסכלת	niph	pft	2ms	סכל	698		act foolishly
16:10	יכעס	qal	wci	3ms	כעס	494		be angry,vexed
	יתנהו	qal	wci	3ms	נתן	678	3ms	give,set
	ירצץ	piel	wci	3ms	רצץ	954		crush,oppress
16:11	כתובים	qal	pptc	mp	כתב	507		write
16:12	יחלא	qal	wci	3ms	חלא	316		be sick
	דרש	qal	pft	3ms	דרש	205		resort to,seek
	רפאים	qal	ptc	mp	רפא	950		heal
16:13	ישכב	qal	wci	3ms	שכב	1011		lie,lie down
	ימת	qal	wci	3ms	מות	559		die
	מלכו	qal	infc		מלך	573	3ms	be king,reign
16:14	יקברהו	qal	wci	3mp	קבר	868	3ms	bury
	כרה	qal	pft	3ms	כרה	500		dig
	ישכיבהו	hiph	wci	3mp	שכב	1011	3ms	lay
	מלא	piel	pft	3ms	מלא	569		fill
	מרקחים	pual	ptc	mp	רקח	955		be mixed
	ישרפו	qal	wci	3mp	שרף	976		burn
17:1	ימלך	qal	wci	3ms	מלך	573		be king,reign
	יתחזק	hith	wci	3ms	חזק	304		strengthen self
17:2	יתן	qal	wci	3ms	נתן	678		give,set
	בצרות	qal	pptc	fp	בצר	130		cut off
	יתן	qal	wci	3ms	נתן	678		give,set
	לכד	qal	pft	3ms	לכד	539		capture
17:3	יהי	qal	wci	3ms	היה	224		be,become
	הלך	qal	pft	3ms	הלך	229		walk,go
	דרש	qal	pft	3ms	דרש	205		resort to,seek
17:4	דרש	qal	pft	3ms	דרש	205		resort to,seek
	הלך	qal	pft	3ms	הלך	229		walk,go
17:5	יכן	hiph	wci	3ms	כון	465		fix,prepare
	יתנו	qal	wci	3mp	נתן	678		give,set
	יהי	qal	wci	3ms	היה	224		be,become
17:6	יגבה	qal	wci	3ms	גבה	146		be high
	הסיר	hiph	pft	3ms	סור	693		take away
17:7	מלכו	qal	infc		מלך	573	3ms	be king,reign
	שלח	qal	pft	3ms	שלח	1018		send
	למד	piel	infc		למד	540		teach
17:9	ילמדו	piel	wci	3mp	למד	540		teach
	יסבו	qal	wci	3mp	סבב	685		surround
	ילמדו	piel	wci	3mp	למד	540		teach
17:10	יהי	qal	wci	3ms	היה	224		be,become
	נלחמו	niph	pft	3cp	לחם	535		wage war
17:11	מביאים	hiph	ptc	mp	בוא	97		bring in
	מביאים	hiph	ptc	mp	בוא	97		bring in
17:12	יהי	qal	wci	3ms	היה	224		be,become
	הלך	qal	ptc	ms	הלך	229		walk,go
	יבן	qal	wci	3ms	בנה	124		build
17:13	היה	qal	pft	3ms	היה	224		be,become
17:16	מתנדב	hith	ptc	ms	נדב	621		offer freely
17:17	נשקי	qal	ptc	mp	נשק	676		be armed with
17:18	חלוצי	qal	pptc	mp	חלץ	323		equipped
17:19	משרתים	piel	ptc	mp	שרת	1058		minister,serve
	נתן	qal	pft	3ms	נתן	678		give,set

ChVs	Form	Stem	Tnse	PGN	Root	BDB	Sfx	Meaning
18:1	יהי	qal	wci	3ms	היה	224		be,become
	יתחתן	hith	wci	3ms	חתן	368		be son-in-law
18:2	ירד	qal	wci	3ms	ירד	432		come down
	יזבח	qal	wci	3ms	זבח	256		slaughter
	יסיתהו	hiph	wci	3ms	סות	694	3ms	incite,allure
	עלות	qal	infc		עלה	748		go up
18:3	יאמר	qal	wci	3ms	אמר	55		say
	תלך	qal	impf	2ms	הלך	229		walk,go
	יאמר	qal	wci	3ms	אמר	55		say
18:4	יאמר	qal	wci	3ms	אמר	55		say
	דרש	qal	impv	ms	דרש	205		resort to,seek
18:5	יקבץ	qal	wci	3ms	קבץ	867		gather,collect
	יאמר	qal	wci	3ms	אמר	55		say
	נלך	qal	impf	1cp	הלך	229		walk,go
	אחדל	qal	impf	1cs	חדל	292		cease
	יאמרו	qal	wci	3mp	אמר	55		say
	עלה	qal	impv	ms	עלה	748		go up
	יתן	qal	jusm	3ms	נתן	678		give,set
18:6	יאמר	qal	wci	3ms	אמר	55		say
	נדרשה	qal	coh	1cp	דרש	205		resort to,seek
18:7	יאמר	qal	wci	3ms	אמר	55		say
	דרוש	qal	infc		דרש	205		resort to,seek
	שׂנאתיהו	qal	pft	1cs	שׂנא	971	3ms	hate
	מתנבא	hith	ptc	ms	נבא	612		prophesy
	יאמר	qal	wci	3ms	אמר	55		say
	יאמר	qal	jusm	3ms	אמר	55		say
18:8	יקרא	qal	wci	3ms	קרא	894		call,proclaim
	יאמר	qal	wci	3ms	אמר	55		say
	מהר	piel	impv	ms	מהר	554		hasten
18:9	יושבים	qal	ptc	mp	ישב	442		sit,dwell
	מלבשים	pual	ptc	mp	לבש	527		be clothed
	ישבים	qal	ptc	mp	ישב	442		sit,dwell
	מתנבאים	hith	ptc	mp	נבא	612		prophesy
18:10	יעשׂ	qal	wci	3ms	עשׂה	793		do,make
	יאמר	qal	wci	3ms	אמר	55		say
	אמר	qal	pft	3ms	אמר	55		say
	תנגח	piel	impf	2ms	נגח	618		thrust at
	כלותם	piel	infc		כלה	477	3mp	complete,finish
18:11	נבאים	niph	ptc	mp	נבא	612		prophesy
	אמר	qal	infc		אמר	55		say
	עלה	qal	impv	ms	עלה	748		go up
	הצלח	hiph	impv	ms	צלח	852		cause to thrive
	נתן	qal	wcp	3ms	נתן	678		give,set
18:12	הלך	qal	pft	3ms	הלך	229		walk,go
	קרא	qal	infc		קרא	894		call,proclaim
	דבר	piel	pft	3ms	דבר	180		speak
	אמר	qal	infc		אמר	55		say
	יהי	qal	jus	3ms	היה	224		be,become
	דברת	piel	wcp	2ms	דבר	180		speak
18:13	יאמר	qal	wci	3ms	אמר	55		say
	יאמר	qal	impf	3ms	אמר	55		say
	אדבר	piel	impf	1cs	דבר	180		speak
18:14	יבא	qal	wci	3ms	בוא	97		come in
	יאמר	qal	wci	3ms	אמר	55		say
18:14	נלך	qal	impf	1cp	הלך	229		walk,go
	אחדל	qal	impf	1cs	חדל	292		cease
	יאמר	qal	wci	3ms	אמר	55		say
	עלו	qal	impv	mp	עלה	748		go up
	הצליחו	hiph	impv	mp	צלח	852		cause to thrive
	ינתנו	niph	jusm	3mp	נתן	678		be given
18:15	יאמר	qal	wci	3ms	אמר	55		say
	משׁביעך	hiph	ptc	ms	שׁבע	989	2ms	cause to swear
	תדבר	piel	impf	2ms	דבר	180		speak
18:16	יאמר	qal	wci	3ms	אמר	55		say
	ראיתי	qal	pft	1cs	ראה	906		see
	נפוצים	niph	ptc	mp	פוץ	806		be scattered
	רעה	qal	ptc	ms	רעה	944		pasture,tend
	יאמר	qal	wci	3ms	אמר	55		say
	ישובו	qal	jusm	3mp	שׁוב	996		turn,return
18:17	יאמר	qal	wci	3ms	אמר	55		say
	אמרתי	qal	pft	1cs	אמר	55		say
	יתנבא	hith	impf	3ms	נבא	612		prophesy
18:18	יאמר	qal	wci	3ms	אמר	55		say
	שׁמעו	qal	impv	mp	שׁמע	1033		hear
	ראיתי	qal	pft	1cs	ראה	906		see
	יושב	qal	ptc	ms	ישב	442		sit,dwell
	עמדים	qal	ptc	mp	עמד	763		stand,stop
18:19	יאמר	qal	wci	3ms	אמר	55		say
	יפתה	piel	impf	3ms	פתה	834		entice
	יעל	qal	impf	3ms	עלה	748		go up
	יפל	qal	impf	3ms	נפל	656		fall
	יאמר	qal	wci	3ms	אמר	55		say
	אמר	qal	ptc	ms	אמר	55		say
	אמר	qal	ptc	ms	אמר	55		say
18:20	יצא	qal	wci	3ms	יצא	422		go out
	יעמד	qal	wci	3ms	עמד	763		stand,stop
	יאמר	qal	wci	3ms	אמר	55		say
	אפתנו	piel	impf	1cs	פתה	834	3ms	entice
	יאמר	qal	wci	3ms	אמר	55		say
18:21	יאמר	qal	wci	3ms	אמר	55		say
	אצא	qal	impf	1cs	יצא	422		go out
	הייתי	qal	wcp	1cs	היה	224		be,become
	יאמר	qal	wci	3ms	אמר	55		say
	תפתה	piel	impf	2ms	פתה	834		entice
	תוכל	qal	impf	2ms	יכל	407		be able
	צא	qal	impv	ms	יצא	422		go out
	עשׂה	qal	impv	ms	עשׂה	793		do,make
18:22	נתן	qal	pft	3ms	נתן	678		give,set
	דבר	piel	pft	3ms	דבר	180		speak
18:23	יגשׁ	qal	wci	3ms	נגשׁ	620		draw near
	יך	hiph	wci	3ms	נכה	645		smite
	יאמר	qal	wci	3ms	אמר	55		say
	עבר	qal	pft	3ms	עבר	716		pass over
	דבר	piel	infc		דבר	180		speak
18:24	יאמר	qal	wci	3ms	אמר	55		say
	ראה	qal	ptc	ms	ראה	906		see
	תבוא	qal	impf	2ms	בוא	97		come in
	החבא	niph	infc		חבא	285		hide oneself

ChVs	Form	Stem	Tnse	PGN	Root	BDB	Sfx	Meaning
18:25	יאמר	qal	wci	3ms	אמר	55		say
	קחו	qal	impv	mp	לקח	542		take
	השיבהו	hiph	impv	mp	שוב	996	3ms	bring back
18:26	אמרתם	qal	wcp	2mp	אמר	55		say
	אמר	qal	pft	3ms	אמר	55		say
	שימו	qal	impv	mp	שים	962		put,set
	האכלהו	hiph	impv	mp	אכל	37	3ms	cause to eat
	שובי	qal	infc		שוב	996	1cs	turn,return
18:27	יאמר	qal	wci	3ms	אמר	55		say
	שוב	qal	infa		שוב	996		turn,return
	תשוב	qal	impf	2ms	שוב	996		turn,return
	דבר	piel	pft	3ms	דבר	180		speak
	יאמר	qal	wci	3ms	אמר	55		say
	שמעו	qal	impv	mp	שמע	1033		hear
18:28	יעל	qal	wci	3ms	עלה	748		go up
18:29	יאמר	qal	wci	3ms	אמר	55		say
	התחפש	hith	infa		חפש	344		disguise self
	בוא	qal	infa		בוא	97		come in
	לבש	qal	impv	ms	לבש	527		put on,clothe
	יתחפש	hith	wci	3ms	חפש	344		disguise self
	יבאו	qal	wci	3mp	בוא	97		come in
18:30	צוה	piel	pft	3ms	צוה	845		command
	אמר	qal	infc		אמר	55		say
	תלחמו	niph	impf	2mp	לחם	535		wage war
18:31	יהי	qal	wci	3ms	היה	224		be,become
	ראות	qal	infc		ראה	906		see
	אמרו	qal	pft	3cp	אמר	55		say
	יסבו	qal	wci	3mp	סבב	685		surround
	הלחם	niph	infc		לחם	535		wage war
	יזעק	qal	wci	3ms	זעק	277		call,cry out
	עזרו	qal	pft	3ms	עזר	740	3ms	help,aid
	יסיתם	hiph	wci	3ms	סות	694	3mp	incite,allure
18:32	יהי	qal	wci	3ms	היה	224		be,become
	ראות	qal	infc		ראה	906		see
	היה	qal	pft	3ms	היה	224		be,become
	ישבו	qal	wci	3mp	שוב	996		turn,return
18:33	משך	qal	pft	3ms	משך	604		draw,pull
	יך	hiph	wci	3ms	נכה	645		smite
	יאמר	qal	wci	3ms	אמר	55		say
	הפך	qal	impv	ms	הפך	245		turn,overturn
	הוצאתני	hiph	wcp	2ms	יצא	422	1cs	bring out
	החליתי	hoph	pft	1cs	חלה	317		be made sick
18:34	תעל	qal	wci	3fs	עלה	748		go up
	היה	qal	pft	3ms	היה	224		be,become
	מעמיד	hiph	ptc	ms	עמד	763		set up,raise
	ימת	qal	wci	3ms	מות	559		die
	בוא	qal	infc		בוא	97		come in
19:1	ישב	qal	wci	3ms	שוב	996		turn,return
19:2	יצא	qal	wci	3ms	יצא	422		go out
	יאמר	qal	wci	3ms	אמר	55		say
	עזר	qal	infc		עזר	740		help,aid
	שנאי	qal	ptc	mp	שנא	971		hate
	תאהב	qal	impf	2ms	אהב	12		love
19:3	נמצאו	niph	pft	3cp	מצא	592		be found
19:3	בערת	piel	pft	2ms	בער	128		burn,consume
	הכינות	hiph	wcp	2ms	כון	465		fix,prepare
	דרש	qal	infc		דרש	205		resort to,seek
19:4	ישב	qal	wci	3ms	ישב	442		sit,dwell
	ישב	qal	wci	3ms	שוב	996		turn,return
	יצא	qal	wci	3ms	יצא	422		go out
	ישיבם	hiph	wci	3ms	שוב	996	3mp	bring back
19:5	יעמד	hiph	wci	3ms	עמד	763		set up,raise
	שפטים	qal	ptc	mp	שפט	1047		judge
	בצרות	qal	pptc	fp	בצר	130		cut off
19:6	יאמר	qal	wci	3ms	אמר	55		say
	שפטים	qal	ptc	mp	שפט	1047		judge
	ראו	qal	impv	mp	ראה	906		see
	עשים	qal	ptc	mp	עשה	793		do,make
	תשפטו	qal	impf	2mp	שפט	1047		judge
19:7	יהי	qal	jus	3ms	היה	224		be,become
	שמרו	qal	impv	mp	שמר	1036		keep,watch
	עשו	qal	impv	mp	עשה	793		do,make
19:8	העמיד	hiph	pft	3ms	עמד	763		set up,raise
	ישבו	qal	wci	3mp	שוב	996		turn,return
19:9	יצו	piel	wci	3ms	צוה	845		command
	אמר	qal	infc		אמר	55		say
	תעשון	qal	impf	2mp	עשה	793		do,make
19:10	יבוא	qal	impf	3ms	בוא	97		come in
	ישבים	qal	ptc	mp	ישב	442		sit,dwell
	הזהרתם	hiph	wcp	2mp	זהר	264		teach
	יאשמו	qal	impf	3mp	אשם	79		offend
	היה	qal	wcp	3ms	היה	224		be,become
	תעשון	qal	impf	2mp	עשה	793		do,make
	תאשמו	qal	impf	2mp	אשם	79		offend
19:11	חזקו	qal	impv	mp	חזק	304		be strong
	עשו	qal	impv	mp	עשה	793		do,make
	יהי	qal	jus	3ms	היה	224		be,become
20:1	יהי	qal	wci	3ms	היה	224		be,become
	באו	qal	pft	3cp	בוא	97		come in
20:2	יבאו	qal	wci	3mp	בוא	97		come in
	יגידו	hiph	wci	3mp	נגד	616		declare,tell
	אמר	qal	infc		אמר	55		say
	בא	qal	ptc	ms	בוא	97		come in
20:3	ירא	qal	wci	3ms	ירא	431		fear
	יתן	qal	wci	3ms	נתן	678		give,set
	דרוש	qal	infc		דרש	205		resort to,seek
	יקרא	qal	wci	3ms	קרא	894		call,proclaim
20:4	יקבצו	niph	wci	3mp	קבץ	867		assemble,gather
	בקש	piel	infc		בקש	134		seek
	באו	qal	pft	3cp	בוא	97		come in
	בקש	piel	infc		בקש	134		seek
20:5	יעמד	qal	wci	3ms	עמד	763		stand,stop
20:6	יאמר	qal	wci	3ms	אמר	55		say
	מושל	qal	ptc	ms	משל	605		rule
	התיצב	hith	infc		יצב	426		stand oneself
20:7	הורשת	hiph	pft	2ms	ירש	439		c. to possess
	ישבי	qal	ptc	mp	ישב	442		sit,dwell
	תתנה	qal	wci	2ms	נתן	678	3fs	give,set

ChVs	Form	Stem	Tnse	PGN	Root	BDB	Sfx	Meaning
20:7	אהבך	qal	ptc	ms	אהב	12	2ms	love
20:8	ישבו	qal	wci	3mp	ישב	442		sit,dwell
	יבנו	qal	wci	3mp	בנה	124		build
	אמר	qal	infc		אמר	55		say
20:9	תבוא	qal	impf	3fs	בוא	97		come in
	נעמדה	qal	coh	1cp	עמד	763		stand,stop
	נזעק	qal	impf	1cp	זעק	277		call,cry out
	תשמע	qal	impf	2ms	שמע	1033		hear
	תושיע	hiph	impf	2ms	ישע	446		deliver,save
20:10	נתתה	qal	pft	2ms	נתן	678		give,set
	בוא	qal	infc		בוא	97		come in
	באם	qal	infc		בוא	97	3mp	come in
	סרו	qal	pft	3cp	סור	693		turn aside
	השמידום	hiph	pft	3cp	שמד	1029	3mp	exterminate
20:11	גמלים	qal	ptc	mp	גמל	168		deal out,ripen
	בוא	qal	infc		בוא	97		come in
	גרשנו	piel	infc		גרש	176	1cp	drive out
	הורשתנו	hiph	pft	2ms	ירש	439	1cp	c. to possess
20:12	תשפט	qal	impf	2ms	שפט	1047		judge
	בא	qal	ptc	ms	בוא	97		come in
	נדע	qal	impf	1cp	ידע	393		know
	נעשה	qal	impf	1cp	עשה	793		do,make
20:13	עמדים	qal	ptc	mp	עמד	763		stand,stop
20:14	היתה	qal	pft	3fs	היה	224		be,become
20:15	יאמר	qal	wci	3ms	אמר	55		say
	הקשיבו	hiph	impv	mp	קשב	904		give attention
	ישבי	qal	ptc	mp	ישב	442		sit,dwell
	אמר	qal	pft	3ms	אמר	55		say
	תיראו	qal	jusm	2mp	ירא	431		fear
	תחתו	qal	jusm	2mp	חתת	369		be shattered
20:16	רדו	qal	impv	mp	ירד	432		come down
	עלים	qal	ptc	mp	עלה	748		go up
	מצאתם	qal	wcp	2mp	מצא	592		find
20:17	הלחם	niph	infc		לחם	535		wage war
	התיצבו	hith	impv	mp	יצב	426		stand oneself
	עמדו	qal	impv	mp	עמד	763		stand,stop
	ראו	qal	impv	mp	ראה	906		see
	תיראו	qal	jusm	2mp	ירא	431		fear
	תחתו	qal	jusm	2mp	חתת	369		be shattered
	צאו	qal	impv	mp	יצא	422		go out
20:18	יקד	qal	wci	3ms	קדד	869		bow down
	ישבי	qal	ptc	mp	ישב	442		sit,dwell
	נפלו	qal	pft	3cp	נפל	656		fall
	השתחות	hish	infc		חוה	1005		bow down
20:19	יקמו	qal	wci	3mp	קום	877		arise,stand
	הלל	piel	infc		הלל	237		praise
20:20	ישכימו	hiph	wci	3mp	שכם	1014		rise early
	יצאו	qal	wci	3mp	יצא	422		go out
	צאתם	qal	infc		יצא	422	3mp	go out
	עמד	qal	pft	3ms	עמד	763		stand,stop
	יאמר	qal	wci	3ms	אמר	55		say
	שמעוני	qal	impv	mp	שמע	1033	1cs	hear
	ישבי	qal	ptc	mp	ישב	442		sit,dwell
	האמינו	hiph	impv	mp	אמן	52		believe
20:20	תאמנו	niph	impf	2mp	אמן	52		be confirmed
	האמינו	hiph	impv	mp	אמן	52		believe
	הצליחו	hiph	impv	mp	צלח	852		cause to thrive
20:21	יועץ	niph	wci	3ms	יעץ	419		consult
	יעמד	hiph	wci	3ms	עמד	763		set up,raise
	משררים	pol	ptc	mp	שיר	1010		sing
	מהללים	piel	ptc	mp	הלל	237		praise
	צאת	qal	infc		יצא	422		go out
	חלוץ	qal	pptc	ms	חלץ	323		equipped
	אמרים	qal	ptc	mp	אמר	55		say
	הודו	hiph	impv	mp	ידה	392		praise
20:22	החלו	hiph	pft	3cp	חלל	320		begin,profane
	נתן	qal	pft	3ms	נתן	678		give,set
	מארבים	piel	ptc	mp	ארב	70		liers-in-wait
	באים	qal	ptc	mp	בוא	97		come in
	ינגפו	niph	wci	3mp	נגף	619		be smitten
20:23	יעמדו	qal	wci	3mp	עמד	763		stand,stop
	ישבי	qal	ptc	mp	ישב	442		sit,dwell
	החרים	hiph	infc		חרם	355		ban,destroy
	השמיד	hiph	infc		שמד	1029		exterminate
	כלותם	piel	infc		כלה	477	3mp	complete,finish
	יושבי	qal	ptc	mp	ישב	442		sit,dwell
	עזרו	qal	pft	3cp	עזר	740		help,aid
20:24	בא	qal	pft	3ms	בוא	97		come in
	יפנו	qal	wci	3mp	פנה	815		turn
	נפלים	qal	ptc	mp	נפל	656		fall
20:25	יבא	qal	wci	3ms	בוא	97		come in
	בז	qal	infc		בזז	102		plunder
	ימצאו	qal	wci	3mp	מצא	592		find
	ינצלו	piel	wci	3mp	נצל	664		strip off
	יהיו	qal	wci	3mp	היה	224		be,become
	בזזים	qal	ptc	mp	בזז	102		plunder
20:26	נקהלו	niph	pft	3cp	קהל	874		assemble
	ברכו	piel	pft	3cp	ברך	138		bless
	קראו	qal	pft	3cp	קרא	894		call,proclaim
20:27	ישבו	qal	wci	3mp	שוב	996		turn,return
	שוב	qal	infc		שוב	996		turn,return
	שמחם	piel	pft	3ms	שמח	970	3mp	gladden
	אויביהם	qal	ptc	mp	איב	33	3mp	be hostile to
20:28	יבאו	qal	wci	3mp	בוא	97		come in
20:29	יהי	qal	wci	3ms	היה	224		be,become
	שמעם	qal	infc		שמע	1033	3mp	hear
	נלחם	niph	pft	3ms	לחם	535		wage war
	אויבי	qal	ptc	mp	איב	33		be hostile to
20:30	תשקט	qal	wci	3fs	שקט	1052		be quiet
	ינח	hiph	wci	3ms	נוח	628		give rest,put
20:31	ימלך	qal	wci	3ms	מלך	573		be king,reign
	מלכו	qal	infc		מלך	573	3ms	be king,reign
	מלך	qal	pft	3ms	מלך	573		be king,reign
20:32	ילך	qal	wci	3ms	הלך	229		walk,go
	סר	qal	pft	3ms	סור	693		turn aside
	עשות	qal	infc		עשה	793		do,make
20:33	סרו	qal	pft	3cp	סור	693		turn aside
	הכינו	hiph	pft	3cp	כון	465		fix,prepare

ChVs	Form	Stem	Tnse	PGN	Root	BDB	Sfx	Meaning
20:34	כתובים	qal	pptc	mp	כתב	507		write
	העלה	hoph	pft	3ms	עלה	748		be taken up
20:35	אתחבר	hith	pft	3ms	חבר	287		unite oneself
	הרשיע	hiph	pft	3ms	רשע	957		condemn, be evil
	עשׂות	qal	infc		עשׂה	793		do, make
20:36	יחברהו	piel	wci	3ms	חבר	287	3ms	unite
	עשׂות	qal	infc		עשׂה	793		do, make
	לכת	qal	infc		הלך	229		walk, go
	יעשׂו	qal	wci	3mp	עשׂה	793		do, make
20:37	יתנבא	hith	wci	3ms	נבא	612		prophesy
	אמר	qal	infc		אמר	55		say
	התחברך	hith	infc		חבר	287	2ms	unite oneself
	פרץ	qal	pft	3ms	פרץ	829		break through
	ישׁברו	niph	wci	3mp	שׁבר	990		be broken
	עצרו	qal	pft	3cp	עצר	783		restrain
	לכת	qal	infc		הלך	229		walk, go
21:1	ישׁכב	qal	wci	3ms	שׁכב	1011		lie, lie down
	יקבר	niph	wci	3ms	קבר	868		be buried
	ימלך	qal	wci	3ms	מלך	573		be king, reign
21:3	יתן	qal	wci	3ms	נתן	678		give, set
	נתן	qal	pft	3ms	נתן	678		give, set
21:4	יקם	qal	wci	3ms	קום	877		arise, stand
	יתחזק	hith	wci	3ms	חזק	304		strengthen self
	יהרג	qal	wci	3ms	הרג	246		kill
21:5	מלכו	qal	infc		מלך	573	3ms	be king, reign
	מלך	qal	pft	3ms	מלך	573		be king, reign
21:6	ילך	qal	wci	3ms	הלך	229		walk, go
	עשׂו	qal	pft	3cp	עשׂה	793		do, make
	היתה	qal	pft	3fs	היה	224		be, become
	יעשׂ	qal	wci	3ms	עשׂה	793		do, make
21:7	אבה	qal	pft	3ms	אבה	2		be willing
	השחית	hiph	infc		שחת	1007		spoil, ruin
	כרת	qal	pft	3ms	כרת	503		cut, destroy
	אמר	qal	pft	3ms	אמר	55		say
	תת	qal	infc		נתן	678		give, set
21:8	פשׁע	qal	pft	3ms	פשׁע	833		rebel, sin
	ימליכו	hiph	wci	3mp	מלך	573		cause to reign
21:9	יעבר	qal	wci	3ms	עבר	716		pass over
	יהי	qal	wci	3ms	היה	224		be, become
	קם	qal	pft	3ms	קום	877		arise, stand
	יך	hiph	wci	3ms	נכה	645		smite
	סובב	qal	ptc	ms	סבב	685		surround
21:10	יפשׁע	qal	wci	3ms	פשׁע	833		rebel, sin
	תפשׁע	qal	impf	3fs	פשׁע	833		rebel, sin
	עזב	qal	pft	3ms	עזב	736		leave, loose
21:11	עשׂה	qal	pft	3ms	עשׂה	793		do, make
	יזן	hiph	wci	3ms	זנה	275		commit harlotry
	ישׁבי	qal	ptc	mp	ישׁב	442		sit, dwell
	ידח	hiph	wci	3ms	נדח	623		thrust out
21:12	יבא	qal	wci	3ms	בוא	97		come in
	אמר	qal	infc		אמר	55		say
	אמר	qal	pft	3ms	אמר	55		say
	הלכת	qal	pft	2ms	הלך	229		walk, go
21:13	תלך	qal	wci	2ms	הלך	229		walk, go
21:13	תזנה	hiph	wci	2ms	זנה	275		commit harlotry
	ישׁבי	qal	ptc	mp	ישׁב	442		sit, dwell
	הזנות	hiph	infc		זנה	275		commit harlotry
	הרגת	qal	pft	2ms	הרג	246		kill
21:14	נגף	qal	ptc	ms	נגף	619		smite, strike
21:15	יצאו	qal	impf	3mp	יצא	422		go out
21:16	יער	hiph	wci	3ms	עור	734		rouse, stir up
21:17	יעלו	qal	wci	3mp	עלה	748		go up
	בקעוה	qal	wci	3mp	בקע	131	3fs	cleave, break
	ישׁבו	qal	wci	3mp	שׁבה	985		take captive
	נמצא	niph	ptc	ms	מצא	592		be found
	נשׁאר	niph	pft	3ms	שׁאר	983		be left
21:18	נגפו	qal	pft	3ms	נגף	619	3ms	smite, strike
21:19	יהי	qal	wci	3ms	היה	224		be, become
	צאת	qal	infc		יצא	422		go out
	יצאו	qal	pft	3cp	יצא	422		go out
	ימת	qal	wci	3ms	מות	559		die
	עשׂו	qal	pft	3cp	עשׂה	793		do, make
21:20	היה	qal	pft	3ms	היה	224		be, become
	מלכו	qal	infc		מלך	573	3ms	be king, reign
	מלך	qal	pft	3ms	מלך	573		be king, reign
	ילך	qal	wci	3ms	הלך	229		walk, go
	יקברהו	qal	wci	3mp	קבר	868	3ms	bury
22:1	ימליכו	hiph	wci	3mp	מלך	573		cause to reign
	יושׁבי	qal	ptc	mp	ישׁב	442		sit, dwell
	הרג	qal	pft	3ms	הרג	246		kill
	בא	qal	ptc	ms	בוא	97		come in
	ימלך	qal	wci	3ms	מלך	573		be king, reign
22:2	מלכו	qal	infc		מלך	573	3ms	be king, reign
	מלך	qal	pft	3ms	מלך	573		be king, reign
22:3	הלך	qal	pft	3ms	הלך	229		walk, go
	היתה	qal	pft	3fs	היה	224		be, become
	יועצתו	qal	ptc	fs	יעץ	419	3ms	advise, counsel
	הרשׁיע	hiph	infc		רשׁע	957		condemn, be evil
22:4	יעשׂ	qal	wci	3ms	עשׂה	793		do, make
	היו	qal	pft	3cp	היה	224		be, become
	יועצים	qal	ptc	mp	יעץ	419		advise, counsel
22:5	הלך	qal	pft	3ms	הלך	229		walk, go
	ילך	qal	wci	3ms	הלך	229		walk, go
	יכו	hiph	wci	3mp	נכה	645		smite
22:6	ישׁב	qal	wci	3ms	שׁוב	996		turn, return
	התרפא	hith	infc		רפא	950		get healed
	הכהו	hiph	pft	3cp	נכה	645	3ms	smite
	הלחמו	niph	infc		לחם	535	3ms	wage war
	ירד	qal	pft	3ms	ירד	432		come down
	ראות	qal	infc		ראה	906		see
	חלה	qal	ptc	ms	חלה	317		be weak, sick
22:7	היתה	qal	pft	3fs	היה	224		be, become
	בוא	qal	infc		בוא	97		come in
	באו	qal	infc		בוא	97	3ms	come in
	יצא	qal	pft	3ms	יצא	422		go out
	משׁחו	qal	pft	3ms	משׁח	602	3ms	smear, anoint
	הכרית	hiph	infc		כרת	503		cut off, destroy
22:8	יהי	qal	wci	3ms	היה	224		be, become

ChVs	Form	Stem	Tnse	PGN	Root	BDB	Sfx	Meaning
22:8	השפט	niph	infc		שפט	1047		plead
	ימצא	qal	wci	3ms	מצא	592		find
	משרתים	piel	ptc	mp	שרת	1058		minister,serve
	יהרגם	qal	wci	3ms	הרג	246	3mp	kill
22:9	יבקש	piel	wci	3ms	בקש	134		seek
	ילכדהו	qal	wci	3mp	לכד	539	3ms	capture
	מתחבא	hith	ptc	ms	חבא	285		hide oneself
	יבאהו	hiph	wci	3mp	בוא	97	3ms	bring in
	ימתהו	hiph	wci	3mp	מות	559	3ms	kill
	יקברהו	qal	wci	3mp	קבר	868	3ms	bury
	אמרו	qal	pft	3cp	אמר	55		say
	דרש	qal	pft	3ms	דרש	205		resort to,seek
	עצר	qal	infc		עצר	783		restrain
22:10	ראתה	qal	pft	3fs	ראה	906		see
	מת	qal	pft	3ms	מות	559		die
	תקם	qal	wci	3fs	קום	877		arise,stand
	תדבר	piel	wci	3fs	דבר	180		speak
22:11	תקח	qal	wci	3fs	לקח	542		take
	תגנב	qal	wci	3fs	גנב	170		steal
	מומתים	hoph	ptc	mp	מות	559		be killed
	תתן	qal	wci	3fs	נתן	678		give,set
	מינקתו	hiph	ptc	fs	ינק	413	3ms	nurse
	תסתירהו	hiph	wci	3fs	סתר	711	3ms	hide
	היתה	qal	pft	3fs	היה	224		be,become
	המיתתהו	hiph	pft	3fs	מות	559	3ms	kill
22:12	יהי	qal	wci	3ms	היה	224		be,become
	מתחבא	hith	ptc	ms	חבא	285		hide oneself
	מלכת	qal	ptc	fs	מלך	573		be king,reign
23:1	התחזק	hith	pft	3ms	חזק	304		strengthen self
	יקח	qal	wci	3ms	לקח	542		take
23:2	יסבו	qal	wci	3mp	סבב	685		surround
	יקבצו	qal	wci	3mp	קבץ	867		gather,collect
	יבאו	qal	wci	3mp	בוא	97		come in
23:3	יכרת	qal	wci	3ms	כרת	503		cut,destroy
	יאמר	qal	wci	3ms	אמר	55		say
	ימלך	qal	impf	3ms	מלך	573		be king,reign
	דבר	piel	pft	3ms	דבר	180		speak
23:4	תעשו	qal	impf	2mp	עשה	793		do,make
	באי	qal	ptc	mp	בוא	97		come in
23:6	יבוא	qal	jusm	3ms	בוא	97		come in
	משרתים	piel	ptc	mp	שרת	1058		minister,serve
	יבאו	qal	impf	3mp	בוא	97		come in
	ישמרו	qal	impf	3mp	שמר	1036		keep,watch
23:7	הקיפו	hiph	wcp	3cp	נקף	668		surround
	בא	qal	ptc	ms	בוא	97		come in
	יומת	hoph	impf	3ms	מות	559		be killed
	היו	qal	impv	mp	היה	224		be,become
	באו	qal	infc		בוא	97	3ms	come in
	צאתו	qal	infc		יצא	422	3ms	go out
23:8	יעשו	qal	wci	3mp	עשה	793		do,make
	צוה	piel	pft	3ms	צוה	845		command
	יקחו	qal	wci	3mp	לקח	542		take
	באי	qal	ptc	mp	בוא	97		come in
	יוצאי	qal	ptc	mp	יצא	422		go out
23:8	פטר	qal	pft	3ms	פטר	809		remove,set free
23:9	יתן	qal	wci	3ms	נתן	678		give,set
23:10	יעמד	hiph	wci	3ms	עמד	763		set up,raise
23:11	יוציאו	hiph	wci	3mp	יצא	422		bring out
	יתנו	qal	wci	3mp	נתן	678		give,set
	ימליכו	hiph	wci	3mp	מלך	573		cause to reign
	ימשחהו	qal	wci	3mp	משח	602	3ms	smear,anoint
	יאמרו	qal	wci	3mp	אמר	55		say
	יחי	qal	jus	3ms	חיה	310		live
23:12	תשמע	qal	wci	3fs	שמע	1033		hear
	רצים	qal	ptc	mp	רוץ	930		run
	מהללים	piel	ptc	mp	הלל	237		praise
	תבוא	qal	wci	3fs	בוא	97		come in
23:13	תרא	qal	wci	3fs	ראה	906		see
	עומד	qal	ptc	ms	עמד	763		stand,stop
	תוקע	qal	ptc	ms	תקע	1075		thrust,clap
	משוררים	pol	ptc	mp	שיר	1010		sing
	מודיעים	hiph	ptc	mp	ידע	393		declare
	הלל	piel	infc		הלל	237		praise
	תקרע	qal	wci	3fs	קרע	902		tear,rend
	תאמר	qal	wci	3fs	אמר	55		say
23:14	יוצא	hiph	wci	3ms	יצא	422		bring out
	פקודי	qal	pptc	mp	פקד	823		attend to,visit
	יאמר	qal	wci	3ms	אמר	55		say
	הוציאוה	hiph	impv	mp	יצא	422	3fs	bring out
	בא	qal	ptc	ms	בוא	97		come in
	יומת	hoph	impf	3ms	מות	559		be killed
	אמר	qal	pft	3ms	אמר	55		say
	תמיתוה	hiph	impf	2mp	מות	559	3fs	kill
23:15	ישימו	qal	wci	3mp	שים	962		put,set
	תבוא	qal	wci	3fs	בוא	97		come in
	ימיתוה	hiph	wci	3mp	מות	559	3fs	kill
23:16	יכרת	qal	wci	3ms	כרת	503		cut,destroy
	היות	qal	infc		היה	224		be,become
23:17	יבאו	qal	wci	3mp	בוא	97		come in
	יתצהו	qal	wci	3mp	נתץ	683	3ms	pull down
	שברו	piel	pft	3cp	שבר	990		shatter
	הרגו	qal	pft	3cp	הרג	246		kill
23:18	ישם	qal	wci	3ms	שים	962		put,set
	חלק	qal	pft	3ms	חלק	323		divide,share
	העלות	hiph	infc		עלה	748		bring up,offer
	כתוב	qal	pptc	ms	כתב	507		write
23:19	יעמד	hiph	wci	3ms	עמד	763		set up,raise
	יבא	qal	impf	3ms	בוא	97		come in
23:20	יקח	qal	wci	3ms	לקח	542		take
	מושלים	qal	ptc	mp	משל	605		rule
	יורד	hiph	wci	3ms	ירד	432		bring down
	יבאו	qal	wci	3mp	בוא	97		come in
	יושיבו	hiph	wci	3mp	ישב	442		cause to dwell
23:21	ישמחו	qal	wci	3mp	שמח	970		rejoice
	שקטה	qal	pft	3fs	שקט	1052		be quiet
	המיתו	hiph	pft	3cp	מות	559		kill
24:1	מלכו	qal	infc		מלך	573	3ms	be king,reign
	מלך	qal	pft	3ms	מלך	573		be king,reign

ChVs	Form	Stem	Tnse	PGN	Root	BDB	Sfx	Meaning
24:2	יעשׂ	qal	wci	3ms	עשׂה	793		do,make
24:3	ישׂא	qal	wci	3ms	נשׂא	669		lift,carry
	יולד	hiph	wci	3ms	ילד	408		beget
24:4	יהי	qal	wci	3ms	היה	224		be,become
	היה	qal	pft	3ms	היה	224		be,become
	חדשׁ	piel	infc		חדשׁ	293		renew,repair
24:5	יקבץ	qal	wci	3ms	קבץ	867		gather,collect
	יאמר	qal	wci	3ms	אמר	55		say
	צאו	qal	impv	mp	יצא	422		go out
	קבצו	qal	impv	mp	קבץ	867		gather,collect
	חזק	piel	infc		חזק	304		make strong
	תמהרו	piel	impf	2mp	מהר	554		hasten
	מהרו	piel	pft	3cp	מהר	554		hasten
24:6	יקרא	qal	wci	3ms	קרא	894		call,proclaim
	יאמר	qal	wci	3ms	אמר	55		say
	דרשׁת	qal	pft	2ms	דרשׁ	205		resort to,seek
	הביא	hiph	infc		בוא	97		bring in
24:7	פרצו	qal	pft	3cp	פרץ	829		break through
	עשׂו	qal	pft	3cp	עשׂה	793		do,make
24:8	יאמר	qal	wci	3ms	אמר	55		say
	יעשׂו	qal	wci	3mp	עשׂה	793		do,make
	יתנהו	qal	wci	3mp	נתן	678	3ms	give,set
24:9	יתנו	qal	wci	3mp	נתן	678		give,set
	הביא	hiph	infc		בוא	97		bring in
24:10	ישׂמחו	qal	wci	3mp	שׂמח	970		rejoice
	יביאו	hiph	wci	3mp	בוא	97		bring in
	ישׁליכו	hiph	wci	3mp	שׁלך	1020		throw,cast
	כלה	piel	infc		כלה	477		complete,finish
24:11	יהי	qal	wci	3ms	היה	224		be,become
	יביא	hiph	impf	3ms	בוא	97		bring in
	ראותם	qal	infc		ראה	906	3mp	see
	בא	qal	wcp	3ms	בוא	97		come in
	יערו	piel	impf	3mp	ערה	788		lay bare
	ישׂאהו	qal	impf	3mp	נשׂא	669	3ms	lift,carry
	ישׁיבהו	hiph	impf	3mp	שׁוב	996	3ms	bring back
	עשׂו	qal	pft	3cp	עשׂה	793		do,make
	יאספו	qal	wci	3mp	אסף	62		gather
24:12	יתנהו	qal	wci	3ms	נתן	678	3ms	give,set
	עושׂה	qal	ptc	ms	עשׂה	793		do,make
	יהיו	qal	wci	3mp	היה	224		be,become
	שׂכרים	qal	ptc	mp	שׂכר	968		hire
	חצבים	qal	ptc	mp	חצב	345		hew out,dig
	חדשׁ	piel	infc		חדשׁ	293		renew,repair
	חזק	piel	infc		חזק	304		make strong
24:13	יעשׂו	qal	wci	3mp	עשׂה	793		do,make
	עשׂי	qal	ptc	mp	עשׂה	793		do,make
	תעל	qal	wci	3fs	עלה	748		go up
	יעמידו	hiph	wci	3mp	עמד	763		set up,raise
	יאמצהו	piel	wci	3mp	אמץ	54	3ms	make firm
24:14	כלותם	piel	infc		כלה	477	3mp	complete,finish
	הביאו	hiph	pft	3cp	בוא	97		bring in
	יעשׂהו	qal	wci	3ms	עשׂה	793	3ms	do,make
	יהיו	qal	wci	3mp	היה	224		be,become
	מעלים	hiph	ptc	mp	עלה	748		bring up,offer
24:15	יזקן	qal	wci	3ms	זקן	278		be old
	ישׂבע	qal	wci	3ms	שׂבע	959		be sated
	ימת	qal	wci	3ms	מות	559		die
24:16	יקברהו	qal	wci	3mp	קבר	868	3ms	bury
	עשׂה	qal	pft	3ms	עשׂה	793		do,make
24:17	באו	qal	pft	3cp	בוא	97		come in
	ישׁתחוו	hish	wci	3mp	חוה	1005		bow down
	שׁמע	qal	pft	3ms	שׁמע	1033		hear
24:18	יעזבו	qal	wci	3mp	עזב	736		leave,loose
	יעבדו	qal	wci	3mp	עבד	712		work,serve
	יהי	qal	wci	3ms	היה	224		be,become
24:19	ישׁלח	qal	wci	3ms	שׁלח	1018		send
	השׁיבם	hiph	infc		שׁוב	996	3mp	bring back
	יעידו	hiph	wci	3mp	עוד	729		testify,warn
	האזינו	hiph	pft	3cp	אזן	24		hear
24:20	לבשׁה	qal	pft	3fs	לבשׁ	527		put on,clothe
	יעמד	qal	wci	3ms	עמד	763		stand,stop
	יאמר	qal	wci	3ms	אמר	55		say
	אמר	qal	pft	3ms	אמר	55		say
	עברים	qal	ptc	mp	עבר	716		pass over
	תצליחו	hiph	impf	2mp	צלח	852		cause to thrive
	עזבתם	qal	pft	2mp	עזב	736		leave,loose
	יעזב	qal	wci	3ms	עזב	736		leave,loose
24:21	יקשׁרו	qal	wci	3mp	קשׁר	905		bind
	ירגמהו	qal	wci	3mp	רגם	920	3ms	stone
24:22	זכר	qal	pft	3ms	זכר	269		remember
	עשׂה	qal	pft	3ms	עשׂה	793		do,make
	יהרג	qal	wci	3ms	הרג	246		kill
	מותו	qal	infc		מות	559	3ms	die
	אמר	qal	pft	3ms	אמר	55		say
	ירא	qal	jus	3ms	ראה	906		see
	ידרשׁ	qal	jusm	3ms	דרשׁ	205		resort to,seek
24:23	יהי	qal	wci	3ms	היה	224		be,become
	עלה	qal	pft	3ms	עלה	748		go up
	יבאו	qal	wci	3mp	בוא	97		come in
	ישׁחיתו	hiph	wci	3mp	שׁחת	1007		spoil,ruin
	שׁלחו	piel	pft	3cp	שׁלח	1018		send away,shoot
24:24	באו	qal	pft	3cp	בוא	97		come in
	נתן	qal	pft	3ms	נתן	678		give,set
	עזבו	qal	pft	3cp	עזב	736		leave,loose
	עשׂו	qal	pft	3cp	עשׂה	793		do,make
24:25	לכתם	qal	infc		הלך	229	3mp	walk,go
	עזבו	qal	pft	3cp	עזב	736		leave,loose
	התקשׁרו	hith	pft	3cp	קשׁר	905		conspire
	יהרגהו	qal	wci	3mp	הרג	246	3ms	kill
	ימת	qal	wci	3ms	מות	559		die
	יקברהו	qal	wci	3mp	קבר	868	3ms	bury
	קברהו	qal	pft	3cp	קבר	868	3ms	bury
24:26	מתקשׁרים	hith	ptc	mp	קשׁר	905		conspire
24:27	qירב	qal	impf	3ms	רבה	915		be many,great
	כתובים	qal	pptc	mp	כתב	507		write
	ימלך	qal	wci	3ms	מלך	573		be king,reign
25:1	מלך	qal	pft	3ms	מלך	573		be king,reign
	מלך	qal	pft	3ms	מלך	573		be king,reign

ChVs	Form	Stem	Tnse	PGN	Root	BDB	Sfx	Meaning
25: 2	יעשׂ	qal	wci	3ms	עשׂה	793		do,make
25: 3	יהי	qal	wci	3ms	היה	224		be,become
	חזקה	qal	pft	3fs	חזק	304		be strong
	יהרג	qal	wci	3ms	הרג	246		kill
	מכים	hiph	ptc	mp	נכה	645		smite
25: 4	המית	hiph	pft	3ms	מות	559		kill
	כתוב	qal	pptc	ms	כתב	507		write
	צוה	piel	pft	3ms	צוה	845		command
	אמר	qal	infc		אמר	55		say
	ימותו	qal	impf	3mp	מות	559		die
	ימותו	qal	impf	3mp	מות	559		die
	ימותו	qal	impf	3mp	מות	559		die
25: 5	יקבץ	qal	wci	3ms	קבץ	867		gather,collect
	יעמידם	hiph	wci	3ms	עמד	763	3mp	set up,raise
	יפקדם	qal	wci	3ms	פקד	823	3mp	attend to,visit
	ימצאם	qal	wci	3ms	מצא	592	3mp	find
	בחור	qal	pptc	ms	בחר	103		choose
	יוצא	qal	ptc	ms	יצא	422		go out
	אחז	qal	ptc	ms	אחז	28		grasp
25: 6	ישׂכר	qal	wci	3ms	שׂכר	968		hire
25: 7	בא	qal	pft	3ms	בוא	97		come in
	אמר	qal	infc		אמר	55		say
	יבא	qal	jus	3ms	בוא	97		come in
25: 8	בא	qal	impv	ms	בוא	97		come in
	עשׂה	qal	impv	ms	עשׂה	793		do,make
	חזק	qal	impv	ms	חזק	304		be strong
	יכשׁילך	hiph	impf	3ms	כשׁל	505	2ms	cause to fall
	אויב	qal	ptc	ms	איב	33		be hostile to
	עזור	qal	infc		עזר	740		help,aid
	הכשׁיל	hiph	infc		כשׁל	505		cause to fall
25: 9	יאמר	qal	wci	3ms	אמר	55		say
	עשׂות	qal	infc		עשׂה	793		do,make
	נתתי	qal	pft	1cs	נתן	678		give,set
	יאמר	qal	wci	3ms	אמר	55		say
	תת	qal	infc		נתן	678		give,set
	הרבה	hiph	infa		רבה	915		make many
25: 10	יבדילם	hiph	wci	3ms	בדל	95	3mp	divide
	בא	qal	pft	3ms	בוא	97		come in
	לכת	qal	infc		הלך	229		walk,go
	יחר	qal	wci	3ms	חרה	354		be kindled,burn
	ישׁובו	qal	wci	3mp	שׁוב	996		turn,return
25: 11	התחזק	hith	pft	3ms	חזק	304		strengthen self
	ינהג	qal	wci	3ms	נהג	624		drive
	ילך	qal	wci	3ms	הלך	229		walk,go
	יך	hiph	wci	3ms	נכה	645		smite
25: 12	שׁבו	qal	pft	3cp	שׁבה	985		take captive
	יביאום	hiph	wci	3mp	בוא	97	3mp	bring in
	ישׁליכום	hiph	wci	3mp	שׁלך	1020	3mp	throw,cast
	נבקעו	niph	pft	3cp	בקע	131		be cleft
25: 13	השׁיב	hiph	pft	3ms	שׁוב	996		bring back
	לכת	qal	infc		הלך	229		walk,go
	יפשׁטו	qal	wci	3mp	פשׁט	832		strip off
	יכו	hiph	wci	3mp	נכה	645		smite
	יבזו	qal	wci	3mp	בזז	102		plunder

ChVs	Form	Stem	Tnse	PGN	Root	BDB	Sfx	Meaning
25: 14	יהי	qal	wci	3ms	היה	224		be,become
	בוא	qal	infc		בוא	97		come in
	הכות	hiph	infc		נכה	645		smite
	יבא	hiph	wci	3ms	בוא	97		bring in
	יעמידם	hiph	wci	3ms	עמד	763	3mp	set up,raise
	ישׁתחוה	hish	impf	3ms	חוה	1005		bow down
	יקטר	piel	impf	3ms	קטר	882		make sacrifices
25: 15	יחר	qal	wci	3ms	חרה	354		be kindled,burn
	ישׁלח	qal	wci	3ms	שׁלח	1018		send
	יאמר	qal	wci	3ms	אמר	55		say
	דרשׁת	qal	pft	2ms	דרשׁ	205		resort to,seek
	הצילו	hiph	pft	3cp	נצל	664		snatch,deliver
25: 16	יהי	qal	wci	3ms	היה	224		be,become
	דברו	piel	infc		דבר	180	3ms	speak
	יאמר	qal	wci	3ms	אמר	55		say
	יועץ	qal	ptc	ms	יעץ	419		advise,counsel
	נתנוך	qal	pft	1cp	נתן	678	2ms	give,set
	חדל	qal	impv	ms	חדל	292		cease
	יכוך	hiph	impf	3mp	נכה	645	2ms	smite
	יחדל	qal	wci	3ms	חדל	292		cease
	יאמר	qal	wci	3ms	אמר	55		say
	ידעתי	qal	pft	1cs	ידע	393		know
	יעץ	qal	pft	3ms	יעץ	419		advise,counsel
	השׁחיתך	hiph	infc		שׁחת	1007	2ms	spoil,ruin
	עשׂית	qal	pft	2ms	עשׂה	793		do,make
	שׁמעת	qal	pft	2ms	שׁמע	1033		hear
25: 17	יועץ	niph	wci	3ms	יעץ	419		consult
	ישׁלח	qal	wci	3ms	שׁלח	1018		send
	אמר	qal	infc		אמר	55		say
	לך	qal	impv	ms	הלך	229		walk,go
	נתראה	hith	cohm	1cp	ראה	906		look at each
25: 18	ישׁלח	qal	wci	3ms	שׁלח	1018		send
	אמר	qal	infc		אמר	55		say
	שׁלח	qal	pft	3ms	שׁלח	1018		send
	אמר	qal	infc		אמר	55		say
	תנה	qal	impv	ms	נתן	678		give,set
	תעבר	qal	wci	3fs	עבר	716		pass over
	תרמס	qal	wci	3fs	רמס	942		trample
25: 19	אמרת	qal	pft	2ms	אמר	55		say
	הכית	hiph	pft	2ms	נכה	645		smite
	נשׂאך	qal	pft	3ms	נשׂא	669	2ms	lift,carry
	הכביד	hiph	infc		כבד	457		make heavy
	שׁבה	qal	impv	ms	ישׁב	442		sit,dwell
	תתגרה	hith	impf	2ms	גרה	173		excite oneself
	נפלת	qal	wcp	2ms	נפל	656		fall
25: 20	שׁמע	qal	pft	3ms	שׁמע	1033		hear
	תתם	qal	infc		נתן	678	3mp	give,set
	דרשׁו	qal	pft	3cp	דרשׁ	205		resort to,seek
25: 21	יעל	qal	wci	3ms	עלה	748		go up
	יתראו	hith	wci	3mp	ראה	906		look at each
25: 22	ינגף	niph	wci	3ms	נגף	619		be smitten
	ינסו	qal	wci	3mp	נוס	630		flee,escape
25: 23	תפשׂ	qal	pft	3ms	תפשׂ	1074		seize,grasp
	יביאהו	hiph	wci	3ms	בוא	97	3ms	bring in

ChVs	Form	Stem	Tnse	PGN	Root	BDB	Sfx	Meaning
25:23	יפרץ	qal	wci	3ms	פרץ	829		break through
25:24	נמצאים	niph	ptc	mp	מצא	592		be found
	ישב	qal	wci	3ms	שוב	996		turn,return
25:25	יחי	qal	wci	3ms	חיה	310		live
25:26	כתובים	qal	pptc	mp	כתב	507		write
25:27	סר	qal	pft	3ms	סור	693		turn aside
	יקשרו	qal	wci	3mp	קשר	905		bind
	ינס	qal	wci	3ms	נוס	630		flee,escape
	ישלחו	qal	wci	3mp	שלח	1018		send
	ימיתהו	hiph	wci	3mp	מות	559	3ms	kill
25:28	ישאהו	qal	wci	3mp	נשא	669	3ms	lift,carry
	יקברו	qal	wci	3mp	קבר	868		bury
26:1	יקחו	qal	wci	3mp	לקח	542		take
	ימליכו	hiph	wci	3mp	מלך	573		cause to reign
26:2	בנה	qal	pft	3ms	בנה	124		build
	ישיבה	hiph	wci	3ms	שוב	996	3fs	bring back
	שכב	qal	infc		שכב	1011		lie,lie down
26:3	מלכו	qal	infc		מלך	573	3ms	be king,reign
	מלך	qal	pft	3ms	מלך	573		be king,reign
26:4	יעש	qal	wci	3ms	עשה	793		do,make
	עשה	qal	pft	3ms	עשה	793		do,make
26:5	יהי	qal	wci	3ms	היה	224		be,become
	דרש	qal	infc		דרש	205		resort to,seek
	מבין	hiph	ptc	ms	בין	106		understand
	ראת	qal	infc		ראה	906		see
	דרשו	qal	infc		דרש	205	3ms	resort to,seek
	הצליחו	hiph	pft	3ms	צלח	852	3ms	cause to thrive
26:6	יצא	qal	wci	3ms	יצא	422		go out
	ילחם	niph	wci	3ms	לחם	535		wage war
	יפרץ	qal	wci	3ms	פרץ	829		break through
	יבנה	qal	wci	3ms	בנה	124		build
26:7	יעזרהו	qal	wci	3ms	עזר	740	3ms	help,aid
	ישבים	qal	ptc	mp	ישב	442		sit,dwell
26:8	יתנו	qal	wci	3mp	נתן	678		give,set
	ילך	qal	wci	3ms	הלך	229		walk,go
	בוא	qal	infc		בוא	97		come in
	החזיק	hiph	pft	3ms	חזק	304		make firm,seize
26:9	יבן	qal	wci	3ms	בנה	124		build
	יחזקם	piel	wci	3ms	חזק	304	3mp	make strong
26:10	יבן	qal	wci	3ms	בנה	124		build
	יחצב	qal	wci	3ms	חצב	345		hew out,dig
	היה	qal	pft	3ms	היה	224		be,become
	כרמים	qal	ptc	mp	כרם	501		tend vineyard
	אהב	qal	ptc	ms	אהב	12		love
	היה	qal	pft	3ms	היה	224		be,become
26:11	יהי	qal	wci	3ms	היה	224		be,become
	עשה	qal	ptc	ms	עשה	793		do,make
	יוצאי	qal	ptc	mp	יצא	422		go out
26:13	עושי	qal	ptc	mp	עשה	793		do,make
	עזר	qal	infc		עזר	740		help,aid
	אויב	qal	ptc	ms	איב	33		be hostile to
26:14	יכן	hiph	wci	3ms	כון	465		fix,prepare
26:15	יעש	qal	wci	3ms	עשה	793		do,make
	חושב	qal	ptc	ms	חשב	362		think,devise
26:15	היות	qal	infc		היה	224		be,become
	ירוא	qal	infc		ירא	432		shoot w/arrows
	יצא	qal	wci	3ms	יצא	422		go out
	הפליא	hiph	pft	3ms	פלא	810		do wondrously
	העזר	niph	infc		עזר	740		be helped
	חזק	qal	pft	3ms	חזק	304		be strong
26:16	גבה	qal	pft	3ms	גבה	146		be high
	השחית	hiph	infc		שחת	1007		spoil,ruin
	ימעל	qal	wci	3ms	מעל	591		act faithlessly
	יבא	qal	wci	3ms	בוא	97		come in
	הקטיר	hiph	infc		קטר	882		make sacrifices
26:17	יבא	qal	wci	3ms	בוא	97		come in
26:18	יעמדו	qal	wci	3mp	עמד	763		stand,stop
	יאמרו	qal	wci	3mp	אמר	55		say
	הקטיר	hiph	infc		קטר	882		make sacrifices
	מקדשים	pual	ptc	mp	קדש	872		be consecrated
	הקטיר	hiph	infc		קטר	882		make sacrifices
	צא	qal	impv	ms	יצא	422		go out
	מעלת	qal	pft	2ms	מעל	591		act faithlessly
26:19	יזעף	qal	wci	3ms	זעף	277		be vexed
	הקטיר	hiph	infc		קטר	882		make sacrifices
	זעפו	qal	infc		זעף	277	3ms	be vexed
	זרחה	qal	pft	3fs	זרח	280		rise,appear
26:20	יפן	qal	wci	3ms	פנה	815		turn
	מצרע	pual	ptc	ms	צרע	863		be leprous
	יבהלוהו	hiph	wci	3mp	בהל	96	3ms	dismay,hasten
	נדחף	niph	pft	3ms	דחף	191		hasten oneself
	צאת	qal	infc		יצא	422		go out
	נגעו	piel	pft	3ms	נגע	619	3ms	strike
26:21	יהי	qal	wci	3ms	היה	224		be,become
	מצרע	pual	ptc	ms	צרע	863		be leprous
	ישב	qal	wci	3ms	ישב	442		sit,dwell
	מצרע	pual	ptc	ms	צרע	863		be leprous
	נגזר	niph	pft	3ms	גזר	160		be cut off
	שופט	qal	ptc	ms	שפט	1047		judge
26:22	כתב	qal	pft	3ms	כתב	507		write
26:23	ישכב	qal	wci	3ms	שכב	1011		lie,lie down
	יקברו	qal	wci	3mp	קבר	868		bury
	אמרו	qal	pft	3cp	אמר	55		say
	מצורע	pual	ptc	ms	צרע	863		be leprous
	ימלך	qal	wci	3ms	מלך	573		be king,reign
27:1	מלכו	qal	infc		מלך	573	3ms	be king,reign
	מלך	qal	pft	3ms	מלך	573		be king,reign
27:2	יעש	qal	wci	3ms	עשה	793		do,make
	עשה	qal	pft	3ms	עשה	793		do,make
	בא	qal	pft	3ms	בוא	97		come in
	משחיתים	hiph	ptc	mp	שחת	1007		spoil,ruin
27:3	בנה	qal	pft	3ms	בנה	124		build
	בנה	qal	pft	3ms	בנה	124		build
27:4	בנה	qal	pft	3ms	בנה	124		build
	בנה	qal	pft	3ms	בנה	124		build
27:5	נלחם	niph	pft	3ms	לחם	535		wage war
	יחזק	qal	wci	3ms	חזק	304		be strong
	יתנו	qal	wci	3mp	נתן	678		give,set

ChVs	Form	Stem	Tnse	PGN	Root	BDB	Sfx	Meaning
27:5	השיבו	hiph	pft	3cp	שוב	996		bring back
27:6	יתחזק	hith	wci	3ms	חזק	304		strengthen self
	הכין	hiph	pft	3ms	כון	465		fix,prepare
27:7	כתובים	qal	pptc	mp	כתב	507		write
27:8	היה	qal	pft	3ms	היה	224		be,become
	מלכו	qal	infc		מלך	573	3ms	be king,reign
	מלך	qal	pft	3ms	מלך	573		be king,reign
27:9	ישכב	qal	wci	3ms	שכב	1011		lie,lie down
	יקברו	qal	wci	3mp	קבר	868		bury
	ימלך	qal	wci	3ms	מלך	573		be king,reign
28:1	מלכו	qal	infc		מלך	573	3ms	be king,reign
	מלך	qal	pft	3ms	מלך	573		be king,reign
	עשה	qal	pft	3ms	עשה	793		do,make
28:2	ילך	qal	wci	3ms	הלך	229		walk,go
	עשה	qal	pft	3ms	עשה	793		do,make
28:3	הקטיר	hiph	pft	3ms	קטר	882		make sacrifices
	יבער	hiph	wci	3ms	בער	128		cause to burn
	הריש	hiph	pft	3ms	ירש	439		c. to possess
28:4	יזבח	piel	wci	3ms	זבח	256		sacrifice
	יקטר	piel	wci	3ms	קטר	882		make sacrifices
28:5	יתנהו	qal	wci	3ms	נתן	678	3ms	give,set
	יכו	hiph	wci	3mp	נכה	645		smite
	ישבו	qal	wci	3mp	שבה	985		take captive
	יביאו	hiph	wci	3mp	בוא	97		bring in
	נתן	niph	pft	3ms	נתן	678		be given
	יך	hiph	wci	3ms	נכה	645		smite
28:6	יהרג	qal	wci	3ms	הרג	246		kill
	עזבם	qal	infc		עזב	736	3mp	leave,loose
28:7	יהרג	qal	wci	3ms	הרג	246		kill
28:8	ישבו	qal	wci	3mp	שבה	985		take captive
	בזזו	qal	pft	3cp	בזז	102		plunder
	יביאו	hiph	wci	3mp	בוא	97		bring in
28:9	היה	qal	pft	3ms	היה	224		be,become
	יצא	qal	wci	3ms	יצא	422		go out
	בא	qal	ptc	ms	בוא	97		come in
	יאמר	qal	wci	3ms	אמר	55		say
	נתנם	qal	pft	3ms	נתן	678	3mp	give,set
	תהרגו	qal	wci	2mp	הרג	246		kill
	הגיע	hiph	pft	3ms	נגע	619		reach,arrive
28:10	אמרים	qal	ptc	mp	אמר	55		say
	כבש	qal	infc		כבש	461		subdue
28:11	שמעוני	qal	impv	mp	שמע	1033	1cs	hear
	השיבו	hiph	impv	mp	שוב	996		bring back
	שביתם	qal	pft	2mp	שבה	985		take captive
28:12	יקמו	qal	wci	3mp	קום	877		arise,stand
	באים	qal	ptc	mp	בוא	97		come in
28:13	יאמרו	qal	wci	3mp	אמר	55		say
	תביאו	hiph	impf	2mp	בוא	97		bring in
	אמרים	qal	ptc	mp	אמר	55		say
	הסיף	hiph	infc		יסף	414		add,do again
28:14	יעזב	qal	wci	3ms	עזב	736		leave,loose
	חלוץ	qal	pptc	ms	חלץ	323		equipped
28:15	יקמו	qal	wci	3mp	קום	877		arise,stand
	נקבו	niph	pft	3cp	נקב	666		be marked
28:15	יחזיקו	hiph	wci	3mp	חזק	304		make firm,seize
	הלבישו	hiph	pft	3cp	לבש	527		clothe
	ילבשום	hiph	wci	3mp	לבש	527	3mp	clothe
	ינעלום	hiph	wci	3mp	נעל	653	3mp	give sandals
	יאכלום	hiph	wci	3mp	אכל	37	3mp	cause to eat
	ישקום	hiph	wci	3mp	שקה	1052	3mp	give to drink
	יסכום	qal	wci	3mp	סוך	691	3mp	anoint,pour
	ינהלום	piel	wci	3mp	נהל	624	3mp	lead,refresh
	כושל	qal	ptc	ms	כשל	505		stumble,totter
	יביאום	hiph	wci	3mp	בוא	97	3mp	bring in
	ישובו	qal	wci	3mp	שוב	996		turn,return
28:16	שלח	qal	pft	3ms	שלח	1018		send
	עזר	qal	infc		עזר	740		help,aid
28:17	באו	qal	pft	3cp	בוא	97		come in
	יכו	hiph	wci	3mp	נכה	645		smite
	ישבו	qal	wci	3mp	שבה	985		take captive
28:18	פשטו	qal	pft	3cp	פשט	832		strip off
	ילכדו	qal	wci	3mp	לכד	539		capture
	ישבו	qal	wci	3mp	ישב	442		sit,dwell
28:19	הכניע	hiph	pft	3ms	כנע	488		humble,subdue
	הפריע	hiph	pft	3ms	פרע	828		make unruly
	מעול	qal	infa		מעל	591		act faithlessly
28:20	יבא	qal	wci	3ms	בוא	97		come in
	יצר	hiph	wci	3ms	צרר	864		distress,cramp
	חזקו	qal	pft	3ms	חזק	304	3ms	be strong
28:21	חלק	qal	pft	3ms	חלק	323		divide,share
	יתן	qal	wci	3ms	נתן	678		give,set
28:22	הצר	hiph	infc		צרר	864		distress,cramp
	יוסף	hiph	wci	3ms	יסף	414		add,do again
	מעול	qal	infc		מעל	591		act faithlessly
28:23	יזבח	qal	wci	3ms	זבח	256		slaughter
	מכים	hiph	ptc	mp	נכה	645		smite
	יאמר	qal	wci	3ms	אמר	55		say
	מעזרים	hiph	ptc	mp	עזר	740		help
	אזבח	piel	impf	1cs	זבח	256		sacrifice
	יעזרוני	hiph	impf	3mp	עזר	740	1cs	help
	היו	qal	pft	3cp	היה	224		be,become
	הכשילו	hiph	infc		כשל	505	3ms	cause to fall
28:24	יאסף	qal	wci	3ms	אסף	62		gather
	יקצץ	piel	wci	3ms	קצץ	893		cut off
	יסגר	qal	wci	3ms	סגר	688		shut
	יעש	qal	wci	3ms	עשה	793		do,make
28:25	עשה	qal	pft	3ms	עשה	793		do,make
	קטר	piel	infc		קטר	882		make sacrifices
	יכעס	hiph	wci	3ms	כעס	494		vex,provoke
28:26	כתובים	qal	pptc	mp	כתב	507		write
28:27	ישכב	qal	wci	3ms	שכב	1011		lie,lie down
	יקברהו	qal	wci	3mp	קבר	868	3ms	bury
	הביאהו	hiph	pft	3cp	בוא	97	3ms	bring in
	ימלך	qal	wci	3ms	מלך	573		be king,reign
29:1	מלך	qal	pft	3ms	מלך	573		be king,reign
	מלך	qal	pft	3ms	מלך	573		be king,reign
29:2	יעש	qal	wci	3ms	עשה	793		do,make
	עשה	qal	pft	3ms	עשה	793		do,make

ChVs	Form	Stem	Tnse	PGN	Root	BDB	Sfx	Meaning
29:3	מלכו	qal	infc		מלך	573	3ms	be king,reign
	פתח	qal	pft	3ms	פתח	834		open
	יחזקם	piel	wci	3ms	חזק	304	3mp	make strong
29:4	יבא	hiph	wci	3ms	בוא	97		bring in
	יאספם	qal	wci	3ms	אסף	62	3mp	gather
29:5	יאמר	qal	wci	3ms	אמר	55		say
	שמעוני	qal	impv	mp	שמע	1033	1cs	hear
	התקדשו	hith	impv	mp	קדש	872		consecrate self
	קדשו	piel	impv	mp	קדש	872		consecrate
	הוציאו	hiph	impv	mp	יצא	422		bring out
29:6	מעלו	qal	pft	3cp	מעל	591		act faithlessly
	עשו	qal	pft	3cp	עשה	793		do,make
	יעזבהו	qal	wci	3mp	עזב	736	3ms	leave,loose
	יסבו	hiph	wci	3mp	סבב	685		cause to turn
	יתנו	qal	wci	3mp	נתן	678		give,set
29:7	סגרו	qal	pft	3cp	סגר	688		shut
	יכבו	piel	wci	3mp	כבה	459		extinguish
	הקטירו	hiph	pft	3cp	קטר	882		make sacrifices
	העלו	hiph	pft	3cp	עלה	748		bring up,offer
29:8	יהי	qal	wci	3ms	היה	224		be,become
	יתנם	qal	wci	3ms	נתן	678	3mp	give,set
	ראים	qal	ptc	mp	ראה	906		see
29:9	נפלו	qal	pft	3cp	נפל	656		fall
29:10	כרות	qal	infc		כרת	503		cut,destroy
	ישב	qal	jus	3ms	שוב	996		turn,return
29:11	תשלו	niph	jusm	2mp	שלה	1017		be negligent
	בחר	qal	pft	3ms	בחר	103		choose
	עמד	qal	infc		עמד	763		stand,stop
	שרתו	piel	infc		שרת	1058	3ms	minister,serve
	היות	qal	infc		היה	224		be,become
	משרתים	piel	ptc	mp	שרת	1058		minister,serve
	מקטרים	hiph	ptc	mp	קטר	882		make sacrifices
29:12	יקמו	qal	wci	3mp	קום	877		arise,stand
29:15	יאספו	qal	wci	3mp	אסף	62		gather
	יתקדשו	hith	wci	3mp	קדש	872		consecrate self
	יבאו	qal	wci	3mp	בוא	97		come in
	טהר	piel	infc		טהר	372		cleanse
29:16	יבאו	qal	wci	3mp	בוא	97		come in
	טהר	piel	infc		טהר	372		cleanse
	יוציאו	hiph	wci	3mp	יצא	422		bring out
	מצאו	qal	pft	3cp	מצא	592		find
	יקבלו	piel	wci	3mp	קבל	867		take,receive
	הוציא	hiph	infc		יצא	422		bring out
29:17	יחלו	hiph	wci	3mp	חלל	320		begin,profane
	קדש	piel	infc		קדש	872		consecrate
	באו	qal	pft	3cp	בוא	97		come in
	יקדשו	piel	wci	3mp	קדש	872		consecrate
	כלו	piel	pft	3cp	כלה	477		complete,finish
29:18	יבואו	qal	wci	3mp	בוא	97		come in
	יאמרו	qal	wci	3mp	אמר	55		say
	טהרנו	piel	pft	1cp	טהר	372		cleanse
29:19	הזניח	hiph	pft	3ms	זנח	276		reject
	הכנו	hiph	pft	1cp	כון	465		fix,prepare
	הקדשנו	hiph	pft	1cp	קדש	872		consecrate
29:20	ישכם	hiph	wci	3ms	שכם	1014		rise early
	יאסף	qal	wci	3ms	אסף	62		gather
	יעל	qal	wci	3ms	עלה	748		go up
29:21	יביאו	hiph	wci	3mp	בוא	97		bring in
	יאמר	qal	wci	3ms	אמר	55		say
	העלות	hiph	infc		עלה	748		bring up,offer
29:22	ישחטו	qal	wci	3mp	שחט	1006		slaughter
	יקבלו	piel	wci	3mp	קבל	867		take,receive
	יזרקו	qal	wci	3mp	זרק	284		toss,scatter
	ישחטו	qal	wci	3mp	שחט	1006		slaughter
	יזרקו	qal	wci	3mp	זרק	284		toss,scatter
	ישחטו	qal	wci	3mp	שחט	1006		slaughter
	יזרקו	qal	wci	3mp	זרק	284		toss,scatter
29:23	יגישו	hiph	wci	3mp	נגש	620		bring near
	יסמכו	qal	wci	3mp	סמך	701		lean,support
29:24	ישחטום	qal	wci	3mp	שחט	1006	3mp	slaughter
	יחטאו	piel	wci	3mp	חטא	306		purify
	כפר	piel	infc		כפר	497		cover,atone
	אמר	qal	pft	3ms	אמר	55		say
29:25	יעמד	hiph	wci	3ms	עמד	763		set up,raise
29:26	יעמדו	qal	wci	3mp	עמד	763		stand,stop
29:27	יאמר	qal	wci	3ms	אמר	55		say
	העלות	hiph	infc		עלה	748		bring up,offer
	החל	hiph	pft	3ms	חלל	320		begin,profane
	החל	hiph	pft	3ms	חלל	320		begin,profane
29:28	משתחוים	hish	ptc	mp	חוה	1005		bow down
	משורר	pol	ptc	ms	שיר	1010		sing
	מחצצרים k	hiph	ptc	mp	חצצר	348		sound w/clarion
	מחצרים q	hiph	ptc	mp	חצר	348		sound w/clarion
	כלות	qal	infc		כלה	477		finished,spent
29:29	כלות	piel	infc		כלה	477		complete,finish
	העלות	hiph	infc		עלה	748		bring up,offer
	כרעו	qal	pft	3cp	כרע	502		bow down
	נמצאים	niph	ptc	mp	מצא	592		be found
	ישתחוו	hish	wci	3mp	חוה	1005		bow down
29:30	יאמר	qal	wci	3ms	אמר	55		say
	הלל	piel	infc		הלל	237		praise
	יהללו	piel	wci	3mp	הלל	237		praise
	יקדו	qal	wci	3mp	קדד	869		bow down
	ישתחוו	hish	wci	3mp	חוה	1005		bow down
29:31	יען	qal	wci	3ms	ענה	772		answer
	יאמר	qal	wci	3ms	אמר	55		say
	מלאתם	piel	pft	2mp	מלא	569		fill
	גשו	qal	impv	mp	נגש	620		draw near
	הביאו	hiph	impv	mp	בוא	97		bring in
	יביאו	hiph	wci	3mp	בוא	97		bring in
29:32	יהי	qal	wci	3ms	היה	224		be,become
	הביאו	hiph	pft	3cp	בוא	97		bring in
29:34	היו	qal	pft	3cp	היה	224		be,become
	יכלו	qal	pft	3cp	יכל	407		be able
	הפשיט	hiph	infc		פשט	832		strip off
	יחזקום	piel	wci	3mp	חזק	304	3mp	make strong
	כלות	qal	infc		כלה	477		finished,spent
	יתקדשו	hith	impf	3mp	קדש	872		consecrate self

ChVs	Form	Stem	Tnse	PGN	Root	BDB	Sfx	Meaning
29:34	התקדש	hith	infc		קדש	872		consecrate self
29:35	תכון	niph	wci	3fs	כון	465		be established
29:36	ישמח	qal	wci	3ms	שמח	970		rejoice
	הכין	hiph	pft	3ms	כון	465		fix,prepare
	היה	qal	pft	3ms	היה	224		be,become
30:1	ישלח	qal	wci	3ms	שלח	1018		send
	כתב	qal	pft	3ms	כתב	507		write
	בוא	qal	infc		בוא	97		come in
	עשות	qal	infc		עשה	793		do,make
30:2	יועץ	niph	wci	3ms	יעץ	419		consult
	עשות	qal	infc		עשה	793		do,make
30:3	יכלו	qal	pft	3cp	יכל	407		be able
	עשתו	qal	infc		עשה	793	3ms	do,make
	התקדשו	hith	pft	3cp	קדש	872		consecrate self
	נאספו	niph	pft	3cp	אסף	62		assemble
30:4	יישר	qal	wci	3ms	ישר	448		be straight
30:5	יעמידו	hiph	wci	3mp	עמד	763		set up,raise
	העביר	hiph	infc		עבר	716		cause to pass
	בוא	qal	infc		בוא	97		come in
	עשות	qal	infc		עשה	793		do,make
	עשו	qal	pft	3cp	עשה	793		do,make
	כתוב	qal	pptc	ms	כתב	507		write
30:6	ילכו	qal	wci	3mp	הלך	229		walk,go
	רצים	qal	ptc	mp	רוץ	930		run
	אמר	qal	infc		אמר	55		say
	שובו	qal	impv	mp	שוב	996		turn,return
	ישב	qal	jus	3ms	שוב	996		turn,return
	נשארת	niph	ptc	fs	שאר	983		be left
30:7	תהיו	qal	jusm	2mp	היה	224		be,become
	מעלו	qal	pft	3cp	מעל	591		act faithlessly
	יתנם	qal	wci	3ms	נתן	678	3mp	give,set
	ראים	qal	ptc	mp	ראה	906		see
30:8	תקשו	hiph	jusm	2mp	קשה	904		harden
	תנו	qal	impv	mp	נתן	678		give,set
	באו	qal	impv	mp	בוא	97		come in
	הקדיש	hiph	pft	3ms	קדש	872		consecrate
	עבדו	qal	impv	mp	עבד	712		work,serve
	ישב	qal	jus	3ms	שוב	996		turn,return
30:9	שובכם	qal	infc		שוב	996	2mp	turn,return
	שוביהם	qal	ptc	mp	שבה	985	3mp	take captive
	שוב	qal	infc		שוב	996		turn,return
	יסיר	hiph	impf	3ms	סור	693		take away
	תשובו	qal	impf	2mp	שוב	996		turn,return
30:10	יהיו	qal	wci	3mp	היה	224		be,become
	רצים	qal	ptc	mp	רוץ	930		run
	עברים	qal	ptc	mp	עבר	716		pass over
	יהיו	qal	wci	3mp	היה	224		be,become
	משחיקים	hiph	ptc	mp	שחק	965		utter mockery
	מלעגים	hiph	ptc	mp	לעג	541		mock,deride
30:11	נכנעו	niph	pft	3cp	כנע	488		humble self
	יבאו	qal	wci	3mp	בוא	97		come in
30:12	היתה	qal	pft	3fs	היה	224		be,become
	תת	qal	infc		נתן	678		give,set
	עשות	qal	infc		עשה	793		do,make
30:13	יאספו	niph	wci	3mp	אסף	62		assemble
	עשות	qal	infc		עשה	793		do,make
30:14	יקמו	qal	wci	3mp	קום	877		arise,stand
	יסירו	hiph	wci	3mp	סור	693		take away
	הסירו	hiph	pft	3cp	סור	693		take away
	ישליכו	hiph	wci	3mp	שלך	1020		throw,cast
30:15	ישחטו	qal	wci	3mp	שחט	1006		slaughter
	נכלמו	niph	pft	3cp	כלם	483		be humiliated
	יתקדשו	hith	wci	3mp	קדש	872		consecrate self
	יביאו	hiph	wci	3mp	בוא	97		bring in
30:16	יעמדו	qal	wci	3mp	עמד	763		stand,stop
	זרקים	qal	ptc	mp	זרק	284		toss,scatter
30:17	התקדשו	hith	pft	3cp	קדש	872		consecrate self
	הקדיש	hiph	infc		קדש	872		consecrate
30:18	הטהרו	hith	pft	3cp	טהר	372		purify oneself
	אכלו	qal	pft	3cp	אכל	37		eat,devour
	כתוב	qal	pptc	ms	כתב	507		write
	התפלל	hith	pft	3ms	פלל	813		pray
	אמר	qal	infc		אמר	55		say
	יכפר	piel	jusm	3ms	כפר	497		cover,atone
30:19	הכין	hiph	pft	3ms	כון	465		fix,prepare
	דרוש	qal	infc		דרש	205		resort to,seek
30:20	ישמע	qal	wci	3ms	שמע	1033		hear
	ירפא	qal	wci	3ms	רפא	950		heal
30:21	יעשו	qal	wci	3mp	עשה	793		do,make
	נמצאים	niph	ptc	mp	מצא	592		be found
	מהללים	piel	ptc	mp	הלל	237		praise
30:22	ידבר	piel	wci	3ms	דבר	180		speak
	משכילים	hiph	ptc	mp	שכל	968		look at,prosper
	יאכלו	qal	wci	3mp	אכל	37		eat,devour
	מזבחים	piel	ptc	mp	זבח	256		sacrifice
	מתודים	hith	ptc	mp	ידה	392		confess
30:23	יועצו	niph	wci	3mp	יעץ	419		consult
	עשות	qal	infc		עשה	793		do,make
	יעשו	qal	wci	3mp	עשה	793		do,make
30:24	הרים	hiph	pft	3ms	רום	926		raise,lift
	הרימו	hiph	pft	3cp	רום	926		raise,lift
	יתקדשו	hith	wci	3mp	קדש	872		consecrate self
30:25	ישמחו	qal	wci	3mp	שמח	970		rejoice
	באים	qal	ptc	mp	בוא	97		come in
	באים	qal	ptc	mp	בוא	97		come in
	יושבים	qal	ptc	mp	ישב	442		sit,dwell
30:26	תהי	qal	wci	3fs	היה	224		be,become
30:27	יקמו	qal	wci	3mp	קום	877		arise,stand
	יברכו	piel	wci	3mp	ברך	138		bless
	ישמע	niph	wci	3ms	שמע	1033		be heard
	תבוא	qal	wci	3fs	בוא	97		come in
31:1	כלות	piel	infc		כלה	477		complete,finish
	יצאו	qal	pft	3cp	יצא	422		go out
	נמצאים	niph	ptc	mp	מצא	592		be found
	ישברו	piel	wci	3mp	שבר	990		shatter
	יגדעו	piel	wci	3mp	גדע	154		hew off
	ינתצו	piel	wci	3mp	נתץ	683		tear down
	כלה	piel	infc		כלה	477		complete,finish

ChVs	Form	Stem	Tnse	PGN	Root	BDB	Sfx	Meaning
31:1	ישׁובו	qal	wci	3mp	שׁוב	996		turn,return
31:2	יעמד	hiph	wci	3ms	עמד	763		set up,raise
	שׁרת	piel	infc		שׁרת	1058		minister,serve
	הדות	hiph	infc		ידה	392		praise
	הלל	piel	infc		הלל	237		praise
31:3	כתוב	qal	pptc	ms	כתב	507		write
31:4	יאמר	qal	wci	3ms	אמר	55		say
	יושׁבי	qal	ptc	mp	ישׁב	442		sit,dwell
	תת	qal	infc		נתן	678		give,set
	יחזקו	qal	impf	3mp	חזק	304		be strong
31:5	פרץ	qal	infc		פרץ	829		break through
	הרבו	hiph	pft	3cp	רבה	915		make many
	הביאו	hiph	pft	3cp	בוא	97		bring in
31:6	יושׁבים	qal	ptc	mp	ישׁב	442		sit,dwell
	מקדשׁים	pual	ptc	mp	קדשׁ	872		be consecrated
	הביאו	hiph	pft	3cp	בוא	97		bring in
	יתנו	qal	wci	3mp	נתן	678		give,set
31:7	החלו	hiph	pft	3cp	חלל	320		begin,profane
	יסוד	qal	infc		יסד	413		establish
	כלו	piel	pft	3cp	כלה	477		complete,finish
31:8	יבאו	qal	wci	3mp	בוא	97		come in
	יראו	qal	wci	3mp	ראה	906		see
	יברכו	piel	wci	3mp	ברך	138		bless
31:9	ידרשׁ	qal	wci	3ms	דרשׁ	205		resort to,seek
31:10	יאמר	qal	wci	3ms	אמר	55		say
	יאמר	qal	wci	3ms	אמר	55		say
	החל	hiph	infc		חלל	320		begin,profane
	ביא	hiph	infc		בוא	97		bring in
	אכול	qal	infa		אכל	37		eat,devour
	שׂבוע	qal	infa		שׂבע	959		be sated
	הותר	hiph	infa		יתר	451		leave,spare
	ברך	piel	pft	3ms	ברך	138		bless
	נותר	niph	ptc	ms	יתר	451		be left,remain
31:11	יאמר	qal	wci	3ms	אמר	55		say
	הכין	hiph	infc		כון	465		fix,prepare
	יכינו	hiph	wci	3mp	כון	465		fix,prepare
31:12	יביאו	hiph	wci	3mp	בוא	97		bring in
31:14	תת	qal	infc		נתן	678		give,set
31:15	תת	qal	infc		נתן	678		give,set
31:16	התיחשׂם	hith	infc		יחשׂ	405	3mp	be registered
	בא	qal	ptc	ms	בוא	97		come in
31:17	התיחשׂ	hith	infc		יחשׂ	405		be registered
31:18	התיחשׂ	hith	infc		יחשׂ	405		be registered
	יתקדשׁו	hith	impf	3mp	קדשׁ	872		consecrate self
31:19	נקבו	niph	pft	3cp	נקב	666		be marked
	תת	qal	infc		נתן	678		give,set
	התיחשׂ	hith	infc		יחשׂ	405		be registered
31:20	יעשׂ	qal	wci	3ms	עשׂה	793		do,make
	יעשׂ	qal	wci	3ms	עשׂה	793		do,make
31:21	החל	hiph	pft	3ms	חלל	320		begin,profane
	דרשׁ	qal	infc		דרשׁ	205		resort to,seek
	עשׂה	qal	pft	3ms	עשׂה	793		do,make
	הצליח	hiph	pft	3ms	צלח	852		cause to thrive
32:1	בא	qal	pft	3ms	בוא	97		come in
32:1	יבא	qal	wci	3ms	בוא	97		come in
	יחן	qal	wci	3ms	חנה	333		decline,encamp
	בצרות	qal	pptc	fp	בצר	130		cut off
	יאמר	qal	wci	3ms	אמר	55		say
	בקעם	qal	infc		בקע	131	3mp	cleave,break
32:2	ירא	qal	wci	3ms	ראה	906		see
	בא	qal	pft	3ms	בוא	97		come in
32:3	יועץ	niph	wci	3ms	יעץ	419		consult
	סתום	qal	infc		סתם	711		stop up
	יעזרוהו	qal	wci	3mp	עזר	740	3ms	help,aid
32:4	יקבצו	niph	wci	3mp	קבץ	867		assemble,gather
	יסתמו	qal	wci	3mp	סתם	711		stop up
	שׁוטף	qal	ptc	ms	שׁטף	1009		overflow
	אמר	qal	infc		אמר	55		say
	יבואו	qal	impf	3mp	בוא	97		come in
	מצאו	qal	wcp	3cp	מצא	592		find
32:5	יתחזק	hith	wci	3ms	חזק	304		strengthen self
	יבן	qal	wci	3ms	בנה	124		build
	פרוצה	qal	pptc	fs	פרץ	829		break through
	יעל	hiph	wci	3ms	עלה	748		bring up,offer
	יחזק	piel	wci	3ms	חזק	304		make strong
	יעשׂ	qal	wci	3ms	עשׂה	793		do,make
32:6	יתן	qal	wci	3ms	נתן	678		give,set
	יקבצם	qal	wci	3ms	קבץ	867	3mp	gather,collect
	ידבר	piel	wci	3ms	דבר	180		speak
	אמר	qal	infc		אמר	55		say
32:7	חזקו	qal	impv	mp	חזק	304		be strong
	אמצו	qal	impv	mp	אמץ	54		be strong
	תיראו	qal	jusm	2mp	ירא	431		fear
	תחתו	qal	jusm	2mp	חתת	369		be shattered
32:8	עזרנו	qal	infc		עזר	740	1cp	help,aid
	הלחם	niph	infc		לחם	535		wage war
	יסמכו	niph	wci	3mp	סמך	701		support oneself
32:9	שׁלח	qal	pft	3ms	שׁלח	1018		send
	אמר	qal	infc		אמר	55		say
32:10	אמר	qal	pft	3ms	אמר	55		say
	בטחים	qal	ptc	mp	בטח	105		trust
	ישׁבים	qal	ptc	mp	ישׁב	442		sit,dwell
32:11	מסית	hiph	ptc	ms	סות	694		incite,allure
	תת	qal	infc		נתן	678		give,set
	מות	qal	infc		מות	559		die
	אמר	qal	infc		אמר	55		say
	יצילנו	hiph	impf	3ms	נצל	664	1cp	snatch,deliver
32:12	הסיר	hiph	pft	3ms	סור	693		take away
	יאמר	qal	wci	3ms	אמר	55		say
	אמר	qal	infc		אמר	55		say
	תשׁתחוו	hish	impf	2mp	חוה	1005		bow down
	תקטירו	hiph	impf	2mp	קטר	882		make sacrifices
32:13	תדעו	qal	impf	2mp	ידע	393		know
	עשׂיתי	qal	pft	1cs	עשׂה	793		do,make
	יכול	qal	infa		יכל	407		be able
	יכלו	qal	pft	3cp	יכל	407		be able
	הציל	hiph	infc		נצל	664		snatch,deliver
32:14	החרימו	hiph	pft	3cp	חרם	355		ban,destroy

ChVs	Form	Stem	Tnse	PGN	Root	BDB	Sfx	Meaning
32: 14	יכול	qal	pft	3ms	יכל	407		be able
	הציל	hiph	infc		נצל	664		snatch,deliver
	יוכל	qal	impf	3ms	יכל	407		be able
	הציל	hiph	infc		נצל	664		snatch,deliver
32: 15	ישיא	hiph	jusm	3ms	נשא	674		beguile
	יסית	hiph	jusm	3ms	סות	694		incite,allure
	תאמינו	hiph	jusm	2mp	אמן	52		believe
	יוכל	qal	impf	3ms	יכל	407		be able
	הציל	hiph	infc		נצל	664		snatch,deliver
	יצילו	hiph	impf	3mp	נצל	664		snatch,deliver
32: 16	דברו	piel	pft	3cp	דבר	180		speak
32: 17	כתב	qal	pft	3ms	כתב	507		write
	חרף	piel	infc		חרף	357		reproach
	אמר	qal	infc		אמר	55		say
	אמר	qal	infc		אמר	55		say
	הצילו	hiph	pft	3cp	נצל	664		snatch,deliver
	יציל	hiph	impf	3ms	נצל	664		snatch,deliver
32: 18	יקראו	qal	wci	3mp	קרא	894		call,proclaim
	יראם	piel	infc		ירא	431	3mp	terrify
	בהלם	piel	infc		בהל	96	3mp	hasten,dismay
	ילכדו	qal	impf	3mp	לכד	539		capture
32: 19	ידברו	piel	wci	3mp	דבר	180		speak
32: 20	יתפלל	hith	wci	3ms	פלל	813		pray
	יזעקו	qal	wci	3mp	זעק	277		call,cry out
32: 21	ישׁלח	qal	wci	3ms	שׁלח	1018		send
	יכחד	hiph	wci	3ms	כחד	470		hide,efface
	ישׁב	qal	wci	3ms	שׁוב	996		turn,return
	יבא	qal	wci	3ms	בוא	97		come in
	הפילהו	hiph	pft	3cp	נפל	656	3ms	cause to fall
32: 22	יושׁע	hiph	wci	3ms	ישׁע	446		deliver,save
	ישׁבי	qal	ptc	mp	ישׁב	442		sit,dwell
	ינהלם	piel	wci	3ms	נהל	624	3mp	lead,refresh
32: 23	מביאים	hiph	ptc	mp	בוא	97		bring in
	ינשׂא	hith	wci	3ms	נשׂא	669		lift self up
32: 24	חלה	qal	pft	3ms	חלה	317		be weak,sick
	מות	qal	infc		מות	559		die
	יתפלל	hith	wci	3ms	פלל	813		pray
	יאמר	qal	wci	3ms	אמר	55		say
	נתן	qal	pft	3ms	נתן	678		give,set
32: 25	השׁיב	hiph	pft	3ms	שׁוב	996		bring back
	גבה	qal	pft	3ms	גבה	146		be high
	יהי	qal	wci	3ms	היה	224		be, become
32: 26	יכנע	niph	wci	3ms	כנע	488		humble self
	ישׁבי	qal	ptc	mp	ישׁב	442		sit,dwell
	בא	qal	pft	3ms	בוא	97		come in
32: 27	יהי	qal	wci	3ms	היה	224		be,become
	הרבה	hiph	infa		רבה	915		make many
	עשׂה	qal	pft	3ms	עשׂה	793		do,make
32: 29	עשׂה	qal	pft	3ms	עשׂה	793		do,make
	נתן	qal	pft	3ms	נתן	678		give,set
32: 30	סתם	qal	pft	3ms	סתם	711		stop up
	יישׁרם	piel	wci	3ms	ישׁר	448	3mp	make straight
	יצלח	hiph	wci	3ms	צלח	852		cause to thrive
32: 31	מליצי	hiph	ptc	mp	ליץ	539		deride
32: 31	משׁלחים	piel	ptc	mp	שׁלח	1018		send away,shoot
	דרשׁ	qal	infc		דרשׁ	205		resort to,seek
	היה	qal	pft	3ms	היה	224		be,become
	עזבו	qal	pft	3ms	עזב	736	3ms	leave,loose
	נסותו	piel	infc		נסה	650	3ms	test,try
	דעת	qal	infc		ידע	393		know
32: 32	כתובים	qal	pptc	mp	כתב	507		write
32: 33	ישׁכב	qal	wci	3ms	שׁכב	1011		lie,lie down
	יקברהו	qal	wci	3mp	קבר	868	3ms	bury
	עשׂו	qal	pft	3cp	עשׂה	793		do,make
	ישׁבי	qal	ptc	mp	ישׁב	442		sit,dwell
	ימלך	qal	wci	3ms	מלך	573		be king,reign
33: 1	מלכו	qal	infc		מלך	573	3ms	be king,reign
	מלך	qal	pft	3ms	מלך	573		be king,reign
33: 2	יעשׂ	qal	wci	3ms	עשׂה	793		do,make
	הורישׁ	hiph	pft	3ms	ירשׁ	439		c. to possess
33: 3	ישׁב	qal	wci	3ms	שׁוב	996		turn,return
	יבן	qal	wci	3ms	בנה	124		build
	נתץ	piel	pft	3ms	נתץ	683		tear down
	יקם	hiph	wci	3ms	קום	877		raise,build,set
	יעשׂ	qal	wci	3ms	עשׂה	793		do,make
	ישׁתחו	hish	wci	3ms	חוה	1005		bow down
	יעבד	qal	wci	3ms	עבד	712		work,serve
33: 4	בנה	qal	wcp	3ms	בנה	124		build
	אמר	qal	pft	3ms	אמר	55		say
	יהיה	qal	impf	3ms	היה	224		be,become
33: 5	יבן	qal	wci	3ms	בנה	124		build
33: 6	העביר	hiph	pft	3ms	עבר	716		cause to pass
	עונן	poel	wcp	3ms	ענן	778		soothsay
	נחשׁ	piel	wcp	3ms	נחשׁ	638		divine
	כשׁף	piel	wcp	3ms	כשׁף	506		practice magic
	עשׂה	qal	wcp	3ms	עשׂה	793		do,make
	הרבה	hiph	pft	3ms	רבה	915		make many
	עשׂות	qal	infc		עשׂה	793		do,make
	הכעיסו	hiph	infc		כעס	494	3ms	vex,provoke
33: 7	ישׂם	qal	wci	3ms	שׂים	962		put,set
	עשׂה	qal	pft	3ms	עשׂה	793		do,make
	אמר	qal	pft	3ms	אמר	55		say
	בחרתי	qal	pft	1cs	בחר	103		choose
	אשׂים	qal	impf	1cs	שׂים	962		put,set
33: 8	אוסיף	hiph	impf	1cs	יסף	414		add,do again
	הסיר	hiph	infc		סור	693		take away
	העמדתי	hiph	pft	1cs	עמד	763		set up,raise
	ישׁמרו	qal	impf	3mp	שׁמר	1036		keep,watch
	עשׂות	qal	infc		עשׂה	793		do,make
	צויתים	piel	pft	1cs	צוה	845	3mp	command
33: 9	יתע	hiph	wci	3ms	תעה	1073		cause to err
	ישׁבי	qal	ptc	mp	ישׁב	442		sit,dwell
	עשׂות	qal	infc		עשׂה	793		do,make
	השׁמיד	hiph	pft	3ms	שׁמד	1029		exterminate
33: 10	ידבר	piel	wci	3ms	דבר	180		speak
	הקשׁיבו	hiph	pft	3cp	קשׁב	904		give attention
33: 11	יבא	hiph	wci	3ms	בוא	97		bring in
	ילכדו	qal	wci	3mp	לכד	539		capture

ChVs	Form	Stem	Tnse	PGN	Root	BDB	Sfx	Meaning
33: 11	יאסרהו	qal	wci	3mp	אסר	63	3ms	tie,bind
	יוליכהו	hiph	wci	3mp	הלך	229	3ms	lead,bring
33: 12	הצר	hiph	infc		צרר	864		distress,cramp
	חלה	piel	pft	3ms	חלה	318		pacify,appease
	יכנע	niph	wci	3ms	כנע	488		humble self
33: 13	יתפלל	hith	wci	3ms	פלל	813		pray
	יעתר	niph	wci	3ms	עתר	801		be supplicated
	ישמע	qal	wci	3ms	שמע	1033		hear
	ישיבהו	hiph	wci	3ms	שוב	996	3ms	bring back
	ידע	qal	wci	3ms	ידע	393		know
33: 14	בנה	qal	pft	3ms	בנה	124		build
	בוא	qal	infc		בוא	97		come in
	סבב	qal	pft	3ms	סבב	685		surround
	יגביהה	hiph	wci	3ms	גבה	146	3fs	make high,exalt
	ישם	qal	wci	3ms	שים	962		put,set
	בצרות	qal	pptc	fp	בצר	130		cut off
33: 15	יסר	hiph	wci	3ms	סור	693		take away
	בנה	qal	pft	3ms	בנה	124		build
	ישלך	hiph	wci	3ms	שלך	1020		throw,cast
33: 16	יכןk	hiph	wci	3ms	כון	465		fix,prepare
	יבןq	qal	wci	3ms	בנה	124		build
	יזבח	qal	wci	3ms	זבח	256		slaughter
	יאמר	qal	wci	3ms	אמר	55		say
	עבוד	qal	infc		עבד	712		work,serve
33: 17	זבחים	qal	ptc	mp	זבח	256		slaughter
33: 18	מדברים	piel	ptc	mp	דבר	180		speak
33: 19	העתר	niph	infc		עתר	801		be supplicated
	בנה	qal	pft	3ms	בנה	124		build
	העמיד	hiph	pft	3ms	עמד	763		set up,raise
	הכנעו	niph	infc		כנע	488	3ms	humble self
	כתובים	qal	pptc	mp	כתב	507		write
33: 20	ישכב	qal	wci	3ms	שכב	1011		lie,lie down
	יקברהו	qal	wci	3mp	קבר	868	3ms	bury
	ימלך	qal	wci	3ms	מלך	573		be king,reign
33: 21	מלכו	qal	infc		מלך	573	3ms	be king,reign
	מלך	qal	pft	3ms	מלך	573		be king,reign
33: 22	יעש	qal	wci	3ms	עשה	793		do,make
	עשה	qal	pft	3ms	עשה	793		do,make
	עשה	qal	pft	3ms	עשה	793		do,make
	זבח	piel	pft	3ms	זבח	256		sacrifice
	יעבדם	qal	wci	3ms	עבד	712	3mp	work,serve
33: 23	נכנע	niph	pft	3ms	כנע	488		humble self
	הכנע	niph	infc		כנע	488		humble self
	הרבה	hiph	pft	3ms	רבה	915		make many
33: 24	יקשרו	qal	wci	3mp	קשר	905		bind
	ימיתהו	hiph	wci	3mp	מות	559	3ms	kill
33: 25	יכו	hiph	wci	3mp	נכה	645		smite
	קשרים	qal	ptc	mp	קשר	905		bind
	ימליכו	hiph	wci	3mp	מלך	573		cause to reign
34: 1	מלכו	qal	infc		מלך	573	3ms	be king,reign
	מלך	qal	pft	3ms	מלך	573		be king,reign
34: 2	יעש	qal	wci	3ms	עשה	793		do,make
	ילך	qal	wci	3ms	הלך	229		walk,go
	סר	qal	pft	3ms	סור	693		turn aside
34: 3	מלכו	qal	infc		מלך	573	3ms	be king,reign
	החל	hiph	pft	3ms	חלל	320		begin,profane
	דרוש	qal	infc		דרש	205		resort to,seek
	החל	hiph	pft	3ms	חלל	320		begin,profane
	טהר	piel	infc		טהר	372		cleanse
34: 4	ינתצו	piel	wci	3mp	נתץ	683		tear down
	גדע	piel	pft	3ms	גדע	154		hew off
	שבר	piel	pft	3ms	שבר	990		shatter
	הדק	hiph	pft	3ms	דקק	200		pulverize
	יזרק	qal	wci	3ms	זרק	284		toss,scatter
	זבחים	qal	ptc	mp	זבח	256		slaughter
34: 5	שרף	qal	pft	3ms	שרף	976		burn
	יטהר	piel	wci	3ms	טהר	372		cleanse
34: 7	ינתץ	piel	wci	3ms	נתץ	683		tear down
	כתת	piel	pft	3ms	כתת	510		beat to pieces
	הדק	hiph	infc		דקק	200		pulverize
	גדע	piel	pft	3ms	גדע	154		hew off
	ישב	qal	wci	3ms	שוב	996		turn,return
34: 8	מלכו	qal	infc		מלך	573	3ms	be king,reign
	טהר	piel	infc		טהר	372		cleanse
	שלח	qal	pft	3ms	שלח	1018		send
	מזכיר	hiph	ptc	ms	זכר	269		c. to remember
	חזק	piel	infc		חזק	304		make strong
34: 9	יבאו	qal	wci	3mp	בוא	97		come in
	יתנו	qal	wci	3mp	נתן	678		give,set
	מובא	hoph	ptc	ms	בוא	97		be brought
	אספו	qal	pft	3cp	אסף	62		gather
	שמרי	qal	ptc	mp	שמר	1036		keep,watch
	ישביk	qal	ptc	mp	ישב	442		sit,dwell
	ישבוq	qal	wci	3mp	שוב	996		turn,return
34: 10	יתנו	qal	wci	3mp	נתן	678		give,set
	עשה	qal	ptc	ms	עשה	793		do,make
	מפקדים	hoph	ptc	mp	פקד	823		be appointed
	יתנו	qal	wci	3mp	נתן	678		give,set
	עושי	qal	ptc	mp	עשה	793		do,make
	עשים	qal	ptc	mp	עשה	793		do,make
	בדוק	qal	infc		בדק	96		repair
	חזק	piel	infc		חזק	304		make strong
34: 11	יתנו	qal	wci	3mp	נתן	678		give,set
	בנים	qal	ptc	mp	בנה	124		build
	קנות	qal	infc		קנה	888		get,buy
	קרות	piel	infc		קרה	900		lay beams
	השחיתו	hiph	pft	3cp	שחת	1007		spoil,ruin
34: 12	עשים	qal	ptc	mp	עשה	793		do,make
	מפקדים	hoph	ptc	mp	פקד	823		be appointed
	נצח	piel	infc		נצח	663		act as director
	מבין	hiph	ptc	ms	בין	106		understand
34: 13	מנצחים	piel	ptc	mp	נצח	663		act as director
	עשה	qal	ptc	ms	עשה	793		do,make
34: 14	הוציאם	hiph	infc		יצא	422	3mp	bring out
	מובא	hoph	ptc	ms	בוא	97		be brought
	מצא	qal	pft	3ms	מצא	592		find
34: 15	יען	qal	wci	3ms	ענה	772		answer
	יאמר	qal	wci	3ms	אמר	55		say

ChVs	Form	Stem	Tnse	PGN	Root	BDB	Sfx	Meaning
34: 15	מצאתי	qal	pft	1cs	מצא	592		find
	יתן	qal	wci	3ms	נתן	678		give,set
34: 16	יבא	hiph	wci	3ms	בוא	97		bring in
	ישב	hiph	wci	3ms	שוב	996		bring back
	אמר	qal	infc		אמר	55		say
	נתן	niph	pft	3ms	נתן	678		be given
	עשים	qal	ptc	mp	עשה	793		do,make
34: 17	יתיכו	hiph	wci	3mp	נתך	677		pour out
	נמצא	niph	ptc	ms	מצא	592		be found
	יתנוהו	qal	wci	3mp	נתן	678	3ms	give,set
	מפקדים	hoph	ptc	mp	פקד	823		be appointed
	עושי	qal	ptc	mp	עשה	793		do,make
34: 18	יגד	hiph	wci	3ms	נגד	616		declare,tell
	אמר	qal	infc		אמר	55		say
	נתן	qal	pft	3ms	נתן	678		give,set
	יקרא	qal	wci	3ms	קרא	894		call,proclaim
34: 19	יהי	qal	wci	3ms	היה	224		be,become
	שמע	qal	infc		שמע	1033		hear
	יקרע	qal	wci	3ms	קרע	902		tear,rend
34: 20	יצו	piel	wci	3ms	צוה	845		command
	אמר	qal	infc		אמר	55		say
34: 21	לכו	qal	impv	mp	הלך	229		walk,go
	דרשו	qal	impv	mp	דרש	205		resort to,seek
	נשאר	niph	ptc	ms	שאר	983		be left
	נמצא	niph	pft	3ms	מצא	592		be found
	נתכה	niph	pft	3fs	נתך	677		be poured
	שמרו	qal	pft	3cp	שמר	1036		keep,watch
	עשות	qal	infc		עשה	793		do,make
	כתוב	qal	pptc	ms	כתב	507		write
34: 22	ילך	qal	wci	3ms	הלך	229		walk,go
	שומר	qal	ptc	ms	שמר	1036		keep,watch
	יושבת	qal	ptc	fs	ישב	442		sit,dwell
	ידברו	piel	wci	3mp	דבר	180		speak
34: 23	תאמר	qal	wci	3fs	אמר	55		say
	אמר	qal	pft	3ms	אמר	55		say
	אמרו	qal	impv	mp	אמר	55		say
	שלח	qal	pft	3ms	שלח	1018		send
34: 24	אמר	qal	pft	3ms	אמר	55		say
	מביא	hiph	ptc	ms	בוא	97		bring in
	יושביו	qal	ptc	mp	ישב	442	3ms	sit,dwell
	כתובות	qal	pptc	fp	כתב	507		write
	קראו	qal	pft	3cp	קרא	894		call,proclaim
34: 25	עזבוני	qal	pft	3cp	עזב	736	1cs	leave,loose
	יקטירוk	hiph	wci	3mp	קטר	882		make sacrifices
	יקטרוq	piel	wci	3mp	קטר	882		make sacrifices
	הכעיסני	hiph	infc		כעס	494	1cs	vex,provoke
	תתך	qal	impf	3fs	נתך	677		pour forth
	תכבה	qal	impf	3fs	כבה	459		be quenched
34: 26	שלח	qal	ptc	ms	שלח	1018		send
	דרוש	qal	infc		דרש	205		resort to,seek
	תאמרו	qal	impf	2mp	אמר	55		say
	אמר	qal	pft	3ms	אמר	55		say
	שמעת	qal	pft	2ms	שמע	1033		hear
34: 27	רך	qal	pft	3ms	רכך	939		be tender,timid

ChVs	Form	Stem	Tnse	PGN	Root	BDB	Sfx	Meaning
34: 27	תכנע	niph	wci	2ms	כנע	488		humble self
	שמעך	qal	infc		שמע	1033	2ms	hear
	ישביו	qal	ptc	mp	ישב	442	3ms	sit,dwell
	תכנע	niph	wci	2ms	כנע	488		humble self
	תקרע	qal	wci	2ms	קרע	902		tear,rend
	תבך	qal	wci	2ms	בכה	113		weep
	שמעתי	qal	pft	1cs	שמע	1033		hear
34: 28	אספך	qal	ptc	ms	אסף	62	2ms	gather
	נאספת	niph	wcp	2ms	אסף	62		assemble
	תראינה	qal	impf	3fp	ראה	906		see
	מביא	hiph	ptc	ms	בוא	97		bring in
	ישביו	qal	ptc	mp	ישב	442	3ms	sit,dwell
	ישיבו	hiph	wci	3mp	שוב	996		bring back
34: 29	ישלח	qal	wci	3ms	שלח	1018		send
	יאסף	qal	wci	3ms	אסף	62		gather
34: 30	יעל	qal	wci	3ms	עלה	748		go up
	ישבי	qal	ptc	mp	ישב	442		sit,dwell
	יקרא	qal	wci	3ms	קרא	894		call,proclaim
	נמצא	niph	ptc	ms	מצא	592		be found
34: 31	יעמד	qal	wci	3ms	עמד	763		stand,stop
	יכרת	qal	wci	3ms	כרת	503		cut,destroy
	לכת	qal	infc		הלך	229		walk,go
	שמור	qal	infc		שמר	1036		keep,watch
	עשות	qal	infc		עשה	793		do,make
	כתובים	qal	pptc	mp	כתב	507		write
34: 32	יעמד	hiph	wci	3ms	עמד	763		set up,raise
	נמצא	niph	ptc	ms	מצא	592		be found
	יעשו	qal	wci	3mp	עשה	793		do,make
	ישבי	qal	ptc	mp	ישב	442		sit,dwell
34: 33	יסר	qal	wci	3ms	סור	693		turn aside
	יעבד	hiph	wci	3ms	עבד	712		cause to serve
	נמצא	niph	ptc	ms	מצא	592		be found
	עבוד	qal	infc		עבד	712		work,serve
	סרו	qal	pft	3cp	סור	693		turn aside
35: 1	יעש	qal	wci	3ms	עשה	793		do,make
	ישחטו	qal	wci	3mp	שחט	1006		slaughter
35: 2	יעמד	hiph	wci	3ms	עמד	763		set up,raise
	יחזקם	piel	wci	3ms	חזק	304	3mp	make strong
35: 3	יאמר	qal	wci	3ms	אמר	55		say
	מביניםq	hiph	ptc	mp	בין	106		understand
	תנו	qal	impv	mp	נתן	678		give,set
	בנה	qal	pft	3ms	בנה	124		build
	עבדו	qal	impv	mp	עבד	712		work,serve
35: 4	הכונוk	niph	impv	mp	כון	465		be established
	הכינוq	hiph	impv	mp	כון	465		fix,prepare
35: 5	עמדו	qal	impv	mp	עמד	763		stand,stop
35: 6	שחטו	qal	impv	mp	שחט	1006		slaughter
	התקדשו	hith	impv	mp	קדש	872		consecrate self
	הכינו	hiph	impv	mp	כון	465		fix,prepare
	עשות	qal	infc		עשה	793		do,make
35: 7	ירם	hiph	wci	3ms	רום	926		raise,lift
	נמצא	niph	ptc	ms	מצא	592		be found
35: 8	הרימו	hiph	pft	3cp	רום	926		raise,lift
	נתנו	qal	pft	3cp	נתן	678		give,set

ChVs	Form	Stem	Tnse	PGN	Root	BDB	Sfx	Meaning
35: 9	הרימו	hiph	pft	3cp	רום	926		raise,lift
35: 10	תכון	niph	wci	3fs	כון	465		be established
	יעמדו	qal	wci	3mp	עמד	763		stand,stop
35: 11	ישחטו	qal	wci	3mp	שחט	1006		slaughter
	יזרקו	qal	wci	3mp	זרק	284		toss,scatter
	מפשיטים	hiph	ptc	mp	פשט	832		strip off
35: 12	יסירו	hiph	wci	3mp	סור	693		take away
	תתם	qal	infc		נתן	678	3mp	give,set
	הקריב	hiph	infc		קרב	897		bring near
	כתוב	qal	pptc	ms	כתב	507		write
35: 13	יבשלו	piel	wci	3mp	בשל	143		boil,cook
	בשלו	piel	pft	3cp	בשל	143		boil,cook
	יריצו	hiph	wci	3mp	רוץ	930		bring quickly
35: 14	הכינו	hiph	pft	3cp	כון	465		fix,prepare
	העלות	hiph	infc		עלה	748		bring up,offer
	הכינו	hiph	pft	3cp	כון	465		fix,prepare
35: 15	משררים	pol	ptc	mp	שיר	1010		sing
	סור	qal	infc		סור	693		turn aside
	הכינו	hiph	pft	3cp	כון	465		fix,prepare
35: 16	תכון	niph	wci	3fs	כון	465		be established
	עשות	qal	infc		עשה	793		do,make
	העלות	hiph	infc		עלה	748		bring up,offer
35: 17	יעשו	qal	wci	3mp	עשה	793		do,make
	נמצאים	niph	ptc	mp	מצא	592		be found
35: 18	נעשה	niph	pft	3ms	עשה	793		be done
	עשו	qal	pft	3cp	עשה	793		do,make
	עשה	qal	pft	3ms	עשה	793		do,make
	נמצא	niph	ptc	ms	מצא	592		be found
	יושבי	qal	ptc	mp	ישב	442		sit,dwell
35: 19	נעשה	niph	pft	3ms	עשה	793		be done
35: 20	הכין	hiph	pft	3ms	כון	465		fix,prepare
	עלה	qal	pft	3ms	עלה	748		go up
	הלחם	niph	infc		לחם	535		wage war
	יצא	qal	wci	3ms	יצא	422		go out
	קראתו	qal	infc		קרא	896	3ms	meet,encounter
35: 21	ישלח	qal	wci	3ms	שלח	1018		send
	אמר	qal	infc		אמר	55		say
	אמר	qal	pft	3ms	אמר	55		say
	בהלני	piel	infc		בהל	96	1cs	hasten,dismay
	חדל	qal	impv	ms	חדל	292		cease
	ישחיתך	hiph	jusm	3ms	שחת	1007	2ms	spoil,ruin
35: 22	הסב	hiph	pft	3ms	סבב	685		cause to turn
	הלחם	niph	infc		לחם	535		wage war
	התחפש	hith	pft	3ms	חפש	344		disguise self
	שמע	qal	pft	3ms	שמע	1033		hear
	יבא	qal	wci	3ms	בוא	97		come in
	הלחם	niph	infc		לחם	535		wage war
35: 23	ירו	hiph	wci	3mp	ירה	434		shoot,teach
	ירים	qal	ptc	mp	ירה	434		throw,shoot
	יאמר	qal	wci	3ms	אמר	55		say
	העבירוני	hiph	impv	mp	עבר	716	1cs	cause to pass
	החליתי	hoph	pft	1cs	חלה	317		be made sick
35: 24	יעבירהו	hiph	wci	3mp	עבר	716	3ms	cause to pass
	ירכיבהו	hiph	wci	3mp	רכב	938	3ms	cause to ride
35: 24	יוליכהו	hiph	wci	3mp	הלך	229	3ms	lead,bring
	ימת	qal	wci	3ms	מות	559		die
	יקבר	niph	wci	3ms	קבר	868		be buried
	מתאבלים	hith	ptc	mp	אבל	5		mourn
35: 25	יקונן	pol	wci	3ms	קין	884		hant a dirge
	יאמרו	qal	wci	3mp	אמר	55		say
	שרים	qal	ptc	mp	שיר	1010		sing
	שרות	qal	ptc	fp	שיר	1010		sing
	יתנום	qal	wci	3mp	נתן	678	3mp	give,set
	כתובים	qal	pptc	mp	כתב	507		write
35: 26	כתוב	qal	pptc	ms	כתב	507		write
35: 27	כתובים	qal	pptc	mp	כתב	507		write
36: 1	יקחו	qal	wci	3mp	לקח	542		take
	ימליכהו	hiph	wci	3mp	מלך	573	3ms	cause to reign
36: 2	מלכו	qal	infc		מלך	573	3ms	be king,reign
	מלך	qal	pft	3ms	מלך	573		be king,reign
36: 3	יסירהו	hiph	wci	3ms	סור	693	3ms	take away
	יענש	qal	wci	3ms	ענש	778		punish,fine
36: 4	ימלך	hiph	wci	3ms	מלך	573		cause to reign
	יסב	hiph	wci	3ms	סבב	685		cause to turn
	לקח	qal	pft	3ms	לקח	542		take
	יביאהו	hiph	wci	3ms	בוא	97	3ms	bring in
36: 5	מלכו	qal	infc		מלך	573	3ms	be king,reign
	מלך	qal	pft	3ms	מלך	573		be king,reign
	יעש	qal	wci	3ms	עשה	793		do,make
36: 6	עלה	qal	pft	3ms	עלה	748		go up
	יאסרהו	qal	wci	3ms	אסר	63	3ms	tie,bind
	הליכו	hiph	infc		הלך	229	3ms	lead,bring
36: 7	הביא	hiph	pft	3ms	בוא	97		bring in
	יתנם	qal	wci	3ms	נתן	678	3mp	give,set
36: 8	עשה	qal	pft	3ms	עשה	793		do,make
	נמצא	niph	ptc	ms	מצא	592		be found
	כתובים	qal	pptc	mp	כתב	507		write
	ימלך	qal	wci	3ms	מלך	573		be king,reign
36: 9	מלכו	qal	infc		מלך	573	3ms	be king,reign
	מלך	qal	pft	3ms	מלך	573		be king,reign
	יעש	qal	wci	3ms	עשה	793		do,make
36: 10	שלח	qal	pft	3ms	שלח	1018		send
	יבאהו	hiph	wci	3ms	בוא	97	3ms	bring in
	ימלך	hiph	wci	3ms	מלך	573		cause to reign
36: 11	מלכו	qal	infc		מלך	573	3ms	be king,reign
	מלך	qal	pft	3ms	מלך	573		be king,reign
36: 12	יעש	qal	wci	3ms	עשה	793		do,make
	נכנע	niph	pft	3ms	כנע	488		humble self
36: 13	מרד	qal	pft	3ms	מרד	597		rebel
	השביעו	hiph	pft	3ms	שבע	989	3ms	cause to swear
	יקש	hiph	wci	3ms	קשה	904		harden
	יאמץ	piel	wci	3ms	אמץ	54		make firm
	שוב	qal	infc		שוב	996		turn,return
36: 14	הרבו	hiph	pft	3cp	רבה	915		make many
	מעולk	qal	infc		מעל	591		act faithlessly
	מעלq	qal	infc		מעל	591		act faithlessly
	יטמאו	piel	wci	3mp	טמא	379		defile
	הקדיש	hiph	pft	3ms	קדש	872		consecrate

ChVs	Form	Stem	Tnse	PGN	Root	BDB	Sfx	Meaning
36: 15	ישלח	qal	wci	3ms	שלח	1018		send
	השכם	hiph	infa		שכם	1014		rise early
	שלוח	qal	infa		שלח	1018		send
	חמל	qal	pft	3ms	חמל	328		spare
36: 16	יהיו	qal	wci	3mp	היה	224		be, become
	מלעבים	hiph	ptc	mp	לעב	541		jest
	בוזים	qal	ptc	mp	בזה	102		despise
	מתעתעים	htpp	ptc	mp	תעע	1073		mock
	עלות	qal	infc		עלה	748		go up
36: 17	יעל	hiph	wci	3ms	עלה	748		bring up, offer
	יהרג	qal	wci	3ms	הרג	246		kill
	חמל	qal	pft	3ms	חמל	328		spare
	נתן	qal	pft	3ms	נתן	678		give, set
36: 18	הביא	hiph	pft	3ms	בוא	97		bring in
36: 19	ישׂרפו	qal	wci	3mp	שׂרף	976		burn
	ינתצו	piel	wci	3mp	נתץ	683		tear down
	שׂרפו	qal	pft	3cp	שׂרף	976		burn
	השחית	hiph	infc		שחת	1007		spoil, ruin
36: 20	יגל	hiph	wci	3ms	גלה	162		lead into exile
	יהיו	qal	wci	3mp	היה	224		be, become
	מלך	qal	infc		מלך	573		be king, reign
36: 21	מלאות	piel	infc		מלא	569		fill
	רצתה	qal	pft	3fs	רצה	953		be pleased
	השמה	hoph	infc		שמם	1030	3fs	be desolate
	שבתה	qal	pft	3fs	שבת	991		cease, desist
	מלאות	piel	infc		מלא	569		fill
36: 22	כלות	qal	infc		כלה	477		finished, spent
	העיר	hiph	pft	3ms	עור	734		rouse, stir up
	יעבר	hiph	wci	3ms	עבר	716		cause to pass
	אמר	qal	infc		אמר	55		say
36: 23	אמר	qal	pft	3ms	אמר	55		say
	נתן	qal	pft	3ms	נתן	678		give, set
	פקד	qal	pft	3ms	פקד	823		attend to, visit
	בנות	qal	infc		בנה	124		build
	יעל	qal	jus	3ms	עלה	748		go up

EZRA

ChVs	Form	Stem	Tnse	PGN	Root	BDB	Sfx	Meaning
1: 1	כלות	qal	infc		כלה	477		finished, spent
	העיר	hiph	pft	3ms	עור	734		rouse, stir up
	יעבר	hiph	wci	3ms	עבר	716		cause to pass
	אמר	qal	infc		אמר	55		say
1: 2	אמר	qal	pft	3ms	אמר	55		say
	נתן	qal	pft	3ms	נתן	678		give, set
	פקד	qal	pft	3ms	פקד	823		attend to, visit
	בנות	qal	infc		בנה	124		build
1: 3	יהי	qal	jus	3ms	היה	224		be, become
	יעל	qal	jus	3ms	עלה	748		go up
	יבן	qal	jus	3ms	בנה	124		build
1: 4	נשאר	niph	ptc	ms	שאר	983		be left
	גר	qal	ptc	ms	גור	157		sojourn
	ינשׂאוהו	piel	jusm	3mp	נשׂא	669	3ms	lift up
1: 5	יקומו	qal	wci	3mp	קום	877		arise, stand
	העיר	hiph	pft	3ms	עור	734		rouse, stir up
	עלות	qal	infc		עלה	748		go up
1: 5	בנות	qal	infc		בנה	124		build
1: 6	חזקו	piel	pft	3cp	חזק	304		make strong
	התנדב	hith	infc		נדב	621		offer freely
1: 7	הוציא	hiph	pft	3ms	יצא	422		bring out
	הוציא	hiph	pft	3ms	יצא	422		bring out
	יתנם	qal	wci	3ms	נתן	678	3mp	give, set
1: 8	יוציאם	hiph	wci	3ms	יצא	422	3mp	bring out
	יספרם	qal	wci	3ms	ספר	707	3mp	count
1: 11	העלה	hiph	pft	3ms	עלה	748		bring up, offer
	העלות	niph	infc		עלה	748		be brought up
2: 1	עלים	qal	ptc	mp	עלה	748		go up
	הגלה	hiph	pft	3ms	גלה	162		lead into exile
	ישובו	qal	wci	3mp	שוב	996		turn, return
2: 2	באו	qal	pft	3cp	בוא	97		come in
2: 41	משררים	pol	ptc	mp	שיר	1010		sing
2: 59	עלים	qal	ptc	mp	עלה	748		go up
	יכלו	qal	pft	3cp	יכל	407		be able
	הגיד	hiph	infc		נגד	616		declare, tell
2: 61	לקח	qal	pft	3ms	לקח	542		take
	יקרא	niph	wci	3ms	קרא	894		be called
2: 62	בקשו	piel	pft	3cp	בקש	134		seek
	מתיחשים	hith	ptc	mp	יחש	405		be registered
	נמצאו	niph	pft	3cp	מצא	592		be found
	יגאלו	pual	wci	3mp	גאל	146		be desecrated
2: 63	יאמר	qal	wci	3ms	אמר	55		say
	יאכלו	qal	impf	3mp	אכל	37		eat, devour
	עמד	qal	infc		עמד	763		stand, stop
2: 65	משררים	pol	ptc	mp	שיר	1010		sing
	משררות	pol	ptc	fp	שיר	1010		sing
2: 68	בואם	qal	infc		בוא	97	3mp	come in
	התנדבו	hith	pft	3cp	נדב	621		offer freely
	העמידו	hiph	infc		עמד	763	3ms	set up, raise
2: 69	נתנו	qal	pft	3cp	נתן	678		give, set
2: 70	ישבו	qal	wci	3mp	ישב	442		sit, dwell
	משררים	pol	ptc	mp	שיר	1010		sing
3: 1	יגע	qal	wci	3ms	נגע	619		touch, strike
	יאספו	niph	wci	3mp	אסף	62		assemble
3: 2	יקם	qal	wci	3ms	קום	877		arise, stand
	יבנו	qal	wci	3mp	בנה	124		build
	העלות	hiph	infc		עלה	748		bring up, offer
	כתוב	qal	pptc	ms	כתב	507		write
3: 3	יכינו	hiph	wci	3mp	כון	465		fix, prepare
	איעלk	hiph	wci	3ms	עלה	748		bring up, offer
	qיעלו	hiph	wci	3mp	עלה	748		bring up, offer
3: 4	יעשׂו	qal	wci	3mp	עשׂה	793		do, make
	כתוב	qal	pptc	ms	כתב	507		write
3: 5	מקדשים	pual	ptc	mp	קדש	872		be consecrated
	מתנדב	hith	ptc	ms	נדב	621		offer freely
3: 6	החלו	hiph	pft	3cp	חלל	320		begin, profane
	העלות	hiph	infc		עלה	748		bring up, offer
	יסד	pual	pft	3ms	יסד	413		be founded
3: 7	יתנו	qal	wci	3mp	נתן	678		give, set
	חצבים	qal	ptc	mp	חצב	345		hew out, dig
	הביא	hiph	infc		בוא	97		bring in

ChVs	Form	Stem	Tnse	PGN	Root	BDB	Sfx	Meaning
3:8	בואם	qal	infc		בוא	97	3mp	come in
	החלו	hiph	pft	3cp	חלל	320		begin,profane
	באים	qal	ptc	mp	בוא	97		come in
	יעמידו	hiph	wci	3mp	עמד	763		set up,raise
	נצח	piel	infc		נצח	663		act as director
3:9	יעמד	qal	wci	3ms	עמד	763		stand,stop
	נצח	piel	infc		נצח	663		act as director
	עשׂה	qal	ptc	ms	עשׂה	793		do,make
3:10	יסדו	piel	pft	3cp	יסד	413		found,establish
	בנים	qal	ptc	mp	בנה	124		build
	יעמידו	hiph	wci	3mp	עמד	763		set up,raise
	מלבשׁים	pual	ptc	mp	לבשׁ	527		be clothed
	הלל	piel	infc		הלל	237		praise
3:11	יענו	qal	wci	3mp	ענה	777		sing
	הלל	piel	infc		הלל	237		praise
	הודת	hiph	infc		ידה	392		praise
	הריעו	hiph	pft	3cp	רוע	929		raise a shout
	הלל	piel	infc		הלל	237		praise
	הוסד	hoph	pft	3ms	יסד	413		be founded
3:12	ראו	qal	pft	3cp	ראה	906		see
	יסדו	qal	infc		יסד	413	3ms	establish
	בכים	qal	ptc	mp	בכה	113		weep
	הרים	hiph	infc		רום	926		raise,lift
3:13	מכירים	hiph	ptc	mp	נכר	647		regard,notice
	מריעים	hiph	ptc	mp	רוע	929		raise a shout
	נשמע	niph	pft	3ms	שׁמע	1033		be heard
4:1	ישמעו	qal	wci	3mp	שׁמע	1033		hear
	בונים	qal	ptc	mp	בנה	124		build
4:2	יגשו	qal	wci	3mp	נגשׁ	620		draw near
	יאמרו	qal	wci	3mp	אמר	55		say
	נבנה	qal	cohm	1cp	בנה	124		build
	נדרושׁ	qal	impf	1cp	דרשׁ	205		resort to,seek
	זבחים	qal	ptc	mp	זבח	256		slaughter
	מעלה	hiph	ptc	ms	עלה	748		bring up,offer
4:3	יאמר	qal	wci	3ms	אמר	55		say
	בנות	qal	infc		בנה	124		build
	נבנה	qal	impf	1cp	בנה	124		build
	צונו	piel	pft	3ms	צוה	845	1cp	command
4:4	יהי	qal	wci	3ms	היה	224		be,become
	מרפים	piel	ptc	mp	רפה	951		let fall
	kמבלהים	piel	ptc	mp	בלה	117		trouble
	qמבהלים	piel	ptc	mp	בהל	96		hasten,dismay
	בנות	qal	infc		בנה	124		build
4:5	סכרים	qal	ptc	mp	סכר	698		hire
	יועצים	qal	ptc	mp	יעץ	419		advise,counsel
	הפר	hiph	infc		פרר	830		break,frustrate
4:6	כתבו	qal	pft	3cp	כתב	507		write
	ישׁבי	qal	ptc	mp	ישׁב	442		sit,dwell
4:7	כתב	qal	pft	3ms	כתב	507		write
	כתוב	qal	pptc	ms	כתב	507		write
	מתרגם	pual	ptc	ms	תרגם	1076		be interpreted
4:8	כתבו	peal	pft	3mp	כתב	1098		write
4:10	הגלי	haph	pft	3ms	גלה	1086		take into exile
	הותב	haph	pft	3ms	יתב	1096		cause to dwell
4:11	שׁלחו	peal	pft	3mp	שׁלח	1115		send
4:12	ידיע	peal	pptc	ms	ידע	1095		know
	להוא	peal	jusm	3ms	הוה	1089		become,be
	סלקו	peal	pft	3mp	סלק	1104		come up
	אתו	peal	pft	3mp	אתה	1083		come
	בנין	peal	ptc	mp	בנה	1084		build
	kאשׁכללו	ish	pft	3mp	כלל	1097		e completed i
	qשׁכלילו	shap	pft	3mp	כלל	1097		complete
	יחיטו	aph	impf	3mp	חוט	1092		repair
4:13	ידיע	peal	pptc	ms	ידע	1095		know
	להוא	peal	jusm	3ms	הוה	1089		become,be
	תתבנא	htpe	impf	3fs	בנה	1084		be built
	ישׁתכללון	hish	impf	3mp	כלל	1097		be completed
	ינתנון	peal	impf	3mp	נתן	1103		give
	תהנזק	haph	impf	3fs	נזק	1102		injure
4:14	מלחנא	peal	pft	1cp	מלח	1100		eat salt
	מחזא	peal	infc		חזה	1092		see,behold
	שׁלחנא	peal	pft	1cp	שׁלח	1115		send
	הודענא	haph	pft	1cp	ידע	1095		inform
4:15	יבקר	pael	impf	3ms	בקר	1085		inquire,seek
	תהשׁכח	haph	impf	2ms	שׁכח	1115		find
	תנדע	peal	impf	2ms	ידע	1095		know
	מהנזקת	haph	ptc	fs	נזק	1102		injure
	עבדין	peal	ptc	mp	עבד	1104		make,do
	החרבת	hoph	pft	3fs	חרב	1093		be waste
4:16	מהודעין	haph	ptc	mp	ידע	1095		inform
	תתבנא	htpe	impf	3fs	בנה	1084		be built
	ישׁתכללון	hish	impf	3mp	כלל	1097		be completed
4:17	שׁלח	peal	pft	3ms	שׁלח	1115		send
	יתבין	peal	ptc	mp	יתב	1096		sit,dwell
4:18	שׁלחתון	peal	pft	2mp	שׁלח	1115		send
	מפרשׁ	pael	pptc	ms	פרשׁ	1109		make distinct
	קרי	peil	pft	3ms	קרא	1111		be read
4:19	שׂים	peil	pft	3ms	שׂים	1113		be made
	בקרו	pael	pft	3mp	בקר	1085		inquire,seek
	השׁכחו	haph	pft	3mp	שׁכח	1115		find
	מתנשׂאה	htpa	ptc	fs	נשׂא	1103		make a rising
	מתעבד	htpe	ptc	ms	עבד	1104		be done
4:20	הוו	peal	pft	3mp	הוה	1089		become,be
	מתיהב	htpe	ptc	ms	יהב	1095		be given
4:21	שׂימו	peal	impv	mp	שׂים	1113		make,set
	בטלא	pael	infc		בטל	1084		make to cease
	תתבנא	htpe	impf	3fs	בנה	1084		be built
	יתשׂם	htap	impf	3ms	שׂים	1113		be made
4:22	זהירין	peal	pptc	mp	זהר	1091		be warned
	הוו	peal	impv	mp	הוה	1089		become,be
	מעבד	peal	infc		עבד	1104		make,do
	ישׂגא	peal	impf	3ms	שׂגא	1113		grow great
	הנזקת	haph	infc		נזק	1102		injure
4:23	קרי	peil	pft	3ms	קרא	1111		be read
	אזלו	peal	pft	3mp	אזל	1079		go,go off
	בטלו	pael	pft	3mp	בטל	1084		make to cease
4:24	בטלת	peal	pft	3fs	בטל	1084		cease
	הות	peal	pft	3fs	הוה	1089		become,be

ChVs	Form	Stem	Tnse	PGN	Root	BDB	Sfx	Meaning
4:24	בטלא	peal	ptc	fs	בטל	1084		cease
5:1	התנבי	htpa	pft	3ms	נבא	1127		prophesy
5:2	קמו	peal	pft	3mp	קום	1110		arise
	שׁריו	pael	pft	3mp	שׁרא	1117		begin
	מבנא	peal	infc		בנה	1084		build
	מסעדין	pael	ptc	mp	סעד	1104		support,sustain
5:3	אתא	peal	pft	3ms	אתה	1083		come
	אמרין	peal	ptc	mp	אמר	1081		say,tell
	שׂם	peal	pft	3ms	שׂים	1113		make,set
	בנא	peal	infc		בנה	1084		build
	שׁכללה	shap	infc		כלל	1097		complete
5:4	אמרנא	peal	pft	1cp	אמר	1081		say,tell
	בנין	peal	ptc	mp	בנה	1084		build
5:5	הות	peal	pft	3fs	הוה	1089		become, be
	שׂבי	peal	ptc	mp	שׂיב	1114		be hoary
	בטלו	pael	pft	3mp	בטל	1084		make to cease
	יהך	peal	impf	3ms	הלך	1090		go
	יתיבון	aph	impf	3mp	תוב	1117		restore,return
5:6	שׁלח	peal	pft	3ms	שׁלח	1115		send
5:7	שׁלחו	peal	pft	3mp	שׁלח	1115		send
	כתיב	peil	pft	3ms	כתב	1098		be written
5:8	ידיע	peal	pptc	ms	ידע	1095		know
	להוא	peal	jusm	3ms	הוה	1089		become, be
	אזלנא	peal	pft	1cp	אזל	1079		go, go off
	מתבנא	htpe	ptc	ms	בנה	1084		be built
	מתשׂם	htap	ptc	ms	שׂים	1113		be made
	מתעבדא	htpe	ptc	fs	עבד	1104		be done
	מצלח	aph	ptc	ms	צלח	1109		prosper
5:9	שׁאלנא	peal	pft	1cp	שׁאל	1114		ask,request
	שׂביא	peal	ptc	mp	שׂיב	1114		be hoary
	אמרנא	peal	pft	1cp	אמר	1081		say,tell
	שׂם	peal	pft	3ms	שׂים	1113		make,set
	מבניה	peal	infc		בנה	1084		build
	שׁכללה	shap	infc		כלל	1097		complete
5:10	שׁאלנא	peal	pft	1cp	שׁאל	1114		ask,request
	הודעותך	haph	infc		ידע	1095	2ms	inform
	נכתב	peal	impf	1cp	כתב	1098		write
5:11	התיבונא	haph	pft	3mp	תוב	1117	1cp	restore,return
	ממר	peal	infc		אמר	1081		say,tell
	בנין	peal	ptc	mp	בנה	1084		build
	הוא	peal	pft	3ms	הוה	1089		become, be
	בנה	peal	pptc	ms	בנה	1084		build
	בנהי	peal	pft	3ms	בנה	1084	3ms	build
	שׁכללה	shap	pft	3ms	כלל	1097	3ms	complete
5:12	הרגזו	haph	pft	3mp	רגז	1112		enrage
	יהב	peal	pft	3ms	יהב	1095		give
	סתרה	peal	pft	3ms	סתר	1104	3ms	destroy
	הגלי	haph	pft	3ms	גלה	1086		take into exile
5:13	שׂם	peal	pft	3ms	שׂים	1113		make,set
	בנא	peal	infc		בנה	1084		build
5:14	הנפק	haph	pft	3ms	נפק	1103		bring forth
	היבל	haph	pft	3ms	יבל	1094		bear along
	הנפק	haph	pft	3ms	נפק	1103		bring forth
	יהיבו	peil	pft	3mp	יהב	1095		be given
5:14	שׂמה	peal	pft	3ms	שׂים	1113	3ms	make,set
5:15	אמר	peal	pft	3ms	אמר	1081		say,tell
	שׂא	peal	impv	ms	נשׂא	1103		carry away
	אזל	peal	impv	ms	אזל	1079		go, go off
	אחת	aph	impv	ms	נחת	1102		deposit
	יתבנא	htpe	jusm	3ms	בנה	1084		be built
5:16	אתא	peal	pft	3ms	אתה	1083		come
	יהב	peal	pft	3ms	יהב	1095		give
	מתבנא	htpe	ptc	ms	בנה	1084		be built
	שׁלם	peal	pptc	ms	שׁלם	1115		be complete
5:17	יתבקר	htpa	jusm	3ms	בקר	1085		be sought
	שׂים	peil	pft	3ms	שׂים	1113		be made
	מבנא	peal	infc		בנה	1084		build
	ישׁלח	peal	jusm	3ms	שׁלח	1115		send
6:1	שׂם	peal	pft	3ms	שׂים	1113		make,set
	בקרו	pael	pft	3mp	בקר	1085		inquire,seek
	מהחתין	haph	pptc	mp	נחת	1102		be deposited
6:2	השׁתכח	htpe	pft	3ms	שׁכח	1115		be found
	כתיב	peil	pft	3ms	כתב	1098		be written
6:3	שׂם	peal	pft	3ms	שׂים	1113		make,set
	יתבנא	htpe	jusm	3ms	בנה	1084		be built
	דבחין	peal	ptc	mp	דבח	1087		sacrifice
	מסובלין	saph	pptc	mp	יבל	1094?		bear along
6:4	תתיהב	htpe	jusm	3fs	יהב	1095		be given
6:5	הנפק	haph	pft	3ms	נפק	1103		bring forth
	היבל	haph	pft	3ms	יבל	1094		bear along
	יהתיבון	haph	jusm	3mp	תוב	1117		restore,return
	יהך	peal	jusm	3ms	הלך	1090		go
	תחת	aph	impf	2ms	נחת	1102		deposit
6:6	הוו	peal	impv	mp	הוה	1089		become, be
6:7	שׁבקו	peal	impv	mp	שׁבק	1114		leave, let alone
	שׂבי	peal	ptc	mp	שׂיב	1114		be hoary
	יבנון	peal	jusm	3mp	בנה	1084		build
6:8	שׂים	peil	pft	3ms	שׂים	1113		be made
	תעבדון	peal	impf	2mp	עבד	1104		make,do
	שׂבי	peal	ptc	mp	שׂיב	1114		be hoary
	מבנא	peal	infc		בנה	1084		build
	תהוא	peal	jusm	3fs	הוה	1089		become, be
	מתיהבא	htpe	ptc	fs	יהב	1095		be given
	בטלא	pael	infc		בטל	1084		make to cease
6:9	להוא	peal	impf	3ms	הוה	1089		become, be
	מתיהב	htpe	ptc	ms	יהב	1095		be given
6:10	להון	peal	impf	3mp	הוה	1089		become, be
	מהקרבין	haph	ptc	mp	קרב	1111		bring near
	מצלין	pael	ptc	mp	צלא	1109		pray
6:11	שׂים	peil	pft	3ms	שׂים	1113		be made
	יהשׁנא	haph	impf	3ms	שׁנא	1116		change
	יתנסח	htpe	jusm	3ms	נסח	1103		be pulled away
	זקיף	peal	pptc	ms	זקף	1091		raise, lift up
	יתמחא	htpe	jusm	3ms	מחא	1099		be smitten
	יתעבד	htpe	jusm	3ms	עבד	1104		be done
6:12	שׁכן	pael	pft	3ms	שׁכן	1115		cause to dwell
	ימגר	pael	jusm	3ms	מגר	1099		overthrow
	ישׁלח	peal	impf	3ms	שׁלח	1115		send

ChVs	Form	Stem	Tnse	PGN	Root	BDB	Sfx	Meaning
6: 12	השניה	haph	infc		שנא	1116		change
	חבלה	pael	infc		חבל	1091		destroy,hurt
	שמת	peal	pft	1cs	שים	1113		make,set
	יתעבד	htpe	jusm	3ms	עבד	1104		be done
6: 13	שלח	peal	pft	3ms	שלח	1115		send
	עבדו	peal	pft	3mp	עבד	1104		make,do
6: 14	שבי	peal	ptc	mp	שיב	1114		be hoary
	בנין	peal	ptc	mp	בנה	1084		build
	מצלחין	aph	ptc	mp	צלח	1109		prosper
	בנו	peal	pft	3mp	בנה	1084		build
	שכללו	shap	pft	3mp	כלל	1097		complete
6: 15	שיציא	shap	pft	3ms	יצא	1115		finish
6: 16	עבדו	peal	pft	3mp	עבד	1104		make,do
6: 17	הקרבו	haph	pft	3mp	קרב	1111		bring near
6: 18	הקימו	haph	pft	3mp	קום	1110		set up,appoint
6: 19	יעשו	qal	wci	3mp	עשה	793		do,make
6: 20	הטהרו	hith	pft	3mp	טהר	372		purify oneself
	ישחטו	qal	wci	3mp	שחט	1006		slaughter
6: 21	יאכלו	qal	wci	3mp	אכל	37		eat,devour
	שבים	qal	ptc	mp	שוב	996		turn,return
	נבדל	niph	ptc	ms	בדל	95		separate self
	דרש	qal	infc		דרש	205		resort to,seek
6: 22	יעשו	qal	wci	3mp	עשה	793		do,make
	שמחם	piel	pft	3ms	שמח	970	3mp	gladden
	הסב	hiph	pft	3ms	סבב	685		cause to turn
	חזק	piel	infc		חזק	304		make strong
7: 6	עלה	qal	pft	3ms	עלה	748		go up
	נתן	qal	pft	3ms	נתן	678		give,set
	יתן	qal	wci	3ms	נתן	678		give,set
7: 7	יעלו	qal	wci	3mp	עלה	748		go up
	משררים	pol	ptc	mp	שיר	1010		sing
7: 8	יבא	qal	wci	3ms	בוא	97		come in
7: 9	בא	qal	pft	3ms	בוא	97		come in
7: 10	הכין	hiph	pft	3ms	כון	465		fix,prepare
	דרוש	qal	infc		דרש	205		resort to,seek
	עשת	qal	infc		עשה	793		do,make
	למד	piel	infc		למד	540		teach
7: 11	נתן	qal	pft	3ms	נתן	678		give,set
7: 12	גמיר	peal	pptc	ms	גמר	1086		complete
7: 13	שים	peil	pft	3ms	שים	1113		be made
	מתנדב	htpa	ptc	ms	נדב	1102		offer freely
	מהך	peal	infc		הלך	1090		go
	יהך	peal	impf	3ms	הלך	1090		go
7: 14	שליח	peal	pptc	ms	שלח	1115		send
	בקרא	pael	infc		בקר	1085		inquire,seek
7: 15	היבלה	haph	infc		יבל	1094		bear along
	התנדבו	htpa	pft	3mp	נדב	1102		offer freely
7: 16	תהשכח	haph	impf	2ms	שכח	1115		find
	התנדבות	htpa	infc		נדב	1102		offer freely
	מתנדבין	htpa	ptc	mp	נדב	1102		offer freely
7: 17	תקנא	peal	impf	2ms	קנא	1111		acquire,buy
	תקרב	pael	impf	2ms	קרב	1111		offer
7: 18	ייטב	peal	impf	3ms	יטב	1095		be good
	מעבד	peal	infc		עבד	1104		make,do
7: 18	תעבדון	peal	impf	2mp	עבד	1104		make,do
7: 19	מתיהבין	htpe	ptc	mp	יהב	1095		be given
	השלם	haph	impv	ms	שלם	1115		finish
7: 20	יפל	peal	impf	3ms	נפל	1103		fall
	מנתן	peal	infc		נתן	1103		give
	תנתן	peal	impf	2ms	נתן	1103		give
7: 21	שים	peil	pft	3ms	שים	1113		be made
	ישאלנכון	peal	impf	3ms	שאל	1114	2mp	ask,request
	יתעבד	htpe	jusm	3ms	עבד	1104		be done
7: 23	יתעבד	htpe	jusm	3ms	עבד	1104		be done
	להוא	peal	impf	3ms	הוה	1089		become,be
7: 24	מהודעין	haph	ptc	mp	ידע	1095		inform
	פלחי	peal	ptc	mp	פלח	1108		pay reverence
	מרמא	peal	infc		רמא	1113		cast,throw
7: 25	מני	pael	impv	ms	מנה	1101		appoint
	שפטין	peal	ptc	mp	שפט	1117		judge
	להון	peal	impf	3mp	הוה	1089		become,be
	דאנין k	peal	ptc	mp	דין	1088		judge
	דאינין q	peal	ptc	mp	דין	1088		judge
	ידעי	peal	ptc	mp	ידע	1095		know
	ידע	peal	ptc	ms	ידע	1095		know
	תהודעון	haph	impf	2mp	ידע	1095		inform
7: 26	להוא	peal	impf	3ms	הוה	1089		become,be
	עבד	peal	ptc	ms	עבד	1104		make,do
	להוא	peal	jusm	3ms	הוה	1089		become,be
	מתעבד	htpe	ptc	ms	עבד	1104		be done
7: 27	ברוך	qal	pptc	ms	ברך	138		kneel,bless
	נתן	qal	pft	3ms	נתן	678		give,set
	פאר	piel	infc		פאר	802		beautify
7: 28	הטה	hiph	pft	3ms	נטה	639		turn,incline
	יועציו	qal	ptc	mp	יעץ	419	3ms	advise,counsel
	התחזקתי	hith	pft	1cs	חזק	304		strengthen self
	אקבצה	qal	wci	1cs	קבץ	867		gather,collect
	עלות	qal	infc		עלה	748		go up
8: 1	התיחשם	hith	infc		יחש	405	3mp	be registered
	העלים	qal	ptc	mp	עלה	748		go up
8: 3	התיחש	hith	infc		יחש	405		be registered
8: 15	אקבצם	qal	wci	1cs	קבץ	867	3mp	gather,collect
	בא	qal	ptc	ms	בוא	97		come in
	נחנה	qal	wci	1cp	חנה	333		decline,encamp
	אבינה	qal	wci	1cs	בין	106		discern
	מצאתי	qal	pft	1cs	מצא	592		find
8: 16	אשלחה	qal	wci	1cs	שלח	1018		send
	מבינים	hiph	ptc	mp	בין	106		understand
8: 17	אוצאה k	hiph	wci	1cs	יצא	422		bring out
	אצוה q	piel	wci	1cs	צוה	845		command
	אשימה	qal	wci	1cs	שים	962		put,set
	דבר	piel	infc		דבר	180		speak
	הביא	hiph	infc		בוא	97		bring in
	משרתים	piel	ptc	mp	שרת	1058		minister,serve
8: 18	יביאו	hiph	wci	3mp	בוא	97		bring in
8: 20	נתן	qal	pft	3ms	נתן	678		give,set
	נקבו	niph	pft	3cp	נקב	666		be marked
8: 21	אקרא	qal	wci	1cs	קרא	894		call,proclaim

ChVs	Form	Stem	Tnse	PGN	Root	BDB	Sfx	Meaning
8:21	התענות	hith	infc		ענה	776		humble oneself
	בקש	piel	infc		בקש	134		seek
8:22	בשתי	qal	pft	1cs	בוש	101		be ashamed
	שאול	qal	infc		שאל	981		ask,borrow
	עזרנו	qal	infc		עזר	740	1cs	help,aid
	אויב	qal	ptc	ms	איב	33		be hostile to
	אמרנו	qal	pft	1cp	אמר	55		say
	אמר	qal	infc		אמר	55		say
	מבקשיו	piel	ptc	mp	בקש	134	3ms	seek
	עזביו	qal	ptc	mp	עזב	736	3ms	leave,loose
8:23	נצומה	qal	wci	1cp	צום	847		fast
	נבקשה	piel	wci	1cp	בקש	134		seek
	יעתר	niph	wci	3ms	עתר	801		be supplicated
8:24	אבדילה	hiph	wci	1cs	בדל	95		divide
8:25	אשקולהk	qal	wci	1cs	שקל	1053		weigh
	אשקלהq	qal	wci	1cs	שקל	1053		weigh
	הרימו	hiph	pft	3cp	רום	926		raise,lift
	יעציו	qal	ptc	mp	יעץ	419	3ms	advise,counsel
	נמצאים	niph	ptc	mp	מצא	592		be found
8:26	אשקלה	qal	wci	1cs	שקל	1053		weigh
8:27	מצהב	hoph	ptc	ms	צהב	843		be gleaming
8:28	אמרה	qal	wci	1cs	אמר	55		say
8:29	שקדו	qal	impv	mp	שקד	1052		watch,wake
	שמרו	qal	impv	mp	שמר	1036		keep,watch
	תשקלו	qal	impf	2mp	שקל	1053		weigh
8:30	קבלו	piel	pft	3cp	קבל	867		take,receive
	הביא	hiph	infc		בוא	97		bring in
8:31	נסעה	qal	wci	1cp	נסע	652		pull up,set out
	לכת	qal	infc		הלך	229		walk,go
	היתה	qal	pft	3fs	היה	224		be,become
	יצילנו	hiph	wci	3ms	נצל	664	1cp	snatch,deliver
	אויב	qal	ptc	ms	איב	33		be hostile to
	אורב	qal	ptc	ms	ארב	70		lie in wait
8:32	נבוא	qal	wci	1cp	בוא	97		come in
	נשב	qal	wci	1cp	ישב	442		sit,dwell
8:33	נשקל	niph	pft	3ms	שקל	1053		be weighed
8:34	יכתב	niph	wci	3ms	כתב	507		be written
8:35	באים	qal	ptc	mp	בוא	97		come in
	הקריבו	hiph	pft	3cp	קרב	897		bring near
8:36	יתנו	qal	wci	3mp	נתן	678		give,set
	נשאו	piel	pft	3cp	נשא	669		lift up
9:1	כלות	piel	infc		כלה	477		complete,finish
	נגשו	niph	pft	3cp	נגש	620		draw near
	אמר	qal	infc		אמר	55		say
	נבדלו	niph	pft	3cp	בדל	95		separate self
9:2	נשאו	qal	pft	3cp	נשא	669		lift,carry
	התערבו	hith	pft	3cp	ערב	786		exchange,share
	היתה	qal	pft	3fs	היה	224		be,become
9:3	שמעי	qal	infc		שמע	1033	1cs	hear
	קרעתי	qal	pft	1cs	קרע	902		tear,rend
	אמרטה	qal	wci	1cs	מרט	598		make bare
	אשבה	qal	wci	1cs	ישב	442		sit,dwell
	משומם	poel	ptc	ms	שמם	1030		be astonished
9:4	יאספו	niph	impf	3mp	אסף	62		assemble
9:4	ישב	qal	ptc	ms	ישב	442		sit,dwell
	משומם	poel	ptc	ms	שמם	1030		be astonished
9:5	קמתי	qal	pft	1cs	קום	877		arise,stand
	קרעי	qal	infc		קרע	902	1cs	tear,rend
	אכרעה	qal	wci	1cs	כרע	502		bow down
	אפרשה	qal	wci	1cs	פרש	831		spread out
9:6	אמרה	qal	wci	1cs	אמר	55		say
	בשתי	qal	pft	1cs	בוש	101		be ashamed
	נכלמתי	niph	pft	1cs	כלם	483		be humiliated
	הרים	hiph	infc		רום	926		raise,lift
	רבו	qal	pft	3cp	רבה	915		be many,great
	גדלה	qal	pft	3fs	גדל	152		be great,grow
9:7	נתנו	niph	pft	1cp	נתן	678		be given
9:8	היתה	qal	pft	3fs	היה	224		be,become
	השאיר	hiph	infc		שאר	983		leave,spare
	תת	qal	infc		נתן	678		give,set
	האיר	hiph	infc		אור	21		cause to shine
	תתנו	qal	infc		נתן	678	1cp	give,set
9:9	עזבנו	qal	pft	3ms	עזב	736	1cp	leave,loose
	יט	hiph	wci	3ms	נטה	639		turn,incline
	תת	qal	infc		נתן	678		give,set
	רומם	pol	infc		רום	926		raise,rear
	העמיד	hiph	infc		עמד	763		set up,raise
	תת	qal	infc		נתן	678		give,set
9:10	נאמר	qal	impf	1cp	אמר	55		say
	עזבנו	qal	pft	1cp	עזב	736		leave,loose
9:11	צוית	piel	pft	2ms	צוה	845		command
	אמר	qal	infc		אמר	55		say
	באים	qal	ptc	mp	בוא	97		come in
	רשתה	qal	infc		ירש	439	3fs	possess,inherit
	מלאוה	piel	pft	3cp	מלא	569	3fs	fill
9:12	תתנו	qal	jusm	2mp	נתן	678		give,set
	תשאו	qal	jusm	2mp	נשא	669		lift,carry
	תדרשו	qal	impf	2mp	דרש	205		resort to,seek
	תחזקו	qal	impf	2mp	חזק	304		be strong
	אכלתם	qal	wcp	2mp	אכל	37		eat,devour
	הורשתם	hiph	wcp	2mp	ירש	439		c. to possess
9:13	בא	qal	ptc	ms	בוא	97		come in
	חשכת	qal	pft	2ms	חשך	362		withhold
	נתתה	qal	pft	2ms	נתן	678		give,set
9:14	נשוב	qal	impf	1cp	שוב	996		turn,return
	הפר	hiph	infc		פרר	830		break,frustrate
	התחתן	hith	infc		חתן	368		be son-in-law
	תאנף	qal	impf	2ms	אנף	60		be angry
	כלה	piel	infc		כלה	477		complete,finish
9:15	נשארנו	niph	pft	1cp	שאר	983		be left
	עמוד	qal	infc		עמד	763		stand,stop
10:1	התפלל	hith	infc		פלל	813		pray
	התודתו	hith	infc		ידה	392	3ms	confess
	בכה	qal	ptc	ms	בכה	113		weep
	מתנפל	hith	ptc	ms	נפל	656		throw oneself
	נקבצו	niph	pft	3cp	קבץ	867		assemble,gather
	בכו	qal	pft	3cp	בכה	113		weep
	הרבה	hiph	infa		רבה	915		make many

ChVs	Form	Stem	Tnse	PGN	Root	BDB	Sfx	Meaning
10:2	יען	qal	wci	3ms	ענה	772		answer
	יאמר	qal	wci	3ms	אמר	55		say
	מעלנו	qal	pft	1cp	מעל	591		act faithlessly
	נשב	hiph	wci	1cp	ישב	442		cause to dwell
10:3	נכרת	qal	cohm	1cp	כרת	503		cut,destroy
	הוציא	hiph	infc		יצא	422		bring out
	נולד	niph	ptc	ms	ילד	408		be born
	יעשה	niph	jusm	3ms	עשה	793		be done
10:4	קום	qal	impv	ms	קום	877		arise,stand
	חזק	qal	impv	ms	חזק	304		be strong
	עשה	qal	impv	ms	עשה	793		do,make
10:5	יקם	qal	wci	3ms	קום	877		arise,stand
	ישבע	hiph	wci	3ms	שבע	989		cause to swear
	עשות	qal	infc		עשה	793		do,make
	ישבעו	niph	wci	3mp	שבע	989		swear
10:6	יקם	qal	wci	3ms	קום	877		arise,stand
	ילך	qal	wci	3ms	הלך	229		walk,go
	ילך	qal	wci	3ms	הלך	229		walk,go
	אכל	qal	pft	3ms	אכל	37		eat,devour
	שתה	qal	pft	3ms	שתה	1059		drink
	מתאבל	hith	ptc	ms	אבל	5		mourn
10:7	יעבירו	hiph	wci	3mp	עבר	716		cause to pass
	הקבץ	niph	infc		קבץ	867		assemble,gather
10:8	יבוא	qal	impf	3ms	בוא	97		come in
	יחרם	hoph	impf	3ms	חרם	355		be banned
	יבדל	niph	impf	3ms	בדל	95		separate self
10:9	יקבצו	niph	wci	3mp	קבץ	867		assemble,gather
	ישבו	qal	wci	3mp	ישב	442		sit,dwell
	מרעידים	hiph	ptc	mp	רעד	944		tremble
10:10	יקם	qal	wci	3ms	קום	877		arise,stand
	יאמר	qal	wci	3ms	אמר	55		say
	מעלתם	qal	pft	2mp	מעל	591		act faithlessly
	תשיבו	hiph	wci	2mp	ישב	442		cause to dwell
	הוסיף	hiph	infc		יסף	414		add,do again
10:11	תנו	qal	impv	mp	נתן	678		give,set
	עשו	qal	impv	mp	עשה	793		do,make
	הבדלו	niph	impv	mp	בדל	95		separate self
10:12	יענו	qal	wci	3mp	ענה	772		answer
	יאמרו	qal	wci	3mp	אמר	55		say
	עשות	qal	infc		עשה	793		do,make
10:13	עמוד	qal	infc		עמד	763		stand,stop
	הרבינו	hiph	pft	1cp	רבה	915		make many
	פשע	qal	infc		פשע	833		rebel,sin
10:14	יעמדו	qal	jusm	3mp	עמד	763		stand,stop
	השיב	hiph	pft	3ms	ישב	442		cause to dwell
	יבא	qal	jusm	3ms	בוא	97		come in
	מזמנים	pual	ptc	mp	זמן	273		be appointed
	שפטיה	qal	ptc	mp	שפט	1047	3fs	judge
	השיב	hiph	infc		שוב	996		bring back
10:15	עמדו	qal	pft	3cp	עמד	763		stand,stop
	עזרם	qal	pft	3cp	עזר	740	3mp	help,aid
10:16	יעשו	qal	wci	3mp	עשה	793		do,make
	יבדלו	niph	wci	3mp	בדל	95		separate self
	ישבו	qal	wci	3mp	ישב	442		sit,dwell
10:16	דריוש	qal	infc		דרש	205		resort to,seek
10:17	יכלו	piel	wci	3mp	כלה	477		complete,finish
	השיבו	hiph	pft	3cp	ישב	442		cause to dwell
10:18	ימצא	niph	wci	3ms	מצא	592		be found
	השיבו	hiph	pft	3cp	ישב	442		cause to dwell
10:19	יתנו	qal	wci	3mp	נתן	678		give,set
	הוציא	hiph	infc		יצא	422		bring out
10:24	משררים	pol	ptc	mp	שיר	1010		sing
10:44	נשאו	qal	pft	3cp	נשא	669		lift,carry
	ישימו	qal	wci	3mp	שים	962		put,set
NEHEMIAH								
1:1	יהי	qal	wci	3ms	היה	224		be,become
	הייתי	qal	pft	1cs	היה	224		be,become
1:2	יבא	qal	wci	3ms	בוא	97		come in
	אשאלם	qal	wci	1cs	שאל	981	3mp	ask,borrow
	נשארו	niph	pft	3cp	שאר	983		be left
1:3	יאמרו	qal	wci	3mp	אמר	55		say
	נשארים	niph	ptc	mp	שאר	983		be left
	נשארו	niph	pft	3cp	שאר	983		be left
	מפרצת	pual	ptc	fs	פרץ	829		broken down
	נצתו	niph	pft	3cp	יצת	428		be kindled
1:4	יהי	qal	wci	3ms	היה	224		be,become
	שמעי	qal	infc		שמע	1033	1cs	hear
	ישבתי	qal	pft	1cs	ישב	442		sit,dwell
	אבכה	qal	wci	1cs	בכה	113		weep
	אתאבלה	hith	wci	1cs	אבל	5		mourn
	אהי	qal	wci	1cs	היה	224		be,become
	צם	qal	ptc	ms	צום	847		fast
	מתפלל	hith	ptc	ms	פלל	813		pray
1:5	אמר	qal	wci	1cs	אמר	55		say
	נורא	niph	ptc	ms	ירא	431		be feared
	שמר	qal	ptc	ms	שמר	1036		keep,watch
	אהביו	qal	ptc	mp	אהב	12	3ms	love
	שמרי	qal	ptc	mp	שמר	1036		keep,watch
1:6	תהי	qal	jus	3fs	היה	224		be,become
	פתוחות	qal	pptc	fp	פתח	834		open
	שמע	qal	infc		שמע	1033		hear
	מתפלל	hith	ptc	ms	פלל	813		pray
	מתודה	hith	ptc	ms	ידה	392		confess
	חטאנו	qal	pft	1cp	חטא	306		sin
	חטאנו	qal	pft	1cp	חטא	306		sin
1:7	חבל	qal	infc		חבל	287		act corruptly
	חבלנו	qal	pft	1cp	חבל	287		act corruptly
	שמרנו	qal	pft	1cp	שמר	1036		keep,watch
	צוית	piel	pft	2ms	צוה	845		command
1:8	זכר	qal	impv	ms	זכר	269		remember
	צוית	piel	pft	2ms	צוה	845		command
	אמר	qal	infc		אמר	55		say
	תמעלו	qal	impf	2mp	מעל	591		act faithlessly
	אפיץ	hiph	impf	1cs	פוץ	806		scatter
1:9	שבתם	qal	wcp	2mp	שוב	996		turn,return
	שמרתם	qal	wcp	2mp	שמר	1036		keep,watch
	עשיתם	qal	wcp	2mp	עשה	793		do,make

ChVs	Form	Stem	Tnse	PGN	Root	BDB	Sfx	Meaning
1:9	יהיה	qal	impf	3ms	היה	224		be,become
	נדחכם	niph	ptc	ms	נדח	623	2mp	be banished
	אקבצם	piel	impf	1cs	קבץ	867	3mp	gather together
	kהבואתים	hiph	wcp	1cs	בוא	97	3mp	bring in
	הביאותים	hiph	wcp	1cs	בוא	97	3mp	bring in
	בחרתי	qal	pft	1cs	בחר	103		choose
	שכן	piel	infc		שכן	1014		establish
1:10	פדית	qal	pft	2ms	פדה	804		ransom
1:11	תהי	qal	jus	3fs	היה	224		be,become
	יראה	qal	infc		ירא	431		fear
	הצליחה	hiph	impv	ms	צלח	852		cause to thrive
	תנהו	qal	impv	ms	נתן	678	3ms	give,set
	הייתי	qal	pft	1cs	היה	224		be,become
2:1	יהי	qal	wci	3ms	היה	224		be,become
	אשא	qal	wci	1cs	נשא	669		lift,carry
	אתנה	qal	wci	1cs	נתן	678		give,set
	הייתי	qal	pft	1cs	היה	224		be,become
2:2	יאמר	qal	wci	3ms	אמר	55		say
	חולה	qal	ptc	ms	חלה	317		be weak,sick
	אירא	qal	wci	1cs	ירא	431		fear
	הרבה	hiph	infa		רבה	915		make many
2:3	אמר	qal	wci	1cs	אמר	55		say
	יחיה	qal	jusm	3ms	חיה	310		live
	ירעו	qal	impf	3mp	רעע	949		be evil
	אכלו	qalp	pft	3cp	אכל	37		be consumed
2:4	יאמר	qal	wci	3ms	אמר	55		say
	מבקש	piel	ptc	ms	בקש	134		seek
	אתפלל	hith	wci	1cs	פלל	813		pray
2:5	אמר	qal	wci	1cs	אמר	55		say
	טוב	qal	pft	3ms	טוב	373		be pleasing
	ייטב	qal	impf	3ms	יטב	405		be good
	תשלחני	qal	impf	2ms	שלח	1018	1cs	send
	אבננה	qal	cohm	1cs	בנה	124	3fs	build
2:6	יאמר	qal	wci	3ms	אמר	55		say
	יושבת	qal	ptc	fs	ישב	442		sit,dwell
	יהיה	qal	impf	3ms	היה	224		be,become
	תשוב	qal	impf	2ms	שוב	996		turn,return
	ייטב	qal	wci	3ms	יטב	405		be good
	ישלחני	qal	wci	3ms	שלח	1018	1cs	send
	אתנה	qal	wci	1cs	נתן	678		give,set
2:7	אומר	qal	wci	1cs	אמר	55		say
	טוב	qal	pft	3ms	טוב	373		be pleasing
	יתנו	qal	jusm	3mp	נתן	678		give,set
	יעבירוני	hiph	impf	3mp	עבר	716	1cs	cause to pass
	אבוא	qal	impf	1cs	בוא	97		come in
2:8	שמר	qal	ptc	ms	שמר	1036		keep,watch
	יתן	qal	impf	3ms	נתן	678		give,set
	קרות	piel	infc		קרה	900		lay beams
	אבוא	qal	impf	1cs	בוא	97		come in
	יתן	qal	wci	3ms	נתן	678		give,set
2:9	אבוא	qal	wci	1cs	בוא	97		come in
	אתנה	qal	wci	1cs	נתן	678		give,set
	ישלח	qal	wci	3ms	שלח	1018		send
2:10	ישמע	qal	wci	3ms	שמע	1033		hear
2:10	ירע	qal	wci	3ms	רעע	949		be evil
	בא	qal	pft	3ms	בוא	97		come in
	בקש	piel	infc		בקש	134		seek
2:11	אבוא	qal	wci	1cs	בוא	97		come in
	אהי	qal	wci	1cs	היה	224		be,become
2:12	אקום	qal	wci	1cs	קום	877		arise,stand
	הגדתי	hiph	pft	1cs	נגד	616		declare,tell
	נתן	qal	ptc	ms	נתן	678		give,set
	עשות	qal	infc		עשה	793		do,make
	רכב	qal	ptc	ms	רכב	938		mount,ride
2:13	אצאה	qal	wci	1cs	יצא	422		go out
	אהי	qal	wci	1cs	היה	224		be,become
	שבר	qal	ptc	ms	שבר	960		inspect
	kמפרוצים	pual	ptc	mp	פרץ	829?		broken down
	qפרוצים	qal	pptc	mp	פרץ	829		break through
	אכלו	qalp	pft	3cp	אכל	37		be consumed
2:14	אעבר	qal	wci	1cs	עבר	716		pass over
	עבר	qal	infc		עבר	716		pass over
2:15	אהי	qal	wci	1cs	היה	224		be,become
	עלה	qal	ptc	ms	עלה	748		go up
	אהי	qal	wci	1cs	היה	224		be,become
	שבר	qal	ptc	ms	שבר	960		inspect
	אשוב	qal	wci	1cs	שוב	996		turn,return
	אבוא	qal	wci	1cs	בוא	97		come in
	אשוב	qal	wci	1cs	שוב	996		turn,return
2:16	ידעו	qal	pft	3cp	ידע	393		know
	הלכתי	qal	pft	1cs	הלך	229		walk,go
	עשה	qal	ptc	ms	עשה	793		do,make
	עשה	qal	ptc	ms	עשה	793		do,make
	הגדתי	hiph	pft	1cs	נגד	616		declare,tell
2:17	אומר	qal	wci	1cs	אמר	55		say
	ראים	qal	ptc	mp	ראה	906		see
	נצתו	niph	pft	3cp	יצת	428		be kindled
	לכו	qal	impv	mp	הלך	229		walk,go
	נבנה	qal	cohm	1cp	בנה	124		build
	נהיה	qal	impf	1cp	היה	224		be,become
2:18	אגיד	hiph	wci	1cs	נגד	616		declare,tell
	אמר	qal	pft	3ms	אמר	55		say
	יאמרו	qal	wci	3mp	אמר	55		say
	נקום	qal	cohm	1cp	קום	877		arise,stand
	בנינו	qal	wcp	1cp	בנה	124		build
	יחזקו	piel	wci	3mp	חזק	304		make strong
2:19	ישמע	qal	wci	3ms	שמע	1033		hear
	ילעגו	hiph	wci	3mp	לעג	541		mock,deride
	יבזו	qal	wci	3mp	בזה	102		despise
	יאמרו	qal	wci	3mp	אמר	55		say
	עשים	qal	ptc	mp	עשה	793		do,make
	מרדים	qal	ptc	mp	מרד	597		rebel
2:20	אשיב	hiph	wci	1cs	שוב	996		bring back
	אומר	qal	wci	1cs	אמר	55		say
	יצליח	hiph	impf	3ms	צלח	852		cause to thrive
	נקום	qal	impf	1cp	קום	877		arise,stand
	בנינו	qal	wcp	1cp	בנה	124		build
3:1	יקם	qal	wci	3ms	קום	877		arise,stand

ChVs	Form	Stem	Tnse	PGN	Root	BDB	Sfx	Meaning
3:1	יבנו	qal	wci	3mp	בנה	124		build
	קדשוהו	piel	pft	3cp	קדשׁ	872	3ms	consecrate
	יעמידו	hiph	wci	3mp	עמד	763		set up,raise
	קדשוהו	piel	pft	3cp	קדשׁ	872	3ms	consecrate
3:2	בנו	qal	pft	3cp	בנה	124		build
	בנה	qal	pft	3ms	בנה	124		build
3:3	בנו	qal	pft	3cp	בנה	124		build
	קרוהו	piel	pft	3cp	קרה	900	3ms	lay beams
	יעמידו	hiph	wci	3mp	עמד	763		set up,raise
3:4	החזיק	hiph	pft	3ms	חזק	304		make firm,seize
	החזיק	hiph	pft	3ms	חזק	304		make firm,seize
	החזיק	hiph	pft	3ms	חזק	304		make firm,seize
3:5	החזיקו	hiph	pft	3cp	חזק	304		make firm,seize
	הביאו	hiph	pft	3cp	בוא	97		bring in
3:6	החזיקו	hiph	pft	3cp	חזק	304		make firm,seize
	קרוהו	piel	pft	3cp	קרה	900	3ms	lay beams
	יעמידו	hiph	wci	3mp	עמד	763		set up,raise
3:7	החזיק	hiph	pft	3ms	חזק	304		make firm,seize
3:8	החזיק	hiph	pft	3ms	חזק	304		make firm,seize
	צורפים	qal	ptc	mp	צרף	864		refine,test
	החזיק	hiph	pft	3ms	חזק	304		make firm,seize
	יעזבו	qal	wci	3mp	עזב	738		restore,repair
3:9	החזיק	hiph	pft	3ms	חזק	304		make firm,seize
3:10	החזיק	hiph	pft	3ms	חזק	304		make firm,seize
	החזיק	hiph	pft	3ms	חזק	304		make firm,seize
3:11	החזיק	hiph	pft	3ms	חזק	304		make firm,seize
3:12	החזיק	hiph	pft	3ms	חזק	304		make firm,seize
3:13	החזיק	hiph	pft	3ms	חזק	304		make firm,seize
	ישבי	qal	ptc	mp	ישׁב	442		sit,dwell
	בנוהו	qal	pft	3cp	בנה	124	3ms	build
	יעמידו	hiph	wci	3mp	עמד	763		set up,raise
3:14	החזיק	hiph	pft	3ms	חזק	304		make firm,seize
	יבננו	qal	impf	3ms	בנה	124	3ms	build
	יעמיד	hiph	wci	3ms	עמד	763		set up,raise
3:15	החזיק	hiph	pft	3ms	חזק	304		make firm,seize
	יבננו	qal	impf	3ms	בנה	124	3ms	build
	יטללנו	piel	wci	3ms	טלל	378	3ms	cover over
	יעמידו k	hiph	wci	3mp	עמד	763		set up,raise
	יעמיד q	hiph	wci	3ms	עמד	763		set up,raise
	יורדות	qal	ptc	fp	ירד	432		come down
3:16	החזיק	hiph	pft	3ms	חזק	304		make firm,seize
	עשויה	qal	pptc	fs	עשׂה	793		do,make
3:17	החזיקו	hiph	pft	3cp	חזק	304		make firm,seize
	החזיק	hiph	pft	3ms	חזק	304		make firm,seize
3:18	החזיקו	hiph	pft	3cp	חזק	304		make firm,seize
3:19	יחזק	piel	wci	3ms	חזק	304		make strong
	עלת	qal	infc		עלה	748		go up
3:20	החרה	hiph	pft	3ms	חרה	354		burn
	החזיק	hiph	pft	3ms	חזק	304		make firm,seize
3:21	החזיק	hiph	pft	3ms	חזק	304		make firm,seize
3:22	החזיקו	hiph	pft	3cp	חזק	304		make firm,seize
3:23	החזיק	hiph	pft	3ms	חזק	304		make firm,seize
	החזיק	hiph	pft	3ms	חזק	304		make firm,seize
3:24	החזיק	hiph	pft	3ms	חזק	304		make firm,seize
3:25	יוצא	qal	ptc	ms	יצא	422		go out
3:26	היו	qal	pft	3cp	היה	224		be,become
	ישבים	qal	ptc	mp	ישׁב	442		sit,dwell
	יוצא	qal	ptc	ms	יצא	422		go out
3:27	החזיקו	hiph	pft	3cp	חזק	304		make firm,seize
	יוצא	qal	ptc	ms	יצא	422		go out
3:28	החזיקו	hiph	pft	3cp	חזק	304		make firm,seize
3:29	החזיק	hiph	pft	3ms	חזק	304		make firm,seize
	החזיק	hiph	pft	3ms	חזק	304		make firm,seize
	שמר	qal	ptc	ms	שׁמר	1036		keep,watch
3:30	החזיק	hiph	pft	3ms	חזק	304		make firm,seize
	החזיק	hiph	pft	3ms	חזק	304		make firm,seize
3:31	החזיק	hiph	pft	3ms	חזק	304		make firm,seize
	רכלים	qal	ptc	mp	רכל	940		trade,gossip
3:32	החזיקו	hiph	pft	3cp	חזק	304		make firm,seize
	צרפים	qal	ptc	mp	צרף	864		refine,test
	רכלים	qal	ptc	mp	רכל	940		trade,gossip
3:33	יהי	qal	wci	3ms	היה	224		be,become
	שמע	qal	pft	3ms	שׁמע	1033		hear
	בונים	qal	ptc	mp	בנה	124		build
	יחר	qal	wci	3ms	חרה	354		be kindled,burn
	יכעס	qal	wci	3ms	כעס	494		be angry,vexed
	הרבה	hiph	infa		רבה	915		make many
	ילעג	hiph	wci	3ms	לעג	541		mock,deride
3:34	יאמר	qal	wci	3ms	אמר	55		say
	יאמר	qal	wci	3ms	אמר	55		say
	עשים	qal	ptc	mp	עשׂה	793		do,make
	יעזבו	qal	impf	3mp	עזב	738		restore,repair
	יזבחו	qal	impf	3mp	זבח	256		slaughter
	יכלו	piel	impf	3mp	כלה	477		complete,finish
	יחיו	piel	impf	3mp	חיה	310		preserve,revive
	שרופות	qal	pptc	fp	שׂרף	976		burn
3:35	יאמר	qal	wci	3ms	אמר	55		say
	בונים	qal	ptc	mp	בנה	124		build
	יעלה	qal	impf	3ms	עלה	748		go up
	פרץ	qal	wcp	3ms	פרץ	829		break through
3:36	שמע	qal	impv	ms	שׁמע	1033		hear
	היינו	qal	pft	1cp	היה	224		be,become
	השב	hiph	impv	ms	שׁוב	996		bring back
	תנם	qal	impv	ms	נתן	678	3mp	give,set
3:37	תכס	piel	jus	2ms	כסה	491		cover
	תמחה	niph	jusm	3fs	מחה	562		be wiped out
	הכעיסו	hiph	pft	3cp	כעס	494		vex,provoke
	בונים	qal	ptc	mp	בנה	124		build
3:38	נבנה	qal	wci	1cp	בנה	124		build
	תקשר	niph	wci	3fs	קשׁר	905		be bound
	יהי	qal	wci	3ms	היה	224		be,become
	עשות	qal	infc		עשׂה	793		do,make
4:1	יהי	qal	wci	3ms	היה	224		be,become
	שמע	qal	pft	3ms	שׁמע	1033		hear
	עלתה	qal	pft	3fs	עלה	748		go up
	החלו	hiph	pft	3cp	חלל	320		begin,profane
	פרצים	qal	pptc	mp	פרץ	829		break through
	הסתם	niph	infc		סתם	711		be stopped up

ChVs	Form	Stem	Tnse	PGN	Root	BDB	Sfx	Meaning
4:1	יחר	qal	wci	3ms	חרה	354		be kindled, burn
4:2	יקשרו	qal	wci	3mp	קשר	905		bind
	בוא	qal	infc		בוא	97		come in
	הלחם	niph	infc		לחם	535		wage war
	עשות	qal	infc		עשה	793		do, make
4:3	נתפלל	hith	wci	1cp	פלל	813		pray
	נעמיד	hiph	wci	1cp	עמד	763		set up, raise
4:4	יאמר	qal	wci	3ms	אמר	55		say
	כשל	qal	pft	3ms	כשל	505		stumble, totter
	הרבה	hiph	infa		רבה	915		make many
	נוכל	qal	impf	1cp	יכל	407		be able
	בנות	qal	infc		בנה	124		build
4:5	יאמרו	qal	wci	3mp	אמר	55		say
	ידעו	qal	impf	3mp	ידע	393		know
	יראו	qal	impf	3mp	ראה	906		see
	נבוא	qal	impf	1cp	בוא	97		come in
	הרגנום	qal	wcp	1cp	הרג	246	3mp	kill
	השבתנו	hiph	wcp	1cp	שבת	991		destroy, remove
4:6	יהי	qal	wci	3ms	היה	224		be, become
	באו	qal	pft	3cp	בוא	97		come in
	ישבים	qal	ptc	mp	ישב	442		sit, dwell
	יאמרו	qal	wci	3mp	אמר	55		say
	תשובו	qal	impf	2mp	שוב	996		turn, return
4:7	אעמיד	hiph	wci	1cs	עמד	763		set up, raise
	אעמיד	hiph	wci	1cs	עמד	763		set up, raise
4:8	ארא	qal	wci	1cs	ראה	906		see
	אקום	qal	wci	1cs	קום	877		arise, stand
	אמר	qal	wci	1cs	אמר	55		say
	תיראו	qal	jusm	2mp	ירא	431		fear
	נורא	niph	ptc	ms	ירא	431		be feared
	זכרו	qal	impv	mp	זכר	269		remember
	הלחמו	niph	impv	mp	לחם	535		wage war
4:9	יהי	qal	wci	3ms	היה	224		be, become
	שמעו	qal	pft	3cp	שמע	1033		hear
	אויבינו	qal	ptc	mp	איב	33	1cp	be hostile to
	נודע	niph	pft	3ms	ידע	393		be made known
	יפר	hiph	wci	3ms	פרר	830		break, frustrate
	נשוב k	qal	wci	1cp	שוב	996		turn, return
	נשב q	qal	wci	1cp	שוב	996		turn, return
4:10	יהי	qal	wci	3ms	היה	224		be, become
	עשים	qal	ptc	mp	עשה	793		do, make
	מחזיקים	hiph	ptc	mp	חזק	304		make firm, seize
4:11	בונים	qal	ptc	mp	בנה	124		build
	נשאים	qal	ptc	mp	נשא	669		lift, carry
	עמשים	qal	ptc	mp	עמס	770		load, carry
	עשה	qal	ptc	ms	עשה	793		do, make
	מחזקת	hiph	ptc	fs	חזק	304		make firm, seize
4:12	בונים	qal	ptc	mp	בנה	124		build
	אסורים	qal	pptc	mp	אסר	63		tie, bind
	בונים	qal	ptc	mp	בנה	124		build
	תוקע	qal	ptc	ms	תקע	1075		thrust, clap
4:13	אמר	qal	wci	1cs	אמר	55		say
	הרבה	hiph	infa		רבה	915		make many
	נפרדים	niph	ptc	mp	פרד	825		divide
4:14	תשמעו	qal	impf	2mp	שמע	1033		hear
	תקבצו	niph	impf	2mp	קבץ	867		assemble, gather
	ילחם	niph	impf	3ms	לחם	535		wage war
4:15	עשים	qal	ptc	mp	עשה	793		do, make
	מחזיקים	hiph	ptc	mp	חזק	304		make firm, seize
	עלות	qal	infc		עלה	748		go up
	צאת	qal	infc		יצא	422		go out
4:16	אמרתי	qal	pft	1cs	אמר	55		say
	ילינו	qal	jusm	3mp	לון	533		lodge, remain
	היו	qal	wcp	3cp	היה	224		be, become
4:17	פשטים	qal	ptc	mp	פשט	832		strip off
5:1	תהי	qal	wci	3fs	היה	224		be, become
5:2	אמרים	qal	ptc	mp	אמר	55		say
	נקחה	qal	coh	1cp	לקח	542		take
	נאכלה	qal	coh	1cp	אכל	37		eat, devour
	נחיה	qal	cohm	1cp	חיה	310		live
5:3	אמרים	qal	ptc	mp	אמר	55		say
	ערבים	qal	ptc	mp	ערב	786		take on pledge
	נקחה	qal	coh	1cp	לקח	542		take
5:4	אמרים	qal	ptc	mp	אמר	55		say
	לוינו	qal	pft	1cp	לוה	531		borrow
5:5	כבשים	qal	ptc	mp	כבש	461		subdue
	נכבשות	niph	ptc	fp	כבש	461		be subdued
5:6	יחר	qal	wci	3ms	חרה	354		be kindled, burn
	שמעתי	qal	pft	1cs	שמע	1033		hear
5:7	ימלך	niph	wci	3ms	מלך	576		counsel
	אריבה	qal	wci	1cs	ריב	936		strive, contend
	אמרה	qal	wci	1cs	אמר	55		say
	נשאים	qal	ptc	mp	נשא	673		be creditor
	אתן	qal	wci	1cs	נתן	678		give, set
5:8	אמרה	qal	wci	1cs	אמר	55		say
	קנינו	qal	pft	1cp	קנה	888		get, buy
	נמכרים	niph	ptc	mp	מכר	569		be sold
	תמכרו	qal	impf	2mp	מכר	569		sell
	נמכרו	niph	pft	3cp	מכר	569		be sold
	יחרישו	hiph	wci	3mp	חרש	361		be silent
	מצאו	qal	pft	3cp	מצא	592		find
5:9	יאמר k	qal	wci	3ms	אמר	55		say
	אמר q	qal	wci	1cs	אמר	55		say
	עשים	qal	ptc	mp	עשה	793		do, make
	תלכו	qal	impf	2mp	הלך	229		walk, go
	אויבינו	qal	ptc	mp	איב	33	1cp	be hostile to
5:10	נשים	qal	ptc	mp	נשה	674		lend
	נעזבה	qal	coh	1cp	עזב	736		leave, loose
5:11	השיבו	hiph	impv	mp	שוב	996		bring back
	נשים	qal	ptc	mp	נשה	674		lend
5:12	יאמרו	qal	wci	3mp	אמר	55		say
	נשיב	hiph	impf	1cp	שוב	996		bring back
	נבקש	piel	impf	1cp	בקש	134		seek
	נעשה	qal	impf	1cp	עשה	793		do, make
	אומר	qal	ptc	ms	אמר	55		say
	אקרא	qal	wci	1cs	קרא	894		call, proclaim
	אשביעם	hiph	wci	1cs	שבע	989	3ms	cause to swear
	עשות	qal	infc		עשה	793		do, make

ChVs	Form	Stem	Tnse	PGN	Root	BDB	Sfx	Meaning
5:13	נערתי	qal	pft	1cs	נער	654		shake out
	אמרה	qal	wci	1cs	אמר	55		say
	ינער	piel	jusm	3ms	נער	654		shake utterly
	יקים	hiph	impf	3ms	קום	877		raise,build,set
	יהיה	qal	jusm	3ms	היה	224		be,become
	נעור	qal	pptc	ms	נער	654		shake out
	יאמרו	qal	wci	3mp	אמר	55		say
	יהללו	piel	wci	3mp	הלל	237		praise
	יעשׂ	qal	wci	3ms	עשׂה	793		do,make
5:14	צוה	piel	pft	3ms	צוה	845		command
	היות	qal	infc		היה	224		be,become
	אכלתי	qal	pft	1cs	אכל	37		eat,devour
5:15	הכבידו	hiph	pft	3cp	כבד	457		make heavy
	יקחו	qal	wci	3mp	לקח	542		take
	שׁלטו	qal	pft	3cp	שׁלט	1020		domineer
	עשׂיתי	qal	pft	1cs	עשׂה	793		do,make
5:16	החזקתי	hiph	pft	1cs	חזק	304		make firm,seize
	קנינו	qal	pft	1cp	קנה	888		get,buy
	קבוצים	qal	pptc	mp	קבץ	867		gather,collect
5:17	באים	qal	ptc	mp	בוא	97		come in
5:18	היה	qal	pft	3ms	היה	224		be,become
	נעשׂה	niph	ptc	ms	עשׂה	793		be done
	ברורות	qal	pptc	fp	ברר	140		purify,polish
	נעשׂו	niph	pft	3cp	עשׂה	793		be done
	הרבה	hiph	infa		רבה	915		make many
	בקשׁתי	piel	pft	1cs	בקשׁ	134		seek
	כבדה	qal	pft	3fs	כבד	457		be heavy
5:19	זכרה	qal	impv	ms	זכר	269		remember
	עשׂיתי	qal	pft	1cs	עשׂה	793		do,make
6:1	יהי	qal	wci	3ms	היה	224		be,become
	נשׁמע	niph	pft	3ms	שׁמע	1033		be heard
	איבינו	qal	ptc	mp	איב	33	1cp	be hostile to
	בניתי	qal	pft	1cs	בנה	124		build
	נותר	niph	pft	3ms	יתר	451		be left,remain
	העמדתי	hiph	pft	1cs	עמד	763		set up,raise
6:2	ישׁלח	qal	wci	3ms	שׁלח	1018		send
	אמר	qal	infc		אמר	55		say
	לכה	qal	impv	ms	הלך	229		walk,go
	נועדה	niph	coh	1cp	יעד	416		gather
	חשׁבים	qal	ptc	mp	חשׁב	362		think,devise
	עשׂות	qal	infc		עשׂה	793		do,make
6:3	אשׁלחה	qal	wci	1cs	שׁלח	1018		send
	אמר	qal	infc		אמר	55		say
	עשׂה	qal	ptc	ms	עשׂה	793		do,make
	אוכל	qal	impf	1cs	יכל	407		be able
	רדת	qal	infc		ירד	432		come down
	תשׁבת	qal	impf	3fs	שׁבת	991		cease,desist
	ארפה	hiph	impf	1cs	רפה	951	3fs	slacken,abandon
	ירדתי	qal	wcp	1cs	ירד	432		come down
6:4	ישׁלחו	qal	wci	3mp	שׁלח	1018		send
	אשׁיב	hiph	wci	1cs	שׁוב	996		bring back
6:5	ישׁלח	qal	wci	3ms	שׁלח	1018		send
	פתוחה	qal	pptc	fs	פתח	834		open
6:6	כתוב	qal	pptc	ms	כתב	507		write
6:6	נשׁמע	niph	pft	3ms	שׁמע	1033		be heard
	אמר	qal	ptc	ms	אמר	55		say
	חשׁבים	qal	ptc	mp	חשׁב	362		think,devise
	מרוד	qal	infc		מרד	597		rebel
	בונה	qal	ptc	ms	בנה	124		build
	הוה	qal	ptc	ms	הוה	217		become
6:7	העמדת	hiph	pft	2ms	עמד	763		set up,raise
	קרא	qal	infc		קרא	894		call,proclaim
	אמר	qal	infc		אמר	55		say
	ישׁמע	niph	impf	3ms	שׁמע	1033		be heard
	לכה	qal	impv	ms	הלך	229		walk,go
	נועצה	niph	coh	1cp	יעץ	419		consult
6:8	אשׁלחה	qal	wci	1cs	שׁלח	1018		send
	אמר	qal	infc		אמר	55		say
	נהיה	niph	pft	3ms	היה	224		be done
	אומר	qal	ptc	ms	אמר	55		say
	בודאם	qal	ptc	ms	בדא	94	3mp	devise
6:9	מיראים	piel	ptc	mp	ירא	431		terrify
	אמר	qal	infc		אמר	55		say
	ירפו	qal	impf	3mp	רפה	951		sink,relax
	תעשׂה	niph	impf	3fs	עשׂה	793		be done
	חזק	piel	impv	ms	חזק	304		make strong
6:10	באתי	qal	pft	1cs	בוא	97		come in
	עצור	qal	pptc	ms	עצר	783		restrain
	יאמר	qal	wci	3ms	אמר	55		say
	נועד	niph	cohm	1cp	יעד	416		gather
	נסגרה	qal	coh	1cp	סגר	688		shut
	באים	qal	ptc	mp	בוא	97		come in
	הרגך	qal	infc		הרג	246	2ms	kill
	באים	qal	ptc	mp	בוא	97		come in
	הרגך	qal	infc		הרג	246	2ms	kill
6:11	אמרה	qal	wci	1cs	אמר	55		say
	יברח	qal	impf	3ms	ברח	137		go thru,flee
	יבוא	qal	impf	3ms	בוא	97		come in
	חי	qal	wcp	3ms	חיה	310		live
	אבוא	qal	impf	1cs	בוא	97		come in
6:12	אכירה	hiph	wci	1cs	נכר	647		regard,notice
	שׁלחו	qal	pft	3ms	שׁלח	1018	3ms	send
	דבר	piel	pft	3ms	דבר	180		speak
	שׂכרו	qal	pft	3ms	שׂכר	968	3ms	hire
6:13	שׂכור	qal	pptc	ms	שׂכר	968		hire
	אירא	qal	impf	1cs	ירא	431		fear
	אעשׂה	qal	impf	1cs	עשׂה	793		do,make
	חטאתי	qal	wcp	1cs	חטא	306		sin
	היה	qal	wcp	3ms	היה	224		be,become
	יחרפוני	piel	impf	3mp	חרף	357	1cs	reproach
6:14	זכרה	qal	impv	ms	זכר	269		remember
	היו	qal	pft	3cp	היה	224		be,become
	מיראים	piel	ptc	mp	ירא	431		terrify
6:15	תשׁלם	qal	wci	3fs	שׁלם	1022		be complete
6:16	יהי	qal	wci	3ms	היה	224		be,become
	שׁמעו	qal	pft	3cp	שׁמע	1033		hear
	אויבינו	qal	ptc	mp	איב	33	1cp	be hostile to
	יראו	qal	wci	3mp	ראה	906		see

ChVs	Form	Stem	Tnse	PGN	Root	BDB	Sfx	Meaning
6:16	יפלו	qal	wci	3mp	נפל	656		fall
	ידעו	qal	wci	3mp	ידע	393		know
	נעשׂתה	niph	pft	3fs	עשׂה	793		be done
6:17	מרבים	hiph	ptc	mp	רבה	915		make many
	הולכות	qal	ptc	fp	הלך	229		walk,go
	באות	qal	ptc	fp	בוא	97		come in
6:18	לקח	qal	pft	3ms	לקח	542		take
6:19	היו	qal	pft	3cp	היה	224		be,become
	אמרים	qal	ptc	mp	אמר	55		say
	היו	qal	pft	3cp	היה	224		be,become
	מוציאים	hiph	ptc	mp	יצא	422		bring out
	שׁלח	qal	pft	3ms	שׁלח	1018		send
	יראני	piel	infc		ירא	431	1cs	terrify
7:1	יהי	qal	wci	3ms	היה	224		be,become
	נבנתה	niph	pft	3fs	בנה	124		be built
	אעמיד	hiph	wci	1cs	עמד	763		set up,raise
	יפקדו	niph	wci	3mp	פקד	823		be visited
	משׁררים	pol	ptc	mp	שׁיר	1010		sing
7:2	אצוה	piel	wci	1cs	צוה	845		command
	ירא	qal	pft	3ms	ירא	431		fear
7:3	יאמרk	qal	wci	3ms	אמר	55		say
	אמרq	qal	wci	1cs	אמר	55		say
	יפתחו	niph	jusm	3mp	פתח	834		be opened
	חם	qal	infc		חמם	328		be warm
	עמדים	qal	ptc	mp	עמד	763		stand,stop
	יגיפו	hiph	jusm	3mp	גוף	157		close
	אחזו	qal	impv	mp	אחז	28		grasp
	העמיד	hiph	infa		עמד	763		set up,raise
	ישׁבי	qal	ptc	mp	ישׁב	442		sit,dwell
7:4	בנוים	qal	pptc	mp	בנה	124		build
7:5	יתן	qal	wci	3ms	נתן	678		give,set
	אקבצה	qal	wci	1cs	קבץ	867		gather,collect
	התיחשׂ	hith	infc		יחשׂ	405		be registered
	אמצא	qal	wci	1cs	מצא	592		find
	עולים	qal	ptc	mp	עלה	748		go up
	אמצא	qal	wci	1cs	מצא	592		find
	כתוב	qal	pptc	ms	כתב	507		write
7:6	עלים	qal	ptc	mp	עלה	748		go up
	הגלה	hiph	pft	3ms	גלה	162		lead into exile
	ישׁובו	qal	wci	3mp	שׁוב	996		turn,return
7:7	באים	qal	ptc	mp	בוא	97		come in
7:44	משׁררים	pol	ptc	mp	שׁיר	1010		sing
7:61	עולים	qal	ptc	mp	עלה	748		go up
	יכלו	qal	pft	3cp	יכל	407		be able
	הגיד	hiph	infc		נגד	616		declare,tell
7:63	לקח	qal	pft	3ms	לקח	542		take
	יקרא	niph	wci	3ms	קרא	894		be called
7:64	בקשׁו	piel	pft	3cp	בקשׁ	134		seek
	מתיחשׂים	hith	ptc	mp	יחשׂ	405		be registered
	נמצא	niph	pft	3ms	מצא	592		be found
	יגאלו	pual	wci	3mp	גאל	146		be desecrated
7:65	יאמר	qal	wci	3ms	אמר	55		say
	יאכלו	qal	impf	3mp	אכל	37		eat,devour
	עמד	qal	infc		עמד	763		stand,stop
7:67	משׁררים	pol	ptc	mp	שׁיר	1010		sing
	משׁררות	pol	ptc	fp	שׁיר	1010		sing
7:69	נתנו	qal	pft	3cp	נתן	678		give,set
	נתן	qal	pft	3ms	נתן	678		give,set
7:70	נתנו	qal	pft	3cp	נתן	678		give,set
7:71	נתנו	qal	pft	3cp	נתן	678		give,set
7:72	ישׁבו	qal	wci	3mp	ישׁב	442		sit,dwell
	משׁררים	pol	ptc	mp	שׁיר	1010		sing
	יגע	qal	wci	3ms	נגע	619		touch,strike
8:1	יאספו	niph	wci	3mp	אסף	62		assemble
	יאמרו	qal	wci	3mp	אמר	55		say
	הביא	hiph	infc		בוא	97		bring in
	צוה	piel	pft	3ms	צוה	845		command
8:2	יביא	hiph	wci	3ms	בוא	97		bring in
	מבין	hiph	ptc	ms	בין	106		understand
	שׁמע	qal	infc		שׁמע	1033		hear
8:3	יקרא	qal	wci	3ms	קרא	894		call,proclaim
	מבינים	hiph	ptc	mp	בין	106		understand
8:4	יעמד	qal	wci	3ms	עמד	763		stand,stop
	עשׂו	qal	pft	3cp	עשׂה	793		do,make
	יעמד	qal	wci	3ms	עמד	763		stand,stop
8:5	יפתח	qal	wci	3ms	פתח	834		open
	היה	qal	pft	3ms	היה	224		be,become
	פתחו	qal	infc		פתח	834	3ms	open
	עמדו	qal	pft	3cp	עמד	763		stand,stop
8:6	יברך	piel	wci	3ms	ברך	138		bless
	יענו	qal	wci	3mp	ענה	772		answer
	יקדו	qal	wci	3mp	קדד	869		bow down
	ישׁתחו	hish	wci	3mp	חוה	1005		bow down
8:7	מבינים	hiph	ptc	mp	בין	106		understand
8:8	יקראו	qal	wci	3mp	קרא	894		call,proclaim
	מפרשׁ	pual	ptc	ms	פרשׁ	831		made distinct
	שׂום	qal	infa		שׂים	962		put,set
	יבינו	hiph	wci	3mp	בין	106		understand
8:9	יאמר	qal	wci	3ms	אמר	55		say
	מבינים	hiph	ptc	mp	בין	106		understand
	תתאבלו	hith	jusm	2mp	אבל	5		mourn
	תבכו	qal	jusm	2mp	בכה	113		weep
	בוכים	qal	ptc	mp	בכה	113		weep
	שׁמעם	qal	infc		שׁמע	1033	3mp	hear
8:10	יאמר	qal	wci	3ms	אמר	55		say
	לכו	qal	impv	mp	הלך	229		walk,go
	אכלו	qal	impv	mp	אכל	37		eat,devour
	שׁתו	qal	impv	mp	שׁתה	1059		drink
	שׁלחו	qal	impv	mp	שׁלח	1018		send
	נכון	niph	ptc	ms	כון	465		be established
	תעצבו	niph	jusm	2mp	עצב	780		be pained
8:11	מחשׁים	hiph	ptc	mp	חשׁה	364		show silence
	אמר	qal	infc		אמר	55		say
	תעצבו	niph	jusm	2mp	עצב	780		be pained
8:12	ילכו	qal	wci	3mp	הלך	229		walk,go
	אכל	qal	infc		אכל	37		eat,devour
	שׁתות	qal	infc		שׁתה	1059		drink
	שׁלח	piel	infc		שׁלח	1018		send away,shoot

ChVs	Form	Stem	Tnse	PGN	Root	BDB	Sfx	Meaning
8:12	עשות	qal	infc		עשה	793		do,make
	הבינו	hiph	pft	3cp	בין	106		understand
	הודיעו	hiph	pft	3cp	ידע	393		declare
8:13	נאספו	niph	pft	3cp	אסף	62		assemble
	השכיל	hiph	infc		שכל	968		look at,prosper
8:14	ימצאו	qal	wci	3mp	מצא	592		find
	כתוב	qal	pptc	ms	כתב	507		write
	צוה	piel	pft	3ms	צוה	845		command
	ישבו	qal	impf	3mp	ישב	442		sit,dwell
8:15	ישמיעו	hiph	impf	3mp	שמע	1033		cause to hear
	יעבירו	hiph	impf	3mp	עבר	716		cause to pass
	אמר	qal	infc		אמר	55		say
	צאו	qal	impv	mp	יצא	422		go out
	הביאו	hiph	impv	mp	בוא	97		bring in
	עשת	qal	infc		עשה	793		do,make
	כתוב	qal	pptc	ms	כתב	507		write
8:16	יצאו	qal	wci	3mp	יצא	422		go out
	יביאו	hiph	wci	3mp	בוא	97		bring in
	יעשו	qal	wci	3mp	עשה	793		do,make
8:17	יעשו	qal	wci	3mp	עשה	793		do,make
	שבים	qal	ptc	mp	שוב	996		turn,return
	ישבו	qal	wci	3mp	ישב	442		sit,dwell
	עשו	qal	pft	3cp	עשה	793		do,make
	תהי	qal	wci	3fs	היה	224		be,become
8:18	יקרא	qal	wci	3ms	קרא	894		call,proclaim
	יעשו	qal	wci	3mp	עשה	793		do,make
9:1	נאספו	niph	pft	3cp	אסף	62		assemble
9:2	יבדלו	niph	wci	3mp	בדל	95		separate self
	יעמדו	qal	wci	3mp	עמד	763		stand,stop
	יתודו	hith	wci	3mp	ידה	392		confess
9:3	יקומו	qal	wci	3mp	קום	877		arise,stand
	יקראו	qal	wci	3mp	קרא	894		call,proclaim
	מתודים	hith	ptc	mp	ידה	392		confess
	משתחוים	hish	ptc	mp	חוה	1005		bow down
9:4	יקם	qal	wci	3ms	קום	877		arise,stand
	יזעקו	qal	wci	3mp	זעק	277		call,cry out
9:5	יאמרו	qal	wci	3mp	אמר	55		say
	קומו	qal	impv	mp	קום	877		arise,stand
	ברכו	piel	impv	mp	ברך	138		bless
	יברכו	piel	jusm	3mp	ברך	138		bless
	מרומם	pola	ptc	ms	רום	926		be lifted up
9:6	עשית	qal	pft	2ms	עשה	793		do,make
	מחיה	piel	ptc	ms	חיה	310		preserve,revive
	משתחוים	hish	ptc	mp	חוה	1005		bow down
9:7	בחרת	qal	pft	2ms	בחר	103		choose
	הוצאתו	hiph	pft	2ms	יצא	422	3ms	bring out
	שמת	qal	pft	2ms	שים	962		put,set
9:8	מצאת	qal	pft	2ms	מצא	592		find
	נאמן	niph	ptc	ms	אמן	52		be confirmed
	כרות	qal	infa		כרת	503		cut,destroy
	תת	qal	infc		נתן	678		give,set
	תת	qal	infc		נתן	678		give,set
	תקם	hiph	wci	2ms	קום	877		raise,build,set
9:9	תרא	qal	wci	2ms	ראה	906		see
9:9	שמעת	qal	pft	2ms	שמע	1033		hear
9:10	תתן	qal	wci	2ms	נתן	678		give,set
	ידעת	qal	pft	2ms	ידע	393		know
	הזידו	hiph	pft	3cp	זיד	267		boil,presume
	תעש	qal	wci	2ms	עשה	793		do,make
9:11	בקעת	qal	pft	2ms	בקע	131		cleave,break
	יעברו	qal	wci	3mp	עבר	716		pass over
	רדפיהם	qal	ptc	mp	רדף	922	3mp	pursue
	השלכת	hiph	pft	2ms	שלך	1020		throw,cast
9:12	הנחיתם	hiph	pft	2ms	נחה	634	3mp	lead,guide
	האיר	hiph	infc		אור	21		cause to shine
	ילכו	qal	impf	3mp	הלך	229		walk,go
9:13	ירדת	qal	pft	2ms	ירד	432		come down
	דבר	piel	infc		דבר	180		speak
	תתן	qal	wci	2ms	נתן	678		give,set
9:14	הודעת	hiph	pft	2ms	ידע	393		declare
	צוית	piel	pft	2ms	צוה	845		command
9:15	נתתה	qal	pft	2ms	נתן	678		give,set
	הוצאת	hiph	pft	2ms	יצא	422		bring out
	תאמר	qal	wci	2ms	אמר	55		say
	בוא	qal	infc		בוא	97		come in
	רשת	qal	infc		ירש	439		possess,inherit
	נשאת	qal	pft	2ms	נשא	669		lift,carry
	תת	qal	infc		נתן	678		give,set
9:16	הזידו	hiph	pft	3cp	זיד	267		boil,presume
	יקשו	hiph	wci	3mp	קשה	904		harden
	שמעו	qal	pft	3cp	שמע	1033		hear
9:17	ימאנו	piel	wci	3mp	מאן	549		refuse
	שמע	qal	infc		שמע	1033		hear
	זכרו	qal	pft	3cp	זכר	269		remember
	נפלאתיך	niph	ptc	fp	פלא	810	2ms	be wonderful
	עשית	qal	pft	2ms	עשה	793		do,make
	יקשו	hiph	wci	3mp	קשה	904		harden
	יתנו	qal	wci	3mp	נתן	678		give,set
	שוב	qal	infc		שוב	996		turn,return
	עזבתם	qal	pft	2ms	עזב	736	3mp	leave,loose
9:18	עשו	qal	pft	3cp	עשה	793		do,make
	יאמרו	qal	wci	3mp	אמר	55		say
	העלך	hiph	pft	3ms	עלה	748	2ms	bring up,offer
	יעשו	qal	wci	3mp	עשה	793		do,make
9:19	עזבתם	qal	pft	2ms	עזב	736	3mp	leave,loose
	סר	qal	pft	3ms	סור	693		turn aside
	הנחתם	hiph	infc		נחה	634	3mp	lead,guide
	האיר	hiph	infc		אור	21		cause to shine
	ילכו	qal	impf	3mp	הלך	229		walk,go
9:20	נתת	qal	pft	2ms	נתן	678		give,set
	השכילם	hiph	infc		שכל	968	3mp	look at,prosper
	מנעת	qal	pft	2ms	מנע	586		withhold
	נתתה	qal	pft	2ms	נתן	678		give,set
9:21	כלכלתם	pilp	pft	2ms	כול	465	3mp	support
	חסרו	qal	pft	3cp	חסר	341		lack
	בלו	qal	pft	3cp	בלה	115		wear out
	בצקו	qal	pft	3cp	בצק	130		swell
9:22	תתן	qal	wci	2ms	נתן	678		give,set

ChVs	Form	Stem	Tnse	PGN	Root	BDB	Sfx	Meaning
9:22	תחלקם	qal	wci	2ms	חלק	323	3mp	divide,share
	יירשׁו	qal	wci	3mp	ירשׁ	439		possess,inherit
9:23	הרבית	hiph	pft	2ms	רבה	915		make many
	תביאם	hiph	wci	2ms	בוא	97	3mp	bring in
	אמרת	qal	pft	2ms	אמר	55		say
	בוא	qal	infc		בוא	97		come in
	רשׁת	qal	infc		ירשׁ	439		possess,inherit
9:24	יבאו	qal	wci	3mp	בוא	97		come in
	יירשׁו	qal	wci	3mp	ירשׁ	439		possess,inherit
	תכנע	hiph	wci	2ms	כנע	488		humble,subdue
	ישׁבי	qal	ptc	mp	ישׁב	442		sit,dwell
	תתנם	qal	wci	2ms	נתן	678	3mp	give,set
	עשׂות	qal	infc		עשׂה	793		do,make
9:25	ילכדו	qal	wci	3mp	לכד	539		capture
	בצרות	qal	pptc	fp	בצר	130		cut off
	יירשׁו	qal	wci	3mp	ירשׁ	439		possess,inherit
	חצובים	qal	pptc	mp	חצב	345		hew out,dig
	יאכלו	qal	wci	3mp	אכל	37		eat,devour
	ישׂבעו	qal	wci	3mp	שׂבע	959		be sated
	ישׁמינו	hiph	wci	3mp	שׁמן	1031		make fat
	יתעדנו	hith	wci	3mp	עדן	726		luxuriate
9:26	ימרו	hiph	wci	3mp	מרה	598		rebel
	ימרדו	qal	wci	3mp	מרד	597		rebel
	ישׁלכו	hiph	wci	3mp	שׁלך	1020		throw,cast
	הרגו	qal	pft	3cp	הרג	246		kill
	העידו	hiph	pft	3cp	עוד	729		testify,warn
	השׁיבם	hiph	infc		שׁוב	996	3mp	bring back
	יעשׂו	qal	wci	3mp	עשׂה	793		do,make
9:27	תתנם	qal	wci	2ms	נתן	678	3mp	give,set
	יצרו	hiph	wci	3mp	צרר	864		distress,cramp
	יצעקו	qal	impf	3mp	צעק	858		cry out
	תשׁמע	qal	impf	2ms	שׁמע	1033		hear
	תתן	qal	impf	2ms	נתן	678		give,set
	מושׁיעים	hiph	ptc	mp	ישׁע	446		deliver,save
	יושׁיעום	hiph	wci	3mp	ישׁע	446	3mp	deliver,save
9:28	נוח	qal	infc		נוח	628		rest
	ישׁובו	qal	impf	3mp	שׁוב	996		turn,return
	עשׂות	qal	infc		עשׂה	793		do,make
	תעזבם	qal	wci	2ms	עזב	736	3mp	leave,loose
	איביהם	qal	ptc	mp	איב	33	3mp	be hostile to
	ירדו	qal	wci	3mp	רדה	921		rule
	ישׁובו	qal	wci	3mp	שׁוב	996		turn,return
	יזעקוך	qal	wci	3mp	זעק	277	2ms	call,cry out
	תשׁמע	qal	impf	2ms	שׁמע	1033		hear
	תצילם	hiph	impf	2ms	נצל	664	3mp	snatch,deliver
9:29	תעד	hiph	wci	2ms	עוד	729		testify,warn
	השׁיבם	hiph	infc		שׁוב	996	3mp	bring back
	הזידו	hiph	pft	3cp	זיד	267		boil,presume
	שׁמעו	qal	pft	3cp	שׁמע	1033		hear
	חטאו	qal	pft	3cp	חטא	306		sin
	יעשׂה	qal	impf	3ms	עשׂה	793		do,make
	חיה	qal	wcp	3ms	חיה	310		live
	יתנו	qal	wci	3mp	נתן	678		give,set
	סוררת	qal	ptc	fs	סרר	710		be stubborn
9:29	הקשׁו	hiph	pft	3cp	קשׁה	904		harden
	שׁמעו	qal	pft	3cp	שׁמע	1033		hear
9:30	תמשׁך	qal	wci	2ms	משׁך	604		draw,pull
	תעד	hiph	wci	2ms	עוד	729		testify,warn
	האזינו	hiph	pft	3cp	אזן	24		hear
	תתנם	qal	wci	2ms	נתן	678	3mp	give,set
9:31	עשׂיתם	qal	pft	2ms	עשׂה	793	3mp	do,make
	עזבתם	qal	pft	2ms	עזב	736	3mp	leave,loose
9:32	נורא	niph	ptc	ms	ירא	431		be feared
	שׁומר	qal	ptc	ms	שׁמר	1036		keep,watch
	ימעט	qal	jusm	3ms	מעט	589		be small,few
	מצאתנו	qal	pft	3fs	מצא	592	1cp	find
9:33	בא	qal	ptc	ms	בוא	97		come in
	עשׂית	qal	pft	2ms	עשׂה	793		do,make
	הרשׁענו	hiph	pft	1cp	רשׁע	957		condemn,be evil
9:34	עשׂו	qal	pft	3cp	עשׂה	793		do,make
	הקשׁיבו	hiph	pft	3cp	קשׁב	904		give attention
	העידת	hiph	pft	2ms	עוד	729		testify,warn
9:35	נתת	qal	pft	2ms	נתן	678		give,set
	נתת	qal	pft	2ms	נתן	678		give,set
	עבדוך	qal	pft	3cp	עבד	712	2ms	work,serve
	שׁבו	qal	pft	3cp	שׁוב	996		turn,return
9:36	נתתה	qal	pft	2ms	נתן	678		give,set
	אכל	qal	infc		אכל	37		eat,devour
9:37	מרבה	hiph	ptc	fs	רבה	915		make many
	נתתה	qal	pft	2ms	נתן	678		give,set
	משׁלים	qal	ptc	mp	משׁל	605		rule
10:1	כרתים	qal	ptc	mp	כרת	503		cut,destroy
	כתבים	qal	ptc	mp	כתב	507		write
	חתום	qal	pptc	ms	חתם	367		seal
10:2	חתומים	qal	pptc	mp	חתם	367		seal
10:29	משׁררים	pol	ptc	mp	שׁיר	1010		sing
	נבדל	niph	ptc	ms	בדל	95		separate self
	יודע	qal	ptc	ms	ידע	393		know
	מבין	hiph	ptc	ms	בין	106		understand
10:30	מחזיקים	hiph	ptc	mp	חזק	304		make firm,seize
	באים	qal	ptc	mp	בוא	97		come in
	לכת	qal	infc		הלך	229		walk,go
	נתנה	niph	pft	3fs	נתן	678		be given
	שׁמור	qal	infc		שׁמר	1036		keep,watch
	עשׂות	qal	infc		עשׂה	793		do,make
10:31	נתן	qal	impf	1cp	נתן	678		give,set
	נקח	qal	impf	1cp	לקח	542		take
10:32	מביאים	hiph	ptc	mp	בוא	97		bring in
	מכור	qal	infc		מכר	569		sell
	נקח	qal	impf	1cp	לקח	542		take
	נטשׁ	qal	impf	1cp	נטשׁ	643		leave,forsake
10:33	העמדנו	hiph	wcp	1cp	עמד	763		set up,raise
	תת	qal	infc		נתן	678		give,set
10:34	כפר	piel	infc		כפר	497		cover,atone
10:35	הפלנו	hiph	pft	1cp	נפל	656		cause to fall
	הביא	hiph	infc		בוא	97		bring in
	מזמנים	pual	ptc	mp	זמן	273		be appointed
	בער	piel	infc		בער	128		burn,consume

ChVs	Form	Stem	Tnse	PGN	Root	BDB	Sfx	Meaning
10:35	כתוב	qal	pptc	ms	כתב	507		write
10:36	הביא	hiph	infc		בוא	97		bring in
10:37	כתוב	qal	pptc	ms	כתב	507		write
	הביא	hiph	infc		בוא	97		bring in
	משרתים	piel	ptc	mp	שרת	1058		minister,serve
10:38	נביא	hiph	impf	1cp	בוא	97		bring in
	מעשרים	piel	ptc	mp	עשר	797		give tenth
10:39	היה	qal	wcp	3ms	היה	224		be,become
	עשר	hiph	infa		עשר	797?		take tithe
	יעלו	hiph	impf	3mp	עלה	748		bring up,offer
10:40	יביאו	hiph	impf	3mp	בוא	97		bring in
	משרתים	piel	ptc	mp	שרת	1058		minister,serve
	משררים	pol	ptc	mp	שיר	1010		sing
	נעזב	qal	impf	1cp	עזב	736		leave,loose
11:1	ישבו	qal	wci	3mp	ישב	442		sit,dwell
	הפילו	hiph	pft	3cp	נפל	656		cause to fall
	הביא	hiph	infc		בוא	97		bring in
	שבת	qal	infc		ישב	442		sit,dwell
11:2	יברכו	piel	wci	3mp	ברך	138		bless
	מתנדבים	hith	ptc	mp	נדב	621		offer freely
	שבת	qal	infc		ישב	442		sit,dwell
11:3	ישבו	qal	pft	3cp	ישב	442		sit,dwell
	ישבו	qal	pft	3cp	ישב	442		sit,dwell
11:4	ישבו	qal	pft	3cp	ישב	442		sit,dwell
11:6	ישבים	qal	ptc	mp	ישב	442		sit,dwell
11:12	עשי	qal	ptc	mp	עשה	793		do,make
11:17	יהודה	hiph	impf	3ms	ידה	392		praise
11:19	שמרים	qal	ptc	mp	שמר	1036		keep,watch
11:21	ישבים	qal	ptc	mp	ישב	442		sit,dwell
11:22	משררים	pol	ptc	mp	שיר	1010		sing
11:23	משררים	pol	ptc	mp	שיר	1010		sing
11:25	ישבו	qal	pft	3cp	ישב	442		sit,dwell
11:30	יחנו	qal	wci	3mp	חנה	333		decline,encamp
12:1	עלו	qal	pft	3cp	עלה	748		go up
12:10	הוליד	hiph	pft	3ms	ילד	408		beget
	הוליד	hiph	pft	3ms	ילד	408		beget
12:11	הוליד	hiph	pft	3ms	ילד	408		beget
	הוליד	hiph	pft	3ms	ילד	408		beget
12:12	היו	qal	pft	3cp	היה	224		be,become
12:22	כתובים	qal	pptc	mp	כתב	507		write
12:23	כתובים	qal	pptc	mp	כתב	507		write
12:24	הלל	piel	infc		הלל	237		praise
	הודות	hiph	infc		ידה	392		praise
12:25	שמרים	qal	ptc	mp	שמר	1036		keep,watch
12:27	בקשו	piel	pft	3cp	בקש	134		seek
	הביאם	hiph	infc		בוא	97	3mp	bring in
	עשת	qal	infc		עשה	793		do,make
12:28	יאספו	niph	wci	3mp	אסף	62		assemble
	משררים	pol	ptc	mp	שיר	1010		sing
12:29	בנו	qal	pft	3cp	בנה	124		build
	משררים	pol	ptc	mp	שיר	1010		sing
12:30	יטהרו	hith	wci	3mp	טהר	372		purify oneself
	יטהרו	piel	wci	3mp	טהר	372		cleanse
12:31	אעלה	hiph	wci	1cs	עלה	748		bring up,offer
12:31	אעמידה	hiph	wci	1cs	עמד	763		set up,raise
12:32	ילך	qal	wci	3ms	הלך	229		walk,go
12:37	עלו	qal	pft	3cp	עלה	748		go up
12:38	הולכת	qal	ptc	fs	הלך	229		walk,go
12:39	עמדו	qal	pft	3cp	עמד	763		stand,stop
12:40	תעמדנה	qal	wci	3fp	עמד	763		stand,stop
12:42	ישמיעו	hiph	wci	3mp	שמע	1033		cause to hear
	משררים	pol	ptc	mp	שיר	1010		sing
12:43	יזבחו	qal	wci	3mp	זבח	256		slaughter
	ישמחו	qal	wci	3mp	שמח	970		rejoice
	שמחם	piel	pft	3ms	שמח	970	3mp	gladden
	שמחו	qal	pft	3cp	שמח	970		rejoice
	תשמע	niph	wci	3fs	שמע	1033		be heard
12:44	יפקדו	niph	wci	3mp	פקד	823		be visited
	כנוס	qal	infc		כנס	488		collect
	עמדים	qal	ptc	mp	עמד	763		stand,stop
12:45	ישמרו	qal	wci	3mp	שמר	1036		keep,watch
	משררים	pol	ptc	mp	שיר	1010		sing
12:46	משררים	pol	ptc	mp	שיר	1010		sing
	הדות	hiph	infc		ידה	392		praise
12:47	נתנים	qal	ptc	mp	נתן	678		give,set
	משררים	pol	ptc	mp	שיר	1010		sing
	מקדשים	hiph	ptc	mp	קדש	872		consecrate
	מקדשים	hiph	ptc	mp	קדש	872		consecrate
13:1	נקרא	niph	pft	3ms	קרא	894		be called
	נמצא	niph	pft	3ms	מצא	592		be found
	כתוב	qal	pptc	ms	כתב	507		write
	יבוא	qal	impf	3ms	בוא	97		come in
13:2	קדמו	piel	pft	3cp	קדם	869		meet,confront
	ישכר	qal	wci	3ms	שכר	968		hire
	קללו	piel	infc		קלל	886	3ms	curse
	יהפך	qal	wci	3ms	הפך	245		turn,overturn
13:3	יהי	qal	wci	3ms	היה	224		be,become
	שמעם	qal	infc		שמע	1033	3mp	hear
	יבדילו	hiph	wci	3mp	בדל	95		divide
13:4	נתון	qal	pptc	ms	נתן	678		give,set
13:5	יעש	qal	wci	3ms	עשה	793		do,make
	היו	qal	pft	3cp	היה	224		be,become
	נתנים	qal	ptc	mp	נתן	678		give,set
	משררים	pol	ptc	mp	שיר	1010		sing
13:6	הייתי	qal	pft	1cs	היה	224		be,become
	באתי	qal	pft	1cs	בוא	97		come in
	נשאלתי	niph	pft	1cs	שאל	981		ask for self
13:7	אבוא	qal	wci	1cs	בוא	97		come in
	אבינה	qal	wci	1cs	בין	106		discern
	עשה	qal	pft	3ms	עשה	793		do,make
	עשות	qal	infc		עשה	793		do,make
13:8	ירע	qal	wci	3ms	רעע	949		be evil
	אשליכה	hiph	wci	1cs	שלך	1020		throw,cast
13:9	אמרה	qal	wci	1cs	אמר	55		say
	יטהרו	piel	wci	3mp	טהר	372		cleanse
	אשיבה	hiph	wci	1cs	שוב	996		bring back
13:10	אדעה	qal	wci	1cs	ידע	393		know
	נתנה	niph	pft	3fs	נתן	678		be given

ChVs	Form	Stem	Tnse	PGN	Root	BDB	Sfx	Meaning
13: 10	יברחו	qal	wci	3mp	ברח	137		go thru,flee
	משררים	pol	ptc	mp	שיר	1010		sing
	עשי	qal	ptc	mp	עשה	793		do,make
13: 11	אריבה	qal	wci	1cs	ריב	936		strive,contend
	אמרה	qal	wci	1cs	אמר	55		say
	נעזב	niph	pft	3ms	עזב	736		be left
	אקבצם	qal	wci	1cs	קבץ	867	3mp	gather,collect
	אעמדם	hiph	wci	1cs	עמד	763	3mp	set up,raise
13: 12	הביאו	hiph	pft	3cp	בוא	97		bring in
13: 13	אוצרה	hiph	wci	1cs	אצר	69		make treasurer
	נאמנים	niph	ptc	mp	אמן	52		be confirmed
	נחשבו	niph	pft	3cp	חשב	362		be thought
	חלק	qal	infc		חלק	323		divide,share
13: 14	זכרה	qal	impv	ms	זכר	269		remember
	תמח	hiph	jus	2ms	מחה	562		blot out
	עשיתי	qal	pft	1cs	עשה	793		do,make
13: 15	ראיתי	qal	pft	1cs	ראה	906		see
	דרכים	qal	ptc	mp	דרך	201		tread,march
	מביאים	hiph	ptc	mp	בוא	97		bring in
	עמסים	qal	ptc	mp	עמס	770		load,carry
	מביאים	hiph	ptc	mp	בוא	97		bring in
	אעיד	hiph	wci	1cs	עוד	729		testify,warn
	מכרם	qal	infc		מכר	569	3mp	sell
13: 16	ישבו	qal	pft	3cp	ישב	442		sit,dwell
	מביאים	hiph	ptc	mp	בוא	97		bring in
	מכרים	qal	ptc	mp	מכר	569		sell
13: 17	אריבה	qal	wci	1cs	ריב	936		strive,contend
	אמרה	qal	wci	1cs	אמר	55		say
	עשים	qal	ptc	mp	עשה	793		do,make
	מחללים	piel	ptc	mp	חלל	320		pollute
13: 18	עשו	qal	pft	3cp	עשה	793		do,make
	יבא	hiph	wci	3ms	בוא	97		bring in
	מוסיפים	hiph	ptc	mp	יסף	414		add,do again
	חלל	piel	infc		חלל	320		pollute
13: 19	יהי	qal	wci	3ms	היה	224		be,become
	צללו	qal	pft	3cp	צלל	853		grow dark
	אמרה	qal	wci	1cs	אמר	55		say
	יסגרו	niph	wci	3mp	סגר	688		be shut
	אמרה	qal	wci	1cs	אמר	55		say
	יפתחום	qal	impf	3mp	פתח	834	3mp	open
	העמדתי	hiph	pft	1cs	עמד	763		set up,raise
	יבוא	qal	impf	3ms	בוא	97		come in
13: 20	ילינו	qal	wci	3mp	לון	533		lodge,remain
	רכלים	qal	ptc	mp	רכל	940		trade,gossip
	מכרי	qal	ptc	mp	מכר	569		sell
13: 21	אעידה	hiph	wci	1cs	עוד	729		testify,warn
	אמרה	qal	wci	1cs	אמר	55		say
	לנים	qal	ptc	mp	לון	533		lodge,remain
	תשנו	qal	impf	2mp	שנה	1040		do again,repeat
	אשלח	qal	impf	1cs	שלח	1018		send
	באו	qal	pft	3cp	בוא	97		come in
13: 22	אמרה	qal	wci	1cs	אמר	55		say
	יהיו	qal	impf	3mp	היה	224		be,become
	מטהרים	hith	ptc	mp	טהר	372		purify oneself
13: 22	באים	qal	ptc	mp	בוא	97		come in
	שמרים	qal	ptc	mp	שמר	1036		keep,watch
	קדש	piel	infc		קדש	872		consecrate
	זכרה	qal	impv	ms	זכר	269		remember
	חוסה	qal	impv	ms	חוס	299		pity
13: 23	ראיתי	qal	pft	1cs	ראה	906		see
	השיבו	hiph	pft	3cp	ישב	442		cause to dwell
13: 24	מדבר	piel	ptc	ms	דבר	180		speak
	מכירים	hiph	ptc	mp	נכר	647		regard,notice
	דבר	piel	infc		דבר	180		speak
13: 25	אריב	qal	wci	1cs	ריב	936		strive,contend
	אקללם	piel	wci	1cs	קלל	886	3mp	curse
	אכה	hiph	wci	1cs	נכה	645		smite
	אמרטם	qal	wci	1cs	מרט	598	3mp	make bare
	אשביעם	hiph	wci	1cs	שבע	989	3mp	cause to swear
	תתנו	qal	impf	2mp	נתן	678		give,set
	תשאו	qal	impf	2mp	נשא	669		lift,carry
13: 26	חטא	qal	pft	3ms	חטא	306		sin
	היה	qal	pft	3ms	היה	224		be,become
	אהוב	qal	pptc	ms	אהב	12		love
	היה	qal	pft	3ms	היה	224		be,become
	יתנהו	qal	wci	3ms	נתן	678	3ms	give,set
	החטיאו	hiph	pft	3cp	חטא	306		cause to sin
13: 27	נשמע	niph	pft	3ms	שמע	1033		be heard
	עשת	qal	infc		עשה	793		do,make
	מעל	qal	infc		מעל	591		act faithlessly
	השיב	hiph	infc		ישב	442		cause to dwell
13: 28	אבריחהו	hiph	wci	1cs	ברח	137	3ms	cause to flee
13: 29	זכרה	qal	impv	ms	זכר	269		remember
13: 30	טהרתים	piel	pft	1cs	טהר	372	3mp	cleanse
	אעמידה	hiph	wci	1cs	עמד	763		set up,raise
13: 31	מזמנות	pual	ptc	fp	זמן	273		be appointed
	זכרה	qal	impv	ms	זכר	269		remember

ESTHER

ChVs	Form	Stem	Tnse	PGN	Root	BDB	Sfx	Meaning
1: 1	יהי	qal	wci	3ms	היה	224		be,become
	מלך	qal	ptc	ms	מלך	573		be king,reign
1: 2	שבת	qal	infc		ישב	442		sit,dwell
1: 3	מלכו	qal	infc		מלך	573	3ms	be king,reign
	עשה	qal	pft	3ms	עשה	793		do,make
1: 4	הראתו	hiph	infc		ראה	906	3ms	show,exhibit
1: 5	מלואת	qal	infc		מלא	569		be full,fill
	עשה	qal	pft	3ms	עשה	793		do,make
	נמצאים	niph	ptc	mp	מצא	592		be found
1: 6	אחוז	qal	pptc	ms	אחז	28		grasp
1: 7	השקות	hiph	infc		שקה	1052		give to drink
	שונים	qal	ptc	mp	שנה	1039		change
1: 8	אנס	qal	ptc	ms	אנס	60		compel
	יסד	piel	pft	3ms	יסד	413		found,establish
	עשות	qal	infc		עשה	793		do,make
1: 9	עשתה	qal	pft	3fs	עשה	793		do,make
1: 10	טוב	qal	infc		טוב	373		be pleasing
	אמר	qal	pft	3ms	אמר	55		say
	משרתים	piel	ptc	mp	שרת	1058		minister,serve

ChVs	Form	Stem	Tnse	PGN	Root	BDB	Sfx	Meaning
1:11	הביא	hiph	infc		בוא	97		bring in
	הראות	hiph	infc		ראה	906		show,exhibit
1:12	תמאן	piel	wci	3fs	מאן	549		refuse
	בוא	qal	infc		בוא	97		come in
	יקצף	qal	wci	3ms	קצף	893		be angry
	בערה	qal	pft	3fs	בער	128		burn
1:13	יאמר	qal	wci	3ms	אמר	55		say
	ידעי	qal	ptc	mp	ידע	393		know
	ידעי	qal	ptc	mp	ידע	393		know
1:14	ראי	qal	ptc	mp	ראה	906		see
	ישבים	qal	ptc	mp	ישב	442		sit,dwell
1:15	עשות	qal	infc		עשה	793		do,make
	עשתה	qal	pft	3fs	עשה	793		do,make
1:16	יאמר	qal	wci	3ms	אמר	55		say
	עותה	qal	pft	3fs	עוה	731		do wrong
1:17	יצא	qal	impf	3ms	יצא	422		go out
	הבזות	hiph	infc		בזה	102		cause to hate
	אמרם	qal	infc		אמר	55	3mp	say
	אמר	qal	pft	3ms	אמר	55		say
	הביא	hiph	infc		בוא	97		bring in
	באה	qal	pft	3fs	בוא	97		come in
1:18	תאמרנה	qal	impf	3fp	אמר	55		say
	שמעו	qal	pft	3cp	שמע	1033		hear
1:19	טוב	qal	pft	3ms	טוב	373		be pleasing
	יצא	qal	jusm	3ms	יצא	422		go out
	יכתב	niph	jusm	3ms	כתב	507		be written
	יעבור	qal	impf	3ms	עבר	716		pass over
	תבוא	qal	impf	3fs	בוא	97		come in
	יתן	qal	jusm	3ms	נתן	678		give,set
1:20	נשמע	niph	wcp	3ms	שמע	1033		be heard
	יעשה	qal	impf	3ms	עשה	793		do,make
	יתנו	qal	impf	3mp	נתן	678		give,set
1:21	ייטב	qal	wci	3ms	יטב	405		be good
	יעש	qal	wci	3ms	עשה	793		do,make
1:22	ישלח	qal	wci	3ms	שלח	1018		send
	היות	qal	infc		היה	224		be,become
	שרר	qal	ptc	ms	שרר	979		rule
	מדבר	piel	ptc	ms	דבר	180		speak
2:1	שך	qal	infc		שכך	1013		abate,crouch
	זכר	qal	pft	3ms	זכר	269		remember
	עשתה	qal	pft	3fs	עשה	793		do,make
	נגזר	niph	pft	3ms	גזר	160		be cut off
2:2	יאמרו	qal	wci	3mp	אמר	55		say
	משרתיו	piel	ptc	mp	שרת	1058	3ms	minister,serve
	יבקשו	piel	jusm	3mp	בקש	134		seek
2:3	יפקד	hiph	jus	3ms	פקד	823		set,entrust
	יקבצו	qal	jusm	3mp	קבץ	867		gather,collect
	שמר	qal	ptc	ms	שמר	1036		keep,watch
	נתון	qal	infa		נתן	678		give,set
2:4	תיטב	qal	impf	3fs	יטב	405		be good
	תמלך	qal	jusm	3fs	מלך	573		be king,reign
	ייטב	qal	wci	3ms	יטב	405		be good
	יעש	qal	wci	3ms	עשה	793		do,make
2:5	היה	qal	pft	3ms	היה	224		be,become
2:6	הגלה	hoph	pft	3ms	גלה	162		led into exile
	הגלתה	hoph	pft	3fs	גלה	162		led into exile
	הגלה	hiph	pft	3ms	גלה	162		lead into exile
2:7	יהי	qal	wci	3ms	היה	224		be,become
	אמן	qal	ptc	ms	אמן	52		nourish
	לקחה	qal	pft	3ms	לקח	542	3fs	take
2:8	יהי	qal	wci	3ms	היה	224		be,become
	השמע	niph	infc		שמע	1033		be heard
	הקבץ	niph	infc		קבץ	867		assemble,gather
	תלקח	niph	wci	3fs	לקח	542		be taken
	שמר	qal	ptc	ms	שמר	1036		keep,watch
2:9	תיטב	qal	wci	3fs	יטב	405		be good
	תשא	qal	wci	3fs	נשא	669		lift,carry
	יבהל	piel	wci	3ms	בהל	96		hasten,dismay
	תת	qal	infc		נתן	678		give,set
	ראיות	qal	pptc	fp	ראה	906		see
	תת	qal	infc		נתן	678		give,set
	ישנה	piel	wci	3ms	שנה	1039	3fs	change,alter
2:10	הגידה	hiph	pft	3fs	נגד	616		declare,tell
	צוה	piel	pft	3ms	צוה	845		command
	תגיד	hiph	impf	3fs	נגד	616		declare,tell
2:11	מתהלך	hith	ptc	ms	הלך	229		walk to and fro
	דעת	qal	infc		ידע	393		know
	יעשה	niph	impf	3ms	עשה	793		be done
2:12	הגיע	hiph	infc		נגע	619		reach,arrive
	בוא	qal	infc		בוא	97		come in
	היות	qal	infc		היה	224		be,become
	ימלאו	qal	impf	3mp	מלא	569		be full,fill
2:13	באה	qal	ptc	fs	בוא	97		come in
	תאמר	qal	impf	3fs	אמר	55		say
	ינתן	niph	impf	3ms	נתן	678		be given
	בוא	qal	infc		בוא	97		come in
2:14	באה	qal	ptc	fs	בוא	97		come in
	שבה	qal	ptc	fs	שוב	996		turn,return
	שמר	qal	ptc	ms	שמר	1036		keep,watch
	תבוא	qal	impf	3fs	בוא	97		come in
	חפץ	qal	pft	3ms	חפץ	342		delight in
	נקראה	niph	pft	3fs	קרא	894		be called
2:15	הגיע	hiph	infc		נגע	619		reach,arrive
	לקח	qal	pft	3ms	לקח	542		take
	בוא	qal	infc		בוא	97		come in
	בקשה	piel	pft	3fs	בקש	134		seek
	יאמר	qal	impf	3ms	אמר	55		say
	שמר	qal	ptc	ms	שמר	1036		keep,watch
	תהי	qal	wci	3fs	היה	224		be,become
	נשאת	qal	ptc	fs	נשא	669		lift,carry
	ראיה	qal	ptc	mp	ראה	906	3fs	see
2:16	תלקח	niph	wci	3fs	לקח	542		be taken
2:17	יאהב	qal	wci	3ms	אהב	12		love
	תשא	qal	wci	3fs	נשא	669		lift,carry
	ישם	qal	wci	3ms	שים	962		put,set
	ימליכה	hiph	wci	3ms	מלך	573	3fs	cause to reign
2:18	יעש	qal	wci	3ms	עשה	793		do,make
	עשה	qal	pft	3ms	עשה	793		do,make

ChVs	Form	Stem	Tnse	PGN	Root	BDB	Sfx	Meaning
2:18	יתן	qal	wci	3ms	נתן	678		give,set
2:19	הקבץ	niph	infc		קבץ	867		assemble,gather
	ישב	qal	ptc	ms	ישב	442		sit,dwell
2:20	מגדת	hiph	ptc	fs	נגד	616		declare,tell
	צוה	piel	pft	3ms	צוה	845		command
	עשה	qal	ptc	fs	עשה	793		do,make
	היתה	qal	pft	3fs	היה	224		be,become
2:21	ישב	qal	ptc	ms	ישב	442		sit,dwell
	קצף	qal	pft	3ms	קצף	893		be angry
	שמרי	qal	ptc	mp	שמר	1036		keep,watch
	יבקשו	piel	wci	3mp	בקש	134		seek
	שלח	qal	infc		שלח	1018		send
2:22	יודע	niph	wci	3ms	ידע	393		be made known
	יגד	hiph	wci	3ms	נגד	616		declare,tell
	תאמר	qal	wci	3fs	אמר	55		say
2:23	יבקש	pual	wci	3ms	בקש	134		be sought
	ימצא	niph	wci	3ms	מצא	592		be found
	יתלו	niph	wci	3mp	תלה	1067		be hanged
	יכתב	niph	wci	3ms	כתב	507		be written
3:1	גדל	piel	pft	3ms	גדל	152		cause to grow
	ינשאהו	piel	wci	3ms	נשא	669	3ms	lift up
	ישם	qal	wci	3ms	שים	962		put,set
3:2	כרעים	qal	ptc	mp	כרע	502		bow down
	משתחוים	hish	ptc	mp	חוה	1005		bow down
	צוה	piel	pft	3ms	צוה	845		command
	יכרע	qal	impf	3ms	כרע	502		bow down
	ישתחוה	hish	impf	3ms	חוה	1005		bow down
3:3	יאמרו	qal	wci	3mp	אמר	55		say
	עובר	qal	ptc	ms	עבר	716		pass over
3:4	יהי	qal	wci	3ms	היה	224		be,become
	אמרם	qal	infc		אמר	55	3mp	say
	שמע	qal	pft	3ms	שמע	1033		hear
	יגידו	hiph	wci	3mp	נגד	616		declare,tell
	ראות	qal	infc		ראה	906		see
	יעמדו	qal	impf	3mp	עמד	763		stand,stop
	הגיד	hiph	pft	3ms	נגד	616		declare,tell
3:5	ירא	qal	wci	3ms	ראה	906		see
	כרע	qal	ptc	ms	כרע	502		bow down
	משתחוה	hish	ptc	ms	חוה	1005		bow down
	ימלא	niph	wci	3ms	מלא	569		be filled
3:6	יבז	qal	wci	3ms	בזה	102		despise
	שלח	qal	infc		שלח	1018		send
	הגידו	hiph	pft	3cp	נגד	616		declare,tell
	יבקש	piel	wci	3ms	בקש	134		seek
	השמיד	hiph	infc		שמד	1029		exterminate
3:7	הפיל	hiph	pft	3ms	נפל	656		cause to fall
3:8	יאמר	qal	wci	3ms	אמר	55		say
	מפזר	pual	ptc	ms	פזר	808		be scattered
	מפרד	pual	ptc	ms	פרד	825		be divided
	שנות	qal	ptc	fp	שנה	1039		change
	עשים	qal	ptc	mp	עשה	793		do,make
	שוה	qal	ptc	ms	שוה	1000		be even,smooth
	הניחם	hiph	infc		נוח	628	3mp	give rest,put
3:9	טוב	qal	pft	3ms	טוב	373		be pleasing
3:9	יכתב	niph	jusm	3ms	כתב	507		be written
	אבדם	piel	infc		אבד	1	3mp	destroy
	אשקול	qal	impf	1cs	שקל	1053		weigh
	עשי	qal	ptc	mp	עשה	793		do,make
	הביא	hiph	infc		בוא	97		bring in
3:10	יסר	hiph	wci	3ms	סור	693		take away
	יתנה	qal	wci	3ms	נתן	678	3fs	give,set
	צרר	qal	ptc	ms	צרר	865		show hostility
3:11	יאמר	qal	wci	3ms	אמר	55		say
	נתון	qal	pptc	ms	נתן	678		give,set
	עשות	qal	infc		עשה	793		do,make
3:12	יקראו	niph	wci	3mp	קרא	894		be called
	יכתב	niph	wci	3ms	כתב	507		be written
	צוה	piel	pft	3ms	צוה	845		command
	נכתב	niph	ptc	ms	כתב	507		be written
	נחתם	niph	ptc	ms	חתם	367		be sealed
3:13	נשלוח	niph	infa		שלח	1018		be sent
	רצים	qal	ptc	mp	רוץ	930		run
	השמיד	hiph	infc		שמד	1029		exterminate
	הרג	qal	infc		הרג	246		kill
	אבד	piel	infc		אבד	1		destroy
	בוז	qal	infc		בזז	102		plunder
3:14	הנתן	niph	infc		נתן	678		be given
	גלוי	qal	pptc	ms	גלה	162		uncover
	היות	qal	infc		היה	224		be,become
3:15	רצים	qal	ptc	mp	רוץ	930		run
	יצאו	qal	pft	3cp	יצא	422		go out
	דחופים	qal	pptc	mp	דחף	191		hasten
	נתנה	niph	pft	3fs	נתן	678		be given
	ישבו	qal	pft	3cp	ישב	442		sit,dwell
	שתות	qal	infc		שתה	1059		drink
	נבוכה	niph	pft	3fs	בוך	100		be confused
4:1	ידע	qal	pft	3ms	ידע	393		know
	נעשה	niph	pft	3ms	עשה	793		be done
	יקרע	qal	wci	3ms	קרע	902		tear,rend
	ילבש	qal	wci	3ms	לבש	527		put on,clothe
	יצא	qal	wci	3ms	יצא	422		go out
	יזעק	qal	wci	3ms	זעק	277		call,cry out
4:2	יבוא	qal	wci	3ms	בוא	97		come in
	בוא	qal	infc		בוא	97		come in
4:3	מגיע	hiph	ptc	ms	נגע	619		reach,arrive
	יצע	hoph	impf	3ms	יצע	426		be spread
4:4	kתבואינה	qal	wci	3fp	בוא	97		come in
	qתבואנה	qal	wci	3fp	בוא	97		come in
	יגידו	hiph	wci	3mp	נגד	616		declare,tell
	תתחלחל	htpp	wci	3fs	חול	296		writhe
	תשלח	qal	wci	3fs	שלח	1018		send
	הלביש	hiph	infc		לבש	527		clothe
	הסיר	hiph	infc		סור	693		take away
	קבל	piel	pft	3ms	קבל	867		take,receive
4:5	תקרא	qal	wci	3fs	קרא	894		call,proclaim
	העמיד	hiph	pft	3ms	עמד	763		set up,raise
	תצוהו	piel	wci	3fs	צוה	845	3ms	command
	דעת	qal	infc		ידע	393		know

ChVs	Form	Stem	Tnse	PGN	Root	BDB	Sfx	Meaning
4:6	יצא	qal	wci	3ms	יצא	422		go out
4:7	יגד	hiph	wci	3ms	נגד	616		declare,tell
	קרהו	qal	pft	3ms	קרה	899	3ms	encounter,meet
	אמר	qal	pft	3ms	אמר	55		say
	שׁקול	qal	infc		שׁקל	1053		weigh
	אבדם	piel	infc		אבד	1	3mp	destroy
4:8	נתן	niph	pft	3ms	נתן	678		be given
	השׁמידם	hiph	infc		שׁמד	1029	3mp	exterminate
	נתן	qal	pft	3ms	נתן	678		give,set
	הראות	hiph	infc		ראה	906		show,exhibit
	הגיד	hiph	infc		נגד	616		declare,tell
	צוות	piel	infc		צוה	845		command
	בוא	qal	infc		בוא	97		come in
	התחנן	hith	infc		חנן	335		seek favor
	בקשׁ	piel	infc		בקשׁ	134		seek
4:9	יבוא	qal	wci	3ms	בוא	97		come in
	יגד	hiph	wci	3ms	נגד	616		declare,tell
4:10	תאמר	qal	wci	3fs	אמר	55		say
	תצוהו	piel	wci	3fs	צוה	845	3ms	command
4:11	יודעים	qal	ptc	mp	ידע	393		know
	יבוא	qal	impf	3ms	בוא	97		come in
	יקרא	niph	impf	3ms	קרא	894		be called
	המית	hiph	infc		מות	559		kill
	יושׁיט	hiph	impf	3ms	ישׁט	445		extend
	חיה	qal	wcp	3ms	חיה	310		live
	נקראתי	niph	pft	1cs	קרא	894		be called
	בוא	qal	infc		בוא	97		come in
4:12	יגידו	hiph	wci	3mp	נגד	616		declare,tell
4:13	יאמר	qal	wci	3ms	אמר	55		say
	השׁיב	hiph	infc		שׁוב	996		bring back
	תדמי	piel	jusm	2fs	דמה	197		liken,think
	המלט	niph	infc		מלט	572		escape
4:14	החרשׁ	hiph	infa		חרשׁ	361		be silent
	תחרישׁי	hiph	impf	2fs	חרשׁ	361		be silent
	יעמוד	qal	impf	3ms	עמד	763		stand,stop
	תאבדו	qal	impf	2mp	אבד	1		perish
	יודע	qal	ptc	ms	ידע	393		know
	הגעת	hiph	pft	2fs	נגע	619		reach,arrive
4:15	תאמר	qal	wci	3fs	אמר	55		say
	השׁיב	hiph	infc		שׁוב	996		bring back
4:16	לך	qal	impv	ms	הלך	229		walk,go
	כנוס	qal	impv	ms	כנס	488		collect
	נמצאים	niph	ptc	mp	מצא	592		be found
	צומו	qal	impv	mp	צום	847		fast
	תאכלו	qal	jusm	2mp	אכל	37		eat,devour
	תשׁתו	qal	jusm	2mp	שׁתה	1059		drink
	אצום	qal	impf	1cs	צום	847		fast
	אבוא	qal	impf	1cs	בוא	97		come in
	אבדתי	qal	pft	1cs	אבד	1		perish
	אבדתי	qal	pft	1cs	אבד	1		perish
4:17	יעבר	qal	wci	3ms	עבר	716		pass over
	יעשׂ	qal	wci	3ms	עשׂה	793		do,make
	צותה	piel	pft	3fs	צוה	845		command
5:1	יהי	qal	wci	3ms	היה	224		be,become

ChVs	Form	Stem	Tnse	PGN	Root	BDB	Sfx	Meaning
5:1	תלבשׁ	qal	wci	3fs	לבשׁ	527		put on,clothe
	תעמד	qal	wci	3fs	עמד	763		stand,stop
	יושׁב	qal	ptc	ms	ישׁב	442		sit,dwell
5:2	יהי	qal	wci	3ms	היה	224		be,become
	ראות	qal	infc		ראה	906		see
	עמדת	qal	ptc	fs	עמד	763		stand,stop
	נשׂאה	qal	pft	3fs	נשׂא	669		lift,carry
	יושׁט	hiph	wci	3ms	ישׁט	445		extend
	תקרב	qal	wci	3fs	קרב	897		approach
	תגע	qal	wci	3fs	נגע	619		touch,strike
5:3	יאמר	qal	wci	3ms	אמר	55		say
	ינתן	niph	jusm	3ms	נתן	678		be given
5:4	תאמר	qal	wci	3fs	אמר	55		say
	טוב	qal	pft	3ms	טוב	373		be pleasing
	יבוא	qal	jusm	3ms	בוא	97		come in
	עשׂיתי	qal	pft	1cs	עשׂה	793		do,make
5:5	יאמר	qal	wci	3ms	אמר	55		say
	מהרו	piel	impv	mp	מהר	554		hasten
	עשׂות	qal	infc		עשׂה	793		do,make
	יבא	qal	wci	3ms	בוא	97		come in
	עשׂתה	qal	pft	3fs	עשׂה	793		do,make
5:6	יאמר	qal	wci	3ms	אמר	55		say
	ינתן	niph	jusm	3ms	נתן	678		be given
	תעשׂ	niph	jus	3fs	עשׂה	793		be done
5:7	תען	qal	wci	3fs	ענה	772		answer
	תאמר	qal	wci	3fs	אמר	55		say
5:8	מצאתי	qal	pft	1cs	מצא	592		find
	טוב	qal	pft	3ms	טוב	373		be pleasing
	תת	qal	infc		נתן	678		give,set
	עשׂות	qal	infc		עשׂה	793		do,make
	יבוא	qal	jusm	3ms	בוא	97		come in
	אעשׂה	qal	impf	1cs	עשׂה	793		do,make
	אעשׂה	qal	impf	1cs	עשׂה	793		do,make
5:9	יצא	qal	wci	3ms	יצא	422		go out
	ראות	qal	infc		ראה	906		see
	קם	qal	pft	3ms	קום	877		arise,stand
	זע	qal	pft	3ms	זוע	266		quake
	ימלא	niph	wci	3ms	מלא	569		be filled
5:10	יתאפק	hith	wci	3ms	אפק	67		restrain self
	יבוא	qal	wci	3ms	בוא	97		come in
	ישׁלח	qal	wci	3ms	שׁלח	1018		send
	יבא	hiph	wci	3ms	בוא	97		bring in
	אהביו	qal	ptc	mp	אהב	12	3ms	love
5:11	יספר	piel	wci	3ms	ספר	707		recount
	גדלו	piel	pft	3ms	גדל	152	3ms	cause to grow
	נשׂאו	piel	pft	3ms	נשׂא	669	3ms	lift up
5:12	יאמר	qal	wci	3ms	אמר	55		say
	הביאה	hiph	pft	3fs	בוא	97		bring in
	עשׂתה	qal	pft	3fs	עשׂה	793		do,make
	קרוא	qal	pptc	ms	קרא	894		call,proclaim
5:13	שׁוה	qal	ptc	ms	שׁוה	1000		be even,smooth
	ראה	qal	ptc	ms	ראה	906		see
	יושׁב	qal	ptc	ms	ישׁב	442		sit,dwell
5:14	תאמר	qal	wci	3fs	אמר	55		say

ChVs	Form	Stem	Tnse	PGN	Root	BDB	Sfx	Meaning
5:14	אהביו	qal	ptc	mp	אהב	12	3ms	love
	יעשׂו	qal	jusm	3mp	עשׂה	793		do,make
	אמר	qal	impv	ms	אמר	55		say
	יתלו	qal	jusm	3mp	תלה	1067		hang
	בא	qal	impv	ms	בוא	97		come in
	ייטב	qal	wci	3ms	יטב	405		be good
	יעשׂ	qal	wci	3ms	עשׂה	793		do,make
6:1	נדדה	qal	pft	3fs	נדד	622		retreat,flee
	יאמר	qal	wci	3ms	אמר	55		say
	הביא	hiph	infc		בוא	97		bring in
	יהיו	qal	wci	3mp	היה	224		be,become
	נקראים	niph	ptc	mp	קרא	894		be called
6:2	ימצא	niph	wci	3ms	מצא	592		be found
	כתוב	qal	pptc	ms	כתב	507		write
	הגיד	hiph	pft	3ms	נגד	616		declare,tell
	שׁמרי	qal	ptc	mp	שׁמר	1036		keep,watch
	בקשׁו	piel	pft	3cp	בקשׁ	134		seek
	שׁלח	qal	infc		שׁלח	1018		send
6:3	יאמר	qal	wci	3ms	אמר	55		say
	נעשׂה	niph	pft	3ms	עשׂה	793		be done
	יאמרו	qal	wci	3mp	אמר	55		say
	משׁרתיו	piel	ptc	mp	שׁרת	1058	3ms	minister,serve
	נעשׂה	niph	pft	3ms	עשׂה	793		be done
6:4	יאמר	qal	wci	3ms	אמר	55		say
	בא	qal	pft	3ms	בוא	97		come in
	אמר	qal	infc		אמר	55		say
	תלות	qal	infc		תלה	1067		hang
	הכין	hiph	pft	3ms	כון	465		fix,prepare
6:5	יאמרו	qal	wci	3mp	אמר	55		say
	עמד	qal	ptc	ms	עמד	763		stand,stop
	יאמר	qal	wci	3ms	אמר	55		say
	יבוא	qal	jusm	3ms	בוא	97		come in
6:6	יבוא	qal	wci	3ms	בוא	97		come in
	יאמר	qal	wci	3ms	אמר	55		say
	עשׂות	qal	infc		עשׂה	793		do,make
	חפץ	qal	pft	3ms	חפץ	342		delight in
	יאמר	qal	wci	3ms	אמר	55		say
	יחפץ	qal	impf	3ms	חפץ	342		delight in
	עשׂות	qal	infc		עשׂה	793		do,make
6:7	יאמר	qal	wci	3ms	אמר	55		say
	חפץ	qal	pft	3ms	חפץ	342		delight in
6:8	יביאו	hiph	jusm	3mp	בוא	97		bring in
	לבשׁ	qal	pft	3ms	לבשׁ	527		put on,clothe
	רכב	qal	pft	3ms	רכב	938		mount,ride
	נתן	niph	pft	3ms	נתן	678		be given
6:9	נתון	qal	infa		נתן	678		give,set
	הלבישׁו	hiph	wcp	3cp	לבשׁ	527		clothe
	חפץ	qal	pft	3ms	חפץ	342		delight in
	הרכיבהו	hiph	wcp	3cp	רכב	938	3ms	cause to ride
	קראו	qal	wcp	3cp	קרא	894		call,proclaim
	יעשׂה	niph	impf	3ms	עשׂה	793		be done
	חפץ	qal	pft	3ms	חפץ	342		delight in
6:10	יאמר	qal	wci	3ms	אמר	55		say
	מהר	piel	impv	ms	מהר	554		hasten
6:10	קח	qal	impv	ms	לקח	542		take
	דברת	piel	pft	2ms	דבר	180		speak
	עשׂה	qal	impv	ms	עשׂה	793		do,make
	יושׁב	qal	ptc	ms	ישׁב	442		sit,dwell
	תפל	hiph	jus	2ms	נפל	656		cause to fall
	דברת	piel	pft	2ms	דבר	180		speak
6:11	יקח	qal	wci	3ms	לקח	542		take
	ילבשׁ	hiph	wci	3ms	לבשׁ	527		clothe
	ירכיבהו	hiph	wci	3ms	רכב	938	3ms	cause to ride
	יקרא	qal	wci	3ms	קרא	894		call,proclaim
	יעשׂה	niph	impf	3ms	עשׂה	793		be done
	חפץ	qal	pft	3ms	חפץ	342		delight in
6:12	ישׁב	qal	wci	3ms	שׁוב	996		turn,return
	נדחף	niph	pft	3ms	דחף	191		hasten oneself
	חפוי	qal	pptc	ms	חפה	341		cover
6:13	יספר	piel	wci	3ms	ספר	707		recount
	אהביו	qal	ptc	mp	אהב	12	3ms	love
	קרהו	qal	pft	3ms	קרה	899	3ms	encounter,meet
	יאמרו	qal	wci	3mp	אמר	55		say
	החלות	hiph	pft	2ms	חלל	320		begin,profane
	נפל	qal	infc		נפל	656		fall
	תוכל	qal	impf	2ms	יכל	407		be able
	נפול	qal	infa		נפל	656		fall
	תפול	qal	impf	2ms	נפל	656		fall
6:14	מדברים	piel	ptc	mp	דבר	180		speak
	הגיעו	hiph	pft	3cp	נגע	619		reach,arrive
	יבהלו	hiph	wci	3mp	בהל	96		dismay,hasten
	הביא	hiph	infc		בוא	97		bring in
	עשׂתה	qal	pft	3fs	עשׂה	793		do,make
7:1	יבא	qal	wci	3ms	בוא	97		come in
	שׁתות	qal	infc		שׁתה	1059		drink
7:2	יאמר	qal	wci	3ms	אמר	55		say
	תנתן	niph	jusm	3fs	נתן	678		be given
	תעשׂ	niph	jus	3fs	עשׂה	793		be done
7:3	תען	qal	wci	3fs	ענה	772		answer
	תאמר	qal	wci	3fs	אמר	55		say
	מצאתי	qal	pft	1cs	מצא	592		find
	טוב	qal	pft	3ms	טוב	373		be pleasing
	תנתן	niph	jusm	3fs	נתן	678		be given
7:4	נמכרנו	niph	pft	1cp	מכר	569		be sold
	השׁמיד	hiph	infc		שׁמד	1029		exterminate
	הרוג	qal	infc		הרג	246		kill
	אבד	piel	infc		אבד	1		destroy
	נמכרנו	niph	pft	1cp	מכר	569		be sold
	החרשׁתי	hiph	pft	1cs	חרשׁ	361		be silent
	שׁוה	qal	ptc	ms	שׁוה	1000		be even,smooth
7:5	יאמר	qal	wci	3ms	אמר	55		say
	יאמר	qal	wci	3ms	אמר	55		say
	מלאו	qal	pft	3ms	מלא	569	3ms	be full,fill
	עשׂות	qal	infc		עשׂה	793		do,make
7:6	תאמר	qal	wci	3fs	אמר	55		say
	אויב	qal	ptc	ms	איב	33		be hostile to
	נבעת	niph	pft	3ms	בעת	129		be terrified
7:7	קם	qal	pft	3ms	קום	877		arise,stand

ChVs	Form	Stem	Tnse	PGN	Root	BDB	Sfx	Meaning
7:7	עמד	qal	pft	3ms	עמד	763		stand,stop
	בקש	piel	infc		בקש	134		seek
	ראה	qal	pft	3ms	ראה	906		see
	כלתה	qal	pft	3fs	כלה	477		finished,spent
7:8	שב	qal	pft	3ms	שוב	996		turn,return
	נפל	qal	ptc	ms	נפל	656		fall
	יאמר	qal	wci	3ms	אמר	55		say
	כבוש	qal	infc		כבש	461		subdue
	יצא	qal	pft	3ms	יצא	422		go out
	חפו	qal	pft	3cp	חפה	341		cover
7:9	יאמר	qal	wci	3ms	אמר	55		say
	עשה	qal	pft	3ms	עשה	793		do,make
	דבר	piel	pft	3ms	דבר	180		speak
	עמד	qal	ptc	ms	עמד	763		stand,stop
	יאמר	qal	wci	3ms	אמר	55		say
	תלהו	qal	impv	mp	תלה	1067	3ms	hang
7:10	יתלו	qal	wci	3mp	תלה	1067		hang
	הכין	hiph	pft	3ms	כון	465		fix,prepare
	שככה	qal	pft	3fs	שכך	1013		abate,crouch
8:1	נתן	qal	pft	3ms	נתן	678		give,set
	צרר	qal	ptc	ms	צרר	865		show hostility
	בא	qal	pft	3ms	בוא	97		come in
	הגידה	hiph	pft	3fs	נגד	616		declare,tell
8:2	יסר	hiph	wci	3ms	סור	693		take away
	העביר	hiph	pft	3ms	עבר	716		cause to pass
	יתנה	qal	wci	3ms	נתן	678	3fs	give,set
	תשם	qal	wci	3fs	שים	962		put,set
8:3	תוסף	hiph	wci	3fs	יסף	414		add,do again
	תדבר	piel	wci	3fs	דבר	180		speak
	תפל	qal	wci	3fs	נפל	656		fall
	תבך	qal	wci	3fs	בכה	113		weep
	תתחנן	hith	wci	3fs	חנן	335		seek favor
	העביר	hiph	infc		עבר	716		cause to pass
	חשב	qal	pft	3ms	חשב	362		think,devise
8:4	יושט	hiph	wci	3ms	ישט	445		extend
	תקם	qal	wci	3fs	קום	877		arise,stand
	תעמד	qal	wci	3fs	עמד	763		stand,stop
8:5	תאמר	qal	wci	3fs	אמר	55		say
	טוב	qal	pft	3ms	טוב	373		be pleasing
	מצאתי	qal	pft	1cs	מצא	592		find
	כשר	qal	pft	3ms	כשר	506		be proper
	יכתב	niph	jusm	3ms	כתב	507		be written
	השיב	hiph	infc		שוב	996		bring back
	כתב	qal	pft	3ms	כתב	507		write
	אבד	piel	infc		אבד	1		destroy
8:6	אוכל	qal	impf	1cs	יכל	407		be able
	ראיתי	qal	wcp	1cs	ראה	906		see
	ימצא	qal	impf	3ms	מצא	592		find
	אוכל	qal	impf	1cs	יכל	407		be able
	ראיתי	qal	wcp	1cs	ראה	906		see
8:7	יאמר	qal	wci	3ms	אמר	55		say
	נתתי	qal	pft	1cs	נתן	678		give,set
	תלו	qal	pft	3cp	תלה	1067		hang
	שלח	qal	pft	3ms	שלח	1018		send

ChVs	Form	Stem	Tnse	PGN	Root	BDB	Sfx	Meaning
8:8	כתבו	qal	impv	mp	כתב	507		write
	חתמו	qal	impv	mp	חתם	367		seal
	נכתב	niph	ptc	ms	כתב	507		be written
	נחתום	niph	infa		חתם	367		be sealed
	השיב	hiph	infc		שוב	996		bring back
8:9	יקראו	niph	wci	3mp	קרא	894		be called
	יכתב	niph	wci	3ms	כתב	507		be written
	צוה	piel	pft	3ms	צוה	845		command
8:10	יכתב	qal	wci	3ms	כתב	507		write
	יחתם	qal	wci	3ms	חתם	367		seal
	ישלח	qal	wci	3ms	שלח	1018		send
	רצים	qal	ptc	mp	רוץ	930		run
	רכבי	qal	ptc	mp	רכב	938		mount,ride
8:11	נתן	qal	pft	3ms	נתן	678		give,set
	הקהל	niph	infc		קהל	874		assemble
	עמד	qal	infc		עמד	763		stand,stop
	השמיד	hiph	infc		שמד	1029		exterminate
	הרג	qal	infc		הרג	246		kill
	אבד	piel	infc		אבד	1		destroy
	צרים	qal	ptc	mp	צור	849		treat as foe
	בוז	qal	infc		בזז	102		plunder
8:13	הנתן	niph	infc		נתן	678		be given
	גלוי	qal	pptc	ms	גלה	162		uncover
	היות	qal	infc		היה	224		be,become
	הנקם	niph	infc		נקם	667		avenge oneself
	איביהם	qal	ptc	mp	איב	33	3mp	be hostile to
8:14	רצים	qal	ptc	mp	רוץ	930		run
	רכבי	qal	ptc	mp	רכב	938		mount,ride
	יצאו	qal	pft	3cp	יצא	422		go out
	מבהלים	pual	ptc	mp	בהל	96		hastened
	דחופים	qal	pptc	mp	דחף	191		hasten
	נתנה	niph	pft	3fs	נתן	678		be given
8:15	יצא	qal	pft	3ms	יצא	422		go out
	צהלה	qal	pft	3fs	צהל	843		neigh,cry
	שמחה	qal	pft	3fs	שמח	970		rejoice
8:16	היתה	qal	pft	3fs	היה	224		be,become
8:17	מגיע	hiph	ptc	ms	נגע	619		reach,arrive
	מתיהדים	hith	ptc	mp	יהד	397		become a Jew
	נפל	qal	pft	3ms	נפל	656		fall
9:1	הגיע	hiph	pft	3ms	נגע	619		reach,arrive
	העשות	niph	infc		עשה	793		be done
	שברו	piel	pft	3cp	שבר	960		wait,hope
	איבי	qal	ptc	mp	איב	33		be hostile to
	שלוט	qal	infc		שלט	1020		domineer
	נהפוך	niph	infa		הפך	245		turn oneself
	ישלטו	qal	impf	3mp	שלט	1020		domineer
	שנאיהם	qal	ptc	mp	שנא	971	3mp	hate
9:2	נקהלו	niph	pft	3cp	קהל	874		assemble
	שלח	qal	infc		שלח	1018		send
	מבקשי	piel	ptc	mp	בקש	134		seek
	עמד	qal	pft	3ms	עמד	763		stand,stop
	נפל	qal	pft	3ms	נפל	656		fall
9:3	עשי	qal	ptc	mp	עשה	793		do,make
	מנשאים	piel	ptc	mp	נשא	669		lift up

ChVs	Form	Stem	Tnse	PGN	Root	BDB	Sfx	Meaning
9:3	נפל	qal	pft	3ms	נפל	656		fall
9:4	הולך	qal	ptc	ms	הלך	229		walk,go
	הולך	qal	ptc	ms	הלך	229		walk,go
9:5	יכו	hiph	wci	3mp	נכה	645		smite
	איביהם	qal	ptc	mp	איב	33	3mp	be hostile to
	יעשׂו	qal	wci	3mp	עשׂה	793		do,make
	שׂנאיהם	qal	ptc	mp	שׂנא	971	3mp	hate
9:6	הרגו	qal	pft	3cp	הרג	246		kill
	אבד	piel	infa		אבד	1		destroy
9:10	צרר	qal	ptc	ms	צרר	865		show hostility
	הרגו	qal	pft	3cp	הרג	246		kill
	שׁלחו	qal	pft	3cp	שׁלח	1018		send
9:11	בא	qal	pft	3ms	בוא	97		come in
	הרוגים	qal	pptc	mp	הרג	246		kill
9:12	יאמר	qal	wci	3ms	אמר	55		say
	הרגו	qal	pft	3cp	הרג	246		kill
	אבד	piel	infa		אבד	1		destroy
	עשׂו	qal	pft	3cp	עשׂה	793		do,make
	ינתן	niph	jusm	3ms	נתן	678		be given
	תעשׂ	niph	jus	3fs	עשׂה	793		be done
9:13	תאמר	qal	wci	3fs	אמר	55		say
	טוב	qal	pft	3ms	טוב	373		be pleasing
	ינתן	niph	jusm	3ms	נתן	678		be given
	עשׂות	qal	infc		עשׂה	793		do,make
	יתלו	qal	jusm	3mp	תלה	1067		hang
9:14	יאמר	qal	wci	3ms	אמר	55		say
	העשׂות	niph	infc		עשׂה	793		be done
	תנתן	niph	wci	3fs	נתן	678		be given
	תלו	qal	pft	3cp	תלה	1067		hang
9:15	יקהלו	niph	wci	3mp	קהל	874		assemble
	יהרגו	qal	wci	3mp	הרג	246		kill
	שׁלחו	qal	pft	3cp	שׁלח	1018		send
9:16	נקהלו	niph	pft	3cp	קהל	874		assemble
	עמד	qal	infa		עמד	763		stand,stop
	נוח	qal	infa		נוח	628		rest
	איביהם	qal	ptc	mp	איב	33	3mp	be hostile to
	הרג	qal	infa		הרג	246		kill
	שׂנאיהם	qal	ptc	mp	שׂנא	971	3mp	hate
	שׁלחו	qal	pft	3cp	שׁלח	1018		send
9:17	נוח	qal	infa		נוח	628		rest
	עשׂה	qal	infa		עשׂה	793		do,make
9:18	נקהלו	niph	pft	3cp	קהל	874		assemble
	נוח	qal	infa		נוח	628		rest
	עשׂה	qal	infa		עשׂה	793		do,make
9:19	ישׁבים	qal	ptc	mp	ישׁב	442		sit,dwell
	עשׂים	qal	ptc	mp	עשׂה	793		do,make
9:20	יכתב	qal	wci	3ms	כתב	507		write
	ישׁלח	qal	wci	3ms	שׁלח	1018		send
9:21	קים	piel	infc		קום	877		confirm
	היות	qal	infc		היה	224		be,become
	עשׂים	qal	ptc	mp	עשׂה	793		do,make
9:22	נחו	qal	pft	3cp	נוח	628		rest
	אויביהם	qal	ptc	mp	איב	33	3mp	be hostile to
	נהפך	niph	pft	3ms	הפך	245		turn oneself
9:22	עשׂות	qal	infc		עשׂה	793		do,make
9:23	קבל	piel	pft	3ms	קבל	867		take,receive
	החלו	hiph	pft	3cp	חלל	320		begin,profane
	עשׂות	qal	infc		עשׂה	793		do,make
	כתב	qal	pft	3ms	כתב	507		write
9:24	צרר	qal	ptc	ms	צרר	865		show hostility
	חשׁב	qal	pft	3ms	חשׁב	362		think,devise
	אבדם	piel	infc		אבד	1	3mp	destroy
	הפיל	hiph	pft	3ms	נפל	656		cause to fall
	המם	qal	infc		המם	243	3mp	confuse,vex
	אבדם	piel	infc		אבד	1	3mp	destroy
9:25	באה	qal	infc		בוא	97	3fs	come in
	אמר	qal	pft	3ms	אמר	55		say
	ישׁוב	qal	jusm	3ms	שׁוב	996		turn,return
	חשׁב	qal	pft	3ms	חשׁב	362		think,devise
	תלו	qal	wcp	3cp	תלה	1067		hang
9:26	קראו	qal	pft	3cp	קרא	894		call,proclaim
	ראו	qal	pft	3cp	ראה	906		see
	הגיע	hiph	pft	3ms	נגע	619		reach,arrive
9:27	קימו	piel	pft	3cp	קום	877		confirm
	קבלk	piel	pft	3ms	קבל	867		take,receive
	קבלוq	piel	pft	3cp	קבל	867		take,receive
	נלוים	niph	ptc	mp	לוה	530		join oneself
	יעבור	qal	impf	3ms	עבר	716		pass over
	היות	qal	infc		היה	224		be,become
	עשׂים	qal	ptc	mp	עשׂה	793		do,make
9:28	נזכרים	niph	ptc	mp	זכר	269		be remembered
	נעשׂים	niph	ptc	mp	עשׂה	793		be done
	יעברו	qal	impf	3mp	עבר	716		pass over
	יסוף	qal	impf	3ms	סוף	692		come to an end
9:29	תכתב	qal	wci	3fs	כתב	507		write
	קים	piel	infc		קום	877		confirm
9:30	ישׁלח	qal	wci	3ms	שׁלח	1018		send
9:31	קים	piel	infc		קום	877		confirm
	קים	piel	pft	3ms	קום	877		confirm
	קימו	piel	pft	3cp	קום	877		confirm
9:32	קים	piel	pft	3ms	קום	877		confirm
	נכתב	niph	ptc	ms	כתב	507		be written
10:1	ישׂם	qal	wci	3ms	שׂים	962		put,set
10:2	גדלו	piel	pft	3ms	גדל	152	3ms	cause to grow
	כתובים	qal	pptc	mp	כתב	507		write
10:3	רצוי	qal	pptc	ms	רצה	953		be pleased
	דרשׁ	qal	ptc	ms	דרשׁ	205		resort to,seek
	דבר	qal	ptc	ms	דבר	180		speak